Lethbridge College - Buchanan Library

CRIMINAL
EVIDENCE

NINTH EDITION

Jefferson L.
INGRAM

University of Dayton

 LexisNexis®

 **anderson publishing**
A member of the LexisNexis Group

John C. Klotter Justice Administration Legal Series

Criminal Evidence, Ninth Edition

Copyright © 1971, 1975 W.H. Anderson Company
1980, 1987, 1992, 1996, 2000, 2004, 2007
Matthew Bender & Company, Inc., a member of the LexisNexis Group

Phone 877-374-2919
Web Site www.lexisnexis.com/anderson/criminaljustice

All rights reserved. No part of this book may be reproduced in any form or by any electronic or mechanical means, including information storage and retrieval systems, without permission in writing from the publisher.

LexisNexis and the Knowledge Burst logo are trademarks of Reed Elsevier Properties, Inc.
Anderson Publishing is a registered trademark of Anderson Publishing, a member of the LexisNexis Group.

Library of Congress Cataloging-in-Publication Data

Ingram, Jefferson L.
    Criminal evidence / by Jefferson L. Ingram. -- 9th ed.
        p. cm.
    Includes index.
    ISBN 978-1-59345-428-9 (softbound)
    1. Criminal evidence -- United States. I. Title.

Cover design by Tin Box Studio, Inc.

EDITOR Elisabeth Roszmann Ebben
ACQUISITIONS EDITOR Michael C. Braswell

Preface

In revising *Criminal Evidence*, Ninth Edition, the author took care to honor John Klotter's extensive work on criminal evidence to continue the excellent approach he followed by updating evidentiary themes, trends, and cases, while remaining true to the original organization and presentation. The book remains primarily a textbook for those involved in the administration of justice and those who are preparing for careers in criminal justice or related areas of study. For that reason, the emphasis continues to be on the rules and principles of evidence that primarily affect criminal cases.

This book has been prepared as a textbook for individuals teaching or learning about the evidentiary framework in the administration of criminal justice. The materials presented cover general evidence law in use by the states and the federal justice system. The text makes frequent reference to the Federal Rules of Evidence as a benchmark of how the law of evidence applies in particular situations. Although differences exist in the way a rule of evidence is administered in different jurisdictions, there is significant uniformity because many states have adopted versions of the Federal Rules of Evidence or the Uniform Rules of Evidence. As state courts follow their individual versions of the Federal Rules of Evidence, they place significant emphasis and reliance on the way the federal courts interpret the Rules.

For the reader or instructor, the book retains its familiar organization with related ancillary materials, including the glossary and the appendices. As a method of organization, the text portion of this book roughly follows the current organizational order of the Federal Rules of Evidence and includes portions of particular rules in box format within the chapters. In Part II, several newer legal cases that explain the evolving principles of evidence law have been added, while some of the older cases in which the judicial writers offered particularly excellent explanations of legal principles have been retained. After Part II, the glossary permits the student to quickly find and learn many of the terms and principles that may be unique to the study of the law of evidence. Appendix I contains a copy of the Federal Rules of Evidence that incorporates the new rule changes that became effective in December 2006.

Constitutional reinterpretations by the Supreme Court of the United States dictate changes in the admissibility of evidence. Forty years ago, the *Miranda* revolution altered the way in which criminal justice professionals could obtain and use some types of evidence. More recently, the Supreme Court of the United States reinterpreted the Sixth Amendment right of confrontation in a way that affects the admissibility of evidence under the Sixth Amendment right of confrontation. The new interpretation may usher in a new era of jurisprudence surrounding the admission of hearsay evidence. Recognizing that the law of evidence evolves, the author made every effort to recognize changes in evidence law and to incorporate the new material into the text discussion of the principles.

The study of criminal evidence involves some understanding of collateral legal subjects like constitutional law and criminal law. The presentation of evidentiary principles are embedded in criminal cases involving murder, robbery, assault, battery, and other crimes. Using a criminal prosecution context, this book presents the traditional rules of evidence that most often affect criminal cases.

To assist the student, this book comes with a Study Guide that focuses on the important parts of each chapter through its learning objectives and discussion outlines.

To assist instructors, an Instructor's Guide and a PowerPoint presentation covering the text section of this book are available.

Jefferson Ingram, University of Dayton, October 2006.

Table of Contents

Chapter 6
Presumptions, Inferences, and Stipulations   135

General Admissibility Tests   **187**

Evidence via Witness Testimony   **273**

PART I

History and
Approach to Study

History and Development of Rules of Evidence

1

The fundamental basis upon which all rules of evidence must rest—if they are to rest upon reason—is their adaptation to the successful development of the truth.

Funk v. United States, 290 U.S. 371 (1933)

Chapter Outline

Key Terms and Concepts

Federal Rules of Evidence   Uniform Rules of Evidence

§ 1.1 Introduction

Observers of criminal trials are often confused by the procedures concerning the admission and exclusion of evidence. The form of the objections offered and the arguments presented only add to the confusion. Logically assuming that the purpose of a trial is to seek the truth, the lay observer is likely to be bewildered by objections to the introduction of apparently relevant evidence. Sometimes evidence that could have a direct bearing on the case is, in fact, excluded at the trial. To understand why certain evidence is admitted and other evidence is excluded, it is necessary to study the history and evolution of the rules of evidence.

§ 1.2 Early Attempts to Determine Guilt or Innocence

Through the ages, humankind has sought fair methods of reaching the truth in criminal cases. Each culture arrived at a method that was congenial to that culture. Some of these systems of determining guilt or innocence were ridiculous and often barbaric. However, history has helped succeeding generations to develop systems that are more workable.

Every tribe and every people devised a system for protecting the lives and property of its citizens. Authorities noted, however, that there were only a few that developed a well-defined, organized, continuous body of legal ideas and methods that could be called a legal system. According to Wigmore, 16 legal systems developed to a stage at which they could be recognized as a legal system: Egyptian, Mesopotamian, Chinese, Hindu, Hebrew, Greek, Maritime, Roman, Celtic, Germanic, Church, Japanese, Mohammedan, Slavic, Romanesque, and Anglican.[1] Although all of these systems had some effect on

---

[1] For a complete, interesting, and informative study of the world's legal systems, *see* WIGMORE, A PANORAMA OF THE WORLD'S LEGAL SYSTEMS (1928).

modern evidence rules, only a few of the older systems have been selected for discussion, because they represent systems that were adopted in part by other cultures and eventually led to our judge-jury system, which in turn was responsible for our rules of evidence. Some of the procedures that developed under these systems are gone, while some remain.

A. *Egyptian Legal System*

In the Egyptian system (the oldest of the systems listed above) the court was made up of 30 judges chosen from the states that constituted Egypt. The defendant was advised in writing of the charges against him or her, and he or she was authorized to answer each charge in writing by: (1) asserting that he or she did not do it; (2) stating that if he or she did it, it was not wrongful; or (3) if it was wrongful, it should bear a lesser penalty than that advocated by his or her accusers. It is interesting to note that at this time (beginning at approximately 4000 B.C.) all formal proceedings of the court were conducted without speeches from advocates. It was believed that speeches of advocates would cloud the legal issues, and those speeches, combined with the cleverness of the speakers, the spell of their delivery, and the tears of the accused, would influence many persons to ignore the strict rules of law and the standards of truth.[2]

The Greek historian Diodorus describes the procedure developed by the Egyptians as follows:

> After the parties had thus twice presented their case in writing, then it was the task of the thirty judges to discuss among themselves their judgment and of the chief justice to hand the image of truth to one or the other of the parties.[3]

B. *Mesopotamian Legal System*

Under the early Mesopotamian system, the king was the fountain of justice, receiving the law from divine guidance. But under King Hammurabi, approximately 2100 B.C., the system envisioned the king as the source of law under which the king could personally administer justice or allow local governors or courts of law to handle the matters.[4] The Mesopotamian system did not operate with police or a prosecutor, but the judges, who were originally royal priests, found the facts from the evidence and applied the law.[5] A record of the trials of this period indicates that the judges called upon the accusers to "produce witnesses or instruments to show guilt." The judges then examined the facts and reached a conclusion as to guilt or innocence. This perhaps was the origin of the modern use of testimony and real evidence.[6]

---

2   WIGMORE, A PANORAMA OF THE WORLD'S LEGAL SYSTEMS (1928).
3   KOCOUREK & WIGMORE, SOURCES OF ANCIENT AND PRIMITIVE LAW, EVOLUTION OF LAW SERIES (1915).
4   99 Mil. L. Rev. 1 (1983).
5   *Id.*
6   WIGMORE, *supra* note 2.

C. Hebrew Legal System

Under the Hebrew legal system, in the early periods rabbis developed the law. The law was tied closely to religion and the judges were considered to act with divine authority. The Pentateuch, which consists of the five books collectively known as the Torah, served as the central foundation of the Hebrew legal system from approximately 1200 B.C. to 300 B.C.[7] When the Jewish people came under the control of the Persian, Greek, and Roman rulers, they continued to have their own court system. Individual jurists made the decisions because there appears to be no record of the use of a jury, or of counsel to represent the defendant.[8]

D. Chinese Legal System

One of the earliest recorded legal systems in the world is the Chinese legal system, beginning before 2500 B.C. It is unique in that it is the only system that survived for approximately 4,500 years, until the country was taken over by the communists during the twentieth century. Under the ancient Chinese system, there was little difference between civil law and criminal law, because the Chinese believed in the existence of the natural order of things, or the law of nature, and considered the written law good only if it was a correct translation of the law of nature. One person—from emperor down to magistrate—made the decision concerning guilt or innocence. Under the Chinese system, there was little distinction between morality and law, and in determining guilt or innocence. The Chinese legal system employed no lawyers as we know them now. There were notaries and brokers, but no licensed professional class. Only judges made the decisions, but higher courts were permitted to review these decisions.[9]

E. Greek Legal System

Unlike the systems previously discussed, under the early Greek legal system a jury determined whether a person charged with a crime was guilty. According to the records, in Athens in approximately 500 B.C., a jury list of about 6,000 names was drawn up. Ordinarily a panel of 201 names was drawn by lot, but for special cases a panel might consist of as many as 1,000 or 1,500 people. At the trial of Socrates in approximately 400 B.C., 501 jurors voted and found a verdict of guilty by a majority of only 60. In one period in Greek history, the decision of guilt or innocence was entirely in the hands of nonprofessionals. The presiding magistrate was selected by lot and the jurors were drafted from the whole citizen body. Under this system, the defendant conducted his or her own defense and presented his or her own evidence. There was no presiding judge to declare the law, and there was no appeal.[10]

---

[7]   Summum v. City of Ogden, 152 F Supp. 2d 1286, 2001 U.S. Dist. LEXIS 12760, n. 10 (2001). *See* The Panorama of the World's Legal Systems at 104 and 107.

[8]   Wigmore, *supra* note 2.

[9]   *Id.*

[10]   *Id.*

F. Roman Legal System

The Roman instinct for constitutional and legal ideas produced the best and most well-developed system of law. Because this system had the greatest influence on modern evidence law, it is discussed in greater detail.

The Roman legal system can be divided into three periods: the Period of the Republic, the Period of the Early Empire, and the Period of the Later Empire. During the Period of the Republic, the Romans began a code that was chiefly procedural. Even this early period, approximately 400 B.C., has influenced the law of the present day. During this period, the lay courts were made up of judges both of law and of fact, there was little judicial discretion, and there was no appeal. Under this early system, the decision of the tribunal that first tried the case was final.

During the Early Empire Period, professional judges and jurors came to the forefront, while the culmination of Roman judicial science was reached in the second and third centuries A.D. By this time, the Roman legal system had developed far beyond that of any earlier civilization. The administration of justice was separated from general political administration, and schools of law were started for the training of lawyers. Also during this period records of cases were kept, and according to Wigmore, these court records were of a type strikingly similar to those later kept in England.

During the Period of the Later Empire (approximately 550 A.D.), Justinian undertook to reduce the enormous bulk of laws to manageable form. The results were the famous Pandects (or Digest), the Code, the Institute[11] and the Novels. *Black's Law Dictionary* defines the Pandects as "[t]he 50 books constituting Justinian's Digest (one of the four works making up the *Corpus Juris Civilis*) first published in A.D. 533."[12] The Code collected the laws and constitutions of the Emperor Justinian and contained 12 books. The Code is one of four works that are part of the *Corpus Juris Civilis*.[13] The Institute was an "elementary treatise on Roman law in four books."[14] The Institute was also one of the four component parts of the *Corpus Juris Civilis*. The Novels are a collection of 168 of the constitutions issued by Emperor Justinian and subsequent emperors that collectively make up the final component of the *Corpus Juris Civilis*.[15]

Jurisprudence had been one of the most advanced of Roman sciences, and it perished with the fall of the Roman government. As other civilizations appeared and evolved, the legal concepts developed by the Romans, including the use and admissibility of evidence, strongly influenced the later legal procedures. As a matter of fact, Quintilian's teachings, recorded about A.D. 68 to 88, contained legal precepts that are pertinent today and reveal how little the nature of legal practice has changed in 2,000 years. Some of the evidence

---

[11] *Id.*
[12] *See* BLACK'S LAW DICTIONARY (2004).
[13] *Id*
[14] *Id.*
[15] *Id.*

rules, such as those relating to the testimony of witnesses and preparation of real and documentary evidence, are still valid today.

Thus we have examples of ancient systems in which guilt or innocence was determined by professional judges without the assistance of a jury, and examples of procedures in which the determination was made entirely by laypersons who were not instructed in the law. In some civilizations, the legal systems were well developed, while in others the administration of justice was a farce, with the person or group in power making decisions concerning life and liberty without guidelines or precedent.

Not only have the experiences of other cultures affected our own evidence rules today, but they have also served as guides for other modern systems and surely will be considered during future attempts to reach just and fair methods of administering justice.

§ 1.3   Modern Legal Systems—Romanesque System

From the world's 16 systems as described by Wigmore, three primary world systems exist today. These systems have spread beyond the country and people of their origin. These are the Romanesque, the Anglican, and the Mohammedan. The two that are most dominant in modern times and of most importance in Western civilization are the Romanesque and Anglican.

Approximately five centuries after the Roman Empire fell, the law texts that were prepared by Roman scholars were resurrected and became the basis of the legal system in Italy, then in many other countries in Europe, and finally far beyond Europe. In Italy, The city of Bologna in Italy became the center of the study of the Roman law, and legal scholars arrived from all over Europe. During the 1200s, 1300s, and 1400s, thousands of foreign students carried the new advanced ideas of the Roman law to the countries of Europe. Faculties of law sprang up in Spain, France, Germany, and the Netherlands. Roman law, or a modification of it, was codified and nationalized.

In the early 1800s, after three centuries of effort, France completed civil, criminal, and commercial codes and developed rules of civil and criminal procedure. Freedom of contract, recognition of private property and family solidarity were the three ideological pillars of the Code Napoleon.[16] Napoleon himself presided at many of the debates and his wishes shaped the code.[17] This so-called Code Napoleon was soon translated into almost every language, and set the fashion in the other European countries. The Code Napoleon of 1804 served as the basis for Louisiana law[18] and remains a strong influence both in principles and in legal terminology. It was adopted in Austria in 1811, the Netherlands in 1838, Italy in 1865, Spain in 1888, Germany in 1898, and

---

[16]   Gallo v. Gallo, 861 So. 2d 168, 173, 2003 La. LEXIS 3448, n.6 (2003).

[17]   Wigmore, A Panorama of the World's Legal Systems (1928), at 1031.

[18]   Madisonville Boatyard, Ltd. v. Poole, 2001 U.S. Dist. LEXIS 20589 (E.D. La. 2001). *See also* Pepper v. Triplet, 864 So. 2d 181, 189, 2004 La. LEXIS 151 (2004).

Switzerland in 1907. The Code had taken eight centuries from the resurrection of the Roman law in the 1100s to the final formation of the Romanesque law in the 1800s.

When the Romanesque system was first developed, the judges established the rules for gathering and admitting evidence and were the finders of fact as well as the law. At first there were few rules of evidence, but eventually a complex set of rules for obtaining and weighing evidence evolved. As often happens, these rules became merely restrictive—that is, they were not guides, but self-sufficient formulas.

The restrictive rules of evidence became so overdeveloped that they were abolished as being a mere hindrance. To replace this system, the continental nations of France, Germany, and Italy adopted a system that allowed a judge to hear and weigh any evidence, without limitations. Although certain rules have developed in recent times to limit the type and amount of evidence to be considered in this judge-directed system, there are no elaborate controlling rules, such as have been developed in the Anglo-American system. A main reason for this is that the judge's discretion, even when a jury is used, largely determines what evidence will be admitted.

The Romanesque system is now used in many countries throughout the world, from Quebec to Cairo and Budapest to Buenos Aires. Millions of people now live under this system, and of the three world systems today, the Romanesque system is the most extensive. In 1928, it governed almost one-sixth of the world's inhabitants.[19]

§ 1.4 —Anglican System

Unlike the other countries of Europe, England rejected the Romanesque legal system. Like other systems, the Anglican legal system developed in several phases. The first of these was the Period of Building a Common Law; the second was the Period of Rejection of the Romanesque Law; the third was the Period of Cosmopolitanization and Expansion.

The early methods of determining guilt or innocence in England were crude by our modern standards. For example, one kind of trial known as "trial by battle" was brought to the British Isles by William the Conqueror in 1066. Instead of a formal trial before a judge, the accused was required to fight his or her victim or the victim's representative. This method of trial continued until the 1800s, when Parliament finally passed an act abolishing it.[20] The case that finally brought trial by battle to the attention of Parliament involved a man who was accused of murdering his sweetheart. He claimed the right of trial by battle. The judges, after considering the law in the matter, agreed that this type of trial had never been abolished. They therefore allowed the accused to select

---

[19]   WIGMORE at Chapter XV.
[20]   TRACY, HANDBOOK OF THE LAW OF EVIDENCE (1952).

this type of trial. The brother of the deceased refused to fight the accused, and the accused went free.

Following the Norman Conquest, the Norman judges organized the jury to assist in their investigation. However, jurors were not selected as unbiased triers of fact, as is the practice today, but were selected because they had knowledge of the case. An ordinance of Henry II in the twelfth century provided that a certain number of jurors should be selected in criminal cases; it specified that jurors be knights.[21] In contrast to modern procedure, the prospective juror was excused if he was ignorant of the facts of the case. The jurors were first left to their own discretion in the use of evidence and were allowed to go among the people in the community and ask for information outside of court. During this period, the jurors were forbidden to call in outside witnesses. However, starting in approximately 1500, witnesses were used more frequently, and gradually the requirement that the triers of the facts possess knowledge of the crime came to be less important. By the end of the 1600s, the jury was allowed to receive no information except that which was offered in court. Initially, the jury served as a substitute for trial by battle, compurgation, and ordeal,[22] but during this period, it evolved into a body that listened to evidence and used logic to render a verdict. Thus, in a period of three or four hundred years, there was a complete reversal of the juror's role.

Given the development of the jury system and the English tradition of protecting the rights of the individual, the need for guidance was obvious. Both the judges and the laymen who participated in the trial recognized that the jurors must have guidance to prevent them from being misled by false testimony or by evidence that was not relevant to the issue. Accordingly, in the 1600s and 1700s, numerous exclusionary rules were developed that kept certain kinds of evidence from the jurors unless the evidence met various tests, as determined by the judge. These rules of admissibility were based upon long judicial experience with parties, witnesses, and jurors. The purpose of these rules was to allow the jury to consider only evidence that was as free as possible from the risks of irrelevancy, confusion, and fraud.[23]

The Anglican system is now followed in England, Scotland, Ireland; Sri Lanka, Hong Kong, and some other countries in Asia; to a great extent in India and some African countries, Canada and, of course, the United States. From the very beginning, the American colonies followed the English law. For example, part of Virginia's plan in 1606 was that "the disposing of all causes happening within the colonies should be done as near to the common law of England and the equity thereof as may be."[24]

---

[21]   *Id.*

[22]   Crist v. Bretz, 437 U.S. 28, 36, 1978 U.S. LEXIS 107, n.12 (1978). Black's Law Dictionary (2004) refers to compurgation as a trial where a defendant could bring friends, frequently numbering 11, to state that they believed the defendant was telling the truth. It explains that ordeal was a "primitive form of trial in which an accused person was subjected to a usually dangerous or painful physical test, the result being considered a divine revelation of the person's guilt or innocence."

[23]   Wigmore on Evidence 5 (1935).

[24]   *Id.*

§ 1.5 Development of the Rules of Evidence in the United States

During the past two centuries, a system of rules for the presentation of evidence has been established in the United States. In some instances, the rules are the result of centuries of deep thought and experience. In other instances, the rules have been established in a haphazard manner without much thought. Although the United States inherited the English system, rules concerning the admissibility of evidence have taken separate developmental paths and are not the same in the two countries. Federal evidence rules are not necessarily the same in the various states within the United States and even states that have adopted a version of the Federal Rules of Evidence have some different interpretations. Due to legislation and court decisions, some of which interpret constitutional provisions, the rules for obtaining and weighing evidence are now more restrictive in the United States than in England.

Certainly the rules are not perfect and are always subject to change— either by the courts or by statute. As stated in *Funk v. United States*:

> The fundamental basis upon which all rules of evidence must rest if they are to rest upon reason is their adaptation to the successful development of the truth. And, since experience is of all teachers the most dependable, and since experience also is a continuous process, it follows that a rule of evidence at one time thought necessary to the ascertainment of the truth should yield to the experience of a succeeding generation whenever that experience has clearly demonstrated the fallacy or unwisdom of the old rule.[25]

The rules of evidence are changed not only by court decisions, but also by congressional or legislative enactments. For example, in 1878, Congress changed federal law to allow a defendant in a federal criminal case to be a witness at his own request, but included a provision that where a defendant did not desire to testify, no negative presumption could be drawn.[26] In Illinois, the legislature provided, under the Sexually Dangerous Persons Act, that evidence of a defendant's prior crimes and punishments, if any, may be admitted against a defendant[27] despite a general rule against admitting a defendant's past criminal acts in a subsequent proceeding. More recently, Congress has enacted specific legislation relating to the admissibility of confessions, wiretap evidence, and eyewitness testimony.[28]

---

[25]   290 U.S. 371 (1933). *See* case in Part II.

[26]   *See* Reagan v. United States, 157 U.S. 301, 305 (1878). "By the Act of March 16, 1878, c. 37, 20 Stat. 30, a defendant in a criminal case may, 'at his own request but not otherwise, be a competent witness.'" The modern version can be found at 18 U.S.C. § 3481 Competency of accused. (2006).

[27]   *See* 725 ILCS 205/5 (2006).

[28]   *See* 18 U.S.C. §§ 2515 and 2518 (2006).

A. *Adoption of the Federal Rules of Evidence*

In an effort to obtain more uniformity in court procedures, the United States Supreme Court in 1972 adopted the *Rules of Evidence for United States Courts and Magistrates*. Congress initially blocked their effective use until it was satisfied with the wording of the rules. Subsequently, in 1987, the scope of these rules was extended to include proceedings before United States bankruptcy judges.[29]

A study of the development and application of this set of rules demonstrates how rules of evidence are changed by legislative action. The Supreme Court order of November 20, 1972, directed the federal district courts and United States magistrates to follow these rules after July 1, 1973. However, in accordance with federal laws, the proposed rules were required to be transmitted to Congress for approval. The House Judiciary Committee wrestled with the provisions for nearly a year, and finally approved a modified version in early 1974 by a vote of 377 to 130. Before approving the Supreme Court draft of the rules of evidence, the House Judiciary Committee changed provisions concerning privileged communications. The current enhancement of the Federal Rules of Evidence became effective in December 2006; however, some revisions are pending but not yet effective.

In explaining the purpose and construction of the Federal Rules of Evidence, the drafters included this comment:

> These rules shall be construed to secure fairness in administration, elimination of unjustifiable expense and delay, and promotion of growth and development of a law of evidence to the end that the truth may be ascertained and proceedings justly determined.[30]

The adoption of the Federal Rules of Evidence has contributed to establishing a uniform body of law. However, there is some doubt that the adoption of the rules has achieved the goal of simplicity that its drafters envisioned.[31]

B. *Uniform Rules of Evidence*

As Congress worked toward adoption of the Federal Rules of Evidence, the National Conference of Commissioners on Uniform State Laws prepared new Uniform Rules of Evidence patterned after the Federal Rules. In 1999, the Commissioners approved an updated draft of the Uniform Rules of Evidence that reflected recent amendments to the Federal Rules. This codification of evidence laws was designed and suggested for adoption by the state legislatures and has been periodically revised to keep it in fair conformity with the Federal Rules,[32] which federal courts have followed since 1975.

---

[29]   Federal Rules of Evidence, Title 28 United States Code (1972). These rules, updated through 2005 by Congress, are included as Appendix I and are referred to throughout this text.

[30]   FED. R. EVID. 102.

[31]   WIGMORE ON EVIDENCE § 6.5 (1988).

[32]   Uniform Rules of Evidence (1999). National Conference of Commissioners on Uniform State Laws. The Table of Contents for the Uniform Rules of Evidence is included in the Appendix.

To avoid confusion and encourage uniformity, the numbering systems for the two sets of rules are consistent. As the Federal Rules have been changed by Congress, the Commissioners on Uniform State Laws have made an effort to bring the Uniform Rules into conformity.

As the evidence rules followed in the federal and state courts of the United States today are products of a combination of legislative acts (as discussed in previous paragraphs) and court decisions, a study of evidence requires an examination of federal and state legislation and the cases interpreting the rules.

§ 1.6 Application of the Rules of Evidence in State and Federal Courts

The history of the United States and the separation of powers concept have influenced the legislative bodies and courts in establishing evidence rules. As a general rule, questions of evidence are governed by the laws of the forum, i.e., the state rules of evidence apply in state courts, and the federal rules apply in federal courts. If the state has jurisdiction over the parties and the cause of action, the rules of evidence and the laws of that state generally will apply.

The United States Constitution gives Congress the power to make regulations guiding the Supreme Court and to create tribunals inferior to the Supreme Court. The rules of evidence established by Congress are to be followed in federal courts. However, no codification of rules can be applied without court interpretation. Therefore, one must carefully examine federal cases, especially United States Supreme Court cases, in applying the law governing the admissibility of evidence in federal courts.

While the legislation of each jurisdiction is supreme, and state rules of evidence provide general guides in state courts, legislation is subject to such limitations as may be prescribed in federal constitutional provisions applicable to the states. For example, the United States Supreme Court has determined that a state rule requiring that a defendant desiring to testify in a criminal case must do so prior to the admission of any other defense testimony violates the Fifth Amendment to the Constitution and the due process clause of the Fourteenth Amendment.[33] Also, where constitutional authority exists, Congress may establish rules relating to the admissibility of evidence in state courts. Demonstrative of such principle is the Omnibus Crime Control and Safe Streets Act of 1968—Title 18 of the United States Code—which provides that evidence relating to wire or oral communications that has been intercepted in violation of that section shall not be used "in or before any court, grand jury, department . . . or other authority of the United States, state or political subdivision thereof." [34]

---

[33]   Brooks v. Tennessee, 406 U.S. 605 (1972).

[34]   For a more thorough discussion of the powers of the federal and state governments, *see* KANOVITZ & KANOVITZ, CONSTITUTIONAL LAW, ch. 1 (10th ed. 2005).

Even though the adoption of the Federal Rules of Evidence and the Uniform Rules of Evidence has not achieved the goal of simplicity that the drafters envisioned, these rules have produced more uniformity and consistency. Because the Federal Rules of Evidence regulate evidentiary matters in all federal courts of the United States, including bankruptcy courts and proceedings held before United States magistrate judges, uniformity has been accomplished to a substantial degree in the federal system. With recognition that our nation is based on a federalist system, there naturally is far less uniformity among the states. At one point, only 36 jurisdictions had adopted evidence codes that followed the model of the Federal Rules and/or the Uniform Rules patterned after the Federal Rules.[35] Currently, 42 states as well as Guam, Puerto Rico, the Virgin Islands, and the United States military have adopted evidence codes based partially or completely on the Federal Rules of Evidence.[36] California, Georgia, Illinois, Kansas, Massachusetts, Missouri, New York, and Virginia have not adopted a version of the Federal Rules.[37] The District of Columbia has not adopted the Federal Rules of Evidence for the District's courts, but the Federal Rules, of course, apply in federal courts sitting within the District of Columbia.[38]

Because the Federal Rules of Evidence have had a major impact on state laws and evidence rules, and because the states have increasingly looked to federal decisions for interpretations, provisions of the Federal Rules of Evidence and federal cases interpreting the Federal Rules are cited throughout this text.[39]

The Federal Rules and the Uniform Rules have generated a reform of the evidence rules. However, the states have not given up their independence on evidence issues. State courts are free to interpret evidentiary rules in a manner different from federal courts and interpretations offered by the courts of sister states. To develop a more comprehensive understanding of the rules, state cases as well as federal cases are cited and examined. Nevertheless, because some state evidence rules differ from both the Federal Rules and the Uniform Rules, it is necessary to consult the laws and decisions of the state that has jurisdiction over the parties.[40]

---

[35] Charles W. Gamble, *Drafting, Adopting and Interpreting the New Alabama Rules of Evidence: A Reporter's Perspective*, 47 ALA. L. REV. 1, n. 55 (1995).

[36] *See* 6-T Weinstein's Federal Evidence, "Table of State and Military Adaptations of Federal Rules of Evidence." (Mathew Bender 2006). The Appendix contains a list of states that have adopted the Uniform Rules of Evidence with the effective dates and the statutory citations.

[37] *Id.*

[38] *Id.*

[39] The Federal Rules of Evidence, as amended, are included in Appendix I.

[40] For a comprehensive coverage of the differences in state rules and interpretations, *see* JOSEPH & SALTZBURG, EVIDENCE IN AMERICA, THE FEDERAL RULES IN THE STATES (1994).

§ 1.7 Future Development of the Rules of Evidence

In studying rules of criminal evidence, it must be recognized that our rules are a product of progressive growth and adaptation to new circumstances. The rules of evidence will continue to change and, in fact, probably will change more rapidly in the next several years as judicial officials and members of legislatures attempt to fashion a more effective system to meet the needs of an evolving society. Evidence rule changes may reflect some new pressing social needs such as allowing admission into evidence of prior sexual offenses by a defendant when other offenses might not be admissible.[41] Alterations to the Dead Man's statutes indicate that the old fears of fraud by witnesses against the dead have been overblown and the usual avenues of cross-examination may work perfectly well.[42] It may be that admitting evidence of prior sex offenses will be seen as unfair and will later be rejected, while changes to the Dead Man's statutes will be seen as appropriate for the ages and will have lasting effects.

Demonstrative of evolutionary development of the rules and interpretations of the rules of evidence is the change made to the marital testimonial privilege recognized by federal courts. Prior to *Trammel v. United States*,[43] both husband and wife were considered holders of the testimonial privilege and could prevent the other from testifying against a defendant spouse. The original theory involved the protection and promotion of marital harmony. The Supreme Court reasoned that if "one spouse is willing to testify against the other in a criminal proceeding—whatever the motivation—their relationship is almost certainly in disrepair; there is probably little in the way of marital harmony for the privilege to preserve."[44] In such a situation, in federal courts, the old rule had to give way to the modern interpretation of the marital testimonial privilege favoring admissibility of the testimony offered by a willing witness spouse.

The application of the rules of evidence to the administration of the law is and should be within the sound discretion of the judiciary. However, contrary to statements made in some cases, recent decisions of reviewing courts appear to require more strict application of the rules of evidence, thus leaving lower courts with less discretion concerning the administration of the business of the court and the admissibility of evidence.

Acts of Congress have effects on the admission of evidence and executive branch orders may have some similar effects in other types of proceedings. Following the attacks of September 11, 2001, Congress passed the USA PATRIOT Act, which changed some of the ways in which the federal government is permitted to collect and use evidence.[45] Although the Patriot Act was

---

[41]   29 HAMLINE L. REV. 177 (2006).
[42]   53 CLEV. ST. L. REV. 75 (2005).
[43]   444 U.S. 40, 1980 U.S. LEXIS 84 (1980).
[44]   *Id.* at 52.
[45]   PUB. L. NO. 107-56, 115 STAT. 272 (2001).

designed to make the nation safer from terrorist activity, some civil libertarians became concerned that the new powers granted to federal law enforcement could have the effect of curtailing some civil rights. Among other things that affect the use or admission of evidence in some cases, the President of the United States issued an Executive Order that limited some indictments, jury trials, and other civil liberties of some non-citizen individuals accused of terrorist activities.[46] The same Executive Order directed that the defense secretary issue orders that purported to limit admission of evidence in special tribunals in cases of trials of international terrorists.[47] However, the Foreign Intelligence Surveillance Act of 1978 authorized some evidentiary searches prior to obtaining a warrant, but the statute anticipated that a warrant would be forthcoming in most cases. The Act excluded the use of any evidence unlawfully obtained through illegal electronic searches and surveillance.[48] Congress passed the Omnibus Crime Control and Safe Streets Act of 1968, which included a Title III section that regulated the manner in which wiretap evidence could be admitted in court. As part of Title III, the Congress provided that evidence seized illegally in violation of the statute would not be admissible in courts or other venues.[49] In another adjustment of search and seizure law, the Congress amended the Foreign Intelligence Surveillance Act by passing relevant provisions of the Patriot Act that had the effect of limiting the use of the Foreign Intelligence Surveillance Act for domestic law enforcement purposes.[50] In summary, the Congress has adjusted the admission of seized evidence through statutory enactments that mirrored public policy initiatives of interest groups and to accommodate the needs of the executive branch. The general thrust has been to allow more evidence to be admitted into court when the legal proceeding involved terrorism or related criminal matters.

Have the restrictive rules of evidence become overdeveloped? Perhaps our society has reached the point where some of the rationales for exclusionary rules are no longer valid and the rules no longer provide appropriate results. However, it would prove unwise to abolish our system entirely, as was done in France in the 1700s. Appropriate changes should be made by the courts and legislatures after careful study and with regard to the objectives to be achieved. Therefore, not only is it necessary that all who are involved in the criminal justice system be aware of the rules of evidence as they exist today, but everyone must also be familiar with the history of the rules, keep up with changes as they occur, and take an active part in recommending improvements when time and events have dictated that changes need to be made to some of the current rules of evidence.

---

[46]   51 AM. U.L. REV. 1081 (2002).

[47]   Id.

[48]   82 B.U.L. REV. 555 (2002).

[49]   Id.

[50]   28 HARV. J.L. & PUB. POL'Y 319 (2005).

§ 1.8   Summary

In every society efforts have been made to determine the guilt or innocence of a person charged with violating the rules of that society. Some of the world's legal systems were built on sound foundations and have continued for many centuries. However, other legal systems disappeared when the governments responsible for developing them were overthrown, or when governments developed other methods for determining guilt or innocence. The experience of history has proven to be a strong teacher that has preserved evidence of prior legal systems so that nations today can harness the knowledge of the past to help the law of evidence evolve in a productive path toward the future.

In England, after centuries of experimentation, a system for determining guilt or innocence developed by utilizing parts of earlier systems. With the development of the jury system, a complex set of rules for determining the admissibility of evidence gradually developed. Although a jury system patterned after that of England was adopted by the United States, the rules for admitting the evidence have been changed by our courts and legislative bodies. Today, the rules of exclusion are stricter in the United States than in England.

The rules for determining the admissibility of evidence have changed and will continue to evolve. In this country, judges, legislators, and other criminal justice personnel must work together to seek better methods for determining guilt and protecting society, while at the same time protecting the rights of the individual.

Approach to the Study
of Criminal Evidence   2

The word "evidence" is applied to that which renders evident; and is defined to be any matter of fact, the effect, tendency, or design of which is to produce in the mind a persuasion, affirmative or disaffirmative, of the existence of some other matter of fact.

State v. Ward, 61 Vt. 153, 17 A. 483 (1889)

Chapter Outline

Key Terms and Concepts

circumstantial evidence	legal evidence
competent evidence	material evidence
corroborative evidence	*prima facie* evidence
cumulative evidence	proof
direct evidence	real evidence
documentary evidence	relevant evidence
evidence	testimony
hearsay evidence	

§ 2.1 Introduction

Before searching the cases and statutes for evidence guidelines on specific issues such as the admissibility of hearsay evidence or the exclusionary effect of evidentiary privileges, developing an understanding of the general concepts and definitions will prove invaluable. Rational thought and history have shaped the rules regulating the admissibility of evidence, while similar reasoning and fairness have provided the justifications for excluding pertinent evidence. The overall goal of the rules of evidence is to produce the truth while reducing the chance for falsehood. A knowledge of these rules and the rationale used by the courts in framing the rules that exclude some evidence assists immeasurably in understanding the specific rules of evidence. Under the Anglican system (with the jury deciding the facts), evidence is not admitted when it would be unfairly prejudicial to the accused.

Although the rules of evidence generally apply in both civil and criminal cases, there are some important differences that are of special interest to those involved in criminal justice. These differences are discussed in this chapter. In addition, the flow and use of evidence from the time it is located, processed and analyzed by the investigator to the time it is considered by the parole board are discussed. In Chapter 4 the use of evidence at the trial is more particularly considered.

§ 2.2 Definitions

In order to fully understand the discussion of the rules of evidence, it is necessary to define some of the words and phrases used. Other words or phrases are defined in future chapters as they are discussed.

A. Evidence

Evidence has been defined as *the means employed for the purpose of proving an unknown or disputed fact*, and it is either judicial or extrajudicial. Every determination of the judgment, whatever its subject may be, is the result of evidence.[1] Evidence is any information upon which a person can base a decision. For example, before a used car is purchased, the car dealer is questioned as to the condition of the car, and in some instances, the car is taken to another mechanic for an inspection. All of this information, or evidence, is then considered before a decision is reached as to whether the purchase will be made.

B. Legal Evidence

Legal evidence is defined in *Black's Law Dictionary* as "[a]ll admissible evidence, both oral and documentary, of such a character that it reasonably and substantially proves the point, rather than merely raising suspicion or conjecture."[2] Legal evidence is that which is used or is intended to be used at the trial or at inquiries before courts, judges, commissioners, referees, etc. To state this more succinctly, evidence as used in law means "that which demonstrates or makes clear or ascertains the truth of the very fact or point in issue, either on the one side or the other."[3]

C. Direct Evidence

Direct evidence is "evidence that is based on personal knowledge or observation and that, if true, proves a fact without inference or presumption."[4] Direct evidence has also been defined as that which immediately points to a question at issue. For example, a witness testifies that he saw the acts that constituted the precise fact to be proved. If, in a homicide case, the witness testifies that he saw the accused stab the victim, this would be direct evidence.

D. Circumstantial Evidence

Circumstantial evidence, sometimes called indirect evidence, is so called because the truth is discovered through inferences of probabilities arising from an association of facts. Circumstantial evidence means that *the existence of a*

---

[1]   RICE, LAW OF EVIDENCE (1893).
[2]   BLACK'S LAW DICTIONARY (8th ed. 2004).
[3]   Leonard v. State, 100 Ohio St. 456, 127 N.E. 464 (1919), quoting Blackstone. (3 BLACKSTONE'S COMMENTARIES 367).
[4]   BLACK'S LAW DICTIONARY (8th ed. 2004).

principal fact is only inferred from the circumstances.[5] One judge stated that the only difference between direct and circumstantial evidence is that direct evidence is more immediate and has fewer links in the chain of connection between the premise and the conclusion. An example of circumstantial evidence would be the testimony of a police officer that he apprehended a subject who had a bag of money that had been covered in red dye from an exploding dye pack. It should be noted that circumstantial evidence has the same value, force, and weight as direct evidence.[6]

E. Testimony

Testimony is evidence that comes to the court through witnesses speaking under oath or affirmation. In some instances, the word *testimony* is used synonymously with the word *evidence*. It is obvious when considering the two words, however, that testimony is limited to that which is oral, while evidence includes writings, physical objects, and other forms. *Evidence* is the broader term and includes *testimony*, which is only one type of evidence.[7]

F. Documentary Evidence

Documentary evidence consists of tangible objects that have the capacity to convey a fact or to establish the truth or untruth of a proposition at issue. Documentary evidence includes all types of traditional documents, records, photographs, pictures, X-ray images, drawings, audio- and videotapes, as well as writings that are not objectionable under the various exclusionary rules.[8] Modern methods of storing information have expanded the concept of documentary evidence to include e-mail, computer diskettes, memory sticks, flash drives, hard drives, and optically stored information. With documentary evidence, it is the object or thing that speaks to offer evidence. "Evidence supplied by a writing or other document, which must be authenticated before the evidence is admissible."[9] A ransom note in a kidnapping case and a printout from a Web site in a child pornography prosecution are examples of documentary evidence.

G. Real Evidence

Real evidence, or "physical" evidence, has been defined as *a fact, the existence of which is perceptible to the senses.* As compared to an intangible concept, real evidence possesses a physical essence and existence that can be observed, touched, and handled. A clearer definition is "physical evidence (such as a knife wound) that itself plays a direct part in the incident in question."[10] Real evidence also includes weapons or implements used in the com-

---

[5]   Twin City Fire Ins. Co. v. Lonas, 255 Ky. 717, 75 S.W.2d 348 (1934).
[6]   United States v. Ortiz, 447 F.3d 28, 32, 2006 U.S. App. LEXIS 10961 (1st Cir. 2006).
[7]   31 C.J.S. EVIDENCE § 3 (1964).
[8]   *See* FED. R. EVID. 1001.
[9]   BLACK'S LAW DICTIONARY (8th ed. 2004).
[10]   *Id.*

mission of a crime as well as evidence of the physical appearance of a place (as obtained by a jury when the members are taken to view a crime scene).

H. *Prima Facie Evidence*

Prima facie evidence is the body of evidence that, if unexplained, uncontradicted, or not called into question, is sufficient to carry a case to the jury and to sustain a verdict in favor of the issue that it supports. This type of evidence, however, may be contradicted by other evidence. The phrase prima facie means "at first sight" or "on the first appearance" or "on the face of it." Prima facie evidence is "evidence that will establish a fact or sustain a judgment unless contradictory evidence is produced."[11] For example, where there was testimony that a defendant was observed at the crime scene, such testimony, if believed, would be prima facie evidence that the defendant was present. Such prima facie evidence exists unless or until contradictory evidence is introduced by the opposing side.

I. *Proof*

Proof is the effect of evidence; that is, it is *the establishment of fact by evidence*. Even though the terms proof and evidence are sometimes used synonymously, they are different. Properly speaking, evidence is only the medium of proof; proof is the effect of evidence. Proof implies persuasion and proof has been defined as "the conviction or persuasion of the mind of a judge or a jury, by the exhibition of evidence, of the reality of a fact alleged."[12]

J. *Cumulative Evidence*

Cumulative evidence is *that which goes to prove what has already been established by other evidence*. In legal phraseology, it means evidence from the same or a new witness that simply repeats, in substance and effect, or adds to, what has already been offered in court. For example, where 10 people witnessed a defendant assault a person on a public street, to have all 10 come to court and render virtually the exact same story identifying the defendant could be considered cumulative evidence. Having two or three witnesses explain what was observed would generally be appropriate and not be considered cumulative evidence.

K. *Corroborative Evidence*

Corroborative evidence is *evidence that is supplementary to evidence already given in court*. It tends to strengthen or confirm previously admitted evidence. It is additional evidence of a different character, but it seeks to prove

---

[11]   BLACK'S LAW DICTIONARY (8th ed. 2004). *See also* People v. Tibbetts, 351 Ill. App. 3d 921, 927, 815 N.E.2d 409, 414, 2004 Ill. App. LEXIS 975 (2004) and State v. Rawlins, 166 N.C. App. 160, 167, 601 S.E.2d 267, 272, 2004 N.C. App. LEXIS 1645 (2004).

[12]   Ellis v. Wolfe-Shoemaker Motor Co., 227 Mo. 508, 55 S.W.2d 309 (1932).

the same point as the earlier evidence. (For example, historically, a conviction cannot stand based solely upon a defendant's confession without corroborating evidence.) Such corroborating evidence may be the testimony of a witness who saw the accused at the scene of the crime. Similarly, evidence from a conspirator made during the existence of the conspiracy may provide corroborating evidence of the crime that will permit the use of the confession.

L. Relevant Evidence

Relevant evidence is *evidence that has any tendency to make the existence of any fact that is of consequence to the determination of the action more probable or less probable than it would be without the evidence.*[13] To be considered relevant, the evidence must help one party prove or disprove a fact while not being unfairly prejudicial to the opposing party's case. Evidence of a past conviction might help the prosecution gain a conviction, but the admission of the evidence of the prior conviction would be not necessarily be fair to a defendant.

M. Material Evidence

Material evidence is *that which goes to the substantial matters in dispute or has a legitimate and effective influence or bearing on the decision of the case.* Material evidence has been defined as "[e]vidence having some logical connection with the facts of consequence or the issues."[14]

N. Competent Evidence

Although the terms *relevancy*, *competency*, and *materiality* are frequently used conjunctively, a matter may be relevant and material to an issue but still be incompetent, and therefore inadmissible under the established rules of evidence. Competent evidence is *evidence that, in legal proceedings, is admissible for the purpose of proving a relevant fact.* The competency of evidence depends on whether it is of the sort or type that may be accepted on any issue to which it is relevant.[15] Evidence may be made competent (or incompetent) by legislation or judicial construction.[16]

O. Hearsay Evidence

Hearsay is *an out-of-court statement, other than one made by the declarant while testifying at the trial or hearing, that is offered in court to prove the truth of the matter asserted.*[17] A witness's statement based upon what someone

---

[13]   FED. R. EVID. 401; For further discussion concerning relevant evidence, *see* Chapter 7.

[14]   BLACK'S LAW DICTIONARY (8th ed. 2004).

[15]   Maddox v. News Syndicate Co., 176 F.2d 897 (2d Cir. 1949).

[16]   Funk v. United States, 290 U.S. 371, 64 S. Ct. 212, 78 L. Ed. 2d 369 (1933).

[17]   FED. R. EVID. 801(c); For further definitions of hearsay and terms related to hearsay evidence, *see* Chapter 12.

else has told him or her, and not from personal observation or knowledge, con-stitutes hearsay evidence. As a general rule, hearsay evidence is not admissi-ble unless it falls under one of the exceptions to the rule excluding hearsay evidence. Where an eyewitness has explained to a police officer that the wit-ness observed the defendant breaking into a store, the officer would generally not be permitted to tell the court what the witness told the officer because such testimony would constitute hearsay evidence if offered by the police officer for proof of its truth.

§ 2.3 Reasons for the Rules of Evidence

By the seventeenth century, the evolution of the jury function was well advanced, and the jury depended on the testimony of witnesses for facts on which to base a verdict. Members of juries were generally ordinary laypeople, impressionable and unacquainted with the law; it was therefore recognized that specific rules for filtering the evidence were necessary. To protect the accused, rules were gradually developed to help assure that evidence was dependable, credible, and trustworthy before it could be considered. Eviden-tiary rules, then, were developed in part to keep out evidence that was untrust-worthy or was unduly prejudicial to the accused. Also, it was obviously necessary for the court to establish rules to carry out the proceedings in an orderly and efficient manner. To achieve these and other lesser objectives, the courts and legislatures have formulated our present-day evidentiary rules.

Efforts have been made to state in more specific terms the reasons for the rules of evidence and to account for the many varied rules that must be inter-preted by the courts. As these rules have been developed by gradual evolution and in fact are still developing, it is difficult to categorize them and to explain why each rule exists. Although it appears that in some instances there is an effort to rationalize or justify an outmoded or outdated rule, there is logic to the explanations given for most of the specific rules of evidence.

§ 2.4 Reasons for Excluding Evidence

Much evidence is excluded even though it would help the jury or the court in determining the true facts concerning the matters at issue. The reasons for excluding the evidence have been numerous and they are phrased in many ways. An effort is made here to categorize these reasons in order to make them more meaningful and understandable. The general reasons for excluding oth-erwise pertinent evidence are listed below.

A. Protect Interests and Relationships

A court weighs the value of having all of the facts before the court against the protection of certain interests and relationships, and it may decide to exclude relevant evidence. Such interests and relationships are regarded, rightly or wrongly, as having sufficient social importance to justify some incidental sacrifice of sources of fact needed in the administration of justice.[18] Protecting interests and relationships by the exclusion of otherwise relevant evidence may also harm the search for the truth. Examples of evidence excluded on the basis of this public policy of protection of relationships are:

1. Evidence protected by the husband and wife confidential communication privilege.
2. Evidence protected by the husband and wife testimonial privilege.
3. Evidence protected by the attorney-client privilege.
4. Evidence protected by the penitent-confessor privilege.[19]

B. Avoid Undue Prejudice to the Accused

Some evidence that would be relevant to the issue is not admitted because of the risk that it might create undue or unfair prejudice to the defendant's case. For example, the criminal record of the accused generally is not admitted, except to impeach the testimony of the accused, because to admit this evidence would unfairly and unduly prejudice the accused in the minds of the jurors. Evidence that might indicate the guilt of the accused would appropriate for admission, but to allow evidence of prior crimes might cause the jury to convict based on the evidence of the prior crimes and not on evidence concerning the case presently in court. In some cases, gruesome photographs should not be admitted into evidence, even though relevant, because to do so might inflame the jury with unfair prejudice against the accused.

C. Prohibit Consideration of Unreliable Evidence

Evidence considered to be unreliable is generally excluded from admission in court, even though it might have a bearing on the case. This category of evidence includes hearsay evidence and most lay witness opinion evidence.[20] To illustrate, the testimony of a police officer that a bystander told him that the accused was driving the car that had been involved in a bank robbery is not admissible. Such evidence is considered hearsay and, although it possesses some relevance, is not considered sufficiently reliable for use in court.

---

[18] McCormick, Evidence § 72 (4th ed. 1992).
[19] Testimonial privileges are discussed in Chapter 10.
[20] These rules are discussed in Chapters 11 and 12.

D. Reduce Violations of Constitutional Safeguards

In order to ensure respect for constitutional provisions regulating search and seizure as well as to ensure respect for other constitutional rights, the Supreme Court of the United States, in the latter half of the twentieth century, developed rules of exclusion to be applied when evidence has been illegally seized. Until the beginning of the previous century, it was almost universally accepted that evidence was admissible even though it was obtained illegally.[21] However, the courts now reason that such evidence as that secured by an illegal search and seizure, evidence obtained in violation of the self-incrimination provisions, or evidence taken in violation of the right-to-counsel provisions, should generally be excluded, even though relevant to the case. In fact, such evidence might provide the only basis for a conviction.[22] The rationale for excluding such evidence has not been consistent, but generally, exclusion has been justified on the ground that by rejecting such evidence, there will be little incentive for law enforcement officials to violate the Constitution in an effort to obtain incriminating evidence.

E. Conserve Time

Cumulative evidence is evidence that is unnecessary and repetitive, and thus may be excluded upon proper objection by one of the parties or upon the court's own motion. The admission of cumulative evidence would otherwise constitute a waste of the court's time as well as the time of the individuals involved. Rejection of cumulative evidence is consistent with and follows the principle of judicial economy.

There have been arguments that some of the historical reasons for excluding relevant evidence have long since disappeared, leaving the technical rules without a logical basis. In some instances, so many exceptions have developed that the rules are no longer meaningful. However, most of the justification for the rules is still valid and should be carefully considered, because understanding the reasons behind the rules can help one to understand their application.

§ 2.5 Rules of Evidence in Criminal Cases Compared to Rules of Evidence in Civil Cases

An early English court stated that there is no distinction between the rules of evidence in criminal and civil cases. The court continued:

> What may be received in the one case, may be received in the other; and what is rejected in the one ought to be rejected in the other. A fact must be established by the same evidence, whether it is to be followed by a criminal or civil consequence.[23]

---

[21]   *See* Weeks v. United States, 232 U.S. 383 (1914).

[22]   Discussed more thoroughly in Chapter 16.

[23]   Rex v. Watson, 2 Stark. 116 (1817); Lord Melville's Case, 29 How. St. Tr. 763 (1806).

In some states, the civil rules of evidence have been made applicable in criminal cases by case law or by statute unless otherwise provided.[24] For example, a Washington statute holds that "[t]he rules of evidence in civil actions, so far as practicable, shall be applied to criminal prosecutions."[25] There are, however, some differences in the current rules and in the application of the rules of evidence that arise solely, or more frequently, in criminal cases. Constitutional law cases that regulate how and when a suspect or arrestee may be questioned have produced rules relating to admission or exclusion of evidence in criminal cases that have no comparable place in civil cases.[26] In addition, evidence produced by searches and seizures may be excluded on federal or state constitutional grounds where police conduct failed to meet constitutional standards.[27]

In civil cases, the contending parties negotiate through the legal process on terms of approximate equality, with no legal presumption favoring the plaintiff or defendant. In criminal cases, the law seeks to protect the person accused of a crime, and a presumption accompanies him or her from the time of apprehension to the moment of conviction: the presumption that he or she is innocent until proven guilty. Throughout the trial, the burden of proof remains on the state, and the prosecution must prove guilt beyond a reasonable doubt, rather than by a preponderance of the evidence.[28] Because of this presumption of innocence, courts have developed special rules for overcoming the presumption.

In addition to requiring the state to meet a higher (or greater) standard of proof in a criminal prosecution, the rules differ in a few other instances. For example, the rule concerning the admission of a dying declaration is different in a criminal case[29] and a doctor-patient privilege may not apply in some types of criminal prosecutions.[30]

The degree of proof must be stronger in a criminal case because, with few exceptions,[31] the accused must be found guilty by all 12 members of the jury, while in a civil case a unanimous decision may not be required. Logic suggests that it should be easier to obtain a money judgment against a defendant in a civil case than to send a defendant to jail or prison in a criminal case. For example, a defendant who has been acquitted in a criminal assault prosecution

---

[24] Mich. Comp. Laws Ann. § 768.22 (1) (2006). "The rules of evidence in civil actions, insofar as the same are applicable, shall govern in all criminal and quasi criminal proceedings except as otherwise provided by law."

[25] Wash. Rev. Code § 10.58.010 (2006).

[26] See Miranda v. Arizona, 384 U.S. 436, 1966 U.S. LEXIS 2817 (1966).

[27] See Mapp v. Ohio, 367 U.S. 643, 1961 U.S. LEXIS 812 (1961).

[28] Apprendi v. New Jersey, 530 U.S. 466 at 483 (2000).

[29] 29 Am. Jur. 2d Evidence § 74. See also Chapter 12.

[30] See State v. Mayl, 106 Ohio St. 3d 207, 2005 Ohio 4629, 833 N.E.2d 1216, 2005 Ohio LEXIS 2063 (2005).

[31] See Johnson v. Louisiana, 406 U.S. 356 (1972), which upheld a conviction in a criminal case in which the state statute provided that 9 of 12 jurors may find the defendant guilty. But see Burch v. Louisiana, 441 U.S. 130 (1979), which held that a state defendant who has been placed on trial for a nonpetty offense and is subsequently convicted by a nonunanimous six-person jury has been denied his right to a trial by jury.

may be found liable for a monetary judgment in a subsequent civil case brought by the original victim based on the conduct that was the subject of the criminal case.

Although the distinction between criminal evidence and civil evidence may be slight when defining the rules, from a practical standpoint there is a great deal of difference. While a jury may accept weak evidence in determining the rights of parties in a civil case, the members of the jury are less likely to accept such evidence when life or liberty is at issue. To the prosecutor, this means that evidence must be presented that will be given great weight by the jury, and sufficient evidence must be presented in court to overcome any reasonable doubt on the part of the jury or judge. In a criminal case, the judge must protect the rights of the defendant. Any act or conduct by the judge that indicates the slightest bias or unfairness may be grounds for reversal.[32]

§ 2.6 Pretrial Flow of Evidence

Although much valuable evidence is made available in court by laypersons who are not connected with the criminal justice process, in most instances police officers and investigators are responsible for discovering, evaluating, protecting, analyzing, and presenting evidence. If the officer does not present the evidence herself, she is still primarily responsible for guiding the flow of evidence, at least until the indictment or information stage.

The officer must develop and preserve the evidence in such a way as to maximize its usefulness in subsequent proceedings. For example, at the beginning of an investigation, if names and addresses of witnesses to a crime are not recorded by the officer, this information may be lost forever. The techniques of sound criminal investigation are outside the scope of this text, but it bears repeating that the failure to properly gather and preserve the available evidence affects all subsequent proceedings.

The Federal Rules of Criminal Procedure and the rules of criminal procedure of all states require an officer making a warrantless arrest to take the arrestee before the nearest available judicial official without unnecessary delay.[33] The officer at this first appearance is not required to present sufficient evidence to convict, but must produce sufficient evidence for the judge or magistrate to determine whether there is probable cause[34] to believe that an offense has been committed and that the accused committed the offense.[35]

Following a review of the evidence, if the judicial official determines that there is probable cause to hold the arrestee for further proceedings or to have

---

[32] State v. Perkins, 130 W. Va. 708, 45 S.E.2d 17 (1947). *See* case in Part II.

[33] County of Riverside v. McLaughlin, 500 U.S. 44 (1991); *See* also FED. R. CRIM. P. 5.

[34] Probable cause has been shown "If the facts and circumstances before the officer are such as to warrant a man of prudence and caution in believing that the offense has been committed, it is sufficient." Carroll v. United States, 267 U.S. 132, 161, 1925 U.S. LEXIS 361 (1925).

[35] *See* Chapter 16 for a discussion of evidence needed to determine probable cause for the issuance of a search warrant.

the case presented to a grand jury in a felony case, the officer must make available all of the evidence that he or she has collected, together with names and pertinent information, to the prosecutor. Although the prosecutor may and should enter into the case at an earlier time, this is usually the step where the prosecutor takes charge.

In many jurisdictions, in order to move the case toward trial, the prosecutor must present the evidence to a grand jury in order to procure an indictment. With the consent of the arrested defendant, the prosecution may be initiated with the use of an information. Prosecutors in many states are not required to obtain a grand jury indictment but may file an information against the defendant. The prosecution must have sufficient evidence to demonstrate probable cause for a grand jury, and in the case of using an information, the prosecutor must believe that the evidence indicates the existence of probable cause. One might argue—and with justification—that the process of determining probable cause before a judge or magistrate and then presenting the evidence to a grand jury for a probable cause determination seems redundant. The first presentation of the evidence involved the judicial system making the initial determination of probable cause rather than allowing a suspect to be held to answer for a crime solely by the executive branch in the absence of judicial involvement.

The prosecutor controls the proceedings in front of the grand jury proceeding, but again, he or she must, in almost every case, call on the officer-investigator and other witnesses to offer testimony before the grand jury. While sufficient evidence must be presented to a grand jury, which will allow the grand jury to conclude that probable cause exists to believe a particular person has committed a particular crime, the formal evidence rules are not followed when presenting evidence to the grand jury.[36] However, sufficient admissible evidence must be presented to convince the grand jury (usually 12 to 23 persons) that an offense against the state has been committed by the person accused.

In some states, where neither the state constitution nor state law requires a grand jury indictment, process by way of information can substitute for the grand jury hearing. The prosecutor, using the evidence presented by officers and other witnesses, evaluates the evidence to determine whether probable cause exists. Where probable cause exists and where the prosecutor concludes that a prosecutable case exists, the prosecutor makes the decision to prepare the information, files it with the proper court, and serves notice to the accused of the specific charge.

Following the return of the indictment or the preparation of the information, the defendant appears personally before the judge. Here, the defendant is arraigned (informed of the charges against him or her), defense counsel may be appointed, and the defendant may enter a plea. Because probable cause is not an issue to be proved at arraignment following a grand jury indictment, there is no need for the judge to admit or evaluate evidence except when the

---

[36]   *See* United States v. John Doe, 481 U.S. 102 (1987).

case originated with the filing of an information. However, at the conclusion of the arraignment, the judge may suggest a time for a preliminary hearing or set a date to hear pretrial motions.

At the pretrial hearing, the defense and the prosecution may present some evidence concerning pretrial motions. Where admission of evidence at trial depends on the manner in which the evidence was seized, both sides will normally present evidence to support their respective positions. Police officers and the defendant may offer evidence of the facts surrounding the search and seizure of evidence so that the judge can determine the legality of the procedure and rule on the trial admissibility of the evidence. Often, the outcome of the suppression hearing determines the fate of both the accused and of the prosecution's case. If, for example, the judge determines that police obtained a confession illegally or that they unconstitutionally seized illegal drugs in the possession of the arrestee, the prosecutor may decide to drop the charge if the judge suppresses the evidence. Conversely, if the judge rules against the defendant at the suppression hearing, the defendant's attorney may advise him or her to consider a negotiated plea or enter a guilty plea. If there are no more pretrial motions or legal issues to be resolved, the case is ready for trial.

§ 2.7 Use of Evidence at the Trial

Even before the trial, the evidence acquired by the police officer, the prosecutor, or by other means, already has been considered several times. Assuming that there has been sufficient evidence to indict the defendant, the case eventually comes before the court and the jury at the trial. By this time, there is a good possibility that some evidence has been found inadmissible by the court. If so, the prosecutor must determine whether there is still enough admissible, relevant evidence to meet the burden of proof beyond a reasonable doubt.

In addition to the parties on each side, the court is made up of the judge, jury, witnesses, prosecutor, and defense attorney.[37] In early English proceedings, the jurors were the only witnesses and were called upon by the judge to give information concerning the case because they had knowledge of the facts. However, the modern juror ideally should have no knowledge of the case, and certainly no firsthand knowledge of the facts. The jury determines what facts have been proved after it has heard the evidence presented by the witnesses, evaluated the facts judicially noticed by the judge, and has considered the inferences and presumptions as instructed by the court.

The trial judge has the duty, upon proper objection, to determine whether a particular item of evidence is relevant, material, and competent, and whether the item should be admitted or excluded from jury consideration. At the close of the case, when all the evidence has been heard, the trial judge's duty is to

---

[37] State v. Perkins, 130 W. Va. 708, 45 S.E.2d 17 (1947). *See* case in Part II. In Chapter 4, the procedure for introducing and considering evidence at trial is presented in more detail.

instruct the jury concerning the law applicable to the case. In a bench trial (without a jury), the judge continues to make evidentiary rulings and takes on the additional role of the trier of fact in determining guilt or innocence.

The prosecutor has the responsibility to evaluate all evidence presented to him or her, to determine the legality of the evidence, to arrange the evidence in sequence so that it is best suited to achieve the objective, to identify the witnesses for the prosecution, to examine the witnesses, and to cross-examine defense witnesses.

Finally, the defense attorney is responsible for seeking evidence with which to present a defense for the accused. The defense attorney also arranges the evidence in the sequence most likely (in his or her opinion) to convey the defendant's legal position to the finders of fact. Defense counsel has the opportunity to introduce, examine, and cross-examine witnesses. Even in a case that from the beginning appears to be hopeless, the defendant has the right to "put the prosecution to its proof" by pleading not guilty and going to trial.

§ 2.8 Consideration of Evidence on Appeal

If the jury or the judge acquits the defendant at the trial, the state has no right to appeal the acquittal in a way that would affect any rights of the defendant.[38] The prohibition against double jeopardy mandates this result. If, however, the defendant is convicted, he or she may appeal the conviction, and the appellate court may examine what occurred in the trial court and reverse the conviction, with or without granting the state the opportunity to retry the defendant. As a general rule, "The presumptions on appeal are all in favor of the validity of the judgment of the trial court,"[39] and, therefore, an appellate court will uphold the guilty verdict unless there were clear legal errors or the evidence was insufficient to meet the government's burden of proof. However, if evidence has been wrongly admitted or improperly excluded in a manner that may have affected the outcome of the trial, an appellate court will often reverse the conviction with directions to retry the case. When a defendant succeeds in having a conviction overturned on appeal, the state may appeal to a higher appellate court in an effort to overturn the lower appellate court and have the trial verdict reinstated. Changes in the application of the rules of evidence change gradually and may result in different outcomes as newer cases reach appellate courts. For example, in *Trammel v. United States*, the Supreme Court approved a change in the old rule that a spouse could not testify against another spouse without that spouse's consent.[40] When the Court revisited the logic behind the rule that a defendant spouse could prevent the other's adverse testimony, it approved the new interpretation offered by the trial court.

---

[38]   *See* Benton v. Maryland, 395 U.S. 784, 1969 U.S. LEXIS 1167 (1969).

[39]   Hoffman v. Gregory, 2005 Ark. LEXIS 135 (Ark. 2005).

[40]   Trammel v. United States, 445 U.S. 40, 1980 U.S. LEXIS 84 (1980). *See* this case in Part II of this book.

§ 2.9 Use of Evidence at the Probation Hearing

Even after the determination of guilt or innocence, the judge may make additional use of evidence in determining whether the person who has been found guilty will be placed on probation or incarcerated. In many jurisdictions, a probation/parole officer will conduct a presentence report. The general rules of evidence that limit the use of evidence at the trial do not apply to the use of the presentence report by the judge. Although this presentence report should be factual, evidence such as hearsay evidence is not excluded from the report. However, it is obvious that this evidence is available only for determining the disposition of the person who has been convicted of a crime and that it cannot be used in determining guilt or innocence. Where a person has been granted probation that may have to be revoked, similar evidentiary policies control the use of evidence at a revocation hearing. When revoking federal probation, the rules of evidence, except those governing privileges, have no application.[41]

While in most states the probation report or presentence investigation report is confidential and available only to the judge, some jurisdictions require that the pre-sentence report be made available for inspection by the offender or by the defense attorney.[42]

§ 2.10 Use of Evidence When Considering Parole

State parole boards consider evidence when determining whether a person who has served time in an institution merits release under the supervision of a parole officer. After making a complete investigation in the field, a parole officer prepares a report that covers the personal position of the convict and his or her history while in custody, among other factors. Although the rules of evidence do not apply to parole revocation hearings[43] or reports,[44] the information compiled serves as important evidence that assists a parole board.

---

[41] United States v. Aspinall, 389 F.3d 332, 344, 2004 U.S. App. LEXIS 23954 (2d Cir. 2004) and FED. R. EVID. 1101(d)(3).

[42] *See* CARLSON, CRIMINAL JUSTICE PROCEDURE (7th ed. 2005).

[43] State v. Abd-Rahmaan, 154 Wn.2d 280, 111 P.3d 1157, 2005 Wash. LEXIS 461 (2005). *See* this case in Part II of this book.

[44] Simpson v. Florida Parole Commission, 2006 U.S. Dist. LEXIS 18068 (2006).

§ 2.11　Summary

In a criminal case, the objective is to gather all of the evidence, whether favorable or unfavorable to the prosecution, that will help the trial court and the reviewing courts to reach the truth and dispose of the case according to law. Although it would appear that all relevant evidence should be admitted, after long empirical investigation, the courts have determined that certain evidence should be excluded. The rules for excluding evidence are generally justified on the grounds that they prevent waste of time and confusion, protect certain interests and relationships, avoid undue and unfair prejudice to the accused, prevent the jury from considering unreliable evidence, and enforce constitutional safeguards.

Generally, there is little distinction between the rules of criminal evidence and rules of civil evidence. However, because the prosecution must prove the accused guilty beyond a reasonable doubt and because the jury verdict usually must be unanimous, a higher degree of evidence is required for proof of guilt in a criminal case.

The importance of recognizing, protecting, preserving, and evaluating evidence begins at the time that the crime is committed. Even prior to trial, the evidence plays a very important part in determining whether there are sufficient grounds for the judicial official to bind the defendant over to the grand jury and for the grand jury to determine whether there is sufficient evidence for an indictment. In some jurisdictions, an information may be filed by the prosecutor as an alternative to an indictment.

The evidence has been filtered, challenged, and evaluated prior to the time that the trial begins, but it is at the trial that evidence is of greatest importance. In a criminal case, the prosecution must introduce sufficient evidence that, together with facts judicially noticed and legal presumptions and inferences, will justify the fact finders in finding the defendant guilty beyond a reasonable doubt. At the trial, the judge, jury, witnesses, prosecutor, and defense attorney are all concerned with the admissibility and weight of evidence.

Even after the trial, reviewing courts often consider the record of evidence presented at the trial in order to determine whether a conviction should be set aside for one reason or another. A reviewing court does not reweigh the evidence, but generally confines its review to matters of law.

Evidence that could not be admitted in court, as well as legally acquired evidence, may be considered by the judge to determine whether a defendant who has been convicted should be placed on probation. This evidence may also influence the judge in determining the conditions on which probation should be granted. Although the strict rules of evidence do not apply to the probation officer when obtaining information for the judge, evidence should be acquired that will help the judge to make an intelligent decision concerning the advisability of granting probation.

Finally, in jurisdictions that still allow early release on parole, evidence is again considered by the parole board in making a determination concerning whether the person who has served time in institutional custody should be granted early release. Once again, the evidence considered by the board need not meet the rules of evidence followed by a court in a trial on the merits. According to the Supreme Court of the United States, the federal exclusionary rule, which helps enforce the Fourth Amendment, does not prohibit a state parole board's use of evidence seized in violation of a parolee's rights.[45]

In the chapters that follow, the many general admissibility tests and special tests for the use of evidence are discussed more comprehensively.

---

[45] Pennsylvania Board of Probation and Parole v. Scott, 524 U.S. 357 (1998). *And see* O'Neal v. Renico, 2005 U.S. Dist. LEXIS 31045 (E.D. Mich. 2005).

Proof by Evidence
and Substitutes

Burden of Proof 3

The term "burden of proof" imports the duty of ultimately establishing any given proposition. This phrase marks the peculiar duty of him who has the risk of any given proposition on which the parties are at issue, who will lose the case if he does not make this proposition out, when all has been said and done.

THAYER, EVIDENCE (1898)

Chapter Outline

Key Terms and Concepts

affirmative defense	burden of proof
alibi	clear and convincing evidence
beyond a reasonable doubt	preponderance of the evidence
burden of going forward	self-defense
burden of persuasion	sufficiency of evidence

§ 3.1 Introduction

In approaching the study of evidence logically and progressively, one starting point is to consider the task of producing evidence with which to prove the truth of a given proposition. No attorney takes a civil or criminal case to court unless there is a good chance that the ultimate proposition can be established by the proper level of proof. In a criminal case, the state has the burden of proving the guilt of the accused beyond a reasonable doubt. Therefore, the "burden of proof" is on the prosecution throughout the trial and this burden never shifts. The term denotes the duty of establishing the truth of the charge against the accused. Ascertaining the truth then becomes an important, if not the most important, objective of the court and jury.

In the criminal justice process, it is necessary that those involved understand the considerations and obligations of the parties in presenting sufficient evidence and the consequences of failing to do so. Failure on the part of the prosecution to introduce sufficient evidence, or failure to properly explain the evidence, will make it impossible for the jury (or judge, when the case is tried without a jury) to determine the truth and thus will result in a miscarriage of justice. Therefore, a thorough knowledge of the concept of *burden of proof* is an essential starting point on which to build an understanding of the rules of evidence.

In a civil case, the party who has the burden of establishing the truth of a given proposition is a private individual, corporation or, in some instances, a governmental unit. In a criminal case, however, the prosecution has the responsibility of establishing the truth of the charges stated in the indictment or information. The rule that imposes the burden of proving guilt of the accused beyond a reasonable doubt upon the state in criminal cases does not apply in civil actions. Therefore, the burden of proof becomes even more important when considering criminal cases than when considering civil cases.

In a criminal case, the investigator must compile evidence sufficient to convince the jury not only that the accused is guilty by a "preponderance of the evidence" but "beyond a reasonable doubt"—that is, the prosecution or the state has the burden of proving the existence of every element of the crime charged.

Recognizing this requirement, the defense can be expected to deliver an attack against the weak links in the chain, because the defense knows that if even one of the elements is not proved beyond a reasonable doubt, there can be no conviction on that specific charge.

Because there has been some confusion concerning the term *burden of proof*, the pertinent terms are comprehensively defined and explained in the following sections of this chapter. In other sections of the chapter, the obligation of the prosecution to prove guilt and the obligation of the accused to produce evidence in a criminal trial are discussed.

In Chapters 4, 5, and 6, rules relating to the process for establishing or ascertaining truth at the trial are defined, explained, and considered.

§ 3.2 Definitions and Distinctions

A statement of what the burden of proof *is not* makes it easier to frame a positive definition. First, the burden of proof does not relate to the number of witnesses, but rather to the merit and weight of the evidence produced—whether by one or many witnesses. Second, the fact that evidence is admissible in conformity with the general principles regarding admissibility, relevancy, materiality, and competency does not necessarily mean that it will be given such weight as to sustain the burden of proof. The testimony of one well-prepared, reliable witness or evidence of a documentary or real nature may result in better proof than testimony from a large number of witnesses whose credibility is suspect.

Generally, the phrase *burden of proof* denotes the duty of establishing the truth of a given proposition or issue. Because the term has been used somewhat loosely by some courts, the definition of burden of proof as used in law requires further explanation. To avoid confusion, the phrases *burden of going forward* and *burden of persuasion* are also defined.

A. Burden of Proof

This term is defined as "[a] party's duty to prove a disputed assertion or charge."[1] The burden of proof may also be defined as the duty upon one party to establish the truth of an issue that is important to the case by the quantum

---

[1]   BLACK'S LAW DICTIONARY (8th ed. 2004).

of evidence demanded by law. *Black's Law Dictionary* notes that the burden of proof also "includes both the *burden of persuasion* and the *burden of production*."[2] The burden of persuasion means that one party must convince the judge or jury to see the facts in a manner that favors the party who introduced the evidence, while the burden of production means that the party has a duty to introduce evidence to attempt to prove a particular point or issue. In a criminal case, the burden of proof means that the prosecution has the duty of proving the guilt of the accused beyond a reasonable doubt. This duty or burden never shifts during the course of the trial, but remains with the prosecution throughout the trial. The emphasis is on the ultimate result rather than on individual issues or questions within the case.

B. Burden of Going Forward

At the start of a criminal trial, the prosecution has the obligation to introduce evidence that will move toward meeting the burden of proof. The burden of going forward has been defined as "[a] party's duty to introduce enough evidence on an issue to have the issue decided by the factfinder, rather than decided against the party. . ."[3] This is a way of saying that the government possesses the initial burden of going forward by initiating its presentation of evidence. In a sense, at the beginning of the legal contest, the government begins the case and must start by introducing evidence that will build toward and eventually reach the level of proof beyond a reasonable doubt. If the prosecution meets the burden of going forward with the evidence and survives a defendant's request for a directed verdict, the burden of going forward with the evidence shifts to the defense to begin building its case. Demonstrative of the principle that the burden of going forward was met is a case in which the defendant had been accused of rape of a child. The prosecution, during its case-in-chief, had introduced evidence that the defendant had blood on his clothes, the child had blood in her diaper, the victim had torn flesh in the private area, and technicians found the defendant's DNA profile on a diaper. At the close of the prosecution's case, the defendant requested a directed verdict of acquittal on the theory that the prosecution had failed to meet its burden of going forward with the evidence. The reviewing court upheld the trial court's denial of the motion because the evidence, both circumstantial and direct, was sufficient for conviction of child rape if a jury would choose to believe the evidence.[4] If the defendant, in meeting the burden of going forward with the evidence, succeeds in creating a reasonable doubt in the prosecution's case, the burden of going forward will shift to the prosecution at the close of the defendant's case-in-chief. In the case of a defendant who pleads an affirmative defense such as alibi, self-defense, mistake of fact, insanity, or another legal theory, the burden of going forward with the evidence supporting the defense

---

[2]   *Id.*
[3]   BLACK'S LAW DICTIONARY (8th ed. 2004).
[4]   Terry v. State, 2006 Ark. LEXIS 326 (Ark. 2006).

initially rests on the defendant. Similarly, in a case involving a felon in possession of a firearm,[5] the defendant had the burden of going forward with evidence that he had been pardoned or had otherwise had his right to bear firearms restored. If the defendant succeeds in going forward with evidence sufficient to meet any burden of proof for that affirmative defense, the burden of going forward shifts to the prosecution to negate the defendant's proof of the defense. This is often expressed by the term *burden of evidence.*[6]

C. Burden of Persuasion

The burden of persuasion refers only to the burden of convincing the factfinder of the collective truth of evidence produced by one side or the other. When the burden of persuasion has been met, the attorney will be able to refer to the evidence during closing arguments to assist the jury in understanding why his or her party should prevail and to demonstrate that his or her client's version is the truth.

When the term *burden of proof* is used in the following sections, the definition as stated in subsection A, *supra*, is applied.

In meeting the burden of proof, the amount of evidence varies depending on whether the case is criminal or civil and whether the case involves an affirmative defense. Generally, in a civil case, the party who initiated the lawsuit possesses the duty of establishing the truth of specific propositions and must do so by a preponderance of the evidence. However, there are some issues in civil cases that must be proved by higher degrees of proof—clear and convincing or beyond a reasonable doubt.

For example, in a civil case in which a state wants to keep a mentally ill person in custody following the end of a criminal sentence, the burden of proof required in order to meet minimal due process requirements must be greater than a preponderance of the evidence that an offender remains a dangerous person.[7] Minnesota permits sexually dangerous predators to be committed to civil custody beyond a prison term when there was clear and convincing evidence that the subject had demonstrated a "habitual course of misconduct in sexual matters and an utter lack of power to control sexual impulses."[8] Viewing matters a bit differently, Kansas chose to use the criminal burden of proof in civil cases in which it desired to commit dangerous pedophiles to civil custody beyond their criminal sentences.[9] The Kansas statute committing sexually violent predators uses the same burden of proof that the prosecution has in proving guilt in criminal cases—beyond a reasonable doubt.[10] These three degrees of proof are discussed and distinguished in the following sections.

---

[5]   State v. Kelly, 210 Ariz. 460, 112 P.3d 682, 2005 Ariz. App. LEXIS 70 (Ariz. 2005).
[6]   *Id.* at 464 and 686.
[7]   Addington v. Texas, 411 U.S, 418, 432, 1979 U.S. LEXIS 93 (1979).
[8]   In re Civil Commitment of Barber, 2005 Minn. LEXIS 355 (Minn. 2005).
[9]   In re Care and Treatment of Ward, 131 P.3d 540, 547, 2006 Kan. App. LEXIS 296 (Kan. 2006).
[10] Kohlsaat v. Parkersburg & Marietta Sand Co., 266 F. 283 (4th Cir. 1920) and In re Winship, 397 U.S. 358 (1970) for proof beyond a reasonable doubt as a federal constitutional requirement.

§ 3.3 Preponderance of the Evidence

The plaintiff in a civil case possesses the burden of proof, which requires that the truth of the plaintiff's claim be established by a fair preponderance of the credible evidence when considered with the defendant's evidence. The preponderance standard means *by the greater weight of evidence* and has been stated to be anything more than 50 percent of the believable evidence, although a mathematical model often does not provide a precise analogy. The concept of preponderance of the evidence does not mean the greater number of witnesses or the greater length of time taken by either side. The phrase *preponderance of the evidence* refers to the quality of the evidence, i.e., its ability to convince and the weight and the effect it has on the jurors' minds.

In order for the civil plaintiff to prevail, the evidence that supports the claim must appear to the jury at least slightly more believable than the evidence presented by the opposing party. If the evidence presented by the plaintiff fails to be more believable than the defendant's evidence, or if the evidence from both sides weighs so evenly that the jurors are unable to say that there is a preponderance on the plaintiff's side, the jury must resolve the question in favor of the defendant. Because the plaintiff has the burden of proof by a preponderance of evidence in civil cases, a failure to meet the burden means that the opposing party prevails due to a failure of proof.

Some civil cases that use the preponderance standard may seem more like criminal cases in some contexts. In determining whether a sexual offender must register under the state version of Megan's Law, Wyoming used the preponderance of the evidence standard to determine at which level of offense a convicted sex offender should be placed for public notification. The Supreme Court of Wyoming rejected the clear and convincing standard against the defendants' argument "that clear and convincing evidence is required in determining the risk of reoffense because the appellant's interests, and the risk of erroneous deprivation of those interests, outweigh any government interest."[11] The court rejected the higher evidentiary standard on the ground that its use would restrict the state government in its ability to protect the public.

Although the preponderance of the evidence standard finds primary application in civil cases, some criminal cases use the standard for different purposes. In a California case in which the defendant pled legal insanity, the burden of persuasion for the defendant to prove insanity was only proof by a preponderance of the evidence, because insanity was not considered an element of the crime. According to the California reviewing court, the civil burden was appropriate even though the defendant argued that the prosecution should have to prove his sanity beyond a reasonable doubt.[12] In the death penalty phase of a capital case, North Carolina permitted the defendant to

---

[11]   In re JJF v. State, 2006 Wyo. 41, 132 P.3d 170, 174, 2006 Wyo. LEXIS 44 (Wyo. 2006).

[12]   People v. Farris, 130 Cal. App. 4th 773, 780 30 Cal. Rptr. 3d 426, 430, 2005 Cal. App. LEXIS 1017 (2005).

bring for jury consideration any evidence of mitigation that had been proved by the defendant by a preponderance of the evidence. This creates a reduced standard that a convicted defendant might more easily meet in avoiding the death penalty.[13] Similarly, in Ohio, to prove insanity as a defense, a defendant must demonstrate insanity by a preponderance of the evidence in order to prevail.[14] In approving the use of the preponderance standard for a defendant's burden in an insanity defense, the Supreme Court in *Patterson v. New York* noted that:

> [O]nce the facts constituting a crime are established beyond a reasonable doubt, based on all the evidence, including the evidence of the defendant's mental state, the State may refuse to sustain the affirmative defense of insanity unless demonstrated by a preponderance of the evidence.[15]

In essence, civil cases primarily use the preponderance of the evidence standard for decision-making purposes, but in a variety of contexts the civil standard has application in criminal cases, especially concerning affirmative defenses.

§ 3.4 Clear and Convincing Evidence

While the level of proof required for civil cases has been described as proof by a preponderance (greater weight) of the evidence, some aspects of civil litigation dictate a greater level of proof known as clear and convincing evidence. As one court noted, "[c]lear and convincing evidence is something more than proof by a preponderance of the evidence but less than proof beyond a reasonable doubt."[16] Clear and convincing evidence is that measure or degree of proof that "will produce in the mind of the trier of facts a firm belief or conviction as to the facts sought to be established."[17] Another way of describing the clear and convincing standard suggests that the level of proof should be evidence that:

> produces in the mind of the trier of fact a firm belief or conviction as to the truth of the allegations sought to be established, evidence so clear, direct and weighty and convincing as to enable [the factfinder] to come to a clear conviction, without hesitancy, of the truth of the precise facts in issue.[18]

13   State v. McNeill, 360 N.C. 231, 249, 624 S.E.2d 329, 341, 2006 N.C. LEXIS 1 (2006).
14   State v. Hancock, 108 Ohio St. 3d 57, 62, 2006 Ohio 160, 840 N.E.2d 1032, 1043, 2006 Ohio LEXIS 215 (2006). *See also* Martin v. Ohio, 480 U.S. 228 (1987).
15   Patterson v. New York, 432 U.S. 197, 206 (1977).
16   United States v. Smith, 2006 U.S. Dist. LEXIS 50535 (N.D. Ind. 2006).
17   State v. Hudak, 2006 Ohio 3830, 2006 Ohio App. LEXIS 3839 (2006), quoting Cross v. Ledford, 161 Ohio St. 469, 120 N.E.2d 118 (Ohio 1954).
18   In re Westchester County Medical Center on behalf of O'Connor, 72 N.Y.2d 517, 534 N.Y.S.2d 886, 892, 531 N.E.2d 607, 613 (1988).

Clear and convincing evidence does not imply clear and *unequivocal* evidence. According to a law review article written in 1987, the concept of clear and convincing roughly translates as "much-more-likely-than-not."[19] The use of the clear and convincing standard of proof was first applied to actions for fraud or deceit.[20] The rationale for employing a higher standard of proof in civil cases in which fraud or criminal conduct has been alleged implicates other concerns. Alleged civil fraud or other wrongdoing suggests that more than money may be involved in a civil case. For example, the defendant's reputation may be at risk in a defamation case or a state may be attempting to terminate parental rights to an allegedly abused or neglected child based on this standard.[21]

In the case of *Addington v. Texas*, Chief Justice Warren Burger wrote "the intermediate standard, which usually employs some combination of the words 'clear,' 'cogent,' 'unequivocal,' and 'convincing,' is less commonly used, but nonetheless is no stranger to civil law."[22]

In distinguishing between the levels of proof, the Supreme Court of New Jersey noted that the state's rules of evidence set forth at least "three standards of proof: a preponderance of the evidence, clear and convincing evidence, and proof beyond a reasonable doubt."[23] The court mentioned that, as a general rule, the preponderance standard applies in civil cases in which the litigant must show that the desired inference is more likely than not to be true.[24] According to the court, the second standard, clear and convincing, denotes a higher standard than proof by a preponderance and less than proof beyond a reasonable doubt.[25] This second standard should produce in the mind of the finder of fact a firm belief concerning the facts sought to be proven. In defining the beyond a reasonable doubt standard, a different court stated that it means that the evidence is sufficient that the facts asserted are almost certainly true. [26]

Lawsuits involving significant interests beyond money, such as a suit to correct a mistake in a deed or other writing, disputes involving an oral contract to make a will, to establish the terms of a lost will, and for the specific performance of an oral contract frequently dictate that sufficient proof requires clear and convincing evidence. In some states, the termination of parental rights may require proof by clear and convincing evidence.[27] Involuntary civil commitments of people who are alleged to pose a continuing risk of sexually reoffending typically require the state to use a heightened level of

---

[19]   72 CORNELL L. REV. 1115, 1119 (1987).

[20]   *Appellate Review in the Federal Courts of Findings Requiring More Than a Preponderance of the Evidence*, 60 HARV. L. REV. 119 (1946).

[21]   ALASKA STAT. § 47.10.088, Involuntary termination of parental rights and responsibilities. (2006).

[22]   Addington v. Texas, 441 U.S. 418, 99 S. Ct. 1804, 60 L. Ed. 2d 323 (1979).

[23]   *See* N.J. R. EVID. 101(b)(1).

[24]   Liberty Mutual Ins. Co. v. Land, 186 N.J. 163, 169, 892 A.2d 1240, 1243, 2006 N.J. LEXIS 375 (N.J. 2006).

[25]   *Id.*

[26]   Riley Hill General Contractor v. Tandey Corp., 757 P.2d 595 (Or. 1987).

[27]   State v. Sonya, 270 Neb. 870, 880, 708 N.W.2d 786, 795, 2006 Neb. LEXIS 5 (Neb. 2006). A higher standard of proof beyond a reasonable doubt is required for termination of parental rights for Indian children. *See* R.R.S. NEB. § 43-279.01 (2006).

proof such as clear and convincing evidence.[28] In 1984, Congress passed the Insanity Defense Reform Act, which requires federal criminal defendants to prove the affirmative defense of insanity by clear and convincing evidence.[29]

§ 3.5 Beyond a Reasonable Doubt

In criminal cases, where freedom or life itself may hang in the balance, the federal constitution has been interpreted to require the highest level of proof, known as proof beyond a reasonable doubt.[30] This demanding level of certainty requires that the prosecution prove that the accused is guilty by introducing strong and overwhelming evidence of guilt beyond a reasonable doubt. The proof presented by the prosecution must have sufficient believability and substance to rebut the strong constitutional presumption of innocence. In legal theory this means that each and every element of the offense charged in the indictment, as well as any aggravating circumstances that affect a sentence, must be proved beyond a reasonable doubt.[31] Otherwise, the accused generally must be acquitted of the charge.[32] The reality is that a jury considers all the evidence together and reaches a verdict without close judicial scrutiny concerning what the jury found on each and every element.

In 1970, the United States Supreme Court traced the history of the "beyond a reasonable doubt" requirement and concluded that this standard of proof is indispensable to command the respect and confidence of the community in applications of criminal law. In recognizing this constitutional requirement, the Court emphasized:

> Lest there remain any doubt about the constitutional stature of the reasonable-doubt standard, we explicitly hold that the Due Process Clause protects the accused against conviction except upon proof beyond a reasonable doubt of every fact necessary to constitute the crime with which he is charged.[33]

---

[28] *See* Commonwealth v. Allen, 269 Va. 262, 609 S.E.2d 4, 2005 Va. LEXIS 23 (2005).

[29] 18 U.S.C. §§ 17, 4241-4247, *and see* § 3.11.

[30] Clark v. Arizona, ___ U.S. ___, 2006 U.S. LEXIS 5184 (2006), quoting In re Winship, 397 U.S. 358, 1970 U.S. LEXIS 56 (1970).

[31] *See* Ring v. Arizona, 536 U.S. 584, 2002 U.S. LEXIS 4651 (2002), Scalia, J., concurring.

[32] An acquittal is not always required in federal courts where the error was harmless beyond a reasonable doubt. In *Neder v. United States*, 527 U.S. 1, 1999 U.S. LEXIS 4007 (1999), the Court held that failure to include an element of the crime in the charge to the jury did not necessarily result in an unfair trial.

[33] In re Winship, 397 U.S. 358, 90 S. Ct. 1068, 25 L. Ed. 2d 368, 1970 U.S. LEXIS 56 (1970). *See* case in Part II. *See also* Clark v. Arizona, ___ U.S. ___, 2006 U.S. LEXIS 5 (2006) in which the Court notes that all elements of criminal cases and juvenile adjudications that involve acts that would be crimes if committed by adults must be proved beyond a reasonable doubt.

As Justice Kennedy noted in supporting the current burden of proof for criminal cases, "We would not allow a State to evade its burden of proof by replacing its criminal law with a civil system in which there is no presumption of innocence and the defendant has the burden of proof. "[34]

In some states, the exact wording of the charge to the jury dealing with the criminal standard of proof is stated by statute. In other states, there is no such requirement, and in fact the judge does not have to explain the term at all.[35] However, where a state statute contains an appropriate jury instruction, if a court reads it to a jury, it should be read exactly as it appears in the statute. For example, one California statute that explains the concept of reasonable doubt provides that:

> It is not a mere possible doubt; because everything relating to human affairs, and depending on moral evidence, is open to some possible or imaginary doubt. It is that state of the case, which, after the entire comparison and consideration of all the evidence, leaves the minds of jurors in that condition that they cannot say they feel an abiding conviction, to a moral certainty, of the truth of the charge.[36]

In explaining the reasonable doubt concept to a jury, the Michigan Supreme Court voiced approval for an instruction that phrased the criminal burden of proof as:

> A reasonable doubt is exactly what it infers. A reasonable doubt is a fair, honest doubt growing out of the evidence or lack of evidence in this case; or growing out of any reasonable or legitimate inferences drawn from the evidence or lack of evidence. It is not merely an imaginary doubt or a flimsy, fanciful doubt. But, rather, it is a fair, honest doubt based upon reason and common sense.[37]

However, other courts, even the Supreme Court of Michigan, hold that there is also no error in refusing to give an instruction explaining the reasonable doubt concept. In one case, the Supreme Court of Michigan noted that the phrase *beyond a reasonable doubt* was not of such an unknown or uncommon meaning that a trial judge must give it additional explanation. The court stated:

---

[34] Foucha v. Louisiana, 504 U.S. 71 at 94 (1992).

[35] People v. Mayo, 140 Cal. App. 4th 535, 548, 44 Cal. Rptr. 3d 497, 508, 2006 Cal. App. LEXIS 873 (Cal. 2006), noting that the United States Constitution does not require trial courts to define reasonable doubt, as long as the jury is informed of the proper standard of proof. *See also* Ex parte Gillentine, 2006 Ala. Crim. App. LEXIS 107 (2006), in which the court held that a trial judge must give an instruction on reasonable doubt and failure to do so constitutes reversible error.

[36] CAL. PEN. CODE § 1096 (Deering 2006).

[37] Michigan v. Allen, 466 Mich. 86, 87, n. 1, 643 N.W.2d 227, 229, n.1 (2002).

> If a trial court gives a deficient definition of reasonable doubt, it cannot be presumed that the jury has, in fact, found guilt beyond a reasonable doubt, whereas, if the trial court instructs on the need to find guilt beyond a reasonable doubt, without more, it can be presumed that the jury has, in fact, found guilt beyond a reasonable doubt.[38]

Alabama takes an opposite position on offering jury instructions concerning reasonable doubt. In a case in which the trial judge failed to offer a jury instruction covering the concept of reasonable doubt, the defendant was convicted on lesser homicide offenses. The circuit court eventually vacated his conviction on the ground that the original trial contained "structural error" and was a nullity because the trial court failed to give the reasonable doubt instruction. The reviewing court affirmed the circuit court decision, sending the case back for a new trial.[39] When the Michigan and Alabama views on reasonable doubt are considered, the result is that state courts are nowhere near a consensus on the correct way to deal with the concept of reasonable doubt in jury instructions.

Where a court offers a reasonable doubt jury instruction, whether it is required to do so by a state law or rule, the court must give the jury an instruction that meets federal constitutional standards. In *Sullivan v. Louisiana*, the United States Supreme Court decided that giving a constitutionally flawed reasonable doubt instruction is not subject to a harmless-error standard of review and requires a reversal.[40] In this first-degree murder case, the prosecution agreed that the instruction did not comply with the requisite instruction mandated by a previous case,[41] but argued that the error was harmless.

The Supreme Court first reaffirmed that:

> What the factfinder must determine to return a verdict of guilty is prescribed by the Due Process Clause. The prosecution bears the burden of proving all elements of the offense charged, . . . and must persuade the factfinder "beyond a reasonable doubt" of the facts necessary to establish each of these elements. This beyond-a-reasonable-doubt requirement, which was adhered to by virtually all common law jurisdictions, applies in state, as well as federal, proceedings.

> It is self evident, we think, that the Fifth Amendment requirement of proof beyond a reasonable doubt and the Sixth Amendment requirement of a jury verdict are interrelated. It would not satisfy the Sixth Amendment to have a jury determine that the defendant is probably guilty, and then leave it to the judge to determine whether he is guilty beyond a reasonable doubt. In other words, the jury verdict required by the Sixth Amendment is a jury verdict of guilty beyond a reasonable doubt.[42]

---

[38]   People v. Allen, 466 Mich. 86, 92, 643 N.W.2d 227, 232, 2002 Mich. LEXIS 722 (2002).
[39]   Ex parte Gillentine, 2006 Ala. Crim. App. LEXIS 107 (2006).
[40]   Sullivan v. Louisiana, 508 U.S. 275, 113 S. Ct. 2078, 124 L. Ed. 2d 182 (1993).
[41]   Cage v. Louisiana, 498 U.S. 39, 111 S. Ct. 328, 112 L. Ed. 2d 339 (1990).
[42]   *Sullivan* at 227, 228.

Rejecting the prosecution's argument that the reasonable doubt instruction error was harmless, the Supreme Court reversed the judgment of the Louisiana court and remanded the case. If a federal constitutional error is to be held harmless, the reviewing court must be able to declare its conviction that the error was harmless beyond a reasonable doubt. Where a court has not been convinced beyond a reasonable doubt, the conviction under review must be reversed.

Referring to the landmark case of *In re Winship*, and reiterating that the government must prove beyond a reasonable doubt every element of a charged offense, the United States Supreme Court in 1994 acknowledged that this ancient and honored aspect of our criminal justice system defies easy explanation. In *Victor v. Nebraska*, the court noted that both *In re Winship* and *Cage v. Louisiana* involved appeals arising from two attempts to define the concept of reasonable doubt.[43] The United States Supreme Court first stated that the "beyond a reasonable doubt" standard is a requirement of due process, but the Constitution neither prohibits trial courts from defining a reasonable doubt nor requires them to do so as a matter of course.[44] The Constitution does not require any particular form or words to be used in advising the jury of the government's burden of proof. However, when a court gives a jury instruction, it must correctly convey the concept of reasonable doubt to the jury. In addition, a jury instruction must not have the effect of shifting the burden of proof to the defendant because such an instruction relieves the prosecution of proving the case beyond a reasonable doubt.[45]

One defendant in the *Victor* case reviewed objected to the use of the phrases "moral evidence" and "moral certainty" in the instruction. After discussing the history of this language, the Supreme Court held that in the context of the instruction as a whole, the use of the phrase did not render the instruction unconstitutional.

In *Victor v. Nebraska*, the instruction included, "[y]ou may find the accused guilty upon the strong probabilities of the case, provided such probabilities are strong enough to exclude any doubt of his guilt that is reasonable." The instruction also included, "A reasonable doubt is an actual and substantial doubt arising from the evidence." In evaluating the merits of the defendant's objection to the jury instruction, the Court noted:

> So long as the court instructs the jury on the necessity that the defendant's guilt be proved beyond a reasonable doubt, the Constitution does not require that any particular form of words be used in advising the jury of the government's burden of proof. Rather, "taken as a whole, the instructions [must] correctly convey the concept of reasonable doubt to the jury.[46]

---

[43]   Victor v. Nebraska, 511 U.S. 1, 114 S. Ct. 1239, 127 L. Ed. 2d 583 (1994). *See* case in Part II.
[44]   *Id.* The syllabus of this case is included in Part II. The instructions to the jurors are included in the case.
[45]   Sandstrom v. Montana, 442 U.S. 510, 523 (1979).
[46]   *Victor*, at 5.

On appeal, the defendant contended that this wording violated the due process clause. Finding that this instruction did not violate due process, the court concluded with this paragraph:

> The Due Process Clause requires the government to prove a criminal defendant's guilt beyond a reasonable doubt, and trial courts must avoid defining reasonable doubt so as to lead the jury to convict on a lesser showing than due process requires. In these cases, however, we conclude that taken as a whole, the instructions correctly conveyed the concept of reasonable doubt to the jury.[47]

A state or federal prosecutor is not required to prove the defendant guilty beyond all possible doubt and the Constitution of the United States does not require that any particular form or words be used in advising the jury of the government's burden of proof or to advise the jury at all concerning the reasonable doubt standard. However, if the jury is erroneously instructed in such a manner that effectively relieves the prosecution of its burden to establish every element of guilt, automatic reversal is often required, "because it is constitutionally mandated that the prosecution prove guilt beyond a reasonable doubt, an erroneous jury instruction on reasonable doubt is never harmless."[48] In a Maryland case, the reviewing court reversed the defendant's conviction of first-degree murder because his trial attorney failed to object to an erroneous jury instruction. The way the judge phrased the jury instruction on reasonable doubt, it could have permitted the jury to convict the defendant by a preponderance of the evidence standard or some standard lower than proof beyond a reasonable doubt.[49]

From the time a law enforcement official begins investigating and preparing a criminal case, the focus is directed toward gathering sufficient evidence to meet the trial evidentiary standard of proof beyond a reasonable doubt. The standard not only applies at the trial, but also influences appellate courts reviewing a case, because they may reverse a conviction where the appropriate burden of proof appears to be lacking. The high level of proof necessary in criminal cases constitutes one of the fundamental differences between criminal and civil cases, and it must be thoroughly understood by all who are involved in the criminal justice system.[50]

§ 3.6 Burden on the Prosecution

From the initiation of the prosecution and throughout the trial, the government has the burden of proof and the obligation to convince the jury or the court of the guilt of a defendant beyond a reasonable doubt. Because the due

---

[47] *Id.* at 31.
[48] State v. McClellan, 2006 Md. App. LEXIS 103 (2006).
[49] *Id.*
[50] Jackson v. Virginia, 443 U.S. 307, 99 S. Ct. 2781, 61 L. Ed. 2d 560 (1979).

process clause of the Fifth and the Fourteenth Amendment requires the prosecution to prove a defendant's guilt beyond a reasonable doubt, trial judges must be vigilant in offering jury instructions concerning proof beyond a reasonable doubt lest the instructions contain defects that might allow a jury to convict on a lower standard of proof. Although not all jurisdictions require that a trial judge give a detailed definition of proof beyond a reasonable doubt, where a judge is required or decides to offer such an instruction, it must properly explain the concept of reasonable doubt. The explanation of the standard must be offered to the jury in a way that ensures that a jury does not convict a defendant where the prosecution has introduced insufficient proof.[51] Where the crime requires proof of criminal intent, or *mens rea*, the responsibility rests with the prosecution to introduce evidence to prove intent. No defendant has any burden to prove innocence and a prosecutor must not imply that the defendant has any duty to disprove the case. For example, in a New York prosecution for driving while impaired, the prosecutor asked the defendant whether he asked to take a breath test in order to prove his innocence. The trial court judge overruled the defendant's objection to the question. The reviewing court reversed the conviction because the prosecutor's question improperly implied that the defendant had a burden to prove his innocence.[52] The prosecutor has a duty that prevents the government from effectively reducing its burden of proof. With the exceptions of affirmative defenses, no defendant possesses a burden of proof in a criminal trial and no defendant ever has a duty to prove that he or she did not commit the crime. Defendants do have some responsibilities during criminal trials—these will be discussed in future sections.

If the defendant pleads not guilty to a criminal charge, the defendant's plea necessarily imposes upon the government the burden of introducing proof of all the elements of the crime beyond a reasonable doubt.[53] The due process clause of the federal Constitution requires that the prosecution bear the burden of proving all of the elements of each offense charged.[54] In addition to the elements, the prosecutor must prove that the court has jurisdiction of the case and that the case is being tried in the proper venue.[55] Additionally, there must be proof that the alleged crime violated the law of the particular jurisdiction and the defendant was the person who committed the crime.[56]

The burdens on the prosecution become most clear when a defendant appeals a conviction and alleges that the government failed to meet a standard of proof for an item of evidence. An appellate court reviews the points of law

---

[51] Arizona v. Fulminante, 499 U.S. 279, 291 (1991).

[52] People v. Handwerker, 2006 N.Y. Slip Op. 26119, 12 Misc. 3d 19, 816 N.Y.S.2d 824, 2006 N.Y. Misc. LEXIS 662 (2006).

[53] In re Winship, 397 U.S. 358 (1970); State v. Sullivan, 34 Idaho 68, 199 P. 647 (1921). *See also* UNIF. R. EVID. 303(b) (1999).

[54] Sullivan v. Louisiana, 508 U.S. 275, 113 S. Ct. 2078, 124 L. Ed. 2d 182 (1993). *See also* Perkins v. State, 441 S.E.2d 511 (Ga.1994).

[55] State v. Miller, 2003 Utah App. 76, 2003 Utah App. LEXIS 247 (2003).

[56] *See* People v. Moreland, 226 Ill. Dec. 814, 686 N.E.2d 597 (1997).

argued by a defendant, especially where a defendant alleges that the prosecution failed to attain proof beyond a reasonable doubt. As one court phrased the review process, "When reviewing the sufficiency of the evidence to support a conspiracy conviction, we will affirm if the record, viewed most favorably to the government, contains substantial evidence supporting the jury's verdict, which means evidence sufficient to prove the elements of the crime beyond a reasonable doubt."[57]

§ 3.7 Burden to Prove All Elements of the Crime

"As a matter of due process the prosecution must prove beyond a reasonable doubt every fact necessary to constitute the crime with which the defendant is charged."[58] To win a conviction, the prosecutor must introduce sufficient believable evidence that proves all the elements of the charged crime beyond a reasonable doubt. For example, in the common law crime of burglary, there are seven elements: (1) trespass, (2) breaking, (3) entering, (4) the dwelling house, (5) of another, (6) at night, and (7) with intent to commit a felony. Meeting the duty of the prosecutor involves introducing proof of each of these elements of common law burglary with sufficient evidentiary weight the meet the burden of proof. Evidence that the defendant interfered in the property rights of another would meet the "trespass" standard, as proof that the defendant applied force to make entry shows a "breaking." But where the evidence also demonstrated that the defendant had permission to stay the night at the bed and breakfast inn, the element of "trespass" would be negated and no common law burglary prosecution could be maintained.

Both state and federal courts have consistently reversed convictions after determining that the prosecution did not prove one of the elements of the crime charged. For example, in an Illinois case, *People v. Gordon*, the reviewing court reversed the conviction of a defendant who had been convicted of possession of a stolen vehicle because the state failed to show that the defendant possessed the car "knowing" that it was stolen.[59] The Illinois statute makes it unlawful for a person not entitled to possession of a vehicle or an essential part of a vehicle to receive, possess, conceal, sell, dispose of, or transfer it, knowing it to have been converted or stolen. On appeal, Gordon claimed that the state failed to prove the essential element, knowing, beyond a reasonable doubt. Citing other decisions, the Illinois reviewing court repeated that "the burden is always upon the state to prove the defendant's guilt beyond a reasonable doubt, and to prove each and every element of the crime." Determining that the state had not proven knowledge on the defendant's part that the vehicle was stolen, the court reversed Gordon's conviction.

---

[57] United States v. Lopez, 443 F.3d 1026, 1030, 2006 U.S. App. LEXIS 9560 (8th Cir. 2006).

[58] 29 AM. JUR. 2d *Evidence* § 168

[59] People v. Gordon, 204 Ill. App. 3d 123, 561 N.E.2d 1164 (1990). *See also* Hay v. Ash, 638 A.2d 633 (Conn. 1994) and Victor v. Nebraska, 511 U.S. 1, 114 S. Ct. 1239, 127 L. Ed. 2d 583 (1994).

In a Georgia case, the police chased a suspicious man into a bathroom where illegal drugs were found following the defendant's exit. A search of the defendant's place of residence disclosed a gun that had been stolen more than two years previously. The jury found the defendant guilty of possessing cocaine, possessing marijuana, and theft by receiving the stolen gun. On appeal, the defendant contended that the evidence was insufficient to prove guilt beyond a reasonable doubt concerning the offense of theft by receiving stolen property. The prosecution did not dispute that the defendant had possession of the stolen gun, but there was no evidence that the defendant knew that the gun was stolen. The reviewing court reversed the gun theft conviction because the court agreed that there had been absolutely no evidence that the defendant had knowledge that the gun was stolen and the court noted that even the "possession of *recently* stolen property is not, by itself, sufficient to sustain a conviction for receiving stolen property."[60] Where one of the elements of a crime cannot be proved beyond a reasonable doubt, a reviewing court must reverse the conviction.

Many jurisdictions will reverse a conviction where one element has not been proved, where the existence of the element was in dispute, and a trial court omitted a jury instruction requiring proof of the element. In a Connecticut case, a defendant had been charged with possession of cocaine in his automobile and in a jacket alleged to belong to the defendant. The defendant disputed the allegation that the cocaine was in his possession and the trial court omitted to instruct the jury on the element that the defendant had to have knowledge that the substance was cocaine. The reviewing court reversed the trial court and held that harmless error could not be found because the issue of knowledge was in dispute.[61] On different facts, a Kentucky appellate court upheld a conviction for robbery in the first degree that required a threat while armed with a deadly weapon. The judge failed to instruct the jury that it first had to find that the defendant's gun was a deadly weapon before it could convict him of first-degree robbery. Over the defendant's objection that his case was not proved beyond a reasonable doubt because one element was missing, the Supreme Court of Kentucky held that the jury would most certainly have found that the gun was a deadly weapon and it applied the harmless error standard of review to uphold the conviction.[62]

In contrast to state practices, federal courts treat a neglected element somewhat differently. In one case in which the trial court failed to instruct the jury that the element, materiality, in a mail and wire fraud case was an element of both crimes, the Supreme Court allowed the conviction to stand. According to the Court, a jury instruction that omits an element of the crime does not necessarily result in a fundamentally unfair trial and should be judged on the harmless error standard. Even though the jury did not consider all the ele-

---

[60]   Crowder v. State, 271 Ga. App. 177, 609 S.E.2d 134, 2004 Ga. App. LEXIS 1657 (2004).
[61]   State v. Gooden, 89 Conn. App. 307, 319, 873 A.2d 243, 251, 2005 Conn. App. LEXIS 202 (2005).
[62]   Thacker v. Commonwealth, 194 S.W.3d 287, 2006 Ky. LEXIS 174 (2006).

ments in the case, the Court upheld the convictions that resulted.[63] Normally, factors that must be found for sentence enhancements must be determined by the jury and are treated like elements of the crime. In federal prosecutions, where the government must prove sentencing factors beyond a reasonable doubt and fails to do so, they can be treated just like elements of the crime that were not proven and can be measured by the harmless error standard. In a case in which the jury in a domestic assault case found that the defendant had assaulted his wife with a deadly weapon, the trial court enhanced the sentence because the proof in the case showed that the deadly weapon was a firearm even though the jury verdict form only mentioned a "deadly weapon." The Supreme Court believed that even though the jury had not specifically found that a firearm was used, and the verdict was for a "deadly weapon," the harmless error standard should be applied and the defendant should have been sentenced as if the jury had found that he used a firearm.[64]

If the prosecution fails to prove one element of the crime beyond a reasonable doubt, the accused may sometimes be found guilty of a lesser degree of that crime or a lesser included offense. For example, under some statutes, a person may be found guilty of burglary in the second degree if the prosecution failed to prove that the breaking and entering occurred at night. In such instances, of course, the penalty is less severe. Similarly, if a sentencing factor is not proved in a state case, the sentence enhancement should not be imposed.

§ 3.8 Burden on the Accused

A defendant has no duty to present any evidence, to introduce any witnesses, or to testify personally because a defendant has no burden to prove or disprove anything.[65] A defendant need not prove anything in order to prevail in a criminal trial. In fact, a strong general rule exists that "[i]t is improper for a prosecutor to suggest that a defendant shoulders the burden of proof in a criminal trial."[66] This concept is such a universal principle of American criminal justice that if a prosecutor were to hint or inadvertently imply during opening or closing statements that any burden rests on the defense, that suggestion could result in a reversal of a conviction on appeal. In an Illinois case involving alleged driving under the influence of alcohol, the prosecutor made improper remarks during the trial that emphasized that the defendant had failed to prove to the arresting officer that he was not guilty of the charged offense by refusing a breath test. The prosecutor repeated the remarks that the defendant missed a chance to prove his innocence by not taking a breath test during closing arguments. On appeal, the defendant contended that the remarks by the prosecutor created the inference that the defendant had some

---

[63]   Neder v. United States, 527 U.S. 1 (1999).
[64]   Washington v. Fecuenco, 548 U.S. ___, 2006 U.S. LEXIS 5164 (2006).
[65]   Generally, a defendant has no burden of proof unless an affirmative defense is at issue.
[66]   Stephenson v. State, 742 N.E.2d 463 (Ind. 2001).

duty to prove his innocence and the prosecutor's remarks shifted the burden of proof from the prosecution. The Supreme Court of Illinois refused to reverse the conviction because the defendant had failed to object at the proper time and the court believed that the outcome was not affected. However, the court did agree that the prosecutor's remarks were improper when it noted, "we feel strongly that the argument here, which implied that defendant might have proven his innocence by submitting to a breath test, is in conflict with the constitutional principle that a defendant is innocent until proven guilty. This type of argument should not be countenanced."[67] The court upheld the principle that a defendant does not have to prove anything and that it was error for the prosecution to imply that the defendant had any burden of proof.

An accused, in constructing a defense, may make some issues logically and legally relevant by pleading an affirmative defense where the burden of proof at some level may rest on the defendant. In the case of an insanity defense, the defendant may have the burden of proof by a preponderance, by clear and convincing evidence, or the defendant may merely have to raise the issue of insanity and introduce some slight evidence of insanity to meet the required affirmative burden. Once the defendant has met whatever burden was required in the jurisdiction, the burden of going forward with the evidence will fall on the prosecution to negate insanity or to introduce evidence to contradict the defendant's claim.

When pleading an affirmative defense, such as coercion, self-defense, entrapment, or mistake, all of which would absolve a defendant of liability, the defendant generally has the responsibility of "going forward with the evidence." Because the allocation of the burden of persuasion varies in many jurisdictions, the burden of proving affirmative defenses may fall on either the government or the defendant as determined by state or federal statute or court decision. For example, New York requires an affirmative defense to be proved by the defendant by a preponderance of the evidence.[68] Arizona handles affirmative defenses differently from New York. In an Arizona case in which a felon was alleged to be in possession of a firearm while under a disability, the defendant bore the burden of going forward with evidence that his gun rights had been restored, but once the defendant had made his proof, the prosecution had the burden of proof to prove nonrestoration of gun rights.[69] Even where the burden of proof has been allocated to the defendant who asserts an affirmative defense, the reality is that, in order to prevail, the defendant need only introduce sufficient believable evidence to create a reasonable doubt. To warrant submission of the defense to the jury, the defendant must produce substantial evidence to support the particular defense theory sufficient to create a reasonable doubt.[70]

---

[67]   People v. Johnson, 218 Ill. 2d 125, 140, 842 N.E.2d 714, 723, 2005 Ill. LEXIS 2072 (2005).
[68]   See N.Y. C.L.S. PENAL § 25.00 Defenses; burden of proof (2006).
[69]   State v. Kelly, 210 Ariz. 460, 464, 112 P.3d 682, 686, 2005 Ariz. App. LEXIS 70 (2005).
[70]   State v. Babers, 514 N.W.2d 79 (Iowa 1994).

The Supreme Court of California explained that where a defendant presented sufficient evidence that, if believed by the jury, could support an affirmative defense, the trial court must offer the jury an instruction explaining the concept of affirmative defenses and how they operate. The court reversed a conviction for selling unregistered securities because one defendant offered a sufficient evidentiary foundation that he personally did not know that the securities he was selling were required to be registered prior to sale. Because the defendant made a proper showing of evidence that could support an affirmative defense, the trial court committed reversible error in not giving the jury an instruction on affirmative defenses.[71] If the defense introduces a sufficient foundation showing an affirmative defense, the defendant is entitled to an appropriate jury instruction on the affirmative defense.

Because the government has the burden of proof on each element of the crime, the burden cannot lawfully be shifted to the defendant to demonstrate that one element of the crime has not been proven. For example, a city ordinance prohibited waving at traffic to stop passersby for the purpose of selling drugs as well as doing the same thing to pedestrians. The ordinance contained a rebuttable presumption that a person who performs the prohibited behaviors has the specific intent to engage in the drug-related activity. A reviewing court held that the rebuttable presumption in the ordinance shifted part of the burden of proof from the prosecution to the defendant.[72] The ordinance violated the federal Constitution by requiring the defendant to disprove an element of the crime, specific intent, in order to prevail.

Similar wording has been attacked in cases in which the wording of the statute had the arguable effect of shifting part of the burden of proof in an unconstitutional manner. The Supreme Court decided to review the procedure by accepting the case, *Sandstrom v. Montana*.[73] In this murder case, the state charged the defendant with deliberate homicide, and the question of the defendant's intent was an important element of the crime. At the trial, the defendant's attorney informed the jury that, although his client admitted to killing the victim, he did not do so "purposely or knowingly," and he was, therefore, not guilty of a deliberate crime but rather of a lesser crime. The defendant's counsel objected to the instruction that "the law presumes that a person intends the ordinary consequences of his voluntary act." He argued that this instruction had the effect of shifting the burden of proof on the issue of purpose or knowledge to the defendant, and it was therefore impermissible because it was in violation of the constitutional guarantee of due process of law. The Supreme Court, in reversing the decision, reasoned that:

> [A] reasonable jury could have interpreted the presumptions as "conclusive," i.e., not technically as a presumption at all, but rather an irrebuttable direction by the court to find intent once convinced

---

[71] People v. Salas, 37 Cal. 4th 967; 127 P.3d 40, 38 Cal. Rptr. 3d 624, 2006 Cal. LEXIS 1900 (2006).

[72] State v. Ashford, 2005 Ohio 2880; 2005 Ohio App. LEXIS 2705 (2005).

[73] Sandstrom v. Montana, 442 U.S. 510, 1979 U.S. LEXIS 113 (1979).

of the facts triggering the assumption. Alternatively, the jury may
have interpreted the instruction as a direction to find intent upon
proof of the defendant's voluntary actions, unless the defendant
proved the contrary.[74]

Under either interpretation, according to the Court, the burden of persuasion on the element of intent effectively shifted to the defendant. The Court
then stated:

> We conclude that under either of the two possible interpretations of
> the instruction set out above, precisely that effect (relieving the state
> of the burden of proof) would result, and that the instruction there-
> fore represents constitutional error.[75]

To summarize, the defendant has the burden of going forward with the
evidence to show an affirmative defense such as alibi or insanity; however, an
instruction that tends to require the defendant to prove his or her innocence, or
any instruction that relieves the prosecution of proving an element of the
crime, violates the due process requirement that the prosecution must prove
every element of the offense beyond a reasonable doubt.

§ 3.9 Burden of Proving Affirmative Defenses—General

Once the prosecution has introduced sufficient evidence that, if believed,
would permit a finding of guilt beyond a reasonable doubt on every element
of the charge, in order to avoid a conviction, the accused may be obliged to
respond with evidence that raises or permits a reasonable doubt that he or she
is guilty as charged.[76] In most instances, the defense has only to introduce sufficient evidence to raise a reasonable doubt in the minds of the jury.

In one group, states follow a slightly different path and allocate a higher
burden to the prosecution where a defendant introduced evidence in support
of an affirmative defense. Where a defendant offers some credible evidence
supporting the applicability of the affirmative defense, the prosecution has the
burden of going forward with the evidence and has the ultimate burden of
proof. States in this category hold that the prosecution bears the burden of
proving the defendant's guilt beyond a reasonable doubt concerning to the
issue raised by evidence supporting the affirmative defense. Some jurisdictions allocate the burden clearly on the defendant to prove the affirmative
defense by a preponderance of the evidence with no burden on the prosecution. In a federal prosecution for illegally purchasing firearms, the defendant

---

[74]   *Id.* at 517.
[75]   *Id.* at 521.
[76]   People v. Gonzalez, 275 Cal. Rptr. 729, 800 P.2d 1159 (1990).

contended that her affirmative evidence of duress should force the prosecution to disprove duress beyond a reasonable doubt. The Supreme Court rejected her position because a majority of the Court presumed that the Congress intended a defendant accused of firearms offenses to bear the burden of proving duress by a preponderance of the evidence.[77] In a prosecution for illegally purchasing firearms, this was especially the case because the elements of the crime, if proved, show guilt, while duress constitutes an excuse for the crime, but does not negate an element of the crime.

Allocating the burden of proving an affirmative defense by statute does not violate due process even where the burden is placed on the defendant to prove insanity by clear and convincing evidence. When Congress reformed the federal insanity defense, it allocated the burden of proof on the defendant by the standard of clear and convincing evidence.[78] In allocating the burden of proof, the Supreme Court has held that a state may constitutionally place an even higher burden of proof of the insanity defense on the defendant by specifying the standard of proof beyond a reasonable doubt.[79]

In the sections that follow, some of the more common affirmative defenses are discussed, including alibi, self-defense, justification, excuse, and other affirmative defenses, with special emphasis on the question of burden of proof.

§ 3.10   —Alibi

In the alibi defense, the defendant does not dispute the fact that the crime occurred, but alleges that he or she was not present to commit the crime because he or she was at a different location and otherwise had no connection to the alleged crime, whether in planning or in execution. Some jurisdictions hold that the presentation of an alibi constitutes an affirmative defense, and that when it is asserted, the defendant has the burden of proof by a preponderance of the evidence.[80] Georgia law takes an opposite view and in a case in which the indictment charged that the defendant was present at the crime scene, even if the defendant introduced alibi evidence, the burden of proof remained on the prosecution to prove the defendant's presence beyond a reasonable doubt.[81] Because the defense of alibi denies any connection with the crime, a defendant who successfully asserts an alibi defense must be acquitted.

Some states require by rule or statute that the defense give the prosecution pretrial notice of an intention to offer an alibi defense. For example, Connecticut requires that the defendant give notice to the prosecution 20 days after the prosecution has stated the time, date, and place where it alleged the crime

---

[77]   Dixon v. United States, ___ U.S. ___, 2006 U.S. LEXIS 4894 (2006).

[78]   United States v. Freeman, 804 F.2d 1574 (11th Cir. 1986). *See also* People v. Spry, 68 Cal. Rptr. 2d 691 (1997). As of 2006, the Supreme Court has never accepted a case to review the constitutionality of the federal insanity defense statute.

[79]   Leland v. Oregon, 343 U.S. 790 (1952).

[80]   State v. Stump, 254 Iowa 1181, 119 N.W.2d 210 (1963).

[81]   Morton v. State, 276 Ga. App. 421, 423, 623 S.E.2d 239, 241, 2005 Ga. App. LEXIS 1266 (2005).

occurred.[82] Where the defense fails to offer prior notice of alibi and the names and addresses of alibi witnesses are not furnished, the alibi witnesses may be prevented from testifying.[83] The reasons for this exclusion, as expressed in a Connecticut case, is that exclusion is a sanction for failure to obey the notice rules; that otherwise, the state would suffer surprise at trial because it would not have time to investigate the witnesses; and that it was proper for the trial court to view late identification of alibi witnesses with suspicion.[84]

Such a statute requiring pretrial notice, however, cannot be used to prohibit a defendant from testifying on his or her own behalf even if he or she has not given the notice to the prosecution.[85] In *State v. Hibbard*, the court pointed out that the state already has the burden of proving beyond a reasonable doubt that the defendant was at the scene of the crime during the time in question. Accordingly, the court held that the trial court erred in denying the appellant the opportunity to testify concerning his whereabouts at the time that the crime occurred.[86]

In explaining the burden of proof requirement in alibi cases, an Oklahoma court pointed out that in requiring the defendant to introduce evidence when he or she claims alibi, the burden of proof does not shift to the defendant to disprove an element of the crime.[87] The court continued by explaining that all that is demanded of the defendant who presents an alibi defense is that he or she demonstrate a state of facts that creates a reasonable doubt concerning presence of the accused at the time and place where the crime was committed.

In *Dat Pham v. Beaver*, a New York court charged the jury that the government had to prove that the defendant was the individual who committed the crime and that the government had to disprove the defendant's alibi beyond a reasonable doubt. The appeals court approved the jury charge and refused to disturb the defendant's conviction[88] because the charge correctly explained New York law, which required the prosecution to rebut evidence of alibi by proof beyond a reasonable doubt.

A defendant is entitled to an alibi instruction, even if not wholly believed, when there is evidence supported by law and when the defense has some foundation in the evidence presented by the defendant.[89] However, an alibi instruc-

---

[82]   *See* CONN. PRACTICE BOOK § 40-21. Defense of Alibi; Notice by Defendant. (2006).

[83]   FLA. R. CRIM. P. 3.200 Notice of Alibi (2006). *See also* McEwing v. State, 2006 Ark. LEXIS 332 (Ark. 2006).

[84]   *See* State v. Salters, 89 Conn. App. 221; 872 A.2d 933; 2005 Conn. App. LEXIS 200 (2005). *See also* State v. Lewis, 391 N.W.2d 726 (Iowa 1986), which held that a trial court's exclusion of the defendant's alibi witness was an abuse of discretion when the defense counsel filed a notice of alibi one day after he heard of the existence of witnesses, witnesses were made available for all informal interviews or depositions before the trial, and the state had one week before the trial to investigate the alibi defense, but chose to do nothing, even declining interviews with witnesses.

[85]   People v. Williams, 2006 Mich. App. LEXIS 2227 (Mich. 2006).

[86]   State v. Hibbard, 273 N.W.2d 172 (S.D. 1978). *See also* Commonwealth v. Ellis, 700 P.2d 948 (Pa. 1997).

[87]   Ashinsky v. State, 780 P.2d 201 (Okla. 1989).

[88]   2006 U.S. Dist. LEXIS 46109 (W.D. Ny. 2006).

[89]   United States v. White, 443 F.3d 582, 587, 2006 U.S. App. LEXIS 8168 (7th Cir. 2006).

tion is appropriate only when the defense evidence demonstrates the defendant's presence elsewhere for the entire period of time during which the government's evidence shows he or she was involved in criminal activity.[90]

§ 3.11 —Insanity

A defendant is presumed to be mentally fit to stand trial, plead, and be sentenced, but may be found unfit to stand trial if, because of mental or physical condition, he or she is unable to understand the nature and purpose of the proceedings against him or her or to assist in his or her defense.[91]

There are two distinct and divergent rules respecting the degree of evidence necessary to rebut the presumption of sanity normally prevailing in a criminal case. Under the first rule, the ultimate burden of proof of sanity is, like any other element of the crime, on the prosecution, and sanity must be shown beyond a reasonable doubt. However, the matter of the defendant's insanity must be made an issue by the defendant before the duty of the prosecution to prove sanity beyond a reasonable doubt will arise. Under this approach, some evidence of insanity will suffice to dissipate the presumption of sanity and put the burden of proof on the prosecution. To raise the issue of sanity, the defendant has the burden of introducing evidence sufficient to evoke the possibility that, as a result of mental disease or defect, he or she lacked a substantial capacity to appreciate the wrongfulness of his or her conduct or to conform his or her conduct to the requirements of the law.

The rule followed by most state courts (and federal courts until 1984) requires that when the defendant introduces substantial evidence of his or her insanity, the issue of his or her capacity to commit the offense becomes a question of proof, and the prosecution's burden of going forward with the evidence requires it to introduce sufficient evidence on the issue of sanity to preclude a verdict of acquittal for the defendant.[92] However, the defendant must introduce sufficient evidence to meet the burden of proof required in that particular jurisdiction to prove insanity. In a prosecution in which the defendant alleged legal insanity as a defense and offered proof, the judge rejected the defense because, as a matter of law, the evidence directed toward proving insanity failed to meet the clear and convincing level of proof. According to the reviewing court, "[t]he clear and convincing standard requires a quantum of proof greater than a preponderance of the evidence, but less than proof beyond a reasonable doubt"[93] and requiring clear and convincing proof did not violate standards of due process.

---

[90] Bright v. United States, 698 A.2d 450 (D.C. App. 1997).
[91] People v. Straub, 685 N.E.2d 429 (Ill. 1997).
[92] United States v. Westerhausen, 283 F.2d 844 (7th Cir. 1960).
[93] People v. Clay, 361 Ill. App. 3d 310, 332, 836 N.E.2d 872, 882, 2005 Ill. App. LEXIS 994 (2005).

A considerable number of courts take a different approach and hold that insanity is an affirmative defense that must be shown by the defendant by a preponderance of the evidence. The statutes in several states allocate the burden of proof for legal insanity to the defendant[94] by a preponderance of the evidence.[95] For example, in California, when a defendant pleads not guilty by reason of insanity, a separate proceeding that is part of the criminal trial is empaneled in which the defendant has the burden of proof by a preponderance of the evidence to prove that he or she was insane at the time he or she committed the act.[96] The United States Supreme Court in several instances has determined that placing this burden on the defendant does not violate the Constitution of the United States[97] even where the burden is on the defendant to prove insanity beyond a reasonable doubt.[98]

In 1984, as part of the Comprehensive Crime Control Act, Congress enacted legislation titled "Insanity Defense Reform Act of 1984." Section 17 of Title 18 of the United States Code defines the scope of the insanity defense for federal offenses and shifts the burden of proof to the defendant. This section provides:

(a) Affirmative Defense. It is an affirmative defense to a prosecution under any Federal statute that, at the time of the commission of the acts constituting the offense, the defendant, as a result of a severe mental disease or defect, was unable to appreciate the nature and quality or the wrongfulness of his acts. Mental disease or defect does not otherwise constitute a defense.

(b) Burden of Proof. The defendant has the burden of proving the defense of insanity by clear and convincing evidence.[99]

The clear and convincing evidence standard is a higher standard than a mere preponderance of the evidence and remains lower than Oregon's current standard for its insanity defense of proof beyond a reasonable doubt.[100] The design of the revised federal insanity defense was to eliminate the confusing spectacle of competing expert witnesses testifying to directly contradictory conclusions as to the ultimate legal issue to be found by the trier of fact. Under the revised insanity defense, expert psychiatric testimony is limited to presenting and explaining the diagnosis of the psychiatrist. In federal criminal trials,

---

[94] CAL. EVID. CODE § 522 (2006). *See also* Turner v. Arkansas, 2005 Ark. App. LEXIS 237 (2005).

[95] A.C.A. § 5-1-111 (d)(1) (2006).

[96] People v. Harris, 130 Cal. App. 4th 773, 30 Cal. Rptr. 3d 426, 2005 Cal. App. LEXIS 1017 (Calif. 2005).

[97] Patterson v. New York, 432 U.S. 197, 97 S. Ct. 2319, 53 L. Ed. 2d 281 (1977). Leland v. Oregon, 343 U.S. 790, 72 S. Ct. 1002, 96 L. Ed. 1302 (1952). *See also* Fleenor v. State, 622 N.E.2d 140 (Ind. 1993), in which the court held that instructing the jury that a capital murder defendant was required to prove insanity at the time of the offense by a preponderance of the evidence, if the state proved that the defendant knowingly killed the victim, was proper.

[98] *See* Leland v. Oregon, 343 U.S. 790 (1952).

[99] 18 U.S.C. § 17 (2006).

[100] People v. Clay, 361 Ill. App. 3d 310, 325, 836 N.E.2d 872, 885, 2005 Ill. App. LEXIS 994 (2005).

expert witnesses may not "state an opinion as to whether the defendant did or did not have the mental conditions constituting an element of the crime charged. Such ultimate issues are matters for the trier of fact alone."[101]

Another provision of the Crime Control Act relates to the disposition of a person found not guilty by reason of insanity.[102] This section of the Act provides:

> If a person is found not guilty only by reason of insanity at the time of the offense charged, he shall be committed to a suitable facility until such time as he is eligible for release pursuant to subsection (e).

Subsection (d) of the Act relates to burden of proof. It provides that:

> In a hearing pursuant to subsection (c) of this section, a person found not guilty only by reason of insanity of an offense involving bodily injury to, or serious damage to property of, another person, or involving a substantial risk of such injury or damage, has the burden of proving by clear and convincing evidence that his release would not create a substantial risk of bodily injury to another person or serious damage of property of another due to present mental disease or defect. With respect to any other offense, the person has the burden of proof by the preponderance of the evidence.

The federal courts have been consistent in holding that the provisions of the Insanity Defense Reform Act, which shift to the defendant the burden of proving the affirmative defense of insanity by clear and convincing evidence, do not violate due process.[103] Illinois follows the federal standard by requiring defendants who plead an insanity defense "to prove by clear and convincing evidence that the defendant is not guilty by reason of insanity."[104] However, the burden of proof remains on the prosecution to prove every element beyond a reasonable doubt.

In *United States v. Byrd*, a bank robbery case, the judges of the Eighth Circuit Court of Appeals rejected the defendant's argument that shifting the burden of proving insanity to the defendant effectively gave him the burden of disproving an element of the offense. Explaining their decision, the court stated:

> Willfulness constitutes the only element going to *mens rea* in the crime charged to Byrd. Consequently, the burden of proving insanity properly resides with the defendant, who may raise the issue for the first time as an affirmative defense.

In 1984, when Congress was considering the amendments to the United States Code relating to the insanity defense, the committee considering the

---

[101] FED. R. EVID. § 704(b).

[102] 18 U.S.C. § 4243 (2006).

[103] United States v. Amos, 803 F.2d 419 (8th Cir. 1986); United States v. Byrd, 834 F.2d 145 (8th Cir. 1987).

[104] *See* § 720 ILCS 5/6-2. Insanity (2006).

modifications found that more than one-half of the states placed the burden of proving insanity on the defendant. Most of the states that place the burden on the defendant require that the defendant prove severe mental disease or defect by a preponderance of the evidence, while the federal law now places the burden on the defendant to prove this by clear and convincing evidence.

To summarize, Congress established the burden of proof in federal criminal trials as requiring the defendant to prove insanity by clear and convincing proof. In some states, the issue of a defendant's capacity to commit the offense becomes a question of proof and the prosecution must introduce evidence sufficient to preclude a verdict of acquittal for the defendant. In other states, the burden is on the accused to prove insanity by a preponderance of the evidence, while in a third group of states and in the federal courts, the burden of proof is on the defendant under a standard of clear and convincing evidence. To have any chance of prevailing on an insanity defense, the defendant who claims insanity has at least a minimal burden to go forward with evidence to overcome the presumption of sanity and may have the burden completely placed on him- or herself by proof beyond a reasonable doubt.

§ 3.12 —Self-Defense

In criminal prosecutions involving violence to the alleged victim, justifiable self-defense may be set up as a complete defense to, or exoneration from, liability for the act charged. Preservation from harm, whether the danger rises to the level of defense of life or of defense from lesser physical harms, is generally recognized as proper conduct if the defender is not committing any wrong.[105] As a general rule, during the presentation of a homicide case, the prosecution has the burden of establishing the death of a human caused by the defendant under circumstances in which it did not appear that the defendant acted in self-defense. If the defendant alleged self-defense in this hypothetical homicide case, the burden of proving this affirmative defense requires the defendant to go forward with proof of facts that indicate that the defendant had a right of self-defense and used no more force than was appropriate under the circumstances. Proof of the defense dictates that the defendant must introduce proof that the he or she did not provoke the incident and killed the other while under an actual or reasonable apprehension of death or serious bodily injury from the aggressor.[106]

A few states place the ultimate burden of proof for affirmative defenses squarely on the defendant. For example, Ohio law states "[t]he burden of going forward with the evidence of an affirmative defense, and the burden of proof, by a preponderance of the evidence, for an affirmative defense, is upon the accused."[107] An Ohio woman had been convicted of killing her husband

---

[105] *See* People v. Lee, 131 Cal. App. 4th 1413, 32 Cal. Rptr. 3d 745, 2005 Cal. App. LEXIS 1278 (2005), where victim fired gun at two menacing dogs.

[106] 40 AM. JUR. 2D *Homicide* § 141 (2006).

[107] OHIO REV. CODE ANN. 2901.05 Burden and degree of proof. (2006).

with a firearm despite her argument of self-defense. She appealed, contending that the Ohio procedure that required her to prove her affirmative defense by a preponderance violated the due process clause of the Fourteenth Amendment. The Supreme Court rejected her contention and held that the burden of proof did not require that she prove her innocence. Ohio's definition of aggravated murder required the prosecution to prove that she had both purposely and with prior calculation and design caused her husband's death. According to the Supreme Court, the fact that evidence offered to support self-defense might negate a purposeful killing by prior calculation and design does not mean that elements of the crime and self-defense impermissibly overlap. Evidence that could create a reasonable doubt about one element of the crime necessary for a finding of guilt could easily fall far short of proving self-defense by a preponderance of the evidence.[108] Where a reasonable doubt appears, the defendant would have to be acquitted. The United States Supreme Court agreed that neither Ohio law nor the instructions concerning self-defense violate the due process clause of the Fourteenth Amendment by shifting to the petitioner the state's burden of proving the elements of the crime. The court went on to note that the "mere fact that all but two States have abandoned the common-law rule that affirmative defenses, including self-defense, must be proved by the defendant does not render the rule unconstitutional."

While a state statute requiring the defendant to prove self-defense does not have an unconstitutional burden-shifting result, some states require only that the defendant raise some evidence tending to prove self-defense. For example, in Illinois, once the defendant has presented some evidence, the burden of proof falls on the prosecution to establish beyond a reasonable doubt that the defendant did not act in self-defense.[109] In the case of *People v. Young*, a reviewing court noted that once a defendant raised the issue of self-defense and introduced some evidence in support of self-defense, the burden fell to the prosecution to prove beyond a reasonable doubt that the defendant did not act in self-defense. The prosecution, to win the case, was required to prove the elements of the crime charged, prove beyond a reasonable doubt that the defendant did not act in self-defense, and that the defendant's use of force was unreasonable.[110] In the case of *Rogers v. State*, the Court of Appeals noted:

> Self defense is established if a defendant: (1) was in a place where he had a right to be; (2) did not provoke, instigate, or participate willingly in the violence; and (3) had a reasonable fear of death or great bodily harm.[111]

The court continued by explaining that the state may negate self-defense by rebutting the defense directly by disproving one of the above elements of self-

---

[108] Martin v. Ohio, 480 U.S. 228, 107 S. Ct. 1098, 94 L. Ed. 2d 267 (1987). *See* case in Part II.
[109] People v. Young, 347 Ill. App. 3d 909, 920, 807 N.E.2d 1125, 1134, 2004 Ill. App. LEXIS 338 (2004).
[110] *Id.*
[111] Rogers v. State, 814 N.E.2d 695, 702, 2004 Ind. App. LEXIS 17 (2004).

defense, by demonstrating that the defendant did not act in self-defense, or, in some cases, the evidence during the prosecution's case-in-chief may prove sufficient to negate self-defense. In evaluating an appeal involving self-defense, the appellate court followed prior law when it noted "[t]he standard of review for a challenge to the sufficiency of evidence to rebut a claim of self-defense is the same as the standard for any insufficiency of the evidence claim."[112] Finally, the court admonished that a defendant's conviction in spite of a claim of self-defense would be reversed only if no reasonable person could say that self-defense was not negated by the state beyond a reasonable doubt.

An Alaska decision followed prior case law in applying the rule that when a defendant has presented some evidence of self-defense, it becomes the prosecution's duty to disprove the defendant's evidence of self-defense beyond a reasonable doubt.[113] In this case, the prosecution's evidence showed that the defendant had hit the victim in the forehead with his hand, punched her in the face, dragged her to the floor, and choked her. The defendant's evidence was that the woman was the aggressor and that he held her on the floor to prevent her from harming him. The self-defense claim failed, but the defendant's evidence was sufficient to force the prosecution to disprove self-defense beyond a reasonable doubt and to obtain a jury instruction on self-defense.[114]

To summarize, in some states when the accused offers the affirmative defense of self-defense and produces evidence in support of the self-defense theory, the burden is on the prosecutor to prove beyond a reasonable doubt that the accused did not act in self-defense. Procedurally, the defendant must raise the issue and offer some evidence that shifts the burden of proof to the prosecution. In other states, the accused not only has the initial burden of going forward with evidence of self-defense, but also carries the ultimate burden of proof by a preponderance of the evidence that he or she acted in self-defense. While imposing any burden of proof on a defendant might appear to raise constitutional issues, state statutes allocating the ultimate burden of proof to the defense have been determined not to run afoul of the requirements of the Constitution.

§ 3.13 Sufficiency of Evidence

Once a court or jury has rendered a decision, there is a strong presumption of regularity and that the case was properly determined. When a defendant appeals a conviction, he or she must contend that serious defects exist in the case sufficient to warrant a reversal of the judgment. "When determining if sufficient evidence was presented to sustain a conviction, a court must view the evidence in a light most favorable to the prosecution. It must determine whether any rational trier of fact could have found that the essential elements

---

[112] *Id.* at 702.

[113] Ross v. State, 2006 Alaska App. LEXIS 41 (2006).

[114] *Id.*

of the crime were proven as required."[115] A reviewing court, on appeal or in a habeas corpus action, may determine that the evidence was insufficient to support the finding of guilty even though, technically, an appellate court does not reweigh the evidence or reconsider the credibility of the witnesses.[116] In *Jackson v. Virginia*, the United States Supreme Court, in confirming the authority of a federal court to review a state court decision on the sufficiency of the evidence, made this comment:

> Yet a properly instructed jury may occasionally convict even when it can be said that no rational trier of fact could find guilt beyond a reasonable doubt, and the same may be said of a trial judge sitting as a jury.[117]

Once it is recognized that a reviewing court can look behind the decision of the jury to determine whether there was sufficient evidence to justify a finding of guilt beyond a reasonable doubt, the question then becomes: What is the test of sufficiency?

In *Jackson*, the United States Court of Appeals for the Fourth Circuit applied the *Thompson v. Louisville*[118] sufficiency-of-the-evidence rule and refused to reverse the state court conviction. Under the *Thompson* rule, a reviewing court must affirm a state court decision if there is any evidence in the record to support it. Under *Thompson*, if there is absolutely no evidence to justify the jury in finding guilt, then the court will reverse the conviction as a violation of due process. But if there is any evidence to support the conviction, as there was in *Jackson*, the case will be affirmed.

The defendant in Jackson appealed to the United States Supreme Court, claiming that the "any evidence rule" was inadequate to protect against misapplication of the constitutional standards of reasonable doubt. The United States Supreme Court agreed, stating that the rule that should have been applied was not the "any evidence rule," but rather the rule that was stated in *In re Winship*,[119] which held that a federal habeas corpus court must consider not whether there was any evidence to support a state conviction, but whether there was sufficient evidence to justify a rational trier of fact to find guilt beyond a reasonable doubt. The Supreme Court in *Jackson* first held that the *Thompson* "no evidence" rule is simply inadequate to protect against misapplications of the constitutional standard of reasonable doubt. That Court then insisted:

> Instead the relevant question is whether after reviewing the evidence in the light most favorable to the prosecution, any rational trier of fact could have found the essential elements of the crime beyond a reasonable doubt.

---

[115] People v. Tombs, 472 Mich. 446, 697 N.W.2d 494, 2005 Mich. LEXIS 622 (2005). *See also* Jackson v. Virginia, 443 U.S. 307, 99 S. Ct. 2781, 61 L. Ed. 2d 560 (1979).

[116] 2006 U.S. App. LEXIS 15848 (3d Cir. 2006).

[117] *Id.*

[118] Thompson v. Louisville, 362 U.S. 199, 80 S. Ct. 624, 4 L. Ed. 2d 654 (1960).

[119] In re Winship, 397 U.S. 358, 90 S. Ct. 1068, 25 L. Ed. 2d 368 (1970). *See* case in Part II.

In affirming that a federal court can and will apply the Winship sufficiency rule, the Court in *Jackson* made this conclusion as to the rules to be followed:

> We hold that in a challenge to a state criminal conviction . . . the appellant is entitled to habeas corpus relief if it is found that upon the record evidence adduced at the trial no rational trier of fact could have found proof of guilt beyond a reasonable doubt.

After asserting that the Supreme Court has this authority and after stating the rule, the Court then found that when applying the rule to the facts of this case, *Jackson* still had no cause of action. The Court said that from the evidence in the record, it was clear that the judge could reasonably have found beyond a reasonable doubt that the petitioner did possess the necessary intent at or before the time of the killing to justify the first-degree murder conviction.

To summarize the sufficiency-of-the-evidence rule, in a criminal case the prosecutor must introduce relevant and otherwise admissible evidence sufficient for the trier of fact to find the defendant guilty beyond a reasonable doubt. The reviewing court may set aside a conviction even after the trier of fact has rendered a guilty verdict if that reviewing court finds that no rational trier of fact could logically have found the defendant guilty beyond a reasonable doubt.

§ 3.14 Summary

The ultimate burden of proof rests on the prosecution from the beginning of a trial and it never shifts to the defendant. A defendant may, depending on the jurisdiction, have an ultimate burden of proof where a defendant asserts one or more affirmative defenses. The burden of going forward with the evidence initially rests on the prosecution but may shift to the defense if the prosecution succeeds in introducing believable prima facie evidence of guilt. To avoid an adverse result, the defendant must meet the burden of going forward with the evidence. The higher level of proof that the federal Constitution requires in criminal cases constitutes the major difference between civil and criminal cases because plaintiffs only need to meet the burden of proving their case by a preponderance of the evidence.

Depending upon the nature of the case, there are three degrees of proof required. These are: a preponderance of the evidence, clear and convincing evidence, and beyond a reasonable doubt. While in a civil case the plaintiff is usually only required to establish his or her claim by a preponderance of the evidence. Some civil cases go beyond this standard and require proof by clear and convincing evidence because other important interests, like reputation, may be at stake. The use of the higher beyond a reasonable doubt standard in criminal cases has been justified because freedom and liberty may be at risk—not merely money. In a criminal case, however, there is no doubt that the accused retains the presumption of innocence until his or her guilt is established beyond a reasonable doubt.

The burden is on the prosecution in a criminal case to show affirmatively the existence of every material fact, including each element of the crime, the identity of the person who committed the crime, and that the crime was perpetrated in violation of the penal laws of the place where it took place.

Even though the primary burden in a criminal case rests with the prosecution, the accused may have the burden of proof when he or she claims an affirmative defense. For example, when claiming an affirmative defense such as coercion, self-defense, entrapment, or mistake, the burden of proof may rest with the defendant to prove the defense, usually by a preponderance of the evidence. Some jurisdictions require that a defendant raise the issue of an affirmative defense and present some evidence in order to require the prosecution to disprove the affirmative defense beyond a reasonable doubt. However, any jury instruction by the court or prosecutor's comment that might reasonably imply that a defendant must prove his or her innocence, or that relieves the prosecution of the duty of proving an element of the crime, violates the due process clause of the Fourteenth Amendment in a state prosecution.

Even though alibi, strictly speaking, is not an affirmative defense, because the defendant merely offers evidence to rebut evidence introduced by the prosecution that the defendant was at the scene of the crime, the defendant must affirmatively introduce evidence to substantiate this alibi claim. If the defense is insanity, the law in some jurisdictions requires that the defendant prove his or her legal insanity by a preponderance of the evidence or by clear and convincing evidence, but constitutionally proof beyond a reasonable doubt has been approved. Also, when evidence is introduced to show self-defense to justify an otherwise criminal act, the defendant may be constitutionally required to offer proof by a preponderance of the evidence that he or she did act in self-defense.

All criminal justice personnel, starting with the law enforcement investigator must recognize the additional evidentiary burden on the prosecution that criminal cases present and must be aware that sufficient evidence should be gathered to convince the jury or the judge not only that the accused is probably guilty of the offense charged, but also that he is guilty beyond a reasonable doubt. Those involved in the criminal justice process should also recognize the fact that the defense will make every effort to create a doubt in the minds of the jury and need that doubt concerning one element for the defense to prevail.

A study of the burden of proof accentuates the need to become familiar with other evidence rules that bear upon the admissibility of evidence. Much of the remainder of the book is devoted to a discussion of these rules.

Proof via Evidence 4

At the trial of a person charged with murder, the fact of death is provable by circumstantial evidence, notwithstanding that neither the body nor any trace of the body has been found and that the accused has made no confession of any participation in the crime. Before he can be convicted, the fact of death should be proved by such circumstances as render the commission of the crime morally certain and leave no ground for possible doubt; the circumstantial evidence should be so cogent and compelling as to convince a jury that upon no rational hypothesis other than murder can the facts be accounted for.

Rex v. Horry, 1952 N.Z.L.R. 111

Chapter Outline

Key Terms and Concepts

case in chief	proof
objection	rebuttal
pretrial motion	rejoinder

§ 4.1 Introduction

In the previous chapter, cases were cited and discussed that leave no doubt that the burden of proving guilt in a criminal case is on the prosecution. How does the prosecutor go about meeting this burden? Must each fact or each bit of knowledge used by the jury or other factfinder in determining guilt or innocence be placed before the jury in the form of direct evidence?

Although the parties have the responsibility of introducing evidence to verify the claims presented, it is not necessary that all facts before the court be in the form of direct evidence. To save time and to avoid placing an unnecessary burden on the parties, the judge may take judicial notice of certain facts and may advise the jury that they may make certain presumptions and inferences. The factfinders may also consider facts stipulated by the parties. Therefore, the jury or other factfinders may make a decision from: (1) facts presented in the form of evidence; (2) information judicially noticed by the judge; (3) legal presumptions; (4) judicially approved inferences; and (5) accepted stipulations. In this chapter, emphasis is on the first of these—facts presented in the form of evidence.

After considering the procedure relating to pretrial motions to exclude evidence, this chapter discusses general admissibility tests. This is followed by a section describing the order of presenting evidence at the trial. Also, the role of the judge, jury, witness, prosecuting attorney, and legal counsel for the defense in relation to the introduction and evaluation of evidence is explained. Finally, the rules relating to the admissibility and weight of direct and circumstantial evidence are comprehensively considered.

In Chapters 5 and 6, "substitutes for evidence"—judicial notice, presumptions, inferences, and stipulations—are defined and examples of each are offered.

§ 4.2 Pretrial Motions Pertaining to Evidence

Rule 104

Preliminary Questions

(a) Questions of admissibility generally

Preliminary questions concerning the qualification of a person to be a witness, the existence of a privilege, or the admissibility of evidence shall be determined by the court, subject to the provisions of subdivision (b). In making its determination, it is not bound by the rules of evidence except those with respect to privileges.

(b) Relevancy conditioned on fact

When the relevancy of evidence depends upon the fulfillment of a condition of fact, the court shall admit it upon, or subject to, the introduction of evidence sufficient to support a finding of the fulfillment of the condition.[1]

* * *

Even before a trial begins, either party may challenge the evidence that an opposing party is expected to introduce at the trial. As a general rule, any procedural defense or evidentiary objection that can be determined without a trial of the general issues should be raised by a pretrial motion. The rationale behind resolving some procedural or evidentiary issues during the pretrial stage is that the resolution could make a trial unnecessary but, in any event, it resolves issues that are appropriate to determine without disrupting the later flow of the trial. These pretrial motions include challenges to the court's jurisdiction, competence or fairness of the tribunal, the statement of the charges, the competency of the defendant to stand trial, the legality of the way in which police gathered evidence, flaws in a grand jury indictment, and constitutional challenges, such as multiple prosecutions or failure to grant a speedy trial.

As a general rule, the motion to suppress evidence must be made before the plea is entered or within a reasonable time after entry of the plea, by leave of the court, but the failure to challenge the evidence in a timely manner may be excused by the court for good cause. If a motion is made to suppress evidence, a hearing will be scheduled within a reasonable time so that the attorneys for each party may present evidence and argue the merits of their respective positions. When the judge agrees with the defendant, the evidence, even if relevant to the issues, will not be admitted at the trial.

One of the most common pretrial motions to exclude evidence is that which challenges the use of evidence illegally seized in violation of either the Fourth Amendment to the United States Constitution or the search and seizure provisions of state constitutions. For example, if the defendant alleges that law enforcement officials obtained evidence by conducting an illegal search and seizure in violation of the defendant's Fourth Amendment rights, the defense

---

[1]   FED. R. EVID. 104(a) and (b).

attorney will file a pretrial motion to suppress the evidence. At the hearing, the prosecutor will contend that the search and seizure were performed lawfully and the defense counsel will present evidence to support the seizures as having been unlawful. If the accused can demonstrate that the evidence was obtained by an unlawful search and seizure, and such evidence does not come within an exception recognized by the courts, the evidence will be suppressed and excluded from the trial.[2] But if the prosecutor can show that the evidence was obtained without violating the defendant's rights under the Constitution, or that the search was within one of the recognized exceptions to the exclusionary rule,[3] or that the social costs of applying the rule outweigh the benefits,[4] the motion to suppress will be denied, and the evidence will be admitted unless excluded for some other evidentiary reason.

Evidence may also be challenged as having been secured in violation of other constitutional provisions. For example, if the self-incrimination provisions of the Fifth Amendment, the right-to-counsel provisions of the Sixth Amendment, or the due process clause of the Fifth or Fourteenth Amendments have been violated by law enforcement personnel in obtaining evidence, the evidence may be inadmissible.[5]

§ 4.3   General Approach to Admissibility

The rules of evidence for all practical purposes are rules of exclusion. Therefore, all evidence offered carries a presumption of admissibility unless, upon objection, the evidence is subject to exclusion. When one party asks a question of a witness and his or her adversary has an objection to it, it will be found that the adversary's objection is based either on the form of the question that was asked or on the substance of the answer solicited. One way to approach the rules of evidence is to keep these simple tests of form and substance in mind as each rule is discussed.

A. *Objections as to Form*

In order to avoid confusing the witness, the court will require that a question be clear and intelligent. Judges will not permit questions to be asked of witnesses where the questions are confusing, compound, improperly phrased, misleading, or argumentative where an objection has been raised by opposing counsel. In fact, the judge will often ask that such questions be rephrased. Questions that are phrased in such a way that there can be no definite answer will, of course, mislead the witness as well as the jury.

---

[2]   Mapp v. Ohio, 367 U.S. 643 (1961), Wong Sun v. United States, 371 U.S. 471, 1963 U.S. LEXIS 2431 (1963).

[3]   *See* Massachusetts v. Sheppard, 468 U.S. 981, 1984 U.S. LEXIS 154 (1984) and Dickerson v. United States, 530 U.S. 428, 2000 U.S. LEXIS 4305 (2000).

[4]   Hudson v. Michigan, 2006 U.S. LEXIS 4677, 74 U.S.L.W. 4311 (2006).

[5]   *See* Chapter 16 for more comprehensive coverage of the exclusion of illegally obtained evidence.

Questions that have two parts, called compound questions, are generally objectionable as to form because it may impossible to answer both parts with one answer and if one answer is given, there is no way to know to which question the answer responded. Other questions that are sometimes objectionable as to form, especially during direct examination, are classified as leading questions.[6] Such questions generally suggest the desired answer by the manner in which they are phrased.

B. Objections as to Substance

If there is no objection as to form, or if an objection is made and settled, the test of substance is then applied. One easy way to understand the test of substance is to imagine three hurdles erected between the evidence and the court. Before the evidence can be admitted into court, all three hurdles must be cleared. They are: relevancy, materiality, and competency.

The concept of relevancy concerns whether the information has a tendency to prove or disprove one or more of the facts at issue in the case. To be relevant, the information must have a tendency to establish or disprove matters at issue in the case.[7] In other words, will the matter at issue be more or less likely to be believed or disbelieved if the jury hears the evidence than if it does not hear the evidence? If the evidence affects the probabilities of belief, it will be considered relevant evidence. Materiality involves the relative importance of evidence. Evidence is material only when it affects a fact or issue of the case in a significant way. The definition of competency is more elusive. Competent evidence is that which is legally adequate and sufficient. The competency test is a catch-all for the exclusionary rules. For example, evidence obtained by an illegal search in violation of the Constitution is inadmissible not because it is immaterial or irrelevant, but because of its legal inadequacy or incompetency.

If the proposed evidence meets the tests of form and substance, it is admitted into court. The weight or the importance to be given to the evidence by the jury or the judge depends on many other factors.

§ 4.4 Order of Presenting Evidence at the Trial[8]

The judge has a great deal of discretion in establishing court procedures, but he or she generally follows the procedures that have been developed over a period of years and have become standard. The usual order of procedure in presenting the case is as follows:[9]

---

[6] Leading questions are discussed in Chapter 9.
[7] The relevancy and materiality rules and examples are comprehensively discussed in Chapter 7.
[8] For a more comprehensive explanation of criminal procedure from arrest to final release, *see* CARLSON, CRIMINAL JUSTICE PROCEDURE (7th ed. 2005).
[9] MCCORMICK, EVIDENCE 7.

1. Prosecution's case-in-chief.
2. Defendant's case-in-chief.
3. Prosecution's case in rebuttal.
4. Defense's case in rejoinder.

Each of these steps is discussed in some depth to point out its scope and limitations.

A. Prosecution's Case-in-Chief

At the beginning of the trial, because the prosecution has the burden of going forward with the evidence and has the ultimate burden of proof, it introduces evidence on behalf of the state. The prosecutor may call as many witnesses as necessary and may introduce exhibits, photographs, documents, or other types of evidence that may help the jury in determining the guilt or innocence of the accused—provided that the evidence meets the admissibility tests. During this phase of the procedure, the prosecutor is "carrying the ball," "calling the plays," and going forward with the presentation of evidence. The lead prosecutor determines which of the potential witnesses for the government will actually testify, decides the order in which the witnesses are presented to the court, and guides the flow of evidence. Each prosecution witness is questioned by the prosecutor first[10] and subsequently the defense has an opportunity to cross-examine the prosecution witnesses. At this stage, the defense cannot introduce its own witnesses and—according to the majority view—must limit cross-examination to subject matters mentioned during the direct examination.

When the prosecuting attorney has presented the case-in-chief and has met the burden of going forward with the evidence or what he or she feels is sufficient evidence to make a case against the defendant by proof beyond a reasonable doubt, he or she signifies the completion of the case-in-chief by stating, "The prosecution rests," or other words to that effect.

B. Defendant's Case-in-Chief

After the prosecution rests, if the defense believes that the prosecution evidence failed to meet the government's burden of proof, the defense may ask the judge for a "directed verdict" of acquittal. If the judge believes that no rational jury could convict on the basis of the evidence presented, the judge will order an acquittal. Is this situation, the case ends and no retrial is possible because the judge's decision operates as a verdict on the merits of the case. If this motion by the defense attorney fails, the defense has the opportunity to present its evidence or case-in-chief. However, the defendant is not required to put on a defense, because the burden of proof remains with the prosecution. The defendant may present evidence in denial of the prosecution's claim; he or she may introduce evidence designed to destroy the prosecutor's proof of

---

[10] The procedure to be followed in the examination of witnesses is discussed in Chapter 9, *infra*.

one of the elements of the offense; the defendant may attempt to establish an alibi or one of the other affirmative defenses through the use of witnesses. The defendant has a Fifth Amendment privilege not to become a witness in his or her own behalf, but all defendants have an opportunity to personally become a witness. If so, the defendant is usually the first witness to take the stand at this stage of the proceedings.[11] As in the case of the prosecution, the defense counsel conducts direct examination of each defense witness and then immediately following the direct examination of each witness, he or she may be cross-examined by the prosecution. When the defense counsel has completed the presentation of the evidence, the defendant's attorney states, "The defense rests."

C. State's Case in Rebuttal

The prosecution now has the opportunity to rebut or refute the evidence presented by the defense. At this stage, the prosecution may not present witnesses that merely support the allegations of the indictment. That should have been done when the prosecution presented its case-in-chief. At this point, the prosecution is limited to the introduction of testimony or other evidence that is directed toward refuting the evidence that has been offered by the defense. New witnesses may be called at this time, but only if they can rebut, contradict, or cast doubt upon the evidence presented by the defendant. For example, if the defense raises the question of insanity, the prosecution may offer evidence to show that the defendant was not insane as defined by law. In this stage, as in other stages, the witness may not only be examined directly, but may also be cross-examined by opposing counsel.

D. Defense's Case in Rejoinder

The defense also has the opportunity to introduce evidence contrary to that introduced by the prosecution during its case in rebuttal. This phase of the trial is called the defense case in rejoinder. With a view to narrowing the subject matter, the evidence is limited to refuting or discrediting the evidence presented by the prosecution during the state's case in rebuttal. Returning to the example above, where the state has offered evidence to demonstrate that the defendant may not have been legally insane, the defendant has the opportunity to offer testimony to correct the evidence offered by the prosecution that the defendant was insane, according to the legal definition. If the prosecution managed to introduce new evidence that "opened the door" to new material, the defense is permitted to rebut the new material with relevant evidence during this stage of the case.

---

[11]   In 1972, the United States Supreme Court held that requiring the defendant to testify before other defense witnesses violates the self-incrimination provisions of the Constitution. Brooks v. Tennessee, 406 U.S. 605, 92 S. Ct. 1891, 32 L. Ed. 2d 358 (1972). State v. Glover, 636 So. 2d 976 (La. 1994).

There are instances when the case may continue with the prosecution and the defense each having the opportunity to refute the evidence presented by the other. However, it is obvious that this becomes more and more limited and, in the usual case, both parties will have presented all the evidence that they intend to present by the end of the defendant's rejoinder.

When both parties have announced that they have rested their cases, the hearing on the facts comes to an end, and the trial proceeds with the arguments of counsel and the court's instructions to the jury.

§ 4.5   Procedure for Offering and Challenging Evidence

Rule 103

Rulings on Evidence

(a) **Effect of erroneous ruling.** Error may not be predicated upon a ruling which admits or excludes evidence unless a substantial right of the party is affected, and

    (1) **Objection.** In case the ruling is one admitting evidence, a timely objection or motion to strike appears of record, stating the specific ground of objection, if the specific ground was not apparent from the context; or

    (2) **Offer of proof.** In case the ruling is one excluding evidence, the substance of the evidence was made known to the court by offer or was apparent from the context within which questions were asked.

(b) **Record of offer and ruling.** The court may add any other or further statement which shows the character of the evidence, the form in which it was offered, the objection made, and the ruling thereon. It may direct the making of an offer in question and answer form.[12]

* * *

For a variety of reasons and in the interests of justice, courts will not admit all evidence offered by either party. The courts follow a complex set of rules in determining what evidence should be admitted and what evidence should be excluded. A significant portion of the remainder of this book will be devoted to the rules that have been developed for judicial application in determining the admissibility of evidence. Most of these rules are rules of exclusion, which the parties will argue are inapplicable in a particular situation, depending on which side desires the admission of the evidence.

---

[12]   FED R. EVID. 103. The Federal Rules of Evidence, effective Jan. 2, 1975 (Pub. L. No. 93-595), apply to United States federal courts, judge magistrate proceedings, and bankruptcy courts. Portions of these rules, as well as the committee comments thereto, are inserted when relevant to the text discussion. The complete rules as approved through 2006 appear in the Appendix, *infra*.

The usual way of offering and eliciting oral testimony involves placing the witness on the stand and asking the witness a question or series of questions. If either the prosecution or the defense believes a question is improper, an objection is made and the court then decides whether the answer should be allowed. The party making the objection must state the ground for the objection, unless the context makes it clear. The opposing counsel is permitted to offer to the judge reasons why the objection should not be sustained. When the judge sustains on objection, that keeps evidence from being presented, the attorney for that party should make an offer of proof (a proffer) of what the evidence, if it had been allowed, would have shown. "An offer of proof must show three things: "(1) what the evidence will be; (2) the purpose and object of the evidence; and (3) each fact essential to establishing the admissibility of the evidence."[13] The offer of proof allows the trial court to properly consider the argument for admissibility and preserves the record for appeal.

If the judge makes what one party considers an erroneous ruling, this can be challenged on appeal, provided that the opposing counsel made a proper and timely objection. In general, however, reversible error will not be predicated upon an erroneous ruling unless the error was sufficiently substantial to have affected the outcome of the trial. If an error did not rise to this level, it does not constitute "reversible error" and is called "harmless error."

In some states, it is still necessary to "except." That is, after the judge's adverse ruling excluding the evidence or overruling the objection, the counsel comments, "We except." In essence, the exception serves as a protest, recorded by the court reporter, against the correctness of the ruling of the judge and preserves the matter for appellate review. To avoid an unnecessary expenditure of trial time, the rules in many states provide that the formal exception procedure is unnecessary,[14] but the objecting attorney must have made an appropriate objection, stating the legal grounds, in order to preserve the trial record for appellate purposes.

In the case of real evidence, such as bullets, guns, articles of clothing, and the like, the party offering the evidence, after having it identified or authenticated by a witness, submits it to the opposing counsel for inspection. When this has been done, it is presented to the judge and, depending upon the type of evidence, to each juror individually or to the jury as a whole.

In emphasizing the requirement of Rule 103 that the opposing party must make a timely objection, the Court of Appeals for the First Circuit noted that merely uttering the word, "objection," may not preserve the issue for appeal.[15] Federal courts have indicated that objections to the admission of evidence are preserved for appeal only if they are timely,[16] correct, and state the specific

---

[13] State v. Peters, 186 S.W.3d 774, 2006 Mo. App. LEXIS 54 (2006) quoting State v. Hirt, 16 S.W.3d 628, 633 (Mo. App. 2000).

[14] Texas Rules of Appellate Procedure, Rule 33(c), Preservation of Appellate Complaints. (Matthew Bender 2006).

[15] Microfinancial v. Premier, 385 F.3d 72, 81, 2004 U.S. App. LEXIS 20777 (1st Cir. 2004)

[16] United States v. Varela-Rivera, 279 F.3d 1174, 1177, 2002 U.S. App. LEXIS 2242 (9th Cir. 2002).

grounds for the objection,[17] unless the grounds are apparent from the context. In a case in which a party failed to make an appropriate objection where and when it should have, an appellate court used the concept of "plain error" as the standard for review.[18]

After discussing the requirements noted in Rule 103, the United States Court of Appeals for the Eleventh Circuit explained that the purpose of the rule concerning a timely objection and related requirements serves to alert the trial court and the opposing counsel to the thrust of the excluded evidence, enabling them to take appropriate action and to construct the record appropriate for appellate review.[19]

§ 4.6 Role of the Trial Judge in Evidence Matters

In the English and American systems, the trial judge is responsible for ensuring that the trial is administered in an orderly way and that it progresses efficiently and smoothly. When a defendant has requested a jury trial, the jury decides which facts have been established beyond a reasonable doubt by the evidence and makes a decision on the facts; however, the judge still plays an important role in relation to the admission and exclusion of evidence. Some of these duties are enumerated and explained below. The judge:

- *Determines before trial whether some of the evidence will be admissible at the trial*—In the first instance, the judge determines, after listening to arguments from both sides, what evidence will be admitted during the trial and what evidence will be suppressed. If a motion to suppress is made before the trial starts, generally the judge's decision stands for the duration of the trial. In unusual situations, the parties, and more likely, the prosecution may appeal the ruling on a suppression motion to a higher court. Where the pretrial ruling effectively ends the prosecution's case, the pretrial decision may be immediately appealable by the prosecution.

- *Acts on motions and objections regarding evidence during the trial*— During the trial, if a party challenges the admission of evidence as being irrelevant, immaterial, incompetent, or otherwise excludable under the rules of evidence, the judge makes the decision concerning admissibility and announces that ruling in court.

---

[17]   In United States v. Thomas, 138 Fed. App. 759, 762 (6th Cir. 2005), the Sixth Circuit held that raising an issue at sentencing was sufficient to preserve a sentencing error for appeal. The defendant had been given a mandatory sentence when the new interpretation called the sentencing guidelines advisory rather than mandatory.

[18]   FED. R. EVID. 103(d). According to the Sixth Circuit, "To establish plain error, a defendant must show that: (1) an error occurred in the district court; (2) the error was obvious or clear; (3) the error affected defendant's substantial rights; and (4) this adverse impact seriously affected the fairness, integrity, or public reputation of the judicial proceedings." United States v. Emuegbunam, 268 F.3d 377, 406 (6th Cir. 2001)

[19]   United States v. Sheffield, 992 F.2d 1164 (11th Cir. 1993).

As a general rule, trial judges have the inherent power to admit or exclude evidence at trial and a trial judge's decisions concerning the admissibility of evidence are reviewable only under the abuse of judicial discretion standard.[20] Putting this in somewhat different terms, a federal appeals court observed that a trial judge has broad discretion in ruling on the admissibility of evidence, and an appellate court will not reverse a trial judge's decision unless a clear abuse of discretion was demonstrated.[21]

- *Makes decisions concerning the constitutionality of law enforcement activities*—A motion to exclude evidence obtained in violation of the Constitution generally must be made at a pretrial hearing on a motion to suppress or may be made during the trial if the issue first surfaces at that point. To decide this challenge properly, the judge must be familiar with the decisions regarding such matters as search and seizure, confessions, right to counsel, self-incrimination, and due process. If a motion is made to exclude evidence because these provisions were violated and the judge admits the evidence that has been obtained in violation of the Constitution, the reviewing court on appeal can and probably will reverse the decision unless the error is harmless.

- *Protects the witnesses from overzealous examination and cross-examination by counsel*—Overzealous counsel sometimes browbeat witnesses by continuing to ask questions or by harshly or unnecessarily cross-examining a witness. The judge exercises discretion in maintaining control over the courtroom and examination processes and may intervene on his or her own motion or from objections made by counsel for the parties.

- *Takes judicial notice*—The judge plays a very important role in judicially noticing facts that may be considered by the jury in making the decision.[22] Some facts are so well known that to require proof via witnesses would constitute a waste of a trial court's time. For example, requiring proof that water boils at 100 degrees Centigrade is a universally known scientific fact. Having a physicist or other expert prove the boiling point of water would certainly waste the court's resources. The judge may accept without proof that water boils at 100 degrees and both parties would generally have no legal objection.

- *Determines competency of the witness to testify*—The judge determines whether the witness is competent to testify.[23] "The general rule is that every witness is presumed to be competent to be a witness"[24] unless the opposing party can demonstrate otherwise. When one party challenges

[20] Jones v. State, 780 N.E.2d 373 at 376 (Ind. 2002). *See also* Grace v. City of Cheyenne, 2006 U.S. App. LEXIS 15182 (10th Cir. 2006).
[21] United States v. Fuller, 2006 U.S. App. LEXIS 14852 (5th Cir. 2006).
[22] Judicial notice is discussed in Chapter 5.
[23] Competency of witnesses is discussed in Chapter 9, *and see* Commonwealth v. Judd, 2006 Pa. Super. 84, 2006 Pa. Super. LEXIS 538 (2006).
[24] *Id.*

the competency of a witness, the test of competency focuses on whether a witness has the capacity of memory and perception as well as whether the witness possesses a sense of obligation to testify truthfully and clearly. In a case in which a witness was alleged to have been incompetent but the judge allowed the testimony, there was proof that the challenged witness knew the difference between telling the truth and telling a lie and he promised to tell the truth. Where the witness possessed sufficient memory of the facts and would tell the truth, the appellate court held that the trial court did not abuse its discretion in holding that the challenged witness was competent to testify.[25] Only where the trial judge abused his or her discretion will a reviewing court consider reversing a conviction.

• *Rules on issues of law*—In addition, the judge makes the decisions concerning the law to be applied in the case, advises the jury as to what facts may be considered, and provides alternatives with respect to lesser included offenses in returning their verdict.

• *Acts a finder of fact in some cases*—Finally, when a trial takes place without a jury, such as when the defendant waives his or her right to a jury, the judge also acts as the factfinder. In this instance, the judge performs a dual role; he or she acts in the normal capacity as a judge managing the case and ruling on evidentiary matters, and he or she also performs the function of the jury in determining the facts of the case.

     While the trial judge in the criminal case has wide latitude in making decisions, the judge must maintain a neutral attitude and avoid any conduct or words that might impair the appearance of impartiality.[26] Generally, a trial judge has discretion to comment on the evidence presented at trial and to make other comments during the course of a trial, but the judge must make it clear that the jury will determine the facts.[27] However, judicial comments to the jury that relate to evidence must be done with great care so that unfair prejudice to either party is avoided.[28]

During deliberations, when a jury appears to be confused about a legal issue and needs additional guidance, and when a resolution of the question is not apparent from earlier instructions, a trial judge has a responsibility to give the jury guidance by a clear statement of relevant legal criteria.[29] The trial court, in the proper exercise of its supervisory role, may participate even-handedly in the proceedings in order to clarify the issues and facilitate the expeditious and orderly progress of the trial.[30] While a trial judge must avoid any actual or apparent partisanship to, for, or against a party, the judge must be engaged and actively overseeing the trial. A judge abandoned this role

---

[25]   People v. Watson, 245 Mich. App. 572 at 583, 629 N.W.2d 411 at 420 (2001).
[26]   State v. Hudson, 950 S.W.2d 543 (Mo. 1997).
[27]   United States v. Zidar, 2006 U.S. App. LEXIS 11858 (9th Cir. 2006).
[28]   United States v. Frederick, 406 F.3d 754, 2005 U.S. App. LEXIS 7770 (6th Cir. 2005)
[29]   United States v. Evans, 431 F.3d 343, 347, 2005 U.S. App. LEXIS 27403 (8th Cir. 2005).
[30]   People v. Jones, 662 N.Y.S. 2d 79 (1997).

where he made jokes, light-hearted comments, and generally had an irreverent attitude throughout a murder case. He joked about not wanting to be there and told lawyer jokes during trial. The appellate court, in reversing a murder conviction that resulted, noted that:

> The trial judge has primary responsibility for maintaining order and decorum in the courtroom and must control criminal proceedings so as to insure that justice is done. We recognize that the trial judge's intent in the instant case may have been to create a casual atmosphere to put jurors at ease and make them feel welcome; however, the trial judge not only failed to maintain order and decorum but also actively contributed to creating an aura of jocularity inappropriate to the gravity of the proceedings.[31]

§ 4.7 Function of the Jury

In a jury trial in a criminal case, the function of the jury is to determine the truth from the facts that have been presented through evidence introduced by both parties. When evaluating the evidence and rendering a decision, the jury faces a variety of challenges because in almost every case contradictory, and sometimes confusing, evidence has been introduced by the parties. The criminal justice system has given the jurors the challenge of determining which witnesses to believe and what evidence should be given the most weight. The ultimate goal is to ascertain whether the defendant is guilty of the crime for which the defendant is being tried. Following the presentation of all of the evidence by the prosecution and the defense and after the attorneys have presented their closing arguments, the jury retires to deliberate. No judge, attorney, or other court employee meets with the jury; the case decision rests entirely with the jury.

The jury need not resolve difficult questions of law because it is the duty of the judge to make legal decisions and resolve legal disputes during the trial. During the latter part of the trial, the judge explains the law to be applied by giving the jury what amounts to a lesson in law that covers the case the jury has just heard. The charge by the judge, or jury instruction, attempts to educate the jury concerning the law and the jury instruction needs to have sufficient particularity that the jury can understand and apply the law. In a nutshell, the jury receives the law from the judge and applies it to the facts that it has found.[32] In jury trials, the jurors have the exclusive responsibility to find the facts, and the trial court may not interfere with this function.

In determining what actually happened, the jurors must have the opportunity to see and hear the accuser and, in some jurisdictions, jurors are permitted, with careful regulation, to ask questions of witnesses,[33] including the

---

[31]　State v. Langley, 896 So. 2d 200, 207, 2004 La. App. LEXIS 3177 (2004).

[32]　47 AM. JUR. 2D *Jury* § 15 (West 2003). *See also* State v. Helton, 2004 N.C. App. LEXIS 840 (2004).

[33]　United States v. Canon, 141 Fed. Appx. 398, 401, 2005 U.S. App. LEXIS 12001 (6th Cir. 2005).

defendant if the defendant has been a witness. Based on the questions asked by counsel, the answers given by the witnesses, the documentary and real evidence, the demeanor of the witnesses, and their own knowledge of people, the jurors must reach a decision based on the evidence and substitutes for evidence that have been made available at the trial. Jurors must make decisions only on the evidence obtained by virtue of courtroom presentations and a juror's private investigation beyond the courtroom can be grounds for a reversal.[34]

In one case, a defendant argued that his conviction for homicide should be reversed because of alleged juror misconduct by using knowledge that had not been introduced at court. In determining the defendant's intent, there was some evidence that the defendant had fired a gun at one of the victims but two of the jurors noted that when a gun is fired it does move upward and to the left, evidence that had never been introduced at trial. The reviewing court held that the jurors had not conducted themselves improperly, they were just relying on their knowledge and common sense in evaluating the evidence.[35] A reversal is not appropriate if the juror's conduct constituted nothing more than applying everyday perceptions and common sense to evaluating the issues presented at trial. In a different case, at least two jurors drove past the crime scene and one may have done so with some regularity, while a third juror may have patronized the actual bank that was the site of the robbery. The trial court, in refusing to disturb the conviction, held that such conduct would not have influenced the jury impermissibly and did not affect the ultimate outcome of the case.[36]

§ 4.8 Role of Witnesses

In presenting evidence in a criminal trial, witness testimony proves to be an absolute necessity because absolutely no actual evidence can be introduced without a witness.[37] Witnesses may be classified as either lay or expert, with lay witnesses generally answering "who," "what," and "when" types of questions while expert witnesses are permitted to offer opinions. In many instances, criminal justice personnel act as witnesses in criminal cases due to the fact that they may possess firsthand knowledge of the important facts of a case. This is especially true of police investigators, but correctional officers and probation and parole officers often serve as witnesses. The witness plays a very important part; in fact, if there were no witnesses, there could be no trial. The witnesses offer the court and jury the important facts and assist in introducing narrative evidence of what they observed at the crime scene or other relevant location. The witnesses are essential to facilitate the introduction of physical evidence into the trial. Because the jury was not present as the crime occurred, the witnesses serve as the eyes and ears of the court in recre-

---

34   State v. Cook, 2006 Kan. LEXIS 361, (2006).
35   Robinson v. Woodford, 2006 U.S. App. LEXIS 6009 (9th Cir. 2006).
36   United States v. Morrow, 412 F. Supp. 2d 146, 168, 2006 U.S. Dist. LEXIS 6274 (D.D.C.2006).
37   A court may take judicial notice of facts as a substitute for evidence. *See* Chapter 5, Judicial Notice.

ating the operative facts of the crime. The jury must evaluate the testimony of the witness for truthfulness, and it is, therefore, important to recognize that it is not only what is said by the witness, but also how it is said and the demeanor with which it is said, that is evaluated. For this reason, the trial witness must be aware not only of what evidence to present, but also of his or her demeanor, the method of presenting the facts, his or her voice, and even his or her dress. In addition to giving oral testimony, the witness is called upon to introduce real evidence or documentary evidence. This evidence is of little value if the witness does not properly explain each piece of evidence in context so that the jury can understand its significance.[38]

The importance of witnesses in the judicial process has long been recognized by the courts. Under constitutional and statutory provisions, including the Sixth Amendment to the federal Constitution, persons accused of crime have the right to have compulsory process for obtaining the attendance of witnesses on their behalf. The defendant, with a few exceptions, had the Sixth Amendment right to confront and cross-examine adverse witnesses.[39] A defendant's fundamental right to present witnesses in his or her defense is violated if improper influences are exerted on the defense witnesses, causing them to be unavailable, to testify untruthfully, or to refuse to testify.[40] The constitutional guarantee includes the right to have the government's assistance in compelling the attendance of favorable witnesses at the trial, the right to offer such witnesses' testimony, and the right to interrogate such favorable witnesses.[41]

§ 4.9 Prosecuting Attorney's Responsibilities

In a criminal case, the prosecutor has extensive powers and responsibilities. In a federal prosecution, the court noted that the courts have no authority to interfere with a prosecutor's decision to prosecute and that the decision to move a case for prosecution rests with the prosecutor alone. In addition, a prosecutor can choose to add charges to a prosecution by the use of a superseding indictment without any judicial intervention.[42] In a landmark case, the Supreme Court of the United States held that a prosecutor could actually procure an additional indictment under the habitual offender statute where the defendant refused to accept a plea bargain that had been offered.[43] A California Court of Appeals recognized prosecutorial discretion when it noted that, as a general rule, "where the facts support a special circumstance allegation, the prosecutor has the discretion to seek the death penalty" or to pursue a charge with a lesser punishment.[44] In fact, some prosecutors have the discretion to

---

38   *See* Chapter 9 for a discussion of the examination of witnesses.
39   State v. Mozee, 112 S.W.3d 102, 108, 2003 Mo. App. LEXIS 940 (2003).
40   People v. Muschio, 278 Ill. App. 3d 525, 663 N.E.2d 93 (1996).
41   21A AM. JUR. 2D *Criminal Law* §1161 (West 2003).
42   United States v. Banner, 442 F.3d 1310, 1315, 2006 U.S. App. LEXIS 5967 (11th Cir. 2006).
43   *See* Bordenkircher v. Hayes 434 U.S. 357, 1978 U.S. LEXIS 56 (1978).
44   People v. Superior Court of San Diego County, 129 Cal. Rptr. 324, 2003 Cal. App. LEXIS 40 (2003).

charge offenders who have committed the same crimes under separate statutes that provide for different punishments.[45]

In a criminal case, a prosecuting attorney represents a state government or the government of the United States and has the burden of introducing the evidence to prove guilt beyond a reasonable doubt. To carry out this responsibility, the prosecutor's duties include the collection of physical evidence, interviewing witnesses, discussing the case with the investigator, and preparing the case for trial.

With respect to evidence, the prosecutor must decide not only what evidence is to be introduced, but how that evidence is to be produced and consider the appropriate time during the trial when each item should be introduced. Legal cases that support admission should be available to present to the court in the event that opposing counsel challenges an item of evidence as violating one of the many rules of exclusion.

The prosecutor guides the case for the state by putting prosecution witnesses on the stand and proving the state's case-in-chief. After asking questions, the prosecutor must be so familiar with the evidence that appropriate follow-up questions may be directed to the witness to clear up any possible misconceptions. It is not enough for prosecutors to be familiar with the state's case—the prosecutor should be aware of the accused's defense and have questions prepared for cross-examination of the defendant's witnesses.

Finally, the prosecutor has the right to make opening and closing remarks. In the opening remarks to the jury, the prosecutor explains what the state intends to prove and how the state will go about presenting its proof. It is often said that the prosecutor should provide a "road map" for the jury during the opening statement. In the closing statement or argument, the prosecutor summarizes the evidence that has been presented in such a way as to cast it in the light most favorable to the prosecution. The prosecutor must anticipate the defense closing argument and because, following the closing argument of the defense, the prosecution has a chance to counter it during the prosecution's final closing rebuttal.

Before leaving the responsibilities of the prosecutor, it should be mentioned that the prosecutor has an overall duty to do justice for all parties—not to win at all costs. Constitutionally, the prosecutor had a responsibility to the defense, and to a possibly innocent defendant, to make exculpatory evidence available upon request. This duty to disclose evidence also includes evidence that might help impeach a prosecution witness. It is reversible error for the prosecutor to use evidence that he or she knows—or should know—is untrue, to use evidence that was acquired in violation of the law, or to withhold evidence favorable to the defense.[46] In the 1963 case of *Brady v. Maryland*, the United States Supreme Court held that suppression by the prosecution of evidence favorable to the accused, upon request, violates due process where the

---

[45]   People v Wilkinson, 102 Cal. App. 4th 72, 125 Cal. Rptr. 2d 294 (2002).
[46]   Maddox v. Montgomery, 718 F.2d 1033 (11th Cir. 1983). *See* case in Part II. Brady v. Maryland, 373 U.S. 83, 83 S. Ct. 1194, 10 L. Ed. 2d 215 (1963).

evidence is material either to guilt or to punishment, irrespective of good faith or bad faith on the part of the prosecution. In interpreting the *Brady* decision in a 1999 case, the United States Supreme Court noted that:

> There are three components of a true *Brady* violation: The evidence at issue must be favorable to the accused, either because it is exculpatory, or because it is impeaching; that evidence must have been suppressed by the State, either willfully or inadvertently; and prejudice must have ensued.[47]

The Court pointed out that in order to prevail on a claim under *Brady*, it must be shown that the prosecution violated its duty to disclose information favorable to the defendant, which affected the outcome of the trial. A "*Brady* violation does not exist unless the nondisclosure was so serious that there [was] a reasonable probability that the suppressed evidence would have produced a different verdict."[48]

In a 1985 case, *United States v. Young*, the Supreme Court of the United States, in a comprehensive opinion, discussed the responsibilities of the prosecution and those of the defense counsel.[49] In this case, the defendant was charged with defrauding a refinery by submitting false certifications that oil purchased by the refinery from the defendant's company was crude oil, when in fact it was a less valuable fuel oil. At the trial, the defense counsel first challenged the integrity of the prosecutor and then charged that the prosecutor did not believe in the government's case. His exact words were, "I submit to you that there's not a person in this courtroom, including those sitting at this table, who thinks that Billy Young intended to defraud Apco."[50] In response, the prosecutor said that the defendant's action was fraudulent, and that the defendant did not act with honor and integrity.

The defendant was found guilty on several counts of mail fraud and of falsifying testimony. When the defendant appealed, the Court of Appeals reversed the conviction and remanded for retrial. The court held that the prosecutor's statements constituted misconduct and were sufficiently egregious to constitute plain error. The Court of Appeals rejected the government's contention that the statements were invited by the defense counsel's own closing arguments.[51] The prosecution then appealed to the United States Supreme Court. The Supreme Court, quoting from other cases, discussed the standard of conduct for prosecutors with these words:

---

[47]   Strikler v. Greene, 527 U.S. 263, 281-282 (1999).

[48]   *Id.* at 282.

[49]   United States v. Young, 470 U.S. 1, 105 S. Ct. 1038, 84 L. Ed. 2d 1 (1985). *See also* United States v. Skarda, 845 F.2d 1508 (8th Cir. 1988).

[50]   *Id.* Young at 5.

[51]   *Id.*

> Nearly a half century ago, this Court counselled prosecutors to "refrain from improper methods calculated to produce a wrongful conviction. . . ." The Court made clear, however, that the adversary system permits the prosecutor to "prosecute with earnestness and vigor." In other words, "while he may strike hard blows, he is not at liberty to strike foul ones."[52]

In referring to the defense counsel's conduct, the Court explained that the defense counsel, like the prosecutor, must refrain from interjecting personal beliefs into the presentation of the case, warning that defense counsel, like his or her adversary, must not be permitted to make unfounded and inflammatory attacks on the opposing advocate.

While determining that the prosecutor's remarks in the *Young* case might be considered improper, the Supreme Court held that they could not be said to rise to the level of plain error. The Court concluded, therefore, that the remarks made by the prosecutor were not of such character as to undermine the fundamental fairness of the trial and contribute to the miscarriage of justice. The Supreme Court accordingly reversed the judgment of the Court of Appeals and reinstated the conviction.[53]

The duty to disclose exculpatory evidence becomes demonstrably critical, both for the defendant and for the non-disclosing attorney. In a New Orleans murder case, a man and his date were leaving a restaurant in the French Quarter when one of three subjects shot the man in the face, resulting in his death. When police questioned his date, she indicated that she had not been wearing her contacts or her glasses and as a result she did not get a good look at the killer and could only see patterns and shapes. However, three weeks later, she made a positive identification of the eventual defendant by picking him from a police lineup. The prosecutor shared the woman's story about not seeing the perpetrator well on the night of the murder and the defense had one police report that the witness needed corrective lenses to see properly, but a second police report three days later that expanded on her need for corrective lenses was never shared with the defense. The defendant's conviction and death sentence were reversed and the prosecutor received sanctions from the Louisiana bar for violating the Rules of Professional Conduct because he had failed to share exculpatory impeachment evidence with the defense, possibly causing the wrong person to be convicted of murder.[54] Finding that the prosecutor had improperly withheld exculpatory evidence from the defendant that there existed a reasonable probability that the conviction might not have resulted but for the prosecutor's wrongdoing, the Supreme Court of Louisiana sanctioned the prosecuting attorney. The Court noted that:

---

[52] *Id.* at 7.

[53] United States v. Young, 470 U.S. 1, 20 (1985).

[54] In re Roger W. Jordan, 913 So. 2d 775; 2005 La. LEXIS 2104 (2005).

> By withholding material exculpatory evidence from a criminal defendant, respondent violated a duty owed to the public. As a prosecutor, respondent is charged with a high ethical standard and may not carelessly skirt his obligation. [Citation omitted.] Although neither *Brady [v. Maryland]* or Rule 3.8 [of Professional Responsibility] incorporates a mental element, Rule XIX, § 10(C) does. Based on the testimony of respondent and the character evidence discussed below, we find that respondent knowingly withheld *Brady* evidence. As to the element regarding actual injury, this Court reversed [the defendant's] conviction on other grounds and granted him a new trial. However, this Court's actions in reversing the conviction does not vitiate the potential injury to the criminal justice system, or to [the defendant], caused by respondent's actions, and warrants serious consideration and discipline by this Court.[55]

Although the defendant's conviction had been reversed prior to the sanction applied to the prosecutor by the Supreme Court of Louisiana, the Court noted that a prosecutor's duty "to disclose is imbedded in the principle that a criminal defendant is deprived of a fair trial when the state withholds exculpatory evidence that is material to guilt or punishment."[56]

Thus, where a state prosecutor failed to share information that was important to either guilt or innocence with the defendant, a violation of the due process clause of the Fourteenth Amendment occurs. Although the defendant had his murder conviction reversed on other grounds other than the misconduct of the prosecutor, the prosecutor's conduct created a reasonable probability that the verdict might have been different if the material had been properly shared. Even when the prosecutor has a duty to share exculpatory evidence and merits a disciplinary sanction, a reviewing court will not reverse a conviction unless the false evidence was material to guilt or punishment and a different result would probably have occurred but for the error.

§ 4.10 Defense Attorney's Responsibilities

When the Bill of Rights was adopted as part of our Constitution in 1791, the right to counsel was included as part of the Sixth Amendment. The Amendment reads in part:

> In all criminal prosecutions the accused shall enjoy the right. . . . to have the assistance of counsel for his defense.

In addition to the federal Constitution, all of the states require by their respective constitutions that the accused shall have the right to appear in person and be represented by counsel.

---

[55] *Id.*
[56] *Id.*

The right to counsel entitles criminal defendants to have effective assistance of counsel, a standard that contemplates the services of an attorney with the customary skills and diligence that a reasonably competent attorney would perform under similar circumstances.[57] According to the Supreme Court, "In assessing attorney performance, all the Federal Courts of Appeals and all but a few state courts have now adopted the "reasonably effective assistance" standard in one formulation or another."[58] In a landmark case, *Strickland v. Washington*, Justice O'Connor wrote, "The benchmark for judging any claim of ineffectiveness must be whether counsel's conduct so undermined the proper functioning of the adversarial process that the trial cannot be relied on as having produced a just result."[59] *Strickland* required a complaining defendant to demonstrate that (1) the defense counsel's performance was deficient and (2) that the deficient performance prejudiced the defense in a way that deprived the defendant of a fair trial.[60] The primary function of the defense attorney at the trial is to make certain that all of the rights of the defendant are properly protected. As in the case of the prosecutor, the defense attorney should have the case prepared and ready for trial, including, where necessary, pretrial conferences with the defendant and interviews with all the witnesses expected to be called on behalf of the defendant.

Although the defense attorney should not tell the defendant what to say in his or her testimony before the jury, he or she can prepare the defendant by explaining how the case will unfold and advise the defendant on witness stand demeanor and suggest topics over which the defendant might have a constitutional or evidentiary right not to answer. Proper preparation of the defendant as a witness, including previewing expected questions and answers, is an essential defense counsel task. The defense attorney, if he or she fulfills the obligations of the defense counsel, will have investigated the case, will have prepared questions for the defendant and other witnesses, and will be ready to introduce the witnesses in a manner that the evidence has its maximum force and impact for the defense. He or she has a responsibility to cross-examine the prosecution's witnesses and to introduce evidence to rebut the testimony of such witnesses and, where possible, to impeach their credibility.

Failure on the part of defense counsel to effectively assist the defendant can result in a new trial. In one New York case, the defendant sought review of his first-degree robbery conviction, among other offenses. His first counsel withdrew 13 months prior to the trial and the court appointed a new attorney to try the case. During the initial investigatory stage, the defendant offered several statements to police that indicated his guilt. There existed legal reasons that might have led to a successful motion to suppress his police statements. The attorney made no effort to suppress the defendant's statements and the lack of effort was not a strategic plan. The defense attorney admitted on the

---

[57]   United States v. Boone, 437 F.3d 829, 839, 2006 U.S. App. LEXIS 3531 (8th Cir. 2006).
[58]   Strickland v. Washington, 466 U.S. 668 at 683, 1984 U.S. LEXIS 79 (1984).
[59]   *Id.* at 686.
[60]   *Id.* at 687.

first day of trial that he had not known the statements existed until the prosecutor made the opening statement. In New York, the standard of review to measure ineffective assistance of counsel is "whether, under the circumstances of the case, the defendant received meaningful representation."[61] In ordering a new trial, the reviewing court noted, "the record makes clear, counsel's failure to timely move for suppression of the statements was not a strategic decision at all, but the consequence of a failure to adequately prepare for trial as demonstrated by his ignorance of the fact that his client had made statements to law enforcement officials."[62] The appellate court granted a new trial because the attorney failed to meet his obligations to appropriately defend the client.

In explaining the right to have effective counsel, one court commented that the Sixth Amendment right to counsel guarantees more than just a warm body to stand next to the accused during the critical stages of the proceedings; the accused is entitled to an attorney who plays the role necessary to ensure that the proceedings are fair.[63] A New Jersey appellate court noted that "[t]he benchmark for judging ineffective assistance of counsel claims is whether the defense attorney's professional errors 'materially contributed' to the defendant's conviction."[64] As a general rule, in order to obtain a reversal of a conviction due to ineffective assistance of counsel, the defendant must demonstrate that counsel's performance was deficient and that that deficient performance created such prejudice to the case that the defendant was deprived of a fair trial.[65] In order to prevail on an ineffective assistance of counsel claim, "The defendant must show that there is a reasonable probability that, but for counsel's unprofessional errors, the result of the proceeding would have been different. A reasonable probability is a probability sufficient to undermine confidence in the outcome."[66] Just because the attorney was appointed a few weeks prior to trial does not demonstrate ineffective assistance of counsel.[67] Ineffective assistance of counsel was not demonstrated in a multiple murder case in which the evidence clearly established that defendants were busy stealing cattle from a couple's farm at the time the defendants killed the farmer and his wife. Counsel's failure to request that some information about a prior conviction be removed from a police report before it was introduced as evidence did not qualify as ineffective assistance of counsel.[68] In other words, if a case had been tried with adequate representation and the outcome of the case would have been different, the error was not harmless and a

---

[61] People v. Noll, 2005 NY Slip Op 9746, 24 A.D.3d 688, 808 N.Y.S.2d 381, 382, 2005 N.Y. App. Div. LEXIS 14293 (2005).

[62] *Id.*

[63] Patrasso v. Nelson, 121 F.3d 297 (7th Cir. 1997).

[64] New Jersey v. Velez, 329 N.J. Super. 128 at 134, 746 A.2d 1073 at 1077 (2000).

[65] State v. Brownlow, 2003 Ohio 1819, 2003 Ohio App. LEXIS 1721 (2003), quoting State v. Cassano, 96 Ohio St 3d. 94, 2002 Ohio 3751 (2002).

[66] *Strickland* at 694.

[67] *Id.*

[68] Rousan v. Roper, 436 F.3d 951, 959, 2006 U.S. App. LEXIS 3003 (8th Cir. 2006).

new trial should be ordered. However, where there would have been no change in outcome with different counsel, the harmless error rule should be applied and the conviction sustained.

In an overall sense, the Sixth Amendment demands that defense counsel effectively represent the defendant in a criminal case by taking advantage of the available legal tools. In a case involving allegedly illegal firearms sales, the defendant was accused of aiding two gun sellers make illegal gun sales on several occasions.[69] The sellers, who testified for the government, had severe credibility problems and gave contradictory testimony that failed to solidly connect the defendant to the illegal gun sales. Even though the jury returned a verdict of guilty, the trial judge indicated that some post-conviction motions for relief might be appropriate and he encouraged the attorney to file them. The attorney missed the seven-day deadline[70] and filed post-conviction motions 41 days after the conviction. On appeal, the defendant contended that his trial counsel was ineffective because he failed to timely file the motions for post-conviction relief and he demonstrated prejudice to his case because the motions would probably have been granted. The reviewing court noted, "Not filing a dispositive motion, particularly when directed to do so by the district court, is a classic dereliction of an attorney's obligation to provide his client with the type of performance required."[71] The reviewing court granted the defendant's motion for a new trial on the ground that the attorney's performance fell below the level of adequacy by missing the filing deadline.

Finally, the defense attorney has the responsibility to make opening statements following the prosecution's opening statements. The defense counsel may defer an opening statement until the start of the defense case-in-chief so that the preview of the defense theory or "road map" of the case will be presented to the jury at a more appropriate time. The defense attorney also has the right to give a closing statement immediately prior to the final statement given by the prosecutor. In the closing statement, the defense attorney reviews and summarizes the evidence presented by defense witnesses, emphasizes inconsistencies in the prosecution's case, focuses on credibility issues of the prosecution's witnesses, and explains the evidence in such a way as to be most favorable to the defendant.

§ 4.11   Admissibility and Weight of Direct and Circumstantial Evidence

The responsibilities of the prosecutor and the defense attorney include introducing evidence at the trial in an effort to cause the factfinders to be convinced that certain acts occurred or did not occur or that facts did or did not exist. In a criminal case, the prosecutor has the responsibility to prove beyond

---

[69]   United States v. Hilliard, 392 F.3d 981, 2004 U.S. App. LEXIS 26887 (8th Cir. 2004).

[70]   FED. R. CRIM. PROC. 33(b)(2).

[71]   *Hilliard*, at 986.

a reasonable doubt that the defendant committed the acts charged, and that these acts violated the law. Similarly, the defense attorney has a duty to introduce sufficient evidence that will produce a reasonable doubt in the mind of the factfinders.

In the process of introducing sufficient proof of guilt, the prosecutor may use both direct and circumstantial evidence. A combination of direct evidence and circumstantial evidence or either one alone may prove sufficient to meet the burden of proof because most courts hold that direct and circumstantial evidence carry equal weight.[72] Demonstrative of this equality is the fact that in considering a defendant's motion for acquittal following the prosecution's case-in-chief, courts give equal weight to direct and circumstantial evidence.[73]

Historically, the question has been debated in both state and federal courts. While some doubt may exist in the minds of legal scholars as to the admissibility, weight, and sufficiency of circumstantial evidence, many cases have reached a judgment of guilt in the absence of direct evidence. In any event, the education of a student in the law of evidence would be incomplete if he or she could not distinguish between direct and circumstantial evidence and give some examples of each.

> The basic distinction between direct and circumstantial evidence is that in the former instance the witnesses testify directly of their own knowledge as to the main facts to be proved, while in the latter case proof is given of facts and circumstances from which the jury may infer other connected facts which reasonably follow, according to common experience.[74]

There is a classic story that helps explain the difference. In a case in which a witness testified that he observed a fight where one man was accused of "biting off" the other fighter's ear. When he testified that the one man "bit off" the other man's ear, the testimony was that he was present when it happened and he saw the fight. On cross-examination, the witness was asked whether he actually observed the one bite the other's ear, he stated that he did not actually see it being bitten but that he saw the defendant spit out the ear. Although he did not see the biting event, circumstantial evidence told him and the court that the defendant must have bitten the ear during the fight because there is no other logical explanation concerning how it got in the one man's mouth. In this context, it is difficult to argue that circumstantial evidence would not have the full force and effect of direct evidence.

The mere fact that evidence is characterized as either direct or circumstantial may suggest that one type may be superior to the other type of evidence with respect to reliability. California seems to indicate a slight distrust of circumstantial evidence in that its jury instructions state that:

---

[72]   United States v. Wiggins, 146 Fed. Appx. 437; 2005 U.S. App. LEXIS 19120 (11th Cir. 2005).
[73]   United States v. Bailey, 169 Fed. Appx. 815, 821, 2006 U.S. App. LEXIS 3402 (5th Cir. 2006).
[74]   See 29 AM. JUR. 2D Evidence § 313 (1994).

a finding of guilt as to any crime may not be based on circumstantial evidence unless the proved circumstances are not only (1) consistent with the theory that the defendant is guilty of the crime, but (2) cannot be reconciled with any other rational conclusion.[75]

Taking a different view in rejecting any distinction between the two types of evidence, the Supreme Court of Ohio noted:

> Circumstantial evidence and direct evidence inherently possess the same probative value. . . . Since circumstantial evidence and direct evidence are indistinguishable so far as the jury's fact-finding function is concerned, all that is required of the jury is that it weigh all of the evidence, direct and circumstantial, against the standard of proof beyond a reasonable doubt. Nothing more should be required of a factfinder.[76]

Although it is true that, all things being equal, direct evidence probably carries more weight with juries, circumstantial evidence has a definite place in the trial of criminal cases because the case law is replete with examples of convictions based exclusively on circumstantial evidence and many cases in which direct evidence proved insufficient for a conviction.

The need for circumstantial evidence appears obvious because criminals generally like cover and often do not commit their activities in plain view. An investigator or police officer would be very pleased if most crimes were witnessed by someone who could testify that he or she directly observed the acts that made up the crime. However, in stealth-type crimes, such as burglary, larceny, and embezzlement, a prosecutor would have a difficult task in obtaining convictions without the use of circumstantial evidence.

There is often the mistaken belief that circumstantial evidence fails to carry sufficient weight to result in a criminal conviction, or at least calls into question a conviction based wholly on circumstantial evidence. In a sexual assault-murder case, the perpetrator left the victim dead. Footprints in snow matched the defendant's shoes while police caught the defendant in possession of the victim's purse. Investigators identified a bloody fingerprint inside the victim's home as matching a print from the defendant. The defendant's DNA profile matched DNA found inside the victim and the defendant exhibited injuries that could be consistent with the victim's efforts at self-defense. Even though no one alive saw the defendant sexually assault or murder the victim, the Supreme Court of North Dakota found that the circumstantial evidence was sufficient to uphold the convictions by proof beyond a reasonable doubt.[77]

Before continuing with the discussion of admissibility, weight, and sufficiency of direct and circumstantial evidence, some definitions and explanations are in order.

---

[75]   *See* Caljic 2.01, California Jury Instructions. (2005).
[76]   *See* State v. Jenks, 574 N.E.2d 492, 502 (Ohio 1991).
[77]   State v. Charette, 2004 ND 187, 687 N.W.2d 484, 488, 2004 N.D. LEXIS 316 (2004).

A. *Direct Evidence*

Evidence, where credible, that proves a fact without deduction or inference is called *direct evidence*. It is evidence that is applied immediately and directly to the fact to be proved—without the aid of any intervening fact or reasoning process. For example, in a trial for murder, a witness positively testifies that he saw the accused inflict the fatal wound. Evidence is declared to be direct and positive when the very acts in dispute are communicated by persons who have actual knowledge of the facts by means of their senses. When direct evidence is introduced, it is not necessary that the factfinders make any inferences or deductions of fact, or that there be any presumptions flowing from the evidence to connect it with the crime. The sole determination that the trier of fact must make is whether the evidence is true,[78] which involves an evaluation of the credibility of the witness who offered the direct evidence. Where the witness is believable, the factfinder will find that the existence of the fact has been established, unless and until other contrary evidence of equal credibility is introduced.

B. *Circumstantial Evidence*

"Circumstantial evidence is *evidence that, if found to be true, proves a fact from which an inference of the existence of another fact may be drawn.*"[79] Another definition of circumstantial evidence is "evidence that, without going directly to prove the existence of a fact, gives rise to a logical inference that such fact does exist."[80] Circumstantial evidence is "testimony not based on actual personal knowledge or observation of the facts in controversy, but of other facts from which deductions are drawn, showing indirectly the facts sought to be proved."[81] While circumstantial evidence may not always be given the recognition by a jury that it deserves in all situations, Justice Kennedy noted that, "[c]ircumstantial evidence may be as probative as testimonial evidence."[82] Echoing Justice Kennedy, but writing much earlier, Justice Clark observed that, "Circumstantial evidence . . . is intrinsically no different from testimonial evidence."[83]

After observing the differences between direct evidence and circumstantial evidence, it must be noted that all that is required of the jury is that it weigh all of the evidence—direct and circumstantial—against a standard of reasonable doubt. This was made clear in an Ohio case in which the defendant contended that the evidence presented by the state was insufficient because it was based on circumstantial evidence of intent. The appellate court noted:

---

[78]   State v. Frantzel, 717 S.W.2d 863 (Mo. Ct. App. 1986).

[79]   Caljic 2.00, Calfifornia Jury Instructions. (2005).

[80]   Bland v. Fox, 172 Neb. 662, 111 N.W.2d 537 (1961), quoting C.J.S. *Evidence* §2.

[81]   Ajaxo, Inc. v. E'Trade, 135 Cal. App. 4th 21, 51, 37 Cal. Rptr. 3d 221, 244, 2005 Cal. App. LEXIS 1950 (2005).

[82]   Siegert v. Gilley, 500 U.S. 226 at 236 (1991), Justice Kennedy concurring.

[83]   Holland v. United States, 348 U.S. 121, 140, 1954 U.S. LEXIS 2740 (1954).

> The elements of an offense may be established by direct evidence, circumstantial evidence, or both. Circumstantial and direct evidence are of equal probative value. When reviewing the value of circumstantial evidence, we note that the weight accorded an inference is fact-dependent and can be disregarded as speculative only if reasonable minds can come to the conclusion that the inference is not supported by the evidence.[84]

There is no doubt that, under the existing decisions, some circumstantial evidence may be equally reliable to—or more reliable than—direct evidence. It would be wholly irrational to impose an absolute bar on the use of circumstantial evidence to prove any fact, including a fact from which another fact is to be inferred. Therefore, either direct evidence or circumstantial evidence may be used to prove the fact in issue, and likewise, either direct or circumstantial evidence may fail to prove the fact in issue.

When evaluating whether the weight and sufficiency of circumstantial evidence should justify a determination of guilt, the United States Supreme Court in the landmark case of *Holland v. United States*[85] clearly stated that circumstantial evidence alone will support a conviction. In unambiguous language, the *Holland* Court did more than reject the jury instruction that, in circumstantial evidence cases, the evidence must be such as to exclude every reasonable hypothesis other than that of guilt; it clearly stated that "where the jury is properly instructed on the standards for reasonable doubt, such an additional instruction on circumstantial evidence is confusing and incorrect."[86] In a recent case that followed the rationale indicated in the *Holland* case, a federal district court in a habeas corpus case refused to disturb a conviction for attempted aggravated kidnapping. The defendant alleged that the prosecution failed to prove its case because the evidence was circumstantial when it showed him chasing two children and attempting to grab one child's leg. The court noted that, "Circumstantial evidence alone, however, may be sufficient to support a criminal conviction."[87] In fact, even where the circumstance evidence reasonably justifies the verdict of guilt but the circumstances could be reconciled with a contrary view, a reviewing court will not disturb the judgment, as a general rule.[88]

In an older case that has never been overturned, the Indiana Court of Appeals set out two principles that should guide the reviewing court in determining the sufficiency of the evidence in circumstantial evidence cases.[89] In that case, a police officer testified that he walked into a public restroom and saw the defendant kneeling in front of another man's groin area. A few sec-

---

84   Ohio v. Thomas, 2002 Ohio 7333, 2002 Ohio App. LEXIS 7226 (2002).

85   *Holland, supra.*

86   *Holland, supra,* 139.

87   Sparrow v. Lindamood, 2006 U.S. Dist. LEXIS 9640 (M.D. Tenn. 2006).

88   People v. Campbell, 2003 Cal. App. Unpub. LEXIS 3270 (2003), quoting People v. Akins, 56 Cal. App. 4th 331, 336-337 (1997).

89   Knowlton v. State, 178 Ind. App. 420; 382 N.E.2d 1004; 1978 Ind. App. LEXIS 1096 (Ind. Ct. App. 1978).

onds later, the defendant's companion spotted the police officer and pulled away from the kneeling defendant, thus exposing the first man's open pants and erect penis. The jury found the defendant guilty of having committed an act of fellatio on the basis of this circumstantial evidence.

When the case was appealed to the Indiana Court of Appeals, that court established two principles that control the review of the sufficiency of evidence in circumstantial evidence cases. These are:

1. Convictions should not be overruled or overturned simply because this court determined that the circumstances do not exclude every reasonable hypothesis of innocence.

2. Convictions should not be sustained when the inference of guilt is based on "mere suspicion, conjecture, conclusion, guess, opportunity, or scintilla."

In the concluding paragraph, the court stated: "We hold that eyewitness testimony of such circumstantial evidence is . . . sufficient to support a charge of sodomy by fellatio."[90]

The federal courts have consistently held that the proof of guilt by the use of circumstantial evidence alone "may be sufficient to support a conviction, and it is not necessary that the evidence preclude every reasonable hypothesis except that of guilt."[91] Recently the Eighth Circuit Court of Appeals noted with approval, that "It is well-settled that the jury is entitled to consider circumstantial evidence exactly as it would direct evidence."[92]

When intent is an element of the offense charged, it must be proved by the prosecution beyond a reasonable doubt. Because no person can absolutely know what another person was thinking at the time of the alleged crime, proof of a "criminal defendant's intent or state of mind is seldom capable of proof by direct evidence."[93] In determining whether circumstantial evidence is sufficient to support a conviction in which intent is an element, one court, in the context of a jury instruction, gave this example of being able to use circumstantial evidence to prove intent:

You remember when you were in school, there was one kid who was a bully. Every school had a bully. He'd step on some other kid's foot, and then he'd laugh, and if he was caught he'd say: Oh, that's an accident. Well, the direct evidence was that he claimed his intent was an accident, and yet everybody knew from the circumstantial evidence what he really intended. Well, ladies and gentlemen, grown-up life is much the same. Thus, it should be clear that direct

90 *Knowlton* at 429.
91 United States v. Hardman, 2005 U.S. Dist. LEXIS 28923 (M.D. Tenn. 2005) and United States v. Barnett, 398 F.3d 516, 522, 2005 U.S. App. LEXIS 2644 (6th Cir. 2005).
92 Sera v. Norris, 400 F.3d 538, 544, 2005 U.S. App. LEXIS 3730 (8th Cir. 2005), quoting United States v. Lam, 338 F.3d 868, 871, (8th Cir. 2003).
93 Robinson v. State, 353 Ark. 372, 108 S.W.3d 622, 2003 Ark. LEXIS 303 (2003).

evidence is never required to prove intent or knowledge. Direct evidence, in fact, on that particular score is often misleading. Here circumstantial evidence is quite sufficient, but it's one of those things, ladies and gentlemen, that must be proved beyond a reasonable doubt.[94]

Although most states follow the reasoning of the federal courts that circumstantial evidence is of equal weight to direct evidence, some states still hold that the jury instruction must contain the language "it must exclude every other reasonable hypothesis consistent with innocence," only if the case rests wholly on circumstantial evidence. In *Terry v. State*, an Arkansas case involving the rape of a child, the father appealed his conviction on the ground that the trial court erred when it refused to grant his motion for a directed verdict based on a failure of proof. The father had been left alone with his infant daughter, who was in good health. When the child's mother returned after a short absence, the father was standing over the infant with blood on his chest and on the victim's clothing. He stated that he had cut his cuticle, but the baby had a significant amount of red blood in her private area when her mother checked. A medical exam indicated tears in her private area and the doctor suspected sexual abuse. Two semen stains on the baby's diaper matched the defendant's DNA profile. Following his conviction and life sentence, he appealed, contending that circumstantial evidence used to convict must exclude every other reasonable hypothesis consistent with innocence and that only conjecture by the jury that he was the perpetrator supported the conviction. According to the Supreme Court of Arkansas:

> Circumstantial evidence may constitute substantial evidence to support a conviction. The longstanding rule in the use of circumstantial evidence is that, to be substantial, the evidence must exclude every other reasonable hypothesis than that of the guilt of the accused. The question of whether the circumstantial evidence excludes every other reasonable hypothesis consistent with innocence is for the jury to decide. Upon review, this court must determine whether the jury resorted to speculation and conjecture in reaching its verdict. [Internal citations omitted.][95]

The Supreme Court of Arkansas affirmed his conviction over his contention that there was no direct proof of what caused the baby's trauma. The reviewing court noted that the jury could have found the circumstantial evidence to be substantial and there was DNA evidence that the defendant was the guilty party.[96]

Some states follow a slightly different view of the manner in which circumstantial evidence should be evaluated. Florida holds that a judgment of acquittal should be granted in a case in which proof of one or more of the ele-

---

[94]   United States v. Yousef, 327 F.3d 56, 131, 2003 U.S. App. 6437 (2d Cir. 2003).
[95]   Terry v. State, 2006 Ark. LEXIS 326 (2006).
[96]   *Id.*

ments of an offense depends completely on circumstantial evidence. The prosecutor does not have to rebut every conceivable variation of events that could potentially be inferred from the facts presented; it need just present evidence that is inconsistent with the defendant's reasonable hypothesis of innocence. In a case that applied the above principle, Florida charged a defendant with uttering a forged check drawn on another person's account. The account holder took the witness stand and denied writing the check. The defendant's testimony was that he had performed automobile repairs for a person who had been referred to him by another client. The new customer paid with a check that the defendant tried to cash that turned out to be a forgery. The prosecution's theory was that the defendant knew the check was forged and that he tried to cash it, while the defendant's position was that he had a reasonable explanation concerning why and how he had acquired the check. Even though nothing in the prosecution's completely circumstantial proof contradicted the defendant's story, the trial court denied defendant's motion for acquittal and the defendant's conviction resulted. On appeal, the reviewing court reversed the conviction on the strength of the Florida rule that requires a prosecutor to present evidence to contradict a defendant's hypothesis of innocence in a circumstantial evidence prosecution. The reviewing court ruled that the trial court should have granted the defendant's motion for acquittal.[97]

In addressing the use of circumstantial evidence, California holds that a criminal conviction cannot be based on circumstantial evidence unless the evidence proves that the circumstances are consistent with the theory that the defendant is guilty of a crime and that those circumstances cannot be reconciled with any other logical conclusion. When the circumstantial evidence has two reasonable interpretations, one that points to a defendant's guilt and another that points to innocence, a jury should adopt the interpretation that points toward innocence. If a jury determines that, of two possible circumstantial interpretations, one appears more reasonable and the other seems unreasonable, the jury should adopt the reasonable interpretation of the circumstantial evidence, regardless of whether it points toward guilt or innocence.[98]

Notwithstanding some disagreement concerning the "hypothesis of innocence" instruction, courts all hold that a conviction may be based solely on circumstantial evidence. Whether a prosecutor introduced sufficient evidence to meet the constitutional standard for "the sufficiency of the evidence is whether, upon viewing the evidence in the light most favorable to the prosecution, any rational trier of fact could conclude that the state proved the essential elements of the crime beyond a reasonable doubt."[99] This measure of evidence sufficiency applies in cases involving both direct and circumstantial evidence.

---

[97] Linn v. State, 921 So. 2d 830, 2006 Fla. App. LEXIS 3040 (2006).
[98] People v. Morales, 25 Cal. 4th 34 at 40, 41, 18 P.3d 11 at 15 (2001).
[99] State v. Singleton, 922 So. 2d 647, 650, 2006 La. App. LEXIS 115 (La. 2006).

§ 4.12 Summary

The prosecutor in a criminal case has the responsibility of introducing evidence sufficient to prove guilt beyond a reasonable doubt. The defense attorney has the responsibility to introduce evidence that challenges the sufficiency of the state's evidence while offering evidence to substantiate the defendant's claims. Over the years, courts and legislatures have established rules for the admissibility of evidence and for the procedure to be followed in presenting evidence in court.

To promote a smooth and orderly flow of evidence at trial, pretrial evidentiary motions may be made by the parties to exclude or suppress certain types of evidence. When a motion to suppress is presented, the burden is on the party making the motion to show that there is a legal reason the evidence should not be admitted.

For all practical purposes, the rules of evidence are rules of exclusion. All evidence is admissible as a general rule unless it is excluded based on an objection or upon the court's own motion. Objections may be based on the form of the question. For example, if the attorney's questions are confusing, improperly phrased, misleading, argumentative, or compound, the opposing party may object based on the form. Objections may also be made based upon the substance of the question asked by the opposing counsel. If the objection is made because the evidence is irrelevant, immaterial, or incompetent, the complaining party will usually be asked to state why such a claim is being made.

The usual order for presenting evidence is for the state to present its case-in-chief, followed by the defendant's case-in-chief. The prosecution then has the opportunity to introduce evidence to rebut the evidence presented by the defense. The defense may, if it deems necessary, follow up with evidence contrary to that introduced by the prosecution during the rebuttal. When both parties have rested their cases, the hearing on the facts comes to an end, and the trial proceeds with the closing arguments and the court's instructions to the jury.

The customary method of offering evidence involves having the party place its witness on the stand and conducting direct examination by asking a series of non-leading questions. The opposing party, through counsel, may challenge any question before an answer is given by making a specific objection. The attorneys must be ready to promptly offer grounds for their respective positions. The court considers the contentions of both parties and then determines whether the answer should be allowed into evidence. In order to preserve an objection to admission or exclusion of evidence for appeal, the objection or motion must have been timely and made with sufficient specificity that the trial judge was aware of the complaint and the court must have actually made a ruling on the objection or motion. In some cases, the attorney who lost the objection or motion may make an offer of proof to further preserve the record for appeal.

In English and American courts, the trial judge, jury, witnesses, prosecuting attorney, and defense attorney all have specific functions. The judge determines whether evidence is admissible and gives instructions to the jury. The jury determines the facts from the evidence and applies the law to the facts, using the instructions given by the judge. The witnesses are the eyes and ears of the court. The prosecuting attorney guides the case for the state by producing witnesses on behalf of the state, and the defense attorney represents the accused by challenging prosecution witnesses and by presenting evidence designed to counter the prosecutor's case.

Although a few American jurisdictions question the weight and sufficiency of circumstantial evidence as compared to direct evidence, most jurisdictions hold that circumstantial evidence has equal weight when compared to direct evidence. A case built entirely upon circumstantial evidence may meet the prosecutor's burden of proof beyond a reasonable doubt. Juries may give circumstantial evidence somewhat less weight than direct evidence, but as long as the jury is satisfied that the total weight of all the evidence demonstrates the defendant's guilt beyond a reasonable doubt, a conviction is appropriate.

All who are involved in the criminal justice process, whether they are directly or indirectly involved in collecting, preserving, presenting, or evaluating the evidence, should be aware of the process by which evidence is introduced, challenged, and evaluated during the trial.

Judicial Notice 5

Judicial notice takes the place of proof, and is of equal force. As a means of establishing facts, it is therefore superior to evidence. In its appropriate field, it displaces evidence, since, as it stands for proof, it fulfills the object which evidence is designed to fulfill, and makes evidence unnecessary.

State v. Maine, 69 Conn. 123, 36 L.R.A. 623,
61 Am. St. Rep. 30, 37 A. 80 (1897)

Chapter Outline

Key Terms and Concepts

adjudicative facts   judicial notice

§ 5.1 Introduction

Near the close of a criminal trial, the judge has the duty to educate the jury concerning the law to be applied to the particular facts that will be determined by the jury. In this phase of the trial, it is said that the judge "instructs the jury," which means that the judge explains to the members of the jury that they are to determine, from the facts presented at the trial consistent with the explanations of the applicable law given by the judge, the guilt or innocence of the accused. Generally, the prosecution and the defense have the burden of establishing facts by producing sworn witnesses, authenticated documents, or real evidence. However, the courts, recognizing that it would be unreasonable to require the opposing parties to introduce evidence for every fact considered by the jury or the judge in a bench trial, have made some exceptions. Criminal trials can be lengthy affairs under our present system, and it would be less than wise to require the parties to prove, for example, that the excess alcohol consumption degrades human motor skills, or that gravity causes an object to fall to earth.

To save the time of the court and for procedural convenience, by virtue of legislative enactment and through case law, formal procedures that serve as substitutes for evidence have evolved. The first substitute for evidence is *judicial notice*. The principle of judicial notice authorizes the court to accept appropriate facts as true without requiring one of the parties to offer formal proof and not permitting the other party to introduce evidence that would dispute the judicially noticed fact.

The second substitute for evidence is the category called *presumptions* and *inferences*. Based on court decisions and through statutory enactment, when a particular basic fact has been proven, the existence of another fact may be deduced from the proof of the basic fact, thereby relieving parties of the burden of presenting evidence to prove a particular fact. One way to consider the difference between a presumption and an inference is to consider that in the case of a presumption, once the basic fact has been proven, the deduction of fact must be made, while in the case of an inference, once the basic fact has been proven, the trier of fact may make the deduction, but is not required to do so. In any event, in a criminal case, a jury or judge does not have to make the deduction of fact and may choose to ignore it.

Stipulations are the third substitute for evidence. The stipulation serves the goal of judicial economy by saving the court's time and by allowing the court to continue its business without requiring proof of a fact or issue over which the parties have no disagreement. The agreed stipulation renders proof unnecessary as to the matters stipulated. The remainder of this chapter is devoted to a discussion of specific examples of judicial notice of facts and judicial notice of laws. In the following chapter, the other substitutes for evidence—presumptions, inferences and stipulations—are explained.

§ 5.2 Judicial Notice Defined

Judicial notice may be defined as *the recognition and acceptance of certain facts that are reasonably undisputable that a judge, under the rules of evidentiary procedure, may properly take or act upon without proof*—either because the facts noticed are indisputable as a matter of notorious common knowledge or are capable of being immediately verified by consultation with standard reference works.[1] Facts that are well-known to the general population, or are well-known to those within the relevant field of knowledge, or are common knowledge within the jurisdiction's geographic area may be the proper subject of judicial notice as long as there is virtually no uncertainty about the fact. To say that a court will take judicial notice of a fact is merely another way of saying that the usual forms of evidence will not be required as proof if the fact is one of public knowledge or is of sufficient notoriety to be known generally by all well-informed persons and generally not subject to serious dispute.

Judicial notice involves the acceptance as true of certain facts and laws without the necessity of introducing evidence. To say this another way, judges will not shut their minds to truths that that other reasonable people see and understand, but the judge does not necessarily have to have personal knowledge of a fact judicially noticed.[2] When a fact is judicially noticed by the court as true, the party requesting judicial notice need not introduce any evidence in support of the fact and the opposing party is generally prevented from introducing evidence to contradict the judicially noticed fact.

In explaining the doctrine of judicial notice, one court commented that judicial notice is a substitute for evidence and is intended to avoid the neces-

---

[1] 29 AM. JUR. 2d *Evidence* § 24.

[2] A judge may not use her personal experience as a substitute for evidence that was not a proper subject for judicial notice. *See* State v. Sarnowski, 2005 WI App 48, 280 Wis. 2d 243, 251, 694 N.W.2d 498, 502, 2005 Wisc. App. LEXIS 150 (2005).

sity for formal introduction of evidence in cases in which there is no real need for it, because the fact is so well established as to be a matter of common knowledge.[3] However, where evidence was available, but was never introduced and could have been introduced by either the prosecution or the defense, where discretionary, a court may refuse to take judicial notice of the evidence when one party requests it during jury deliberations.[4] In federal courts, judicial notice may be taken at any time during any stage of a proceeding.[5]

What passes for common knowledge will vary with the geographic area where the court sits and does not necessarily depend upon the actual knowledge of the judge. A court may take judicial notice of a fact if that fact is not subject to reasonable dispute in that it is either generally known within the territorial jurisdiction of the trial court or capable of accurate and ready determination by resort to sources whose accuracy cannot reasonably be questioned.[6] For instance, a judge might not understand the exact science involved in DNA testing, but could judicially notice the accuracy of the scientific principle where there was general acceptance of the principle by those with knowledge in the field. In other fields of knowledge, a judge may consult authoritative sources to verify the validity of taking judicial notice. For example, in making a judicial notice decision, a court could review such relevant material as historical works, science and art books, language and medical journals and dictionaries, calendars, encyclopedias, commercial lists and directories, maps and charts, and statutes and legislative reports.[7]

Although the judge has great discretion in taking judicial notice, the power of judicial notice must be exercised with great caution. If there is any doubt whatever, either as to the fact itself or as to its being a matter of common knowledge, evidence should be required.[8] Generally speaking, matters of judicial notice meet at least two basic requisites and one final consideration: (1) a matter must be of common and general knowledge to those in the relevant field of knowledge; and (2) it must be authoritatively settled, not subject to reasonable dispute, and not uncertain.[9] Finally, because judicial notice is a substitute for evidence and only relevant evidence is admissible, a court will not take judicial notice of facts that are not relevant in the particular case.[10]

The judge may take judicial notice upon the request of either party, or upon his or her motion, even in the absence of a request. In deciding whether to judicially notice a fact, the judge may consult statutes and case law, as well as review legal encyclopedias, in seeking sources of information regarding the appropriateness of taking judicial notice. A judge may seek assistance in

---

[3]   Commonwealth v. Birdeye, 637 A.2d 1036 (Pa. 1994).

[4]   United States v. Neill, 964 F. Supp. 438 (D.D.C. 1997).

[5]   FED. R. EVID. 201(f).

[6]   Fawcett v. State, 697 A.2d 385 (Del. 1997).

[7]   United States v. Neill, 964 F. Supp. 438 (D.D.C. 1997).

[8]   Fawcett v. State, 697 A.2d 385 (Del. 1997).

[9]   State v. Shanks, 640 A.2d 155 (Conn. 1994).

[10]   People v. Young, 34 Cal. 4th 1149, 1171, 105 P.3d 487, 499, 24 Cal. Rptr. 3d 112, 126, 2005 Cal. LEXIS 1017 (2005).

reaching the decision by consulting any authoritative source of information that serves the purpose. Also, in taking judicial notice, the judge may request assistance from counsel and, in the absence of such assistance, may decline to notice the desired fact.[11] In the case of *People v. Maxwell*, the court asserted that a court is not required to seek indisputable sources of information on its own initiative when a request for judicial notice is made. The court further explained that, in some cases, the original source document may be required to provide the court with sufficient information, but if the information supplied is insufficient, the trial judge is entitled to refuse to take judicial notice of the matter.[12]

With respect to the topics of proper judicial notice in criminal cases, one North Carolina court noted that generally there are a wide range of miscellaneous facts that may properly be the subject of judicial notice, including:

> the laws of nature; human impulses, habits, functions and capabilities; the prevalence of a certain surname; established medical and scientific facts; well-known practices in farming, construction work, transportation, and other businesses and professions; the characteristics of familiar tools and appliances, weapons, intoxicants, and poisons; the use of highways; the normal incidence of the operation of trains, motor vehicles, and planes; prominent geographical features such as railroads, water courses, and cities and towns; population and area as shown by census reports; the days, weeks, and months of the calendar; the effect of natural conditions on the construction of public improvements; the facts of history; important current events; general economic and social conditions; matters affecting public health and safety; the meaning of words and abbreviations; and the results of mathematical computations.[13]

While these categories are not all-inclusive, they represent many topics on which courts take judicial notice of facts on an ongoing basis. For convenience, the rules concerning judicial notice are often categorized as judicial notice of facts and judicial notice of laws. In the following sections, the two categories are discussed and distinguished.

---

[11] People v. Maxwell, 78 Cal. App. 2d 124, 144 Cal. Rptr. 95 (1978).

[12] *Id.*

[13] Haynes Mall v. Central Carolina, 2006 N.C. App. LEXIS 175 (N.C. 2006), quoting 1 KENNETH S. BROUN, BRANDIS AND BROUN ON NORTH CAROLINA EVIDENCE § 27, at 104-09 (5th ed. 1998).

§ 5.3 Judicial Notice of Facts

Rule 201

Judicial Notice of Adjudicative Facts

(a) **Scope of rule.** This rule governs only judicial notice of adjudicative facts.

(b) **Kinds of facts.** A judicially noticed fact must be one not subject to reasonable dispute in that it is either (1) generally known within the territorial jurisdiction of the trial court or (2) capable of accurate and ready determination by resort to sources whose accuracy cannot reasonably be questioned.

(c) **When discretionary.** A court may take judicial notice, whether requested or not.

(d) **When mandatory.** A court shall take judicial notice if requested by a party and supplied with the necessary information.[14]

* * *

Rule 201 of the Federal Rules of Evidence limits the scope of the rule to the judicial notice of "adjudicative facts." Adjudicative facts are facts that concern the dispute between the parties and may be determinative of the outcome of the case. Adjudicative facts are customarily established through the introduction of formal proof, but may be established by judicial notice pursuant to this rule.[15] In accordance with Subdivision (b) of Rule 201, the court may take judicial notice of the facts that are well-known within the territorial jurisdiction of the trial court, or the judge determines by reference to an authoritative source that the fact is not subject to reasonable dispute.

As indicated in Subdivision (c) of Rule 201, a court may take judicial notice without a formal request from either counsel. According to the general rule, a judge may take judicial notice at any time, whether during the trial or even during the appellate process,[16] so long as judicial notice would have been appropriate at the trial. The judge is required to take judicial notice if asked by a party and supplied with the necessary information. In a California case, the court agreed that the burden is on the party requesting judicial notice to supply the court with sufficient, reliable, and trustworthy sources of information about the matter. The court is not required to seek out, on its own initiative, indisputable sources of information.[17] The court continued by warning that if the information supplied is insufficient, the trial court is entitled to refuse to take judicial notice of the matter requested. In a California case where the defendant alleged that a constitutional flaw existed in death penalty legislation, the court refused to take judicial notice of the flaw because the defendant

---

[14] FED. R. EVID. 201.

[15] *See* WEISSENBERGER, FEDERAL EVIDENCE 3D (1998).

[16] Central Green Co. v. United States, 531 U.S. 425 at 435 (2001).

[17] People v. Moore, 69 Cal. Rptr. 2d 56 (1997).

failed to demonstrate on the record, or through sources of which the court could have taken judicial notice, that his claims were empirically accurate.[18]

In most states, the code or statute pertaining to evidence provides the rules that must be followed by the court relating to judicial notice of facts.[19]

Judicial notice of facts is not the same as the extrajudicial or personal knowledge of the judge; what the judge knows and what facts the judge may judicially notice are not identical, and the private knowledge of the judge is not a sufficient basis for taking judicial notice of facts.[20] In *State v. Vejvoda*, the reviewing court, after explaining the limits on the use of judicial notice, decided that the trial court improperly took judicial notice of the fact that the defendant was driving in a city within the county of prosecution when the arresting officer's testimony referred only to street names, but not their location. The fact that the judge was aware that the streets were probably in the county of prosecution did not cure the failure to introduce evidence. In a different case, a reviewing court reversed a conviction for failing to support defendant's children because the trial judge committed error in using her personal experience that there were plenty of jobs for carpenters in the area. Because the judge had trouble hiring a carpenter in the relevant period, she assumed that the failure to obtain work sufficient to support his children was the deliberate decision by the defendant, who was a carpenter by trade.[21]

Courts do not always reach predictable results when asked to take judicial notice. California appellate courts appear reluctant to take judicial notice when a trial court either refused to do so or when the trial court was never presented with a request. Other jurisdictions seem quite comfortable in taking judicial notice wherever appropriate, even at the appellate level. Even though courts are not in complete agreement as to what facts must be judicially noticed and when to take notice and what facts may be judicially noticed on request, some matters traditionally have been considered proper topics for consideration. These are discussed in the sections that follow. However, the examples given are merely demonstrative of the general principles and are not meant to be exhaustive.

§ 5.4 —Matters of General Knowledge

While it is accepted practice to take judicial notice of facts of common knowledge, and such facts need not be proved by the opposing party, the following question arises: What facts are common knowledge? A fact is said to be generally recognized or known when it is not open to reasonable dispute.

---

[18] People v. Michaels, 28 Cal. 4th 486, 541, 49 P.3d 1032, 122 Cal. Rptr. 2d 285 (2002).
[19] *See* Appendix II for a list of states that follow the Uniform Rules of Evidence.
[20] State v. Vejvoda, 231 Neb. 668, 438 N.W.2d 461 (1989). *See* case in Part II. *See also* United States v. Lewis, 833 F.2d 1380 (9th Cir. 1987) and Vaughn v. Shelby-Williams of Tenn., Inc., 813 S.W.2d 132 (Tenn. 1991).
[21] State v. Sarnowski, 2005 Wis. App. 48; 280 Wis. 2d 243, 250, 694 N.W.2d 498, 502, 2005 Wis. App. LEXIS 150 (2005).

For example, the fact that whiskey and rum are intoxicating liquors is generally known and their qualities are not subject to any reasonable dispute.[22] This does not mean that everyone must be aware of the fact; scarcely any fact is known by everyone. All that is necessary is that a matter be familiar to the majority of humankind or to those persons familiar with a particular matter in question. When the matter depends upon uncertain testimony and becomes a disputable item in court, it ceases to fall under the heading of common knowledge and will not be judicially recognized. For example, in a case in which a trial court had taken judicial notice that a federal penitentiary in Puerto Rico was located within the jurisdiction of the United States, judicial notice was not appropriately taken under the matters of general or common knowledge theory because the location of the prison within the special jurisdiction of the United States would not be one that a reasonable person would know from memory.[23]

Facts judicially noticed may be of purely local knowledge, such as the character of the location where an accident occurred, the name of a street, or the location of a business area. For example, a federal court sitting in Georgia took judicial notice of the identity of the new county sheriff in a civil rights case where the new sheriff's name had to be substituted for name of the former sheriff.[24] Sometimes, well-known facts, which seem appropriate for judicial notice at first look, will fail when carefully considered. A decision to find that "McDowell Road is a heavily traveled east-west street in the City of Phoenix," would seem appropriate by a judge who was familiar with the area, but the appellate court reversed a conviction based on the theory that a judge could not take notice of that fact, when at the time of day and season of the year in question, the road might not be well-known as a heavily traveled road.[25]

Courts may take judicial notice of notorious nationally known facts that are not the subject of reasonable dispute. For example, one court took judicial notice that the E-Bay auction process was a matter of common knowledge concerning how it worked.[26] Another court took judicial notice that, in litigation concerning the *Star Wars* series of movies, Luke Skywalker was nurtured by Obi-Wan Kenobi.[27] Because it is a well-known fact that tobacco products pose disease-related risks, including lung cancer, it is proper for a court to take notice of the harm of tobacco.[28] While it might not be proper to take judicial notice that all pit bull terriers are dangerous,[29] because there are alternative

---

[22]   *See* State v. Aiken, 121 Ohio Misc. 2d 7, 2002 Ohio 6436, 779 N.E.2d 1105, 2002 Ohio Misc. LEXIS 44 (Ohio 2002).

[23]   United States v. Bello, 194 F.3d 18, 1999 U.S. App. LEXIS 26461 (1999).

[24]   Young v. Graham, 2005 U.S. Dist. LEXIS 20882 (2005).

[25]   United States v. Mariscal, 285 F.3d 1127 at 1131, 2002 U.S. App. LEXIS 5354 (9th Cir. 2002).

[26]   Action Tapes, Inc. v. Weaver, 2005 U.S. Dist. LEXIS 29312, n.2, (N.D. Tex. 2005).

[27]   Twentieth Century Fox Film Corp. v. Marvel Enterprises, 155 F. Supp. 2d 1, 41, 2001 U.S. Dist. LEXIS 11568 (S. Dist. N.Y. 2001).

[28]   Spain v. Brown and Williamson Tobacco, 363 F.3d 1183, 1194, 2004 U.S. App. LEXIS 5792 (11th Cir. 2004).

[29]   Yuzon v. Collins, 116 Cal. App. 4th 149, 168, 10 Cal. Rptr. 3d 18, 33, 2004 Cal. App. LEXIS 228 (2004).

opinions on the subject of their propensities, a court can take judicial notice of legal opinions that mention problems and vicious tendencies of the breed.[30]

Other examples of instances in which courts have taken judicial notice of matters of general knowledge are these: guns are the tools of the trade to substantial dealers in narcotics,[31] a pistol is a deadly weapon,[32] a full-choke shotgun scatters less than a modified-choke shotgun, and an open-bore shotgun splatters more than either of them, provided that the distance is not extremely short;[33] the capitol building of the state of Utah is located on State Street,[34] witnesses are often unable to accurately remember dates;[35] and a defendant nearly always wants his or her trial to be postponed.[36]

Concerning the proper subjects of judicial notice, the courts have held that the prevailing prime interest rate and the average rate for 30-year fixed mortgages are proper subjects for judicial notice,[37] and that a court may take judicial notice of the fact that telephone lines carry interstate calls.[38] In state cases, the courts have held that the judge may take judicial notice of mortality tables as proof of life expectancy,[39] and that judicial notice may be taken of the fact, that at one time in history, there are many qualified corporate bonds and public utility stocks that provide a rate of return between 10 and 15 percent.[40]

In discussing judicial notice, a Georgia court explained that the courts will generally take judicial notice of a fact if the fact is of common knowledge that all people of average intelligence are presumed to know and that is certain and indisputable.[41] A Maryland court noted that it was appropriate for a court to take judicial notice that most men do not carry purses.[42] A Florida court took judicial notice that a well-known local Christian school was a school for purposes of state law because the trial judge should not be compelled to force the school's principal to spend valuable time at the courthouse confirming a status that seemed to be common knowledge.[43]

For purposes of determining whether the search of a vehicle was appropriate as part of a police/community caretaking function following the arrest of the owner, the court held that it could take judicial notice that an expensive vehicle such as a Porsche is especially vulnerable in New York City.[44] Courts

---

[30] Warboys v. Prouix, 303 F. Supp. 2d 111, 119, 2004 U.S. Dist. LEXIS 1562 (D. Conn. 2004).
[31] United States v. Crespo, 834 F.2d 267, 271 (2d Cir. 1987), *cert. denied*, 485 U.S. 1007, 99 L. Ed. 2d 700, 108 S. Ct. 1471 (1988).
[32] State v. Taylor, 182 S.W. 159 (Mo. 1916).
[33] Sanders v. Allen, 65 U.S. 220, 56 S. Ct. 69 (1911).
[34] Utah Gospel Mission v. Salt Lake City, 316 F. Supp. 2d 1201, 2004 U.S. Dist. LEXIS 12966 (2004).
[35] People v. Berne, 51 N.E.2d 578 (Ill. 1943).
[36] Sam v. State, 265 P. 609 (Ariz. 1928).
[37] In re Marriage of Dudley, 2003 Ml 848, 2003 Mont. Dist. LEXIS 3446 (Mont. 2003).
[38] Havens Steel Co. v. Randolph Eng. Co., 813 F.2d 186 (9th Cir. 1987); United States v. Deckard, 816 F.2d 428 (8th Cir. 1987).
[39] Clement v. Fulton, 110 P3d 927, 933, 2005 Alas. LEXIS 45, n.1 (Alaska 2005).
[40] Stewart v. State, 394 So. 2d 1337 (Miss. 1981); Svetenko v. Svetenko, 306 N.W.2d 607 (N.D. 1981).
[41] Weems v. State, 485 S.E.2d 767 (Ga. 1997).
[42] Ransome v. State, 2003 Md. LEXIS 39 (Md. Ct. App. 2003).
[43] Cox v. Florida, 764 So. 2d 711, 713, 2000 Fla. App. LEXIS 7516 (2000).
[44] United States v. Mundy, 806 F. Supp. 373 (E.D.N.Y. 1992).

can lawfully take judicial notice of the high interest rates prevailing in the late 1970s and early 1980s over those in previous years.[45] However, it was error to take judicial notice of the fact that HIV cannot be transferred via saliva, because there is disagreement among experts concerning this matter.[46]

On the other hand, the courts have held that certain facts are not presumed to be known by the court. Bringing case law to a court's attention has been held *not* to be a proper topic for judicial notice.[47] Courts have refused to take judicial notice of: a pardon,[48] that all of the detainees from Iraq and Afghanistan at Guantanamo Bay were "enemy combatants,"[49] and that a non-law-abiding citizen is always a perjurer.[50] A Florida court held that a mother's lesbianism was not a proper subject of which the court could take judicial notice.[51] Another Florida court improperly took judicial notice of the value of a non-working motor vehicle because the standard reference value books considered only vehicles that were operable.[52] A court should not take judicial notice of the age of a juvenile that was an element of the charge of underage alcohol consumption.[53] Because many people have knowledge of events around them that may affect everyday lives, judicial notice of contemporary happenings and events may be the subject of judicial notice. For instance, it is common knowledge that there has been an increase in the number of serious crimes committed by persons less than 18 years of age. The judge may take judicial notice of economic facts, such as the constant increase in the cost of living and the decrease in the purchasing power of the dollar. In such instances, the facts are noticed judicially without proof by either side.

§ 5.5 —History and Historical Facts

The collection of historical facts that make up the history of the states and our nation are either well-known to contemporary members of society or have been recorded in works of history. As such, these facts are either common knowledge or are subject to ready verification by consulting standard reference works. In taking judicial notice of historical facts or events, courts simply recognize the reasonably unrefutable facts of our history that, if proof were required by a court, would constitute a waste of time. Most Americans vividly remember the historic events that occurred on September 11, 2001. In a case where a parole hearing was not held in a timely fashion on September 11,

---

[45] Harris Trust and Savings Bank v. John Hancock Mutual Life Ins. Co., 767 F. Supp. 1269 (S.D.N.Y. 1991).
[46] Weeks v. State, 834 S.W.2d 559 (Tex. 1992).
[47] Hyde v. Paskett, 383 F. Supp. 2d 1256, 2005 U.S. Dist. LEXIS 23165 (D. Idaho 2005).
[48] State v. Garrett, 188 S.W. 58 (Tenn. 1916).
[49] Rasul v. Bush, 215 F. Supp. 2d 55, 67, 2002 U.S. Dist. LEXIS 14031 (D.D.C. 2002).
[50] State v. Baird, 195 S.W. 1010 (Mo. 1917).
[51] Mardie v. Mardie, 680 So. 2d 538, 540 (Fla. Dist. Ct. App. 1996).
[52] Walentukonis v. Florida, 2006 Fla. App. LEXIS 9766 (2006).
[53] State v. K.N., 124 Wn. App. 875, 103 P.3d 844, 2004 Wash. App. LEXIS 3135 (2004).

2001 due to the terrorist attacks in Pennsylvania and the governor's response, a court took judicial notice of the events of that day in recognizing that a sufficient reason existed for the hearing to be rescheduled later than the time demanded by administrative regulations.[54] According to a case cited by the court, "matters of history, if sufficiently notorious to be subject to general knowledge, will be judicially noticed."[55] The financial history of the United States, including events such as the 1929 stock market collapse and the depression of the 1930s, are matters proper for judicial notice. In a bankruptcy matter, a court can take judicial notice of the average rate of a 30-year mortgage at a particular time by consulting the *Wall Street Journal*.[56] The price of listed stocks on recognized exchanges constitutes historical data that cannot be subject to any serious dispute and can be the subject of judicial notice.[57] The day of the week on which a particular date fell, the date on which war was declared or ended, the destructive character of a flood or other disaster—all can be matters of judicial notice. The court, in an action to declare life insurance policies in force, judicially noticed the flight of refugees from Castro's Cuba to Miami, Florida, and their acceptance, encouragement, and support by the United States.[58]

In criminal cases as well as civil cases, the court may take judicial notice of historical facts of a national character, such as the fact that a state of war existed in Korea in 1950,[59] that a political disturbance and civil war existed in Croatia after it declared independence in 1991[60] and, in a modern environmental suit, that the decade following 1953 was one of heightened military concern in the United States.[61]

The judge does not have to be personally aware of historical facts to take judicial notice of them. It would be asking too much for the judge to be aware of all the details of history. He or she may refer to properly authenticated official public documents, encyclopedias, history books, periodicals, or even newspaper articles. However, such judicial knowledge is generally limited to what a judge may properly know in a judicial capacity, and he or she cannot take judicial notice of a historical fact of which only he or she is aware.

Although a court may take judicial notice of historical facts, the court is not required to do so unless the party so requesting supplies the necessary information. For example, where a defendant wanted the court to take judicial notice of municipal ordinances that had been passed prior to trial, the court refused because it was under no obligation to take judicial notice when it had not been supplied with the necessary information.[62]

---

[54] Wiley v. Commonwealth, 801 A.2d 644, 2002 Pa. Commw. LEXIS 510 (2002).

[55] *See generally* Fatemi v. Fatemi, 371 Pa. Super. 101, 537 A.2d 840 (Pa. Super. 1988).

[56] In re Chaing, 274 B.R. 295, 305, 2002 Bankr. LEXIS 170 (Dist. Mass. 2002).

[57] Grimes v. Navigant Consulting, 185 F. Supp.2d 906, 913, 2002 U.S. Dist. LEXIS 1708 (N.D. Ill. 2002).

[58] Blanco v. Pan-American Life Ins. Co., 221 F. Supp. 219 (S.D. Fla. 1963); Perez v. Department of Revenue, 778 P.2d 326 (Colo. Ct. App. 1989).

[59] Gagliormella v. Metropolitan Life Ins. Co., 122 F. Supp. 246 (D.C. Mass. 1954).

[60] Abrambasic v. Ashcroft, 403 F. Supp. 2d 951, 958, 2005 U.S. Dist. LEXIS 31713 (D. S.D. 2005).

[61] Gould Electronics v. United States, 2002 U.S. Dist. LEXIS 262 (E.D. Pa. 2002).

[62] State v. Hofland, 151 N.H. 322, 327, 857 A.2d 1271, 1276, 2004 N.H. LEXIS 146 (N.H. 2004).

§ 5.6 —Geography and Geographical Facts

Although the prosecutor must introduce evidence to show that the court has jurisdiction in the case during the initial stages, he or she does not have to introduce evidence to show, for example, that Chicago is in Cook County, Illinois. Courts can take judicial notice of: (1) "of the prominent geographical and natural features of the country, such as the large lakes and rivers; the division of the country into states; the existence, location, and population of political subdivisions; and distances between well-known points. Courts also judicially notice the territorial limits of the United States"[63] and (2) the prominent geographical and natural features of the country that are common knowledge, such as lakes and other bodies of water, and whether the body of water is tidal water or whether it can be navigated;[64] In a similar way, a federal district has the power to take judicial notice of whether particular streets were located within a city within the court's jurisdiction.[65] In a cocaine case involving possession too close to a school, a Texas court noted that courts "may take judicial notice of the location of cities, counties, boundaries, dimensions, and distances, because geographical facts such as these are easily ascertainable and capable of verifiable certainty."[66] Similarly, Texas law, under the water code, requires that courts "shall take judicial notice of the creation of the [water] district and of its boundaries.[67]

Topography of the land and geographic features change very slowly, which makes judicial notice quite appropriate in many cases. Municipal boundaries may change more frequently due to annexation and consolidation, but the exact area and location of a municipal border can be discerned by reference to topographical maps, reference works, and common knowledge. "Trial courts are generally permitted to take judicial notice of any geographic facts that are common knowledge within its jurisdiction."[68] In one case, the court took judicial notice that "Suffolk County . . . is the easternmost county on Long Island, separated from Connecticut on the north by Long Island Sound and bordered on the west by Nassau County."[69] In a New York impaired driving case, the judge took judicial notice when he observed "that Elmwood Avenue is a significant traffic artery in the Town of Brighton. It is also heavily residential, involving vehicles regularly entering and exiting the road, and pedestrians crossing, biking, and otherwise using the street, all requiring the ability of motorists to stop easily and quickly as needed."[70] A court may take

---

[63]　23 FLA. JUR. *Evidence and Witnesses* § 40 (2005).

[64]　*Id.* § 41.

[65]　United States v. Connor, 153 Fed. Appx. 600, 2005 U.S. App. LEXIS 23361 (11th Cir. 2005).

[66]　Lovelady v. State, 65 S.W.3d 810, 813, 2002 Tex. App. LEXIS 378 (2002) and New Process Steel, L.P. v. Sharp Freight System, n.5, 2006 Tex. App. LEXIS 2967 (2006).

[67]　TEX. WATER CODE § 49.066(a) (2005).

[68]　State v. Davis, 2004 Ohio 5680, 2004 Ohio App. LEXIS 5144 (2004).

[69]　Town of Suffolk v. Town of East Hampton, 406 F. Supp. 2d 227, 232, 2005 U.S. Dist. LEXIS 41036 (2005).

[70]　People v. D'Ambrosia, 192 Misc. 2d 560, 746 N.Y.S.2d 556, 2002 N.Y. Misc. LEXIS 1043 (2002).

judicial notice that the town of Foristell is located in St. Charles County, Missouri, because the fact is not subject to reasonable dispute.[71] In these cases, the facts were notorious and well-known within the judicial district or were subject to verification by unimpeachable sources.

A court may take judicial notice that a geographical area of a city has a well-known reputation as a location for particular purposes. A Colorado trial court took judicial notice that a particular section of a city street constituted a "notorious location for drug dealing."[72] However, a judicial notice of negative associations and influences of a neighborhood were held not to be the proper subject of judicial notice where the attendant geographical facts were not well-known within the jurisdiction of the court.[73] Other geographical facts that have been judicially noticed include the fact that a pawn shop was located within the jurisdiction of the court and the location was proper for venue purposes, [74] that a traffic stop occurred within the jurisdiction of the police officer,[75] and how a street intersection within the jurisdiction functions.[76]

While some courts have decided that a judge should not take judicial notice of the exact length of time it takes to travel from one point to another, a court may take judicial notice of the fact that a trip of 31 nautical miles between the island of Rota (in the Trust Territory of the Pacific Islands) and Guam must have involved travel through international waters.[77] Similarly, a federal magistrate judge holding court within a national park properly took judicial notice of a geographical fact that to travel between two points in the park along a park road required travel entirely within Yosemite National Park.[78]

§ 5.7 —Facts Relating to Nature and Science

Generally, courts may take judicial notice of facts that, although not specifically known by the general public, can be readily determined by reference to sources whose accuracy cannot reasonably be disputed. In reaching the level of acceptance required before judicial notice is appropriate, scientific principles and facts involving novel areas of science must have their validity established by expert testimony. As a particular scientific fact or process gains general acceptance and becomes undisputed by those in the field, judicial notice of the reliability of the scientific process or principle becomes appropriate and a court may dispense with formal proof. In some cases, trial and appellate courts have taken judicial notice of scientific literature even when

---

[71]   United States v. Vincente-Hernandez, 2004 U.S. Dist. LEXIS 26722 (E.D. Mo. 2004). *See* FED. R. EVID. 201(b). and 29 AM. JUR. 2D *Evidence* §§ 75-82 (1994).
[72]   People v. Archuleta, 980 P.2d 509, 1999 Colo. LEXIS 202 (1999).
[73]   Ottinger v. Ottinger, 1998 Tenn. App. LEXIS 574 (Tenn. 1998).
[74]   United States v. Connor, 153 Fed. Appx. 600, 603, 2005 U.S. App. LEXIS 23361 (2005).
[75]   State v. Burkhalter, 2006 Ohio 1623, 2006 Ohio App. LEXIS 1520 (2006).
[76]   Torres v. State, 2002 Tex. App. LEXIS 6312 (2002).
[77]   United States v. Perez, 769 F.2d 1336 (9th Cir. 1985).
[78]   United States v. Coutchavlis, 260 F.3d 1149, 2001 U.S. App. LEXIS 18363 (9th Cir. 2001).

the literature was not presented by either party.[79] Such practice, however, may pose a danger if the court misapplies the principle or the scientific conclusion. Consistent with the proper use of judicial notice, courts frequently take notice of the elementary principles of physics, such as the force of gravity or the laws of thermodynamics. Also, facts relating to the climate of the state and the climate elsewhere may be judicially noticed. Of special significance in criminal cases is the fact that the courts may take judicial notice of scientific facts that have a bearing on the case, and scientific facts that have been well established by authoritative scientists and are generally accepted as irrefutable. For example, judicial notice was properly taken of the fact that appropriate expert testimony founded upon epidemiological data would be reliable because epidemiology is a well-established branch of science and medicine.[80] However, one court distinguished between climate and the weather on a particular day by holding that because of the fluctuating nature of weather, weather on any particular date is not the type of fact normally subject to judicial notice.[81]

The scope of judicial notice in scientific areas changes as human knowledge expands. A number of these scientific areas are of special interest in the criminal justice process. For example, ballistic identification for firearms was once unacceptable, but presently ballistic identification techniques are the proper subject of judicial notice. Likewise, when testing for human DNA first evolved, courts were reluctant to admit the evidence, but as the science became accepted in the relevant scientific community, courts recognized the principle that human DNA is unique to each person.[82] A California court, when faced with an appeal contending that the principles of DNA testing were not proved, noted just the opposite and observed the acceptability of DNA evidence by stating, "the record provides no basis to conclude that a challenge to the admissibility of the DNA evidence would have been successful."[83] In the California case, representative of state cases everywhere, the court took judicial notice of the accuracy of the PCR [polymerase chain reaction] method of using DNA to make accurate identifications.[84] When a newer method of identifying DNA arose, one court required testimony to develop evidence that the capillary electrophoresis method of separating multiple-sourced DNA samples was accepted in the scientific community. When this was established, the court took judicial notice of the particular method of DNA identification and the evidence produced by the process was properly admitted.[85] A Hawaii court judicially noticed the reliability of the identification of hair samples because the scientific principles involved are well-known and of proven reliability.[86] Judicial notice may be taken of the validity of techniques for identifying ques-

---

[79]   Mata v. State, 46 S.W.3d 902, 910, 2001 Tex. Crim. App. LEXIS 45 (Tex. 2001).

[80]   Berry v. CSX, 709 So. 2d 552, 1998 Fla. App. LEXIS 2243 (Fla. Dist. Ct. App. 1998).

[81]   Weems v. State, 485 S.E.2d 767 (Ga. 1997).

[82]   DNA profiles are unique except for identical twins.

[83]   Campbell v. Rice, 408 F.3d 1166, 1171, 2005 U.S. App. LEXIS 9221 (9th Cir. 2005).

[84]   Id.

[85]   State v. Butterfield, 2001 UT 59, 27 P.3d 1133, 1144, 2001 Utah LEXIS 92 (2001).

[86]   State v. Fukusaku, 946 P.2d 32, 44 (Haw. 1997).

tioned handwriting and typewriting.[87] Judicial notice is appropriate to recognize the validity of the principle underlying the horizontal gaze nystagmus (HGN) test, used as a diagnostic tool to discover alcohol-impaired drivers. According to a Connecticut court, conducting a hearing on the reliability of the HGN test was not necessary because it had already been proved that the HGN test had been scientifically validated as accurate, making the test a proper subject for judicial notice.[88] As a general rule, courts have been unwilling to take judicial notice of the scientific validity of the polygraph or to admit the results in criminal cases due to concerns about reliability or relevancy.[89] Going against the majority view, a reviewing court in New Jersey reversed a trial court decision excluding polygraph evidence, citing an older case upholding judicial notice of the reliability of the polygraph because the polygraph is used extensively by law enforcement agencies.[90]

Judicial notice "is generally limited to matters of public record and to matters of common knowledge that cannot reasonably be disputed."[91] Subjects of judicial notice could include notice of a date on a calendar, principles of gravity, or an unquestioned law of mathematics. [92] Notice should be taken of scientific principles and authoritative treatises that are generally known and accepted or are readily verifiable from sources of indisputable accuracy. However, courts generally will not take judicial notice of scientific facts or principles that remain of questionable validity. For example, in an assault case, an Ohio appellate court refused to take judicial notice of a defendant's offering of a complicated scientific formula that he alleged computed the rate of the acceleration of falling objects, which the prosecution contended injured other people. The court believed that the formula did not represent a proven scientific principle that was so well understood as to be part of the common knowledge of every person.[93]

In explaining the law concerning scientific evidence, one court cautioned that the test for the admissibility of novel scientific evidence is whether the procedure or technique in question has reached the scientific stage of verifiable certainty.[94] The court further noted that once a procedure has been recognized in a substantial number of courts, the trial judge may judicially notice, without receiving evidence, that the procedure has been established with verifiable certainty, or that it rests upon the laws of nature.

---

[87]   Fenelon v. State, 195 Wis. 416, 217 N.W. 711 (1928); United States v. Hiss, 107 F. Supp. 128 (S.D.N.Y. 1952).
[88]   State v. Balbi, 89 Conn. App. 567, 572, 874 A.2d 288, 291, 2005 Conn. App. LEXIS 236 (Conn. 2005).
[89]   Unites States v. Ramirez-Robles, 386 F.3d 1234, 1248, 2004 U.S. App. LEXIS 21847 (9th Cir. 2004). The Fourth Circuit Court of Appeals continues to enforce a per se ban on polygraph evidence. *See* United States v. Prince-Oyibo, 320 F.3d 494, 501, 2003 U.S. App. LEXIS 3568 (4th Cir. 2003).
[90]   State v. Domicz, 377 N.J. Super. 515, 557, 873 A.2d 630, 656, 2005 N.J. Super. LEXIS 161 (2005). (Both parties stipulated to admissibility.)
[91]   Timm v. Reitz, 39 P.3d 1252, 1258, 2001 Colo. App. LEXIS 2019 (2001).
[92]   Johnson v. Commonwealth, 12 S.W.3d 258, 267, 1999 Ky. LEXIS 159 (1999).
[93]   State v. Mendez, 2004 Ohio 3107, 2004 Ohio App. LEXIS 2755 (2004).
[94]   Gentry v. State, 443 S.E.2d 667 (Ga. Ct. App. 1994).

In the absence of a hearing, only scientific methods proven "inherently reliable" will allow a court to take judicial notice of the accuracy of scientific testimony and avoid the requirement for an evidentiary hearing on the reliability of such testimony.[95]

Courts may take judicial notice of the scientific reliability of blood-alcohol concentration tests.[96] In approving the admission of evidence under the "silent witness" theory, an Alabama court noted that a photograph or similar recording of an image is admissible even in the absence of an observing or sensing witness because the process of taking the picture ensures that it has been produced with reliability and trustworthiness.[97]

§ 5.8 —Language, Abbreviations, and Symbols

Because judges possess an above-average educational level and are members of society able to understand the usual terms and definitions used by ordinary people, judges may take judicial notice of commonly used words, phrases, slang words having a clearly fixed meaning,[98] and symbols. The personal knowledge of judges does not qualify them to take judicial notice merely because they have extensive knowledge of words and phrases; they may take judicial notice of usual words that are known by the community, even if not known personally by the judge. Where a word or phrase is known generally to those in the relevant field, but not understood by the judge, resort to standard dictionaries or other similar reference works, whose accuracy cannot reasonably be questioned, allows judicial notice to be taken of common words as defined in standard and specialized dictionaries.

Ordinarily, the court may not take judicial notice of the meaning of obscure slang words or expressions common to a small group. However, if the word has come into such frequent use as to convey a particular meaning, and it no longer can be considered as simply the language of slang that is understood only by a certain segment of the population, the court may take judicial notice of the word. For example, the court may take judicial notice of the meanings of such terms as "cold check" and "hot check," as they are in common use in Texas.[99] Idioms that have acquired a special meaning may be judicially noticed. The term "Democrat" may be judicially noticed as meaning the members and candidates of the Democratic party, and the court may take judicial notice that "pig" has come to be used as a derogatory name for the police.[100]

The use of symbols has occasionally been the proper subject of judicial notice. Trademarks, logos, and similar graphic representations convey identifying messages to interested persons. Corporations frequently use symbols to

---

[95] State v. Foret, 628 So. 2d 1116 (La. 1993).
[96] Commonwealth v. Wirth, 936 S.W.2d 78 (Ky. 1996); State v. Van Sickle, 813 P.2d 910 (Idaho 1991).
[97] Straughn v. Alabama, 2003 Ala. Crim. App. LEXIS 138 (Ala. 2003).
[98] Still v. Secretary of the Commonwealth, 73 Pa. D. & C. 106, 1950 Pa. D. & C. LEXIS 247 (1950).
[99] Elder v. Evatt, 154 S.W.2d 684 (Tex. 1941).
[100] St. Petersburg v. Waller, 261 So. 2d 151 (Fla. 1972).

make a company image recognizable to the public. Police officers carry badges in varying forms that identify them as members of a particular law enforcement entity. In an unpublished opinion in a case alleging impersonation of an officer, one court took judicial notice of the design, writing, and symbols incorporated into a genuine badge carried by a bona fide police officer.[101]

The courts may take judicial notice of the meaning of abbreviations generally known and in common use, such as abbreviations for days and months. But judicial notice may not be taken of the meaning of abbreviations, symbols, or initials when the meaning is not generally known or when they have no meaning without explanation. A court, for example, may take judicial notice that the initials "M.D." refer to a physician,[102] and that "Chas." is an abbreviation for "Charles,"[103] or that the abbreviation "G.I." refers to a soldier.[104]

§ 5.9 Judicial Notice of Laws

While courts often take judicial notice of facts, judicial notice of law follows from the same basic premise of allowing for the notice of undisputable facts. It would be time-consuming and useless to require the opposing parties to introduce evidence to prove that laws that are known, or ought to be generally known, are in fact laws of the jurisdiction. A court must take judicial notice of the laws applicable in its own individual jurisdiction as well as the laws of the state in which it sits. Many states permit judicial notice of the laws of sister states and some will allow notice of foreign law on a proper occasion. The normal method of finding the applicable law, common as well as statutory, is by informal investigation. To facilitate judicial notice of law, counsel usually brings the judge's attention to statutes or citations in references to decisions applicable to the case being tried. An Ohio court noted that it could take judicial notice of a sister state's public statutory or case law within the United States and "may inform itself in such manner as it deems proper."[105]

State trial courts judicially notice federal law, and a federal court will judicially notice the law of every state. In fact, when sitting in a diversity jurisdiction case, the federal court is acting as if it were a state court and will follow state law concerning judicial notice as precisely as possible. However, when the United States Supreme Court reviews the decision of a state court, it will not take judicial notice of the law of another state unless the state court below could have done so.[106]

---

[101] People v. Diaz, 2005 Cal. App. Unpub. LEXIS 3559 (2005).
[102] State v. Brady, 223 Or. 433, 354 P.2d 811 (1960).
[103] Cumbol v. State, 205 Tenn. 260, 326 S.W.2d 454 (1959).
[104] Still v. Secretary of the Commonwealth, 73 Pa. D. & C. 106; 1950 Pa. D. & C. LEXIS 247 (1950).
[105] Ohio v. Turner, 105 Ohio St. 3d 331, 341, 2005 Ohio 1938, 826 N.E.2d 266, 278, 2005 Ohio LEXIS 961 (2005).
[106] Hanley v. Donoghue, 116 U.S. 1, 6 S. Ct. 242, 29 L. Ed. 535 (1885).

The following sections (§§ 5.10 through 5.16), specifically discuss the extent to which courts take judicial notice of laws prevailing within the forum, the laws of other states, and foreign nations.

§ 5.10 —Law of the Forum

It is axiomatic that all courts must take judicial notice of the law prevailing within the forum, i.e., the law that exists within the state or that applies to the particular federal jurisdiction. One of the reasons for having state and federal laws is that they are to be used and adjudicated by the courts. It would be foolish to permit courts to take judicial notice of federal laws and laws of other states and countries without taking judicial notice of their own laws. A state court must judicially notice the law of the forum, whether that law is statutory law or has been derived from case law. In addition to notice of laws, courts generally take judicial notice of their own court records and from court records generated by other courts in the state. For example, California courts may judicially notice the records of any court in the state.[107] Similarly, a Colorado trial court properly took judicial notice that a defendant's two prior criminal convictions were felonies because classification of a prior offense is a matter of law.[108] A California court took judicial notice of various legislative materials relating to the legislature's enactment of a statute relating to refiling of criminal complaints that had previously been dismissed.[109] Court rulings, records, files, and transcripts can properly be the subject of judicial notice in a particular case when a party makes a request.[110] The only limitation to judicial recognition of the law of the forum is that it be public law.[111] Generally speaking, a strictly private act is not judicially noticed.

If the trial court has established precedent by case law, the court is not required to hold a pretrial hearing before taking judicial notice. For example, an Illinois appeals court determined that it was unnecessary to hold a pretrial hearing prior to admitting deoxyribonucleic acid (DNA) identification testimony if case law had been established in a previous case.[112] The court could take judicial notice of DNA identification as an accepted scientific procedure based on prior rulings, where the trial court had made an independent finding regarding the witness's qualifications as an expert in DNA identification.

---

[107] *See* People v. Young, 34 Cal. 4th 1149; 105 P.3d 487; 24 Cal. Rptr. 3d 112; 2005 Cal. LEXIS 1017 (2005) (In n.3, the court noted its power to judicial notice of all state court records under the authority of CAL. EVID. CODE § 452(d).

[108] People v. Frost, 5 P.3d 317, 1999 Colo. App. LEXIS 239 (1999).

[109] People v. Konow, et al., 32 Cal. 4th 995, 1014, 88 P.3d 36, 46, 12 Cal. Rptr. 3d 301, 313, 2004 Cal. LEXIS 3385 (2004).

[110] People v. Lawley, 27 Cal. 4th 102, n. 2, 38 P.3d 461, 115 Cal. Rptr. 2d 614, n. 2 (2002).

[111] State v. Miller, 778 S.W.2d 292 (Mo. 1989) (court took judicial notice that driving while intoxicated was an offense under state law). *See also* Moten v. State, 640 A.2d 222 (Md. 1994).

[112] People v. Johnson, 199 Ill. Dec. 931, 634 N.E.2d 1285 (1994). *See also* United States v. Martinez, 3 F.3d 1191 (8th Cir. 1993).

§ 5.11 —Federal Law

Article VI of the United States Constitution provides that the "Constitution, and the laws of the United States which shall be made in Pursuance thereof, and all Treaties made, or which shall be made under the Authority of the United States, shall be the supreme Law of the Land; the Judges in every State shall be bound thereby . . ." Accordingly, all federal and state courts must take judicial notice of the provisions of the federal Constitution, its amendments, and the laws of the United States made pursuant to the Constitution. In regard to congressional enactments, judicial notice is not limited to their existence, wording, and interpretation, but extends to all matters connected therewith.[113]

§ 5.12 —Law of Sister States

Many states have adopted a version of the Uniform Judicial Notice of Foreign Law Act, which provides that "every court in the state shall take judicial notice of the common law and statutes of every state, territory, and other jurisdiction of the United States."[114] "The court may inform itself of such laws in such manner as it may deem proper, and it may call upon counsel to aid it in obtaining such information."[115] Ohio law serves as a typical model where it requires a party who plans to rely on the law of a sister American state to give notice in the pleadings or other reasonable written notice. The court may consider any reasonable source to determine the substance of foreign law.[116] The reasonable notice requirement is to assure fairness and avoid undue surprise to the opponent when a party plans to rely on laws of other jurisdictions by using judicial notice. For example, under Florida law, the courts may take judicial notice of the "decisional, constitutional, and public statutory law of every other state, territory, and jurisdiction of the United States,"[117] subject to the mandate that a court must must take judicial notice where a party has given a written request and sufficient information has been given to the court to enable the opposing party to prepare to meet the request.[118]

Public laws of general application are clearly included within the term "statutes." This term also fairly includes other states' constitutions and rules of procedure having force of law throughout each such state, although such rules were adopted by the highest court of the state rather than its legislature. These materials are usually accessible through state codes, and being that they are of

---

[113] Gardner v. Barney, 73 U.S. (6 Wall.) 499, 18 L. Ed. 890 (1868).

[114] WIS. STAT. § 902.02(1) (2006).

[115] *Id.* at § 902.02(2).

[116] State v. Turner, 105 Ohio St. 3d 331, 341, 2005 Ohio 1938, 826 N.E.2d 266, 2005 Ohio LEXIS 961 (2005).

[117] *See* FLA. STAT. ANN. § 90.202(2) (Matthew Bender 2006).

[118] *See* FLA. STAT. ANN. § 90.203(1), (2) (Matthew Bender 2006).

the general nature of public laws, these laws should be judicially noticed.[119] In a Texas case involving the extradition to Massachusetts of an escaped prisoner, the Texas court took judicial notice that escape was a crime under the laws of Massachusetts and that to be charged with escape under Massachusetts law, the accused must have been in the custody of or committed to a Massachusetts penal institution.[120] Although not a sister state, a federal court may take judicial notice of state law where appropriate. In a federal drug prosecution, where the defendant was attempting to suppress evidence, a federal district court took notice of the Nebraska and California requirements for display of vehicle license plates, which helped determine whether a vehicle stop was legal.[121]

§ 5.13 —Law of Foreign Countries

As a strong general rule, the federal courts of the United States treat foreign law as facts that must be proven by the parties before the court,[122] but judges do possess the discretionary power to judicially notice the laws of foreign nations, at least in civil cases.[123] Proving foreign law has been the custom since the 1940s, but some federal courts do take judicial notice even when it is not requested.[124] Following modern logic, federal courts may be required to take judicial notice where a federal law or a treaty specifically requires it.[125] Massachusetts also takes a progressive approach and requires its courts to take judicial notice of the "law . . . of a foreign country whenever the same shall be material."[126] Ohio law serves as a typical model where it requires a party who plans to rely on the law of a foreign country to give notice in the pleadings or other reasonable notice. The court may consider any reasonable source to determine the substance of foreign law.[127] Although many state courts will not be required to take judicial notice of laws in foreign countries,[128] some states allow their courts to judicially notice foreign law as a substitute for proof. Demonstrative of modern practice, a California court applied California law when interpreting a contract, rather than taking judicial notice of Hong Kong contractual law on the particular point. The parties had neither requested judicial notice of the foreign law nor supplied the court with evidence of the relevant aspects of Hong Kong law. Had a request been made for the court to take judicial notice of foreign law, the California court appeared to have been ready

---

[119] Litsinger Sign Co. v. American Sign Co., 11 Ohio St. 2d 1, 40 Ohio Op. 2d 30, 227 N.E.2d 609 (1967). *See also* Mayo v. State, 681 N.E.2d 689 (Ind. 1997).

[120] Ex parte Stephen S. Delorenzo, 2001 Tex. App. LEXIS 1941 (Tex. 2001).

[121] United States v. Molson, 2006 U.S. Dist. LEXIS 2292 (D. Neb. 2006).

[122] *See* Black Diamond Steamship Corp. v. Robert Stewart & Sons, 336 U.S. 386, 397, 93 L. Ed. 754, 69 S. Ct. 622 (1949).

[123] *See* FED. R. CIV. P. 44.1.

[124] Castro-Perez v. Gonzales, 409 F.3d 1069, 1071, 2005 U.S. App. LEXIS 9974 (9th Cir. 2005).

[125] Baxter v. Baxter, 423 F.3d 363; 2005 U.S. App. LEXIS 19825 (3d Cir. 2005), n. 4.

[126] Anno. Laws Mass. GL ch. 233, § 70 (Mathew Bender 2006).

[127] OHIO CIV. R. 44.1 is incorporated by OHIO CRIM. R. 27. (Matthew Bender 2006).

[128] Kearney v. Savannah Foods, 350 F. Supp. 85 (S.D. Ga. 1972).

to consider Chinese law.[129] In Texas, when the law of a foreign jurisdiction could have been introduced in the pleadings or requested on motion, but was not, the courts take an interesting approach by assuming that the foreign jurisdiction's laws are the same as Texas law.[130] Going in a different direction than seems to be the trend allowing judicial notice of foreign nation law, Wisconsin holds that the laws of a foreign nation shall not be subject to the state provisions concerning judicial notice.[131] As a practical matter, the laws of foreign nations do not normally possess relevance that affects the adjudication of criminal cases in either state or federal courts.

§ 5.14 —Municipal Ordinances

A municipal court may be required by commonwealth or state law to take judicial notice of the ordinances in effect within the jurisdiction of the court.[132] In some jurisdictions, other superior state courts may be required to exercise that same judicial notice over municipal ordinances as is required for the municipal courts themselves. The court may obtain information sufficient to take judicial notice of ordinances in any manner it may deem appropriate and may consult with counsel for assistance in obtaining the information. As a general rule, when municipal courts are permitted to take judicial notice, they do so under the same rules that apply to courts of general jurisdiction and appellate courts.[133]

Generally, judicial notice may be taken of municipal ordinances only when the case is being tried in a municipal court. In some jurisdictions, in courts other than municipal courts, municipal ordinances must be pleaded and proved because they are not the subject of judicial notice.[134] Recent statutory amendments in some states now allow every court to take judicial notice of municipal ordinances. Ohio requires that criminal courts take judicial notice of the rules of the supreme court of the state and of the decisional, constitutional, and public statutory law of the state, including municipal ordinances. The party desiring that a court take judicial notice shall give the opposing party notice of the intent to request judicial notice of a municipal ordinance or local rule of court in the pleadings or otherwise.[135] The modern practice of allowing judicial notice of municipal ordinances and rules enhances the concept of judicial economy and appears to demonstrate a trend in this direction.

---

[129]   Washington Mutual Bank v. Superior Court, 24 Cal. 4th 906, 15 P.3d 1071 (Cal. 2001).

[130]   Gerdes v. Kennamer, 155 S.W.3d 541, 548, 2004 Tex. App. LEXIS 10945 (2004).

[131]   WIS. STAT. § 902.02, Uniform judicial notice of foreign law act. (2006).

[132]   42 PA. CONS. STAT. § 6107 (Judicial notice of certain Pennsylvania local government ordinances) (2005).

[133]   See PA. R. EVID. 201 (Judicial Notice of Adjudicative Facts) (2006).

[134]   Honiker v. State, 230 Ga. App. 597, 497 S.E.2d 70 (Ga. 1998).

[135]   OHIO R. CIV. P. 44.1 (Anderson 2006). Ohio Rule of Criminal Procedure 27 notes that it incorporates Civil Rules 44 and 44.1 involving judicial notice.

The Court of Appeals for the First Circuit noted in 2004 that municipal ordinances and private codes to which statutes refer have traditionally not been included within the concept of judicial notice by courts of general jurisdiction. Under this view, municipal ordinances must be pleaded and proved as any other fact.[136] Louisiana has a different approach from actually requiring proof and allows judicial notice to be taken of parish ordinances when a copy of the ordinance is filed with the court with a judicial notice request.[137]

A Georgia appellate court reiterated the traditional view that neither the Georgia Supreme Court, nor any appellate or superior court, can take judicial notice of municipal[138] or county ordinances.[139] When a prosecutor or defendant wants to rely on the provisions of a municipal ordinance, it must be alleged and proved in the trial court because it is a well-established principle that judicial notice cannot be taken by superior and appellate courts.[140]

A municipal court that has exclusive jurisdiction of cases involving the violation of traffic ordinances of a city situated within its territorial jurisdiction may take judicial notice of those ordinances.[141]

§ 5.15   —Administrative Regulations

Under the Federal Rule of Evidence 201(b), administrative regulations fall within the category of facts that are capable of accurate and simple determination by consulting sources whose accuracy cannot reasonably be questioned[142] and for which judicial notice proves appropriate. In addition, the Uniform Rules of Evidence provide that judicial notice may be taken of the published regulations of governmental subdivisions or agencies of the state. Administrative regulations published in the Federal Register must be judicially noticed by all federal courts and many state courts also notice such regulations in the interest of judicial economy. In an unpublished opinion, the Tenth Circuit observed that a federal court sitting under its diversity jurisdiction may judicially notice that state's administrative regulations.[143] Naturally, a federal court can take judicial notice of reports of the federal Department of Health and Human Services and of relevant Ohio Administrative Code provisions.[144] that had been entered in related proceedings.[145]

---

[136]   Getty Petroleum v. Capital Terminal, 391 F.3d 312, 320, 2004 U.S. App. LEXIS 25586 (1st Cir. 2004).

[137]   Bayou Liberty Association v. St. Tammany Parish Council, 2006 La. App. LEXIS 1378 (2006).

[138]   Calloway v. State, 227 Ga. App. 775, 490 S.E.2d 521 (1997).

[139]   Strykr v. Long County, 277 Ga. 624, 626, 593 S.E.2d 348, 350, 2004 Ga. LEXIS 187 (2004).

[140]   Flippen Alliance v. Brannan, 267 Ga. App. 134, 136, 601 S.E.2d 106, 109, 2004 Ga. App. LEXIS 460 (2004).

[141]   People v. Cowles, 142 Cal. App. 2d 865, 298 P.2d 732 (1956); Cook v. Superior Court, 261 Cal. Rptr. 706 (1989).

[142]   Toth v. Grand Trunk Railroad, 306 F.3d 335, 2002 U.S. App. LEXIS 19169 (6th Cir. 2002).

[143]   Samson Resources v. Wamsutter, 117 Fed. Appx. 641, 644, 2004 U.S. App. LEXIS 22795 (10th Cir. 2004).

[144]   Gamble v. Ohio Department of Job and Family Services, 2006 U.S. Dist. LEXIS 968 (S.D. Ohio 2006).

[145]   Missouri Pacific Railroad Co. v. United Transportation Union, General Committee of Adjustment, 580 F. Supp. 1490 (D.C. Mo. 1984).

In 2003, a federal district court in a case involving conduct by a former Pennsylvania state police officer, the court took judicial notice of the Pennsylvania State Police directives and an internal state police administrative regulation.[146] In California, a trial court took judicial notice of regulations requiring death row prisoners to provide blood and saliva samples containing DNA to the California Department of Justice pursuant to state law. The action of the trial court concerning judicial notice was not altered by the appellate court.[147] Similarly, in a driving while intoxicated prosecution, an Ohio reviewing court concluded that it could properly take judicial notice of standards for the horizontal gaze nystagmus test promulgated by the National Highway Traffic Safety Administration.[148] In a challenge to the proper promulgation of the Indiana Administrative Code in a driving under the influence case, the reviewing court upheld the manner in which the administrative rule had been established and held that the trial court acted properly in taking judicial notice of the administrative code provisions.[149]

In the Commonwealth of Virginia, tax regulations promulgated and published pursuant to law are to be accorded judicial notice by the courts.[150] Similarly, in Texas judicial notice is required for all administrative determinations and regulations concerning retroactive tax benefits.[151] Where courts have taken judicial notice of state and federal administrative rules and regulations, logic dictates that such notice is appropriate because the rules and regulations are capable of easy verification from official printed sources whose accuracy cannot reasonably be disputed.

§ 5.16 —Jurisdiction of Courts

A criminal conviction cannot be permitted to stand unless the evidence or substitutes for proof provide a foundation or evidence that the offense was committed within the jurisdiction of the court. A court will take judicial notice of the limits of its jurisdiction and the extent of the territory included therein where there are geographical facts that are matters of common knowledge or the jurisdiction can be determined from maps in common usage.[152] However, a juvenile court cannot take judicial notice of its jurisdiction where part of the requirement of jurisdiction depends on the age of the juvenile; the juvenile's

---

[146] Haber v. Evans, et al., 268 F. Supp. 2d 507, 512, 2003 U.S. Dist. LEXIS 10199 (E.D. Pa. 2003).
[147] Alfaro v. Terhune, 98 Cal. App. 4th 492, 120 Cal. Rptr. 2d 197, 2002 Cal. App. LEXIS 4116 (2002).
[148] State v. Stritch, 2005 Ohio 1376, 2005 Ohio App. LEXIS 1337 (2005).
[149] Disabato, et al., v. State, 840 N.E.2d 1, 4, 2005 Ind. App. LEXIS 2390 (2005).
[150] Chesapeake Hospital Authority v. Commonwealth of Virginia, 262 Va. 551, 554 S.E.2d 55, 2001 Va. LEXIS 143 (2001).
[151] *See* Occidental Permian Ltd. v. R.R. Comm'n of Texas, 47 S.W.3d 801 (Tex. Ct. App. 2001).
[152] Keesee v. Commonwealth of Virginia, 216 Va. 174, 175, 217 S.E.2d 808, 810, 1975 Va. LEXIS 265 (1975).

age must be proven in the case as part of jurisdiction.[153] In a criminal or a delinquency case, the prosecution must prove that offense was committed within the territorial jurisdiction of the court and a failure to prove jurisdiction or have judicial notice taken of jurisdiction may reverse the case.[154] A court may also take judicial notice of the fact that a particular milepost or interchange of an interstate highway is within the court's territorial jurisdiction.[155]

The courts have been consistent in holding that a court may take judicial notice of its own jurisdiction. In one case, an officer observed a driver speeding on the opposite side of the road. When he stopped the speeder and when he initially observed him, the speeder was in a different city because the city and court boundary ran down the middle of the road. The officer cited the driver for speeding as well as driving while intoxicated, but the trial court took judicial notice that he had never been in the city over which it had territorial jurisdiction. When the defendant requested that the judge take judicial notice that the defendant had committed no offense within the court's jurisdiction, the court agreed and dismissed the case due to the judicial notice it took concerning the limits of its jurisdiction.[156]

The court of appeals held that insufficient evidence had been presented by the state for the jury to find venue, and therefore reversed the defendant's conviction. The Supreme Court of Oregon, after noting the fact that the city of Coos Bay located in Coos County is a proper matter subject to judicial notice under the Oregon statute, found it would have been better if the trial court had taken judicial notice that the city was located in Coos County. However, the court held that there was sufficient evidence presented so that the jury could reasonably infer that the acts took place in the jurisdiction. Accordingly, the Supreme Court reversed the Court of Appeals and held that the trial court did not err in denying defendant's motion for a judgment of acquittal.

---

[153] State v. K.N., 124 Wash. App. 875, 877, 103 P.3d 844, 845, 2004 Wash. App. LEXIS 3135 (2004).
[154] In the Interest of A. C., 263 Ga. App. 44, 45, 587 S.E.2d 210, 211, 2003 Ga. App. LEXIS 1087 (2003).
[155] State v. Scott, 3 Ohio App. 2d 239, 32 Ohio Op. 2d 360, 210 N.E.2d 289 (1965).
[156] City of North Ridgeville v. Stack, 2006 Ohio 1177, 2006 Ohio App. LEXIS 1063 (2006).

§ 5.17 Judicial Notice Process

Rule 201

Judicial Notice of Adjudicative Facts

* * *

(e) Opportunity to be heard. A party is entitled upon timely request to an opportunity to be heard as to the propriety of taking judicial notice and the tenor of the matter noticed. In the absence of prior notification, the request may be made after judicial notice has been taken.

(f) Time of taking notice. Judicial notice may be taken at any stage of the proceeding.

(g) Instructing jury. In a civil action or proceeding, the court shall instruct the jury to accept as conclusive any fact judicially noticed. In a criminal case, the court shall instruct the jury that it may, but is not required to, accept as conclusive any fact judicially noticed.[157]

Adjudicative facts are the kinds of facts whose existence or nonexistence must be determined by the jury. These types of facts normally concern questions about who did what, to whom, where it happened, and how was it accomplished. These facts can be determined by a jury or, in some cases, can be accepted by the jury under judicial notice. A California court explained that judicial notice is a substitute for evidence that does away with the necessity for evidence on the point and must be considered conclusive on the fact judicially noticed.[158] How does the jury become aware that it may consider facts judicially noticed by the court? When the judge decides that a certain fact or a certain law will be judicially noticed, he or she states in open court that such fact is noticed. If a party requests that a fact be judicially noticed and the judge agrees with the party, the jury will be so advised. Also, the court may of its own volition determine that the fact will be judicially noticed and so advise the jury.

Once a matter is judicially noticed, evidence generally will not be admitted to dispute the fact noticed. To allow evidence to contradict judicially noticed facts would be contrary to the rationale for the rule in the first place. A fact should not be judicially noticed if it is doubtful, uncertain, or subject to reasonable dispute. However, in a criminal case, the jury is not required to accept the fact as conclusive and generally must be instructed that they are not bound by any fact judicially noticed and may ignore the fact or principle judicially noticed by the court.[159]

Prior to the decision, the party is entitled, on timely request, to have a chance to be heard—outside the hearing of the jury—on the propriety of taking judicial notice and on the nature of the matter proposed to be judicially noticed.

---

[157] FED. R. EVID. 201.

[158] People v. Nava, 17 Cal. App. 4th 1807, 1817, 22 Cal. Rptr. 2d 600, 604 (Cal. 1993).

[159] *See* OHIO R. EVID. 201(G) Judicial Notice of Adjudicative Facts (Matthew Bender 2006).

In some states, the rules relating to the procedure followed in judicial notice situations are spelled out by rule or statute. For example, in Oregon, the procedures for taking judicial notice are stated as follows:

OREGON REVISED STATUTES, TITLE 4. EVIDENCE AND WITNESSES CHAPTER 40. EVIDENCE CODE

JUDICIAL NOTICE

40.060 Rule 201(a). Scope. ORS 40.060 to 40.085 govern judicial notice of adjudicative facts. ORS 40.090 governs judicial notice of law.

40.065 Rule 201(b). Kinds of facts. A judicially noticed fact must be one not subject to reasonable dispute in that it is either:

(1) Generally known within the territorial jurisdiction of the trial court; or

(2) Capable of accurate and ready determination by resort to sources whose accuracy cannot reasonably be questioned.

40.070 Rules 201(c) and 201(d). When mandatory or discretionary.

(1) A court may take judicial notice, whether requested or not.

(2) A court shall take judicial notice if requested by a party and supplied with the necessary information.

40.075 Rule 201(e). Opportunity to be heard. A party is entitled upon timely request to an opportunity to be heard as to the propriety of taking judicial notice and the tenor of the matter noticed. In the absence of prior notification, the request may be made after judicial notice has been taken.

40.080 Rule 201(f). Time of taking notice. Judicial notice may be taken at any stage of the proceeding.

40.085 Rule 201(g). Instructing the jury.

(1) In a civil action or proceeding, the court shall instruct the jury to accept as conclusive any fact or law judicially noticed.

(2) In a criminal case, the court shall instruct the jury that it may, but is not required to, accept as conclusive any fact judicially noticed in favor of the prosecution.[160]

§ 5.18 Judicial Notice in Criminal Cases

As a general rule, criminal trial courts may take judicial notice of court records,[161] the hour of sunrise on a particular day,[162] the scientific accuracy of laser speed detection,[163] the fact that a defendant has been on probation,[164] legislative history of state law,[165] and a variety of other verifiable facts. However, some courts are more reluctant to permit the use of judicial notice in criminal cases than in civil cases. In a Florida case, a court improperly took judicial

---

[160] OR. REV. STAT. §§ 40.60-40.85 (2006).

[161] Burgess v. Florida, 831 So. 2d 137 at 141, 2002 Fla. LEXIS 2178 (2002); *See also* FLA. STAT. § 90.202(6) (1997).

[162] Swafford v. Florida, 828 So. 2d 966 at 967, 2002 Fla. LEXIS 789 (2002).

[163] State v. Lloyd, 2002 Ohio 3017, 2002 Ohio App. LEXIS 3027 (2002).

[164] Werley v. Florida, 814 So. 2d 1159 at 1163, 2002 Fla. App. LEXIS 4789 (2002).

[165] People v. Acosta, 29 Cal. 4th 105 at 120, 52 P.3d 624 at 634, 124 Cal. Rptr. 2d 435 at 447 (2002).

notice of a document that had been used in a prior domestic violence case involving the same defendant. At trial, although the document had not been entered as an exhibit or entered in evidence, the prosecution had been permitted to use the judicially noticed document during direct examination. The state supreme court held that the improper use of the judicially noticed document constituted reversible error.[166] In a New York criminal case, the defendant had been convicted of grand larceny of an automobile, but there had been no proof of value of the vehicle. On appeal, the court took judicial notice that the vehicle had a value in excess of $500 by consulting a national listing of car values. New York's top court reversed on the theory that an appellate court could not properly take judicial notice of the value of the car because there had been no proof of its condition, marketability, or mileage. The conviction was reversed because the Court of Appeals determined that some evidence concerning the value of the car should have been admitted so the jury could make the valuation decision.[167]

This is not to say that the judge in a criminal case will not take judicial notice of facts and laws. Judicial notice has been taken of the fact fingerprint evidence and analysis have generally been accepted as accurate[168] and that individual fingerprints are unique,[169] and of the accuracy of radar devices.[170] Also, as the preceding paragraphs indicate, there are numerous instances in which the courts will take judicial notice of other well-established facts.

Judicially noticed facts are treated differently depending on whether the case is civil or criminal. Rule 201(g) of the Federal Rules of Evidence notes that a court shall instruct the jury to accept as conclusive any fact judicially noticed in civil cases, but in criminal cases requires that a court instruct the jury that it may, but is not required to, accept as conclusive any fact judicially noticed. Recognizing that judges are hesitant to take judicial notice of facts and laws in criminal cases, especially in borderline situations, and accepting the fact that juries are instructed that they are not required to accept as conclusive any fact judicially noticed in criminal cases, justice personnel are cautioned not to place too much reliance on the judicial notice concept. Rather than taking a chance that judicial notice will not be taken, traditional evidence should be prepared and made ready to introduce in the event that the judge fails to take judicial notice of facts and to ensure that a jury will actually hear the evidence.

---

[166] Stoll v. Florida, 762 So. 2d 870, 2000 Fla. LEXIS 1457 (2000).
[167] People v. Alicea, 25 N.Y.2d 685, 686, 254 N.E.2d 915, 916, 306 N.Y.S.2d 686, 688 (1969).
[168] United States v. Janis, 387 F.3d 682, 689, 2004 U.S. App. LEXIS 22599 (8th Cir. 2004).
[169] United States Sullivan, 246 F. Supp. 2d 700, 702, 2003 U.S. Dist. LEXIS 3016 (E.D. Ky. 2003).
[170] State v. Palmer, 2006 Ohio 2712; 2006 Ohio App. LEXIS 2555 (2006).

§ 5.19   Summary

Although the usual procedure is for the parties to introduce evidence to prove a fact in dispute, in some instances such evidence is unnecessary because the court will take judicial notice of certain facts. This procedure is necessary and reasonable in order to save the time of the court, the parties, and the attorneys.

Judicial notice involves the court recognizing the existence of certain facts and laws without requiring the parties to introduce proof. For convenience, the rules concerning judicial notice are often categorized as judicial notice of facts and judicial notice of laws. Rule 201 of the Federal Rules of Evidence relates only to the taking of judicial notice of adjudicative facts.

The general rule is that the trial judge may take judicial notice without motion of counsel or take judicial notice of fact following a request by counsel. The judge, in fact, is given a great deal of discretion concerning judicial notice, and an appellate court will not disturb the taking of judicial notice unless there is a clear abuse of discretion. Where a trial court did not take judicial notice, an appellate court may take judicial notice of any matter that a trial court could have noticed but did not notice. Many appellate courts will not judicially notice a fact where a trial court could have done so, but declined for appropriate reasons within the limits of a trial court's discretion.

In the interests of judicial economy, it is obvious that there are many facts that are commonly known and need not be proved in court. Examples of these include historical facts, geographical facts, scientific facts, and other facts that are generally known to the ordinary person. A judge may take notice of facts that may be ascertained by consulting standard reference works. In addition to facts, the judge may take judicial notice of certain laws, such as the Constitution of the United States, administrative regulations, laws of the several states, and in some instances, municipal ordinances.

All of the persons involved in the criminal justice process must be aware that a judge may take notice of certain facts and certain laws, but it is a grave mistake to assume that the judge hearing the case will always take judicial notice of even well-known facts, especially in criminal cases. If there is any doubt as to the character of the fact to be introduced or proved in court, evidence should be acquired and made ready for court presentation. Also, the astute investigator must recognize that even though a judge may judicially notice certain matters, the opposing party may challenge the propriety of such actions, and failure to prepare documented information to educate the court to take judicial notice of certain facts can result in a court's refusal to judicially notice important facts.

Presumptions, Inferences, and Stipulations   6

The use of presumptions and inferences to prove an element of the crime is indeed treacherous, for it allows men to go to jail without any evidence on one essential ingredient of the offense. It thus implicates the integrity of the judicial system.

Barnes v. United States, 412 U.S. 837, 93 S. Ct. 2357 (1973)
(Douglas, J., dissenting)

Chapter Outline

Key Terms and Concepts

inference	presumption of law
presumption	stipulation
presumption of facts	

§ 6.1 Introduction

Chapter 4 described the process of introducing evidence in criminal cases. In the typical criminal case, to the extent that a party has a burden of proof,[1] each party has the obligation of introducing evidence to establish facts from which a judge or jury will make a decision. However, in some instances, the jury may consider information other than that derived from actual evidence specifically introduced by the parties. One way of distinguishing this information source is to designate it as a substitute for evidence.

Judicial notice, discussed in Chapter 5, is one of several substitutes for evidence. The chapter included discussion of the legal reasoning that permits a trial or appellate judge to take notice of certain facts and laws. In addition, case decisions and statutes limiting the use of judicial notice were noted. This chapter introduces and explains three other substitutes for evidence—presumptions, inferences, and stipulations.

"Inferences and presumptions are a staple of our adversary system of factfinding. It is often necessary for the trier of fact to determine the existence of an element of the crime—that is, an 'ultimate' or 'elemental' fact—from the existence of one or more 'evidentiary' or 'basic' facts."[2] In some instances, facts may be presumed, thereby relieving the parties of the burden of presenting evidence to prove them, and under traditional common law principles, some facts can be inferred or deduced from other basic facts presented in court.

---

[1] Generally, a defendant has no burden of proof and the burden of proof beyond a reasonable doubt rests with the prosecution. Where a defendant pleads an affirmative defense such as self-defense, insanity, alibi, mistake of fact, or some other affirmative defense, there may be a burden of proof on a defendant if he or she expects to prevail on the selected defense.

[2] County Court of Ulster County v. Allen, 442 U.S. 140, 156 (1979).

In this chapter, presumptions, inferences, and stipulations are defined and distinguished. In addition, the chapter discusses the reasons for the presumptions and inferences, as well as the types of presumptions recognized by the courts. Also, this chapter gives detailed attention to specific examples of presumptions and inferences and explains how they play an important role in the trial process. Finally, this chapter defines and explains the remaining substitute for evidence, the stipulation, and demonstrates some significant specific examples of how attorneys use stipulations.

§ 6.2   Definitions and Distinctions

Rule 301

**Presumptions in General
in Civil Actions and Proceedings**

In all civil actions and proceedings not otherwise provided by Acts of Congress or by these rules, a presumption imposes on the party against whom it is directed the burden of going forward with evidence to rebut or meet the presumption, but does not shift to such party the burden of proof in the sense of the risk of nonpersuasion, which remains throughout the trial upon the party on whom it was originally cast.[3]

* * *

A. Presumptions

When the Federal Rules of Evidence were being written, the committee that considered Rule 301 intended to limit the scope of the rule to civil actions and proceedings to effectuate the intent of Rule 301. The committee did not wish to deal with the thorny questions of presumptions in criminal cases and therefore limited Rule 301 to civil actions. In criminal cases, the parties must look to state statutes and state court decisions as well as federal court decisions for answers to questions relating to presumptions.

The term *presumption* has been used by courts and legal writers to describe several different consequences that flow from the introduction of evidence in a trial. A California statute defines a presumption as "an assumption of fact that the law requires to be made from another fact or group of facts found or otherwise established in the action."[4] As the Supreme Court of Illinois recently defined the concept: "A presumption is a legal device that permits or requires the fact finder to assume the existence of an ultimate fact, after certain predicate or basic facts have been established."[5] A presumption is a rule of law that allows a jury in a criminal case to infer or deduce the exis-

---

[3]   FED. R. EVID. 301.

[4]   CAL. EVID. CODE § 600 (Matthew Bender 2006).

[5]   People v. Pomykala, 2003 Ill. LEXIS 7 (2003).

tence of a second fact from the proof of the first, or basic, fact. For example, where evidence shows that a person has been missing for three years with no explanation [the basic fact], the presumed fact arises that the person is deceased as of the end of the three-year period.[6] In another example, in stolen property cases, proof that a person possesses recently stolen property, the basic fact, allows but does not require, a jury or judge to infer or presume that the person in possession knew that the property was stolen. In other words, a presumption draws a particular inference as to the existence of one fact, not actually known, arising from its usual connection with another particular fact or facts that are known or proved. In a California case involving possession of stolen property, the court instructed the jury that conscious possession of recently stolen property with corroborating evidence of guilt would be suffi-cient for a conviction; however, a conviction would not be appropriate if the only evidence was possession of recently stolen property.[7]

A federal court, in discussing the use of the presumption, indicated that a presumption is an evidentiary device that allows the trier of fact to deter-mine the existence of an element of the crime—that is, an ultimate or essen-tial fact—from the existence of one or more evidentiary or basic facts.[8] For example, in a burglary case, a state court told a jury that burglary with an assault on one of the occupants of the building is an act that is inherently dan-gerous to human life and the conscious disregard for life allows malice to be presumed.[9]

In an older case, a court described a presumption in another way: a pre-sumption may be an inference that common sense, enlightened by human knowledge and experience, draws from the connection, relation, and coinci-dence of facts and circumstances with each other.[10] Some courts argue that a true legal presumption is in the nature of evidence and is to be weighed as such. Others hold (probably more properly) that a presumption is not evi-dence, but is a substitute for evidence[11] and may be treated as if it were evi-dence and accepted as fact or disregarded.

Mandatory presumptions in criminal cases are generally unconstitutional because they relieve the prosecution of having to prove all the elements beyond a reasonable doubt and have the effect of calling into question the pre-sumption of innocence. Therefore, a statutory presumption that considered that a renter of personal property, who did not return it within five days after receiving a demand for the return of the property, had unlawfully converted it to his own use could not stand because of its mandatory nature.[12]

---

[6]   *See* In the Matter of the Estate of Joseph Cosentino, an Absentee, 177 Misc. 2d 629, 676 N.Y.S.2d 856 (1998).

[7]   People v. Mendoza, 24 Cal. 4th 130, 176, 6 P.3d 150, 178, 99 Cal. Rptr. 2d 485, 515, 2000 Cal. LEXIS 6118 (2000).

[8]   United States v. Skinner, 973 F. Supp. 975 (W.D. Wash. 1997).

[9]   Cruz v. Maloney, 152 Fed. Appx. 1, 2005 U.S. App. LEXIS 22911 (1st Cir. 2005).

[10]   Commercial Credit Co. v. Maxey, 289 Ill. App. 209, 7 N.E.2d 155 (1937).

[11]   Siler v. Siler, 152 Tenn. 379, 277 S.W. 886 (1925); Amend v. Bell, 89 Wash. 2d 124, 570 P.2d 138 (1978).

[12]   Sherrod v. State, 280 Ga. 275, 275, 627 S.E.2d 36, 37, 2006 Ga. LEXIS 145 (Ga. 2006).

B. Inferences

In a criminal case, an "inference is a deduction of fact that may logically and reasonably be drawn from another fact or group of facts established by the evidence."[13] Phrased in a slightly different manner, an inference has been defined as a deduction of fact that a jury may make but that a criminal jury cannot be required to make. "Whether the inferred fact is found to exist will be decided by the trier of fact."[14] It also has been defined as a deduction that the jurors may draw from facts shown without the law directing them to make such a deduction.

Although the terms *presumption* and *inference* are sometimes used synonymously, the courts have attempted to distinguish between them as to both their origin and effect. According to some courts, an inference should be recorded as a permissible deduction from the evidence before the court, which the jury may accept or reject. A presumption, as contrasted with an inference, is a rule of law, relatively fixed or relatively definite in scope and effect, that attaches to certain evidentiary facts and produces a specific procedural consequence. To state this more simply, a presumption is a mandatory deduction that the law expressly requires, while an inference is no more than a permissible deduction that the trier of fact may adopt. However, any criminal jury is free to disregard the finding of the deduced or inferred fact because the jury has the sole power to determine what facts have been proven and to decide which allegations have not been proven. Concerning the historical facts of the case, it would almost be true to state that in criminal cases, only inferences may exist because presumptions of fact cannot be enforced. In adopting this view concerning inferences and presumptions, the Supreme Court of Pennsylvania noted that:

> Inferences and presumptions are staples of our adversary system of factfinding. It is often necessary for the trier of fact to determine the existence of an element of the crime—that is, an 'ultimate' or 'elemental' fact—from the existence of one or more 'evidentiary' or 'basic' facts.[15]

> Nevertheless, to the extent that these logical tools impede rather than assist in the jury's exercise of its factfinding function, they cannot be employed to prove the elements of a crime. Hence, "virtually all so-called 'criminal presumptions' are really no more than . . . inferences."[16]

---

[13] Tak Sun Tan v. Runnels, 413 F.3d 1101, 1118, 2005 U.S. App. LEXIS 13461 (9th Cir. 2005).

[14] CHARLES W. EHRHARDT, FLORIDA EVIDENCE § 301.1 at 89-90 (2003 ed.), quoted in Palmas y Bambu v. E.I Dupont, 881 So. 2d 565; 2004 Fla. App. LEXIS 7372 (Fla. 2004).

[15] Commonwealth v. Salter, 2004 Pa. Super. 318, 858 A.2d 610, 2004 Pa. Super. LEXIS 2687 (2004), quoting Commonwealth v. MacPherson, 561 Pa. 571, 752 A.2d 384, 389 (2000).

[16] *Id.*, quoting Commonwealth v. DiFrancesco, 458 Pa. 188, 329 A.2d 204, 1974 Pa. LEXIS 706, n.3 (1974).

In the case of *Commonwealth v. DiFrancesco*, the court held that an "inference is merely a logical tool which permits the trier of fact to proceed from one fact to another, whereas a 'presumption' is a procedural device which not only permits an inference of the 'presumed' fact, but also shifts to the opposing party the burden of producing evidence to disprove the presumed fact."[17]

In a criminal case, a North Carolina court noted that a permissive inference suggests to the jury a possible conclusion to be drawn if the prosecution proves the existence of the basic fact, but does not require the jury to come to that conclusion. If the court failed to instruct the jury that it could draw an inference from proof of the basic fact but that it did not have to make the deduction, error has occurred because a jury is free to ignore the conclusion to an inference.[18] In another case, the court made this distinction concerning the difference between an inference and a presumption:

> Presumptions are one thing; inferences another. Presumptions are assumptions of fact which the law requires to be made from another fact or group of facts; inferences are logical deductions or conclusions from an established fact. Presumptions deal with legal processes, whereas inferences deal with mental processes.[19]

In the court's view, an inference is simply a logical deduction or conclusion that the law allows, but does not require, following the establishment of the basic facts.

A jury or trial court may "draw inferences from circumstantial evidence so long as the inferences are rationally related to the proven fact."[20] That is, a rational connection must exist between the initial fact proven and the fact later inferred. According to the Supreme Court of the United States, a jury may properly infer from one fact the existence of another fact that is essential to guilt, if reason and experience support the inference.[21] However, finding an inferred fact from an earlier inferred fact has its limits because, at some point, inferences become so removed from the original fact that supported the first inference that the final conclusion may not be accurate. A federal court of appeals cautioned that "reasonable inferences supported by other reasonable inferences which have an evidentiary basis may warrant a conviction. Nonetheless, where a conviction appears to be based on multiple and successive inferences, we must exercise caution"[22] to ensure that a conviction rests upon more than conjecture.

---

[17]   Commonwealth v. DiFrancesco, 458 Pa. 188, 329 A.2d 204, 1974 Pa. LEXIS 706 (1974).

[18]   State v. Smith, 170 N.C. App. 461, 469, 613 S.E.2d 304, 311, 2005 N.C. App. LEXIS 1075 (2005).

[19]   State v. Jackson, 112 Wash. 2d 867, 774 P.2d 1211 (1989). *See* case in Part II. *See also* State v. Parks, 245 Neb. 205, 511 N.W.2d 774 (1994), in which the court held that a "presumption" is a fact inferred from another proved or established fact or facts, while an "inference" is a conclusion on the existence of a particular fact reached by considering other facts in the usual course of human reasoning, and thus an "inference" is a deduction that the factfinder may draw in his discretion, but is not required to draw as a matter of law.

[20]   State v. Germany, 2006 Wash. App. LEXIS (Wash. 2006).

[21]   Tot v. United States, 319 U.S. 463, 63 S. Ct. 1241, 87 L. Ed. 2d 1519 (1943).

[22]   United States v. Michel, 446 F.3d 1122, 1128, 2006 U.S. App. LEXIS 11665 (10th Cir. 2006).

When revising a state evidence code, a state legislature may create statutory inferences and presumptions; however, the facts proven must bear a rational relationship to the fact to be inferred, and if they do not, a statutory inference or presumption cannot stand.[23] For example, if a state decided to allow a prosecutor to make an adverse comment on the fact that a defendant did not testify in his or her defense in order to allow the jury to infer guilt, such an inference would be overturned on appeal. A defendant has a constitutional right not to testify, and, in asserting the right by not testifying, no adverse inference of guilt will be permitted by allowing a prosecutor's comment.[24]

While a court may give instructions regarding inferences that can be drawn from proven facts, an instruction that permits the jurors to infer an element of the crime charged is constitutional only if the presumed fact follows beyond a reasonable doubt from the proven fact. In the case of *State v. Jackson*, the Supreme Court of Washington held that, when the charge is attempted burglary, a trial court cannot instruct the jury that it may infer that the defendant acted with intent to commit a crime within a building when the evidence supports the finding that the defendant may have attempted to enter the building, when there exist other equally reasonable conclusions that follow from the circumstances.[25] In this case, an officer saw the defendant kicking the front door of a shop. When the defendant spotted the officer, he proceeded to walk away briskly. When the door was examined, it was found that about 10 inches of Plexiglas had been pushed inward and that part of the wood stock around the Plexiglas was broken out of its frame. The defendant was charged with second degree burglary. In the instruction to the jury, the judge stated that the jury may infer that the defendant acted with intent to commit a crime within the building. In reversing the conviction, the court noted that an inference shall not arise when other reasonable conclusions exist that could follow from the circumstances. Applying this reasoning, the court determined that the instruction that the jury may infer that the defendant intended to commit a crime within the building merely because he had repeatedly kicked the door prior to the officer's approach was improper.

A jury instruction that seems to imply that a presumption must be drawn from proof of a basic fact or bundle of facts may face appellate hurdles. In an Alabama murder case[26] involving the use of a firearm and a knife, there was proof that the defendant committed the killings due to his confession and eyewitness testimony. Among other jury instructions, the trial judge instructed the jury that in:

> every intentional and unlawful killing of a human being is presumed
> to be done with malice aforethought unless the circumstances that
> surround the killing rebut the idea of malice. Every intentional and

---

23   Commonwealth v. Sattazahn, 428 Pa. Super. 413, 631 A.2d 597 (1993).
24   People v. Carter, 36 Cal. 4th 1114, 1191, 117 P.3d 476, 32 Cal. Rptr. 3d 759, 820, 2005 Cal. LEXIS 8908 (2005).
25   State v. Jackson, *supra* note 19.
26   Jones v. Campbell, 436 F.3d 1285, 2006 U.S. App. LEXIS 1381 (11th Cir. 2006).

unlawful killing of a human being with a deadly weapon, such as a pistol or with a knife, is presumed to be done with malice unless the evidence that proved the killing rebuts the presumption of malice.[27]

Upon appeal to the Supreme Court of Alabama, the court noted that the instruction did not actually require the jury to infer or draw the presumption that malice existed. The basic facts supporting the inference involved proof of the defendant's intentional killing of the victims by using a gun and knife. From that bundle of facts in conjunction with other facts in the case, the jury could have developed the inference that malice was involved. The words "presume" or "presumption" present the danger that the inference or presumption is mandatory, but the Eleventh Circuit did not believe that the seemingly mandatory language produced a mandatory presumption when other jury instructions in the case were properly considered. In other cases, when the jury instruction seemed to require that a presumption or inference had to be drawn, the convictions were reversed.[28]

C. Stipulations

As another substitute for evidence, the stipulation is less difficult to define and understand than presumptions and inferences. When the parties stipulate to a fact, it simply means that they *have agreed that proof of the matter will not be required*. A stipulation implies that both parties have conceded to the existence or nonexistence of a fact, the contents of a document, the testimony of a witness, or other matter that has an important connection to the case. When the parties have agreed to a stipulation, the effect is to remove the fact as an issue in the case because the parties no longer have any dispute as to the fact, document, principle, or testimony. A stipulation may be written or oral, and normally the trial judge will consent to allowing the stipulation.[29] As a general rule, the liberal use of stipulations is generally encouraged in the interests of judicial economy. Once parties have agreed to stipulate to a particular fact, what a witness would say if she testified, to admit certain evidence, or any other agreement of fact, the stipulation remains binding on both parties. Where the parties have stipulated as to a fact, such agreement authorizes the court to find the existence of such a fact and to consider that fact without any further proof. The triers of fact are not, however, bound to accept the fact as true and may find to the contrary if persuaded by other evidence. Interestingly, a court is not bound to accept a fact or principle that has been the subject of a stipulation. In one case, the defendant stipulated to the admissibility of a polygraph test result, but the appellate court determined that the parties could not

---

[27]   *Id.* at 1300.

[28]   *See* Francis v. Franklin, 471 U.S. 307, 1985 U.S. LEXIS 4 (1985). The court upheld the reversal of a murder conviction based partly on impermissible mandatory presumptions. *See also* Sandstrom v. Montana, 442 U.S. 510, 1979 U.S. LEXIS 113 (1979).

[29]   People v. Sorenson, 196 Ill. 2d 425, 429, 752 N.E.2d 1078, 1083 (2001).

stipulate concerning admissibility because the use of polygraph results impinged on the integrity of the judicial system.[30]

When the parties have stipulated concerning a fact or facts, such agreement authorizes the court to find the existence of such a fact and to consider the fact proven beyond a reasonable doubt. In a murder case, the defendant and the prosecution agreed to a stipulation of facts in the case, including the fact that the defendant admitted to committing the killings. As part of the stipulation agreement, the prosecution dismissed some collateral charges and the court found the defendant guilty of the murders. The stipulations of fact indicated that the defendant and the prosecution were in agreement concerning the facts of the case and no proof was necessary.[31] In a different case, the prosecution and the defense stipulated concerning the substance of what a government expert witness would testify. The parties agreed that the expert witness would tell the court that the substances he tested were identified as cocaine base.[32] A stipulation was proper in such a case because neither party had any doubt concerning the identity of the substance.

While the general rule is that parties are bound by their stipulations, a trial court has the discretion to consider issues not raised in a pretrial stipulation. Alternatively, a trial court may disregard issues of law stipulated by parties as a way of granting a party relief from the stipulation in order to prevent "manifest injustice."[33] A court, for good cause shown, may allow a party to withdraw a stipulation where new facts operate to make the stipulation create unfairness to a party or where a stipulation otherwise impairs a fair trial.

§ 6.3 Reasons for Presumptions and Inferences

The use of presumptions and inferences in criminal trials plays an important part in expediting the judicial process even though some confusion and lack of clarity concerning the use of presumptions remains among attorneys, judges, and police. As a substitute for evidence, presumptions take the place of actual proof and possess the same theoretical evidentiary weight as direct evidence. As many courts have noted, circumstantial evidence by itself will support a conviction for the most heinous crime,[34] which it could not do if the weight of presumptions and inferences were lower than direct evidence. Naturally, in criminal cases, the finder of fact may choose to ignore any presumption or inference. In the final analysis, when presented with an inference or presumption, most jury members will probably make the deduction of fact suggested by proof of the basic fact because much everyday reasoning and decision making follows a similar path of logic.

---

[30]   People v. Jackson, 202 Ill. 2d 361, 368, 781 N.E.2d 278, 282 (2002).
[31]   Johnson v. Wilson, 2006 U.S. App. LEXIS 15479 (6th Cir. 2006).
[32]   United States v. Anderson, 450 F.3d 294, 2006 U.S. App. LEXIS 14177 (7th Cir. 2006).
[33]   G.I.C. Corp. v. United States, 121 F.3d 1447 (11th Cir. 1997).
[34]   Jones v. State, 2006 Ala. Crim. App. LEXIS 2 (2006).

A. Procedural Technique

One court stated that a presumption is no more than a procedural technique designed for trial convenience in order to facilitate the production of proof by requiring the party with easier means of access to come forward with the evidence.[35] Without a presumption, it would be difficult in some instances for the trial to go forward. One purpose of the presumption is to place the burden on the party who alone is in possession or in control of the facts with respect thereto. To make it possible to go forward with the trial, the presumption assumes a certain condition to exist until the contrary is shown.

The use of a presumption as a substitute for evidence alters the burden of offering evidence. The effect of a presumption is that the existence of the presumption shifts the burden of going forward with the evidence to the opposing party.[36] Once the presumption exists, the existence of the presumed fact remains proved unless and until the opposing party introduces evidence that contradicts or casts doubt on the truth of the presumed fact. When rebuttal evidence is introduced, the finder of fact must determine whether the rebuttal evidence was sufficiently strong as to cast doubt on the existence of the presumed fact and ignore the presumption, or decide whether the presumed fact remains.[37] As one court noted, "Whenever evidence contradicting the presumption is offered the latter disappears entirely, and the triers of fact are bound to follow the usual rules of evidence in reaching their ultimate conclusion of fact. . . ."[38] Therefore, despite some reasoning to the contrary, a better conclusion is that a presumption is not evidence but rather a rule of procedure or an administrative assumption that is overcome when evidence to the contrary is introduced.[39]

B. Public Policy

Some presumptions of law are sanctioned by the courts and legislatures for public policy purposes. Maryland law states, "[t]here is a rebuttable presumption that the child is the legitimate child of the man to whom its mother was married at the time of conception."[40] The public policy strives to find children legitimate and this presumption serves that purpose. Similarly, when a child is born or conceived during wedlock, the child is presumed to be legitimate, with the husband of the wife being the presumed father.[41]

An example of a presumption of law that was determined by the courts and legislatures for public policy reasons is that all persons are presumed to

---

[35]   Waugh v. Commonwealth, 394 Pa. 166, 146 A.2d 297 (1958).

[36]   City of Wilmington v. Minella, 879 A.2d 656, 2005 Del. Super. LEXIS 275 (2005).

[37]   Barnes v. Yoshikawa, 2002 Cal. App. Unpub. LEXIS 12095 (Cal. 2002).

[38]   Mullin v. Brown, 210 Ariz. 545, 547, 115 P.3d 139, 141, 2005 Ariz. App. LEXIS 83 (2005), quoting Seiler v. Whiting, 52 Ariz. 542, 84 P.3d 452, 1938 Ariz. LEXIS 190 (1938).

[39]   Green v. Ransor, Inc. 175 S.W.3d 513, 516, 2005 Tex. App. LEXIS 8125 (2005).

[40]   MD. FAMILY LAW CODE ANN. § 5-1027 (Matthew Bender 2006).

[41]   Stubbs v. Colandrea et al., 154 Md. App. 673, 682, 841 A.2d 361, 366, 2004 Md. App. LEXIS 9 (Md. 2004).

know the law.[42] Likewise, defendants in criminal cases are initially presumed to be innocent until the contrary may be proved.[43] When a government agent has authority to exercise discretion, it is presumed that the agent's acts are based on public policy when exercising that discretion.[44] Therefore, there is a presumption that a prosecutor has legitimate grounds for the action he or she takes and is acting with regularity.[45]

C. Allowance of Normal Governmental Activities

Presumptions such as honest and proper conduct by public officials allow normal governmental activities to be accepted at face value. Without this presumption, it would be burdensome, if not impossible, for criminal litigants to prove affirmatively each and every routine record that is material to a case. Consequently, there is a general presumption "that public officers perform their duties correctly, fairly, in good faith, and in accordance with law and governing regulations. . . ."[46] It would be virtually impossible to prove a record when, for example, the clerk who made the entry has died, or due to the heavy caseload of the trial court, no one in the court or clerk's office can personally remember anything about the case in question.

§ 6.4 Presumptions of Law

A presumption of law is an inference or deduction that, in the absence of direct evidence on the subject, the law requires to be drawn from the existence of certain established facts.[47] Presumptions of law may be rebutted by the introduction of evidence that contradicts the original presumption and effectively replaces that presumption with a different conclusion. Examples of presumptions of law are the presumption of innocence, the presumption in favor of sanity, and the presumption that people do not act with criminal intent. Naturally, every person is presumed to intend the natural and probable consequences of his or her acts, but such a presumption may be rebutted.

Generally, there is a strong presumption that regularly enacted laws are constitutional.[48] Following a similar rationale, a trial judge is presumed to be fair and impartial in the absence of contrary evidence by the wronged party making the allegation.[49]

---

[42]   Bakody Homes v. City of Omaha, 516 N.W.2d 244 (Neb. 1994).

[43]   People v. Bayette, 29 Cal. 4th 381, 58 P.3d 391, n. 10 (2002).

[44]   Demery v. United States, 357 F.3d 830; 2004 U.S. App. LEXIS 1828 (8th Cir. 2004).

[45]   Hartman et al. v. Moore, 126 S. Ct. 1695, 1705, 164 L. Ed. 2d 441, 456, 2006 U.S. LEXIS 3450 (2006).

[46]   Hampton v. Nicholson, 2006 U.S. App. Vet. Claims LEXIS 168 (U.S. App. Vet. Claims, 2006), quoting Haley v. Dept. of the Treasury, 977 F.2d 553, 558 (Fed. Cir. 1992).

[47]   Waugh v. Commonwealth, 394 Pa. 166, 146 A.2d 297 (1958).

[48]   Smith v. Doe, 538 U.S. 84, 110, 2003 U.S. LEXIS 1949 (2003).

[49]   Manila School Dist. No. 15 v, Wagner, 357 Ark. 20, 26, 159 S.W.3d 285, 290, 2004 Ark. LEXIS 222 (Ark. 2004).

A presumption of law is a rule of law that allows a judge or jury to assume that a fact is true until such time as the opposing party introduces other evidence that disproves or outweighs the presumed fact. When a presumption of law exists, it is considered prima facie correct and will sustain the burden of evidence until conflicting facts on point are shown.[50]

In distinguishing between a presumption of law and a presumption of fact, one reviewing court noted, "There can be presumptions of law or presumptions of fact. Presumptions can be artificial or logical. Artificial presumptions are those created because of considerations of public policy. Logical presumptions are those where there is a 'rational connection' on the basis of 'logical probability' between the elemental fact and the evidentiary fact."[51]

§ 6.5 Presumptions of Fact

Presumptions of fact are not the subject of a fixed rule, but are merely natural presumptions, such as appear from common experience and logic that arise from the particular circumstances of any case. The terms *presumption of fact* and *inference* seem to be used more frequently when the deduced fact is permissive in nature and rebuttable by contrary facts. In one case, the court said that a presumption of fact is the mental process by which the existence of one fact is inferred from proof of some other fact or facts that experience shows is usually associated by succession or coexistence.[52]

Some argue that a presumption of fact is really not a presumption because it amounts to no more than an inference.[53] In any event, the presumption or inference of fact must not be drawn from propositions that are uncertain, but must be founded on facts established by direct evidence. Presumptions may not be founded on other presumptions. To say this another way, presumptions do not create their own foundations. Presumptions of fact are derived from circumstances in a particular case, by means of the common experience of mankind.

Presumptions of fact may be permissible "if there is a sound and rational connection between the proved and inferred facts and when proof of one fact renders the existence of another fact so probable that it is sensible and timesaving to assume the truth of the inferred fact until the adversary disproves it. . . ."[54] Destroying the presumption may be accomplished by refuting the basic fact upon which the presumption of fact rests or by demonstrating that the fact presumed is not true. For example, where a person has not been seen by her usual associates for the statutory period (the basic fact) such proof gives rise to the

---

[50]   In re Wood's Estate, 374 Mich. 278, 132 N.W.2d 35 (1965).

[51]   Wasserman v. Parciasepe, 377 N.J. Super. 191, 198, 871 A.2d 781, 784, 2004 N.J. Super. LEXIS 4 (N.J. 2004).

[52]   Cox v. Nance, 24 Tenn. App. 304, 143 S.W.2d 897 (1940).

[53]   Hoge v. George, 27 Wyo. 423, 200 P. 96 (1921).

[54]   USX Corp. v. Barnhart, 395 F.3d 161, 171, 2004 U.S. App. LEXIS 26868 (3d Cir. 2004), quoting Sec'y of Labor v. Keystone, 331 U.S. App. D.C. 422 (D.C. Cir. 1998).

presumption of fact that the individual is dead (the presumed fact). The presumption of death may be rebutted by clear proof that the individual is presently alive or by rebutting the basic fact. Where proof existed that someone had seen the individual within the statutorily required absence, the basic fact has been rebutted and the presumption of the fact of death is extinguished.

§ 6.6 Classes of Presumptions

For purposes of discussion, presumptions are further divided into conclusive (irrebuttable) presumptions and rebuttable presumptions. A conclusive presumption (*presumption juris et de jure*) is a rule of substantive law, rather than a rule of evidence. A disputable or rebuttable presumption is a species of evidence that may be accepted and on which reliance may be placed when there is no other evidence to refute the contention it stands for.

A statute may make a presumption conclusive; in which case, the presumption cannot be destroyed or overcome by evidence. However, in criminal cases, conclusive presumptions have been held to violate the Constitution and no longer may be used in criminal cases. In *Sandstrom v. Montana*, the United States Supreme Court held that mandatory conclusive presumptions are unconstitutional, because they conflict with the presumption of innocence.[55] In California, a conclusive presumption once existed where:

> Intent to commit theft by fraud is presumed if one who has leased or rented the personal property of another pursuant to a written contract fails to return the personal property to its owner within 20 days after the owner has made written demand by certified or registered mail following the expiration of the lease or rental agreement for return of the property so leased or rented. Cal. Penal Code Ann. § 484(b) (West 1988).

The Supreme Court of the United States reversed a California conviction of grand theft auto because the statute created an impermissible mandatory conclusive presumption in violation of the due process clause of the Fourteenth Amendment as prohibited by *Sandstrom v. Montana*. When faced with the proof of the basic fact that a defendant had not returned personal property within the statutory time limit, a conclusive presumed fact arose that the defendant possessed an intent to commit theft by fraud.[56]

Another example of a traditional conclusive presumption holds that a child born in wedlock is conclusively presumed to be a legitimate child.[57] To preserve the father-child relationship and to foster family integrity, tradition-

---

[55]   Sandstrom v. Montana, 442 U.S. 510, 523 (1979).

[56]   *See* Carella v. California, 491 U.S. 263 (1989).

[57]   *See* G.M.H. v. J.L.H., 700 S.W.2d 506 (Mo. Ct. App. 1985), which reaffirmed that at common law the presumption that a child born in wedlock is conclusively presumed to be legitimate, but indicated that today the presumption is rebuttable, is an evidentiary presumption, and is overcome by a showing of substantial evidence to the contrary.

ally courts would uphold the conclusive presumption and not permit the husband or another man to introduce evidence to contest or to support the possibility of paternity. All modern evidence codes allow the admission of contrary evidence of paternity when certain conditions are present, thus turning the conclusive presumption into a rebuttable one. The advent of irrefutable genetic testing required the courts and legislatures to review the rationale behind the conclusive presumption.[58] The original rationale for having conclusive presumptions was that the public policy of preservation of the family unit overrode the general requirement that courts should search for the truth. Also, the fact that a non-biological father has played the role of father arguably should be preserved rather than have a biological father, who has not played that role, intervene in a child's life. In one Alabama case, the biological father, after DNA testing, sought to be declared the child's legal father when the child had lived completely with the husband of the mother. Ultimately, the appellate court reversed a lower court holding that the biological father was the father. The court held that a biological father, who had no standing to bring a suit to declare a child illegitimate, could not rebut the policy supporting the Alabama presumption of paternity of children born to a married couple.[59] The reviewing court appeared interested in keeping the existing family intact and excluding the biological father.

A rebuttable presumption (*presumption juris tantum*) requires the trier of fact to consider the deduction as true until disproved by contrary evidence. An example of a rebuttable presumption of law is the presumption that states that an accused person is presumed to be innocent, but the prosecutor may introduce evidence that overcomes and negates the presumption of innocence. In Florida, proof that a defendant had possession of a controlled substance gave rise to the presumption that he knew about the illicit nature of the substance. However, the presumption is rebuttable and the defendant may introduce evidence of his ignorance concerning the illegality of the substance in order to rebut the presumption.[60]

In some jurisdictions, presumptions are evidentiary devices that are categorized into two groups—mandatory and permissive. According to a Florida appeals court, a "mandatory presumption" in a criminal case is generally unconstitutional when it relieves the state of its burden of proof and violates the due process clause by shifting the burden of persuasion to the criminal defendant.[61] However, a "permissive inference" or a "permissive presumption" in a criminal case is generally permissible because the finder of fact is not required to make the deduction.

A "permissive inference" or presumption allows but does not require the finder of fact to infer the fact suggested by proof of the basic fact. The inferred fact places no burden on the defendant to rebut it because the judge or jury can

---

[58] D.F. v. Department of Revenue, 823 So. 2d 97, 98, 2002 Fla. LEXIS 1162 (2002).

[59] P.G. and J.G. v. G.H., 857 So. 2d 823, 2002 Ala. Civ. App. LEXIS 553 (Ala. 2002).

[60] Scott v. Florida, 808 So. 2d 166, 2002 Fla. LEXIS 4 (2002).

[61] People v. Tirado, 254 Ill. App. 3d 497, 626 N.E.2d 1114 (1993).

accept the existence of the inferred fact or reject it. In a Florida burglary case in which the defendant was found in possession of property taken from the victim's residence, the judge charged the jury that "Proof of possession of recently stolen property, unless satisfactorily explained, gives rise to an inference that the person in possession of the property knew or should have known that the property had been stolen."[62] The standard jury instruction, despite the defendant's allegation, did not create a mandatory presumption by suggesting to the jury that it might infer that the defendant knew the property was stolen but was free to decide otherwise. A Georgia court upheld a similar jury instruction in a theft case, ruling that "such an instruction is permissible when a defendant is found to be in possession of stolen goods, for the defendant can always rebut the inference by explaining to the jury the reason for the defendant's possession, though the jury is certainly free to accept or reject the defendant's explanation."[63] Regardless of whether a presumption is categorized as conclusive, rebuttable, mandatory, or permissive, a presumption will generally be considered unconstitutional if it relieves the prosecution from having to prove every element of the crime.[64] For example, where a statute notes that a person who fails to return a rental car within five days after the lease expires, a presumption arises that the person embezzled the vehicle, such mandatory presumption violates the due process clause of the Fourteenth Amendment because it relieves the prosecution of proving part or all of the crime.[65] A mandatory presumption may not shift the burden of proof on any element of the offense; to do so conflicts with the overriding presumption of innocence and invades the fact-finding function of the judge or jury.

§ 6.7 Specific Presumption Situations

By studying the most common specific presumptions and developing an understanding of the context in which they operate, a clear understanding of the presumption as a substitute for evidence emerges. In studying the specific presumptions, it is important to appreciate the reasons for presumptions and their origins. State legislatures have created some presumptions by statute while others have developed as a result of court decisions. Where presumptions have been created as examples of public policy by a state legislature, some of them may be rebutted when substantial evidence of contrary facts is introduced, while others may appear to be conclusive and cannot be easily overcome by contradictory evidence.

---

62   Walker v. State, 896 So. 2d 712, 714, 2005 Fla. LEXIS 361 (Fla. 2005), quoting Fla. Std. Jury Instr. (Crim.) 14.1.

63   Martin v. State, 254 Ga. App. 40, 42, 561 S.E.2d 154, 156, 2002 Ga. App. LEXIS 250 (Ga. 2002).

64   United States v. Haberek, 2006 U.S. Dist. LEXIS 44670 (N.D. Ill. 2006), United States v. Edelkind, 2006 U.S. Dist. LEXIS 41056 (W.D. La. 2006).

65   People v. Laughlin, 137 Cal. App. 4th 1020, 1024, 40 Cal. Rptr. 3d 737, 739, 2006 Cal. App. LEXIS 388 (2006).

One view of presumptions holds that a presumption is not evidence of anything and merely determines which party should go forward and produce evidence pertaining to the matters at issue. Along with this position is the collateral view that a presumption should not be treated as evidence and should not be placed on the scale of justice to be weighed with actual evidence when making a decision.[66] As a Pennsylvania court held, "[a]ffirmative evidence of a material element of the crime charged may never be displaced by a mere evidentiary presumption; nor may that presumption substitute for evidence."[67] The principle that a presumption is not evidence has not gained universal acceptance because some jurisdictions hold that a presumption actually serves as a substitute for evidence. In such a situation, "a presumption substitutes for evidence of the presumed fact until the trier of fact finds from credible evidence that the presumed fact does not exist."[68] Some courts have held that "a presumption has the effect of evidence"[69] and must be given the same force and effect unless rebutted or called into question.

Presumptions are used sparingly in criminal cases and are scrutinized very carefully by reviewing courts to determine whether they place an unreasonable burden on the accused. Moreover, statutory presumptions must not, under the guise of regulating the presentation of evidence, operate to preclude the accused from presenting his or her defense.[70]

The number of statutory presumptions and judicial presumptions is extensive. A high percentage of these do not find their way into criminal cases, and therefore they will not be discussed in detail. Some examples of presumptions that are not given further attention are: (1) a private transaction has been fair and regular; (2) the ordinary course of business has been followed; (3) a promissory note or a bill of exchange was given or endorsed for a sufficient consideration; and (4) a writing is accurately dated.

Although presumptions possess a more limited usage in criminal cases than in civil cases, they are not without importance. The following sections discuss and demonstrate the most significant and important presumptions related to criminal cases.

§ 6.8   —Innocence

As a matter of well-settled law, it is uniformly agreed that the defendant in a criminal case is presumed innocent from the time the prosecution begins and retains this presumption forever or until a finder of fact returns a guilty verdict. This rebuttable presumption of innocence places upon the prosecution

---

[66]   Mullin v. Brown, 210 Ariz. 545, 548, 115 P.3d 139, 142, 2005 Ariz. App. LEXIS 83 (2005).

[67]   Commonwealth v. Salter, 2004 Pa. Super. 318, 858 A.2d 610, 614 2004 Pa. Super. LEXIS 2687 (Pa. 2004)

[68]   Roberts v. N.D. Dep't of Human Services, 2005 ND 50, 692 N.W.2d 922, 927, 2005 N.D. LEXIS 50 (N.D. 2005).

[69]   People v. Niene, 8 Misc. 3d 649, 652, 798 N.Y.S.2d 891, 894, 2005 N.Y. Misc. LEXIS 981 (N.Y. 2005).

[70]   State v. Kelly, 218 Minn. 247, 15 N.W.2d 554 (1944).

the burden of proving the defendant guilty beyond a reasonable doubt. This presumption exists until the time the finder of fact determines that the defendant has been proven guilty beyond a reasonable doubt.[71] Of course, when jury deliberations result in a guilty verdict, a defendant's presumption of innocence ends because it has been overcome by the evidence presented by the government.[72]

The so-called presumption of innocence is not, strictly speaking, a presumption in the sense of a deduction from a given premise or basic fact. It does not involve the proof of a basic fact from which a deduction may be drawn; it is a fact that exists until sufficient proof to the contrary appears. More accurately, the "presumption of innocence serves as a procedural doctrine that allocates the burden of proof in criminal trials."[73] Any deviation from the presumption of innocence has the effect of undermining procedural fairness.[74] A federal court, in an effort to explain the presumption of innocence, noted that:

> It is not a mere belief at the beginning of the trial that the accused is probably innocent. It is not a will-o'-the-wisp, which appears and disappears as the trial progresses. It is not a matter which jurors may disregard, in accordance with whim or fancy. It is a legal presumption which the jurors must consider along with the evidence and the inferences arising from the evidence, when they come finally to pass upon the case. In this sense, the presumption of innocence does accompany the accused through every stage of the trial.[75]

In the 2003 decision of *United States v. Dufresne*, the defendant appealed on several grounds, including the contention that the trial court improperly instructed the jury on the presumption of innocence. The court told the jury that:

> [T]he defendants are presumed by the law to be innocent and therefore the law does not require a defendant to prove his innocence or produce any evidence at all. The Government bears the burden of proving the defendants guilty beyond a reasonable doubt. If the Government has failed to do so you must find the defendants not guilty.
>
> The law presumes a defendant to be innocent of all crimes charged. Thus a defendant, although accused, begins this trial as any other with a clean slate, with no evidence against him. The law permits nothing but legal evidence in support of any charges against an accused. So, the presumption of innocence also is sufficient to acquit a defendant unless you the jurors are satisfied that the Gov-

[71] State v. Halls, 2006 Utah App. 142, 549 Utah Adv. Rep. 21, 2006 Utah App. LEXIS 136 (2006).
[72] United States v. Medina, et al., 430 F.3d 869, 2005 U.S. App. LEXIS 26772 (2005).
[73] United States v. Scott, 2006 U.S. App. LEXIS 14182 (9th Cir. 2006).
[74] Adkins v. Tennessee, 911 S.W.2d 334, 1994 Tenn. Crim. App. LEXIS 785 (Tenn. 1994).
[75] Dodson v. United States, 23 F.2d 401 (4th Cir. 1928); United States v. Thaxton, 483 F.2d 1071 (5th Cir. 1973); United States v. Friday, 404 F. Supp. 1343 (E.D. Pa. 1975).

> ernment again has proven the defendant's guilt beyond a reasonable
> doubt after careful and impartial consideration of all the evidence in
> the case.[76]

According to the *Dufresne* court, as long as the court informed the jury about the concept of guilt beyond a reasonable doubt, including properly informing them of the presumption of innocence in the jury instruction, the Constitution does not require any additional instruction.[77] The court did stress that the presumption of innocence can be sufficient to attain an acquittal where the prosecution's evidence does not establish a prima facie case.

Generally, in a criminal case, the judge instructs the jury on the presumption of innocence. In earlier decisions, some courts had held that failure to give a specific instruction on the presumption of innocence was reversible error. However, in 1979, the United States Supreme Court in *Kentucky v. Whorton* held that failure to give a requested instruction on the presumption of innocence does not in and of itself violate the Constitution.[78] In this case, the defendant was charged with committing several armed robberies in three separate indictments. At the conclusion of all the evidence, the defendant's counsel asked that the jury be instructed on the presumption of innocence. The instruction requested was:

> The law presumes an accused to be innocent of crime. He begins a
> trial with a clean slate, with no evidence against him. And the law
> permits nothing but legal evidence presented before the jury to be
> considered in support of any charge against the accused. So the pre-
> sumption of innocence alone is sufficient to acquit an accused
> unless the jury members are satisfied beyond a reasonable doubt of
> the accused's guilt from all of the evidence in the case.

The judge refused this instruction, but gave one to the effect that the jury could return a verdict of guilty only if they found beyond a reasonable doubt that the defendant with the requisite criminal intent had committed the acts charged in the indictment.

The jury found the defendant guilty of 10 counts of first-degree robbery, two counts of first-degree wanton endangerment, and two counts of first-degree attempted robbery. He was sentenced to consecutive terms of imprisonment, totaling 230 years. The defendant appealed. The Supreme Court of Kentucky held that the failure to give the instruction concerning the presumption of innocence was reversible error. The prosecutor for the Commonwealth appealed to the United States Supreme Court.

---

[76] United States v. Dufresne, ___ F.3d ___, 2003 U.S. App. LEXIS 2126 (3d Cir. 2003), *cert. denied*, 538 U.S. 1064, 2003 U.S. LEXIS 4193 (2003).

[77] *Id.*

[78] Kentucky v. Whorton, 441 U.S. 786, 99 S. Ct. 2088, 60 L. Ed. 2d 640 (1979).

In reversing the Supreme Court of Kentucky and reinstating the convictions, the Supreme Court of the United States found that an instruction on the presumption of innocence is not required in all cases. Accordingly, the *Whorton* Court held that:

> In short, the failure to give a requested instruction on the presumption of innocence does not in and of itself violate the Constitution.[79]

The Court went on to explain that failure to give a specific instruction on innocence should be evaluated in light of the totality of the circumstances, including: all of the instructions to the jury, the arguments of counsel, whether the weight of evidence was overwhelming, and other relevant factors. As the Court later explained in a different case, "[a] jury instruction on the presumption of innocence is not constitutionally required in every case to satisfy due process, because such an instruction merely offers an additional safeguard beyond that provided by the constitutionally required instruction on reasonable doubt."[80] A dissenting opinion in Whorton differed with both views and offered the opinion that the due process clause of the Fourteenth Amendment mandated that an instruction on the presumption of innocence be given if it had been requested, unless there was clearly presented evidence that failure to give the instruction constitutes harmless error.[81]

While a precise jury instruction supporting the presumption of innocence need not be given in every case to meet federal due process standards, trial courts strive to offer jury instructions that are fair, even if not all instructions speak directly to the presumption of innocence. In a habeas corpus case,[82] a federal judge reviewed the trial proceedings of a state case involving a murder at a crack house. Evidence in the case included eyewitness testimony and proved overwhelming. Both the prosecutor and the defendant's attorney had received proposed jury instructions from the judge in which the judge omitted any mention of the presumption of innocence. Despite his lack of objection, the defendant contended that the writ of habeas corpus should be granted because of the trial court's inadvertent omission of the presumption of innocence. The trial judge did charge the jury on the burden of proof, which in some ways performs a similar task to an instruction on the presumption of innocence. The trial judge stated:

> The standard of proof required in every criminal case is proof of guilt beyond a reasonable doubt. . . . So, proof of guilt beyond a reasonable doubt, what is it? It does not require the People to prove an accused guilty beyond all possibility of doubt or beyond a shadow of a doubt. It requires the People to establish the accused guilty beyond a reasonable doubt. Therefore, before you may convict the

---

[79] *Id.* at 789.
[80] Arizona v. Fulminante, 499 U.S. 279, 291, 1991 U.S. LEXIS 1854 (1991).
[81] *Id.* at 791.
[82] Williams v. McGinnis, 2006 U.S. Dist. LEXIS 29400 (E.D. N.Y. 2006).

accused, each of you must be satisfied that the credible evidence, the evidence that you accept, is sufficient to convince you beyond a reasonable doubt that the accused is, in fact, guilty and that the accused is, in fact, the person who committed the crimes charged. Therefore, before you may convict the accused, each of you must be satisfied that the credible evidence, the evidence that you accept, is sufficient to convince you beyond a reasonable doubt that the accused is, in fact, guilty and that the accused is, in fact, the person who committed the crimes charged.[83]

The federal district court refused to grant the writ on the grounds that, while the presumption of innocence was not explicitly stated, the jury charge, taken as a whole, was more than sufficient to give the defendant due process. The district court was following the reasoning of the *Kentucky v. Whorton* case, in which the jury instruction must be viewed in its entirety. By requiring the state prosecutor to prove guilt beyond a reasonable doubt, by implication, the defendant is presumed to be innocent until proven otherwise.

Emphasizing the importance of giving a clear instruction on the presumption of innocence, one judge cautioned that the natural inclination of some jurors may be to assume that, because the defendant has been selected for prosecution, he or she must be guilty, and one of the trial judge's greatest responsibilities is his or her duty to overcome that inclination by impressing upon the jury the importance of the presumption of innocence and of the government's burden to prove guilt beyond a reasonable doubt.[84] Courts have upheld jury instructions covering the presumption of innocence that have been not been models of clarity. Where such jury instructions have been approved, the information received by the jury during the trial, coupled with the jury instructions at the close of the trial, have permitted the jury to have a clear understanding of the presumption of innocence. If a trial court failed to instruct the jury on the prosecution's burden of proving the defendant's guilt beyond a reasonable doubt and on the defendant's presumption of innocence, reversal will often be the result.[85]

The universal rule is that following a conviction and upon appeal, a defendant "no longer enjoys the presumption of innocence."[86] When an appellate court reviews a case, it begins its work with the presumption that the trial court was correct in its verdict and that the defendant is guilty. In the case of *State v. Giddens*, a Tennessee reviewing court explained that a guilty verdict removes a defendant's presumption of innocence and actually raises a presumption of guilt on appeal so that a defendant bears the burden of demonstrating that the evidence was insufficient to support a guilty verdict.[87] The court further explained that on appeal of the jury's conviction, the Court of

---

[83]　*Id.*

[84]　United States v. Doyle, 130 F.3d 523 (2d Cir. 1997).

[85]　People v. Phillips, 69 Cal. Rptr. 2d 532 (1997).

[86]　Golden v. State, 276 Ga. App. 538, 623 S.E.2d 727, 729, 2005 Ga. App. LEXIS 1309 (2005). *See also* Reedy v. Wright, 2002 Va. Cir. LEXIS 64 (Va. 2002).

[87]　State v. Giddens, 2006 Tenn. Crim. App. LEXIS 215 (2006).

Criminal Appeals does not re-weigh the evidence or re-evaluate the credibility of the witnesses, but merely considers whether the evidence is sufficient to support the conviction.

§ 6.9 —Sanity

"The presumption of sanity is equally universal in some variety or other, being (at least) a presumption that a defendant has the capacity to form the *mens rea* necessary for a verdict of guilt and the consequent criminal responsibility," according to the Supreme Court of the United States.[88] Therefore, a prosecutor does not have to prove sanity as one of the elements in every crime. On the strength of this rebuttable presumption, a judge may offer a jury instruction that states that every person is presumed sane until the contrary is shown by the evidence. Where the defense introduces no evidence of insanity, the prosecution has no obligation to address a defendant's mental status other than to prove *mens rea*. The presumption of sanity is a rule of law that stands in the place of evidence unless evidence is introduced to rebut the presumption.

The concept of competency to stand trial, while related to legal insanity, involves some different considerations. Most certainly, there is a presumption of capacity to stand trial. As long as a defendant understands the nature and importance attached to a trial and is able to materially assist in his or her defense in a meaningful manner, sufficient competency has been demonstrated. The inquiry concerning competency involves an assessment of the level of mental ability and the state of mind that exists at or near the time of trial rather than the mental status of the defendant that existed at the time the alleged crime was committed. In evaluating competency, expert medical testimony will usually be required for appropriate evaluation. Criminal law presumes that individuals are competent, and a finding of competency, once made, continues to be presumably correct until the defendant or the prosecution offer some good reason to doubt it.[89]

Under the provisions of the 1984 Comprehensive Crime Control Act, mental disease or defect does not constitute a defense in federal criminal trials unless the defendant proves by clear and convincing evidence that, at the time of the commission of the acts, and as a result of severe mental disease or defect, the defendant was unable to appreciate the nature and quality of the acts or understand the wrongfulness of the acts. This Act makes it clear that, in federal court, the burden of proving the defense of insanity by clear and convincing evidence is on the accused. If the accused does not meet this burden, then, in effect, the presumption of sanity prevails[90] because the defendant failed to meet the burden of proof.

---

[88]   Clark v. Arizona, 2006 U.S. LEXIS 5184 (2006).
[89]   Garrett v. Groose, 99 F.3d 283 (8th Cir. 1996).
[90]   Insanity Defense Reform Act of 1984, Pub. L. No. 98-473, 18 U.S.C. § 17.

While federal law now states that a defendant has the burden of proving the defense of insanity by clear and convincing evidence, the law applies only in federal courts. The states are free to enact their respective insanity defenses and related presumptions without regard to the way the federal government approaches the issue. In some states, when the issue of the defendant's sanity has been raised concerning a defense to the alleged crime, the issue of sanity becomes a question of proof that the prosecution must meet. Under this view, the prosecution has the burden of proving sanity after the defendant, who claims insanity as a defense, has come forward with evidence to rebut the presumption of sanity.[91] In those states, if the evidence is legally sufficient to raise the issue of insanity and rebut the presumption and the prosecution offers no evidence of sanity, there is no factual issue for the jury, and the defendant is entitled to a directed verdict of acquittal.

The nature and quantum of evidence that the prosecution must produce to meet the burden of proof of sanity, in order to justify an instruction to the jury on the issue of sanity, varies with both the jurisdiction and with the nature and quantum of evidence indicating mental illness. For example, in Pennsylvania, insanity is considered an affirmative defense so, to prevail, the defendant must raise the issue and prove insanity by a preponderance of the evidence.[92] California takes a similar position to Pennsylvania under its penal code, which states:

> In any criminal proceeding, including any juvenile court proceeding, in which a plea of not guilty by reason of insanity is entered, this defense shall be found by the trier of fact only when the accused person proves by a preponderance of the evidence that he or she was incapable of knowing or understanding the nature and quality of his or her act and of distinguishing right from wrong at the time of the commission of the offense.[93]

In support of an insanity defense, lay testimony may be sufficient to satisfy the defendant's burden of proving sanity according to the Supreme Court of New Hampshire.[94] In New Hampshire, the defendant has an affirmative burden of proving insanity by clear and convincing evidence.[95] According to a different court, while expert opinion may make a strong argument for rebutting the presumption of sanity, it may not be conclusive and the finder of fact may reject it, even where it has not been contested.[96]

In some states, there is a general presumption of sanity and the defendant bears the burden of proving, by a preponderance of the evidence, insanity at the time of the conduct charged.[97] In these states, the law also presumes the

---

[91]   In the case of People v. Brown, 252 Ill. App. 3d 377, 425 N.E.2d 100 (1993), the court held that once a bona fide doubt of the defendant's fitness to stand trial is raised, there is no longer a presumption of fitness.

[92]   Commonwealth v. Mitchell, 576 Pa. 258, 274, 839 A.2d 202, 211, 2003 Pa. LEXIS 2553 (2003).

[93]   CAL. PENAL CODE § 25(b). (Matthew Bender 2006).

[94]   State v. Fichera, 2006 N.H. LEXIS 76 (N.H. 2006).

[95]   N.H. REV. STAT. ANN. 628:2, II. (Matthew Bender 2006).

[96]   Jones v. Indiana, 825 N.E.2d 926; 2005 Ind. App. LEXIS 644 (2005).

[97]   Martinez v. State, 867 S.W.2d 30 (Tex. 1993).

defendant's sanity at the time of trial and the defendant has the burden of proving by a preponderance of the evidence that, as a result of mental disease or defect, he or she lacked the capacity to understand the proceedings against him or her or to assist in his or her defense.[98]

In 1984, Congress completed a comprehensive overhaul of the insanity defense as applied in the federal courts. Under the provisions of the Insanity Defense Reform Act, Congress gave defendants the burden of proving the defense of insanity by clear and convincing evidence.[99] Placing the burden of proof on the defense sparked litigation concerning the constitutionality of the Act because the prior law did not allocate a burden of proof on any defendant using the insanity defense. Legal challenges often contended that the new insanity defense violates the due process clauses of the Fifth and Fourteenth Amendments.[100] In a case heard before the United States Court of Appeals for the Eleventh Circuit, the defendant alleged that placing the burden of proof of insanity by clear and convincing evidence violated his rights under the Fifth Amendment. The Eleventh Circuit noted that several states had constitutionally placed the burden of insanity defenses on defendants with no observable due process violations. Two other federal circuits that had addressed the due process claim involving state insanity cases had also rejected the theory that placing a burden on an insanity defendant violated the federal constitution.[101] Similar to the federal insanity defense, Illinois presumes that sanity is the normal state for offenders and requires that defendants who allege the defense rebut the presumption of sanity. Illinois law provides that when "the defense of insanity has been presented during the trial, the burden of proof is on the defendant to prove by clear and convincing evidence that the defendant is not guilty by reason of insanity."[102] Against a defendant's contention that the elevated burden of proof needed to rebut the presumption of sanity violated due process by being "irrational, unfair, and contrary to contemporary practice," an Illinois reviewing court affirmed his conviction. It held that the Illinois statute did not violate due process, even if only seven jurisdictions used such a high burden of proof in insanity cases.[103]

§ 6.10 —Suicide

The presumption against suicide stems from and is raised by our common knowledge and experience that most sane persons possess a natural love of life and an instinct for self-protection that effectively deter them from suicide or the self-infliction of serious bodily injury. Most jurisdictions recognize the

---

[98]   State v. Bibb, 626 So. 2d 913 (La. 1993).

[99]   18 U.S.C. § 17(b) and §4242(b).

[100] United States v. Freeman, 804 F.2d 1574 (11th Cir. 1986); United States v. Amos, 803 F.2d 419 (8th Cir. 1986).

[101] United States v. Wattleton, 296 F.3d 1184, 2002 U.S. App. LEXIS 13686 (11th Cir. 2002).

[102] ILL. COMP. STAT. ANN. 720 ILCS 5/6-2 (Matthew Bender 2006).

[103] People v. Clay, 361 Ill. App. 3d 310, 836 N.E.2d 872, 2005 Ill. App. LEXIS 994 (Ill. 2005), *appeal denied*, 2006 Ill. LEXIS 164 (Ill. 2006).

existence of an affirmative presumption of death by accidental means that arises under appropriate circumstances and recognize a presumption against suicide,[104] but the presumption is not universally recognized.[105]

The presumption against suicide may be overcome by affirmative evidence of suicide, which effectively rebuts the presumption. When it was shown that a prisoner died two days after his arrival at a federal prison transfer center, the prison contended that he had committed suicide. The guards found the decedent's blood-soaked body hanging in his cell from torn bed sheets affixed to a ceiling vent. Oklahoma has a presumption against suicide but it has been described as a procedural tool for ordering proof and is not considered affirmative evidence. In a suit between the federal government and the estate of the deceased, the government offered sufficient evidence to rebut the presumption against suicide by showing that the deceased had been locked alone in a cell and his injuries appeared to be self-inflicted.[106] In a similar manner, the presumption against suicide was rebutted in a case in which the decedent voluntarily leapt from a tall building, where there was some evidence of his suicidal tendencies, and in which the decedent had a preexisting deteriorating health condition, there was sufficient evidence to overcome the presumption against suicide.[107]

The presumption against suicide and in favor of accidental or other means of causing death is not generally considered evidence and should not be weighed as such. However, courts in several states follow the minority view that the presumption is itself evidence or has evidentiary weight.[108] This presumption against suicide and in favor of accident or natural cause operates procedurally once the insurance company has set up the defense of suicide. The presumption serves to place the burden of coming forward with evidence of suicide on the insurer to rebut the presumption against suicide. In one case in which the deceased died from ingesting hydrocodone and ethanol, the insurer contended that the death was suicide rather than an accidental overdose of drugs. The court held that the presumption against suicide had the effect of evidence that the defendant insurance company had to rebut by a preponderance of the evidence, which it failed to do. In effect, the preponderance had the force and effect of actual evidence, and that, in order to prevail, the insurance company had to prove suicide.[109]

---

[104] Estate of Norman Holly v. American Family Life Assurance, 2005 Ohio 2281, 2005 Ohio App. LEXIS 2190 (2005).

[105] New Mexico does not recognize a presumption against suicide. Solorzano v. Bristow, 136 N.M. 658 N.M. 658, 662, 2004 NMCA 136; 103 P.3d 582, 586, 2004 N.M. App. LEXIS 121 (2004).

[106] Estate of Trentadue ex rel. Aguilar v. United States, 397 F.3d 840, 863, 2005 U.S. App. LEXIS 1811 (10th Cir. 2005).

[107] Garcia v. Workmen's Compensation Appeal Board, 503 Pa. 342, 469 A.2d 585 (Pa. 1983).

[108] Under North Dakota law, the presumption that death was accidental has the weight of affirmative evidence. Dick v. New York Life Ins. Co., 359 U.S. 437, 79 S. Ct. 921, 3 L. Ed. 2d 935 (1959).

[109] Wood v. Valley Forge Life Ins. Co., 2006 U.S. Dist. LEXIS 18581 (E.D. Ark. 2006).

In the majority of cases, when substantial credible contrary evidence regarding the means of causing death is produced, the presumption against suicide has been rebutted and the case must be decided on the evidence produced at trial.[110]

§ 6.11 —Possession of Fruits of Crime

When the evidence establishes that the accused possesses recently stolen property, and there is no satisfactory explanation for such possession consistent with innocence, the jury may be instructed that inferences of guilty knowledge may be drawn from the unexplained possession of the stolen goods.

In *Dobson v. Commonwealth*, a case in which the defendant possessed a recently stolen Hertz rental automobile, the jury received the following instruction:

> Proof of the exclusive personal possession by the defendant of recently stolen goods is a circumstance from which you may reasonably infer that the defendant was the thief unless the defendant offers a reasonable account of possession consistent with innocence which the Commonwealth has failed to prove untrue. The term "recently" is a relative term. The longer the period of time since the theft the more doubtful becomes the inference which may reasonably be drawn from unexplained possession.[111]

The defendant argued that the jury instruction violated his due process rights under the Fourteenth Amendment because it had the effect of reversing the burden of proof so that he had to prove he was not the thief rather than the Commonwealth having to prove beyond a reasonable doubt that he was the wrongdoer. In rejecting his contentions, the court noted that the due process clause does not prohibit the use of a permissive inference as a procedural device that shifts to a defendant the burden of going forward with the evidence or producing some evidence contesting a fact that may otherwise be inferred. The inference must not shift the burden of proof and as long as the prosecution retains the ultimate burden of proof beyond a reasonable doubt, no constitutional problems arise from the use of the presumption.[112]

The strength of such a presumption, which the possession of stolen property raises, depends upon the circumstances surrounding the case. The defendant's possession must be exclusive, and it must have occurred within a relatively short time after commission of the crime. The longer the period from

---

[110] Carson v. Metropolitan Life Ins. Co., 165 Ohio St. 238, 59 Ohio Op. 310, 135 N.E.2d 259 (1956); Kettlewell v. Prudential Ins. Co., 4 Ill. 2d 383, 122 N.E.2d 817 (1954); Ziegler v. Equitable Life Assur. Soc., 284 F.2d 661 (7th Cir. 1960).

[111] Dobson v. Commonwealth, 260 Va. 71, 74, 531 S.E.2d 569, 571 (2000).

[112] *Id.* at 75 and 572.

the crime to the point at which the defendant was found in possession of the stolen property, the weaker the presumption becomes.

Although some researchers believe that the presumption of an accused party's guilt arising from the doctrine of recent possession does not hold the validity that it once held,[113] this presumption is still accepted in the courtroom. For example, in the 2004 case of *Covil v. Commonwealth*, the Supreme Court of Virginia approved using the presumption that a person in possession of recently stolen property is presumed to know that the property was stolen.[114] Police observed Covil driving a stolen rental car and had complete possession of the car until his arrest. He told an incredible story that other people were aware that he needed to rent a car and two men who he had never met approached him to loan the car for 50 dollars. The Virginia court refused to reverse his conviction for grand larceny and noted:

> The inference of guilty knowledge arising from an accused's possession of recently stolen property may be repelled by a credible explanation, but the trier of fact is under no obligation to accept an account it finds unworthy of belief. In cases of this kind, when a defendant's "hypothesis of innocence" is rejected as unreasonable, evidence of his possession of recently stolen goods is sufficient to support a conviction.[115]

The court noted that the presumption that the defendant knowingly possessed stolen property could be properly applied because the defendant was spotted in exclusive control of the recently stolen vehicle, even though he alleged that another person had given him the car to rent. The trial court found his story to be incredible. The court upheld the conviction based on the prima facie presumption of guilty knowledge by virtue of his possession of the recently stolen rental car.

In *State v. Cunningham*, an Ohio Court of Appeals approved of the use of the principle that possession of recently stolen property, if not satisfactorily explained, may give rise to an inference that the person in possession knew that the property had been stolen. In *Cunningham*, police found the defendant in possession of an automobile stolen two days prior to his arrest and for which he had no readily believable explanation. The trial court noted that possession of stolen property may be sufficient for a conviction.

> Possession of property recently stolen if not satisfactorily explained, is ordinarily a circumstance from which you may reasonably draw the inference and find in light of surrounding circumstances shown by the evidence in the case that the person in possession of the property knew or had reasonable cause to believe the property had been stolen.

---

[113]   WIGMORE, EVIDENCE § 2513 (Cladbourn Rev. 1981).
[114]   Covil v. Commonwealth, 268 Va. 692, 604 S.E.2d 79, 2004 Va. LEXIS 143 (2004).
[115]   *Id.* at 895 and 82.

> If you find beyond a reasonable doubt from the evidence in this case that the motor vehicle was stolen and that while recently stolen, the property was in the possession of the defendant, you may or may not, depending upon the facts, draw the inference that the property was possessed by the defendant with the knowledge or having reasonable cause to believe that the property was stolen.[116]

The Court of Appeals followed the common law rule concerning possession of recently stolen property and ruled that the permissible inference has long been rooted in the common law. According to the court, the inference does not have the effect of forcing a defendant to take the witness stand against his will in violation of the Fifth Amendment in order to avoid a conviction.[117]

In contrast to the above cases, California treats the presumption relating to recently stolen property as having a much weaker evidentiary effect. California courts instruct juries that mere possession, without more, is not sufficient to prove that a defendant had knowledge that the property recently had been the subject of theft, robbery, or burglary. The typical California jury instruction counsels jurors that:

> If you find that a defendant was in [conscious] possession of recently [stolen] [extorted] property, the fact of that possession is not by itself sufficient to permit an inference that the defendant is guilty of the crime of [which crime]. Before guilt may be inferred, there must be corroborating evidence tending to prove defendant's guilt. However, this corroborating evidence need only be slight, and need not by itself be sufficient to warrant an inference of guilt.[118]

The Supreme Court of California in *People v. Mendoza*[119] rejected the challenge to the above jury instructions saying that, as long as some corroboration evidence existed, allowing the use of an inference concerning the possession of recently stolen property was appropriate. In this case, the defendant had been accused of, among other crimes, a variety of robberies and burglaries, both crimes that may require some proof that the defendant knew the property was stolen. Because a person's intent often can be derived from considering his or her conduct, the trial court gave a jury instruction covering the possession of recently stolen property. The jury instruction explained to the jury that knowing possession of recently stolen property was not enough evidence to permit an inference that the defendant was guilty of robbery or burglary. The instruction noted that some corroborating evidence of guilt was necessary to prove knowledge that the property was stolen. The judge explained that the required corroboration evidence need only be slight to be sufficient to warrant an inference of knowledge that the property was stolen and that the defendant

---

[116]   State v. Cunningham, 2002 Ohio 4312, 2002 Ohio App. LEXIS 4394 (2002).
[117]   *Id.*
[118]   CALJIC 2.15, Possession of Stolen Property. (West Group 2005).
[119]   People v. Mendoza, 24 Cal. 4th 130, 176, 6 P.3d 150, 178, 99 Cal. Rptr. 2d 485, 515 (Cal. 2000).

was guilty of robbery and burglary. According to the trial court, under the California jury instructions the jury could consider as corroboration:

> (1) "the attributes of possession—time, place and manner"; (2) "that the defendant had the opportunity to commit the crime charged"; (3) "the defendant's conduct"; (4) "his false or contradictory statements, if any"; (5) "other statements he may have made with reference to the property"; (6) "a false account of how he acquired possession of the stolen property"; and (7) "any other evidence which tends to connect the defendant with the crime charged."[120]

The net effect of the California jury instruction covering possession of recently stolen property weakened the traditional inference or presumption concerning knowledge that property was stolen, but still permits the jurors to use natural and logical reasoning.

In summary, where the presumption or inference concerning recently stolen property is applied, these conditions must be met: (a) the possession must be unexplained by any innocent origin; (b) the possession must be fairly recent; and (c) the possession must be exclusive,[121] as a general rule, although many jurisdictions will find that joint possession is sufficient. As noted above, some states require some corroboration with the inference in order to allow a conviction.

§ 6.12 —That a Person Intends the Ordinary Consequences of His or Her Voluntary Acts

In a variety of factual contexts, several federal and state courts have considered the effect of an instruction to the jury in a criminal case that "the law presumes that a person intends the ordinary consequences of his voluntary acts."[122] The United States Supreme Court considered the effects of this type of jury instruction in the case of *Sandstrom v. Montana* in 1979,[123] in which the Court recognized the principle that a jury instruction that shifts to the defendant the burden of proof on a required element of the crime violates due process. Sandstrom had been charged and convicted of deliberate homicide in that he purposely or knowingly caused the victim's death. At the trial, the defendant argued that although he killed the victim, he did not do so purposely or knowingly, and therefore was not guilty of deliberate homicide.

---

[120] *Id.*
[121] Constructive possession is sufficient to allow the presumption. *See* Ahmed v. Yates, 2006 U.S. Dist. LEXIS 18549 (N.D. Cal. 2006) and Ferguson v. State, 920 So. 2d 838, 840, 2006 Fla. App. LEXIS 2283 (2006).
[122] United States v. Wharton, 433 F.2d 451 (D.C. Cir. 1970) and cases cited.
[123] Sandstrom v. Montana, 442 U.S. 510, 99 S. Ct. 2450, 61 L. Ed. 2d 39 (1979).

The trial court instructed the jury that "the law presumes that a person intends the ordinary consequences of his voluntary acts."[124] The jury was not told that the presumption could be rebutted. The defendant's attorney argued that the instruction had the effect of shifting the burden of proof on the issue of purpose or knowledge to the defense and that the instruction was impermissible under the federal Constitution as a violation of due process of law.

Despite the defendant's constitutional objections, the jury found the defendant guilty and he appealed to the Supreme Court of Montana. That court upheld the conviction, conceding that cases cited by the defense prohibited shifting the burden of proof to the defendant by means of the presumption, but held that the cited cases "do not prohibit allocation of some burden of proof to the defendant under certain circumstances."[125] The court also found that, because the defendant had only the burden of producing some evidence that he did not intend the ordinary consequences of his voluntary act, but not to disprove that he acted purposely or knowingly, the burden of proof had not shifted.

The Supreme Court of the United States, after consideration of previous decisions, reasoned that the jury could interpret this instruction as conclusive on the issue of intent. The Court agreed that the instruction violated the Fourteenth Amendment's requirement that the state prove every element of a criminal offense beyond a reasonable doubt. The Court therefore found that the instruction "that the law presumes a person intends the ordinary consequences of his voluntary acts"[126]—in this case, at least—was improper and unconstitutional.

In *Sandstrom v. Montana*, the United States Supreme Court held that the due process clause of the Fourteenth Amendment was violated by a jury instruction inferring that the law presumes that a person intends the ordinary consequences of his voluntary acts in the absence of an instruction that noted that the presumption could be rebutted. The Court expressly left open the question whether, if a jury is so instructed, the error can be held harmless.

Following *Sandstrom*, courts took different approaches to the harmless error problem, and the Supreme Court considered the matter again in 1983 in *Connecticut v. Johnson*.[127] In the *Johnson* case, the defendant was convicted of attempted murder, kidnapping in the second degree, robbery in the first degree, and sexual assault in the first degree. The defendant appealed to the Supreme Court of Connecticut on the grounds that the charge to the jury was improper.

The trial court's charge to the jury, which was challenged, began with general instructions regarding the presumption of innocence and the state's burden of proving beyond a reasonable doubt the existence of every element of the crime charged. The jury was then advised on the issue of intent: "a person's intention may be inferred from his conduct and every person is conclusively presumed to intend the natural and necessary consequences of his

---

[124]   *Id.* at 515.
[125]   Sandstrom v. Montana, 176 Mont. 492, 497, 580 P.2d 106, 109 (1978).
[126]   Sandstrom v. Montana, 442 U.S. 510, 525, 99 S. Ct. 2450, 61 L. Ed. 2d 39 (1979).
[127]   Connecticut v. Johnson, 460 U.S. 73, 103 S. Ct. 969, 74 L. Ed. 2d 823 (1983).

act."[128] The court then gave specific instructions on the elements of each crime. With respect to attempted murder, the court again spoke of a conclusive presumption. Also, on the charge of kidnapping in the second degree, the instructions of the court referred to intent as largely a matter of inference from the facts of the case.

The respondent argued on appeal that the conclusive presumption language in the jury instructions on intent rendered the instructions unconstitutional under *Sandstrom*. The state argued on appeal that the error, if any, was harmless. The Supreme Court of Connecticut affirmed the conviction for kidnapping and sexual assault, but reversed the convictions for attempted murder and robbery on the grounds that the instructions concerning the conclusive presumption shifted the burden of proof as to intent. The court concluded that the "unconstitutional conclusive presumption language in the general instruction was not cured by the specific instructions on attempted murder and robbery." In upholding the conviction for sexual assault, the Supreme Court of Connecticut ruled that sexual assault was a "specific intent" crime and that, consequently, the jury was not influenced by the erroneous general instructions concerning the presumption of intent.

When the defendant appealed to the United States Supreme Court, that Court agreed with the lower court that the proposition, "every person is conclusively presumed to intend the natural and necessary consequences of his act," constituted error violating the Fourteenth Amendment's due process clause. The Supreme Court further explained that "an erroneous presumption on a disputed element of the crime renders irrelevant the evidence on the issue because the jury may have relied upon presumptions rather than upon that evidence." If the instruction is given on the presumption, especially the conclusive presumption, the concern is that the jury will look no further in determining the intent, which is an element of the crime.

In a different case involving an identical jury charge, the Supreme Court indicated that "there may be rare situations in which the reviewing court can be confident that a *Sandstrom* error did not play any part in the jury's verdict. For example, if the instruction had no bearing on the offense for which the defendant . . . was convicted, it would be appropriate to find the error harmless."[129] However, the Court explained that, in this case, the conclusive presumption instruction permitted the jury to convict the respondent using what amounted to a conclusive presumption. According to the Court, such an error deprived the respondent of "constitutional rights so basic to a fair trial that their infraction can never be treated as harmless error."[130]

In a Medicare fraud case in which a chiropractor had been accused of performing uncovered medical procedures but billing them under covered procedure codes so that he could be paid, the doctor complained about a jury instruction. According to the allegation, the instruction violated due process

---

[128]   Connecticut v. Johnson, 460 U.S. 73, 78 (1983).
[129]   Connecticut v. Johnson, 460 U.S. 73, 87,1983 U.S. LEXIS 131 (1983).
[130]   *Id.* at 88, citing Chapman v. California, 386 U.S. 18, 23 (1967).

and constituted reversible error because the instruction had the effect of reversing the burden of proof. The trial court charged the jury that "You may infer, but certainly are not required to infer, that a person intends the natural and probable consequence of acts knowingly done or knowingly omitted."[131] The Court of Appeals rejected the defendant's arguments, which appeared to invite a reversal based on the impermissible creation of a mandatory presumption. The reviewing court determined that the language used by the trial court did not shift the burden of proof because it was clear that the prosecution had to prove all the elements of the case.[132]

Sandstrom and related cases held that the due process clause bars the state from using evidentiary presumptions that effectively relieve the state of its burden of persuasion beyond a reasonable doubt as to every essential element of the crime. A permissive presumption, which suggests a possible conclusion but does not require it to be drawn, does not shift the burden of proof and is permissible as long as the conclusion follows logically from the predicate. But a mandatory presumption, even a rebuttable one, is prohibited if it relieves the state of the burden of persuasion as to an element of the offense.

While United States Supreme Court decisions involving inferences or presumptions of ordinary consequences have not proved to be models of clarity, the decisions appear to indicate that where jury instructions relating to intent create a mandatory presumption that unconstitutionally shifts the burden of persuasion on the element of intent to the defendant, the instruction violates due process. As a general rule, such decisions will not survive judicial scrutiny. However, where the inference is clearly rebuttable and does not change the ultimate burden of proof, a jury instruction may not always, in every case, be objectionable and some state courts may not be following the *Sandstrom* case properly. As an Arkansas court observed, "Intent or state of mind is seldom capable of proof by direct evidence and must usually be inferred from the circumstances of the crime."[133]

Accordingly, courts have generally allowed the prosecution to introduce indirect evidence to show intent. For example, an Arkansas appeals court held that "A presumption exists that a person intends the natural and probable consequence of his acts."[134] A Virginia court permitted the measuring a defendant's intent by considering the natural and probable consequences of the defendant's acts.[135] A Georgia appeals court agreed that an instruction stating that every person is presumed to intend the natural and probable consequences of his or her conduct, particularly if that conduct is unlawful and dangerous to safety or the lives of others, was sufficient.[136] In an unpublished opinion in an attempted murder case, a Minnesota court permitted a jury instruction that

---

[131]   United States v. Lawrence, 405 F.3d 888, 899, 2005 U.S. App. LEXIS 6725 (10th Cir. 2005).
[132]   *Id.* at 900.
[133]   Taylor v. State, 77 Ark. App. 144, 150, 72 S.W.3d 882, 885 (Ark. 2002).
[134]   Russell v. State, 2005 Ark. App. LEXIS 744 (Ark. 2006).
[135]   Thornburgh v. Commonwealth, 2006 Va. App. LEXIS 90 (Va. 2006).
[136]   Scott v. State, 225 Ga. App. 729, 484 S.E.2d 780 (1997).

allowed the jury to infer that the defendant intended the natural and probable consequences of his act.[137] And a Kentucky court held that intent may be inferred from actions because a person is presumed to intend the logical and probable consequences of his conduct, and the person's state of mind may be inferred from actions preceding and following the charged offense.[138] From a review of the above cases, it may become somewhat apparent that many courts regularly come dangerously close to violating the principles announced in *Sandstrom v. Montana*. However, because most cases are not litigated to the state supreme court level and almost never reach the Supreme Court of the United States, some deviation from the black-letter case law occurs.

§ 6.13 —Knowledge of the Law

A society that operates on the rule of law requires that the individuals within the society make strong efforts to obey the law, whether civil or criminal. "The general rule that ignorance of the law or a mistake of law is no defense to criminal prosecution is deeply rooted in the American legal system."[139] Therefore, as a legal principle, all persons are presumed to know the general public laws of the nation, state, and locality where they reside and to know the legal effects of their acts. The maxim that everyone is presumed to know the law, "is founded on public policy and necessity."[140] The rationale for the rule is that "one's acts must be considered as having been done with knowledge of the law, for otherwise the evasion of the law would be facilitated, and the courts would be burdened with collateral inquiries into the content of men's minds.[141] For example, a federal court held that the defendant was presumed to know that money posted for bail was subject to liens in favor of the government[142] and federal courts can include the phrase, "ignorance of the law is no excuse" in jury instructions.[143] While a number of decisions have held that the presumption that one knows the law is a conclusive presumption, it is recognized that no single person knows all the law or even comes close to understanding all its meanings. One federal court of appeals noted that the concept, "everyone knows the law," is based on an "embarrassing tenacity of legal fictions."[144] Because not everyone knows the law exactly, judicial decisions are often reversed based on someone's legal error and not every arrest results in a prosecutable case.

---

[137]   State v. Johnson, 2006 Minn. App. Unpub. LEXIS 560 (Minn. 2006).

[138]   Parker v. Commonwealth, 952 S.W.2d 209 (Ky. 1997).

[139]   United States v. Hancock, 231 F.3d 557, 561, 2000 U.S. App. LEXIS 26827 (9th Cir. 2000), quoting Cheek v. United States, 498 U.S. 192, 199, 1991 U.S. LEXIS 348 (1991).

[140]   Atlas Realty Corp. v. House, 123 Conn. 74, 192 A. 564 (1937).

[141]   *Id.*

[142]   United States v. Cannistraro, 694 F. Supp. 62 (D.N.J. 1988).

[143]   United States v. Turcotte, 405 F.3d 515, 525, 2005 U.S. App. LEXIS 6710 (7th Cir. 2005).

[144]   Atwell v. Lisle Park District, 286 F.3d 987, 2002 U.S. App. LEXIS 6775 (8th Cir. 2002).

As a general rule, trial judges are presumed to know the law and to follow it properly in rendering decisions,[145] and "police officers are charged with knowledge of the law"[146] and are presumed to understand the laws they are charged with enforcing.[147]

While the presumption extends to judicial decisions, persons are not presumed to know how the courts will construe the law or what laws will be held unconstitutional.[148] In one case, an Illinois police officer was permitted to follow and enforce an Illinois law that was later ruled unconstitutional. Even though a police officer is presumed to know the law, the officer cannot foresee how a court will construe the law in future litigation.[149] In fact, even "prisoners are not exempt from the principle that everyone is presumed to know the law and is subject to the law whether or not he is actually aware of the particular law of which he has run afoul."[150] Consequently, when prisoners miss filing deadlines dictated by statutory requirements for appeals and habeas corpus, such failures are not generally excused and may have severe consequences.[151]

A person is not presumed to know the laws of a sister state or foreign country, but he or she is presumed to know that laws are subject to change, and is presumed to know of the changes.[152]

§ 6.14 —Flight or Concealment

Human conduct may prove ambiguous, because the same act in one situation may not result in the same inference when the act occurs in a different context. Although many law enforcement officers assume that flight following the crime or concealment thereafter raises a presumption of consciousness of guilt, the facts may give rise to different interpretations. This evidence rule deserves careful attention because the factual situation of each crime might result in different conclusions being drawn from similar conduct. Although there are some older cases in certain jurisdictions indicating that flight before arrest raises a presumption of guilt, the better—and majority—rule is that the flight of the accused or his or her concealment does not raise a legal presumption or inference of guilt. However, flight or concealment may constitute evidence of a consciousness of guilt[153] and "evidence of flight is generally admissible as evidence of 'consciousness of guilt' and of guilt itself."[154] Alternatively, a suspect's flight from a crime scene or from a police officer could

[145] Webster v. Hartman, 309 Ill. App. 3d 459, 461, 722 N.E.2d 266, 269 (1999). *See also* State v. Leim, 944 P.2d 1222 (Ariz. 1997).
[146] Sneed v. State, 876 So. 2d 1235, 1238, 2004 Fla. App. LEXIS 8390 (Fla. 2004).
[147] United States v. Hernandez, 55 F.3d 443 (9th Cir. 1995).
[148] Screws v. United States, 32 U.S. 91, 65 S. Ct. 103, 89 L. Ed. 1495 (1945).
[149] *See* Illinois v. Krull, 480 U.S. 340 (1987).
[150] Baker v. Norris, 2003 U.S. App. LEXIS 3367 (8th Cir. 2003).
[151] Dean v. Houston, 2006 U.S. Dist. LEXIS 2544 (D. Neb. 2006).
[152] *See* 31A C.J.S. *Evidence* § 147 (1996).
[153] State v. Rodriguez, 23 N.M. 156, 167 P. 426 (1918).
[154] United States v. Tinker, 185 F.3d 871, 1999 U.S. App. LEXIS 26149 (9th Cir. 1999).

indicate a consciousness of guilt of some completely different offense or of a desire not to be involved in a police investigation. Evidence of flight need not prove that a suspect fled immediately following the alleged crime but evidence that a person fled months later when the police were focusing on the crime may be sufficient for a jury to consider. This evidence may be presented as a circumstance tending to indicate guilt, and may become especially significant when corroborating evidence is introduced. The strength of the evidence of flight depends upon all the facts and circumstances, because flight may show consciousness of guilt or may indicate nothing. When, however, the state introduces evidence to show flight or concealment, the defendant is entitled to introduce evidence to explain why he or she fled or concealed himself or herself.[155]

In a federal prosecution involving a felon in possession of a firearm and ammunition, state agents attempted to serve a search warrant, which the defendant initially resisted. The eventual search revealed a gun and ammunition and indicated that the defendant was the only resident. He admitted to owning the gun and the ammunition. The gun's presence resulted in a referral for federal prosecution, and, after agreeing to surrender in Rhode Island, the defendant absconded and was not arrested for several years. The federal judge permitted the prosecutor to introduce evidence of flight only after defense evidence was introduced that appeared to make the delay in the prosecution seem like the government was "trumping up" the charge. The fact that the defendant had agreed to surrender and did not and then fled, permitted the trial judge to allow evidence of flight without unfairly prejudicing the defense. In approving the admission of flight evidence, the Court of Appeals noted.

> In the case at hand, the appellant's resistance to the execution of the search warrant, his admissions on that occasion, and the unfulfilled promise of self-surrender formed a sufficient factual predicate for the introduction of the flight evidence. This predicate substantially diminished the possibility that the jury might infer guilt solely on the basis of the appellant's flight. To cinch matters, the court's cautionary instructions, twice repeated, mitigated any risk that the jury might give the flight evidence undue weight.[156]

Here, the evidence of flight explained the delay from the date of indictment to holding the trial and added to the inference of consciousness of guilt and helped impeach defense witnesses who did nothing to exonerate the defendant while he was out of the jurisdiction.[157]

When contesting the constitutionality of a jury instruction concerning flight following a crime, a California defendant contended that a flight instruction violated his right to due process. In *People v. Mendoza*,[158] the defendant,

---

[155] Hines v. Commonwealth, 136 Va. 728, 117 S.E. 843 (1923).

[156] United States v. Benedetti, 433 F.3d 111, 116, 2005 U.S. App. LEXIS 28490 (1st Cir. 2005).

[157] *Id.* at 118.

[158] People v. Mendoza, 24 Cal. 4th 130, 179, 180, 6 P.3d 150, 180, 99 Cal. Rptr. 2d 485, 517, 518 (Cal. 2000).

when confronted by a victim concerning the recent theft of three guns from his home, ran from police through the house, out a side door, and over a fence. Where there is evidence of flight, California law requires the judge to offer a jury instruction covering unexplained flight.

The trial court here gave the standard instruction, CALJIC No. 2.52 (1979 rev.), which reads:

> The flight of a person immediately after the commission of a crime, or after he is accused of the crime, is not sufficient in itself to establish his guilt, but is a fact which, if proved, may be considered by you in light of all other proved facts in deciding the question of his guilt or innocence. The weight to which such circumstance is entitled is a matter for the jury to determine.[159]

The defendant contended that the flight instruction violated his right to due process because it created an unconstitutional permissive inference of guilt. According to the defendant, because it cannot be said with substantial assurance that the presumed or inferred fact of guilt is more likely than not to flow from the proved fact of flight on which it is made to depend, the reading of the instruction to the jury violated due process because of its lack of logic. According to the California Supreme Court, a permissive inference involving flight violates the due process clause only if the suggested conclusion is not one that common sense and logic justify when due consideration is given for facts proved to the jury.[160] The conviction was affirmed.

While California law requires a flight instruction in cases in which flight has occurred, many judges in other states must determine when and if flight instructions are proper in particular cases. The answer generally depends upon the facts of the case and whether flight actually occurred. In one case, the court noted that the government is entitled to a flight instruction when the evidence in the case supports the following inferences: (1) from defendant's behavior to flight; (2) from flight to consciousness of guilt; (3) from consciousness of guilt to consequences of guilt concerning the crimes charged; and (4) from consciousness of guilt concerning the crime charged to actual guilt of the crime charged.[161]

In referring to flight instructions, a federal district court instructed the jury that it could consider a defendant's flight from police to infer consciousness of guilt.[162] Police noticed the defendant driving without a buckled safety belt and attempted a traffic stop. The defendant, who had prior felony convictions, sped away, but was eventually captured. The interior of the car contained a large bag of marijuana and a semi-automatic pistol. As a general rule, a flight instruction may be given when the evidence warrants it. The trial court told the

---

[159] *Id.*

[160] *Id.*

[161] United States v. Cook, 580 F. Supp. 948 (N.D.W. Va. 1983), *aff'd*, 782 F.2d 1037 (4th Cir. 1983); *see also* State v. Woodall, 385 S.E.2d 253 (W. Va. 1989).

[162] United States v. Webster, 442 F.3d 1065, 1066, 2006 U.S. App. LEXIS 8061 (8th Cir. 2006).

jury, "You may also consider any evidence of flight by the defendant, along with all of the evidence in the case, and you may consider whether this evidence shows a consciousness of guilt and determine the significance to be attached to any such conduct."[163] Fleeing police by a convicted felon in possession of a firearm with a large quantity of marijuana could indicate a guilty conscience. Because the instruction allowed an inference of guilt, but did not require such a deduction, the reviewing court held that the giving of the flight instruction was proper.

In a different federal case, the evidence indicated that the defendants, upon observing an FBI agent in an unmarked car, drove out of an apartment complex, ran a stop light, ran two additional stop lights without making any effort to slow down, passed three cars while going uphill in a no-passing zone, and drove at speeds of 50-60 miles per hour.[164] The reviewing court upheld an instruction that flight can be considered evidence of guilt. In another case, the court indicated that evidence that the defendant ran from the scene of the crime, ducked into his girlfriend's apartment when police spotted him and quickly exited out the back, entered two other apartments, and changed his clothes, was sufficient to warrant a flight instruction.[165] Evidence that the defendant, while in another state six weeks after the crime, gave a fictitious name and address to a detective, coupled with testimony of the defendant's employer that on the date of the crime the defendant called to tell him that he would not be returning to work, was also sufficient to support a jury instruction on flight as consciousness of guilt.[166]

If evidence of flight is relied upon by the prosecution to infer consciousness of guilt and the supportive evidence has been introduced, a flight instruction may be given by the court. Reciprocal fairness would seem to dictate that an instruction on lack of flight should be given, but case law does not require a lack of flight instruction.[167] In an unpublished opinion, a California court noted that, "A defendant has no right to an instruction on the absence of flight, even when there is some evidence to support the instruction."[168] Courts have broad discretion to give an instruction on absence of flight when it is supported by evidence and is of sufficient relevance in the context of the case. One court noted that the benefit of the flight instruction, which is available to the Commonwealth with respect to an accused's guilty behavior, should also be available to the accused with regard to another's guilty behavior when the accused defends on that basis.[169]

---

[163] *Id.* at 1067.

[164] United States v. Beard, 775 F.2d 1577 (11th Cir. 1985), *cert. denied*, 475 U.S. 1030, 106 S. Ct. 1235, 89 L. Ed. 2d 343 (1985).

[165] State v. Weible, 142 Ariz. 113, 688 P.2d 1005 (1984).

[166] Garrett v. State, 59 Md. App. 97, 474 A.2d 931 (1984).

[167] State v. Williams, 2004 Tenn. Crim. App. LEXIS 191 (Tenn. 2004).

[168] People v. Monroe, 2001 Cal. App. Unpub. LEXIS 175 (Cal. 2001). *See also* People v. Aguirre, 2005 Cal. App. Unpub. LEXIS 6669 (Cal. 2005).

[169] Commonwealth v. Milligan, 693 A.2d 1313 (Pa. 1997).

In determining whether a flight instruction is proper there must be unexplained actual flight and the flight instructions may be given only where the evidence of flight has considerable probative value. Evidence of flight should not be admitted when there is an independent justification for flight for reasons that cannot be explained to the jury because of a separate prejudicial effect.[170] Typically, the trial judge will advise the jury that flight may be prompted by a variety of motives, and best practice suggests that the judge should admonish the jury to consider all evidence before making an inference of guilt from the fact of flight.

§ 6.15 —Unexplained Absence as Death

At common law, when a person left his or her home or usual place of residence for parts unknown, and was not heard from or known to be living for a period of seven years, the legal presumption arose that he or she was dead. Many states have enacted "presumed decedents laws" that provide that a presumption of death will arise in situations in which a person has been absent for unexplained reasons for a specific number of years. Upon a petition by an interested party and upon proof of absence, that no person has seen the missing person, and that there is no explanation other than death, a court will enter a decree finding a presumption of death.[171] Absentee individuals who have been declared dead prior to the statutory time have often been involved in suicide, accidents, shipwrecks, aircraft accidents, or similar occurrences in which the body would not likely have been found and in which there was a high likelihood of death.

In one New York case, the trial court ruled that the missing person was deceased. The evidence showed that he had told his business partner and his wife that he was intent on ending his life. When he left the marital home, he did not take his driver's license, credit cards, or any personal effects. Medically, he had terminal heart disease, suffered from shortness of breath, and had been diagnosed as an alcoholic. The court took testimony that about 70 percent of individuals with his heart disease do not live five years. Significantly, the missing man's diagnosis was a late-term diagnosis of cardiomyopathy that indicated he needed a heart transplant. A search of all the usual databases, including Social Security, Board of Elections, and others disclosed no activity. The court concluded that the missing man was dead as of the date of his disappearance.[172]

The cases are not in agreement with respect to the presumed death of a fugitive from justice because that person, if alive, has a good reason to be absent. In an action on a life insurance policy, an Illinois court held that the

---

[170]   Walker v. State, 913 So. 2d 198, 232, 2005 Miss. LEXIS 216 (Miss. 2005).

[171]   Cavanagh v. Lentz, 2005 Conn. Super. LEXIS 2731 (Conn. 2005). Due to proof that a woman's husband was missing, had severe mental problems, and had tried to commit suicide at a prior time, the coroner was ordered to prepare a presumptive death certificate.

[172]   Matter of Bennett, 2006 N.Y. Slip Op. 50889U (N.Y. 2006).

fact that the absent person was a fugitive from justice did not preclude the application of the presumption.[173] A good reason or motive for a person's absence may provide a satisfactory reason sufficient to determine that the individual is not deceased. Absence to avoid a criminal prosecution may constitute a sufficient reason to conclude that a person has not died but is absent to avoid potential incarceration.[174] A surety on a defendant's bail bond attempted to avoid forfeiture of bail and introduced evidence that the defendant had disappeared after leaving his car at an airport, and that an intensive search failed to locate him. Other evidence indicated that the defendant had been indicted, was a member of a group on whom a murderous assault had been made, and had a good reason for flight. The court upheld the forfeiture on the ground that, where a motive or where doubt about the reason for the absence exists, the presumption of continued life remains.[175]

The legal effect that the presumption that a person, missing seven years, with his or her location being unknown and undetermined, is dead can have important consequences for those who would inherit by will or intestate distribution. In many states and in Washington, "the presumption of death attaches where a party has been absent for seven years without tidings of his or her existence."[176] During the first seven years of absence, Washington presumes that the person remains alive. Under the statute, the presumptive heirs and legatees may petition for a distribution of the presumed deceased person's estate. Where the court is satisfied that the statutory requirements have been met, the estate will be distributed.[177]

In many states the statutory period has been shortened to five years of absence. A shortened period may follow the logic that in the present environment with large computer databases and the Internet, disappearing is more difficult than ever, in the absence of death. In many jurisdictions, there is a presumption that the death occurred at the end of the statutory period,[178] which may create problems for insurance eligibility. New York has shortened the period for a presumption of death to a continuous absence of three years but allows proof of death in fewer than three years.[179]

---

[173]   Blodgett v. State Mutual Life Assurance Co., 32 Ill. App. 2d 155, 177 N.E.2d 1 (1961).

[174]   Starr et al. v. Old Line Life Insurance Co., 104 Cal. App. 4th 487, 496, 128 Cal. Rptr. 2d 282, 288, 2002 Cal. App. LEXIS 5174 (2002).

[175]   People v. Niccoli, 102 Cal. App. 2d 814, 228 P.2d 827 (1951).

[176]   Nelson v. Schubert, 98 Wn. App. 754, 759, 994 P.2d 225, 229, 2000 Wash. App. LEXIS 3 (2000).

[177]   REV. CODE WASH. § 11.80.100 (Matthew Bender 2006).

[178]   See CAL. PROB. CODE § 12401 (2006).

[179]   See NY CLS EPTL § 2-1.7 (Matthew Bender 2006).

§ 6.16 —Regularity of Official Acts

"The government is always presumed to act in good faith,"[180] and that presumption extends to its appointed and elected officials. This rebuttable presumption of regularity supports the official acts of public officials and police officers, and courts presume that public officials have properly discharged their official duties, in the absence of clear evidence to the contrary.[181] The strong presumption that public officials will discharge their duties in good faith and observe civil and criminal law proves difficult to overcome, whether it is an argument of malfeasance or quasi-criminal wrongdoing. To rebut the presumption of proper conduct, the moving party will have to meet the burden by clear and convincing evidence to the contrary.[182]

As a general rule, the presumption that governmental officials have acted properly extends to grand jury proceedings.[183] For example, in *United States v. Exson*,[184] the reviewing court refused to dismiss the indictment on the strength of the defense allegation that the prosecution misled the grand jury on material matters. According to the Court of Appeals, even if there were some irregularities in grand jury proceeding, a dismissal would not be appropriate. The court noted that:

> The proceedings of a grand jury are afforded a strong presumption of regularity, and a defendant faces a heavy burden to overcome that presumption when seeking dismissal of an indictment. See *United States v. Hintzman*, 806 F.2d 840, 843 (8th Cir. 1986). Dismissal due to errors in grand jury proceedings is appropriate only if the defendant shows actual prejudice, see *United States v. Kouba*, 822 F.2d 768, 774 (8th Cir. 1987), and "the petit jury's guilty verdict rendered [any] errors harmless." *Id.*[185]

The presumption of regularity attending official acts applies to the acts of most public officials. One court may presume that another court properly performed its duties until the contrary has been shown and therefore a rebuttable presumption of regularity attaches to a defendant's prior convictions.[186] A federal court in Indiana determined that where there is no evidence of tampering with seized evidence, a presumption of regularity attends the official acts of the public officers in custody of the evidence, as the courts presume they did

---

[180]　Long Lane Limited Partnership v. Bibb, 159 Fed. Appx. 189; 2005 U.S. App. LEXIS 26912 (Fed. Cir. 2005).

[181]　Butler v. Principi, 244 F.3d 1337, 201 U.S. App. LEXIS 5270 (Fed. Cir. 2001); United States v. Chemical Foundation, Inc., 272 U.S. 1, 47 S. Ct. 1, 71 L. Ed. 131 (1926); Charleston Television, Inc. v. South Carolina Budget and Control Bd., 373 S.E.2d 890 (S.C. 1988).

[182]　Tecom, Inc. v. United States, 66 Fed. Cl. 736, 768, 2005 U.S. Claims LEXIS 195 (2005). *See also* Am-Pro v. United States, 281 F.3d 1234, 2002 U.S. App. LEXIS 3047 (Fed. Cir. 2002).

[183]　United States v. Diaz, 2006 U.S. Dist. LEXIS 46315 (N.D. Ga. 2006) and United States v. Lucarelli, 2006 U.S. Dist. LEXIS 39664 (D. Conn. 2005).

[184]　United States v. Esxon, 328 F.3d 456, 459, 2003 U.S. App. LEXIS 8836 (8th Cir. 2003).

[185]　*Esxon* at 459.

[186]　Montana v. Kvislen, 2003 Mont. 27, 314 Mont. 176, 2003 Mont. LEXIS 26 (2003).

their jobs correctly.[187] And courts may presume that public officers have properly discharged their official duties; the acts of postal workers and their superiors are included in this presumption of regularity.[188] Trial jurors are considered public officials for purposes of this presumption and are presumed to have followed jury instructions properly and in good faith.[189] Likewise, absent evidence that a member of the grand jury acted with malice, hatred, or ill will, or fraud, or otherwise violated the oath taken by grand jurors, it is presumed that the grand jurors did not improperly or illegally act in returning" an indictment.[190] A prosecuting attorney acts as an officer of the court and is presumed to have acted constitutionally when interviewing a criminal suspect.[191]

§ 6.17   Constitutionality Tests for Presumptions and Inferences

Criminal cases require the prosecution to prove all the elements of any charged crime beyond a reasonable doubt, but where inferences and presumptions are presented in a case, the prosecution may be proving one fact and not actually proving the inferred fact. Due process clauses in the Fifth and Fourteenth Amendments require that fundamental fairness prevail in a criminal trial. In meeting the fundamental fairness standard, generally requiring a jury to make a mandatory deduction from proof of the basic fact violates due process. Even allowing the deduction or inference constitutionally requires a close logical connection between the basic fact and the presumed fact. Early decisions of the United States Supreme Court set forth a number of different standards to measure the validity of statutory presumptions. One test was whether there was a "rational connection" between the basic fact and the presumed fact. A second was whether the legislature might have made it a crime to do the thing from which the presumption authorized an inference. A third was whether it would be more convenient for the defendant or for the prosecution to adduce evidence of the presumed fact.

However, in *Tot v. United States*,[192] the Court singled out one of these tests as controlling, and the *Tot* rule has been followed in the two subsequent cases in which the issue has been presented. The *Tot* Court had before it a federal statute that, as construed, made it a crime for a person previously convicted of a crime of violence to receive any firearm or ammunition that had been transported in interstate or foreign commerce. The statute further provided that "the possession of a firearm or ammunition by any such person shall be presump-

---

[187]   United States v. Kelly, 14 F.3d 1169 (7th Cir. 1994).

[188]   United States Postal Service v. Gregory, 534 U.S. 1, 10, 2001 U.S. LEXIS 10307 (2001).

[189]   United States v. Mc Cuiston, 2006 U.S. App. LEXIS 16292 (5th Cir. 2006).

[190]   Culp v. State, 2005 Miss. LEXIS 828 (Miss. 2005). *See also* Michael B. v. Superior Court, 103 Cal. App. 4th 1384, 1396, 127 Cal. Rptr. 2d 454, 464 (Cal. 2002).

[191]   Cooper Cameron Corp. v. United States, 280 F.3d 539, 550, 2002 U.S. App. LEXIS 839 (5th Cir. 2002).

[192]   Tot v. United States, 319 U.S. 463, 1943 U.S. LEXIS 531 (1943).

tive evidence that such firearm or ammunition was shipped or transported or received, as the case may be, by such person in violation of this Act."[193] Proof of possession and a prior violent crime equaled guilt with the presumption carrying half the burden of proof. The *Tot* Court noted that the "due process clauses of the Fifth and Fourteenth Amendments set limits upon the power of Congress or that of a state legislature to make the proof of one fact or group of facts evidence of the existence of the ultimate fact on which guilt is predicated."[194]

The Court held the presumption unconstitutional and decided that the controlling test for determining the validity of a statutory presumption was that there be a rational connection between the fact proved and the fact presumed. The Court stated:

> Under our decisions a statutory presumption cannot be sustained if there be no rational connection between the fact proved and the ultimate fact presumed, if the inference of the one from proof of the other is arbitrary because of lack of connection between the two in common experience. This is not to say that a valid presumption may not be created upon a view of relation broader than that a jury might take in a specific case. But where the inference is so strained as not to have a reasonable relation to the circumstances of life as we know them, it is not competent for the legislature to create it as a rule governing the procedure of courts.[195]

Two subsequent cases in which the Supreme Court ruled upon the constitutionality of criminal presumptions, *United States v. Gainey*[196] and *United States v. Romano*,[197] involved companion sections of the Internal Revenue Code dealing with illegal alcohol stills. The presumption in *Gainey* that the person's presence at an illegal distillery permitted, but did not require, a jury to infer that Jackie Gainey was "carrying on" the business of a distiller, unless the defendant explained being present at the still to the satisfaction of the jury. The Court held that the *Gainey* presumption should be tested by the "rational connection" standard announced in the *Tot* case, and sustained the statutory presumption and the conviction. The presumption of "carrying on" the business carried weight because few illegal distillers would allow strangers to observe the illegal still. The *Gainey* Court recognized that, in enacting the statutory presumption, Congress allowed the unexplained evidence to have its natural probative value.

The presumption under attack in the *Romano* case was identical to that in *Gainey*, except that the former authorized the jury to infer from the defendant's presence at an illegal still that he or she had possession, custody, or control of the still. The Court held this presumption invalid on the ground that

---

[193] 15 U. S. C. 902 (f).
[194] Tot at 467.
[195] *Id.* at 467-468.
[196] United States v. Gainey, 380 U.S. 63, 1965 U.S. LEXIS 1733 (1965).
[197] United States v. Romano, 382 U.S. 136, 1965 U.S. LEXIS 207 (1965).

"absent some showing of the defendant's function at the still, its connection with possession is too tenuous to permit a reasonable inference of guilt; the inference of the one from proof of the other is arbitrary"[198] and not based on good probabilities. In effect, presence did not indicate possession, although sometimes presence might indicate possession. Though quite similar to the Gainey presence at the still, the Romano case had a different outcome based on the manner in which the Supreme Court interpreted the two presumptions.

A "statutory presumption for criminal cases must be regarded as 'irrational' or 'arbitrary' and hence unconstitutional, unless it can at least be said with substantial assurance that the presumed fact is more likely than not to follow from the proof of the proved fact on which it is made to depend."[199] This was spelled out by the Supreme Court in *Leary v. United States*, in which the Court overturned a federal statute that authorized juries to infer from the defendant's possession of marijuana that the defendant knew that the marijuana was illegally brought into the United States. The presumption of knowing that marijuana was imported from proof of mere possession was invalid under the due process clause because there was no proof that typical marijuana possessors are generally aware that their marijuana was locally grown or aware that their marijuana was likely to have been imported or knew that it actually was imported.[200]

In the year following the *Leary* decision, the Supreme Court considered the constitutionality of instructing a jury that it may infer from the defendant's possession of heroin and cocaine that the defendant knew that the drugs had been illegally imported.[201] The Court noted that there was a reason for the logic of the presumption of knowledge of importation from proof of possession.

> "It may be that the ordinary jury would not always know that heroin illegally circulating in this country is not manufactured here. But Turner and others who sell or distribute heroin are in a class apart. Such people have regular contact with a drug which they know cannot be legally bought or sold; their livelihood depends on its availability; some of them have actually engaged in the smuggling process."[202]

The Court held that the inference with regard to heroin was valid, judged by either of the two tests stated in the *Tot* decision.

In a case involving similar reasoning, police approached a vehicle that was being refuelled and that matched the description of a car whose occupants were suspected of criminal activity. When the driver, who was pumping gasoline, saw the officer approaching, he attempted to get into the car to leave. A struggle ensued and the police prevailed. At that time an officer discovered a handgun wedged between the driver's seat and the console. Under New York

---

[198] Tot v. United States, 319 U.S. 463, 467, 1943 U.S. LEXIS 531 (1943).
[199] Leary v. United States, 395 U.S. 6, 36, 1969 U.S. LEXIS 3271 (1969).
[200] *Id.*
[201] Turner v. United States, 396 U.S. 398, 1970 U.S. LEXIS 3146 (1970).
[202] *Id.* at 416.

law, the presence of a firearm in an automobile is presumptive evidence of its illegal possession by all persons then occupying the vehicle. The officers testified that none of the defendants was ever observed actually handling the gun, but they observed the defendant as one of the occupants of the vehicle. The driver's testimony that he alone possessed the gun failed to rebut the presumption of New York law that implicated the passengers in possession. The evidence showed that the occupants of the car had been travelling together for several weeks and must have known about the gun. The Appellate Division of the Supreme Court believed that the presumption of possession by all of the vehicle occupants was entirely rational. Because it was more likely than not that all occupants possessed the gun and the presumption had not been rebutted, the reviewing court upheld the conviction for criminal possession of a gun.[203] The result followed the *Tot* rationale covering the constitutionality of presumptions,[204] and a jury could have determined that the passenger did not have possession of the firearm, if it believed that the evidence rebutted the presumption and that the defendant-passenger was not in possession of the gun.

Taking a contrary view, an Illinois court reversed a conviction for unlawful use of a weapon when police discovered a firearm on the rear floor of the defendant's car when the defendant was unaware that the gun was present.[205]

As a general rule when dealing with statutory presumptions that declare that, on proof of one fact, another fact may be inferred or presumed, such a statute is probably constitutional, provided that no constitutional right of the accused is harmed or destroyed by the operative effect of the presumption, that the presumption is subject to rebuttal, and that there is a fairly strong rational connection between the basic fact proved and the ultimate fact presumed.[206]

In an Illinois case involving a presumption that a driver had been proven to be under the influence of alcohol, the Supreme Court reversed a double homicide conviction. In accordance with then-existing Illinois law, the trial court instructed the jury with language from 9-3(b) of the Illinois code and rephrased it into a jury instruction that stated: "If you find from your consideration of all the evidence that the defendant was under the influence of alcohol at the time of the alleged violation, such evidence shall be presumed to be evidence of a reckless act unless disproved by evidence to the contrary."[207] Other jury instructions assisted the jury in finding that the defendant was under the influence of alcohol when there had been proof that his blood-alcohol level was .08 or greater, but the instructions did not require such a finding. The court instructed the jury that:

[203] People v. Tabb, 12 A.D.3d 951, 952, 785 N.Y.S.2d 193, 194, 2004 N.Y. App. Div. LEXIS 14284 (N.Y. 2004), Appeal denied, 4 N.Y.3d 768, 2005 N.Y. LEXIS 419 (2005).
[204] *See* County Court v. Allen, 442 U.S. 140, 165, 166, 99 S. Ct. 2213, 2228, 2229, 60 L. Ed. 2d 777, 796, 797 (1979).
[205] People v. Seibech, 141 Ill. App. 3d 45, 489 N.E.2d 1138 (Ill. 1986).
[206] Finney v. State, 686 N.E.2d 133 (Ind. 1997).
[207] People v. Pomykala, 2003 Ill. LEXIS 7 (2003).

> If you find beyond a reasonable doubt that at the time the defendant drove a vehicle that the amount of alcohol concentration in the defendant's blood or breath was 0.08 or more, you may presume that the defendant was under the influence of alcohol. You never are required to make this presumption. It is for the jury to determine whether the presumption should be drawn. You should consider all the evidence in determining whether the defendant was under the influence of alcohol. Illinois Pattern Jury Instructions, Criminal, No. 23.30 (4th ed. 2000).[208]

According to the Supreme Court of Illinois, because a reasonable juror could conclude that the jury instruction mandated a finding of recklessness without any factual connection between the intoxication and the reckless act, the statute had created a mandatory presumption. The effect of this mandatory presumption improperly and unconstitutionally shifted the burden of disproving recklessness to the defendant, which required a reversal of the homicide convictions.[209]

A question raised in some cases involved the constitutionality of a state statute making the fact that a defendant was armed with a pistol, for which he had no license as required by that particular state, prima facie evidence of his intent to commit a felony against another person. A California court held that such a statute included in a jury instruction violated due process. The appellate court felt that to apply a rebuttable presumption against a defendant in a criminal case violates due process "unless it can at least be said with *substantial assurance* that the presumed fact is more likely than not to flow from the proved fact on which it is made to depend."[210] Similarly, an Indiana court concluded that the fact that a person was armed with an unlicensed gun was irrelevant to the question of whether that person intended to commit a crime of violence.[211] Taking an opposing view, a Washington state court, in analyzing a similar presumption involving a firearm, held such a statute constitutional, as the court found a rational connection between carrying pistols without a license and intending crimes of violence.[212]

In a Virginia case, the law provided that a person who possessed rental property and failed to return the property within five days of the agreed date of return will be deemed guilty of larceny.[213] In one case, a defendant rented a car from Rent-a-Wreck and failed to return it consistent with the rental agreement. He told the company that he was in a hospital following a suicide attempt and could not return it, but told the company where to find it. The car was recovered six days past the rental period when a company employee happened to see it at an apartment complex. Following his conviction, the defen-

---

[208] *Id.*

[209] *Id.*

[210] People v. Bedolla, 94 Cal. App. 3d 1, 156 Cal. Rptr. 171 (Cal. 1979), quoting Leary v. United States, 395 U.S. 6, 36 (1969).

[211] Everett v. State, 208 Ind. 145, 195 N.E. 77 (1935).

[212] State v. Thomas, 58 Wash. 2d 746, 364 P.2d 930 (1961).

[213] VA. CODE ANN. § 18.2-117 (Matthew Bender 2006).

dant appealed, contending that Virginia law concerning the presumption of his fraudulent intent to commit larceny, based on a failure return the car, had been rebutted by his hospitalization for attempted suicide. The Court of Criminal Appeals rejected the defendant's contention and noted that the statute operated to allow a prima facie presumption of fraudulent intent upon failure to return and that the evidence failed to rebut the deduction contemplated by the statute.[214]

One California case appeared to create a mandatory presumption that would be inconsistent with due process and the Supreme Court decided cases dealing with this presumption. A trial court proceeding resulted in the conviction of a California defendant for possessing hydriodic acid with intent to manufacture the illegal drug, methamphetamine. State law provided that where a person possessed sufficient amounts of red phosphorus and iodine, the person would be deemed to have possessed hydriodic acid, even if no acid had ever been synthesized. The defendant contended on appeal that the statute created a mandatory presumption that if one possesses the two precursor chemicals that one was guilty of possessing hydriodic acid. The effect of the law permitted the government to convict for possession of hydriodic acid without any proof of possession of hydriodic acid. In a decision by the Supreme Court of California, the court held that there was no presumption at issue but that the language that appeared to be a mandatory presumption was really a "valid exercise of the Legislature's power to create substantive law and define crimes."[215] The defendant's intent to manufacture methamphetamine required proof of possession of hydriodic acid, which she did not possess. The Supreme Court of California upheld the conviction[216] and the Supreme Court of the United States refused to review the decision.[217]

To summarize, when determining the constitutionality of statutory presumptions, the court must find a rational connection between the basic fact and the presumed fact, and it must find that there is a reasonable possibility in the ordinary course of events that the conclusion required by the presumption is in accord with human experience. Second, a presumption that has the effect of shifting the burden to the defense to disprove an element of the crime is unconstitutional.

§ 6.18 Stipulations

The stipulation is another substitute for evidence that has the effect removing some issues from the lawsuit because the parties have no disagreement or dispute concerning those issues. A stipulation amounts to a concession by both

---

[214] Newport v. Commonwealth, 2005 Va. App. LEXIS 152 (Va. 2005). For an opposite judicial view, *see*, Carella v. California, 491 U.S. 263, 109 S. Ct. 2419, 105 L. Ed. 2d 218 (1989).

[215] People v. McCall, 32 Cal. 4th 175, 179, 82 P.3d 351, 354, 8 Cal. Rptr. 3d 337, 340, 2004 Cal. LEXIS 8 (Cal. 2004).

[216] *Id.*

[217] McCall v. California, 542 U.S. 923, 2004 U.S. LEXIS 4451 (2004).

parties to the existence or nonexistence of a fact, an agreement concerning the contents of a document, or an agreement over what a witness would have said if the witness actually testified. A California court suggested that "A stipulation is an agreement between counsel respecting business before the court, and like any other agreement or contract, it is essential that the parties or their counsel agree to its terms."[218] California juries are told that stipulations between the parties are binding on the jury concerning the fact or matter stipulated.[219] In making a stipulation, the parties may make it orally or in writing, but it must clearly be part of the court record. California juries are told that stipulations between the parties are binding on the jury concerning the fact or matter stipulated. While stipulations may be encouraged, the opposing side is not obligated to stipulate, which would otherwise have the effect of preventing that party from presenting part of its case with actual evidence. In one case involving aggravated domestic violence, the defendant complained that the trial court erred when it permitted the prosecution to introduce evidence of his two prior domestic violence convictions when he had offered to stipulate to the earlier convictions. The reviewing court held that the prosecution did not have to stipulate to the prior convictions, and, in any event, the earlier convictions were elements of proof needed by the prosecution for the aggravated domestic violence charge. Therefore, the defendant was not entitled to prevent the jury from hearing that evidence.[220]

Generally, no party can force another to stipulate even if the parties agree on an issue. In a 2005 case, the prosecution wanted a defendant at a sentencing proceeding to stipulate concerning his prior convictions. The defendant's conviction records had somehow been destroyed. The defendant knew about his prior offenses and the prosecution had a sentencing worksheet concerning the prior offenses but that evidence was insufficient to prove the earlier criminal convictions. Because the sentencing judge allowed the insufficient record of past convictions, the reviewing court sent the case back for a resentencing proceeding. Even though there was no serious doubt that both parties knew the truth concerning the defendant's past record, the defendant could not be forced to agree to the stipulation.[221]

A stipulation regarding a fact authorizes the court to find the existence of such a fact and to consider that fact without any further proof. A judge does not have to allow the stipulation when the stipulation would create a potential for unfair prejudice to one party. The triers of fact are not, however, bound to accept the stipulated fact as true; they may find to the contrary if persuaded by other evidence or for any reason at all in a criminal case.

---

[218] People v. Wagoner, 2002 Cal. App. Unpub. LEXIS 1169 (Cal. 2002), quoting Palmer v. City of Long Beach, 33 Cal. 2d 134, 199 P.2d 952 (1948).

[219] CALJIC 1.02, California Jury Instructions (West Group 2005).

[220] State v. Newman, 208 Ariz. 507, 95 P.3d 950, 2004 Ariz. App. LEXIS 118 (2004).

[221] State v. English, 171 N.C. App. 277, 614 S.E.2d 405, 407, 408, 2005 N.C. App. LEXIS 1211 (N.C. 2005).

Stipulated testimony merely amounts to a mutual agreement by both parties that if a certain person were present, he or she would testify under oath to the facts contained within the agreed stipulation. In the case of *Barnes v. State*, a Maryland court held that when evidence is offered by way of "stipulation," the parties do not necessarily agree to the facts that the evidence seeks to establish, but that the stipulation goes only to the content of the testimony of a particular witness if he or she were to appear and testify.[222] However, once a stipulation is agreed upon, as a general rule, the stipulation may not be withdrawn without the consent of both parties and the judge or for cause, such as fraud, mistake, or undue influence.[223] Demonstrative of this principle is a Texas murder case in which a defendant entered a written stipulation at his first trial that he had stabbed and killed his wife, among other facts. When, the trial court declared a mistrial, an issue for the second murder trial involved whether the stipulation from the first trial should be binding on the defendant for the second trial on the same issues. The trial judge admitted the stipulation at the second trial, noting that it had originally been made for trial and it would be admitted as a valid stipulation. On appeal, the reviewing court upheld the trial court decision that admitted the stipulation at the second trial,[224] noting that the defendant had placed no limitation on its use and the stipulation had never been withdrawn. In contrast, in a North Carolina case, the court was presented with the question of whether a stipulation entered into by the prosecutor at the defendant's first sentencing hearing could bind the state at the resentencing proceedings.[225] The reviewing court decided that the prosecutor was not bound by the original stipulation because circumstances had changed and the prosecutor had evidence that had not been possessed at the original sentencing proceeding and had the evidence been possessed originally, the prosecutor would not have entered into the stipulation.

While the courts have indicated that stipulations should be encouraged, it is error for the trial court to require one of the parties to a lawsuit to stipulate with his or her adversary.[226] In the Tennessee case of *State v. Ford*, the reviewing court decided that the trial court had erred in requiring a motorist to stipulate to the use of the court's summary of a defense witness's testimony rather than allowing the witness's live testimony, when both the motorist and the state objected to the stipulation. The reviewing court noted that the trial court has neither the duty nor function to require one of the parties to a lawsuit to stipulate with his adversary. However, a court in a different jurisdiction held that sometimes a party may be required to stipulate. In a case involving a felon who possessed a gun under a disability and who was charged with aggravated assault, the defendant offered to stipulate that he was not permitted to possess firearms due to his prior felony conviction. The prosecution refused because

[222] Barnes v. State, 354 A.2d 499 (Md. 1976).
[223] Harlan v. Harlan, 544 N.E.2d 553 (Ind. 1989).
[224] Carrasco v. State, 154 S.W.3d 127, 128, 2005 Tex. Crim. App. LEXIS 76 (2005).
[225] State v. Adams, 490 S.E.2d 220 (N.C. 1997).
[226] State v. Ford, 725 S.W.2d 689 (Tenn. 1986).

it wanted to introduce evidence of his prior aggravated assault convictions rather than allow the defendant to merely admit that he was a felon. The reviewing court reversed the conviction because the facts underlying the prior felony proved to be unduly prejudicial when the probative value was considered and where the defendant admitted to being a felon.[227] The rule seems to be that where an element of a crime requires proof of a prior felony and the defendant offers to stipulate to the felony, a prosecutor may be forced to agree to a stipulation of the felony where some prejudice to the defendant's case might otherwise result.

A stipulation is also used as a means of determining whether certain evidence will be admitted into court. In criminal cases in which the parties have stipulated to the admissibility of certain evidence, that evidence is admissible to corroborate other evidence of the defendant's participation in the crime charged. In the absence of any claim that the stipulation was entered into by mistake, inadvertence, fraud, or misrepresentation, counsel may stipulate regarding evidence that may be received. As a general rule, once a stipulation has been accepted by a trial court the parties will not be permitted to withdraw a stipulation unless the withdrawing party offers a strong reason demonstrating that the original matter stipulated is not true. Many courts also require that the application for withdrawal be made in a timely manner.[228]

There are limitations on the use of stipulations. It is clear that a stipulation amounting to a complete concession by the defense to the prosecutor's case would be inconsistent with a plea of not guilty and should not be permitted. A stipulation that is clearly erroneous should not be accepted, and its acceptance probably would be justification for reversal on constitutional grounds. Also, the court is not required to admit a stipulation as a substitute for evidence that may be detrimental to the defendant's case.[229].

It is obvious that stipulations can have adverse effects on the prosecutor's case or the defendant's case. For example, where a stipulation was read to the jury and established that the defendant had tested negative for the herpes virus while the rape victim had tested positive, sufficiently supported the defendant's theory that he could not have transmitted the herpes virus to the victim; therefore, it was within the trial court's discretion to disallow further inquiry into the rape victim's past sexual conduct.[230]

As a general rule, a stipulation may be withdrawn, but doing so generally requires the trial court's consent. Once withdrawn, a stipulation ceases to be effective for any purpose. The withdrawal of a stipulation, however, would be a reasonable basis for a continuance in order for the opposing party to have time to prepare evidence concerning matters formerly embraced by the stipulation and avoid undue surprise.

---

[227]   Ferguson v. State, 2005 Ark. LEXIS 361 (Ark. 2005).
[228]   People v. Calvert, 326 Ill. App. 3d 414, 760 N.E.2d 1024 (Ill. 2001).
[229]   United States v. Grassi, 602 F.2d 1192 (5th Cir. 1979).
[230]   State v. Vatars, 123 N.M. 446, 942 P.2d 189 (1997).

§ 6.19 —Polygraph Tests

An example of the use of a stipulation occurs when the parties agree to the admission of the results of a polygraph examination. Although it is generally held that polygraph tests are not judicially acceptable because of their unreliability and possible dangers of unfair prejudice, some jurisdictions make an exception when there is a stipulation by both parties; then the results of the test may be admitted. Courts from many jurisdictions have found a valid exception for the admissibility of stipulated polygraph test results.[231]

A majority of jurisdictions hold that polygraph evidence is inadmissible per se. Representative of the majority view, Louisiana holds that polygraph evidence is not admissible in either a civil or criminal trial because of the decisive nature of the evidence and the danger that the trier of fact might give too much weight to the evidence.[232] An Illinois appellate court reversed a conviction for first-degree murder on the ground that prejudicial error occurred when the trial judge permitted the prosecution, during its case-in-chief, to mention that the defendant had been driven by police to take a polygraph examination. During the drive to the polygraph testing location, when she feared that the test results would prove her undoing, the defendant made some inculpatory statements to the officer. The results of the test or if she ever took it were not admitted; the facts surrounding the defendant's ride to the testing location and what she stated were admitted at the trial. The general rule in Illinois is that evidence regarding polygraph examinations and their results are not admissible because of concerns about reliability, questions about whether the test will determine guilt or innocence, and problems with the prejudicial value of the evidence outweighing the probative value. In reversing the conviction, the reviewing court noted, "The State's suggestion of reliability of the defendant's statement based on her anticipated failure of the polygraph test is an improper purpose for the admission of polygraph evidence."[233]

A substantial minority of courts admit polygraph evidence upon stipulation of the parties.[234] For example, the Arkansas code prohibits the admission of polygraph examination evidence,[235] but case law allows an exception where both parties stipulate to the admissibility of the polygraph results in writing.[236] Georgia generally prohibits the admission of polygraph evidence but recognizes some exceptions. Where the parties stipulate to admission or where the evidence explains a defendant's conduct or motive, polygraph evidence may

---

[231] State v. Chambers, 451 P.2d 27 (Ariz. 1969); State v. McNamara, 252 Iowa 19, 104 N.W.2d 568 (1960); Herman v. Eagle Star Ins. Co., 283 F. Supp. 33 (C.D. Cal. 1966).

[232] Cook v. State, 928 So. 2d 589; 2006 La. App. LEXIS 242 (La. 2006).

[233] People v. Washington, 363 Ill. App. 3d 13, 20, 842 N.E.2d 1193, 1199, 2006 Ill. App. LEXIS 24 (Ill. 2006).

[234] For a list of states following the per se exclusion rule and another list of states following the court admission upon stipulation rule, *see* Giannelli, *Forensic Science: Polygraph Evidence: Part II*, 30 CRIM. L. BULL. 366 (1994). *See also* § 15.5 for a discussion of the use of the results of polygraph examinations.

[235] A.C.A. § 12-12-704 (2006).

[236] Rollins v. State, 2005 Ark. LEXIS 293 (Ark. 2005), quoting Ramaker v. State, 345 Ark. 225, 234, 46 S.W.3d 519, 525, 2001 Ark. LEXIS 352 (2001).

be allowed at the judge's discretion. In one Georgia murder case, the defendant signed a stipulation allowing admission of the results prior to taking the examination. She knew that a failed exam could be used against her and her attorney had so advised. The polygraph had the effect of corroborating her boyfriend's account of the murder that strengthened the evidence supporting her conviction. The Supreme Court of Georgia affirmed her murder conviction.[237] Some states have statutes that provide for the admissibility of polygraph results by stipulation, while others accomplish this result by court decision.

The California Code provides that:

> Notwithstanding any other provision of law, the result of a polygraph examination, the opinion of a polygraph examiner, or any reference to offer to take, failure to take, or taking of a polygraph examination shall not be admitted into evidence in any criminal proceeding unless all parties stipulate to the admission of such results.[238]

A California court held that this stipulation statute, which requires all parties to consent, does not violate the defendant's constitutional rights.[239] The defendant alleged that the statute violated her due process right to introduce relevant evidence, including the results of a polygraph. The Supreme Court of California rejected her offer to introduce evidence proving the reliability of the polygraph that, if proven, would call into question the constitutionality of the California law making polygraph evidence inadmissible.

When a judge allows evidence of the results of polygraph testing, the jury should be instructed that it is for them to determine what corroborative weight and effect such testimony should be given.[240]

§ 6.20 Summary

To save the time of the court and to achieve results that the courts and legislatures have determined are necessary in the administration of justice, presumptions and inferences are utilized. The presumption takes the place of evidence in certain instances and, until facts that overcome the presumption are shown, the presumptive facts are accepted as true.

Presumptions are classified as rebuttable presumptions and conclusive presumptions. A rebuttable presumption may be overcome by evidence to the contrary; a conclusive presumption cannot be rebutted.

---

[237] Thornton v. State, 279 Ga. 676; 620 S.E.2d 356; 2005 Ga. LEXIS 634 (Ga. 2005).
[238] Cal. Evid. Code § 351.1 (2006).
[239] People v. Wilkinson, 33 Cal. 4th 821; 94 P.3d 551; 16 Cal. Rptr. 3d 420; 2004 Cal. LEXIS 6833 (Ca. 2004), *cert. denied*, 543 U.S. 1064, 2005 U.S. LEXIS 59 (2005).
[240] State v. Souel, 372 N.E.2d 1318 (Ohio 1978).

There are many specific examples of both rebuttable and conclusive presumptions. Presumptions are used sparingly in criminal cases and are looked at very carefully by reviewing courts to determine whether they place an unreasonable burden on the accused. Some of the specific presumptions that are prevalent in criminal cases are: the presumption that a person is innocent until proven guilty beyond a reasonable doubt; the presumption that a person is sane; the presumption that a person in possession of recently stolen property knows that the property was stolen; and the presumption that all people know the general public laws of the state and country in which they reside.

Legislative bodies are not without controls when determining what presumptions are effective in law. The due process clauses of the Fifth and Fourteenth Amendments set limits upon legislatures when making proof of one fact or a group of facts serve as proof of a deduced or presumed fact. There is the danger that a presumption may subtly shift the burden of proof in an unconstitutional manner. Particularly in recent years, statutory presumptions have been subject to review on the grounds that they are unconstitutional. A presumption that wass arbitrary, irrational, or shifted the burden of proof would violate the due process clauses of the Constitution.

Another means of relieving the parties of the necessity of introducing evidence is the use of the stipulation. The stipulation, which should be used more often by the courts, indicates that the parties are willing to agree to the truth of certain allegations, leaving only the truly disputed facts to be determined by the jury or court.

It is a mistake for those involved in the criminal justice process to rely heavily on presumptions. Countervailing evidence may be offered when the presumption is in favor of the prosecution, and the prosecution must be prepared to reinforce the presumption. Also, the prosecution must be prepared to rebut presumptions that are favorable to the defense.

Although stipulations are excellent ways of assuring judicial economy, their improper use can lead to acquittal of guilty individuals and retrials for some. Many prosecutors have gone to trial unprepared because of misinterpretation of the effect of a stipulation. To avoid this pitfall, the investigator and prosecutor should be prepared with admissible evidence in the event that the opposing party disputes the fact that a stipulation was made, or if mistake or fraud is claimed.

General Admissibility
Tests

Relevancy and Materiality   7

There is a principle—not so much a rule of evidence as a presupposition involved in the very conception of a rational system, as contrasted with the old formal and mechanical systems—which forbids receiving anything irrelevant, not logically probative. . . . The two leading principles should be brought into conspicuous relief, (1) that nothing is to be received which is not logically probative of some matter requiring to be proved; and (2) that everything which is thus probative should come in, unless a clear ground of policy or law excludes it.

THAYER, EVIDENCE (1898)

Chapter Outline

Key Terms and Concepts

exculpatory circumstances   motive
incriminating circumstances   relevancy
materiality   unfair prejudice

§ 7.1 Introduction

This chapter and Chapter 8 focus on general admissibility tests (relevancy, materiality, and competency) for evidence that are applied by the courts when considering whether to admit or exclude evidence. This chapter concerns the concepts of general relevancy and materiality and their effect on admission and exclusion of evidence, while Chapter 8 explains competency of evidence and witnesses.

Because the primary objective and purpose in a criminal trial is to determine the truth regarding the issues presented, the general rule considers all evidence admissible unless, upon proper objection, it is subject to exclusion under the established evidence rules. The usual procedure followed in making a general objection to the evidence is for the attorney to object on the grounds that the evidence is irrelevant, immaterial, and incompetent. Better practice suggests that the objecting party offer a specific objection such as a hearsay objection, an objection to a compound question, or an objection that a question assumes facts not yet in evidence, so that the judge has a clear basis for making a ruling. Unless the reason for the objection is obvious from the context, the judge may ask that the challenger offer a reason and explain the claim that the evidence should be excluded from trial consideration.

For those involved in the criminal justice process, it is important to understand these relevancy and materiality rules. In many instances, evidence that has been laboriously obtained and prepared for introduction is excluded because it does not meet the relevancy and materiality tests.

§ 7.2   Relevancy and Materiality Defined

Rule 401

Definition of "Relevant Evidence"

"Relevant evidence" means evidence having any tendency to make the existence of any fact that is of consequence to the determination of the action more probable or less probable than it would be without the evidence."[1]

Lawyers and judges frequently treat the terms *relevant* and *material*—and particularly their opposites, *irrelevant* and *immaterial*—as interchangeable. Although *relevant* is a broad term that is often used to mean both relevant and material, the distinction between the two concepts is significant. Federal Rule of Evidence 401 does not mention materiality or consider the concept.

Another way to consider the concept of relevancy involves dividing it into two separate concepts: logical relevancy and legal relevancy. "To be admissible, logically relevant evidence also must be legally relevant."[2] An item of evidence may meet the logical relevancy test if it sways the trier of fact in any direction concerning the existence or nonexistence of any important fact. Despite having the tendency to prove or disprove a fact, a logically relevant item of evidence may be excluded where it lacks legal relevancy. For example, a gruesome color photograph might be logically relevant because it proves death, but where the fact of death has not been disputed, the introduction of the photograph may be excluded because it may have the tendency to inflame the jury and cause the jury to render a decision based on emotion rather than logic. Thus, the photograph can be classified as logically relevant because it proves death, but can be excluded as legally irrelevant because the photograph presents the unfair danger of inflaming the jury.

As one Connecticut court explained the relationship between logical and legal relevancy:

> It is not logical relevance alone, however, that secures the admission of evidence. Logically relevant evidence must also be legally relevant . . . that is, not subject to exclusion for any one of the following prejudicial effects: (1) where the facts offered may unduly arouse the jury's emotions, hostility or sympathy, (2) where the proof and answering evidence it provokes may create a side issue that will unduly distract the jury from the main issues, (3) where the evidence offered and the counterproof will consume an undue amount of time, and (4) where the defendant, having no reasonable ground to anticipate the evidence, is unfairly surprised and unprepared to meet it.[3]

---

[1]   FED. R. EVID. 401.

[2]   Missouri v. Kennedy, 2003 Mo. App. LEXIS 265 (2003).

[3]   Connecticut v. Crnkovic, 68 Conn. App. 757, 793 A.2d 1139, 2002 Conn. App. LEXIS 159 (2002), quoting Connecticut v. Joly, 219 Conn. 234, 593 A.2d 96 (1991).

As a general rule, logically relevant evidence may be excluded by a judge as legally irrelevant where the probative value is substantially outweighed by the danger of unfair prejudice, confusion of the issues, or misleading the jury, or by considerations of undue delay, waste of time, or needless presentation of cumulative evidence.

A. Relevant Evidence

Black's Law Dictionary defines relevant evidence as "[e]vidence tending to prove or disprove a matter in issue."[4]

Relevant evidence has also been described as "evidence that in some degree advances the inquiry, and thus has probative value and is prima facie admissible."[5]

In *Corpus Juris Secundum*, logical relevancy is defined as "the existence of such a relationship in logic between the fact of which evidence is offered and a fact in issue that the existence of the former renders probable or improbable the existence of the latter."[6]

A simpler definition from a Georgia case is: "Relevancy is a logical relationship between evidence and a fact in issue or to be established."[7]

Other definitions include:

- Evidence that is "relevant" will, by definition "prejudice" the other side.[8]

- Testimony is "relevant" if a reasonable inference can be drawn therefrom regarding, or if any light is shed upon, a contested matter.[9]

- Real evidence is relevant if it sheds any light on the circumstances.[10]

- Relevant evidence is evidence having any tendency in reason to prove any material fact.[11]

One court determined that where a defendant missed a pretrial hearing and went from Texas to Mexico, the prosecution was correct in introducing evidence of her flight as showing a consciousness of guilt. To prove relevancy, the prosecution had to demonstrate that her flight had some connection to the offense being prosecuted. To avoid evidence of flight being considered relevant, the defendant had to show that her flight was in relation to some other transaction or motivation. Relevancy was established due to evidence that the defendant had no intention of returning from Mexico to face a murder charge.[12] In a different case, discussing the definition of relevancy, the Court

---

[4]   BLACK'S LAW DICTIONARY (8th ed. 2004).
[5]   McCORMICK, LAW OF EVIDENCE 319.
[6]   31A C.J.S. *Evidence* § 198 (1996).
[7]   Continental Trust Co. v. Bank of Harrison, 36 Ga. App. 149, 136 S.E. 319 (1926).
[8]   United States v. Kapp, 2003 U.S. Dist. LEXIS 4178 (N.D. Ill. 2003).
[9]   State v. Smith, 5 Wash. App. 237, 487 P.2d 277 (1971).
[10] State v. Jones, 56 N.C. App. 259, 289 S.E.2d 383 (1982).
[11] Kansas Annotated Statutes, K.S.A. § 60-401 (2006).
[12] Villegas v. State, 2004 Tex. App. LEXIS 308 (2004).

of Appeals for the Ninth Circuit held that the trial court had allowed irrelevant evidence to be admitted against a defendant in a case in which the defendant had been charged with interstate travel to have sexual relations with a minor. A police detective had been chatting with the defendant in an Internet chat room and the defendant agreed to meet the "police officer/child" in Las Vegas. The police arrested the defendant and discovered numerous stories of adults having sex with children, especially incest, on the defendant's PDA (personal digital assistant). The trial court admitted five of these stories against the defendant. On appeal, the Ninth Circuit held that the sex stories on the PDA were not relevant because the stories were not inextricably linked to the charged crimes and the stories were not part of the activity that led to the defendant's arrest.[13]

A trial court's decision concerning logical relevancy, and consequently admissibility or exclusion based on legal relevancy, falls under judicial discretion. The decision to admit or exclude evidence will not be disturbed on appeal absent proof of an abuse of judicial discretion. In a child sex abuse case, a trial judge admitted evidence that explicit photographs, sexual devices, and pornographic videos were found in the home that the defendant shared with his current girlfriend. The alleged sex abuse occurred six years earlier when the defendant was married to the complaining witnesses' mother. On appeal, the defendant contended that the recent photographs, sexual toys, and pornographic videos should not have been admitted because they were irrelevant to any issue in a six-year-old child abuse case. In reversing the conviction, the appellate court noted that "[t]he evidence of items seized six years after the alleged abuse ended and not connected to the alleged abuse through testimony or otherwise at trial is irrelevant to issues of abuse occurring between 1991 and 1997. The district court abused its discretion in admitting the photographs into evidence."[14] The evidence could have been excluded on the ground that there was absolutely no logical relevancy (no connection) that existed between alleged abuse and explicit photographs, sexual devices and pornographic videos found years later in a different house.

B. Material Evidence

Black's Law Dictionary defines material evidence as "[e]vidence having some logical connection with the facts of consequence or the issues."[15] Evidence that does not have a clear relationship to a matter at issue is immaterial.

Materiality concerns the importance of evidence. Evidence is material only when it significantly affects the matter or issue in a case. As one court noted, "[t]he concept of materiality does not relate to the weight of evidence. Rather, it involves the relationship between the proposition that the evidence is offered to prove the issues in the case.[16] The concept boils down to this ques-

---

[13]   United States v. Curtin, 443 F.3d 1084, 1093, 2006 U.S. App. LEXIS 8071 (9th Cir. 2006).

[14]   *See* State v. Zuke, 2006 Iowa App. LEXIS 161 (Iowa 2006).

[15]   BLACK'S LAW DICTIONARY (8th ed. 2004).

[16]   In re Estate of Bean, 2005 Tenn. App. LEXIS 754 (Tenn. 2005).

tion: Would the evidence offer a substantially important fact in this case to prove or disprove a charge against the defendant without being unfairly prejudicial to the defendant?

In describing material evidence, courts have noted that:

- "Material evidence" is that which is relevant and goes to substantial matters in dispute, or has legitimate and effective influence or bearing on the decision of the case.[17]

- For purposes of a motion for a new trial based upon newly discovered evidence, "material evidence" is evidence that is relevant and goes to the substantial matters in dispute or has a legitimate and effective influence or bearing on the decision of the case.[18]

- Material evidence may include evidence that is wholly impeaching if the result of the proceeding would have been different had the evidence been disclosed.[19]

Material evidence that would otherwise be considered relevant may lose its probative value when it becomes too far removed from the event in question. For example, the fact that a testifying defendant had a poor reputation for truthfulness 25 years ago may be excluded as not having any current probative value concerning his present reputation for honesty. However, the determination of remoteness is a matter within the discretion of the trial court.[20]

C. *Materiality and Relevancy Distinguished*

In one case, the court distinguished between materiality and relevancy by stating, "As used with respect to evidence, 'material' has a wholly different meaning from 'relevant.' To be relevant means to relate to the issue. To be material means to have probative weight, that is, reasonably likely to influence the tribunal in making the determination required to be made"[21] without creating undue prejudice to either party.

Although evidence may be relevant, it is not necessarily material.[22] If a proposition of fact is not required to be proved under applicable rules of substantive law governing a case, that evidence is not material under Rule 401 and should be excluded from admission to evidence. Thus, any evidence introduced solely to prove or disprove a relatively inconsequential fact, directly or indirectly, is irrelevant and should be excluded.[23] Although evidence may be

---

[17]   Hill v. State, 159 Ga. App. 489, 283 S.E.2d 703 (1981).

[18]   United States v. Riggs, 495 F. Supp. 1085 (M.D. Fla. 1980).

[19]   State v. Macdonald, 122 Wash. App. 804, 810, 95 P.3d 1248, 1251, 2004 Wash. App. LEXIS 1859 (Wash. 2004).

[20]   State v. Glenn, 492 S.E.2d 393 (S.C. 1997).

[21]   Weinstock v. United States, 231 F.2d 699 (D.C. Cir. 1956).

[22]   Another way to say the same thing is to say that an item of evidence may be logically relevant but not legally relevant.

[23]   Blue Cross & Blue Shield v. Phillip Morris, Inc., 138 F. Supp. 357, 2001 U.S. Dist. LEXIS 4837 (E.D.N.Y. 2001).

relevant because it relates to or has some bearing on the case, it may have such slight relevancy as to be immaterial.

In making these fine distinctions between relevancy and materiality, it is important to note that in actual practice the distinction is not always clear and in most cases whether evidence is characterized as irrelevant or immaterial makes little difference in effect.[24]

§ 7.3 Admissibility of Relevant Evidence

Rule 402

Relevant Evidence Generally Admissible; Irrelevant Evidence Inadmissible

All relevant evidence is admissible, except as otherwise provided by the Constitution of the United States, by Act of Congress, by these rules, or by other rules prescribed by the Supreme Court pursuant to statutory authority. Evidence which is not relevant is not admissible.[25]

The general rule that all relevant evidence is admissible has a variety of exceptions. If the evidence logically bears on any point in issue, it should be admitted to help the finder of fact determine what took place. If the evidentiary proposition advanced by either party tends to prove or disprove a proposition at issue, then the evidence is normally considered logically relevant and should be admitted. However, if the evidence does not logically assist the jury or judge in determining an important fact at issue or creates the risk of confusion of issues or of facts or wastes time, the judge should exclude the evidence from consideration as irrelevant.

Unless the constitution of the federal or a state government, a statute, or a rule of law excludes evidence for a specific reason, all relevant evidence is admissible.[26] If an objection is made to the admissibility of relevant evidence, the burden is on the party making the objection to show the reason for the exclusion.[27]

When a court reviews an alleged erroneous admission of evidence by a trial judge, the appellate court considers whether the trial judge abused his or her discretion in allowing the evidence.[28] A federal reviewing court cautioned that the trial judge is in a superior position to weigh the true potency of proffered evidence and, because his or her decision is made in the rapid-fire tempo

---

[24]   Holmes v. State, 40 Ala. App. 251, 112 So. 2d 511 (1959).
[25]   FED. R. EVID. 402.
[26]   Clem v. Arkansas, 351 Ark. 112, 121, 90 S.W.3d 428, 432 (2002).
[27]   United States v. D.K.G., 630 F. Supp 1540 (E.D. Tex.), aff'd, 828 F.2d 532 (5th Cir.), *cert. denied*, 485 U.S. 976, 108 S. Ct. 1270, 99 L. Ed. 2d 481 (1986).
[28]   People v. Szymanski, 2005 Mich. App. LEXIS 650 (Mich. 2005).

of trial, it ought not to be judged too harshly with the advantage of hindsight.[29] The reviewing court agreed that a decision as to relevancy should stand unless there is clear evidence of abuse of judicial discretion or plain error.

The Federal Rules of Evidence make clear that evidence should be admitted unless a specific rule forbids the admission of the evidence. The wording of Federal Rule 402 has been adopted by many states in formulating their own rules. Some states have adopted the rule with modifications. For example, the Iowa Code provides that "[a]ll relevant evidence is admissible, except as otherwise provided by the Constitution of the United States or the State of Iowa, by statute, by these rules, or other rules of the Iowa Supreme Court. Evidence which is not relevant is not admissible."[30]

When interpreting federal evidence provisions, recent decisions of federal courts have followed the reasoning that all evidence should be admissible unless it comes within one of the specific exceptions. In a federal prosecution for murder and use of a firearm while involved in a drug conspiracy, the defendants objected that guns found at their residence, none of which was the murder weapon, had been improperly admitted against them, causing unfair prejudice. Although they argued that there was not a sufficient connection between the charged crimes and guns at the home, the court held that possession of guns was admissible because gun possession was an element of one of the charges and possession was part of the alleged overt act needed to be proved for the drug conspiracy charge.[31] Evidence that helps establish elements of the crime or a defense is generally considered relevant and admissible. Following similar logic, where the prosecutor desired to prove that a defendant had possession of illegal document-making equipment, which included a personal computer, the judge properly excluded defendant's proffered evidence of other lawful uses for which a computer and its software may be used. What other people did with personal computers had no proper relevancy to the uses that the defendant made of his personal computer.[32] In contrast, where evidence might not initially seem relevant, because not directly connected to the case, a judge may properly admit the evidence. In a prosecution for possession of a firearm by a felon, when the defendant stated that he thought a .30 caliber rifle was a .177 caliber BB gun, the judge properly allowed the prosecutor to introduce BB gun ammunition and .30 caliber ammunition for the jury's inspection even though none of the ammunition had been taken from the defendant. In deciding that the ammunition had relevance, the court believed that the contrast in ammunition styles would make it more likely that the defendant's assertion that he thought the gun was a BB gun was not a truthful statement.[33]

---

[29]   United States v. Johnson, 585 F.2d 119 (5th Cir. 1978). *See also* United States v. Rubin, 37 F.3d 49 (2d Cir. 1994).

[30]   IOWA R. EVID. 5.402 (2005).

[31]   United States v. Smallwood, 306 F. Supp. 582 (E.D. Va. 2004).

[32]   United States v. Cabrera, 208 F.3d 309, 2000 U.S. App. LEXIS 6226 (1st Cir. 2000).

[33]   Unites States v. Scott, 267 F.3d 729 (7th Cir. 2001).

§ 7.4 Reasons for Exclusion of Relevant and Material Evidence

---

Rule 403

Exclusion of Relevant Evidence on Grounds of Prejudice, Confusion, or Waste of Time

Although relevant, evidence may be excluded if its probative value is substantially outweighed by the danger of unfair prejudice, confusion of the issues, or misleading the jury, or by considerations of undue delay, waste of time, or needless presentation of cumulative evidence.[34]

Although relevant evidence is generally admissible, there are some rules of exclusion. Evidence that may be described as logically relevant may be excluded as legally irrelevant when there is the danger of unfair prejudice, the admission of the evidence could confuse the issues being litigated, the jury could become confused by the evidence, or the presentation of the evidence would be unduly time-consuming or constitute a waste of time. The Federal Rules of Evidence enumerate and codify some of these exclusions, but the practitioner must look to the cases for explanations that apply to specific fact situations. Some of the reasons for excluding relevant evidence are discussed here.

A. The Probative Value is Substantially Outweighed by the Danger of Unfair Prejudice

Probative value refers to the tendency of an item of evidence to help prove or disprove a disputed fact, issue, or position. Where the probative value of the evidence is slight and the danger of unfair prejudice is great, the judge, upon proper objection, may refuse to allow the admission of the evidence. Such exclusion of evidence based on prejudice does not apply to a bench trial because a judge would have to hear the evidence in order to rule on the objection in the first place.[35] Relevance alone does not require that evidence be admitted; even relevant evidence must be excluded if it will confuse the issue, mislead the jury, waste time, or cause delay, or if its probative value is substantially outweighed by the danger of unfair prejudice.[36] The crucial aspect of evaluating prejudice involves "undue prejudice," because most relevant evidence offered by one party is designed to harm the merits of the opposing side's case. Under Rule 403, concern is directed only at prejudice that is unfair

---

[34] FED. R. EVID. 403.

[35] Schultz v. Butcher, 24 F.3d 626 (4th Cir. 1994); The alleged prejudicial admission of evidence in a bench trial seldom produces sufficient grounds for reversing a verdict because presumably the trial judge can mentally exclude improper inferences from his or her analysis of the evidence. *See* Bic Corporation v. Far Eastern, 23 Fed. Appx. 36, 2001 U.S. App. LEXIS 22416 (2d Cir. 2001).

[36] United States v. Johnson, 904 F. Supp. 1303 (M.D. Ala. 1995).

under the circumstances.[37] The concept of "undue prejudice" "applies to evidence which uniquely tends to evoke an emotional bias against the defendant as an individual and which has very little effect on the issues."[38]

In one Tennessee murder case, the trial court committed error when it permitted gruesome photographs of the deceased to be admitted at the capital sentencing proceeding for the purpose of demonstrating the presence of an aggravating factor. The reviewing court noted that the photographs were extremely unpleasant and gruesome in varying degrees in that they depicted the victim's body in a state of decomposition. The court held that the prejudicial value of the photographs outweighed the probative effect, but it did not overturn the sentence. The reviewing court viewed the photographic evidence as harmless error that did not affect the judgment of the jury because it did not sentence the defendant to death.[39] In another case, involving prosecution for possession of sexually explicit photographs of minors, the trial court erred in admitting two sexually explicit violent narratives involving rape and torture found on the defendant's computer. The probative value of the explicit literary narratives was outweighed by prejudicial effect because the defendant had been charged with possession of child pornography found on his computer; however, the porn pictures did not involve violence, but had illegal sexual content only.[40] In the Tennessee murder case and the child pornography case, the evidence was arguably logically relevant to each prosecution, but the unfair harm to each defendant's case outweighed the effect that the evidence could have presented.

In interpreting the unfair prejudice portion of Ohio Rule of Evidence 403, an Ohio court of appeals approved a trial judge's decision to admit evidence of the defendant's prior rape and murder conviction of his wife at his trial for conspiracy to commit murder of his wife's sister. Normally, a defendant's prior criminal acts would not be logically relevant to proof of a new crime or, if the prior acts were considered logically relevant, the prejudicial value would exclude the evidence. Allegedly, the defendant, who was in prison, wanted his wife's sister murdered in the exact same way that he had previously killed his wife, so that it would look as if he were not guilty of his wife's death. The trial judge admitted the prior crime evidence to show the defendant's motive and plan for engaging in the conspiracy to have the sister murdered. The reviewing court upheld allowing the prior crime evidence because it held that the probative value to help prove the conspiracy outweighed any unfair prejudicial effect on the defendant's case.[41] In a prosecution for aiding and abetting the distribution of crack cocaine, evidence of other related crimes was admitted after the judge conducted an on-the-record review of the case law, evaluated the probative value of the evidence, and weighed the potential prejudice to the defendant. A second federal court, in interpreting this provision, explained

---

[37]   United States v. Bennafield, 287 F.3d 320, 202 U.S. App. LEXIS 8009 (4th Cir. 2002), *cert. denied*, United States v. Bennafield, 537 U.S. 961, 2002 LEXIS 7487 (2002).

[38]   People v. Cotton, 2002 Cal. App. Unpub. LEXIS 421 (2002).

[39]   State v. Banks, 2004 Tenn. Crim. App. LEXIS 793 (2004).

[40]   United States v. Grimes, 244 F.3d 375 (5th Cir. 2001).

[41]   State v. Bloomfield, 2004 Ohio 749, 2004 Ohio App. LEXIS 692 (2004).

that in the context of the balancing test for exclusion of evidence whose probative value is outweighed by its prejudicial effect, "unfair prejudice" means the undue tendency to suggest a decision on an improper basis.[42]

Unfair prejudice, which may justify exclusion of otherwise probative evidence, speaks to the capacity of some concededly relevant evidence to lure the fact-finder into declaring guilt on different grounds from proofs specific to the offense charged. The critical issue is the degree of unfairness of the prejudicial evidence and whether it tends to support a decision on an improper basis.[43] In the federal prosecution of a leader of the Outlaws motorcycle gang, the government managed, over the defendant's objection, to have portions of the gang's constitution shown to the jury. The Outlaws' constitution mentioned that membership was open only to white men, an irrelevant fact that the defendant believed would create an unfair prejudice to his case in the minds of the jury. The federal court of appeals held that the probative value of allowing the jury to see racism of the gang's policies did not outweigh the clear danger of unfair prejudice. Despite the error, the conviction was not reversed, because under the circumstances of the case, the error was held to have been harmless.[44]

While the trial judge has broad authority in weighing the testimony's probative value against the possible prejudicial effect, his or her determination is subject to review by an appeals court. For example, the Ninth Circuit Court of Appeals held that where the evidence possesses very slight, if any, probative value, it is an abuse of discretion to admit it if there is even a modest likelihood of unfair prejudice or small risk of misleading the jury.[45]

B. Introduction of the Evidence Would Confuse the Issues

The right of a defendant to introduce relevant evidence favorable to himself that is logically relevant has been clearly established but it is not without any limit and may be restricted or curtailed where the evidence would detract from the main issues of the case.[46] Where collateral or confusing evidence may introduce unimportant side issues in a criminal case, that evidence may be excluded from a jury trial at the discretion of the court. However, an objection on the ground that evidence would be confusing would not normally be offered in a bench trial because the implication would be that the attorney seeks to prevent the judge from becoming confused, a suggestion that would not help the client's case.[47] Evidence of prior crimes by the accused is often inadmissible even though material and logically relevant because such evidence would tend to confuse the issues by bringing up an earlier case. In our

[42] United States v. Sills, 120 F.3d 917 (8th Cir. 1997).
[43] United States v. Payne, 119 F.3d 637 (8th Cir. 1997).
[44] United States v. Bowman, 302 F.2d 1228, 1239, 1240, 2002 U.S. App. LEXIS 17165 (2002).
[45] United States v. Hitt, 981 F.2d 422 (9th Cir. 1992).
[46] Clark v. Arizona, ___ U.S. ___, 2006 U.S. LEXIS 5184 (2006).
[47] People v. Rogelio, 2005 Cal. Unpub. LEXIS (Cal. 2005), in which the court noted, "The trial court observed that in a bench trial, factors such as the inflammatory nature of the crime, confusion of the issues, and the consumption of time involved in addressing the prior offenses were less significant than they would have been in a jury trial."

system of trial by jury, the courts have attempted to ensure that the evidence introduced does not distract the jury from the case being tried or to lure the jury to find guilt for the wrong reason. Under this rationale, some evidence, although relevant, is excluded.[48]

When considering the "confusion of the issues" provision of Rule 403 in a prosecution involving conspiracy to possess a large quantity of hashish found in the trunk of a vehicle, a trial court properly excluded evidence of small amounts of marijuana and hashish found in the interior ashtray of the defendant's automobile. Because the prosecutor failed to demonstrate that the marijuana and hashish inside the car were connected to the contraband in the trunk, introduction of the interior drugs might have had the tendency to confuse the jury concerning the primary issue in the case.[49] In a different case, in which the defendant attempted to point the blame at another person, judicial exclusion of evidence indicating that the third party had "failed" a polygraph test was not an abuse of discretion. The trial court voiced concern about the examiner's inability to conclusively provide accuracy rates for the polygraph examinations he had previously conducted. This factor, which reduced the reliability of the polygraph while it added to the potential for prejudice, confusion and misleading jury cause the judge to reject the polygraph evidence.[50]

C. The Evidence Would Mislead the Jury

Where evidence might have the tendency to mislead the jury to an incorrect conclusion or decision, the trial judge should refuse to admit the evidence. For example, in a federal court in 1996, the judge properly refused to allow defense evidence to be introduced that the prosecution had tried to contact the defendant's cellmate to determine whether the defendant had made any incriminating statements. The judge believed that the value of the evidence had marginal utility and possessed a strong probability of jury confusion that could mislead the jury if the evidence were admitted.[51]

However, in a case in which the possibility of the jury being misled by evidence seemed strong, the state trial judge allowed evidence to be presented. In that case, which involved a capital murder prosecution, the trial judge allowed the prosecution to introduce evidence that the defendant tried to get a witness to have a sexual relationship with the defendant's girlfriend. The argument could be made that the evidence could possibly confuse the jury about why the defendant would want a witness to have a sexual relationship with his girlfriend, when the real issue was whether a murder had been committed by the defendant. However, the Supreme Court of Delaware agreed with the trial judge that the evidence was properly admitted,[52] despite the chance for misleading the jury with collateral matters.

---

[48]   United States v. Harris, 70 Cal. Rptr. 2d 689 (1997).
[49]   United States v. Wexler, 630 F. Supp. 249 (E.D. Pa 1986).
[50]   United States v. Lea, 1249 U.S. 632 (7th Cir. 2001).
[51]   United States v. Ailsworth, 948 F. Supp. 1485 (D. Kan. (1996).
[52]   Capano v. State, 781 A.2d 556 (Del. 2001).

D. The Evidence Would Unduly Delay the Trial of the Case, Waste Time, or Needlessly Present Cumulative Evidence

Evidence that might be relevant and might assist the jury in making a decision may still be excluded where a judge determines that admission of the evidence could cause a delay in the trial proceedings. In a criminal case involving criminal nonpayment of customs duties, the defendant attempted to introduce stipulations made by the government in another case involving the parties. The trial judge properly excluded the stipulations from the previous case that some of plaintiff's shipments were duty-free, on the grounds that stipulations would confuse jury and bring new issues for consideration. The trial judge concluded that admission of the stipulations would have opened door to collateral and confusing issues that, in turn, would have caused undue delay in the trial.[53]

The judge, at his or her discretion, may exclude relevant evidence if it unnecessarily delays the case or presents evidence that has already been covered sufficiently by other evidence.[54] For example, in a mail fraud and computer fraud case, the prosecution alleged that the defendant had committed the crimes while working for the government as a civilian computer specialist. One of the defendant's supervisors testified how the defendant's fraudulent schemes operated. In an effort to impeach the supervisor, the defendant wanted to cross-examine the supervisor concerning the supervisor's financial problems 10 years ago. At that time, the defendant had lent money to the supervisor, violating government policy. In an unpublished opinion, the reviewing court held that the exclusion of this line of cross-examination by the trial court was proper because the evidence would have been a waste of time even if it could have been somewhat relevant.[55] Against a defendant's argument under Rule 403 that the trial court had allowed the government to introduce cumulative evidence against him, the appellate court upheld the ruling of the trial judge. In a drug-selling prosecution, police had arrested a defendant after he threw a bag of cocaine out a window. Subsequently, police arrested him again for dropping a jar of rock cocaine out a window as police were entering the apartment. Later, the defendant was arrested a third time after police observed a known drug seller enter an apartment occupied by the defendant. At his trial for possession with intent to distribute 50 grams or more of cocaine base, he contended that bringing evidence of the first and third arrests for drug possession was improper because the government had more than sufficient evidence to prove the case and, therefore, the proof of the other crimes was unfairly prejudicial. The Court of Appeals for the Eighth Circuit held that the evidence was not improperly cumulative because the other crime evidence helped establish knowledge that he possessed cocaine base and that it tended to prove that he had the intent to distribute cocaine products.[56] Evidence can

---

53   United States v. Vitek Supply Corporation, 144 F.3d 476 (7th Cir. 1998).
54   Thompson v. American Steel & Wire Co., 317 Pa. 7, 175 A. 541 (1934). *See also* Germain v. Breaux, 702 So. 2d 691 (La. 1997).
55   United States v. Benjamin, 125 Fed. Appx. 438, 440, 2005 U.S. App. LEXIS 3943 (2005).
56   United States v. Gipson, 446 F.3d 828, 2006 U.S. App. LEXIS 11040 (2006).

be described as cumulative if it is repetitive of evidence already before the jury. When determining when cumulative evidence should be excluded, a federal court of appeals offered the following method for making a decision:

> Evidence is "cumulative" when it adds very little to the probative force of the other evidence in the case, so that if it were admitted its contribution to the determination of truth would be outweighed by its contribution to the length of trial, with all the potential for confusion, as well as prejudice to other litigants, who must wait longer for their trial, that a long trial creates.[57]

In a case in which the court was considering, under Rule 403, whether the "needless presentation of cumulative evidence" provision applied to keep evidence sought to be offered by the defendant's wife that she feared the Internal Revenue Service officers and agents. The court determined that the evidence was properly excluded because the defendant's wife had already testified on cross-examination about her apprehension of agents and that she thought the agents were strange people who were going to kill her or rob her.[58]

E. The Evidence Would Unfairly and Harmfully Surprise a Party Who Has Not Had Reasonable Opportunity to Anticipate That Such Evidence Would Be Offered

In the interests of fairness and due process, many courts will refuse to admit evidence where the opposing party had a duty and failed to give prior notice of an intention to introduce unanticipated evidence such as evidence of an affirmative defense.[59] Some courts advocate the exclusion of evidence if the opposing party is caught by unfair surprise. The reasoning behind this is that if the opponent has been unfairly surprised by unanticipated evidence and has received no warning or could not have logically anticipated that such evidence would be offered, then the evidence should be excluded, even though relevant. Confusion surrounding this rule has generated concern by many writers who suggest that the situation should be addressed by judicial instructions offered to the jury at the trial stage. In some jurisdictions, if an allegation of unfair surprise occurs, the complaining party must ask for a continuance or the objection concerning surprise is deemed to have been waived.[60]

As indicated in the previous section, the trial judge possesses considerable latitude in making decisions concerning the admissibility of relevant evidence. If the evidence is relevant, it should be admitted unless a stronger opposing evidentiary rule that demands exclusion. As a matter of public policy, the

---

[57]   United States v. Kizeart, 102 F.3d 320 (7th Cir. 1996), citing Judge Posner in United States v. Williams, 81 F.3d 1434, 1443 (7th Cir. 1996).

[58]   United States v. Streich, 759 F.2d 579 (7th Cir. 1985).

[59]   See Payne v. Tennessee, 501 U.S. 808 (1991) and Ransom v. State, 919 So. 2d 887, 888, 2005 Miss. LEXIS 595 (Miss. 2005), cert. denied, 2006 U.S. LEXIS 4985 (2006).

[60]   Burns v. State, 2005 Tex. App. LEXIS 1772 (Tex. 2005).

factfinders should have the opportunity to evaluate the weight to be given to the evidence. However, the mere fact that evidence is admissible because it meets the threshold of relevancy does not mean that the evidence establishes the fact or principle for which it was introduced. If the totality of the evidence received falls short of satisfying the burden of persuasion, then the jury has a responsibility to find against the party who bears the burden. On the other hand, the jury should have the benefit of hearing as much of the evidence as possible in determining whether the evidence received justifies finding for the party who has the burden of proof or burden of persuasion.

For example, in a case in which a woman who was on trial for solicitation for capital murder, she objected to the use of impeachment evidence that she had previously defrauded the government of welfare benefits. She claimed unfair surprise because her attorney had just been given the welfare fraud report that morning. The trial judge properly allowed the introduction of the fraud documents for impeachment purposes and noted that the defense attorney had received some notice concerning the use of the welfare fraud evidence because a prosecution witness list contained the name of a person who knew of the fraud.[61] While there may have been some surprise, there was not "unfair surprise." Similarly, no unfair surprise existed in a murder trial in which the state disclosed evidence that a cellmate was prepared to tell how the defendant had confessed to the cellmate concerning the two murders. The prosecution had disclosed the existence of the tape-recorded statement of the cellmate to the defense counsel seven days prior to the cellmate's actual testimony. The reviewing court agreed with the trial court that it was proper not to grant a continuance and it held that no unfair prejudice occurred despite the defense argument that it needed more time to develop potential impeachment evidence against the former cellmate-witness. The court of appeals affirmed the conviction.[62]

§ 7.5 Relevancy of Particular Matters

In previous sections of this chapter, the focus of the material centered on the general concepts relating to relevancy and materiality and how those concepts affected admission and exclusion of evidence. These rules apply in situations in which a party to a criminal action offers evidence for introduction. However, there are some particular instances in which not only the general rules apply, but also specific rules that relate to particular situations.

Evidence necessary to prove the essential elements of a case, as well as the preliminary facts, such as identity, jurisdiction of the court, and the mental condition of the accused must generally be admitted under one legal theory or another. However, trial and appellate challenges to admissibility or exclusion frequently occur regarding character evidence, evidence of prior crimes,

---

[61] People v. Birdsley, 2002 Cal. App. Unpub. LEXIS 597 (2002).

[62] Mendez v. State, 2004 Tex. App. LEXIS 11216 (Tex. 2004), *cert. denied*, Mendez v. Texas, ___ U.S. ___, 2005 U.S. LEXIS 7926 (2005).

identification issues, scientific testing evidence, the use of real evidence (especially in criminal cases), and other particular matters are discussed in detail in the sections that follow.

Logically relevant evidence is sometimes excluded by rape shield laws that are designed to protect complaining witnesses from having prior or subsequent sexual history divulged in court and to encourage the reporting of sexual crimes. Legislatures in many states have made legislative determinations that inquiries into sexual history that might be somewhat logically relevant carry a significant danger of unfairly prejudicing and misleading a jury and should be deemed to be legally irrelevant or immaterial. This is not to say that the prior history of a victim of a sexual assault can never be determined to be legally relevant or material, but a defendant must make a strong showing of both logical and legal relevance to have such evidence admitted. In one unreported Michigan case, the reviewing court reversed a defendant's conviction of first-degree criminal sexual assault because the trial court refused to allow evidence concerning the source of another man's DNA on the complaining victim's underwear. The victim had some private area injury, and the fact that another man was involved made the evidence both logically and legally relevant (material) to the issue of which man caused the victim's injuries.[63]

§ 7.6 —Identity of Persons

In order to ensure that the proper persons are tried and, if guilty, have appropriate sentences imposed, it is essential that those who are prosecuted in criminal cases be positively identified as the perpetrators. Therefore, courts allow a great deal of latitude in admitting evidence designed to prove identity. Any fact, however slight, that tends to satisfy a person of ordinary prudence and caution regarding identity is admissible if other rules are met.[64]

When evaluating the admissibility of evidence to prove identity, the court must consider not only the relevancy test, but in some instances constitutional grounds, like due process violations at lineups or the lack of counsel at a lineup, or other similar arguments. If the proposed evidence relates to the actual observation of the accused or others by the witness, the evidence is generally admissible. For example, the witness proposes to testify that, "I know the accused—I saw him enter the bank and exit with some bags that appeared to be money bags." This is relevant evidence and generally admissible. Other challenges may be in order, such as the credibility of the witness, but the testimony would probably not be challenged on constitutional grounds.

Identification may become more complicated when the witness did not know the person he or she saw at the crime scene but indicates that he or she could identify him at a lineup, a showup, a photographic array, or a PowerPoint

[63]   State v. Command, 2006 Mich. App. LEXIS 1558 (2006).
[64]   United States v. Zeiler, 296 F. Supp. 224 (W.D. Pa. 1969); Commonwealth v. Rivera, 397 Mass. 244, 490 N.E.2d 1160 (1986).

presentation. Here the evidence must meet the relevancy test, but it may be challenged if law enforcement agents performed the pretrial identification procedure in an unduly suggestive manner that may have contaminated the in-court identification of the witness.[65] The witness may be testifying from his or her memory of the identification procedure and not the crime scene observation.

In a landmark case concerning eyewitness identification decided by the U.S. Supreme Court, *Neil v. Biggers*, the Court offered a five-factor test to determine whether an identification has been made accurately. The *Neil* test considered "the opportunity of the witness to view the criminal at the time of the crime, the witness' degree of attention, the accuracy of the witness' prior description of the criminal, the level of certainty demonstrated by the witness at the confrontation, and the length of time between the crime and the confrontation."[66] In the *Neil* case, the rape victim had been with her attacker for a considerable length of time, had paid attention to his appearance, had given police an accurate prior description, had not misidentified any other person, was very certain of her identification, and the elapsed time since the crime had been about six months. She made her identification at a one-person "walk by" in the police station. The *Neil* Court approved the identification process under the five-factor test and held that the woman's identification of her attacker satisfied relevancy and due process standards when the totality of the circumstances were considered.[67] In another case, a woman was properly permitted to identify her rapist following the rape, but the identification occurred on a public street immediately following the attack. When she ran for help following the rape, she encountered a man who helped find her clothing and called police. Subsequently, she observed her attacker leave the basement and enter another apartment. Her spontaneous identification was held to have been properly made, done without undue suggestiveness, and was accomplished without any police involvement.[68]

When a pretrial identification procedure has been unnecessarily suggestive; involves "steering" by police—in which a suspect appeared in successive lineups or photo arrays; or was otherwise unfair, the identification evidence at the trial is not challenged with arguments concerning relevancy, but with the possible violation of due process.

Is evidence of a suspect's past activities admissible to show identity, even though this may include evidence of other crimes? In an Alabama case, when police were questioning a suspect about one murder, he told authorities about a second murder in which he had been involved. At trial of the second murder case, the prosecution introduced evidence of the first murder for the purpose of proving that the defendant was the person who did the act in the second

---

[65] *See* Neil v. Biggers, 409 U.S. 188, 1972 U.S. LEXIS 6 (1972) for five factors used to evaluate the accuracy of eyewitness identification. *See also* KLOTTER, WALKER, AND HEMMENS, LEGAL GUIDE FOR POLICE: CONSTITUTIONAL ISSUES (7th ed. 2005), Chapter 8, for a comprehensive discussion of pretrial identification procedures.

[66] Neil v. Biggers, 409 U.S. 188, 199-200, 1972 U.S. LEXIS 6 (1972).

[67] *Id.*

[68] State v. McElroy, 29 Kan. App. 2d 990, 992-993, 35 P.3d 283, 286-287 (2001).

murder. On appeal, the introduction of the other crime was upheld because the other murder was committed in a novel or unusual manner so that proof of the guilty party in one case tended to prove the identity of the guilty party in the second case. As the reviewing court noted, "[w]hen extrinsic offense evidence is introduced to prove identity, the likeness of the offenses is the crucial consideration. In other words, the physical similarity must be such that it marks the offenses as the handiwork of the accused."[69] In this case, the defendant was acquainted with both victims, the victims were of similar age, both were shot in the head after being taken to isolated areas, both appeared to be victims of robbery, both vehicles were burned, and the bodies were removed significant distances from where the vehicles were discovered.[70] The court determined that the evidence was properly admitted to prove identity.

More than mere general similarity between factual situations being compared will be required to use a separate crime in order to show identity under the similar crimes theory of proving identity.[71] There must be identifiable points of similarity that pervade both fact situations and demonstrate significant similarity, and the points of similarity must have some special character or be so unusual as to point to the defendant's identity. In one Alabama murder case, the trial court properly allowed evidence of other murders committed by the defendant to be introduced against him for the purpose of showing identity. The reviewing court noted that "[s]pecifically, all three murders were residential robbery/murders, two perpetrators were involved in each case, the same weapon was used in all three murders, all the victims were shot in the head, a cash register was taken during the Houston County murder and a safe was taken in the Dale County murders, and [the defendant's] fingerprints were found at each crime scene. The circuit court correctly allowed evidence of the Dale County murders to be introduced." The court held that collateral crime evidence of murder committed by the defendant was relevant to the issue of identity and was sufficiently similar to his commission of the other murders to be admissible at his current murder trial.[72]

The results of scientific tests may be considered relevant in proving a defendant's identity. In a California case, blood found at the murder scene matched the DNA profile of the defendant and blood found on the defendant's clothes matched the DNA of the child murder victim. The defendant was included as a possible donor of the crime scene blood and the DNA match of the blood found on the defendant's clothing could not exclude the victim as the source. Additionally, DNA from the defendant was discovered under the fingernails of the 13-year-old victim. The DNA profile that emerged indicated that the perpetrator was African-American even though there was no other evidence of the race of the defendant. The use of racial typing and the overall use of the DNA to identify the perpetrator was upheld by the Supreme Court of

---

[69]   Irvin v. State, 2005 Ala. Crim. App. LEXIS 132 (2005).
[70]   *Id.*
[71]   Wimberly v. State, 2005 Ala. Crim. App. LEXIS 103 (2005).
[72]   *Id.*

California for the purpose of helping establish the identity of the perpetrator.[73] Naturally, the testing must be conducted by properly trained technicians, conducted according to accepted standards, and introduced in court by a qualified witness. When properly done, DNA results offer circumstantial evidence that the defendant's identity has been properly established.[74]

§ 7.7 —Identity of Things

Subject to some exceptions, evidence that helps prove the identity of things or objects connected to a crime is generally considered relevant by a court. Items of personal property associated with a victim or a defendant may be relevant because they may have the effect of placing a particular person at a particular place. For example, for the purpose of identifying the accused as the guilty party, evidence that the defendant had the victim's distinctive money clip following an armed robbery helped prove that the defendant was the person who committed the crime.[75] When a clothing company's merchandise tag, found on the floor of a savings and loan association after a robbery, led officers to the defendant, who was identified by the victims as wearing a dark business suit, two dark suits of clothing identified by the defendant's wife as belonging to the defendant were relevant and material as evidence.[76] In an unpublished California case in which the defendant denied that he was one of the robbers, he was found in possession of all the proceeds of the robbery while wearing the jacket and pants worn by the actual robber, and had the gun used to intimidate the robbery victims, the evidence was sufficient to establish his identity as the perpetrator.[77]

Other examples of relevant, tangible evidence against a defendant are found in the following cases: In a North Carolina capital murder case, the reviewing court held that blood found on the defendant's pants that he wore on the night of the homicide, which matched the blood type of the decedent, was not improperly admitted. In addition, the fact that evidence technicians recovered DNA evidence from the pants of the defendant that indicated that the decedent was the source of the DNA also helped tie the defendant to the crime scene and helped prove the government's case.[78] Bite mark evidence offered by qualified experts[79] has been admitted in many cases in which scientific,

---

[73] People v. Wilson, 38 Cal. 4th 1237, 1250, 2006 Cal. LEXIS 8228 (2006).

[74] Commonwealth v. Gaynor, 443 Mass. 245, 266, 820 N.E.2d 233, 251, 2005 Mass. LEXIS 7 (2005).

[75] People v. Hinds, 2004 Mich. App. LEXIS 785 (2004).

[76] United States v. Alloway, 397 F.2d 105 (6th Cir. 1968).

[77] People v. Wardell, 2005 Cal. App. Unpub. LEXIS 11539 (2005).

[78] Daughtry v. Polk, 2006 U.S. App. LEXIS 17962 (4th Cir. 2006). *See also* 2002 Fulton County D. Rep. 3059, 2002 Ga. App. LEXIS 1286 (2002) and Missouri v. Thompson, 2001 Mo. App. LEXIS 903 (2001) for an example of the relevancy of blood comparisons.

[79] Meadows v. Commonwealth, 178 S.W.3d 527, 536, 2005 Ky. App. LEXIS 131 (2005). "Forensic dentists are experts on identifying persons based on unique characteristics of their teeth, which may include determining the identity of an unknown deceased person based on dental records, determining the age of a person based on his or her teeth, and determining who made a bite based on an analysis of the bite mark and the suspect's teeth."

technical, or other specialized knowledge would assist the trier of fact. In an Indiana case, expert testimony concerning bite marks made on the victim were compared with the defendant's mouth by a forensic odontologist. The bite mark evidence indicated that the defendant had been an active participant rather than an observer in the beating and confinement of the victim. The Supreme Court of Indiana approved the admission of the bite mark evidence to prove the identity of the mouth that made the impression, which revealed the identity of the defendant.[80] The Mississippi Supreme Court in the case of *Stubbs v. State* found that the reliability of a bite mark as a means of identification had been sufficiently established in the scientific community and had been recognized in Mississippi so as to make such evidence relevant and admissible in criminal cases. The court admitted bite mark evidence without separately establishing the scientific reliability in each even though it noted that bite mark evidence has been criticized.[81]

In *United States v. Carrasco*, the Ninth Circuit approved the admission of drug scales with narcotic residue, a bag full of pink baggies, and a glass methamphetamine pipe in a prosecution for knowingly possessing a revolver and ammunition under the disability of a prior felony conviction. Even though the court found that the defendant only had a small quantity of drugs and money in his possession, the Court of Appeals held that the district court properly admitted the drug scale and baggies as relevant evidence for the purpose of showing that the defendant knowingly possessed the revolver and ammunition.[82] In an Eighth Circuit case, the court upheld the introduction into evidence of scales that were present in the defendant's trailer home that the prosecution used to prove the defendant's intention to distribute 50 or more grams of cocaine. Police found pre-bagged rock cocaine in the home that also helped establish the intent to distribute cocaine.[83]

§ 7.8 —Circumstances Preceding the Crime

The preparation, planning, and calculation undertaken by a defendant prior to the criminal act will generally be relevant in establishing criminal intent. Following a crime, efforts to escape detection or apprehension, if planned prior to the crime, may also have the effect of proving the proper *mens rea* for the crime. The purchase of items necessary for the commission of the crime and arranging to arrive at the appropriate place at the proper time will be of interest to the prosecution. Similarly, any efforts to disguise the crime or the crime scene or destroy evidence, as well as efforts involving escape or escape of detection, may assist a prosecutor in proving consciousness of guilt. Conduct that is inconsistent with innocence and affirmative actions that tend

---

[80]   Carter v. State, 766 N.E.2d 377, 380, 2002 Ind. LEXIS 330 (2002).

[81]   2003 Miss. LEXIS 115 (2003).

[82]   United States v. Carrasco, 257 F.3d 1045, 2001 U.S. App. LEXIS 16502 (9th Cir. 2001).

[83]   United States v. Johnson, 439 F.3d 947, 955, 2006 U.S. App. LEXIS 6040 (8th Cir. 2006).

to demonstrate a consciousness of guilt will normally be relevant and admissible against the accused. Witnesses may have observed the crime as it occurred and other witnesses may have overheard threats directed toward a victim. Other witnesses may have conveyed a firearm or sold the defendant items used in the commission of the crime. Most of these types of evidence, whether they involve physical objects, human conduct, or oral evidence, should be considered relevant and generally admissible against an accused individual.

The best test of the relevance of testimony about antecedent circumstances that may shed light on the alleged crime is whether a particular fact, necessary to be proved in the case, tends to render the existence of that fact more or less probable than would be the case without the evidence.[84] In an unpublished California case, evidence that tended to prove attempted murder, that the defendant had the specific intent to kill, was shown by the fact that the defendant procured a sharp knife from the kitchen of his former wife and brought it to the bedroom where he repeatedly stabbed her.[85] The prior obtaining of the knife demonstrated that he had the sufficient mental state for the crime.

Evidence of prior planning in a California case indicated that the defendant, who had recently escaped from a prison, had obtained a knife and a hatchet from a neighbor's home and used the weapons to kill four people. The court emphasized that taking the weapons before using them demonstrated prior calculation sufficient for premeditated murder. Following the killings, the defendant committed larceny of the family automobile in order to escape from the police. The trial court held that the evidence of the planning, including the killings and the theft of the car, was relevant because it demonstrated both an intention to murder and design to escape.[86]

Activities that precede the crime may occur very briefly prior to the actual act and still be considered relevant evidence of planning the crime. In an unpublished Michigan case, evidence that preceded the crime of murder helped prove both premeditation and malice on the part of the defendant. In rejecting the defendant's appeal that the jury should have been instructed on manslaughter, the court noted that the defendant had a chance to reflect or decide to control his passions after he obtained a kitchen knife during his walk to his girlfriend's bedroom. His acts of slashing her throat and windpipe demonstrated that he had the intent to kill and had time during his walk to the bedroom to premeditate. His behavior helped prove two elements of the crime of first-degree murder.[87]

In a Missouri case, the court admitted testimony that the defendant had discussed killing women who caused problems for his family, that he fantasized about having sexual relations with them while they died, and that he made statements that could have meant that he intended to have sexual rela-

---

[84]   State v. Hymore, 9 Ohio St. 2d 122, 38 Ohio Op. 2d 298, 224 N.E.2d 126 (1967); United States v. Gipson, 385 F.2d 341 (7th Cir. 1967). *See also* State v. Hemphill, 699 S.W.2d 83 (Mo. Ct. App. 1985).

[85]   People v. Dinh, 2006 Cal. App. Unpub. LEXIS 2603 (Cal. 2006).

[86]   Cooper v. Calderon, Warden, 255 F.3d 1104, 2001 U.S. App. LEXIS 15400 (9th Cir. 2001).

[87]   People v. Benore, 2005 Mich. App. LEXIS 2718 (Mich. 2005).

tions with the victim. This evidence, according to the court, provided background information that helped the jury understand the main facts in issue.[88]

Evidence of prior difficulties between one of the defendants and a property owner was admissible in a prosecution for burglary and criminal damage to property. The prosecution's evidence of events occurring prior to the crime was admissible to show motive and intent.[89] Similarly, where the defendant had received numerous threats of serious injury directed toward both him and his family members from the decedent over a period of time when they lived in the same trailer home, such evidence was considered relevant regarding self-defense and defense of another, and was also relevant evidence of the defendant's subjective mental state.[90]

The defendant may also introduce evidence of events preceding the crime. For example, a defendant in a murder case may offer evidence of prior attacks upon her in an effort to make a case for self-defense. In *State v. Paddio*, the defendant was permitted to introduce relevant evidence that she had been injured by the deceased such that she had to seek medical care and that others had observed victim-inflicted injuries to her many times.[91] Following similar reasoning, in different case involving a stabbing and ultimate death of the victim, a Missouri appellate court reversed a manslaughter conviction where the trial court excluded evidence that the victim had a reputation for violent and bizarre behavior. The reviewing court held that a defendant in a murder trial may introduce evidence of a victim's reputation for violence because that evidence meets the test for logical and legal relevance and should have been admitted to prove that the alleged victim may have been the aggressor.[92]

§ 7.9 —Subsequent Incriminating or Exculpatory Circumstances

Following suspicious activity, the actions or conduct of a suspect may assist in establishing a defense or may provide the prosecution with evidence that helps prove guilt. As one Kentucky court noted, the "common-law rule is based on the inference that the guilty run away but the innocent remain."[93] For example, evidence of flight, resisting arrest, concealment, assuming a false name, and criminal conduct during flight for the purpose of financing and accomplishing further flight is admissible in a criminal prosecution. As one Ohio court noted, "the fact of an accused's flight, escape from custody, resistance to arrest, concealment, assumption of a false name, and related conduct, are [all] admissible as evidence of consciousness of guilt, and thus of guilt

---

[88]   State v. Davis, 877 S.W.2d 669 (Mo. 1994).
[89]   Watkins v. State, 190 Ga. App. 429, 379 S.E.2d 227 (1989).
[90]   People v. Davis, 2002 Cal. App. Unpub. LEXIS 4371 (2002).
[91]   State v. Paddio, 832 So. 2d 1120, 2002 La. App. LEXIS 3737 (2002).
[92]   State v. Gonzales, 153 S.W.3d 311, 312, 2005 Mo. LEXIS 8 (Mo. 2005).
[93]   Rodriguez v. Commonwealth, 107 S.W.3d 215, 219, 2003 Ky. LEXIS 138 (Ky. 2003).

itself."[94] While flight and other such conduct does not raise a legal presumption of guilt, the jury may consider these circumstances together with other
· facts in evidence and give the evidence the weight it thinks the evidence deserves, given the facts presented.[95]

Where an individual sees police officers and flees immediately, such conduct may be relevant to criminality and deserves some investigation by police to determine whether the flight reflected a consciousness of guilt.[96] As Chief Justice Rehnquist noted, "Headlong flight—wherever it occurs—is the consummate act of evasion: it is not necessarily indicative of wrongdoing, but it is certainly suggestive of such."[97] According to a South Carolina court, "Evidence of flight has been held to constitute evidence of the defendant's guilty knowledge and intent."[98] In one South Carolina case, police attempted to stop a vehicle that was traveling with its lights turned off while pulling out of a parking lot. The officer thought that some investigation was necessary, but the defendants attempted to evade being pulled over and one of the men ran when the car eventually stopped. The evidence of flight was properly admitted because there was proof that "the defendant had knowledge that he was being sought by the authorities."[99] As a general rule, unexplained flight can be admissible as evidence to infer consciousness of guilt, according to a Connecticut court. In a case in which an accused fled to Puerto Rico within three or four days following the victim's allegations against him for sexual abuse and before police could interview him, evidence of flight was properly admitted. The defendant testified in his own defense but he offered no rebuttal explanation of why he needed to go to Puerto Rico at that specific time and why he remained there for six years.[100]

There are limitations on the weight of such evidence. In a very old case, the United States Supreme Court in *Hickory v. United States*[101] set aside a conviction because the trial judge had charged the jury that flight created a presumption of guilt. The Court concluded that flight and concealment "are mere circumstances to be considered and weighed in connection with other proof with that caution and circumspection which their inconclusiveness when standing alone require." Flight following a criminal act constitutes a type of circumstantial evidence of consciousness of guilt, but its probative value usually depends on all of the surrounding facts and circumstances. The inference of consciousness of guilt upon flight has been subject to considerable judicial criticism on the ground that common experience does not always support the assumption. In recognition of this concept and consistent with the *Hickory* case above, one court charged the jury that "the government bore the burden

[94]   Ohio v. Stedman, 2001 Ohio App. LEXIS 4912 (2001).
[95]   Connecticut v. Beverly, 72 Conn. App. 91, 104, 805 A.2d 95, 104 (2002).
[96]   Illinois v. Wardlow, 528 U.S. 119 (2000).
[97]   *Id.* at 124.
[98]   State v. Crawford, 362 S.C. 627, 635, 608 S.E.2d 886, 890, 2005 S.C. App. LEXIS 24 (S.C. 2005).
[99]   *Id.* at 636, 891.
[100] State v. Gonzalez, 272 Conn. 515, 530, 864 A.2d 847, 857, 2005 Conn. LEXIS 20 (Conn. 2005).
[101] 160 U.S. 408, 16 S. Ct. 327, 40 L. Ed. 474 (1896).

of showing that the appellant had intentionally fled and that flight does not create a presumption of guilt but, to the contrary, may be completely consistent with innocence."[102] Essentially, it was up to the jury to make the determination of what inference, if any, to draw from proof of flight.

The length of time between the crime and the flight may have a bearing on both the admissibility and the weight of the flight evidence. Where a defendant in a murder case fled from police at a traffic stop seven days after the crime, the court held that evidence of consciousness of guilt could still exist and was not too remote in time to be properly associated with the crimes of murder and kidnapping. Defendant's explanation of flight seven days after the crime was held to go to the weight of flight evidence rather than its admissibility.[103]

When evidence of flight has been introduced in a case, the judge normally will give a jury instruction concerning evaluation of the evidence. In Connecticut, the trial judge should consider the instructions on flight to determine whether they are correct in both law and fact so that no injustice can be done by erroneous instructions. In reviewing a jury charge, an appellate court should neither microscopically dissect nor should the individual instructions be read or judged in isolation with a view to discovering any minute error or inaccuracy. The reviewing court should read the instructions as a whole, while considering their likely effect on the jury.[104]

In further amplification of jury instructions regarding flight, in a federal prosecution for having a firearm under a disability, the trial court permitted the prosecution to introduce evidence that when the defendant was ordered to stop his car for a seatbelt violation, he sped away in an attempt to elude the officer. When the police viewed the interior of the car, they found a bag of marijuana and a semi-automatic pistol. The judge charged the jury that:

> You may also consider any evidence of flight by the defendant, along with all of the evidence in the case, and you may consider whether this evidence shows a consciousness of guilt and determine the significance to be attached to any such conduct.
>
> Whether or not evidence of flight shows a consciousness of guilt and the significance to be attached to any such evidence are matters exclusively within the province of the jury. In your consideration of the evidence of flight you should consider that there may be reasons for this which are fully consistent with innocence.[105]

The Eighth Circuit Court of Appeals approved the jury instruction because it allowed the jury to either infer or not whether the defendant had a consciousness of guilt after it considered the defendant's explanation concerning an

---

[102]   United States v. Benedetti, 433 F.3d 111, 116, 2005 U.S. App. LEXIS 28490 (1st Cir. 2005).

[103]   United States v. Young, 2003 U.S. App. LEXIS 7432 (8th Cir. 2003).

[104]   Connecticut v. Crnkovic, 68 Conn. App. 757, 766-767, 793 A.2d 1139, 1147, 2002 Conn. App. LEXIS 159 (2002).

[105]   United States v. Webster, 442 F.3d 1065, 1067, 2006 U.S. App. LEXIS 8061 (8th Cir. 2006).

innocent reason for flight.[106] In the opposite situation, jurors are permitted to infer that a person refusing to flee from crime, even though he or she had the opportunity to flee, does so because of no consciousness of guilt.[107]

Just as evidence of escape may be admitted to allow a jury to consider whether an inference of consciousness of guilt should be drawn,[108] a suicide attempt may be admissible for any weight a jury might want to give it. In a case involving an allegation that the defendant had committed several sexual offenses against his 10-year-old stepdaughter, the defendant wrote a suicide note and shot himself in the head on the morning his trial was to have started. As a general rule, evidence of an attempted suicide may be considered by a finder of fact as evidence that might indicate a consciousness of guilt and a jury should evaluate the suicide attempt evidence within the whole context of the case. According to the reviewing court, "[t]he note was evidence of attempted suicide, was relevant as possibly indicating a consciousness of guilt, and was properly admitted for the jury's consideration."[109] Attempts by a defendant to "influence testimony, or induce perjury is also admissible as evidence of consciousness of guilt," according to a Michigan appellate court.[110] More direct threats made by a defendant against witnesses or other persons who are cooperating with the prosecution are typically admissible against a defendant to show consciousness of guilt.[111]

In some instances, comments made by the defendant following the charged crime are admissible. Demonstrative of this point is the case in which the defendant possessed an awareness of guilt as evidenced by his words to a law enforcement officer. While under arrest for murder, the defendant refused to speak after hearing his *Miranda* warnings, except to say that, "I have nothing to say, I'm going to get the death penalty anyway." The court allowed the statement to be admitted for the purpose of demonstrating that the defendant had a consciousness of having committed a homicide.[112] However, post-arrest silence following *Miranda* warnings cannot be used a evidence of consciousness of guilt and the prosecutor may not generally comment on a defendant's silence. Implicit in the *Miranda* warning is the message that an arrestee will not be penalized by exercising the right to remain silent.[113]

Other instances in which courts have considered the activities of the suspect following the crime are: (1) the use of a false name after the commission of a crime; (2) the suspect's refusal to consent to the entry of his home; and (3) the growth of a beard to change appearance. In the case of *Connecticut v. Young*, the defendant offered a false name at the point of arrest and attempted

---

[106]   *Id.*

[107]   WIGMORE, EVIDENCE § 276 (1979); State v. Milam, 108 Ohio App. 254, 9 Ohio Op. 2d 252, 156 N.E.2d 840 (1959).

[108]   Bigby v. Dretke, 402 F.3d 551, 557, 2005 U.S. App. LEXIS 3815 (5th Cir. 2005).

[109]   Duncan v. Georgia, 269 Ga. App. 4,6, 602 S.E.2d 908, 910, 2004 Ga. App. LEXIS 1052 (2004).

[110]   People v. Radley, 2005 Mich. App. LEXIS 3100 (2005).

[111]   Mendiola v. State, 2005 Ark. App. LEXIS 654 (2005).

[112]   United States v. Bushyhead, 270 F.3d 905, 908, 909, 2001 U.S. App. LEXIS 23400 (9th Cir. 2001).

[113]   United States v. Rodriguez, 260 F.3d 416, 2001 U.S. App. LEXIS 16956 (5th Cir. 2001).

to alter and conceal evidence of a crime, factors that the court noted have commonly been accepted as being relevant on the issue of consciousness of guilt.[114] Similarly, in a Pennsylvania murder case, the defendant initially gave police an alias rather than his real name, and the defendant's lie concerning his name was presented to the jury. In upholding the admission of the alias, the reviewing court noted that the use of the alias evidence did not violate the rules of evidence or the Fifth Amendment privilege against self-incrimination.[115] In another case, however, a defendant was merely exercising his rights under the Fourth Amendment when he refused to consent to a search of his home where the police had no search warrant. The refusal to consent was not admissible as any evidence of consciousness of guilt.[116] In one bank robbery case, the accused gained weight after his arrest, shaved his beard, and began to wear glasses in an apparent effort at frustrating courtroom identification by tellers. The court charged the jury that it could consider the defendant's change of appearance to indicate a fear of being identified by tellers and that the change could help prove consciousness of guilt,[117] but it was up to the jurors to determine how much weight to give the evidence.

§ 7.10   —Defenses

While relevancy is the requirement for admitting evidence against a defendant, the same standards generally apply when the defense wants to negate or rebut the prosecution's case. Although a criminal defendant need not introduce any evidence in order to prevail, most defendants attempt to challenge the prosecution's evidence with proof that attempts to rebut the prosecution's case. Alternatively, a defendant may choose to present evidence of an affirmative defense, such as alibi, entrapment, or insanity, and on these generally, the defendant has the burden of proof in many jurisdictions. As a general rule, defense evidence must meet the same tests for relevancy and materiality as the prosecution's evidence. Such evidence is usually admissible if it meets general admissibility tests, but there may be some additional requirements in some situations. Several commonly offered defenses are discussed here.[118]

---

[114]   68 Conn. App. 10, 791 A.2d 581, n.9, 2002 Conn. App. LEXIS 83 (2001).

[115]   Nelson v. Vaughn, 2004 U.S. Dist. LEXIS 4708 (E.D. Pa. 2004). *See also* Adkins v. Commonwealth, 96 S.W.3d 779, 2003 Ky. LEXIS 13 (2003).

[116]   People v. Keener, 148 Cal. App. 3d 73, 195 Cal. Rptr. 733 (1983).

[117]   United States v. Carr, 362 U.S. App. D. C. 303, 373 F.3d 1350, 1353, 2004 U.S. App. LEXIS 14305 (D.C. Cir. 2004). Post-conviction relief denied at United States v. Carr, 2006 U.S. Dist. LEXIS 6368 (D.D.C. 2006).

[118]   *See* KLOTTER, CRIMINAL LAW (7th Ed. 2004) for a discussion of defenses in criminal cases. And *see* Abbe Smith, *Promoting Justice through Interdisciplinary Teaching, Practice, and Scholarship: The Difference in Criminal Defense and the Difference it Makes*, 11 WASH. U. J.L. & POLICY 83 (2003). *See also* Daniel S. Medwed, *Actual Innocents: Considerations in Selecting Cases for a New Innocence Project*, 81 NEB. L. REV. 1097 (2003).

A. *Insanity*

A defendant's mental state becomes relevant when there is an issue concerning responsibility for the alleged crime and when there is concern that a defendant may not be able to assist his or her attorney in presenting a defense. The first issue of mental health focuses on the defendant's state of mind at the time the alleged crime occurred. Evidence that proves the defendant met or failed to meet the jurisdiction's test for legal insanity will be relevant and admissible to either prove or disprove the mental condition of the defendant. Many jurisdictions place the burden of proof of legal insanity on the defendant. The second issue concerning mental health occurs at the time of trial and concerns the defendant's mental competency to meaningfully assist his or her attorney in presenting a defense.

The concept of legal insanity is recognized as a defense in most jurisdictions, while temporary insanity is recognized as a defense in some jurisdictions. Some jurisdictions allow a verdict of guilty, but insane.[119] Arizona recently restricted the insanity defense under the traditional *M'Naghten* rule by removing part of the test that addressed cognitive capacity and leaving the basic "right-wrong" part of the test.[120] Evidence regarding an accused's mental condition just before and after the alleged offense, if not unreasonably far removed in time, is usually admissible because of relevancy to the question of mental condition at the time of the offense.[121] Some states recognize a type of temporary insanity caused by voluntary intoxication but use it in mitigation of the penalty attached to the offense for which the defendant has been convicted.[122] As a general rule, to qualify for the defense of temporary insanity based on alcohol consumption, one state statute requires that there be evidence that the defendant, due to severe alcohol intoxication, either did not know that his conduct was wrong or that he was incapable of conforming his conduct to the requirements of the law.[123]

B. *Voluntary Intoxication*

Intoxication is a voluntary insanity, and, as a general rule, will not excuse a person from criminal responsibility. The Texas Code is representative of most jurisdictions when it states, "[v]oluntary intoxication does not constitute a defense to the commission of crime."[124] It is generally accepted that a defendant's voluntary intoxication is neither an excuse for the commission of crime, nor a defense to a prosecution for it.[125] This general rule of the common law is contained in the statutes of many states and exists by judicial deci-

---

[119] *See* OR. REV. STAT. §§ 161.319, 161.325 (2006).

[120] *See* Clark v. Arizona, ___ U.S. ___, 2006 U.S. LEXIS 5184 (2006).

[121] Beardslee v. United States, 387 F.2d 280 (8th Cir. 1967). *See* § 3.11 of this book for a discussion of the burden of proving sanity. *See also* 18 U.S.C. § 17 (2006), Insanity Defense, for the text of the insanity defense available in federal criminal trials.

[122] TEX. PENAL CODE § 8.04(b) (2005).

[123] Wilson v. Cockrell, 2002 U.S. Dist. LEXIS 19002 (N.D. Tex. 2002).

[124] TEX. PENAL CODE § 8.04 (a) (2005).

[125] Leppla v. State, 277 Ga. App. 804, 811, 627 S.E.2d 794, 800, 2006 Ga. App. LEXIS 75 (Ga. 2006).

sion in the federal courts, but some state and federal jurisdictions recognize limited exceptions.

One exception to the general rule that voluntary intoxication does not serve as a defense exists in some jurisdictions when a defendant has been accused of a crime that involves some specific intent or requires the operation of a more complicated mental process such as deliberation or premeditation. If the evidence discloses that a defendant was extremely intoxicated to the point that the correct *mens rea* or criminal intent could not be formed, some jurisdictions will take the lack of *mens rea* of a specific intent crime into consideration either as demonstrating that a particular crime has not been committed or will use intoxication as a mitigating factor. Under this limited exception, drunkenness may be taken into account to indicate that a necessary mental element of a crime[126] was absent.

Not all jurisdictions agree that voluntary intoxication may operate as a mitigator or as a partial defense. In Arizona, the statute states that "[t]emporary intoxication resulting from the voluntary ingestion, consumption, inhalation or injection of alcohol, an illegal substance . . . or other psychoactive substances or the abuse of prescribed medications does not constitute insanity and is not a defense for any criminal act or requisite state of mind."[127] Where an intoxicated driver, fleeing from police, killed a police officer involved in the pursuit, the defendant argued in a habeas corpus petition that the state must prove *mens rea* and must give consideration to his intoxicated state. According to Missouri law, proof of voluntary intoxication does not, by itself, establish that the defendant was incapable of forming the proper *mens rea*. In a prosecution for two sex offenses against a minor committed in South Dakota, there was significant evidence that the defendant was under the influence of alcohol. Over the defendant's objection, the trial judge instructed the jury that voluntary intoxication was not a defense or a mitigating factor in a sexual assault prosecution. The reviewing court approved the instruction even though only general criminal intent is necessary to prove the crime of rape. The appellate court did caution that federal courts should generally "refrain from giving voluntary intoxication instructions in cases involving rape, a general intent crime,"[128] but where there was significant evidence of intoxication, such an instruction should not be considered unfairly prejudicial. As long as there is proof that the intoxicated defendant had the correct mental state, the conviction will stand in South Dakota federal courts. The approach demonstrated by these two examples is consistent with the position of the U.S. Supreme Court under its holding that a state can prohibit a criminal defendant from offering evidence of voluntary intoxication to negate the requisite *mens rea* without violating the due process clause of the Fourteenth Amendment.[129]

---

[126] United States v. Veach, 2006 U.S. App. LEXIS 19283; 2006 Fed. Appx. 0266P (6th Cir. 2006).

[127] ARIZ. REV. STAT. § 13-503 (2006). Effect of alcohol or drug use.

[128] United States v. Medicine Horn, 447 F.3d 620, 624, 2006 U.S. App. LEXIS 12161 (8th Cir. 2006).

[129] Montana v. Egelhoff, 518 U.S. 37, 56, 1996 U.S. LEXIS 3878 (1996).

Where intoxication is established as a defense to a specific intent crime, the result may not always be acquittal, but rather conviction of a lesser degree of the offense for which no proof of specific intent is necessary. In a prosecution for a felony failure to appear in court, an acquittal may result from voluntary intoxication where the defendant became so drunk that he passed out and missed his felony drunk driving court appearance.[130] In support of allowing voluntary intoxication as a defense, the United States Virgin Islands holds that voluntary intoxication may be a defense to a crime requiring a specific *mens rea* but not to a crime requiring only a general *mens rea*.[131]

C. Other Defenses

Evidence of other affirmative defenses may be relevant if introduced for the purpose of establishing defenses such as entrapment, alibi, self-defense, defense of others, mistake of fact, mistake of law, and others. These, of course, must meet the other tests of admissibility in addition to the relevancy and materiality tests.

§ 7.11 —Character Evidence

Rule 404

Character Evidence Not Admissible to Prove Conduct; Exceptions; Other Crimes

(a) Character evidence generally. Evidence of a person's character or a trait of character is not admissible for the purpose of proving action in conformity therewith on a particular occasion, except:

(1) Character of accused. Evidence of a pertinent trait of character offered by an accused, or by the prosecution to rebut the same; * * *.

(2) Character of victim. Evidence of a pertinent trait of character of the alleged victim of the crime offered by an accused, or by the prosecution to rebut the same, or evidence of a character trait of peacefulness of the victim offered by the prosecution in a homicide case to rebut evidence that the victim was the first aggressor; * * *.

(3) Character of witness. Evidence of the character of a witness, as provided in rules 607, 608, and 609.[132]

* * *

The character of a defendant should assist a jury or judge in making determinations about a defendant. In ordinary social and business situations, people make judgments about others based on character, a trait of character, or

---

[130] *See* Hutchinson v. Alaska, 27 P.3d 774, 2001 Alaska App. LEXIS 121 (2001).
[131] George v. Sively, 254 F.3d 438, 443, 444, 2001 U.S. App. LEXIS 12401 (3d Cir. 2001).
[132] FED. R. EVID. 404.

reputation. This approach works quite well in ordinary human affairs where money or relationships may be involved. However, when evaluating whether someone might be guilty of a crime, reliance on character evidence could mislead a finder of fact into making an erroneous decision that affects the freedom of the accused. Merely because a person has a bad reputation for a particular character trait does not necessarily mean that the subject always follows that trait or that he or she followed the trait on a particular occasion. Alternatively, justice might not be served if we partially substitute character for more demanding and more reliable evidence of criminality. If the state were permitted to prove that a person's character is bad, it could be contended that this fact would have some slight probative value in determining whether that person actually committed the charged offense. The reputation of an accused for a particular character trait arguably might be relevant, but the jury might use the reputation for that trait to convict in a close case where, in the absence of the evidence, it would have acquitted. As is sometimes stated in legal circles, proof of character might prove too much and the jury might convict to punish the defendant for his bad character rather than the issues presented at trial. In order to protect the accused from the possibility of conviction based on bad character, a general rule has evolved that evidence showing the bad character of the accused is usually not admitted.

Rule 404(a) codifies the basic rule that evidence that tends only to show a propensity to act in a particular manner or shows evidence of a criminal defendant's general bad character is not admissible.[133] This basic prohibition is often called the "propensity" rule. Under this rule and under the general evidence provisions, a person's character or propensities to act in a certain way may not be offered as a basis for the inference that on a specific occasion a person acted in conformity with the propensity or the character trait. Rule 404(a) is especially applied to exclude evidence in a criminal case. The prosecution may not use evidence of a negative character trait of a defendant to show that the defendant may have a propensity to commit the crime for which the defendant is currently on trial.[134] However, as indicated in the text of Rule 404(a), as well as in case law, the rule generally excluding character evidence has exceptions.[135]

While the prosecution generally cannot introduce evidence of the bad character of the accused, the courts apply a different rule when the criminal defendant wishes to make his or her character an issue in the case. Because a jury might give a defendant with good character the benefit of the doubt in a close case, he or she has the opportunity to introduce evidence of general good character to show that it was improbable that he or she committed the charged crime. There are dangers associated with making a defendant's character an issue because once the accused has introduced such evidence, the prosecution may rebut it with the same type of evidence. In this situation, the defendant is

---

[133] Hinton v. Georgia, 253 Ga. App. 69, 70, 557 S.E.2d 481, 483 (2001).

[134] Ohio v. Bronner, 2002 Ohio 4248; 2002 Ohio App. LEXIS 4413 (2002).

[135] *See* WEISSENBER, FEDERAL EVIDENCE 3D (1998) and FED. R. EVID. 404(b).

said to have "opened the door," and the prosecution may then go into the matter by using the same type of evidence.[136]

As a strong general rule, the prosecution cannot offer evidence of bad character unless the defendant has previously offered his or her good character or a character trait as relevant evidence. Therefore, if the defendant chooses to place his or her general character or a particular character trait at issue, in fairness, the prosecution may introduce evidence that rebuts the defendant's evidence.[137] In a Delaware case in which the defendant had been convicted of aggravated harassment, the prosecution had been permitted to introduce evidence that the defendant violated a prior protection order in a different state and that the defendant had previously harassed the witness. The prosecution also asked if the defendant had a harassment conviction in Delaware, to which he answered he did not remember. Normally, inquiring into specific acts that reflect on the defendant's character traits would have been inadmissible under Rule 404(a) and similar state rules. In this case, the defendant "opened the door" to the evidence when he took the witness stand and told the prosecutor that he always treated "the ladies" nicely, including two daughters of his own. The prosecutor's follow-up questions to a former girlfriend of the defendant indicated that he had a character trait of being harassing to women whom he had dated. The reviewing court held that Rule 404 does not prevent a prosecutor from presenting rebuttal evidence where a defendant has given false testimony to a jury about his own conduct with women, which was at issue in the harassment case.[138]

Even when the defendant has not "opened the door" to his or her character and the prosecution improperly reveals to the jury that the defendant had a prior felony conviction, any resulting conviction will not automatically be reversed. If there is overwhelming evidence of guilt or if the judge issues an immediate curative jury instruction, the conviction will not be disturbed based solely on a violation of erroneous admission of character evidence against an accused.[139]

While the prosecution generally cannot introduce adverse character evidence about the defendant during its case-in-chief, a defendant may bring forth relevant evidence of the alleged victim's character for a particular trait. Federal Rule 404 generally excludes character evidence from admission, but provides an exception for "evidence of a pertinent trait of character of the victim of the crime offered by an accused."[140] For example, when a defendant wife claimed self-defense in a domestic homicide case, the trial judge refused to allow her to introduce evidence that her deceased husband had a reputation as a violent and dangerous man. On appeal, the defendant contended that the

---

[136] 1 WIGMORE, EVIDENCE § 58 (1983); *See also* FED. R. EVID. 405(a).

[137] United States v. Tran Trong Cuong, 18 F.3d 1132 (4th Cir. 1994); United States v. Clark, 26 Fed. Appx. 422, 426, 427 (2001); *but see* State v. McCarty, 271 Kan. 510, 23 P.3d 829, 2001 Kan. LEXIS 385 (2001), in which evidence of prior crime was relevant for a different purpose from proof of character.

[138] Baumann v. State, 891 A.2d 146, 147, 2005 Del. LEXIS 493 (Del. 2005).

[139] Nickleson v. State, 2005 Tex. App. LEXIS 6658 (2005).

[140] FED. R. EVID. 404(a)(1).

trial court erred when it prevented her from introducing proof that her husband had a violent character. Specifically, the court excluded evidence that the victim-husband, who was previously angry at a car dealership, broke several windows of cars held as inventory on the dealer's lot. In self-defense cases, the victim's violent character becomes relevant only to the extent that it relates to the defendant's fear of harm from the victim. The reviewing court granted the defendant a new trial because the trial court should have allowed the introduction of evidence of the victim's violent character, including specific instances of violence because it was clearly relevant to the issue of self-defense.[141]

The character of the ordinary witness—one who is not accused, including the victim—can also be shown by evidence if it bears upon the case. As a general rule, every person who testifies as a witness places his or her character for truthfulness at issue. If a defendant testifies, the credibility of the defendant becomes relevant and subject to impeachment. As in the case of other types of character evidence, once the door is opened, the other side may introduce evidence to rebut the evidence introduced by the first party.

Evidence of a defendant's good general character may be sufficient to create reasonable doubt concerning whether a defendant is guilty of the crime charged. For that reason, a defendant is always permitted to introduce relevant evidence of his or her good character. The defendant is permitted to present evidence that he or she possesses a positive general reputation, but the defendant cannot introduce evidence that is irrelevant to general reputation. For example, a trial judge properly excluded a defendant's offer, through his witnesses, to prove that he was an honest person when the defendant had not taken the witness stand and the case involved a murder prosecution.[142]

In referring to Alaska's version of Rule 404(a)(1), a state trial court noted that the accused in a criminal case has an option to introduce evidence of his or her good character by personal testimony or through other defense witnesses, but the prosecution may meet the evidence of defendant's good general character with proof of specific incidents that have the effect of rebutting the defendant's evidence.[143] In the case involving sexual abuse of girls, the defendant had testified that he had a benevolent nonsexual attitude toward children and had been employed as a counselor to teenagers who had been victims of sexual abuse. The trial court properly allowed the Alaska prosecutor to introduce evidence that the defendant had made sexual comments about 10- to 14-year-old girls as rebuttal evidence.[144] Every defendant who testifies places his or her credibility at issue and is subject to efforts to impeach like any other testifying witness, but merely testifying does not place at issue all other sorts of character traits or the defendant's general reputation.[145]

[141]　State v. Everett, 630 S.E.2d 703, 2006 N.C. App. LEXIS 1302 (2006).
[142]　Marschke v. State, 185 S.W.3d 295, 307, 2006 Mo. App. LEXIS 280 (2006).
[143]　Bryant v. State, 115 P.3d 1249, 1253, 2005 Alas. App. LEXIS 62 (2005).
[144]　Id. at 1254.
[145]　Gage v. State, 2005 Tex. App. LEXIS 531 (2005).

§ 7.12 —Proof of Other Crimes, Wrongs, or Acts

Rule 404
Character Evidence not Admissible to Prove
Conduct; Exceptions; Other Crimes

* * *

(b) Other crimes, wrongs, or acts.

Evidence of other crimes, wrongs, or acts is not admissible to prove the character of a person in order to show action in conformity therewith. It may, however, be admissible for other purposes, such as proof of motive, opportunity, intent, preparation, plan, knowledge, identity, or absence of mistake or accident, provided that upon request by the accused, the prosecution in a criminal case shall provide reasonable notice in advance of trial, or during trial if the court excuses pretrial notice on good cause shown, of the general nature of any such evidence it intends to introduce at trial.[146]

* * *

Rule 404(b) in essence restates the general rule that evidence of other crimes, wrongs, or acts may not be admissible to prove the character of a person in order to show action and conformity therewith. It may, however, be admissible against a defendant for other purposes, such as proof of motive, opportunity, intent, preparation, plan, knowledge, identity, or absence of mistake or accident.[147] Federal Rule 404(b) was amended in 1991 to provide for a notice requirement to criminal defendants where use of character evidence was contemplated.

When a trial court is faced with deciding whether to admit prior acts against a defendant currently on trial, the judge must make sure that the prior acts are not admitted to prove that the defendant has a predisposition to commit the charged crime or that the evidence proves the defendant is a bad person. In a District of Columbia prosecution against a defendant who had been selling counterfeit compact discs, the prosecution wanted to prove that the defendant knew that the discs were counterfeit. The jewel cases that contained the discs had a thin piece of paper inside that indicated the artist for each disc and the jewel cases were wrapped in plastic wrap. Because the defendant had previously been convicted of selling compact discs without a vending license from the district under circumstances in which it was clear that he knew the compact discs were counterfeit, the prosecution wanted to admit the prior offense. The reviewing court noted that admission of prior acts and crimes were presumptively inadmissible due to the danger of unfair prejudice, but in this case, the court approved the admission of prior crime evidence because it tended to show that the defendant had knowledge that the compact discs were

---

[146] FED. R. EVID. 404(b).
[147] Idaho v. Siegel, 137 Idaho 538, 541, 50 P.3d 1033, 1036, 2002 Idaho App. LEXIS 30 (2002).

counterfeit.[148] The two crimes were so similar in many aspects that proof of one tended to prove the other.

As a general rule, evidence of prior misconduct is inadmissible as part of the evidence to suggest that the defendant might be guilty of a crime for which the defendant is presently standing trial. In a case in which a minor adopted child had accused her father of sexual offenses, it was error to permit allegations by the defendant's adult daughters from a prior marriage that, 30 years ago, the defendant had sexually abused them by touching them inappropriately. In reversing the convictions, the reviewing court noted that "[e]vidence is legally relevant if its probative value outweighs its costs."[149] In this case, the earlier allegations took place too long ago and allegedly involved only touching, while in the present prosecution the allegation involved statutory rape and sodomy. To be admissible, evidence of prior uncharged sexual activities must be nearly identical to the crime charged in the current case and so unusual that the prior acts operate as a virtual signature of the defendant's method of committing the crime. Here, the long lapse of time and the fact that the present facts were quite different, created unfair prejudice to the defendant and did not connect the old uncharged acts with the different present alleged activity. The prejudicial value of the prior 30-year-old uncharged acts outweighed any probative effect in the present case, so the appellate court reversed the convictions.[150] In a murder prosecution, where the defendant had not opened the door to use of impeachment evidence by the use of prior crimes, had not placed his general reputation at issue, and had not offered proof of good character, it was reversible error for the prosecution to ask witnesses if the defendant had ever threatened someone with an AK-47 rifle.[151]

Evidence of other crimes or prior misconduct by the defendant is generally not admissible to prove that a defendant is guilty of a crime for which he or she is currently on trial. Where an exception to this general rule applies, the evidence of prior crimes may be admissible if the evidence demonstrates a defendant's knowledge sufficient to commit the crime, common scheme or plan, motive, intent, or lack of mistake. In a prosecution for selling crack cocaine, a South Carolina trial court allowed evidence against the defendant that he had made unrelated crack cocaine sales to a government witness at different times previously. The reviewing court reversed the conviction on the theory that the admission of the prior sales under the common scheme or plan exception did not apply. The court noted that:

> The foundation for admissibility transcends mere similarity, for the admission of such evidence under the common scheme or plan exception requires a connection between the extraneous crimes and

---

[148]   Jackson v. United States, 856 A.2d 1111, 1114, 2004 D.C. App. LEXIS 413 (D.D.C. 2004). *See* case in Part II.

[149]   State v. Berwald, 186 S.W.3d 349, 359, 2005 Mo. App. LEXIS 1917 (2005).

[150]   *Id.*

[151]   Robertson v. Florida, 829 So. 2d 901, 912, 2002 Fla. LEXIS 1969 (2002).

the crime charged so that proof of the former tends to prove the latter. Succinctly stated, prior bad act evidence must be relevant to prove the alleged crime.

Here, the earlier crimes were similar—both involved the sale of crack cocaine and the present prosecution was for basically the same crime. In reversing the defendant's conviction, the appellate court did not see a continuing plan from the earlier sales that linked to the present sale and so it viewed the earlier sales as completely unrelated.[152] It should be noted that many courts would take a different view and would hold that the crimes are so similar that the earlier crime evidence should have been admitted.

When evidence of other crimes, wrongs, or acts committed by the defendant are introduced by the prosecution, the government has the burden of demonstrating a clear, logical, and legal relevance between the alleged earlier offense or misconduct and the case being tried.[153] For example, in a case in which the defendant had been charged with third-degree rape, the government introduced evidence that the defendant at prior times had engaged in intercourse with the victim and that he had done similar acts on numerous occasions with another underage female. These prior acts were not the subject of the prosecution but were permitted to be introduced—not to show that the defendant was a bad person—but to show his common scheme, plan, or motive in committing the presently charged crime. The court permitted the prosecution to introduce evidence of the prior acts with one victim to show that the defendant had a lustful disposition toward that victim. The trial court found the earlier acts had been proved by a preponderance of the evidence and that the probative value outweighed any danger of unfair prejudice. The reviewing court found no error in the use of the prior act evidence under Washington's version of Rule 404 and upheld the conviction.[154]

The United States Court of Appeals for the Eleventh Circuit declared that the trial judge must employ a two-part test in determining the admissibility of extrinsic evidence. It must first be determined that such evidence is relevant to an issue other than the defendant's character, and there must be sufficient proof to allow a jury to find by a preponderance of the evidence that the defendant committed the extrinsic act. Finally, it must be determined that the evidence has probative value not substantially outweighed by undue prejudice.[155] In applying this rule, another court held that in a murder case where the current victim and the prior victim had both been bound with their arms and ankles drawn up behind them, where both victims had gags placed in their mouths and had objects tied around their necks, and that the materials used to tie the women were similar, and that both women were of nearly the same height and weight, and that the underwear of both victims were removed, such

[152] State v. Tuffour, 364 S.C. 497, 613 S.E.2d 814, 2005 S.C. App. LEXIS 127 (2005).
[153] Colorado v. Rath, 44 P.3d 1033, 1038, 2002 Colo. LEXIS 271 (2002).
[154] State v. Harshbarger, 2005 Wash. App. LEXIS 505 (2005).
[155] United States v. Clemons, 32 F.3d 1504, 1508 (11th Cir. 1994).

similarities permitted the prior crime evidence to be introduced to show identity, common plan, and intent.[156]

In 1988, the Supreme Court was asked to clarify the application of Rule 404(b).[157] In this case, the petitioner was charged under federal law with knowledge of the possession and sale of stolen videotapes. At the trial, the district court allowed the government to introduce, as evidence of "similar acts" under Rule 404(b), evidence of the petitioner's involvement in a series of sales of allegedly stolen televisions and appliances from the same suspicious source as the tapes. On appeal, the defendant conceded that "similar acts" evidence was admissible to show his knowledge that the tapes had been stolen, but he argued that the grave potential of "similar acts" evidence for causing undue prejudice calls for a preliminary determination by the court that the defendant committed such acts before the jury should be allowed to hear that evidence. In a footnote to that case, the Supreme Court noted that there was inconsistency in the circuit courts, because six circuits apparently required a preliminary finding of the trial court that the government has proven commission of the similar act.

The United States Supreme Court then decided that the evidence of the prior acts was properly admitted by the trial court. According to the Court, there is no need for a preliminary finding by the trial court that the government has proven the commission of the similar acts and that such a requirement is inconsistent with the legislative history behind Rule 404(b). In referring to the relevancy issue, the court included this statement:

> Evidence is admissible under Rule 404(b) only if it is relevant. "Relevancy is not an inherent characteristic of any item of evidence but exists only as a relation between an item of evidence and a matter properly provable in the case." In Rule 404(b) context, similar act evidence is relevant only if the jury can reasonably conclude that the act occurred and that the defendant was the actor.[158]

Most states have adopted rules that are either identical or similar to Federal Rule 404. Each year, cases that interpret these rules reach state reviewing courts. Some of these decisions, which state the rules of the respective states and explain the reasoning of the courts in applying the rules, are included in Part II of this book.

The philosophy underlying the general rule excluding evidence of other crimes or other bad acts committed by the accused "is meant to prevent the State from punishing people for their character."[159] If most prior misconduct is allowed into evidence, its admission "endangers the defendant of being convicted because he or she is a person of bad character generally, or has crimi-

---

[156]   Kansas v. Higgenbotham, 271 Kan. 582, 589, 590, 23 P.3d 874, 879, 880 (2001).

[157]   Huddleston v. United States, 485 U.S. 681, 108 S. Ct. 1496, 96 L. Ed. 2d 771 (1988).

[158]   *Id.*

[159]   Bassett v. State, 795 N,E.2d 1050, 1053, 2003 Ind. LEXIS 750 (2003).

nal tendencies.[160] As one court, when speaking of uncharged crimes, succinctly stated, "[i]f the trial court does not clearly perceive the connection between the prior bad act and the crime charged, then the defendant should be given the benefit of the doubt, and the evidence should be rejected."[161] However, evidence of other, uncharged misconduct may be admitted if it has a legitimate tendency to prove a specific crime charged and it tends to establish motive, intent, absence of mistake or accident, a common scheme or plan embracing the commission of two or more crimes so related to each other that proof of one tends to establish the other, or to prove the identity of the person charged with commission of the crime.[162] For prior misconduct to be admissible, the prosecution must identify a proper purpose for admitting the evidence, there must be sufficient proof that the defendant committed the prior crime, and there must be a sufficient similarity between the prior act and the offense for which the defendant is standing trial.[163] The decision to admit prior crime evidence rests with the trial court in the exercise of judicial discretion and appellate courts will disturb a conviction only upon clear proof of abuse of discretion.[164]

Applying these general rules, an Arkansas trial court allowed evidence of a defendant's prior robbery conviction involving a nighttime break-in at an elderly woman's home to be introduced at his trial for aggravated robbery. In the crime for which he was on trial, the defendant entered an elderly woman's home, knocked her down, took her wallet, and fled the scene of the crime. The woman suffered a broken leg and died a month later. At the trial, the judge admitted evidence of the defendant's prior robbery offense as proof of modus operandi where he previously robbed an elderly woman who lived alone, at night, struck her in the face, and left with her wallet. In affirming the conviction, the court of appeals rejected the theory of *modus operandi* to admit the first conviction, but held that proof of the prior robbery should have been admitted on the theory that it proved the defendant had the same intent, motive, and plan to rob as he had in the prior case involving the first elderly woman.[165]

However, prior crimes and misconduct may be excluded when the connection to the charged crime is largely irrelevant and unfairly prejudicial. In an Indiana case in which the victim, wearing brass knuckles, initiated a fight with the defendant, who used a knife to puncture the victim's heart, the defendant objected to the use of prior act evidence at his homicide trial. The trial judge permitted the prosecutor to introduce evidence that the defendant used marijuana, had rolling papers, had Xanax and alcohol in his blood, and that he wanted to cut another man's throat at a different time. In reversing the homicide conviction, the appellate court held that the other crime and misconduct

---

[160] Samaniego-Hernandez v. State, 839 N.E.2d 798, 802, 2005 Ind. App. LEXIS 2450 (2005).
[161] State v. Gaines, 2002 Mo. App. LEXIS 1865 (2002).
[162] State v. Lancaster, 954 S.W.2d 27 (Mo. 1997).
[163] Robbins v. State, 277 Ga. App. 843, 844, 627 S.E.2d 810, 812, 2006 Ga. App. LEXIS 157 (2006).
[164] State v. Wililams, 209 Ariz. 228, 234, 99 P.3d 43, 49, 2004 Ariz. App. LEXIS 155 (2004).
[165] Medlock v. State, 79 Ark. App. 447; 89 S.W.3d 357; 2002 Ark. App. LEXIS 621 (2002), *aff'd*, 2004 Ark. LEXIS 527 (2004).

evidence was not properly admitted to show the defendant's state of mind or to refute self-defense. The other evidence involved different people and occurred at different times from the fatal altercation and had the effect of unfairly showing that the defendant had a criminal propensity and may have engaged in the illegal conduct.[166]

§ 7.13 —Experimental and Scientific Evidence

While the progress of science and its application to crime-solving in the criminal justice field cannot be overemphasized, the concepts involving relevancy and materiality require additional attention to assure the admission of scientific results into evidence. Probably the most prominent recent development in science that has positively influenced criminal justice professionals involves versions of DNA testing for identification purposes. It is imperative that the individuals conducting criminal investigations become solidly aware of the rules regarding the care, custody, and admissibility of scientific evidence and evidence resulting from experiments. This includes tests covering such evidence as weapons, bullets, fingerprints, DNA collection and care protocols, photographs, motion pictures, X-rays, tape recordings, maps, drawings, blood-alcohol tests, and results from computer hard drive examinations. While most experiments and scientific tests will be conducted by experts and introduced in court by expert witnesses, in some situations, specifically trained technicians who may not precisely fit the traditional definition of expert may present the evidence in court. These types of evidence will be discussed more thoroughly in other chapters under specific headings, especially in Chapter 14, Real Evidence.

The admissibility of all scientific or technical evidence arguably should be a foregone conclusion because its results contain no bias and only reveal truth. The contention could be made that the introduction of scientific evidence (e.g., the testing of firearms to show patterns of powder and shot made upon the object at different distances, tests of the speed of motor vehicles, blood tests, etc.) should always be admissible as relevant in criminal cases. Each scientific result must meet individual tests of relevancy and materiality prior to being considered for admission. However, in some instances the trial judge in his or her discretion may exclude the evidence to avoid possible unfair prejudice to the accused. Moreover, the court may impose a limit on the prosecution's demonstrations to avoid procedures that may unduly arouse, mislead, or confuse the jury. The admission or exclusion of scientific or technical evidence rests with the trial judge, whose decision will not be disturbed by an appellate court unless it finds a clear abuse of discretion.

As a preliminary matter concerning the admissibility of the results of scientific tests or experiments, the trial court must determine whether the results will meet the tests for relevancy. According to Federal Rule of Evidence 702,

---

[166]   Gillespie v. State, 832 N.E.2d 1112, 1117, 2005 Ind. App. LEXIS 1505 (2005).

"[I]f scientific, technical, or other specialized knowledge will assist the trier of fact to understand the evidence or to determine a fact in issue, a witness qualified as an expert by knowledge, skill, experience, training, or education, may testify thereto in the form of an opinion or otherwise." The burden of proof that the test is reliable rests on the party offering the scientific evidence; that is, in a criminal case, the prosecution has the burden of proving that the evidence is reliable if the prosecution is introducing it.[167] As a general rule, before scientific evidence is admitted, the party seeking to introduce the evidence must lay a foundation for the evidence such as introducing proof that [1.] "the underlying theory is generally accepted as valid; [2.] the procedures used are generally accepted as reliable if performed properly; [and] [3.] the procedures were applied and conducted properly in the present instance."[168]

After reviewing the *Frye* test[169] for admissibility for scientific evidence as established in previous cases, the United States Supreme Court in 1994 reconsidered an old legal standard regulating scientific testing in many federal courts. Until *Daubert v. Merrell Dow Pharmaceuticals*,[170] the *Frye v. United States* standard,[171] which required that a scientific principle and its related test have gained "general acceptance" in the particular field before a court should consider admitting the scientific results gradually gained acceptance in federal and state jurisdictions. Many trial judges followed this procedure when faced with the task of screening scientific evidence for relevancy and reliability.[172] Following *Daubert*, federal judges may follow Federal Rules of Evidence, which wisely allow trial judges to exercise broad discretion when evaluating the admissibility of scientific evidence.[173]

Daubert established the following nonexclusive list of factors to guide lower federal courts in assessing the reliability of scientific evidence:

1. Whether a scientific theory or technique can be (or has been) tested;

2. Whether the theory or technique has been subjected to peer review or publication;

3. The known or potential rate of error and the existence and maintenance of standards controlling the technique's operation;

4. Whether the technique is generally accepted.

The Court in *Daubert* emphasized that the inquiry in determining the reliability of scientific evidence is flexible, focusing on the principles and methodology proffered as evidence, rather than the conclusions they generate.[174]

---

[167] State v. Woodall, 385 S.E.2d 253 (W. Va. 1989).
[168] State v. Escobido-Ortiz, 109 Haw. 359, 367, 126 P.3d 402, 410, 2005 Haw. App. LEXIS 520 (2005).
[169] *See* Frye v. United States, 54 D.C. App. 46, 293 F. 1013, 1923 U.S. App. LEXIS 1712 (1923).
[170] Daubert v. Merrell Dow Pharmaceuticals, Inc., 509 U.S. 579, 1993 U.S. LEXIS 4408 (1993).
[171] Frye v. United States, 54 App. D.C. 46, 47, 293 F. 1013, 1014 (1923).
[172] Daubert v. Merrell Dow Pharmaceuticals, Inc., 509 U.S. 579, 1993 U.S. LEXIS 4408 (1993).
[173] United States v. Scheffer, 523 U.S. 303, 322, 1998 U.S. LEXIS 2303 (1998).
[174] *See* Chapter 15 for a comprehensive discussion of the admissibility of the results of examinations and tests.

When considering the admissibility of scientific evidence, only the scientific validity—not the scientific precision—is required for admissibility of such scientific evidence. Courts are not to be concerned only with the reliability of conclusions generated by valid methods, principles, and reasoning, but need to determine whether the principles and methodology underlying the testimony itself are valid.[175]

§ 7.14 Summary

In a criminal trial, the primary objective is to determine the truth as to the issues presented. Over the years, the courts have developed rules of exclusion, including rules concerning relevancy and materiality. If the evidence does not meet the tests of relevancy and materiality, it will not be admitted. Evidence that has even a slight tendency to prove or disprove a pertinent fact in issue will be considered relevant, but some relevant evidence may be excluded if its tendency to prove or disprove a fact at issue is unfairly prejudicial. Evidence that goes to substantial matters in dispute and has an effective influence or bearing on the decision of the case is material.

The trial court has great latitude in determining the admissibility of the evidence and whether it has legal relevancy or materiality. The court's interpretation as to what evidence is relevant is usually given great weight, and its determination will be final unless there is a clear abuse of discretion.

State constitutions and the federal constitution, along with state and federal court decisions and relevant statutes, must be considered in determining what evidence meets the relevancy and materiality tests. The following general rules have been developed through this procedure:

- Evidence that tends to establish the identity of persons involved is admissible as being relevant and material. This, of course, is subject to the other rules of admissibility.

- Evidence that concerns the identity of things connected with the crime is considered relevant, although there are some exceptions.

- Evidence that helps prove or disprove elements of the crime will be considered relevant and material.

- Generally, evidence that relates to the circumstances and events that precede or follow the crime is admissible as relevant to the issues.

- Evidence relating to the defenses claimed by the defendant, such as mental disease, coercion, self-defense, and alibi is generally admissible if it meets the other admissibility tests in addition to the relevancy and materiality tests.

---

[175] United States v. Prince-Oyibo, 320 F.3d 494, 498, 499, 2003 LEXIS 3568 (4th Cir. 2003).

- Although evidence regarding the character and reputation of the accused, as well as other evidence concerning the commission of other crimes, is sometimes recognized as relevant and material, it is often excluded because of overriding dangers of unfair prejudice to the defendant's case. For this reason, only certain evidence of this type is admissible.

- Evidence of other crimes, wrongs, or acts is not admissible to show criminal propensity, but may be admissible to show the existence of a continuing or common plan, scheme, motive, intent, identity, lack of mistake, lack of knowledge, or conspiracy of which the crime charged is a part.

- Evidence concerning experimental and scientific evidence is also usually considered relevant, but it must pass other tests before it can be admitted into court.

It is obvious that even though the parties may succeed in excluding evidence that is irrelevant and immaterial, there is certainly no reciprocal assurance that evidence that is relevant and material necessarily will be admitted. In future chapters, some of the other requirements will be discussed, and relevancy and materiality as they relate to specific types of evidence will be explored in more detail.

Competency of Evidence and Witnesses   8

The terms "relevancy," "competency," and "materiality" are frequently used conjunctively in such manner as to suggest that they are synonymous, yet it is obvious upon second thought that a matter which may be relevant to an issue of the case may be rendered incompetent and inadmissible as to the established rules of evidence, such as the rule which excludes hearsay evidence or requires the production of the best evidence. . . . In other words evidence must be not only logically relevant, but of such a character as to be receivable in courts of justice.

20 AM. JUR. *Evidence* 253

Chapter Outline

Key Terms and Concepts

competency of evidence   negative evidence
competency of witnesses

§ 8.1 Introduction

While the preceding chapters discussed some of the rules concerning relevancy and materiality, the focus of this chapter involves competency of both witnesses and evidence. Even when evidence has been deemed to be relevant and material or logically relevant and legally relevant, it still must cross the third hurdle of competency before it can be considered admissible. Evidence is inadmissible if it is incompetent, but evidence may admissible when it is competent[1] and when it meets the standards of relevancy and materiality.[2]

Evidence that is competent, relevant, and material is admissible. The application of the rules concerning competency of evidence and witnesses has troubled courts, judges, and attorneys with its complexity, and for that reason, many writers and even some legal encyclopedias fail to adequately explain the competency restrictions. Therefore, this chapter will consider the rules relating not only to the competency of witnesses, but also to the competency of evidence. The fact that a witness meets the threshold of competency to testify does not necessarily mean that the evidence that the witness may offer meets the standard of competency. Similarly, evidence may meet the tests of relevancy, materiality, and competency, but the witness who wishes to offer the evidence may not be competent as a witness.[3]

---

[1]   Peterson v. State, 274 Ga. 165, 167 (2001); State v. Stanley, 131 N.M. 368, 373, 37 P.3d 85, 91 (2001).

[2]   State v. Martinez, 149 N.C. App. 553, 560, 561 S.E.2d 528, 533 (2002); Robbins v. State, 88 S.W.3d 256, 259, 2002 Tex. Crim. App. LEXIS 208 (2002).

[3]   *See* ILL. COMP. STAT. ANNO. § 735 ILCS 5/8-201. Dead-Man's Act (Matthew Bender 2006) and CAL. VEH. CODE § 40803 Admissibility of speed trap evidence. (Matthew Bender 2006).

§ 8.2 Definitions

Black's Law Dictionary defines competent evidence as "evidence that is relevant and is of such a character (e.g., not unfairly prejudicial or based on hearsay) that the court should receive it."[4] Competent evidence is also defined as evidence that tends to establish the fact in issue and does not rest on mere surmise or conjecture.[5]

Perhaps the definition of competent evidence can be better understood if incompetent evidence is defined. In *Black's Law Dictionary*, incompetent evidence is defined as "evidence that is for any reason inadmissible."[6] A Kentucky court recognized that evidence was defective and thus incompetent where the proof indicated that a defendant was a persistent felony offender. Because the evidence proving the persistent offender status had not been properly authenticated at the trial and the incompetent evidence had been introduced against the defendant, the penalty had to be reversed.[7] Here, if the trial judge had determined that the evidence failed the test of competency, the court would have excluded the evidence from admission.

In seeking answers about what evidence should be deemed incompetent, and therefore inadmissible, many avenues are open and volumes of material are available. Much of this book is devoted to determining what evidence is considered incompetent and therefore inadmissible in court.

§ 8.3 General Categories of Incompetent Evidence

If evidence is found to be incompetent, it is usually because the courts have found that it comes within one of the three general categories discussed below.

A. *Wrongfully Obtained Evidence*

Evidence that has been obtained in violation of the Constitution, such as that obtained by an illegal search, often will not be admitted because the courts have reasoned that admitting such evidence would encourage the state to disregard the constitutional rights of citizens. Demonstrative of principle, the Supreme Court held that where the police operated roadblocks to screen all drivers for crime, in the absence of individualized suspicion, the practice violated the Fourth Amendment.[8] Evidence obtained directly or indirectly as a result of an involuntary confession should not be admitted because the process used in obtaining the evidence violated the due process clauses of the Consti-

---

[4]   BLACK'S LAW DICTIONARY (8th ed. 2004).
[5]   31A C.J.S. *Evidence* § 3 (1996).
[6]   BLACK'S LAW DICTIONARY (8th ed. 2004).
[7]   Merriweather v. Commonwealth, 99 S.W.3d 448, 2003 Ky. LEXIS 39 (2003). *See also* Young v. Commonwealth, 47 Va. App. 616; 625 S.E.2d 691; 2006 Va. App. LEXIS 42 (2006).
[8]   *See* City of Indianapolis v. Edmond, 531 U.S. 32 (2000). *See also* Mapp v. Ohio, 357 U.S. 643 (1961).

tution.[9] A conviction cannot stand where police violate the principles of *Miranda v. Arizona* to obtain evidence in a manner that is inconsistent with the intent of the required custody warnings.[10] Evidence seized due to illegal police activity is inadmissible, not because it is irrelevant or immaterial, but because it is incompetent as determined by the courts.

B. *Statutory Incompetency*

Some evidence is admissible as competent evidence because a statute provides that it is competent evidence and, similarly, some evidence is not admissible because a state or federal statute prohibits the admission of the evidence. For example, § 2515 of the Omnibus Crime Control and Safe Streets Act of 1968,[11] as amended, provides that evidence obtained by wiretapping or eavesdropping, when conducted in violation of the statute, is inadmissible in any court or other official proceeding. Similarly, an Ohio statute provides that a police officer is incompetent to testify as a witness in a misdemeanor prosecution against a driver charged with violating the vehicle or traffic laws if the officer, at the time of the arrest or citation, was using a motor vehicle that was not properly marked and did not have a flashing light mounted outside the police vehicle.[12] Some states have statutes that protect the interests of decedents' estates when the law specifically states that some people are not competent as witnesses in listed legal actions.[13] Evidence produced in contravention of these and similar statutes will be excluded from court use, not because it is irrelevant or immaterial, but because the statutes specifically provide that the evidence is not admissible or usable in court.

C. *Evidence Excluded Because of a Court-Established Rule*

Although many rules of evidence have now been codified, most evidence is excluded because the courts, over a period of years, have established certain rules regarding the admissibility of evidence. Some excellent examples, which will be discussed more thoroughly in forthcoming chapters, are rules that prohibit the admission of certain opinion testimony, hearsay evidence, and privileged communications. The Federal Rules of Evidence prevent a judge who is sitting in the case from being a witness in that case, and a juror who is hearing a case is considered incompetent as a witness in the same case.[14] Where court rules exclude evidence, the courts generally have a sound reason for

---

[9]   *See* Arizona v. Fulminante, 499 U.S. 279 (1991); the exclusion of illegally obtained evidence is discussed in Chapter 16. *See also* KANOVITZ & KANOVITZ, CONSTITUTIONAL LAW (10th ed. 2005) and KLOTTER, WALKERR, & HEMMENS., LEGAL GUIDE FOR POLICE: CONSTITUTIONAL ISSUES (7th ed. 2005).

[10] State v. Seibert, 542 U.S. 600, 2004 U.S. LEXIS 4578 (2004).

[11] Title III of the Omnibus Crime Control and Safe Streets Act of 1968, 18 U.S.C. § 2510 *et seq.*

[12] City of Parma Heights v. Nugent, 92 Ohio Misc. 2d 67, 700 N.E.2d 430, 1998 Ohio Misc. LEXIS 32 (1998); *see* OHIO REV. CODE § 4549.14 in conjunction with OHIO REV. CODE § 4549.13 (Matthew Bender 2006) and OHIO EVID. R. 601(C) (Matthew Bender 2006).

[13] *See* BURNS IND. CODE ANN. § 34-45-2-4, When executor or administrator is party.

[14] *See* FED. R. EVID. 605 and 606.

rejecting the evidence, whether the purpose involves the public policy of supporting confidential relationships or preventing the admission of evidentiary errors involving hearsay evidence.

§ 8.4 Competency of Evidence— Documentary Evidence

Legal evidence includes not only oral testimony given under oath by witnesses in open court and physical objects introduced in evidence by witnesses, but also all kinds of documents and records. The concept of document includes traditional writings, as well as films, videotapes, CD and DVD data, electronically stored documents, jump drive documents, Web pages, and stored cell phone data. These methods of storing information and of observing them are roughly classified as documentary evidence. Evidence meeting the definition of documentary evidence is subject to the same rules of relevancy, materiality, and competency as other types of evidence. Documentary evidence must pass all of the competency tests, such as the hearsay test, the opinion evidence test, and the various constitutional tests. In addition, documentary evidence must meet other qualifications before it is admissible. The party desiring to offer documentary evidence must authenticate the document by demonstrating that it is genuine. Documentary evidence must also meet the requirements of the best evidence rule and comply with requirements that are peculiar to "questioned documents."[15]

§ 8.5 —Tests and Experiments

The results of scientific tests and experiments may assist the trier of fact in evaluating the evidence in a criminal case and assist the jury in reaching a correct verdict. Evidence showing the outcome of an experiment or test may be admissible to aid in determining the issues in a case in which it is shown that the conditions under which the experiment or test was made are substantially similar to the circumstances prevailing at the time of the occurrence. Evidence obtained as a result of tests and experiments made during a trial or conducted out of the courtroom has been challenged as being incompetent evidence based on alleged improper administration, improper conduct, and testing under different circumstances.[16] Generally, where it is necessary to show the condition or quality of a certain article or substance, the item itself may be introduced in evidence to supplement the testimony of the witness, or as direct evidence when properly identified. Some scientific tests are designed to reveal the identity of a substance, a chemical, or drug, while other tests reconstruct how an

---

[15]   The rules relating to the admissibility of documentary evidence are discussed fully in Chapter 13.

[16]   Holt v. State, 2006 Tenn. Crim. App. LEXIS 107 (2006).

event occurred or connect people or objects to a crime. The actual objects tested may be introduced as evidence, but in some cases, only the results of testing are available. For instance, most drug analysis tests and some experiments may prove destructive to the item being tested, a factor that will prevent the actual object or item from being introduced as physical evidence.

Making the determination of whether the results of a test or experiment should be admitted as evidence requires a trial court to evaluate whether the test will produce relevant evidence that is reliable and fair. Until the Supreme Court of the United States decided the *Daubert v. Merrell Dow Pharmaceuticals* case (1993), a great number of courts, both federal and state, followed the old *Frye* standard. The *Frye* case (1923) generated a test for admissibility of scientific evidence suggested by the District of Columbia Court of Appeals that other state and federal courts often adopted. In determining whether to admit scientific evidence and tests, the *Frye* Court considered that:

> Just when a scientific principle or discovery crosses the line between the experimental and demonstrable stages is difficult to define. Somewhere in this twilight zone, the evidential force of the principle must be recognized, and while courts will go a long way in admitting expert testimony deduced from a well-recognized scientific principle or discovery, the thing from which the deduction is made must be sufficiently established to have gained general acceptance in the particular field in which it belongs.[17]

In *Daubert v. Merrell Dow Pharmaceuticals*, the issue arose concerning whether the *Frye* standard governed in federal cases or whether the Federal Rules of Evidence should take precedence because the Federal Rules were enacted long after the *Frye* decision. According to *Daubert*, Federal Rule 702 generally controls the admissibility of scientific or technical knowledge in federal courts.[18] Rule 702, Testimony of Experts, states:

> If scientific, technical, or other specialized knowledge will assist the trier of fact to understand the evidence or to determine a fact in issue, a witness qualified as an expert by knowledge, skill, experience, training, or education, may testify thereto in the form of an opinion or otherwise, if (1) the testimony is based upon sufficient facts or data, (2) the testimony is the product of reliable principles and methods, and (3) the witness has applied the principles and methods reliably to the facts of the case.

Even though the *Frye* test was displaced upon adoption of the Federal Rules of Evidence, it did not mean that Rule 702 placed no limits on the admissibility of scientific evidence and tests. The trial judge must be certain that any and all scientific evidence admitted is both relevant and reliable. While Rule 702

---

[17]   54 D.C. App. at 47, 293 F. at 1014, 1923 U.S. App. LEXIS 1712 (D.C.C.A. 1923).
[18]   Daubert v. Merrell Dow Pharmaceuticals, Inc., 509 U.S. 579, 1993 U.S. LEXIS 4408 (1993).

does not mention the "general acceptance" standard of *Frye*, many of the evaluations performed by a judge in deciding whether to admit evidence of scientific tests and experiments under Rule 702 will consider some of the following factors as a commonsense approach: (1) whether the scientific evidence has been tested and the methodology by which it has been tested; (2) whether the evidence has been subjected to peer review or publication; (3) whether the potential rate of error is known; (4) whether the evidence is generally accepted in the scientific community; and (5) whether the experts' research in the field has been conducted independent of litigation.[19] Consistent with the concept of federalism, courts that follow a state adoption of the Federal Rules of Evidence are free to interpret them differently from the *Daubert* decision and could follow a state version of the *Frye* standard or some other version consistent with due process. Examples of scientific tests and experiments that may be admissible are: blood grouping tests, blood-alcohol testing, fingerprint comparisons, ballistics experiments, and DNA tests.[20]

§ 8.6 —Conduct of Trained Dogs

Evidence produced by observing the conduct of trained dogs may be admissible against a defendant in a variety of contexts. Law enforcement officials may use dogs to discover the identity of a suspect, to actually find the suspect, to find lost objects, to detect the presence of controlled substances, to alert to the presence of arson accelerants, to discover cadavers, and to identify objects containing explosives.

The conduct of a dog in tracking a suspect, as interpreted by the animal's handler, has been held to produce competent and admissible evidence in both civil and criminal cases.[21] "[M]any courts have ruled that in general, evidence of tracking a defendant is admissible, subject to establishment of a proper foundation"[22] to assist in proving identity as long as a proper foundation regarding the animal's training and the handler's skills with the dog have been proven. For example, Washington requires that the party offering the dog tracking evidence establish foundation requirements. A precondition for dog tracking evidence to be admitted requires that:

> (1) the handler was qualified by training and experience to use the dog, (2) the dog was adequately trained in tracking humans, (3) the dog has, in actual cases, been found by experience to be reliable in

---

[19]   State v. Begley, 956 S.W.2d 471 (Tenn. 1997).

[20]   The rules relating to admissibility of evidence concerning tests and experiments are discussed in detail in Chapter 15.

[21]   Washington v. Loucks, 98 Wash. 2d 563, 656 P.2d 480, 1983 Wash. LEXIS 1333 (1983); *see also* Washington v. Hunotte, 2001 Wash. App. LEXIS 1941 (2001) and Commonwealth v. Hill, 52 Mass. App. 147, 153 (2001).

[22]   *See* Jay M. Zitter, Annotation, *Evidence of Trailing by Dogs in Criminal Cases*, 81 A.L.R. 5TH 563 (Updated 2004).

pursuing human track, (4) the dog was placed on track where circumstances indicated the guilty party to have been, and (5) the trail had not become so stale or contaminated as to be beyond the dog's competency to follow.[23]

Washington courts generally require that the dog tracking evidence have some minimal corroboration to be admissible. Dog tracking evidence should include a cautionary jury instruction that dog tracking evidence by itself cannot support a conviction in the absence of other evidence.[24]

Evidence of the conduct of a dog in tracking the accused from the scene of a crime to the place where the police arrested him has been found competent and admissible. The evidence could be treated as circumstantial or corroborative evidence of identity where other circumstances pointed to the defendant's guilt of the crime charged. The Court of Appeals for the Ninth Circuit approved the use of canine evidence of identification in a bank robbery context in *United States v. Hornbeck*, in which the appeals court quoted the district court:

> We have received information that the K-9 Trainer has been doing so [working in the field successfully alerting police to defendants] for the past eight years and the bloodhound had been used in 22 criminal investigations. And accordingly, the foundation has been established, the reliability of the dog and the handler has been established, and therefore I see no impediments to allowing those matters to be received into evidence.[25]

The appellate court also noted that the district court had reviewed the reliability of the evidence concerning the foundation for the dog and the handler and had determined that the prosecutor had established the proper foundation for admissibility of the scent-tracking evidence offered by the handler.

In a similar context, a reviewing court agreed that the proper foundation had been established where a state trooper testified that he and his dog had received extensive training in tracking a human scent, that they had undergone in-service training and recertification, that the dog had successfully tracked people both in actual cases and in training exercises, and that the dog had been placed on the trail where circumstances indicated that the perpetrator had recently been. Evidence that his dog had tracked a human scent from the place where a rapist entered the victim's house to the defendant's house was properly admitted.[26] In some states, no amount of proper foundation for tracking dogs will allow the evidence to be admitted.[27] One Illinois reviewing court

---

[23] State v. Lathim, 2006 Wash. App. LEXIS 936 (2006).

[24] State v. Burnice, 2006 Wash. App. LEXIS 45 (2006).

[25] 2003 U.S. App. LEXIS 8043 (9th Cir. 2003).

[26] State v. Cole, 695 A.2d 1180 (Maine 1997). *See also* Thomas v. State, 226 Ga. App. 441, 487 S.E.2d 75 (1997), and People v. Brooks, 950 P.2d 649 (Colo. 1997).

[27] *Id.*, 81 A.L.R. 5th 563, sec. 4.

noted that bloodhound tracking evidence had never been admitted in state courts since 1914 and the court decided to stand by the rule of exclusion.[28]

The Court of Criminal Appeals of Alabama approved the use of trained dogs for identifying persons suspected of a store burglary. The owner of the store fired several shots at the departing men he knew to be the guilty parties. Shoes and socks believed to belong to the culprits were found in the parking lot and were used to give the canines a sniff of the goal of their search. Four miles down the road, the dogs identified the defendant's odor as matching the scent from the clothing at the parking lot. The prosecution appealed a trial court order suppressing the canine identifications on the ground that dog tracking evidence cannot establish probable cause to arrest. In overturning the trial court's decision on the motion to suppress, the reviewing court held that such evidence could equal probable cause if the training and reliability of the dog is established, the trainer/handler has proper qualifications, and the circumstances indicate reliability of the evidence. Citing cases that extended over a century the court held that dog tracking evidence was admissible for identification purposes. [29]

Canine identification of accelerants used in arson has been approved in appropriate cases. In a California case, the trial court conducted a hearing to consider whether canine evidence should be admitted through the animal's handler. The deputy-handler testified that the dog had been trained to alert to accelerants, had been involved in more than 280 fire cases, plus an additional 100 to 150 training fires, that she and the dog had been trained in connection with accelerant detection, that the dog underwent continued training and retraining, and that the animal did not give false alerts when accelerants were missing. The trial judge approved the admission into evidence of the handler's testimony concerning the dog's conduct in detecting accelerants at the crime scene in question.[30]

§ 8.7 —Telephone Conversations

The substance of telephone conversations may be considered competent and admissible as evidence, provided the contents of the conversation are relevant and material and there has been authentication of the voices. The concept of authentication means that the party wishing to introduce evidence of a telephone conversation must be able to prove who was actually talking on the telephone and, in some cases, prove the identities of all parties to the conversation. Identification of the speakers may occur by the use of either direct evidence offered by one of the parties to the conversation who knew with whom

[28]   People v. Lefler, 294 Ill. App. 3d 305, 308, 689 N.E.2d 1209, 1212, 1998 Ill. App. LEXIS 34 (1998). The court held that all dog tracking evidence had to be excluded, even if tracking were done with a trained German Shepard canine.

[29]   State v. Montgomery, 2006 Ala. Crim. App. LEXIS 36 (2006).

[30]   People v. Perez, 2003 Cal. App. Unpub. LEXIS 558 (2003).

he or she was speaking, or by facts and circumstantial proof that indicates the identity of one or more of the speakers. In addition, where the conversation evidence has been obtained by wiretap, relevant federal and state laws must have been properly observed or the evidence may be excluded.[31] Beyond the data generated by traditional phones, newer phone systems and cell phones generate tremendous amounts of nonverbal data and metadata that are routinely stored for long periods either by the cell phone carrier or in the handset. Many cell phones store text messages, pictures, Web pages, information on personal contacts, as well as calendar and appointment data. Police and prosecutors have just begun to mine this nonverbal data and that process and the results will generate new admissibility issues as these new technologies are exploited.

For evidence of telephone conversation contents to be admitted, the identities of participants must be authenticated. Such identity may be proved through voice identification, where the recipient is familiar with the caller's voice, or through circumstantial evidence, where the caller gives sufficient specific information that only he or she would know, such as a name, telephone number, address, and Social Security number.[32] Where a call was made to a number assigned to a particular person, and that person purportedly answered, such conduct tends to show that the person answering was the person who was the intended recipient. Similarly, when one calls a business under similar circumstances and where the answering voice indicates that the intended business has been reached, such conduct tends to authenticate the conversation as genuinely coming from the business. Telephone conversations may be authenticated and made competent where one party to the conversation recognizes a person based on distinctive accents or speech patterns, or from proof of the contents or substance of a conversation. The requirement of direct voice recognition is not an inexorable or mechanical rule, but where the caller or the person called can recognize the other, this tends to authenticate the other person on the line. The party desiring the introduction of telephone conversation evidence is not required to eliminate all possibilities inconsistent with authenticity, or to prove beyond a reasonable doubt that the person with whom the person spoke is actually the intended recipient of the conversation; the standard is rather low.[33] Thus, conflicts in information to establish the identity of a telephone caller go to the weight and not the admissibility of the evidence.

When a caller places a call to another person who does not recognize the caller's voice, the fact that the caller self-identified does not serve as sufficient authentication of the identity of the caller.[34] Caller Identification (Caller ID), a device that, for the person called, displays the number and other data related to the incoming call, may play a role in authenticating a caller. Although Caller ID may be admitted to prove the source of the call, a foundation is necessary

---

[31]   18 U.S.C. § 2511 *et seq.*, Title III of the Omnibus Crime Control and Safe Streets Act of 1968, as periodically amended, generally prohibits the interception of wire, electronic, and oral communications by anyone, unless done in compliance with the Act.

[32]   Angleton v. State, 686 N.E.2d 803 (Ind. 1997).

[33]   Kalola v. Eisenberg, 344 N.J. Super. 198, 205, 781 A.2d 77, 81, 2001 N.J. Super. LEXIS 368 (2001).

[34]   Wells v. Liddy, 37 Fed. Appx. 53, 2002 U.S. App. LEXIS 3356 (4th Cir. 2002).

to establish the proper functioning of the device,[35] and while Caller ID cannot authenticate the identity of the caller, it may be admissible to prove the location and source of the call. Demonstrative of this principle is a Virginia case in which the defendant allegedly abducted his girlfriend after a quarrel. The father of the abducted female had Caller ID, which recorded the telephone numbers of incoming callers. The victim's father was permitted to testify that he received a phone call from his daughter and that his Caller ID device displayed the telephone assigned to the phone his daughter was using. The telephone number on the caller ID device proved to be the appellant's telephone number. The Virginia court held that this combination of information was sufficient to authenticate the daughter's call as having come from the home of her boyfriend and that there was no error in allowing the father/witness to testify concerning the number that was displayed on his Caller ID device. This evidence proved where the call originated and was corroborative of the victim's testimony that she telephoned her parents from the quarrelling boyfriend's home.[36] Thus, in conjunction with other information, Caller ID may provide the additional information necessary to authenticate a caller and make the evidence competent.

Circumstantial evidence may be sufficient to authenticate the identity of the speaker. In *State v. Marshall*, the reviewing court concluded that the telephone conversation purported to have been with the defendant was sufficiently authenticated to be admitted in evidence. At a prior time, the defendant rented some appliances from a rent-to-own company, but refused to pay the current rent or return the items. Store employees called the telephone number given by the defendant on his rental agreement and the defendant identified himself as being the person who had the property. The appeals court held that the identity of the defendant as being the person talking on the phone had been properly authenticated because the defendant self-identified by refusing to return the property and he clearly was aware of the topic of the conversation.[37] However, the mere identification of the person called by the person who has placed a telephone call does not suffice to authenticate the statements and make them admissible against the person so identified. In the above case, the party against whom the evidence was to be introduced had special knowledge of the facts that identified him as the person who had rented the property.

In a prosecution for second-degree rape of a child, the defendant appealed his conviction based on the admission of a telephone conversation that he allegedly had with one of his young victims. When adults became aware of allegations that the defendant had consummated sexual relations with one or more children, one adult had one of the victims call the defendant's telephone number and engage him in incriminating conversation that implicated him in the crimes for which he was convicted. The trial court permitted the adult to

[35] *See* 31 WRIGHT & GOLD, FEDERAL PRACTICE AND PROCEDURE: EVIDENCE § 7110 n. 42 (2000).
[36] Tatum v. Commonwealth of Virginia, 17 Va. App. 585, 440 S.E.2d 133, 1994 Va. App. LEXIS 30 (1994).
[37] State v. Marshall, 2005 Ohio 5585; 2005 Ohio App. LEXIS 5054 (2005).

relate to the jury the substance of the conversation that the adult witness over-heard between the victim and the defendant. The appellate court agreed that the adult could authenticate the defendant as being the voice on the telephone making incriminating statements because the defendant and the adult witness were neighbors, the witness was familiar with the quality of the defendant's voice, and the victim dialed the defendant's number in full view of the adult witness.[38]

§ 8.8 Negative Evidence as Competent Evidence

In Black's Law Dictionary, negative evidence is defined as "evidence suggesting that an alleged fact does not exist, such as a witness's testifying that he or she did not see an event occur."[39] Evidence is positive when the witness states that a certain thing did or did not happen, or did or did not exist, and negative when the witness states that he or she did not see or know of the existence of a certain circumstance or fact.[40] Trial courts have broad discretion to admit evidence that something did not happen[41] and must determine whether the probative value outweighs the prejudicial nature of the evidence. Testimony concerning negative evidence is admissible where the circumstances demonstrate that the negative evidence has some probative force; the proponent establishes the competency of the witness; and the witness has personal knowledge that something *did not* occur.[42]

Although a foundation must be laid before negative testimony will be considered relevant and competent, testimony as to the nonexistence of a fact or as to the witness's lack of knowledge of its existence is admissible where the situation of the witness was such that if the fact had existed, he or she probably would have known it.[43]

An effective use of negative evidence involves allowing an opposing witness to testify freely and completely concerning matters within his or her knowledge and noting, for later cross-examination purposes, matters that he or she would logically have related to others at a prior time. If the witness adds testimony covering new topics that he or she had not discussed earlier, bringing out his or her previous silence on that topic, or absence of evidence, has the effect of impeaching the witness's direct testimony. The prior silence appears to be inconsistent with the recent trial testimony, suggesting that the trial testimony might be a recent contrivance by the witness. Questions arise when the witness fails to mention the substance of the testimony at a time when it would have been natural to speak on the topic. Therefore, the absence

---

[38]   State v. Brown, 2006 Wash. App. LEXIS 1092 (2006).
[39]   BLACK'S LAW DICTIONARY (8th ed. 2004).
[40]   31A C.J.S. *Evidence* § 165 (1994).
[41]   Brown v. Classic Inns, 2002 Wis. App 134, 255 Wis. 2d 832, 646 N.W.2d 854 (2002).
[42]   29A AM JUR. 2d *Evidence* § 318 (1994).
[43]   31A. C.J.S. *Evidence* § 165 (1994).

of evidence—negative evidence—may be relevant and competent to prove a recent fabrication by the witness.[44]

Not all negative evidence will be admissible if a court rules that the probative value is not strong. In a Hawai'i case, the state supreme court held that it was error for a victim's father to testify concerning the victim's reputation for peacefulness by offering evidence that he never saw his son attack his own family, friends, or anyone else during the son's youth. The negative evidence of violence was not probative of whether the victim launched an attack on another person six years later and required a reversal of the defendant's conviction.[45]

Some writers and courts have noted that, as a general rule of evidence, all other things being equal, positive evidence carries more weight than negative evidence,[46] but to instruct the jury that positive evidence should be given greater weight is error.[47] To indicate that negative evidence carries less weight than positive evidence invades the province of the jury. One court indicated that where there are two witnesses of equal credibility in direct contradiction on a question of fact, the positive testimony will be given preference.[48]

In summary, while negative evidence is regarded by some authorities as entitled to less weight than positive evidence, negative evidence is valuable and admissible when a proper foundation has been laid, provided that the competency of the witness and his or her knowledge of the matter are established. Negative evidence has probative value and, in the right situation, may be adequate to help form a factual determination.[49]

§ 8.9 Evidence Competent for Some Purposes but Not for Others

Where evidence may be admissible on one theory and excludable under another, generally courts have decided that the fact that "evidence is admissible for one purpose, but not another, does not make it inadmissible."[50] If, on the other hand, the evidence has so strong a prejudicial value as to upset the balance of the advantages of receiving the evidence, a judge has discretion in deciding whether to admit or refuse it. When evidence is logically relevant and admissible under one theory but inadmissible under a different theory, in admitting the evidence, the judge should advise the jury in an instruction dur-

[44] Connecticut v. Vines, 71 Conn. App. 359, 371 A.2d 918, 926, 2002 Conn. App. LEXIS 406 (2002).
[45] State v. Dean, 2005 Haw. LEXIS 584 (2005).
[46] 29A AM. JUR. Evidence § 1438 (1994); see also Randall v. Norfolk S. Ry. Co., 800 N.E.2d 951, 959, 2003 Ind. App. LEXIS 2406 (2003).
[47] Tafoya v. Chapin, 2003 Neb. App. LEXIS 64 (2003).
[48] State v. Bentley, 499 So. 2d 581 (La. 1987); 29A AM. JUR. 2d Evidence § 318 (1994).
[49] See Brown v. District of Columbia, 700 A.2d 787, 1997 D.C. App. LEXIS 229 (1997).
[50] People v. McGhee, 268 Mich. App. 600, 639, 709 N.W.2d 595, 620, 2005 Mich. App. LEXIS 2753 (2005).

ing the trial that the evidence can be considered for one purpose but not for another.[51] A second cautionary instruction should be requested by the defendant's counsel prior to the jury retiring to deliberate. Trials conducted under the Federal Rules of Evidence suggest that when evidence is admissible for one purpose but not another, "the court, upon request, shall restrict the evidence to its proper scope and instruct the jury accordingly."[52] Demonstrative of this rule, in an Iowa case, the prosecution played audio recordings of the defendant's interrogation by law enforcement officials. The defendant's answers were considered evidence but the questions and comments of the police officers were not evidence that could be considered for the truth. The questions and comments of the police interrogators were admissible only to give context to the defendant's statements. Because the evidence was admissible for one purpose and not for other purposes, the judge erred by not giving a limiting instruction to the jury not to consider as evidence what the police said.[53]

Constitutional reasons may have the effect of excluding evidence when offered for one purpose but permitting admission of that evidence as competent when used for a different purpose. In a New York criminal case, the prosecution was prevented from using the defendant's statements made after his arrest due to a *Miranda* warning violation. When the defendant took the witness stand in his own defense and offered a story that was inconsistent with his post-arrest statement, the prosecution could introduce the inconsistent post-arrest statement only for the purpose of impeaching the defendant.[54] According to Chief Justice Burger, "[t]he shield provided by *Miranda* cannot be perverted into a license to use perjury by way of a defense, free from the risk of confrontation with prior inconsistent utterances."[55] Excluding the post-arrest statement from use as impeachment evidence would have permitted the defendant to commit perjury without suffering any adverse consequences.

Before moving to the discussion of the competency of witnesses, it should be mentioned that there are many other evidentiary rules of exclusion that are not addressed here, not because they are not pertinent, but because they are discussed in detail in other chapters.

---

[51]   Mackey v. Russell, 148 Fed. Appx. 355, 2005 U.S. App. LEXIS 16933 (6th Cir. 2005). *See also* OHIO EVID. R. 105, which states, "When evidence which is admissible as to one party or for one purpose but not admissible as to another party or for another purpose is admitted, the court, upon request of a party, shall restrict the evidence to its proper scope and instruct the jury accordingly."

[52]   FED. R. EVID. 105.

[53]   State v. Esse, 2005 Iowa App. LEXIS 1199 (Iowa 2005).

[54]   *See* Harris v. New York, 401 U.S. 222 (1971).

[55]   *Id.* at 226.

§ 8.10　Competency of Witnesses

Rule 601

General Rule of Competency

Every person is competent to be a witness except as otherwise provided in these rules. However, in civil actions and proceedings, with respect to an element of a claim or defense as to which State law supplies the rule of decision, the competency of a witness shall be determined in accordance with State law.[56]

The Federal Rules of Evidence start with the presumption that all witnesses are competent to offer testimony unless a particular rule of evidence provides otherwise or there exists some defect in the four elements of competency of the witness that renders the witness incapable of offering proper evidence.[57] Because federal courts often sit as state civil courts in diversity of citizenship cases, Rule 601 defers to state law to determine whether a witness is competent when adjudicating state cases. The Supreme Court of Pennsylvania stated the competency rule that applies in many state courts when it noted that, "[i]n general, a witness's competency to testify at trial is presumed and the burden falls on the objecting party to demonstrate the witness's incompetence."[58] In the interests of clarity, a distinction must be made between the competency of a witness and the competency of evidence. A witness may meet the tests of competency and yet not be authorized to testify concerning evidence that is incompetent, such as certain hearsay evidence or illegally seized evidence.

One of the common tests of witness competency looks to see if four factors have been met. Every witness must take the oath, have original perception, be able to remember the facts, and have an ability to communicate to the court. A collateral test of the competency of a witness requires that the witness be able to communicate relevant material and that the witness have the ability to understand that there is an obligation to communicate truthfully. The competency of a witness is determined exclusively by the trial judge, whose "determination will be upheld in the absence of a clear abuse of discretion."[59] The question of competency is almost always one of fact, and thus will not be reversed unless clearly erroneous.[60] Although witness competency involves a

---

[56]　FED. R. EVID. 601.

[57]　*Id.*

[58]　Commonwealth v. Harvey, 812 A.2d 1190, 202 Pa. LEXIS 2833 (2002).

[59]　People v. Avila, 38 Cal. 4th 491, 589, 133 P.3d 1076, 1144, 43 Cal. Rptr. 3d 1, 81 2006 Cal. LEXIS 5867 (Cal. 2006).

[60]　Commonwealth v. Garmache, 35 Mass. App. 805, 626 N.E.2d 616 (1994). *See also* United States v. Gates, 10 F.3d 765 (11th Cir. 1993), in which the court held that the court has the power to rule that the witness is incapable of testifying, and in an appropriate case it has a duty to hold a hearing to determine that issue.

question of law for the judge to determine, credibility is a fact issue that only the jury has the power to evaluate.[61]

In determining whether the witness is competent to testify at the trial, the better practice is to make the determination prior to the trial and out of the hearing of the jury[62] in order to avoid a chance that a jury might believe that a court had determined that a witness was believable rather than merely competent. Where the trial is to the judge, a determination of witness competency may be done at the time the witness is called to the witness stand.[63]

When a person has been called as a witness to give testimony in front of a grand jury, the usual tests for competency apply, but a witness's competency is rarely contested because a grand jury meets in secret and constitutes an ex parte proceeding. In one New York case, an indictment was quashed because the prosecutor made no attempt to determine whether the four-year-old complaining witness met the requirements of competency,[64] even though a prosecutor has the power to make a ruling on the competency of a grand jury witness.[65] As one court noted, "[a] more stringent standard than that applied to trial proceedings certainly cannot be applied to determine competency of a witness to testify before a Grand Jury, whose function is primarily investigative."[66] In the grand jury context, one state considers children competent to testify without taking the oath, so long as the jurors are aware that the witness was not under oath but met the other requirements for competency.[67] The tests for determining competency of a witness before a grand jury are: (1) the witness must understand the obligation of an oath and the obligation to tell the truth before the grand jury; and (2) the witness must be capable of giving a reasonably correct account of the matters that he or she has seen or heard in reference to the questions being asked. Where the competency of a grand jury witness has been raised, these two issues must be determined by the court's own examination and upon the testimony of witnesses who may be called by the prosecution or by the witness's counsel. This is a duty that the court cannot avoid merely by referring to or quoting from the statements of the medical experts. The court must make its own determination and its own examination. The court must be assured that the physical and mental health of the witness will not be damaged, impaired, or harmed in any significant way.[68] Because the defendant has no representation at a grand jury proceeding, questions about the competency of grand jury witnesses do not frequently arise, and where they do, the witness often raises the issue.

---

[61]   Lewis v. State, 269 Ga. App. 94, 96, 603 S.E.2d 492, 494, 2004 Ga. App. LEXIS 1085 (2004).
[62]   Norman v. Georgia, 269 Ga. App. 219, 223, 603 S.E.2d 737, 742, 2004 Ga. App. LEXIS 1120 (2004).
       See also, Medina v. Diguglielmo, 373 F. Supp. 2d 526; 2005 U.S. Dist. LEXIS 10672 (E.D. Pa. 2005).
[63]   See Ohio v. Cotterman, 2001 Ohio App. LEXIS 3322 (2001).
[64]   People v. Esaw, 2002 N.Y. Slip Op. 40045U, 2002 N.Y. Misc. LEXIS 201 (N.Y. 2002).
[65]   See NY CLS CPL § 190.30(6), Grand jury; rules of evidence. (Matthew Bender 2006).
[66]   In re Loughran, 276 F. Supp. 393, 430, 1967 U.S. Dist. LEXIS 7589 (C.D. Cal. 1967).
[67]   People v. Miller, 295 A.D.2d 746, 747, 746 N.Y.S.2d 50, 51, 2002 N.Y. App. Div. LEXIS 6511 (2002).
[68]   Id.

Where the competency of expert witnesses is at issue, courts generally have broad discretion in determining whether to allow the testimony. Where a court decides that the proposed expert witness possesses sufficient qualifications by virtue of study, skill, research, practice, training, or education and that expert testimony would be helpful to the jury's understanding of the case, a trial judge has the authority to rule that a witness is qualified to offer expert testimony.[69] Naturally, an expert witness must have special knowledge beyond the knowledge possessed by a lay witness and be able to meet the usual requirements for a competent witness.

In the sections immediately following, the specific grounds for challenging the competency of witnesses are discussed.

§ 8.11   —Mental Incapacity

The basic standard or rule applied when considering the mental capacity of the witness to testify is the one first announced by the United States Supreme Court in *District of Columbia v. Armes*:

> The general rule is that a lunatic or a person affected with insanity is admissible as a witness if he has sufficient understanding to apprehend the obligation of an oath, and to be capable of giving a correct account of the matters which he has seen or heard in reference to the questions at issue; and whether he has that understanding is a question to be determined by the court, upon examination of the party himself, and any competent witnesses who can speak to the nature and extent of his insanity. [70]

In *Armes*, the Court upheld the admissibility of the testimony of an acute melancholic who was confined to an asylum and had attempted suicide several times by sticking a fork into his neck. The Court stressed that "the existence of partial insanity does not prevent individuals so affected . . . from giving a perfectly accurate and lucid statement of what they have seen or heard."[71]

In a Hawai'i case, the state supreme court reversed a conviction for kidnapping and rape because the trial court failed to hold a hearing to establish the competency of the complaining witness. The hearing was a necessary step because the female victim, who suffered from Down Syndrome, functioned at the cognitive level of a four- to seven-year-old child. According to the court, where there was a question about competency, the trial court had a duty to determine whether the proposed witness was capable of expressing herself and whether she knew the duty to tell the truth. The mental illness was not dis-

---

[69]   Bonner v. Iowa, 2002 Iowa App. LEXIS 1328 (2001).

[70]   107 U.S. 519, 2 S. Ct. 840, 27 L. Ed. 618 (1882).

[71]   *Id. See* Juvilier, *Psychiatric Opinions As To The Credibility of Witnesses: A Suggested Approach*, 48 CAL. L. REV. 648 (1960).

qualifying by itself, but if the mental state removed the elements of competency, the testimony should have been excluded.[72]

Even where a trial court accepts arcane psychiatric concepts of mental condition or illness as a basis for measuring criminal capacity and responsibility, a court will not blindly accept such theoretical concepts when evaluating the competency of witnesses. Despite mental difficulties, the test of a witness's competency includes the capacity to communicate relevant material and to understand the obligation to do so truthfully. In approving the testimony of a somewhat mentally retarded female rape victim, a state appeals court concurred with the trial court that allowed her to testify concerning the sexual acts in which her father had required her to engage from the age of 12 until she was 14. The young victim could not recall the exact years in which the crimes occurred, but she was able to give fairly complete details of vaginal intercourse, anal intercourse, and other details clearly derived from personal memory.[73]

Most courts in state and federal cases allow testimony of a witness even though the witness has been found to be drug addicted and taking psychiatric medicine for her mental problems. This has been reflected in the Federal Rules of Evidence as interpreted by various courts. For example, in one federal trial, a prosecution witness was permitted to testify that she was a drug addict and she admitted to having smoked significant quantities of crack cocaine on the day that she was a witness to several crimes. The witness had suffered from a gunshot to her head and had auditory and visual hallucinations. She was also under a doctor's care, which resulted in multiple psychiatric medications being prescribed. With all of these problems that might relate to her competency, the trial court properly permitted her to testify against the defendant.[74] In federal courts, feeble-mindedness and insanity alone are not enough to prevent a witness from being considered competent. One federal court noted that "[a] witness wholly without capacity is difficult to imagine."[75] In one federal case, the trial court erred when it ruled that a witness was incompetent to testify, "because he had been found to be criminally insane and incompetent to stand trial, and was subject to hallucinations."[76] The Fourth Circuit Court of Appeals advised that the trial court could have conducted an in camera examination of the witness to determine whether he or she was capable of testifying. In referring to the determination of witness competency, a Maryland court, interpreting its version of federal Rule 601, noted that holding a competency hearing outside of the hearing of the jury is not required but comes within the discretion of the trial judge. The court believed that as long as the trial judge was satisfied with the competency of a challenged witness, competency was sufficiently established.[77]

---

[72]   Hawai'i v. Kelekolio, 74 Haw. 479, 849 P.2d 58, 1993 Haw. LEXIS 25 (1993); *see also* Ohio v. Papalevich, 2001 Ohio 4087, 2001 Ohio App. LEXIS 5063 (2001), in which a court may have allowed an incompetent prosecution witness to testify.

[73]   State v. Grahek, 2003 Ohio 2650, 2003 Ohio App. LEXIS 2390 (2003).

[74]   United States v. Williams, 445 F.3d 724, 728 2006 U.S. App. LEXIS 9639 (4th Cir. 2006).

[75]   Bornstad v. Honey Brook Twp., 2005 U.S. Dist. LEXIS 19573 (E.D. Pa. 2006).

[76]   United States v. Lightly, 677 F.2d 1027 (4th Cir. 1982).

[77]   *See* Perry v. State, 381 Md. 138, 848 A.2d 631, 2004 Md. LEXIS 246 (2004).

In determining the competency of a witness, one court referred to a previous case that concerned the competency of a witness who had a history of psychological disturbances. The court held that the government witness was competent, even though he suffered from the traumatic effects of a bullet wound to his head, because there was no indication that he had a prolonged history of mental illness. The court explained that the witness had been responsive to questions and made it plain that he understood the importance of his oath to testify truthfully.[78]

Mental illness and psychiatric problems are not factors that automatically exclude a potential witness from being considered competent to give testimony,[79] but they are not totally irrelevant in making a competency decision. In a case involving a juvenile adjudication of delinquency for an act that would have been rape if committed by an adult, the trial court committed error when it failed to conduct a more complete competency hearing.[80] The complaining witness was a 12-year-old girl who attended special education classes, had imaginary friends, had been previously diagnosed with schizophrenia, and her ability to remember even routine information proved to be limited. The juvenile court conducted an examination of the witness, but failed to follow up on answers that might have been enlightening to the court to properly consider her competency as a witness. In reversing the adjudication, the reviewing court noted:

> There is no indication in the record that the court questioned B.D. regarding her capacity to recount the events accurately or even that she understood the nature of the proceedings. After the trial court questioned B.D. regarding routine questions such as the day, month, and year and received inaccurate or confusing responses from her, the court merely proceeded to the next set of questions without delving further into the key issue of competency.

> The lack of more detailed evidence supporting or refuting B.D.'s competency should be clear on the record. Since such evidence is lacking, we find that the trial court abused its discretion in failing to conduct a more complete competency hearing.[81]

The trial judge must make a preliminary determination concerning competency, and where the judge permits a witness to offer evidence, the jury must evaluate credibility of the witness and the value to be assigned to the testimony.[82]

In summary, a witness is competent to testify unless evidence is introduced to show that incompetency exists. Where one party has concerns that an adverse witness may lack some of the elements of competency, "[t]he party requesting a determination of the competency of a witness to testify has the

---

[78]   United States v. Bloome, 773 F. Supp. 545 (E.D.N.Y. 1991).
[79]   State v. Shellhouse, 202 Tenn. Crim. App. LEXIS 839 (2002).
[80]   In re J.M., 2006 Ohio 1203; 2006 Ohio App. LEXIS 1088 (2006).
[81]   Id.
[82]   United States v. Phibbs, 999 F.2d 1053 (6th Cir. 1993). See case in Part II.

burden of proof."[83] To meet that burden, the challenging party must establish the inability to understand the obligation of the oath and to comprehend the obligation imposed by it, or a lack of understanding of the consequences of false swearing, or the inability to perceive accurate impressions and to retain them.

§ 8.12 —Children

Where the competency of a child to be a witness becomes an issue for either party, the trial judge has the duty to evaluate whether the child possesses the elements of competency. Even where neither party objects to the competency of a child witness, the trial judge generally has the discretion to determine whether competency exists.[84] As one court noted, "trial judges are required to make a preliminary determination as to the competency of all witnesses, including children, and that absent an abuse of discretion, competency determinations of the trial judge will not be disturbed on appeal."[85] According to a reviewing court, one trial judge conducted a proper examination of a six-year-old child witness when the judge's questions to the child were:

> sufficient to establish the child was capable of "receiving just impressions of the fact and transactions" and "relating them truly." Although [she] showed some confusion about the actual terms "right" and "wrong" and "truth" and "lie", she clearly demonstrated she knew the difference between telling the truth and telling a lie, and knew the consequences of telling a lie.[86]

In a state case, the Supreme Court of Arkansas noted that everyone is presumed to be competent and applied the principle to a child witness. According to that court, "[c]hild witnesses are treated no differently than adults in determining competency. The age of a child is not determinative of competency. We apply the same presumption and standards in deciding the capacity of a child witness to testify as are applied in determining the competency of any witness."[87] It is not necessary to show that the child witness has religious beliefs or a detailed knowledge of the nature of the oath. Generally, an appellate court will not find an abuse of discretion in allowing children to testify as long as the record shows that a reasonable judge could find a moral awareness in the child to tell the truth, that the child has firsthand knowledge, and that the witness could remember and relate the facts.[88]

---

[83]   People v. Cookson, 335 Ill. App. 3d 786, 789, 780 N.E.2d 807, 809, 2002 Ill. App. LEXIS 1179 (Ill. 2002). *See also* ILL. COMP. STAT. ANN., 725 ILCS 5/115-14 (2006).

[84]   Haycraft v. State, 760 N.E.2d 203, 209, 2001 Ind. App. LEXIS 2225 (2001).

[85]   In re J.M., 2006 Ohio 1203, 2006 Ohio App. LEXIS 1088 (2006).

[86]   State v. Patterson, 2005 Ohio 6703; 2005 Ohio App. LEXIS 6050 (2005).

[87]   Modlin v. State, 2003 Ark. LEXIS 215 (Ark. 2003).

[88]   Clem v. Arkansas, 351 Ark. 112, 124, 90 S.W.3d 428, 434, 2002 Ark. LEXIS 598 (2002).

Although some statutes are similar to Ohio's in providing that "children under ten years of age, who appear incapable of receiving just impressions of the facts respecting which they are examined, or of relating them truly"[89] are incompetent as witnesses, there is no fixed age at which a child is considered to be a competent witness. In *Wheeler v. United States*,[90] the United States Supreme Court said:

> That the boy was not by reason of his youth [five and one-half years], as a matter of law, absolutely disqualified as a witness is clear. While no one would think of calling as a witness an infant only two or three years old, there is no precise age which determines the question of competency. This depends on the capacity and intelligence of the child, his appreciation of the difference between truth and falsehood, as well as of his duty to tell the former. The decision of this question rests primarily with the trial judge, who sees the proposed witness, notices his manner, his apparent possession or lack of intelligence, and may resort to any examination which will tend to disclose his capacity and intelligence as well as his understanding of the obligations of an oath. As many of these matters cannot be photographed into the record the decision of the trial judge will not be disturbed on review, unless from that which is preserved, it is clear that it was erroneous.

Interpreting Rule 601 of the Indiana statute, which is identical to the federal rule, the Indiana court admonished that under the evidence rule providing that all persons are competent to be witnesses, the trial court is still required to conduct an inquiry of whether the child: (1) understands the difference between telling a lie and telling the truth, (2) knows he or she is under compulsion to tell the truth, and (3) knows what a true statement actually is.[91] The court in this case agreed that a seven-year-old child's testimony that she knew the difference between right and wrong, and that one was punished for telling a lie, was insufficient foundation to establish her competency as a witness where the child was not asked to provide an example of someone telling a lie or otherwise asked to demonstrate that she truly knew the difference between the truth and a lie. In a later Indiana case, the court held that because Rule 601 did not presumptively exclude children as witnesses and did not prohibit a special inquiry into the competency of children, the rule should be read as requiring a court to inquire into the competency of children.[92]

In a variety of cases, children much younger than 10 years of age have been considered competent witnesses while other cases have refused to allow some young children to testify. A determination of competency of child witnesses depends upon the facts in each case and on the maturity of the individual child. In Pennsylvania, all witnesses are considered competent, including

---

[89]   OHIO R. EVID. 601(A) (Matthew Bender 2006).
[90]   159 U.S. 523, 16 S. Ct. 93, 40 L. Ed. 244 (1895).
[91]   Newsome v. State, 686 N.E.2d 868 (Ind. 1997).
[92]   Alridge v. Indiana, 779 N.E.2d 607, 609, 2002 Ind. App. LEXIS 2050 (2002).

children, but witnesses under 14 years of age may face special scrutiny. In one case involving juvenile sexual abuse by an adult, the trial court permitted a six-year-old girl to testify.[93] Against the presumption of competency, the defendant must first demonstrate some defect in competency to cause the court to hold a "taint" hearing. This process examines whether events or other people have tainted the child's memory and perception. In evaluating whether a defendant has presented evidence sufficient to hold the "taint" hearing, the court considers the totality of the circumstances surrounding the child's allegations, including:

> (1) the age of the child; (2) the existence of a motive hostile to the defendant on the part of the child's primary custodian; (3) the possibility that the child's primary custodian is unusually likely to read abuse into normal interaction; (4) whether the child was subjected to repeated interviews by various adults in positions of authority; (5) whether an interested adult was present during the course of any interviews; and (6) the existence of independent evidence regarding the interview techniques employed.[94]

Where a defendant fails to produce sufficient evidence to warrant a "taint" hearing, the trial court will permit the child's testimony without additional analysis or consideration.

In contrast to the Pennsylvania case above, in a Washington case, a trial court held that a six-year-old witness who was four years old at the time of the event was not competent as a witness. According to the court, the competency of a child depends upon three factual inquiries: "(1) whether the witness is describing an event that she had the capacity to accurately perceive, (2) whether the witness is describing an event that she has the capacity to accurately recall, and (3) whether the witness is describing an event that she has the capacity to accurately relate."[95] The judge excluded the victim's testimony because it had been subject to post-event suggestion, tainted questioning, and exposure to pornography, in addition to the victim having been very young at the time of the alleged events.[96] Children who were somewhat older than those in the above cases have been regularly determined to be competent as witnesses. In a Wyoming case, where three female children (aged ten, eleven, and twelve) had complained to relatives of sexual abuse by their father, the Supreme Court of Wyoming approved the use of their testimony after reviewing the standard elements of competency and determining that the victims had not had their stories tainted by interrogators, relatives, or each other.[97]

The child's ability to receive just impressions of the facts relates to the time that the events occurred, while his or her capacity to state them relates to

---

[93]   Commonwealth v. Judd, 2006 Pa. Super. 84, 897 A.2d 1224, 2006 Pa. Super. LEXIS 538 (2006).
[94]   Id., at 1230.
[95]   State v. Ramirez, 2002 Wash. App. LEXIS 546 (2002).
[96]   Id.
[97]   Billingsley v. State, 2003 Wyo. 61, 2003 Wyo. LEXIS 74 (2003).

the time of the trial. For example, in a case in which the father had been accused of the sexual abuse of his five-year-old daughter and an audiotape had been made at the time of her original complaint, the trial court could play the tape to determine her ability to originally perceive as of the time of the crime. A separate inquiry had to be conducted at the time of trial to determine her competency as an eight-year-old witness. In reversing a trial court determination against competency at the time of trial, the appellate court closely scrutinized the information from the time of the alleged crime and considered the girl's interaction with the trial judge and other persons to conclude that her original perception was appropriate and that she presently was competent as a witness.[98] Of crucial importance is the child's competency or incompetency as of the date that the child is offered as a witness, and not at the time that the incidents originally occurred. In a Wyoming case, the judge conducted an inquiry into the competency of a child witness that included questioning concerning "the mental capacity[,] at the time of the occurrence concerning which he is to testify, to receive an accurate impression" of the events which the child witness was to offer the court.[99] This inquiry assured the court that the child possessed original perception and, in conjunction with other judicial interrogatories, assured the court that the child met the requirements for competency at the time of his testimony.

On occasion, courts have permitted very young children to serve as witnesses following a determination of competency. In the case of a four-year-old witness whose father had repeatedly shot her in an effort to kill her, the Louisiana trial court permitted the child to testify against her father at his attempted murder trial. On appeal, the defendant challenged the competency of his daughter as a witness. The appeals court upheld the trial judge's determination after it reviewed the steps taken by the judge to assure competency of the child. Among other steps taken to assure competency in this case:

> Before allowing Ashley Annunciation to testify, the trial judge questioned the child out of the jury's presence. Ashley correctly stated her age, date of birth, grade in school, school attended, and her teacher's name. At the judge's request, she correctly spelled and wrote her name. Although she hesitated, and denied knowing the difference between the truth and a lie, she ably remonstrated the judge when he purposely misidentified the color of her dress, telling him that if he said her pink dress was blue, "It would be a lie."[100]

According to the appellate court, even where a child seems hesitant or sometimes gives unresponsive answers, such conduct does not indicate a lack of competency but may reflect the unfamiliar surroundings or indicate stress. Competency may be found under such circumstances especially when the

---

[98]   Commonwealth v. D.J.A., 2002 Pa. Super. 176, 800 A.2d 965, 2002 Pa. Super. LEXIS 1130 (2002).

[99]   Beaugureau v. State, 2002 Wyo. 160, 56 P.3d 626, 631, 2002 Wyo. LEXIS 180 (2002).

[100] State v. Deutor, 842 So.2d 438, 2003 La. App. LEXIS 724 (2003).

child witness understands the more specific types of questions and offers responsive answers.[101]

A Mississippi court noted that the test for admissibility of child testimony required that the trial judge: "determine that the child witness (1) has the ability to perceive and remember events, (2) understand and answer questions intelligently, and (3) comprehend and accept the importance of truthfulness."[102] In that case, the child had been six years of age at the time of the crime but was eight at the time of the proposed testimony and knew her birthday, where she went to school, her teachers' names, and she recounted her home telephone number. Additionally, the girl stated that it was a bad thing to tell a lie. Not only did the judge observe the child answering the questions, he observed her carriage and demeanor, all factors in reaching the conclusion that the child was competent as a witness.[103]

The preferable course is apparently to accept a child's testimony if the competency tests are met. However, the testimony should not be allowed if evidence indicates that the child lacks competency. For example, a reviewing court held that a trial court had properly found that a four-year-old child was not competent to testify at a trial, as she was unresponsive to questions in open court from both the prosecution and the court, and she could not state what it meant to tell the truth or a lie.[104]

To be considered a competent witness, a child need not understand the concept of perjury but must know the difference between telling a lie and telling the truth. In an Arkansas prosecution for sexual crimes against a child who was five years old at the time of the offense and seven at the time of trial, the judge conducted a competency hearing with the child. Outside of the presence of the jury, the prosecutor asked the child witness about the difference between a lie and the truth and gave several examples that the child understood. From the prosecutor's questions, it appeared that the child knew her colors, the difference between a dog and a cat, understood the need to tell the truth, and seemed to understand the significance of an oath. In upholding the trial judge's decision to allow the child to testify, the appellate court noted that, "As long as the record is one upon which the trial judge could find a moral awareness of the obligation to tell the truth and an ability to observe, remember, and relate facts, we will not hold there has been a manifest error or abuse of discretion in allowing the testimony."[105]

In summary, children as witnesses present challenges to determine whether they are competent. Individual determinations based on the unique facts of each child and each case will assist the court in evaluating each pro-

---

[101] *Id.*

[102] Borsarge v. State, 786 So.2d 426, 430, 2001 Miss. App. LEXIS 227 (2001).

[103] *Id.*

[104] People v. District Court of El Paso County, 776 P.2d 1083 (Colo. 1989); *see A Legal & Psychological Critique of the Present Approach to the Assessment of the Competency of Child Witnesses*, 38 OSGOODE HALL L.J. 409 (2000), for a review of the historical evolution of competency of child witnesses in the United States and Canada.

[105] Warner v. State, 2005 Ark. App. LEXIS 875 (Ark. 2005).

posed child witness. When the child meets the elements of competency of original perception and recollection, and is able to communicate the story to the finder of fact, the judge should rule that the particular child is a competent witness. In the case of children, the final element of competency, the oath, is excused as long as the judge is satisfied that the child understands the duty to tell the truth.

§ 8.13 —Husband and Wife

The common law rule held that husbands and wives were incompetent as witnesses for or against each other because the spouse had an interest in the case and could not serve as an unbiased witness. The rule appears to have its genesis in medieval times and seems to have developed "from two canons of medieval jurisprudence: first, the rule that an accused was not permitted to testify in his own behalf because of his interest in the proceeding; second, the concept that husband and wife were one, and that since the woman had no recognized separate legal existence, the husband was that one."[106] Additional justification suggested by the Supreme Court in *Hawkins v. United States* that, "the rule rested mainly on a desire to foster peace in the family and on a general unwillingness to use the testimony of witnesses tempted by strong self-interest to testify falsely."[107]

Because a defendant was barred as a witness in his or her own behalf because of interest, it was quite natural to bar his or her spouse in view of the prevailing legal fiction that husband and wife were one person.[108] Courts began to erode this early rule, however, when its logic and philosophy began to fail and when the rule gave protection to the wrong interests. Thus, in the 1839 federal case of *Stein v. Bowman*, the United States Supreme Court noted that the rule of spousal incompetency "is subject to some exceptions; as where the husband commits an offence against the person of his wife."[109]

Modern law in virtually all states permits one spouse to be considered competent to testify against the other where one spouse has been charged with a crime against the person or property of the other or has been charged with a crime against a child of either or the child's property.[110]

In 1933, the United States Supreme Court rejected the common law rule that excluded testimony by spouses in favor of each other,[111] but the new interpretation of the common law rule applied only to federal actions. In *Hawkins v. United States*, the Court:

---

[106] People v. Sinohui, 28 Cal. 4th 205, 210, 47 P.3d 629, 2002 Cal. LEXIS 3777 (2002), quoting Trammel v. United States, 445 U.S. 40, 44 (1980).

[107] Hawkins v. United States, 358 U.S. 74, 75, 1958 U.S. LEXIS 115 (1958).

[108] 1 Coke, COMMENTARY UPON LITTLETON 6b (19th ed. 1832). *See* Chapter 10 for a discussion of the husband-wife testimonial privilege.

[109] 38 U.S. 209, 221, 1839 U.S. LEXIS 431 (1839).

[110] WIS. STAT. § 905.05(3)(b) (2006) and VA. CODE ANN. § 8.01-398 (2006).

[111] Funk v. United States, 290 U.S. 371, 54 S. Ct. 212, 78 L. Ed. 369 (1933). *See* this case in Part II in Cases Relating to Chapter 1.

recognized that the basic reason underlying the exclusion [of one spouse's testimony on behalf of the other] had been the practice of disqualifying witnesses with a personal interest in the outcome of a case. Widespread disqualifications because of interest, however, had long since been abolished both in this country and in England in accordance with the modern trend which permitted interested witnesses to testify and left it for the jury to assess their credibility. Certainly, since defendants were uniformly allowed to testify in their own behalf, there was no longer a good reason to prevent them from using their spouses as witnesses. With the original reason for barring favorable testimony of spouses gone the Court concluded that this aspect of the old rule should go too.[112]

While spouses were considered competent to testify as interested individuals, the jury could evaluate the value of the testimony and the credibility of the spouse-witness, recognizing that the evidence came from an interested individual.

Marriage does not make the spouse incompetent in civil or criminal cases, and spouses may testify freely unless prevented by defects in the elements of competency: oath, original perception, recollection, and an ability to communicate. Typical of the modern trend, the Maine Revised Statutes hold that, "[t]he husband or wife of the accused is a competent witness except in regard to marital communications."[113] What has emerged is that the spouses are generally considered competent for all purposes, but some marital privileges exist that may have the effect of allowing one spouse to refuse to give testimony. In some instances a defendant spouse may still be able to prevent the other from testifying even when the proposed witness spouse is fully willing to testify against the defendant spouse.[114] Competency seems assured but concepts involving privilege may prevent spousal testimony. For example, in a murder case in which the defendant spouse had been accused of killing the victim and his DNA had been found on the woman's body, the prosecution wanted his then-current wife to testify against him concerning his whereabouts on the night of the victim's death. It was a foregone conclusion that the then-wife was a competent witness, but the defendant argued that a marital privilege, the confidential communication privilege, prevented her from telling the jury that he left their home in the middle of the relevant night. The trial court held that the defendant's act of leaving the marital home did not qualify as a confidential communication with his then-wife because it was not much of a communication and it was not done in confidence because other people outside the marital home would have been able to view his presence outside the home. Thus, the wife was competent as a witness and no privilege prevented her testimony.[115]

---

[112] 358 U.S. 74, 76 (1958).

[113] 15 M.R.S. § 1315 (2005).

[114] This is most likely to occur in a situation in which the defendant spouse has communicated with the proposed witness spouse under circumstances in which the defendant spouse was relying on the intimate and close marital relationship.

[115] State v. Bates, 2003 Me. 67; 822 A.2d 1129; 2003 Me. LEXIS 77 (2003).

In a California case in which a defendant had committed false imprisonment against his wife while at the same time kidnapping and murdering a second person, the trial court compelled the falsely imprisoned wife to testify against her defendant husband. The alleged error, rejected by the trial court and the state supreme court, was that because the defendant had not been charged with a crime against his spouse in the murder case, that the crime against a spouse exception for allowing testimony did not apply. It was held that because the crime against the wife was part of the plan and facilitated the crime against the deceased, they were part of one continuous course of criminal conduct that permitted the defendant's wife to be considered competent to testify against him.[116]

Statutes in many states permit spouses to testify against each other in prosecutions for only certain types of crimes. For example, under Ohio law, a husband and wife are competent to testify on behalf of each other in all criminal prosecutions and against each other pursuant to the law that recognizes exceptions to statutory privileges. Under Ohio law, spouses are considered competent witnesses who may give testimony against each other in: (1) prosecutions for personal injury of either by the other, rape of one by the other, other sexual offenses against each other, and in cases involving personal protection orders; (2) prosecutions for bigamy; and (3) prosecutions for failure to provide for, for neglect of, or for cruelty to their minor children under 18 or their physically or mentally handicapped children under 21 years of age.[117]

Following a similar legal theory, the state of Georgia has a statute that provides that one spouse is competent to testify against the other, but the statute does not compel adverse spousal testimony unless the husband or wife has been charged with a crime against a minor child.[118] In interpreting this statute, the Court of Appeals of Georgia noted that the trial court committed error when it virtually required a wife to testify against her spouse in a case in which her husband had been accused of assaulting his girlfriend. Under the Georgia statute, the witness spouse is considered competent to give evidence against a spouse but cannot be compelled to do so.[119] In another case, the court permitted testimony from a spouse who had a statutory right not to testify, but the judge failed to advise the testifying spouse of her legal rights. The defendant contended that the trial court committed error by failing to inform his wife that Georgia law did not require her testimony. The reviewing court indicated that the lower court did not err in failing to advise the defendant's wife that she could not be compelled to testify against her husband. Generally, trial judges have no duty to inquire concerning whether a witness might possess a legal right to refuse to give testimony.[120] According to Georgia law, as interpreted,

---

[116] People v. Sinohui, 47 P.2d 629 (Cal. 2002).
[117] OHIO REV. CODE ANN. § 2945.42 (Matthew Bender 2006).
[118] GA. CODE ANN. § 24-9-23 (2006).
[119] Phillips v. State, 278 Ga. App. 439, 441 629 S.E.2d 130, 132 2006 Ga. App. LEXIS 350 (2006).
[120] Ingram v. State, 262 Ga. App. 304, 307, 585 S.E.2d 211, 215 2003 Ga. App. LEXIS 914 (2003).

the spouse is competent to testify against the accused in a criminal case, but to require such testimony would constitute error.

The Texas Rules of Evidence grant a privilege to the spouse of the accused not to be called as a witness for the prosecution, but does not prohibit the voluntary testimony of the witness on behalf of the prosecution because only the witness spouse is a holder of the privilege.[121] The rule allows the spouse to testify voluntarily for the state about non-confidential matters—even over the objection of the accused.[122] In *Jackson v. State*, the prosecution won a conviction against the defendant, who contended that error had occurred when his wife was forced to testify against him for criminal trespass of her individual apartment. He contended that the apartment was community property under state law and he had an equal right to possession. The reviewing court held that he had no property interest in his wife's separate apartment because she had the lease in her name only, they did not live together, and because the crime was against her property, the privilege not to testify against her husband had no application.[123] Under the current Texas rule of evidence, the wife was competent as a witness and was properly compelled to testify against her husband.

In Pennsylvania criminal proceedings, competent spouses have a privilege not to testify against a current spouse but the witness spouse may waive the testimonial privilege. However, the privilege does not apply in some circumstances involving an alleged crime against the spouse or children or their property committed by the defendant spouse or when the defendant spouse has been charged with murder or rape.[124] Neither spouse is considered competent to testify to any confidential communication made by one spouse to the other, unless the privilege is waived,[125] but confidential communication has been limited to oral or written communication and does not include acts done in confidence in front of the witness spouse. In one Pennsylvania case, in which the defendant killed another person's child in the view of his spouse and disposed of the murder weapons, the witness spouse was permitted to testify to the defendant's acts of murder and disposal.[126] An Iowa court followed a different theory from that of Pennsylvania when a reviewing court held that a trial court committed reversible error in compelling a defendant's wife to testify after she had invoked the marital confidential communication privilege. The court held that the marital privilege not to testify against one's spouse belongs to the spouse whose testimony is sought and not the defendant spouse. According to the reviewing court, the wife was improperly compelled to testify about her husband's abuse of a child, but the child was not a child of either spouse and neither was a caregiver for the child. The theory that the wife should not have been forced to testify against her husband because the abuse of a non-family

---

[121]   TEX. R. EVID. 504(b) Husband-Wife Privileges. (Matthew Bender 2006).

[122]   *Id.*

[123]   2005 Tex. App. LEXIS 3631 (Tex. 2005).

[124]   42 PA. CONS. STAT. § 5913 (2005).

[125]   *Id.*, at § 5914.

[126]   Commonwealth v. Burrows, 2001 Pa. Super. 164; 779 A.2d 509, 518, 2001 Pa. Super. LEXIS 643 (Penn. 2001), *appeal denied*, 572 Pa. 732, 815 A.2d 632, 2002 Pa. LEXIS 337 (2002).

member did not directly undermine the marital relationship, the witness spouse should not have been compelled to testify against her husband.[127]

Explaining the application of the federal rules, a federal court of appeals noted that the marital privilege recognized by federal courts really involves two privileges. The first is the marital testimonial privilege, which permits a witness spouse from having to testify against the defendant spouse during the existence of the marriage; the second privilege allows one spouse to prevent the other from giving testimony relating to confidential communications made between them during the existence of the marriage.[128] As one Indiana court noted, the purpose of the marital privileges are "grounded at least in significant part not on a policy of promoting disclosure but on concern for the health of the ongoing relationship between husband and wife and the policy of preventing further conflict between them by forcing one to testify against the other."[129]

In one federal case, the trial court had required the defendant's spouse to testify concerning his possession of an unregistered firearm silencer. The government was not able to prove that the witness spouse knew that the object she had observed was a firearm silencer, and because she was not an active and knowing participant in the crime of possession of an unregistered silencer, she should not have been forced to testify against her husband. Because federal courts hold that confidential marital communications are not covered by any privilege when the spousal communication concerns the commission of a crime in which both spouses are participants, had the prosecution demonstrated that the wife was a willing participant in the criminal possession, the marital confidential communication privilege would not have existed.[130]

Modern legal theory holds that spouses are competent to testify for or against each other. Even though legal competency exists, through the exercise of the marital privilege, either or both spouses may refuse to testify against the other. The ability to exercise a privilege to testify for or against the other spouse depends on case law and the provisions of federal or state statutes. Although spouses may testify for each other in all jurisdictions, some jurisdictions do not require one spouse to testify against the other spouse in any criminal case, while in others the spouse is required by statute to testify against the accused spouse only when the spouse is accused of certain crimes. If the statute makes wives and husbands competent to testify against each other regarding a specific crime, and there is no privilege to assert, then a spouse may be compelled to testify. Under these circumstances, if the spouse refuses to testify, he or she may be found to be in civil contempt of court.

---

[127] State v. Anderson, 636 N.W.2d 26, 36, 2001 Iowa Sup. LEXIS 217 (2001).
[128] United States v. Montague, 421 F.3d 1099, 1103, 2005 U.S. App. LEXIS 14593 (10th Cir. 2005).
[129] Glover v. State, 836 N.E.2d 414, 421, 2005 Ind. LEXIS 983 (2005).
[130] United States v. Foresman, 63 Fed. Appx. 138, 2003 U.S. App. LEXIS 9476 (4th Cir. 2003).

§ 8.14 —Conviction of Crime

Under English common law, a person convicted of a felony was considered incompetent to testify as a witness in court.[131] Nevada followed this theory and refused to admit testimony from felons during the 1800s.[132] Over time, states gradually removed this disability to testify.

Pursuant to state law and in agreement with the common law, a Tennessee appellate court reversed a conviction for assault with intent to commit murder because one of the prosecution witnesses had previously been convicted of petit larceny. The appellate court ordered a new trial in 1872 because the state of the law at that time was such that people who had been convicted of specific crimes were deemed to be incompetent as witnesses in courts. "The rule of exclusion grew out of the common law doctrine that a party to the record, or one interested in the result, with certain exceptions, which were engrafted upon the rule from supposed necessity, was not competent as a witness, because of the temptation to perjury."[133] Virtually all states had laws similar to Tennessee, but as times changed, the legal theory supporting legal incompetency evolved. More than 88 years ago, the United States Supreme Court decided that "the dead hand of the common law rule," disqualifying a witness who had been convicted of crime, should no longer be applied in criminal cases in the federal courts.[134] Since that time, virtually every state jurisdiction has enacted legislation that expressly removes any witness disqualification that formerly existed in the common law and the laws of many states. The older theory held that a person who had been convicted of a crime was not morally trustworthy as a witness because the person had been evil enough to commit a crime. Under modern legislation, states have acted legislatively and have removed any defect in competency from those who have criminal records. Demonstrative of this principle, the state of Arizona provides that "[a] person shall not be incompetent to testify because he is a party to an action or proceeding or interested in the issue tried, or because he has been indicted, accused or convicted of a crime . . ."[135] A potential witness may be deemed as presumptively competent through legislation, but the immediate question of whether a witness meets the four elements of competency is generally an issue to be determined by the trial judge. Naturally, issues relating to credibility are matters to be determined by the trier of fact. Because some crimes may, by their nature, lead to questions about a person's honesty or credibility, proof of some prior crimes committed by a witness may be permitted because it may have a legitimate bearing on the jury's perception of the witness's truthfulness. Most jurisdictions permit a showing of the fact of a witness's felony conviction or conviction of a crime of moral turpitude for the purpose of impeach-

[131] Logan v. United States, 144 U.S. 263, 1892 U.S. LEXIS 2080 (1892).
[132] State v. Foley, 15 Nev. 64, 1880 Nev. LEXIS 16 (1880).
[133] State v. Kennedy, 85 S.C. 146, 150, 67 S.E. 152, 1910 S.C. LEXIS 219 (1910).
[134] Rosen v. United States, 245 U.S. 467, 1918 U.S. LEXIS 2150 (1918).
[135] ARIZ. REV. STAT. § 12-2201 (Matthew Bender 2006).

ing the credibility of the witness.[136] Many defendants prefer, as a matter of trial strategy, not to take the witness stand in their own defense because prior felony convictions become relevant and admissible and they are believed to be assist the jury in evaluating credibility.[137]

In interpreting federal and state statutes during the past half-century, courts have made it quite clear that a criminal conviction does not render a witness incompetent to testify. For example, in a Connecticut case, the court held that the fact that the principal witness had been treated for chronic alcoholism and drug abuse in several mental institutions, and had an extensive criminal record, did not render the witness incompetent to testify.[138] In an older California case, a defendant contended that a prosecution witness was incompetent and should have not been permitted to testify for the government because he had two prior narcotics convictions and was awaiting trial on a third charge. In speaking of the government witness, the reviewing court noted that "[i]t is regrettable that the state must stoop to partnership with the odious agent provocateur,"[139] but the argument that the witness lacks competency due to prior felony convictions was erroneous. In a federal case, the court agreed that "the government cannot be expected to depend exclusively upon the virtuous in enforcing the law,[140] and so long as a reasonable jury could believe an informant's testimony, after hearing relevant impeachment evidence regarding his or her reliability, the government may rely upon such testimony" even though the witness had been previously convicted.[141] The general rule is that prior convictions of a witness affect the weight and credibility of the witness's testimony, but do not disqualify the witness.[142]

§ 8.15 —Religious Belief

Old practice in many American jurisdictions prevented those who had no religious belief from serving as witnesses in court. The Supreme Court of Kansas noted in an old case that, "[u]nder the common law, as well as in some of the states, atheists and persons without religious belief are deemed insensible to the obligations of an oath and incompetent as witnesses."[143] But the Supreme Court of Alabama noted in an earlier (1841) case that oaths had nothing to do with Christianity because they were more ancient than the Chris-

---

[136] For the rules regarding impeachment of witness, *see* Chapter 9.

[137] Morrow v. Ignacio, 2006 U.S. App. LEXIS 14199 (9th Cir. 2006).

[138] State v. Valeriano, 191 Conn. 659, 468 A.2d 936, 1983 Conn. LEXIS 623 (1983), *cert. denied*, 466 U.S. 974, 104 S. Ct. 2531, 80 L. Ed. 2d 824 (1983).

[139] People v. Empie, 196 Cal. App. 2d 648, 650, 16 Cal. Rptr. 755, 757, 1961 Cal. App. LEXIS 1624 (1961).

[140] Lockhart v. Texas, 150 Tex. Crim. 230, 200 S.W.2d 164, 1947 Tex. Crim. App. LEXIS 868 (1947).

[141] United States v. Richardson, 764 F.2d 1514 (11th Cir. 1985).

[142] United States v. Reynolds, 2006 U.S. App. LEXIS 18115 (4th Cir. 2006). *See also* People v. Hinton, 37 Cal. 4th 839, 887, 126 P.3d 981, 1018, 38 Cal. Rptr. 3d 149, 193, 2006 Cal. LEXIS 336 (Cal. 2006).

[143] Atchison, T. & S. F. R. Co. v. Potter, 60 Kan. 808, 811, 58 P. 471, 1899 Kan. LEXIS 143 (1899).

tian religion.[144] Under modern law in most jurisdictions, state constitutions or statutes affirmatively provide that no person shall be rendered incompetent to testify as a witness on account of his or her religious opinions or for want of any religious belief.[145] As one Alaska court noted, "Today the theological underpinnings of the oath requirement have largely been removed, both through statutory provisions for affirmation, and by holdings to the effect that religious belief is not an essential prerequisite of the witness' competency."[146] However, not all inquiries about the religion of a witness are forbidden if an aspect of religion might have an effect on bias or motive for impeachment purposes.[147] Massachusetts allows persons other than Christians to be sworn as witnesses according to the ceremonies of their respective religion. However, a person with a belief in some notion of a supreme being and a person who has no belief "in any religion shall be required to testify under the penalties of perjury" and the "evidence of his disbelief in the existence of God may not be received to affect his credibility as a witness."[148]

The courts and state statutes have been consistent in providing that one's religious belief or lack thereof should not be a basis upon which a court or jury should evaluate testimonial capacity or credibility.[149] Consistent with this view is Federal Rule of Evidence 610, which holds "[e]vidence of the beliefs or opinions of a witness on matters of religion is not admissible for the purpose of showing that by reason of their nature the witness' credibility is impaired or enhanced." If the witness is able to understand the obligation of an oath and the consequences of false swearing, the witness is competent, even if there is no evidence that he or she has a religious background.[150]

§ 8.16   Competency of Judge as Witness

Rule 605

Competency of Judge as Witness

The judge presiding at the trial may not testify in that trial as a witness. No objection need be made in order to preserve the point.[151]

---

[144] Blocker v. Burness, 2 Ala. 354, 355, 1841 Ala. LEXIS 357 (Ala. 1841).

[145] Gillars v. United States, 182 F.2d 962 (D.C. Cir. 1950). Under Rule 610, Religious Beliefs or Opinions, evidence of the beliefs or opinions of a witness on matters of religion is not admissible for the purpose of showing that by reason of their nature the witness's credibility is impaired or enhanced. *See also* United States v. Teicher, 987 F.2d 112 (2d Cir. 1993).

[146] Flores v. State, 443 P.2d 73, 77 1968 Alaska LEXIS 172 (1968).

[147] Slagle v. Bagley, 2006 U.S. App. LEXIS 20240; 2006 Fed. Appx. 0283P (6th Cir. 2006).

[148] MASS. GEN. LAWS, ch. 233, § 19 (Mathew Bender 2006).

[149] *See* MICH. COMP. LAWS, § 600.1436 (Mathew Bender 2006), which removed any religious test for competency and provided that religion-related interrogation of the witness could not be the subject of inquiry.

[150] Chapell v. State, 710 S.W.2d 214 (Ark. 1986).

[151] FED. R. EVID. 605.

For some years, the matter of whether a judge should be incompetent to testify as a witness in a trial over which he or she presides has been debated. The argument has been offered that where a judge both sits as a judge in the very case where the judge will serve as a witness calls into question the impartiality of the judge.[152] Some authorities advocate that this matter should be left to the discretion of the judge, and in some states this is the rule that is followed.[153] Additional issues would arise when a judge served as a witness, especially those involving who should rule on objections, who would compel the judge to answer questions, and what would occur during cross-examination. However, these issues have been rendered moot by 28 U.S.C. § 455, which mandates that federal judges disqualify themselves in cases in which they are or have been material witnesses or in which they may have bias or prejudice.[154] Rule 605 of the Federal Rules of Evidence follows the federal statute that deems federal judges incompetent to testify in cases in which they are sitting. This rule has been so well followed that a Texas court was prompted to state, "[n]ot surprisingly, there are few reported federal or state cases involving Rule 605 violations."[155]

In one Kentucky case, the appellant argued that because the judge vigorously questioned certain trial witnesses at length, the trial judge had effectively become a material witness and should have recused himself at a post-conviction hearing. The Supreme Court of Kentucky disagreed because the judge's conduct could not have influenced the finder of fact in a bench trial.[156]

Many states have adopted the federal rule either by statute or by court decision. A Nebraska court, referring to the Nebraska statute, decided that a judge presiding at a trial may not testify in that trial as a witness and added that no objection need be made in order to preserve the error.[157] When there is only a remote possibility that a judge will be called as a witness, the judge need not disqualify him- or herself solely on the eventuality that one side might call the judge as a witness.[158] Judges are considered competent witnesses in cases over which they are not presiding. In one case in which the parties came to a settlement in the presence of the judge, but the agreement was not immediately reduced to a writing, the judge can be called as a witness in a separate proceeding to give evidence concerning the agreement.[159]

---

[152] Elmore v. State, 13 Ark. App. 221, 227, 682 S.W.2d 758, 762, 1985 Ark. App. LEXIS 1735 (1985). The failure of a witness judge to recuse him- or herself does not always constitute reversible error. *See also* 22 A.L.R.3d 1198 (2003).

[153] *See* cases collected in Annotation, *Judge as a Witness in a Case on Trial Before Him*, 157 A.L.R. 315. *See also* MORRIS, FEDERAL PRACTICE, including the advisory committee's note on Rule 605.

[154] 28 U.S.C. § 455 (2006). Disqualification of justice, judge, or magistrate (magistrate judge).

[155] Bradley v. State ex rel. White, 990 S.W.2d 245, 248, 1999 Tex. LEXIS 33 (1999).

[156] Bowling v. Commonwealth, 80 S.W.3d 405, 419, 2002 Ky. LEXIS 52 (2002). *See also* Henderson v. State, 2005 Tenn. Crim. App. LEXIS 667 (2005).

[157] State v. Livingston, 509 N.W.2d 205 (Neb. 1993); State v. Rodriguez, 509 N.W. 2d 1 (Neb. 1993).

[158] In re Disqualification of Bond, 94 Ohio St. 3d 1221, 2001 Ohio 4102, 763 N.E.2d 593, 2001 Ohio LEXIS 3351 (2001).

[159] McMillin v. Davidson Industries, 2005 Ohio 224; 2005 Ohio App. LEXIS 221 (2005).

Having a sitting judge serve as a witness in a case in which he or she is presiding presents significant logistical and practical problems that are not easily resolved. The judge does not readily become just another ordinary witness and the jury may view the judge's testimony as more credible than that of a typical witness. Problems would arise when an attorney needed to object to the judge's testimony, to cross-examine the judge, or to impeach the judge when the attorney will practice before that judge in the future.[160] This reasoning was reiterated in a 1997 decision, which held that a judge presiding at a trial is considered incompetent to testify in the trial as a witness, and the prohibition applies not only to formal testimony, but also whenever the judge assumes the role of a witness.[161] The court cautioned that the judge's taking the role of a witness in the trial before him or her is manifestly inconsistent with the judge's customary role of impartiality.

§ 8.17 Competency of Juror as Witness

Rule 606

Competency of Juror as Witness

(a) At the trial.—A member of the jury may not testify as a witness before that jury in the trial of the case in which the juror is sitting. If the juror is called so to testify, the opposing party shall be afforded an opportunity to object out of the presence of the jury.

(b) Inquiry into validity of verdict or indictment.—Upon an inquiry into the validity of a verdict or indictment, a juror may not testify as to any matter or statement occurring during the course of the jury's deliberations or the effect of anything upon that or any other juror's mind or emotions as influencing the juror to assent to or dissent from the verdict or indictment or concerning the juror's mental processes in connection therewith, except that a juror may testify on the question whether extraneous prejudicial information was improperly brought to the jury's attention or whether any outside influence was improperly brought to bear upon any juror. Nor may a juror's affidavit or evidence of any statement by the juror concerning a matter about which the juror would be precluded from testifying be received for these purposes.[162]

Although many older cases are to the contrary, the general rule is that a juror may not testify as a witness in the trial of a case in which he or she is sitting. "Considerations that bear upon the permissibility of testimony are similar to those invoked when a judge is called as a witness."[163] The juror could argue against any personally impeaching evidence and rehabilitate his or her

---

[160] Sommers v. Concepcion, 20 S.W.3d 27, 40, 2000 Tex. App. LEXIS 1206 (2000).

[161] State v. Vidales, 6 Neb. App. 163, 571 N.W.2d 117 (1997). *See also* State v. Whitfield, 939 S.W.2d 361 (Mo. 1997).

[162] Fed. R. Evid. 606.

[163] Notes of Advisory Committee on Rules. Subdivision (a). of Rule 606.

testimony in the perception of other jurors in a way not open to other witnesses. A witness juror would have an unfettered opportunity to unfairly sway the jurors with personal historical knowledge of the case that may have been inadmissible at trial. The chances are too great that the testimony of the juror would have an undue influence on verdict. This rule of exclusion was codified in the Federal Rules of Evidence, which, without exception, prohibit the members of a jury from testifying in the case in which they sit as jurors. If an attorney attempted to call a sitting juror, objection may be made outside the hearing of the jury.[164]

In an Indiana case, when an alternate juror was permitted to accompany the duly seated jury into deliberations, one regular juror asked the opinion of the alternate juror concerning a particular point of evidence. The argument in the case questioned whether the alternate juror had effectively testified to the jury. The reviewing court held that the situation did not violate the rule against juror testimony because the alternate juror had been subject to all the same evidence and influence as the regular jurors and so did not add any new evidence to what the regular jurors already possessed.[165]

Section (b) of Federal Rule 606 generally holds that jurors are incompetent as witnesses; however, the Rule allows jurors to testify about whether outside influences improperly affected jury deliberations. This rule makes a juror incompetent to testify not only concerning the facts to prove the case, but also covers activities that took place during the jury's deliberations. This incompetency stems from the old maxim that "a juror may not impeach his own verdict." The rule has been justified on a variety of theories including the need for the preservation of the secrecy of internal jury deliberations and to protect the verdict against attack for corrupt reasons.[166] Additional reasoning asserts that jurors should not be harassed and beset by the defeated party in an effort to discover misconduct sufficient to set aside a verdict.[167] Were this rule to permit inquiry into the mental deliberations and processes of the jurors, every verdict would be susceptible to being undermined by post-trial jury tampering and harassment of jurors. Under federal decisions, the protection to the jurors extends to each of the components of the deliberation, including arguments, statements, discussions, mental and emotional reactions, and any other feature of the deliberation process.[168] Interestingly, where the inquiry of reasoning and deliberation concern the judge and improper extraneous factors used in reaching a verdict in a bench trial, no prohibition on an investigation of judicial reasoning exists.[169]

---

[164] FED. R. EVID. 606(a).

[165] Sanchez v. State, 794 N.E.2d 488; 2003 Ind. App. LEXIS 1570 (Ind. 2003). *See also* Griffin v. State, 754 N.E.2d 899, 2001 Ind. LEXIS 814 (2001).

[166] People v. Grider, 246 Cal. App. 2d 149, 153, 54 Cal. Rptr. 497, 501, 1966 Cal. App. LEXIS 1013 (1966).

[167] McDonald v. Pless, 238 U.S. 264, 35 S. Ct. 785, 59 L. Ed. 1300 (1915).

[168] United States v. Crosby, 294 F.2d 928 (2d Cir. 1961).

[169] Stewart v. Southwest Foods, 688 So. 2d 733, 735, 1996 Miss. LEXIS 643 (1996).

Rule 606(b) makes an exception that authorizes the juror to testify on the question of whether extraneous prejudicial information was improperly brought to the jury's attention or whether any outside influence was improperly brought to bear upon any juror. The purpose of this is to allow the courts to determine whether there were any irregularities, such as the introduction of a prejudicial newspaper account into the jury room, or statements by the bailiff concerning the case. Mistakes and misconduct of the jury during its deliberations that do not involve external influences are not generally subject to inquiry.[170]

In a Wisconsin case, there was an allegation that some of the jury members had become extrajudicially aware that the defendant had prior criminal convictions. At post-conviction relief hearings, the defense counsel alleged that there had been jury misconduct that required a reversal and new trial. As the reviewing court noted, pursuant to Wisconsin law "the party seeking to impeach the verdict must demonstrate that a juror's testimony is admissible by establishing that: (1) the juror's testimony concerns extraneous information (rather than the deliberative process of the jurors), (2) the extraneous information was improperly brought to the jury's attention, and (3) the extraneous information was potentially prejudicial."[171] Under this daunting procedure, if the appellant establishes that the juror is permitted to testify, the appellant then must next demonstrate that one or more jurors heard the statements or engaged in the alleged conduct and, finally, the court must then determine whether sufficient prejudice occurred to justify overturning the conviction.[172] In this case, the defendant managed to meet the first three hurdles, but the court did not find by clear and convincing evidence that any jurors were exposed to the prejudicial information about the defendant's prior convictions. Therefore, the reviewing court refused to disturb the jury verdict. Under Wisconsin case law, jurors are permitted to testify for the purpose of deciding whether a juror has been untruthful concerning biases during voir dire, whether extraneous information was brought to the jury's attention, and whether outside influences were used to alter any juror's thinking.[173] Simply stated, the process to overturn a jury verdict based on outside influence almost always proves unsuccessful to any criminal appellant.

Irrational juror conduct may not be a basis for a reversal of a conviction where no external influence had been involved. In a non-published decision, the Ninth Circuit Court of Appeals affirmed the denial of a writ of habeas corpus where the defendant had evidence that one juror made his decision to vote for a guilty verdict based on a coin toss. The juror's testimony was still an effort to impeach a jury verdict based on internal juror behavior. Prior case law did not support granting the writ based on irrationality of jury behavior such as juror intoxication or that a conviction was the result of a bargain in the jury room.[174]

---

[170]   Williams v. Price, 343 F.3d 223, 2003 U.S. App. LEXIS 18662 (3d Cir. 2003).
[171]   State v. Searcy, 288 Wis. 2d 804; 709 N.W.2d 497; 2005 Wisc. App. LEXIS 1124 (2005).
[172]   *Id.*, at 828, 507.
[173]   State v. Hennings, 2002 Wis. App. 1, 249 Wis. 2d 489, 639 N.W.2d 224, 2001 Wis. App. LEXIS 1160 (2002).
[174]   Reyes v. Seifert, 125 Fed. Appx. 788; 2005 U.S. App. LEXIS 33 (9th Cir. 2005).

In a suit for damages allegedly at the hands of the police, one officer, who had been found civilly liable, wanted to introduce an affidavit from a juror that concerned internal juror misconduct. The court first considered whether the affidavit concerned the type of misconduct for which evidence may be entertained under Federal Rule of Evidence 606(b). The officer alleged that the jury improperly determined a verdict amount concerning punitive damages in the first phase and that decision constituted an "extraneous influence" that affected the second phase jury deliberations. Because the allegations of misconduct did not allege that outside influence was brought to bear upon any juror and no extraneous evidence or information was allegedly brought to the jury's attention, the court determined that no evidentiary hearing was necessary to determine whether a new trial was needed.[175]

Juror misconduct had been alleged in an organized crime case where all jurors had been asked if they could render a fair and impartial verdict and whether a person being of Italian descent might have any bearing on their view of guilt or innocence. No juror answered affirmatively, but an allegation was later made that one of the jurors mentioned that the police would not arrest and bring to trial any person who was innocent. In support of his claim of juror misconduct, the defendant produced an affidavit of a person who swore that the juror had discussed the case with him during trial and had told him that the juror stated that law enforcement officers would never arrest and bring a person to trial if he or she were not guilty. The trial court held that such an allegation involving outside prejudicial information might have been brought to influence other jurors or the fact that one juror held such views was sufficiently strong to require the court to hold a hearing at which time the suspect juror could testify in conformity with Rule 606(b). The juror would not be giving evidence concerning any material or statement made by jurors during deliberations, but would be offering information about improper outside influences being brought to bear against the juror.[176]

In deciding a Ninth Circuit case involving alleged juror misconduct involving an untruthful story told to the trial judge, a defendant moved that the judge hold a hearing to determine whether there had been juror misconduct. During the trial, a juror determined that, because of religious reasons, she could not judge a fellow human and had been having a hard time continuing to serve as a juror. The trial judge, in the presence of the attorneys, questioned the juror and, with no objection from either party, excused the juror for cause because she felt unable to continue to serve consistent with her deeply held religious views and with the oath she had taken. Following a conviction, a relative of one of the defendants had a conversation with the dismissed juror in which the relative alleged that the juror stated that she wanted off of the case because other jurors were badgering her to vote for conviction and made some vague statement that racial reasons were present to make serving difficult. The trial judge refused to have the dismissed juror testify at a motion for a new trial

---

[175]   Helena v. City of San Francisco, 2006 U.S. Dist. LEXIS 27 (N.D. Cal. 2006).

[176]   Ida v. United States, 191 F. Supp. 2d 426, 2002 U.S. Dist. LEXIS 5004 (S.D.N.Y. 2002).

because of the provisions of Federal Rule of Evidence 606(b) and the supporting case law. Defense counsel had an opportunity to question the juror at the time the judge excused her and under Rule 606(b), it would be improper to question the dismissed juror's deliberations up to the time she left the jury. The Court of Appeals noted that at most, the relative stated that the dismissed juror "claimed that the dismissed juror 'implied' that she felt racial pressure because she was a 'holdout.' While the dismissed juror and the appellants are African-American, this fact alone does not warrant piercing the secrecy and sanctity of jury deliberations or disrupting the finality of the process."[177] The Court of Appeals held that alleged evidence of juror misconduct involving racial pressure was insufficient to pierce the sanctity of the jurors' deliberations. In order for a court to inquire into a jury verdict, the alleged misconduct generally must involve jury deliberations tainted by extraneous factors. In a different case, the defendant requested a hearing to determine whether jury misconduct had occurred in a jury trial where the defendant was charged with defrauding the United States. The defendant submitted two post-trial affidavits from jurors in the case that alleged that during jury deliberations, one juror inquired of the others concerning how would things look and "what kind of message will it send to the . . . investors if we do not convict?"[178] The Court of Appeals affirmed the trial court's denial of the motion to hold a hearing on the grounds that the juror comments were not extraneous to jury deliberations.

As a general rule, jurors can be prevented from talking about the case to each other until deliberations begin. During deliberations, judges routinely order jurors to discuss the case with no one other than fellow jurors during regularly scheduled deliberations. Once a trial has concluded and the jurors have been officially discharged, they are free to speak with attorneys in the case as well as print, broadcast, and Internet media, or to choose not to speak with anyone or any organization. In this context, information concerning the internal deliberations, discussions, and behaviors of the jury may be revealed at the individual discretion of the juror. Courts are under no general duty to make jurors available to interested persons and may take some affirmative steps to protect personal matters of the jurors from unwarranted harassment.[179]

Because discharged jurors have the right to refuse any comment on a case, states are permitted to keep much juror information private and can refuse to disclose it unless a defendant-appellant makes a strong case for disclosure. In one California case,[180] the appellant wanted to discover the name and address of a juror who served on his capital jury because he had reason to suspect that the juror had committed misconduct. The trial court refused to disclose the personal information of the juror because it found a compelling need to keep the juror's identity secret under a California statute.[181] The statute allows some

---

[177]   United States v. Decoud, 2006 U.S. App. LEXIS 19599 (9th Cir. 2006).

[178]   United States v. Wintermute, 443 F.3d 993, 1001, 2006 U.S. App. LEXIS 8786 (8th Cir. 2006).

[179]   See, United States v. Scrushy, 2005 U.S. Dist. LEXIS 42127 (N.D. Ala. 2006).

[180]   People v. Avila, 38 Cal. 4th 491, 133 P.3d 1076, 43 Cal. Rptr. 3d 1, 2006 Cal. LEXIS 5867 (2006).

[181]   CAL. CODE CIV. PROC. § 237, Names of qualified jurors made available to public; Petition for access to records; Notice; Hearing; Violations (Matthew Bender 2006).

protection for jurors against unreasonable contact with the defendant or some-one working on behalf of the defendant because the identity is sealed unless a judge orders a different result.[182] Similarly, Florida requires that a party wish-ing to have the trial court interview jurors after the trial relative to misconduct must present factual allegations, which demonstrates that the verdict might be subject to challenge.[183] Essentially, following the trial, jurors are free to dis-cuss the case at any and all levels or to remain silent. Some jurisdictions limit contact, unless judicially approved, if the initiator is the defendant, counsel, or another person connected to the original case.

§ 8.18 Summary

To be admissible in a trial in a criminal case, evidence must be competent in that it meets the tests of logical and legal relevancy. The item of evidence must help prove or disprove a fact in issue and the probative value of the evi-dence must be greater than its prejudicial effect. The evidence is then consid-ered competent. Even though the evidence has passed the relevancy and materiality tests, it will be excluded if the court finds that it is incompetent for other legal reasons, such as a statutory or constitutional violation.

Care must be taken to avoid confusion concerning the rules regarding com-petency of the evidence and competency of the witness. A witness may be com-petent by meeting the four elements of competency, and yet the evidence to be introduced by the witness may be ruled incompetent, and thus excludable.

From a general point of view, evidence is incompetent if: (1) law enforce-ment officials have obtained it wrongfully or illegally; or (2) a statute declares it to be incompetent; or (3) it has been declared incompetent by the courts, or (4) it has insufficient or no connection to the case.

Documentary evidence must meet the usual competency tests so that it possesses sufficient connection to the case, but it also must comply with spe-cial requirements. For example, it must be authenticated to show that it is gen-uine. Likewise, real evidence may be excluded as incompetent if specific requirements are not met.

Through court decisions and statutes, rules have evolved that require a witness to meet the four elements of competency: oath (or a substitute), orig-inal perception, recollection, and an ability to communicate prior to being per-mitted to testify in court. While competency rules have been liberalized in recent years, there are still certain requirements that, if not met, may make a witness incompetent to testify in court or may prevent a prospective witness from testifying through reliance on a privilege.

Even though a person may not have normal mental capacity, he or she may be allowed to testify if he or she can understand the obligation of an oath and can give a correct account of the matters seen or heard. Some jurisdictions

---

[182] *Id.*
[183] *See* FLA. R. CRIM. P. 3.575, Motion to Interview Juror (Matthew Bender 2006).

hold that a child is generally presumed competent to testify, while other jurisdictions hold that below a specified age, the presumption is against competency. As a general rule, a child can be proved to be competent where the child demonstrates the capacity to observe events and to recollect and communicate them, and has the ability to understand questions and to make intelligent answers with the understanding of the duty to speak the truth.

At common law, neither husband nor wife was permitted to testify for or against the other. All states by statute have made both husband and wife competent to testify on behalf of an accused spouse, but with some exceptions that vary depending on the jurisdiction. It is generally provided that the prosecution may not force a spouse to testify against the accused spouse.

A criminal conviction for a felony generally does not render a witness or a defendant incompetent to testify. While considered competent to testify, a defendant who has been previously convicted of a crime, especially a felony, can choose to forgo testifying because it opens the door to evidence of prior felonies and misdemeanors, involving moral turpitude, being introduced as an impeachment device. However, certain convictions may be relevant if they are introduced to show that the defendant had a common scheme or plan, motive, intent, identity, knowledge sufficient to commit the crime, or lack of mistake in committing the crime.

The competency of the presiding judge to testify as a witness in a case the judge is presently hearing has severe limitations. Under the modern rules of evidence, and consistent with Rule 605 of the Federal Rules of Evidence, judges in federal courts and states that have adopted a state version of the Federal Rules are incompetent to testify as to any matter in a trial over which the judge presides. A juror is incompetent to act as a witness at the trial of a case while serving as a juror in that case. Under Federal Rule 606, jurors also may not testify about the verdict or the manner in which the jury decided the case except when the inquiry relates to external influence or external prejudicial information that may have been improperly brought to the jurors' attention.

As a practical matter, justice personnel should be fully aware of the rules that make testimony or other evidence inadmissible because of competency rules. In some instances, a case may be resolved based on one piece of real evidence or testimony that an attorney attempts to get the court to admit or exclude.

Evidence via Witness Testimony

Examination
of Witnesses

9

For two centuries past, the policy of the Anglo-American system of Evidence has been to regard the necessity of testimony by cross-examination as a vital feature of the law. The belief that no safeguard for testing the value of human statements is comparable to that furnished by cross-examination, and the conviction that no statement (unless by special exception) should be used as testimony until it has been probed and sublimated by that test, has found increasing strength in lengthening experience.

WIGMORE, EVIDENCE, Vol. 5, § 1367 (3d ed. 1940)

Chapter Outline

Key Terms and Concepts

affirmation
cross-examination
direct examination
hostile witness
impeachment of witness
judicial control
leading question

oath
past recollection recorded
present memory revived
prior inconsistent statement
recross-examination
redirect examination
sequestration

§ 9.1 Introduction

All evidence in criminal trial arrives through the testimony of witnesses who either directly testify to the historical facts or provide testimony that allows physical evidence to be introduced to the trier of fact. In a very real sense, without witnesses, there could be no trials in the criminal justice system. The function of the witness is facilitate the introduction of evidence from which the trier of fact can make a determination of what happened, who did the criminal act, and whether the person should be held accountable. Because the purpose of a criminal trial is to determine whether the accused is guilty of the crime charged, it would seem logical to assume that all testimony of witnesses and all physical evidence would be admissible. However, for various statutory and public policy reasons, trial witnesses are limited not only in what they may reveal, but also in how they may reveal it.

In conducting the criminal trial, the normal procedure is first for the prosecution to present evidence that tends to prove the offense charged beyond a reasonable doubt. In so doing, the prosecution calls a series of witnesses and then proceeds to ask questions of the witnesses. After the prosecution has presented its case, the defense has an opportunity to put witnesses on the stand and introduce evidence that follows the defense's theory of the case. Before either the prosecution witnesses or the defense witnesses can testify, however, they must meet certain requirements, including having personal knowledge and taking the oath to tell the truth. Even after the witnesses have been qualified, their testimony is subject to many rules that will be discussed in this chapter and in future chapters.

This chapter focuses on the general rules regulating the qualification of witnesses and witness examination by the prosecution and the defense. Specifically, the sections in this chapter cover the qualifications of the witnesses, the requirement of the oath or affirmation, separation of witnesses, direct and cross-examination of witnesses, and the process of witness impeachment and rehabilitation. Later chapters will discuss in great detail the rules that limit the admissibility of testimonial evidence, while giving due recognition to some of the more complex and arcane rules and their exceptions. This category includes the testimonial privileges, opinion testimony, and the hearsay rule, with its exceptions.

§ 9.2   Essential Qualities of a Witness

Rule 602

Lack of Personal Knowledge

A witness may not testify to a matter unless evidence is introduced sufficient to support a finding that the witness has personal knowledge of the matter. Evidence to prove personal knowledge may, but need not, consist of the witness' own testimony. This rule is subject to the provisions of Rule 703, relating to opinion testimony by expert witnesses.[1]

In order to meet the threshold witness requirements and to be eligible to testify, a witness must have a personal connection with the relevant occurrence, coupled with mental and physical facilities sufficient to be able to observe and understand the events at the time of their occurrence and to recollect and relate them to the jury or a court in a manner that renders the testimony relevant.[2] In other words, the witness must be qualified. Normally, "in any criminal trial every person is competent to be a witness,"[3] but when an issue arises that questions the competency of a particular witness, the witness may be required to demonstrate that the witness had original perception, remembers what happened, can communicate this knowledge and is willing to take the oath or a substitute. When a judge makes a determination about competency, the witness is either competent or incompetent, because there are no degrees of competency where one witness would have more competency than another.[4]

The rationale for Federal Rule 602 appears to consider that lay testimony that is not based on personal information is useless, and a witness cannot pro-

---

[1]   FED. R. EVID. 602. Rule 703, which is referred to in Rule 602, provides that the expert witness need not have personal knowledge of facts or dates.

[2]   People v. Hooker, 253 Ill. App. 3d 1075, 625 N.E.2d 1081 (1993).

[3]   A.R.S. § 13-4061 Competency of witness (Ariz. 2006). *See also* FED. R. EVID. R 601.

[4]   Hawai'i v. Jones, 98 Haw. 294, 2002 Haw. App. LEXIS 65 (2002).

vide information about a matter about which the witness has no knowledge.[5] In a revocation of a community control order for a convicted defendant, the trial court impermissibly allowed witnesses to testify concerning matters about which they had no knowledge. One of the witnesses stated that she had been informed that the defendant left the secure facility without finishing his treatment, while another offered evidence that the defendant had left the facility against medical advice. Because neither witness had any firsthand knowledge, their information was worthless and should not have considered as the basis for the revocation of community control.[6]

The requirement of firsthand knowledge or original knowledge will prevent a person from being considered competent as a witness for a particular case. In a case in which an altercation arose in a parking garage, a security guard was watching a video console where he could observe the altercation in real time.[7] Other security guards watched the tape later and concluded that the defendant was one of the perpetrators of the violence. A few days later, the defendant and his attorney viewed the videotape, but the portion containing the incident had been taped over with a television show. The trial court allowed the security guards who had only observed a replay of the tape to testify against the defendant over his objection that they were incompetent because they did not observe the incident, but only later watched it on a security playback monitor. Essentially, the argument was that the guards possessed no personal knowledge. The appellate court reversed the judgment on the ground that none of the security guards who observed the videotape were competent witnesses and because they had been permitted to testify, the verdict had to be reversed.

As a general rule, the party offering the testimony must prove that the witness had an opportunity to observe the incident about which he or she is testifying. This does not necessarily mean that a witness must have observed every facet of the event in question. For example, in a stabbing altercation outside an apartment complex, the court permitted a responding police officer to testify that the victim's stab wounds were consistent with someone fleeing an aggressor.[8] An emergency room doctor testified to the same conclusion, although neither the doctor nor the officer observed the fight. They obtained their personal knowledge by observing the situation and the victim and coming to a conclusion. The appellate court approved the admission of evidence by the two witnesses on the theory that each one was an expert and was properly allowed to offer a conclusion even though neither one observed the fight. The police officer had specific training as a police officer and had additional training as a military police officer.

Consistent with the requirement of personal knowledge, an appellate court approved allowing a federal officer to testify concerning deportation procedures because the agent had sufficient personal knowledge under Rule 602.

[5]   United States v. Allen, 10 F.3d 405 (7th Cir. 1993).
[6]   Wilson v. State, 1842 So. 2d 237, 2003 Fla. App. LEXIS 4814 (2003).
[7]   Frazer v. El-Amin, 2004 Minn. App. LEXIS 1015 (2004).
[8]   Vasquez v. State, 2006 Tex. App. LEXIS 500 (2006).

The immigration officer had worked at the deportation facility for 30 days and had personal knowledge about how deportation orders operated.[9]

In criminal cases, witnesses are frequently called upon to testify about events that they only casually observed, such as when making an identification or recounting events that were not thought to be important at the time of observation. It is permissible under the firsthand knowledge requirement for a witness to testify that to the best of the witness's belief, the defendant committed the criminal act, while acknowledging that he or she may be mistaken as to the identity of the defendant. Where a witness has testified to an event about which he or she possessed no firsthand knowledge, without objection from the opposing side, the evidence is admitted. In a Minnesota case, an impaired driver failed to object when a police officer testified that the defendant had been given access to a phone to call an attorney, even though the police officer merely deduced that this event occurred. Even though the officer had no firsthand knowledge, the court admitted the evidence because the defendant failed to object.[10]

§ 9.3   Oath or Affirmation Requirement

> **Rule 603**
>
> **Oath or Affirmation**
>
> Before testifying, every witness shall be required to declare that the witness will testify truthfully, by oath or affirmation administered in a form calculated to awaken the witness' conscience and impress the witness' mind with the duty to do so.[11]

As one of the elements of competency, every witness, including children, is required to state that he or she will testify truthfully or in some fashion indicate that the witness understands the duty to tell the truth. The purpose of the formal oath or affirmation serves to impress upon the witness's mind and conscience the importance of telling the truth and only the truth at the trial. To further impress upon the witness the responsibility of telling the truth, the courts require that the prospective witness take an oath[12] or offer some form of affirmation that is "calculated to awaken the witness' conscience and impress the witness' mind with the clear duty"[13] to tell the truth. Using an affirmation in place of an oath does not itself weaken the weight of the testimony of a wit-

---

[9]   United States v. Ambriz-Vasquez, No. 01-10144, 2002 U.S. App. LEXIS 8597 (9th Cir. 2002).

[10] Minnesota v. Pederson, 2002 Minn. App. LEXIS 119 (2002).

[11] FED. R. EVID. 603.

[12] The person administering the oath generally must be someone empowered under local law to administer oaths or the statements offered thereafter will not be deemed to be under oath. *See* State v. Lawson, 2002 Tenn. Crim. App. LEXIS 468 (2002).

[13] Esguerra v. State, 2005 Alaska App. LEXIS 2 (2005).

ness, but it may have some bearing on the weight given that testimony by some members of a jury.

Because of First Amendment protection of the freedom of religion, it is not proper to require the witness to affirm God in the court's administered oath. In *United States v. Looper*,[14] the United States Court of Appeals for the Fourth Circuit stated that, at common law, there was neither a requirement of affirming God's name, nor a requirement of raising a hand for a valid oath. In that case, a witness refused to affirm God in making the oath based upon his religious belief in the Church of God. The trial court denied him the right to testify, but the reviewing court set aside the conviction.

Most states have statutes that allow the witness to make an affirmation rather than an oath. The affirmation need not take a particular form; the concept of affirmation is designed to afford some flexibility when dealing with religious adults or children.[15] This alternative to the formal oath is provided for those who lack the requisite belief in God, and for those who are forbidden by conscientious scruples to take an oath. Under these statutes, the witness must explicitly state that the scruple exists.

If the witness claims a First Amendment right not to be sworn, the court's interest in administering the precise form of oath must yield to the witness's First Amendment rights.[16] In the case of *United States v. Ward*, the reviewing court held that the defendant had a right to substitute the phrase "fully integrated honesty" for the word "truth" in taking the oath and that the rule governing the form of the oath was sufficiently flexible to permit modifications of the oath. Rule 603 and similar state statutes were developed with a view to affording flexibility when dealing with adults, atheists, conscientious objectors, mentally challenged persons, and children.[17]

When a potential witness refuses to take an oath to tell the truth and completely refused to testify in any form, trial courts face a problem. If the potential witness made an out-of-court statement, that statement might provide needed evidence. However, a constitutional problem arises under this situation because the defendant is denied the right under the Sixth Amendment to confront the adverse witness. These types of situations have no easy answer and may result in evidence that is inadmissible.[18]

In the exercise of judicial discretion, a court may dispense with the formal oath when one of the parties presents a young child as a witness. As a substitute for the oath, the court must be satisfied that a young witness understands the consequences of not telling the truth. As one court phrased the standard, the primary issue was whether the "six-year-old victim had the ability to understand the necessity of telling the truth while testifying in the proceed-

---

[14]   419 F.2d 1405 (4th Cir. 1969).
[15]   North Carolina v. Beane, 146 N.C. App. 220, 225, 226, 552 S.E.2d 193, 196, 197, 2001 N.C. App. LEXIS 852 (2001).
[16]   United States v. Ward, 989 F.2d 1015 (9th Cir. 1992).
[17]   *See* the advisory Notes accompanying Federal Rule 603.
[18]   *See* Crawford v. Washington, 541 U.S. 36, 2004 U.S. LEXIS 1838 (2004).

ings."[19] The competency of a child witness can be demonstrated by testimony that the child understands the importance of telling the truth and understands the concept of a lie. One court noted that it was not necessary that a child understand the nature of an oath, the legal concept of false swearing or why someone holds up a hand as long as the child demonstrates a moral awareness of the obligation to tell the truth.[20]

An oath may not be required in some other judicial proceedings that do not involve young children. For example, in a capital case, an Ohio court permitted a death-eligible convicted defendant to offer an unsworn statement to the court in an effort to present mitigating evidence to avoid the death penalty.[21] Under the criminal rules in Ohio, any criminal defendant has a right to make an unsworn statement at the time of sentencing or to present other unsworn evidence of mitigation of punishment.[22]

Rule 603 of the Federal Rules of Evidence requires that every witness declare "that he or she will testify truthfully by oath or affirmation, administered in a form calculated to awaken the witness' conscience and impress the witness' mind with the duty to do so."[23] Most states have adopted this or a similar rule. Generally, this requirement is satisfied by an oath or affirmation given in any manner designed to impress the witness that he must tell the truth and that failure carries serious consequences.[24] Where a witness has neither taken the oath nor otherwise affirmed to tell the truth, a failure to object by the opposing party has generally been viewed as a waiver. As one court noted, "[d]espite the constitutional nature of the oath requirement, our appellate courts have consistently held that where the trial court fails to administer the oath to a witness, the defendant's failure to object waives appellate review of the court's error."[25] A party may not permit the trial to proceed and raise the question after the verdict because, if the error had been brought to the attention of the trial court, it could have corrected the oversight by having the witness re-testify under oath.[26]

---

[19]   State v. Ledbetter, 2003 Tenn. Crim. App. LEXIS 677 (2003).

[20]   Warner v. State, 2005 Ark. App. LEXIS 875 (2005). *See* § 8.12 for a discussion of the competency of child witnesses.

[21]   State v. Turner, 105 Ohio St. 3d 331, 2005 Ohio 1938, 826 N.E.2d 266, 2005 Ohio LEXIS 961 (2005).

[22]   OHIO CRIM. R. 32 (2006).

[23]   FED. R. EVID. 603.

[24]   Larson v. State, 686 P.2d 583 (Wyo. 1984).

[25]   North Carolina v. Beane, 146 N.C. App. 220, 225, 552 S.E.2d 193, 196, 2001 N.C. App. LEXIS 852 (2001).

[26]   *Id.*

§ 9.4   Judicial Control of Testimony

Rule 611

**Mode and Order of Interrogation
and Presentation**

(a) **Control by court.** The court shall exercise reasonable control over the mode and order of interrogating witnesses and presenting evidence so as to (1) make the interrogation and presentation effective for the ascertainment of the truth, (2) avoid needless consumption of time, and (3) protect witnesses from harassment or undue embarrassment.[27]

*   *   *

The responsive answer by a sworn witness to the questions posed by one party's attorney serves as the usual manner of introducing evidence in a criminal trial. Whether the testimony takes the form of a narrative response to a fairly open-ended question or an individual response to specific questions is ultimately a matter to be decided by the trial judge under the particular circumstances. Usually, the judge does not interfere with the attorney's approach unless there is some danger that improper or incompetent evidence might be admitted. The judge has the authority and, in fact, the responsibility to exercise reasonable control over the mode and order of interrogating witnesses and presenting evidence. Proper judicial oversight and control facilitate the interrogation process and assists in a presentation effective for the ascertainment of the truth, for avoiding needless consumption of time, and for the protection of witnesses from undue harassment.

The trial judge enjoys wide discretion in ruling on the forms of questions and how the attorneys examine the witnesses. The judge may not only rule on objections to questions, but also may instruct a witness to answer the questions as asked. A judge may order that witnesses not argue with the attorneys or the judge and give answers that are responsive to the actual question asked. The judge has the ultimate responsibility for the orderly reception or rejection of evidence, and a reviewing court will usually uphold judicial decisions in relation to the control of testimony unless there is a clear abuse of discretion.

Under Federal Rule of Evidence 614 and similar state rules, judges have the right to ask questions of witnesses and to call witnesses in the exercise of judicial discretion. Following this procedure, in a federal prosecution for selling cocaine base, the trial judge asked questions of two prosecution witnesses.[28] The judge interjected questions during the defense cross-examination of the government's drug purchaser, but the questions appeared to be of a clarifying nature. The judge also asked questions of a police officer involved in the sting drug purchase about how the police officer originally met the coop-

---

[27]   Fed. R. Evid. 611.

[28]   *See* United States v. McCray, 437 F.3d 639, 2006 U.S. App. LEXIS 3116 (7th Cir. 2006).

erating drug purchaser. The reviewing court held that the questions were not the kind that would have prejudiced the defendant unfairly, even though it expressed some concern that the judge placed the defense counsel in an awkward position to accept the judge's questions or to challenge the judge's impartiality in front of the jury.

In a North Carolina case in which the defendant contended that the judge failed to control the examination of witnesses to ensure justice for both sides, the appellate court approved the practice of the trial judge in assuring that the jury did not hear some arguments concerning admissibility of evidence when the arguments might have unfairly swayed the jury. In addition, where the trial judge had asked questions of the witnesses and of the prosecutor to clarify the admissibility of evidence, the appellate court did not view that questioning as assisting the prosecution in providing a proper foundation for the admission of evidence. The reviewing court held that "the trial court was acting within permissible bounds of supervising and controlling the examination of [a witness] to insure justice for both parties by clarifying testimony as well as eliciting pertinent facts."[29]

A federal appellate court recently observed "[f]ederal judges have wide discretion to determine the role that they will play during the course of a trial."[30] Wide discretion in controlling court activity does not imply unfettered freedom, and appellate courts may reverse if the discretion is abused. For example, in an Eighth Circuit case, the defense counsel wished to inquire about a mental disability of a prosecution witness. It was known to the defense attorney that the witness had a short-term memory problem. When the witness answered that he had "diabetes" as a disability, the trial court refused to allow additional inquiry relative to mental disability. The court refused to hear any evidence of the witness's mental disability and limited the cross-examination by the defendant. On appeal, the court held that the refusal to inquire about a mental disability of the prosecution witness violated the defendant's right of confrontation necessitating a reversal of the conviction[31] under the abuse of discretion standard.

A trial judge abused his discretion in the conduct of a trial when the court refused to allow the defendant's DNA expert to testify on the ground that the defendant had not notified the court and the prosecution about the witness within the proper amount of time. The sanction for failure to timely notify was exclusion of the evidence. On appeal, the court held that the trial court abused its discretion because the defense attorney had only been hired two days prior to trial and immediately gave notice that he would probably use a DNA expert or two. Because the attorney had just been hired and there had been no failure to notify as a tactic to gain unfair advantage, the trial court abused its discretion in trial management by excluding the DNA expert's evidence.[32]

---

[29]   North Carolina v. Callicutt, 2003 N.C. App. LEXIS 813 (2003).

[30]   United States v. Washington, 417 F.3d 780, 783-784 (7th Cir. 2005).

[31]   United States v. Love, 2003 U.S. App. LEXIS 10756 (8th Cir. 2003).

[32]   People v. Kelly, 288 A.D.2d 695, 696, 697, 732 N.Y.S.2d 484, 486, 487, 2001 N.Y. App. Div. LEXIS 11148 (2001).

Rule 611 of the Federal Rules of Evidence and similar adoptions by the states make it clear that the judge exercises control over the examination of witnesses in determining what evidence shall be admitted and in what order. In a North Carolina murder case, the court permitted the prosecutor to question a prosecution witness on entirely new matters that had not been addressed during either the direct or cross-examination. The general rule is that a party cannot usually question a witness on new material on redirect examination. In allowing the line of questions concerning the fear that the murder victim had about the defendant being likely to kill him, the judge admitted evidence that had a probative value that outweighed the danger of unfair prejudice to the defendant. The appellate court held that the judge did not abuse his discretion under Rule 611 and upheld the original verdict.[33]

§ 9.5   Separation of Witnesses

Rule 615

Exclusion of Witnesses

At the request of a party, the court shall order witnesses excluded so that they cannot hear the testimony of other witnesses, and it may make the order of its own motion. This rule does not authorize exclusion of (1) a party who is a natural person, or (2) an officer or employee of a party which is not a natural person designated as its representative by its attorney, or (3) a person whose presence is shown by a party to be essential to the presentation of the party's cause, or (4) a person authorized by statute to be present.[34]

Statutes or rules court in all jurisdictions authorize trial judges to exclude witnesses from the courtroom except when that witness is testifying. Some court orders may allow witnesses who have testified to remain within the courtroom following their testimony. The procedure is variously called separation, exclusion, sequestration, or "putting witnesses under the rule." The Federal Rules of Evidence and state derivatives take the position that sequestration of witnesses is a matter of right; the rule states "[a]t the request of a party the court shall order witnesses excluded so that they cannot hear the testimony of other witnesses."[35] The purpose of the sequestration rule is to prevent witnesses from hearing the testimony of other witnesses and subsequently adjusting their testimony,[36] whether consciously or inadvertently. Other purposes of Rule 615 are "to discourage and expose fabrication, inac-

---

[33] North Carolina v. Castor, 150 N.C. App. 17, 24, 562 S.E.2d 574, 579, 2002 N.C. App. LEXIS 360 (2002).

[34] FED. R. EVID. 615.

[35] *Id.*

[36] Tennessee v. Coleman, 2002 Tenn. Crim. App. LEXIS 84 (2002).

curacy, and collusion and to minimize the opportunity that each witness will have to tailor testimony to the testimony of other witnesses."[37]

Several categories of persons are excluded from an order of sequestration. Natural persons who are parties to the action cannot excluded from the courtroom because excluding them would raise serious Sixth Amendment right of confrontation and Fifth or Fourteenth Amendment due process problems. In most instances, police officers who have been in charge of an investigation are allowed to remain in court despite the fact that they may be called as witnesses. In a federal prosecution, where the judge had placed the other witnesses "under the rule" by ordering them to be sequestered, the defendant complained at trial and on appeal that one of the arresting officers had been permitted to stay at the counsel table with the federal prosecutors.[38] The defendant argued that the officer was not indispensable to the government's case. In rejecting the defendant's argument, the Court of Appeals for the First Circuit held that Rule 615 permitted the government to designate the officer as the officer or an employee of a party that is not a natural person and to remain in the courtroom.

In interpreting Rule 615 of the Kentucky rules of evidence, the Supreme Court of Kentucky held that reversible error had occurred in a robbery case when the trial court permitted two investigating officers to remain in the courtroom during the presentation of the commonwealth's case-in-chief. Rule 615 automatically allows one officer to remain under subsection (2) of the rule, but a second officer's presence cannot be justified under subsection (3), which allows a "person whose presence is shown by a party to be essential to the presentation of the party's case." In this case, one officer testified first, while the second (and improperly present) officer was able to observe the testimony of the first and make any needed adjustments to his future testimony. When the second officer took the stand, his memory would have been completely refreshed concerning all the minute and important details. The Supreme Court of Kentucky reversed the conviction.[39]

In another case, an undercover agent who was the prosecuting witness in a cocaine distribution conspiracy trial was permitted to sit at the government counsel's tables, even though he was also to be a witness in the case.[40] And Federal Rule of Evidence 615 did not require the exclusion of a testifying government agent from the trial during the testimony of other witnesses, because the agent was an officer for the government.[41]

---

[37]   *See Exclusion of Witnesses under Rule 615 of Federal Rules of Evidence*, 181 A.L.R. FED. 549 (March 2003).

[38]   United States v. Charles, 456 F.3d 249; 2006 U.S. App. LEXIS 19619 (1st Cir. 2006).

[39]   Mills v. Commonwealth, 95 S.W.3d 838, 840, 841, 2003 Ky. LEXIS 11 (2003).

[40]   United States v. Adamo, 882 F.2d 1218 (7th Cir. 1989).

[41]   United States v. Thomas, 835 F.2d 219 (9th Cir.), *cert. denied*, 486 U.S. 1010, 108 S. Ct. 1741, 100 L. Ed. 2d 204 (1987). *See also* United States v. Gonzalez, 918 F.2d 1129 (8th Cir. 1990), in which the court decided that the trial court did not abuse its discretion when it denied the defendant's motion to sequester the government's case agent, even though the case agent later testified against defendant and his codefendants, inasmuch as the case agent functioned as the government's designated representative.

In determining whether a government agent qualifies as an essential witness in accordance with Rule 615, much depends upon the nature of the case and the quality and quantity of the evidence. For example, in a case reviewed by the Sixth Circuit Court of Appeals, A DEA Special Agent and an FBI Special Agent were qualified as essential witnesses who could remain in the courtroom during the trial so that they could assist with the drug prosecution because of the expected length of the trial, the number of defendants, and the large amount of evidence, some of which was not readily accessible.[42]

For a witness to meet the requirements of the exception to sequestration indicated in Rule 615(3), a party must demonstrate that the presence of a witness is essential to the presentation of the party's case. In one case, for example, a defendant failed to demonstrate to the satisfaction of the court that his girlfriend possessed such specialized expertise or intimate knowledge of the facts of the case that counsel could not effectively function without her presence to the extent that exemption from sequestration was warranted.[43] In a pretrial order, pursuant to a defense motion under Rule 615, a federal judge decreed that the prosecution could have only one representative (the case agent) in the courtroom with the rest of the prosecution's witnesses removed from court except when testifying.[44] The judge rejected the prosecution's suggestion that it be allowed to have two agents present in the courtroom and noted that the weight of authority allows only one representative.

As a penalty for disregarding the judge's order, a reviewing court held that a trial court acted within its discretion in refusing to allow a defense witness to testify when the witness had remained in court despite a sequestration order issued under Rule 615 of the Federal Rules of Evidence.[45]

Under the theory of judicial discretion, reviewing courts will normally uphold the decision of a lower court in determining whether a witness who has failed to follow the court's sequestration order should be allowed to testify. In criminal cases, the defense witnesses will generally be allowed to testify even if they failed to follow the rules, although courts may consider sanctions.[46] For example, in one federal case, some of the prosecution's witnesses violated the sequestration order through no fault of the government.[47] The district court judge prevented the prosecution from admitting some evidence through a witness who had not testified and could have received courtroom information and the judge allowed the parties to explore the violation of the sequestration order during cross-examination. The judge also instructed the jury that in considering witness credibility, they could consider the fact of the violation of the sequestration order. Even though the defense contended that the judge should have taken stronger action, the appellate court affirmed the trial judge's actions. In

---

[42]   United States v. Phibbs, 999 F.2d 1053 (6th Cir. 1993).

[43]   United States v. Agnes, 581 F. Supp. 462 (E.D. Pa. 1984).

[44]   United States v. Blackman, 2006 U.S. Dist. LEXIS 70147 (E.D.N.C. 2006).

[45]   United States v. Gibson, 675 F.2d 825 (6th Cir.), *cert. denied*, 459 U.S. 972, 103 S. Ct. 305, 74 L. Ed. 2d 285 (1982). *See also* United States v. Lamp, 779 F.2d 1088 (5th Cir.), *cert. denied*, 476 U.S. 1144, 106 S. Ct. 2255, 90 L. Ed. 2d 700 (1986).

[46]   People v. Melendez, 102 P.3d 315; 2004 Colo. LEXIS 1006 (2004). See case in Part II.

[47]   United States v. Ruiz Solorio, 337 F.3d 580, 592, 2003 U.S. App. LEXIS 14585 (6th Cir. 2003).

summary, where there has been a violation of a judge's sequestration order that is not affirmatively attributable to either the prosecution or the defense, a trial court will be reluctant to exclude the testimony, especially where the exclusion may do more harm to justice than any other remedy. If an exclusion effectively removes a defendant's ability to mount a defense, a trial court will be most reluctant to apply such a remedy and would generally seek a less drastic sanction.

§ 9.6 Direct Examination of Witnesses

When a witness is called to offer testimony and where there is no objection to the competency of the witness, as a general rule the witness will be allowed to give evidence in response to questions. Where there is an initial objection to the witness's competency or other challenge to giving testimony,[48] the judge will have to make an inquiry and make a determination concerning competency. After the court has determined that a witness is qualified to testify, the witness has observed any sequestration order as required, and the witness has been administered the oath or affirmation, the direct examination of the witness begins. Direct examination usually begins by having the party who called the witness ask the witness his or her name, address, and occupation. Even though everyone in the courtroom may know this information, it is necessary to complete the court records. After these preliminary background questions are completed, the general questioning of the witness begins.

If the witness cannot understand or speak English or for some other reason is not able to communicate in the usual manner, a language or sign interpreter will to assist in helping the witness to communicate with the attorneys and the jury. According to Rule 604, the interpreter must meet the qualifications of an expert and must take an oath to make a correct translation. An interpreter may also translate documentary evidence for admission into evidence.[49] The interpreter is not permitted to give his or her individual conclusions with respect to the answers of the witness, but must give a literal interpretation of the language employed by the witness.[50]

Even after the case has progressed to this stage, there are still rules that apply during the direct examination of the witness. For example, leading questions, those that suggest the desired answer, are usually not authorized on direct examination, although some leading questions may be permitted concerning preliminary matters and when speaking with child witnesses. Limiting procedures have evolved regarding allowing a witness to refer to records in an effort to revive memory, or to use memoranda of past recollection as a substitute for memory. These are discussed in the sections that follow.

---

[48] Other challenges to a witness could involve one of the marital privileges, attorney-client privilege, Fifth Amendment privilege, or a challenge under the Fourth Amendment.

[49] Boim v. Quranic Literacy Inst., 340 F. Supp. 2d 885, 916, 2004 U.S. Dist. LEXIS 22745 (N.D. Ill. 2004).

[50] FED. R. EVID. 604.

§ 9.7 —Leading Questions

Rule 611

Mode and Order of Interrogation and Presentation

(c) Leading questions. Leading questions should not be used on the direct examination of a witness except as may be necessary to develop the witness' testimony. Ordinarily leading questions should be permitted on cross-examination. When a party calls a hostile witness, an adverse party, or a witness identified with an adverse party, interrogation may be by leading questions.[51]

The use of leading questions on direct or redirect examination is, with certain exceptions, forbidden, and the opposing counsel has the right to object to such questions.[52] The reason for this rule is that the suggestive powers of leading questions have the effect of allowing the questioner to testify by having a witness adopt the substance of the examiner's questions. However, courts have some discretion in allowing the use of leading questions on direct examination[53] where necessary to develop a particular witness's testimony. This is especially true where the witness is an adverse party, a hostile witness, or a witness identified with an adverse party.[54]

A question is generally considered leading where the wording has been framed in a manner that suggests the answer what the questioner desires of the witness.[55] In order to elicit the facts, a trial lawyer may find it necessary to direct the attention of a witness to the specific matter about which his or her testimony is desired, and if the question does not suggest the answer, it is not leading. Even though the question may call for a "yes" or "no" answer, it is not impermissibly leading[56] unless it is so worded that, by permitting the witness to answer yes or no, the witness would be testifying in the language of the interrogator rather than his or her own language.[57] A leading question suggests to the witness "how to answer or puts into his mouth words to be echoed back."[58]

---

[51] FED. R. EVID. 611.

[52] For reasons that will be explained in later sections, leading questions are permitted on cross-examination.

[53] Williams v. State, 733 N.E.2d 919, 922 (2000).

[54] Lamkins v. State, 778 N.E.2d 1248, 1250, 2002 Ind. LEXIS 892 (2002).

[55] Nebraska v. Sabella, 2003 Neb. App. LEXIS 68 (2003).

[56] Goudeau v. Texas, 2002 Tex. App. LEXIS 5612 (2002).

[57] *See* Newsome v. State, 829 S.W.2d 260 (Tex. 1992), in which the court held that the mere fact that a question may be answered by a simple "yes" or "no" will not render it impermissibly leading. The question is impermissibly "leading" only when it suggests which answer is desired or when it puts into the witness's mouth words to be echoed back.

[58] Ohio v. Boden, 2002 Ohio 5043, 2002 Ohio App. LEXIS 5060 (2002), quoting BLACK'S LAW DICTIONARY (6th ed. 1990) 888.

The alternative form of question, "State whether or not . . ." or "Did you or did you not . . ." is free of this defect of form because both affirmative and negative answers are presented for the witness's equal choice. Nevertheless, such a question may become leading, insofar as it rehearses lengthy details that the witness may not otherwise have mentioned, and thus supplies him or her with full suggestions, which he or she would incorporate—without any effort—by the simple answer, "I did" or "I did not." Such a question may or may not be improper, according to the amount of palpably suggestive detail that it embodies.[59]

As a general rule the "decision whether to permit leading questions on direct examination is left to the discretion of the trial court,[60]" but the general rule against leading questions allows the trial judge discretion for the purposes of allowing an attorney an opportunity to develop a witness's testimony.[61] However, the fact that a prosecutor used several leading questions on direct examination that sparked objections that the judge sustained, does not constitute sufficient prosecutorial misconduct sufficient to require a retrial.[62] In one case, when a prosecutor conducted the state's case-in-chief by consistently using leading questions by paraphrasing the testimony of the witnesses as he moved to the next leading question, such tactic coupled with other errors can contribute to a reversal of a criminal conviction.[63]

Although the general rule is that leading questions may not be used on direct examination, there are well-known exceptions to this rule. These exceptions are based upon necessity, and the right to lead is given only to the extent reasonably required to meet the necessity. The best-known exceptions are as follows:

A. Introductory Matters

Only questions relating to the name of the witness, his or her address, or other matters that are introductory are authorized. One North Carolina court noted that has held that "leading questions on direct examination should be permitted if the witness . . . is recalling preliminary or introductory testimony."[64] These permissible, introductory leading questions, however, must always stop short of the disputed facts.

B. Hostile Witnesses

Anyone who has watched television court battles recognizes the rule that leading questions are authorized whenever the party has called a hostile witness, an adverse party, or a witness identified with an adverse party, even though he

---

59   State v. Scott, 20 Wash. 2d 696, 149 P.2d 152 (1944).
60   State v. Laveck, 2005 Ohio 62, 2004 Ohio App. LEXIS 6743 (2004).
61   Moore v. State, 2005 Ark. LEXIS 245 (2005).
62   State v. Serrano, 91 Conn. App. 227, 232, 880 A.2d 183, 188, 2005 Conn. App. LEXIS 390 (2005).
63   Chambers v. State, 924 So.2d 975, 977, 2006 Fla. App. LEXIS 5058 (2006).
64   North Carolina v. McElvine, 2002 N.C. App. LEXIS 2174 (2002).

or she is the witness of the party that called the witness.[65] Where the witness has manifested an intent to evade and an unwillingness to testify, the court may authorize the use of leading questions to the extent deemed necessary.[66]

The rule permitting leading questions of hostile witnesses is of special significance in criminal matters in which the state must often rely on reluctant or hostile witnesses to prove its case. As a general rule, the trial judge must rule that the witness is hostile or reluctant before leading questions may be asked, but "where the record shows that a witness has reason to be adverse to the calling party, no formal declaration of a witness's hostility is required."[67]

The rule, as explained by a Mississippi appeals court, is that when a party must call a witness as its own but the witness is really allied and supports the other side, the party may ask the judge for a ruling that the witness is hostile.[68] Alternatively, when an opposing party makes an objection that the party who called the witness is using leading questions, the attorney may ask that the judge rule that the witness be considered hostile. In the Mississippi case, the government prosecuted the defendant for carjacking, kidnapping, and armed robbery and the prosecution had to call the defendant's girlfriend as a government witness. Under such circumstances, a judge commits no error in allowing leading questions[69] because the girlfriend did not want to help the prosecution.

In determining whether a witness is an unwilling or a hostile witness, the judge takes into consideration many factors. In some instances, it is apparent that the witness is hostile and the determination is not difficult; in others, the judge must take into consideration the demeanor and actions of the witness. For example, in a rape prosecution, the trial judge did not abuse his discretion by allowing the prosecutor to ask leading questions of the commonwealth's own witness, who was the defendant's girlfriend.[70] The judge properly allowed leading questions because of the witness's demeanor and the manner in which she answered the questions.

C. Obviously Erroneous Statements

Where it appears that the witness has inadvertently answered a question incorrectly, or that he or she did not understand the question, a leading question may be used on direct examination to afford the witness an opportunity to correct the mistake.[71] For example, if a police witness, in answer to a question, inadvertently gave the date as 1989 the prosecutor would be allowed to say, "You mean 1999, don't you?" According to a federal district court, "[a] trial

---

[65]   Lampkins v. Indiana, 778 N.E.2d 1248, 1250, 2002 Ind. LEXIS 892 (2002).

[66]   *See* Hayes v. State, 493 S.E.2d 169 (Ga. 1997), in which the reviewing court held that the trial court has the discretion to allow leading questions on direct examination, when a witness is nervous, reluctant, or hostile.

[67]   North Carolina v. Robinson, 2002 N.C. App. LEXIS 2403 (2002).

[68]   Brassfield v. State, 905 So. 2d 754, 760, 2004 Miss. App. LEXIS 1108 (2004).

[69]   *Id.*

[70]   Commonwealth v. Caldwell, 634 N.E.2d 124 (Mass. 1994).

[71]   See State v. White, 259 S.E.2d 281 (N.C. 1979), which held that a witness may be interrogated with leading questions on direct examination when it appears that the witness has exhausted his or her memory or has trouble understanding the questions.

court has discretion to permit a prosecutor to ask leading questions on direct examination to develop and clarify testimony."[72]

Applying this rationale, a North Carolina court determined that a trial judge using discretion may allow the prosecutor, during the direct examination of a hostile witness, to ask leading questions as if on cross-examination, for the purpose of refreshing his or her recollection or awakening his or her conscience, thus enabling him or her to testify correctly.[73]

The exception to the rule that disallows leading questions also applies when the questions are asked by the defense attorney. When the witness made erroneous statements in a federal case, the reviewing court found no problem with the lower court allowing defense counsel to ask leading questions on cross-examination of the defendant when the prosecution had been "particularly egregious" in questioning the witness, causing the witness to misunderstand the prosecutor's questions.[74]

D. Child Witnesses, Mentally Handicapped Witnesses, and Witnesses with Slight Command of the English Language

While most witnesses who do not regularly testify in court find themselves stressed, worried, and feeling out of their element in the unusual and unfamiliar setting of a courtroom, this discomfort applies especially to children who have been victims of sexual or other crimes and persons with mental disabilities or illness. Extremely shy witnesses or witnesses who will be asked embarrassing questions may have difficulty giving testimony when questioned under direct examination. Out of necessity, virtually all courts will allow use of leading questions in order to obtain testimony from children or witnesses who have difficulty testifying in the absence of the prompting leading questions.[75]

In a Michigan case, the court allowed the prosecutor to question the complaining child witness in a sexual abuse case through the use of leading questions. In the absence of leading questions, the victim-witness had offered only cryptic testimony that had not proved productive.[76] Included in this category where leading questions may be used are witnesses who are mentally handicapped but not incompetent to testify. In a Tennessee case, the trial court allowed the use of leading questions in a sexual battery case where the victim possessed extremely limited speech ability. The victim's lack of speech may have stemmed from a high fever during childhood and the victim also had mental deficiencies. The prosecutor contended that both the limited speech and the mental condition suggested that the court authorize leading questions on direct examination. The court of appeals agreed with the prosecution's contention

---

[72]   Williams v. Senkowski, 2001 U.S. Dist. LEXIS 10843 (S.D.N.Y. 2001).

[73]   State v. Smith, 289 N.C. 143, 221 S.E.2d 247 (1976).

[74]   Woods v. Lecureux, 110 F.3d 1215 (6th Cir. 1997).

[75]   *See* Wallace v. Arkansas, 2003 Ark. App. LEXIS 15 (2003), in which the court approved using leading questions directed to a child victim of sexual abuse.

[76]   Michigan v. Lyons, 2003 Mich. App. LEXIS 757 (2003).

"that the trial court acted within its discretion in allowing the State to lead the victim during her testimony."[77] The exception is limited to the leading questions reasonably necessary to overcome the obstacle of securing testimony.[78]

A Mississippi appellate court ruled that the trial court did not abuse its discretion when it permitted a child who was almost five years of age to testify through the use of leading questions.[79] The defendant, who had been charged with murdering the child-witness's brother, contended that he did not get a fair trial because the prosecution used more than 40 leading questions to develop the child's testimony. The reviewing court found no unfair prejudice to the defendant and noted that the situation involving children is a classic example of a situation where leading questions may be necessary.

After explaining the reason for the exception to the leading question rule, a New York court determined that the victim's language difficulty justified the decision by the trial court to pose its own questions and to permit the prosecutor to pose some leading questions in a prosecution for second degree robbery.[80]

§ 9.8 —Refreshing Memory—Present Memory Revived

Rule 612

Writing Used To Refresh Memory

Except as otherwise provided in criminal proceedings by section 3500 of Title 18, United States Code, if a witness uses a writing to refresh memory for the purpose of testifying, either—

    (1) while testifying, or

    (2) before testifying, if the court in its discretion determines it is necessary in the interests of justice,

an adverse party is entitled to have the writing produced at the hearing, to inspect it, to cross-examine the witness thereon, and to introduce in evidence those portions which relate to the testimony of the witness. If it is claimed that the writing contains matters not related to the subject matter of the testimony, the court shall examine the writing *in camera*, excise any portions not so related, and order delivery of the remainder to the party entitled thereto. Any portion withheld over objections shall be preserved and made available to the appellate court in the event of an appeal. If a writing is not produced or delivered pursuant to order under this rule, the court shall make any order justice requires, except that in criminal cases when the prosecution elects not to comply, the order shall be one striking the testimony or, if the court in its discretion determines that the interests of justice so require, declaring a mistrial.[81]

---

[77]   Tennessee v. Stewart, 2003 Tenn. Crim. App. LEXIS 482 (2003).

[78]   United States v. Nabors, 762 F.2d 642 (8th Cir. 1985). *See also* Clark v. State, 952 S.W.2d 882 (Tex. 1997), in which the court explained that in cases dealing with child witnesses, the rule against leading questions on direct examination is somewhat relaxed.

[79]   Osborne v. State, 2006 Miss. App. LEXIS 134 (2006).

[80]   People v. Williams, 662 N.Y.S.2d 118 (1997).

[81]   Fed. R. Evid. 612.

To a greater or to a lesser extent, all memory fades with the passage of time and many court witnesses experience difficulty recalling all the relevant details that were once fresh in the mind. Despite preparation by the attorneys, trial witnesses frequently do not remember all the facts, especially after a long period between the events and the trial. It is also apparent that referring to a written statement may revive the memory of an experience. In other words, by referring to statements or other past experiences, the recollection of the witness may be refreshed to the point that a witness is able to testify from present memory. If the witness has absolutely no recollection regarding the matters being contested, he or she obviously is not competent to testify concerning those matters. However, if the witness remembers the transaction in general but not the essential details, or if he or she remembers that he or she recorded the transaction, some evidence concerning the transaction is admissible. This process involves two concepts that have become known as present memory revived or present memory refreshed and past memory recorded or past recollection recorded. These two concepts differ in theory and therefore the tests for admissibility differ. In the first instance, where present memory has been refreshed, the witness is able to testify from present memory, which is the evidence and not the not the writing or other reference used to refresh memory. In the second instance, where the witness originally recorded the event in writing at a time when it was fresh in the witness's memory, the writing is the evidence and not the oral testimony.

In this section, the first of these two concepts—present memory revived or as it is sometimes called, present memory refreshed—will be discussed. In the next section, the concept of past recollection recorded will be discussed.

In many instances, the trial court allows a witness to refer to records, accounting sheets, or reports while testifying. Generally, doctors, engineers, accountants, and other experts, as well as criminal justice officials, are allowed to refer to data on their reports while they are testifying as a means of refreshing their memory. As a practical matter, it is impossible for law enforcement personnel, who make daily investigations of alleged violations of law, to remember the names, dates, and what took place without referring to notes made by them at the time or immediately thereafter. However, trial courts must exercise caution to assure that the witness is testifying from present memory that has recently been refreshed. The court should be careful to ensure that the memorandum is not a written summary made specifically for use in court and that the law enforcement officer is not merely testifying from the written record but from a refreshed memory.

When a witness has a lapse of memory while testifying, the court allows him or her to refer to some form of memorandum to refresh or revive his or her recollection of the facts. A witness is "permitted to refresh and assist his memory, by the use of a written instrument, memorandum or entry in a book, and may be compelled to do so if the writing is present in court. It does not seem to be necessary that the writing should have been made by the witness himself, nor that it should be an original writing, provided, after inspecting it, he can speak to the facts from his own recollection."[82] After the witness's memory is revived or refreshed and he or she presently recollects the facts and swears to them, his or her testimony, and not the writing, is the evidence. When a party uses an earlier statement of his or her own witness to refresh the witness's memory, the only evidence recognized as such is the testimony so refreshed.

Documents shown to a witness for the purpose of reviving his or her recollection may not be read by the witness to the court under the pretext of refreshing the memory of the witness or shown to the jury, because the documents themselves are not evidence and have no independent evidentiary value. The fact that a defense attorney might seek to introduce that material on cross-examination rather than the prosecutor on direct examination is not a difference of significance. The fact that a tape recording rather than a written document is involved also does not affect the result.[83]

In one case involving aggravated sexual abuse of a child, the trial court allowed the nine-year-old complaining witness to read a transcript of her preliminary hearing testimony. The court permitted the defense to inspect the transcript and to cross-examine the girl about it. Prior to reading the transcript, the victim was not able to recall precisely or in great detail what the defendant had done to her, but after to reading her original transcript, she was able to give evidence about exactly what the defendant had done to her, how he removed her underpants, and how he engaged her in prohibited sexual contact. The Utah Supreme Court approved the use of the transcript to refresh her memory, which allowed her to testify from present memory.[84] In another use of present memory refreshed, an Ohio murder defendant complained that both the coroner and a DNA expert both consulted their written reports during their direct examination by the prosecutor.[85] The coroner referred to his report to refresh his memory of the decedent's age while the DNA expert consulted his report concerning the genetic profile obtained from an examination of the defendant's right shoe. When a convicted defendant makes a contention of this nature, the court must determine whether the witness had an independent recollection of the event and was merely using the memorandum to refresh details or is using a memorandum as a testimonial crutch for something beyond the witness's recollection. In both cases the witnesses testified from present memory that had been refreshed. According to the reviewing court, the defense attorney was not deficient in not objecting at trial and the failure to object did not prove any ineffective assistance of counsel.

In a Hawai'i case involving the testimony of a police officer who had stopped a driver under suspicion of driving while impaired, the officer testified that the defendant took nine steps away and ten steps back during a field sobriety test. Similar detail caused the defense to complain that the officer was

---

[82]   Brockenbrough v. Commonwealth, 2003 Va. App. LEXIS 243 (2003), quoting Harrison v. Middleton, 52 Va. 527, 544 (1854).

[83]   United States v. McKeever, 271 F.2d 669 (2d Cir. 1959); *see also* United States v. Booz, 451 F.2d 719 (3d Cir. 1971); People v. Parks, 485 P.2d 257 (Cal. 1971).

[84]   Utah v. Pritchett, 2003 Utah 24, 473 Utah Adv. Rep. 45, 2003 Utah LEXIS 52 (2003).

[85]   State v. Neeley, 2006 Ohio 418 2006 Ohio App. LEXIS 349 (2006).

testifying from a record made at the time of arrest and not from present memory. The officer was able to remember other details of the case and of the defendant, such as the type of vehicle he was driving, from present memory. Although the officer did admit to reviewing police records prior to trial, he stated that much of what he offered from the witness stand was from present memory refreshed. Applying this reasoning, the court decided that an officer's use of the notes he took of the defendant's arrest was for the purpose of refreshing recollection to facilitate accurate testimony and did not indicate that he was using past recollection recorded to offer evidence. The officer's recounting of the events of the arrest of the driver was based on memory and was independent of his notes, thus demonstrating extensive independent recall sufficient to testify from present memory.[86] Not all jurisdictions desire to admit evidence as present memory refreshed when the witness has been hypnotized.

In some cases in which a witness or victim possesses no present recollection, the use of hypnosis has been approved. For example, the Louisiana Supreme Court has determined that the testimony of a witness who has had his memory refreshed through hypnosis should be treated as other "recollection refreshed" testimony and the fact of hypnosis affects the weight and not the admissibility of the evidence.[87] While the requirements for hypnotically enhanced testimony vary among jurisdictions, the Ninth Circuit Court of Appeals requires that "a complete stenographic record of the hypnosis interview be maintained."[88] A different set of guidelines, mentioned by the Supreme Court of the United States, suggests that hypnosis be performed by a psychologist or psychiatrist who has received special training and who is independent of the investigation, that the hypnosis procedure occur in a neutral setting, and only the subject and the hypnotist should be present.[89] Although the court has discretion in determining whether hypnotically refreshed testimony is admitted, a per se rule excluding all hypnotically refreshed testimony infringes impermissibly on a criminal defendant's right to testify on his or her own behalf.[90]

In a New Jersey case, the trial court initially approved the use of hypnotically enhanced identification of a sexual predator-burglar by the victim.[91] During the attack, the victim had seen her attacker when she opened her eyes once and had a difficult time making an identification. A licensed clinical psychologist placed her under hypnosis after meeting with her privately. The interview was tape-recorded in all important respects and succeeded in refreshing her memory. Later, the victim selected the defendant from a photo array and identified his jacket from her hypnotically induced refreshed memory. At the trial, the court permitted the playing of substantial portions of the tape to the jury

---

[86]   Hawai'i v. Yamamoto, 98 Haw. 294, 2002 Haw. App. LEXIS (2002).

[87]   Louisiana v. Smith, 809 So. 2d 556, 565, 2002 La. App. LEXIS 221 (2002).

[88]   Mancuso v. Olivarez, 292 F.3d 939, 2002 U.S. App. LEXIS 11135 (9th Cir. 2002).

[89]   *See* Rock v. Arkansas, 483 U.S. 44, 107 S. Ct. 2704, 97 L. Ed. 2d 37 (1987).

[90]   *Id.*

[91]   *See* State v. Moore, 188 N.J. 182, 902 A.2d 1212; 2006 N.J. LEXIS 1168 (2006). This case contains an excellent discussion of the issues related to the use of hypnotically refreshed memory and related concerns.

and the jury convicted the defendant. Through the appellate process, the defendant eventually earned a new trial, at which time the trial court refused to permit the use of hypnotically refreshed memory because of reliability problems. Although the Supreme Court of the United States has determined that a defendant may use hypnotically refreshed memory at trial, the trial court, supported by the Supreme Court of New Jersey, determined that the prosecution cannot use hypnotically refreshed memory in criminal trials even though a defendant could do so under a ruling from the Supreme Court of the United States. In rejecting the admission of hypnotically refreshed memory evidence, the Supreme Court of New Jersey cited the fact that guidelines from earlier cases were not often followed by the psychologists, the subject often believes too strongly in what the hypnotic session reveals, and hypnotically refreshed memory has never gained acceptance in the scientific field.

In an effort to regulate hypnotic-related evidence, California, by statute, provides that hypnotic evidence for recollection can be admitted where it follows the state law. Among other things, California requires that the pre-hypnotic memory be preserved in some written or taped form; that a written record is made of the memory of the event prior to hypnosis; that the witness gave consent; that the pre- and post-hypnosis interviews be videotaped; and that the sessions be conducted by a licensed medical doctor, psychologist, or social worker trained in hypnosis.[92]

In all cases of refreshed memory, the trial judge has a duty to prevent a witness from putting into the record the contents of an otherwise inadmissible writing under the guise of refreshing recollection. Counsel should lay a foundation for the necessity of refreshing the witness's memory, show the witness the writing, remove the writing from the witness, and ask questions about the refreshed memory. Under this theory, showing the witness the writing should be all that is required to refresh the memory.[93] When using a writing to refresh memory, the defendant has the right to compel the production of the document used to refresh the witness's memory. Where the document is not produced, the judge may order the refreshed memory testimony to be stricken, even where the document could not be introduced as evidence.

Although the court may allow witnesses to refer to records or reports to refresh memory while testifying, it is preferable to testify without this assistance. If the witness prepares adequately, he or she will need to refer to written statements only in rare instances. If the question concerns a situation in which the jury would normally expect the witness to remember the facts without the aid of the writing, use of the writing lessens the weight of the testimony.

In interpreting Rule 612 of the Federal Rules of Evidence, which provides in general terms that the adverse party is entitled to have the writing produced, a federal district court explained that it is not every time a witness looks at any document in preparation for the trial that such document must be disclosed to the other side. In determining whether the document must be disclosed, the

---

[92]   *See* Schall v. Lockheed, 37 Cal. App. 4th 1484, 44 Cal. Rptr. 2d 191, 1995 Cal. App. LEXIS 834 (1995), quoting § 795 of the California Code.

[93]   Tennessee v. Pylant, 2003 Tenn. Crim. App. LEXIS 405 (2003).

court should consider the extent to which the documents were consulted and relied upon, and the extent to which the opinions and conclusions were reflected therein, as opposed to factual recitations.[94] The judge has much discretion in exercising control over the introduction of such evidence and in interpreting the rules.[95]

In the case of *United States v. Blas*, a federal court of appeals noted that the purpose of the rule as codified in Rule 612 is "to promote the search of credibility in memory."[96] In interpreting the rule, which provides that the adverse party is entitled to have the writing produced at a hearing to inspect it, to cross-examine the witness about it, and to introduce into evidence the portions that relate to the testimony of the witness, the court cautioned that this does not include the opportunity to test evidence "in whatsoever way, and to whatsoever extent the defense might wish."

Accordingly, a denial of the defendant's request for the production of the police report and other documents reviewed by law enforcement officers prior to testifying was not an abuse of discretion. Where the defendant had other avenues open to him to test the accuracy of the officer's testimony, the defendant had no absolute right to inspect the notes or memoranda not used by the witness in court.

Referring to Federal Rule of Evidence 612, the Tenth Circuit Court of Appeals held that the defendant in a perjury prosecution is not entitled to require disclosure of the entire transcript of a perjury prosecution witness's prior testimony before a grand jury; rather, disclosure of the grand jury transcript is properly confined to those pages actually used by the government in examining the witness.[97]

§ 9.9 —Past Recollection Recorded

Rule 803

Hearsay Exceptions; Availability of Declarant Immaterial

The following are not excluded by the hearsay rule, even though the declarant is available as a witness:

(5) Recorded recollection.—A memorandum or record concerning a matter about which a witness once had knowledge but now has insufficient recollection to enable the witness to testify fully and accurately, shown to have been made or adopted by the witness when the matter was fresh in the witness' memory and to reflect that knowledge correctly. If admitted, the memorandum or record may be read into evidence but may not itself be received as an exhibit unless offered by an adverse party.[98]

---

[94] In re Comair Air Disaster Litigation, 100 F.R.D. 350 (1983).
[95] United States v. Terry, 729 F.2d 1063 (6th Cir. 1984).
[96] United States v. Blas, 947 F.2d 1320, 1327 (7th Cir. 1991).
[97] United States v. Larranaga, 787 F.2d 489 (10th Cir. 1986); *see also* United States v. Sai Keung Wong, 886 F.2d 252 (9th Cir. 1989).
[98] FED. R. EVID. 803(5).

When a witness's memory cannot be refreshed by any technique and where the evidence has been recorded by some permanent method, the recording or writing may become a substitute for the witness's memory, and where it meets all the requirements, be introduced as substantive proof of the facts that it contains. However, the proponent of the recorded memory must lay a foundation before the writing will be admitted.

A memorandum of past recollection recorded may be admissible in evidence when the witness who made it, or under whose direction it was made, testifies that he or she at one time had firsthand personal knowledge of the facts, and that the writing, when made, was an accurate record of the event, that the writing was made within a reasonable time following the event, and that after seeing the writing, he or she does not have sufficient present independent recollection of the facts to testify accurately to those facts.[99] To meet the accepted standards of admissibility, an Ohio court noted that:

> foundational requirements for the use of a past recollection recorded include a showing that: (1) the witness has insufficient memory to accurately testify to crucial information; (2) that the witness can show through their testimony that the past recollection recorded was made or adopted when the matter was fresh in the witness's memory; and (3) that the past recollection recorded correctly reflects the knowledge the witness had at the time it was recorded.[100]

The trial judge must be satisfied that the writing was made from firsthand knowledge at a time when the events were fresh in the writer's mind, and the witness must verify the writing's authenticity and truthfulness. If the witness cannot say that there is insufficient memory to testify fully, the foundation has not been made. In a rape case in which the prosecution attempted to have a videotape recollection of a child witness admitted, since the child could not testify that the videotape correctly reflected her knowledge of the events in question on the date it was recorded, and the trial court properly excluded the record under the state version of Rule 803(5) dealing with past recollection recorded.[101] Similarly, to be admissible, the document or writing must concern a matter about which the witness at one time possessed knowledge and could not qualify when a police officer's report had been compiled from observations of other people at the scene.[102]

In *Parker v. Reda*, the court permitted a correctional officer to read from a memorandum that he had prepared following an altercation with a prison inmate. The officer did not possess sufficient memory of the incident to testify from present memory, but he noted that the words written were from firsthand information and were recorded subsequent to the events in question

---

[99] United States v. Porter, 986 F.2d 1014 (6th Cir.), *cert. denied*, 510 U.S. 933, 114 S. Ct 347, 126 L. Ed. 2d 312 (1993).

[100] Ohio v. Perry, 147 Ohio App. 3d 164, 170, 171, 768 N.E.2d 1259, 1264, 2002 Ohio App. LEXIS 1169 (2002).

[101] *Id.*

[102] *See* Cahill v. Gagnon, 794 A.2d 451, 452, 2002 R.I. LEXIS 55 (2002).

when the events were fresh in his mind. The officer testified that he had written the words himself and that they correctly reflected the prison altercation, which the words described. The court of appeals upheld the trial court's admission of the evidence against a challenge that the trial court had abused its discretion in admitting the memorandum under Rule 803(5).[103]

Under modern police practice, the document may not have ever been written in the traditional manner; it may have originally been an entry by an officer on a computer system. In *North Carolina v. Love*, the complaining witness spouse told police that her husband had repeatedly threatened to beat her. This information as well as other relevant data was recorded by a police officer using a computer. He allowed the witness to review what she had told him in order to correct any errors in typing by the officer. She stated at the time that the report was accurate and that she did not wish to change anything. At trial, the witness could not remember what she had told the officer, but she did remember making a statement to police that was read back to her and she stated that it was true when made. The appellate court approved the trial court decision allowing the officer to read to the trier of fact the statement made by the complaining witness.[104]

Neither the federal rules nor federal courts have developed a set rule concerning precisely when the evidence must be recorded following the event.[105] An Iowa appellate court approved the use of past recollection recorded when the witness recorded the information in a writing 31 days after observing the facts of the case.[106] In one federal case, the officer interviewed the defendants but did not make a written memorandum of the interview until 11 days later. The trial court allowed the officer to read from the memorandum and the court of appeals approved. As the appellate court noted:

> Rule 803(5) requires that the memorandum be made by the witness "when the matter was fresh in the witness' memory," but we have declined to adopt any bright-line rule to measure whether a particular delay is too long. Instead, we have held that the trial court may consider the lapse of time along with other circumstances that may be relevant in determining the likelihood that the witness had an accurate memory of the event at the time the record was prepared.[107]

The doctrine of past recollection recorded has "long been favored by the federal courts and practically all of the state courts that have had occasion to decide the question."[108] The application of this doctrine does not deprive the accused of the opportunity to cross-examine the witness as guaranteed by the

---

[103]   Parker v. Reda, 327 F.3d 211, 2003 U.S. App. LEXIS 8011 (2d Cir. 2003).

[104]   North Carolina v. Love, 576 S.E.2d 709, 712, 713, 2003 N.C. LEXIS 114 (2003)

[105]   *See* Isler v. United States, 2003 D.C. App. LEXIS 291 (2003), in which the appeals court permitted admission of past recollection recorded when it was first recorded at the first trial of the issue some five months after the event occurred.

[106]   Iowa v. Stevenson, 2001 Iowa App. LEXIS 752 (2001).

[107]   United States v. Green, 258 F.3d 683, 688, 2001 U.S. App. LEXIS 16770 (7th Cir. 2001).

[108]   United States v. Kelly, 349 F.2d 720, 770 (2d Cir. 1965).

Sixth Amendment[109] because the witness with the faulty memory will be in court and testifying about the making of the writing. Cross-examination may be somewhat limited given the faulty memory of the witness, but the right to confront and cross-examine the witness will generally not pose a problem of constitutional dimensions. In applying the rule concerning past recollection recorded, the Supreme Court of Oregon held that a checklist used by a police officer in the operation of a breath analysis machine was admissible in a prosecution for drunk driving, although the witness had a present recollection of the subject matter, of which the checklist was a record.[110] The witness had identified the checklist, had recalled making it at the time of the event—when his recollection was fresh—and had testified to its accuracy. And the trial court properly allowed parts of the witness's statement to be read into the record where the witness had remembered making a statement, but did not remember what she had said when the record was made at a time when the matter was fresh in her memory and reflected her knowledge correctly.[111] The United States Court of Appeals for the Seventh Circuit held that a memorandum of a telephone conversation between an Internal Revenue Service (IRS) agent and a tax defendant was properly admitted at trial.[112] The court indicated that it "would seem, as the government argues, that the report satisfies the criteria for admissibility as a recorded recollection under F.R. Ev. 803(5)." The agent, in laying a foundation, had testified that the history sheet was prepared immediately after the conversation, but that he no longer recalled the details of conversation.

§ 9.10 Cross-Examination of Witnesses

Rule 611

Mode and Order of Interrogation and Presentation

* * *

(b) Scope of cross-examination. Cross-examination should be limited to the subject matter of the direct examination and matters affecting the credibility of the witness. The court may, in the exercise of discretion, permit inquiry into additional matters as if on direct examination.[113]

* * *

---

[109] United States v. Kelly, 349 F.2d 720 (2d Cir. 1965); People v. Banks, 50 Mich. App. 622, 213 N.W.2d 817 (1974); People v. Hobson, 369 Mich. 189, 119 N.W.2d 581 (1963).

[110] State v. Sutton, 450 P.2d 748 (Or. 1969).

[111] United States v. Porter, 986 F.2d 1014 (6th Cir. 1993), *cert. denied*, 510 U.S. 933, 114 S. Ct. 347, 126 L. Ed. 2d 312 (1993).

[112] United States v. Sawyer, 607 F.2d 1191 (7th Cir. 1979); *see also* United States v. Ray, 768 F.2d 991 (8th Cir. 1985).

[113] FED. R. EVID. 611(b).

The right to confront and question adverse witnesses is a critical component in fact-finding at trial[114] and the right of confrontation is guaranteed by the Sixth Amendment to the Constitution of the United States.[115] The rationale for allowing comprehensive cross-examination of witnesses has been noted in both federal and state cases and is designed, among other things, to assist in discerning whether witnesses have been truthful in their testimony. In a Florida case, the court explained that all witnesses who testify at the trial place their credibility at issue and, regardless of the subject matter of the witness's testimony, parties on close examination may inquire into the matters that affect the truthfulness of the witness's testimony.[116] A Georgia court held that the permissible purposes of cross-examination include attempting to bring out facts that might show the witness's testimony as either unbelievable, biased, or partial to one party.[117] As the Supreme Court noted in an old case, cross-examination as part of the confrontation in a lawsuit presupposes:

> personal examination and cross-examination of the witness in which the accused has an opportunity, not only of testing the recollection and sifting the conscience of the witness, but of compelling him to stand face to face with the jury in order that they may look at him, and judge by his demeanor upon the stand and the manner in which he gives his testimony whether he is worthy of belief.[118]

The right to observe or to see one's accusers is of little value unless one can question the accuser. For that reason, the right of cross-examination is included in the Sixth Amendment right of an accused to confront adverse witnesses.[119] No one experienced in trying lawsuits would deny the critical value of cross-examination in exposing falsehood and revealing the facts. The fact that this right appears in the Sixth Amendment to the Constitution reflects the framers' belief in those liberties and safeguards whereby confrontation was a fundamental right essential to a fair trial in a criminal prosecution.

A full cross-examination of a witness on the subjects of his or her direct examination is an absolute right and not a mere privilege of the party against whom the witness is called. The denial of this right is reversible error except in certain limited circumstances. For example, the denial of this right is not reversible error when a witness, having given his or her direct testimony, dies prior to cross-examination. The judge often allows the direct examination to stand and gives precautionary instructions to the jury in such cases. Where the cross-examination has been curtailed following proper direct examination covering material issues because of a witness's valid claim of privilege, the

---

[114]   United States v. McKeithan, 2002 U.S. App. LEXIS 23408 (3d Cir. 2002).
[115]   The Sixth Amendment applies to the states. South Carolina v. Mizzell, 349 S.C. 326, 563 S.E.2d 315, 2002 S.C. LEXIS 68 (2002), quoting Pointer v. Texas, 380 U.S. 400, 402 (1965).
[116]   Chandler v. State, 702 So. 2d 186 (Fla. 1997).
[117]   Carswell v. State, 491 S.E.2d 343 (Ga. 1997).
[118]   Mattox v. United States, 156 U.S. 237, 242, 15 S. Ct. 337, 339, 39 L. Ed. 409, 411, 1895 U.S. LEXIS 2131 (1895).
[119]   United States v. Villarman-Oviedo, 325 F.3d 1, 2003 U.S. App. LEXIS 5694 (1st Cir. 2003).

trial court may strike the witness's direct testimony in an effort to preserve the Sixth Amendment right of confrontation and cross-examination.[120]

The extent of cross-examination, with respect to an appropriate subject of inquiry, is within the sound discretion of the trial judge. He or she may exercise reasonable judgment in determining when the subject is exhausted or when it moves in an improper direction. The court has discretion regarding how long and in what direction a cross-examination may proceed. As a general rule, a cross-examiner possesses fairly wide latitude, but it does not mean that the cross-examiner may make all the decisions about examination.[121]

However, effective cross-examination in a criminal case is the primary means by which the credibility and truthfulness of witnesses can be tested. The trial judge does not have the discretion to grant or withhold such right completely.[122] The determination of whether and to what extent to cross-examine a particular witness rests with the defendant's counsel. Where the attorney for the defendant chooses, as a part of trial strategy, not to cross-examine a witness, the effect is to waive the Sixth Amendment right of cross-examination. [123]

Cross-examination is generally limited in scope to the subject matter of the direct examination of the witness, but also extends to matters affecting the credibility of the witness.[124] A long-established rule has been that cross-examination of a witness is limited to the scope of the direct examination. One exception to this rule is that cross-examination may be permitted to test the capacity of the witness to observe, remember, and recount, and to test the sincerity and truthfulness of the witness. This may be done with respect to subjects not strictly relevant to the testimony given by the witness on direct examination. Inquiry may be made concerning bias, interest, or prejudice of the witness as long as it goes to testing credibility.

Although under the traditional rules of the limited scope of cross-examination the prosecution usually may not cross-examine on matters not brought out on direct examination, the attorney may and should make the opposing witness the prosecution's witness at the proper time, and ask additional questions of the witness if necessary to get all the facts before the court. However, Rule 611(b) allows a trial court, in the exercise of discretion, to permit questioning on matters beyond the scope of direct examination, but the questioner must inquire as if on direct examination. When direct examination opens a particular subject, the consequent cross-examination may probe into any related area covered on direct examination and may inquire into specific facts developed by the opposing counsel on direct examination. The cross-examination is not restricted to identical details developed during the direct examination, but extends to the entire related subject matter limited by the concepts or relevance.[125] A limitation placed on the prosecution in a criminal proceed-

[120]   Combs v. Kentucky, 74 S.W.3d 738, 744, 2002 Ky. LEXIS 98 (2002).
[121]   North Carolina v. Jenkins, 2002 N.C. App. LEXIS 2356 (2002).
[122]   State v. Toole, 640 A.2d 965 (R.I. 1994).
[123]   United States v. McKeithan, 2002 U.S. App. LEXIS 23408 (3d Cir. 2002).
[124]   Illinois v. Millbratz, 323 Ill. App. 3d 206, 211, 751 N.E.2d 650, 2001 Ill. App. LEXIS 541 (2001).
[125]   Stotler v. Florida, 834 So. 2d 940, 943, 2003 Fla. App. LEXIS 445 (2003).

ing prevents the government from establishing, either by cross-examination of the defendant or by the independent testimony of other witnesses that it is likely that the accused is guilty of the offense with which he or she is presently charged because he or she has committed prior criminal acts.[126]

The extent to which cross-examination on collateral matters will be permitted is a matter peculiarly within the discretion of the trial judge. An appellate court will not reverse the trial court decision unless there has been a plain abuse of discretion on his or her part. Although shutting off cross-examine is not a practice that should be encouraged, a trial judge does not abuse his or her discretion when he or she shuts off a continuation of extended cross-examination into collateral and immaterial matters.[127]

In a case before the United States Court of Appeals for the Seventh Circuit, the court agreed that the trial court has the discretion to impose reasonable limitations on cross-examination of witnesses in a criminal trial, based upon concerns regarding harassment, confusion of issues, and repetitive or marginally relevant interrogation.[128] The court cautioned that, even though the Sixth Amendment guarantees a defendant the right to cross-examine hostile witnesses and defense counsel should be afforded every opportunity to effectively cross-examine a government witness, this does not mean that the right to cross-examination is unlimited. In this case, after the defense counsel had cross-examined the witness for most of the afternoon and evening, and had exposed facts showing virtually every possible motive or bias that the witness might have for testifying against the defendant, the court properly terminated the cross-examination.

The trial court may not preclude all inquiry into a subject appropriate for cross-examination, but it may and should exercise such control over the scope of the examination as is necessary to prevent the parties from unduly burdening the record with cumulative or irrelevant matters.[129] To enable the court to discharge this duty, when a question is objected to as irrelevant, counsel conducting the inquiry should advise the court of the question's purpose. If he or she fails to do so, and the question is not "inevitably and patently material," the objection may be sustained without error.[130]

In the case of *People v. McKinney*, the court held that cross-examination is limited to the scope of direct examination and to matters that explain, qualify, discredit, or destroy the witness's direct testimony. Once a matter is brought up on direct examination, it often opens the door to more extensive cross-examination. For example, once a police officer is asked on direct exam-

---

[126] United States v. Hall, 342 F.2d 849 (4th Cir. 1965); Unbaugh v. Hutto, 486 F.2d 904 (8th Cir. 1973).

[127] United States v. Mills, 366 F.2d 512 (6th Cir. 1966).

[128] United States v. Spivey, 841 F.2d 799 (7th Cir. 1988). *See* case in Part II. *See also* State v. Jackson, 212 Wis. 2d 203, 567 N.W.2d 920 (1997), in which the court held that reasonable limits may be placed upon inquiry into matters affecting the prosecution witness's credibility based on concerns about, among other things, harassment, prejudice, confusion of the issues, witness safety, or repetitiveness, especially when the attack on the witness's credibility falls under the rape shield law.

[129] FED. R. EVID. 611(b).

[130] Harris v. United States, 371 F.2d 365 (9th Cir. 1967).

ination about his or her high rate of speed in pursuing a driver in an attempt to prove that the officer violated a vehicle code, cross-examination of the officer about whether he or she activated his or her siren and warning lights was relevant and within the scope of direct examination.[131]

One common exception to the rule that cross-examination should be limited to subject matter brought out on direct examination is the exception that permits cross-examination on matters relating to the names and addresses of witnesses. The witness's name and address open countless avenues of in-court examination and out-of-court investigation.

This principle was well stated in *Alford v. United States*,[132] in which the Supreme Court reversed a federal conviction because the trial judge had sustained objections to questions by the defense seeking to elicit the "place of residence" of a prosecution witness over the insistence of the defense counsel that "the jury was entitled to know who the witness is, where he lives and what his business is." The reviewing court said:

> The question, "Where do you live?" was not only an appropriate preliminary to the cross-examination of the witness, but on its face, without any such declaration of purpose as was made by counsel here, was an essential step in identifying the witness with his environment, to which cross-examination may always be directed.

In conducting cross-examination, the name and address of the witness generally must be given when the witness testifies at trial. In *Smith v. Illinois*, the Supreme Court held that when "the credibility of a witness is in issue, the very starting point in 'exposing falsehood and bringing out the truth' through cross-examination must necessarily be to ask the witness who he is and where he lives. The witness's name and address open countless avenues of in-court examination and out-of-court investigation. To forbid this most rudimentary inquiry at the threshold is effectively to "emasculate the right of cross-examination itself."[133] Under almost all circumstances, the true name of the witness must be disclosed when the prosecution plans to call them as trial witnesses.[134] For example, in a California capital murder case, the trial court had ordered that neither the name nor the address of a crucial prosecution witness had to be divulged at trial or prior to trial. The witness was serving time in a California penal institution and arguably could have been subject to "prison justice" by fellow prisoners if it became known that they testified. The appellate court reversed the trial court decision and ordered that the names and addresses of all witnesses be given to the defendant because the proposed witnesses were present at the prison homicide and had necessary information.[135]

---

[131]   Foster v. City of Pittsburgh, 639 A.2d 929 (Pa. 1994).

[132]   282 U.S. 687, 51 S. Ct. 218, 75 L. Ed. 624 (1931).

[133]   Smith v. Illinois, 390 U.S. 129, 131 (1968).

[134]   State v. Craft, 149 Ohio App. 3d 176, 180, 776 N.E.2d 546, 548, 2002 Ohio App. LEXIS 4647 (2002).

[135]   Alvarado v. Superior Court, 23 Cal. 4th 1121, 1146, 5 P.3d 203, 220 (2000), *cert. denied*, 532 U.S. 990, 2001 U.S. LEXIS 3196 (2001).

As in the above case, where a witness resides in a penal institution, this fact must be disclosed. The purpose of the inquiry regarding the witness's address and present employment is to make known to the jury the setting or context in which to judge the character, veracity, or bias of the witness, and it is necessary to show that the witness was in custody in order to make such inquiry, even if there may be some danger to the witness or his family.

As is true with many rules of evidence, this rule is not without alternatives. Where there is a threat to the life of the witness, the pretrial right of the defendant to have the witness's true name, address, and place of employment is not absolute.[136] However, the threat to the witness must be actual and not the result of conjecture. When a threat to the life of a witness is shown, the prosecution must disclose relevant information to the judge in his or her chambers. Judges and the states have various tools to prevent or minimize threats to witnesses, such as the use of housing relocation, establishing new identities, state witness protection programs, and transfer of an incarcerated witness to a different prison or one out of state. States may use a state witness protection program. Typical of many state laws, to protect California witnesses, a statute enhances murder convictions to life without parole when a witness has been killed to prevent testimony or in retaliation for having served as a witness.[137] When a request has been made to keep a witness's identity private, a trial judge must determine whether the witness's true name, address, and place of employment must be disclosed in order to protect the right to effective cross-examination. If the trial judge concludes that the defendant does not have the right to ask the witness's exact address and place of employment, the defendant is entitled to ask any other relevant questions that may aid the jury in weighing the witness's credibility.[138]

The rules relating to cross-examination for purposes of impeachment are discussed in other sections of this chapter.

§ 9.11 Redirect and Recross-Examination

After a witness has been cross-examined, the party calling the witness may, by redirect examination, afford the witness the opportunity to make a full explanation of his or her testimony during cross-examination, allowing him or her to rebut the discrediting effect of his or her testimony on cross-examination and to correct any improper impressions that may have been created. On redirect examination, a witness may give the reasons for his or her actions in order to refute unfavorable inferences from matters brought out on cross-examination. He or she may state the circumstances of the inquiry covered on cross-examination, even where the facts revealed on redirect examination may

---

[136] United States v. Varelli, 407 F.2d 735 (7th Cir. 1969); United States v. Smaldone, 484 F.2d 311 (10th Cir. 1973); *see* e.g. OHIO CRIM. R. 16 (2006).
[137] CAL. PENAL CODE § 190.2 (10) (2006).
[138] United States v. Palermo, 410 F.2d 468 (7th Cir. 1969).

be detrimental to the other party. As explained in a Florida case, under the doctrine of completeness, redirect testimony is admissible to qualify, limit, or explain testimony given on cross-examination.[139]

For example, in a case in which the defendant was being prosecuted for possession of cocaine, defense counsel opened the door to redirect examination by asking a police officer on cross-examination whether the defendant had ever changed her position concerning whether she knew she possessed cocaine on the day of the arrest.[140] Because the defense had asked questions of the police officer concerning events that occurred on the day of her arrest, the prosecution was allowed to conduct a redirect examination about the defendant's statement to the officer on the night of the arrest that she knew that cocaine was in her car, although that statement had not been disclosed until the morning of the trial.

The scope and extent to which the redirect examination of a witness will be permitted is a matter largely within the discretion of the trial judge, and his or her ruling will not be disturbed unless an abuse of discretion is clearly shown.

While a defendant has a constitutional right to cross-examination of adverse witnesses, such a right does not extend to recross-examination.[141] The decision whether to allow recross-examination is typically left to judicial discretion and is normally limited to new matters brought out on redirect examination. If a court refused to allow recross-examination on new matters developed during redirect examination, the party is effectively denied any cross-examination covering the new matter. While a court should not by rule prohibit recross-examination of a witness about new matters brought out on redirect examination, a court should refuse to permit recross-examination where no new material was developed on redirect examination.[142]

Redirect examination may be appropriate where the "door has been opened" by an attorney for one of the parties on cross-examination, by pursuing a line of inquiry that exceeded the scope of the direct examination. For example, in a prosecution for felony driving while intoxicated that caused a death, the prosecutor neglected to ask a trial witness—a police officer—whether he had given a ticket to the defendant for causing the accident. However, a defense question "opened the door" and allowed the prosecutor to ask the officer about the ticket during redirect examination. In "opening the door," the defense counsel on cross-examination asked the officer whether he had given the defendant a ticket for leaving the scene of the accident. This question allowed the prosecution on redirect examination to ask questions concerning tickets in general, which allowed the question about the ticket for causing the accident.[143]

---

[139] Pacheco v. State, 698 So. 2d 393 (Fla. 1997).
[140] United States v. Deisch, 20 F.3d 139 (5th Cir. 1994).
[141] Ohio v. Henderson, 2003 Ohio 312 (2003).
[142] Kelly v. Florida, 843 So. 2d 223, 2003 Fla. App. LEXIS 4732 (2003).
[143] Havard v. Mississippi, 800 So. 2d 1193, 1196, 1197, 2001 Miss. App. LEXIS 308 (2001).

§ 9.12 Impeachment of Witnesses

Rule 607

Who May Impeach

The credibility of a witness may be attacked by any party, including the party calling the witness.[144]

In judging the credibility of witnesses, the task rests with the trier of fact, whether it is a judge or a jury. The task of giving the trier of fact the information necessary to evaluate the testimony of each witness falls to the parties, who must offer sufficient information concerning the believability and reliability of each witness. The judge or jury must determine whether to believe any witnesses and to decide which witnesses to believe.[145] One case referred to McCormick on Evidence, which suggests:

> Impeachment is a technique used to attack the truth-telling capacity of a witness. Impeachment may be accomplished by demonstrating the witness' bias, self-contradiction, poor character, defect in perceptive capacity, prior convictions or bad acts, or by contradicting the witness on specific facts in her testimony.[146]

Impeachment has also been defined as the process of attempting to diminish the credibility of a witness by convincing the jury or court that the testimony of the particular witness should be considered untruthful or unreliable.[147] Every witness who takes the oath to tell the truth places his or her credibility at issue and relevant evidence that affects the credibility should generally not be excluded.[148] There are various methods and techniques of impeaching adverse witnesses, some of which will be discussed in the following sections.

A party's decision to impeach a witness in a criminal case is subject to a discretionary limitation by the trial judge.[149] In determining whether the trial judge abused his or her discretion in limiting a defendant's impeachment of the complaining witness, the pertinent issue is whether the rejection of a defendant's efforts to impeach the credibility of the complaining witness withholds from the jury information necessary to make a discriminating appraisal of the witness's trustworthiness to the prejudice of a defendant's substantial

---

[144] FED. R. EVID. 607.

[145] Brown v. Maryland, 368 Md. 320, 327, 793 A.2d 561, 565, 2002 Md. LEXIS 95 (2002).

[146] Colorado v. Trujillo, 49 P.3d 316, 2002 Colo. LEXIS 569 (2002), citing 1 JOHN W. STRONG, McCORMICK ON EVIDENCE § 33 (5th ed. 1999).

[147] State v. Dale, 874 S.W.2d 446 (Mo. 1994). *See also* State v. Johanesen, 319 Or. 128, 873 P.2d 1065 (1994), in which the court stated that "impeachment" refers to elicitation or presentation of any matter for the purpose of impairing or destroying the credibility of the witness in the estimation of the trier of fact.

[148] Commonwealth v. Maddox, 955 S.W.2d 718 (Ky. 1997).

[149] Connecticut v. Abernathy, 72 Conn. App. 831, 836, 837, 806 A.2d 1139, 1145, 1146, 2002 Conn. App. LEXIS 519 (2002).

rights. Thus, denying impeachment of the complaining witness in a prosecution for robbery by referring to the complaining witness's prior convictions for assault and rape was not an abuse of discretion affecting substantial rights of the defendant. However, impeachment of the witness with three convictions for the crimes of auto theft, robbery, and burglary—each crime having an element of dishonesty—was properly permitted.[150]

A witness may not be impeached by evidence that merely contradicts his or her testimony on a matter that is collateral (and not material) to any issue in the trial.[151] For example, where a prosecution witness has stated that the defendant was wearing a blue shirt at the crime scene, impeachment by a defense witness that the defendant was wearing a red shirt demonstrates an example of collateral evidence that could be excluded. The rule precluding impeachment of a witness by otherwise admissible evidence directed to collateral issues serves policies such as the prevention of confusion, waste of time, and surprise. Such policies have peculiar force when the attempt to impeach serves to discredit a witness by means of introducing purported misconduct short of a conviction.[152]

Every criminal defendant who takes the stand to testify in his or her own defense becomes subject to cross-examination to the same extent as any other witness[153] and must face the possibility of impeachment as may any other witness[154] unless, under the particular circumstances of the case, specific questions should be excluded because their probative value as to the issue of the defendant's credibility is negligible when compared with their possible prejudicial impact on the jury[155] or where there are overriding constitutional or statutory provisions that limit such impeachment.[156] For example, the defendant may have a Fifth Amendment privilege with respect to other uncharged crimes, the questions may relate to illegally seized wiretap evidence, or may involve a confidential marital communication.

§ 9.13   —Own Witness

The traditional rule holds that a party vouches for the credibility of witnesses it may call to offer evidence. Under this theory, a party may not impeach his or her own witness under the theory that a party would not call a

---

[150] Davis v. United States, 409 F.2d 453 (D.C. Cir. 1969); *see also* United States v. Frankenthal, 582 F.2d 1102 (7th Cir. 1978).

[151] Byomin v. Alvis, 169 Ohio St. 395, 8 Ohio Op. 2d 420, 159 N.E.2d 897 (1959); Kilpatrick v. State, 285 So. 2d 516 (Ala. 1973).

[152] Lee v. United States, 368 F.2d 834 (D.C. Cir. 1966).

[153] North Carolina v. Boekenoogen, 147 N.C. App. 292, 297, 554 S.E.2d 848, 851, 2001 N.C. App. LEXIS 1143 (2001).

[154] Robinson v. Texas, 2000 Tex. App. LEXIS 5792 (2000) and Hampton v. Texas, 2003 Tex. App. LEXIS 3984 (2003).

[155] Raffel v. United States, 271 U.S. 494, 46 S. Ct. 566, 70 L. Ed. 1054 (1926); Sharp v. United States, 410 F.2d 969 (5th Cir. 1969); United States v. McMurray, 20 F.3d 831 (8th Cir. 1994). *See also* Chandler v. State, 702 So. 2d 186 (Fla. 1997).

[156] Lopez v. Texas, 990 S.W.2d 770, 777, 1999 Tex. App. LEXIS 871 (1999).

witness if there were doubts about credibility. However, modern evidence theories as well as Rule 607 of the Federal Rules of Evidence permit any party to attack the credibility of its own witnesses without showing any proof of surprise, hostility on the part of the witness, or that the witness is allied with the opposing side.

With respect to state evidence law, some jurisdictions follow provisions identical or similar to Rule 607, while other states follow the traditional rule.[157] A federal appeals court, following the reasoning of Rule 607, stated that in determining the admissibility of testimony that the government elicits to impeach its own witness, the government's motive in eliciting such testimony is irrelevant.[158] A Florida appeals court held that the evidence code provision of that state allows any party, including the party calling the witness, to impeach the credibility of the witness without regard to whether the testimony of the witness construes surprise or affirmative harm.[159] In contrast, a New York statute follows the traditional rule and does not permit the party who called the witness to impeach unless the witness in a criminal case gives evidence that tends to be adverse to the party calling the witness. In that event, the surprised party may introduce evidence that the witness has previously given an oral or written statement that contradicts his or her in-court testimony.[160] In New York "[a] party may impeach its own witness only if that witness gives testimony upon a material issue or fact which 'tends to disprove the party's position or affirmatively damages the party's case.'"[161] The reality seems to be that a party may impeach a witness when unexpected hostility or surprise becomes evident, with the result that under either general theory, it will be a rare case in which the outcome is based on the type of policy that is followed regarding the impeachment of one's own witness.

One technique that appears to involve impeaching one's own witness may be considered damage control rather than impeachment. When a prosecutor plans to place a witness on the stand and the witness has been cooperative in exchange for certain leniencies from the government, the prosecutor may wish to disclose a plea bargain or other favorable deal between the prosecution's witness and the government. This has the effect of displaying honesty on the part of the prosecution so the jury does not learn of a plea bargain or prior conviction of crime for the first time when disclosed by the defense counsel on cross-examination.[162] Thus, through open disclosure, the prosecutor takes the wind out of the sails of potential impeachment by the defense. Open disclosure may benefit either party in a criminal case and is usually the most appropriate path to follow when using a witness who has prior legal problems.

---

[157] For example, compare N.Y. CRIM. PROC. LAW § 60.35(1) (demonstrating the limited situations in which a party may impeach its own witness), with FED. R. EVID. 607 (allowing any party to impeach any witness—including its own—for any reason or no reason).

[158] United States v. Logan, 121 F.3d 1172 (8th Cir. 1997).

[159] Collins v. State, 698 So. 2d 1337 (Fla. 1997).

[160] N.Y. CRIM. PROC. LAW § 60.35 (2006).

[161] New York v. Andujar, 290 A.D.2d 654, 656, 736 N.Y.S.2d 159, 161, 2002 N.Y. App. Div. LEXIS 68 (2002).

[162] United States v. Valuck, 286 F.3d 221 (5th Cir. 2002).

In a criminal case, the government may impeach its own witness by presenting his or her prior inconsistent statements; however, there are limits on this authority. A trial judge should not permit the government to call a witness for the primary purpose of impeaching that witness with a view to getting evidence before the court that would not normally be admissible.[163] The government also may not impeach its own witness merely because the witness refused to give testimony that the government hoped he or she would give.[164]

Impeachment of one's own witnesses is not permissible if the questioning is a means of subterfuge to expose the jury to otherwise inadmissible evidence.[165] However, the state may impeach its own witness to lessen the blow of a cross-examination by the defense attorney. For example, where the government informant's past would likely have come out on cross-examination, the government had a legitimate reason to explore the subject on direct examination.[166]

§ 9.14 —Bias or Prejudice

One of the most effective ways to impeach a witness is to show bias on the part of that witness. "Bias is a term used in the 'common law of evidence' to describe the relationship between a party and a witness which might lead the witness to slant, unconsciously or otherwise, his testimony in favor of or against a party. Bias may be induced by a witness' like, dislike, or fear of a party, or by the witness' self-interest."[167] In criminal cases, great latitude is generally permitted in cross-examination of a witness in order to test his or her credibility and to develop facts that may tend to show bias, prejudice, or any other motive that the witness may have for giving testimony. If a witness denies facts that show bias or prejudice, his or her denial may be rebutted with extrinsic evidence,[168] because bias is always relevant. Although it is error for the trial judge to exclude a defendant's testimony that would reasonably show bias or prejudice, the trial court retains the normal discretion to limit the extent of proof even when bias or prejudicial interests are involved.[169] Examples of situations in which cross-examination was allowed to show bias follow.

In a Michigan case involving a defendant charged with criminal sexual conduct with a minor, the prosecutor was properly permitted to introduce evidence that a defense witness had been acquitted of charges involving criminal sexual conduct with a child under the age of 13. The theory concerned the fact that a person who had been acquitted of similar conduct could have a bias or

---

[163] Busiello v. McGinnis, 235 F. Supp. 2d 179, 185 (2002).
[164] United States v. Ince, 21 F.3d 576 (4th Cir. 1994).
[165] *Id.*
[166] *Id.*
[167] Coles v. United States, 808 A.2d 485, 489, 2002 D.C. App. LEXIS 556 (2002).
[168] United States v. Frankenthal, 582 F.2d 1102 (7th Cir. 1978).
[169] Wynn v. United States, 397 F.2d 621 (D.C. Cir. 1967); *see also* Austin v. United States, 418 F.2d 456 (D.C. Cir. 1969). *See also* State v. Lee, 640 A.2d 553 (Conn. 1994), in which the court held that cross-examination concerning motive, interest, bias, or prejudice is a matter of right and may not be unduly restrictive.

interest in seeing another person acquitted of the charges, especially where both defendants have made claims of innocence.[170] And in Texas a reviewing court held that evidence implying that the defendant and the defense witness were affiliated with a gang was admissible to show bias on the part of the defense witness.[171]

Courts have generally agreed that a prosecution witness may be cross-examined to show bias if promises of leniency were made by the prosecution. For example, a court in Tennessee decided that the defendant has a right to cross-examine the prosecution witness to impeach credibility or to establish motive or prejudice of the witness and this includes the right to cross-examine the prosecution witness regarding any promises of leniency, promises to help the witness, or any other favorable treatment offered to the witness.[172] As a general rule, the attorney attempting to impeach a witness by demonstrating bias must have a reasonable and well-founded suspicion that the evidence of bias has a basis in fact. The bias should be reasonably inferable from the facts presented by the attorney.[173]

Examples of cases in which evidence has been allowed to show bias are many. A few are briefly summarized here. When a defense witness who possessed exculpatory evidence prior to trial and knew of the defendant's legal difficulties immediately and never attempted to convey the information to the police and only offered the evidence at trial, that witness could be impeached by a showing of bias in favor of the defendant based on recent fabrication of exculpatory evidence.[174] Evidence that the defendant and the defense witness whose credibility was crucial to the resolution of the case were affiliated with the same street gang was admissible to show bias on the part of the witness toward the defendant, and the evidence was not unfairly prejudicial.[175]

Because a trial court has discretion in admitting impeachment evidence concerning bias, it may refuse to admit evidence for which a case could be made. In an aggravated assault case, the defendant wanted to call the victim's mother as a witness to question her about her offer, on her son's behalf, to receive $25,000 in exchange for her son (the assault victim) dropping all charges against the defendant. The court refused to allow the evidence of the monetary offer to show the witness's bias against the defendant. The bias theoretically developed because the defendant rejected the offer to compromise the criminal case and no money changed hands. The court reasoned that the offer could have been to settle civil issues between the victim and the defendant and therefore had no bearing on the criminal case.[176]

---

[170]   Michigan v. Layher, 464 Mich. 756, 765, 631 N.W.2d 281, 286, 2001 Mich. LEXIS 1192 (2001).
[171]   McKnight v. State, 874 S.W.2d 745 (Tex. 1994).
[172]   State v. Spurlock, 874 S.W.2d 602 (Tenn. 1993). *See also* Commonwealth v. Dawson, 702 A.2d 864 (Pa. 1997).
[173]   Joyner v. United States, 818 A2d 166, 172, 2003 D.C. App. LEXIS 133 (2003).
[174]   Massachusetts v. Cintron, 435 Mass. 509, 522, 759 N.E.2d 700, 711, 2001 Mass. LEXIS 771 (2001).
[175]   United States v. McCoy, 131 F.3d 760 (8th Cir. 1997).
[176]   Gavin v. Mississippi, 767 So. 2d 1072, 1077, 2000 Miss. App. LEXIS 454 (2000).

Evidence of a complainant's prior consensual sexual acts may be admitted to show that the complainant is biased or has a motive to fabricate rape charges; in such cases, issues of the complainant's bias and credibility are not collateral, and the rape shield law must give way to the defendant's Sixth Amendment rights.[177]

In a Georgia case, the defense counsel was entitled to thoroughly examine a police officer about the circumstances surrounding the defendant's confessions and to attempt to show bias that might have affected the officer's testimony.[178] The reviewing court noted that the trial court abused its discretion by refusing to allow the defense counsel to play a videotape of the defendant's first statement, in which he denied committing the murder.

§ 9.15 —Character and Conduct

Rule 608

Evidence of Character and Conduct of Witness

(a) Opinion and reputation evidence of character. The credibility of a witness may be attacked or supported by evidence in the form of opinion or reputation, but subject to these limitations: (1) the evidence may refer only to character for truthfulness or untruthfulness, and (2) evidence of truthful character is admissible only after the character of the witness for truthfulness has been attacked by opinion or reputation or otherwise.

(b) Specific instances of conduct. Specific instances of the conduct of a witness, for the purpose of attacking or supporting the witness' credibility, other than conviction of crime as provided in Rule 609, may not be proved by extrinsic evidence. They may, however, in the discretion of the court, if probative of truthfulness or untruthfulness, be inquired into on cross-examination of the witness (1) concerning the witness' character for truthfulness or untruthfulness, or (2) concerning the character for truthfulness or untruthfulness of another witness as to which character the witness being cross-examined has testified.

The giving of testimony, whether by an accused or by any other witness, does not operate as a waiver of the accused's or the witness' privilege against self-incrimination when examined with respect to matters that relate only to character for truthfulness.[179]

As a general rule, the prosecution may not introduce evidence of a defendant's character or habit. However, if a defendant places his or her general reputation at issue by introducing what is loosely described as a "character" witness, or from the witness stand personally offers character evidence, he or

---

[177] State v. Jackson, 212 Wis. 2d 203, 567 N.W.2d 920 (1997).

[178] Carswell v. State, 491 S.E.2d 343 (Ga. 1997).

[179] FED. R. EVID. 608.

she places his or her character at issue and is said to have "opened the door" for the prosecution to test the credibility of the witness. The prosecution may inquire on cross-examination whether the witness had knowledge of specific facts that, if known generally, would tend to detract from the summary of the defendant's reputation offered by the character witness. Allowing the character witness's knowledge of the defendant's character to be tested by such means is fraught with great danger. Unless circumscribed by rules of fairness and grounded in good faith on the part of the prosecution, the result may be unfairly prejudicial to the defendant, thus causing a miscarriage of justice.

If the prosecution attempts to attack the observations offered by a character witness or to cast doubt on the credibility of the defendant's character witnesses, there should be a prior demonstration, out of the hearing of the jury, establishing to the trial judge's satisfaction the truth of the basis for such inquiry. Moreover, cautionary instructions should be given to the jury, preferably at the time of the inquiry and in the jury instructions at the close of the case.

In *Michelson v. United States*,[180] the United States Supreme Court carefully considered the manner and extent of cross-examination of character witnesses in criminal cases. The Court stated:

> Wide discretion is accompanied by heavy responsibility on trial courts to protect the practice from any misuse. The trial judge was scrupulous to so guard it in the case before us. He took pains to ascertain, out of the presence of the jury, that the target of the question was an actual event, which would probably result in some comment among acquaintances if not injury to defendant's reputation. He satisfied himself that counsel was not merely taking a random shot at a reputation imprudently exposed or asking a groundless question to waft an unwarranted innuendo into the jury box.

Where the defendant's character witnesses have been cross-examined through inquiry about whether the witnesses had knowledge of specific facts that, if generally known, would tend to detract from the character testimony, the jury must be carefully cautioned that the testimony refers solely to reputation and not to the truth of collateral facts.[181] The prosecution may explore the basis and scope of the witness's knowledge of the defendant's reputation by asking the witness whether he or she has heard various reports about the defendant, provided that the questions have a foundation; for example, in the sense that arrests or accusations have been rumored and discussed. Past instances of misconduct mentioned on cross-examination must directly concern truthfulness or untruthfulness. If the prior conduct was merely improper, illegal, or immoral, then the evidence should not be permitted under Rule 608(b). For example, cross-examination of a witness concerning whether she ever attempted to strike another person with a stick should not be allowed, because the act, even if it occurred, has nothing to do with the honesty or

---

[180] 335 U.S. 469, 69 S. Ct. 213, 93 L. Ed. 168 (1948).
[181] Gross v. United States, 394 F.2d 216 (8th Cir. 1968); United States v. Lewis, 482 F.2d 632 (D.C. Cir. 1973).

believability of the witness.[182] The prosecution's cross-examination regarding specific instances of conduct has limitations. It is permitted to evaluate only the character witness's credibility and knowledge of a defendant and cannot be used to prove the prosecution's case against a defendant.[183] The prosecutor may not simply ask a question without any basis in fact; the government must have a good faith belief that the specific instances of misconduct occurred. The danger lurking in this impeachment process is that in constructing an intelligible question, the cross-examiner's query often gives details of specific misconduct affecting general reputation, which would not otherwise be admissible.[184]

Because a defendant's character witnesses generally convey the collective community opinion concerning the defendant's overall character, the prosecutor may inquire on cross-examination whether a defendant's character witness "has heard" of the defendant's prior arrests or convictions. Such cross-examination is not admitted to establish the truth that such events took place, but only to test the foundations and reliability of the witness's testimony. Under Rule 608 it is inadmissible to establish the defendant's bad character or his or her propensity to commit the crime charged, but the evidence might be admissible under a different legal theory. The typical rationale for permitting such questions, even when they refer to a defendant's prior arrests, is that they enable the jury to better evaluate the character testimony that has been offered. If a witness has heard these damaging rumors and adheres to his or her statement that the defendant's reputation is good, some light and some doubt will have been shed upon the standards the witness has employed; alternatively, if he or she has not heard of these rumors that have some basis in fact, some doubt will have been cast upon his or her ability to speak on behalf of the collective opinion of the community.

In one case in which the prosecution's character witness was to be cross-examined, the court found no prejudicial error in refusing to permit questions concerning whether the witness had been involved in drug dealing because "drug dealing is not the type of conduct that necessarily bears on a witness's character for truthfulness."[185] Alternatively, when a defendant had testified on direct examination, the prosecutor properly used the defendant's prior convictions for writing a check on insufficient funds, defrauding an innkeeper, writing a check when he had no bank account, and tax fraud for impeachment evidence.[186] In a different case, the court approved the admission of evidence of misdemeanor convictions against a defendant witness. The defendant had testified, "I ain't done nothing wrong for awhile [sic]." The prosecutor obtained testimony from appellant concerning misdemeanor convictions, not

---

[182] Tennessee v. Neblett, 2003 Tenn. Crim. App. LEXIS 429 (2003).

[183] Unites States v. Chan, 2002 U.S. Dist. LEXIS 1221 (S.D.N.Y. 2002).

[184] *See* North Carolina v. Calloway, 2002 N.C. App. LEXIS 2438 (2002), in which the appellate court held that cross-examination concerning prior acts of the defendant was not proper under Rule 608(b), but was admissible under North Carolina Evidence Rule 404(b), dealing with exceptions to proof of other crimes to prove conduct.

[185] United States v. Walker, 47 Fed. Appx. 639, 2002 U.S. App. LEXIS 19817 (4th Cir. 2002).

[186] United States v. Arhebamen, 2006 U.S. App. LEXIS 24564 (6th Cir. 2006).

in an effort to impeach appellant's credibility by showing conviction of a misdemeanor, but to show that appellant had not been truthful in his testimony. By showing that the defendant had not been truthful about his recent misdemeanor convictions, the evidence tended to impeach his testimony.[187]

The credibility of a witness may be attacked or supported by evidence in the form of reputation or opinion, but this is subject to several limitations. Under Rule 608(a), the evidence may refer only to character for truthfulness or untruthfulness, and evidence of truthful character is admissible only after the truthfulness of the witness has been attacked by opinion or reputation evidence or otherwise. Where a witness denies specific instances of personal misconduct, other than for conviction of crime, the examiner is stuck with the answer and the party may not, as a general rule, prove the misconduct by extrinsic evidence under Rule 608(b).[188]

In applying the rules relating to the admissibility of evidence concerning character and conduct of the witness, the time element is normally given consideration when the conviction occurred more than 10 years prior. However, in a federal prosecution, the judge ruled that a defendant attorney's older convictions involving income tax issues would be permitted to be introduced by the prosecution. As a tactic, the defendant introduced them during his direct examination. On appeal, the court held that the defendant had waived his right to complain by introducing the impeaching evidence on his direct examination, despite the fact that the judge had stated that the prosecution could use the more-than-10-year-old convictions as impeachment evidence.[189] In a case in which a police officer lied to the defendant during interrogation, the trial court properly refused to allow cross-examination concerning the officer's lies. Generally, a witness's credibility may be attacked by specific instances of conduct if they are probative of the witness's character for truthfulness or untruthfulness. In this case, the trial court held that because the use of false statements by police during questioning is a routine practice, the evidence was not admissible to impeach the police officer's testimony at trial. According to the court, it had not found any authority suggesting that use of deception as a police interrogation tactic implicated an officer's credibility under oath.[190]

In further defining the limits placed on the use of character evidence, a Pennsylvania federal court refused to allow the prosecution to impeach an embezzlement defendant using a prior felony car theft conviction as a method of questioning his character for honesty if the defendant took the witness stand. The trial judge had concerns that proof of the car theft conviction would have little probative value concerning whether the defendant committed embezzlement. The objection to using the earlier felony was that the jurors might base their decision on something other than the evidence presented in

---

[187]   Ohio v. Walker, 2002 Ohio 7372, 2002 Ohio App. LEXIS 7228 (2002).

[188]   FED. R. EVID. 608, *and see* State v. Neblett, 2003 Tenn. Crim. App. LEXIS 429 (2003).

[189]   United States v. McConnet, 2006 U.S. App. LEXIS 23230 (10th Cir. 2006).

[190]   Minnesota v. Martinez, 657 N.W.2d 600, 602, 603, 2003 Minn. App. LEXIS 252 (2003).

the case.[191] Other judges might weigh this case differently because dishonesty is involved in both embezzlement and theft.

If evidence of prior crimes is admissible to impeach, the defendant cannot prevent the prosecution from introducing evidence to that effect by offering to stipulate to the existence of the prior felony convictions. In another case involving a felon in possession of a firearm, the defendant stipulated that he had prior felony convictions. [192] Once the defendant became a witness in his own defense, he placed his character trait for honesty at issue and the district court did not abuse its discretion in allowing the prosecution to cross-examine the defendant concerning his prior felony convictions.

In interpreting Rule 608 of the Federal Rules, the United States Court of Appeals for the Second Circuit agreed with the lower court in allowing cross-examination of the witness concerning the truthfulness of his character.[193] In this prosecution for possession and distribution of heroin, the court ruled that the government was entitled to use the defendant's otherwise unexplained or unexplainable sources of income to prove illegal dealings and to cross-examine the defendant regarding his lavish expenditures; the government could further cross-examine the defendant regarding his false credit card application to show general lack of credibility.

§ 9.16 —Conviction of Crime

Rule 609

Impeachment by Evidence of
Conviction of Crime

(a) General rule. For the purpose of attacking the credibility of a witness,

    (1) evidence that the witness other than an accused has been convicted of a crime shall be admitted, subject to Rule 403, if the crime was punishable by death or imprisonment in excess of one year under the law under which the witness was convicted, and evidence that an accused has been convicted of such a crime shall be admitted if the court determines that the probative value of admitting this evidence outweighs its prejudicial effect to the accused; and

    (2) evidence that any witness has been convicted of a crime shall be admitted if it involved dishonesty or false statement, regardless of the punishment.

(b) Time limit. Evidence of a conviction under this rule is not admissible if a period of more than ten years has elapsed since the date of the conviction or of the release of the witness from the confinement imposed for that conviction, whichever is the later date, unless the court determines, in the interests of justice, that the probative value of the conviction supported by

---

[191] United States v. Miller, 2004 U.S. Dist. LEXIS 23299 (E.D. Pa. 2006).

[192] United States v. Kilgore, 151 Fed. Appx. 799, 802, 2005 U.S. App. LEXIS 20690 (11th Cir. 2005).

[193] United States v. Sperling, 726 F.2d 69 (2d Cir. 1984).

specific facts and circumstances substantially outweighs its prejudicial effect. However, evidence of a conviction more than 10 years old as calculated herein, is not admissible unless the proponent gives to the adverse party sufficient advance written notice of intent to use such evidence to provide the adverse party with a fair opportunity to contest the use of such evidence.

(c) Effect of pardon, annulment, or certificate of rehabilitation. Evidence of a conviction is not admissible under this rule if (1) the conviction has been the subject of a pardon, annulment, certificate of rehabilitation, or other equivalent procedures based on a finding of the rehabilitation of the person convicted, and that person has not been convicted of a subsequent crime which was punishable by death or imprisonment in excess of one year, or (2) the conviction has been the subject of a pardon, annulment, or other equivalent procedure based on a finding of innocence.

(d) Juvenile adjudications. Evidence of juvenile adjudications is generally not admissible under this rule. The court may, however, in a criminal case allow evidence of a juvenile adjudication of a witness other than the accused if conviction of the offense would be admissible to attack the credibility of an adult and the court is satisfied that admission in evidence is necessary for a fair determination of the issue of guilt or innocence.

(e) Pendency of appeal. The pendency of an appeal therefrom does not render evidence of a conviction inadmissible. Evidence of the pendency of an appeal is admissible.[194]

As a general rule, because a case should be decided on relevant evidence that either proves or fails to prove the crime charged, it would be unfair to introduce evidence to show that a suspect in a criminal case had previously committed other crimes. The concern when a judge admits evidence of a prior crime or crimes is that a jury might, in a close case, convict the defendant because the defendant had committed prior crimes. A jury might determine that if the defendant had committed one prior crime, then he or she might be guilty of the crime presently charged. The concern with prior crime evidence is that juries might use a defendant's prior convictions as evidence of the defendant's propensity to commit crime.[195] Whenever a defendant decides to testify at trial, he or she places his or her trait for credibility directly at issue.[196] In such a case, if a defendant testifies in his or her own defense, evidence that the defendant committed certain prior crimes may be admitted, not to prove that the defendant committed the crime for which he or she is being tried, but to reflect on the defendant's credibility as a witness.[197] The reason for exposing a criminal record is to call into question the reliability and credibility of the witness for telling the truth.

[194] FED. R. EVID. 609.
[195] North Dakota v. Stewart, 2002 N.D. 102, 646 N.W.2d 712, 715, 2002 N.D. LEXIS 140 (2002).
[196] United States v. Murphy, 172 Fed. Appx. 461, 462, 2006 U.S. App. LEXIS 7827 (3d Cir. 2006).
[197] *See* United States v. McMurray, 20 F.3d 831 (8th Cir. 1994); *see also* State v. Lewis, 2003 Minn. App. LEXIS 255 (2003), in which a court allowed evidence of a prior sexual conviction to be admitted against a testifying defendant as a challenge to his credibility.

The ordinary witness may usually be asked, for purposes of impeachment, whether he or she has been convicted of a felony, infamous crime, or crime involving moral turpitude. For purposes of attacking the credibility of the witness, some courts have limited the evidence to certain types of crimes. The California Supreme Court left no doubt about this issue. That court wrote:

> The case law is clear. The only relevant consideration is whether the prior conviction contains as a necessary element the intent to deceive, defraud, lie, cheat, steal, etc.[198]

In applying this rule to the offense of possession of heroin for sale, the court indicated that one who possesses heroin, intending to sell it illegally to another, may fairly and properly be deemed a dishonest person and may reasonably be deemed "unworthy of belief." Evidence of a previous conviction for possession of heroin intended for sale was properly admitted for impeachment purposes. However, not all jurisdictions hold that drug possession or sale offenses constitute crimes for which honesty can be called into question.

Criminal offenses that are remote in time to the current trial may be excluded where they are older than 10 years or are considered too remote in time, even if within the 10-year period. In an unpublished opinion, a court of appeals in the state of Washington held that a victim-witness in a robbery case could not be impeached by the use of two convictions involving sexually oriented crimes with minors, in which one conviction was more than 10 years old and the other conviction was less than 10 years old. The court noted that the crimes, communicating with a minor and taking indecent liberties with a minor, were completely different from any crime involving dishonesty and refused to admit evidence of the crimes to impeach the robbery victim-witness.[199]

As a general rule, a witness may not be impeached by inquiry into prior misdemeanors unless those misdemeanors involve moral turpitude. In a Virginia case, the appellate court held that a trial court erred when it allowed the prosecution to impeach the defendant with a crime not involving moral turpitude. According to the court, a prior conviction of contributing to the delinquency of a minor was not a crime involving moral turpitude and evidence of the prior crime should not have been admitted into evidence.[200] Where a prior misdemeanor involved a crime of moral turpitude such as theft, such a crime involves dishonesty and may be used for impeachment purposes. According to an Illinois appellate court, in a case in which the credibility of the defendant was crucial to guilt or innocence, "theft is a crime that speaks directly to a person's truthfulness," and the jury should have been allowed to fully assess his credibility.[201] In a federal prosecution for having a firearm under a disability, the defendant wanted to introduce the driving while intoxicated convictions

[198]   People v. Spearman, 157 Cal. 883 (1979).
[199]   Washington v. Walker, 2002 Wash. App. LEXIS 1792 (2002).
[200]   Jarrell v. Commonwealth of Virginia, 2002 Va. App. LEXIS 353 (2002).
[201]   Illinois v. Diehl, 335 Ill. App. 3d 693, 704, 783 N.E.2d 640, 650, 2002 Ill. App. LEXIS 1060 (2003).

for both of the officers who were the primary witnesses in the case. One of the officers lied about drinking when initially stopped by the other police. The judge excluded the DUI evidence on the theory that the police officer's misdemeanor convictions were not relevant to their credibility.[202] A Washington court authorized the use of evidence of a misdemeanor under a state statute similar to Rule 609(a)(2) of the Federal Rules of Evidence. The court in that case indicated that some crimes of theft, such as embezzlement, involve an element of deceit or untruthfulness; thus, they are admissible under subdivision (a)(2) of Rule 609 for the purpose of attacking the credibility of a witness.[203]

Impeachment evidence does not generally include conviction of crimes not involving dishonesty that are punishable by one year of incarceration or less. In an Arizona felony prosecution, the Supreme Court of Arizona held that evidence of prior drug convictions that did not involve any incarceration could not be used as impeachment evidence because under Arizona's version of Rule 609 the prior crimes did not involve incarceration of more than one year and did not involve dishonesty when the prior crimes were only drug possession or use offenses.[204]

A witness generally may not be impeached by the introduction of evidence regarding a pending charge that has not been tried. When the prosecutor asked a defense witness questions concerning the fact that he was about to stand trial for murder, kidnapping, and robbery, the question was not only erroneous, but also unduly prejudicial to the defendant. His constitutional right to a fair trial was violated.[205] However, in some cases a witness's credibility may be impeached by introducing evidence that he or she has pending criminal charges and is cooperating with the prosecution.[206] The fact that a witness is facing criminal charges and cooperating with the prosecution may indicate bias and is something a jury should be permitted to evaluate.

In federal cases, the district court judge initially determines whether the probative value of admitting evidence outweighs its prejudicial effect (Rule 609 (a)(1)). The trial judge's decision will not be disturbed unless there is a clear abuse of discretion.

For example, the Eighth Circuit Court of Appeals upheld the admission of prior felonies against a defendant for the purpose of impeachment.[207] The defendant had been charged with being a felon in possession of a firearm based on a shooting at a home where he had been attending a party. The judge permitted prosecutors to question the defendant concerning the fact of his three prior violent felonies during cross-examination. Although the judge did not make a record of balancing the probative value of the impeachment evi-

---

[202] United States v. Edwards, 156 Fed. Appx. 954, 956, 2005 U.S. App. LEXIS 26786 (9th Cir. 2005). *Contra* North Carolina v. Gregory, 154 N.C. App 718, 722, 572 S.E.2d 838, 840, 841, 2002 N.C. App. LEXIS 1534 (2002).

[203] State v. Burton, 676 P.2d 975 (Wash. 1984).

[204] State ex rel. Fomley v. Martin, 69 P.3d 1000, 2003 Ariz. LEXIS 80 (2003).

[205] Moore v. Commonwealth, 634 S.W.2d 426 (Ky. 1982).

[206] Stevens v. Hall, 294 F.3d 210, 224, 2002 U.S. App. LEXIS 12849 (1st Cir. 2002).

[207] United States v. Headbird, 461 F.3d 1074, 2006 U.S. App. LEXIS 22326 (8th Cir. 2006).

dence against the danger of unfair prejudice, the reviewing court assumed that the judge made the appropriate analysis. However, in a prosecution for conspiracy to defraud the United States by preparing and submitting false federal income tax returns, a Colorado court decided that evidence of a prior state conviction for theft of rental property was inadmissible for impeachment purposes absent a showing that the probative value of the conviction outweighed the prejudice to the defendant.[208]

The trial judge has broad discretion to determine the admissibility of evidence relating to prior convictions. Rule 609 must be read by the trial court in conjunction with Rule 403, which requires that the trial judge balance the probative value of the impeachment evidence against the risk of unfair prejudice. In a case involving Rule 609, a trial court refused to permit a defendant to attempt to impeach a government witness concerning the witness's past criminal activity, and the appellate court upheld the decision.[209] The government's witness had a misdemeanor conviction that was more than 10 years old and did not involve dishonesty. The felony conviction similarly dated more than a decade ago and the district court determined that the probative value of admitting the witness's prior felony was exceeded by the danger of unfair prejudice to the government. Courts are especially hesitant to admit evidence relating to convictions of witnesses that occurred long before the crime that is the subject of a current trial. The Seventh Circuit Court of Appeals has established a five-part test to be used by courts in determining whether to admit evidence of a prior crime as impeachment evidence. Pursuant to Rule 609, the trial court should evaluate:

> (1) the impeachment value of the prior crime; (2) the point in time of the conviction and the defendant's subsequent history; (3) the similarity between the past crime and the charged crime; (4) the importance of the defendant's testimony; and (5) the centrality of the credibility issue.[210]

As expressed by the Seventh Circuit, deciding whether convictions that are within the 10-year period should be used to impeach calls for careful consideration by the trial judge, using the five factors suggested above.[211] The Federal Rules of Evidence provide that such evidence is not admissible if more than 10 years have elapsed since the date of conviction or from the confinement imposed for that conviction unless the court determines that the probative value substantially outweighs its prejudicial effect. By relying on the provisions of Rule 609, the Seventh Circuit Court of Appeals held that, in a prosecution for conspiracy to extort for the purpose of collecting a gambling debt, the trial court did not abuse its discretion in excluding evidence of the prior criminal record of a government witness.[212] In that case the prior crimi-

---

[208] United States v. Reece, 797 F. Supp. 843 (D. Colo. 1992), aff'd, 28 F.3d 114 (10th Cir. 1993).

[209] Unites States v. Loma, 2006 U. S. App. LEXIS 24599 (9th Cir. 2006).

[210] United States v. Smith, 181 F. Supp. 2d 904, 909, 2002 U.S. Dist. LEXIS 4602 (N.D. Ill. 2002), quoting United States v. Smith, 80 F. 3d 1188, 1193 (1997).

[211] United States v. Hernandez, 106 F. 3d 737, 739, 740 (1997).

[212] United States v. Muscarella, 585 F.2d 242 (7th Cir. 1978).

nal record comprised of misdemeanors and juvenile convictions that were more than ten years old.

State courts have followed much of this same theory and philosophy when interpreting their respective versions of Rule 609. In an Alaska theft case, a trial court permitted the prosecutor to introduce the defendant-witness's prior conviction for theft by receiving stolen equipment.[213] The defendant had taken the stand in his own defense to explain that his company allowed any employee to borrow equipment at any time. The appellate court found no abuse of discretion under Rule 609 and upheld the admission on cross-examination of the defendant's prior crime involving a prior conviction for theft of property. Once a defendant takes the stand in his or her defense, the defendant places the defendant's credibility at issue.

Below are a few examples of cases in which criminal convictions were used for the purpose of attacking a witness's credibility. In a prosecution for possession of more than five grams of cocaine, the trial court did not abuse its discretion in admitting the defendant's prior conviction for conspiracy to import heroin and aiding and abetting the distribution of heroin.[214] There was no abuse of discretion in admitting evidence of two prior convictions for possession of unauthorized weapons when the defendant was on trial for two counts of distributing crack cocaine.[215] According to the Supreme Court of North Dakota, evidence of the defendant witness's prior convictions for felony unauthorized use of a motor vehicle, unlawful possession of a firearm by a felon, and reckless endangerment were considered probative of the defendant's character for truthfulness and admissible for impeachment purposes in a prosecution for driving under the influence and aggravated reckless driving involving a death.[216] A Minnesota court properly admitted evidence of a defendant's prior robbery conviction that occurred less than six years before as impeachment evidence in a trial for attempted second-degree murder. The appellate court noted that the evidence of the robbery conviction helped the jury obtain a better view of the whole person in assessing his truthfulness.[217]

Although subject to many exceptions, Rule 609 generally prohibits the use of evidence of a conviction when the person has been pardoned or the conviction is the subject of annulment or certificate of rehabilitation. In *United States v. McMurrey*, convictions for which the witness had been pardoned to restore rights of citizenship were inadmissible as impeachment evidence even though the pardons were not based on rehabilitation or innocence.[218] However, according to the comments associated with Rule 609, a pardon granted solely for the purpose of restoring the defendant's civil rights lost by virtue of a felony conviction has no relevance where a party desires to inquire into the

[213] Damitz v. State, 2005 Alaska App. LEXIS 26 (2005).
[214] United States v. Conway, 53 Fed. Appx. 872, 876, 877, 2002 U.S. App. LEXIS 26341 (10th Cir. 2002).
[215] United States v. Broadwater, 2003 U.S. App. LEXIS 10873 (7th Cir. 2003).
[216] North Dakota v. Stewart, 2002 N.D. 102, 646 N.W.2d 712, 715, 716, 2002 N.D. LEXIS 140 (2002).
[217] State v. Flores, 2006 Minn. App. Unpub. LEXIS 390 (2006).
[218] United States v. McMurrey, 827 F. Supp. 424 (S.D. Tex. 1993), aff'd, 48 F.3d 149 (1993). *See also* State v. Baker, 956 S.W.2d 8 (Tenn. 1997).

character of the pardoned individual. If the pardon or other proceeding includes a finding of rehabilitation, the result under federal Rule 609, and many state jurisdictions, is to render the conviction inadmissible for impeachment purposes.[219] An alternative policy could allow each party to introduce proof of the conviction and rehabilitation, but this procedure presents challenges with respect to reasons of policy, economy of time, and difficulties of evaluating the pardon and whether rehabilitation has occurred. Due process requires that federal courts give full credit to state pardons.

The examiner, in his or her inquiries about a conviction, generally may not go beyond the name of the crime, the time and place of conviction, and the punishment. Additional details, such as the name of the victim and aggravating circumstances, may not be included in the inquiry. A substantial number of states, while not opening the door to a retrial of the previous conviction, permit the witness to make a brief and general statement of explanation, mitigation, or denial of guilt, and other states recognize the discretion of the trial judge to permit the witness to do so.[220]

§ 9.17 —Prior Inconsistent Statements

Rule 613

Prior Statements of Witnesses

(a) **Examining witness concerning prior statement.** In examining a witness concerning a prior statement made by the witness, whether written or not, the statement need not be shown nor its contents disclosed to the witness at that time, but on request the same shall be shown or disclosed to opposing counsel.

(b) **Extrinsic evidence of prior inconsistent statement of witness.** Extrinsic evidence of a prior inconsistent statement by a witness is not admissible unless the witness is afforded an opportunity to explain or deny the same and the opposite party is afforded an opportunity to interrogate the witness thereon, or the interests of justice otherwise require. This provision does not apply to admissions of a party-opponent as defined in Rule 801(d)(2).[221]

The testimony of a witness may be impeached by showing prior declarations, statements, or testimony from another case that contradict or are inconsistent with the witness's testimony offered at trial. Prior inconsistent statements include written statements actually signed by the maker, statements adopted or approved by a witness or a party-witness, mechanical recordings of

---

[219] FED. R. EVID. 609: History; Ancillary Laws and Directives.
[220] Wittenberg v. United States, 304 F. Supp. 744 (D. Minn. 1969); United States v. Bray, 445 F.2d 178 (5th Cir. 1971).
[221] FED. R. EVID. 613.

statements or their exact transcription, and accurate statements recited in a continuous narrative form.[222] One of the fundamental rules regarding this avenue of impeachment is that the person whom the party seeks to impeach must have uttered the prior inconsistent statement—not another person.[223] Under the Federal Rules, the statement need not be shown to the witness, but on request shall be shown or disclosed to opposing counsel. The witness should be informed of the statements and the conditions, time, place, and circumstances under which they were made. In a 2002 Wyoming case involving the larceny of three horses, a prosecution witness, allied with the defendant, testified that she had no knowledge of the disposition of the animals, when earlier she had told the actual owner of the horses about their sale at auction. The witness was properly impeached when she was informed of the circumstances of her earlier statement and given an opportunity to explain or deny the statements. When she denied making earlier inconsistent statements, the court permitted the state to call the person to whom the inconsistent statement had been addressed to offer the substance of the prior inconsistent statement.[224]

In interpreting a state version of Rule 613 in a prosecution for two counts of rape, the defendant contented that the prosecution failed to notify the defense attorney that the victim once told a police officer that the defendant "did not put anything in her" when her position at trial was that the defendant had completed the rapes.[225] The appellate court reversed the rape convictions because it believed that the impeachment evidence, if offered in court, created a reasonable probability that the result of the trial would have been different if the complaining witness had been impeached with the prior inconsistent statement.

Previous contradictory statements introduced for the purpose of impeachment generally are not admissible as substantive evidence due to their nature as hearsay evidence. Many jurisdictions hold that it is incumbent on the defendant to request a cautionary statement from the judge that the prior inconsistent statement can only be used to evaluate the credibility of that particular witness.[226] However, contradictory statements may become substantive evidence if the witness recants the testimony that he or she gave at trial and admits that his or her prior statements reflect the true facts. Such an admission would make the prior statements a part of the witness's present testimony[227] and the witness would be available for cross-examination. In an exception to the general rule holding that prior inconsistent statements are for impeachment use only, Colorado permits the use of a prior inconsistent statement as substantive proof if the witness, while testifying, "was given an opportunity to explain or deny the statement or is still available to give further testimony in

---

[222] Ohio v. Linder, 2002 Ohio 5077, 2002 Ohio App. LEXIS 5113 (2002).

[223] Colorado v. Trujillo, 49 P.3d 316, 2002 Colo. LEXIS 569 (2002).

[224] Willis v. Wyoming, 2002 Wyo. 79, 46 P.3d 890, 896, 2002 Wyo. LEXIS 81 (2002).

[225] State v. Scheidel, 165 Ohio App. 3d 131; 2006 Ohio 195; 844 N.E.2d 1248; 2006 Ohio App. LEXIS 166 (2006).

[226] Polk v. Indiana, 783 N.E.2d 1253, 1267, 1258, 2003 Ind. App. LEXIS 313 (2003).

[227] Tripp v. United States, 295 F.2d 418 (10th Cir. 1961).

the trial"[228] and the previous inconsistent statement purports to contain information within the witness's personal knowledge.

State courts generally construe their adaptations of the Federal Rules of Evidence with similar reasoning and often follow the logic and jurisprudence advanced by federal court decisions. After stating that the trial court is vested with broad discretion regarding what evidence may be admitted as a prior inconsistent statement for impeachment purposes, a Connecticut appeals court noted that one of the roles of the trial court is to determine whether two statements are inconsistent, including content and considering omission, and whether the prior statement should be admitted.[229]

§ 9.18 —Defects of Recollection or Perception

An effective method of impeaching a witness involves demonstrating to the judge or jury that a witness had a defect in perception, recordation of facts, recollection, narration, or perception concerning matters about which he or she testified. For example, a witness whose hearing or eyesight is impaired may be impeached by calling the impairment to the attention of the jury or judge or by demonstrating it in court. The opposing party may attempt to impeach the witness's testimony by showing that he or she has a poor memory and was unable to recall events of similar importance. The use of contradiction to impeach, while different from prior inconsistent statement as an impeachment tool, involves evidence that shows a different prior witness's testimony may not be accurate due to misperception or an erroneous conclusion derived from observed facts.[230] As in other matters involving impeachment of a witness, the trial judge has a great deal of discretion in determining whether to admit or exclude such evidence[231] and the judge or jury "has the duty to determine the impeachment value of inconsistencies or contradictions as well as testimonial defects of perception, memory, and sincerity."[232]

In determining that the witness's ability to perceive what took place was impaired, evidence may be introduced to show that the witness was under the influence of drugs or alcohol at the time that he or she perceived the events or when he or she testified. However, evidence showing that the witness is a chronic alcoholic, without more evidence to show influence at a specific time, is not admissible on the issue of the witness's credibility.[233]

In attempting to impeach a witness, the party is permitted to test the credibility of that witness by delving into the testimony of the witness to test the

---

[228] COLO. REV. STAT. 16-10-201. Inconsistent statement of witness—competency of evidence (2006).
[229] Connecticut v. Francis D., 75 Conn. App. 1, 17, 18, 815 A.2d 191, 203, 204, 2003 Conn. App. LEXIS 64 (2003).
[230] McCarter v. Commonwealth of Virginia, 38 Va. App 502, 506, 507, 566 S.E.2d 868, 869, 870, 2002 Va. App. LEXIS 393 (2002).
[231] State v. Vigliano, 232 A.2d 129 (N.J. 1969).
[232] Lett v. State, 902 So. 2d 630, 2005 Miss. App. LEXIS 157 (2005).
[233] Wilson v. United States, 232 U.S. 563 (1914).

witness's ability to perceive and to test the ability to remember the facts. However, judges have wide latitude in determining limits in the attempt to impeach a witness to prevent harassment of the witness, prejudice to either party, or confusion of the issues.[234]

§ 9.19 —Use of Confession for Impeachment Purposes

A free and voluntary confession, properly offered, that has been recanted prior to or at trial allows the prosecution to use the earlier confession as an impeachment tool and as substantive evidence as an exception to the hearsay rule.[235] Since the *Miranda v. Arizona* decision in 1966, a body of law has developed concerning the use of improperly taken confessions when offered solely for impeachment purposes. In the *Miranda* case, the Supreme Court of the United States held that when an individual is taken into custody and is not free to leave under circumstances in which police wish to question the person, the police must inform the arrestee that he or she has the right to consult with an attorney and does not have to speak with police about the reason for the arrest.[236] In that decision, the Court indicated that unless such warnings were properly given at the time when custody and the desire to interrogate coexisted, and when proper waiver has been demonstrated by the prosecution at trial, no direct evidence and most derivative evidence obtained as a result of interrogation may be used against the defendant. When a defendant understands the warning and remains silent, that silence cannot be used against him or her at trial because the defendant was merely following the *Miranda* principles by remaining silent.[237] Were the decision otherwise, the defendant would be informed that he has the right of silence, but the reality of the silence would be that the exercise of that right would prove costly if the prosecution could use the fact of silence as a tool against the defendant by asking a testifying police officer about the defendant's silence or mentioning it during a closing argument.

When a defendant in custody made an unwarned confession in violation of *Miranda* and realized the prosecution could not use the confession to prove guilt, the defendant believed he could tell a different story at trial, secure in the knowledge that his prior inconsistent confession would not be admitted.

---

[234] Newton v. Kemna, 354 F.3d 776, 781, 2004 U.S. App. LEXIS 232 (8th Cir. 2004).

[235] A voluntary confession is generally admissible against a defendant, whether as an exception to the hearsay rule or as non-hearsay by definition. Under Federal Rule 801, a voluntary confession or a prior statement by definition is not considered hearsay and will be admitted unless some other legal doctrine calls for exclusion under the circumstances.

[236] Miranda v. Arizona, 384 U.S. 436, 86 S. Ct. 1602, 16 L. Ed. 2d 694 (1966). The Supreme Court reaffirmed the *Miranda* case in 2000 when it ruled that the warnings were required by the constitution and that Congress could not overturn the *Miranda* decision by changing federal law. Dickerson v. United States, 530 U.S. 428, 2000 U.S. LEXIS 4305 (2000).

[237] Doyle v. Ohio, 426 U.S. 610, 96 S. Ct. 2240, 49 L. Ed. 2d 91 (1976).

The prosecution used his earlier unwarned confession to impeach him. However, in upholding the conviction, in *Harris v. United States*, the Supreme Court determined that an extrajudicial confession obtained without properly administering the *Miranda* warnings could be used for impeachment purposes.[238] The Court reasoned that a defendant, having voluntarily taken the stand, has an obligation to speak truthfully and accurately, and the prosecution properly introduced the non-Mirandized confession as impeachment evidence. If the trial court had excluded the unwarned statement, it would have given the defendant immunity from perjury when he told one story to police and a separate untruthful story to the court.

If a confession has been taken in violation of *Miranda* or has been secured from the arrestee by less than free and voluntary means, it may not be used for impeachment purposes or as substantive proof. In *Mincey v. Arizona* (1978) the Supreme Court refused to extend the *Harris* reasoning to a confession obtained in violation of the free and voluntary rule.[239] If a voluntary confession has been obtained without administering the *Miranda* warnings, it may be used only for impeachment purposes when the defendant takes the witness stand and directly contradicts the confession. The evidence will be received not as substantive evidence of guilt, but solely as impeachment evidence. If the statement has been obtained involuntarily, it is inadmissible for any purpose due to doubts concerning its reliability.

While the *Miranda* case excludes unwarned custodial answers to questions, police may not make an end run around the warning requirement. For example, in one case an officer interrogated the suspect without giving any warnings while the subject was in custody. After she confessed to murder, the officer took a break for a short time and returned to give the *Miranda* warnings for the first time. The officer managed to get the subject to confess to murder for a second time. This process violated *Miranda* and the confession, though voluntary by traditional standards, violated the requirement mandated by the original *Miranda* case.[240]

A defendant's post-*Miranda* silence cannot be used to impeach or otherwise call into question his or her assertion of a constitutional right, but the silence must be the exercise of a constitutional right and not a conspiracy of silence among criminals. The concept was followed in case in which one arrestee told a confederate to remain silent when the police attempted to question the confederate. Such speech did not constitute silence and could be admitted against the speaker. Introducing evidence that one defendant tried to silence another defendant does not indicate the exercise of the rights under *Miranda*; instead, it demonstrated the opposite, a desire not to remain silent. The appellate court approved the trial court's admission of evidence that one drug arrestee tried to influence the other to remain silent in the face of police

---

238   Harris v. New York, 401 U.S. 222, 91 S. Ct. 643, 28 L. Ed. 2d 1 (1971); *see also* Oregon v. Hass, 420 U.S. 714, 915 S. Ct. 1215, 43 L. Ed. 2d 570 (1975).

239   Mincey v. Arizona, 437 U.S. 385, 1978 U.S. LEXIS 115 (1978).

240   Missouri v. Seibert, 542 U.S. 600, 2004 U.S. LEXIS 4578 (2004).

attempts at interrogation.[241] In a similar case, a defendant shouted to his wife, as she was being arrested, to "not say anything" to police. The couple had been arrested with a quantity of cocaine and police wanted to interrogate them. The appellate court held that the statement was admissible against the defendant because the husband was not invoking his right to silence; he was talking. Thus, the rule that silence cannot impeach does not apply to cross-examination involving prior inconsistent statements or acts.

The principle that post-arrest, post-*Miranda* silence cannot be used to convict was succinctly stated in a federal case in which the court explained that the prosecutor may not impeach the defendant by showing that his testimony at the trial was inconsistent with his post-arrest, post-*Miranda* silence. However, if the defendant speaks to the government agents after having received the *Miranda* warnings or speaks under circumstances in which *Miranda* warnings were not necessary, the prosecutor may impeach the defendant by pointing out inconsistencies between the story he told the police and the story he told the jury.[242]

Not every instance in which a government witness or prosecutor mentions that a defendant remained silent after being given the *Miranda* warnings will result in the reversal of a conviction. In a child abuse case, police asked some questions of the accused, who was not in custody.[243] During the interview, the accused told police that he wanted to talk to his father before speaking further. The mention of this type of silence did not run afoul of the rule prohibiting comment on silence because the accused was not in custody and was not subject to *Miranda* warnings. However, later in the trial, the prosecutor asked a special agent on the witness stand if the defendant had declined to be interviewed after his arrest and after the *Miranda* warnings had been given. The agent answered in the affirmative. This type of exchange violated the principle that post-arrest, post-*Miranda* evidence of silence cannot be admitted against that defendant. However, in this case, the judge immediately issued a cautionary instruction to the jury, admonished the witness and the prosecutor, and told the jury to disregard the question and answer. The reviewing court held that this use of silence evidence constituted harmless error.

The use of statements and confessions taken properly for impeachment purposes presents no problem when the statement is admitted against the person who uttered it. However, if the statement has been taken in violation of the principles of *Miranda* or has been taken involuntarily, the admission or confession is prohibited from admission to prove guilt. Where the statement was voluntarily offered, even though the *Miranda* warnings should have been offered, the statement may only be used for impeachment purposes when the

---

[241] United States v. Lopez-Lopez, 282 F.3d 1, 2002 U.S. App. LEXIS 2896 (1st Cir. 2002).

[242] United States v. Scott, 47 F.3d 904 (7th Cir. 1995), *cert. denied*, 516 U.S. 857, 116 S. Ct. 162, 133 L. Ed. 2d 104 (1995). *See also* United States v. Toro-Peiaez, 104 F.3d 819 (10th Cir. 1997), in which the court held that a prosecutor's use of a properly Mirandized defendant's post-arrest silence or partial silence for impeachment purposes violates that defendant's privilege against self-incrimination.

[243] United States v. One Star, 2006 U.S. App. LEXIS 25417 (8th Cir. 2006).

defendant gives a contradictory statement during the defense case-in-chief. The fact that a subject exhibited silence before the *Miranda* warnings were necessary is admissible, but after the warnings, the fact of silence should not bring a comment from a government witness or prosecutor because it constitutes error.

§ 9.20 Rehabilitation of Witness

When evidence has been offered to impeach a witness, other evidence that is consistent with the witness's trial testimony may be offered to counteract the effects of the impeaching evidence. For example, in Pennsylvania, a court may permit the introduction of a prior consistent statement of a witness for the purpose of rehabilitation where the statement is being presented to rebut an inference of recent fabrication, improper motive, or faulty memory.[244] For example, when a defendant impeached a prosecution witness with a number of prior inconsistent statements, the trial court permitted the prosecution to play a videotape of one of the defendant's prior statements to police that was consistent with his trial testimony as a method of rehabilitating the prosecution witness.[245] In a federal racketeering prosecution involving a homicide, a prosecution witness had been impeached by allegations that he and a cellmate concocted a story while housed together in jail that was adverse to the defendants. The appellate court approved the trial use of the witness's prior statement, which had been made long before the witness had been housed with his cellmate. Because the prior statement was consistent with the witness's trial testimony, the trial court properly admitted the prior consistent statement as rehabilitation evidence.[246]

In a murder trial in which the defendant's credibility was critical, the defendant had the right to give a full explanation of his prior inconsistent statements, and failure to admit such testimony was reversible error.[247] In this case, the defendant had been prohibited from testifying that he altered his prior statements at the conclusion of the polygraph examination because police authorities had assured him that they believed that he had told the truth when he stated that he did not shoot his wife. Failure to allow the defendant to explain the inconsistencies called into question his credibility and was reversible error.

Rehabilitation may be appropriate when the defendant implies that a prosecution witness has recently fabricated portions of his or her testimony. At a trial involving a potential death sentence for murder and rape, the defense suggested that a statement made by a witness, quoting the defendant as saying, "I'd like to have a piece of that," was untrue and had been recently devised. The prosecution was properly permitted to introduce evidence (as a prior con-

---

244 *See* PA. R. EVID. 613 Prior statements of witnesses (2006).
245 *See* People v. Elie, 2006 Colo. App. LEXIS 1487 (2006).
246 United States v. Rivera, 51 Fed. Appx. 47, 2002 U.S. App. LEXIS 24036 (2d Cir. 2002).
247 Crumpton v. Commonwealth, 384 S.E.2d 339 (Va. Ct. App. 1989).

sistent statement) that the witness had made nearly identical statements to an investigating police officer immediately after the murder occurred.[248]

In some instances, the court may admit evidence of the defendant's reputation for truthfulness as part of the rehabilitation process when there been an attack on the defendant's credibility. For example, a defendant whose evidence had been impeached by the use of witness testimony that contradicted his evidence attempted to introduce evidence of his reputation for truthfulness. Merely contradicting a witness's testimony does not constitute an attack on the credibility of the witness. The Oregon Court of Appeals refused to approve the introduction of evidence of the defendant's character for truthfulness because it had nothing to do with the statements made by prosecution witness that contradicted the defendant's evidence.[249] In another case, the defendant's counsel exposed several inconsistencies between a state trooper's testimony at the trial and statements he made following a shooting. In rebuttal, the state, over the defendant's objection, called two highway patrol officers to testify to the trooper's reputation for honesty. The reviewing court found that the trial court erred in admitting evidence of the trooper's reputation for truthfulness because his character for truthfulness was never attacked.[250] However, in a Nebraska case, the reviewing court indicated that the admission of evidence of a witness's reputation for truthfulness after impeachment because of prior inconsistent statements made by the witness is within the discretion of the trial court.[251]

If evidence indicates that a witness made an out-of-court statement after he testified that he could not recall making any statement, the impeached witness must be given an opportunity to explain the inconsistencies.[252]

In discussing the rule relating to the rehabilitation of a witness, one court explained the rule by stating, "[w]hen a party has attacked a witness' credibility, rehabilitation evidence is admissible."[253] Credibility has been attacked when the defense counsel, during opening arguments, referred to some of the expected government's witnesses as "snitches," "criminals," "masters of manipulation," and informants with an "axe to grind."[254] Rehabilitation of a witness by the use of appropriate evidence may be viewed as according due process to the opposing side with a view to ensuring each party a fundamental opportunity to meet the evidence offered by the other side.

---

[248]   Woodall v. Kentucky, 63 S.W.3d 104, 131, 2001 Ky. LEXIS 142 (2002).

[249]   Oregon v. Dugan, 177 Or. App. 546, 550, 551, 34 P.3d 726, 729, 730, 2001 Or. App. LEXIS 1622 (2001). In this case the defendant did not testify at the trial, but introduced a transcript from his first trial that the court admitted as an exception to the hearsay rule.

[250]   State v. Johnson, 784 P.2d 1135 (Utah 1989).

[251]   State v. King, 197 Neb. 729, 250 N.W.2d 655 (Neb. 1977).

[252]   Johnson v. Garlow, 478 S.E.2d 347 (W. Va. 1996). *See also* State v. Harris, 560 N.W.2d 672 (Minn. 1997).

[253]   United States v. Scott, 267 F.3d 729, 735, 2001 U.S. App. LEXIS 21476 (7th Cir 2001).

[254]   Unites States v. Cano, 289 F.3d 1354, 1366, 2002 U.S. App. LEXIS 8590 (11th Cir. 2002).

§ 9.21 Summary

Although the testimony of witnesses is essential in criminal cases, not all witnesses who have information about the facts of the case are permitted to testify. Moreover, witnesses who are authorized to testify are limited as to the manner and extent of the testimony they may give. The trial judge has a responsibility to apply the rules of evidence in determining whether a witness may testify at all and, if so, the extent of his or her testimony. Usually the trial judge has a great deal of discretion in making this determination and a reviewing court will not reverse a trial judge except on abuse of discretion.

Generally, to be eligible to testify, a witness must have a personal connection with the relevant occurrence, coupled with mental and physical faculties sufficient to observe the events at the time of their occurrence, and must be able to recollect and relate the events to the jury or court in a manner that renders the testimony relevant. Before the witness gives substantive information, he or she is required to state under oath or affirmation that he or she will testify truthfully.

To prevent witnesses from being influenced by the testimony of other witnesses, the judge has the discretion to separate the witnesses during the trial so they are in the courtroom only when called upon to testify and cannot coordinate their testimony with other witnesses. As a general rule, police officers and other government agents are considered officers of the court and are allowed to remain in the courtroom despite the fact that they will be called as witnesses. This is not an absolute rule, however.

After a witness has been sworn, the attorney representing the party calling him or her as a witness will conduct the questioning. This is direct examination of the witness. As a general rule, leading questions are not permitted on direct examination, although there are exceptions. For example, leading introductory questions, such as a witness's address, are allowed, and hostile witnesses may be asked leading questions. In addition, leading questions may be permitted on direct examination in order to correct an obviously erroneous statement, and children of tender years and others who have difficulty expressing themselves may, when necessary, be asked leading questions on direct examination.

Although it is preferable for witnesses to testify from memory in all situations, it is clear that witnesses do not always remember the facts after a substantial period of time has passed. Recognizing this human limitation, witnesses are allowed in some instances and under very controlled conditions to refresh their memories by referring to written statements. This is known as refreshing memory or, in some courts, "present memory revived."

When the witness has no present recollection of the events or has a deficient memory that does not allow the witness to testify properly and fully concerning what occurred at the time, and the information has been preserved, the writing may be admissible. Where the witness remembers that he or she recorded the facts concerning the action, the writing or memorandum of past recollection is admitted when the proponent has laid a proper foundation.

The right of cross-examination has for years been considered a constitutional right coexistent with the right of confrontation. The purpose of cross-examination is to give the opposing party an opportunity to challenge the credibility of statements given by the witness on direct examination. With some exceptions, cross-examination of the witness is limited to the scope of matters brought out on direct examination. On rare occasions, especially in cases involving sex offenses and small children, direct confrontation may be curtailed as long as the overall right of confrontation and its purposes have been met.

After a witness has been cross-examined, the party calling him or her may ask questions on redirect examination to explain matters brought out on cross-examination. Following this, the opposing party may then ask questions on recross-examination, but such questions are limited to new matters brought out on redirect examination.

Impeachment is the process of attempting to diminish the credibility of a witness by convincing the jury or court that the testimony may not be truthful or is unreliable. Common techniques in the impeachment process are to show bias, interest, or prejudice on the part of the witness, to introduce evidence of conviction of certain crimes, and to introduce evidence of prior inconsistent statements. In some instances, a confession may be used for impeachment purposes even though the *Miranda* warnings were not administered. However, if a confession was not made freely and voluntarily, it will not be admitted even for impeachment purposes due to questions concerning the truthfulness of the confession.

An impeached witness may be rehabilitated and evidence may be admitted to contradict the impeaching testimony.

Those involved in the criminal justice process are often confused and disappointed when they are not allowed to testify about what they think is pertinent, but the rules of evidence have created methods of achieving fundamental fairness while accommodating socially important goals. If the rules of evidence are fully understood and if justice personnel are familiar with the reasons for limiting the use of evidence, they will be more confident and better prepared for giving testimony.

Privileges 10

For more than three centuries it has now been recognized as a fundamental maxim that the public . . . has a right to every man's evidence. When we come to examine the various claims of exemption, we start with the primary assumption that there is a general duty to give what testimony one is capable of giving, and that any exemptions which may exist are distinctly exceptional, being so many derogations from a positive general rule.

United States v. Bryan, 339 U.S. 323, 331 (1950)
(quoting 8 J. WIGMORE, EVIDENCE § 2192)

Chapter Outline

Key Terms and Concepts

assertion and waiver (of privilege)	privileged communications
duration (of privilege)	scope (of privilege)
exception	

§ 10.1 Introduction

Rule 501

General Rule

Except as otherwise required by the Constitution of the United States or provided by Act of Congress or in rules prescribed by the Supreme Court pursuant to statutory authority, the privilege of a witness, person, government, State, or political subdivision thereof shall be governed by the principles of the common law as they may be interpreted by the courts of the United States in the light of reason and experience. However, in civil actions and proceedings, with respect to an element of a claim or defense as to which State law supplies the rule of decision, the privilege of a witness, person, government, State, or political subdivision thereof shall be determined in accordance with State law.[1]

Although the admission of all relevant evidence would help to discover the truth and uncover falsity, courts exclude some relevant evidence for social policy reasons. The inevitable result may obscure the truth and occasionally result in a different party prevailing than the party that would have prevailed had all the relevant evidence been admitted. The reasons for privileges that exclude evidence come from state and federal legislatures, state and federal constitutional provisions, and court decisions interpreting the common law. In many cases, courts refuse to admit otherwise relevant evidence due to the operation of legal privileges that have developed to protect and foster particularly important relationships, interests, and rights. According to the Supreme Court, "[t]he lawyer-client privilege rests on the need for the advocate and counselor

---

[1] FED. R. EVID. 501.

to know all that relates to the client's reasons for seeking representation if the professional mission is to be carried out."[2] The rule that protects the rights of persons in certain relationships to refuse to give information acquired as the result of the relationship and to refuse to disclose the identity of an informant in some instances is known in law as the testimonial privilege rule, or the privileged communications rule. However, most privileges come from a legislative enactment or have developed through case law. For example, there is no privilege under the First Amendment that would allow journalists to refuse to identify sources or that would permit a news reporter to refuse to divulge information given in confidence by a source.[3]

In most instances in which the law recognizes a privilege, one person has communicated information to another person that was intended to be kept confidential by both parties and the privilege not to disclose generally serves an important social interest. For example, where a penitent confesses to a priest or rabbi as part of religious faith and practice and the information was intended to be kept private, society allows this confidentiality because it recognizes the benefit to society of religious teachings and practices. A society hostile to religion would reject this confidence and order the information to be disclosed in a court proceeding. Similarly, police are often permitted to decline a defense request to reveal the identity of secret informants. Society values the informant who is willing to assist law enforcement and, as an encouragement, permits the identity to remain secret to protect the informant and to encourage additional assistance in the future. In both of these examples, it is believed that the balance of benefits to society is on the positive side of the ledger and that to refuse to recognize such a privilege would not serve society as well.

The privileged communications rule includes information beyond items gathered from informant sources and may cover the identity of the person who gave the privileged information. It can be more accurately stated that there are really three categories of privileges: (1) those that protect privileged communications resulting from relationships, such as husband-wife and attorney-client; and (2) those relating to disclosing the identity of persons who made the communications, such as not revealing the identity of an informant, and (3) those that permit a defendant to not give the prosecutor constitutionally protected information and allows governments to keep from divulging secrets that are deemed essential or otherwise confidential. The privilege that exists between spouses actually involves two distinct privileges: one covering confidential communications[4] made to each other during the marriage and the other involving a privilege of the potential witness spouse not to testify against the

---

[2]   Trammel v. United States, 445 U.S. 40, 51 (1980).

[3]   Atlanta Journal-Constitution v. Jewell, 251 Ga. App. 808, 810, 555 S.E.2d 175, 179, 2001 Ga. App. LEXIS 1153 (2001).

[4]   Communication includes speech and, in some jurisdictions, it includes conduct that one spouse performs in full view of the other while relying on the confidentiality of the relationship. When a husband killed a man in full view of his wife, the acts were not deemed to constitute confidential communication. *See* Roland v. State, 882 So. 2d 262, 265, 2004 Miss. App. LEXIS 911 (2004).

other during the duration of the marriage. The second category permits the peace officer and the prosecutor to refuse to divulge the name of an informant and, in some jurisdictions, may allow news reporters the privilege of not revealing the identity of their confidential information sources.[5]

The rules regarding privileges have evolved over a long period through case law and legislative enactments.[6] Concern with privileges and their effects have energized critics who have been both numerous and vocal. Some authorities argue that the reasons for excluding valuable testimony because of these privilege rules are no longer valid and should be abandoned, or at least modified. As the late Chief Justice Burger once observed, "Whatever their origin these exceptions to the demand for everyman's evidence are not lightly created nor expansively construed, for they are in derogation of the search for truth."[7] Those who oppose the use of the privilege argue that prohibiting the use of some evidence because of certain relationships alters the normal mode of proof in a trial by denying the trier of fact some of the information that he or she otherwise would have been able to present to the court. These arguments have had some influence on judicial behavior and because these rules are either in derogation of the common law or are statutory enactments, there is a tendency on the part of the courts to construe the rules narrowly.[8] Courts are reluctant to expand the particular privileges to relationships other than those already covered by constitutions, common law, or existing statutes.[9]

The general rule that holds that privileges should be narrowly construed[10] seems to be based on the fact that the use of privileges artificially restricts the admission of evidence while frequently frustrating the search for the truth. However, a contrary view[11] exists that indicates that statutes creating privileges should be liberally construed because they have been founded on principles that represent prevailing public policy. In a North Dakota case, the trial court held that privilege rules should be narrowly construed because they are by nature in derogation of the search for the truth.[12] In a California case in which the prosecution wanted a wife, estranged for 17 years, to testify against her husband, the court narrowly construed the law consistent with the intent of the legislature and allowed her to refuse to testify against her husband in a

---

[5]   Persky v. Yeshiva University, 2002 U.S. Dist. LEXIS 23740 (S.D.N.Y. 2002) *and see* United States v. Hively, 202 F. Supp. 886, 889, 890 (E.D. Ark. 2002) for a brief discussion of the news reporters' privilege in federal courts.

[6]   For example, *see* 10 D EL. C ODE § 4322 (2006), which allows reporters to refuse to reveal source identities and to decline to testify concerning the substantive content of the information derived from the confidential source. The Act requires courts to balance the public's interest in having the reporter's testimony presented in a particular case against the public's interest in keeping the reporter's confidences.

[7]   United States v. Nixon, 418 U.S. 683, 94 S. Ct. 3090, 41 L. Ed. 2d 1039 (1974).

[8]   *See* Cavallaro v. United States, 153 F. Supp. 2d 52, 58, 2001 U.S. Dist. LEXIS 11232 (D. Mass. 2001).

[9]   Rudh v. Rudh, 517 N.W.2d 632 (N.D. 1994). This case held that the rules of privilege are narrowly construed because they derogate the search for the truth. *See also* State v. Szemple, 135 N.J. 406, 640 A.2d 817 (1994), which held that, as a general proposition, privileges are to be narrowly construed.

[10]   State v. Clark, 570 N.W.2d 195 (N.D. 1997).

[11]   State v. Anderson, 636 N.W.2d 26, 35, 2001 Iowa Sup. LEXIS 217 (2001).

[12]   State v. Clark, 570 N.W.2d 195 (N.D. 1997).

double homicide case.[13] As the court stated, "privileges and their exceptions are statutory creations which cannot be altered by judicial interpretation."[14] A Washington court held that a conversation between a woman and her social agency counselor could be divulged by the counselor to the court when the substance of the counseling involved the woman's admissions of child neglect. Washington had a counselor-patient privilege, but that privilege did not survive when the court looked at the exceptions contained in another part of the Washington code.[15] In a Pennsylvania case, the court refused to recognize the privilege when a rape victim made statements to a counseling agency.[16]

Under the common law, there was no accountant-client privilege, so where such a privilege exists, it does so based on statutory enactments. Similarly, there is not an accountant-client privilege under federal law,[17] except for the limited privilege granted under the Internal Revenue Code.[18] States that have an accountant-client privilege generally follow a statutory framework that allows a public accountant to refuse to divulge information in court that has been obtained by virtue of the employment relationship. Because statutory privileges are narrowly construed, the accountant-client privilege dictates that to be considered confidential and covered by a privilege, the communication must arise from actual accounting services and not have been generated from consulting or other related activities.[19]

The United States Supreme Court, when drafting the Rules of Evidence for Federal Courts and Magistrates in 1972, included comprehensive rules relating to privileges. The draft included guidelines relating to traditional privileges, such as the lawyer-client privilege, husband-wife privilege, and communications to clergy. In addition, these guidelines set limits on the use of evidence regarding the political vote, trade secrets, identity of informers, and state secrets.[20] When the draft of the Federal Rules of Evidence reached Congress, it ran into legislative opposition, with the result that Congress scrapped the proposed rules covering privileges and enacted Rule 501 in place of the proposed rules covering privileges. Congress determined that the federal case law respecting privileges was not to be frozen by detailed federal rules, but allowed to develop on a case-by-case basis. As a result, Congress never enacted the proposed comprehensive codifications and only a general provision regarding privileges remained in the version that was finally adopted by both houses of Congress.[21]

---

[13]   Jurcoane v. Superior Court, 93 Cal. App. 4th 886, 895, 896, 113 Cal. Rptr. 2d 483, 490, 2001 Cal. App. LEXIS 1562 (2001).

[14]   *Id.*

[15]   Hamilton v. Department of Social and Health Services, 109 Wash. App 718, 730, 37 P.3d 1227, 1233, 2001 Wash. App. LEXIS 2810 (2001).

[16]   In re Pittsburgh Action Against Rape, 494 Pa. 15, 428 A.2d 126 (1981).

[17]   United States v. Bisanti, 414 F.3d 168, 170, 2005 U.S. App. LEXIS 13575 (1st Cir. 2005).

[18]   *See* 26 U.S.C. § 7525, Confidentiality privileges relating to taxpayer communications.

[19]   PepsiCo, Inc. v. Baird, Kurtz & Dobson LLp, 305 F. 3d 813, 815, 2002 U.S. App. LEXIS 192 (8th Cir. 2002).

[20]   MOORE'S RULES PAMPHLET, Federal Rules of Evidence, as effective July 1, 1975.

[21]   Trammel v. United States, 445 U.S. 40, 47, 1980 U.S. LEXIS 84 (1980). *See* case in Part II, Cases Relating to Chapter 2.

Notwithstanding the fact that Congress rejected the draft prepared by the Supreme Court and deleted the articles relating to privileges, the definitions and requirements developed in the document are well worth studying. Some of these definitions are used in this chapter.

In the sections that follow, the relationships recognized by law in which the exchange of confidential information is encouraged are discussed first. These relationships include: (1) attorney-client, (2) physician-patient, (3) husband-wife and (4) communications to clergy. A later section examines the law relating to privileges that protect the identity of informants and the news media-informant privilege.

§ 10.2   Reasons for Privileged Communications

The theoretical basis for privileges involving communication reflects concern for the protection of important personal relationships and the recognition of significant other legal rights and social interests that may be at stake. When the protection and importance of these relationships philosophically outweigh the need for the evidence, courts tend to uphold the privilege and exclude the evidence to protect perceived higher social values. Few privileges were recognized at common law, but a number of privileges have been created by statutory enactment. In general, a statute conferring a privilege should be strictly and narrowly construed,[22] a view recently cited with approval by the United States Supreme Court.[23]

The rationale for the privileged communication rules is that when people occupy certain confidential relations, the law, on public policy grounds, will not compel, or in some instances even allow, one of them to violate the confidence reposed in him or her by the other. This rule of privileged communications is not a rule of substantive law, but rather a rule of evidence that does not affect the general competency of a witness but merely renders him or her incompetent to testify about particular matters covered by the privilege.

In explaining the application of the privilege rules, one court noted that paramount in deciding whether to recognize an evidentiary privilege is weighing the need for truth against the importance of the relationship or policy sought to be furthered by the privilege, and the likelihood that recognition of the privilege will in fact protect that relationship in the factual setting of the case.[24]

Traditionally, the courts recognize and protect the following relationships: (1) husband-wife, (2) attorney-client, (3) physician-patient, and (4) clergy-penitent. Some jurisdictions by statute recognize confidential communication privileges involving counselor-client, accountant-client, psychologist-client,

---

[22]   See Mims v. Wright, 578 S.E.2d 606 (N.C. 2003), strictly construing doctor-patient privilege; see Perras v. Allstate Ins. Co. 2002 Conn. Super. LEXIS 3128 (2002), strict application of the attorney-client privilege.

[23]   Pierce County v. Guillen, 537 U.S. 129, 123 S. Ct. 720, 730, 154 L. Ed. 2d 610, 625, 626, 2003 U.S. LEXIS 747 (2003).

[24]   In re August, 1993, Regular Grand Jury, 854 F. Supp. 1403 (S.D. Ind. 1994).

and news reporter-source. In each instance there are specific rules regarding the scope of the privilege, who is considered a "holder" of the privilege, who is eligible to claim the privilege, and when, how, and in what context the privilege may be asserted. There are also some general requirements that apply in all instances. First, the exchange must be between two people whose relationship is recognized by law. Second, the communication must have been exchanged because of the confidential nature of the relationship. Third, the communication must be such that the interests of society will be benefited to a greater degree than the opposing party by keeping information secret rather than by revealing it.

A communication is not privileged merely because either party or all parties regard it as confidential. A confidential relationship that is recognized by the courts or by statute must exist and a communication intended to remain confidential must have occurred between the proper parties.

One other general principle is that when a third party who was not a member of the privileged relationship overhears the privileged communication, whether by accident or design, that person in most cases may testify about the substance of the communication. However, some jurisdictions allow the communication to remain privileged when the two parties reasonably believed that their communication was not likely to be heard by an eavesdropper.

In the sections that follow, the specific rules that apply to the respective privileged communications are explored.

§ 10.3 Communications Between Husband and Wife

Protection of confidential communications between spouses has origins in the common law and is based on considerations of public policy and the need to preserve peace and harmony, and to foster confidentiality in marital relationships.[25] As an early Supreme Court case noted:

> This rule is founded upon the deepest and soundest principles of our nature. Principles which have grown out of those domestic relations, that constitute the basis of civil society, and which are essential to the enjoyment of that confidence which should subsist between those who are connected by the nearest and dearest relations of life. To break down or impair the great principles which protect the sanctities of husband and wife, would be to destroy the best solace of human existence.[26]

Common law rules that become obsolete in practice or for which a questionable basis emerges, are subject to judicial revision or rejection. For example, in the case of *Funk v. United States*,[27] the United States Supreme Court

---

[25]   Commonwealth of Pennsylvania v. Spetzer, 813 A.2d 707, 718, 2002 Pa. LEXIS 3116 (2002).

[26]   Stein v. Bowman, 38 U.S. (13 Pet.) 209, 223, 10 L. Ed. 129 (1839).

[27]   290 U.S. 371, 54 S. Ct. 212, 78 L. Ed. 369 (1933). *See* case in Part II, in Cases Relating to Chapter 1.

stated that a rule of evidence thought necessary at one time should yield to the experience of a succeeding generation whenever experience has clearly demonstrated the fallacy of the proposition or where changed circumstances suggest an invalidation of the old rule. At no place is this more evident than in the law relating to the husband-wife testimonial privilege. In a 1980 case,[28] *Trammel v. United States,* the Supreme Court set aside rules for federal courts that had been established in the 1958 case of *Hawkins v. United States.*[29] As a result of *Trammel* and its influence on state jurisprudence, it is necessary to approach the husband-wife privilege from two perspectives.

A. *Statement of the Rules*

Rule 1. Information privately disclosed between husband and wife while relying on the confidence of the marital relationship is privileged.[30] This rule is followed in both federal and state courts and was not changed by the decision in *Trammel,* which applied only to federal courts.

Rule 2. A witness spouse cannot testify against a defendant spouse regarding any acts observed or regarding any nonconfidential communication that occurred before or during the marriage unless both spouses agree. Under this theory, both spouses hold the marital testimonial privilege and may assert it to prevent the witness spouse from giving testimony. This rule was established for federal courts in *Hawkins v. United States,*[31] but the *Trammel* case had the effect of reversing the *Hawkins* decision and viewed only the witness spouse as being a holder of the privilege with the right to refuse to testify against a defendant spouse.[32] The *Hawkins* rule is still followed in some states.[33]

B. *Scope of the Privilege*

At common law, neither spouse possessed competency as a witness to give testimony, either for or against the other. This rule was based on the premise that husband and wife were one, and at common law, where one was a party to a suit, whether civil or criminal, the other was not permitted to be a witness. This restrictive rule was gradually abolished by court decisions and statutes, and it was replaced by the rule that a spouse may testify for the other in a criminal proceeding, but in some instances a spouse may not testify against the other if either spouse objects.

The *Trammel* case involved a husband who had been indicted on federal drug charges while his wife had been named in the indictment as an unindicted conspirator. The trial court ruled that confidential communications between Mr. Trammel and his wife were privileged and therefore inadmissible, but the wife was permitted to testify to any act she observed before or during the marriage

---

[28] Trammel v. United States, 445 U.S. 40, 100 S. Ct. 906, 63 L. Ed. 2d 145 (1980).
[29] Hawkins v. United States, 358 U.S. 74, 79 S. Ct. 136, 3 L. Ed. 2d 125 (1958).
[30] Blau v. United States, 340 U.S. 332, 71 S. Ct. 301, 95 L. Ed. 306 (1950).
[31] Hawkins v. United States, *supra* note 29.
[32] *See* the footnotes by the court in the *Trammel* case cited *supra* note 28.
[33] For example, *see* MINN. STAT. § 595.02 (2002).

and to any communication made in the presence of a third person. The Court in *Trammel* referred to studies which revealed that in 1958, when *Hawkins* was decided, 31 states allowed a defendant the privilege of preventing adverse spousal testimony, but the Court indicated that the number had declined to 24 in 1980. The Court then said, "Here we must decide whether the privilege against adverse spousal testimony promotes sufficiently important interests to outweigh the need for probative evidence in the administration of criminal justice."[34] With respect to nonconfidential communications within a marriage, the Supreme Court decided "that the existing rule should be modified so that in federal courts, the witness-spouse alone has a privilege to refuse to testify adversely; the witness may be neither compelled to testify nor foreclosed from testifying. This modification—vesting the privilege in the witness-spouse—furthers the important public interest in marital harmony without unduly burdening legitimate law enforcement needs."[35] *Trammel* affected only federal courts.

Prior to *Trammel*, in the case of *Blau v. United States*,[36] the Supreme Court reaffirmed the rule that confidential communications between husband and wife are privileged. The *Trammel* Court noted that the *Trammel* case did not change the *Blau* recognition of the marital confidential communication privilege in federal courts.[37] This meant that neither spouse could be required to testify concerning these communications, nor would the other be permitted to testify if the other objected. This case did not decide, however, the issue of whether the spouse may be permitted to testify to an act observed before or during the marriage, nor did it settle the issue of communications made in the presence of a third party. The lower court in *Trammel* agreed that confidential communications between husband and wife were privileged and therefore inadmissible, but the privilege permitted the wife to testify about any acts that she observed before and during the marriage, and about any communications made in the presence of a third person.

After discussing the arguments for and against permitting a spouse to testify about criminal acts observed during a marriage or non-confidential communications, the Court concluded:

> Accordingly, we conclude that the existing rule should be modified so that the witness spouse alone has the privilege to refuse to testify adversely: the witness may be neither compelled to testify nor foreclosed from testifying. This modification—vesting the privilege in the witness spouse—furthers the important public interest in marital harmony without unduly burdening legitimate law enforcement needs.[38]

---

[34]   Trammel v. United States, *supra* note 28.

[35]   *Id.*

[36]   Blau v. United States, *supra* note 30.

[37]   *See* Trammel v. United States, note 5 of the Court's decision.

[38]   Trammel v. United States, *supra* note 28. *See also* United States v. Ramos-Osequera, 120 F.3d 1028 (9th Cir. 1997), in which the court held that the federal common law recognizes two different marital privileges: one bars testimony concerning statements privately and confidentially communicated between spouses and may be invoked by the testifying or non-testifying spouse; and the other permits a person to refuse to testify against his or her spouse about anything.

In some jurisdictions, written communications between spouses[39] and physical acts done in full view of the spouse may constitute confidential communications from which a testimonial privilege may arise. Private communications between spouses does not always occur behind closed doors and may be made openly when other persons are not able to hear or observe. In a murder prosecution, the trial court admitted conversations between the witness spouse and the defendant spouse in which the defendant spouse made incriminating confidential statements to the wife. In reversing the conviction, the Supreme Court of Kentucky noted that some of the conversations were completely private, one occurring in a hay barn away from other people. The court held that the trial court should not have allowed the wife to testify concerning those private conversations. The court also questioned the trial court ruling that permitted the testimony of the wife concerning her feeling a gun when she hugged her husband, because that communication could be considered conduct as well as privileged communication.[40]

To summarize, the general rule in both state and federal courts is that information privately disclosed between husband and wife in reliance on the confidential nature of the marital relationship is protected from disclosure. In most jurisdictions, the "marital communications privilege protects confidential communications made between spouses while they are married and it survives the marriage."[41] Federal courts recognize two separate marital privileges: the marital confidential communications privilege and the adverse marital testimonial privilege.[42] In federal courts and some state courts, the witness-spouse alone has the privilege to testify or refuse to testify adversely regarding criminal acts observed and nonconfidential communications occurring during the marriage. In other states, where the rule has not been changed by statute or court decision, an accused may object not only to a spouse testifying about confidential communications, but also to that spouse's testimony about any act observed before or during the marriage. However, with respect to the marital confidential communication privilege, generally both spouses are holders of this privilege and each may assert it independently of the other.

The part of the marital confidential communication privilege that concerns confidential communications during the marriage has periodically come under scrutiny. It has been argued that if the marriage is in "utter shambles," the force behind the rule no longer exists, and the spouse should be required to testify. In a federal prosecution on three counts of making false statements to a federally insured financial institution, the defendant contended that the trial court erred in allowing her estranged husband to testify concerning documents and conversations indicating falsity that he had acquired while visiting the former marital residence. During the visit, the estranged husband

[39]   United States v. Montgomery, 384 F. 3d 1050, 1056, 2004 U. S. App. LEXIS 19322 (2004).

[40]   St. Clair v. Commonwealth, 174 S.W. 2d 474, 480, 2005 Ky. LEXIS 334 (2005). *See* case in Part II.

[41]   Arizona v. Harrod, 200 Ariz. 309, 315, 26 P.3d 492, 498, 2001 Ariz. LEXIS 104 (2001), *cert. granted*, 536 U.S. 953, 122 S. Ct. 2653, 153 L. Ed. 2d 830, 2002 U.S. LEXIS 4892 (2002), remanded for resentencing, 65 P.3d 948, 2003 Ariz. LEXIS 31 (2003).

[42]   United States v. Espino, 317 F.3d 788, 795, 2003 U.S. App. LEXIS 261 (8th Cir. 2003).

searched for papers related to his prior divorce from another woman, and inadvertently stumbled upon documents indicating that his wife had filed the materially false loan applications for which she was eventually convicted. After the husband observed the incriminating documents, he took his information to federal authorities and agreed to wear a concealed recording device to record any incriminating statements his wife might make. At an arranged meeting, the wife made several statements to the husband that indicated her consciousness of guilt in making the false statements. Over the objection of the wife, who alleged a violation of the marital confidential communication privilege, the trial court allowed the husband to testify to confidential matters he learned while in the wife's home and from meeting with her. The trial court held that the marital communication privilege should not be applied to communications made while the spouses, while still technically married, were living separate lives with no reasonable expectation of reconciliation or reunification as a happily married couple.[43]

However, current Arizona law holds that neither a husband nor a wife can testify for or against the other without the consent of the other spouse. This applies during the marriage, as well as afterward, concerning events occurring during and any communication made by one spouse to the other during the marriage. Naturally these prohibitions against testimony do not apply in a criminal action or proceeding for a crime committed by one spouse against the other or against intimate family members or crimes like non-support or civil proceedings involving the marriage.[44] Arizona courts have interpreted the statute to forbid any testimony by a spouse concerning any communication between them that occurred during the marriage, whether the marriage is intact at the time of the testimony or not, unless the other spouse gives consent to the testimony.[45] However, Arizona courts do not hold that the communication privilege protects nonconfidential communications or noncommunicative acts done when the other spouse may be in a position to observe. In one Arizona case involving a conspiracy to commit murder, the wife was properly permitted to testify about conduct of the defendant observed during the marriage when the acts were not intended as confidential communicative activities.[46] While the principle that the marital confidential communication privilege should not apply if a marriage is in utter shambles is probably still a minority view, the trend appears to be in that direction, especially in the federal courts.

An essential prerequisite for the assertion of the marital communication privilege is the existence of a valid marriage.[47] People who cohabitate and who do not qualify for common law marriage status or who are of the same gender

---

43   United States v. Singleton, 260 F.3d 1295, 1297, 1298, 2001 U.S. App. LEXIS 17694 (11th Cir. 2001).

44   ARIZ. REV. STAT. § 13-4062 (2006).

45   State ex rel. Woods v. Cohen, 173 Ariz. 497, 501, 502, 844 P.2d 1147, 1151, 1152, 1992 Ariz. LEXIS 104 (1992).

46   Arizona v. Harrod, 200 Ariz. 309, 26 P.3d 492, 498, 499, 2001 Ariz. LEXIS 104 (2001).

47   People v. Badgett, 30 Cal. Rptr. 2d 152 (1994).

are generally not considered married and cannot assert marital privileges.[48] The marriage is considered valid if there has been a formal ceremony as recognized by a state and the marriage has not been dissolved. If a couple or one member of a couple contends that the two have matured a common law marriage, the marriage must have been initiated in a state that recognized common law marriages and the burden to prove the existence of the marriage rests with the person making the allegation of marriage.[49] In the states that permit common law marriages to come into existence, certain requirements must be met. If those requirements are followed and the common law marriage is recognized in that state, a defendant in a criminal case could invoke either the marital communication privilege or the marital testimonial privilege in that state or any other.

In the absence of proof of a common law or formal marriage, no marital privilege attaches to any communication between a particular man and woman. When a valid common law marriage exists, other states are generally bound to recognize the marriage and treat it as equal to a marriage contracted in a traditional ceremony. For example, in Texas, where common law marriages are recognized, there was a common law marriage between the defendant and the witness, and the defendant could invoke the marital communication privilege.[50] The court decided that because the defendant and witness had lived together in Texas and held themselves out to the public as a married couple, and as the witness testified that she and the defendant agreed to live together as husband and wife and indicated on an employment application and tax records that she was married, and because the defendant and witness exchanged wedding rings, this was sufficient indication of a common law marriage and the defendant could invoke the marital communication privilege.

In another case, however, the common law relationship did not exist between the defendant and his girlfriend at the time the defendant made inculpatory statements regarding the murder of his wife, and there was no evidence that the defendant had divorced his wife or that his wife was dead.[51] Courts generally are under no obligation to inform a possible common law wife that she has a privilege not to testify because once a spouse takes the stand and offers testimony, the presumption arises that she has waived any marital privilege that she may have possessed.[52] One court refused to recognize a purported marriage because the "wife" of the defendant was still married to her first husband and could not be legally married to the defendant. The court held that there was no marital privilege of any type because there was nothing but a bigamous "marriage," which did not qualify as a legitimate marriage.[53]

---

[48]   *See* A.L.R.4th 422 (2006).
[49]   Perrotti v. Meredith, 2005 PA Super 57, 868 A.2d 1240, 1243, 2005 Pa. Super. LEXIS 148 (2005).
[50]   People v. Badgett, 30 Cal. Rptr. 2d 152 (1994).
[51]   Duran v. State, 881 S.W.2d 569 (Tex. 1994).
[52]   Smith v. Georgia, 254 Ga. App. 107, 108, 561 S.E.2d 232, 233, 2002 Ga. App. LEXIS 274 (2002).
[53]   Arboleda v. Newland, Warden, 2003 U.S. Dist. LEXIS 513 (N.D. Cal. 2003).

In a 1997 case, the court held that, despite the fact that a couple claimed that they were legally married, the spousal communication privilege protecting confidential communications between husband and wife during the marriage did not extend to homosexuals in "spousal relationships."[54] This type of limitation on privileges of married couples may be affected by the Supreme Court's decision in *Lawrence v. Texas*, in which laws regulating private sexual activity between persons of the same sex were ruled to be unconstitutional.[55] Spousal privileges or some similar legal theory may eventually be statutorily devised or created by case law that protects same-gender relationships, although the early litigation seems to indicate that extension of this type of privilege may be a long way into the future.[56]

C. Exceptions

1. The privilege is generally limited to confidential communications

The marital privilege protects information privately disclosed between husband and wife that at the time was intended to be a confidential communication and can generally be asserted by either spouse.[57] Where no other people are able to hear a communication between spouses, the husband-wife confidential communication privilege should be recognized. In an Arkansas case, the husband and wife were in a car when the husband shot at people in a nearby car. While he paused, the wife asked him what he was doing and he told her that he was reloading to kill another person. The appellate court noted that the trial court committed error when it permitted the defendant's wife to testify concerning their roadside conversation. The court determined that a valid marital privilege existed that should have prevented the admission of the wife's testimony about his intent because the street discussion occurred in reliance on the confidential nature of their marital relationship.[58] The presence of unnecessary third parties prevents confidential communication between spouses, such as where a prisoner sends a letter to his wife.[59] One court admitted an incriminating message left by a defendant for his wife on an answering machine. Because the answering machine was not in the exclusive control of the wife and other people shared the machine, no confidential communication existed.[60] If other persons are present at the time of the communication, including immediate family members or children, no confidential communi-

---

54 Greenwald v. H & P 29th Street Associates, 659 N.Y.S.2d 473 (N.Y. 1997). A*nd see* Hernandez v. Robles, 2005 N.Y. Slip Op. 9436, 805 N.Y.S.2d 354, 2005 N.Y. App. Div. LEXIS 13892 (2005) determining that same-sex individuals were not eligible in New York to obtain marriage licenses.

55 *See* Lawrence v. Texas, 539 U.S. 558, 2003 U.S. LEXIS 5013 (2003).

56 *See* Wilson v. Ake, 354 F. Supp. 2d 1298; 2005 U.S. Dist. LEXIS 755 (2005) and Li v. State, 338 Or. 376, 110 P.3d 91, 2005 Or. LEXIS 490 (2004).

57 United States v. Montgomery, 384 F. 3d 1050, 1057, 2004 U.S. App. LEXIS 19322 (2004). The court noted (n.1) that 33 states and the District of Columbia allow either spouse to assert the confidential communication privilege.

58 Walker v. State, 2005 Ark. App. LEXIS 471 (2005).

59 United States v. Griffin, 440 F.3d 1138, 2006 U.S. App. LEXIS 6393 (9th. Cir. 2006).

60 Wong-Wing v. State, 156 Md. App. 597, 847 A.2d 1206, 2004 Md. App. LEXIS 65 (2004).

cation occurs if the children are old enough to comprehend what the spouses are communicating. In a West Virginia case, the defendant's conversation with his wife in an automobile where their eight-month-old infant was present remained covered by the marital confidential communication privilege because the child was not a comprehending party. Even if the wife later told another person, the confidence of the communication remained and was not waived by her conduct.[61]

2. Communications overheard by third parties or made to third parties

Another exception to the marital privilege, concerns the testimony of a third party who was in a position to overhear communications between spouses. As a general rule, when a third party has overheard the conversation between the husband and wife, that person may testify about the communication, even where the spouses hoped that the conversation was private.[62] The reasoning for this is that the justification for the privilege rule does not exist completely under the circumstances. Another rationale for this exception is that by failing to take precautions to prevent others from hearing, the spouses are deemed to have waived the right to secrecy.[63] However, according to the Supreme Court of Mississippi and courts in other states, when a spouse who received or made a confidential communication to the other spouse communicates the message to a third party at a later time, the confidence may remain and the third party may not testify concerning the substance of the original confidential communication.[64]

In determining whether the marital confidential communication privilege should be recognized in a particular case, courts generally consider several factors that support the basis of the privilege. Some states that recognize this privilege apply it whenever it the facts meet the standards, while other states use a balancing test and do not always recognize the privilege. For example, under Tennessee law, before communications between husband and wife may be recognized as privileged in a criminal proceeding, a court must conduct an evaluation of the following statutory factors: "(A) the communications must originate in a confidence that they will not be disclosed; (B) the element of confidentiality is essential to the full and satisfactory maintenance of the relationship between the parties; (C) the relationship must be one which, in the opinion of the community, ought to be sedulously [diligently] fostered; and (D) the injury to the relation by disclosure of the communications outweighs the benefit gained for the correct disposal of litigation."[65] A given requirement

---

[61] West Virginia v. Bohon, 211 W. Va. 277, 279, 565 S.E.2d 399, 401, 2002 W. Va. LEXIS 51 (2002).

[62] United States v. Espino, 317 F.3d 788, 795, 796, 2003 U.S. App. LEXIS 261 (8th Cir. 2002).

[63] People v. Melski, 10 N.Y.2d 78, 176 N.E.2d 81 (1961); *see* People v. Gomez, 134 Cal. App. 3d 874, 185 Cal. Rptr. 155 (1982), which held that if the facts show that the communication was not intended to be kept confidential, the communication is not privileged.

[64] In re Miss. Rules of Evidence, 2003 Miss. LEXIS 152 (2003), (2006), *See* Comment to MISS. R. EVID. 504, (2006).

[65] TENN. CODE. ANN. § 24-1-201, Husband and Wife (2005). Tennessee allows both spouses to be holders of this privilege.

for the above test is the existence of a valid marriage at the time of the communication. In applying such a test in a murder prosecution, a Tennessee appellate court upheld a trial court decision denying a husband's assertion of the marital confidential privilege. He made his incriminating statement in front of several witnesses, including his spouse. However, he was separated from his spouse while he lived with his girlfriend during weekdays. The appellate court noted that the statement failed to have been made in confidence with his spouse because there was no real confidential relationship with his wife. The court held that recognizing the existence of the privilege would not foster his relationship with his wife and that disclosure outweighed any benefit gained from nondisclosure, so the court refused to hold that a confidential privilege existed.[66]

The privilege protecting confidential marital communication does not exist where the communication was not made to the spouse or was made in the presence of an unnecessary third party. In a Minnesota case, a husband returned to his marital home where his wife was present and she observed blood spatters on his clothes that came from the murder victim. The wife had overheard her husband plotting to rob the victim at an earlier time and heard the husband talking with his partner in crime subsequent to the killing. The wife's father overheard much of the same speech and conduct and both the wife and her father testified at the husband's murder trial over his objection. The appellate court upheld the trial court ruling that no confidential privilege had existed since the defendant made statements in his home in anger concerning the events at the murder scene, he was indifferent to the presence of his wife, and he had no expectation that she would even be awake. According to the Supreme Court of Minnesota, because the communication did not originate in a confidential manner and an unnecessary third party (her father) easily overheard the angry husband's statements, both the wife and her father properly testified against the defendant.[67]

3. Prosecution against one spouse for acts against the other spouse or their child

It would be a miscarriage of justice and inconsistent with the rationale for the marital privilege for the rule to prevent one spouse from testifying against the other when the spouse was the victim of the aggressor spouse or their child[68] or a person living in their household.[69] This exception applies in prosecutions for child abuse, bigamy, adultery,[70] and cases involving criminal injury to the person or property of a family member. A Wisconsin court per-

---

[66] *See* State v. Evans, 2006 Tenn. Crim. App. LEXIS 387 (2006). For another case where the court balanced the factors to deny the existence of a confidential communication privilege, *see* State v. Powers, 2002 Tenn. LEXIS 768 (2002), *cert. denied*, Powers v. Tennessee, 538 U.S. 1038, 2003 U.S. LEXIS 3797 (2003).

[67] State v. Palubicki, 700 N.W.2d 476, 484, 2005 Minn. LEXIS 418 (2005).

[68] Jackson v. State, 2005 Tex. App. LEXIS 3631 (2005) a*nd see* Texas Rules of Evidence, Rule 504)b)(4)(A) (2006).

[69] Kentucky Rules of Evidence, Rule 504(c)(2) (2005).

[70] United States v. Taylor, 62 M.J. 636, 2006 CCA LEXIS 9 (2006).

mitted a wife to testify against her husband in a prosecution for sexual assault charges involving the defendant's niece. The defendant had become sexually involved with his 15-year old niece, who had been babysitting for the family. The defendant and his wife had a conversation concerning a sexual toy for which the defendant had a dubious explanation. The court ruled that no husband-wife privilege of any sort existed and it approved permitting the wife to relate to the court what the defendant had told his spouse concerning the toy, a story that implicated the defendant in committing the crime of adultery against his wife.[71]

In a ruling consistent with the exception concerning criminal acts committed against a spouse, children, or their property, a Texas court agreed that a wife who was separated from her husband at the time he committed criminal trespass into her private apartment could testify against him. Although the court noted that the spouse of an accused generally has a privilege not to be called as a witness against him or her, this privilege does not exist where one spouse (or spousal property) has been the subject of a crime by the defendant spouse.[72] An Ohio court ruled that a husband charged with kidnapping and abduction, who bound his wife with duct tape after he had beaten her, had not been making confidential communications with her. The couple had been celebrating their wedding anniversary but an argument ensued resulting in the violent encounter. The trial court required the wife to testify against the husband despite her effort to invoke the spousal testimonial privilege and rejected her argument that a confidential communication had been made because personal injury was not considered an essential element of kidnapping. The appellate court approved the admission of the wife's testimony, saying:

> This Court is not persuaded by appellant's argument. [Ohio law] in no way provides that the injury to the testifying spouse must be an element of the crime of which the defendant spouse is charged. It is irrelevant whether [the wife] suffered her injuries while she was actually restrained by appellant or whether she sustained injuries as a part of appellant's continuous course of conduct of which his restraint of [her] was a part.[73]

The marital privilege not to testify has a recognized exception when the criminal victim is the child of a defendant or witness spouse. In an Ohio case involving numerous rapes and sexual batteries by the husband on the couple's daughter, neither the marital confidential communication privilege nor the marital testimonial privilege applied because of the injury to the daughter; the trial court properly allowed the wife to testify against the husband. Under Ohio law, "Husband and wife are competent witnesses to testify in behalf of each other in all criminal prosecutions and to testify against each other in all

---

[71]   State v. Richard G.B., 2003 Wis. App. 13, 259 Wis. 2d 730, 735, 656 N.W.2d 469, 471 2002 Wis. App. LEXIS 1372 (2003).

[72]   Jackson v. State, 2005 Tex. App. LEXIS 3631 (2005).

[73]   State v. Purvis, 2006 Ohio 1555, 2006 Ohio App. LEXIS 1493 (2006).

actions, prosecutions, and proceedings for personal injury of either by the other, bigamy, or failure to provide for, neglect of, or cruelty to their children under 18 years of age or their physically or mentally handicapped child under 21 years of age."[74] Although the sexual abuse had been in private, the defendant confessed to his wife in the presence of his daughter-victim. The court's ruling, upheld on appeal, allowed the defendant's wife to testify because no marital privilege of any kind existed due to the crimes against a family member.[75]

Although a spouse may not be prohibited from testifying against the other spouse when the crime involves an alleged criminal act against the spouse, a Georgia court held that the wife of a defendant charged with kidnapping her had the right to invoke the marital testimonial privilege not to testify against her husband.[76] In opposition to this view is the position of California, where a wife was required to testify against her husband concerning her own false imprisonment and the homicide of her former boyfriend, both committed by her husband against her and a third-party victim. In this case the court found that little marital harmony remained to be protected because the wife had resumed dating, and because she was also a victim, her testimony about her own false imprisonment and the murder could be compelled over a claim of invoking the marital testimonial privilege.[77]

Interestingly, some defendant spouses may prevent the adverse use of their spouse's voluntary statements when the statements have been offered prior to trial. In a case in which the wife made a tape-recorded statement to police that implicated her husband in criminal activity, the prosecution had been permitted to play the tape at trial. Over the husband's objection and the wife's refusal to testify about the alleged assault with intent to commit murder of a third party, the trial court allowed the wife's evidence to be recounted during the trial. The defendant raised a Sixth Amendment objection, contending that he was unable to confront cross-examine his wife at his trial because she refused to testify. The Supreme Court of the United States reversed the conviction and sent the case back to the trial court. The Court held that by playing the wife's tape-recorded statement at the trial, when the defense was unable to cross-examine the defendant's wife, violated the defendant's constitutional rights under the confrontation clause of the Sixth Amendment. According to the Court, the confrontation clause demanded that the testimonial evidence from the wife given to police had to be tested by the crucible of cross-examination. When testimonial evidence was at issue and where there was no prior opportunity to cross-examine the wife, the admission of her police-recorded statement constituted reversible error under the Sixth Amendment as applied to the states.[78]

---

[74]   OHIO REV. CODE ANN. § 2945.42. Competency of witnesses, (Matthew Bender 2006)

[75]   State v. Wilson, 2006 Ohio 2000; 2006 Ohio App. LEXIS 1860 (2006).

[76]   Carter v. State, 275 Ga. App. 483, 486, 621 S.E.2d 503, 506, 2005 Ga. App. LEXIS 1003 (2005).

[77]   California v. Sinohui, 28 Cal. 4th 205, 47 P.3d 629, 2002 Cal. LEXIS 3777 (2002); *See also* Wisconsin v. Richard G. B., 259 Wis. 2d 730, 656 N.W.2d 469, 2002 Wisc. App. LEXIS 1372 (2002) for an interesting approach to a crime against a spouse requiring collateral testimony by the spouse as an exception to the rule excluding spousal testimony.

[78]   *See* Crawford v. Washington, 541 U.S. 36, 2004 U.S. LEXIS 1838 (2004).

4. Conspiracy

Where a husband and wife jointly have engaged in a criminal conspiracy, the defendant spouse cannot claim the marital testimonial privilege to prevent adverse testimony by the other spouse in a federal prosecution. In an Eighth Circuit case, the court allowed the testimony of a defendant's spouse in a prosecution for conspiracy to distribute methamphetamine. The defendant and his wife had engaged in drug trafficking but the prosecution offered her a possibility of a reduced sentence in her personal drug prosecution if she testified against her husband. In permitting the wife to testify, the trial court was careful to prevent any confidential communications that had occurred between her and her husband from being introduced but allowed the witness-wife to testify about their ongoing drug conspiracy and the defendant's actions, when it involved drug trafficking.[79]

A federal circuit court of appeals approved allowing a spouse who had conspired with her husband to testify against him by relying on the federal common law relating to marital privileges. The trial court rejected any role that the Nebraska state law of privilege might have because the trial involved a federal violation of conspiracy to distribute and possess methamphetamine. The trial court ruled that the federal common law interpreting marital privileges was the appropriate standard, and the case of *Trammel v. United States*[80] held that the privilege not to testify against a spouse-defendant resided with the other spouse. In this case, the wife had participated in a conspiracy with her husband and others, so there was no argument that a confidential communication privilege covered the wife's testimony and the holder of the federal testimonial privilege is the witness-spouse who, in this case, could testify if she chose to do so, whether because of an agreement with the prosecution or otherwise.[81]

Minnesota has taken a completely different route concerning criminal conspiracies between spouses. According to Minnesota law, "A husband cannot be examined for or against his wife without her consent, nor a wife for or against her husband without his consent, nor can either, during the marriage or afterwards, without the consent of the other, be examined as to any communication made by one to the other during the marriage."[82] In offering an interpretation of the law, the state's top court held that a wife, over her husband's objection, should not be required to testify against her husband. In this case, the two spouses allegedly engaged in a conspiracy to commit a murder of a potential witness against them in a separate criminal proceeding. Minnesota requires the consent of the witness-spouse and of the defendant-spouse prior to offering any testimony concerning matters adverse to a defendant-spouse as long as the crime was not against the other, their children, or property.[83]

---

[79] United States v. Espino, 317 F.3d 788, 795, 796, 2003 U.S. App. LEXIS 261 (8th Cir. 2003).

[80] 445 U.S. 40, 47, 1980 U.S. LEXIS 84 (1980).

[81] United States v. Espino, 317 F.3d 788, 794, 2003 U.S. App. LEXIS 261 (8th Cir. 2003).

[82] MINN. STAT. § 595.02 , subd. 1(a) (2005).

[83] Minnesota v. Gianakos, 644 N.W.2d 409, 418, 419, 2002 Minn. LEXIS 350 (2002). The defendant was later convicted in a related federal prosecution involving the same conduct. *See* United States v. Gianakos, 404 F.3d 1065 (2005), which was later reversed, 414 F.3d 912 (2005).

D. Duration of the Privilege

The Supreme Court opinion in *Trammel*[84] allowing the witness-spouse to decide whether to testify adversely makes the question of the duration of the marital testimonial privilege less important in federal trials. The majority of the states appear to have adopted the view that only the witness-spouse is a holder of the marital testimonial privilege. However, when the marital confidential communication privilege is implicated, the better view is that both marriage partners are holders and may assert the privilege in an appropriate setting. Generally, the privilege exists during the marriage and for an indefinite time after the marriage and may continue following the death of one of the marital partners.[85] In an Iowa case in which a defendant had been accused of having sex with an underage female, the Supreme Court reversed the conviction because the trial court had permitted his ex-wife to give testimony against the defendant. The applicable Iowa rule of evidence does not appear to require that a marital communication be accomplished in confidence. The ex-wife had erroneously been permitted to offer evidence that involved confidential communications with the defendant that covered incriminating matters with the underage female. Thus, in Iowa, the marital communication privilege, like that of many states, survives the termination of the marriage and may be asserted in subsequent criminal trials.[86]

Although in most American jurisdictions, the marital privilege continues after divorce with respect to statements made in confidence during the existence of the marriage,[87] an argument could be made that the reason for the rule no longer applies after the divorce. When spouses are divorced at the time of the trial, allowing a willing former spouse to testify against the defendant spouse would not affect any present relationship. In Michigan, a former spouse was permitted to testify concerning the murder of her then-husband's girlfriend when the husband had confided in his then-wife about the details of the homicide. The Supreme Court of Michigan did not want to hear the case[88] and a federal district court found no problem with allowing the confidential communication testimony of the former wife to be admitted against the former husband.[89] Taking an opposite position, a Washington court made it clear that even a former spouse cannot be examined regarding any confidential communications made by one to the other during the marriage.[90] A common-sense approach allows a spouse or former spouse to testify about nonconfidential matters and also allows a defendant spouse to prohibit a spouse or

---

[84]   Trammel v. United States, *supra* note 28.

[85]   *See*, for example, IOWA CODE § 622.9 (2005).

[86]   Iowa v. Anderson, 636 N.W.2d 26, 32, 33, 2001 Iowa Sup. LEXIS 217 (2001).

[87]   Commonwealth of Pennsylvania v. Weiss, 565 Pa. 504, 776 A.2d 958, 2001 Pa. LEXIS 1574 (2001), in which the court held that disclosure of confidential communications made during a marriage is prohibited even following the dissolution of the marriage.

[88]   People v. Bean, 469 Mich. 1004, 674 N.W.2d 380, 2004 Mich. LEXIS 252 (2004).

[89]   Bean v. Ludwick, 2005 U.S. Dist. LEXIS 34209 (2005).

[90]   State v. Modest, 944 P.2d 417 (Wash. 1997).

former spouse from testifying against a defendant with respect to confidential matters discussed or communicated during the marriage.[91]

The protection offered by either spousal privilege does not extend to acts or utterances, whether confidential or not, made prior to the marriage or after divorce.[92] Moreover, the privilege does not apply when the defendant is merely living with the person who is called as a witness[93] unless there is a recognized common law marriage.[94] Even where some technical details concerning the marriage have not been met, such as not filing the marriage license following the ceremony or not obtaining a marriage license, courts may uphold the marriage as having validity and the marriage will support the assertion of the marital confidential communication privilege.[95] In a state that considers marriages between first cousins "void," that state generally will recognize marriages between first cousins as valid where the marriage occurred in a state that approves of first-cousin marriages,[96] a prerequisite for permitting an assertion of a marital privilege.

§ 10.4 Communications Between Attorney and Client

A. *Statement of the Rule*

Confidential communications made in the course of professional employment between an attorney or one reasonably believed to be an attorney and his or her client may not be divulged by the attorney without the consent of the client and neither the attorney nor the client can be compelled to testify regarding such communications. The privilege applies when a potential client initially consults an attorney, even though no professional relationship develops, and it also applies when someone consults a person who is reasonably believed to be an attorney, but who is in fact not an attorney.

The privilege regarding confidential communications between client and attorney, as in the case of the marital communications privilege, was recognized at common law. As a general rule, the privilege applies only when statements are made to an attorney where there is an expectation that the information will remain confidential, but the privilege does not exist when a defendant spoke in such a loud voice that other people could hear him.[97] The purpose of the privilege is to facilitate full and complete communication

---

[91] Louisiana v. Nash, 821 So. 2d 678, 683, 684, 2002 La. App. LEXIS 1928 (2002).

[92] Pereira v. United States, 347 U.S. 1, 74 S. Ct. 358, 98 L. Ed. 435 (1954).

[93] Dermody v. State, 2002 Tex. App. LEXIS 6639 (2002); *see also* Arboleda v. Newland, Warden, 2003 U.S. Dist. LEXIS 513 (N.D. Cal. 2003).

[94] *See* Bevan v. Bevan, 2006 Ohio 2775, 2006 Ohio App. LEXIS 2605 (2006) for the essentials of common law marriage.

[95] Washington v. Denton, 97 Wash. App. 267, 271, 983 P.2d 693, 695, 1999 Wash. App. LEXIS 1582 (1999); *contra*, In re Khalil, D.C. Civ. App. No. 2001/183, 2003 U.S. Dist. LEXIS 6229 (N.D. Cal. 2003).

[96] Cook v. Cook, 209 Ariz. 487; 104 P.3d 857; 2005 Ariz. App. LEXIS 6 (2005).

[97] People v. Urbano, 128 Cal. App. 4th 396, 26 Cal. Rptr. 3d 871, 2005 Cal. App. LEXIS 572 (2005).

between attorneys and their clients. Sound public policy recognized that the attorney's assistance could be effectively offered only when the client was free from the consequences of apprehension or discovery by reason of subsequent statements of the lawyer. In a case involving representation on a criminal or civil matter, the privilege prevents the attorney from being required to be an adverse witness. In fact, in the absence of the attorney-client privilege, the Sixth Amendment right to counsel would become a hollow shell. Although the privilege has the effect of preventing significant evidence from being offered in the search for the truth, good public policy holds that the interests protected by the privilege outweighs the desirability of placing all facts known to the attorney before the jury.

A Connecticut court, in an unreported case, accepted the government's argument that by filing a habeas corpus case alleging ineffective assistance of trial counsel, the defendant had waived his attorney-client privilege concerning documents desired by the state. Confidences are maintained until the interests of justice would be frustrated by the exercise of the privilege and then it must give way.[98]

In a 1981 case, the United States Supreme Court clarified the reason for the privilege and the extent of the privilege in federal courts.[99] According to the Court, the attorney-client privilege encourages "full and frank communication between attorneys and their clients and thereby promote[s] broader public interests in the observance of law and administration of justice."[100] The Court explained that the attorney-client privilege has been recognized in federal courts not only to protect professional advice given to those who can act upon it, but also the privilege gives information to a lawyer to enable him or her to give sound and informed advice. The protections extend only to communications with the attorney and not to facts known by the client so that the client need not disclose what the attorney was told but might have to reveal facts known to the client that are not otherwise privileged.

A party cannot conceal a fact under a claim of privilege merely by revealing it to his or her lawyer and a party who is testifying cannot refuse to answer questions concerning facts related to the case merely because he or she has at one time or another disclosed such facts to his or her lawyer. The witness may refuse to testify on other grounds but not merely because he or she has communicated the facts to his or her attorney.

B. Scope of the Privilege

The privilege is subject to statutory regulations and limitations based on court decisions. While it is desirable to protect communications between an attorney and his or her client, unless the facts demonstrate that such a relationship exists, the rule should not apply. As a general proposition, the burden

---

[98] Breton v. Commissioner, 2006 Conn. Super. LEXIS 1240 (2006). *Contra*, People v. Madera, 112 P.2d 688, 2005 Colo. LEXIS 526 (2005).

[99] Upjohn Co. v. United States, 449 U.S. 383, 101 S. Ct. 677, 66 L. Ed. 2d 584 (1981).

[100] *Id.* at 389.

to prove that an attorney-client relationship has developed rests with the defendant, who must show that an attorney has been hired, that the defendant was the client, that confidential communications involving the seeking or offering of legal advice were made between the two, and that no unnecessary third parties were present. In addition to client-attorney communication, the privilege generally covers other communications made by the client with people who are necessary to support the attorney in the rendition of legal services. These others include office personnel such as secretaries, law clerks, and investigators hired by the attorney. The privilege may also include a client's communications with a medical doctor or accountant employed by his attorney when made for the purpose of enabling the attorney to comprehend the client's fact situation in order to give appropriate legal advice.[101]

A classic comment from a landmark case illuminating the scope and attributes of the privilege is found in *United States v. United Shoe Machinery Corp.*[102] In that case, the Court commented:

> The privilege applies only if (1) the asserted holder of the privilege is or sought to become a client; (2) the person to whom the communication was made (a) is a member of the bar of a court, or his subordinate and (b) in connection with this communication is acting as a lawyer; (3) the communication relates to a fact of which the attorney was informed (a) by his client (b) without the presence of strangers (c) for the purpose of securing primarily either (i) an opinion on law or (ii) legal services or (iii) assistance in some legal proceeding, and not (d) for the purpose of committing a crime or tort; and (4) the privilege has been (a) claimed and (b) not waived by the client.

After referring to previous cases, a federal court reiterated that the attorney-client privilege is intended to be construed within the narrowest possible limits consistent with the logic of its principle. In one case, a defendant had been arrested and released and his attorney moved to withdraw from the case. The client failed to appear at the withdrawal hearing and was indicted for failure to appear. Over his objection, his former attorney testified that she had forwarded notice of the hearing date to the defendant. The court ruled that that she was not testifying in violation of the attorney-client privilege but was testifying concerning non-privileged information.[103] Merely handing documents or telling the attorney material that is known by other people will not cause that information to become privileged. Extraneous information or documents offered to the attorney that are not necessary to the delivery of legal services will not generally be deemed covered by the privilege.

---

[101] In re Grand Jury Subpoenas, 2003 U.S. Dist. LEXIS 9022 (S.D.N.Y. 2003).

[102] 89 F. Supp. 357 (D. Mass. 1950); *see also* United States v. Schmidt, 360 F. Supp. 339 (M.D. Pa. 1973), for a discussion of the scope of the privilege.

[103] State v. Kemper, 158 Ohio App. 3d 185, 187, 2004 Ohio 4050, 814 N.E.2d 540, 541, 2004 Ohio App. LEXIS 3677 (2004).

As generally recognized, the privilege only applies when the person to whom the communication was made was a member of the bar or was reasonably believed to be a member of the bar, or his or her subordinate or agent. It is clear that a statement made to one who is not an attorney, such as a prison inmate, is not privileged.[104] Even when the prison inmate has knowledge of the law and is assigned to the law library to help prisoners with their legal problems by writing letters, preparing pleadings, and giving them other advice, he or she is not a lawyer for the purposes of the privilege. Statements made to him or her are not privileged statements. However, statements made to an attorney's essential employee by a person seeking legal services from the attorney are covered by the privilege.[105] In most situations in which the presence of third parties is necessary, or at least useful to assisting attorney-client communication, the presence of those persons does not destroy the privilege.[106] When a potential homicide defendant asked his girlfriend-attorney questions about criminal problems, the attorney-client relationship may not exist, especially when the attorney was not a criminal attorney and her employment prohibited her from representing private clients. The attorney viewed the exchange as the usual boyfriend-girlfriend type of chatter even though it concerned a homicide, and did not consider it a request for legal advice.[107] However, the reasonable impressions and expectations of the potential client may hold more weight than the perceptions of the putative attorney.

The primary purpose of the privilege is to protect communications between attorney and client; however, the privilege is broad enough to also shield communications made by the client to an agent of the attorney, such as a scientific expert retained to aid in the preparation and presentation of the defense.[108] And information provided to an accountant by a client at the behest of his or her attorney for the purposes of interpretation and analysis is within the attorney-client privilege to the extent that it is provided in connection with the legal representation.[109] However, when the federal government wanted information from a taxpayer's accounting firm, the records were not privileged under the attorney-client rationale because the taxpayer, and not the attorney, had hired the accounting firm to provide accounting services that were not precisely related to the delivery of legal services.[110]

Although the attorney-client privilege has existed for several hundred years and is recognized in all courts, not all of the relationships are protected in all contexts. Some of the situations in which the confidential communication protection does not apply are discussed in the following sections.

---

[104] State v. Spell, 399 So. 2d 551 (La. 1981).

[105] American National Water Mattress Corp. v. Manville, 642 P.2d 1330 (Alaska 1982).

[106] Cavallaro v. United States, 284 F.3d 236, 246, 2002 U.S. App. LEXIS 5366 (1st Cir. 2002).

[107] Jones v. United States, 2003 D.C. App. LEXIS 434 (2003).

[108] State v. DeMarco, 275 N.J. Super 311, 646 A.2d 431 (1994). See case in Part II.

[109] United States v. United Technologies Corp., 979 F. Supp. 108 (D. Conn. 1997).

[110] Cavallaro v. United States, 153 F. Supp. 2d 52, 57, 58, 2001 U.S. Dist. LEXIS 11232 (1st Cir. 2001).

C. Exceptions

1. Identity of client

The identity of the attorney's client has not been considered a privileged matter because it usually reveals little concerning the nature of the relationship or what has been discussed between the two individuals. As a general rule, the mere existence of an attorney-client relationship and the identity of the client is not a privileged communication, unless the identity of the client is the last piece of evidence needed to initiate a criminal prosecution or the disclosure would reveal a confidential communication.[111] The privilege pertains to the subject matter and not the fact of the employment as attorney, and as it presupposes the relationship of attorney and client, it does not attach to the creation of that relationship. The client or the attorney may be permitted or compelled to testify regarding his or her employment as an attorney, the fee or how it was paid, advice given to his or her client about a certain matter, or certain services performed for the client.[112] For example, in a grand jury inquiry regarding the failure of the client to appear for trial and whether the attorney told the client of the trial date, the attorney-client privilege failed to protect an attorney's act of communicating a trial date to her client, whether communicated to the client directly by appellant or by a member of her staff. The attorney appeared to be reluctant to assist in the prosecution of her client on a charge of willfully failing to appear for trial by withholding information about whether she ever informed him of the trial date. Such communication or lack of it did not constitute a privileged communication with the client and the attorney was bound to reveal it to a grand jury.[113]

Absent a unique situation or special circumstances, client identity and fee information are not privileged because neither the fact of employment nor the amount of the fee paid has any bearing on the matters discussed between the client and the attorney. Revealing this sort of information does not curtail or chill the communication between the necessary actors involved in the attorney-client relationship.[114] Thus, in a proceeding to require two attorneys to respond to an administrative summons in connection with the investigation of tax returns of their clients, information as to the amount of fees paid, dates of payment, and by or through whom payments were made was not privileged.[115]

Although the authorities are for the most part uniformly against any privilege as applied to the fact of retainer or identity of the client, there is an exception to this general rule that is as firmly grounded as the rule itself. The exception is that the privilege may be recognized when so much of the actual communication has already been disclosed that identification of the client amounts to a disclosure of the client's motivation for seeking legal advice. The reasons for needing or for seeking legal advice constitute a confidential com-

---

[111]　Nester v. Jernigan, 908 So.2d 145,149, 2005 Miss. LEXIS 467 (2005).
[112]　Morris v. State, 242 A.2d 559 (Md. 1968).
[113]　Moudy v. Superior Court, 964 P. 2d 469, 1998 Alaska App. LEXIS 44 (1998).
[114]　Sony v. Soundview, 2001 U.S. Dist. LEXIS 23220 (D. Conn. 2001).
[115]　In re Wasserman, 198 F. Supp. 564 (D.D.C. 1961).

munication to the attorney. In a case in which the federal government initiated an investigation related to potentially fraudulent tax shelters devised by a national accounting firm and unnamed taxpayers desired to intervene in the case without revealing their identities, the court approved allowing the clients to remain unknown to the government. According to the court, revealing the clients' identities would reveal their motivations in seeking the accounting firm's advise to invest in potentially abusive tax shelters that could create a civil or criminal prosecution once identities were known to the federal government.[116]

Clarifying the general rule that the identity of the attorney's client is not subject to secrecy under the attorney-client privilege, as well commenting on the limitations on this exception, a federal district court noted that the identity of the client and the amount of the fee or the form of payment of the fee are not usually considered privileged.[117] The attorney's time records and billing statements are not considered covered by the attorney-client privilege, at least where the records and statements do not contain detailed accounts of the services performed.[118] In fact, the attorney has a positive duty to protect confidential information from being disclosed unless properly ordered by a court to do so, and even then, only after contesting the disclosure.[119]

2. Advice in furtherance of crime

There is no privilege if either the attorney or the client has involved the other in a criminal endeavor or if the legal advice of the lawyer has been sought or obtained to facilitate or assist anyone in committing or planning a crime or committing a fraud.[120] As one court noted, "Only when a client knowingly seeks legal counsel to further a continuing or future crime does the crime-fraud exception apply."[121] Under such circumstances, the attorney and the "client" may be forced to divulge any communication between them that relates to "covering up" an old crime or embarking on new criminal behavior. The privilege does not exist when the desired advice concerns future criminality, but the privilege will cover legal advice on resolving prior crimes within a lawful context. This exception to the attorney-client privilege prevents the attorney and/or client from giving or obtaining advice about how to commit a new crime or fraud.[122] Simply stated, communications between a client and his or her attorney seeking legal advice in order to initiate or accomplish an ongoing or future fraud do not carry any privilege under the attorney-client relationship.[123] The interests of public justice require that no shield be

---

[116] United States v. Arthur Andersen, 2003 U.S. Dist. LEXIS 11255 (D. Conn. 2003).
[117] Estate of Reiserer v. United States, 229 F.R.D. 172, 179, 2005 U.S. Dist. LEXIS 17597 (W.D. Wash. 2005).
[118] DiBella v. Hopkins, 403 F.3d 102, 120, 2005 U.S. App. LEXIS 5332 (2d Cir. 2005).
[119] Mass. R. Prof. Conduct, ALM Sup. Jud. Ct. Rule 3:07, RPC 1.6 (2006).
[120] For example, see Cal Evid Code § 956 (2006).
[121] United States v. Doe, 429 F.3d 450; 2005 U.S. App. LEXIS 25256 (3d Cir. 2005).
[122] See Hawai'i v. Wong, 97 Haw. 512, 40 P.3d 914, 2002 Haw. LEXIS 100 (2002); and see La. Code Evid. Ann. Art. 506(C)(1)(b), in which attorney-client communications covering new crimes are not considered privileged.
[123] State v. Menard, 844 So. 2d 1117 (La. Dist. Ct. App. 2003).

interposed to protect a person who takes counsel on how he or she can safely commit a new crime. This exception to the attorney-client privilege does not apply when a person has committed a crime, prior to consulting an attorney concerning what the client's legal rights may be and inquired how the crime may be lawfully adjusted. The crime-fraud exception prevents a privilege from being recognized when a "client" who, having committed a crime, seeks advice on how he or she can initiate or complete a "cover-up" of the offense. For example, when a prospective client asked the attorney to hide a murder weapon or otherwise aid in the disposition of a murder weapon, such conduct falls outside of the attorney-client privilege.[124] Further, a client's plan to commit perjury is not protected under the privilege where a client contended that his attorney encouraged him to commit perjury in a murder trial. His lawyer properly was permitted to counter the allegations by the convicted murderer in a subsequent perjury trial because no privilege existed.[125]

The act of a jailed inmate, who calls an attorney on a monitored line and speaks about whether he should trust a fellow inmate to arrange for a hit man to murder witnesses and maybe kill the prosecutor, falls into the crime-fraud exception to the attorney-client privilege. The acts contemplated need not be successful; the mere communication of criminal plans takes the communication outside the protections of the attorney-client privilege.[126]

This exception to the attorney-client privilege was comprehensively explained by the United States Court of Appeals for the Fourth Circuit in the case of *In re Grand Jury Proceedings*, in which an attorney sought a writ requiring the reversal of an order directing him to testify concerning conversations between himself and three individuals.[127] The attorney claimed that his conversations with the three other parties concerning a business relationship were confidential and that they should not be required to testify concerning such confidential communications. The reviewing court first explained that "the attorney-client privilege as traditionally recognized at common law and as now incorporated in the Federal Rules of Evidence controls in all federal judicial proceedings." The court, however, continued by stating that the privilege impedes the full and free discovery of the truth and is in derogation of the public's "right to have every man's evidence." Accordingly, the privilege is to be construed within the narrowest possible limits consistent with the logic of its principle. In discussing the exception to the rule, the court noted that:

> Consonant with this policy, the privilege applies only when the person claiming the privilege has as a client consulted an attorney for the purpose of securing a legal opinion or services and not "for the purpose of committing a crime or tort," and in connection with that consultation has communicated information which was intended to be kept confidential.

---

124   Mixon v. State, 179 S.W.3d 233, 235, 2005 Tex. App. LEXIS 9079 (2005).
125   State v. Buford, 2005 Tenn. Crim. App. LEXIS (2005).
126   United States v. Lentz, 419 F. Supp.2d 820, 829 (E.D. Va 2005).
127   In re Grand Jury Proceedings, 727 F.2d 1352 (4th Cir. 1984).

Although the crime-fraud exception to the attorney-client privilege may have a narrow construction, in order to prevail on an allegation of crime-fraud, the burden of proving the exception rests with the party wishing to invade the attorney-client relationship. Where the prosecution wants to invoke the crime-fraud exception, it must make a prima facie demonstration that (1) the client was committing a fraud or crime and that (2) the communications between the attorney and the client were made in furtherance of the allege crime-fraud.[128] In a case in which the prosecution believed that the client was destroying e-mail communication necessary to a prosecution, the reviewing court found that the crime-fraud exception to the attorney-client privilege applied to the attorney's communication with his defendant regarding the types of e-mails the prosecution was seeking in a discovery request. The communication permitted the client to know which e-mails to destroy from the hard drive to keep them from being turned over to the government. [129]

One court found that the communications between a client and her attorney were not covered by the attorney-client privilege when the government uncovered evidence that a recently convicted defendant was fabricating evidence. Information had been posted on a Web page that was designed to falsely indicate the defendant's innocence and perhaps influence her sentencing. A fax of the Web site had been sent to the defendant's attorney and the implication was that the defendant was attempting to use her relationship with her attorney to further her continued criminal activity or to commit new crimes by attempting to influence her sentencing proceeding. Under the circumstances, there existed no protected communication with her attorney concerning the fraudulent Web page and the crime-fraud exception arguably had application.[130]

3. Communications not intended to be confidential[131]

A communication is considered "confidential" if it is not intended to be disclosed to third parties other than those to whom its disclosure is necessary in rendering professional legal services to the client or to those persons reasonably necessary for the transmission of the communication. Communication will be remain confidential if an attorney or client needs to divulge information to an accountant, a private investigator, or similar person assisting the attorney in understanding or interpreting the facts. If the communication is not intended to be confidential, then the rationale for the attorney-client privilege does not exist. Because the privilege prevents the full and free discovery of the truth, the privilege is strictly enforced and limited to situations in which the communication was intended to remain confidential.[132]

---

[128] In re Grand Jury Proceedings, 445 F.3d 266, 274, 2006 U.S. App. LEXIS 10041 (2006).

[129] Id. at 275.

[130] State v. Cliffords, 2005 ML 120; 2005 Mont. Dist. LEXIS 1239 (2005); see also 178 A.L.R. FED. 87.

[131] See draft of FED. R. EVID. as submitted to Congress in 1972.

[132] United States v. Lentz, 419 F. Supp. 2d 820, 826, 2005 U.S. Dist. LEXIS 41084 (E.D. Va. 2005).

Where an unnecessary third party was present at the time the communications were made, the attorney-client privilege generally does not exist. Demonstrative of this principle is a Florida case in which a jailed defendant called his sister, who called his lawyer on a three-way telephone call. At the jail end of the conversation, an audible warning automatically notified the defendant that the conversation might be monitored and recorded. At trial, the court admitted into evidence a number of taped telephone conversations initiated by the defendant on the monitored line. One of the taped conversations that included incriminating information occurred among the defendant, the man who was his attorney at the time, and his sister on the three-way telephone conversation. The appellate court upheld the admission of the authenticated tape of the incriminating conversation as well as other taped conversations on the theory the attorney-client privilege only covers communications that are neither overheard by nor intended to be disclosed to third persons.[133]

In justifying this exception to the privilege, a federal court in New York noted that a client's disclosure to a third party of a communication made during a confidential consultation with his attorney eliminated whatever privilege the communication may have already possessed.[134] That court explained that the exception applies whether the disclosure is viewed as an indication that confidentiality is no longer intended or as a waiver of the privilege.

4. Statements of the attorney relating to the client's mental or physical condition

The privilege does not extend to information received by the attorney that does not relate to communications, even though it was obtained while he or she was acting as an attorney. For example, testimony at the trial by the defendant's previous counsel from another proceeding concerning the defendant's mental competency does not violate the attorney-client privilege.[135] The court in *Clanton v. United States* stated:

> Here the attorney's testimony did not relate to private, confidential communications with his client during the time of communications prior to and at the entry of the pleas of guilty. He was qualified as a layman to express a view as to his client's mental competency.

However, an attorney has a duty of confidentiality to the client regardless of whether the information is available from other public or private sources. Such duty to preserve confidences extends beyond information that may be covered by a narrow interpretation of the attorney-client privilege.[136]

---

[133]   State v. Black, 920 So. 2d 668, 670, 2006 Fla. App. LEXIS 48 (2006), *reh'g denied*, 2006 Fla. App. LEXIS 3673 (2006)

[134]   Bower v. Weisman, 669 F. Supp. 602 (S.D.N.Y. 1987).

[135]   Clanton v. United States, 488 F.2d 1069 (5th Cir. 1974).

[136]   Sealed Party v. Sealed Party, 2006 U.S. Dist. LEXIS 28392 (2006).

5. Posthumous revelation exception

Does a compelling need for important evidence in criminal cases outweigh the confidentiality claims involving the attorney-client privilege? This issue received national attention in the Monica Lewinsky inquiry when Whitewater prosecutor Kenneth Starr asked a federal grand jury to issue subpoenas for handwritten notes made by the attorney who represented Deputy White House Counsel Vincent W. Foster Jr., who had committed suicide by the time the subpoenas were issued.

A federal grand jury issued subpoenas for the notes and litigation resulted when the district court refused to require that the attorney-client privilege be breached even following the client's death. The court of appeals reversed and held that the notes could be viewed by the grand jury, effectively holding that, in this case, the attorney-client privilege did not survive the death of the client.

The United States Supreme Court disagreed with the reasoning of the Court of Appeals, holding that the petitioner's notes were protected by the attorney-client privilege. The Supreme Court admonished that the relevant case law demonstrated that it has been overwhelmingly, if not universally, accepted for more than a century that the privilege survives the client's death in such a case.[137] After explaining that the Independent Counsel's arguments against the privilege's posthumous survival were invalid, the Supreme Court emphasized that "knowing that communications will remain confidential even after death serves a weighty interest in encouraging a client to communicate fully and frankly with counsel; posthumous disclosure of such communication may be as feared as disclosure during the client's lifetime."[138] "Balancing *ex post* the importance of the information against client interests, even limited to criminal cases, introduces substantial uncertainty into the privilege's application, and therefore must be rejected."[139]

In a more recent decision, an Ohio case involved the disappearance and probable death of a nine-year-old girl, in which authorities believed that a deceased woman had communicated information to her attorney. Her attorney refused to divulge what the client had communicated to her due to an Ohio law[140] that provided a durable attorney-client privilege after death that extended the privilege until consent to release the privilege had been given by a surviving spouse or personal representative. Numerous state and federal courts heard aspects of the case,[141] but the principle that an attorney-client privilege can survive the death of the client-holder of the privilege remained intact. The interests served by extending the attorney-client privilege beyond the life of the holder allows living holders of the privilege security in the knowledge that embarrassing or personal information shared with an attorney in the delivery of legal advice will remain private under most situations.

---

[137] Swidler & Berlin v. United States, 524 U.S. 399, 1998 U.S. LEXIS 4214 (1998).

[138] *Id.*, Headnote.

[139] *Id.*

[140] OHIO REV. CODE § 2317.02 (2006).

[141] Ohio v. Doe, 433 F.3d 502, 2006 U.S. App. LEXIS 481 (6th Cir. 2006).

D. *Assertion and Waiver*

The party who desires to make use of the attorney-client privilege must establish that the privilege existed in the first instance, and that there has been no waiver.[142] Where a court recognizes the existence of the privilege, the privilege prohibits disclosure of information that has been confidentially disclosed to an attorney. The information remains personal to the client or successor and must be asserted by the client-holder of the privilege and not by the attorney.[143] However, if the client is neither present nor available during the proceeding in which the attorney's testimony has been ordered, the attorney must honor the client's wishes and may assert the privilege on behalf of the client, but the attorney is not asserting on his or her behalf.[144] In one case in which the parents of a minor child were present when the child talked to his attorney, a court of appeals held that the presence of the parents as third parties did not waive the attorney-client privilege because the parents were intent on keeping the conference confidential.[145]

Recent decisions have reaffirmed the rule that the waiver of the attorney-client privilege rests solely with the client, not the counsel. The attorney or agent may exercise that power only when acting with the client's authority.[146] Therefore, to allow the district attorney to invoke the attorney-client privilege that existed between a murder victim and his attorney is error.[147] However, while the attorney-client privilege belongs to the client and not the attorney, an attorney may and should assert it if done for the benefit of his or her client.[148]

A convicted defendant generally waives the attorney-client privilege when he or she raises a claim of ineffective assistance of counsel in an appellate setting or in a petition for a writ of habeas corpus. When a convict alleges that his trial attorney provided ineffective assistance of counsel in pursuing a particular defense strategy or in determining what witnesses to call or how to cross-examine, the person seeking habeas relief places at issue any attorney-client privilege that might apply to the substance of conversations that covered trial planning.[149] In a California case, a federal district court, entertaining an application for a writ of habeas corpus, entered an order prohibiting the state prosecutor from turning over to other prosecutors any evidence obtained by

---

[142]   United States v. Ary, 2005 U.S. Dist. LEXIS 21958 (D. Kan. 2005).

[143]   For example, see CAL. EVID. CODE § 951 (2006) and HLC Properties, Ltd. v. Superior Court, 35 Cal. 4th 54, 62, 105 P.3d 560, 565, 2005 Cal. LEXIS 1607 (2005), where the court held that "the attorney-client privilege belongs only to the client, whether the client is a natural person, an unincorporated organization, or some other entity."

[144]   Martin Marietta v. West Virginia, 227 F.R.D. 382, 2005 U.S. Dist. LEXIS 8379 (2005).

[145]   Arizona v. Sucharew, 66 P. 2d 59, 65, 2003 Ariz. App. LEXIS 61 (2003).

[146]   State v. Davis, 116 N.J. 341, 561 A.2d 1082 (1989).

[147]   Smith v. State, 770 S.W.2d 70 (Tex. Ct. App. 1989).

[148]   United States v. Loften, 518 F. Supp. 839 (S.D.N.Y. 1981).

[149]   See In re Lott, 139 Fed. Appx. 658; 2005 U.S. App. LEXIS 12280 (2005). However, in later litigation, the Sixth Circuit Court of Appeals noted that "The Rules of Evidence make it abundantly clear that the attorney-client privilege stands in all federal judicial proceedings, which would include habeas proceedings where petitioners assert actual innocence." In re Lott, 424 F.3d 446, 452, 2005 U.S. App. LEXIS 19429, 2005 Fed. Appx. 383P (6th Cir. 2005).

virtue of the defendant's waiver of the attorney-client privilege. The prosecution appealed the order, arguing that the defendant completely waived the attorney-client privilege and the district court had no authority to prevent the use of the nonprivileged materials to reprosecute the defendant. The Ninth Circuit affirmed the trial court order limiting the waiver to the habeas corpus case. In its opinion the court indicated that it affirmed the district court's order, adopting a narrow waiver rule. The Ninth Circuit held that the scope of the defendant's waiver extended only to the federal habeas petition, and that the privilege was not waived for other legal purposes. To have decided otherwise would have exposed a habeas corpus litigant to making a determination of whether to waive the privilege and have a chance at winning a habeas corpus claim but having all his formerly privileged information available to the state for a retrial, or foregoing any habeas corpus claim, secure that while he was serving time his confidences remained safe.[150] Thus, a total waiver by filing a claim under habeas corpus does not necessarily waive the attorney-client privilege for a case under appellate consideration.

The bare fact that a person has been charged in a subsequent criminal case does not waive the attorney-client privilege arising from a prior criminal case, even when the defendant's mental state may be at issue in the second criminal matter. According to the Supreme Court of Wisconsin, the attorney's opinions, perceptions, and impressions relating to a former client's mental competency arising from an earlier representation are confidential communications within the meaning of the attorney-client privilege. The attorney should not have been permitted to testify about her opinions of his mental state because those opinions were naturally formed from information obtained from privileged communications.[151]

Once a client has effectively waived the attorney-client privilege, the attorney may testify regarding matters otherwise within the scope of the privilege; he or she has no standing to invoke the privilege if the client does not wish to do so.[152] However, an attorney, while testifying as a witness or otherwise, in the absence of a client's consent, may not disclose any privileged communication made to the client or received by the attorney.[153]

Unless a holder of the attorney-client privilege makes a positive effort to assert or claim the privilege, the benefits will be lost because no one other than the holder's own attorney possesses any duty to alert the holder of its existence. Under the general rule, a failure to object constitutes waiver. For a holder of the privilege to avoid waiver, a claim of privilege must be promptly raised or the court will rule that the privilege has been waived. A holder waives the privilege when he or she places a confidential communication at issue that goes directly to a claim or defense, whether at trial or upon appeal.[154]

---

[150] Bittaker v. Woodford, 331 F.3d 715, 2003 U.S. App. LEXIS 11298 (9th Cir. 2003).

[151] Wisconsin v. Meeks, 2002 Wis. App. 65, 251 Wis. 2d 361, 643 N.W.2d 526, 2002 Wis. App. LEXIS 156 (2002), *review granted*, 2002 Wis. 48, 252 Wis. 2d 148, 644 N.W.2d 685, 2002 Wis. LEXIS 246 (2002).

[152] Barnes v. State, 460 So. 2d 126 (Miss. 1983).

[153] Arizona ex rel. Thomas v. Schneider, 130 P.3d 991, 994, 2006 Ariz. App. LEXIS 44 (2006).

[154] Jackson v. City of Chicago, 2005 U.S. Dist. LEXIS 32538 (N. D. Ill. 2005).

Voluntary testimony by the client, with neither compulsion nor complaint or upon the client's request, or by the attorney that discloses a portion of the confidential communication is a waiver as to the remainder of the particular communication. A holder waives the privilege by voluntarily divulging privileged information to a third party,[155] whether in court or otherwise. If a client alleges that his or her attorney's representation in a criminal case constituted ineffective assistance of counsel, the client has waived the attorney-client privilege to the extent of the allegation.[156]

§ 10.5   Communications Between Physician and Patient

A. Statement of the Rule

Unlike the attorney-client privilege and the husband-wife privilege, the physician-patient privilege did not exist at common law but instead is dictated by statute[157] or court decision.[158] Therefore, courts are generally not free to modify the statute's intent or to change its mandates, [159] but federal courts are permitted to define new privileges by interpreting common law principles in light of reason and experience.[160] The purpose of the statutes creating the physician-patient privilege is to encourage patients to reveal all relevant information to their physician without worrying that the information will later be disclosed. As the Supreme Court noted, "the physician must know all that a patient can articulate in order to identify and to treat disease; barriers to full disclosure would impair diagnosis and treatment."[161] While the statutes of the various states are inconsistent in defining which professional groups are covered by the physician-patient privilege, most modern statutes include psychologists and psychotherapists. Some statutes specifically include marriage counselors and social workers. Because state laws differ significantly, it is essential that the prosecutor or law enforcement official consult the statutes and analyze the cases interpreting the statutes. If the relationship is not specifically stated in the statute or covered by case law interpretation, the privilege will not be recognized.

California has a statute that provides that a patient has a privilege to refuse to disclose, and to prevent others from disclosing, any confidential communication made to a physician as long as the privilege is claimed by the patient privi-

---

[155]   United States v. Lentz, 419 F.Supp.2d 820, 827, 2005 U.S. Dist. LEXIS 41084 (E.D. Va. 2005).

[156]   LeCroy v. Secretary, Florida Dept. of Corrections, 421 F.3d 1237, 1253, 2005 U.S. App. LEXIS 18570 (11th Cir. 2005), n. 11.

[157]   Guerrier v. Florida, 811 So. 2d 852, 854, 2002 Fla. App. LEXIS 4087 (2002).

[158]   Jaffee v. Richmond, 518 U.S. 1, 15, 1996 U.S. LEXIS 3879 (1996). The Supreme Court recognized that a psychotherapist-patient privilege existed under Rule 501 for federal courts.

[159]   D'Amico v. Delliquardri, 114 Ohio App. 3d 579, 683 N.E.2d 814 (1996). See also State v. Hardin, 569 N.W.2d 517 (Iowa 1997).

[160]   See FED. R. EVID. 501, Notes of the Committee.

[161]   Trammel v. United States, 445 U.S. 40, 51, 1980 U.S. LEXIS 84 (1980).

lege holder or a person authorized by the holder to claim the privilege. A person who was a physician[162] at the time of the confidential communication may claim the privilege for the life of the patient, unless released by the patient.[163]

At first impression, the California provision appears to totally protect confidential medical communications. However, § 998 of the California Evidence Code, provides that, "there is no privilege under this article in a criminal proceeding" for the doctor-patient privilege.[164] Similarly, there is no application of the medical privilege when the services of a physician were sought to enable a person to commit a tort (civil wrong) or to escape detection or apprehension following the commission of a tort or a crime.[165] When medical information that might prove embarrassing is weighed against the interests of justice and potential loss of freedom to a defendant, the confidential medical evidence will be admitted as a matter of public policy as expressed in California law.

As an example of a state with less protection in medical situations, in Massachusetts a court held that general labels of representatives of the Center for Family Development (CFD), who ran a sexual information and trauma team process under the labels of "Sexual Abuse Clinician," "Sexual Abuse Counselor," "Therapist," and "Evaluator," were insufficient to meet the specific professional requirements to render the CFD records privileged under either psychotherapist-patient privilege, rape counselor-victim privilege, or social worker-client privilege.[166] In contrast to Massachusetts, California psychotherapist-patient privilege law covers many more counselors by including physicians, psychiatrists, psychologists, licensed clinical social workers, school psychologists, licensed marriage and family therapists, and numerous other support workers in the mental health and counseling fields.[167] However, Mississippi permits greater protection of the doctor-patient relationships because it holds that medical and pharmacological records are privileged in criminal proceedings and cannot be divulged without the patient's consent.[168]

The Supreme Court of the United States in 1996 recognized a limited federal doctor-patient confidential communication privilege that protects the confidences of a patient and his or her psychotherapist or licensed clinical social worker pursuant to Federal Rule of Evidence 501. The case involved a police officer who had killed a fight participant and had subsequently sought mental health assistance to deal with the aftermath. The Committee Notes to Rule 501 of the Federal Rules of Evidence contemplated that federal courts would define new testimonial privileges consistent with developing federal common law, in accordance with new experiences and needs. In recognizing the new privilege, the Court observed that all 50 states had previously implemented

---

[162] A physician for purposes of California law is defined as a "person authorized, or reasonably believed by the patient to be authorized, to practice medicine in any state or nation." *See* CAL. EVID. CODE § 990 (2006).

[163] CAL. EVID. CODE § 994 (Matthew Bender 2006).

[164] CAL. EVID. CODE § 998 (Matthew Bender 2006).

[165] CAL. EVID. CODE § 997 (Matthew Bender 2006).

[166] Commonwealth v. Pare, 43 Mass. App. 566, 686 N.E.2d 1025 (1997).

[167] CAL. EVID. CODE § 1010 (Matthew Bender 2006).

[168] Cox v. Mississippi, 2003 Miss. LEXIS 103 (2003)

laws to protect some sort of psychotherapist-patient privilege and that the need and rationale for such a privilege was the same as for the marital and attorney-client privileges.[169]

In *United States v. Romo*,[170] the defendant arranged to speak with a licensed professional counsellor whose job included providing psychological counseling to incarcerated inmates. At the meeting, inmate Romo told the counselor specifically that he had mailed a serious threat on the life of the President of the United States to the White House. The counselor informed him that the counselor would have to report the threat and brought the Secret Service into the picture. Inmate Roma repeated his accusations to the Secret Service agent as well to a corrections officer. The appellate court agreed with the trial court that no federal psychotherapist-patient privilege existed under the circumstances because the contact between Romo and the therapist had not been for diagnosis or treatment. Additionally, the communication had been repeated to unnecessary third parties. Disclosure to other parties appeared to establish that the defendant did not consider the information to be private and confidential, which could mean that the federal psychotherapist-patient privilege never existed or that if it did, the patient had waived the privilege.

B. Scope of the Privilege

The privilege exists for the protection of the patient, not the physician, and for that reason the patient is considered the holder of the privilege and may assert this privilege.[171] However, although not a holder, a physician called to testify should alert the court that a medical privilege exists. The rationale for the rule is to shield the patient from disclosures that might be undesirable. There is no intent to protect third persons or other family members, although others may benefit incidentally. For the privilege to apply, the physician-patient relationship must have existed at the time that the physician acquired the information he or she is called upon to disclose. Interestingly, the federal courts do not recognize a physician-patient privilege, but federal courts do recognize a psychotherapist-patient privilege under federal common law.[172]

In an Oregon case, the court held that the doctor-patient privilege normally protected a juvenile's confidential information from revelation by her psychotherapist when the information was gained in the course of treatment and counseling. However, where a patient may have divulged confidential information relative to the patient's sexual abuse of another child, privilege law denies any privilege for communications between a psychotherapist and a patient. The statute makes no distinction based on the fact that the patient may be a minor and is also the person who allegedly perpetrated the abuse, rather than the victim. When a doctor/therapist receives information concerning

---

[169]   *See* Jaffee v. Richmond, 518 U.S. 1, 116 S. Ct. 1923 (1996).

[170]   United States v. Romo, 413 F.3d 1044, 2005 U.S. App. LEXIS 1331 (9th Cir. 2005).

[171]   State v. Miles, 211 Ariz. 475; 123 P.3d 669, 673, 2005 Ariz. App. LEXIS 161 (2005).

[172]   Doe v. Oberweis Dairy, 2004 U.S. Dist. LEXIS 9204 (D. Ill. 2004) and Sterner v. DEA, 2005 U.S. Dist. LEXIS 18467 (2005).

child abuse, there may be an affirmative duty to report it and there is no privilege to withhold that information in some jurisdictions.[173] In a habeas corpus case, a federal appellate court accepted a state court determination that no physician-patient privilege existed where a patient made incriminating statements to hospital nurses in the presence of police officers. The Oklahoma statute covered nurses and other healthcare providers, but not when police officers, who were not necessary to diagnosis and treatment, were present.[174]

Florida takes a blanket approach and holds that no provision exists under Florida law that would allow any breaching of the confidentiality accorded to doctor-patient confidences. In one case a defendant charged with attempted murder wanted to obtain all of the victim's psychiatric records from her psychiatrist, which he believed were necessary to assist in his defense. The court of appeal held that none of the records needed to be disclosed because Florida law failed to contain any statutory authority for revealing the privileged communication and did not offer any legal standard for determining whether or when to reveal confidential communications with a psychiatrist. According to the court of appeals, "there is neither an Evidence Code provision, nor an applicable constitutional principle, which allows the invasion of the victim's privileged communications with her psychotherapist."[175] Confidentiality under these circumstances may encourage people who need psychological assistance to contact medical resources, but it would also foreclose the discovery of important evidence to prevent a miscarriage of justice.

California distinguishes between the doctor-patient privilege, which may be asserted only in civil actions, and the psychotherapist-patient privilege, which sweeps with a much broader stroke and may be asserted in both civil and criminal cases. Under California law, a patient has the privilege to refuse to reveal (and to prevent the doctor from revealing) a confidential communication between the psychotherapist and the patient.[176] As a limitation on the privilege, a psychotherapist may have a duty to warn or disclose information when the or she reasonably believes that the patient or patients pose a credible and serious threat to another person or persons. As the California statute states, "There is no privilege under this article if the psychotherapist has reasonable cause to believe that the patient is in such mental or emotional condition as to be dangerous to himself or to the person or property of another and that disclosure of the communication is necessary to prevent the threatened danger."[177] Because there would be no privilege under these circumstances, appropriate action, such as notifying police and alerting possible victims, must be initiated if the psychotherapist becomes convinced during the course of treatment that the patient is a menace to himself or others.

[173] State ex rel. Juvenile Department v. Michael Spencer, 198 Or. App. 599, 604 108 P.3d 1189, 1192, 2005 Or. App. LEXIS 346 (2005).
[174] Freeman v. Grubbs, 134 Fed. Appx. 233, 2005 U.S. App. LEXIS 10499 (10th Cir. 2005).
[175] Florida v. Farmiglietti, 817 So. 2d 901, 907, 908, 2002 Fla. App. LEXIS 6199 (2002).
[176] CAL. EVID. CODE § 1014, Psychotherapist—patient privilege. (Matthew Bender 2006). The psychotherapist is considered a holder of the privilege unless released by the patient.
[177] CAL. EVID. CODE § 1024, Patient dangerous to self or others. (Matthew Bender 2006).

C. Exceptions

While many states have created the doctor-patient privilege by statute, the exceptions that have been found necessary in order to obtain information required by the public interest or to avoid fraud are so numerous that the value of the privilege has been reduced in many jurisdictions.[178] In New York, among the exclusions from the statutory doctor-patient privilege, the following have been noted as not giving rise to any medical privilege and for which the doctor or other health worker may be required to testify: cases of communicable diseases, cases of child abuse, children under the age of 16 who have been crime victims, serious burns, and bullet and knife wounds.[179] California, for example, excludes cases in which the patient puts his or her condition in issue, all criminal proceedings (unless covered by the psychotherapist-patient privilege) will and similar contests, malpractice cases, and disciplinary proceedings, as well as certain other situations; thus, the exceptions leave virtually nothing covered by the privilege.

When a physician is required by state law to report to a law enforcement officer a gunshot wound, deadly weapon wounds, severe burns, or domestic violence, the physician may testify, without violating the physician-patient privilege, concerning the condition of the wounded person, the victim's personal information, and the description of the nature and location of such wound and how it occurred. Knowledge in these areas may be obtained by examination, observation, and treatment of the victim.[180]

An example of a privilege with limited coverage is Florida, where the psychotherapist-patient privilege covers medical doctors and licensed psychologists but not other practitioners offering mental counseling and assistance. In one case involving the deaths of two children in a vehicle accident in which the wife had been driving, the prosecution sought information from her husband and her psychotherapist. Because both potential sources of information were covered by either a marital privilege or a psychotherapist privilege, the desired information could not initially be discovered. However, the prosecution added a count involving child abuse and neglect due to reckless driving. Under Florida law, this additional charge theoretically allowed the testimony of the psychotherapist and the defendant's husband despite confidential communications. The relevant statute contained an exception to confidential communications privileges when the communication involved a perpetrator or alleged perpetrator of known or suspected child abuse, abandonment, or neglect. The court approved properly limited questioning of both the husband

---

[178] *See* OHIO REV. CODE ANN. § 2921.22. Failure to report a crime or knowledge of a death or burn injury. All doctors and other people have duties to report the commission of known felonies unless covered by a privilege.

[179] *See* In re New York County, 98 N.Y. 2d 525, 779 N.E.2d 173, 178, 749 N.Y.S.2d 462, 467, 2002 N.Y. LEXIS 3140 (2002).

[180] *See* OHIO REV. CODE ANN. § 2151.421. (2006), Duty to report child abuse or neglect; investigation and followup procedures and § 2317.02., (2006) Privileged communications.

and the psychotherapist concerning the child abuse theory based on the auto-mobile wreck because of the exception in Florida law.[181]

Obtaining illicit drugs is not covered by the physician-patient privilege in most jurisdictions. In a Colorado case, a defendant had obtained numerous controlled substance prescriptions from different doctors. The policed arrested him after his doctor discovered that a local pharmacy had a "narcotics alert" on him due to the large number of pain prescriptions filled in a single month. A state statute criminalized the defendant's conduct of obtaining controlled substances illegally and an exception to the doctor-patient privilege allowed the doctor to testify as an exception to the privilege.[182]

The privilege may be justified only when disclosures are made in confidence. Therefore, when the communication is made in the presence of unnecessary third persons, some jurisdictions hold that the privilege is waived. For example, when the crime victim allowed her sister to be present in the emergency room along with a police officer, no doctor-patient privilege existed due to the presence of nonessential persons who overheard the medical information being divulged.[183] New York holds an opposite position and upholds the privilege under similar circumstances. In a case in which an arrested patient gave incriminating statements in front of a police officer to a nurse gathering necessary medical information, the physician-patient privilege remained intact because the officer was required by law to stay with defendant. The presence of a necessary third-party police officer did not destroy the privilege.[184]

While statements made by a patient to a psychologist in the presence of unnecessary third persons are normally outside the protection of the physician-patient privilege, some jurisdictions permit the presence of third parties whose presence does not destroy a psychotherapist-patient privilege. For example, an Oklahoma statute permits the presence and participation of family members without destroying the physician and psychotherapist patient-doctor privilege.[185]

If a psychiatrist gives information to police regarding the identity of a suspect, the privilege does not apply. In an Arkansas case, the defendant's psychiatrist gave police officers sufficient information about the defendant to enable the officer to identify the defendant and to obtain a warrant to search the defendant's home. In this case, the court agreed that evidence developed as a result of the search was not excluded by the privilege.[186]

---

[181] Hill v. State, 2003 Fla. App. LEXIS 8327 (2003).

[182] People v. Harte, 131 P.3d 1180, 2005 Colo. App. LEXIS 1861 (2005).

[183] State v. Gillespie, 710 N.W.2d 289, 298, 2006 Minn. App. LEXIS 24 (2006).

[184] People v. Jaffarian, 2005 N.Y. Slip Op. 25324, 9 Misc. 3d 455, 458, 799 N.Y.S.2d 733, 735, 2005 N.Y. Misc. LEXIS 1640 (2005).

[185] See 12 OKLA. STAT. § 2503, Physician and Psychotherapist-Patient Privilege. (2005).

[186] Gruzen v. State, 267 Ark. 380, 591 S.W.2d 342 (1979), cert. denied, 449 U.S. 852, 101 S. Ct. 144, 66 L. Ed. 2d 64 (1980).

D. *Assertion and Waiver*

The physician-patient privilege belongs to the patient and the physician may be compelled to testify if the patient has waived the privilege.[187] State statutes creating a physician-patient privilege usually provide that if the patient voluntarily testifies about privileged matters, the physician may be compelled to testify on the same subject. In civil actions, the physician also may be compelled to testify by express consent of his or her patient or, if the patient is deceased, by the express consent of the surviving spouse, executor, or administrator of the estate of the deceased patient.[188] However, the physician may claim the privilege covering his or her patients' records in the absence of evidence that the patient for whom the doctor may serve as witness has waived his or her privilege.[189]

In making certain that the patient-physician privilege belongs to the patient, the Supreme Court of Vermont stated:

> While the defendant has the power to invoke the privilege, it is based on the presumption that he speaks for the patient. Once it is clear that he does not speak for the patient, his power to invoke the privilege ceases.[190]

In this case, the defendant doctor was found guilty of knowingly filing false Medicaid claims. His ground for challenging the conviction was that the court erred in allowing evidence of the medical records of the patients to be admitted. However, as the patients did not object to using the records, the physician was not permitted to invoke the privilege because the law conferred the status of holder only on the patients.

In many jurisdictions, a defendant waives any claim of physician-patient confidentiality or privilege concerning information given to obtain an examination or treatment of mental conditions when the defendant asserts that he or she is not guilty by reason of insanity, or has a mental impairment that might affect culpability or makes an allegation that the defendant is not competent to stand trial.[191] A Colorado appellate court in a murder case agreed that, pursuant to a statute, the defendant who raises a mental defense waives the physician-patient privilege with respect to mental issues because, otherwise, the accused could take all the benefits and have none of the burdens of asserted mental defenses.[192] Similarly, in Connecticut, the assertion of an insanity defense constitutes a waiver of the psychiatrist-patient privilege because a defendant must share psychiatric reports and submit to government psychi-

[187] *See* Wheeler v. Commissioner of Social Services, 662 N.Y.S.2d 550 (1997); *see also* OHIO REV. CODE ANN. § 2317.02(B)(1) Privileged communications, when the patient is clearly the holder of the privilege and the physician may be compelled to testify following waiver. (Anderson 2006).

[188] OHIO REV. CODE ANN. § 2317.02(B)(1)(a) and (b). Privileged communications (Anderson 2006).

[189] People v. Bickham, 89 Ill. 2d 1, 431 N.E.2d 365 (1982).

[190] State v. Chenette, 560 A.2d 365 (Vt. 1989).

[191] *See*, for example, COLO. REV. STAT. §§ 16-8-103.6 (2005).

[192] People v. Herrera, 87 P.3d 240, 248, 2003 Colo. App. LEXIS 2039 (2003).

atric examinations as ordered by the court.[193] Waiver may occur if the defense plans to introduce part of a doctor's report, and, as part of discovery, turns the report over to the prosecution. In a case involving attempted murder, the appellate court held that the trial court correctly ruled that the defendant waived his doctor-patient privilege because his public defender voluntarily turned over the toxicology reports to the prosecution, which bound the defendant.[194]

§ 10.6 Communications to Clergy

A. Statement of the Rule

At common law, there was no privilege for communications or confessions to a spiritual advisor, and in the absence of state statutes the privilege would not exist.[195] At present, all 50 states have enacted privilege statutes that cover confidential communications between religious leaders and followers[196] and have attempted to be inclusive in order to cover genuine religions and faiths. Representative of religious privileges is a statute of Colorado, which provides: "A clergy member, minister, priest, or rabbi shall not be examined without both his or her consent and also the consent of the person making the confidential communication as to any confidential communication made to him or her in his or her professional capacity in the course of discipline expected by the religious body to which he or she belongs."[197] California defines "clergy" to mean a priest, minister, religious practitioner, or similar functionary of a church or of a religious denomination or religious organization.[198]

In an Arizona case involving improper sexual conduct between an adult and a child, a church music director received a confession from the defendant in which she admitted to the details of the crime. The director of music did not ever receive confessions and generally referred all questions involving church doctrine and policies to the regular pastor. The music director forwarded the e-mail confession to the church's actual minister, who sent it on to the child's parents, who contacted police. At the trial, the confession was properly introduced because the director of music did not serve as an actual minister, according to church teachings and, therefore, confidential communications to the music director were not covered by the clergy-penitent privilege.[199]

Although every state has a privilege law covering confidential communications made to clergy or similar religious advisors, the statutes differ from state to state. For example, in Louisiana the code is very comprehensive and not only recognizes religious privileges, but also includes definitions. It provides:

---

[193]   State v. Ross, 269 Conn. 213, 292, 849 A.2d 648, 703, 2004 Conn. LEXIS 214 (2004), rev'd on other grounds.

[194]   State v. Moses, 107 Haw. 282, 285, *112 P.3d 768, 772,* 2005 Haw. App. LEXIS 174 (2005).

[195]   State v. Morehous, 97 N.J.L. 285, 117 A. 296, 1922 N.J. LEXIS 186 (1922).

[196]   *See* 73 N.Y.U. L. REV. 225, 231 (1998), n. 39, noting state statutes that provide for the privilege.

[197]   *See* C.R.S. 13-90-107 (1) (C) (2005).

[198]   CAL. EVID. CODE § 1030 (2006).

[199]   Waters v. O'Connor, 209 Ariz. 380, 103 P.3d 292 (2004).

> a person has a privilege to refuse to disclose and to prevent another person from disclosing a confidential communication by the person to a clergyman in his professional character as a spiritual advisor.[200]

The Louisiana legislature included definitions within the statutory formulation covering the priest-penitent privilege. The legislature noted that "A clergyman is a minister, priest, rabbi, Christian Science practitioner, or other similar functionary of a religious organization or an individual believed so to be by the person consulting him."[201] "A communication is confidential if it is made privately and not intended for further disclosure except to other persons present in furtherance of the purpose of the communication."[202] Under this statute, the privilege may be claimed by the person seeking spiritual advice, his or her legal representative, and may be claimed on behalf of the holder by the clergyperson, even after the person's death. [203]

The Michigan statute is more concise. It provides:

> Any communications between . . . members of the clergy and the members of their respective churches, . . . are hereby declared to be privileged and confidential when those communications were necessary to enable . . . members of the clergy . . . to serve as such . . . member of the clergy.[204]

Only in the Court of Appeals for the Third Circuit has a federal priest-penitent privilege been recognized. The Court of Appeals determined that a federal clergy-communicant privilege exists and that this privilege protects the disclosure of communications from a communicant to a member of the clergy in his or her spiritual or professional capacity, by persons who seek spiritual counseling and who reasonably expect that their words will be kept in confidence.[205]

Similarly, under Washington's law regulating religious privileges, it states that "[a] member of the clergy or a priest shall not, without the consent of a person making the confession, be examined as to any confession made to him or her in his or her professional character, in the course of discipline enjoined by the church to which he or she belongs."[206] In a case in which a stepdaughter sought to obtain a church's report of disciplinary action against her sexually abusive stepfather in a tort action against the church and the stepfather, the appellate court upheld the defendant's assertion of the clergy-penitent privilege. The reviewing court noted that the church's disciplinary proceeding against the stepfather was conducted under church doctrine and the disciplinary counsel members were ordained clergy.[207]

---

[200]   LA. CODE EVID. Art. 5.11(B) (2006).
[201]   LA. CODE EVID. Art. 5.11(A)(1) (2006).
[202]   LA. CODE EVID. Art. 5.11(A)(2) (2006).
[203]   LA. CODE EVID. Art. 5.11(C) (2006).
[204]   MICH. COMP. LAWS ANN. § 767.5 a.(2) (Matthew Bender 2006).
[205]   In re Grand Jury Investigation, 918 F.2d 374 (3d Cir. 1990).
[206]   WASH. REV. CODE § 5.60.060(3) (2006).
[207]   Doe v. Church of Jesus Christ of Latter-Day Saints, 122 Wn. App. 556, 568, 90 P.3d 1147, 1154, 2004 Wash. App. LEXIS 1112 (2004).

B. Scope of the Privilege

In order for a communication of a church member to a clergy member to be privileged, the "communications between the penitent and clergy must be: (1) made to an ordained member of the clergy; (2) a confession . . . in the course of discipline enjoined by the church and (3) confidential"[208] and not be deemed to constitute casual communications. The privilege generally applies to a voluntary confession, as well as to one made under a mandate of the church, and to observations as well as to communications. A statute granting the privilege to a "clergyman or other minister of any religion" does not limit the privilege to priests or clergy of any one denomination.[209] The term "clergyman" as used in the draft of Federal Rule of Evidence 506 and in other statutes includes a minister, priest, rabbi, or other similar functionary of a religious organization.

Although the courts have been liberal in interpreting the definition of "clergyman" and other terms as used in the various statutes, the state of New York's cleric-congregant privilege did not encompass statements to an Alcoholics Anonymous gathering and its leader. While the group was acknowledged as a religious organization, the defendant's communication to the group fell outside the cleric-congregant privilege. The evidence divulged at the Alcoholics Anonymous meeting was properly used to convict the speaker of two homicides.[210]

Explaining that the privilege was not universal, a California court held that the privilege did not apply to a conversation of the defendant with a man who had been trained as an "ethics officer" in the Church of Scientology and was not ordained as an auditor or a minister of the Church of Scientology.[211]

C. Exceptions

In order for a communication to be privileged under most statutes, it must have been made to a clergy member in his or her professional capacity or character. Statements made by priests suspected of child abuse taken by other church priests in the course of conducting "troubled-priest interventions" were not considered privileged because communications to and from the individual priests were routinely shared with third parties. Therefore, when a defendant priest spoke to other clergy members as a "friend" under an intervention program, no privilege resulted concerning the communication.[212]

For example, several individuals alleged in a lawsuit that a probationary Methodist clergy member had molested the individual plaintiffs. The churches involved resisted answering the interrogatories with which they had been served. The trial court had ordered the pretrial discovery of the various state-

208   State v. Martin, 137 Wash. 2d 774, 791, 975 P.2d 1020, 1029, 1999 Wash. LEXIS 287 (1999).
209   In re Swenson, 183 Minn. 602, 237 N.W. 589 (1931).
210   Cox v. Miller, 296 F.3d 89, 2002 U.S. App. LEXIS 14398 (2d Cir. 2002).
211   People v. Thompson, 133 Cal. App. 3d 419, 184 Cal. Rptr. 72, 1982 Cal. App. LEXIS 1727 (1982).
212   Roman Catholic Archbishop of Los Angeles v. Superior Court, 131 Cal. App. 4th 417, 421, 32 Cal. Rptr. 3d 209, 2005 Cal. App. LEXIS 1164 (2005).

ments because it held that the clergy-penitent privilege did not apply under the circumstances. The appellate court reversed the trial court decision insofar as it rejected any application of the religious privilege because the appeals court determined that the trial court had used an incorrect legal standard in arriving at its decision. According to the appellate court, the lower court never determined whether the communications to the youth minister were "penitential communications." In suggesting the correct standard to be applied, the court suggested that:

> in order for a statement to be privileged, it must satisfy all of the conceptual requirements of a penitential communication: (1) it must be intended to be in confidence; (2) it must be made to a member of the clergy who in the course of his or her religious discipline or practice is authorized or accustomed to hear such communications; and (3) such member of the clergy must have a duty under the discipline or tenets of the church, religious denomination or organization to keep such communications secret.[213]

The court explained that the person making the statement to the religious leader may be of any faith because California law does not have any special requirement that the person making the communication have any connection to the church or to the clergy member to whom the communication has been addressed.[214]

When the communication is not made within the requisite nature of the confidential disclosure of a penitent seeking religious advice or consolation from a clergy member, a court should not recognize the privilege. Where an alleged sexual abuser made incriminating statements to an Episcopal priest concerning his relationship with a female, a trial court admitted the priest's testimony over the defendant's objection. The defendant's statements to the priest sought advice on his relationship with the complaining witness and were not for spiritual guidance.[215] Similarly, no priest-penitent privilege existed where the defendant spoke to two preachers, whose wives were present, concerning his sexual activity with an underage female. The defendant made no effort to prevent the other individuals from hearing the preachers discuss his situation and the preachers did not, at the time, consider the communication and discussion as privileged.[216]

D. Assertion and Waiver

The majority of the jurisdictions consider the clergy-penitent privilege to be for the benefit of the penitent. Therefore, the penitent may claim the privilege or waive the privilege as he or she sees fit. The general rule is that if the

---

[213] Doe 2 v. Superior Court, 132 Cal. App. 4th 1504, 1516, 34 Cal. Rptr. 3d 458, 466, 2005 Cal. App. LEXIS 1537 (2005).

[214] *Id.* at 1517, 467.

[215] Richmond v. State, 2004 Iowa App. LEXIS 1083 (2004).

[216] Rogers v. State, 2006 Miss. LEXIS 226 (2006).

penitent waives the privilege, the clergy member may be required to testify about the communication.[217] On the other hand, in some jurisdictions, such as California, the clergy member is deemed to be a holder of the privilege on the theory that the state should neither force a member of the clergy to violate, nor punish him or her for refusing to violate, church doctrine where the church teaching requires clergy to maintain secrecy as to confidential statements made in the course of religious counseling.[218]

Despite the fact that most statutes and decisions consider the clergy-penitent privilege to be for the benefit of the penitent, some states hold quite the opposite view and consider the clergy member to be the holder of the privilege.[219] In a New Jersey case, the court held that clergy alone may elect to waive the priest-penitent privilege in their sole discretion and within the dictates of their religious beliefs, and the penitent need not consent to disclosure of the confession, confidential communication, or confidential relation in order for clergy members to waive the privilege.[220]

Evidence of statements made in confidence to a member of the clergy is subject to admission in court in certain situations under some statutes. For example, in Texas, communications that would normally covered by a priest-penitent privilege are not considered privileged when the case involves a sexual assault against a child.[221] Additionally, most jurisdictions hold that the privilege is waived if the holder of the privilege voluntarily discloses privileged material to non-ordained unnecessary third parties. In a Washington case it was not clear, but if the defendant authorized his attorney to allow the prosecutor to take a deposition about the case from his preacher, the reviewing court noted that such conduct would waive the priest-penitent privilege.[222]

§ 10.7 Confidential Informant Privilege

Because confidential informants have long proved essential to various types of law enforcement activities, a privilege has evolved for the protection of the identities of these informants. The rule against disclosure of their identities recognizes that the informants serve as an important resource in effective law enforcement. This privilege prompts citizen involvement in alerting police to wrongdoing with the general promise that the citizen's identity will remain undiscovered by criminal suspects. Some informants were merely observers, while other informants may have been materially involved in the

---

[217] WIGMORE ON EVIDENCE § 2395 (Supp. 1979). *See also*, REV. CODE WASH. § 5.60.060, "Who are disqualified—Privileged communications." (2006).

[218] CAL. EVID. CODE § 1034 (2006).

[219] Burke v. Burke, 59 Va. Cir. 86, 2002 Va. Cir. LEXIS 330 (2002).

[220] State v. Szemple, 135 N.J. 406, 640 A.2d 817 (1994).

[221] TEX. FAM. CODE § 261.202 (2005), Privileged Communication. "In a proceeding regarding the abuse or neglect of a child, evidence may not be excluded on the ground of privileged communication except in the case of communications between an attorney and client."

[222] State v. Glenn, 115 Wn. App. 540, 551, 62 P.3d 921, 927, 2003 Wash. App. LEXIS 161 (2003).

crime to the point at which they may have to be witnesses in criminal trials. Dealing with two types of confidential informants has created confusion about the confidential informant privileges. Some clarity in this area may be obtained by approaching the topic from two perspectives. One approach is to consider the confidential informant who gives information from which the court can determine "probable cause" for securing an arrest or a search warrant. This is different from the informer who was an integral part of the illegal transaction, whose identity may be demanded by the defense, and who has been called a material witness.

United States Supreme Court decisions have made it clear that in most instances the state does not have to disclose the name of the informant who gave information upon which a court found probable cause for a search warrant. In the 1983 case of *Illinois v. Gates,* the Supreme Court reemphasized that it is not necessary to disclose the identity of an informant who only gives information that helps establish probable cause.[223] In this case, police obtained a search warrant for a residence and an automobile based on an affidavit setting forth facts contained in a letter written to police by an undisclosed informant. Police and federal officers corroborated most of the facts contained in the letter. The *Gates* Court, in reaffirming that an informant's identity may be withheld, quoted an older case,[224] and stated that "the magistrate must be informed of some of the underlying circumstances from which the informant concluded that the narcotics were where he claimed they were, and some of the underlying circumstances from which the officer concluded that the informant, whose identity need not be disclosed . . . was 'credible' or his information 'reliable.'"[225] As a general rule, an informant who provides police with information that the police use to obtain a warrant or to foster an investigation may have his or her identity remain confidential. However, if the informant later testifies at trial, the identity must be disclosed to the defendant for Sixth Amendment confrontation reasons to facilitate cross-examination.

As developed from case law and practice, communications made by informants to public officers engaged in the discovery of crime may be privileged. As the Supreme Court noted in *Roviaro v. United States*:

> The purpose of the privilege is the furtherance and protection of the public interest in effective law enforcement. The privilege recognizes the obligation of citizens to communicate their knowledge of the commission of crimes to law-enforcement officials and, by preserving their anonymity, encourages them to perform that obligation.[226]

This privilege exists in order to conceal the identity of the informant, thereby allowing him or her to continue as a source of future information while protecting the confidential informant from reprisals based on the infor-

---

[223]　Illinois v. Gates, 462 U.S. 213, 103 S. Ct. 2317, 76 L. Ed. 2d 527 (1983).
[224]　Aguilar v. Texas, 378 U.S. 108, 114, 1964 U.S. LEXIS 994 (1964).
[225]　*Gates* at 278.
[226]　353 U.S. 53, 59, 1957 U.S. LEXIS 1125 (1959).

mant's cooperation with law enforcement. The public policy encouraging citizens to assist police in solving crimes outweighs the damage that may be done to any defendant's case unless the defendant's due process rights become compromised. Where the confidential informant's testimony is not relevant to the defendant's guilt or innocence, where the informant will not be a trial witness, and where the informant did not participate in the crime for which defendant has been charged, there is no requirement to reveal the identity of the informant. The policy of informant confidentiality has its limits where non-disclosure rule would frustrate a defendant from fairly presenting a defense; in such a case, the informant's identity may have to be divulged. Where the disclosure is relevant and would be helpful to the defense or might be essential to a fair trial, the government's privilege must give way. In making a decision, trial courts must also consider whether revealing an informant's identity will endanger the informant.[227]

Whether the privilege must yield depends upon the facts and circumstances of the particular case based on the degree of the informant's involvement. The informant who merely observed criminal activity and informed police will rarely have his or her identity revealed while an informant who had an active and strong role in the crime may have his or her identity revealed as essential to a fair trial. Cases that fall between non-involvement and active participation prove to be the hardest to determine whether disclosure of identity should be revealed to a defendant.[228] But if the informer testifies for the state, the privilege may not be invoked by it.[229]

Several examples may help to clarify this exception. In an old, but important case decided by the Supreme Court, the justices ruled that the prosecutor was not privileged to withhold the name of the informant when the informant played a direct and prominent part at the crime scene as the sole participant with the accused, Roviaro, in the very offense for which the latter was being tried.[230] The informant had taken a material part in bringing about petitioner's possession of the drugs and he had been present with petitioner at the occurrence of the alleged crime and at the arrest.

In deciding whether to require an informant's identity to be revealed to the defendant, courts generally make a detailed inquiry into the facts. The primary issue concerns whether the informant really falls into the category of a material witness. If the witness has been an active and "hands on" participant in the offense, the prosecution will almost always have to reveal the identity of the witness because identity will be crucial to the development of a defense. However, if the informant has been primarily an observer who conveyed information and did not actively participate in the offense, the witness probably will not be labeled an essential witness for the defense and will not be deemed a material witness. The usual burden rests with the defendant to demonstrate the

---

[227]   United States v. Smith, 2005 U.S. Dist. LEXIS 3782 (E.D. Pa. 2005).

[228]   United States v. Harrison, 2005 U.S. Dist. LEXIS 6195 (E.D. Pa. 2005).

[229]   Nutter v. State, 8 Md. App. 635, 262 A.2d 80 (1970).

[230]   Roviaro v. United States, 353 U.S. 53, 77 S.Ct. 623, 1 L. Ed. 2d 639 (1957).

materiality of the witness. He or she must provide more evidence than mere speculation that the witness possessed a greater degree of involvement.[231] Most courts conduct a rough balancing test, weighing the public's interest in obtaining necessary information against the individual defendant's right to prepare a defense without undue impediment. Once a court has made a decision not to require the identity of a confidential informant to be revealed, the decision is normally reviewed under an abuse of discretion standard, and infrequently will be reversed.

Consistent with *Roviaro v. United States*, a defendant who desires to have an informant's identity disclosed to him must present evidence that tips the balance toward disclosure. In a New Jersey case, the court noted that it needed to balance the need for the information by the defendant against the public benefit in having informants come forward to assist law enforcement agents. According to the New Jersey Supreme Court the privilege to withhold an informant's identity is inapplicable:

> where the informant's identity is already known to those who might pose a risk of retaliation against the informant; where the identity of the informant is relevant and helpful to the defense or is essential to a fair determination of the case; where the informant is an essential witness to an issue that is basic to the case; where the informant actively participated in the crime for which defendant is charged; where entrapment is a plausible defense; and where disclosure is mandated by fundamental principles of fairness to the accused.[232]

In the New Jersey case the informant identified the defendant concerning a restaurant robbery as one of three men who had guns similar to those used in the robbery and who had coin rolls similar to those taken in the robbery. Because the defendant contended that his description did not meet the one given by the informant, he should have been permitted to learn the identity of the informant to show that the informant had made an error in identification. The informant had not placed the defendant at the scene of the crime and the informant had not participated in the robbery at the McDonald's restaurant and could, at best, have been rather marginal in the identification of the defendant. The informant had done no more than provide some slight information or a tip to police in the early stages of the investigation. A different witness tied the defendant to the robbery—not the confidential informant. According to the court, the identity of the informant did not have to be disclosed to the defendant under New Jersey law or the principles of *Roviaro v. United States*.[233]

In order to obtain the identity of confidential informants, the criminal defendant bears the burden of demonstrating the need for disclosure. In one federal prosecution for distributing controlled substances, the defendant con-

---

[231] Carpenter v. Lock, 257 F.3d 775, 2001 U.S. App. LEXIS 15918 (8th Cir. 2001), *cert. denied*, 534 U.S. 1091, 122 S. Ct. 834, 151 L. Ed. 2d 714, 2002 U.S. LEXIS 394 (2002).

[232] New Jersey v. Williams, 356 N.J. Super. 599, 604, 813 A.2d 1215, 2003 N.J. Super. LEXIS 17 (2003).

[233] *Id.*

tended that he needed to know the identity of the confidential informant to whom he had allegedly sold drugs. Because the informant was the sole witness to the alleged transaction and the defendant alleged that he had no knowledge of the crime whatsoever, the identity of the informant was crucial to the construction of a defense. When the defendant's need was balanced against the government's desire to encourage future confidential informants and the chance of harm to the particular informant, the identity must be disclosed, according to the district court. In this case, the fact that the informant was a material witness to the alleged crime necessitated the release of his identity.[234] In a civil case arising from a failed prosecution for drug dealing, the prosecution-defendant sought to keep the informant's identity secret. The trial court determined that the plaintiff had met the burden of proof and ordered that the prosecution reveal the identity and other relevant details of the informant because:

> The informant used by the defendants was not only an eyewitness to the events . . ., but also helped set the stage for the drug transaction and actively participated in the transaction itself. In fact, the confidential informant was the only person to have direct contact with the suspect during the course of the drug transaction.[235]

Because the general rule holds that the identity of governmental informants may be privileged, the burden is on the party seeking to overcome the privilege claim to establish that the party's interests substantially outweigh any governmental secrecy interest.[236]

If an informant only provides law enforcement officials with the location of the defendants, the trial court need not disclose the identity of the confidential reliable informant.[237] Even when an informant was present during the criminal transaction at issue, the fact that he did not actively participate in the crime favors nondisclosure of his or her identity.[238] In an Ohio case, the defendants desired the official disclosure of the informants' identities and used the nondisclosure as an appellate issue. The trial court decision was affirmed because the defendants had not experienced any prejudice, already knew the identities of the witnesses, and had actually personally threatened them at gunpoint prior to the trial.[239]

If a court decides that disclosure of the informant's identity has been shown to be essential to the defense when a failure to reveal the identity would harm the presentation of a defense, or that the informant was a participant in the crime charged, or that the informant's testimony may be crucial to determining guilt or innocence, the informant's identity must yield to the defen-

---

[234]   United States v. Harrison, 2005 U.S. Dist. LEXIS 6195 (E.D. PA. 2005).

[235]   Carbajal v. Village of Hempstead, 2003 U.S. Dist. LEXIS 23493 (E.D.N.Y. 2003).

[236]   State v. Williams, 925 So. 2d 567, 573, 2006 La. App. LEXIS 593 (2006).

[237]   United States v. Given, 712 F.2d 1298 (8th Cir. 1983).

[238]   United States v. Torbide, 558 F.2d 1053 (2d Cir. 1979); see also United States v. Gonzales, 606 F.2d 70 (5th Cir. 1979).

[239]   Ohio v. Lawson, 2002 Ohio 6925, 2002 Ohio App. LEXIS 6656 (2002).

dant's need for the evidence.[240] At this point, the government must choose between revealing the informant's name—thereby risking his or her safety and its own investigative efficacy—and forfeiting the informant's testimony. The privilege not to reveal the identity of confidential informants belongs to the governmental authority, whether state or federal, not to the informant, and thus only the prosecution has the power to waive the privilege.

§ 10.8 State Secrets and Other Official Information

Sovereign governments all have and use information that would have negative effects if the data were openly revealed. Covert intelligence operations, state-of-the-art weapons systems, and diplomatic and military information can all be, at some levels, considered secret matters. In an early case, the executor of the estate of a United States spy sued to recover money allegedly owed under a contract to the estate due to the deceased's espionage work for President Lincoln against the Confederate States of America. The Court of Claims dismissed the case because it believed that the work under the contract was a secret service and that the facts surrounding the contract and its results were to be clandestinely secured and privately communicated. Public policy required that the case be dismissed. The Supreme Court affirmed, noting that, "[i]t may be stated as a general principle, that public policy forbids the maintenance of any suit in a court of justice, the trial of which would inevitably lead to the disclosure of matters which the law itself regards as confidential, and respecting which it will not allow the confidence to be violated."[241]

Recognizing the importance of governmental privilege to withhold sensitive information, the draft of Rule 509(b) of the Federal Rules of Evidence, provided that:

> The government has a privilege to refuse to give evidence and to prevent any person from giving evidence upon a showing of reasonable likelihood of danger that the evidence will disclose a secret of state or official information, as defined in this rule.[242]

The rule defined *state secret* as "a governmental secret relating to the national defense or the international relations of the United States." It defined official information as "information within the custody or control of a department or agency of the government, the disclosure of which is shown to be contrary to the public interest." While the privilege originally embraced only military secrets, courts now recognize that state secrets include all types of "information that would result in 'impairment of the nation's defense capabil-

---

[240] State v. Francis, 2003 Conn. Super. LEXIS 757 (2003).
[241] Totten v. United States, 92 U.S. 105, 107, 1875 U.S. LEXIS 1732 (1875).
[242] The draft of the rule was prepared by the United States Supreme Court but never adopted by Congress.

ities, disclosure of intelligence-gathering methods or capabilities, and disruption of diplomatic relations with foreign governments.'"[243]

This principle, which protects military and state secrets, was described as "well-established in the law of evidence" in the landmark case of *United States v. Reynolds*.[244] In this case, there were fatalities when a B-29 test aircraft crashed while on a secret test mission that included civilians. The surviving family members sued for damages under the Federal Tort Claims Act. As part of their proof, they wanted a copy of the accident investigation report, among other documents. The Air Force claimed a national secrets privilege that the courts ultimately upheld under a clearly deferential approach to the federal government's assertions. In adjudicating the claim of a state secrets privilege, the court held that:

> The privilege belongs to the Government and must be asserted by it; it can neither be claimed nor waived by a private party. It is not to be lightly invoked. There must be a formal claim of privilege, lodged by the head of the department which has control over the matter, after actual personal consideration by that officer. The court itself must determine whether the circumstances are appropriate for the claim of privilege, and yet do so without forcing a disclosure of the very thing the privilege is designed to protect.[245]

The plaintiff's claim of necessity was lessened when the Air Force offered to reveal the accident report and related information, but not the secret details of the equipment and the mission of the aircraft. The Supreme Court upheld the validity of the governmental secrets claim of privilege under these circumstances.[246]

The policy basis of the rule is the desirability of encouraging complete candor among executive department employees to discuss secret governmental operations with respect to their exchange of views within the executive branch of the federal government. Moreover, the state secrets privilege is consistent with the Freedom of Information Act.[247]

In order for the privilege to be allowed under the rule stated and under the general laws of evidence, the government must make a claim of a state secrets privilege and demonstrate a need for protecting the secret or other official information. The judge, in an *in camera* session, may require a showing of the entire text of the government's statements before granting the privilege. Then, if the privilege is successfully claimed by the government, the effect of such claim makes evidence unavailable as though the witness had died or claimed the privilege against self-incrimination.[248]

---

[243]   Molerio v. FBI, 242 U.S. App. D.C. 137, 749 F.2d 815, 820-21 (D.C. Cir. 1984) (quoting Ellsberg v. Mitchell, 228 U.S. App. D.C. 225, 709 F.2d 51, 57 (D.C. Cir. 1983)).

[244]   345 U.S. 1, 1953 U.S. LEXIS 2329 (1953).

[245]   *Id.* at 7.

[246]   United States v. Reynolds, 345 U.S. 1, 1953 U.S. LEXIS 2329 (1953).

[247]   5 U.S.C. § 552(a) and (b). (Matthew Bender 2006). The Freedom of Information Act (FOIA) and the Privacy Act contain exceptions for classified information. 5 U.S.C. § 552(b)(1) (FOIA); 5 U.S.C. § 552a(k) (Privacy Act).

[248]   For a further discussion of the self-incrimination protection, *see* Chapter 16.

In pointing out the importance of the privilege, the United States Court of Appeals for the District of Columbia Circuit indicated that a ranking of the various privileges recognized in our courts would be a delicate undertaking at best, but that it is quite clear that the privilege to protect state secrets must head that list.[249] In another case, a Fifth Circuit Court of Appeals decision stated that "to the extent that the documents withheld are internal working papers in which opinions are expressed, policies are formulated, and actions are recommended, they are privileged."[250] However, the court went on to say that to the extent that the documents contain purely factual material in a form that can be separated without compromising the privileged portions of the document, the material is not privileged and is subject to discovery.

The state secrets privilege covers matters that, if revealed, might threaten military operations or diplomatic interests of the United States and are absolutely shielded from revelation. The privilege includes a prohibition on revelation of covert operations of intelligence agencies or their future operational plans. The privilege belongs to the federal government, which is the only entity permitted to assert or waive the privilege. The process to assert a state secrets claim begins with the agency or department that has responsibility for the area covered by the request. According to *United States v. Reynolds:*

> There must be a formal claim of [the state secrets] privilege, lodged by the head of the department which has control over the matter, after actual personal consideration by that officer. The court itself must determine whether the circumstances are appropriate for the claim of privilege, and yet do so without forcing a disclosure of the very thing the privilege is designed to protect.[251]

While there should be extreme deference given to the executive department that asserts a privilege, the difficult task is to determine whether the claimed privilege would harm the interests asserted without giving away the secret while at the same time protecting national security. The most strongly articulated need for the information will not, according to the *Reynolds* case, overcome a properly pled government claim of absolute privilege.

A claim of government secrets privilege arose when a covert Central Intelligence Agency Operations Officer sued the Central Intelligence Agency, its director, and 10 unnamed employees under Title VII of the Civil Rights Act that he had experienced unlawful discriminatory practices at the hands of CIA management and that job expectations of him were much higher than that for white CIA agents. The federal government moved to dismiss the case, citing the state secret privilege. The federal district court conducted a hearing to determine the validity of the government's state secrets contention. Following a thorough review of the merits of each side, the court determined that in order for the plaintiff to properly pursue the racial discrimination case, he would

---

[249]   Halkin v. Helms, 598 F.2d 1 (D.C. Cir. 1978).
[250]   Branch v. Phillips Petroleum Co., 638 F.2d 873 (5th Cir. 1981).
[251]   *Reynolds,* 345 U.S. at 8.

have to disclose the nature of his employment and the place of his employment, as well as similar information about fellow employees, including their duty stations. In fact, the names of most of his superiors were classified, which would have rendered proof of discrimination by comparing positions and duties a breach of national security. Because the court held that divulging government secrets would have been crucial to the deciding the core factual questions in the case, the state secrets doctrine compelled dismissal of the case.[252]

In another government secrets case that involved the Central Intelligence Agency, a married couple who had served as spies for the United States in their country of origin filed a suit that alleged the government had defaulted on its promises of financial assistance and support in exchange for their spying activities during the Cold War. The couple alleged that the CIA had eventually permitted them to reside in the United States, providing support for many years, but gradually reduced the support level as the couple's income rose. When the husband lost his job and was precluded from taking some jobs due to CIA requirements, they alleged that the government would no longer live up to its bargain to support them for life. Two lower courts allowed the suit to continue on the theory that the government secrets privilege did not apply, but the Supreme Court, citing the post-Civil War *Totten*[253] case, reversed on the theory that public policy prevents suits based on covert espionage agreements between the federal government and individuals.[254] Even if all the allegations were true, there is no remedy where state secrets would have to be revealed.

Some government secrets cases involve allegations that might form the plot of a thriller movie. In a suit against the CIA and its former director, George Tenet, among other defendants, plaintiff Khaled El-Masri, a German national of Lebanese descent, contended that he was abducted by Macedonian agents while attempting to cross the border between Serbia and Macedonia. Following his abduction, El-Masri alleges the Macedonian authorities imprisoned him for 23 days in order to question him concerning his relationship with Al Qaeda. He contended that he was tortured prior to being flown to Kabul, Afghanistan, under CIA control. Prior to the flight to Kabul, he was sodomized, blindfolded, shackled, and drugged. El-Masri claims he was tortured in a small, cold cell under the control of the CIA. He alleged that he was held for four months, during which time he was interrogated about his alleged association with Mohammed Atta, one of the 9-11 terrorist pilots. During one of his hunger strikes, the CIA, he alleges, force-fed him with a tube in his throat. He claimed that when the CIA realized he was not the right person, the CIA eventually had him taken to Albania and released on the side of a road. All of this mistreatment and some injuries, El-Masri alleged, came at the hands of the CIA or its associates which prompted him to sue the head of the CIA, Director Tenet, and other unknown CIA agents under a variety of legal

---

[252]   Sterling v. Tenet, 416 F.3d 338, 341, 2005 U.S. App. LEXIS 15945 (4th Cir. 2005).

[253]   *See* Totten v. United States, 92 U.S. 105, 107, 1875 U.S. LEXIS 1732 (1875), in which secret spy contracts were deemed unenforceable based on state secrets and public policy.

[254]   Tenet v. Doe, 544 U.S. 1, 3, 2005 U.S. LEXIS 2202 (2005).

theories. He filed his suit in a federal district court that had jurisdiction for civil actions by non-citizens for torts committed in violation of the law of nations or in violation of a treaty of the United States. The United States government intervened in the suit and asserted a state secrets privilege and filed a motion to dismiss the suit. According to settled legal theory, when the federal government validly asserts the state secrets privilege to prevent the release of information during pretrial discovery or the release of any information that, if disclosed, would adversely affect national security, the privilege is absolute.[255] Once the federal government invoked the claim that the state secrets were endangered, the district court had to decide whether the proper official had invoked the privilege and then determine whether the government's assertion qualified as a state secret. According to the district court, the judiciary must not blindly accept the government's assertion at face value, but should independently determine whether the alleged government secrets claim deserves the protection of the privilege. Where the claim, if exposed, would harm the military or national defense, the claim will be accepted without requiring additional investigation. In this case, the government contended that damage to national security could result if the government or the defendants were required to participate in pretrial discovery to admit or deny El-Masri's allegations. Because there was no way to try this case without exposing state secrets, the claim had to be denied and the case dismissed.[256] The result may not deliver justice to the individual litigant, but the larger picture of governmental security will not be compromised by allowing government secrets to be divulged.

If the granting of the privilege excludes evidence that may bear directly upon a substantive defense element of a criminal case, it may be necessary to require dismissal.[257]

The state secret privilege was successfully invoked in a case in which a federal employee in the Department of Defense had been dismissed and sued in the federal court of claims, because he believed that he had been improperly fired in violation of the Whistleblower Protection Act, 5 U.S.C. § 2302. As part of his discovery in his suit, he wanted the government to produce some sensitive documents and the federal officials stated that the matter involved a state secret and that the requested documents contained classified intelligence information. The plaintiff countered that the requested documents did not contain information that, if disclosed, posed a reasonable danger to national security. The trial judge agreed with the government that the items desired under discovery clearly concerned highly sensitive subjects and were covered under the state secrets privilege.[258]

---

[255] *See* Ellsberg v. Mitchell, 228 U.S. App. D.C. 225, 709 F.2d 51, 56 (D.C. Cir. 1983).

[256] *See* El-Masri v. Tenet, et al., 2006 U.S. Dist. LEXIS 34577 (E.D. Va. 2006).

[257] United States v. Andolschek, 142 F.2d 503 (2d Cir. 1944).

[258] Barlow v. United States, 2000 U.S. Claims LEXIS 156 (2000).

When the federal government makes an allegation that evidence that a party wants to introduce, or discover, involves a sensitive state secret, the judge should consider whether the proper official invoked the privilege and whether the allegation could conceivably endanger a crucial government interest. Where the judge is convinced that the claim has been properly made and appears to be valid, the proceeding will have to be dismissed if the evidence was critical to the legal action contemplated. When a court holds that the government secrets privilege applies, it is absolute.

§ 10.9 News Media–Informant Privilege

Members of the print and broadcast media, and Internet news outlets often find themselves in situations that may inform them of facts and evidence that ordinary members of the public would not likely discover. Some of this data makes its way to newspapers, news magazines, or to the broadcast arena, but due to space and interest limitations, some of the news is never publicly disseminated. Internet bloggers are the newest arrivals to the news gathering-dissemination cycle, but they are likely to have a presence in news reporter-source litigation, especially because electronic communication on the Internet leaves a clear trail of file meta data that is often very traceable and legally discoverable. News gatherers may find that not only may the judicial system be interested in their sources but police, legislative bodies, and private tort lawyers may develop an intense interest in a particular news source. The reason frequently offered to deny any news privilege concerns the superior interest that the public possesses in favor of proper administration of the law as opposed to private accommodations that have developed between newsgatherers and their sources.[259] Consistent with the general rule that a court is entitled to everyone's evidence, the traditional position held that news gatherers should offer their facts to a court as readily as any other citizen called to give evidence. An opposite position holds that if a news reporter were required to divulge every bit of news confidential information known to him or her, including news sources, to the police, prosecutors, and the courts, their sources would be reluctant to give information necessary for the public to become informed.[260] The First Amendment[261] as applied to the states and to the federal government arguably gives, or should give, some sort of privilege or shield to gather news without revealing all sources.

In recent years, all sorts of reporters, from the national newspapers and media outlets to reporters for small weekly newsletters, have litigated hundreds of cases confronting the issue of whether a reporter has the privilege to refuse to testify concerning information acquired in connection with that per-

---

[259] See A.L.R.3d 37 (Updated Oct. 2005).
[260] This is the same argument that allows police to shield some informants from disclosure of their identities.
[261] "Congress shall make no law . . . abridging the freedom of speech, or of the press. . . ." Constitution of the United States, Amendment I.

son's employment. Unlike communications between husband and wife and between attorney and client, there is no common law dealing with the news media-informant privilege. Earlier cases clearly indicated that unless a statute creates a privilege, journalists are under the same duty as every other person to testify when properly called to court or to a grand jury.[262] In developing the law relating to the news media-informant privilege, journalists have refused to testify or otherwise reveal information on the grounds that the First Amendment protects such communications and that statutes enacted by the various states enhanced this theoretical First Amendment protection.

The United States Supreme Court first confronted the constitutional issue of whether a reporter has a privilege to shield confidential sources in *Branzburg v. Hayes*.[263] In that case, for which Justice White authored a plurality opinion,[264] the Court acknowledged that news gathering qualified for some First Amendment protection, but found that the First Amendment does not guarantee the press a constitutional right of special access to information not generally available to the public. As Justice White wrote in *Branzburg*:

> we cannot seriously entertain the notion that the First Amendment protects a newsman's agreement to conceal the criminal conduct of his source, or evidence thereof, on the theory that it is better to write about crime than to do something about it. Insofar as any reporter in these cases undertook not to reveal or testify about the crime he witnessed, his claim of privilege under the First Amendment presents no substantial question.[265]

Reporters receive little protection under the federal Constitution and generally must respond to grand jury subpoenas as any other witness must do, and answer a prosecutor's questions relevant to an investigation into the commission of crime.

Justice Douglas in the *Branzburg* case would have found an absolute immunity absent the reporter's personal involvement in the crime. Justice Stewart, writing for himself and two other justices, would have found a qualified privilege. Thus, four justices believed that there was no reporter's privilege, three believed in a qualified privilege, and one believed in an absolute privilege. Justice Powell authored the pivotal opinion, agreeing with the four justices, thereby making a majority, but he implied that there may be a form of privilege that should be considered on a case-by-case basis.

The justices of the Supreme Court disagreed at the time this case was decided, and the judges and justices of the federal courts and state courts continue to disagree on the issue. However, Justice White in the *Branzburg* decision invited Congress and the state legislatures to create statutory reporters' privileges.

---

[262] Clein v. State, 52 So. 2d 117 (Fla. 1951).
[263] Branzburg v. Hayes, 408 U.S. 665, 1972 U.S. LEXIS 132 (1972).
[264] For a discussion of the opinions of the various judges in the case of *Branzburg v. Hayes, see* Liggett v. Superior Court, 260 Cal. Rptr. 161 (1989).
[265] *Branzburg*, 408 U.S. at 692.

Taking Justice White's invitation seriously, 28 states by statute or case law have provided newsgatherers either an absolute or qualified privilege from divulging information received in confidence.[266] These statutes have been labeled "shield laws." Congress has yet to enact a federal shield law, but efforts directed toward a federal law have been introduced in Congress.[267] State laws differ in wording and have been interpreted differently by the respective state courts.

California's shield law was first enacted in 1935. This statute has undergone many amendments, and in 1980 the evidence code section relating to the News Gatherers Shield Law was incorporated into the California Constitution.[268] The California Evidence Code provision provides in pertinent part:

> A publisher, editor, reporter or other person connected with or employed under a newspaper . . . shall not be adjudged in contempt by a judicial, legislative, administrative body or any other body . . . for refusing to disclose the source of any information procured while so connected or employed . . . or refusing to disclose any unpublished information obtained or prepared in gathering, receiving, or processing information for communication to the public.[269]

> As used in this subsection, "unpublished information" includes information not disseminated to the public by the person from whom disclosure is sought, whether or not related information has been disseminated and includes, but is not limited to all notes, out takes, photographs, tapes, or other data of whatever sort not itself disseminated to the public through a medium of communication, whether or not published information based upon or related to such material has been disseminated.[270]

In a case involving online news magazines that had gathered and published information obtained from confidential sources to a mass online audience, the owner of the information wanted to find the magazine's sources. The topic of the story involved some stolen Apple Computer trade secrets to develop and release an electronic device that would assist in making live sound recordings on Apple computers. To find out who had stolen the trade secret material, Apple sued the Web site to obtain the identity of the alleged criminal. Civil subpoenas were issued to force the Web site to divulge its confidential sources. Although a trial court ordered the persons to comply with the subpoena and refused to grant a protective order, an appellate court held that any subpoenas demanding unpublished information from the online magazine's owners or employees would be unenforceable. According to the appeals court, any effort to enforce the subpoenas would run afoul of identi-

---

[266] *See* 38 GONZ. L. REV. 445, 450, and n. 19.
[267] *See* 14 COMM. LAW CONSPECTUS 543.
[268] CAL. CONST. art. I, § 2, cl. (b). Amended June 3, 1980.
[269] CAL. EVID. CODE § 1070 (a). (2006).
[270] CAL. EVID. CODE § 1070 (c). (2006).

cal provisions of the California Constitution and the California Rules of Evidence protecting reporters from having to divulge their secret sources and unpublished confidential material.[271]

Even in states that have shield laws, there are limitations on the application of the laws. To successfully raise a claim to the privilege, information generally must have been imparted to the reporter under a "cloak of confidentiality," and there must have been an understanding, express or implied, that the information would not be disclosed.[272] If a reporter or a newspaper fails to assert that the interview in question was conducted under a cloak of confidentiality, a motion to reveal the reporter's notes, transcriptions, memoranda, or tape recordings will not be denied. In Pennsylvania, which has a shield law that allows news organizations and their staffs to protect confidential news sources from disclosure,[273] one case involved a newspaper reporter's article about a defendant charged with murder, in which the reporter interviewed the defendant. The reporter did not obtain the information from a confidential source and the defendant told only about his own version of the shooting and did not implicate any confidential source. The prosecutor had no other source from which to obtain the original raw interview data offered by the defendant and could not call the defendant to the witness stand to ask him. According to the trial court, because the newspaper reporter was not covered by the shield law and its privilege, the reporter was required to testify concerning the matters related to him by the defendant.[274]

While Pennsylvania law covers confidential sources, New Jersey's law is an example of a law that has greater coverage and offers significantly more protection to the news media[275] than those of Pennsylvania. The New Jersey shield law does not require that a confidential source have been the basis or genesis of a story as long as the individual reporter has been engaged in news gathering, procuring, transmitting, compiling, editing, or disseminating news material. When a person who had been injured by inhalation of insecticide had been videotaped with his consent while in the emergency room for a television program called "Trauma: Life in the E.R.," he had no right later to obtain copies of any and all videotapes of his experience in the emergency room as part of a suit against his employer and the video news gathering company. Under the New Jersey statute, a confidential source was not a prerequisite, so the reporters and videographers were covered by the shield law as members of the news media. As a result, they did not have to provide raw video, edited video, notes, or audiotapes of the victim's emergency room experience.[276]

[271] O'Grady v. Superior Court, 2006 Cal. App. LEXIS 802 (2006).
[272] People v. Bova, 460 N.Y.S.2d 230 (1983).
[273] See 42 PA. CONS. STAT. § 5942 Confidential communications to news reporters (2006).
[274] Commonwealth of Pennsylvania v. Tyson, 2002 Pa. Super. 168, 800 A.2d 327, 2002 Pa. Super. LEXIS 1071 (2002).
[275] See N.J. STAT. § 2A:84A-21 Newspaperman's privilege (2006).
[276] Kinsella v. Welch, 2003 N.J. Super. LEXIS 253 (2003); he could not obtain the footage from the Learning Channel because his footage never aired.

Maryland has taken an approach midway between Pennsylvania and New Jersey in developing a news gatherer shield that protects a news reporter from revealing stories or news or information procured by the reporter/news gatherer. However, Maryland may require disclosure of news sources when a court finds that the news or significant information is relevant to a major legal issue before any judicial, legislative, or administrative body, or any body that has the power to issue subpoenas. A requirement to divulge news or data may be ordered when the news or information cannot be obtained from any other source when there is an overriding public interest in disclosure to the court or other public body. The source of the news remains protected from being divulged.[277] Maryland wants the source to remain private and not to become public while requiring that important information be made public.

While the legislative intent behind the shield laws is to protect the relationship between an informant who desires to give information to a news reporter and a radio, television, or newspaper reporter, trial courts must take into consideration the Sixth Amendment rights of a criminal defendant before ruling that certain evidence is protected by the statute. In determining whether a shield statute protects evidence from disclosure, the court must consider the particular circumstances of the case, the crime charged, the possible defenses, the significance of the informant's testimony, and other factors.[278] In a New York case, the court held that in judging a claimed privilege against compelled disclosure by news media, there must be proper balance between the freedom of the press and the obligation of all citizens to give relevant testimony with respect to criminal conduct.[279]

Vermont has taken a different route from many jurisdictions and has opted to follow the strict view that the government is entitled to every person's evidence. While the state has no statute that protects the news media with a privilege not to disclose sources, reporters were believed to possess some protections. Following a celebration that turned into a riot at the University of Vermont, the police and prosecutor's office became aware that a television station had significant video footage taken at the crime scene. A local court issued a subpoena against the television station to produce the footage so that police could attempt to identify the individual vandals for prosecution. The trial court held that the reporters, even in the absence of statute, held a qualified privilege that could be overcome by the prosecution if it could demonstrate: (1) that the materials sought were material to a person's guilt or innocence and (2) that the identities of the vandals could be found from no other source. Relevancy was virtually a given, but because the government failed to demonstrate that alternative efforts would not produce the desired evidence, the trial court held that the television station and its reporters did not have to give their evidence to the prosecution. The Supreme Court of Vermont reversed the trial court in a resounding holding, saying:

---

[277] MD. CODE ANN. § 9-112, Courts and Judicial Proceedings (Matthew Bender 2003).

[278] State v. Geis, 441 N.E.2d 803 (Ohio Ct. App. 1981).

[279] People v. Korkala, 467 N.Y.S.2d 517 (1983).

> In the circumstances of this case, no privilege, qualified or otherwise, excuses [the station] from furnishing the videotape of the riot. Therefore, the State did not have to show that the materials were available from other sources. The facts here are essentially indistinguishable from those in *Branzburg v. Hayes*, 408 U.S. 665, 33 L. Ed. 2d 626, 92 S. Ct. 2646 (1972), in which the United States Supreme Court held that there is no constitutional privilege under the First Amendment that excuses reporters from appearing and testifying before grand juries investigating criminal conduct, even if the source of their information is confidential.[280]

The Supreme Court of Vermont based its decision on the view that every person's evidence should be available, especially where there is a possibility of criminal conduct. It noted that a grand jury had a duty to inquire everywhere except where a bona fide privilege existed. The Supreme Court of Vermont found no privilege in common law, applicable federal statutes, or the First Amendment, so it ordered the television station to give over its videotape.

While the news media-informant privilege of the journalist's privilege remains unsettled in many jurisdictions, some understanding can be gleaned from a review of two inconsistent recent cases. A federal court held that a reporter did not have to reveal telephone numbers of sources who may have "leaked" information that the federal government was interested in particular Islamic charity organizations. The court noted that the reporters and their sources had placed reliance on their confidential relationships when nationally important matters were being investigated. The district court balanced the First Amendment rights given to a free press and the interests of the government under the situation and held that the balance tipped toward maintaining the secrecy of confidential news sources, even though there is no federal news gatherer-source privilege.[281] In a case that held public attention for a long time in which reporters were held in contempt of court for refusing to testify concerning their alleged confidential sources that related to the "leaking" of the identity of a CIA operative, Valerie Plame, reporters lost their legal arguments to establish a reporter's federal privilege. The case had political overtones and reached into the Office of the Vice President of the United States. The litigants contended that the First Amendment gave them a privilege not to reveal sources and confidential material and that they had a common law privilege, among other theories. The Court of Appeals for the District of Columbia circuit rejected their contentions completely and, relying on the Supreme Court's decision in *Branzburg v. Hayes*, upheld their contempt citations. As the Court of Appeals noted, "The Supreme Court in no uncertain terms rejected the existence of such a privilege. As we said at the outset of this discussion, the Supreme Court has already decided the First Amendment issue before us

---

[280] In re Inquest Subpoena (WCAX), 2005 Vt. 103, 890 A.2d 1240, 1241, 2005 Vt. LEXIS 244 (2005).

[281] New York Times v. Gonzales, 382 F. Supp. 2d 457, 2005 U.S. Dist. LEXIS 2642 (2005).

today."[282] With two differing decisions coming from federal courts in two different circuits, the Supreme Court of the United States may decide to resolve differences and reaffirm that there is no federal reporter confidential source privilege in the First Amendment or elsewhere.

§ 10.10 Summary

From a public policy perspective, society generally desires that all relevant evidence be made available to the trier of fact in a criminal case. However, it is also important that certain rights, interests, and relationships be protected, especially where justice may hang in the balance. In resolving these two considerations, some courts and legislatures have developed rules limiting the admission of some types of evidence while some jurisdictions prefer admission of evidence. In some situations, the protection of the relationship or right is considered more important than the need for the evidence, even if it causes an injustice in another area.

One privilege that has developed over a period of many years is the husband-wife confidential communication privilege. The general rule relating to confidential communications between husband and wife is that testimony pertaining to confidential communications arising out of the marital relationship is forever privileged and a court will not require the conversations to be revealed unless both parties agree to do so. However, there are several exceptions to this rule where crimes have been committed against family members or their property or the case involves divorce or child custody. With respect to the marital testimonial privilege, the clear trend is to remove the defendant spouse as a holder and permit one spouse to decide whether to testify against the other. This procedure makes sense if the relationship between the two spouses is such that there is no longer any harmony or interest in preserving the marriage. Under current interpretations, the marital testimonial privilege prevents a witness spouse from being forced to testify against the defendant spouse, but this privilege ends when the marriage is dissolved.

A second common law privilege protects communications between attorney and client. Confidential communications made in the course of professional employment may not be divulged by the attorney without the client's consent. The privilege may not be claimed when the communication concerns the commission of a crime at some time in the future or how to cover up a prior crime. The client holds the privilege, and he or she may waive the privilege even if the attorney does not agree.

---

[282] In re Grand Jury Subpoena (Miller), 365 U.S. App. D.C. 13, 397 F.3d 964, 2005 U.S. App. LEXIS 2494 (2005).

Although at common law there was no physician-patient privilege, most states have enacted statutes creating this testimonial privilege. Where statutes have been enacted, the privilege prohibits disclosure by the physician and allied support staff, when called to testify, of confidential communications made to him or her or information acquired by him or her, in the course of his or her professional attendance upon the patient. The privilege does not apply when a statute requires reports of gunshot wounds or wounds inflicted by deadly weapons. The privilege generally applies only in civil cases when the disclosures were made in confidence, but some states allow medical privileges to be claimed in criminal cases. The patient must claim the privilege and only the patient may grant a waiver.

At common law, there was no privilege as to communications or confessions to a spiritual adviser but all 50 states now recognize the privilege. The clergy member, priest or rabbi may not disclose, over the objection of the party so confiding, the confessions or admissions made as a part of the practice of the particular church. In order for the communication to be privileged under the statutes, it must be made to the clergy member in a professional capacity. Generally, the privilege may be claimed only by the communicator, but the issue may be raised by the priest or rabbi.

One privilege that is of great concern to criminal justice personnel is the confidential informant privilege. It can be said that, as a general rule, the name of the informant does not have to be disclosed, especially if his or her information relates only to facts from which probable cause can be based. However, if the informant played an integral part in the illegal transaction and his or her disclosure is necessary and relevant to a fair defense, his or her identity may be required to be disclosed. Much discretion in this regard is in the hands of the judge when making a determination concerning whether an informant meets the requirements of a material witness.

Testimony relating to state secrets and other official information is sometimes privileged upon a showing of a reasonable likelihood of danger that the evidence will disclose state secrets or official information. Where this privilege is upheld, it is absolute.

The United States Supreme Court has determined that, in the absence of statutes, communications to a newspaper editor or reporter are not privileged in federal courts. In states recognizing the privilege, some courts apply a balancing test that focuses on the need for the information and potential availability from other sources. If collateral sources make the information available, the news media privilege will likely prevail. Twenty-eight states, by statute or otherwise, have enacted news media privilege laws that attempt to resolve conflicting interests.

Because of the common law privileges, as well as the statutory privileges, it is possible that much relevant evidence may be excluded from trials. However, there are many exceptions that permit much valuable evidence to be obtained, if criminal justice personnel are familiar with the rules and the exceptions.

Courts and legislatures frequently alter the confidential communication privilege rules in order to prevent abuse and to effectuate fair public policy. Changes in evidence rules and laws dictate that law enforcement officials consult the rules of evidence and state case law with a view to ascertaining changes that will affect the practice of criminal justice.

Opinions and
Expert Testimony   11

Opinion evidence, to be of any value, should be based either upon admitted facts or upon facts, within the knowledge of the witness, disclosed in the record. Opinion evidence that does not appear to be based upon disclosed facts is of little or no value.

Balaban & Katz Corp. v. Commissioner of Internal Revenue,
30 F.2d 807 (7th Cir. 1929)

Chapter Outline

Key Terms and Concepts

expert witness	polygraph examination
lay witness	summaries
neutron activation analysis	ultimate issue
opinion evidence	voiceprint identification

§ 11.1 Introduction

When a witness takes the stand and testifies, the testimony is normally restricted to the facts and circumstances within the personal knowledge, observation, or recollection of the witness, as distinguished from opinions, inferences, impressions, and conclusions that the facts may have generated in the same witness. The province of the jury is to reach conclusions based on facts regarding matters presented; therefore, an inference, opinion, or conclusion of the witness based on the same facts will generally be excluded from admission under the opinion rule.

However, the rule that excludes opinion evidence has exceptions that are based on reason and practical necessity. Frequently the only possible or practical method of getting proof of a fact in issue is by means of opinion evidence. If, from the nature of the subject matter, no better evidence can be obtained and opinion evidence will aid the members of the jury in their search for the truth, the judge in his or her discretion may admit the evidence even though it consists of an opinion. As one court noted, "Lay opinion testimony is admissible only to help the jury or the court to understand the facts about which the witness is testifying and not to provide specialized explanations or interpretations . . ."[1] The law does not look with favor on opinion evidence because it invades the province of the fact finder, and, in theory, such evidence should not be admitted unless it is required to prevent a miscarriage of justice.

Over the years, courts and legislatures have approved dozens of exceptions to the opinion evidence rule—to the extent that some opinion evidence is admissible in almost every case. These rules of exception have developed in two areas: (1) opinions of nonexpert or lay witnesses and (2) opinions of expert

---

[1]   United States v. Espino, 317 F.3d 788, 797, 2003 U.S. App. LEXIS 261 (8th Cir. 2003).

witnesses. The rules of evidence treat lay witnesses differently from expert witnesses because lay witnesses are typically discouraged from offering opinions while expert witnesses generally are called to offer opinion evidence.

Occasionally criminal justice personnel testify as expert witnesses when they possess a particular expertise such as familiarity with drug transaction protocols, serial killer profiles, or fingerprint comparisons. However, in most instances criminal justice personnel testify as lay witnesses because they offer testimony covering facts within their personal knowledge, observation, or recollection. There is no bright line between lay and expert testimony because every person evaluates information based on individual experiences. Even a lay witness is capable of expressing opinions outside the normal knowledge held by most people without having to be qualified as an expert. When a juror may not fully understand the evidence or not be able to come to a conclusion concerning a fact at issue without the assistance of a person with specialized knowledge, that witness must then be qualified as an expert witness.[2]

The goals of this chapter focus on the general rules related to admissibility of lay opinion evidence and on the protocols required for the use of expert witnesses.[3] The chapter details some of the specific instances that are commonly presented in criminal justice situations and discusses some of the more common rules governing the admission of opinion evidence in criminal cases.

§ 11.2 Definitions and Distinctions

Before discussing the general rules and the exceptions related to opinion testimony of expert and nonexpert witnesses, some definitions are necessary to understand these rules.

A. *Opinion Evidence*

Opinion evidence is defined in *Black's Law Dictionary*[4] as a "witness's belief, thought, or inference, or conclusion concerning a fact or facts." The term refers to opinions offered by witnesses while testifying in open court and is distinguished from extrajudicial opinions.

B. *Expert Witness*

An expert witness is particularly skilled, learned, or experienced in a particular art, science, trade, business, profession, or vocation, and has gained a thorough knowledge of a subject that is not possessed by the average layperson. *Black's Law Dictionary*[5] defines an expert witness as a "witness qualified

---

[2]   Williams v. State, 2006 Tex. App. LEXIS 1687 (2006) quoting Osbourn v. State, 92 S.W.3d 531, 537 (Tex. Crim. App. 2002). *See* case in Part II.

[3]   *See* 2005 UTAH L. REV. 230 (2005) for a note that clarifies the distinction between lay and expert witnesses with respect to their proper subject matter.

[4]   BLACK'S LAW DICTIONARY (8th ed. 2004).

[5]   BLACK'S LAW DICTIONARY (8th ed. 2004).

by knowledge, skill, experience, training, or education to provide a scientific, technical, or other specialized opinion about the evidence or a fact issue." In one case, an expert witness was defined as one who has acquired the ability to deduce correct inferences from hypothetically stated facts or from facts involving scientific or technical knowledge.[6]

C. Nonexpert Witness

A nonexpert, or lay witness, is one who is not particularly skilled, learned, or experienced in the particular area that is at issue in the court, but who may have knowledge that an average person possesses about many of the things involved in everyday life. A person who is an expert in one field may be considered to be a lay witness when he or she takes the stand to testify about a field in which the witness can claim no expertise. The lay witness bases his or her conclusions on facts personally observed, while the expert witness, who must qualify as such by establishing that he or she has some special skill, knowledge, or experience, may base his or her opinions on facts of his or her own observation or on evidence presented by other witnesses. The lay witness may offer opinions concerning matters about which the average person forms opinions, such as the identity of a person[7] or whether an automobile driver had consumed excessive alcohol.[8] The line between lay and expert testimony is not always easy to discern and the same witness may offer some evidence as a lay witness and also offer evidence as an expert.[9]

§ 11.3 Admissibility of Nonexpert Opinions

> **Rule 701**
>
> **Opinion Testimony by Lay Witnesses**
>
> If the witness is not testifying as an expert, the witness' testimony in the form of opinions or inferences is limited to those opinions or inferences which are (a) rationally based on the perception of the witness, and (b) helpful to a clear understanding of the witness' testimony or the determination of a fact in issue, and (c) not based on scientific, technical, or other specialized knowledge within the scope of Rule 702.[10]

---

[6] City of Chicago v. Lehmann, 262 Ill. 468, 104 N.E. 829 (1914). "Expert witness" will be further defined in later sections of this chapter.

[7] United States v. Beck, 418 F.3d 1008, 2005 U.S. App. LEXIS 16713 (9th Cir. 2005).

[8] McClain v. Texas, 2005 Tex. App. LEXIS 760 (Tex. Crim. App. 2005).

[9] United States v. Ayala-Pizarro, 407 F.3d 25, 2005 U.S. LEXIS 8322 (1st Cir. 2005). *See* State v. Streckfuss, 171 N.C. App. 81; 2005 LEXIS 1190 (2005), in which a police officer was permitted to identify the smell of alcohol and give a lay opinion that the defendant driver was alcohol impaired.

[10] FED. R. EVID. 701.

Although subject to many exceptions, the general rule provides that "non-expert" or lay witnesses must state facts or offer evidence based upon their personal knowledge and observations. With some exceptions, lay witnesses cannot give conclusions or opinions, but this rule is tempered by the fact that many items of evidence that could be considered opinions may not be viewed as such through the eyes of the law. For example, when a person testifies as to what he or she observes, hears, or smells, the testimony may be considered a statement of fact and not a conclusion or opinion—even though the statement is actually an opinion of what he or she saw, heard, or smelled.[11] Much effort has been expended to confine the testimony of witnesses to statements of what they saw, heard, or otherwise observed, as distinguished from inferences or opinions formed as a result of such observations. The legal distinction between opinion and fact has not been characterized as a bright line, but can be viewed as shades of gray. For example, one person may testify that the color of a swimming pool was blue while another might refer to the same pool as having an aqua color. Both persons probably view their respective characterizations of color as fact rather than realizing that each one has testified concerning their opinion of the color of the pool.

Despite occasional appellate disputes about whether it was proper for a lay witness to give an opinion[12] or whether the opinion offered by a particular witness should have been preceded by testimony establishing the witness's qualifications as an expert, the modern trend appears to allow more lay opinion to be introduced. As one court noted, "a lay witness can give opinion testimony if the witness' opinion is rationally based on such witness' perception and it is helpful in providing a clear understanding of the testimony of the witness or a determination of a fact at issue."[13] A trial court has broad discretion on the admission of lay witness testimony and a judge's decision will only be disturbed on appeal for an abuse of discretion.[14] However, when a lay witness clearly crosses the line to offer testimony that requires special expertise, courts tend to prevent the lay witness from giving testimony that is beyond the competency of the witness.[15]

The lay witness may state a relevant opinion if it is: (1) based the original perception of the witness; (2) generally helpful to the finder of fact to obtain a clear understanding of the issues; and (3) not based on the types of evidence that are reserved for expert testimony.[16] The general rule is that as a condition of stating his or her opinion, the witness must state the facts on which such opinion is based, but if the basis is mentioned on direct examination, the witness will be required to offer it if asked on cross-examination. The enumera-

---

[11] *See* Livingston v. Texas, 2006 Tex. App. LEXIS 2234 (2006), in which an appellate court upheld the trial court ruling that permitted a lay witness to testify concerning the identity of odors emanating from a boat that smelled "like cigarettes, stale beer, and sweaty sex."

[12] People v. Souva, 2005 Colorado App. LEXIS 1615 (2005).

[13] Ohio v. Zentner, 2003 Ohio App. LEXIS 2185 (2003).

[14] Colorado v. Caldwell, 43 P.3d 663, 667, 2001 Colo. App. LEXIS 1514 (2001).

[15] *See* State v. Nobach, 2002 Mont. 91, 309 Mont. 342, 46 P.3d 618, 2002 Mont. LEXIS 189 (2002).

[16] FED. R. EVID. 701.

tion of facts not only goes to show the competency of the witness, but also provides an opportunity to test the reasonableness of the inference, because a witness will not be permitted to state an opinion that is inconsistent with or finds no support in the facts.

The purpose of allowing a lay witness to testify concerning his or her opinion is to help the jury or fact finder obtain a clear understanding of the testimony or to help decide a fact at issue. However, opinion testimony may be admissible in some jurisdictions only after a showing that the witness's perceptions cannot adequately be conveyed except through opinions.[17] To allow opinion testimony absent a showing of the inadequacy of other means of expression may invade the province of the jury. This principle was succinctly explained by a Washington court, which held that a witness, whether lay or expert, may not offer an opinion concerning the defendant's guilt, whether by a direct statement or by inference, as such testimony is inherently prejudicial because it invaded the role reserved for the jury.[18] Courts generally hold that neither a lay nor an expert witness may testify as to the guilt of a defendant, even by inference, and such comments directly or indirectly are prohibited.[19] However, some courts allow lay witnesses to come dangerously close to offering an opinion concerning the ultimate issue. In a Texas case, the trial court properly permitted a lay witness to offer opinion evidence on the issue of whether a defendant properly used deadly force to protect another person,[20] an issue that went to the core of the case.

Even if the lay witness can describe some of the circumstances that led to an opinion, the witness may still give an opinion even when it is difficult to articulate all of the factors. For example, in a theft case in a retail store, a loss prevention security guard was permitted to offer lay opinion evidence concerning whether the defendant intended to deprive Wal-Mart of its property. While a lay witness cannot possess personal knowledge of what another person may be thinking, she may possess personal knowledge of facts from which an opinion regarding the mental state of another person may be drawn. The opinion offered by the lay witness in this theft case was based on her personal perceptions and observations and her opinion was rationally based on knowledge of the events observed.[21]

Apparently extending the use of opinion evidence by nonexpert witnesses, Federal Rule of Evidence 701(b) allows opinions or inferences if they are merely "helpful" to clarify the witness's testimony or to aid in the determination of a factual issue. With the addition of 701(c) in 2000, the lay witness may now offer an opinion as long as it is not based on scientific or specialized knowledge traditionally covered by expert testimony. For example, in a major drug trafficking case, a police officer was properly permitted to testify about

---

[17] Kight v. State, 512 So. 2d 922 (Fla. 1987).

[18] State v. Thompson, 950 P.2d 977 (Wash. 1998).

[19] Washington v. Olmedo, 112 Wash. App. 525, 531, 49 P.3d 960, 963, 2002 Wash. App. LEXIS 1705 (2002).

[20] Garcia v. State, 2005 Tex. App. LEXIS 4424 (2005).

[21] Hines v. State, 2006 Tex. App. LEXIS 3256 (2006).

his deciphering of a phone book, ledgers, and a date book to match customers with drug amounts purchased and money owed. The officer did some low-level deciphering of the books but did not embark on code breaking or sophisticated analysis to figure the meaning of the books. The court held that the testimony of the police officer constituted lay testimony for which no special foundation or expertise was necessary.[22] The 2000 amendment to Rule 701 may broaden the circumstances under which a lay witness may give an opinion or inference based upon personal observation,[23] but limits remain on the conclusions that lay witnesses may draw. In a state case, a police officer should not have been permitted to give an opinion concerning why people slide down in their car seats when they see police cars, because a jury is fully capable of forming its own conclusion.[24]

Referring to the proper standards for admissibility of lay opinion testimony, a federal court of appeals commented that lay opinion evidence should be admissible when the witness has had sufficient contact with the facts of the case that would render a lay opinion helpful to the judge or jury. In the case, a defendant's probation officer had been permitted to identify the defendant by looking at a still picture taken by a bank's surveillance system. The probation officer had previous significant contacts with the defendant that were considered sufficient to be able to recognize a picture of his client, the accused bank robber. The Court of Appeals for the Ninth Circuit held that a lay witness probation officer's identification testimony was properly admissible within the meaning of Rule 701, where it was based upon personal observation and recollection of concrete facts.[25]

Although allowing some lay opinion evidence, Rule 701, however, does not allow the introduction of opinion evidence when the facts are clear and the jury can draw its own conclusion from the facts that have been presented. To allow lay opinion evidence under such circumstances would present the risk that the testimony might usurp the function of the jury.[26]

While Rule 701 placed some limits on the admissibility of opinion testimony by lay witnesses, the rule did not have the effect of prohibiting an undercover police officer from testifying concerning the identity of a defendant based on several telephone conversations and from knowledge of his voice gained from personal meetings. The court permitted the officer to offer the opinion that the defendant was the person with whom the officer spoke during the telephonic initiation of several drug transactions.[27]

[22] United States v. Cano, 289 F.3d 1354, 1361, 1362, 2002 U.S. App. LEXIS 8590 (11th Cir. 2002), *cert. denied*, 2003 U.S. LEXIS 433 (2003).
[23] FED. R. EVID. 701 had subsection (c) added in 2000 and became effective on December 1, 2000.
[24] State v. Clark, 136 S.W. 3d 582, 2004 Mo. App. LEXIS 904 (2004).
[25] United States v. Beck, 418 F.3d 1008; 2005 U.S. App. LEXIS 16713 (2005).
[26] United States v. Reneau, 390 F.3d 746, 2004 U.S. App. LEXIS 24837 (2nd Cir. 2004), *cert. denied*, 544 U.S. 1007, 2005 U.S. LEXIS 3660 (2005).
[27] United States v. Bush, 405 F.3d 909, 2005 U.S. App. LEXIS 7114 (10th Cir. 2005).

It is obvious that significant evidence would be unavailable to the fact finders if all lay opinion evidence were excluded from criminal trials. Examples of proper subject matter for lay opinion testimony are discussed in § 11.4.

§ 11.4 Subjects of Nonexpert Opinions

A. Age

Lay witness opinion testimony is admissible when it is rationally based on personal knowledge and helpful to the trier of fact. It is a foregone conclusion that all humans evaluate other humans with respect to the age for various reasons. Because the age of other humans is important and virtually everyone makes this determination, age is a matter on which everyone has experience and may offer courtroom opinion. Competent witnesses with firsthand knowledge will generally be permitted to offer an estimate or opinion as to the age of a person[28] and a witness may give his or her age, although the age of the witness was not personally known by the witness.[29] As one court noted, where age was concerned, it was "particularly appropriate for a lay witness to express an opinion on the subject."[30]

In criminal prosecutions involving possession of child pornography, the prosecution must demonstrate that some of the actors involved are less than 18 years of age. Because many of the films seized do not leave any way to find or discover the actors and their real ages as of the date of the video recording, witnesses for the prosecution will have to offer evidence concerning age. In one child pornography prosecution, the federal government used lay witnesses to date the age of the actors involved over the objection of the defendant that expert witnesses were required to offer proof of age for underage victims. The court of appeals upheld the use of lay witnesses to prove the age of child victims on the theory that lay witnesses with some specialized knowledge could offer opinion evidence concerning the ages of the children in the film where the witnesses had served as postal inspectors and possessed years of training and experience in determining the ages of video actors.[31]

Necessity often requires that the opinion of the witness as to the age of a person be used because it is often impossible to testify to the exact age of another person. For example, a North Carolina court commented:

---

[28] Asplundh Manufacturing Company v. Benton Harbor Engineering, 57 F.3d 1190, 1201, 1202 (3d Cir 1995).
[29] State v. Selmon, 2006 Ohio 65, 2006 Ohio App. LEXIS 50 (2006).
[30] United States v. Yazzie, 976 F.2d 1252, 1256 (9th Cir. 1992).
[31] United States v. Davis, 41 Fed. Appx. 566, 571, 2002 U.S. App. LEXIS 15312 (3d Cir. 2002), and in another pornography case, the trial court properly permitted lay testimony concerning age. *See* United States v. Nelson, 38 Fed. Appx. 386, 392 (9th Cir. 2002).

> The opinion of a lay witness concerning the age of an accused is admissible into evidence when the witness has had adequate opportunity to observe the accused.[32]

Thus, if the witness has had adequate opportunity to observe the accused and if it is impossible to determine the exact age of the person, then opinion evidence of the lay witness concerning age is admissible. If the exact age of an individual is available from documents or the individual in question, however, the use of that evidence is generally appropriate, sufficient,[33] and preferable to estimation of age by a lay or an expert witness.

B. *Appearance*

When individuals experience exciting events, become upset, have frightening experiences, or seem scared of another person or situation, an explanation of all the outward manifestations that give rise to the conclusion that a person has experienced excitement, fear, or another emotion are not easily described by another person. How one person's demeanor appears to another is a matter well within the human experience and would not ordinarily call for expert testimony. Assuming a witness meets the requirements of competency and has personally observed another person, a court normally should admit lay testimony concerning the appearance and demeanor of another. For example, in an assault case in which a man threatened his former girlfriend with a firearm, the trial court admitted testimony of a police officer that the victim appeared "fearful" and "excited" at the time he initially encountered her. The appellate court upheld the admission of the testimony describing the victim on the theory that lay testimony can be offered when it is based on the perception of the witness (the officer) and the testimony would be helpful to a clear understanding of the witness's testimony. The officer had firsthand perception and his statements were based on direct involvement and experience in the case.[34] In a case involving felony driving under the influence, an off-duty police officer had been drinking at a bar with three friends and became intoxicated. Prior to leaving the bar, a waitress noticed the off-duty police officer and concluded that he was "wobbly" and "obviously intoxicated." A waitress in a bar would normally have observed the effects of alcohol on human behavior and have a foundation for her opinion. The trial judge allowed the waitress to offer her opinion or conclusion to the jury over the defendant's objection. According to the appellate court, because the waitress had firsthand knowledge that would be helpful to the jury and her opinion was rationally based on her perception, the trial court properly admitted her lay opinion under Mississippi's adaptation of Rule 701.[35]

---

[32]   State v. Cobb, 295 N.C. 1, 243 S.E.2d 759 (1978).
[33]   Commonwealth of Massachusetts v. Montalvo, 50 Mass. App. Ct. 85, 88, 735 N.E.2d 391, 394, 2000 Mass. App. LEXIS 763 (2000).
[34]   Washington v. Bain, 2002 Wash. App. LEXIS 1863 (2002).
[35]   George v. Mississippi, 812 So. 2d 1103, 1105, 1106, 2001 Miss. App. LEXIS 436 (2001).

In a different case, the trial court did not commit error when it allowed a detective's testimony in an assault case to describe the defendant's physical condition at the time of the incident, he had noticed the defendant was very muscular and had calloused knuckles. This testimony was relevant because it attempted to show, through appearance, that the defendant had the strength and ability to inflict the serious injuries sustained by the victim.[36]

C. Conduct

A lay witness may describe the acts, conduct, and demeanor of a person under investigation if necessary to enable the jury to draw a correct inference. In such a case the witness should be required—as far as is possible—to state the facts on which he or she based his or her opinions. In a prosecution for mail fraud and extorting campaign contributions by the city treasurer, prosecution witnesses, when describing the management style and conduct of the city treasurer, went too far when they testified that they had "no doubt" and had a "personal feeling" that the manager had ordered their supervisor to prevent recalcitrant contractors from receiving future business from the city. The opinion about the treasurer's inferred decisions offered by the lay witnesses was not grounded in any perception and constituted inadmissible speculation.[37]

However, lay opinion as to the mental state of another person may be admissible in some cases. One court properly permitted several law enforcement officers to testify that the defendant "tried to kill" one of the officers involved. The reviewing court held that the lay testimony of the officers "amounted to nothing more than shorthand statements of fact based on their knowledge and observations." The testimony of the officers had the effect of explaining their perceptions and did not directly implicate the guilt or the mental state of the defendant,[38] although the testimony seemed to clearly reflect on the intended conduct of the defendant.

An appellate court approved allowing an eyewitness to a drug-related murder testify that the reason the defendant killed her sister was because her sister sold more drugs at her location than the defendant was selling at his drug point. The witness and the defendant were heavily involved in the drug trade and understood how it operated. Because the witness was subject to intense cross-examination, the trial court was within its discretion to allow the lay opinion concerning the reason for the murder.[39] When describing conduct, the better view would be to have the witness tell what he or she observed, saw, and heard, but the rules of evidence do not preclude the use of words of opinion-description when appropriate and when the opinion does not unnecessarily invade the province of the jury.

---

[36]   State v. Ames, 950 P.2d 514 (Wash. 1998).

[37]   United States v. Santos, 201 F.3d 953, 963, 963, 2000 U.S. App. LEXIS 649 (7th Cir. 2000).

[38]   State v. McVay, 620 S.E.2d 883, 2005 N.C. App. LEXIS 2402 (2005).

[39]   United States v. Vega-Figueroa, 234 F.3d 744, 755, 2000 U.S. App. LEXIS 32127 (1st Cir. 2000).

Testimony concerning observed conduct may prove crucial when investigating a suspected intoxicated automobile driver. In a Texas case, officers conducted field sobriety tests on a subject who was asked to do a one-leg stand test and a walk-and-turn test. The trial court permitted the officers involved to offer lay testimony concerning the tests and their observations of the subject's performance involving coordination, balance, and ability to follow instructions. The tests and their results were considered grounded in the common knowledge that persons who are impaired will not normally perform well on the tests and such observation of the test taking. The appellate court held that police officers could properly testify concerning the results of routine field tests for impairment.[40] In an Ohio case, police officers observed several subjects around a pickup truck and one man on the sidewalk leaning inside the vehicle. One officer testified that from the time of day, the location, the number of people around the vehicle, and considering the defendant's actions and hand movements, the officer believed that a drug transaction was taking place. The appellate court approved of the officers' testimony about the defendant's activities and agreed that they could properly offer their lay opinion that they believed a narcotics deal was being concluded.[41]

A Montana appellate court upheld a trial court decision that permitted police officers to offer lay opinions concerning whether the defendant possessed methamphetamine for the purposes of sale. According to the officers, based on their experience, the quantity of illegal drugs the defendant was carrying indicated possession with the intent to distribute. The officers testified concerning their training, experience, and knowledge of the manner that methamphetamine was typically distributed. The appellate court held that the testimony was rationally based on their perceptions and helped convey a clear understanding of the facts in the case.[42] In a Texas case, involving a similar rationale, the court upheld the admissibility of a detective's lay opinion that a quantity of methamphetamine was being held for purposes of sale because scales, packaging materials, and a large amount of money were present at the defendant's place of residence.[43]

While the recent trend has been to permit more lay opinion testimony, many courts still place some limitations on the use of lay opinion, especially where the testimony leans clearly toward being classified as expert testimony. In a Second Circuit case, where investigators listened to wiretaps of numerous suspects thought to be involved in the drug trade and offered their conclusions and opinions concerning the wiretap and other criminal activity to the court, such testimony was beyond the scope of lay testimony. The court rejected the prosecution's contention that the officer was offering testimony that would be helpful to the jury and concluded that the opinion offered usurped the role of the jury and should not have been admitted at trial.[44]

---

[40] Plouff v. State, 2006 Tex. App. LEXIS 2546 (2006).

[41] State v. Farrow, 2005 Ohio 3005, 2005 Ohio App. LEXIS 2799 (2005).

[42] State v. Frasure, 323 Mont. 479, 100 P.3d 1013, 204 Mont. LEXIS 558 (2004).

[43] Ortiz v. Texas, 2005 Tex. App. LEXIS 6721 (2005).

[44] United States v. Reneau, 390 F.3d 746, 750, 2004 U.S. App. Lexis 24837 (2d Cir. 2004), *cert. denied*, 544 U.S. 1007, 2005 U.S. LEXIS 3660 (2005).

D. Distance and Space

In criminal cases it is often necessary to elicit testimony concerning location, distances, and space between objects. While it is preferable to introduce evidence to show exact distances, in some cases this is not practical, and opinion evidence becomes necessary. As a result, an ordinary witness may give his or her estimate of distances, provided that he or she is cognizant of the facts on which the estimate is based. The lay witnesses must have a sound foundation for offering an opinion concerning the speed of a vehicle. An appellate court approved a lower court's decision not to allow minor nondriver eyewitnesses, ages 10 and 13, respectively, to offer opinions about the actual speed of a truck immediately prior to a collision[45] but a federal district court allowed teenaged girls to give testimony concerning the speed of a vehicle even though they had little experience in driving motor vehicles.[46] In a more appropriate context involving the speed of a vehicle, courts have held that police officers, testifying as lay witnesses, may offer opinions concerning the speed of vehicles they have observed. In one case, an officer who had an unobstructed view saw and heard a defendant's truck proceeding up the street with its engine racing and noticed the bouncing of the vehicle due to speed. The court permitted the officer to give his opinion concerning whether the vehicle was being operated in excess of the posted speed limit.[47] On the other hand, a victim-witness should not be permitted to give an estimate or opinion of the distance that a tractor-trailer truck pushed her car when she was not "sure" and did not "remember" how far the truck pushed her car.[48] In traffic enforcement cases, police are permitted to make an estimate that one vehicle was following another vehicle at too close of a distance and to base a traffic stop on such a conclusion.[49]

E. Time and Duration

Relying on this same rationale, courts have authorized witnesses to make estimates of elapsed time.[50] However, if the witness can give specifics from which the jury can make its own estimate of time, then the opinion evidence regarding the passage of time is inadmissible. In a case in which an alibi defense rested on proof of time, lay witnesses were permitted to offer opinions concerning when the defendant was present at particular locations, some of which supported his alibi with reference to time and some of which did not assist in his alibi defense.[51]

---

[45]   Marshall v. Williams, 153 N.C. 128, 134, 574 S.E.2d 1, 2002 N.C. App. LEXIS 1071 (2001).
[46]   Bradley v. O'Donoghue, 2005 U.S. Dist LEXIS 4716 (2005).
[47]   State v. Barnhill, 166 N.C. 228, 601 N.E. 215. 204 N.C. App LEXIS 1607 (2004).
[48]   Heath v. Rush, 259 Ga. App. 887, 578 S.E.2d 564, 2003 Ga. App. LEXIS 287 (2003).
[49]   Ford v. State, 158 S.W.3d 488, 2005 Tex. Crim. App. LEXIS (2005).
[50]   Allison v. Wall, 121 Ga. 822, 49 S.E. 831 (1905).
[51]   Gonzalez v. Texas, 2000 Tex. App. LEXIS 3032 (2000).

F. Intoxication and Drug Use

When a witness possesses an appropriate foundation to offer lay opinion evidence, the witness may state his or her conclusion without first detailing the facts on which he or she bases such opinion. The subject of the testimony must not encompass topics of a complex nature that would be appropriate only for expert witness testimony. Intoxication is such a matter and is so commonly encountered that almost anyone may discern it.[52] Therefore, a former police officer who observed the defendant speeding, hitting a vehicle, jumping a curb, rolling three times, getting out of the remains of the vehicle after an accident, having slurred speech, and stumbling around was permitted to offer his opinion that the defendant was intoxicated.[53] Because opinion evidence of intoxication is not restricted to expert testimony, a police officer may offer lay evidence that a person was impaired where sufficient basis for the opinion exists. In a driving while impaired prosecution, an officer concluded and was permitted to offer the opinion that the driver of a boat was operating the craft while under the influence of alcohol. The foundation or basis for the officer's opinion was the subject's poor performance on sobriety tests.[54] For any witness to offer an opinion concerning drug or alcohol use, the lay witness must show that he or she had a sufficient firsthand opportunity to observe the defendant while the proponent of the evidence must show that the witness possessed a foundation for the opinion.

While the arresting officer may not give a legal definition of driving while impaired, the officer may give his or her opinion that the defendant was a less safe driver as a result of alcohol consumption, based on the officer's experience with driving under the influence arrests and observations.[55] As a general rule, a police officer may not offer an opinion concerning whether an arrested driver was under the influence of controlled substances because that opinion must be offered by an expert. In a Texas case in which the officer testified that the driver appeared to be under the influence of alcohol or some controlled substance, the court of appeals reversed the driving under the influence conviction because the arresting officer gave no qualified evidence that the defendant was under the influence of a controlled substance and there was no other evidence that supported the conviction.[56]

Montana court first explained the rule to be applied and then applied the rule relating to the admissibility of lay testimony when evidence of intoxication is offered. The court advised that the state complied with the foundational requirement of the evidence rule that requires testimony from personal knowledge and the evidence rule relating to opinion testimony by lay witnesses, and thus, admission of lay witness testimony pertaining to a witness's opinion as

---

[52]   Warren v. State, 164 Md. App. 153, 168, 882 A.2d 934, 943, 2005 Md. App. LEXIS 189 (2004).
[53]   Sloane v. State, 2004 Tex. App. LEXIS 6903 (2004).
[54]   Bowling v. State, 275 Ga. App. 45, 47, 619 S.E.2d 688, 689, 690, 2005 Ga. App. LEXIS 808 (2005). *See* case in Part II.
[55]   Hatcher v. State, 277 Ga. App. 611, 613, 627 S.E.2d 175, 177, 2006 Ga. App. LEXIS 164 (2005).
[56]   Kaleta v. State, 2003 Tex. App. LEXIS 2677 (2003).

to whether the defendant was intoxicated on the night in question was not an abuse of discretion in a prosecution for driving while intoxicated. The court noted that the record made it clear that the witness's opinions as to the defendant's intoxication were rationally based on his perception and personal knowledge, and the state established that the witness knew the objective signs of intoxication, that he had a great deal of experience being around people who have been in varying states of intoxication, and that he had observed the defendant for quite some time before alerting police.[57]

In one case, the defendant was convicted of operating a motor vehicle while under the influence of intoxicants. On appeal, the defendant argued that the trial court erred in allowing a police officer to express an opinion concerning his intoxication. The court held that because the officer's perception was helpful in determining an issue in the case and the officer had a rational basis for his opinion based on significant experience with impaired drivers, he was properly allowed to testify, even though he was offering testimony as a lay witness.[58]

As a result of appellate courts deciding a large number of criminal drug cases, the courts have developed a body of law concerning opinion evidence offered by law enforcement agents and other lay witnesses that has fairly specific application to drug testimony. Although police officers and other lay witnesses are not qualified to express an opinion about matters that are within the scope of the common knowledge and experience of the jury, or that are peculiarly within the specialized knowledge of experts, they are qualified to testify concerning matters related to controlled substances if the opinion testimony satisfies the criteria concerning firsthand knowledge and helpfulness to a clear understanding of the testimony or a fact in issue. Police training always includes experience with narcotics detection and identification that gives police officers a foundation for drug identification.

In a Texas case, a trial court permitted a police officer to testify that she smelled burned marijuana and found a baggie of marijuana inside an automobile that she had stopped for a traffic offense. She mentioned that she had training in the academy regarding what unburned marijuana looked like and had become familiar with the odor of burning marijuana during other training. The judge allowed the officer to testify as a lay witness with respect to the marijuana. Texas law permitted a lay witness to give testimony in the form of opinions where they were rationally based on the witness's perception and were helpful to a clear understanding of the witness's testimony or helped to determine a fact in issue. In affirming the conviction, the appellate court noted, "marihuana has a distinct appearance and odor that are familiar and easily recognizable to anyone who has encountered it. So [the officer]'s opinion that appellant possessed marihuana, based on the odor she smelled and the green, leafy substance she saw, was one that a reasonable person could draw from the circumstances. Her testimony regarding the identification of the marihuana was admissible as a lay opinion."[59]

---

[57]   State v. Carter, 948 P.2d 1173 (Mont. 1997).
[58]   Ohio v. Davis, 2002 Ohio App. LEXIS 7280 (2002).
[59]   Osbourn v. Texas, 92 S.W.3d 531, 537, 2002 Tex. Crim. App. LEXIS 236 (2002). *See* case in Part II.

Where the factual analysis appears more complicated, a court may reverse a conviction where police officer testimony was admitted as lay witness opinion but should have been admitted, if at all, as expert testimony. In a Maryland case, the appellate court held that police officers who had observed conduct that appeared to indicate the illicit sale of controlled substances were offering their opinions based on the officers' specialized knowledge, experience, and training in drug investigations. The officers were not merely identifying a drug from appearance, but were basing their opinion that narcotics sales had occurred based on their evaluation of various factors that would not have caused a lay witness to come to the same conclusion.[60] Following similar logic, a Colorado appellate court reversed a defendant's conviction for possessing pseudoephedrine with intent to manufacture a controlled substance. Police officers had been permitted to testify as lay witnesses that the defendant possessed not only precursor chemicals, but were permitted to explain to the jury how methamphetamine is manufactured and how the precursor chemicals were used. The officers' testimony would have been admissible as expert testimony had the prosecutor qualified the officers as experts, but the admission of the evidence as lay testimony constituted reversible error because the testimony may have substantially influenced the jury.[61]

In another example, one of the prosecution's lay witnesses was permitted identify a quantity of suspected drugs as cocaine due to his personal experience and knowledge of cocaine as well as from the circumstances of the transaction. The witness had consumed cocaine hundreds of times and snorted or smoked two to three grams per day for several years. Due to his personal involvement in cocaine use and his familiarity with the drug, the lay witness was properly permitted to identify the controlled substance that was the subject of the trial as cocaine. The court reasoned that the opinion of the lay witness was helpful to the trier of fact and the prosecutor offered a proper foundation to show that the witness was sufficiently familiar with cocaine to be able to identify it.[62] In a case that had an opposite result, the Supreme Court of Montana reversed the defendant's conviction for driving under the influence of drugs. After a defendant had taken prescription medications for his chronic pancreatitis and low blood pressure caused by atrial fibrillation, a police officer followed him and rescued him after his car left the road and rolled over on its top. When the traditional tests for alcohol intoxication did not indicate that alcohol had been a factor in the wreck, the officer concluded that the defendant was under the influence of drugs. The officer indicated that he noticed shallow breathing, slow responses to questions, and slurred speech, which led him to that conclusion. On appeal, Montana's top court reversed the conviction on the ground that, although the officer had familiarity and training to evaluate alcohol intoxication, he was not sufficiently trained to understand the

---

[60]   Ragland v. State, 385 Md. 706, 870 A.2d 609, 2005 Md. LEXIS 119 (2005).

[61]   People v. Veren, 2005 Colo. App. LEXIS 1957 (2005), *reh'g denied*, 2006 Colo. App. LEXIS 112 (2006).

[62]   State v. Maag, 2005 Ohio 3761, 2005 Ohio App. LEXIS 3461 (2005).

pharmacological effects of particular drugs on motor skills or what levels would cause motor skill degradation such that an individual could not safely operate a vehicle. The court noted that the knowledge to make such determinations would require a qualified expert and that neither the officer nor the general public could make determinations as lay witnesses concerning whether drug intoxication caused the wreck and whether he was driving under the influence of drugs.[63]

G. Sanity or Mental Condition

While both expert and lay opinion may be admissible to assist the trier of fact in determining a person's mental condition or sanity, a jury may accept one version of the evidence over the other. In one case in which the defendant suffered from schizophrenia and killed the victim, he admitted the killing saying that he thought the victim turned into a witch and he was attempting to twist her head off. The defense and prosecution introduced evidence concerning his mental condition that included both lay and expert testimony. The defense experts testified that he was insane at the time of the killing while lay witnesses for the prosecution noted that his behavior seemed normal on the day of the crime prior to the killing. The jury ignored the expert testimony and, relying on the lay testimony, convicted the defendant. According to the appellate court, a jury remains free to disregard expert opinion in favor of lay evidence of the defendant's demeanor before and after the crime.[64]

A nonexpert witness, in response to purely hypothetical questions, may not give an opinion on the question of sanity. Subject to judicial approval, a witness may give testimony concerning another person's sanity when that witness clearly has demonstrated that he or she is acquainted with the person whose mental condition is at issue, and can detail facts and circumstances relating to his or her acquaintance and the conduct and conversation upon which his or her opinion is based.[65] Before a nonexpert witness is competent to testify as to the sanity, mental condition, or retardation of another person, the witness must demonstrate a foundational level of acquaintance involving close contact and duration as to indicate clearly that the testimony would be of value in determining the mental issue. In a North Carolina homicide case, the defendant, who was mentally retarded, shot and killed a co-worker who had been hazing him about his mental condition. The trial court permitted his former live-in girlfriend, with whom he had a child, to testify that the defendant was not retarded. The girlfriend had an intimate relationship with the defendant and had an opportunity to have observed the defendant in a variety of social contexts. She indicated that he performed the typical daily rou-

---

[63] State v. Nobach, 2002 Mont. 91, 309 Mont. 342, 46 P.3d 618, 2002 Mont. LEXIS 189 (2002).

[64] Moler v. Indiana, 782 N.E.2d 454, 2003 Ind. App. LEXIS 119, *transfer denied*, 2003 Ind. LEXIS 119 (2003).

[65] Rupert v. People, 429 P.2d 276 (Colo. 1967); McCall v. State, 408 N.E.2d 1218 (Ind. 1980). *See also* United States v. Santos, 131 F.3d 16 (1st Cir. 1997).

tine and, although he could be quiet sometimes, no one would think that anything was wrong.[66]

In the case above, where lay evidence of mental condition had been admitted, the North Carolina Court of Appeals suggested some specific conditions that must be applied in determining whether a lay witness may properly testify concerning a defendant's mental condition.[67] That court provided that the following factors are to be considered: (1) the witness's opinion must be rationally based on the personal perception of the lay witness; (2) the testimony must be helpful to the determination of a fact in issue; and (3) the subject of mental condition is an appropriate subject for lay opinion.

There is no requirement as to the length of acquaintance. For example, the testimony of two police officers who were with the defendant for approximately ten and four hours respectively was not disqualified on the ground that the witnesses had insufficient opportunity to observe the defendant. The fact that the officers had not known the defendant for a longer period went to the weight of the testimony on the sanity question and not to its admissibility.[68]

H. Identification

Often the only adequate way that a person can be identified is by lay opinion. Therefore, the identification of a person need not be made in absolutely positive terms. A witness may testify that an accused "resembles" or "looks like" the person who committed the crime. He or she may testify that in his or her opinion the accused is the person who perpetrated the crime. Courts generally admit lay opinion concerning identity when a witness is sufficiently familiar with the person in question so that the lay witness is better suited to make the identification than the jury.[69] The sound of a person's voice also may be the basis of an opinion as to a person's identity.[70]

This rule also applies to the identity of things. A person who has tasted alcoholic beverages before may testify as to the nature and odor of a beverage. Police officers are generally permitted to testify concerning the smell of burned marijuana.[71] In a prosecution in which a man had been accused of manufacturing methamphetamine in his trailer home, police became suspicious when they served a warrant in an unrelated matter. Police detected the strong and distinctive chemical odor typical associated with methamphetamine manufacturing and procured a search warrant. The trial court permitted the officers involved to testify concerning the distinctive smell inside the trailer home because they had received training in recognizing methamphetamine manufacturing odors and were trained to recognize materials used in drug production.[72]

---

[66]   State v. McClain, 169 N.C. App. 657, 670, 610 S.E.2d 783, 792, 2005 N. C. App. LEXIS 804 (2005).
[67]   Id.
[68]   Kaufman v. United States, 350 F.2d 408 (8th Cir. 1965).
[69]   United States v. Kornegay, 410 F.3d 89, 94, 2005 U.S. App. LEXIS 10707 (1st Cir. 2005).
[70]   See United States v. Norman, 415 F.3d 466, 2005 U.S. App. LEXIS 13149 (5th Cir. 2005).
[71]   See Ohio v. Bolling, 2001 Ohio App. LEXIS 3248 (2001).
[72]   State v. Lonsinger, 2005 Tenn. Crim. App. LEXIS 12 (2005).

At trial, proper identification of the perpetrator often serves to resolve the primary issue because, in most cases, there is little doubt that a crime has occurred. In a case in which the defendant had been charged with robbery of a federally insured financial institution, he proposed to call an expert forensic anthropologist to refute expected identification testimony from the prosecution. Over the government's objection, the trial judge concluded that the proposed expert was qualified by training and education and would be permitted to offer testimony concerning ear morphology. The court permitted the anthropologist to testify that the defendant could not have been the bank robber because his earlobes were not attached to his neck while the pictures taken of the robber indicated otherwise.[73] In another case in which the identity of the perpetrator proved to be the primary issue, the trial court permitted the victim's boyfriend to make an in-court identification of the defendant. In the crime, the victim's car had been taken in a carjacking when the perpetrator demanded the keys to the vehicle. The victim's boyfriend had a good opportunity to observe the perpetrator when he handed the vehicle keys to him and the boyfriend naturally had paid close attention to the person with the gun. The trial court allowed the victim's boyfriend to make an in-court identification that followed his identification of the defendant from a photographic array. Similarly, the trial court permitted the victim to make a separate identification because she had been present at the carjacking, had an excellent opportunity of view the perpetrator, and was only a few feet from the carjacker at the time the vehicle was taken. The appellate court approved the identification of the defendant by both the victim and her boyfriend because they had an excellent opportunity to view the perpetrator and the photographic arrays used in the case had not been unduly suggestive.[74]

When lay witnesses are able to make identifications based on their familiarity with characteristics of the defendant that are not immediately observable by the jury at the trial, the lay witness testimony is admissible. However, when the trier of fact is equally able to make an identification from the same evidence observed by a police officer, the lay testimony of an officer should not be admitted. In a Ninth Circuit case, a conviction for attempted murder was reversed when the trial court allowed an officer to identify the defendant as the person depicted on a videotape of the crime. The officer had seen the defendant at least two times and had spoken with him, but could not recall any specific occasion. In this situation, the judge or jury was equally as qualified as the officer to make the evaluation of whether the figure in the video was the defendant.[75]

---

[73]   United States v. McClintock, 2006 U.S. Dist. LEXIS 201 (E.D. Pa. 2006).

[74]   Graham v. State, 273 Ga. 187, 189, 614 S. E.2d 815, 818, 2005 Ga. App. LEXIS 442 (2005).

[75]   United States v. Kane, 146 Fed. Appx. 912, 2005 U.S. App. LEXIS 22877 (9th Cir. 2005).

I. *Handwriting*

Assuming a proper foundation, the opinion of a lay witness concerning the identity of an acquaintance's handwriting may be admissible. Although handwriting identification testimony involves a process of mental comparison, the lay witness is not permitted to fortify his or her opinion by making a physical comparison of the contested writing with genuine standards, for the reason that he or she has no more skill in making the comparison than do the jurors.[76] In order for the lay witness to be permitted to identify a handwriting sample, a foundation must be established to show that the witness had an opportunity to become familiar with the handwriting. In a case involving signatures on a car dealership form in an embezzlement case, the victim was permitted to identify the defendant's signature. He had gained familiarity with the defendant's signature because he observed the genuine signature on various car dealership documents during the ordinary course of business. The reviewing court upheld the admission of the lay witness's identification of the signature because he had a basis or foundation for giving his opinion and the court believed that his opinion would be of assistance to the jury.[77] Proof that a witness has a foundation for identifying writing may be accomplished by showing that the witness corresponded with the writer, handled documents written by him or her, or by other means.

While lay witnesses, even with proof of a foundation, are not permitted to offer opinion evidence by comparing a known sample of a signature or more extensive writing, expert witnesses and jurors may be permitted to make such a comparison. In a California case involving insurance fraud, the defendant's genuine driver's license was offered in evidence, as was a fraudulent application for life insurance benefits. According to the prosecutor's theory of the case, both documents were signed by the defendant,. The trial court permitted the jury, composed of laypersons, to compare the admittedly genuine signature with the questioned signature to determine whether the same person made both writings. According to the appellate court, the practice of allowing comparison of signatures was proper when done by a jury.[78]

In an action for misapplying and converting traveler's checks, the Eleventh Circuit Court of Appeals reasoned that the trial court did not err in admitting evidence of two coworkers' identifications of the defendant's handwriting on the converted checks.[79] In this case, both lay witnesses testified that they were familiar with the defendant's handwriting and that, in their opinion, it matched or was similar to the handwriting on the checks. The court explained that this

---

[76] *See* United States v. Saelee, 162 F. Supp. 2d 1097 (2001), in which the trial judge refused to allow a forensic document examiner testify as a layperson because the witness would not be offering testimony based on sensory perception.

[77] Bell v. State, 910 So. 2d 640, 2005 Miss. App. LEXIS 159 (2005).

[78] People v. Rodriguez, 133 Cal. App. 4th 545, 553, 553, 34 Cal. Rptr. 3d 886, 892, 2005 Cal. App. LEXIS 1628 (2005).

[79] United States v. Barker, 735 F.2d 1280 (11th Cir. 1984).

testimony was valid under Federal Rules 701 and 901(b), which allow for the admission of nonexpert opinion as to the genuineness of handwriting based upon familiarity not acquired for the purpose of the litigation.

J. Speed

Most courts admit the testimony of a nonexpert witness relating to the speed of a motor vehicle, provided that the witness had sufficient opportunity to observe the vehicle in motion. Courts routinely allow lay witnesses to offer testimony concerning the speed of motor vehicles provided that the witness has a basis for offering the opinion. A Georgia court upheld the speeding conviction of a juvenile and the admission in evidence of the officer's testimony that the officer observed the defendant speeding. The officer has been on routine patrol and observed the defendant's vehicle traveling at an excessive speed. The foundation for the officer's estimate of the vehicle's speed included eleven years as an officer, his experience in enforcing speed laws, his personal driving experience, and his experience in observing and estimating vehicle speed. As a general rule, the admissibility of an officer's estimate of vehicle speed is so strong that it allows a conviction for speeding, if no contested evidence has been admitted.[80] A California court upheld the admissibility of a police officer's estimate made from an aircraft that the defendant was speeding at 105 miles per hour despite the defendant's objection that the officer had not been trained to visually estimate vehicle speed on the public highway.[81] A trained runner may properly offer an estimate of the speed at which he normally runs where it is based on his experience running on a calibrated treadmill that measured miles per hour.[82] While lay witnesses generally are permitted to express opinion estimates of vehicle speed in terms such as "fast," "slow," "excessive," and the like, some opinions have been found to be conclusory in nature as well as lacking in evidentiary value.[83] The court in its discretion may disallow such opinion evidence.

In a case that was reviewed by a Florida appeals court, the judges advised that an estimate of the speed at which a conveyance or other object was moving at a given time is generally viewed as a matter of common observation rather than expert opinion, such that any person of ordinary ability and intelligence, having the opportunity of observation, is competent to testify to the rate of speed of such a moving object.[84] The court cautioned, however, that lay witness testimony regarding the speed of an object must be grounded in reliability and personal perception rather than speculation, and thus the lay witness's opportunity of observation is critical to the admissibility of testimony regarding speed. Applying this reasoning, the court held that a driver of an

---

[80]   In the Interest of B.D.S., 269 Ga. App. 89, 90, 91, 603 S.E.2d 488, 489, 2004 Ga. App. LEXIS 1084 (2004). *aff'd*, 273 Ga. App. 576, 615 S.E.2d 627, 2005 Ga. App. LEXIS 579 (2005).

[81]   People v. Zunis, 134 Cal. App. 4th Supp. 1, 36 Cal. Rptr. 3d 489, 2005 Cal. App. 1873 (2005).

[82]   Soto v. New York City Transit Authority, 2006 N.Y. LEXIS 518 (2006).

[83]   Catina v. Maree, 498 Pa. 433, 447 A.2d 228 (1982).

[84]   Lewek v. State, 702 So. 2d 527 (Fla. 1997).

automobile who passed by the defendant prior to a fatal accident could give lay testimony in a vehicular homicide prosecution that the defendant was traveling 60 miles per hour in a 45 mile-per-hour zone, when the driver had ample time to observe the defendant and the testimony was not based on speculation but was based on observations at the time of the accident.

§ 11.5 Opinions of Experts

Rule 702

Testimony by Experts

If scientific, technical, or other specialized knowledge will assist the trier of fact to understand the evidence or to determine a fact in issue, a witness qualified as an expert by knowledge, skill, experience, training, or education, may testify thereto in the form of an opinion or otherwise . . .[85]

In order to sustain proof beyond a reasonable doubt, many criminal case presentations require the use of expert witnesses and their special expertise. In the absence of the testimony of experts, it would be difficult for the prosecution to provide the jury with sufficient evidence to meet the burden of proof in cases in which the technical nature of the evidence exceeds the knowledge of the average person. Expert testimony may be admissible when the subject matter at issue involves concepts with which the average person is not sufficiently familiar or in cases in which the expert testimony would assist the jurors in understanding the issues or determining a fact at issue.[86] Over the years, laws relating to the use of expert opinion evidence have developed differently from those relating to the use of nonexpert opinion evidence. While the nonexpert, with some exceptions, may testify only if he or she has firsthand knowledge of the incident, the expert is generally permitted to give an opinion, even if he or she does not have firsthand knowledge. The expert may have analyzed the facts following the event and arrived at an opinion, may have conducted scientific experiments on some of the evidence and drawn a conclusion, or may have testified based on a hypothetical fact pattern offered by a party. An expert may consider reports and results of experiments conducted by other experts when such reliance is usual and customary in that field of expertise. Expert testimony may be presented by a qualified expert when the subject matter is such that the jury cannot necessarily be expected to understand without assistance, especially when the subject matter involves complex technical or scientific evidence. Testimony from a person who has special training, education, and knowledge is thought to assist the judge or jury in making proper decisions.

---

[85]   Fed. R. Evid. 702.

[86]   State v. Nesbitt, 185 N.J. 504, 514, 888 A.2d 472, 478, 2006 N.J. LEXIS 7 (2006).

When the desirability of or need for expert testimony arises, generally the trial judge must make a decision concerning whether expert testimony will assist the trier of fact, regardless of whom the prosecutor or defense counsel proposes to call as the expert witness. In the District of Columbia, the courts hold that for expert testimony to be considered, the subject matter "must be so distinctively related to some science, profession, business or occupation as to be beyond the ken of the average layman" and the proposed expert "witness must have sufficient skill, knowledge, or experience in that field or calling to make it appear that his opinion" will assist the judge or jury, and that expert testimony cannot be admitted where the state of the knowledge does not permit a reasonable opinion to be offered, even by an expert.[87]

If expert testimony is proper and a witness qualified to offer an opinion is available, admissibility of expert testimony will be subject to additional judicial discretion and will focus on the expert personally. The Supreme Court of Nebraska noted that the trial court must evaluate the admissibility of expert testimony in a four-step process. The trial court must first decide whether a witness has the qualifications to testify as an expert through an evaluation of the proposed expert's knowledge, skill, training, and education. The trial judge must next determine whether the reasoning or methodology underpinning the expert testimony is valid and reliable. Then the judge must decide whether the methodology used by the expert was properly applied and that the appropriate protocols were followed and that any tests were performed properly. Finally, the court must evaluate whether the expert evidence and the opinions offered are more probative than unfairly prejudicial.[88]

When a prosecutor or a defense attorney wants to use an expert witness to present evidence, the trial judge has broad discretion in determining whether to admit the evidence. If a judge decides that expert testimony would be helpful and the subject matter is appropriate, a trial judge must still determine whether the proffered witness qualifies as an expert.[89] The judge initially decides whether the opinion evidence of the expert witness would aid the court or jury in reaching a conclusion and whether the particular witnesses offered as experts have the particular knowledge or experience that would make their opinions helpful to the court or jury. For example, the Tenth Circuit approved a trial court's determination that an agent could testify as an expert concerning the manner that drug kingpins use to avoid having their identities and drug activities becoming known to law enforcement. The trial court determined that the special agent was qualified as an expert and it believed that expert testimony would assist the jury in understanding a rather complex drug-selling operation[90]

---

[87]   Hager v. United States, 856 A.2d 1143, 1148, 2004 D.C. App. LEXIS (2004), *cert. denied*, 2006 U.S. LEXIS 2452 (2006).

[88]   State v. Mason, 271 Neb. 16, 709 N.W.2d 638, 2006 Neb. LEXIS 23 (2006).

[89]   Burnett v. State, 815 N.E.2d 201, 205, 2004 Ind. App. LEXIS 1864 (2004), in which the court overruled a defense objection and permitted a police officer to testify as an expert in fingerprints and fingerprint identification. The court noted the officer's long career of study, field work, and training in the area of fingerprints.

[90]   United States v. Walker, 2006 U.S. App. LEXIS 11289 (10th Cir. 2006).

Taking a different opinion in a highly contested area of expertise, a district court permitted the use of an expert in the problems associated with eyewitness identification because the court believed that the expert's testimony could assist the jury in understanding the evidence or deciding a fact in issue.[91]

Whether expert testimony shall be admitted has generally been left to the broad discretion of trial courts[92] and will not be overturned except upon proof of an abuse of judicial discretion.[93] When the court has properly admitted the opinion of an expert, the jury or the judge may consider the credentials of the expert in determining the weight to give to the expert's testimony.[94] Because the fact finder is permitted to determine the weight to accord expert testimony, it may accept it or reject it completely, or anywhere in between.

Other rules for the use of expert testimony have been handed down in various cases. In one case, a North Carolina court held that an expert's opinion may be based on hearsay statements or other reports that may not normally be admissible in evidence. An expert may base an opinion on tests performed and upon reports generated by other persons where such reliance is usual and customary in the field of expertise. The expert witness is usually permitted to disclose the basis for his or her opinion so that the finder of fact may assess the credibility and weight to be granted to the testimony.[95] Some courts have evaluated the admissibility of an expert's testimony on three factors: qualification, reliability, and fit."[96] The expert must have the special expertise required of any expert in the particular field; the expert must have utilized a proper method sufficient to assure reliability; and the expert must offer relevant testimony that is customarily used it the particular field of expertise.

Even though a witness qualifies as an expert, a trial court may refuse to permit the expert to offer testimony when such testimony fails to assist the finder of fact. For example, an expert's testimony will be excluded where there is a sufficient indication that his or her opinion is based on information that does not go beyond the experience and understanding of the average juror. In *United States v. Carter,* a bank robbery case, the defendant had been accused of robbing tellers at two separate federally insured banks. Because law enforcement officials offered a teller two separate photo arrays for identification purposes, Carter argued undue suggestiveness involving the identification process and asked to be permitted to use an expert witness who would explain the difficulties of making accurate eyewitness identifications. The trial court refused to permit expert testimony relative to eyewitness identification challenges. The appellate court upheld the trial court decision that expert testimony was not admissible due to the fact that expert testimony would not have

---

[91]   United States v. Sullivan, 246 F. Supp. 2d 696, 698, 2003 U.S. Dist. LEXIS 3015 (E.D. Ky. 2003).

[92]   State v. Vernes, 2006 Mont. 32, 331 Mont. 129, 132, 133, 130 P.3d. 169, 173, 2006 Mont. LEXIS 41 (2006).

[93]   State v. Tolliver, 268 Neb 920, 921, 689 N.E.2d 567, 573, 2004 Neb. LEXIS 195 (2004).

[94]   United States v. Rutland, 372 F.3d 543, 2004 U.S. App. LEXIS 12432 (3d Cir. 2004).

[95]   State v. Lyles, 615 S.E.2d 890, 893, 894, 2005 N.C. App. LEXIS 1424 (2005).

[96]   Elliot v. Kiesewetter, 112 Fed. Appx. 821, 824, 2004 U.S. 821, 2004 U.S. App. LEXIS 21628 (3d Cir. 2004)

aided the jury and might mislead them in their evaluations concerning identity of the robber. The appellate court noted that jurors understand that memory can be faulty, that stress on the eyewitness can cause problems in accuracy, that eyewitnesses vary in their degree of attention, and that there may be some problems in how police use identification procedures. An expert witness is not necessary to assist the jurors in coming to a conclusion concerning identity under the circumstances, according to the court of appeals.[97] Taking a different opinion in this often-contested area of expertise, a district court permitted the use of an expert in the problems associated with eyewitness identification because the court believed that the expert's testimony could assist the jury in understanding the evidence or deciding a fact in issue.[98]

An expert need not be a university-educated professional, such as a physician or scientist. He or she may be a plumber, carpenter, or police officer, if his or her technical expertise in his or her occupation would help the jury to understand a particular point in evidence. In addition, Federal Rule 702 has no provision that would rank academic training as being superior to demonstrated practical experience. An expert could be an immunized conspirator who understood drug dealing protocols or a law enforcement officer who has intimate knowledge about business practices of drug dealers or the mechanics of drug trafficking.[99] Any specialized knowledge that would not be generally held by the public at large may qualify a person as an expert in that field.

In state jurisdictions that have adopted a variation of the Federal Rules of Evidence, Rule 702 defines the conditions that must be present in order for an expert to testify. The rule states that if the testimony would "assist the trier of fact to understand the evidence or to determine a fact in issue," then an expert witness may testify. Because the expert may testify as to matters that are specialized as well as scientific or technical, the rule makes plain its intention to allow expert testimony on matters that are not necessarily beyond the understanding of laypersons. In interpreting this section, an appellate court approved the admission of the expert testimony of a 17-year veteran police officer, whose background included participation or leading a dozen gambling investigations. The court permitted the officer to describe generalized gambling operations and explain to the jury the gaming terminology used by the defendant because the officer was qualified by experience to understand the specific gambling operation involved. The subject matter involved was considered by the trial court to be beyond the understanding of lay jurors so expert testimony was admissible.[100]

In another case, the Seventh Circuit Court of Appeals approved the use of expert testimony in a case involving a violation of the Endangered Species Act[101] regarding whether exotic animal parts were derived from animals pro-

---

[97]   United States v. Carter, 410 F.3d 942, 949, 2005 U. S. App. LEXIS 10830 (7th Cir. 2006).
[98]   United States v. Sullivan, 246 F. Supp. 2d 696, 698, 2003 U.S. Dist. LEXIS 3015 (E.D. Ky. 2003).
[99]   United States v. Pomranky, 165 Fed. Appx. 259, 260, 2006 U.S. App. LEXIS 2490 (4th Cir. 2006).
[100]   United States v. Anderson, 2006 U.S. App. LEXIS 11581 (8th Cir. 2006).
[101]   16 U.S.C.S. § 1531 *et seq.*

tected under the law.[102] In a prosecution for attempted and actual illegal distribution of Schedule III and IV drugs by a physician, the Eighth Circuit Court of Appeals held that the use of an expert witness physician who explained the protocols and standards of care for writing drug prescriptions was appropriate because the expert witness's testimony was helpful to the jury in understanding the case.[103]

§ 11.6 Qualifications of an Expert

A person who has acquired specialized knowledge of a particular subject matter over which he or she is to testify—either by academic study of the recognized authorities or by practical experience—and who can assist and guide the jury in resolving a problem or issue that the jury may not be able to determine because its knowledge is inadequate, may meet the qualifications as an expert witness.[104] A witness who, by education, training, and experience, has become an expert in any art, science, profession, or calling may be permitted to state his or her opinion as to a matter in which he or she is versed and that is material to the case, and he or she may also state the reasons for such opinion. Whether a witness qualifies as an expert rests within the sound discretion of the trial judge.[105] For example, a trial court erroneously characterized a volunteer acting chief's testimony concerning the cause of a fire as lay testimony rather that expert testimony. The witness had more than 30 years' experience investigating fires, had received training and education in causes of fires, had studied fire investigation according to national standards, and had taken approximately 40 classes offered by the state concerning fire investigation. The Supreme Court of Nebraska reversed a trial court determination that the volunteer fire fighter lacked sufficient knowledge, skill, and training and the fire fighter should have been allowed to testify as an expert in fire causation.[106] The gist of this case illustrates the principle that knowledge is the key to developing expertise and that knowledge can come from any source, even nontraditional learning situations or on-the-job training, and is not relegated to formalized university experiences culminating in a doctoral-level degree

An expert in a criminal case may offer an opinion based wholly upon personal knowledge of the facts disclosed in his or her testimony, or upon facts in evidence assumed in hypothetical questions, but the witness may not properly offer an opinion concerning the ultimate issue to be determined by the trier of fact because that opinion invades the function of the jury.[107] The Supreme

---

[102] United States v. Kapp, 419 F.3d 666, 673, 2005 U.S. App. LEXIS 17606 (7th Cir. 2005).

[103] United States v. Katz, 2006 U.S. App. LEXIS 11462 (8th Cir. 2006).

[104] People v. Miller, 173 Ill. 2d 167, 670 N.E.2d 721 (1996), *See also* United States v. Sosa, U.S. Dist. LEXIS 2254 (2006), for a review of the foundational requirements for expert testimony.

[105] George v. Ellis, 2003 Pa. Super. 121, 820 A.2d 815, 2003 Pa. Super. LEXIS 441 (2003).

[106] Perry Lumber Company v. Durable Services, 271 Neb. 303, 310, 710 N.W.2d 854, 2006 LEXIS 47 (2006).

[107] Missouri v. Churchill, 98 S.W. 3d 536, 2003 Mo. LEXIS 37 (2003).

Court of New Jersey reversed a conspiracy drug conviction in which the trial court permitted an expert witness to improperly give his opinion on the ultimate issue, the guilt of the defendant, when there was clearly a factual issue concerning whether the defendant was actually involved with the drug transaction. The testimony of the expert impermissibly invaded the role of the jury.[108]

However, some courts will permit expert witnesses to testify to ultimate issues and those decisions are not often reversed on this ground.[109] While there is no requirement that the expert express an opinion in terms of percentages or probability, many fields of expertise use mathematical models. Handwriting experts often express their opinions in probabilities, but there is no exclusion of evidence if an expert notes that a forged document "probably" was authored by the defendant, but such an answer could affect the weight of the testimony.[110]

One who has the necessary training, experience, and skill, and who has familiarized him- or herself with the necessary data, can form an expert opinion that is substantially superior to that of the average person and therefore useful to the jury. Expert witnesses may have some similarities in qualifications or possess different backgrounds and not have equal qualifications,[111] but as long as a proposed expert crosses the threshold of being an expert in the relevant field, the trial judge should permit the witness to testify. The duty of the jury is to determine the weight to give the testimony of each expert witness. Any difference or inconsistency between information that an expert possesses as the result of becoming an expert and information acquired from other sources for litigation purposes goes to the weight a jury may attach to the expert's testimony.[112] The absence of certificates, memberships, and the like does not in and of itself detract from the competency of an expert witness.[113] A court may not exclude expert testimony just because the expert lacks a degree or training that the district court thinks most appropriate.[114] The fact that the expert does not have a degree or license in his or her professed speciality goes to the weight of the testimony rather than to its admissibility.[115] The special knowledge necessary to qualify as an expert may be derived from experience as well as study.[116]

When a party offers a witness as an expert on a matter in issue, the judge must preliminarily determine whether the proposed expert's competency, with respect to a special skill or experience, will assist the trier of fact in reaching a determination. In the absence of an admission or a waiver by the adverse party, the judge must make a finding that the witness meets the qualifications

---

[108] State v. Boston, 380 N.J. Super 487, 493, 882 A.2d 987, 991, 2005 N.J. Super. LEXIS 292 (2005).

[109] Jefferson v. Roe, 2002 U.S. Dist. LEXIS 6153 (N.D. Cal. 2002).

[110] United States v. Mornan, 413 F.3d 372, 380, 2005 U.S. App. LEXIS 13043 (3d Cir. 2005).

[111] Panitz v. Behrend, 2001 Pa. Super. 93, 771 A.2d 803, 2001 Pa. Super. LEXIS 372 (2001).

[112] United States v. 60.14 Acres of Land, 362 F.2d 660 (3d Cir. 1966); Ziegler v. Crorfont, 516 P.2d 954 (Kan. 1973); Kline v. Lorillard, 878 F.2d 791 (4th Cir. 1989).

[113] Tank v. Comm'r of Internal Revenue, 270 F.2d 477 (6th Cir. 1959); see also Moran v. Ford Motor Co., 476 F.2d 289 (8th Cir. 1973).

[114] Waldorf v. Shuta, 916 F. Supp. 423 (D.N.J. 1996).

[115] Dickerson v. Cushman, 909 F. Supp. 1467 (M.D. Ala. 1995).

[116] Morrow v. State, 230 Ga. App. 137, 495 S.E.2d 609 (1998).

of an expert in the particular field. When a party offers a witness as an expert, there is no presumption that the witness is competent to give an opinion; it is incumbent upon the party offering the witness to demonstrate that the witness has the necessary learning, knowledge, skill, or practical experience to enable him or her to give opinion testimony.

A Mississippi appellate court, noting the requirements for determining the admissibility of expert testimony, referred to a two-part test: (1) the witness must be qualified as an expert because of the knowledge, skill, experience, training, or education he or she possesses and (2) whether the witness's scientific, technical, or other specialized knowledge will assist the trier of fact.[117] Where a witness has been deemed to be "qualified" as an expert, testimony may be based on facts within the witness's personal knowledge, facts presented to the expert at trial, and/or facts presented out of court and not directly perceived where such facts are reasonably relied upon by other experts in the field.[118]

The weight and value of the testimony of an expert witness depends largely upon his or her qualifications as an expert, and these qualifications may be the subject of intensive inquiry by the opposing counsel.

§ 11.7 Selection of Expert Witness

Rule 706

Court Appointed Experts

(a) Appointment. The court may on its own motion or on the motion of any party enter an order to show cause why expert witnesses should not be appointed, and may request the parties to submit nominations. The court may appoint any expert witnesses agreed upon by the parties, and may appoint expert witnesses of its own selection. An expert witness shall not be appointed by the court unless the witness consents to act. A witness so appointed shall be informed of the witness' duties by the court in writing, a copy of which shall be filed with the clerk, or at a conference in which the parties shall have opportunity to participate. A witness so appointed shall advise the parties of the witness' findings, if any; the witness' deposition may be taken by any party; and the witness may be called to testify by the court or any party. The witness shall be subject to cross-examination by each party, including a party calling the witness.

(b) Compensation. Expert witnesses so appointed are entitled to reasonable compensation in whatever sum the court may allow. The compensation thus fixed is payable from funds which may be provided by law in criminal cases and civil actions and proceedings involving just compensation under the fifth amendment. In other civil actions and proceedings the compensation shall be paid by the parties in such proportion and at such time as the court directs, and thereafter charged in like manner as other costs.

---

[117] Mooneyham v. State, 915 So.2d 1102, 1104, 2005 Miss. App. LEXIS 989 (2005).

[118] FED. R. EVID. 703 *and see* United States v. Stone, 222 F.R.D. 334, 2004 U.S. Dist. LEXIS 12873 (E.D. Tenn. 2004).

(c) Disclosure of appointment. In the exercise of its discretion, the court may authorize disclosure to the jury of the fact that the court appointed the expert witness.

(d) Parties' experts of own selection. Nothing in this rule limits the parties in calling expert witnesses of their own selection.[119]

In an appropriate case, a judge may appoint an expert upon the judge's own motion, but usually the prosecutor, defense attorney, or both may request that experts be appointed by the court to evaluate evidence and testify in a case. To the extent possible, each party will attempt to suggest nominations of an expert who would testify most favorably for his or her side. In some state jurisdictions, and under Federal Rule 706, the judge may appoint expert witnesses based on agreement by the parties or the court may appoint witnesses based on the judge's preference, especially where there is disagreement. Any expert witness who receives an appointment will be informed of the expected duties by the judge in writing, and a copy of the letter of appointment will be filed with the clerk. Alternatively, the notice of appointment will be given to the parties at a conference in which the parties have the opportunity to participate. When an expert is appointed by the court, that expert must advise the parties of the expert's opinions and conclusions. The parties may take a deposition of the expert witness and the expert witness may be called to testify by any party or by the judge. Even though one party may have called the expert to the stand, the expert may be cross-examined by each party. In the interests of fairness and to eliminate bias, the judge, using discretion, may authorize disclosure to the jury that the expert was appointed by the judge and was not selected by a party.[120]

Rule 706 of the Federal Rules of Evidence continues the long-established practice of federal judges having authority to appoint expert witnesses. Section (c) of the rule authorizes federal courts and state courts that have adopted a version of the Federal Rules to disclose to the jury the fact that the court appointed the expert witness. Disclosure to the jury that the court appointed the expert witness should give the expert witness more credibility with the jury.

Noting the provisions of Rule 706, one federal district court[121] commented that:

> The United States Court of Appeals for the Tenth Circuit has explained that "[a] court's authority to appoint an expert under Rule 706 is discretionary and we may only overturn the denial of such a motion for abuse of discretion. Under this standard, a trial court's decision will not be disturbed unless the appellate court has a definite and firm conviction that the lower court made a clear error of

---

[119]   FED. R. EVID. 706.

[120]   *Id.*

[121]   Jama Investments v. Los Alamos, 2006 U. S. Dist. LEXIS 29554 (E.D.N.M. 2006).

judgment or exceeded the bounds of permissible choice in the circumstances." *Cestnik v. Federal Bureau of Prisons,* 84 Fed. Appx. 51, 53, (10th Cir. 2003) (citing *Duckett v. Mullin*, 306 F.3d 982, 999 (10th Cir. 2002)[122]

In a case in which the indigent litigant in a legal malpractice case requested the appointment of an expert witness to evaluate the standard of care for an attorney in an earlier criminal case, the district court exercised its discretion and refused to appoint an expert under Rule 706. As the court noted, "Because plaintiff's claims are straightforward, do not present any complex matters for determination, and are of the type of professional conduct that Kansas law permits to be evaluated by common knowledge without the use of expert testimony, the court concludes that it should not exercise its discretion to appoint an expert in this matter pursuant to Fed. R. Evid. 706."[123]

§ 11.8   Examination of Expert Witness

Rule 703

Bases of Opinion Testimony by Experts

The facts or data in the particular case upon which an expert bases an opinion or inference may be those perceived by or made known to the expert at or before the hearing. If of a type reasonably relied upon by experts in the particular field in forming opinions or inferences upon the subject, the facts or data need not be admissible in evidence in order for the opinion or inference to be admitted.[124]

Rule 704

Opinion on Ultimate Issue

(a) Except as provided in subdivision (b), testimony in the form of an opinion or inference otherwise admissible is not objectionable because it embraces an ultimate issue to be decided by the trier of fact.

(b) No expert witness testifying with respect to the mental state or condition of a defendant in a criminal case may state an opinion or inference as to whether the defendant did or did not have the mental state or condition constituting an element of the crime charged or of a defense thereto. Such ultimate issues are matters for the trier of fact alone.[125]

---

[122]   United States v. Michigan, 680 F. Supp. 928 (W.D. Mich. 1987).
[123]   Ellibee v. Fox, 2006 U.S. Dist. LEXIS 13351 (D. Kan. 2006).
[124]   FED. R. EVID. 703.
[125]   FED. R. EVID. 704.

After the witness has qualified as an expert, he or she is first examined by the party who called the witness. There are two avenues through which expert evidence may be presented to the jury: (1) through testimony of the witness based on his or her personal knowledge and observation or from reports and results of tests performed by other experts when it is usual and customary to do so in the field of expertise,[126] and (2) through testimony of the witness when the expert witness is asked to assume that hypothetical facts (generally based on the case being tried) are true and to offer an opinion based on the hypothetical fact situation.[127] An expert witness may base his or her opinion partly upon personal knowledge of facts disclosed in his or her testimony and may be partially based on factual evidence assumed in a hypothetical question.[128] A hypothetical question need not include all of the facts in evidence, nor facts or theories advanced by opposing counsel. A trial judge may properly accept expert testimony predicated on facts that have been previously admitted in evidence as testimony by witnesses who themselves made relevant observations of primary facts. For example, a doctor called to testify may give his or her expert opinion as to whether facts already in evidence support an inference or causation or support a particular diagnosis or prognosis. Also, the expert witness may base his or her testimony on information from his or her knowledge of textbooks, treatises, articles, and other publications relevant to the particular field of expertise.

As a rule, expert testimony must be based on facts and evidence presented in the record or on hypothetical facts assumed to be true, but a hypothetical cannot be based on facts unsupported by any evidence.[129] The Federal Rules of Evidence provide, however, that if the external facts or data are of a type reasonably and customarily relied upon by experts in the particular field when forming opinions or inferences on the subject, the external facts or data need not be admissible in evidence.[130] In a bank fraud case involving check kiting, among other violations, a trial court permitted a federal law enforcement officer to give expert testimony based on his analysis of data that he had neither personally collected nor prepared. The federal officer had used information taken from bank records and analyzed the records using a computer program. The Court of Appeals for the Sixth Circuit upheld the admission of the opinion of the expert because the practice of permitting forensic financial examiners to analyze data collected by other persons prior to trial and to use the information to form an opinion was consistent with the Federal Rules of Evidence.[131] Similarly, a medical examiner may rely on a report prepared by a different medical examiner because reliance on the data prepared by other professionals was a common and standard protocol.[132]

---

[126]   State v. Ayers, 2005 Tenn. Crim. App. LEXIS 1108 (2005).
[127]   State v. Nesbitt, 185 N.J. 504, 511, 888 A.2d 472, 476, 2006 N.J. LEXIS 7 (2006).
[128]   Lewis v. Virginia, 2004 Va. App. LEXIS 595 (2004).
[129]   Wells v. State, 913 So. 2d 1053, 1057, 2005 Miss. App. LEXIS 434 (2005).
[130]   FED. R. EVID. 703.
[131]   United States v. Abboud, 438 F.3d 554, 586, 2006 U.S. App. LEXIS 3797 (6th Cir. 2006).
[132]   Sauerwin v. State, 2005 Ark. LEXIS 565 (2005).

In order to be admissible, the testimony of an expert witness must meet the other rules of evidence (i.e., the evidence must be relevant).[133] In accordance with the traditional teachings concerning the use of opinion testimony, various jurisdictions still hold to the common law rule that expert opinion testimony should not be admitted where such testimony would invade the province of the jury.[134] The common law rule held that experts may give opinions, but not opinions as to the "ultimate issue"; according to this reasoning, only the jury has that responsibility.[135] For example, Connecticut follows the rule that an expert witness may not give his or her opinion if it embraces an ultimate issue to be decided by the trier of fact.[136] The Federal Rules of Evidence have rejected the traditional view of opinion on the ultimate issue, according to the comments made by those who drafted it. Rule 704 of the Federal Rules of Evidence abolishes the "ultimate issue" rule except for opinions on mental states or conditions in criminal cases. In a federal prosecution for obtaining money through a fraudulent scheme, it was not reversible error to permit a handwriting expert for the government to offer an opinion that the signatures on financial documents were fraudulent, testimony that virtually went to the heart of the case and involved the ultimate issue.[137] Similarly, in a prosecution for drug possession with intent to distribute, a police officer with sufficient experience to be qualified as an expert on drug trafficking was permitted to offer his opinion that the defendant possessed the drugs because he expected to distribute them to other people. While this opinion was one that the jury would have to determine, it was permissible to allow the expert to express an opinion on this ultimate issue.[138]

Notwithstanding the general rule that no witness, layperson, or expert is allowed to testify regarding his or her opinion about the guilt of the defendant, whether by direct statement or inference, some courts allow a witness to come fairly close to expressing an opinion concerning guilt. In a federal prosecution that involved a charge of possession with intent to distribute crack cocaine, a federal officer was permitted to testify as an expert concerning what quantities of crack cocaine would be possessed for personal use and "whether the quantity of the drugs, as well as the possession of a gun along with that quantity, indicated distribution."[139] Although the questions appeared to go to the ultimate issue of distribution, the actual question met the requirements of Rule 704(b) because it did not directly offer an opinion on the defendant's mental state or condition.

---

[133] *See* Richman v. Sheahan, 415 F. Supp. 2d 929, 2006 U.S. Dist. LEXIS 6667 (N.D. Ill. 2006), in which trial court rejected police use of force expert from testifying concerning medical matters because evidence was not relevant. *See also* United States v. Monteiro, 407 F. Supp. 2d 351, 2006 U.S. Dist. LEXIS 227 (D. Mass. 2006), where a trial court excluded expert testimony because the trial judge was not convinced of reliability of the particular theory, rendering the expert testimony irrelevant and inadmissible.
[134] State v. French, 2006 Haw. LEXIS 85 (2006).
[135] People v. Wilson, 25 Cal. 2d 341, 153 P.2d 720 (1944).
[136] State v. Finan, 275 Conn. 60, 63, 881 A.2d 187, 190, 2005 Conn. LEXIS 325 (2005). *Accord*, Smallwood v. Commonwealth, 2005 Va. App. LEXIS 196 (2005).
[137] United States v. Rutland, 372 F.3d 543, 545, 2004 U.S. App. LEXIS 12432 (3rd Cir. 2004).
[138] State v. Walker, 2006 N.J. Super. LEXIS 145 (2006).
[139] Doe Boy v. United States, 2006 U.S. Dist LEXIS 13503 (D. Del. 2006).

§ 11.9 Cross-Examination of Expert Witness

Rule 705

Disclosure of Facts or Data Underlying Expert Opinion

The expert may testify in terms of opinion or inference and give reasons therefor without first testifying to the underlying facts or data, unless the court requires otherwise. The expert may in any event be required to disclose the underlying facts or data on cross-examination.[140]

Following direct examination, an expert witness ordinarily faces a probing inquiry on cross-examination in an attempt to challenge the opinion, as well as the facts and data on which the expert's opinion is based. The rules governing the cross-examination of witnesses generally apply and the trial court has broad discretion in allowing cross-examination of expert witnesses both as to the manner and scope of cross-examination.[141] A California court stated that counsel may cross-examine an expert witness more extensively and searchingly than a lay witness, and the prosecution was entitled to attempt to discredit the expert's opinion.[142] The failure to allow cross-examination may constitute grounds for reversal if the error could have affected the outcome,[143] but a judge may impose reasonable limitations on cross-examination of an expert witness, especially when the facts underlying the expert's opinion are inadmissible for other legal reasons.[144]

On cross-examination, an expert witness may be interrogated concerning the basis for his or her opinion. Cross-examination may include an inquiry relative to the expert's knowledge of textbooks, treatises, articles, and other scholarly publications in the field; he or she may be confronted with excerpts from them and the expert may be asked whether he or she is familiar with them and whether he or she agrees with them. In a situation in which the expert refuses to acknowledge reliance on standard works in the field, the cross-examiner may lay the foundation that the treatise is authoritative and reliable using its own expert and impeach the opposing expert.[145] Rule 705 of the Federal Rules of Evidence allows an expert witness to testify on direct examination by offering opinions and conclusions without first having to disclose underlying facts on which the testimony is based. However, on cross-examination, where the basis for an expert's opinion has been challenged, an expert must explain how the expert developed his or her conclusions or opinions.[146]

---

[140] FED. R. EVID. 705.

[141] Dean v. State, 211 Iowa 143, 233 N.W. 36 (1930).

[142] People v. Dennis, 71 Cal. Rptr. 2d 680, 950 P.2d 1035 (1998).

[143] United States ex rel. Reed v. Gilmore, 1999 U.S. Dist. LEXIS 21525 (N.D. Ill. 1999).

[144] Ward v. Dretke, 420 F.3d 479, 494, 2005 U.S. App. LEXIS 16596 (5th Cir. 2005).

[145] Armstrong v. Brown, 2002 Ohio App. LEXIS 6728 (2002), *appeal denied*, 98 Ohio St. 3d 1539, 2003 Ohio 1946, 786 N.E.2d 902, 2003 Ohio LEXIS 1076 (2003).

[146] United States v. Garcia, 2006 U.S. App. LEXIS 10555 (11th Cir. 2006).

In applying the Texas version of Rule 705, the courts allow a party to request a hearing outside of the presence of the jury, prior to allowing an expert to testify on direct examination. The purpose of this Rule 705 hearing is to allow the court to determine whether the expert witness's opinion has a sufficient basis for its admission. In one case involving severe injuries to a child, the defendant was permitted to extensively inquire concerning the qualifications of the emergency room doctor who treated the injuries and who was prepared to offer opinions regarding the trauma. Following the Rule 705 hearing, the court deemed that the doctor had a proper basis for his opinion and permitted the doctor to explain how such injuries could have been inflicted.[147] In Mississippi, Rule 705 operates similarly to the procedure in Texas, but it allows any party to request foundational data upon which an expert's opinion is expected to be based and such information is to be provided to the requesting opposing party prior to trial. Alternatively, the basis can be revealed on cross-examination by the party against whom the expert testimony is offered.[148] Whether the expert testifies in a federal or state court, the basis for the testimony can be revealed to the parties at trial or earlier so that the trier of fact may give proper weight to the evidence.

In an Ohio case involving cross-examination, one expert stated that he did not rely on any treatise as the basis of his opinion and did not believe that any were authoritative, while the opposing expert identified a couple of treatises as authoritative. When the doctor did not accept any treatise as authoritative, the trial court should have permitted the opposing party to attempt impeachment of the doctor by using excerpts from the treatises recognized as authoritative by the other expert. Under the staff notes to Rule 706, there is clear contemplation that when an expert refuses to recognize a treatise as authoritative, the opposing counsel may lay the foundation that the treatise is authoritative and pursue impeachment of the other expert by referring to the opposing view contained within the treatise.[149]

An expert witness who expresses an opinion that significantly relies on his or her readings of scholarly material may be cross-examined as to that opinion by reference to other reputable works in the field. However, the substance of the treatise or other scholarly writing may be used only to impeach the credibility of an expert witness if the witness has placed reliance on the treatise or has accepted the authoritative nature of the writing. The rationale for this rule is that such cross-examination tests the expert witness's credibility and reliability by inquiring into the extent of the expert's familiarity with the accepted authorities in his or her specialty and by asking the expert whether he or she agrees with the recognized authorities. The excerpts with which the witness is confronted on cross-examination do not, however, become affirmative evidence in the case.[150]

---

[147]　Montgomery v. State, 2006 Tex. App. LEXIS 3377 (2006).

[148]　Lawrence v. State, 2005 Miss. App. LEXIS 552 (2005).

[149]　Armstrong v. Brown, 2002 Ohio App. LEXIS 6728 (2002), *appeal denied*, 98 Ohio St. 3d 1539, 2003 Ohio 1946, 786 N.E.2d 902, 2003 Ohio LEXIS 1076 (2003).

[150]　Hinkle v. Cleveland Clinic, 159 Ohio App. 3d 351, 2004 Ohio 6853, 823 N.E.2d 945, 2004 Ohio App. LEXIS 6382 (2004).

While the federal Constitution's Sixth Amendment confrontation clause guarantees the opportunity for confrontation and cross-examination of adverse witnesses, it does not guarantee that the cross-examination of expert witnesses will be effective or be as extensive as the defense might desire.[151] The problems and constitutional issues surrounding the admission of expert testimony typically concern the fact that an expert may testify to conclusions that may be based on the knowledge of other persons who never testify in the court. The essence of the argument concerns the fact that the person who conducted a test or wrote a treatise is in not in court when the information is mentioned by an expert witness and the outside writer or scientist cannot actually be cross-examined. In a North Carolina case in which a defendant had been accused of committing a variety of drug offenses involving opium and possession of prescription drugs, he complained that reversible error had been committed when the trial judge allowed the prosecution to introduce evidence of the chemical analysis of seized drug material. The analysis had been performed by an expert who never testified and the results were permitted to be introduced by a second expert who had not made the tests. The appellate court upheld the admission of the expert's opinion despite the defendant's argument that his Sixth Amendment right to confront and cross-examine adverse witnesses had been violated. The court noted that the results of outside tests or facts developed concerning information relied upon by an expert is not considered substantive evidence and does not violate the right of confrontation when used to show the basis for the expert's opinion. The court reasoned that it was the expert opinion itself that must be regarded as the substantive evidence and the defendant is permitted to cross examine the testifying witness. Such a procedure is permissible when the tests are of the type reasonably relied upon by experts in the field and violate neither the hearsay rule nor the Sixth Amendment right of confrontation.[152]

The prosecution as well as the defense has the right of cross-examination of adverse witnesses. For example, in a Missouri murder case, the defense on appeal alleged that the prosecutor had engaged in inappropriate cross-examination when the prosecution interrogated the defendant's expert witness concerning whether her diagnosis had taken into consideration all of the facts, whether she had ever testified for the prosecution, whether she had actually reviewed all of the information provided to her, and whether she had adequately interviewed the defendant, among other grounds. The appellate court reviewed the record and held that the prosecutor had engaged in permissible cross-examination directed toward impeachment of an expert witness.[153]

[151] Delaware v. Fensterer, 474 U.S. 15, 106 S. Ct. 292 (1985).
[152] State v. Delaney, 171 N.C. App. 141, 613 S.E.2d 699, 700, 701, 2005 N.C. App. LEXIS 1160 (2005). *See also*, State v. Bunn, 619 S.E.2d 918, 2005 N.C. App. LEXIS 2301 (2005).
[153] Missouri v. Dewey, 86 S.W.3d 434, 440, 2002 Mo. App. LEXIS 2055 (2002).

§ 11.10   Subjects of Expert Testimony

While previous sections of this chapter discussed some of the general rules relating to expert witness testimony, the emphasis of this section relates to considerations of the proper subjects of expertise. There are numerous areas in which experts can meet the qualifications and assist the trier of fact in reaching logical conclusions; if fact, there is no closed list of subjects for which expert testimony might prove helpful. As new scientific and technology developments occur, additional fields of specialized knowledge that require expert testimony will be recognized by the courts. Expert testimony generally will be admissible as long as the testimony has a proper foundation, has been based on reliable principles, and the expert has applied the principles appropriately. Although it would be impossible to discuss all of the areas in which expert testimony would be admissible, especially in criminal cases, the subsections below discuss and illustrate some of the most common areas or subjects that will benefit from expert testimony.

A. *Automobile Accidents*

Expert testimony of police officers and others who may be qualified as accident reconstruction experts may be admissible at criminal or civil trials arising from motor vehicle accidents. In one Florida case, the court properly permitted one police officer, who was a qualified accident reconstruction expert, to give testimony of what he personally observed. In addition, the court permitted the expert to incorporate in his opinion information developed by another officer who was deceased at the time of trial. Pursuant to the Florida version of Rule 705, the trial court permitted the officer-expert to give his opinion without offering prior disclosure of the underlying facts or data upon which he based his opinion. As a general rule, when an expert on direct examination does not specifically mention underlying data, he or she may be asked on cross-examination about the basic facts and data on which the opinion rests.[154] According to one treatise, "During cross-examination, the expert may be required to disclose all of the evidence relied upon regardless of whether it is otherwise admissible."[155] A Florida appellate court reversed a murder conviction where the trial court permitted the prosecution to introduce expert testimony that fiber evidence was found that pointed to the defendant being the driver of the vehicle involved in the death, a fact the defendant disputed. The trial court had rejected the defendant's attempt to introduce the expert opinion testimony of an accident reconstructionist and forensic scientist concerning how the accident happened, how the clothing fibers were released as a result of the wreck, and how they could be distributed as a result of the accident. The appellate court held that an understanding of how fibers are released from clothing, and the possible significance of the presence or absence of fibers in

---

[154]   Carratelli v. Florida, 832 So. 2d 850, 861, 2002 Fla. App. LEXIS 17158 (2002).

[155]   *See* CHARLES W. EHRHARDT, FLORIDA EVIDENCE § 704.1 (2002 ed.).

a particular part of an automobile after an accident were properly the subject of expert testimony. The trial court committed reversible error and abused its discretion in excluding the defendant's expert testimony.[156] In a different case involving a conviction of vehicular homicide, both the prosecution and the defense presented expert testimony concerning how the vehicle left the road. The defendant presented evidence by a mechanical engineer who analyzed skid marks, which supported the defendant's position that the wreck was an accident and that the death was not criminal. Using a more sophisticated approach, the prosecution offered an accident reconstruction expert who used a computer software program—PC-Crash. The prosecution's expert validated the program and testified that it had gained general acceptance in the expert accident reconstruction community. The appellate court upheld the conviction because, even though the two expert witnesses presented opposing conclusions, the jury could determine which version to believe.[157] In a vehicular homicide case in which the vehicle left the highway and broke apart, expert witnesses for the prosecution were permitted to offer expert opinions concerning the speed of the defendant's vehicle at the time of the accident. Their qualifications appeared to be proper and their methodology designed to evaluate a vehicle's speed at the time of the event proved appropriate to the task, including their evaluation of scuff marks and crossover marks on the pavement to help estimate vehicle speed.[158]

In many recent automobile collision cases in which the speed of a defendant's car may be at issue, newer technology, coupled with expert witnesses with cutting edge knowledge, proves decisive. In a Florida double manslaughter case, at issue was the speed of the defendant's Pontiac Trans Am at the time it hit the victims, who were in a car backing into a public street from a private driveway. The vehicle's "black box," or event data recorder, which also operated the defendant's air bag, recorded the speed at 114 m.p.h. in a 30 m.p.h. speed zone. According to the appellate court, using expert testimony was permissible to admit the speed of the vehicle based on the event data recorder because the state's expert testified concerning the reliability of the event data recorder and the fact that they are generally accepted in the accident reconstruction community.[159]

As a general rule, a court does not commit error when it permits a qualified expert witness to reconstruct a motor vehicle accident by basing his or her opinion on photographs, damage repair estimates, personal measurements at the accident scene, police reports, studies of victim injuries, and interviewing witnesses and participants. Where the expert's reconstruction will assist the trier of fact, the expert's testimony should be admitted.[160] In an action arising

---

[156] Barfield v. State, 880 So. 2d 768, 770, 2004 Fla. App. LEXIS 8357 (2004), *reh'g denied* 2004 Fla. App LEXIS 18629 (2004).

[157] *See* State v. Phillips, 123 Wash. App. 761, 98 P.3d 838, 2004 Wash. App. LEXIS 2296 (2004), *reh'g denied*, 2005 Wash. LEXIS 492 (2005).

[158] Maine v. Irving, 2003 Me. 31, 818 A 2d 204, 2003 Me. LEXIS 36 (2003).

[159] Matos v. State, 899 So. 2d 403, 405; 2005 Fla. App. LEXIS 4359 (2005).

[160] Hamilton v. Jones, 2005 Ark. App. LEXIS 92 (2005).

out of the death of an automobile driver in a head-on collision to which there were no eyewitnesses, testimony of a safety engineer, who saw one of the automobiles only after it had been brought into a salvage yard and altered, was admissible when, in his personal examination of the automobile in the salvage yard, he had considered pertinent to the subject of his investigation only the parts of the automobile that were photographed immediately after the collision.[161]

B. Airplane Crashes

Witnesses who have special training, education, or experience may qualify as experts in determining the cause of aircraft accidents.[162] For example, in an airplane crash where the plane had not flown in years, contained old fuel, and had been improperly certified as "airworthy," the inspector had a duty to conduct a more thorough inspection before certification. According to the experts, the crash was caused by engine failure which was, in turn, caused by poor and inadequate maintenance. The expert noted that the inspector did "not indicate that [he] completed the steps necessary to ensure the airworthiness of the fuel system including the carburetor or air intake filter." These conclusions involve evaluation of facts and circumstances that are beyond the knowledge of ordinary witnesses and require an expert to develop an opinion concerning the cause of this crash and apply to similar aircraft mishaps.[163] Naturally, expert testimony may be offered to demonstrate that one party was not negligent in an aircraft disaster. When a plaintiff alleged that the federal government had been negligent in offering some services to a pilot, including altimeter settings, alternative airports, and negligence in sending rescue equipment, an expert witness was properly permitted to offer admissible opinion evidence concerning whether the conduct of federal employees amounted to negligence.[164]

C. Physical and Mental Condition

A general practitioner may usually testify concerning matters within a medical specialty if his or her education or experience, or both, involve demonstrable knowledge of the subject. A skilled medical witness generally has no need to be duly licensed to practice medicine[165] and, in most cases, the expert does not have to be licensed in the particular jurisdiction. However, some jurisdictions require a better match between general knowledge and the specialty than merely possessing a medical degree or license. The general rule is that anyone who is shown to have special knowledge and skill in under-

[161]　Leeper v. Thornton, 344 P.2d 1101 (Okla. 1959)

[162]　See In re Aircraft Accident at Little Rock, Arkansas, June 1, 1999, 231 F. Supp. 2d 852, 2002 U.S. Dist. LEXIS 22881 (E.D. Ark. 2002).

[163]　Mills v. Oberg, 2005 Minn. App. LEXIS 106 (2005).

[164]　Bieberle v. United States, 255 F. Supp. 2d 1190, 1206, 1207, 2003 U.S. Dist. LEXIS 5427 (D. Kan. 2003).

[165]　See Tenet Healthcare Corp. v. Gilbert, 277 Ga. App. 895, 627 S.E.2d 821, 2006 Ga. App. LEXIS 167 (2006), in which an expert's affidavit had to be attached to a complaint to make the case actionable and the court held that the affidavit was sufficient even though the expert possessed no license to practice at the time of the complaint.

standing human ailments may have the foundation to testify as an expert qualified to give an opinion on the particular question in issue. For example, medical doctors who are well-versed in the effects of insulin, hypoglycemia, and how intoxication might result when insulin protocols were not followed, may be permitted to offer testimony to help establish the defense of involuntary intoxication.[166]

While expert medical testimony may prove preferable, it is not always essential that an expert medical witness be a medical practitioner. Thus, nonmedical witnesses who have had experience in electrical work may testify to the effects of electrical shock upon the human body. An expert witness in the field of toxicology was permitted to testify in a driving under the influence prosecution that the defendant was a user of marijuana based on the amount of marijuana metabolite found in his blood. She offered testimony concerning amounts of amphetamine, methamphetamine, and mirtazapine, a depressant, but she found no alcohol in the blood sample. Under questioning by the prosecutor, the expert was not able with certainty to say whether the defendant was under the influence or not based on her analysis of his blood chemistry. Even though the expert testified to medical evidence and she was not a medical doctor, her level of expertise was properly admitted in an effort to illuminate the condition of the defendant.[167]

An expert who gives testimony may carry more weight with a jury when explaining physical attributes or mental conditions. For example, a Tennessee court allowed a physician who was an expert in the area of pharmacology and toxicology to testify concerning the physiological effects of drinking ethylene glycol (automobile antifreeze). The court permitted the doctor to explain how ethylene glycol causes a patient's blood to become acidic while metabolizing into oxalic acid, which binds with calcium, causing kidney failure and death.[168] With the detail offered by the doctor, a trier of fact would most likely place great weight on the testimony. In a child molestation case in which an ordinary medical doctor took a history from the alleged victim and conducted a physical exam of the mouth and the child's privates, the court permitted the doctor to testify as an expert that the results of the overall exam indicated that, in the doctor's opinion, the child had been molested.[169] Evidence from this expert witness would be given much more weight by the trier of fact than would be given to a non-medical child counselor. However, a licensed physician's assistant, who treated the defendant in the hospital's emergency room on the night of the arrest, could be precluded from testifying as an expert about all the medical issues in the case, and his testimony could be limited to the examination and treatment of the defendant at the hospital.[170]

---

[166]   People v. Garcia, 113 P. 3d 775, 2005 Colo. LEXIS 562 (2005).
[167]   State v. Lee, 2005 Tenn. Crim. App. LEXIS 399 (2005).
[168]   Tennessee v. Combs, 2002 Tenn. Crim. App. LEXIS 799 (2002).
[169]   State v. Lente, 2005 NMCA 111, 119 P. 3d 737, 739, 740, 2005 N.M. LEXIS 105 (2005).
[170]   State v. Carlson, 559 N.W.2d 802 (N.D. 1996).

The trial court is given great discretion in deciding how testimony regarding a defendant's mental condition should be characterized following its admission. Some courts limit expert testimony relating to the conclusions drawn by an expert because of the danger that the expert's opinion might invade the province of the jury. Other jurisdictions do not exhibit a concern about whether an expert's conclusion might intrude into an area reserved for jury decision making. In a Florida case in which the defendant had murdered her mother, the trial court limited the testimony of a defense psychiatrist by preventing him from expressing an opinion concerning whether the defendant was "insane." The appellate court expressed the opinion that a medical expert can offer an opinion concerning whether a defendant is "insane" because expert witnesses in Florida are permitted to render an opinion concerning an ultimate issue in a case.[171] The federal rules under Rule 704 are slightly more restrictive that the Florida rules and allow an expert to offer an opinion or inference concerning the ultimate issue unless it relates to a mental state or condition of a criminal defendant.[172]

In a California attempted murder case, the trial court held that expert testimony tending to prove or disprove whether the defendant harbored the necessary mental capacity to form the requisite criminal intent would not be admitted. The appellate court concurred because it believed that an expert would not be able to know what ability to form a specific intent was actually possessed by another human.[173] Finally, in a third case, the appellate court declared that the trial court erred in excluding an "expert opinion that the defendant was severely impaired in his ability to form an intent to kill and an intent to injure."[174]

If the members of the jury can readily observe the defendant's mental condition, expert testimony concerning the condition will be excluded.[175] In *State v. Cortez*, the reviewing court held that the trial court did not err in excluding the psychologist's testimony that the defendant was slow to answer, forgot easily, and did not express himself well, because these aspects of the accused's personality could be readily observed by the jurors when he testified at the trial.

D. Summaries

The Federal Rules of Criminal Procedure interface with the Federal Rules of Evidence when, as a precondition of admission of expert testimony, the criminal rules[176] require that both the prosecution and the defense prepare a written summary of any testimony that either side expects to have admitted under Federal Rule of Evidence 702, 703, or 705. As a general rule, the orig-

[171] Reynolds v. Florida, 837 So. 2d 1044, 2002 Fla. App. LEXIS 19140 (2002).

[172] *See* FED. R. EVID. 704.

[173] California v. Sanchez, 2002 Cal. App. Unpub. LEXIS 11068 (2002); *see* Steele v. State, 97 Wis. 2d 72, 294 N.W.2d 2 (1980).

[174] State v. Edmon, 28 Wash. App. 98, 621 P.2d 1310 (1981). *See also* Commonwealth v. Pallotta, 36 Mass. App. 669, 634 N.E.2d 915 (1994).

[175] State v. Cortez, 935 F.2d 135 (8th Cir. 1991).

[176] FED. R. CRIM PROC. 16.

inals of the testimony summarized must be made available to the opposing party for examination in advance of trial or the expert's testimony may be excluded.[177] In an appeal from a federal conviction involving sexual abuse where the prosecution had not been completely forthcoming concerning the basis of its expert's opinion relative to the presence of semen, the trial court's decision to allow the expert to testify was upheld by the Eighth Circuit Court of Appeals. The trial court's admonition to the prosecution that it should be more forthcoming in the future with respect to pretrial summaries of expert testimony was noted with approval by the Court of Appeals.[178] Trial witnesses may also be permitted to offer summaries of testimony as an aid to the understanding of the jury. For example, summaries of various complex stock sale transactions may be properly admitted in cases involving income tax evasion. An internal revenue agent's summary of the prosecution's evidence was consistent with the Federal Rules of Evidence where the testifying agent had specialized knowledge of the tax transactions at issue and was able to place the transactions in context. The summary witness need not necessarily be an expert witness, but in many cases summary witnesses do carry expert witness qualifications.[179]

E. Handwriting Comparisons

Analysis of handwriting consists of having an expert compare a known specimen of a person's handwriting to a questioned sample in order to determine whether the same person composed both documents. The scientific theory behind handwriting analysis is that each person's writing technique is different and unique from virtually everyone else.[180] Each time a handwriting expert testifies in court, he or she must demonstrate appropriate qualifications as an expert witness. Testimony that a certain person wrote an individual document is an opinion offered by the expert, but the handwriting analysis need not be absolutely certain as long as principles and proper methodology have been followed. To be qualified, he or she must have expert training and experience in handwriting analysis in general or must be intimately familiar with the handwriting of the individual in question. A witness who is not qualified can merely express an untrained comparison of two writings that are in evidence.[181] For example, a trial court committed error when the judge permitted a police officer to testify that the handwriting belonged to the defendant when the officer had no expertise and was not familiar with the defendant's handwriting prior to the trial.[182] However, a jury may be permitted to compare a

---

[177]　United States v. Roy, 2006 U. S. Dist. LEXIS 9583 (2006).

[178]　United States v. Conroy, 424 F.3d 833, 838, 2005 U.S. App. LEXIS 21080 (2005).

[179]　United States v. Pree, 408 F. 3d 855, 869, 2005 U.S. App. LEXIS 9222 (7th Cir. 2005). *See also* § 13.8 *infra*.

[180]　United States v. Prime, 431 F.3d 1147, 1153, 2005 U.S. App. LEXIS 27276 (2005).

[181]　United States v. Tipton, 964 F.2d 650 (7th Cir. 1992). Forensic document examiner qualified as an expert regarding forged documents. *See also* Ryan v. United States, 384 F.2d 379 (1st Cir. 1967).

[182]　Ohio v. Brennan, 2002 Ohio App. LEXIS 5788 (2002).

known sample with a questioned sample of handwriting and come to a conclusion[183] even though the jury has no special expertise. In contrast, comparison handwriting analysis is generally admissible in court when the evidence comes from a qualified expert. The purpose of allowing expert testimony is to assist the jury in deciding the questioned document and to draw the jury's attention to similarities between the known and the unknown writing sample.[184] When a qualified expert had years of experience in the field of handwriting analysis, he was permitted to offer his opinion that the defendant wrote the document in question[185] despite the fact that the jury would have to ultimately decide the same question.

Because handwriting identification cannot be based upon absolute scientific certainty, the opinion of an expert regarding handwriting must meet only the generally accepted standards adopted by questioned document examiners.[186] In a prosecution for mail and wire fraud, the defendant challenged the government's expert witness concerning her "methodology, the bases for her conclusions, and the degrees of certainty with which she was able to reach her conclusions."[187] She testified that her conclusions were within a reasonable degree of scientific certainty that the defendant wrote some of the questioned documents. Her conclusions were not stated in absolute terms but were within the parameters expected of an expert on handwriting comparisons and were, therefore, properly admitted by the trial court. The jury was permitted to accept or reject the expert's testimony.

The Supreme Court of the United States has emphasized that requiring a defendant to provide a handwriting sample for comparison purposes does not violate the privilege against self-incrimination.[188] According to the Court, the use of this type of evidence does not run counter to Fifth Amendment constitutional protections because the quality of the handwriting is used for the sole purpose of comparison with a document of uncertain authorship. A handwriting sample reveals the physical characteristics of writing style and does not require a defendant to give actual adverse testimony. "A mere handwriting exemplar, in contrast to the content of what is written, like the voice or body itself, is an identifying characteristic" that is outside the protection of the Fifth Amendment.[189]

Expert testimony may be admissible to determine authorship of a document based not upon handwriting analysis, but upon an evaluation of the style

---

[183]　People v. Rodriguez, 133 Cal. App. 4th 545, 554, 34 Cal. Rptr. 3d 886, 892 2005 Cal. App. LEXIS 1628 (2005).

[184]　United States v. Smith, 153 Fed. Appx. 187, 2005 U.S. App. LEXIS 23798 (4th Cir. 2005) (forensic document examiner who helped develop standards for handwriting analysis was deemed to be qualified as an expert regarding forged instruments).

[185]　See United States v. Brown, 152 Fed. Appx. 59, 2005 U.S. App. LEXIS 22703 (2d Cir. 2005).

[186]　United States v. Herrera, 832 F.2d 833 (4th Cir. 1987).

[187]　United States v. Mornan, 413 F.3d 372, 380, 2005 U.S. App. LEXIS 13043 (3d Cir. 2005).

[188]　Gilbert v. California, 388 U.S. 263, 265, 1967 U.S. LEXIS 1086 (1967), See also United States v. Dionisio, 410 U.S. 1 (1973), in which the court upheld a federal judge's order that required a suspect to give voice samples for grand jury consideration.

[189]　Hiibel v. Sixth Judicial District Court of Nevada, 542 U.S. 177, 194, 2004 U.S. LEXIS 4385 (2004), quoting United States v. Wade, 388 U.S. 218, 223 (1967).

of word selection and textually unique qualities of a writing.[190] Some courts have admitted the testimony of forensic document examiners[191] who look for common artifacts, style, and linguistic markers in questioned documents, while other courts have been somewhat more reticent to fully take advantage of this modern method of determining authorship of questioned documents.[192] In one federal case, the judge concluded that the principle of uniqueness of handwriting or hand printing failed to satisfy the requirements for reliability because there was no scientific proof that each person writes a document with characteristics unique to that person. However, the same judge allowed evidence of the mechanics of handwriting and comparisons of similarities or dissimilarities and other factors that would assist the jury in determining authorship of questioned documents.[193]

F. Typewriter Comparisons

In past years, experts who could qualify to make handwriting comparisons were more in demand than those who could give testimony regarding the source of typewritten documents. However, as the typewriter became more popular, experts who qualified to testify that typewritten documents were written on a specific typewriter were in demand. The need for experts in the typewriter comparison field, while once robust, has diminished in importance but has not completely evaporated. Because some traditional typewriters are still in use, this expertise retains some marginal utility in civil cases as well as in criminal prosecutions.[194] Today, with the more common use of various computer printers that print in a fairly uniform manner, discerning the source of a document has become somewhat more difficult.

Expert evidence is generally admissible to prove that a document was typed on a particular type of machine, such as an Underwood typewriter, even though the police never obtained the specific typewriter. In order to prove that a document was typed on a particular computer printer/typewriter using a specific daisywheel print wheel, courts frequently admit expert testimony.[195] In making comparisons, the expert usually points out the unique characteristics such as dirt particles changing the printed character, damage to a particular character, and any irregularities specifically unique to a particular print wheel. Sometimes a comparison of documents indicates that they were typed on the same machine even though they purportedly came from separate sources.[196] More modern methods of printing pose unique problems concerning identifi-

---

[190] See Sargur Srihari et al., *Individuality of Handwriting*, 47 J. FORENSIC SCI. 856 (2002).

[191] United States v. Gricco 2002 U.S. Dist. LEXIS 7564 (E.D. Pa. 2002).

[192] United States v. Lewis, 220 F. Supp. 2d 548, 2002 U.S. Dist. LEXIS 17062 (S.D. W.Va. 2002); United States v. Brewer, 2002 U.S. Dist. LEXIS 6689 (N.D. Ill. 2002); United States v. Saelee, 162 F. Supp. 2d 1097 (D. Alaska 2001); United States v. Fujii, 152 F. Supp. 2d 939 (N.D. Ill. 2000).

[193] See United States v. Hildalgo, 229 F. Supp. 2d 961, 2002 U.S. Dist. LEXIS 21633 (D. Ariz. 2002).

[194] Eta-Ndu v. Gonzales, 411 F.3d 977, 981, 982, 2005 U.S. App. LEXIS 12120 (8th Cir. 2005), in which forensic analysis of typewritten letters proved important in a deportation case.

[195] United States v. Johns, 2000 U.S. App. LEXIS 542 (6th Cir. 2000).

[196] Caldron v. Ashcroft, 110 Fed. Appx. 789, 2004 U.S. App. LEXIS 19793 (9th Cir. 2004).

cation, especially with recyclable inkjet print heads and refillable inks containing different chemical compositions from the original factory ink.

Determining the source of printed documents has taken a step forward because several manufacturers of color laser printers have designed hardware that prints the serial number and manufacturer's code in binary form on each sheet of paper printed by the machine. Documents printed by commercial printing companies will usually carry the same identification marks, as will color prints made from desktop laser printers.[197]

In some older cases, courts have allowed the opinion of an expert as to the identification of the operator of the typewriter. In doing so, the expert points out the individual style of the person typing the instrument, taking into consideration the force with which the typist struck particular keys. This identification is primarily predicated on the manner of punctuation, the length of the lines, the depth of the indentation, and other personal style characteristics.[198]

G. Polygraph Examination Results

For a variety of reasons, courts have not generally admitted the results of lie detector, or polygraph, tests because either the scientific principles behind such tests remain in question or the implementation of the testing continues to suffer from questionable reliability. One state court noted, "The general rule in Illinois is to preclude the introduction of evidence regarding polygraph examinations and their results because (1) the evidence is not sufficiently reliable, and (2) the results may be taken as determinative of guilt or innocence despite their lack of reliability."[199] The Fourth Circuit has a policy of banning the admission of polygraph evidence and it continues to refuse admission of test results because of precedent and questions concerning the reliability of the polygraph.[200] In some cases, courts will permit admission of polygraph tests if all parties consent,[201] but when there has been no written stipulation signed by all parties, courts almost uniformly deny the admission of polygraph results.[202] However, when a defendant agrees to take a polygraph test, to be bound by the results, and gives prior consent to the admission of the results, the polygraph operator may testify concerning his or her opinion of what the examination revealed. In a Georgia murder case, a female defendant agreed to take a polygraph and offered a written stipulation that the results could be admitted. The test results proved damaging to her defense and the Supreme Court of Georgia upheld the admission of the polygraph results under the circumstances.[203]

---

[197]   "Investigating Machine Identification Code Technology in Color Laser Printers." Electronic Frontier Foundation. 1 Jun 2006. Available at: http://www.eff.org/Privacy/printers/wp.php.

[198]   Thomas v. State, 197 Okla. 450, 172 P.2d 973 (1946).

[199]   People v. Washington, 363 Ill. App. 3d 13, 842 N.E.2d 1193, 1199, 2006 Ill. App. LEXIS 24 (2006).

[200]   United States v. Prince-Oyibo, 320 F.3d 494, 501, 2003 U.S. App. LEXIS 3568 (4th Cir. 2003) and United States v. Sprague, 134 Fed. Appx. 607, 2005 U.S. LEXIS 10127 (4th Cir. 2005).

[201]   See § 6.19 supra. See also § 15.5 for a general description of polygraph tests.

[202]   See Ohio v. DiBlasio, 2002 Ohio 2466, 2002 Ohio App. LEXIS 2691 (2002); see also J.R.T. II v. State, 783 N.E.2d 300, 2003 Ind. App. LEXIS 171 (2003).

California by statute bans the admission of polygraph evidence and the opinions of examiners from adult and juvenile proceedings, unless all parties stipulate to the admission of the results.[204]

While polygraph evidence generally is excludable absent agreement, the Supreme Court of Georgia held that there may be occasions in which a polygraph might be admissible in the penalty phase of a death penalty case. In one case, a defendant had passed a polygraph exam conducted a few days after the murder, but the polygraph evidence was not admitted at the guilt phase of the trial. The trial court refused to allow the convicted defendant to present the evidence during his portion of the sentencing. However, the state supreme court reversed the sentence, noting, "When the defendant seeks to introduce unstipulated polygraph test results as mitigation evidence, the trial court must exercise its discretion to determine whether those results are sufficiently reliable to be admitted."[205]

Polygraph examination results are admitted only after a proper foundation has been laid and the examiner's qualifications are established. In a Florida case, the reviewing court concluded that the claimant in a forfeiture proceeding failed to properly lay the foundation for the admission of polygraph examinations, in which the claimant sought only to admit the hard copy of the examination.[206] The court noted that there was no proffer to the court relating to the polygraph examiner's qualifications, or procedures and circumstances surrounding the admissions of the examinations.

While polygraph results are generally not admissible, statements made to polygraph operators that do not directly relate to or are not essential to the examination concerning the merits of a case or its important details may be admissible where they qualify as admissions or confessions.[207] Therefore, voluntary statements that a polygraph subject makes before, during, or after the administration of a polygraph test may be admissible as long as the admission of the statements does not run afoul of other rules of evidence or any applicable constitutional provision.[208]

H. Voiceprint Identification

General acceptance of voiceprint identification has not yet gained the scientific level of accuracy and certainty that was once believed to be possible. The theory that allows voice comparisons holds that each person's voice possesses unique tone and cadence characteristics that expert evaluation will indicate whether a given voice sample was produced by a particular person. Some state courts and federal courts have permitted the use of voiceprint evidence

---

[203] Thornton v. State, 279 Ga. 676, 678, 620 S.E.2d 356, 360, 2005 Ga. App. LEXIS 634 (2005).

[204] CAL. EVID. CODE § 351.1 (Matthew Bender 2006)

[205] Height v. State, 278 Ga. 592, 594, 595, 604 S.E.2d 796; 2004 Ga. LEXIS 958 (2004). *Contra*, United States v. Roman, 368 F. Supp. 2d 119, 2005 U.S. Dist. LEXIS 7772 (2005).

[206] United States v. One Parcel of Real Estate, 804 F. Supp. 319 (S.D. Fla. 1992).

[207] *See* Esquibel v. Texas, 2005 Tex. App. LEXIS 6760 (2005)

[208] *See* State v. Damron, 151 S.W. 3d 510, 2004 Tenn. LEXIS 993 (2004).

with proper instructions.[209] For example, in *Alaska v. Coon*, the appellate court held that spectrographic voice analysis evidence, properly prepared, could be used in evidence in a criminal case involving terroristic voice threats that the victim had recorded.[210] The Supreme Court of Alaska determined that the state courts would follow the *Daubert v. Merrell Dow Pharmaceuticals*[211] standard in determining when and under what circumstances to admit expert scientific evidence. However, the Federal Bureau of Investigation, in a report cited in the *Coon* case, noted that problems remained in the validity and reliability of voice analysis and that the use of spectrographic voice analysis appeared to be on the decline. The same report noted that the FBI now has a policy not to provide expert testimony on spectrographic comparisons due to the inconclusive nature and unknown error rate of the technique.[212]

In granting a new trial for murder where police had voiceprint data that indicated voiceprint analysis was not able to identify the defendant's voice from ransom calls, the court seemed to agree that voiceprint analysis was not a proven theory for admissibility in courts. The police knew that the voiceprint analysis could not identify the defendant, but they withheld the information from him despite his request for exculpatory evidence.[213] In a recent federal case, the Fourth Circuit approved a trial court's exclusion of voiceprint analysis on the theory that the proffered evidence would not have assisted the jury and that the evidence did not produce any meaningful scientific analysis.[214]

In an older federal case from Hawai'i that predated the *Daubert* decision, a district court approved the admission of expert testimony of spectrographic voice identification in a prosecution for conspiracy and extortion. The voice sample consisted of 65 words recorded by the victim on an answering machine and proved to be a cornerstone of the government's case against the defendant. The trial court accepted the use of voice recognition evidence under the standard of *Frye v. United States*[215] and noted that spectrographic voice analysis had gained general acceptance in its field and that the defendant had met his burden of establishing the scientific basis and reliability of the proposed expert testimony. Because the trial court believed that the expert testimony would assist the jury in rendering a decision, admitting the evidence was appropriate.[216]

---

[209] *See* § 15.10 for a thorough discussion of the use of voiceprints. *And see* United States v. Maivia, 728 F. Supp. 1471, 1990 U.S. Dist. LEXIS 677 (D. Haw. 1990), in which the trial court allowed the introduction of speech spectrographic analysis through the use of expert witnesses.

[210] Alaska v. Coon, 974 P.2d 386, 1999 Alaska LEXIS 28 (1999).

[211] The *Daubert* standard comes from *Daubert v. Merrell Dow Pharmaceuticals*, 509 U.S. 579 (1993), which altered the federal court legal formula for admitting scientific evidence. To admit scientific testing, some of the questions to be answered include whether the offered scientific theory has been sufficiently tested, whether the method has been the subject of peer review and publication, whether the error rate remains within an acceptable range or frequency, whether quality controls ensure reliability, and whether the methodology has gained general scientific acceptability.

[212] *See* Bruce E. Koenig, *Selected Topics in Forensic Voice Identification*, 20 FBI CRIME LAB. DIGEST 78, 80 (1993), cited in Alaska v. Coon, 974 P.2d 386, 402 n. 88 (1999).

[213] Commonwealth v. Lykus, 20 Mass. L. Rep. 598, 2005 Mass. Super. LEXIS 686 (2005).

[214] United States v. Ricketts, 141 Fed. Appx. 93, 95, 2005 U.S. App. LEXIS 14500 (2005).

[215] 54 App. D.C. 46, 293 F. 1013 (1923).

[216] United States v. Maivia, 728 F. Supp. 1471, 1477, 1478, 1990 U.S. Dist. LEXIS 677 (D. Haw. 1990).

I. *Neutron Activation Analysis*

Although some courts have authorized expert witnesses to testify concerning the results of neutron activation analysis or gunpowder residue testing, some of these courts have expressed doubts concerning expert opinions. For example, in a Minnesota Supreme Court case, the neutron activation analysis was used to show that the defendant, who was accused of shooting a police officer, had fired a pistol shortly before his arrest. After the suspect was taken into custody, but prior to the time he was booked in the county jail, his hands were swabbed with a nitric acid solution. These swabs were sent to the Treasury Department laboratory in Washington for neutron activation analysis, a testing procedure that can determine the presence and amount of certain chemical elements that are normally present on the hand of a person who has recently fired a weapon. Although admitting the testimony of a representative of the Treasury Department, the court expressed concern about the sweeping and unqualified manner in which the expert testimony was offered.[217] The absence of test results may have adverse consequences for a defendant who does not cooperate with the police to a minimal degree. In a case in which a defendant refused to submit a sample for neutron activation testing, a trial court permitted the prosecution to comment, during closing arguments, on the refusal because there was no Fifth Amendment privilege to decline to allow a chemical sample to be taken from the defendant's hand.[218] On the other hand, when an arrestee demands to be subjected to a gunpowder residue test, the prosecution is generally under no obligation to conduct such a test and is certainly not under any duty to conduct a residue test to negate probable cause[219] or conduct a test when overwhelming evidence of guilt is present.[220]

Neutron activation analysis[221] was once used to determine whether a lead bullet came from a particular batch of lead melt from the lead manufacturer. If a crime scene bullet matched a bullet of similar composition in a cartridge found in the defendant's control, the inference would be that the cartridges containing the lead bullet came from the same source or box of ammunition. As science progressed, the theory that the lead in a particular melt was homogenous received strong criticism and appears to be an unsupportable theory, even though neutron activation analysis can reveal the trace elements like silver, copper, antimony, or arsenic that are present in bullet lead.[222] Virtually no court would admit such evidence using neutron activation analysis in the present time.[223]

---

[217] State v. Spencer, 216 N.W.2d 131 (Minn. 1974).

[218] Hubbert v. Mississippi, 759 So. 2d 504, 505, 506, 2000 Miss. App. LEXIS 196 (2000)

[219] Vazquez v. Rossnagle, 163 F. Supp. 2d 494, 2001 U.S. Dist. LEXIS 3974 (3d Cir. 2001).

[220] In re Crossley, 2003 Mich. App. LEXIS 327 (2003).

[221] The process requires access to a nuclear reactor where the lead sample is radiated to reveal the trace components contained within the lead.

[222] *See* Commonwealth v. Daye, 19 Mass L. Rep. 674, 2005 Mass. Super. LEXIS 368 (2005).

[223] The theoretical basis by which neutron activation analysis determines whether one lead specimen matched a different sample depends upon the homogenous nature of lead in the manufacturing process. Scientific research presently holds that lead samples are not homogenous, which dooms other scientific efforts to trace lead based on its composition. For a related discussion, *see* Clemmons v. State, 2006 Md. LEXIS 192 (2006).

J. DNA Deoxyribonucleic Acid Identification

Scientific and technological advances in the past 25 years have made identification of suspects easier and more definite with the application of DNA typing. Deoxyribonucleic acid contains the pattern or unique hereditary "roadmap" for all human beings and determines how humans develop, grow, and mature throughout life. The theory that everyone has unique DNA, except identical twins, has reached scientific certainty and the ability to translate the science from the laboratory to the courtroom has become routine. Suspects who have left samples of their DNA at the crime scene or on a victim may have their known DNA sample compared to recovered specimens. Where a person would never have had the opportunity to have lawfully been in a specific location to have left DNA evidence or would never have normally occupied a position to leave DNA evidence on or in a victim, the match that can be made may prove decisive in proving guilt. Similarly, wrongly convicted individuals may be able to prove that someone else was the criminal, and, in so doing, free themselves from illegal incarceration. Although the scientific principle of DNA has been long accepted in American state and federal courts, alleged errors in statistical application and significance, the application of the science, the handling of DNA samples, issues involving alleged contamination,[224] hearsay allegations, and Sixth Amendment confrontation issues drive the litigation efforts of defendants to keep DNA evidence from being admitted at trial.

In an Ohio case in which the genetic material was collected from the crime scene by police and evidence technicians and transmitted for testing to a crime lab, the trial court permitted the results to be introduced into court by an expert witness who had never observed the testing or viewed the process. The trial expert witness used a copy of the report generated by the lab technician and offered his own conclusions. The appellate court reversed on several grounds and held that the DNA results should not have been admitted because the defendant had not been permitted to cross-examine the lab worker who performed the tests, thus creating a Sixth Amendment right of confrontation violation. The court held that the lab report was testimonial in nature and should have been introduced by the one who performed the testing.[225] Taking an opposite view, a New York trial court admitted DNA evidence against a defendant where one sample had been taken in 1993, stored, and analyzed years later. The technician compared the stored DNA sample to a recent one taken from the defendant and reported a match. An expert witness in forensic biology and DNA typing testified that she supervised and reviewed the records of the DNA profile performed on the defendant's saliva at the medical examiner's office and she also reviewed and compared the DNA profile taken from the victim, which was done at a Virginia laboratory. The trial court permitted her

---

[224] *See* 3 CARDOZO PUB. L. POL'Y & ETHICS J. 847 (2006). *DNA in the Legal System: The Benefits Are Clear, The Problems Aren't Always.*

[225] State v. Crager, 164 Ohio App. 3d 816, 826, 827, 2005 Ohio 6868, 844 N. E. 2d 390, 398, 399, 2005 Ohio App. LEXIS 6188 (2005), *cert. granted*, 109 Ohio St. 3d 1421, 2006 Ohio 1967, 2006 Ohio LEXIS 1037 (2006).

to offer her opinion that the two samples matched. The court found that the admission of the DNA evidence did not violate the defendant's right to confront witnesses and would not result in a reversal of the case on appeal.[226]

DNA analysis using the Restriction Fragment Length Polymorphism (RFLP) testing requires relatively large and non-degraded samples in order to obtain accurate results. The expert usually is able to testify using statistical probability to render an opinion concerning a DNA match. Newer methods, such as the Polymerase Chain Reaction (PCR) process of DNA testing, enable scientists to amplify or copy DNA samples that are too small to subject to the RFLP process prior to amplification.[227] The expert who has conducted the testing, or the expert who will testify in court in reliance on the work of laboratory technicians, will testify concerning the collection of the evidence and its testing and will interpret the results in a form that will be useful for the trier of fact.

K. Fingerprint Identification

The basic theory that everyone has unique fingerprints and that fingerprints do not change with time or age allows identification between a known sample and an unknown impression. The standard methodology used in the United States, ACE-V, stands for analysis, comparison, evaluation, and verification.[228] From the first time it was admitted in court in 1911, these principles have generally been accepted by courts as offering a sound method of making reliable identifications.[229] By implementing these principles, law enforcement officers may make identifications using palm, toe, and heel prints, where suspects have generated print impressions. The police officer or evidence technician must testify concerning the recovery process that was used to obtain the visible impression or latent prints from a crime scene, but the analysis and interpretation of the results must generally be introduced in court by an expert. As required in other fields of expertise, the expert must establish an evidentiary foundation to show that by study, training, and experience he or she has attained sufficient expertise to offer opinion testimony. For example, in a burglary case, despite a defense objection, a judge accepted the prosecution's witness as an expert following her explanation concerning her qualifications. She testified:

---

[226] People v. Brown, 2005 N.Y. Slip Op. 25303, 9 Misc. 3d 420, 423, 801 N.Y.S.2d 709, 711, 2005 N.Y. Misc. LEXIS 1556 (2005).

[227] *See* United States v. Morrow, 374 F. Supp. 2d 51, 2005 U.S. Dist. LEXIS 8327 (D.D.C. 2005).

[228] Commonwealth v. Patterson, 445 Mass. 626, 628 n. 2, 840 N.E.2d 12, 14 n.2, 2005 Mass. LEXIS 765 (2005).

[229] Illinois v. Jennings, 252 Ill. 534, 96 N.E. 1077 (1911). More recently, the Court of Appeals upheld the validity of fingerprint identification in United States v. Crisp, 324 F.3d 261, 2003 U.S. App. LEXIS 6021 (4th Cir. 2003), *cert. denied*, 540 U.S. 888, 2003 U.S. LEXIS 6388 (2003). Utah recently upheld the principle of fingerprint identification validity in State v. Quintana 2004 Utah App. 418, 103 P.2d 168, 169, 2004 Utah App. LEXIS 459 (2004).

that her basic classroom work in "ridgeology" was done at the Hawai'i Criminal Justice Data Center in Honolulu, her advance classroom work was done with the Sacramento Police Department (SPD) in California, and she had a diploma or certificate for ridgeology from the SPD. [She] further testified that she did not receive any "FBI [United States Federal Bureau of Investigation] identification training," did not know if the SPD "had any kind of national accreditation," did not "have any kind of certification with any national or international group," and had not been assigned "any kind of error rate or proficiency" for her work in fingerprinting.[230]

While a person must qualify as an expert at interpreting fingerprints in order to properly testify, police personnel or evidence technicians are assigned to collect and preserve fingerprint evidence. When properly obtained and preserved, other experts offer the evidence in court. The FBI and many large law enforcement agencies have experts trained in fingerprint analysis and schooled in courtroom presentation of that evidence. Some cases may present special challenges to obtaining usable fingerprint evidence. In a Virginia case, a police officer used a mixture of equal parts water, black fingerprint powder, and clear Ivory dish soap and applied it to the reverse side of a vehicle identification strip to reveal a defendant's fingerprints. The judge allowed the evidence to be introduced by a fingerprint analyst who testified that the specially revealed fingerprint matched the defendant's prints.[231]

To assist the jury in understanding fingerprint testimony, the expert normally will use enlarged photographs, PowerPoint presentations, or other means to show the points of similarity in the ridges and lines on which the expert has based his or her conclusion.

In a slightly different context, experts may be permitted to testify that footprints at the crime scene match or have a close resemblance to the shoes worn by the accused in a criminal case. For example, a trial court permitted a forensic technician to testify that shoe prints left in fireproofing dust from a safe cracked during a burglary matched the shoes worn by the defendant. The court observed that qualified expert testimony could be admitted because shoe print identification does not rest on arcane scientific principles, but on visual comparison of physical samples. An expert could recognize small anomalies in shoe design, wear, or physical traits characteristic of a particular shoe that might escape a non-expert. The judge ruled that such information could assist the jury and should be admitted.[232] In a Georgia rape and burglary case, the court admitted evidence of shoe impressions taken from the crime scene. A Georgia Bureau of Identification microanalyst conducted the comparisons between the impression and the actual shoes of the defendant and testified at trial that there was a good match between the wear pattern and tread design of

---

[230] State v. Medeiros, 206 Haw. App. LEXIS 185 (2006).
[231] Hasson v. Commonwealth, 2006 Va. App. LEXIS (2006).
[232] *See* Ratiff v. State, 110 P.3d 982, 2005 Alas. App. LEXIS 39 (2005).

defendant's shoe and the crime scene impressions.[233] However, some jurisdictions do not require an expert to make a shoe print comparison where a footprint has been photographed and compared to shoes a defendant was wearing at the time of apprehension. In one case, the trial court allowed photographs of the impressions and the actual shoes into evidence while allowing the jury to decide whether a match existed.[234]

L. Testimony Relating to Drug Operations

Drug manufacturing and distribution operations generally have significant similarities, such that law enforcement officials who have extensive experience in drug-related crime may be permitted to offer expert testimony concerning the modus operandi of drug traffickers. As a limitation, the expert must be careful to explain the usual pattern of drug operation within his or her area of expertise but not to carry the testimony so far as to offer a personal opinion concerning guilt[235] because that is beyond the area of expertise and intrudes on the province of the jury. Experts involved with investigating illegal drug use and sale can be permitted to respond to hypothetical situations posed by the prosecutor where the hypothetical closely mirrors the facts in the case. In a New Jersey case, an officer was asked to assume that a hypothetical was true and to offer an opinion concerning whether a person in the hypothetical would be possessing drugs for personal use or for sale. The Supreme Court of New Jersey approved allowing the officer to testify as an expert because the officer had extensive experience in investigation drug culture and sales protocols.[236] Expert witnesses may be authorized to testify regarding the identification, use, and value of narcotics, as well as the language used by narcotics dealers.[237] To qualify as an expert, the witness must show that his or her knowledge, skill, training, or experience allows the witness to help the fact finders understand and evaluate the significance of the evidence.[238] Qualified witnesses may be permitted to express their opinions concerning whether a given hypothetical fact pattern would indicate that a person who was engaged in drug transactions for personal use was involved in drug distribution.[239] In one case, the court found that there was no abuse of discretion in allowing a paid informant to testify as an expert witness about drug transactions when the evidence indicated that the informant had participated in more than 50 similar drug sales.[240]

A police officer may testify as an expert regarding drug-related practices if the evidence introduced indicates that the officer is qualified by experience, training, and education. For example, a reviewing court held that the trial court

---

[233] Thrasher v. Georgia, 2003 Ga. App. LEXIS 734 (2003).

[234] Redmond v. Mississippi, 815 So. 2d 1241, 1245, 2002 Miss. App. LEXIS 123 (2002).

[235] New Jersey v. Summers, 176 N.J. 306, 323, 324, 823 A.2d 15, 2003 N.J. LEXIS 567 (2003).

[236] New Jersey v. Nesbitt, 185 N.J. 504, 511, 888 A.2d 472, 478, 2006 N.J. LEXIS 7 (2006).

[237] United States v. Walker, 2006 U.S. App. LEXIS 11280 (6th Cir. 2006)

[238] United States v. Garcia, 2006 U.S. App. LEXIS 10955 (11th Cir. 2006).

[239] New Jersey v. Summers, 350 N.J. Super. 353, 365, 366, 795 A.2d 308, 2002 N.J. Super. LEXIS 195 (2002).

[240] United States v. Anderson, 813 F.2d 1450 (9th Cir. 1987).

did not abuse its discretion in a drug-trafficking prosecution by admitting a police officer's expert testimony regarding countersurveillance techniques employed by a drug dealer to avoid detection.[241] To assist lay jurors, qualified law enforcement officers can testify concerning common practices of drug dealers, how sales occur, and that innocent adults are never permitted to be present at the scene of illegal drug sales.[242]

In a Pennsylvania case, defendants had been making telephone calls to each other in which they would use cryptic language. The question "What can you do for me?" is answered by, "Tomorrow." A second exchange queried, "Ain't nothing jumpin,'" and received the reply, "Goddam boy, whatcha doin'?" The reply to this exchange was, "Just waiting around." The trial court ruling, affirmed on appeal, permitted an expert in drug sales to state that, in his opinion, this type of telephone exchange indicated that one person wanted to buy drugs and that the other person would sell but did not have any drugs to sell but was waiting for a new shipment.[243] In an older federal case, the court held that a detective could testify as an expert regarding the significance of extensive telephone traffic between the defendant and members of an alleged drug ring, because the evidence showed that the detective had specialized knowledge that would assist the trier of fact in understanding the evidence.[244] The court recognized that the detective had worked vice narcotics for seven years and tactical narcotics before that, participating in more than 200 street arrests and investigations.

M.   *Other Subjects of Expert Testimony*

With the continued popularity of the Internet, the trading of child pornography has accelerated. In an effort to reduce the incidence of harm to children, state and federal prosecutors continue to bring many child pornography cases in which the age of the young subjects is an element to be proved. While lay opinion testimony can be admitted, expert testimony may assist the trier of fact in reaching a conclusion. In a California case in which the possession of child pornography was used to revoke probation, revocation required proof that a minor was involved in the depiction and the government had to prove that the probationer knew that the actors were under the age of 18. The trial court approved of the use of two experts who had special knowledge and were qualified to judge the age of persons depicted in the pornography. According to the trial court:

> Here the testimony of both [experts] was regarding developmental factors beyond the normal experience and knowledge of the average fact finder. The age of the actors was an element of the offense and the testimony of the experts was relevant to the conclusion.[245]

---

[241] United States v. deSoto, 885 F.2d 354 (7th Cir. 1989). *See* case in Part II.
[242] United States v. Garcia, 439 F.3d 363, 366, 2006 U.S. App. LEXIS 5032 (7th Cir. 2006).
[243] Commonwealth v. Moss, 2004 Pa. Super 224, 852 A.2d 374, 2004 Pa. Super. LEXIS 1408 (2004).
[244] United States v. Brewer, 1 F.3d 1430 (4th Cir. 1993).
[245] California v. Kurey, 88 Cal. App. 4th 840, 846, 847, 106 Cal. Rptr. 2d 150, 2001 Cal. App. LEXIS 319 (2001). *See also* United States v. Hamilton, 413 F.3d 1138, 1143-1144, 2005 U.S. App. LEXIS 12790 (10th Cir. 2005).

Expert testimony has not been limited to verbal evidence; computer generated animations have been permitted when created by crime scene reconstruction experts. The animations must be properly authenticated as depicting what they purport to depict by presenting a fair and accurate representation of the evidence. To be considered for admission, the probative value of computer generated animations must not outweigh any danger of unfair prejudice to the defendant. In a Pennsylvania case, the trial court permitted the prosecution's expert to offer a frame by frame image of how the expert believed that the killer committed the murder of his wife. In approving the admission of the evidence, the appellate court noted that the use of computer generated animations had to be weighed carefully because of the danger of prejudice. The animation was admissible because it assisted the expert in offering his opinion and served as a graphic representation that illustrated the previously formed opinion of the expert witness.[246]

Some of the many other subjects of expert testimony include modus operandi of offenders,[247] speed of vehicles,[248] cause of a fire,[249] cause of an explosion,[250] meaning of terms,[251] cause of death,[252] DNA profile identification,[253] blood alcohol content,[254] and shoe and tire imprint testimony.[255]

§ 11.11   Experts from Crime Laboratories

Because of the limitations placed on the use of confessions, more reliance is being placed upon the use of real evidence and other evidence obtained by laboratory technicians. With the addition of crime laboratories in all parts of the country, experts from these laboratories have become more readily available. These experts must qualify as do other experts, through experience, training, or knowledge before they can give opinions concerning the significance of laboratory tests and other scientific evidence and the evidence must be useful to the finder of fact. Expert testimony of this type is especially important in the field of ballistics—comparing cartridge cases and bullets found at the scene with those fired from a known weapon. For example, in a murder prosecution, the court permitted the commonwealth's laboratory expert to explain the methodology followed in using a comparison microscope to examine a known shotgun shell and compare it to a shell of unknown origin. The court allowed the ballistics expert to testify that the shell fired at the

[246] Commonwealth v. Serge, 2006 Pa. LEXIS 561 (2006).
[247] Johninson v. State, 878 S.W.2d 727 (Ark. 1994).
[248] Matos v. State, 899 So. 2d 403, 2005 Fla. App. LEXIS 4359 (2005).
[249] Commonwealth v. Lugo, 63 Mass. App. Ct. 204, 824 N.E.2d 481, 2005 Mass. App. LEXIS 296 (2005).
[250] Bitler v. A.O. Smith, 400 F.3d 1227, 2004 U.S. LEXIS 28000 (10th Cir. 2004).
[251] United States v. Walker, 2006 U.S. App. 11280 (10th Cir. 2006).
[252] State v. Vining, 645 A.2d 20 (Me. 1994).
[253] Brown v. State, 270 Ga. App. 176, 605 S.E.2d 885, 2004 Ga. App. LEXIS 1381 (2004).
[254] State v. Taylor, 165 N.C. App. 750; 600 S.E.2d 483, 2004 N.C. App. LEXIS 1519 (2004).
[255] Rodgers v. State, 2006 Tex. Crim. App. LEXIS (2006).

crime came from the defendant's shotgun because it contained the same markings as did the test-fired shell. The judge admitted the evidence linking the shell to the gun because ballistics was a proper subject for expert testimony.[256] No attempt will be made here to list all of the other areas in which a crime laboratory expert can testify, but these include tool mark comparisons and testimony concerning glass and glass fractures, enhancing latent fingerprint evidence with cyanoacrylate fuming, clothing, hairs, and fibers.

§ 11.12   Summary

Most witnesses should confine their testimony to who, what, where, and when types of answers, but as humans often form opinions, there is no absolute bar to admitting opinion evidence. The general rule excluding opinion evidence gives way in a variety of settings for lay witnesses and almost disappears when expert witnesses are concerned. The rule excluding lay opinion evidence is based on the principle that the witnesses are to furnish the facts and the jury has the responsibility of reaching conclusions based on these facts.

There are, however, necessary exceptions to the general rule. These commonsense exceptions have been developed so that the jury will have better information and because the courts have recognized that it is often impossible to give facts to describe all situations. For example, it is difficult to give facts that explain a person's emotional state or to explain that a person was "nervous" or "acted suspiciously."

The rules relating to the exceptions to the opinion rule are discussed in two categories: those relating to nonexpert opinions and those relating to expert opinions. If the ordinary lay witness cannot adequately or accurately describe the facts so as to enable the jurors to draw an intelligent conclusion, the witness may be permitted to offer a lay opinion. For example, a lay witness, in the usual case and with certain limitations, may give opinion testimony as to age, smell, appearance, conduct, distance, mental condition, handwriting, identification, and speed of a vehicle.

Expert witness, when properly qualified, may offer opinions where the opinions will assist the trier of fact in situations where lay opinion would not be permitted. However, this exception possesses a different logical basis; therefore, the rules are different. This opinion testimony is allowed because the expert, due to training, experience, or knowledge, can give information on a specific subject that is substantially superior to the knowledge possessed by the average person. The opinion of the expert witness does not have to be, and usually is not, based on direct observation of prior incidents that brought about the trial. An expert's opinion may be based on scientific testing performed by the expert him- or herself, testing conducted by other experts, questions based on hypothetical assumed facts, or on facts presented by other witnesses in the trial.

---

[256] Commonwealth v. Whitacre, 2005 Pa. Super. 221, 878 A.2d 96, 100, 2005 Pa. Super. LEXIS 1500 (2005).

Examples of subjects of expert testimony are: (1) speed of automobile from tire marks; (2) cause of death; (3) handwriting comparisons; (4) typewriter comparisons; and (5) fingerprint comparisons.

Although sworn justice personnel will not normally present the case in court, because many officers will offer crucial portions of testimony, it is important to understand the lay opinion rule and the exceptions to it. While ordinary law enforcement personnel may actually qualify as expert witnesses due to specialized training and experience, most police officers will be testifying as lay witnesses in criminal trials where opinion evidence has limitations.

Hearsay Rule
and Exceptions   12

The determination that a statement is hearsay does not end the inquiry into admissibility; there must still be a further examination of the need for the statement at trial and the circumstantial guaranty of trustworthiness surrounding the making of the statement.

Zippo Mfg. Co. v. Rogers Imports, Inc.,
216 F. Supp. 670 (S.D.N.Y. 1963)

Chapter Outline

Key Terms and Concepts

dying declaration	pecuniary interest
former testimony	penal interest
hearsay rule	spontaneous utterance
nontestimonial utterance	

---

§ 12.1 Introduction

While virtually everyone has heard of the concept of hearsay evidence, whether from books, films, television shows, and newspapers, most people do not know how it operates in court and fewer still understand the rationale behind the hearsay rule. Even those who have some understanding of the rule are probably unaware that the exceptions to the hearsay rule allow may allow more evidence to be admitted than the rule excludes. When a court recognizes an exception and admits hearsay evidence, there are usually powerful reasons and other justifications for trusting the truthfulness of the evidence. If the hearsay rule were applied without exceptions, it would be very difficult in many criminal cases to present sufficient facts to prove guilt, and certainly much reliable evidence would be excluded from consideration.

As a practical matter, determining what kind of testimony can be considered hearsay provides the starting point for developing an understanding of this rule of exclusion. When an out-of-court statement is repeated in court by a person who overheard another person outside of court make a statement, the evidence may be excluded on the ground that it constitutes hearsay evidence. To be properly considered hearsay evidence, the substance of the out-of-court statement must have been offered in court to prove its truth. When an out-of-court statement is repeated in court and the purpose of offering the statement was merely to demonstrate that a particular person was physically present to be able to make the statement, the internal contents of the statement have not been offered for the proof of the truth contained within the words. In that situation, the out-of-court statement is not considered hearsay evidence. Courts tend to exclude hearsay evidence because subtle alterations in wording, demeanor, or inflection may change the meaning of spoken words. Every time a story is retold to a new person, the essence of the story alters slightly, with a detail added or unconsciously deleted, causing the meaning to shift. The general rule excluding hearsay statements is justified on these and other grounds. It is important to be aware of the historical justifications for the rule in order to understand the exceptions. If the reasons for the rule do not exist in a particular situation, then the evidence should be admitted to assist in determining the facts of the case. Some of the reasons for the exclusion of evidence under the hearsay rule are discussed in the following paragraphs.

1. "Traditionally, testimony that is given by a witness who relates not what he or she knows personally, but what others have said, and that is therefore dependent on the credibility of someone other than the witness."[1]

2. "Hearsay evidence is objectionable because the person who makes the offered statement is not under oath and is not subject to cross-examination."[2] Although the witness in court who has repeated what someone else has said will be under oath, the person who actually made the statement was not under oath so that hearsay statements generally lack trustworthiness.

3. The demeanor or conduct of the person who actually makes the statement cannot be observed by the judge and jury when the witness comes to court to tell what was stated outside the court. Evaluating demeanor proves important when judging credibility of witnesses and is an important aspect of the right of confrontation.[3]

4. There is a danger that the in-court witness who is reporting what was said by an out-of-court declarant may repeat the statement inaccurately. The proponent of the evidence "essentially asks the jury to assume that the out-of-court declarant was not lying or mistaken when the statement was made."[4]

5. One of the principal reasons for the hearsay rule is to exclude declarations whose veracity or truthfulness cannot be tested by cross-examination. Because the declarant's statement was made out of court, the declarant cannot be cross-examined and the adverse party against whom the evidence is offered is deprived of the opportunity to challenge his memory or sincerity.[5]

In explaining the reasons for the hearsay rule, the Supreme Court of Missouri commented that the rationale for exclusion of evidence is to allow only trustworthy evidence into court. The court noted that the general reason courts exclude hearsay evidence is because the out-of-court declarant and the state-

---

[1] BLACK'S LAW DICTIONARY (2004).

[2] Missouri v. Mozee, 2003 Mo. App. LEXIS 940 (2003), quoting State v. Bowens, 964 S.W. 2d 232, 240, 1998 Mo. App. LEXIS 383 (1998).

[3] See In re Kentron D., 101 Cal. App. 4th 1381, 125 Cal. Rptr. 2d 260, 2002 Cal. App. LEXIS 4629 (2002).

[4] Armstead v. State, 255 Ga. App. 385, 389, 565 S.E.2d 579, 582, 2002 Ga. App. LEXIS 633 (2002).

[5] Iowa v. Dullard, 2003 Iowa Sup. LEXIS 169 (2003).

ment cannot always be subjected to cross-examination, the statement was not offered under oath, and neither the judge nor the jury can evaluate the out-of-court declarant's demeanor and credibility as a witness.[6] Similarly, the Supreme Court of Connecticut offered related reasons for the hearsay rule when it stated:

> The declarant might be lying; he might have misperceived the events which he relates; he might have faulty memory; his words might be misunderstood or taken out of context by the listener. And the ways in which these dangers are minimized for in-court statements—the oath, the witness' awareness of the gravity of the proceedings, the jury's ability to observe the witness' demeanor, and, most importantly, the right of the opponent to cross-examine—are generally absent for things said out of court.[7]

Some forms of hearsay evidence prove more reliable than others and for that reason some hearsay will be admitted based on recognized and standardized hearsay exceptions. The courts, in seeking to allow as much evidence into court as possible while sifting out unreliable evidence, have developed many exceptions to the hearsay rule. For each exception, however, there is a clear justification designed to assure the trustworthiness of the evidence. In situations involving hearsay in which none of the well-known hearsay exceptions permits admission of the evidence, the federal rules allow a party to argue that the interests of justice would be promoted by admission of the hearsay evidence where there are guarantees that the evidence sought to be introduced would be trustworthy and probative on the point for which it is offered.[8]

While this chapter emphasizes many hearsay exceptions, some types of evidence that may be challenged as excludable hearsay have been discussed in other chapters of the book. For example, an out-of-court confession that is repeated by another person in a court is, technically, hearsay. However, this evidence is often admissible under one of the exceptions discussed in Chapter 16. The hearsay exception of "past recollection recorded" and its rationale were discussed in Chapter 9. Official records, ancient documents, and learned treatises are generally admissible as hearsay exceptions and will be considered in Chapter 13.

This chapter discusses and defines the hearsay rule of exclusion and introduces the important exceptions that permit hearsay evidence to be admitted in criminal courts. Among the exceptions treated within this chapter are declarations against interest, the business records exception, dying declarations, spontaneous and excited utterances, and family history.

---

[6]　Missouri v. Link, 25 S.W.3d 136, 145, 2000 Mo. LEXIS 56 (2000).

[7]　Connecticut v. Cruz, 260 Conn. 1, 792 A.2d 823, 2002 Conn. LEXIS 127 (2002).

[8]　*See* FED. R. EVID. 807.

§ 12.2 Definitions and Statement of the Hearsay Rule

Rule 801

Definitions

The following definitions apply under this article:

(a) Statement. A "statement" is (1) an oral or written assertion or (2) nonverbal conduct of a person, if it is intended by the person as an assertion.

(b) Declarant. A "declarant" is a person who makes a statement.

(c) Hearsay. "Hearsay" is a statement, other than one made by the declarant while testifying at the trial or hearing, offered in evidence to prove the truth of the matter asserted.

(d) Statements which are not hearsay. A statement is not hearsay if—

(1) Prior statement by witness.—The declarant testifies at the trial or hearing and is subject to cross-examination concerning the statement, and the statement is (A) inconsistent with the declarant's testimony, and was given under oath subject to the penalty of perjury at a trial, hearing, or other proceeding, or in a deposition, or (B) consistent with the declarant's testimony and is offered to rebut an express or implied charge against the declarant of recent fabrication or improper influence or motive, or (C) one of identification of a person made after perceiving the person; or

(2) Admission by party-opponent.—The statement is offered against a party and is (A) the party's own statement in either an individual or a representative capacity or (B) a statement of which the party has manifested an adoption or belief in its truth, or (C) a statement by a person authorized by the party to make a statement concerning the subject, or (D) a statement by the party's agent or servant concerning a matter within the scope of the agency or employment, made during the existence of the relationship, or (E) a statement by a co-conspirator of a party during the course and in furtherance of the conspiracy. The contents of the statement shall be considered but are not alone sufficient to establish the declarant's authority under subdivision (C), the agency or employment relationship and scope thereof under subdivision (D), or the existence of the conspiracy and the participation therein of the declarant and the party against whom the statement is offered under subdivision (E).[9]

During the course of both civil and criminal litigation, many courts have resolved and refined hearsay problems by explaining the concepts and defining hearsay and evaluating the admissibility of hearsay evidence. Although these explanations are worded differently, the general meaning of hearsay concepts emerges. Some of these definitions are included here as examples:

---

[9] FED. R. EVID. 801.

> Evidence of a statement which is made other than by the witness while testifying at a hearing, offered to prove the truth of the matter stated, is hearsay evidence and inadmissible, subject to certain statutory exceptions.[10]

> Hearsay is an out-of-court statement, other than one made by a declarant while testifying at trial, offered to prove the truth of the matter asserted.[11]

> "Hearsay" is a statement, other than one made by the declarant while testifying at the trial or hearing, offered in evidence to prove the truth of the matter asserted.[12]

> "Hearsay testimony" is an out-of-court statement offered to prove the truth of a matter asserted and is dependent on the credibility of the out-of-court declarant.[13]

The federal courts have interpreted and explained the Federal Rules of Evidence as litigants have raised legal questions and identified problems. For example, one court decided that evidence was "not hearsay" as defined in Rule 801(d)(1)(A) when a witness, although present and testifying at the trial, claimed no recollection of either the underlying events described in his prior grand jury testimony or of the giving of the testimony itself.[14] The trial court did not abuse its discretion in admitting the witness's grand jury testimony under Rule 801(d)(1)(A), which pertains to prior inconsistent statements. When prior inconsistent statements come within the rule, they are not considered hearsay and may be admitted as substantive evidence.

Under Rule 801(d)(1)(A), if an out-of-court statement is inconsistent with the declarant's trial testimony and was given under the penalty of perjury at a deposition, trial, hearing, or similar proceeding, the prior statement may be received as evidence and is not considered hearsay. For purposes of this rule, the word "inconsistent" does not include only statements diametrically opposed or logically incompatible, but also evasive answers, silence, changes in position, or in a reported change in memory.[15]

According to one court, the rationale for the admission of prior consistent statements as provided in Rule 801(d)(1)(B) is that the statements are considered relevant and necessary.[16] Where there is a charge of recent fabrication, a witness's prior deposition testimony is admissible to refute these charges of fab-

---

[10] State v. Clark, 949 P.2d 1099 (Kan. 1997).

[11] Iowa v. Amodeo, 2002 Iowa App. LEXIS 1151 (2002).

[12] IND. R. EVID. 801(c) (Matthew Bender 2006).

[13] People v. Schoultz, 224 Ill. Dec. 885, 682 N.E.2d 446 (1997).

[14] United States v. DiCaro, 772 F.2d 1314 (7th Cir. 1985).

[15] United States v. Williams, 737 F.2d 594 (7th Cir. 1984). See also State v. Pusyka, 592 A.2d 850 (R.I. 1991), in which the court held that a witness's prior statement must be sufficiently inconsistent with the witness's in-court testimony to be admissible. This determination is within the sound discretion of the trial judge.

[16] State v. Gardner, 490 N.W.2d 838 (Iowa 1992).

rication.[17] However, a sexual assault victim's videotaped statements were not admissible under this exception for prior statements by the witness when the victim was never subjected to cross-examination about the prior statements.[18]

The purpose of Rule 801(d)(1)(C) is to permit introduction of identifications made by a witness when the witness's memory was fresh and there was less opportunity for influence to be exerted upon him.[19]

The United States Supreme Court has determined that an out-of-court identification by the victim, naming the defendant as the assailant, was admissible as nonhearsay although the victim could not remember seeing the assailant.[20]

Section 801(d)(1)(B) of the Federal Rules of Evidence provides that a statement is not hearsay if consistent with the declarant's testimony and offered to rebut an express or implied charge against the declarant of recent fabrication or improper influence or motive. In a case that reached the United States Supreme Court, *Tome v. United States*, the interpretation of this provision was debated.[21] In *Tome*, the government initiated charges against the defendant involving the sexual abuse of his four-year-old daughter. The prosecution's theory was that the defendant committed the assaults while the child was with the defendant and disclosed the crime when she was spending vacation time with her mother. The defense argued that the allegations were concocted so that the mother would obtain custody and the child would not be returned to her father. After the alleged motive to fabricate arose, the child made out-of-court statements to witnesses. At the trial, the judge permitted the admission of the statements of some of these witness statements, despite the fact that they were introduced after charges of recent fabrication had been made. The United States Supreme Court reversed the conviction, deciding that Rule 801(d)(1)(B) permitted the introduction of a declarant's consistent out-of-court statements to rebut a charge of recent fabrication or improper influence, or motive only when those statements were made before the fabrication, influence, or motive arose.

Determining that the statements made by the child to other witnesses were made after the defendant's charge of fabrication, the Supreme Court remanded the case for further proceedings. The majority explained that to allow the out-of-court statements made after the in-court charge of fabrication would shift the emphasis of the trial to the out-of-court statements rather than the in-court statements.

Rule 801(d)(2)(E) of the Federal Rules, which has been made part of the rules of evidence in many states, provides that a statement is not hearsay if made by a conspirator during the course of and in furtherance of the conspiracy. Changes made to Federal Rule 801(d)(2)(E) in 1997 noted that the contents

17 State v. Deases, 479 N.W.2d 597 (Iowa 1991).
18 State v. Palabay, 844 P.2d 1 (Wash. 1992).
19 United States v. Marchand, 564 F.2d 983 (2d Cir. 1977).
20 United States v. Owens, 484 U.S. 554, 108 S. Ct. 838, 98 L. Ed. 2d 951 (1988).
21 Tome v. United States, 513 U.S. 150, 115 S. Ct. 696, 130 L. Ed. 2d 574 (1995).

of a statement made by a conspirator are insufficient to establish that the conspirator can speak for the other conspirators. While an out-of-court statement made by a conspirator fits the traditional definition of hearsay, this rule of evidence simply declares that it shall not be deemed to be hearsay. In explaining the rule's purpose, a federal court noted that statements made by conspirators during the course of and in furtherance of a conspiracy do not fit within the definition of hearsay; rather, the court views these statements as party admissions.[22] A conspirator's statement is made in furtherance of the conspiracy (so as to be admissible as) when the statement is part of the information flow between the conspirators, intended to help each perform his or her role.[23] However, a mere conversation between the conspirators or merely narrative declarations among them would not constitute conversations made "in furtherance of a conspiracy" and would not be admissible under this provision.[24]

In case in which a doctor wanted to hire a hit man to kill his wife, the trial court refused to allow the doctor's son to testify, under Rule 801(d)(1)(B), that the doctor really only wanted the hit man to follow his wife and conduct some surveillance. The doctor told the son the surveillance story only after being arrested in the plot, and therefore he had a motive to fabricate despite his assertion to the contrary. Because the motive to fabricate arose before the statement to his son, the son could be prohibited from testifying about his father's statement because it would not meet Rule 801's requirements and would be considered inadmissible hearsay.[25]

Rule 802

Hearsay Rule

Hearsay is not admissible except as provided by these rules or by other rules prescribed by the Supreme Court pursuant to statutory authority or by Act of Congress.[26]

As defined in Rule 801 of the Federal Rules of Evidence, hearsay is "a statement other than one made by the declarant while testifying at the trial or hearing offered in evidence to prove the truth of the matter asserted."[27] Another definition is that hearsay evidence is evidence that derives its value not from the credit to be given to the witness upon the stand, but at least in part from the veracity and competency of another person who is not testifying. One court stated that "Hearsay is testimony of an out-of-court statement offered to

---

[22]   United States v. Powell, 973 F.2d 885 (10th Cir. 1992), *cert. denied*, 507 U.S. 1161, 113 S. Ct. 1598, 123 L. Ed. 2d 161 (1992).
[23]   United State v. Godinez, 110 F.3d 448 (7th Cir. 1997).
[24]   United State v. Nazemian, 748 F.2d 552 (9th Cir. 1991).
[25]   United States v. Drury, 2003 U.S. App. LEXIS 18152 (11th Cir. 2003).
[26]   FED. R. EVID. 802.
[27]   *Id.*

establish the truth of the matter asserted therein and whose value thus depends upon the credibility of the out-of-court declarant."[28] For example, if a police officer were to testify concerning the meaning of numbers on a fast food receipt when the officer gathered his understanding of the significance of the numbers by speaking with an employee of the fast food establishment, the officer's testimony would constitute hearsay evidence because it depends on the veracity and credibility of the fast food employee who was not in court or under oath.

While hearsay evidence may be excluded, out-of-court statements that are not offered for their substantive truth may be admissible because they do not meet the definition of hearsay. Where police arrested a suspected drug dealer after observing a sale, they found two cell phones during the post-arrest search of his person. When phones rang on two occasions, the officer answered the calls and had conversations with unknown persons who wanted to buy drugs. The trial court permitted the substance of the conversations to be admitted against the defendant because the statements were not offered to prove their substantive truth, only that other people thought they could buy drugs by phoning the defendant's cell phones. These phone conversations were circumstantial evidence that the defendant had the intent to distribute drugs.[29]

The term "statement," as used in the hearsay definition, consists of: (1) an oral or written assertion or (2) nonverbal conduct of a person, if it is intended by him or her as an assertion or is a substitute for speech. Therefore, a statement may be an actual verbal statement, a written statement, or nonverbal conduct, such as pointing, to identify a suspect in a lineup. The act of pointing to indicate a choice in a lineup context operates as a substitute for speech and when a police officer subsequently testifies in court about the out-of-court witness's indication, the officer has brought the out-of-court, nonverbal assertion into court as a hearsay statement. A "declarant," as used in the hearsay definition, is a person who makes a statement.

Although the rule that hearsay evidence is inadmissible is generally true, significant hearsay evidence is admitted based on exceptions to the general rule of exclusion. The exceptions to the hearsay rule are so numerous that the argument could be made that most hearsay evidence may be admissible while some hearsay evidence may be excluded. This chapter considers some of the well-recognized exceptions and the reasoning for those exceptions in the sections that follow.

---

[28]   Illinois v. Thompson, 327 Ill. App. 3d 1061, 765 N.E.2d 1203, 2002 Ill. App. LEXIS 162 (2002).
[29]   Commonwealth v. Vasquez, 20 Mass. L. Rep. 319; 2005 Mass. Super. LEXIS 656 (Mass. 2005).

§ 12.3   History and Development of the Hearsay Rule

In an article that appeared in the Minnesota Law Review, the authors included a thumbnail sketch of the history of the use of the hearsay rule.[30] This article included the following history:

> The hearsay rule was not the creation of some clever legal philosopher or rules-drafting committee. Rather, it was a byproduct of jury-based common law adjudication. It was molded and remolded over the course of more than four centuries by lawyers pursuing the business of representing clients and by judges seeking to ensure proper verdicts. As a consequence of its incremental development, the rule, like so much in Anglo-American jurisprudence, does not have a single goal or express a single viewpoint. It reflects a variety of objectives sought at different times by participants in the courtroom contests.

> Medieval English jury adjudication was, in essence, based upon hearsay. Juries in the thirteenth and fourteenth centuries decided cases on the basis of rumor, gossip, and community opinion to which they were exposed before the trial commenced. While reservations about hearsay were articulated as early as 1202, it was not until the latter half of the 1500s that serious concerns were voiced about its use in litigation.

The hearsay rule as we know it had its origin in England in the sixteenth century. Prior to that time, juries were permitted to obtain evidence by consulting persons who were not called as witnesses. Jurors did not decide the case on the basis of testimony given in open court, but were in fact chosen because they had some knowledge of the case.

In 1813, Chief Justice Marshall, in explaining the justification for the hearsay rule, stated, "Our lives, our liberty, and our property, are all concerned in the support of these rules, which have been matured by the wisdom of ages, and are now revered from their antiquity and the good sense in which they are founded. One of these rules is that hearsay evidence is by its own nature inadmissible." Justice Marshall went on to say that "[i]ts intrinsic weakness, its incompetency to satisfy the mind of the existence of the fact, and the frauds which might be practiced under its cover, combine to support the rule that hearsay evidence is totally inadmissible."[31]

As jurors began to be chosen only if they had no knowledge of the case that would influence their decision, the hearsay rule began to develop. By 1700, the rule prohibiting the admission of hearsay statements was formulated in criminal cases. Over the centuries, exceptions to the hearsay rule have developed because of the strict exclusionary nature of the rule.

---

[30] Richard F. Rakos and Stephen Landsman, *The Hearsay Rule as the Focus of Empirical Investigation*, 76 MINN. L. REV. 655 (1992).

[31] Mima Queen and Child v. Heburn, 7 U.S. (3 Cranch) 290 (1813). *See also* Donnelly v. United States, 288 U.S. 243, 33 S. Ct. 449, 57 L. Ed. 820 (1913) for a discussion of the history of the rules.

§ 12.4 Exceptions to the Hearsay Rule—General

Although Chief Justice John Marshall argued that hearsay evidence should not be admitted in federal courts because of its intrinsic weakness and incompetency, and despite the fact that he concluded that "[t]his court is not inclined to extend the exceptions further than they have already been carried,"[32] state and federal courts have made exceptions and the exceptions have been extended over the years in all American courts.

In Rules 803 and 804 of the Federal Rules of Evidence there are at least 28 specific exceptions, and Rule 807 contains one broad category of residual exceptions for situations not specifically covered by Rule 803 or Rule 804. Rule 807 provides for recognition of other exceptions when there are "equivalent circumstantial guarantees of trustworthiness."[33]

The reasons for the hearsay rule in the first instance are based on the facts that: (1) the declarant was not under oath to speak the truth; (2) the demeanor of the person who actually made the statement cannot be observed by the judge and jury; (3) there is danger that the statement may be repeated inaccurately; and (4) generally the declarant cannot be cross-examined despite the defendant's rights under the Sixth Amendment. The argument for admitting evidence under exceptions to the rule holds that if the purpose and rationale for excluding evidence under the hearsay rule do not exist in a specific case and if the interests of justice will be best served by admitting the statement into evidence, then the evidence should be admitted as an exception to the hearsay rule.

As a general rule, most hearsay exceptions have been categorized into fairly recognizable and repeating fact patterns addressed by the rules of evidence. Attorneys are able to intelligently argue the advantages and disadvantages of following a well-known exception by arguing the merits of the introduction of hearsay evidence. Thus, when hearsay statements fall within firmly rooted hearsay exceptions, or occur under circumstances with particularized guarantees of trustworthiness,[34] such statements are adequately reliable to be admissible in criminal cases.[35]

In the following sections, the text discusses some of the hearsay exceptions that are most frequently encountered by criminal justice personnel and explains the rationales for the exceptions.

---

[32] Mima Queen and Child v. Hepburn, *supra* note 31.
[33] FED. R. EVID. 807. The exceptions noted in Rules 803 and 804 are not included in this section. Rule 807 covers situations that are not specifically mentioned in Rules 803 and 804. These rules are included in the Appendix, and they should be reviewed before continuing.
[34] *See* FED. R. EVID. 807.
[35] United States v. Barrett, 8 F.3d 1296 (8th Cir. 1993); United States v. Matthews, 20 F.3d 358 (2d Cir. 1994).

§ 12.5   —Spontaneous and Excited Utterances

Rule 803

Hearsay Exceptions; Availability of Declarant Immaterial

* * *

The following are not excluded by the hearsay rule, even though the declarant is available as a witness:

* * *

(2) Excited utterance. A statement relating to a startling event or condition made while the declarant was under the stress of excitement caused by the event or condition.[36]

* * *

Where hearsay evidence will be admitted as substantive evidence, as a general rule facts and circumstances that demonstrate the reliability and trustworthiness of the evidence must be present. Speech prompted in a declarant by an exciting event may be admissible as a hearsay exception if it qualifies as a spontaneous exclamation. The circumstances under which spontaneous declarations or excited utterances occur offer reasons to believe that a statement made under severe stress will be truthful. "Rule 803(2) allows the admission of excited utterances based on the theory that a person speaking about a startling event, while still under the stress of experiencing or observing that event, normally does not have either the capacity or the incentive to prevaricate."[37] The theory of this exception is that circumstances produce a condition of excitement that temporarily halts the capacity for reflection and produces utterances that are free of conscious and considered fabrication. Another way to indicate the spontaneity of such speech is to think of a stimulus that produces an instant human response without an opportunity for significant reflection. As one court properly described this hearsay exception, "An excited utterance is the event speaking and not the speaker."[38] "The crucial question, regardless of the time lapse, is whether, at the time the statement is made, the nervous excitement continues to dominate while the reflective processes remain in abeyance."[39] In order for a spontaneous or excited utterance to be admissible, a Wisconsin court noted that there must be: (a) proof of a startling event or experience, (b) the statement made by the declarant must relate to the startling event or situation, and (c) the statement must be made while the declarant is still under the stress or the excitement caused by the event or condition.[40] The court approved the admission of a victim's spontaneous statement

---

[36]   FED. R. EVID. 803(2).
[37]   United States v. Brito, 427 F.3d 53, 61, 2005 U.S. App. LEXIS 22525 (1st Cir. 2006).
[38]   Pennsylvania v. Zukauskas, 501 Pa. 500, 503, 462 A.2d 236, 237, 1983 Pa. LEXIS 620 (1983).
[39]   Pennsylvania v. Keys, 2003 Pa. Super. 5, 814 A.2d 1256, 1258, 2003 Pa. Super. LEXIS 4 (2003).
[40]   State v. Mayo, 2006 Wis. App. 78, 713 N.W.2d 191, 2006 Wis. App. LEXIS 276 (Wis. 2006).

offered to police after being hit in the head by a tire iron during a robbery perpetrated by the defendant. The victim knew the defendant, experienced the
injury at the hands of the defendant, and gave his account concerning his
injuries to the police within 10 minutes of being injured.[41] Following a similar
rationale, a Washington court noted that for excited utterances to be admissible under the state's adaptation of the Federal Rules of Evidence, "A statement
relating to 'a startling event or condition' made while the declarant was under
the stress of excitement caused by the event or condition' is admissible as an
excited utterance. ER 803(a)(2). An excited utterance has three closely related
elements: First, a startling event or condition must have occurred. Second, the
statement must have been made while the declarant was under the stress or
excitement caused by the startling event or condition. Third, the statement
must relate to the startling event or condition."[42] The statement in this case
qualified as an excited utterance because the declarant had just been assaulted,
had seen her vehicle destroyed, and seen a man's finger nearly bitten away
from the hand. The declarant was under extreme stress and little time passed
between the event and her statement to police officers.[43]

In another case, when a man violated a no-contact domestic protection
order and returned to assault his former girlfriend, a neighbor's 911 call summoned police. The victim had been beaten and kicked. The police arrived
within minutes. In response to police queries, the victim told the story of how
she had been injured while she remained in severe pain and under stress and
in fear of the ex-boyfriend. At the hospital, the victim offered her statement,
which took approximately twenty minutes. She was crying, fearful, in pain,
and her voice had a tremor. The victim remained in the same emotional state
throughout her interview. According to the trial court, it was proper to admit
the victim's spontaneous statement offered at the crime scene and the subsequent statement taken at the hospital, even though a significant amount of time
had elapsed since the violent assault.[44]

Similar to the prior case, when police arrived in response to two 911 calls
involving a domestic disturbance with a gun, the defendant's wife ran out of
the home in a hurry shouting to police that "he's got a gun" and "he's going to
kill me." The wife told the officers that her husband, at one point, had a gun
to her head. During this time she appeared hysterical and in a state of panic.
When the officers could not find the gun in the marital bedroom, they
requested the wife's assistance in securing the firearm, but she was reluctant
to help, appearing frantic and frightened to the officers. She told them that she
did not want to go back in the house. Shortly after, the officers calmed her and
took a detailed statement. At the defendant's federal trial for being a felon in
possession of a firearm, the court admitted the spontaneous statements given
by the wife upon the arrival of the police officers, over the defendant's objec-

---

[41] *Id.*

[42] Washington v. Grzogorek, 2002 Wash. App. LEXIS 598 (2002).

[43] *Id.*

[44] Washington v. Ross, 2002 Wash. App. LEXIS 2422 (2002), *appeal denied*, 149 Wash. 2d 1013, 69 P.3d
876, 2003 Wash. LEXIS 432 (2003).

tion. The Court of Appeals sustained the admission of the wife's excited utterance on the theory that the domestic disturbance constituted an exciting event, especially because the fight generated two 911 calls in rapid succession, the wife's statement was about the events in the home concerning the gun and the husband's threats, and she made them immediately after the events before she had a chance to calm herself or reflect on the events.[45]

In an Indiana case, police arrived at the scene of a reported criminal battery. The victim was crying and shaking, and her appearance and overall demeanor indicated that she was very upset. She was talking rapidly and showed signs of fresh physical injuries, including a bleeding cut above her eye. Her left eye was swollen and she was holding an ice pack to her eye. The attack had left marks on her neck that appeared to have been caused by someone grabbing her around the neck. Over the defendant's objection that the woman's story as told to an officer was not a spontaneous utterance, the trial court permitted the police officer to tell the court what the victim had told him at the scene concerning her injuries. The trial court noted that for a hearsay statement to be admitted as an excited utterance under Indiana's version of Rule 803(2), three elements must be shown: (1) a startling event occurs; (2) a statement is made by a declarant while under the stress of excitement caused by the event; and (3) the statement relates to the event. An Indiana appellate court held that the woman's statement to police met all the requirements and was properly admitted.[46]

The exciting event must affect the declarant with sufficient stress to remove or inhibit reflective ability. In sustaining a conviction for third-degree assault, the reviewing court approved the admission of a series of excited utterances made by the victim to a friend. The husband had been threatening his wife at their joint business when the wife phoned a friend for assistance in leaving the workplace, noting in a fearful voice that she was afraid her husband would hit her. A second call to the same friend requested that the friend rescue the wife immediately because her husband had beaten her and, when the rescuer arrived, the wife was crying and her face and arms were red. The wife did not testify at the trial, but the court permitted the wife's friend to relate virtually everything that the frightened and fearful wife told the rescuing friend about the ordeal at the time of the rescue. The Supreme Court of Colorado approved the admission of the rescuing friend's testimony because there was a startling event with the beating that created stress, the victim's spontaneous statement concerned the events and described them, and the wife related the story to her friend while still under the stress of the beating from her husband.[47]

As a general rule, to be admissible a spontaneous statement need not be completely spontaneous and may be made in response to a question by a police officer or other person.[48] The fact that the statement goes beyond a mere

---

[45]   United States v. Hadley, 431 F.3d 484, 496, 2005 U.S. App. LEXIS 26526 (6th Cir. 2005).

[46]   Cox v. Indiana, 774 N.E.2d 1025, 2002 Ind. App. LEXIS 1533 (2002).

[47]   Compan v. People, 121 P.3d 876, 882, 2005 Colo. LEXIS 873 (2005).

[48]   Washington v. Fikre, 2003 Wash. App. LEXIS 191 (2003); *see also* Massachusetts v. Ivy, 55 Mass. App. 851, 855, 774 N.E.2d 1100, 1104, 2002 Mass. App. LEXIS 1175 (2002).

description of the event may be considered in deciding whether the statement was sufficiently related to the event to be spontaneous, as required by the excited utterance exception to the hearsay rule, or whether the statement was a product of conscious reflection.[49]

The fact that the excited witness was a law enforcement agent does not exclude the admissibility of statements under the excited utterance exception to the hearsay rule.[50] A prostitute who had been kidnapped and held for six hours in the back of a van where she was forced to commit sexual acts with the strangers who had taken her made an excited utterance to several District of Columbia police officers. The woman gained her freedom following a shootout with the police officers after they overcame the resistance of the armed men. She had undergone a stressful kidnapping where the men threatened her with death if she did not have sex with them, forced her to drive the van while they committed at least two robberies, and was present in the van during the shootout. As the reviewing court noted, "Being inside a van that becomes the target of police gunfire certainly qualifies as a serious occurrence."[51] Her first words to an officer involved her rape allegations, even though those acts occurred earlier than the shootout. The trial court admitted her first statement made to police under the excited utterances exception to the hearsay rule on the theory that it was her first opportunity to comment about her ordeal, that there were sufficient events to cause stress, that she had not had an opportunity to fabricate, and that her remarks indicated the spontaneity of her speech. Her comment to another officer a few minutes later that she had been kidnapped and repeatedly raped were not inadmissible due to a lapse of time. The court held that the lapse of time is a factor to consider in determining spontaneity, but in this case, the lapse was rather short for both utterances to the police. Under the circumstances, the reviewing court affirmed the admission of the victim's excited utterances.

According to accepted practice, there is no definite time interval following an exciting event that will make the utterance either fall under the exception to the hearsay rule. The general rule is that an utterance following an exciting event must be made soon enough thereafter so that it can reasonably be considered a product of the stress of the excitement, rather than of reflection or deliberation. In a Massachusetts case, the reviewing court affirmed a conviction of digital rape when the victim awoke to find the defendant's finger inside her private area and his mouth on her breast. She became so upset that her frantic, screaming, and crying awakened everyone in the house and the victim made her statements describing the events while under the stress of the rape. In approving the admissibility of the victim's stressful utterances, the court noted that there was an exciting or startling event (awakening to digital rape) that caused a high degree of agitation in the declarant and that the statements were made while the victim was under the stress or influence of the

---

[49] United States v. More, 791 F.2d 566 (7th Cir. 1986).
[50] Bryant v. United States, 859 A.2d 1093, 1106, 2004 D.C. App. LEXIS 526 (2004).
[51] *Id.*

exciting event (immediately) and before she had time to fabricate. The eye-witnesses universally described the victim as being upset to the point of being frantic. The trial court properly allowed witnesses to testify concerning the substance of what the victim stated following the rape.[52] A different court, in a case with some distinguishing facts, held that when a woman alleged that her husband had beaten her, dragged by the hair, and had held her captive overnight, such information did not fall under the excited utterance exception. The victim had walked eight or ten blocks to find a police officer after she escaped the next morning and told the officer her story. The appellate court reversed the trial court's admission of the officer's rendition of the beating because the court did not concur that the woman's story to the officer met the requirements for a spontaneous utterance. According to the appellate court, the utterances were offered as a narrative of overnight events and were not given as a reaction to a single startling episode and failed as an excited utterance. The reviewing court held that the admission of the statement denied the defendant the right to cross-examine the victim, who did not testify against the defendant.[53]

In making an evaluation concerning whether the elapsed time between the startling event and the declaration to another is too long that the statement is not an excited utterance, the trial court will focus on the declarant's state of mind at the time the alleged excited statement was made. To be deemed admissible, the stress and influence of the event must be present at the time that a declarant makes a statement to a third party. For example, in a case in which the defendant had been charged with lewd conduct with a minor under 16 years of age, the trial court permitted a sister of the victim to tell the court what the victim told her.[54] In a later conversation, the child told her mother substantially the same story. According to the evidence, the conduct occurred while the defendant was babysitting the victim when he placed his finger in her private area. The child stayed at the defendant's home that night, went to school the next day, and returned to stay at the defendant's house the next night. On the second day, the child's father picked her up and drove her to her mother's home. The child disclosed no details of the incident to anyone until the evening when her sister questioned her concerning whether something was wrong. At that time, the child told her sister about the illegal conduct, and subsequently she told her mother about the encounter with the defendant. Over an objection by the defendant's attorney, the judge permitted the sister and the mother of the victim to tell the jury what the victim told them on the theory that the excited utterance exception to the hearsay rule permitted admission of their testimony. In finding error in the admission of the child's story through the sister and mother, the reviewing court noted that an excited utterance requires that the declarant be under the stress of the event when making the statement. The court stated that:

---

[52]   Massachusetts v. Davis, 54 Mass. App. Ct. 756, 762, 767 N.E.2d 1110, 1116, 2002 Mass. App. LEXIS 674 (2002).

[53]   *See* Pennsylvania v. Keys, 2003 Pa. Super. 5, 814 A.2d 1256, 2003 Pa. Super. LEXIS 4 (2003).

[54]   State v. Field, 2006 Idaho App. LEXIS 44 (2006).

"[i]n considering whether a statement constitutes an excited utterance, the totality of the circumstances must be considered, including the nature of the startling condition or event, the amount of time that elapsed between the startling event and the statement, the age and condition of the declarant, the presence or absence of self-interest, and whether the statement was volunteered or made in response to a question."[55]

The reviewing court agreed with the prosecution that the event would be classified as startling or shocking, but that stress would, for the purposes of the excited utterance exception, last for hours but and not days, as was contended in this case. In finding that the declarant was not offering an excited utterance, the court stated that "at some point, the time span between a startling event and a subsequent statement simply becomes too great for the statement to be considered an excited utterance even when the declarant is a child."[56] If the situation indicates a lapse of time sufficient to manufacture or formulate a statement and if a statement lacks spontaneity, a trial court should not admit the alleged spontaneous statement.[57]

§ 12.6 —Business and Public Records

Rule 803

Hearsay Exceptions; Availability of Declarant Immaterial

* * *

The following are not excluded by the hearsay rule, even though the declarant is available as a witness:

* * *

(6) Records of regularly conducted activity. A memorandum, report, record, or data compilation, in any form, of acts, events, conditions, opinions, or diagnoses, made at or near the time by, or from information transmitted by, a person with knowledge, if kept in the course of a regularly conducted business activity, and if it was the regular practice of that business activity to make the memorandum, report, record, or data compilation, all as shown by the testimony of the custodian or other qualified witness, or by certification that complies with Rule 902(11), Rule 902(12), or a statute permitting certification, unless the source of information or the method or circumstances of preparation indicate lack of trustworthiness. The term "business" as used in this paragraph includes business, institution, association, profession, occupation, and calling of every kind, whether or not conducted for profit.

---

[55]   *Id.*
[56]   *Id.*
[57]   North Carolina v. Riley, 54 N.C. App. 692, 695, 572 S.E.2d 857, 859, 2002 N.C. App. LEXIS 1531 (2002).

(7) Absence of entry in records kept in accordance with the provisions of paragraph (6). Evidence that a matter is not included in the memoranda, reports, records, or data compilations, in any form, kept in accordance with the provisions of paragraph (6), to prove the nonoccurrence or nonexistence of the matter, if the matter was of a kind of which a memorandum, report, record, or data compilation was regularly made and preserved, unless the sources of information or other circumstances indicate lack of trustworthiness.

(8) Public records and reports. Records, reports, statements, or data compilations, in any form, of public offices or agencies, setting forth (A) the activities of the office or agency, or (B) matters observed pursuant to duty imposed by law as to which matters there was a duty to report, excluding, however, in criminal cases matters observed by police officers and other law enforcement personnel, or (C) in civil actions and proceedings and against the Government in criminal cases, factual findings resulting from an investigation made pursuant to authority granted by law, unless the sources of information or other circumstances indicate lack of trustworthiness.[58]

* * *

Businesses, organizations, and government agencies collect and compile records generated during their ordinary and usual operations. Because businesses create these records with a view toward accuracy and with no motive to falsify, there is a presumption that they contain true and reliable information. Recognizing the accuracy principle, many states have adopted the Uniform Business Records Act, which facilitates the admission into evidence of records of regularly conducted operations of government and private entities. Demonstrative of the Uniform Business Records Act is the version adopted by the state of Washington, which provides that the "record of an act, condition or event, shall in so far as relevant, be competent evidence if the custodian or other qualified witness testifies to its identity and the mode of its preparation, and if it was made in the regular course of business, at or near the time of the act, condition or event, and if, in the opinion of the court, the sources of information, method and time of preparation were such as to justify its admission."[59]

The purpose of the statute is to provide, as an exception to the hearsay rule, an acceptable substitute for the specific authentication of records kept in the ordinary course of business. The underlying rationale permitting this exception is that business records have the "earmark of reliability" or "probability of trustworthiness," because they reflect events occurring in the day-to-day operations of the enterprise, and business entities rely on their ordinary records in the conduct of business.

---

[58] FED. R. EVID. 803. *See also* FED. R. EVID. 803(9) and (10) in Appendix I.
[59] WASH. REV. CODE § 5.45.020, Uniform Business Records As Evidence Act. (Matthew Bender 2006).
[60] FED. R. EVID. 803.

Under the Federal Rules of Evidence, the uniform law regarding records has been greatly expanded. According to these rules, various business and public records may be the source of evidence as exceptions to the hearsay rule. Some of these are records of regularly conducted activity, public records and reports, records of vital statistics, etc. Not only is information from the records admissible, but evidence also may be introduced to prove the absence of public records or entries or the absence of an entry in records of regularly conducted activities.[60]

All such records are admissible under this rule, but they are subject to exclusion if the sources of the information or other circumstances indicate a lack of trustworthiness. In interpreting the Arizona Rules of Evidence, one court approved the admission as business records of quality assurance records of calibrations for machines that detect alcohol intoxication. Where technicians had calibrated the Intoxilyzer 5000 and kept public records of the results for each machine, the records could be admitted as an exception to the hearsay rule under Rule 803(6). There is every reason to trust the results of the tests because no technician knows whether a given machine will be used and the technician has no motive to falsify or otherwise misstate the truth concerning which machines pass or failed the calibration tests.[61] But where the public record has been prepared in anticipation of litigation by law enforcement officers, it is considered testimonial hearsay even if admitted as a business record. In a Florida DUI case,[62] the defendant objected to a technician testifying to what tests and results a colleague reported from a blood sample. The colleague had retired and the employee technician had not performed the lab work but reported the results obtained by the retired colleague. Another Florida court had determined that "a lab report prepared pursuant to police investigation and admitted to establish an element of a crime is testimonial hearsay even if it is admitted as a business record."[63] The reviewing court concluded that the hearsay evidence should not have been admitted because there was no proof that the retired employee who conducted the tests was unavailable.

Although in a slightly different context, a secondary school might not seem like a business, but an Indiana court held that computer-stored school attendance records were admissible as a record of a regularly conducted activity. The Indiana court noted that "data compilation, in any form" is a sufficiently broad category to include school records stored on a computer system.[64] An Arkansas court held that a state court did not commit error in a theft case by permitting the prosecution to introduce a state sales receipt that purported to establish the value of a stolen vehicle the defendant was alleged to have received. The vehicle was owned by the state and was sold at auction after recovery for fair market value. The office that oversaw Arkansas vehicles regularly kept appropriate records of sales of excess vehicles and had custody

[61] *See* Bohsancurt v. Eisenberg, 129 P.3d 471, 2006 Ariz. App. LEXIS 26 (2006).
[62] Sabota v. State, 2006 Fla. App. LEXIS 12505 (2006).
[63] Johnson v. State, 929 So. 2d 4, 7, 2005 Fla. App. LEXIS 20 (2005).
[64] J.L. v. Indiana, 789 N.E.2d 961, 963, 964, 2003 Ind. App. LEXIS 921 (2003).

of the bill of sale that was properly introduced as a business record kept by a government agency in its regular course of business.[65]

Business records that have been created with litigation in mind do not generally qualify for admission under the business records exception to the hearsay rule. In a prosecution for possession with the intent to manufacture or deliver a controlled substance, police searched the defendant's person, revealing a substance believed to be rock cocaine. A positive field test resulted in the suspected rock cocaine being sent to a state police lab for testing. At the trial, the state police employee who conducted the test was not available, so the drug lab's manager offered the positive results of the drug test to the court, despite the defendant's hearsay objection. The trial judge admitted that the lab results constituted hearsay, but held that the results of the drug test were admissible because the results were business records of regularly conducted activity under Rule 803(6). The reviewing court noted that the hearsay exception for business records had not generally been applied to reports and records prepared in anticipation of litigation because the motivation in making the reports was to prosecute individuals for drug possession. With the evidence of drug possession removed from the commonwealth's proof, there was insufficient evidence to sustain the conviction and the reviewing court reversed the conviction for possession. When evidence appears to meet the requirements of the business record exception, but the result or report has been prepared in anticipation of litigation, the report will often be excluded.[66]

Some types of business records that are routinely created as a usual business practice fail to qualify for admission under the business records exception, especially when they may include hearsay on hearsay. In a prosecution for spousal battery, the trial court permitted the admission of client intake data from a crisis intervention center log. The information included the specific reason the person needed shelter and detailed past crimes and stresses in the client's relationships. Employees routinely took information from women needing shelter from domestic problems and used the information in counseling the women during their stay. The custodian of the records explained the routine of collecting the information and how that data was stored. The appellate court agreed that the admission of the intake forms to prove the truth of the contents was erroneous because the form's contents were derived from hearsay statements that contained multiple layers of hearsay. The client's offering of facts for the form was the first layer of hearsay; the employee's recording of the facts constituted another layer; and the rendering of the form at the trial was a third layer. The trial court should have rejected the records because they failed to meet the business records hearsay exception. [67]

---

[65] Ervin v. State, 2006 Ark. App. LEXIS 95 (2006).

[66] Commonwealth v. Carter, 2004 PA Super 420, 861 A.2d 957, 961, 2004 Pa. Super. LEXIS 3909 (2004).

[67] People v. Ayers, 125 Cal. App. 4th 988, 994, 23 Cal. Rptr. 3d 242, 245, 2005 Cal. App. LEXIS 50 (2005).

Although police reports containing statements concerning the cause of or responsibility for an accident are in a sense business or public records, they are often excluded because the person making the report is relying on what someone else told him or her and the record does not reflect what the officer personally observed from firsthand perception. For example, in a case in which a man was convicted of three counts of violating the animal control ordinance, the trial court refused to allow him to introduce police reports of incidents that he had reported to show that he and his neighbors had problems getting along.[68] Proof of the prior difficulties could show the motivation for the present complaints against him. The appellate court noted that "police reports showing prior incidents are generally, by themselves, inadmissible hearsay with no probative value" and that the narrative parts of a police report do not contain facts that should be admissible under the business records exception to the hearsay rule.[69] Police reports that contain admissible evidence personally observed by the officer, as well as inadmissible evidence obtained from other eyewitnesses and included within the report, can be received in evidence if the inadmissible portions are redacted from the report.[70] Some public record police reports may be admissible where they contain only firsthand information or have been prepared in the usual course of business. For example, when police had prepared typical repair and cost reports concerning damage done to a holding cell by a prisoner, the reports constituted a business record and could be admitted against a defendant because the report had been prepared in the ordinary course of the business of running a jail.[71]

In determining whether a proffered government document is either an investigative report or a compilation of factual findings that do not come within the public record exception of the hearsay rule, the court considers: (1) whether the document contains findings that address materially contested issues in the case; (2) whether the record or report contains factual findings; and (3) whether the report was prepared for advocacy purposes or in anticipation of litigation.[72]

Applying this test, an Indiana court agreed that a diagram of the scene of a single-vehicle accident in which the passenger died, which was prepared by the accident investigator for the state police, did not contain any interpretative factual findings, and thus was admissible under the public records exception to the hearsay rule in the prosecution of a motorist for operating the vehicle while intoxicated. The court explained that the diagram was merely a recording of physical conditions that were observed by the investigator, and the fact that the statute, which makes accident reports filed by persons involved in automobile accidents confidential, did not bar the admission of a Standard Crash Report filed by the officer who investigated the accident, because the statute contains an exception for such reports.

---

[68]   Pless v. State, 2006 Ga. App. LEXIS 523 (2006).
[69]   *Id.*
[70]   Pottorf v. Bray, 2003 Ohio 4255 (2003).
[71]   Williams v. State, 2003 Alaska App. LEXIS 136 (2003).
[72]   Shepherd v. State, 690 N.E.2d 318 (Ind. 1997).

A police report may be admitted as an exception to the hearsay rule where the report is required to be recorded as part of a police department's regularly conducted activities. In Louisiana, a parish sheriff has a duty to seek out and obtain fingerprint evidence and record them as part of criminal investigations. In a case involving attempted armed robbery,[73] a defendant contended that the officer who lifted a latent fingerprint from the crime scene had to personally testify to that fact and that any other expert who so testified would be offering hearsay evidence. In rejecting the defendant's contention that the testifying officer would be offering hearsay, the reviewing court noted that the Supreme Court of Louisiana previously ruled that fingerprints on file with a police agency fall under the public documents exception to the hearsay rule and, in this case, the fingerprint evidence was properly introduced to show that the crime scene fingerprint matched the print of the defendant.

In some jurisdictions, police reports and other public records may be admissible as business or public records in civil cases, but inadmissible in criminal cases.[74] In a Texas case, a criminal defendant wanted the court to admit police records of other similar accidents that occurred on the same road following his vehicle accident. The defendant had been drinking alcohol and subsequently drove into a tree. The accident resulted in criminal charges. The defendant wanted to introduce evidence of other accidents on the wet highway that occurred the same night in order to mitigate his criminal responsibility. The trial court refused to admit any police reports of the other accidents because Texas law excluded police reports from admission in all criminal cases on the ground that such evidence constituted hearsay.[75] An autopsy report may meet the requirements of a business record exception to the hearsay rule but may be excluded on constitutional grounds. In an Alabama homicide case,[76] the defendant objected to the introduction of an autopsy report when it was introduced by a doctor who had not performed the autopsy, but had read the public records generated by the actual autopsy doctor. Under Alabama law, an autopsy report is generally admissible as a business records exception to the hearsay rule.[77] However, the defendant made a Sixth Amendment right of confrontation argument that the actual declarant doctor giving the information was not present in court for cross-examination. In holding that the trial court committed error in admitting the autopsy report, the appellate court noted that the Sixth Amendment confrontation clause prevents a prosecutor from proving an essential element of the crime by hearsay evidence alone. According to the reviewing court, if the prosecution had only to introduce an autopsy report and shift the burden to the defendant to refute the hearsay facts contained within, the report would not be consistent with due

---

[73]   State v. Arita, 900 So.2d 37, 44, 2005 La. App. LEXIS 501 (2005).

[74]   *See* TEX. EVID. R. 803(B) (Matthew Bender 2006).

[75]   McCumber v. Texas, 202 Tex. App. LEXIS 7351 (2002). Police reports may be admissible at suppression hearings because the formal rules of evidence do not apply. *See* Caballero v. State, 2005 Tex. App. LEXIS 1865 (2005).

[76]   Smith v. State, 898 So. 2d 907, 2004 Ala. Crim. App. LEXIS 93 (2004).

[77]   *Id.* at 916.

process of law. So while an autopsy report might be admissible as a business record exception in a civil case, the effect of the Sixth Amendment prevents the admission of an autopsy report in criminal cases when it is not offered by the doctor who performed the procedure.

It is well-known that business and public records are commonly entered and stored on computer systems and that police departments are moving toward generating fewer paper records. Computer records stored on servers or personal computers are unavailable and useless except by accessing the data on a display or printing the data on paper. In admitting computer-generated printouts, which reflect the records stored on the computer, courts are actually following the best evidence rule. This is not departing from the business records hearsay rule, because the data contained must meet any hearsay hurdles that are presented, as well as meeting the requirements of authentication of a writing. In a Virginia case[78] in which the defendants were observed committing theft from a retail store, the trial court admitted a computer-generated inventory report as an exception to the hearsay rule under the business records theory. In the past, Virginia courts have admitted business records into evidence even though the witness did not prepare them, because their trustworthiness or reliability is guaranteed by the regularity of preparation and the records are used by the business in transacting business. As the reviewing court noted, "[t]he evidence proved that Rite-Aid maintained a computerized inventory in the regular course of its business, and regularly used the Telethon device to determine the status of its inventory."[79] Following the observed theft, a loss prevention officer used a hand-held scanner to take inventory of the remaining products on the shelf to determine what items had been stolen and the computer system generated a report that was admitted into evidence.

Computer-generated maps may fall under the definition of business records stored on electronic computing equipment and should admissible in evidence if they are relevant and material, without the necessity of identifying, locating, and producing as witnesses the individuals who made the entries in the regular course of business. In a prosecution for manufacturing crack cocaine within 1,500 feet of a school zone, the trial court allowed the introduction into evidence of a computer-generated map of the jurisdiction purporting to demonstrate that a school existed within 1,500 feet of the crack laboratory. To be admissible as a business record, the evidence must have been made in the regular course of business, that it was the regular course of business to produce this record (a map), and that it must have been prepared at the time described in the report. In this case, the custodian of the map data personally prepared the map from computer-stored data, had sufficient knowledge of the methods used to generate city maps, and was well acquainted with the technology used to produce city maps. Thus, the trial court held that the city map produced by the witness in the usual course of business could be

---

[78]   McDowell v. Commonwealth, 48 Va. App. 104, 628 S.E.2d 542, 2006 Va. App. LEXIS 229 (2006).
[79]   *Id.*

admitted as a hearsay exception under the business records exception to help prove that the crack lab was within 1,500 feet of a school.[80]

The absence of a business record when it normally would have been recorded may constitute negative evidence of an event or evidence that the event most likely did not happen. The foundational showing that the business or entity normally recorded and kept such records and that a due diligence search has not revealed the entry where it would normally have been entered allows the custodian of the records to note the nonexistence of the data.[81]

§ 12.7 —Family History and Records (Pedigree)

Rule 803

Hearsay Exceptions; Availability of Declarant Immaterial

The following are not excluded by the hearsay rule, even though the declarant is available as a witness:

* * *

(11) Records of religious organizations. Statements of births, marriages, divorces, deaths, legitimacy, ancestry, relationship by blood or marriage, or other similar facts of personal or family history, contained in a regularly kept record of a religious organization.

(12) Marriage, baptismal, and similar certificates. Statements of fact contained in a certificate that the maker performed a marriage or other ceremony or administered a sacrament, made by a clergyman, public official, or other person authorized by the rules or practices of a religious organization or by law to perform the act certified, and purporting to have been issued at the time of the act or within a reasonable time thereafter.

(13) Family records. Statements of fact concerning personal or family history contained in family Bibles, genealogies, charts, engravings on rings, inscriptions on family portraits, engravings on urns, crypts, or tombstones, or the like.

(19) Reputation among members of a person's family by blood, adoption, or marriage, or among a person's associates, or in the community, concerning a person's birth, adoption, marriage, divorce, death, legitimacy, relationship by blood, adoption, or marriage, ancestry, or other similar fact of personal or family.[82]

* * *

Evidence of one's family information that occurred or existed prior to the declarant's birth by its nature involves hearsay. No person has an actual awareness of his or her date of birth except through hearsay information, and most

---

[80] *See* Connecticut v. Polanco, 69 Conn. App. 169, 797 A.2d 523, 2002 Conn. App. LEXIS 187 (2002).

[81] Washington v. Knott, 2002 Wash. App. LEXIS 392 (2002).

[82] FED. R. EVID. 803.

family history falls into the same category. Almost all evidence relating to pedigree, genealogy, and family history consists of hearsay but usually will be admissible as an exception to the general rule excluding hearsay evidence. The family history exception to the hearsay rule is based in part on the inherent trustworthiness of a declaration by a family member regarding matters of family history and on the usual unavailability of other evidence. For example, in an incest prosecution, an investigating officer asked the female child-victim who she was and what was her relationship to the defendant. The court permitted the officer to testify that the child-victim stated that the defendant was her father under the theory that the statement given to the officer fell within the hearsay exception of family history.[83] Such evidence is admissible if the declarant is related by blood or marriage to the other person, or has been so intimately associated with the other person's family as to be likely to have accurate information concerning the birth, marriage, divorce, death, ancestry, or relationship.[84]

In one case in which the defendant had been charged with incest and the rape of his daughter, the prosecution sought to prove that the victim was actually his daughter. The defendant had accepted the girl as his daughter; the mother testified that the defendant was the biological father of the victim; the victim called the defendant "Daddy;" and the entire family had accepted the girl as his daughter. In addition, a civil court entered a judgment of paternity against the defendant finding that the victim was his child. According to the trial court, the hearsay exception under the Louisiana equivalent of Federal Rule 803(19) governing reputation concerning family history and family relationship proved that the defendant was the father of the victim sufficient to support a conviction of aggravated incest.[85]

The family history exception does not extend to every facet of a defendant's life or his family history in a way that would allow every piece of exculpatory evidence to be admitted. In a death penalty case, in an effort to have the jury spare the life of her son, the mother of the defendant gave a videotaped interview covering many facts of the family in Cuba, her son's lack of problems with the law, and some additional inculpatory family history evidence. The defendant appealed the exclusion by the trial court of portions of the audio of the video as well the transcript of the same information. According to the defendant, the video contained sound information that should have been admitted under the family history exception of Rule 804. The court noted that the unavailability of the witness (she could not travel from Cuba) was clear, but the exception to the hearsay rule for family matters did not extend so far as to cover testimony about the mother's own medical problems, appellant's difficulties with the Texas Youth Commission, the defendant's desire to leave Cuba, his clean record in Cuba, and child abuse inflicted upon appellant by his

[83] Eads v. State, 2002 Ark. App. LEXIS 75 (2002).
[84] FED. R. EVID. 804(b)(4).
[85] Louisiana v. Scott, 823 So. 2d 960, 968, 2002 La. App. LEXIS 93 (2002), *remedial writ denied*, 843 So. 2d 1122, 2003 La. LEXIS 1653 (2003).

stepfather. The Texas Court of Criminal Appeals affirmed the conviction and death sentence.[86]

Generally, the courts have interpreted "member of the family" broadly. For example, the court in a Virginia case held that for purposes of the pedigree exception to the hearsay rule, the decedent in a wrongful death action is a "member of the family or [a person] related to the family" whose history the decedent's declaration of paternity concerns. Hearsay evidence of the decedent's declaration is admissible provided no better evidence can be obtained.[87]

Oral declarations by a family member regarding matters of family history are admissible as an exception to the hearsay rule, while other evidence of family history may be admissible where the information has been recorded in a manner that suggests reliability. Oral declarations of the names of uncles, aunts, and cousins and their point of origin in Eastern Europe may be accepted as family history sufficient to make a claim to an intestate relative's estate.[88] Virtually no family would record a birth record in a family bible if the birth never occurred, a factor that gives reliability to family histories contained within religious books. Family records contained within the family bible are admissible when a proper showing is made as to the authority or authenticity of entries of the family record, especially when better evidence is not available. Such matters as births, deaths, and marriages are competent as evidence.

Some jurisdictions permit the entry of family history when it has been entered in a family Bible even where the persons who know the history remain alive. In a polygamy investigation, there was some belief that proof of the multiple marriages and sexual activity with underage wives resulting in live births would be found in a family Bible. The result of a search warrant revealed a bible with missing pages that were alleged to contain the intimate and illegal family history. The focus of the prosecution changed to tampering with evidence with the Bible being admitted in evidence against the defendant.[89] In some instances, the absence from the jurisdiction of the person who made the statements or the entries in the Bible, or insanity or illness hindering his or her presence at the trial is enough to make the evidence admissible. In some jurisdictions, entries in family Bibles are declared admissible by statute,[90] while some states recognize the hearsay exception for family records that have been included in family Bibles.[91]

Federal Rule of Evidence 803(11) provides that regularly kept records of a religious organization may be consulted in order to find family information, and if this information meets the legal requirements, it should be admissible as an exception to the hearsay rule. Although many people do not have close ties to organized religion, many people are intimately involved with their reli-

---

[86] *See* Valle v. Texas, 109 S.W.3d 500, 2003 Tex. Crim. App. LEXIS 143 (2003).

[87] Smith v. Givens, 223 Va. 455, 290 S.E.2d 844 (1982).

[88] *See* In re Estate of Doris Rosen, Deceased, 2003 Pa. Super. 96, 819 A.2d 585, 2003 Pa. Super. LEXIS 364 (2003).

[89] State v. Sliwinski, 2004 Mont. 1221, 2004 Mont. Dist. LEXIS 2119 (2004).

[90] FED. R. EVID. 803.

[91] Estate of Earl Wallace, Deceased, 2004 Phila. Ct. Com. Pl. LEXIS 134 (Pa. 2004).

gion in situations in which careful records of church membership, birth, baptism, bar mitzvah, and wedding information are generated. Because there is every desire to accurately record this information and no reason to erroneously enter the information, there is a presumption that the records are accurate. In interpreting this rule, one federal court explained that the exception is limited to personal information and does not authorize evidence of statements of monetary contributions to a church, because these do not fall within the religious records exception to the hearsay rule.[92]

Under Federal Rule of Evidence 803(19) and its state equivalents, family relationships that exist by blood, adoption, or marriage may be proved by persons who have intimate knowledge of the family or by associates of family members concerning family history. For example, a father or mother could give the date of birth of their respective parents, even though they could not possibly know this information from firsthand knowledge. And a father could testify to the birth date of his son or daughter, even thought the father was not present at the birth or even in the geographical area of the birth. In a case in which a defendant was accused of harboring an illegal alien, among other crimes, a trial court permitted the illegal alien's aunt to testify that he was from El Salvador and was not a United States citizen.[93] People who do not have a close association with the family or group are not permitted to offer this sort of hearsay in court. For example, in a prosecution for aggravating driving under the influence of an intoxicant while a person under 15 years of age was in the vehicle,[94] the trial court permitted the arresting officer to relate to the court the fact that he had heard the putative father of the 15-year-old state that the boy passenger was only 13. While the investigation was ongoing, a different adult male came to take charge of the child and noted to the officer that the boy was his 13-year-old son. Police proved unable to locate the boy or his father prior to trial, so the trial judge permitted the police officer to state the age of the child, an element of the aggravating driving under the influence charge. At trial, the defendant entered a hearsay objection that the trial court rejected. The appellate court determined that the trial court committed reversible error in allowing the officer to give an age to the boy by stating that he looked young and that the putative father had stated to the officer that the boy was 13. The officer who testified had no personal knowledge concerning the age of the child, had not been a member of the family community, and was a stranger to the child and his father. Because the family history related to an element of the crime, the appellate court reversed the conviction.

[92]   Hall v. C.I.R., 729 F.2d 632 (9th Cir. 1984).
[93]   United States v. Garcia-Flores, 136 Fed. Appx. 685; 2005 U.S. App. LEXIS 12732 (5th Cir. 2005).
[94]   State v. May, 210 Ariz. 452, 455, 112 P.3d 39, 42, 2005 Ariz. App. LEXIS 73 (2005).

§ 12.8 —Former Testimony

Rule 804

Hearsay Exceptions; Declarant Unavailable

* * *

(b) **Hearsay exceptions.**—The following are not excluded by the hearsay rule if the declarant is unavailable as a witness:

(1) **Former testimony.** Testimony given as a witness at another hearing of the same or a different proceeding, or in a deposition taken in compliance with law in the course of the same or another proceeding, if the party against whom the testimony is now offered, or, in a civil action or proceeding, a predecessor in interest, had an opportunity and similar motive to develop the testimony by direct, cross, or redirect examination.[95]

* * *

Every criminal defendant has a Sixth Amendment right to confront and cross-examine adverse witnesses and not having the opportunity to confront a witness will likely lead to the reversal of a conviction. Therefore, when evidence is introduced against a defendant in a manner that has the effect of preventing meaningful cross-examination, the trial judge should exclude the evidence. A literal construction of the Sixth Amendment would prevent virtually all hearsay evidence from being considered for admission, and have the effect of making trials difficult. Where a substitute for cross-examination exists or where the defendant originally had motive, opportunity, and incentive to conduct cross-examination at a prior proceeding between the same parties, the evidence may be admitted even though it constitutes hearsay testimony. This exception does not require that the defendant have conducted cross-examination of the witness at the earlier proceeding, only that the defendant had the opportunity. As a general rule, to have an opportunity to use testimony given in a prior proceeding, the parties to the lawsuit must be identical, the now-absent witness must have been under oath in the first proceeding, the absent witness must now be unavailable for testimony, and the lawsuit must cover the same issues covered in the first proceeding. Under Rule 804, the declarant must be unavailable for testimony where unavailability may involve an assertion of a constitutional or other privilege, when the witness is beyond the power of the court to command attendance, or when the witness simply refuses to testify through no fault of the offering party, or when the witness testifies to a lack of memory, or when the witness is dead. If a hearsay exception absolutely conflicts with the Sixth Amendment provision that states: "in all criminal prosecutions, the accused shall enjoy the right to be confronted with the witnesses against him," the evidence will not be admissible.

---

[95] FED. R. EVID. 804.

In interpreting the Sixth Amendment right of confrontation and cross-examination, the Supreme Court overruled a case that allowed testimonial evidence without personal confrontation with the adverse witness. The older case, *Ohio v. Roberts*,[96] permitted the admission of prior testimony against the defendant when the witness was unavailable and when the prior testimony bore some "indicia of reliability." Unavailability was a fairly easy determination, but "indicia of reliability" seemed to invite judicial determination on uncertain terms. When the confrontation issue came to the Court in *Crawford v. Washington*,[97] the Court took the opportunity to overrule *Ohio v. Roberts* and to more clearly enforce the original concept of the Sixth Amendment confrontation clause.

In *Crawford*, the defendant had been convicted of assaulting a man who attempted to rape his wife, using evidence given by the wife in a statement to police. The defendant's wife invoked her marital testimonial privilege and did not testify against the defendant, with the result that the trial judge allowed the wife's statement to the police to be used against the defendant. The judge followed the *Ohio v. Roberts* view and allowed the testimony because the judge viewed the defendant's wife as unavailable and considered the wife's out-of-court statement to be "reliable." The statement called into question the defendant's contention of self-defense. The Supreme Court reversed the decision of the Supreme Court of Washington that reinstated the trial court conviction and held that Crawford's Sixth Amendment right to confront and cross-examine adverse witnesses had been violated. The Court found a Sixth Amendment violation because, where testimonial evidence was at issue, the playing of the wife's testimony by audiotape prevented the defendant from confronting or conducting any cross-examination of the wife. The Court held that the Sixth Amendment demanded both unavailability and at least a prior opportunity to cross-examine the witness. In this case, the defendant had no opportunity to ever cross-examine his wife. The rule to be distilled from the *Crawford* case is that when testimonial evidence is involved, there must be a trial opportunity to cross-examine the witness or a proper earlier proceeding where the right of cross-examination existed and there must be proof of unavailability of the witness.[98] The case did not put an end to hearsay exceptions, but reinstated the right to confront and cross-examine witnesses where prior testimony is involved.

In a later Washington case,[99] the alleged victim in a domestic violence case made a 911 call to report an assault by her former boyfriend, who was under a no-contact order and who had just fled the victim's dwelling. The former girlfriend-victim did not testify against her attacker but the trial court admitted an audiotape of the 911 call against the defendant, over his Sixth Amendment objection. The defendant appealed his resulting conviction through Washington courts with unsuccessful results. The Supreme Court of the

---

[96]   Ohio v. Roberts, 448 U.S. 56, 1980 U.S. LEXIS 140 (1980).
[97]   541 U.S. 36, 2004 U.S. LEXIS 1838 (2004).
[98]   *Id.*
[99]   Davis v. Washington, ___ U.S. ___, 2006 U.S. LEXIS 4886 (2006).

United States affirmed after determining that the 911 call was not testimonial in nature and the use of the audiotape did not create a confrontation and cross-examination issue under the Sixth Amendment. The victim was speaking with an emergency operator while the events were in progress, describing current circumstances that necessitated a police response. As the Court noted in making a distinction between testimonial statements and nontestimonial statements, "Statements are nontestimonial when made in the course of police interrogation under circumstances objectively indicating that the primary purpose of the interrogation is to enable police assistance to meet an ongoing emergency. They are testimonial when the circumstances objectively indicate that there is no such ongoing emergency, and that the primary purpose of the interrogation is to establish or prove past events potentially relevant to later criminal prosecution."[100] The victim's statements were not testimonial because the statements were necessary to enable the police to resolve the ongoing emergency rather than to reconstruct what had happened in the past. Because the Court characterized the 911 call as nontestimonial, the Sixth Amendment is not implicated.

In *Hammon v. Indiana*,[101] a companion case to *Davis v. Washington*, police responded to a domestic disturbance at the home of a married couple. The wife told officers that nothing was wrong, but invited the police inside the home, where they separately questioned each spouse. The wife signed a affidavit indicating that she had been the victim of a battery at the hands of her husband. The wife did not appear to testify at the bench trial. Over the defendant-husband's Sixth Amendment cross-examination objection, the trial court admitted the affidavit and other information that the wife had given to one of the officers. The prosecution put the officer who had questioned the wife on the stand and asked him to testify to what the wife-victim told him and to authenticate her affidavit. In relevant parts, the Indiana court all affirmed the conviction. The Supreme Court found that the wife's statements to police were testimonial in nature and the admission of the wife's statements violated the defendant's Sixth Amendment right of confrontation and cross-examination. According to the *Hammon* Court, the officer's questions were directed at determining what had happened and was part of an investigation into alleged criminal conduct. The more formal features of the investigation and the affidavit strengthened the testimonial aspects of the testimony given by police and through the introduction of the affidavit at trial. The Court reversed the defendant's conviction and remanded the case.

In a case in which the witness had disappeared after the first trial and prior to the second trial, the defendant objected, complaining that his rights under the Sixth Amendment to confront and cross-examine adverse witnesses and Federal Rule of Evidence 804(b)(1) were violated.[102] The defendant objected to the prosecution using the transcript of the witness from the first trial. In

---

[100]   *Id.* at ___.

[101]   ___ U.S. ___, 2006 U.S. LEXIS 4886 (2006).

[102]   United States v. Garcia, 117 Fed. Appx. 162, 2004 U.S. App. LEXIS 25480 (2d Cir. 2004).

order for the prior testimony to be used at a second trial, the party against whom the evidence is to be admitted must have had an opportunity and similar motive to conduct cross-examination at the first proceeding. Reviewing courts have looked at transcripts of the original cross-examination to determine whether the trial counsel had a full opportunity to probe and expose the witness's testimony and undermine its credibility where appropriate. In holding that the former testimony could be constitutionally used against the defendant at his second trial on the same issue, the Court of Appeals concluded:

> that this prior cross-examination sufficiently allowed the jury at the second trial to evaluate the truth of [the missing witness'] testimony, and that [the defendant] had a similar motive in both trials. This conclusion is further strengthened by the facts that evidence of [the missing witness'] flight was put before the jury in the second trial, defense counsel emphasized the flight in his summation, and the district court specifically referred to it in the charge to the jury. Therefore, the admission of [the missing witness'] prior testimony at [the defendant's] second trial did not violate [the defendant's] right to confrontation under the Sixth Amendment nor was it contrary to Federal Rule of Evidence 804(b)(1).[103]

In affirming the conviction, the Court of Appeals was satisfied that the defendant had sufficient reason to effectively cross-examine the missing prosecution witness at the prior trial and that it would not be unfair to allow evidence of what the witness said at the first trial into evidence at the second trial.

In one case, the defense wanted to use former testimony in favor of a defendant.[104] The trial issue involved missing witnesses who testified at a grand jury proceeding and then disappeared. The prosecution successfully contended that it did not have the same incentive, motive, and intent to examine the witnesses at the grand jury stage of the criminal process as it would have at a trial. The defendant wanted the grand jury testimony of the two missing witnesses to be admitted at trial because their evidence would deflect the responsibility for the crime from the defendant and place it on a third party. The parties were in agreement that the witnesses were missing and unavailable, but the quality and thrust of the questions asked of the missing grand jury witness was simply different than if the prosecution were to have cross-examined them at trial. The Court of Appeals agreed with the federal prosecutor and upheld the refusal to admit the evidence.[105] Not argued in the case was the concept that the government did not ever cross-examine the witnesses because they were called to the grand jury by the prosecution as grand jury witnesses and the prior grand jury proceeding was not an adversarial one.

The mere possibility that a witness might assert a Fifth Amendment privilege or offer a legally sufficient reason for not testifying at a second trial

---

[103] *Id.* at 164.
[104] United States v. Carson, 455 F.3d 336, 2006 U.S. App. LEXIS 18361 (D.C. Cir. 2006).
[105] *Id.*

failed to constitute a sufficient reason to allow reported testimony evidence from a prior hearing as a hearsay exception in a trial on the merits. Accordingly, the Supreme Court of Virginia held that

> Before concluding that testimony is unavailable, the inquiry must include exploration of the subject matter of the testimony that prompts the reluctance of the witness and the reasons for refusal. Vague assertions of discomfort or generalized statements of fear or concern cannot rise to the same level of significance as evidence of specific threats. While it is the litigants' responsibility to produce the evidence, appropriate judicial pressure should be employed to test the resolve of the witness. At a bare minimum, refusal to testify should be met with an order from the trial court directing the witness to testify.[106]

A Wisconsin court held that a witness who attempts to invoke the Fifth Amendment and who absolutely refuses to testify even in the face of a court order, although present, is "unavailable" for purposes of determining the admissibility of hearsay statements.[107] If the prosecution in a criminal case seeks to offer testimony taken at a previous trial or earlier proceeding, the burden is on the prosecution to establish that efforts have been made to locate the witness, and that the witness is unavailable despite reasonable efforts made in good faith to secure his or her presence at the trial.[108]

Some jurisdictions and legal authorities assert that former testimony is actually not hearsay, because it was given under oath and subject to cross-examination. The Federal Rules of Evidence and derivative state adopters recognize former testimony as hearsay, but hold that it is admissible under an exception to the hearsay rule. Under either approach, when a witness for the prosecution or defense is unavailable and cannot be produced at the present trial or, being present, refuses to testify, courts will generally admit the recorded testimony of such witness from a prior criminal proceeding where it meets the other qualifications for this hearsay exception. A witness who is expected to assert some constitutional or statutory privilege is not considered to be unavailable until the witness is placed on the witness stand and formally asserts a privilege not to testify or simply refuses to testify even though no legal basis exists for the refusal.[109]

In criminal prosecutions, the mere temporary illness or disability of a witness or family member may be insufficient to justify the admission of his or her former testimony; it must appear that the witness is in such a state, either mentally or physically, that in reasonable probability he or she will never be

---

[106] Sapp v. Commonwealth of Virginia, 263 Va. 415, 425, 559 S.E.2d 645, 650, 2002 Va. LEXIS 41 (2002).

[107] Wisconsin v. Tomlinson, 254 Wis. 2d 502, 528, 648 N.W.2d 367, 380, 2002 Wis. LEXIS 494 (2002).

[108] State v. Keairns, 9 Ohio St. 3d 228, 460 N.E.2d 245 (1984). *See also* United States v. Winn, 767 F.2d 527 (9th Cir. 1985), which held that a witness is not "unavailable" within the meaning of the rule governing admission of hearsay when the declarant is unavailable unless the prosecution makes a good faith effort to obtain the witness's presence.

[109] *See* Edmonds v. State, 2006 Miss. App. LEXIS 311 (Miss. 2006).

able to attend the trial. Therefore, the Eleventh Circuit Court of Appeals agreed that the statement made by defense counsel that the defendant's wife was unavailable to testify as a witness due to her child's illness, in and of itself, was insufficient to demonstrate the unavailability of the witness for the purpose of securing the admission of the witness's testimony (given at a pretrial suppression hearing) as an exception to the rule against hearsay.[110]

In admitting reported testimony from a state court proceeding in a federal criminal trial, federal courts have recognized that the witness's testimony in a state court hearing may be admitted by a federal court if the witness cannot be procured to testify in the federal court proceeding. In one federal case in Alaska, the judge allowed the testimony of a deceased police officer to be admitted at a federal suppression hearing. The judge held that, under Rule 804, because the deceased declarant was unavailable, that the former testimony had been given in a motion to suppress, and that the defendant had the same or similar motive and opportunity to cross-examine the now-deceased officer, there was no abuse of discretion in admitting the former testimony.[111]

In an Arkansas criminal case[112] where there was a companion civil case that had been filed, an attorney for the civil plaintiff deposed a witness in the homosexual rape case and the witness died prior to the date of the criminal trial. The judge permitted the evidence from the deceased witness to be admitted into evidence because the declarant was deceased and the court found that the defendant's civil attorney had an opportunity that he did not exercise to cross-examine the now-dead witness. Additionally, the defendant's criminal attorney could have deposed the adverse witness but chose not to do so. In upholding the admission into evidence of the earlier deposition testimony, the reviewing court noted that the civil trial and criminal trial involved the same facts and same participants, giving the defendant's civil attorney proper motive and incentive to cross-examine at the earlier proceeding. An important concept that the appellate court may have missed is that the parties were different in the civil trial from the criminal trial because the plaintiff in the civil trial was the injured party and the plaintiff in the criminal trial was the prosecution.

In summary, when a party wants to admit into evidence earlier testimony offered at prior proceedings, there should be an identity of parties, and identity of issues between the prior proceeding and the present one. There must have been ample motive, incentive, and opportunity for the adverse party to have developed sufficient cross-examination of a witness who must have been under oath for the former testimony exception to be permitted. Where all the statutory and legal issues are met involving former testimony, "[o]nly the absence of an opportunity for the trier to observe the witness's demeanor detracts from the ideal conditions for giving testimony."[113]

---

[110]   United States v. Acosta, 769 F.2d 721 (11th Cir. 1985). *See also* State v. Howell, 868 S.W.2d 238 (Tenn. 1993).

[111]   United States v. Geiger, 263 F.3d 1034, 1038, 2001 U.S. App. LEXIS 19409 (9th Cir. 2001).

[112]   Simmons v. State, 2006 Ark. App. LEXIS 276 (2006).

[113]   5-804 WEINSTEIN'S FEDERAL EVIDENCE § 804.04. Chapter 804 Hearsay Exceptions; Declarant Unavailable (Matthew Bender 2006).

§ 12.9 —Dying Declarations

Rule 80

Hearsay Exceptions; Declarant Unavailable

* * *

(b) Hearsay exceptions.—The following are not excluded by the hearsay rule if the declarant is unavailable as a witness:

* * *

(2) Statement under belief of impending death. In a prosecution for homicide or in a civil action or proceeding, a statement made by a declarant while believing that the declarant's death was imminent, concerning the cause or circumstances of what the declarant believed to be impending death.[114]

To qualify as a dying declaration, the victim must have made a statement concerning the cause and circumstances of his or her own impending death by homicide and the statement must have been made with a clear understanding that death was imminent. The victim must have given up all hope of recovery or living any appreciable length of time. Dying declarations in homicide cases have from ancient times been admitted in evidence either: (1) because of solemnity—the solemnity of the occasion and the fear that one would not want to meet one's maker with a lie on one's lips, or (2) because of necessity— because the victim of the homicide cannot testify, it is necessary to protect the public against homicidal criminals and prevent a miscarriage of justice. Under the common law, the person making the dying declaration must actually die,[115] but the federal courts do not require death in order for the declaration to be admissible. Consistent with the position of many states, a Tennessee appellate court noted the five requirements for the admissibility of a dying declaration:

> (1) The declarant must be dead at the time of the trial; (2) the state-
> ment is admissible only in the prosecution of a criminal homicide;
> (3) the declarant must be the victim of the homicide; (4) the state-
> ment must concern the cause or the circumstances of the death; and
> (5) the declarant must have made the statement under the belief that
> death was imminent.[116]

From the legal perspective, the dying declaration has the same effect and carries the same presumptive weight as if it were testimony given under oath. However, a number of authorities point out that while knowledge of imminent

---

[114] FED. R. EVID. 804.

[115] If the person survived, the individual could personally testify or the statement might be admissible as an excited utterance.

[116] State v. Mayes, 2004 Tenn. Crim. App. LEXIS 9 (2004) and State v. Lewis, 2006 Tenn. Crim. App. LEXIS 237 (2006).

death constitutes a substitute for an oath and provides credibility, the evidentiary weight to be given to the statement falls to the finder of fact. A jury could reject the value of a dying declaration because it is merely hearsay and is not the equivalent of, nor does it have the same value or weight as, testimony that is given under oath in open court and is subject to cross-examination.[117]

In order for a judge to admit a dying declaration, the declarant's statement must describe the circumstances and events immediately surrounding or leading up to the defendant's conduct that caused death of the declarant. Under current hearsay and Sixth Amendment standards, a dying declaration has a better chance of admission when the declarant makes a spontaneous statement rather than answering questions from a police officer.[118] To meet a defendant's objection to the admission of a dying declaration under the Sixth Amendment, the Commonwealth of Virginia takes the position that a defendant forfeits the right of confrontation and cross-examination when there is proof by a preponderance of the evidence that the defendant's act has caused the absence of the dying declarant.[119] Similarly, in Texas, one court permitted a dying declaration to be admitted against the a defendant who was on trial for killing the dying declarant.[120] The person making a dying declaration generally does not have to unequivocally and unambiguously state that the victim knows death is imminent but the awareness of impending death may be inferred from the character of the wounds, the language used by the declarant, from the facts and surrounding circumstances, or from what has been told to the victim by medical personnel. The expectation of imminent demise may be shown by the circumstances of his or her condition or by his or her acts, such as sending for a minister or rabbi before making the declaration or requesting last rites from a minister or priest.

In an old case, *Mattox v. United States*, the Supreme Court of the United States succinctly stated conditions under which the dying declaration exception to the hearsay rule applied in federal criminal trials and set forth the justification for the rule:[121]

> Dying declarations are admissible in a trial for murder, as to the fact of the homicide and the person by whom it was committed, in favor of the defendant as well as against him. . . . But it must be shown by the party offering them in evidence that they were made under a sense of impending death. This may be made to appear from what the injured person said; or from the nature and extent of the wounds inflicted, being obviously such that he must have felt or known that he could not survive; as well as from his conduct at the time and the

---

[117] Commonwealth v. Brown, 388 Pa. 613, 131 A.2d 367 (1957); *see also* Rodriguez v. State, 697 S.W.2d 463 (Tex. App. 1985).

[118] *See* Crawford v. Washington, 541 U.S. 36, 2004 U.S. LEXIS 1838 (2004).

[119] Commonwealth v. Morgan, 69 Va. Cir. 228, 232, 2005 Va. Cir. LEXIS 189 (Va. 2005).

[120] Gonzalez v. State, 195 S.W.3d 114, 2006 Tex. Crim. App. LEXIS 1129 (Tex. 2006). *See* case in Part II.

[121] Mattox v. United States, 146 U.S. 140, 13 S. Ct. 50, 36 L. Ed. 917 (1892).

> communications, if any, made to him by medical advisors, if assented to or understandingly acquiesced in by him. The length of the time elapsing between the making of the declaration and the death is one of the elements to be considered . . .

Approving the admission of the dying declarations in the case, the Court commented further:

> The admission of the testimony is justified on the ground of necessity, and in view of the consideration that certain expectation of almost immediate death will remove all temptation to falsehood and enforce as strict adherence to the truth as the obligation of an oath could impose. But the evidence must be received with the utmost caution, and, if the circumstances do not satisfactorily disclose that the awful and solemn situation in which he is placed is realized by the dying man because of the hope of recovery, it ought to be rejected.

Under the modern Federal Rules of Evidence, the dying declarant need not *actually* die, but many states still hold that or the dying declaration is not admissible unless the declarant has died. Even with the guidelines established by federal and state statutes and the Supreme Court of the United States and state supreme courts, lower courts are required to apply the test to specific cases. For example, are the victim's statements admitted as dying declarations if they are elicited by questions? Must the victim affirmatively state that he or she is dying? Is the length of time the declarant lives after making a dying declaration material? Must the person actually die?

In a New York murder prosecution,[122] the trial court admitted a series of comments and responses to questions as a dying declaration. The decedent's wife heard gunshots and found her husband on the sidewalk bleeding from two shots in his back. He told her that "it hurt" and to call an ambulance. He subsequently told her that "I'm dying" as the police arrived. Police asked his wife to inquire of the decedent as to who shot him because the victim spoke only Spanish. He replied by giving the defendant's name, who he identified by using a nickname. He died a few hours later. At trial, the dying declaration was admitted against the defendant. Years later, on the strength of *Crawford v. Washington*,[123] the defendant contended that the statements should not have been used as a dying declaration because the statements were "testimonial in nature" and he was not be able to exercise his Sixth Amendment right to confront and cross-examine the dead declarant. The New York court that reviewed the defendant's motion to vacate his homicide conviction noted that dying declarations constitute an exception to the ban on testimonial evidence that cannot be subjected to cross-examination. The court mentioned that the

---

[122] People v. Durio, 7 Misc. 3d 729, 731, 794 N.Y.S.2d 863, 685, 2005 N.Y. Misc. LEXIS 398 (N.Y. 2005).

[123] 541 U.S. 36, 2004 U.S. LEXIS 1838 (2004). *See* the material on this case in § 12.8—Former Testimony. The Supreme Court of California held that *Crawford v. Washington* and its Sixth Amendment concerns did not apply to dying declarations. *See* People v. Monterroso, 34 Cal. 743, 22 Cal. Rptr. 3d 1, 101 P.3d 956 (2004).

Supreme Court of the United States recently referred to dying declarations and noted that many dying declarations may not be testimonial in nature but that even those that were could be admitted.[124]

An Illinois court, in deciding whether a dying declarant possessed a belief that imminent death was a virtual certainty, held that a trial court could have inferred that the decedent knew death was approaching when he knew that he had been shot twice, he mentioned that he could not move his legs, he was gasping for air, he appeared to be in pain, and he told a friend that he was dying. At the hospital the dying victim told a doctor that he was not doing well and the doctor agreed with him that he was in "bad shape." At the hospital, the victim gave police a description of the defendant. The victim had been in an altercation the evening prior to the shooting with the defendant after the defendant forced the victim's girlfriend to have sex with him. The defendant was alleged to have shot the victim as the victim answered his front door. The reviewing court agreed with the trial court that the victim's statements were properly admitted as a dying declaration because the victim's words pertained to the cause or circumstances of the victim's receipt of final injuries, the victim knew he was dying, and the victim possessed the mental faculties to offer an accurate statement or statements concerning how his injuries were received.[125] Similarly, in a Minnesota case,[126] in deciding whether the victim realized that death was imminent and a certainty, the trial court agreed with the prosecution and concluded that the victim possessed sufficient awareness of his coming demise. The victim had multiple stab wounds, was bleeding profusely, and was having extreme difficulty breathing. He had been stabbed in the neck, a wound that pierced his larynx, and shot in the chest, severing a major artery. He was bleeding profusely, and he clutched his chest as he spoke. Within a few minutes, the victim was unable to walk and told police he could not breathe. Shortly after, he stopped breathing and the emergency responders could not locate a pulse and he soon died. The Supreme Court of Minnesota agreed that the victim knew that his life was soon coming to an end.[127]

When an injured person does not believe that he or she is going to die or the proof may be uncertain that the victim has that belief, the statement may be admissible as an excited utterance. A Commonwealth of Virginia court admitted a statement that qualified as a dying declaration and as an excited utterance. The victim was still under the influence of being shot with a gun; he offered his statement from first-person knowledge of who shot him; and he otherwise was competent as a witness. There were no indications in this case that the victim had reflected or had a chance to fabricate an answer to a police officer's question. The appellate court held that the statement was properly admitted as an excited utterance.[128]

---

[124]   *Id.*
[125]   People v. Gilmore, 356 Ill. App. 3d 1023, 1031, 828 N.E.2d 293, 301, 2005 Ill. App. LEXIS 314 (2005).
[126]   State v. Martin, 695 N.W.2d 578, 583, 2005 Minn. LEXIS 267 (2005).
[127]   *Id.*
[128]   Commonwealth v. Morgan, 69 Va. Cir. 228, 230, 2005 Va. Cir. LEXIS 189 (2005).

As a matter of logic, a dying declaration must be made between the infliction of the fatal injury and the death of the declarant. A Texas court explained that the length of time a declarant lives after making a dying declaration is immaterial in determining whether the statement is a dying declaration for purposes of the hearsay exception.[129] In a California case, the dying declarant was well aware of his impending death and despite the fact that he lived 11 more days was not material to the determination of whether the statement was admissible as a dying declaration.[130]

While the typical dying declaration is usually offered orally and later reduced to a writing, a dying declaration may be either written or oral but must relate to injuries suffered by the declarant prior to his or her death and may never cover the death of a third party. Due to the typical police response to reported homicides, in many instances the dying statements are made to law enforcement officers and emergency medical responders. Law enforcement officers are generally trained to recognize that while a statement by a declarant may not qualify as a dying declaration, it may be admissible under the hearsay exception known as the excited utterance exception. Police officers should take care to record the substance of a statement and the circumstances under which it was uttered as soon as possible in order to clearly convey the final statements regarding a victim's final injuries. Cross-examination by defense attorneys should also be anticipated at the time the statement is offered by the victim so that the police officer will be prepared to give accurate testimony about what he or she heard.

§ 12.10   —Declarations Against Interest

Rule 804

Hearsay Exceptions; Declarant Unavailable

* * *

(b) Hearsay exceptions.—The following are not excluded by the hearsay rule if the declarant is unavailable as a witness:

* * *

(3) Statement against interest. A statement which was at the time of its making so far contrary to the declarant's pecuniary or proprietary interest, or so far tended to subject the declarant to civil or criminal liability, or to render invalid a claim by the declarant against another, that a reasonable person in the declarant's position would not have made the statement unless believing it to be true. A statement tending to expose the declarant to criminal liability and offered to exculpate the accused is not admissible unless corroborating circumstances clearly indicate the trustworthiness of the statement.[131]

---

[129]   Charles v. State, 955 S.W.2d 400 (Tex. 1997).

[130]   People v. Monterroso, 34 Cal. 4th 743, 763, 101 P.3d 956, 971, 22 Cal. Rptr. 3d 1, 18, 2004 Cal. LEXIS 11763 (2004).

[131]   FED. R. EVID. 804.

A. Declarations Against Pecuniary Interests

Any time a person makes an oral or written statement that could have the effect of harming his or her pecuniary or monetary interests, such statement may qualify as an exception to the hearsay rule. Because most individuals are somewhat self-serving, when people make declarations against pecuniary interests that are out of line with typical statements, they are probably being truthful. A statement qualifying as a declaration against interest may be admissible as an exception to the hearsay rule because declarations against interest have been found to offer a high probability of truthfulness. Admission into evidence has become acceptable out of necessity, because most individuals decline to repeat such statements while under oath in a court of law because admitting a declaration against interest may have an adverse result. The legal theory holds that a person does not make statements against his or her own pecuniary interest unless the statements generally are true and have thus considered such statements trustworthy, even though there may be no opportunity to confront or to cross-examine the witness.

A declaration against interest by a person who is not a party nor in privity with a party to an action is admissible in evidence when: (1) the person making such declaration is either dead or unavailable as a witness due to sickness, insanity, or absence from the jurisdiction; (2) the declarant had peculiar means of knowing the facts that he or she stated; (3) the declaration was against his or her pecuniary or proprietary interest; and (4) he or she had no probable motive to falsify the facts stated.[132] Applying the declaration against interest theory, an Arkansas court revoked a prior judgment ordering a trustee to pay child support to a child beneficiary's custodian.[133] The trustee refused to comply with the court's original order when the trustee gained knowledge that the custodian-father and the non-custodial mother appeared to have colluded to defraud the court and the trust. The mother, who could not be found for the hearing, told the trustee that she and the custodian father had concocted a scheme to get $2,000 per month from the trustee for the benefit of the child and that the mother and father were planning on splitting the $2,000 each month. At the time of the court's hearing, the mother was absent and the statement clearly was against her pecuniary interest because if the trustee acted properly knowing the truth about the fraud, her share of the monthly child support would not likely be paid. She must have known that the statement was against her pecuniary interest when it was made and her absence permitted the hearsay use of her statement. As the appellate court noted in approving the trial court admission of the mother's declaration against interest, "Here, Ms. Salmon was unavailable because no one knew her location and attempts to find her had proved unavailing. Ark. R. Evid. 804(a)(4). Moreover, Ms.

---

[132]   Gichner v. Antonio Troiano Tile Co., 410 F.2d 238 (D.C. Cir. 1969).
[133]   Osborne v. Salmon, 2006 Ark. App. LEXIS 266 (2006).

Salmon's statements that she had colluded with Mr. Osborne (the father) were admissible because such statements were declarations against the pecuniary interest of her estate.[134]

A hearsay statement may qualify as a declaration against interest if the statement, at the time of its original utterance, was contrary to the declarant's pecuniary, proprietary, or social interest, or tended to subject the declarant to civil or criminal liability, or to render invalid the declarant's claim against another, so that a reasonable person in the declarant's position would not have uttered the statement unless that person believed the statement to be true.[135] A statement may qualify as a declaration against the interest when the statement threatens loss of employment or reduces chances for future employment. For example, a hearsay statement made by the lessee's employee to a fire investigator that he and others were smoking on the leased premises a few hours before the fire started was against the employee's pecuniary and proprietary interests, and because the statement also concerned a subject of which the employee was personally cognizant and there was no conceivable motive to falsify, the statement was admitted as a declaration against the interest of the employee. The court in that case agreed, however, that the statement would not be admitted unless the employee was unavailable to testify at the trial.[136]

In a Texas case, the trial court first acknowledged the rule relating to declarations against interest and reviewed the admissibility requirements, including the fact that the statement must have adverse consequences to the one making the statement. When police executed a search warrant of a residence where the defendant was present, the police discovered a quantity of cocaine in the presence of the defendant and a friend. Several days later, after posting bail for an associate, the defendant stated to his girlfriend that he knew the cocaine belonged to the friend who had been present during the search because the defendant admitted selling the cocaine to the same friend. In approving the admission of the declaration made to his girlfriend, the reviewing court noted that: "The voluntary statement, although made several days after the arrest, was not the product of coercion or questioning. . . . McElroy's incriminating statements were made to his live-in girlfriend, and thus, he had no reason to believe that statements made to her would be used against him."[137] In this case, the original declarant, the defendant, was unwilling to repeat his statement on the witness stand and therefore was "unavailable" to testify within the meaning of the statute governing the inadmissibility of declarations against interest.

---

[134]   *Id.*

[135]   New Jersey v. Brown, 170 N.J. 138, 148, 784 A.2d 1244, 1251, 2001 N.J. LEXIS 1409 (2001).

[136]   Gichner v. Antonio Troiano Tile Co., *supra* note 132.

[137]   Risher v. Texas, 85 S.W.3d 839, 842, 2002 Tex. App. LEXIS 6086 (2002).

B. Statements Against Penal Interests—
Confessions and Admissions

Included within the general exception introduced above is the hearsay exception concerning admissions and confessions. A confession, as it is used in criminal law, consists of a suspect admitting responsibility for all the elements of the crime or crimes, and constitutes a complete acknowledgment of guilt by one who has committed a crime or crimes. The confession is the admission of the criminal act itself, not an admission of a fact or circumstances from which guilt may be inferred. An admission, as distinguished from a confession, consists of the suspect admitting to some involvement or having responsibility for some elements of a crime or admitting to facts that, when linked to other facts, may show guilt. However, the statement falls short of a complete confession for the criminal act itself. An admission may consist of a partial confession, but the admission fails to take complete responsibility for committing incriminating acts or conduct that equals guilt. In a Tennessee murder case, police videotaped a voluntary statement of the eventual defendant, in which she admitted being at the scene of the homicide, but denying any involvement. This kind of statement qualifies as an admission, but not a full confession, because it only placed her at the crime scene, and nothing more.[138]

A Maryland case illustrates the importance of a declaration against penal interest in a case in which a husband was convicted of the murder of his wife. His defense suggested that his wife was murdered by a man named Gatton because there was some evidence that the deceased wife and Gatton had been having an affair. Additionally, it was alleged that Gatton had been in the company of the deceased at the home of another woman and in the other woman's presence. The second woman was prepared testify, but the trial court excluded the fact that Gatton had raped the second woman, and to ensure that the second woman kept quiet, Gatton threatened her. The woman was not permitted to offer evidence that Gatton had told her that if she talked about the rape, he would "take care of her" just like he had "taken care of " the deceased. To make his point, Gatton showed the other woman a knife and a gun while making his threats. Under Maryland evidence law, "[a] statement tending to expose the declarant to criminal liability and offered to exculpate the accused is not admissible unless corroborating circumstances clearly indicate the trustworthiness of the statement."[139] The appellate court found that there were sufficient corroborating circumstances to lend credence to Gatton's declaration against penal interest because the murder weapon was of the same caliber shown to the second woman and the deceased had been cut with a knife similar the one shown to the second woman. The court of appeals reversed the conviction on the ground that Gatton's statement to the second woman consti-

---

[138]   State v. Lewis, 2006 Tenn. Crim. App. LEXIS 237 (2006).
[139]   MD. R. EVID. 5-804(b)(3) (Matthew Bender 2006).

tuted a declaration against penal interest and the court should have allowed the second woman to testify on behalf of the defendant.[140]

Consistent with the Maryland practice, under the Federal Rules of Evidence the statement against interest exception includes statements that are against penal interest as well as those against pecuniary and proprietary interests.[141] In a federal prosecution, the defendant had been caught with a firearm under the seat of the car in which he was a passenger and suffered a federal conviction for being a felon in possession of a firearm.[142] One of the points of his appeal involved the fact that the trial court refused to allow his girlfriend to testify that a third-party friend of the defendant admitted to her that the gun belonged to the third party and that the third party admitted placing it under the car seat in which the defendant was riding at the time of his arrest. The appellate court noted that the declaration against interest (penal) was subject to two conditions. The first condition required that the person making the declaration be unavailable for testimony, a fact clearly present in this case because the third party asserted the Fifth Amendment privilege against self-incrimination at the trial. The second requirement for admission failed because the trial court did not find corroborating circumstances that could indicate the trustworthiness of the declaration against interest and the trustworthiness of the declarant. The girlfriend would like to see her boyfriend before he finished a prison term, so there was a motive for her to be less than honest. The third party had denied that he ever admitted to having the gun to his own parole officer. Under the circumstances, the reviewing court agreed with the trial court that the declaration against interest failed the tests of admissibility under the rules of evidence.[143]

When declarants make out-of-court confessions that could subject them to criminal prosecution and who are not defendants in a case, the confessions qualify as hearsay evidence and may be admitted as declarations against the interests of the people making the declarations. Such evidence may be admissible as an exception to the hearsay rule when the evidence meets the requirements of the declaration against interest.[144] The reason for admitting the confession as an exception to the hearsay rule is that a reasonable person in such a position would not have made the incriminating statement constituting a confession unless he believed it to be true, and if the confession is not true, the defendant is free to explain why he or she made a false confession. Confessions are made for a variety of reasons and may involve efforts to protect other people or by an attack of conscience and honesty, and for other unknown reasons.

In interpreting Federal Rule 804(b)(3), Statement against interest, the District of Columbia Court of Appeals observed that the Rule requires a three-

---

[140] *See* Gray v. State, 368 Md. 529, 796 A.2d 697, 2002 Md. LEXIS 159 (2002).
[141] FED. R. EVID. 804(b)(3).
[142] United States v. Johnson, 121 Fed. Appx. 912, 2005 U.S. App. LEXIS 2533 (2d Cir. 2005).
[143] *Id.*

step process to determine whether an admissible statement against penal inter-est has been made.[145] The court should consider whether the alleged declarant actually made a statement, determine whether the declarant actually is unavail-able for testimony, and evaluate whether there are corroborating circumstances that support the trustworthiness of the statement. Of course, the statement must have had the tendency to subject the declarant to some sort of criminal penalty and the declarant must have been aware of that fact. There must be some proof that the declarant understood that the statement was against his or her penal interest at the time it was made. Corroboration need not be as strong as having a second person overhear the declarant; it just must appear that under the circumstances, the statement meets a threshold of believability or plausibility sufficient to admit the statement.[146]

In a case in which the declarant had a motive to falsify a declaration against interest, the trial court properly refused to admit the hearsay statement. During a murder prosecution, the defendant attempted to have the court admit the declaration against penal interest made by his father for jury consideration. In addition to the usual considerations concerning admissibility, the court evaluated whether the out-of-court declaration of the father would have been influenced by any motive to falsify. The father's statement did not fully incrim-inate him, but it was designed to remove suspicion from his son. According to the court, there were inconsistencies in the father's statement that created a credibility question concerning the trustworthiness of his statement. In addi-tion, the father knew that police were looking for his son in connection with the killing, and the court expressed concern that the father's statement was not credible. The effort by the father to accept complete responsibility for attacks on three people half his age whom he did not know, and who were seriously wounded or killed, proved implausible to the court. After considering the appeal, the reviewing court upheld the convictions and agreed that the trial court was correct in refusing to admit the father's alleged declaration against penal interest.[147]

Before leaving the declaration against interest exception to the hearsay rule, a couple of caveats should be noted. First, the federal rule, as well as most state rules, requires corroboration of both the declarant's trustworthiness as well as the statement's trustworthiness. The party who seeks to introduce the unavailable witness's statement against penal interest has a duty to intro-duce sufficient proof that a rational juror could believe in its truth. In order to determine whether a declarant's statement is sufficiently trustworthy, a judge should focus on whether there are corroborating circumstances that clearly demonstrate the trustworthiness of the declarant's statement.[148] In other words,

---

[144] *See* Chapter 16 for a discussion of the constitutional issues concerning confessions and admissions. *See also* Kansas Annotated Statutes, K.S.A. § 60-460(j) Hearsay evidence excluded; exceptions. (2006).
[145] Ingram v. United States, 885 A.2d 257, 264, 2005 D.C. App. LEXIS 533 (2005).
[146] *Id.*
[147] *See* Stewart v. Maryland, 151 Md. App. 425, 827 A.2d 850, 2003 Md. App. LEXIS 75 (2003).
[148] United States v. Franklin, 415 F.3d 537, 547, 2005 U.S. App. LEXIS 14540 (5th Cir. 2005).

the proponent must demonstrate sufficient corroboration of the statement in context with other facts in the case in order for the declaration to be admissible.

Moreover, there is no declaration against penal interest if the declarant has not mentioned facts that, if true, would most assuredly implicate the declarant in crime. Early stage criminal planning or merely thinking about a crime is not a crime in itself. In a Michigan case, the court held that a declarant's statements implicating the defendant in a scheme to burn down the defendant's house were not against the declarant's penal interest as required for admission under the hearsay exception. Because the arson had not yet taken place and significant steps toward completion had not taken place, the statements only demonstrated an intent to commit a crime in the future.[149]

§ 12.11   —Other Exceptions—Residual Exceptions

Rule 807

Residual Exception

A statement not specifically covered by Rule 803 or 804 but having equivalent circumstantial guarantees of trustworthiness, is not excluded by the hearsay rule, if the court determines that (A) the statement is offered as evidence of a material fact; (B) the statement is more probative on the point for which it is offered than any other evidence which the proponent can procure through reasonable efforts; and (C) the general purposes of these rules and the interests of justice will best be served by admission of the statement into evidence. However, a statement may not be admitted under this exception unless the proponent of it makes known to the adverse party sufficiently in advance of the trial or hearing to provide the adverse party with a fair opportunity to prepare to meet it, the proponent's intention to offer the statement and the particulars of it, including the name and address of the declarant.[150]

While there are other specific exceptions, including those listed in Federal Rules 803 and 804, that cover the typical hearsay exceptions, Rule 807 regulates the admission into evidence of hearsay evidence that is not regulated by other rules governing hearsay. The rules have made it clear that merely because some of the exceptions are listed, such listing does not close the door to the use of other non-typical hearsay evidence as exceptions to the hearsay rule. It would be presumptuous to assume that all possible desirable exceptions to the hearsay rule have been catalogued or that accused individuals might never create any new situations in which there is reason to trust hearsay evidence will never arise. Therefore, Rule 807 specifically provides for other exceptions when certain conditions are met.[151]

---

[149]   People v. Brownridge, 225 Mich. App. 291, 570 N.W.2d 672 (1997).

[150]   FED. R. EVID. 807.

[151]   The provisions of former Rule 803 (24) and former Rule 804(b)(5) have effectively been transferred to Rule 807 effective December 1, 1997 and remain in the latest version of the federal rules.

The residual exceptions to the hearsay rule are limited by considerations of general relevancy and trustworthiness. Rules 807 provides that a hearsay statement will be admitted, even if not specifically covered by the other exceptions that are enumerated, if it has equivalent circumstances of trustworthiness when:

> The court determines that: (A) the statement is offered as evidence of a material fact; (B) the statement is more probative on the point for which it is offered than any other evidence that the proponent can procure through reasonable efforts; and (C) the general purposes of these rules and the interests of justice will best be served by admission of the statement into evidence."[152]

In order to admit a statement under Rule 807, one court noted that:

> [T]here must be a showing that (1) the statement has equivalent circumstantial guarantees of trustworthiness to the other hearsay exceptions; (2) the statement is offered as evidence of a material fact; (3) the statement is more probative on the point for which it is offered than any other evidence which the proponent can procure through reasonable efforts; (4) the general purposes of the rules and the interests of justice will best be served by its admission; and (5) adequate notice must be given to the opposing party.[153]

To summarize, admissibility under Rule 807 must overcome five hurdles, including trustworthiness, materiality, probative importance, the interests of justice, and timely notice to the opposing party. In fact, the Second Circuit noted that the residual exception of Rule 807 is to be used "very rarely, and only in exceptional circumstances."[154]

Interpreting the rule authorizing evidence to be admitted under these exceptions, one court agreed with the philosophy of the Second Circuit and stated that the residual exception to the hearsay rule is one of rare application and is not meant to be used as a catch-all for the admission of statements falling just outside the borders of recognized exceptions; rather, courts should undertake independent analysis to determine whether a particular case involves exceptional circumstances. Admission might also be appropriate when a court finds guarantees of trustworthiness equivalent to or exceeding guarantees reflected in present exceptions to the hearsay rule.[155]

In a case in which the defendant attempted to introduce hearsay evidence under Rule 807, the trial judge denied his efforts.[156] In the case, the defendant, who served in the military in Iraq, had been accused of selling military body

---

[152] FED. R. EVID. 807.
[153] United States v. Peneaux, 432 F.3d 882, 891, 2005 U.S. App. LEXIS 28877 (8th Cir. 2005).
[154] McGory v. City of New York, 2002 U.S. Dist. LEXIS 20177 (S.D.N.Y. 2002), quoting Parsons v. Honeywell, 929 F.2d 901, 907 (2d Cir. 1991).
[155] Shakespeare v. State, 827 P.2d 454 (Alaska 1992). *See also* State v. Huntington, 575 N.W.2d 268 (Wis. 1998).
[156] United States v. Avery, 2005 U.S. Dist. LEXIS 15979 (E.D. Pa. 2005).

armor on E-bay. Among other offenses, he had been charged with mail fraud and unauthorized sale of government property. During the investigation, a Defense Department employee interviewed the defendant in Iraq in the presence of two superior noncommissioned officers when the defendant, in response to a question, denied selling government body armor on E-bay. At the trial, the prosecution put one of the noncommissioned officers on the stand and he testified that he had been present when the defendant denied selling the armor. On cross-examination of the witness, when the witness admitted that he could not remember every detail of the meeting, the defense attorney sought to refresh the witness's memory by using a report of the meeting that had been prepared by the Defense Department employee. When the prosecution objected, the judge had the witness silently read the report to himself. The report contained the defendant's assertion that he purchased boots and body armor from a man in North Carolina. Defense counsel attempted to further cross-examine the witness with the Defense Department report in an effort to rebut the prosecutor's theory that the defendant had stolen the armor from the federal government. When the prosecutor complained that the report was hearsay evidence, the judge agreed and would not allow the statement to be used as evidence. The defendant's counsel sought to have the statement admitted under the residual exception covered by Rule 807. The trial court refused on the ground that to be admissible under Rule 807, a statement must meet five requirements: trustworthiness, materiality, probative importance, interests of justice and notice to the opposing party. According to the trial court,

> The trustworthiness of [the] statement is compromised, however, by the fact that his statement concerned events that took place, at the very at least, ten months earlier, and while he was deployed in Iraq. Moreover, [the declarant's] statement is contained in an interview report that he did not himself prepare, and there is no indication that the information he provided during the interview was made under oath and subject to the penalty of perjury.[157]

The court rejected the efforts of the defendant to have the statement-report admitted as an exception to the hearsay rule under Rule 807 because its trustworthiness could not be substantiated.

A Delaware reviewing court agreed with the lower court that a videotaped interview containing a statement by an absent declarant who had told the interviewee that the declarant, rather than the defendant, had shot the murder victim, was admissible under the residual exception to the hearsay rule because the statement was offered as evidence of a material fact.[158] The court explained that the statement made by the absent declarant offered evidence that the defendant had not killed the victim, the statement was more probative on that point than any other evidence procurable by the defendant because the declar-

---

[157]　*Id.*
[158]　Denby v. State, 695 A.2d 1152 (Del. 1997).

ant and interviewee had both invoked the Fifth Amendment privilege, and the purposes of the Delaware Rules of Evidence and interests of justice would be served by admission of the statements. In addition, the admission in favor of the defendant did not have a chance to violate the defendant's Sixth Amendment right to confront and cross-examine because the defendant was the proponent of the evidence.

In a case decided before the present Rule 807 became effective, the United States Supreme Court in *Idaho v. Wright* considered the application of the residual exception to the hearsay rule as it then existed. The rationale offered by the Court should be considered applicable to cases arising under Rule 807 because Rule 807 was designed as a replacement for the earlier provisions in the Federal Rules of Evidence. An Idaho trial court convicted defendant Wright under state law for two counts of lewd conduct with a minor.[159] The trial court admitted under Idaho's residual hearsay exception, which is similar to the federal provision, certain statements that the child made to a pediatrician. Prior to reaching the United States Supreme Court, the state supreme court reversed, finding that the admission of the doctor's testimony under the residual hearsay exception violated the defendant's rights under the confrontation clause. The state asked for a writ of certiorari.

The United States Supreme Court first found that Idaho's residual hearsay exception is not a firmly rooted hearsay exception for confrontation clause purposes. The Court continued by saying that the hearsay exception accommodates ad hoc instances in which statements not otherwise falling within a recognized hearsay exception might be sufficiently reliable to be admissible at trial, and thus does not share the same provision of reliability supporting the admissibility of statements under a firmly rooted hearsay exception. The *Wright* Court advised that to rule otherwise would require that virtually all codified hearsay exceptions be found to assume constitutional stature, something that the Supreme Court has declined to do.

In the *Wright* case, the United States Supreme Court held that the admission of the child's hearsay statements violated the defendant's Sixth Amendment right of confrontation. The Court agreed with the state supreme court that the child's statements did not fall within a traditional hearsay exception, and lacked "particularized guarantees of trustworthiness" because the doctor had conducted the interview without procedural safeguards—he failed to videotape the interview, asked leading questions, and had a preconceived idea of what the child should be disclosing.

In a recent case, *Crawford v. Washington*,[160] the Supreme Court of the United States dealt a harsh blow at prosecution efforts to successfully get evidence admitted under Rule 807 and related state evidence rules. In the *Crawford* case, a trial court convicted the defendant of assault of a man who had tried to rape the defendant's wife. At trial, the court permitted his wife's recorded out-of-court statement given to police to be admitted against him.

---

[159]   Idaho v. Wright, 497 U.S. 805, 110 S. Ct. 3139, 111 L. Ed. 2d 638 (1990).
[160]   Crawford v. Washington, 541 U.S. 36, 52, 2004 U.S. LEXIS 1838 (2004).

The defendant's wife did not testify at trial after defendant invoked his state marital privilege to prevent her testimony, but the prosecution used her out-of-court recorded statements as substantive evidence against him. Because his wife did not testify, he was effectively prevented from confronting and cross-examining her. The Supreme Court reversed the assault conviction with the view that allowing the wife's statement against him that contained testimonial evidence, the trial court prevented the defendant's exercise of his Sixth Amendment right to confront and cross-examine an adverse witness. Only in exceptional situations will testimonial evidence be admitted when confrontation and cross-examination are impossible. In the *Crawford* case, the court noted that statements taken by police during investigations are generally considered testimonial in nature and can be excluded on Sixth Amendment grounds.[161]

Even before the *Crawford* case, courts hesitated to admit evidence under the residual exception unless all of the conditions were met. For example, in a North Dakota federal district court, prosecutors filed a motion pursuant to Rule 807, the residual hearsay rule, to admit the grand jury testimony of the deceased victim into evidence at trial, and to admit her diary and notes obtained by investigators who also interviewed her. The prosecutor contended that the diary and other materials should also be admitted under Rule 807 because the victim had given earlier testimony under oath and some evidence had been corroborated by the police investigation. The evidence was material and the court noted that the prosecution had complied with the notice to the other party as required under Rule 807. In rejecting the evidence, the trial court noted that the elderly woman declarant had some memory problems, that there was no way to conduct cross-examination of a dead witness, the jury could not draw conclusions about her credibility, and the judge noted that there had been no effort to preserve the testimony of the deceased by taking her deposition. For all these reasons, the trial court refused to allow the prosecution to use the evidence against the defendant.[162]

In a federal case that involved the admission of evidence under Rule 807, the defendant had been charged and convicted of kidnapping resulting in death based upon the disappearance of his ex-wife.[163] He filed a motion for a new trial based partly on the fact that the jury had seen and considered some evidence that the judge had not formally admitted into evidence and the defendant argued that it could not have been admitted even under the residual exception of Rule 807. The evidence that is contested by the defendant consisted of two day planner books that belonged to the defendant's ex-wife in which she penned some of her thoughts as an unhappy wife prior to the divorce. According to the trial court, the day planners were intentionally supplied to the jury by the government. The inadmissible evidence included notes within the day planners in which the deceased ex-wife mentioned harassing or threatening telephone calls by the defendant, referred to a protective order that

---

[161] *Id.*

[162] *See* United States v. Noorlun, 2002 U.S. Dist. LEXIS 11862 (D.N.D. 2002).

[163] United States v. Lentz, 2004 U.S. Dist. LEXIS 29650 (E.D. Va. 2004).

she had sought at an earlier time, and included her cryptic notations about conversations she had with the defendant's daughter. The day planners also contained telephone numbers for a police detective who worked with protective orders and the number for a domestic violence support group. The trial judge found that the evidence contained in the day planners was virtually all hearsay and some of it had multiple layers of hearsay to which the defendant could obtain no cross-examination even if they had been admitted by the judge. There were also "moving and powerful" notes in the planners in the decedent's own handwriting. As the judge noted, "[t]his evidence, although compelling, bears no indicia of reliability because these statements do not fall within any of the twenty-three recognized exceptions to the hearsay rule, nor do they indicate any particularized guarantees of trustworthiness."[164] According to the judge's reasoning, the fact that the jury saw and evaluated unadmitted hearsay evidence constituted a violation of the defendant's right to confrontation. In resolving whether the evidence could have been admitted, the judge considered that the decedent was unavailable, that there were no circumstantial guarantees of trustworthiness, that the evidence might relate to a material fact, whether the evidence was probative, whether admission would serve justice, and whether the opposing side had received notice. The court evaluated and rejected the government's contention that the day planner evidence could be admitted under the residual exception of Rule 807 and reversed the conviction.

In a different situation, a trial judge allowed evidence under the residual exception of Rule 807 when one minor was accused of the aggravated sexual battery of another minor.[165] At a bench trial, the judged adjudicated the alleged juvenile aggressor, a minor, as a juvenile delinquent. The evidence against the defendant consisted of some testimony from the minor victim and evidence presented by a forensic examiner who had questioned the victim. The forensic examiner followed proper interrogation protocols in interviewing the minor victim. As is required under Rule 807, the government gave the defendant notice that the forensic examiner would be called as a prosecution witness. Over the defendant's objection, the forensic questioner answered some foundational questions and explained the techniques used in talking to the juvenile victim. Over the juvenile defendant's objections on Rule 807 and Sixth Amendment confrontation grounds, the court allowed the forensic examiner to tell the court what the girl-victim told the forensic examiner concerning when the events occurred and how the defendant's and the victim's private areas had been joined together, among other relevant facts. Specifically, the court considered that the forensic examiner's evidence was material to the case, and, because the victim's testimony was unclear on some matters in court that she had freely mentioned out of court, the forensic examiner's testimony was the most probative available. The court found the examiner's testimony trustworthy when considered with other evidence in the case and proper notice had been given to the defendant. Admitting the evidence under the residual excep-

---

[164]   *Id.*
[165]   United States v. W.B., 452 F.3d 1002, 2006 U.S. App. LEXIS 17378 (8th Cir. 2006).

tion to the hearsay rule appeared to serve the interests of justice, so the court affirmed the juvenile adjudication.

If the reasons for excluding hearsay evidence are not strong and the interests of justice would best be served by admission of a hearsay statement into evidence, the proponent must assert logical rationales that support admitting the evidence under the residual exception theory to the hearsay rule. Admitting evidence under the residual exception rule had a chance of court approval where there are special cases involving unique circumstances.

§ 12.12 Nontestimonial Utterances

The previous sections discussed the hearsay rule and demonstrated some of the well-known exceptions that allow admission of evidence in contravention of the general rule. Courts recognize the legal principle that states that if an out-of-court statement is offered to show what was said, rather than for the truth of the matter stated, the out-of-court statements are not considered hearsay.[166] Demonstrative of this principle is a situation in which an officer believed that stolen property had been hidden in a wooded area, but he was not certain. When he asked the defendant's son where the stolen goods were located, the son pointed to the woods behind a motel, but did not speak. The trial court allowed the officer to testify concerning the one-sided conversation he had with the defendant's son over the defense objection that the evidence constituted inadmissible hearsay. The boy's gesture, or verbal act, conveyed information but the gesture was not used to prove the truth of the matters visually asserted by the boy. His gesture was admitted to show why the officer walked into the wooded area where he found the stolen goods. The court of appeals held that the testimony of the officer explaining the boy's gesture, did not qualify as hearsay because it was not offered for its truth.[167]

A Virginia court advised that whether an out-of-court statement or act constituted hearsay depended on the purpose for which the statement was offered at trial; a statement that was offered for proof of its truth qualified as hearsay, but a statement or act that has been offered to the purpose of explaining or throwing light on the conduct of an individual to whom the statement was directed is not considered hearsay.[168] Where a witness testified that she called police after observing a larcenist leaving her store and mentioned that the reason the man piqued her interest was because another store employee gave her a detailed description of the repeat larcenist. The statement describing the appearance of the repeat larcenist was not offered for proof of its truth; it was offered only to explain why the witness scrutinized the behavior of the particularly described customer.[169] However, "a nod of the head in response to

---

[166] Cormier v. State, 955 S.W.2d 161 (Tex. 1997).
[167] Saunders v. Commonwealth, 2003 Va. App. LEXIS 394 (2003).
[168] Farrar v. Commonwealth, 2006 Va. App. LEXIS 301 (2006).
[169] Id.

a question calling for a "yes" or "no" answer, or a gesture pointing to a particular person when asked to identify a perpetrator, are examples of assertive conduct"[170] that qualifies as hearsay evidence.

A Florida trial court committed reversible error resulting in the wrongful conviction of a defendant for grand theft of a motor vehicle. The defendant's position was that another person told the defendant that the other person was the owner of the van and that the defendant had permission to drive it. If this were true, the defendant's necessary state of mind for larceny would have been lacking. The testimony was not hearsay and should not have been excluded because the defendant did not offer it for the truth of the matter asserted within the statement. The defendant's purpose in offering the evidence was to show that because he heard the statement by the alleged owner, the defendant possessed a good faith belief that the other person owned the van, and that he had lawful permission to drive it.[171]

The hearsay rule does not apply when the proffered evidence has not been offered for its truth. In one case, a defendant contended on appeal that his counsel failed to object to inadmissible hearsay offered by the prosecution. A police officer testified that he asked the defendant for permission to search his apartment and the officer stated that the defendant answered in the affirmative. The defendant's statement could be called a verbal act "because the statement [was] admitted merely to show that it was actually made, not to prove the truth of what was asserted it."[172] The trial court held, and the appellate court agreed, that no hearsay evidence had been permitted in that context because the officer was not offering the defendant's positive answer for its truth, only to indicate that the defendant had made the statement that indicated the officer believed that he had the legal authority to make a lawful entry and search of the apartment.[173]

Under what is sometimes referred to as the verbal act doctrine, a statement that accompanies conduct is admissible because it gives legal significance to the act. The Florida Supreme Court explained a verbal act as:

> an utterance of an operative fact that gives rise to legal consequences. Verbal acts, also known as statements of legal consequence, are not hearsay, because the statement is admitted merely to show that it was actually made, not to prove the truth of what was asserted in it.[174]

The Florida court noted that in order for verbal acts to be admissible, the conduct that is explained by the words must be independently material or important to the issue at hand, the conduct that occurs must be equivocal, and

---

[170] People v. Jurado, 38 Cal. 4th 72, 129, 131 P.3d 400, 438, 41 Cal. Rptr. 3d 319, 365, 2006 Cal. LEXIS 4391 (2006).

[171] Alfaro v. Florida, 837 So. 2d 429, 2002 Fla. App. LEXIS 13992 (2002).

[172] 5-801 WEINSTEIN'S FEDERAL EVIDENCE § 801.11[3] Verbal Acts (Matthew Bender 2006).

[173] Dragani v. Bryant, 2005 U.S. Dist. LEXIS 38057, n. 7 (M.D. Fla. 2005).

[174] Banks v. Florida, 790 So. 2d 1094, 2001 Fla. LEXIS 1411 (2001).

the words uttered must assist in giving legal context or significance to the conduct, and the words must be spoken with the conduct.[175] Where the evidence is offered only to show that words were spoken and not for proof of the truth of what was said, the evidence is not hearsay. For example, in a case in which a trial court convicted the defendant of the sale and delivery of cannabis and possession of cannabis, the case depended upon the testimony of a confidential informant.[176] The trial court refused to allow a separate witness to offer the defendant's response to a question from the confidential informant. One of the witnesses who had been present at the crime scene was prepared to tell the court that when the defendant had been asked to sell marijuana by the prosecution's confidential informant, the defendant told her, "I don't do that kind of stuff."[177] The trial court rejected allowing the witness to tell what the defendant answered to the confidential informant on the ground that it was hearsay. The appellate court held that the trial court should have allowed the witness to state what the defendant had said in response to an offer to commit a crime from the confidential informant. The statement was a verbal act of the defendant that was not hearsay and it should have been admitted just to show that he made the statement. The fact that the defendant would refuse an offer to commit drug selling is material for his defense that he was not involved in the drug sale that occurred within the home. In a different case, a "waitress" at a bar/club came over to where an undercover officer was sitting and rubbed her buttocks on his lap as an invitation to a free lap dance and said that the fun did not have to end there, that there was a private room. The undercover officer paid $50 to the proprietor and the "waitress" said the $50 would pay for oral sex but that a tip would be nice. The appellate court held that the words of the "waitress" were verbal acts because the statements were made merely to demonstrate that the operative words were uttered and not to prove their substantive truth. In this case, the words explain why the undercover officer wanted to go to the private room. The nonverbal conduct of the "waitress" was equivocal, the words spoken were important to understanding the situation, and the words accompanied her conduct and were admissible under the verbal act doctrine.[178]

§ 12.13   Summary

The general rule is that once evidence is identified as hearsay it should not be admissible in court because of the concern that hearsay evidence may not be reliable or truthful and may not have been given under oath. Hearsay evidence is defined as oral testimony or written evidence presented in court from a statement uttered or written out of court, when the statement is offered in

---

[175] *Id.*

[176] Burkey v. State, 922 So. 2d 1033, 1035, 2006 Fla. App. LEXIS 2772 (2006).

[177] *Id.*

[178] Pronesti v. Florida, 847 So. 2d 1165, 1166, 2003 Fla. App. LEXIS 9472 (2003).

court to prove the truth of matters asserted therein. Thus, evidence that relies on the credibility of the out-of-court declarant will be classified as hearsay and excluded. Although this general rule is universally applied and based on sound reasoning, there are many exceptions. If evidence meets the requirements of a recognized exception or the residual exception, it may be admissible, even though it is classified as hearsay.

Examples of exceptions to the hearsay rule include spontaneous and excited utterances, some business and public records, family history and records, former testimony, dying declarations, declarations against interest, and exceptions under the residual exception rule. Under each of the traditional hearsay exceptions evidence may be admitted for substantive proof; however, it must meet the specific requirements that have been established for the particular exception because these requirements help assure trustworthiness.

The Sixth Amendment to the U.S. Constitution guarantees defendants the right to confront and cross-examine the witnesses against them. When out-of-court hearsay statements are admitted as evidence in court, the defendant may not have the opportunity to cross-examine or even confront the adverse declarant whose evidence is introduced by the one who overheard the declarant speak. Since the Supreme Court recently held that testimonial evidence normally requires that actual confrontation and cross-examination must be permitted, some hearsay exceptions have come under more intense scrutiny by trial courts.[179] While preserving of the rights of confrontation for defendants, the interests of justice require that a balance exist between the rights of defendants and the necessities of justice and fairness for society.

The hearsay rule does not exclude evidence when the out-of-court statements are offered solely as evidence that a statement was made, and not for the substantive content of the statement. Witnesses to out-of-court statements who repeat them in court, not for the substantive truth of the statement, but to indicate the person's physical or mental condition, will be permitted to offer evidence.

From the foregoing discussion, it is clear that although some hearsay evidence is not admissible in court, there are many exceptions to the hearsay rule. The exceptions to the rule may result in most evidence classified as hearsay being admitted and very little evidence being excluded, but where courts admit hearsay evidence, the requirements of the exceptions assure truthfulness. In order to offer the greatest level of admissible evidence to the prosecutor, good practice dictates that criminal justice personnel be familiar not only with the rules that exclude hearsay evidence, but also with the hearsay exceptions and their individual requirements, which permit the admission of hearsay evidence in court.

---

[179] *See* Crawford v. Washington, 541 U.S. 36, 2004 U.S. LEXIS 1838 (2004).

Evidence via Documents
and Real Evidence

Documentary Evidence   13

Before any writing will be admitted in evidence, it must be authenticated in some manner, i.e., its genuineness or execution must be proved. Even a competent public record or document must be properly identified, verified or authenticated by some recognized method before it may be introduced in evidence.

City of Randleman v. Hinshaw,
2 N.C. App. 381, 163 S.E.2d 95 (1968)

Chapter Outline

Key Terms and Concepts	
authentication	secondary evidence
best evidence rule	self-authentication

---

§ 13.1 Introduction

Trial evidence consists of three categories: (1) oral testimony offered from the witness stand, (2) documentary evidence introduced by witnesses, and (3) real evidence, which is offered by witnesses who make its introduction possible. While the discussion in previous chapters related primarily to oral evidence, this chapter focuses on the broad category of documentary evidence. This type of evidence encompasses evidence beyond what the term "documentary evidence" would normally bring to mind. Documentary evidence includes evidence furnished by written instruments, inscriptions, and documents of all kinds. The term is broad enough to encompass every form of writing and applies to both public and private documents. Under the Federal Rules of Evidence, a writing or recording has been defined as including "letters, words, or numbers, or their equivalent, set down by handwriting, typewriting, printing, photostating, photographing, magnetic impulse, mechanical or electronic recording, or other form of data compilation."[1] Originally, a document provided a way of storing information in a fairly permanent manner, but that concept has grown to include movies, phonograph records, video- and audiotapes, computers and their mass storage devices, and photographs. Because the general rules of admissibility apply to all types of evidence, documentary evidence must meet these usual requirements. In addition, there are certain rules that apply uniquely to documentary evidence. These rules are discussed in this chapter. In Chapter 14 the rules relating to the introduction of real evidence will be discussed and explained.

A document has a rather expansive definition that includes many things that are not ordinarily considered to be documents. A document may be defined as any message that has been expressed, described, inscribed, embed-

---

[1]   FED. R. EVID. 1001(1).

ded, saved, or recorded in or upon any substance by means of letters, figures, or marks, and intended to be used for the purpose of recording that matter. Examples of private documents are photographs, computer data, videotape data, films, deeds, wills, agreements, and personal and commercial contracts. Birth records, death records, marriage records, registrations of various kinds, some police records, and licensing records are examples of public documents.

To be admitted into evidence, documentary evidence must meet the same rules of evidence as oral testimony concerning relevancy, competency, and materiality. In addition, the party that introduces a document must lay a foundation for the introduction of the documentary evidence to demonstrate that it is genuine and that it is what it purports to be. The proponent must bring sufficient evidence to authenticate, verify, or identify the document offered. Meeting the requirements for authentication and the best evidence rule are two tests that relate primarily to documentary evidence. The following sections of this chapter address the general rules relating to these tests and their requirements, and demonstrate the principles by offering some specific examples.

§ 13.2 Authentication

Rule 901

Requirement of Authentication or Identification

(a) General provision

The requirement of authentication or identification as a condition precedent to admissibility is satisfied by evidence sufficient to support a finding that the matter in question is what its proponent claims.

(b) Illustrations

By way of illustration only, and not by way of limitation, the following are examples of authentication or identification conforming with the requirements of this rule:

(1) Testimony of witness with knowledge

Testimony that a matter is what it is claimed to be.

(2) Nonexpert opinion on handwriting

Nonexpert opinion as to the genuineness of handwriting, based upon familiarity not acquired for purposes of the litigation.

(3) Comparison by trier or expert witness

Comparison by the trier of fact or by expert witnesses with specimens which have been authenticated.

(4) Distinctive characteristics and the like

Appearance, contents, substance, internal patterns, or other distinctive characteristics, taken in conjunction with circumstances.

(5) Voice identification

Identification of a voice, whether heard firsthand or through mechanical or electronic transmission or recording, by opinion based upon hearing the voice at any time under circumstances connecting it with the alleged speaker.

(6) Telephone conversations

Telephone conversations, by evidence that a call was made to the number assigned at the time by the telephone company to a particular person or business, if (A) in the case of a person, circumstances, including self-identification, show the person answering to be the one called, or (B) in the case of a business, the call was made to a place of business and the conversation related to business reasonably transacted over the telephone.

(7) Public records or reports

Evidence that a writing authorized by law to be recorded or filed and in fact recorded or filed in a public office, or a purported public record, report, statement, or data compilation, in any form, is from the public office where items of this nature are kept.

(8) Ancient documents or data compilation

Evidence that a document or data compilation, in any form, (A) is in such condition as to create no suspicion concerning its authenticity, (B) was in a place where it, if authentic, would likely be, and (C) has been in existence 20 years or more at the time it is offered.

(9) Process or system

Evidence describing a process or system used to produce a result and showing that the process or system produces an accurate result.

(10) Methods provided by statute or rule

Any method of authentication or identification provided by Act of Congress or by other rules prescribed by the Supreme Court pursuant to statutory authority.[2]

Evidence in the form of a writing that has not been proven to have a connection to the case cannot fairly assist either side in meeting a burden of proof or refuting any fact in issue. Therefore, under a fundamental rule of evidence, no document or other writing may be admitted into evidence without some proof of authenticity or proof that it is what the proponent says that it is. As one early writer stated, "A writing, of itself, is evidence of nothing, and therefore is not, unless accompanied by proof of some sort, admissible in evidence."[3] Another court later noted that "authentication under Rule 901 requires the presentation of sufficient evidence to make out a prima facie case the proffered evidence is what it purports to be, and once a prima facie showing has been made, the evidence should be admitted and the trier of fact permitted to determine whether the proffered evidence is what it purports to be."[4] The requirement of authentication does not demand that the proponent of a document conclusively prove that the document or article is genuine, but only that the document or article has enough evidence presented by the proponent that supports the finding that the item is what its proponent claims it to be.[5]

---

[2] FED. R. EVID. 901.

[3] Stamper v. Griffin, 20 Ga. 312 (1856).

[4] United States v. Duncan, 166 Fed. Appx. 464; 2006 U.S. App. LEXIS 3266 (11th Cir. 2006). Bruther v. General Elec. Co., 818 F. Supp. 1238 (S.D. Ind. 1993).

[5] State v. Anglemyer, 269 Neb. 237, 243, 691 N.W.2d 153, 160, 2005 Neb. LEXIS 35 (2005).

According to the rationale behind this rule, absent a showing that the evidence is what the proponent alleges, it has no logical or legal relevance. The required proof may be contained within the document itself, in that the document may become, by authority of statute or otherwise, "self-authenticating." Otherwise, outside proof is required to lay a foundation for admission of the documentary evidence. Authentication merely means that there must be preliminary proof of genuineness, authenticity, or identity of the document sufficient to prove that the evidence is what its proponent purports the evidence to be.

Because authentication is a preliminary requirement designed to ensure that a piece of evidence is what it purports to be, a proponent need only introduce evidence that would allow a reasonable juror to conclude that the document or article is the genuine item and that it is what it appears to be.[6] Another way of phrasing the requirement of authentication is to have the proponent "present foundational evidence that is sufficient to constitute a rational basis for a jury to decide that the primary evidence is what its proponent claims it to be."[7] While authentication is necessary for admission of documentary evidence, the proponent may use a variety of evidence to demonstrate its genuine quality, including direct or circumstantial evidence.[8] For example, in an arranged drug purchase, police gave their confidential operative marked money and a hidden cassette recorder prior to the informant making a drug purchase. The informant was outside of the view of the officer at some times, but returned with the recording of the transaction and the purchased drugs. The confidential informant testified under oath that the tape-recording was a genuine and accurate recording of the drug transaction and the officer testified that the recorder had been in the police vault since it was originally returned. The reviewing court upheld the admission of the sound recording because it has been properly authenticated as a writing under the state's version of Rule 901 by the officer and the informant.[9]

Depending on the character of the document that a proponent seeks to have introduced into evidence, the requirements vary concerning authentication. The proponent of documentary evidence usually offers sworn testimony by a witness concerning the source and genuineness of the writing. Having the witness identify the writing and swear to its authenticity while under oath will typically suffice to authenticate a writing. In some instances, however, such specific testimony is not required. For example, a trial court accepted a copy of a different court's record of a defendant's prior convictions when the document had the authentication seal of the court affixed to the documents and the signatory of the authentication notation certified that each document was a true copy of the ones in the official records. The appellate court held that the documents were properly authenticated.[10] In one case, a trial court accepted a

---

6　　Washington v. Payne, 117 Wash. App. 99, 107, 69 P.3d 889, 2003 Wash. App. LEXIS 1061 (2003).

7　　Ohio v. Payton, 2002 Ohio App. LEXIS 496 (2002).

8　　State v. Carpenter, 275 Conn. 785, 856, 882 A.2d 604, 648, 2005 Conn. LEXIS 396 (2005).

9　　Wilkerson v. State, 2005 Ark. App. LEXIS 12 (Ark. 2005). *See* case in Part II.

10　　Conley v. Commonwealth, 2005 Va. App. LEXIS 516 (2005).

copy of a driving record as self-authenticating where the record came from the state's division of motor vehicles along with a notarized certificate of authenticity.[11] Also, in some cases, the formal authenticity requirement may be become unnecessary with the use of a stipulation between the parties if they agree to the genuineness of the writing.

In an effort to promote judicial economy, statutes have been designed to do away with the formal authentication requirements when such requirements obviously serve little purpose. Even when such statutes are in effect, the opposing party is not foreclosed from disputing authenticity by introducing evidence that the documents fail to meet the requirements or are not authentic. Rule 901(b) of the Federal Rules of Evidence lists ten examples of authentication or identification that conform to the rule. Some of these deal with real evidence, which is discussed in the next chapter, while some refer to documentary or oral evidence.

In authenticating written documents under Rule 901(b)(2), state courts have universally agreed that a nonexpert witness may properly identify a signature or handwriting if the witness is sufficiently familiar with the writing of another person so that the testimony would aid the jury. The witness may become familiar with a person's handwriting by observing him or her write on previous occasions, whether the observations were made from a social setting, interactions at work, or through personal correspondence. However, knowledge of another person's writing may be acquired by any means, as long as it is not obtained especially for the trial.[12] Courts have not set a minimum number of occasions or encounters with examples for familiarity to be sufficient for authentication purposes. However, evidence must be introduced to show that the witness possessed sufficient familiarity with the handwriting. In one case, a trial court permitted an employer to authenticate a fraudulent document alleged to have been signed by a dishonest salesman-employee. The prosecution demonstrated that the employer had observed the employee's handwriting on many occasions over a nine-month period prior to the prosecution. The reviewing court found that the employer had sufficient familiarity with the signature to authenticate a signature on a document as belonging to the allegedly dishonest employee.[13] In a Texas case, the trial court permitted the victim of a beating and stabbing to testify that a copy of the defendant's indictment had been sent to her with handwriting placed on the face of the indictment requesting that she not cooperate with the government's prosecution of defendant. The victim had dated the defendant for about 18 months, and based on that relationship she was able to recognize his handwriting on the face of the indictment copy and authenticate the document as having been written by the defendant.[14]

---

[11] United States v. Mirelez, 59 Fed. Appx. 286, 2003 U.S. App. LEXIS 2162 (10th Cir. 2003).

[12] *See* FED. R. EVID. 901(b)(2).

[13] Bell v. State, 910 So. 2d 640, 644, 2005 Miss. App. LEXIS 159 (2005).

[14] Montgomery v. Texas, 2002 Tex. App. LEXIS 5444 (2002).

A nonexpert witness may be cross-examined in order to aid the jury in deciding how much weight to give his or her testimony, and his or her ability to identify the questioned handwriting or signature may be tested by asking him or her to identify a genuine specimen among false copies.

Rule 901(b)(7) provides that the requirement of authentication of a public record or report, as a condition precedent to admissibility, is satisfied if evidence is introduced to show that the writing was authorized by law to be recorded or filed in a public office. Under this section, the proponent of the evidence need only demonstrate that the office from which the party obtained the records served as the legal custodian of the records or served as the official repository. The public records need not be in any particular form in order to be deemed authentic, and minor irregularities in appearance should not preclude admittance if the record is authentic.

Due to the fact that people who could authenticate older documents may be deceased or have memory problems, the rules have been relaxed concerning the authentication of ancient documents. Rule 901(b)(8) of the Federal Rules of Evidence liberalizes the common law "ancient document" rule. It provides that a document may be admitted when requirements pertaining to age, nonsuspicious condition, and appropriate custody are satisfied. Under this rule, a document must be demonstrated to be at least 20 years old before it may be authenticated as an ancient document. Many states that have adopted a state variation of the Federal Rules have used the same requirements for ancient document authentication, including the 20-year period necessary to qualify as an ancient document.[15]

In interpreting the "ancient document" authentication rule, a trial court in Hawai'i properly permitted a lease for land that had been executed in 1872 to be admitted in a trial court in a dispute over title to land on Maui. The opponent contended that the internal language of the document failed to mention a particular parcel of land and that the ancient document dealing with the disputed land was not relevant. The Intermediate Court of Appeals of Hawai'i disagreed and held that under the ancient document rules of Rule 901, the document had been properly authenticated.[16] Most assuredly, no one who was a party to the original lease was alive to help otherwise authenticate the document.

Although the rule requires that documents admitted as ancient documents come from proper custody and be free of suspicion,[17] that suspicion does not go to the content of the documents, but rather to whether the document is genuine.[18] Questions as to the document's content and completeness bear on the weight to be accorded the evidence and do not affect the threshold question of authenticity.

Rule 901(b)(9) provides that evidence describing a process or system used to produce a result and showing that the process or system produced an accurate result satisfies the authentication requirement. Examples of evidence that

---

[15]   *See*, for example, Wis. Stat. § 909.015 (2006).
[16]   Makila Land Co. v. Kapu, 2006 Haw. App. LEXIS 181 (2006).
[17]   29A AM. JUR. 2d *Evidence* § 1204 (2006).
[18]   Threadgill v. Armstrong World Industries, Inc., 928 F.2d 1366 (3d Cir. 1991).

has been held admissible under this subsection are X-rays, computer output, electrocardiograms, surveys and polls, and statistical samples. Typically evidence produced by a process or system is presented to the jury or the judge by means of expert testimony, and usually the witness who conveys the substance of the evidence also lays the necessary foundation.

When computer records and evidence were rare and were not usually introduced as evidence, courts were reluctant to apply this exception to computer printouts.[19] As the business use of computers has become necessary and commercial transactions are virtually always recorded in computer databases, courts have been forced to determine when and under what circumstances computer-generated data should be authenticated. Federal Rule of Evidence 901(B)(9) offers an example of authentication identification conforming to the requirements of this rule. This section states that evidence describing a process or system used to produce a result and showing that the process or system produces an accurate result conforms to the authentication requirements of the rule.

More recently, courts have admitted computer printouts in accordance with this provision. In a federal prosecution involving the illegal sale of firearms by a federal licensee, the federal government wanted to introduce evidence that the defendant had often neglected to contact the Bureau of Alcohol, Tobacco, and Firearms for instant background checks of purchasers and created bogus approval numbers. The trial court permitted the prosecutor to introduce the printouts of computerized records reflecting the actual approval numbers issued by the government agency to the defendant in order to show the numeral discrepancies. The Court of Appeals approved the authentication of the computer printout because it was produced on a regular monthly basis by the government and the printout came from the office where the data was expected to be generated and to be stored.[20] In a different case, in which an automatic teller machine technician had been accused of removing money from the machine, electronically and automatically generated evidence stored on a computer was admitted against him. The trial court rejected his lack of authentication argument. The trial court admitted the computer-generated records as having met the minimum standards for authentication, especially because the records were based on automatic data inputs and were not dependant on human interaction. The appellate court noted that computer business records have a level of trustworthiness that the individually prepared records lack.[21]

Recognizing that evidence generated or gathered by means of a process or system is often highly technical and complex in nature, some courts appear to require a higher level of authentication for computer-generated records when they are offered for admission into evidence. In a bankruptcy case, the judge refuse to allow a creditor to introduce computer-generated records as not properly authenticated. The records custodian gave vague and conclusory testi-

---

[19]　United States v. Fendley, 522 F.2d 181 (5th Cir. 1975).
[20]　United States v. Meienberg, 263 F.3d 1177, 2001 U.S. App. LEXIS 19177 (10th Cir. 2001).
[21]　State v. Huehn, 53 P.3d 733, 737, 2002 Colo. App. LEXIS 21 (2002). *See* case in Part II.

mony concerning how the computer system operated and mainly offered assertions rather than proof for authentication. There was no testimony concerning how errors were eliminated from the system and the witness did not know the brand name of the mainframe computer. On appellate review, the court held that there was no abuse of discretion in refusing to admit the party's monthly billing statements.[22]

§ 13.3   Self-Authentication

Rule 902

Self-Authentication

Extrinsic evidence of authenticity as a condition precedent to admissibility is not required with respect to the following:

(1) Domestic public documents under seal. A document bearing a seal purporting to be that of the United States, or of any State, district, Commonwealth, territory, or insular possession thereof, or the Panama Canal Zone, or the Trust Territory of the Pacific Islands, or of a political subdivision, department, officer, or agency thereof, and a signature purporting to be an attestation or execution.

(2) Domestic public documents not under seal. A document purporting to bear the signature in the official capacity of an officer or employee of any entity included in paragraph (1) hereof, having no seal, if a public officer having a seal and having official duties in the district or political subdivision of the officer or employee certifies under seal that the signer has the official capacity and that the signature is genuine.

(3) Foreign public documents. A document purporting to be executed or attested in an official capacity by a person authorized by the laws of a foreign country to make the execution or attestation, and accompanied by a final certification as to the genuineness of the signature and official position (A) of the executing or attesting person, or (B) of any foreign official whose certificate of genuineness of signature and official position relates to the execution or attestation or is in a chain of certificates of genuineness of signature and official position relating to the execution or attestation. A final certification may be made by a secretary of an embassy or legation, consul general, consul, vice consul, or consular agent of the United States, or a diplomatic or consular official of the foreign country assigned or accredited to the United States. If reasonable opportunity has been given to all parties to investigate the authenticity and accuracy of official documents, the court may, for good cause shown, order that they be treated as presumptively authentic without final certification or permit them to be evidenced by an attested summary with or without final certification.

(4) Certified copies of public records. A copy of an official record or report or entry therein, or of a document authorized by law to be recorded or filed and actually recorded or filed in a public office, including data compi-

---

[22]   *See* In re Vinhnee v. American Express, 336 B.R. 437, 2005 Bankr. LEXIS 2602 (9th Cir. 2005).

lations in any form, certified as correct by the custodian or other person authorized to make the certification, by certificate complying with paragraph (1), (2), or (3) of this rule, or complying with any Act of Congress or rule prescribed by the Supreme Court pursuant to statutory authority.

(5) Official publications. Books, pamphlets, or other publications purporting to be issued by public authority.

(6) Newspapers and periodicals. Printed materials purporting to be newspapers or periodicals.

(7) Trade inscriptions and the like. Inscriptions, signs, tags, or labels purporting to have been affixed in the course of business and indicating ownership, control, or origin.

(8) Acknowledged documents. Documents accompanied by a certificate of acknowledgment executed in the manner provided by law by a notary public or other officer authorized by law to take acknowledgments.

(9) Commercial paper and related documents. Commercial paper, signatures thereon, and documents relating thereto to the extent provided by general commercial law.

(10) Presumptions under Acts of Congress. Any signature, document, or other matter declared by Act of Congress to be presumptively or prima facie genuine or authentic.

(11) Certified domestic records of regularly conducted activity. The original or a duplicate of a domestic record of regularly conducted activity that would be admissible under Rule 803(6) if accompanied by a written declaration of its custodian or other qualified person, in a manner complying with any Act of Congress or rule prescribed by the Supreme Court pursuant to statutory authority, certifying that the record:

(A) was made at or near the time of the occurrence of the matters set forth by, or from information transmitted by, a person with knowledge of those matters;

(B) was kept in the course of the regularly conducted activity; and

(C) was made by the regularly conducted activity as a regular practice.

A party intending to offer a record into evidence under this paragraph must provide written notice of that intention to all adverse parties, and must make the record and declaration available for inspection sufficiently in advance of their offer into evidence to provide an adverse party with a fair opportunity to challenge them.

(12) Certified foreign records of regularly conducted activity. In a civil case, the original or a duplicate of a foreign record of regularly conducted activity that would be admissible under Rule 803(6) if accompanied by a written declaration by its custodian or other qualified person certifying that the record:

(A) was made at or near the time of the occurrence of the matters set forth by, or from information transmitted by, a person with knowledge of those matters;

(B) was kept in the course of the regularly conducted activity; and

(C) was made by the regularly conducted activity as a regular practice.
The declaration must be signed in a manner that, if falsely made, would subject the maker to criminal penalty under the laws of the country where the declaration is signed. A party intending to offer a record into evidence under this paragraph must provide written notice of that intention to all adverse parties, and must make the record and declaration available for inspection sufficiently in advance of their offer into evidence to provide an adverse party with a fair opportunity to challenge them.[23]

Through modifications to the rules of evidence and from court decisions giving content and context to the operation of authentication in a variety of situations, courts have developed a substantial body of decisional law governing instances in which authenticity may be viewed as sufficiently established without extrinsic evidence. Under the early cases and under older rules of evidence, there were only a few self-authenticating documents, such as ancient documents, documents bearing a certificate of acknowledgment, and replies to letters.[24] However, to save the time of the court, the number of types of documents that are self-authenticating has grown. For example, the Federal Rules of Evidence now lists 12 types or categories of writings that are presently considered self-authenticating. Rule 902 of the Federal Rules of Evidence provides that extrinsic evidence of authenticity as a condition precedent to admissibility is not required with respect to the following: (1) domestic public documents under seal; (2) domestic public documents not under seal but certified by the appropriate public officer in charge of them; (3) foreign public documents accompanied by certification as to genuineness of signature and official position of executing or attesting person; (4) copies of public or official records certified by the custodian of the original record; (5) official publications issued by public authority; (6) newspapers and periodicals; (7) trade inscriptions and labels; (8) documents acknowledged by a notary public or other officer authorized by law to take acknowledgments; (9) commercial paper and related documents; (10) documents declared by Congress to be presumptively authentic, (11) certified foreign records of regularly conducted activity, and (12) certified domestic records of regularly conducted activity.[25]

In a prosecution involving the trespass by civilians on a United States military base without permission, the trial court admitted a document that certified that the individual trespasser's name was not on a government list of persons permitted to enter the base. The Certificate of Non-Existence of Record (CNER) signed by the lieutenant commander of the base stated that a diligent search of the records did not reveal the defendant's name. In rejecting the defendant's argument that the document had not been properly authenticated, the court, under Rule 902(1), held that the CNER admitted by the dis-

---

[23] FED. R. EVID. 902.
[24] TRACY, HANDBOOK OF THE LAW OF EVIDENCE (1952).
[25] *See*, generally, FED. R. EVID. 902.

With respect to a written document, if a witness who can state that he or she witnessed the signing of the document, that testimony would authenticate the document. When an eyewitness is not available, an expert may authenticate a document by comparing signatures following an examination. In such instances, a properly qualified handwriting expert may testify after comparing the signature on the document with the signature on another document signed by the person and recognized as the person's true signature.[38] In one case, a defendant had been convicted of attempted carjacking based partly on notes he allegedly wrote to friends from jail indicating that he wanted the friend to "take out" two of the victims in the case. One former friend testified that he received a letter purportedly from the defendant and that he was familiar with the defendant's handwriting because he had watched him write rap songs several times. The Supreme Court of Delaware held that this evidence was sufficient proof of authentication even though there was additional evidence that the distinctive content of the letters indicated that the author was the defendant.[39] In determining admissibility of questioned documents, trial judges have considerable discretion in determining what evidence is admissible for proving the authenticity of a questioned document.

To have a witness authenticate a writing, there must be a foundation presented to show the reasons the witness has familiarity with a signature or writing. The procedure generally followed in qualifying a witness to identify a writing, a signature, or a tape recording is to place the witness on the stand and ask the witness foundational questions that will assure the jury and the judge that the witness is familiar with the writing and demonstrates how the witness gained the familiarity. The witness may be asked, "Will you state whether you are acquainted with the handwriting of the writer?" If the witness answers in the affirmative, the witness will then be asked to look at the letter or signature and tell whether it is the handwriting of the writer. In addition, the witness may be asked questions that could confirm whether he or she is or is not qualified. For example, he or she may be asked whether he or she has had an exchange of correspondence with the person, whether he or she has seen writing that the person has admitted to be his or her own, or whether the witness has become familiar with the person's writing by doing business with him or her on a day-to-day basis.[40]

Similar procedures are followed in authenticating videotapes. Generally, authentication requires evidence to document who operated the recorder that taped the event and when and where the videotaping occurred. In a prosecution for capital murder, in an interrogation room police interviewed the defendant following his arrest while a video camera recorded the events with sound. The appellate court approved the admission of the videotape into evidence and of the playing of the video for the jury. Prior to allowing the jury to view the

---

[38]   Goldberg v. Texas, 95 S.W.3d 345, 372, 2002 Tex. App. LEXIS 6114 (2002); Johnson v. Texas, 2001 Tex. App. LEXIS 3554 (2001).

[39]   Smith v. Delaware, 2006 Del. LEXIS 340 (2006).

[40]   W.T. Rawleigh Co. v. Overstreet, 71 Ga. App. 873, 32 S.E.2d 574 (1944).

trict court clearly exhibited the raised seal of the United States Department of the Navy and carried the signature of the lieutenant commander who certified and swore that the contents of the letter were true. Consistent with the Federal Rule 902, the seal of any executing officer or custodian will generally suffice to authenticate a document under Rule 902(1).[26]

In interpreting Rule 902(3), governing the authentication and admissibility of foreign public documents, a federal appeals court held that non-certified foreign public documents should be treated as presumptively authentic if the parties have been given reasonable opportunity to investigate the authenticity and accuracy of the documents and have demonstrated good cause.[27] In one case, in which a foreign ship had been arrested in Louisiana, one party wanted to introduce a foreign affidavit sworn and dated in front of an honorary Maltese counsel. A federal district court permitted the use of the affidavit because it had been signed, stamped, and initialed by the Maltese counsel, thereby meeting the requirements under Rule 902(3). Newspaper articles reporting that the plaintiff was in bankruptcy were admissible as evidence in accordance with Rule 902(6).[28]

Where a public record may be self-authenticating, it must be presented in proper order with appropriate seals or signatures in order to meet the requirements of Rule 902(4). In a tax suit, the trial court had admitted tax documents introduced by a city and a school district in an effort to collect back property taxes. The tax documents contained an affidavit and were notarized by a tax assessor as being true copies of the original delinquent tax statements. The documents were not considered records under seal and had not been signed by someone authorized within the school district or city under seal who could attest to the signor's authority. The reviewing court reversed the trial court's finding of authentication on the ground that because the tax documents "did not bear a seal or contain a certification under seal from a public officer, the tax statements were not self-authenticating as certified public records"[29] under the Texas version of Rule 901(4).

In a criminal case in which the court admitted copies of the defendant's juvenile adjudications that were certified copies and were given under the hand and seal of the office of the juvenile court clerk, the defendant contended that the documents were not properly presented to be self-authenticating public documents under seal. Even if there were some slight irregularities in the seal of one of the documents, the reviewing court concluded that the proof met the minimum requirements for authentication and were properly admitted against the defendant at his sentencing hearing.[30] The Tenth Circuit held that a copy of a driving record obtained from a state's official repository of records

---

[26]   United States v. Ventura-Melendez, 275 F.3d 9, 14, 2001 U.S. App. LEXIS 26901 (1st Cir. 2001).

[27]   Raphaely Intern., Inc. v. Waterman Corp., 972 F.2d 498 (2d Cir.), cert. denied, 507 U.S. 916, 113 S. Ct. 1271, 122 L. Ed. 2d 666 (1993).

[28]   Price v. Rochford, 947 F.2d 829 (7th Cir. 1991).

[29]   Al-Nayem v. Irving Independent School District, 159 S.W.3d 762, 764, 2005 Tex. App. LEXIS 1919 (2005).

[30]   Hull v. State, 172 S.W.3d 186, 189, 2005 Tex. App. LEXIS 6502 (2005).

constituted an official public record under Rule 902(4) that the court deemed to be self-authentication when accompanied by a notarized certification of the correctness of the record executed by a clerk in the state license bureau.[31]

In a drug conspiracy trial in which the defendants generated hotel, motel, private mailbox rental receipts, and other records made by businesses with which they transacted business, the business records were properly considered to be self-authenticating under Rule 902(11). The prosecution complied with the federal rule requirement that the opposing party give sufficient notice to the other party prior to the time of introduction of the records to avoid unfair surprise. The prosecution and the defense may authenticate a business record through a written declaration by a qualified custodian that the record met the necessary foundational requirements that the business made the record at or near the time of the transaction, proof that the business generated the record in the usual course of business, and proof that the business kept the record in the usual course of business. Because the prosecution followed the evidentiary requirements, the Seventh Circuit Court of Appeals rejected the defendant's argument that authentication of the business records had not been properly established and approved the introduction of the self-authenticating business records because they had been certified by their respective custodians as accurate renditions of the records generated by their respective business organizations.[32]

Under Federal Rule 902 and similar state rules of evidence, extrinsic evidence is not required for documents within the self-authenticating group, and such documents are admissible without further authentication. The opposing party may introduce evidence that disputes a judge's preliminary ruling on authentication and may attempt to have perfectly authenticated documentary evidence rejected based on arguments that the authenticated documents possess insufficient relevancy to the case.

§ 13.4 Methods of Authentication

Because all writings must be authenticated to be admissible as evidence, when written documents are not self-authenticating, the proponent of a writing must offer a sufficient evidentiary foundation to support its admission. Generally, one of four methods may be followed in offering sufficient proof of authenticity: (1) proof of signing, (2) proof of signature, (3) comparison of signatures, and (4) circumstantial evidence.[33] Requirements include proof of the genuineness and proper execution of the document, and that the document correctly states what the party claims.

The most common method of authentication of a written document is offering proof of signing. It is common for the authenticating witness to tes-

---

[31] United States v. Mirelez, 59 Fed. Appx. 286, 2003 U.S. App. LEXIS 2162 (10th Cir. 2003).

[32] United States v. Bledsoe, 70 Fed. Appx. 370, 2003 U.S. App. LEXIS 13312 (7th Cir. 2003). *See also* FED. R. EVID. 902 (11) in Appendix I.

[33] TRACY, HANDBOOK OF THE LAW OF EVIDENCE (1952).

tify that he or she saw the person sign the document in question. The next most common method of authentication is proof of the signature. If the witness did not see the person sign, but is familiar with and can identify the signature, this is sufficient authentication. Such evidence is as competent and valid as the testimony of the writers themselves and is not to be considered secondary evidence.[34] Some written documents may be self-authenticating under Rule 901(7) covering trade inscriptions, sign, and tags. In an Indiana prosecution for possession of methamphetamine precursor chemicals, the trial court approved the admission of several boxes that originally contained pseudoephedrine hydrochloride, a chemical used in the manufacture of methamphetamine. The original packaging contained printed data that told the weight of the drugs within the box and the state offered the labels under the Indiana rule of evidence that allow self-authentication for "inscriptions, signs, tags, or labels purporting to have been affixed in the course of business and indicating ownership, control, or origin."[35]

A tape recording or a 911 call recording constitutes a writing and must be authenticated in order to be introduced at trial. In one case involving a burglary charge the defendant wanted to introduce a recording of a 911 call made by a resident in the apartment building that he was alleged to have burglarized. The trial court refused to admit two unauthenticated recordings of 911 calls for the purpose allowing an excited witness to detail what had he had been observed doing and for the purpose of impeaching a witness. The defendant had not called any witness to prove who was making the 911 calls and the defense had previously passed on an opportunity to ask a witness if she was the one who made one or both of the emergency calls. Because there was no proof of authentication of the 911 calls, the trial court properly excluded them.[36]

In a Texas case, drug investigators prevailed upon an informant to wear an audiotape recorder to provide a voice record of a drug transaction that the police had arranged with a drug dealer. When the prosecutor attempted to introduce the audiotape of the drug sale conversation, the defense objected that the tape had not been properly authenticated. The prosecutor had offered the testimony of the man who wore the wire who identified his own voice, identified the defendant's voice, and identified the voice of another individual and who knew the time, place, and circumstances under which the audio recording had been made. Even though the informant was not able to identify a fourth speaker who was heard on the audiotape, the court held that the process properly authenticated the tape. The reviewing court noted that the Texas version of Federal Rule 901 required only that "the proponent show by sufficient evidence that the matter in question is what its proponent claims" and held that "the informant's identification of the voices on the recording was sufficient to authenticate the tape under Rule 901."[37]

---

[34] United States v. Moreno, 68 U.S. 400 (1863).

[35] Reemer v. State, 835 N.E.2d 1005, 1007, 2005 Ind. LEXIS 955, n.4 (Ind. 2005).

[36] State v. Peay, 96 Conn. App. 421, 435, 900 A.2d 577, 2006 Conn. App. LEXIS 326 (2006).

[37] Jones v. Texas, 80 S.W.3d 686, 688, 689, 2002 Tex. App. LEXIS 4414 (2002).

trict court clearly exhibited the raised seal of the United States Department of the Navy and carried the signature of the lieutenant commander who certified and swore that the contents of the letter were true. Consistent with the Federal Rule 902, the seal of any executing officer or custodian will generally suffice to authenticate a document under Rule 902(1).[26]

In interpreting Rule 902(3), governing the authentication and admissibility of foreign public documents, a federal appeals court held that non-certified foreign public documents should be treated as presumptively authentic if the parties have been given reasonable opportunity to investigate the authenticity and accuracy of the documents and have demonstrated good cause.[27] In one case, in which a foreign ship had been arrested in Louisiana, one party wanted to introduce a foreign affidavit sworn and dated in front of an honorary Maltese counsel. A federal district court permitted the use of the affidavit because it had been signed, stamped, and initialed by the Maltese counsel, thereby meeting the requirements under Rule 902(3). Newspaper articles reporting that the plaintiff was in bankruptcy were admissible as evidence in accordance with Rule 902(6).[28]

Where a public record may be self-authenticating, it must be presented in proper order with appropriate seals or signatures in order to meet the requirements of Rule 902(4). In a tax suit, the trial court had admitted tax documents introduced by a city and a school district in an effort to collect back property taxes. The tax documents contained an affidavit and were notarized by a tax assessor as being true copies of the original delinquent tax statements. The documents were not considered records under seal and had not been signed by someone authorized within the school district or city under seal who could attest to the signor's authority. The reviewing court reversed the trial court's finding of authentication on the ground that because the tax documents "did not bear a seal or contain a certification under seal from a public officer, the tax statements were not self-authenticating as certified public records"[29] under the Texas version of Rule 901(4).

In a criminal case in which the court admitted copies of the defendant's juvenile adjudications that were certified copies and were given under the hand and seal of the office of the juvenile court clerk, the defendant contended that the documents were not properly presented to be self-authenticating public documents under seal. Even if there were some slight irregularities in the seal of one of the documents, the reviewing court concluded that the proof met the minimum requirements for authentication and were properly admitted against the defendant at his sentencing hearing.[30] The Tenth Circuit held that a copy of a driving record obtained from a state's official repository of records

---

[26] United States v. Ventura-Melendez, 275 F.3d 9, 14, 2001 U.S. App. LEXIS 26901 (1st Cir. 2001).

[27] Raphaely Intern., Inc. v. Waterman Corp., 972 F.2d 498 (2d Cir.), *cert. denied*, 507 U.S. 916, 113 S. Ct. 1271, 122 L. Ed. 2d 666 (1993).

[28] Price v. Rochford, 947 F.2d 829 (7th Cir. 1991).

[29] Al-Nayem v. Irving Independent School District, 159 S.W.3d 762, 764, 2005 Tex. App. LEXIS 1919 (2005).

[30] Hull v. State, 172 S.W.3d 186, 189, 2005 Tex. App. LEXIS 6502 (2005).

constituted an official public record under Rule 902(4) that the court deemed to be self-authentication when accompanied by a notarized certification of the correctness of the record executed by a clerk in the state license bureau.[31]

In a drug conspiracy trial in which the defendants generated hotel, motel, private mailbox rental receipts, and other records made by businesses with which they transacted business, the business records were properly considered to be self-authenticating under Rule 902(11). The prosecution complied with the federal rule requirement that the opposing party give sufficient notice to the other party prior to the time of introduction of the records to avoid unfair surprise. The prosecution and the defense may authenticate a business record through a written declaration by a qualified custodian that the record met the necessary foundational requirements that the business made the record at or near the time of the transaction, proof that the business generated the record in the usual course of business, and proof that the business kept the record in the usual course of business. Because the prosecution followed the evidentiary requirements, the Seventh Circuit Court of Appeals rejected the defendant's argument that authentication of the business records had not been properly established and approved the introduction of the self-authenticating business records because they had been certified by their respective custodians as accurate renditions of the records generated by their respective business organizations.[32]

Under Federal Rule 902 and similar state rules of evidence, extrinsic evidence is not required for documents within the self-authenticating group, and such documents are admissible without further authentication. The opposing party may introduce evidence that disputes a judge's preliminary ruling on authentication and may attempt to have perfectly authenticated documentary evidence rejected based on arguments that the authenticated documents possess insufficient relevancy to the case.

§ 13.4 Methods of Authentication

Because all writings must be authenticated to be admissible as evidence, when written documents are not self-authenticating, the proponent of a writing must offer a sufficient evidentiary foundation to support its admission. Generally, one of four methods may be followed in offering sufficient proof of authenticity: (1) proof of signing, (2) proof of signature, (3) comparison of signatures, and (4) circumstantial evidence.[33] Requirements include proof of the genuineness and proper execution of the document, and that the document correctly states what the party claims.

The most common method of authentication of a written document is offering proof of signing. It is common for the authenticating witness to tes-

[31] United States v. Mirelez, 59 Fed. Appx. 286, 2003 U.S. App. LEXIS 2162 (10th Cir. 2003).
[32] United States v. Bledsoe, 70 Fed. Appx. 370, 2003 U.S. App. LEXIS 13312 (7th Cir. 2003). *See also* FED. R. EVID. 902 (11) in Appendix I.
[33] TRACY, HANDBOOK OF THE LAW OF EVIDENCE (1952).

tify that he or she saw the person sign the document in question. The next most common method of authentication is proof of the signature. If the witness did not see the person sign, but is familiar with and can identify the signature, this is sufficient authentication. Such evidence is as competent and valid as the testimony of the writers themselves and is not to be considered secondary evidence.[34] Some written documents may be self-authenticating under Rule 901(7) covering trade inscriptions, sign, and tags. In an Indiana prosecution for possession of methamphetamine precursor chemicals, the trial court approved the admission of several boxes that originally contained pseudoephedrine hydrochloride, a chemical used in the manufacture of methamphetamine. The original packaging contained printed data that told the weight of the drugs within the box and the state offered the labels under the Indiana rule of evidence that allow self-authentication for "inscriptions, signs, tags, or labels purporting to have been affixed in the course of business and indicating ownership, control, or origin."[35]

A tape recording or a 911 call recording constitutes a writing and must be authenticated in order to be introduced at trial. In one case involving a burglary charge the defendant wanted to introduce a recording of a 911 call made by a resident in the apartment building that he was alleged to have burglarized. The trial court refused to admit two unauthenticated recordings of 911 calls for the purpose allowing an excited witness to detail what had he had been observed doing and for the purpose of impeaching a witness. The defendant had not called any witness to prove who was making the 911 calls and the defense had previously passed on an opportunity to ask a witness if she was the one who made one or both of the emergency calls. Because there was no proof of authentication of the 911 calls, the trial court properly excluded them.[36]

In a Texas case, drug investigators prevailed upon an informant to wear an audiotape recorder to provide a voice record of a drug transaction that the police had arranged with a drug dealer. When the prosecutor attempted to introduce the audiotape of the drug sale conversation, the defense objected that the tape had not been properly authenticated. The prosecutor had offered the testimony of the man who wore the wire who identified his own voice, identified the defendant's voice, and identified the voice of another individual, and who knew the time, place, and circumstances under which the audio recording had been made. Even though the informant was not able to identify a fourth speaker who was heard on the audiotape, the court held that the process properly authenticated the tape. The reviewing court noted that the Texas version of Federal Rule 901 required only that "the proponent show by sufficient evidence that the matter in question is what its proponent claims" and held that "the informant's identification of the voices on the recording was sufficient to authenticate the tape under Rule 901."[37]

---

[34]　United States v. Moreno, 68 U.S. 400 (1863).

[35]　Reemer v. State, 835 N.E.2d 1005, 1007, 2005 Ind. LEXIS 955, n.4 (Ind. 2005).

[36]　State v. Peay, 96 Conn. App. 421, 435, 900 A.2d 577, 2006 Conn. App. LEXIS 326 (2006).

[37]　Jones v. Texas, 80 S.W.3d 686, 688, 689, 2002 Tex. App. LEXIS 4414 (2002).

With respect to a written document, if a witness who can state that he or she witnessed the signing of the document, that testimony would authenticate the document. When an eyewitness is not available, an expert may authenticate a document by comparing signatures following an examination. In such instances, a properly qualified handwriting expert may testify after comparing the signature on the document with the signature on another document signed by the person and recognized as the person's true signature.[38] In one case, a defendant had been convicted of attempted carjacking based partly on notes he allegedly wrote to friends from jail indicating that he wanted the friend to "take out" two of the victims in the case. One former friend testified that he received a letter purportedly from the defendant and that he was familiar with the defendant's handwriting because he had watched him write rap songs several times. The Supreme Court of Delaware held that this evidence was sufficient proof of authentication even though there was additional evidence that the distinctive content of the letters indicated that the author was the defendant.[39] In determining admissibility of questioned documents, trial judges have considerable discretion in determining what evidence is admissible for proving the authenticity of a questioned document.

To have a witness authenticate a writing, there must be a foundation presented to show the reasons the witness has familiarity with a signature or writing. The procedure generally followed in qualifying a witness to identify a writing, a signature, or a tape recording is to place the witness on the stand and ask the witness foundational questions that will assure the jury and the judge that the witness is familiar with the writing and demonstrates how the witness gained the familiarity. The witness may be asked, "Will you state whether you are acquainted with the handwriting of the writer?" If the witness answers in the affirmative, the witness will then be asked to look at the letter or signature and tell whether it is the handwriting of the writer. In addition, the witness may be asked questions that could confirm whether he or she is or is not qualified. For example, he or she may be asked whether he or she has had an exchange of correspondence with the person, whether he or she has seen writing that the person has admitted to be his or her own, or whether the witness has become familiar with the person's writing by doing business with him or her on a day-to-day basis.[40]

Similar procedures are followed in authenticating videotapes. Generally, authentication requires evidence to document who operated the recorder that taped the event and when and where the videotaping occurred. In a prosecution for capital murder, in an interrogation room police interviewed the defendant following his arrest while a video camera recorded the events with sound. The appellate court approved the admission of the videotape into evidence and of the playing of the video for the jury. Prior to allowing the jury to view the

---

[38]   Goldberg v. Texas, 95 S.W.3d 345, 372, 2002 Tex. App. LEXIS 6114 (2002); Johnson v. Texas, 2001 Tex. App. LEXIS 3554 (2001).

[39]   Smith v. Delaware, 2006 Del. LEXIS 340 (2006).

[40]   W.T. Rawleigh Co. v. Overstreet, 71 Ga. App. 873, 32 S.E.2d 574 (1944).

video, the trial court heard evidence from one of the officers who was present when the police videotaped the interrogation. He stated that the video showed what it purported to show, that it was a reliable depiction of what happened during the interrogation of the defendant-appellant, and that it had not been altered or changed in any way. The appellate court found no error in admitting the video of the defendant's interrogation.[41] In a case in which a defendant attempted to elude a marked police car, the officer in pursuit turned on the lights and a videotape recorder that captured what was observable by the officer through the cruiser's windshield. At the trial, the defendant complained that the videotape played during the prosecution's case had not been properly authenticated. The appellate court rejected the argument because the officer in the chase cruiser testified in court that he had previously reviewed the tape and it was a true and accurate copy of the one he had made during the car chase on the date of the offense and depicted exactly what he had originally observed.[42]

In a case involving a different kind of writing, the reviewing court held that the district court did not abuse its discretion in allowing an expert witness to testify that the defendant's fingerprint was discovered on a package of cocaine found in his apartment, notwithstanding that the police officer did not testify that he personally lifted the fingerprints, which permitted him to identify the print as that of the defendant.[43] In this case, the officer testified that all the prints identified were lifted by him or his assistant, all at the same time, in the same room, on the same day, and that they discussed how to label the lifted prints to reflect various packages on which they were found. The court fount that this process and testimony demonstrated a sufficient foundation of authentication.

§ 13.5   Specific Examples of Documentary Evidence

Human social and business interactions in the modern world produce a wide variety of evidentiary items that are classified as "writings" but do not fall into the category of traditional documents. From electronic checks, computer data, Web pages, to actual paper documents, these "writings" preserve and explain much of human activity. Although memories may have faded, documents created in the course of human events remain to assist in the reconstruction of the recent past. When the activities involve crimes, these documents may help prove or disprove a criminal case. Even though the primary amount of evidence introduced into courts consists of oral evidence, documentary evidence plays an important part in recreating the full picture for the finder of fact. Documentary evidence includes written proof of laws; judi-

---

[41]   Harrison v State, 869 So. 2d 509, 2002 Ala. Crim. App. LEXIS 232 (2002). *cert. denied*, 2004 U.S. LEXIS 162 (2004).

[42]   Ball v. State, 2005 Tex. App. LEXIS 2575 (2005).

[43]   United States v. Vasquez, 858 F.2d 1387 (9th Cir. 1988).

cial records and proceedings; public records; private documents such as business records, account books, corporate records, letters, telegrams, and other correspondence; books; church records; hospital records; hotel registers; and many others. In each instance, the general rules of evidence, as well as the authentication requirements discussed in this chapter, must be considered when arguing for or against admission. Court decisions and statutes in various states must be consulted for more precise rules concerning the introduction of documentary evidence.

In order to develop a better understanding of some of the rules relating to documentary evidence, examples of specific types of such evidence are included here. These examples have been selected as those most likely to be encountered by criminal justice personnel[44] and are not exclusive to problems related to the admission of documentary evidence.

A. *Public Records and Documents*

Writings that have been deposited in public offices or were created by those public offices are generally easier to authenticate than some private writings. In many cases, because a public official is under a duty to keep records or make reports of acts or transactions occurring in the course of his or her official duty, records or reports so made by or under the supervision of the public official are admissible as prima facie evidence of facts stated.[45] A public officer may be a county recorder, coroner, tax assessor, member of a board of elections, or a law enforcement official.

Even though a document has been labeled as a "public document" or "public record" does not make the document admissible in court. A publicly recorded document may include opinion, conclusions, and hearsay evidence and, although properly authenticated, it may be excluded on relevancy grounds. The fact that a document contains opinions and conclusions may create particular problems for the admission of some police records because hearsay evidence commonly is included in police reports.

In a variety of situations, police officers and law enforcement personnel may have a duty record or may create records of transactions that occur in the usual course of their work. The official records and writings made by such officers, or under their supervision, are of a public nature and are ordinarily admissible in evidence as proof of their contents, even though not proved by the person who actually made the entries. The extraordinary degree of confidence reposed in such documents is founded principally upon the fact that they have been made by authorized, accredited officers and deputies appointed for that purpose. In one Ohio case, a trial court refused to allow a police officer, who was the custodian of records for the police agency, to testify that a certificate showing that a public record revealed that a police officer had been certified to operate a machine that checked blood-alcohol content. The officer

[44] *See* Chapter 14 for a discussion of the use of photographs, diagrams, maps, and models.
[45] People v. Hudson, 655 N.Y.S.2d 219 (1997).

had been prepared to testify that the certificate was a true copy of the original. The appellate court reversed the suppression of the certificate and noted that certified copies of public records do not generally require extrinsic evidence of authenticity because they are deemed to be self-authenticating.[46] In a Texas prosecution, in order to obtain a sentence enhancement, the prosecutor needed to prove prior criminal acts of a defendant who had been convicted in a different state. A Texas court ruled that an informational penitentiary packet obtained from a Florida correctional facility and certified as containing correct information could be considered self-authenticated where it bore an insignia of the Florida Department of Corrections and carried a certification of correctness along with the signature and seal of the correctional services director. The prosecution then compared defendant's prints taken from the crime scene, at the point of arrest, and from the penitentiary packet to determine that the defendant was the same person.[47]

When properly authenticated and relevant, police training and policy manuals may be admissible under the public document provisions of statutes. In a murder prosecution resulting in a conviction for the manslaughter of a police officer, the police department manual was admissible to demonstrate that the victim, an off-duty police officer who had been shot during a robbery attempt, was under a duty to apprehend felons at all times.[48] A Mississippi court held that certificates attesting to proper calibration of Intoxilyzer machines were considered public records for which authentication existed as a matter of law. The government only needed to demonstrate that the certificates had been prepared by the state agency pursuant to statute under authority granted to the department of public safety and had to comply with the requirements of that law in order to be considered authenticated for evidentiary purposes.[49]

Many public records, including death certificates and autopsy reports, contain undisputed facts that have occurred; they are generally considered public documents that may be admissible as self-authenticating. However, a statement contained within such a record that amounts to an opinion or belief is not admissible because it violates other rules of evidence, including rules excluding hearsay evidence.[50] However, when the official records are not being used to prove their truth, a hearsay objection is not a problem and authentication proves to be the major hurdle. Admitting court records of prior convictions for violating domestic relations no-contact orders was proper even if the records did not have the seal of the court as required. The appellate court noted that there was no abuse of discretion in admitting the certified records and there was evidence the court found the records sufficiently authenticated.[51]

---

[46]   Ohio v. Mustafa, 2001 Ohio App. LEXIS 5661 (2001).
[47]   Aragon v. Texas, 2003 Tex. App. LEXIS 2380 (2003).
[48]   Michell v. State, 689 So. 2d 1118 (Fla. 1997).
[49]   Pulliam v. Mississippi, 2003 Miss. App. LEXIS 299 (2003).
[50]   Carson v. Metropolitan Life Ins. Co., 156 Ohio St. 104, 45 Ohio Op. 103, 100 N.E.2d 197 (1951). *See also* Baulch v. Johns, 70 F.3d 813 (5th Cir. 1995).
[51]   State v. Lux, 2005 Wash. App. LEXIS 980 (2005).

In some states, the state statute as interpreted by the courts expressly provides for the authentication and use of certified copies. In a Washington case involving an allegation of underage possession of alcoholic spirits, a trial court admitted, over the defendant's objection, certified copies of public records that established the age of the underage defendant. In rejecting the defendant's argument that the public records were not properly authenticated and should not have been admitted, the reviewing court held that certified copies under the circumstances were self-authenticating and admissible without any additional authentication. The appellate court stated that, "Ordinarily, the proponent of tangible evidence such as documents must first establish a foundation by presenting sufficient evidence to show that the item is what the proponent claims it is. But here, the documents in question were certified copies of official public records. Such documents are self-authenticating and admissible without further foundational showing."[52]

In a different case[53] involving a prosecution for unlawful imprisonment, the prosecution wanted the defendant to be required to register under the Sexual Offender Registration Act because the victim was under 17 years of age at the time of the crime. The court rejected the offer of proof of the birth certificate and passport from the Dominican Republic because both documents were in Spanish, there was no certified transcript of the documents, and the Dominican Republic had never signed an international convention that would have assisted in a finding of self-authentication. Due to the failure to authenticate the birth certificate, the defendant had no duty to register as a sex offender. Similarly, a Texas court held that an Illinois "penitentiary packet" accompanying the defendant that contained an order that sentenced the defendant to an Illinois prison, a fingerprint card, and an Illinois offender report was not self-authenticating because it bore no certification by an Illinois official and had no Illinois state seal. Even though the fingerprints on the card matched those of the defendant, that fact could not authenticate the entire "penitentiary pack."[54]

While most public records and documents are generally admissible without extrinsic evidence of authenticity, most comply with the requirements as set out in state and federal rules of evidence. The statutes for the respective states must be examined to determine whether there are any additional conditions that must be met to assure admissibility, such as giving reasonable notice of intent to use the evidence or by delivering a copy to the adverse party in a reasonable time before the trial.[55]

---

[52]   Washington v. Daley, 2003 Wash. App. LEXIS 234 (2003).

[53]   *See* People v. Vazquez, 2006 NY Slip Op 26225 (N.Y. 2006). *See also* United States v. Torres-Reyes, 46 Fed. Appx. 925 (2002).

[54]   Banks v. State, 158 S.W.3d 649, 653, 2005 Tex. App. LEXIS 1838 (2005).

[55]   *See* FED. R. EVID. 1005 for an example of other requirements that may assist in admission of evidence. Meeting the hearsay rules also may influence the admission of evidence under Rule 902.

B. Private Writings

Written documents classified as "private writings" encompass a wide variety of documents. They include personal correspondence, e-mail, text messages, many business records, and individual business contracts. Credit card receipts, ATM receipts, telephone bills, as well as cash register tapes from retail stores qualify as private writings. In order for a private writing to be admissible in court, it must be proven to be genuine and also that it is what it appears to be. The genuineness may be proven by the testimony of anyone who saw the writing executed, by indirect or circumstantial evidence, or from testimony that an automated process generated the writing. However, if circumstantial evidence is used to establish the authenticity of a document, it must be of such force and character that the person's authorship or the identity of the person responsible for the creation of the writing can be legitimately deduced from its contents or from attendant circumstances.

Circumstantial evidence in one murder case authenticated a letter written by the defendant to his brother in which the defendant admitted to being the person who shot the deceased.[56] The letter named the judge hearing the murder case; named and discussed a friend, who had turned state's witness; mentioned two witnesses who could identify the defendant; and was signed using the defendant's name and jail address. It was dated and postmarked on days the defendant was in custody. With all of this evidence, the trial judge properly ruled that the letter had been sufficiently authenticated to be admissible against the defendant.

Expert and lay witnesses may testify to their opinions respecting authorship or genuineness of writings provided that they are properly qualified and the proponent has offered a proper foundation. A lay witness must be sufficiently familiar with the handwriting of the person whose authorship of the contested document is at issue.[57] The proponent of the document usually establishes that the witness gained the necessary familiarity with the handwriting by observing the person write or by receiving letters or other written material from the purported author. If a party offers an expert witness to authenticate a document, the expert must be qualified as having expertise with handwriting prior to offering opinions concerning the known sample and the questioned sample of writing. In a murder case[58] in which the defendant had been accused of killing his mother, he argued that the judge abused the court's discretion by admitting into evidence a letter purportedly written by the defendant. The defendant's sister testified that she was sure the handwriting belonged to the defendant, even though she had not seen his writing in several years. Her knowledge of her brother's writing was not acquired for litigation purposes and her level of certainty was high. In approving the authentication, the court of appeals noted that there was also evidence that the letter purport-

---

[56] State v. Townshend, 2005 Ohio 6945, 2005 Ohio App. LEXIS 6239 (2005).

[57] FED. R. EVID. 901(b)(2). This federal rule specifies that the familiarity not be acquired for purposes of the litigation when a lay witness provides the authentication.

[58] People v. Schuster, 2004 Mich. App. LEXIS 2680 (2004).

edly written by the defendant had been found in the home of the deceased.[59] In a Pennsylvania case,[60] two juveniles engaged in a dispute over a DVD and the defendant juvenile severely injured the other in an unprovoked attack. The trial court permitted the state to introduce a computerized instant text message allegedly sent by the defendant to the victim that contained threats of physical injury. The messages were authenticated by the defendant's consistent use of a instant message name, by the defendant's mention of an alleged stolen DVD, and by the fact that the threatened behavior contained in the instant message actually occurred with the defendant doing what he threatened in front of witnesses. The instant messages were properly authenticated as having come from the defendant and there was no need to engage the defendant's Internet service provider to obtain meta data that would have additionally authenticated the message.

Documents on private computers can be properly authenticated by a variety of methods. In one case[61] in which a father allegedly sexually abused his own daughter, the court allowed the prosecution to introduce two letters that police found on the defendant's computer hard drive. The evidence of authentication showed that each person in the household had an individual computer and they did not use another family member's computer. Properly trained police examined the hard drive of the defendant's computer, finding two relevant letters that indicated the time and date of creation and copying to floppy disks and telephone records from the home when the defendant was alone indicated that he was the one home when the computer letters were written. The subject of the computer letters involved details related to the sexual assaults of his daughter. The appellate court concluded that there was no error in admitting the text of the letters against the defendant because they had been properly authenticated.

Business records that are generated in the ordinary and usual course of business may be authenticated and introduced in court. In one case[62] in which the defendant was alleged to have violated a restraining order of "no contact" by calling the victim's cell phone and regular phone, an employee of the cell phone provider was permitted to lay a foundation for introducing evidence of the times that the defendant violated the order by making reference to computer-generated calling records of the phone calls between the defendant's phone and the phones of the victim. The regularly and automatically generated phone records also may be considered as self-authenticating because they are records of regularly conducted business operations.[63]

---

[59] *Id.*

[60] In the Interest of F.P., 2005 Pa. Super. 220, 878 A.2d 91, 93, 2005 Pa. Super. LEXIS 1499 (2005).

[61] State v. John L., 85 Conn. App. 291, 299, 856 A.2d 1032, 1038, 2004 Conn. App. LEXIS 407 (Conn. 2004).

[62] Smith v. State, 839 N.E.2d 780, 785, 2005 Ind. App. LEXIS 2442 (2005).

[63] *Id.*

§ 13.6   Best Evidence Rule

Rule 1002

Requirement of Original

To prove the content of a writing, recording, or photograph, the original writing, recording, or photograph is required, except as otherwise provided in these rules or by Act of Congress.[64]

Documentary evidence and evidence contained within the concept of a "writing" must be authenticated before such evidence will be admitted for proof of its contents. Authentication may not suffice to permit documentary evidence to be admitted in court unless it meets the other rule peculiar to documentary evidence, the best evidence rule.[65] In order for the best evidence rule to apply, the internal content of the writing must be at issue.[66] As the rule has commonly, but imperfectly, been stated, *the best evidence that is obtainable under the circumstances of the case must be presented to prove any disputed fact.* The label "best evidence" is not exactly correct because the rule does not require the best possible evidence; it only signifies a preference for the original of the document or writing.[67] Where proof is to be made of a fact that is recorded in a writing, the best evidence and probably the most accurate rendition of the contents of the writing involves the production of the original document. Any proof of a lower degree is secondary evidence that will only be received as proof when nonproduction of the original writing is properly excused, usually through no fault of the party offering the secondary evidence. A Florida reviewing court noted that when the best evidence rule requires the original or a qualified substitute, a court should accept no secondary evidence if the secondary evidence serves merely as a substitute for the original.[68] The best evidence rule rests upon the principle that if original evidence is available, the original must be produced to assure the court that there has been no alteration of the information contained within the writing.

The justices of the Ninth Circuit Court of Appeals, in discussing the application of the best evidence rule, included this comment:

---

[64]   FED. R. EVID. 1002.

[65]   *See* FED. R. EVID. 1002.

[66]   Hasson v. Commonwealth, 2006 Va. App. LEXIS 225 (Va. 2006).

[67]   In re Santaella, Debtor, 2002 Bankr. LEXIS 1420 (2002).

[68]   McKeehan v. State, 838 So. 2d 1257, 1259, 2003 Fla. App. LEXIS 3367 (2003). *See* case in Part II. *But see* Commonwealth v. Leneski, 66 Mass. App. Ct. 291, 294, 846 N.E.2d 1195, 1198, 2006 Mass. App. LEXIS 525 (2006), in which the court noted that the best evidence rule does not apply in that jurisdiction to photographs, videotapes, or films. In referring to the best evidence rule in Ohio, one court noted that "This rule has been generally abrogated, though, by Evid. R. 1003, which states: '[a] duplicate is admissible to the same extent as an original unless (1) a genuine question is raised as to the authenticity of the original or (2) in the circumstances it would be unfair to admit the duplicate in lieu of the original.'" *See* State v. Dobrovich, 2005 Ohio 1441, 2005 Ohio App. LEXIS 1405 (2005).

The best evidence rule embodied in Rules 1001-1008 represents a codification of a long-standing common law doctrine. Dating back to 1700, the rule requires not, as the name implies, the best evidence in every case, but rather the production of an original document instead of a copy. Many commentators refer to the rule not as the best evidence rule but as the original document rule.[69]

Drafters of the Federal Rules of Evidence included this note regarding the best evidence rule:

> Traditionally the rule requiring the original centered upon the accumulations of data and expressions affecting legal relations set forth in words and figures. This meant that the rule was one essentially relating to writings. Present day techniques have expanded methods of storing data, yet the essential form which the information ultimately assumes for useable purposes is words and figures. Hence the considerations underlying the Rule dictate its expansion to include computers, photographic systems and other modern developments.[70]

The real purpose of, and reasons for, the best evidence rule were well stated by Dean Wigmore:[71]

> (1) As between a supposed literal copy and the original, the copy is always liable to errors on the part of the copyist, whether by wilfulness or by inadvertence; this contingency wholly disappears when the original is produced. Moreover, the original may contain, and the copy will lack, such features of handwriting, paper, and the like, as may afford the opponent valuable means of learning legitimate objections to the significance of the document. (2) As between oral testimony, based on recollection, and the original, the added risk, almost the certainty, exists, of errors of recollection due to the difficulty of carrying in the memory literally the tenor of the document.

Consistent with Dean Wigmore, the Eleventh Circuit noted that:

> The purpose of the best evidence rule is to prevent inaccuracy and fraud when attempting to prove the contents of a writing. However, where the original of a recording has been lost or destroyed, the original is not required and other evidence of its content is admissible, unless the proponent lost or destroyed the original in bad faith. Once the terms of Rule 1004 are satisfied, the party seeking to prove the contents of the recording . . . may do so by any kind of secondary evidence.[72] (Citations omitted.)

---

[69]   Siler v. Lucasfilm, Ltd., 979 F.2d 1504 (9th Cir. 1986).

[70]   These original drafters' comments were included with Rule 1001 of the Federal Rules of Evidence.

[71]   IV WIGMORE, EVIDENCE § 1179 (3d ed. 1940). *See also* United States v. Holton, 116 F.3d 1536 (D.C. Cir. 1997).

[72]   United States v. Ross, 33 F.3d 1507, 1513, 1994 U.S. App. LEXIS 28195 (11th Cir. 1994), *cert. denied*, 537 U.S. 1113, 154 L. Ed. 2d 787, 123 S. Ct. 944, 2003 U.S. LEXIS 707 (2003).

The focus of the best evidence rule concerns only the substantive content of a writing and does not regulate other evidence that may modify or surround the creation of a writing. Therefore, testimony as to other facts about a writing, such as its existence, identity, the date of creation, or how or why it was created, may be admissible. Thus, in a case in which the defendant had engaged in a crippling fight with the victim at a coin laundry, a videotape of the incident would normally be admitted. In this case, the owner of the laundry viewed the surveillance videotape of the crime but did not preserve it. The trial court permitted the laundry owner, who was not present at the crime scene, to tell the jury what he saw on the tape when he late viewed it. Because the original was not available and there was an explanation for its nonproduction, the court permitted secondary evidence—the laundry owner's rendition of what he saw on the video. The appellate court sustained the defendant's objection to the use of secondary evidence because the laundry owner's testimony would have been, at best, a summary of what he remembered seeing on the video and would not be an accurate portrayal of the original videotape recording of the crime as it occurred.[73]

"The [best evidence] rule is inapplicable when content is not at issue."[74] In a South Dakota criminal prosecution, a defendant on trial for felony theft objected to a store clerk and other employees testifying about the price of a DVD player the defendant had allegedly stolen. The defendant alleged that the best evidence rule required production of the in-store signs setting the price of the DVD player and on which the testimony was based. In rejecting the defendant's contention, the court noted that the prosecution was not trying to prove the contents of the department store's price labels and signs, but attempting to show how the employees learned the price of the DVD player. The price on the store tag sufficed to provide adequate evidence of market value and was not disputed by either side.[75] Similarly, in a Texas case, the police transferred two marked bills to the defendant in a cocaine deal and the bills were recovered and photocopied carefully following the arrest. The bills were reused by the police in other drug cases and were not kept for the defendant's prosecution. Over the defendant's objection, on best evidence rule grounds, the trial court allowed the admission of the photocopies of the money into evidence on the theory that the substantive content of the writing of the two bills was not at issue; the evidence of the drug transaction and the recovery of the bills from the defendant and the linkage of the bills to the police as bait bills was offered to demonstrate that the defendant was the person who sold cocaine to the undercover police officer. Because the evidence of the photocopied currency was not offered to prove the contents of the currency, the best evidence rule did not apply.[76]

---

[73] People v. Jimenez, 2005 N.Y. Slip Op. 25219, 8 Misc. 3d 803, 804, 796 N.Y.S.2d 232, 233, 2005 N.Y. Misc. LEXIS 1114 (N.Y. 2005).

[74] 6 JACK B. WEINSTEIN ET AL., WEINSTEIN'S FEDERAL EVIDENCE § 1002.05[1] (2d ed 2002).

[75] South Dakota v. Downing, 2002 S.D. 148, 654 N.W.2d 793, 2002 S.D. LEXIS 165 (2002).

[76] Bryant v. Texas, 2003 Tex. App. LEXIS 6687 (2003), accord, California v. Page, 2003 Cal. App. Unpub. LEXIS 6732 (2003).

Where a document exists but witnesses possess the same knowledge that was incorporated into the writing, witnesses may testify independently of the introduction of the document as long as they do so from personal knowledge. In a trial for felony theft of pistols, the trial court allowed one of the prosecution witnesses to testify about the substantive contents of a confession made by the defendant. The defendant had previously orally offered his confession to a detective who tape-recorded the confession, but neither the taped confession nor a writing was ever introduced at the defendant's trial. The trial court decision held that the best evidence rule was not implicated because the detective gave the testimony concerning the confession from the witness stand from his own memory and did not rely upon the writing/tape recording. The Supreme Court of Arkansas agreed on the theory that because the prosecution did not introduce a writing of the confession, the best evidence rule did not apply.[77]

With respect to letters written by the use of carbon paper,[78] courts have found that because they are made by the same mechanical act as the original they are generally not excluded under the best evidence rule.[79] For example, if the carbon copy is mailed and the original typed letter retained, the one mailed would certainly be considered a duplicate original letter, as much so as the original letter. Therefore, carbon impressions are not considered copies, but duplicate originals.[80] A retained carbon copy of a letter was not subject to exclusion under the best evidence rule when the carbon copy was signed as was the original by the person who prepared it. The retained copy, as well as the copy sent, was considered to be a counterpart or duplicate.[81]

In one case, a defendant contested whether the police officer had proper certification as a law enforcement officer. The officer testified that he had completed the police academy and that he had received certification as a police officer and held that status at the time of the defendant's stop and arrest. The trial court rejected the defendant's argument that the paper certificate should have been introduced to prove that that officer possessed proper state certification and that failure to introduce the certificate violated the best evidence rule. The court of appeals also rejected the defendant-appellant's argument and noted that "[t]he content of the certificate attesting to his certification was not in issue: in issue was whether the officer was certified, which was a fact that existed independent of the written certification even though his successful completion of training and certification had been reduced to and was evidenced by a writing."[82]

---

[77]   Gamble v. Arkansas, 351 Ark. 541, 550, 95 S.W.3d 755, 761, 2003 Ark. LEXIS 44 (2003).

[78]   Carbon paper was used for many years to use the original impression of a typewriter or handwriting to create a duplicate imprint on a second sheet of paper placed beneath the first, top paper. The use of carbonless business forms, copy machines, and laser printers have largely made carbon paper obsolete.

[79]   See FED. R. EVID. 1001(4).

[80]   Davis v. Williams Bros. Constr. Co., 207 Ky. 404, 269 S.W. 289 (1925); Hartstock v. Strong, 21 Md. App. 110, 318 A.2d 237 (1974).

[81]   Bruce v. United States, 361 F.2d 318 (5th Cir. 1965).

[82]   Clinkscale v. Arkansas, 2002 Ark. App. LEXIS 614 (2002).

§ 13.7   Secondary Evidence

> ### Rule 1003
>
> ### Admissibility of Duplicates
>
> A duplicate is admissible to the same extent as an original unless (1) a genuine question is raised as to the authenticity of the original or (2) in the circumstances, it would be unfair to admit the duplicate in lieu of the original.[83]

A duplicate, or as it is often called, a duplicate original, as defined in Rule 1001(4), "is a counterpart produced by the same impression as the original or from the same matrix, or by means of photography, including enlargements and miniatures, or by mechanical or electronic re-recording, by chemical reproduction, or by other equivalent techniques that accurately reproduce the original." If the original has been lost or destroyed through no fault of the proponent of the evidence, secondary evidence may be admitted where the loss or destruction of the original was not the fault of the proponent and where there is no reason to doubt the accuracy of the secondary evidence or duplicate original.[84] In ruling that a duplicate original could be admitted into evidence, a federal district court permitted the introduction of secondary evidence of voice recordings. The originals had been recorded on a digital chip by the government and transferred to audiotape and to an audio compact disc. The judge ruled that the copies appeared to be duplicates and fully admissible under Rule 1001 and Rule 1003, governing the admissibility of duplicates.[85] Similarly, in a case from Mississippi, a trial court admitted a duplicate, though slightly edited, videotape of the criminal drug sale. The defendant allegedly sold marijuana to an informant while the act was videotaped. The original tape contained evidence of other crimes, so the prosecution had the other crimes edited out of the version shown to the jury over the defendant's best evidence rule objection. The eyewitness-informant testified that the edited videotape recording accurately depicted the original version. The appellate court affirmed the admissibility of the edited tape by noting that Mississippi Rule of Evidence 1003 provides that "a duplicate is admissible to the same extent as an original unless (1) a genuine question is raised as to the authenticity of the original or (2) in the circumstances it would be unfair to admit the duplicate in lieu of the original."[86] The rationale for Rule 1003 is that when the only concern is with introducing the words or other contents before the court with accuracy and precision, a counterpart serves equally as well as the original if the counterpart or duplicate original is the product of a method that ensures accuracy and authenticity.[87]

---

[83]   *See* FED. R. EVID. 1003.
[84]   Luebbert v. Simmons, 98 S.W.3d 72, 75, 76, 2003 Mo. App. LEXIS 74 (2003).
[85]   United States v. Capanelli, 257 F. Supp. 2d 678, 680, 2003 U.S. Dist. LEXIS 5243 (S.D.N.Y. 2003).
[86]   Griffin v. State, 918 So. 2d 882, 884, 2006 Miss. App. LEXIS 12 (Miss. 2006).
[87]   Notes of the Advisory Committee on the Proposed Rules.

Applying this rationale, a federal district court in Minnesota allowed the admission of a digitally enhanced surveillance videotape against a defendant charged with arson of a commercial building. An expert converted the original video recording to a digital format and contrast-enhanced as well as corrected to real-time images. The defendant objected under the best evidence rule that the enlargement of selected images with adjusted brightness and contrast rendered the new version untrustworthy and inadmissible. The trial judge held that the new version was admissible because the images remain accurate renditions of what happened at the crime scene and did not distort reality any more than a black-and-white surveillance camera distorts by not recording color images.[88] In a Georgia case, a trial court permitted the prosecution to introduce a copy of the original printout from an Intoxilyzer blood-alcohol test over the defendant's objection that the best evidence rule required the original printout or an excuse for its nonproduction. In reviewing the case, the appellate court observed that the prosecution made no effort to explain why the original was missing or how it became lost or destroyed and so secondary evidence (the copy) was not admissible. The appellate court reversed the driving under the influence of alcohol conviction on the ground that the best evidence rule had been violated and there was no other evidence on the record against the defendant.[89]

Copies of a defendant's confession that were made at the same time as the original can be admitted against a defendant over his best evidence rule objection. In a murder case, the defendant tried to keep any copies of his confession from admission because the prosecution had lost the first original. The defendant signed all three originals, but the prosecution or police lost or misplaced the first original. A government witness testified that the second original had the same contents as the first original, but the defendant contended that there was a faint line across the second original and that on page two, the page number had been circled by blue ink. The trial court judge ruled that the other evidence of the defendant's confession would be admitted on the ground that it qualified as a duplicate original that had the same validity as the first original produced.[90]

Rule 1004

Admissibility of Other Evidence of Contents

The original is not required, and other evidence of the contents of a writing, recording, or photograph is admissible if—

(1) Originals lost or destroyed. All originals are lost or have been destroyed, unless the proponent lost or destroyed them in bad faith; or

(2) Original not obtainable. No original can be obtained by any available judicial process or procedure; or

---

88 Unites States v. Siefert, 351 F. Supp. 2d 926, 927, 2005 U.S. Dist. LEXIS 747 (D.C. Minn. 2005).

89 Lumley v. State, 2006 Ga. LEXIS 755 (Ga. 2006).

90 State v. Rizzo, 2005 Conn. Super. LEXIS 1685 (Conn. 2005).

> **(3) Original in possession of opponent.** At a time when an original was under the control of the party against whom offered, that party was put on notice, by the pleadings or otherwise, that the contents would be a subject of proof at the hearing, and that party does not produce the original at the hearing; or
>
> **(4) Collateral matters.** The writing, recording, or photograph is not closely related to a controlling issue.[91]

When the original writing has been lost or destroyed, secondary evidence of its contents may become admissible when the original has not been lost or destroyed through the fault of the offering party. To facilitate the admission of the secondary evidence, a reasonable search should be made for the lost writing in the place where it was last known to have been, and inquiry should be made of persons most likely to have custody or who may have some knowledge of its whereabouts. As a general rule, before secondary evidence may be introduced in evidence, there must be proof that the writing was lost or destroyed without fraudulent intent or culpable responsibility on the part of the proponent and that the proponent offered satisfactory explanation for the failure to produce the original.[92] In an unpublished opinion, an Arkansas appellate court ruled that the original surveillance tape from a convenience store should have been introduced in court against a defendant accused of shoplifting. The clerk-witness did not observe the theft directly, but immediately played the surveillance tape that revealed the theft by the defendant. The defendant objected to the clerk-witness testifying concerning what the videotape recording showed, contending that the clerk-witness had no personal knowledge and that the videotape was the original copy that had to be produced because its contents were at issue in the case. The court of appeals reversed the conviction on the ground that the original writing (the videotape) must be admitted, rather than secondary evidence, because the original had not been lost or destroyed and the prosecution had not accounted for its absence.[93] In a Texas case, an aerial videotape of a defendant's vehicle during a chase was admitted even when the police officer was not sure if it was a copy and did not know who made the tape. The officer authenticated the events in the tape as accurately depicting events on the ground and the court properly admitted the videotape of the crime regardless of whether the tape was the original or a duplicate.[94]

Where the original and duplicate original copies have all been destroyed prior to trial, a judge has discretion to allow secondary evidence of what the original videotape contained. In an unpublished Minnesota case,[95] an original

---

[91]   FED. R. EVID. 1004.

[92]   Bank One, N.A. v. Bettinger, 2003 Ohio App. LEXIS 2974 (2003).

[93]   Bradley v. State, 2003 Ark. App. LEXIS 756 (2003). *See also* People v. Jimenez, 796 N.Y.S.2d 232; 2005 N.Y. Misc. LEXIS 1114 (2005).

[94]   Lemelle v. Texas, 2003 Tex. App. LEXIS 5913 (2003).

[95]   *See* State v. Mack, 2006 Minn. App. Unpub. LEXIS 53 (2006).

videotape was copied and made available to the police, the prosecution, and the defense and all parties had a chance to view it. For unexplained reasons, the case took a significant time to come to trial, with the result that all parties had destroyed all versions of the videotape through inadvertence or through planned recycling. The defendant made no allegation that the videotape was lost through the prosecutor's fault, fraud, or bad faith. The trial court held that under Rule 1004, allowing other evidence of the contents, there was no abuse of judicial discretion to permit a police officer to explain some of what he had observed on the videotape as secondary evidence.

While the best evidence rule does not mandate production of the original writing when the testimony shows that the original item has been lost or destroyed and there has been no bad faith by the proponent, a Tennessee court admitted a transcript of an original tape recording and an officer's recollection of what the defendant originally stated. In this prison assault case, in which a correctional officer had been injured and the defendant prisoner had originally made a taped confession of his statement concerning the crime, the original tape had been lost following its transcription. The state offered the excuse that a disgruntled former employee may have been responsible for the missing tape and original transcript. The appellate court upheld the trial court decision under the Tennessee version of Rule 1004 to admit the secondary evidence because the defendant had been furnished a copy of the transcript of the tape and had the opportunity to vigorously cross-examine the correctional officer who testified regarding the contents of the original confession.[96]

As a general rule, if the original document or the primary evidence is not available, secondary evidence may be admitted. Rule 1004 of the Federal Rules of Evidence provides that the original is not required and secondary evidence of the contents of a writing (or recording or photograph) is admissible if: (1) originals are lost or destroyed (not in bad faith); (2) the original is not obtainable; (3) the original is in the possession of an opponent; or (4) the writing, recording, or photograph is not related to the controlling issue.

The state of Nevada, as well as most other states, has codified the common law best evidence rule.[97] Nevada's statute is identical to Rule 1004 of the Federal Rules of Evidence. In *Tomlinson v. State*, a defendant who had been convicted of robbery argued that all four of the requirements established in the state statute should be met before other secondary evidence could be admissible.[98] The Supreme Court of Nevada, however, agreed with the state that only one of the four requirements is necessary for the nonoriginal evidence to be admissible.

While all states allow the admission of secondary evidence, the proponent of the evidence must lay a foundation that explains why the original evidence disappeared and support the admission of secondary evidence. The party must satisfy the judge that the original evidence has been lost, destroyed, or is oth-

---

[96]   Tennessee v. Terry, 2000 Tenn. Crim. App. LEXIS 295 (2000).

[97]   NEV. REV. STAT. § 52.255 (Matthew Bender 2006).

[98]   Tomlinson v. State, 878 P.2d 311 (Nev. 1994).

erwise unavailable through no fault of the moving party and that one of the reasons contained in Rule 1004 applies. In a Texas case,[99] the police or the judiciary lost the last page of an affidavit for a search warrant at some point after the warrant had been served. An unsworn but true copy of the last page of the affidavit was offered as secondary evidence of the terms of the original writing. The secondary evidence did not have the magistrate's signature or the affiant officer's signature but was admitted into evidence. The appellate court approved the admission of secondary evidence of the affidavit because there was no proof of bad faith as the reason for the loss or destruction of the original writing and the reviewing court did not address the issue of prosecutorial or police negligence in mishandling the affidavit page.

When the original writing cannot be located and appropriate justifications have been proffered, proper secondary evidence may be admissible. A common misconception concerns the type of secondary evidence that should be admitted in place of the original. Although some support for the next best evidence may be found in some cases, generally any type of secondary evidence may be admitted as long as it meets the authentication and relevancy tests.

Modern developments with the use of desktop computers and the use of network server computers have created additional challenges concerning what really constitutes the original, the duplicate original, and what serves as secondary evidence. In at least one case, data and records stored on magnetic and optical media have been held to fall within the bounds of "best evidence" because they represent a "writing." Printouts or computer screen output are the best evidence because of the impossibility in practice of reading the original, which is a piece of magnetic disc, a compact disc, or videodisc.[100]

The rules relating to best and secondary evidence generally apply to recordings and photographs as well as documents. For example, when an original tape recording was available and would normally be the best evidence, one trial court nevertheless permitted introduction of a copy that was conceded to be accurate. The court reasoned that when a copy is proven accurate and serves to prove the substance of the original in a more easily understood form, the spirit of the rule permits the admission of the copy.[101]

The proven fact that a person recorded a conversation does not automatically implicate the best evidence rule or serve to exclude oral testimony concerning the issue. The best evidence rule does not require that a party prove the loss of a recording before offering testimony about the conversation.[102] In *United States v. Rose*, the government sought to prove the contents of a conversation, the court explained, not the contents of the tape recording. A court may admit a transcript of a tape recording when the original or duplicate original audiotape has been admitted for jury consideration. While this may seem

[99] McCormick v. State, 2006 Tex. App. LEXIS 1619 (2006).
[100] FED. R. EVID. 1004 and 1001(4).
[101] Johns v. United States, 323 F.2d 421 (5th Cir. 1963); *see also* People v. Marcus, 107 Cal. Rptr. 264, 31 Cal. App. 3d 208 (1973).
[102] United States v. Rose, 590 F.2d 232 (7th Cir. 1978), *cert. denied*, 442 U.S. 929 (1979).

to violate the best evidence rule, a trial court generally has discretion to admit a transcript under these circumstances as an aid to assist the jury, especially when the audiotape may be of less than perfect quality. Under the circumstances, the transcript would not be offered as evidence to prove the contents of the tape, so it would not be prohibited by the best evidence rule.[103] As would be required in all such cases, the proponent offering the transcript would have to lay a foundation demonstrating the accuracy of the transcript.

When a fact may be subject to proof in more than one manner, the proponent may choose the method that best suits the party. In the course of introducing evidence sufficient to demonstrate that a defendant had committed a robbery, the prosecutor had a police officer introduce photographs of the actual currency seized from the defendant. Over an objection that the money was a writing and the originals should have been introduced, the defendant contended that the admission of the money violated the best evidence rule and secondary evidence of the money should not have been permitted. In approving the trial court's admission of the photographs, the appellate court noted that a witness can testify concerning tangible objects (such as money) without introducing the actual objects and without violating the best evidence rule.[104] Another way of considering a case like this is to note that, other than the fact that the writing on the currency denoted its value, it was the fact that money was taken in a robbery, and not precisely how much, that was important.

§ 13.8 Summaries

Rule 1006

Summaries

The contents of voluminous writings, recordings, or photographs which cannot conveniently be examined in court may be presented in the form of a chart, summary, or calculation. The originals, or duplicates, shall be made available for examination or copying, or both, by other parties at a reasonable time and place. The court may order that they be produced in court.[105]

The evidentiary rule allowing the use of summaries is consistent with the common law and permits the use of summaries of evidence when that method may be the only practical way to present the evidence to a court.[106] The admissibility of summary evidence is a matter that rests within the sound discretion of the trial court, but standards have evolved to guide courts in exercising their discretion. As a general rule, a proper foundation must be offered with regard

---

[103]   Washington v. Miles, 2001 Wash. App. LEXIS 2349 (2001).
[104]   Wingfield v. State, 2005 Ark. 574 (2006).
[105]   FED. R. EVID. 1006.
[106]   Washington v. Dudley, 2003 Wash. App. LEXIS 1551 (2003).

to the admissibility of the originals. The Sixth Circuit holds that there are five requirements for admission of a summary under Rule 1006.

> . . . Rule 1006 imposes five requirements for the admission of a summary: (1) the underlying documents must be so voluminous that they cannot be conveniently examined in court, (2) the proponent of the summary must have made the documents available for examination or copying at a reasonable time and place, (3) the underlying documents must be admissible in evidence, (4) the summary must be accurate and nonprejudicial, and (5) the summary must be properly introduced through the testimony of a witness who supervised its preparation.[107]

Failure to meet these or similar requirements in other jurisdictions may result in summary evidence being refused by the trial judge.

According to one New Jersey court, there are three kinds of evidentiary summaries that are often admitted in court. The first can be called a primary evidence summary and is used to condense large amounts of material that could not otherwise be grasped by a court or jury. The second type of summary involves a pedagogical device summary, which serves as a demonstrative aid to present or clarify drawings, charts, calculations, or models, and can simplify evidence already admitted in a case. The final type can be called a secondary evidence summary because it is a combination of the first two types of summaries. This summary assists the jury in accurately understanding complex evidence that they would otherwise have difficulty placing in context or understanding its importance.[108]

Just as a scientist might read an abstract of a scientific study to assist in understanding the complete study, a summary of a large body of evidence serves a similar purpose for a jury. The purpose of an evidentiary summary under Rule 1006 serves as an aid to the jury in its examination of evidence already admitted.[109] Summaries of voluminous writings, recordings, or photographs that cannot conveniently be examined in court must be accurate and nonprejudicial in order to be admissible,[110] although in preparing a summary certain editorial discretion must be exercised or the summary would contain all the evidence and frustrate the purpose of the summary.

The preparation and submission to the jury of summaries prepared by an expert is almost indispensable to the understanding of a long and complicated set of facts. When summaries are used and physically given to the jury, the court must ascertain with certainty that they are based upon, and fairly represent, competent evidence already before the jury. Such summaries, if given to

---

[107] United States v. Jamieson, 427 F.3d 394, 409, 2005 U.S. App. LEXIS 23337 (6th Cir. 2005), quoting United States v. Modena, 302 F.3d 626, 633 (6th Cir. 2002).

[108] *See* Heinzerling v. Goldfarb, 359 N.J. Super. 1, 8, 818 A. 2d 345, 349, 2002 N.J. Super. LEXIS 531 (2002).

[109] United States v. Winn, 948 F.2d 145 (5th Cir. 1991).

[110] Daniel v. Ben E. Keith Co., 97 F.3d 1329 (10th Cir. 1996). *See also* United States v. Petty, 132 F.3d 373 (7th Cir. 1997).

the jury, must be accompanied by appropriate instructions concerning their nature and use. The jury should be advised that the summaries do not, in and of themselves, constitute evidence in the case, but only purport to summarize the documentary and detailed evidence already admitted; that the jury should examine the basis upon which the summaries rest and be satisfied that they accurately reflect other evidence in the case; and that, if the jury is not so satisfied, the summaries should be disregarded. In addition, broad cross-examination should be permitted upon the summaries to afford a thorough test of their accuracy.

Summaries may used to assist the jury in understanding large amounts of information or to place large amounts of data in perspective, but the summaries are generally not considered evidence unless specifically admitted.[111] In a case in which the defendant had been charged with transporting fraudulently obtained merchandise across state lines, the prosecution presented summaries of some of the evidence. According to the government, the defendant would add himself as an authorized user to store credit cards and charge goods that he sold in interstate commerce. During the prosecution's case-in-chief, the government introduced more than 220 exhibits, including receipts for bogus credit card purchases, fraudulent additions to credit card account applications, and related evidence that it condensed into several summaries for use during trial as a way to place the evidence in context. On appeal, the defendant argued that the government failed to offer an adequate foundation for the summaries because it failed to allow the defendant to view the underlying records prior to trial. The Seventh Circuit rejected the defendant's contentions, noting that there was nothing in the record that indicated that the defense had not been permitted to view and inspect the underlying data and the defendant failed to object at trial. The court found no error in the use of summaries under the circumstances.[112]

Courts "cannot rationally expect an average jury to compile summaries and to create sophisticated flow charts to reveal patterns that provide important inferences about the defendant's guilt."[113] Furthermore, Rule 1006 does not provide that it is literally impossible to examine all of the underlying records before a summary chart may be utilized, but only that in-court examinations would be an inconvenience. To further assist a jury in its deliberations, [i]f a summary or chart is introduced solely as a pedagogical device, the court should instruct the jury that the chart or summary is not to be considered as evidence, but only as an aid in evaluating evidence.[114]

In interpreting Rule 1006, the Fifth Circuit Court of Appeals approved the use of summary charts in a case involving mail fraud in conjunction with perjury in receiving workers' compensation. The defendant was collecting disability payments for a back injury while he worked as a pilot for several charter airline companies. The government presented summaries in the form

---

[111]   United States v. Green, 428 F.3d 1131, 1134, 2005 U.S. App. LEXIS 24583 (8th Cir. 2005).

[112]   United States v. Murry, 395 F.3d 712, 717, 2005 U.S. App. LEXIS 8 (7th Cir. 2005).

[113]   United States v. Buck, 324 F.3d 786, 791, 2003 U.S. App. LEXIS 4820 (5th Cir. 2003).

[114]   Maine v. Corbin, 2000 Me. 167, 759 A.2d 727, 729, 730, 2000 Me. LEXIS 176 (2000).

of a timeline chart comparing the dates that the defendant worked and payments received, to the dates of fraudulent forms filed with the government to continue his disability benefits. The defendant claimed that the trial court erred when it admitted the timeline summary chart along with a government witness who explained the summary chart. The reviewing court noted that summary evidence is admissible based on the court's discretion and past practice permits a summary witness in a limited way to explain voluminous records. The court rejected the defendant's complaints because pursuant to the defendant's trial objection, the chart was never admitted into evidence and the court did not allow the summary chart to go to the jury room. In affirming the conviction, the Court of Appeals found no error in the use of the summary under Rule 1006.[115] However, when summary charts are erroneously admitted in a manner that substantially affects the legal rights of a defendant, such admission may result in a reversal of a trial jury decision and the awarding of a new trial.[116]

Interpreting a state evidence rule similar to Federal Rule 1006, a Utah court approved the use of summaries. In this case, the court decided that when the original consists of numerous accounts or other documents that cannot be examined in court without great loss of time, and the evidence sought from the account is only the general result of the whole, the evidence may be admitted.[117] The court reasoned that summaries are admissible if they are submitted in writing and if the proponent has laid the foundation for admissibility of the underlying documents.

Obviously, the admission of summary exhibits must be conditioned on the requirement that the items of evidence upon which they rest must be admissible. For example, in a federal case[118] involving conspiracy to import and harbor illegal aliens, the defendant contended that the summary spreadsheet exhibit offered by the prosecution, which tracked the status of illegal aliens working on the farms of defendant's clients, was unnecessary because the data was not voluminous, his counsel had not been permitted a chance to examine the underlying documents, and the items of evidence on which the summary spreadsheet was based involved inadmissible hearsay. The reviewing court rejected the defendant's arguments and noted, "[t]he spreadsheet was introduced to establish the alienage of the workers. As the government demonstrates, however, even without the admission of the summary exhibit, the evidence of the alienage of the persons involved was uncontested."[119] Even if there was any error, which the court did not find, any error was harmless.

While Rule 1006 allows the use of summaries when all of the conditions are met, a court should exclude summaries when the proponent of the summary fails to meet the requirements or where hearsay evidence has been

---

[115] United States v. Harms, 442 F.3d 367, 375, 2006 U.S. App. LEXIS 6622 (5th Cir. 2006).

[116] United States v. Hart, 295 F.3d 451, 2002 U.S. App. LEXIS 11246 (2002).

[117] Harvester Co. v. Pioneer Tractor & Implement, Inc., 626 P.2d 418 (Utah 1981).

[118] United States v. Matousek, 131 Fed. Appx. 641, 2005 U.S. App. LEXIS 9063 (10th Cir. 2005).

[119] *Id.*

included as one of the bases of the summary. In a prosecution for selling cocaine base, the trial court permitted the federal government to introduce summaries of the numbers of defendant's cell phone calls, and to whom they were made, when the evidence that supported the summaries was never authenticated. In addition, some of the evidence was hearsay; the government failed to make the cell phone records available for examination and copying; and the government failed to give written notice to the defendant that it was going to use cell phone records in a summary. The reviewing court noted that the summaries should not have been admitted because the summaries did not meet the requirements for admission. However, in affirming the conviction, the court viewed the other evidence as sufficiently strong that the admission of the summaries constituted harmless error. [120]

When a trial court authorizes the use of summary charts as a teaching device rather than as substantive evidence as provided in Rule 1006, the preferred practice is for the court to give limiting instructions regarding the purpose of the summaries.[121] In a case that came close to reversal, the appellate court grudgingly allowed a verdict to stand where the prosecution had permitted one of its own witnesses to summarize trial testimony just before the government rested its case. The Court of Appeals noted that under Rule 1006 there is no provision that addresses summary witnesses who summarize trial testimony, but some courts have permitted summary testimony in a limited capacity. The court took the position that while the use of summary evidence often serves an important purpose, one of the purposes of Rule 1006 is to not permit the prosecution to repeat its entire case-in-chief shortly before jury deliberations and prior to final arguments.[122]

§ 13.9 Learned Treatises

Medical books or treatises, even though properly identified and authenticated and shown to be recognized as standard authorities on the subjects to which they relate, are not generally admissible in evidence due to their hearsay status. According to the common law rule, proponents of evidence are not permitted to use learned treatise passages as substantive proof of their contents.[123] For example, according to Pennsylvania case law, "learned writings which are offered to prove the truth of the matters therein are hearsay and may not properly be admitted into evidence for consideration by the jury."[124] Similarly, in Ohio, a learned treatise may be part of the basis for an expert opinion and can

[120] United States v. Laguerre, 119 Fed. Appx. 458, 2005 U.S. App. LEXIS 213 (4th Cir. 2005).
[121] United States v. Howard, 774 F.2d 838 (7th Cir. 1985).
[122] United States v. Fullwood, 342 F.3d 409, 2003 U.S. App. LEXIS 16309 (5th Cir. 2003), *cert. denied*, 540 U.S. 1111 (2004).
[123] Aldridge v. Edmunds, 561 Pa. 323, 331, 750 A.2d 292, 296, 2000 Pa. LEXIS 1059 (2000).
[124] Calandra v. St. Agnes Med. Ctr., 2005 Phila. Ct. Com. Pl. LEXIS 254 (2005).

be used to impeach a witness, but it cannot be used for substantive evidence.[125] However, the federal courts do not exclude learned treatises from use as substantive evidence to the extent that an expert witness relies upon the treatise, as long as the treatise is established as a reliable authority by admission by that witness or another witness or by the use of judicial notice.[126]

A few states have adopted the rule that a published treatise, periodical, or pamphlet on a subject of history, science, or art may be admitted in evidence in some limited types of cases to prove the truth of a matter stated therein if the judge takes judicial notice or an expert witness in the subject area testifies that the writer of the treatise, periodical, or pamphlet is a recognized authority on the subject. Under a Massachusetts statute,[127] as a prerequisite to the admission of a medical treatise as evidence in medical malpractice actions, the proponent of such evidence must demonstrate for the trial judge that the offered treatise statements are relevant and that the writer of such statements is recognized in his profession or calling as an expert on the subject.[128]

§ 13.10 Summary

In addition to oral testimony, documentary evidence may be used in court to assist the jury and judge in determining the ultimate facts. Documentary evidence includes all kinds of documents, records, and writings. The concept of a writing proves to be an expansive idea and many jurisdictions include computer data wherever and however stored, movies, videotapes, digital video disc and compact disc storage, as well as almost anything that contains data under the definition of a writing. To be admissible, documentary evidence must meet the same requirements of relevancy, competency, and materiality, as does oral evidence, in addition must meet other requirements specifically related to writings. As a prerequisite to admission, documentary evidence must also be authenticated by one of several processes. As a rule, competent evidence must be introduced to show that the writing is what it purports to be.

In the interests of judicial economy, courts have recognized practical and simplified methods of authentication that are to be used in specific instances. Domestic public documents under seal are often deemed to be self-authenticating, while documents that have been certified as accurate copies of documents on file by the official custodian are similarly considered to be self-authenticating. Official publications by government agencies, including statutes and official regulations, may be self-authenticating because the concept of authentication is only a threshold consideration that the document is what it purports to be. Given that authentication is a rather low standard, the

---

[125] *See* Beard v. Meridia Huron Hospital, 106 Ohio St. 3d 237, 239, 2005 Ohio 4787, 834 N.E.2d 323, 326, 2005 Ohio LEXIS 2077 (2005).

[126] *See* FED. R. EVID. 803(18).

[127] Annotated Laws of Massachusetts, ALM GL ch. 233, § 79C (Matthew Bender 2006).

[128] Lasalvia v. Johnson, 15 Mass. 622, 2003 Mass. Super. LEXIS 9 (2003).

opposing party may introduce evidence that disputes the judge's initial determination that a document has been authenticated and the ultimate decision concerning whether the document has evidentiary value belongs to the finder of fact.

Although these are not necessarily exclusive, there are four general methods of authenticating a document: (1) proof of signing; (2) proof of signature; (3) comparison of signatures, usually by an expert; and (4) circumstantial evidence. The degree of proof varies with the type of document. As a general rule, public records and documents are admissible into evidence as exceptions to the hearsay rule without the same degree of authenticity as is required for private writings. This is allowed because of the extraordinary degree of confidence reposed in documents drafted by authorized and accredited officers or required by law to be filed publicly. This same degree of confidence is not placed in private writings, and such writings must be proven by slightly more exacting standards to be genuine before they are admissible as evidence.

To prevent the admission of forgeries, fabrications, and false writings, the best evidence rule accepts the principle of law that there is a decided preference for the original document where the contents of the writing are at issue. Although the rule permits several types of secondary evidence to be considered acceptable to the courts, many jurisdictions recognize several significant exceptions to producing the original. When the original cannot be obtained through any judicial process or has been lost or destroyed through no fault of the proponent, courts will frequently accept secondary evidence. The historical basis for this rule assumes that a copy is more likely to have errors and that a typewritten or computer-generated copy and will lack such features as handwriting and original paper impressions and could be more easily manipulated. Without individual characteristics of the original, an opponent has few means to detect alteration or fraud on secondary evidence. Currently, most modern writings are produced in ways that allow many duplicate originals that have not been produced by the human hand and are indistinguishable from each other. For this reason, many of the rationales for requiring the original are no longer valid, and exceptions have been included in statutes and codes, consistent with the interests of justice.

Real Evidence 14

Stains of blood, found upon the person or clothing of the party accused, have always been recognized among the ordinary indicia of homicide. The practice of identifying them by circumstantial evidence and by the inspection of witnesses and jurors has the sanction of immemorial usage in all criminal tribunals. . . . the degree of force to which it is entitled may depend upon a variety of circumstances to be considered and weighed by the jury in each particular case; but its competency is too well settled to be questioned in a court of law.

People v. Gonzalez, 35 N.Y. 49 (1866)

Chapter Outline

Key Terms and Concepts

admissibility of evidence   gruesome photographs

chain of custody   weight of evidence

§ 14.1 Introduction

Real evidence is *evidence that is addressed directly to the senses such as by sight, hearing, or taste, and it is without the intervention of witnesses.* This type of evidence has a physical and tangible existence as compared to oral testimony alone. Real evidence has often been referred to by the terms, "demonstrative" or "physical" evidence. Some authorities distinguish between demonstrative and real evidence by defining real evidence as that which involves the introduction of an object that had a direct part in the incident, such as the exhibition of injured parts of the body or an actual gun or knife used in a crime. On the other hand, demonstrative evidence involves the production in court of such things as models made for the trial, maps, photographs taken for use in litigation, X-rays, films, and weapons that are used only for demonstrative purposes and were not actually used in the crime. The term "demonstrative real evidence" generally refers to a physical object that had no historical connection to the crime, but will be used to show how a similar item was actually used in the crime or how a similar object reacted to events or forces that occurred during the crime.[1] Demonstrative items of evidence possess no probative value themselves[2] but serve merely as visual aids to assist the triers of fact in understanding the verbal testimony of a witness.[3] When demonstrative evidence is admitted, the decision is based on judicial discretion and is reviewable under the standard of abuse of discretion.[4] For example, in a murder prosecution in which a man had been killed while in his girlfriend's bed, the trial court permitted the government to bring a mannequin head to help the jury understand the testimony of the medical examiner. To further the jury's understanding, the court permitted a wooden dowel to be inserted in the man-

---

[1]   Torres v. Texas, 2003 Tex. App. LEXIS 6580 (2003).

[2]   *Id.*

[3]   32 C.J.S. *Evidence* § 602 (1996).

[4]   Washington v. Fairbanks, 2003 Wash. App. LEXIS 2050 (2003).

nequin's head to demonstrate the trajectory of the bullet. The medical examiner authenticated the head and dowel representing the trajectory as accurately depicting the original crime scene. The Supreme Court of Georgia approved of using this demonstrative real evidence because the mannequin head served to illustrate the medical examiner's testimony.[5] In this and the following chapter, real evidence includes both types.

In admitting real evidence, courts must carefully weigh the probative value against the risk of unfair prejudice because real evidence is generally considered an especially persuasive class of evidence. In a Texas case, the court permitted the prosecution to dress a dummy in the bloody clothes of the deceased over the objection of the defendant that the danger of unfair prejudice outweighed any probative value of the dummy. Demonstrative real evidence must accurately depict what it purports to depict, and in this case the dummy appeared much smaller than the size of the deceased. Even though the defense unsuccessfully contended that having the dummy in court in the defendant's bloody clothes would prejudice the defendant, it failed to mention the size discrepancy. The reviewing court upheld the original trial court ruling.[6] Recent court decisions have emphasized the necessity of developing more sophisticated methods of obtaining and utilizing real evidence in criminal cases. Because of the constitutional limitations placed upon the use of confessions, more emphasis is placed upon the use of real evidence. For example, in the case of *Schmerber v. California*,[7] the United States Supreme Court held that the Fifth Amendment self-incrimination protection applied to evidence of a testimonial or communicative nature, but not to real evidence. In that case the Court stated:

> On the other hand, both federal and state courts have usually held that it [the Fifth Amendment] offers no protection against compulsion to submit to fingerprinting, photographing, or measurements, to write or speak for identification, to appear in court, to stand, to assume a stance, to walk, or to make a particular gesture.

The Court also noted that:

> Compulsion which makes a suspect or accused the source of real or physical evidence does not violate it [the Fifth Amendment].

In rendering the *Schmerber* decision, the Court clarified the use of real evidence that may be derived from the suspect personally. Because the suspect may be required to offer real evidence without violating the suspect's Fifth

---

[5]   Moss v. Georgia, 274 Ga. 740, 559 S.E.2d 433, 2002 Ga. LEXIS 48 (2002).

[6]   Runnels v. State, 193 S.W.3d 105, 107, 2006 Tex. App. LEXIS 17 (Tex. 2006). The trial court might not have admitted the dummy if the defense had objected to its use because it did not properly depict the size of the victim.

[7]   384 U.S. 757, 86 S. Ct. 1826, 16 L. Ed. 2d 908 (1966). *See* case in Part II. *See* Chapter 16 for discussion of constitutional safeguards that regulate the admissibility of evidence,

Amendment privilege, evidence that merely offers or confirms the existence of physical facts involves no compulsory testimony and is fully admissible provided no other rule of evidence excludes it.

The sections that follow discuss the tests for general admissibility relating to real evidence and offer some examples of the types of real evidence of particular concern to criminal justice personnel. In Chapter 15, emphasis is placed on the use of results of experiments and tests conducted in and out of court.

§ 14.2 Admissibility Requirements

To be admissible, real evidence must generally meet the same requirements of relevancy, competency, and materiality as documentary evidence and oral testimony. In addition, a foundation proving authenticity must be laid before real evidence is admissible. Generally, the foundation is laid by an attorney calling a witness and asking questions relating to the real evidence to be introduced. To provide a proper foundation, the real evidence offered must be identified as being the same evidence or object involved in the alleged crime and it must be shown that the object has not undergone any important or material change.[8] In many instances criminal justice personnel are most familiar with the evidence and can most correctly connect the evidence with the crime and the accused by using several authentication techniques. Occasionally, a defendant may be willing to stipulate facts that support admission of adverse evidence.[9] Finally, the prosecuting attorney may call upon the victim to take the stand to establish the identity and relevance of the real evidence.

As a general rule for real evidence to be admissible at trial, the proponent must show that it is sufficiently connected with case through the defendant, the victim, or the crime.[10] The state must demonstrate a reasonable probability that tampering, substitution, or alteration of the evidence did not occur. Trial courts may assume and appellate courts will concur, "absent a showing of bad faith or ill will, that the officials charged with custody of the evidence properly discharged their duties and did not tamper with the evidence."[11]

The party offering an item in evidence bears the burden of presenting evidence sufficient to support a finding that the matter in question is what the party claims, and in satisfying its burden the party may authenticate the item either by having a witness visually identify the item as the one that was involved in the crime or by establishing a chain of custody that indirectly establishes the identity and integrity of the evidence by tracing its continuous location. During a trial, a decision concerning whether an item of evidence has been sufficiently authenticated for admission rests with the trial judge, whose

---

[8] State v. McClure, 2006 N.C. App. LEXIS 47 (N.C. 2006).

[9] *See* People v. Garth, 353 Ill. App. 3d 108, 817 N.E.2d 1085, 2004 Ill. App. LEXIS 1192 (2004).

[10] People v. Hogan, 114 P.3d 42, 51, 2004 Colo. App. LEXIS 2001 (Colo. 2004), *reh'g denied*, 2005 Colo. LEXIS 597 (Colo. 2005).

[11] State v. Goff, 191 S.W.3d 113, 116, 2006 Mo. App. LEXIS 712 (2006).

decision is subject to review on the basis of an abuse of discretion standard.[12] Once the proponent of the real evidence has laid a minimally sufficient foundation, "a lack of positive identification or a defect in the chain of custody goes to the weight of the evidence rather than the admissibility."[13]

Four general rules regarding the admissibility of real evidence are often applied. They are: (1) establishment of a chain or continuity of custody; (2) necessity; (3) relationship to crime; and (4) proper identification.

A. *Establishment of a Chain or Continuity of Custody*

In establishing a chain of custody, the proponent of the evidence must demonstrate where the evidence has been stored or housed since the evidence originally came into the possession of the police or the evidence may be excluded from use at trial.[14] Chain of custody applies to defendants as well, but normally the issue is one for the prosecution because it will be introducing most of the real evidence. The necessity of proving chain of custody exists because many people may handle the evidence from the time of its original collection. Proof of where the evidence has been minimizes the chances that someone tampered with the evidence, substituted evidence, lost and replaced it, or otherwise allowed it to be altered in some manner.[15] A failure to make a chain of custody objection at the time the evidence is introduced generally waives any chain of custody argument.[16] Proving the chain of custody assures authenticity of the evidence, and without authentication the evidence would be inadmissible. While it is preferable to introduce evidence to show that the chain of custody was not broken at any time, in offering proof of the chain of custody, the prosecution need not eliminate each and every possibility of tampering with the evidence. As one court noted, "Minor uncertainties in the proof of chain of custody are matters to be argued by counsel and weighed by the jury, but they do not render the evidence inadmissible as a matter of law."[17] In one case in which the officer testified about collecting contraband, the officer stated that it was in the same condition except for some changes that occurred during chemical testing. The chemist in the case indicated similar guarantees of control and custody and the judge held that the drug evidence could be admitted due to proof of the chain of custody.[18] In proving sufficient chain of custody, the prosecutor is not "required to foreclose every possibility of tampering; it need only show reasonable assurance of the identity of the evidence."[19]

---

[12]   People v. Lee, 2005 Mich. App. LEXIS 3186 (2005).
[13]   State v. Housley, 922 So.2d 659, 665, 2006 La. App. LEXIS 116 (2006).
[14]   State v. Cowans, 336 Ill. App. 3d 173, 782 N.E.2d 779, 2002 Ill. App. LEXIS 1170 (2002), *appeal denied*, 2003 Ill. LEXIS 649 (2003). *See* case in Part II.
[15]   Tennessee v. Woods, 2001 Tenn. Crim. App. LEXIS 797 (2001).
[16]   Miller v. State, 2004 Tex. App. LEXIS 11547 (Tex. 2004).
[17]   Green v. State, 2006 Ark. LEXIS 167 (Ark. 2006).
[18]   In the Matter of Kassan D., 287 A.D.2d 564, 565, 566, 731 N.Y.S.2d 487, 2001 N.Y. App. Div. LEXIS 9594 (2001).
[19]   Franklin v. State, 2006 Ga. App. LEXIS 1111 (2006).

In the case of *New York v. Lanza*,[20] the appellate court reviewed the standards for chain of custody and held that, under the circumstances of the case, the chain had been properly proven. In *Lanza*, the defendant sold crack cocaine to an undercover police officer on two occasions. Each time, the undercover officer acquired the drug and handed the substance to another officer, who placed the suspected drug in a plastic evidence bag, labeled the bag, and locked it in a special police drug locker. Subsequently, the sample was removed and transported in two separate containers to the crime lab where he watched an evidence receiving technician weigh each bag, mark them, and place them in a safe storage area within a different plastic bag. At trial, a chemist identified a certified copy of the crime lab record for the two, bagged items of suspected crack cocaine. The court noted the procedure followed by the chemist, in which:

> she retrieved the two bags from the vault and placed them in a locked box to which only she had access. Approximately two weeks later, she removed the bags from the locked box, opened them and took a small amount of material from each for testing. We conclude that this evidence, including the certified Crime Lab record, was sufficient to establish a complete chain of custody (citations omitted). In addition, defendant does not dispute that the substance contained in the two exhibits admitted at trial was the substance sold by him, as demonstrated by the undisputed testimony of the undercover officer and Kane, and the forensic chemist testified that those two exhibits were the ones from which she obtained the substance for testing.[21]

According to the appellate court in *Lanza*, the chain of custody had been clearly shown at the trial proceeding by appropriate evidence. In this case, the prosecution proved that the defendant possessed crack cocaine and sold it to the undercover officer, who had it properly analyzed, and the lab expert properly explained the identity of the controlled substance. Chain of custody need not be perfect in every respect; it is sufficient that once the prosecution introduces evidence that strongly suggests the presence of virtually every link in the chain, any gaps go to the weight rather than to the admissibility of the evidence.[22]

When the chain of custody covers an extended period, but the chain has been sufficiently proved to be unbroken, the evidence should be admitted. In 1994, the brother of a female marijuana dealer found that someone had killed her by cutting her throat. Police found blood on a washcloth on the back fence that contained blood. They properly tagged it and sent it to an Atlanta lab. At the time, the amount of DNA that was collected was insufficient for testing, so the samples were stored properly in a secured cold room until 2001, when

---

[20] New York v. Lanza, 299 A.D.2d 649, 650, 749 N.Y.S.2d 618, 620, 2002 N.Y. App. Div. LEXIS 10780 (2002).

[21] *Id.*

[22] Troxell v. Indiana, 778 N.E.2d 811, 814, 2002 Ind. LEXIS 888 (2002), *and see* Hawkins v. Arkansas, 105 S.W.3d 397, 2003 Ark. App. LEXIS 334 (2003).

the science had advanced to permit new testing that disclosed that the defendant's and the victim's DNA were present in the washcloth sample.[23] At the defendant's murder trial, police officers, crime scene technicians, lab officials who conducted the DNA testing, and other individuals who had been involved in the case testified concerning the chain of custody of the blood samples from the time of the original collection to the introduction of the results at trial. The defendant objected to the introduction of the DNA evidence based on alleged, but not clearly specified, problems with the chain of custody of the blood sample. The trial judge admitted the evidence because he found that a proper chain of custody had been proven even though a significant period had elapsed between the crime and the trial. In upholding the murder conviction, the appellate court observed that as long as the blood samples had been handled in a routine manner and there was no reason to raise a suspicion that the blood-based results were not from the original blood sample, a sufficient chain of custody was properly proven.[24] The length and duration of the chain of custody, where properly demonstrated, will not prevent the introduction of evidence when the custody of the evidence has been unbroken.

However, the failure to properly follow chain-of-custody procedures or a failure to allege and prove them in court will have serious consequences for the prosecution. For example, an Illinois appeals court reversed a probation revocation based on the defendant's delivery of a controlled substance within 1,000 feet of a church where a defendant had sold crack cocaine to an undercover police agent. The officer stated that when he received the crack he inventoried the item, but offered no further evidence concerning chain of custody. The parties stipulated to the fact of what a state forensic scientist would testify concerning the crack cocaine and the state rested its case. The defense asked for a directed verdict because the prosecution had failed to prove a chain of custody for the crack cocaine and failed to demonstrate that the sample tested by the state was the crack cocaine allegedly taken from the defendant. Following his probation revocation based on the crack cocaine sale, the defendant appealed on the lack of chain of custody proof. In analyzing the requirements for the chain of custody, the appellate court noted that:

> When contraband is sought to be introduced, it is the State's burden to establish "a chain of custody of sufficient completeness to render it improbable that the [evidence] has been tampered with, exchanged, or contaminated." The State must show that the police took reasonable protective measures to ensure that the substance taken from the defendant was the same as the substance tested by the forensic chemist. This requires proof of delivery, presence, and safekeeping. Unless the defendant produces evidence of actual tampering, substitution, or contamination, the State is only required to establish that reasonable protective measures were employed to pro-

---

[23]   Schmerber v. California, 384 U.S. 757, 1966 U.S. LEXIS 1129 (1966) held that the use of a defendant's own blood does not violate the Fifth Amendment privilege against self-incrimination. *See* case in Part II.

[24]   Paschal v. State, 280 Ga. 430, 432, 628 S.E.2d 586, 589, 2006 Ga. LEXIS 202 (2006).

tect the evidence from the time that it was seized and that it is improbable that the evidence was altered. Once the State has done so, the evidence is admissible and any remaining deficiencies in the chain of custody merely go to the weight of the evidence. Finally, where there is a link in the chain missing, but testimony has described the condition of the evidence when it was seized and that description matches the condition of the evidence when examined, a continuous chain of custody is established. (citations omitted.) [25]

In this case, because the prosecution failed to present any evidence concerning the handling and safekeeping of the evidence between the time the state received the crack from the defendant and the delivery of some substance to the state forensic scientist, proof of the chain of custody failed. It was important for the prosecution to establish that some reasonable protective measures had been employed from the time the evidence was seized to demonstrate that it was improbable that the evidence was altered. Because the state failed to follow the proper procedures or failed to prove that it followed them, the appellate court reversed the case.[26]

Notwithstanding the fact that the courts have been reluctant to prohibit the use of evidence even if there has been a gap in the chain of custody, it is quite clear that unless the prosecution can to show that the item has not been contaminated or tampered with, it will not be admitted. Evidence may be admitted with slight deficiencies in the chain of custody, but a court or jury will give less weight to such evidence.

B. Necessity

Because of the weight that may be placed upon the use of real evidence, courts have reasoned that it should not be admitted unless a valid reason for its admission is offered. While real evidence does not require absolutely perfect links in the chain of custody to qualify for admission in evidence,[27] the admission or exclusion of real evidence rests largely within the sound discretion of the trial judge.[28] In some instances, the party offering a demonstration of the real evidence is required to give good reason for its acceptance into evidence. As one court stated, the evidence should be admitted when it is both relevant and highly probative, better evidence cannot reasonably be anticipated, and the dangers are small in comparison to the advantages.[29]

While the admission of certain evidence is not improper merely because it may tend to influence the emotions, it should be excluded when it appears to be designed to appeal to the emotional and sympathetic tendencies of a judge or jury. In a trial for having her husband murdered, the court initially

---

[25] Illinois v. Moore, 335 Ill. App. 3d 616, 781 N.E.2d 493, 2002 Ill. App. LEXIS 1058 (2002).

[26] Id.

[27] People v. Conner, 2005 Mich. App. LEXIS 653 (2005).

[28] See Washington v. Delgado, 2003 Wash. App. LEXIS 87 (2003), which held that a judge in his or her discretion may admit or exclude real evidence in the form of photographs.

[29] Commonwealth v. Inhabitants of Holliston, 107 Mass. 232 (1871).

excluded a sexually suggestive photograph of the defendant, found in the possession of the defendant's paramour, as being unfairly prejudicial and cumulative.[30] The jury might become motivated for unfair reasons. The trial court later reversed its ruling and admitted the explicit photo after the defendant testified that she had not had a consensual sexual relationship with the government witness who hired the hit man to kill her husband. Once her testimony was on the record as denying her relationship with her lover, the photograph became more relevant and less prejudicial to explain her relationship with her paramour, who hired the hit man.

When photographs of a murder victim serve only to inflame the passion of the jury, their prejudicial effect outweighs their probative value and admission is improper.[31] Applying this rule, the court held that the prejudicial effect of photographs of the murder victim outweighed their probative value and the admission in a murder trial was improper under Illinois law. The court noted that the photographs were both grisly and cumulative of testimony and it was difficult to understand how photographs showing the gunshot wound to the victim's penis explained the testimony describing the wound.

C. Relationship to Crime

Evidence may be excluded at the discretion of the judge when facts that the prosecution seeks to prove are only remotely connected to the issues. In other words, the evidence that a party seeks to have admitted must tend to prove or disprove a fact at issue in the case and when the effects of an item of evidence are marginal, it should be excluded. In addition, if the evidence would be likely to mislead or confuse the jury, a judge may refuse to allow the evidence.[32] In a drug sale case in which the defendant wanted the jury to view the scene, the judge refused to allow a jury view of the crime scene because the physical area in which the alleged drug sale occurred had changed significantly since the time of the defendant's arrest.[33]

In cases in which the prosecution wants to introduce a physical object (such as a weapon) connected with the commission of a crime, it may properly be admitted into evidence only after it has been satisfactorily identified and shown to have a sufficient connection to the crime charged. In a case involving a series of car thefts in which firearms were used, a witness positively identified a distinctive gun used by the defendants, connecting the gun and the defendants and assuring its admissibility.[34] If there is insufficient evidence to show that the article is connected with the crime, it should not be admitted. For example, in a child sexual misconduct case, the prosecution had a plastic bag containing hair taken from the defendant's possession marked as an exhibit, but

---

[30]   United States v. Brudette, 86 Fed. Appx. 121, 2004 U.S. App. LEXIS 804 (6th Cir. 2004).

[31]   United States ex rel. Gonzalez v. DeTella, 918 F. Supp. 1214 (N.D. Ill. 1996).

[32]   32 C.J.S. *Evidence* § 602.

[33]   Sherman v. Arkansas, 2005 Ark. App. LEXIS 141 (2005).

[34]   Attaway v. Georgia, 259 Ga. App. 822, 826, 827, 578 S.E.2d 529, 533, 2003 Ga. App. LEXIS 270 (2003).

it never introduced the bag of hair into evidence.[35] The prosecution had planned to ask the defendant about the hair if he took the witness stand, but the opportunity never arose. A reviewing court concluded that the bag of hair did not make any fact that was of consequence to the case more or less probable than it would have been without it. The reviewing court concluded the hair was improperly introduced because it may have encouraged jury speculation, but the appellate court thought that the hair evidence constituted harmless error and did not reverse the convictions. A federal court reasoned that evidence that a .38-caliber shell found in the parking lot near the defendant's apartment was admissible in a prosecution for armed robbery when the expert testimony linked the shell to a box of cartridges found in the defendant's car and linked the box of cartridges to bullets recovered from the crime scene.[36]

Although the burden is on the party introducing the evidence to show that it complies with the requirements, in most instances the court will admit real evidence if it has any logical bearing upon the case. The judge has the discretion as to whether the evidence is related to the crime, and his or her decision is not subject to review unless there has been a clear abuse of this discretion.

D. Proper Identification

When the prosecution wants to introduce an object, article, tool, weapon, or similar tangible item in evidence to prove a fact to which it is connected from a previous time or event, the item is not competent evidence unless it is first identified as being the same object that was originally recovered and is shown to be in substantially the same condition as it was during the time or event to which it is claimed to be related.[37] A Texas court noted that in identifying evidence, "[t]he chain of custody is conclusively proven if an officer is able to identify that he or she seized the item of physical evidence, put an identification mark on it, placed it in the property room, and then retrieved the item being offered on the day of trial."[38] The requirement that physical objects be identified or authenticated as genuine serves to prevent the introduction of false evidence or evidence that has been subjected to tampering. In a case in which the defendant had been accused of having a firearm under a disability, he contended that the prosecution had not properly authenticated or identified the gun in court as the one originally taken from the defendant. The evidence showed that one officer recovered the gun and his radio transmissions gave

---

[35] State v. Jacobson, 87 Conn. App. 440, 450, 866 A.2d 678, 687, 2005 Conn. App. LEXIS 64 (2005).

[36] United States v. Davis, 103 F.3d 660 (8th Cir. 1996), *cert. denied*, 520 U.S. 1258, 117 S. Ct. 2424, 138 L. Ed. 2d 187 (1997).

[37] Gutman v. Industrial Comm., 71 Ohio App. 383, 50 N.E.2d 187 (1942); *see also* State v. Campbell, 103 Wash. 2d 1, 691 P.2d 929, *cert. denied*, 471 U.S. 1094, 105 S. Ct. 2169, 85 L. Ed. 2d 526 (1984), which held that before a physical object connected with the commission of a crime may properly be admitted into evidence, it must be satisfactorily identified and shown to be in substantially the same condition as it was when the crime was committed. The factors to be considered include the nature of the article, circumstances surrounding its preservation and custody, and the likelihood of intermeddlers tampering with it.

[38] Bridges v. State, 2005 Tex. App. LEXIS 10389 (Tex. 2005).

verification, while another officer accepted the gun and logged it into the property room using a voucher and the gun's serial number. The officer at trial testified that the serial number of the gun at trial matched the recorded number on the property room voucher. The trial court held that the gun in court had been sufficiently identified as the actual gun taken from the defendant and denied the motion to set aside the guilty verdict.[39] The identification requirement prevents the chance of incorrect evidence being introduced against a defendant.

Generally, physical evidence is properly admitted if it is readily identifiable by some unique feature or other identifying mark.[40] When a real or physical object is offered as evidence in a criminal prosecution, an adequate foundation for admission requires testimony that the one is the same object that was involved in the alleged incident, and the condition of the object is substantially unchanged.[41]

The state met the identification requirement in a Michigan case in which the 7-11 store pre-positioned a $2 bill that had a recorded serial number in the cash register.[42] This $2 bill was to be given out to robbers and, following a robbery, an arrested defendant possessed a $2 bill with the same pre-recorded serial number, which was recovered by police. The serial number sufficiently identified the $2 bill as having been taken in a robbery and it was properly admitted into evidence at the defendant's robbery trial.

Articles are sometimes admitted into evidence even though a slight alteration or change has occurred, e.g., a court admitted a serrated blade of a knife discovered at a murder scene after a fire when a surviving victim stated that the defendant had cut his throat with a complete knife;[43] clothing worn by the deceased was washed by his widow after having been returned by the police;[44] a murder weapon was dusted for fingerprints by the police and then wiped clean;[45] two mangled bullets recovered from a wall that a ballistics expert stated were fired from the same gun;[46] and laquer was removed from counterfeit bank bill plates.[47]

In the case of *Washington v. Commonwealth*, the appellate court held that the trial court did not err in admitting a shirt into evidence in a prosecution for capital murder even though the shirt had been worn, washed, ironed, and folded after the crime had been committed. The fact that bloodstains found on the shirt had been cut out for laboratory analysis, leaving small holes, did nothing to impair the admissibility or probative value of the exhibit because the changes were sufficiently explained to avoid any confusion of the jury.[48]

[39] United States v. Stukes, 2004 U.S. Dist. LEXIS 21486 (S.D.N.Y. 2004), *aff'd*, 2006 U.S. App. LEXIS (2d Cir. 2006).
[40] United States v. Abreu, 952 F.2d 1458 (1st Cir.), *cert. denied*, 503 U.S. 994, 112 S. Ct. 1695, 118 L. Ed. 2d 406 (1992).
[41] United States v. Miller, 994 F.2d 441 (8th Cir. 1993).
[42] People v. Grandberry, 2005 Mich. App. LEXIS 2099 (2005).
[43] Commonwealth v. Edwards, 2006 Pa. LEXIS 1529 (2006).
[44] Davidson v. State, 208 Ga. 834, 69 S.E.2d 757 (1952).
[45] State v. Cooper, 10 N.J. 532, 91 A.2d 786 (1952).
[46] Grayson v. King, 2006 U.S. App. LEXIS 21215 (11th Cir. 2006).
[47] State v. Stewart, 1 Ohio App. 2d 260, 204 N.E.2d 397 (1963).
[48] Washington v. Commonwealth, 228 Va. 535, 323 S.E.2d 577, *cert. denied*, 471 U.S. 1111, 105 S. Ct. 2347, 85 L. Ed. 863 (1984).

§ 14.3   Exhibition of Person

When the prosecution of the defendant is based on physical harm to the victim, it would seem that the best evidence of such harm would be the exhibition of the person of the victim to the jury. Such a witness would be more valuable in determining what happened than would oral testimony, photographs, or even X-rays, in some instances. Courts as a rule will allow the display of injuries to the jury—often in spite of the fact that the injury is gruesome.

The trial judge has a great deal of discretion in determining whether the physical display of the injury is so inflammatory as to unduly influence the jury. Such decisions are seldom overruled, unless there is a clear abuse of discretion. However, if the judge determines that the display of the person and the injury is so inflammatory that it may prejudice the jury, the judge may refuse to allow the display of a crime-related injury. In a California case, a judge permitted the jury to view a videotape of a man who was in a hospital after being attacked with a hammer by the defendant. He was in poor condition after the attack and was so elderly that he died prior to the defendant's trial. There were questions concerning the reliability of the witness's statement, but the judge allowed the jury to observe the man and hear his story on videotape, which had been recorded after the attack.[49]

Although the judge in his or her discretion may permit the witness to be exhibited at the trial in a criminal case in order to determine the extent of injury, the judge runs the risk of committing reversible error if he or she compelled a defendant to appear at a trial in handcuffs or shackles. In one case, upheld on appeal, the trial court required the defendant to wear wrist restraints at trial because the defendant refused to take his medication, refused to change out of prison clothes, and there was evidence that he might be trying to escape and hurt people.[50] Where a defendant consented to being shackled out of the jury's sight as a condition of serving as his own attorney, no constitutional due process violation occurred.[51] If a prosecutor is able to develop, on the record, facts that indicate a particularized need for restraints, restraints may not constitute a violation of due process.[52] Therefore, if the prosecutor presents clear justifications for restraining a defendant, mechanical prisoner restraints may be permitted without violating the defendant's rights.[53] In the penalty phase of a death penalty case, the court ordered that the defendant be shackled with visible leg irons, handcuffs, and a belly chain without taking any evidence or showing special circumstances that might have suggested that restraint was actually needed. The Supreme Court of the United States reversed the death

---

[49]   *See* California v. Tatum, 108 Cal. App. 4th 288, 133 Cal. Rptr. 2d 267, 2003 Cal. App. LEXIS 629 (2003).

[50]   United States v. Montgomery, 152 Fed. Appx. 822, 826, 2005 U.S. App. LEXIS 21893 (11th Cir. 2005).

[51]   Overton v. Mathes, 425 F.3d 518, 520, 2005 U.S. App. LEXIS 21885 (8th Cir. 2005).

[52]   United States v. Salehi, 2006 U.S. App. LEXIS 16285 (3d Cir. 2006).

[53]   New Jersey v. Grant, 361 N.J. Super. 349, 358, 825 A.2d 577, 2003 N.J. Super. LEXIS 222 (2003), in which an indictment was dismissed upon appeal when the target testified at a grand jury proceeding while in visible restraints.

penalty, noting that the restraints almost certainly affected the jury's perception of the defendant's character. Although a court may not compel a defendant to wear jail or prison clothes during the defendant's jury trial, a failure to object to being tried in custodial clothing is sufficient to negate an actionable constitutional violation.[54]

§ 14.4   Articles Connected with the Crime

Real evidence that includes weapons, tools, devices, and instruments that an accused person has employed in committing the alleged crime are admissible in evidence provided that the prosecutor can properly connect each item of evidence to the defendant and to the crime. That is to say, the real evidence must be authenticated to demonstrate that it is the genuine article and show that there was or is a connection between the article, the accused, and the crime.[55] Federal Rule of Evidence 901(a) notes that "authentication or identification as a condition precedent to admissibility is satisfied by evidence sufficient to support a finding that the matter in question is what its proponent claims." Examples of types of articles that have been acquired by investigators and submitted for consideration are discussed in the paragraphs that follow.

A. Weapons

In a bank robbery prosecution in which the defendant was charged with violating a federal statute stating that it is a crime to take money from a bank by intimidation, the trial court admitted into evidence the component parts of a nonexplosive simulated bomb consisting of a brown paper bag, a small box, a short length of wire, and an ordinary alarm clock. Although counsel for the defendant argued that these items were irrelevant to proving any element of the crime, the Eighth Circuit Court of Appeals upheld the use of the real evidence on the theory that the introduction of such evidence helps to demonstrate the method by which the crime was committed.[56]

In order to prove a defendant guilty of a homicide committed with a stolen firearm, the prosecutor presented evidence from police officers concerning the location from which a gun had been recovered. The firearm was of the correct caliber, it was near the location of the homicide, and contained six fired shell casings. The connection of the gun to the case was completed

---

[54]   Tolliver v. Greiner, 2005 U.S. Dist. LEXIS 32402 (N.D.N.Y. 2005). *See also* United States v. Salehi, 2006 U.S. App. LEXIS 16285 (3d Cir. 2006).

[55]   Davis v. United States, 700 A.2d 229 (D.C. App. 1997).

[56]   Caldwell v. United States, 338 F.2d 385 (8th Cir. 1964). In Evans v. United States, 122 F.2d 461 (10th Cir. 1941), the court admitted a string and broom used in the commission of a homicide. In State v. Fulcher, 20 N.C. App. 259 (1973), a hammer found at the scene of a murder was admitted into evidence in view of bruise marks on the victim's body, even though there was no evidence particularly identifying the hammer as the murder weapon.

when the owner of the gun identified it as having been the one stolen from him a few days earlier. The trial court held that the gun could be admitted in court as real evidence.[57]

In a case from the District of Columbia, a defendant contended that the prosecution failed to authenticate a firearm that the defendant allegedly had possessed while under a disability. The gun that the defendant threw away during a chase was tagged, bagged, and sealed, along with 11 cartridges. At the trial, it was discovered that the bag had been opened and two rounds of ammunition were missing, but the gun was present. There was no explanation why the bag had become unsealed, but a police officer testified that the gun appeared to be the one he had recovered after the defendant threw it away and he recalled the make, model, and color of the gun he originally seized. He testified that the serial number on the gun matched the serial number that he recorded at the time he seized the gun. The reviewing court upheld the admission into evidence of the gun and ammunition, because the prosecution only had to prove that as a matter of reasonable probability, there was no misidentification of the gun in order to properly authenticate it using the chain of custody theory.[58]

Weapons admitted in criminal cases must be authenticated and should have a sufficient relationship to the case to be properly admitted. In a case in which the prosecution failed to establish that a firearm had been used in an assault, no sufficient connection existed to allow the weapon into evidence. However, the trial court permitted a police officer to explain how, during the defendant's arrest, the officer discovered a handgun on the defendant's person. The court, in the absence of an objection, allowed the officer to describe the non-crime-related pistol and its holster in great detail and admitted the pistol into evidence. The appellate court noted that the admission of the second weapon that had no connection to the case was error, but the court considered the error to be harmless under the circumstances.[59]

A weapon that appears to have virtually no connection with a homicide can be excluded from evidence when it lacks relevance to the facts of a case. Under the circumstances, a judge may refuse to permit it to be authenticated and introduced into evidence. In a Mississippi homicide case, police arrested the defendant, who was wearing bloody clothes and sleeping on top of a .32 pistol and a .380 handgun. At the trial, the defendant wanted to introduce evidence that he also possessed the .380 handgun at the time of his arrest.[60] The deceased had been fatally shot with the .32 caliber pistol possessed by the defendant, but there was never any evidence that the .380 handgun had been present at the murder scene. In arguments to the trial judge, the defendant's counsel contended that the .380 had been at the murder scene, but neither party introduced any actual evidence that the .380 handgun had any role in the homicide. The Supreme Court of Mississippi upheld the trial judge's exclusion

57 Andrews v. Texas, 78 S.W.3d 13, 18, 2002 Tex. App. LEXIS 1056 (2002).
58 United States v. Goddard, 2006 U.S. App. LEXIS 6970 (D.C. Cir. 2006).
59 Davis v. Arkansas, 2003 Ark. App. LEXIS 386 (2003).
60 Flora v. State, 925 So. 2d 797, 813, 2006 Miss. LEXIS 49 (2006).

of the extra firearm, noting that the judge did not abuse his discretion. In this case, it might be argued that the defendant wanted to "muddy the waters" in an effort to create some confusion on the part of the jury.

For many types of weapons, proof of a chain of custody will not be the only method of proving a sufficient connection to a particular crime. All modern firearms must have serial numbers stamped on the frame of the weapon, so that a firearm identified at the crime scene by a serial number may be authenticated at trial by reference to the same number. Even when the serial number has not been used, the failure to establish a chain of custody is not essential if the weapon introduced is clearly identified by one or more witnesses or through expert ballistics evidence. Demonstrative of these principles for authentication, in an Arkansas aggravated robbery case, a witness identified a .22 Ruger pistol that the prosecution introduced by its appearance as the gun that the witness had given the defendant.[61] The witness testified that the serial number on the .22 Ruger was the identical number that had been on the pistol the witness had transferred to the defendant. In this case, the witness was able to identify the gun by its overall appearance as well as by its serial number, sufficiently authenticating the gun for use as evidence against a suspected armed robber.

In addition, if the weapon to be introduced is properly identified, it may be admitted into evidence even though it is inaccurately described by the person who seized it. For example, in a federal case, a sawed-off shotgun was properly admitted into a cocaine distribution prosecution, even though the agent inaccurately described the type of shotgun, because he was able to identify it as the one he seized by identifying his signature on the evidence tag that he placed on the gun after its seizure.[62]

In addition to firearms, other weapons used to commit crimes may be introduced into evidence if properly identified. For example, a knife was properly introduced when its authenticity was established by two witnesses who identified the knife as the one used by the defendant, even though the knife's chain of custody was not established.[63] And the admission of a handheld crossbow found in the defendant's possession at the time of his arrest was not an abuse of discretion given the context of the case, including the defendant's flight from a detective and the alleged assault on the detective with a crossbow.[64]

B. Instruments Used in the Crime

Instruments associated with crimes, such as burglary tools, screwdrivers, explosives, lock picks and other implements adapted to crime, especially burglary, are admissible if reasonably identified, although more weight will be given to the evidence if identification is certain. If the witness is unable to

---

[61]   Looney v. State, 2005 Ark. LEXIS 326 (Ark. 2005).
[62]   United States v. Abreu, 952 F.2d 1458 (1st Cir.), *cert. denied*, 503 U.S. 994, 112 S. Ct. 1695, 118 L. Ed. 2d 406 (1992).
[63]   Ex parte Works, 640 F.2d 1056 (11th Cir. Ala. 1994).
[64]   United States v. Mosby, 101 F.3d 1278 (8th Cir. 1996).

state with certainty that the object shown at the trial is the same instrument associated with the crime, the witness's uncertainty goes only to the weight of the physical evidence and not to its admissibility.[65]

In a Hawai'i case, an apartment manager observed a subject with a bicycle and a backpack attempting to gain entry into the apartment's parking garage by prying on the steel-framed locked door.[66] When asked why he did not use a key, the subject noted that he did not have a key. Upon additional inquiry, the manager realized the subject was an interloper who had a rope, a cord, and a chisel in his hand. A shoving match between the two men followed, in which the backpack fell to the ground, revealing screwdrivers, pliers, and a pair of scissors. The defendant argued on appeal that physical evidence did not support the proof of possession of burglar tools and that the eyewitness did not give believable testimony. The reviewing court rejected the defendant-appellant's contention because it thought that reasonable minds could find guilt beyond a reasonable doubt based on the manager's testimony concerning the real evidence.

In a prosecution for having or making burglary tools and second-degree burglary, a defendant had been found inside a fenced compound where recreational vehicles had been stored and where she had no permission to enter. In her possession were tools commonly used and possessed by burglars—a flashlight and a drill. The burglary had taken place at night in the area where she was found and some of the items stolen from the property had been physically disassembled or detached from some of the structures. Despite the defendant's claim that she was using the tools for disassembling her own property, the trial verdict, upheld on appeal, was that she was guilty of possession of burglary tools.[67]

In a case in which the defendant was charged with burglary, after the prosecution introduced proof that the burglary had occurred, the prosecution properly introduced evidence that the defendant had burglary tools or implements in his possession soon after the time of the commission of the offense.[68] Such evidence proved sufficient for conviction.

Evidence that has a strained chain of custody or may be difficult to identify may be admitted against a defendant when it meets the threshold of authenticity. In a commercial burglary of a bar, a bar owner caught the defendant, who he recognized, inside the building with a crowbar while standing near a lottery vending machine.[69] As the defendant with the crowbar approached the bar owner, the bar owner shot the defendant in the leg. The defendant dropped the crowbar and made a successful initial escape, but police eventually arrested him. The bar owner produced the crowbar at the request of the prosecutor about a week prior to the trial. The defendant object-

[65]   Scott v. State, 632 N.E.2d 961 (Ind. 1994); State v. Erossette, 634 So. 2d 1309 (La. 1994).
[66]   State v. Tetu, 2005 Haw. App. LEXIS 435 (Haw. 2005).
[67]   Washington v. Baker, 2002 Wash. App. LEXIS 2998 (2002).
[68]   State v. Coleman, 699 A.2d 91 (Conn. 1997). *See also* Commonwealth v. Casavant, 426 Mass. 368, 688 N.E.2d 945 (1998), in which a five-inch perfume aerosol can was admissible in a sex-related first-degree murder trial.
[69]   State v. Boydston, 2006 Mo. App. LEXIS 1246 (2006).

ed to the introduction of the crowbar because the prosecution never properly offered a foundation for the crowbar as being the one that the burglar dropped after being shot. The reviewing court rejected the defendant's arguments, noting that a specific objection had not been tendered at trial and the court did not find plain error in the admission of the crowbar that the bar owner claimed to have taken from the real burglar.

C. Clothing

Clothing that a witness identifies as having been worn by the accused or the victim during the commission of the crime may be submitted to the jury for inspection. For example, in one case, clothing that had been taken in a robbery from a retail store was admitted against an accused robber.[70] Police recovered the stolen clothing from a garbage bag that was discovered in the defendant's bedroom closet. The defendant's accomplices in the robbery testified about how they had packaged the stolen goods and delivered them to the defendant. The testimony sufficiently connected the stolen goods to the possession of the defendant at his place of residence and the clothing was in substantially the same condition when presented at trial as it was at the time police recovered it. As a general rule, any deficiency in the chain of custody with respect to an item of evidence affects the weight of the evidence, but not its admissibility.

In a capital murder case, the prosecution introduced some bloody clothing that the murder victim had been wearing at the time of her death.[71] The evidence disclosed that a crime scene technician collected the bloody clothing from the morgue from the gurney on which the deceased's body had been processed, placed it in a secured box, and properly stored the clothing in the police property room. At the trial, the same evidence technician opened the box, outside the presence of the jury, and labeled each item. The judge admitted the clothes into evidence because the prosecution had established a proper chain of custody for admission into evidence. The reviewing court approved the admission of the bloody clothes as it noted that it was a well-established principle that clothing that was demonstrated to have been worn by the victim at the time a crime was committed is considered to be admissible evidence.

Police may seize clothing and other tangible personal articles belonging to an arrestee following a lawful arrest and may hold the clothing as evidence without violating the arrestee's Fourth Amendment right to be free from unlawful searches and seizures. Similarly, when police encountered a person who seemed to have been a crime victim at a hospital emergency room and observed evidence in plain view, they may lawfully seize it. In an Illinois case, police had been called to an emergency room because a patient had a gunshot wound, where they observed and seized the defendant's bloody pants and

---

[70] People v. Green, 2006 N.Y. Slip Op. 6014, 818 N.Y.S.2d 862, 2006 N.Y. App. Div. LEXIS 9719 (N.Y. 2006).

[71] State v. Chapman, 359 N.C. 328, 352, 611 S.E.2d 794, 814, 2005 N.C. LEXIS 361 (2005).

shoes.[72] After additional investigation, police sent the articles of clothing for DNA testing that disclosed that some of the blood on the items of clothing belonged to a homicide victim as well as to the defendant. The defendant attempted to have the evidence suppressed, but the trial court refused. The real evidence, consisting of the clothing, shoes, and the DNA evidence, was properly introduced because a patient at an emergency room has no expectation of privacy and the real evidence was in plain view of the officers. In a different case, a Washington trial court noted in a case in which a defendant alleged that he had an expectation of privacy in his shoes held by the police, "The United States Supreme Court has held, under the Fourth Amendment, that a defendant has no reasonable expectation of privacy in property jail personnel seize from a defendant upon arrival after a lawful arrest."[73] Therefore, when the police possessed the defendant's shoes following an arrest for rape, they could properly maintain the chain of custody and use the shoes for identification purposes and to obtain a shoeprint to assist in the rape prosecution without violating any of the defendant's constitutional rights. In a similar situation, police arrested a man for the murder of his ex-wife. Because he seemed unconcerned about the shooting death of his ex-wife and because police were aware of his rocky relationship with her, they developed probable cause for his arrest. Following the arrest, police tested his clothing for evidence of gunshot residue. The tests revealed the presence of chemicals indicating that the wearer of the clothing had recently fired a gun. On appeal, the reviewing court approved of the warrantless seizure and scientific testing of the clothing as evidence and held that the evidence had been properly admitted by the trial court.[74]

In order to be admissible, clothing and other articles must meet relevancy and materiality tests. In the case of *State v. Atkins*, a Missouri court of appeals agreed with the trial court that the victim's robe, nightgown, and bedsheets were relevant in a rape case.[75] In this case, the defendant was convicted of first-degree burglary, forcible rape, and armed criminal action. The evidence indicated that the defendant forcibly entered the victim's apartment through a window. It was alleged that, after a struggle with the victim, the defendant overcame her will to resist by threatening to stab her with a knife, which he displayed, and that he then forcibly raped her.

The defendant argued on appeal that the trial court erred by admitting into evidence the victim's robe, nightgown, and bedsheets, claiming that the items failed to support any material fact. Disagreeing with the defendant's contention, the reviewing court decided:

[72] People v. Hillsman, 362 Ill. App. 3d 623, 626, 839 N.E.2d 1116, 1120, 2005 Ill. App. LEXIS 1209 (2005).
[73] Washington v. Cheatam, 112 Wash. App. 778, 785, 51 P.3d 138, 143, 2002 Wash. App. LEXIS 1832 (2002).
[74] Colorado v. Rogers, 68 P.3d 486, 2002 Colo. App. LEXIS 1627 (2002).
[75] State v. Atkins, 697 S.W.2d 226 (Mo. Ct. App. 1985).

> Evidence is relevant and admissible if it tends to logically prove or dis-
> prove facts in issue, or if it corroborates other material evidence. . . .
> The articles were found by the police at the crime scene. The robe and
> sheets contained seminal stains while the nightgown was torn and
> bloody. This evidence corroborated the victim's story that she had been
> raped and that her lip had been cut during the struggle with Atkins.

The court concluded by indicating that the evidence was relevant and material and affirmed the trial court's decision.

A Texas appeals court did not disturb a trial court holding admitting the
underwear that the defendant had been wearing on the night that a child in his
exclusive care had been raped.[76] From a single stain on defendant's underwear,
experts determined that the stain tested positive for blood from the infant victim and semen from the defendant. The trial court also admitted a washcloth
used at an emergency room that had been used to wipe the infant's private area
that contained presence of semen. Because the real evidence in the case
appeared to meet all the requirements of authentication by chain of custody, the
appeals court affirmed the conviction for aggravated sexual assault on a child.

In a California homicide case, the trial court admitted various items of
bloody clothing that police found the victim had been wearing during the
attack that took her life. The defendant objected, claiming that admission of
the victim's bloody clothes failed to meet the tests of relevancy because their
prejudicial value outweighed the probative value. The trial court admitted
bloodstain evidence matching the victim's blood type that had been taken from
the defendant's jeans and that tended to place him at the crime scene at or near
the time of death. The appellate court held that the gruesome bloodstained
clothing removed from the victim after her death had been properly admitted
because the prejudicial value did not outweigh the probative value and the
court ruled that the defendant's bloody jeans containing the blood of the
deceased were properly admitted.[77]

In a Florida case, the victim's bloody shorts and shirt, which were used by
an expert in a bloodstain pattern analysis to discover how the murders
occurred, were properly admitted into evidence at a murder trial.[78] The court
upheld the introduction of this evidence because it was consistent and tied in
with other evidence detailing the manner of the commission of the crime.

D. Bloodstains

The discovery of the presence of blood on the person or clothing of the
accused party or the victim has been recognized as being among the ordinary
indicia of homicide and lesser criminal injury. Blood-related evidence left by
the perpetrator at the scene of the crime, whether that of the defendant or the
victim, tends to prove who has been present and may indicate by its patterns

---

[76]   Smith v. State, 2004 Tex. App. LEXIS 11851 (2004).

[77]   California v. Navarette, 30 Cal. 4th 458, 511, 66 P.3d 1182, 1204, 2003 Cal. LEXIS 2638 (2003).

[78]   Hannon v. State, 638 So. 2d 39 (Fla. 1994).

what occurred and how long ago the acts took place. Blood evidence may be visible to law enforcement officers or may require enhancement by chemicals introduced at the scene. Police and evidence technicians have used Luminol[79] as a screening test to detect latent evidence of blood since 1955, when it was first used in the investigation of a crime scene and introduced in court.[80] Even a recent challenge to the use of Luminol was deflected by a court, noting that the science in this area is not new and has been universally accepted as a presumptive test for blood.[81]

The practice of identifying blood and criminals by circumstantial evidence and by the inspection of witnesses and jurors has had the sanction of immemorial usage in criminal tribunals.[82] With the development of twentieth-century blood testing, science generated new data on types and subtypes of blood, yielding additional information from blood analysis. Most recently, the use of deoxyribonucleic acid (DNA) as a method of identifying the source of blood left at crime scenes opened new avenues of identification of criminals as well as screening the innocent away from prosecution. The testing has also evolved to the point at which extremely small samples of blood may be used to reveal DNA information that previously would not have been available. Blood is only one type of body fluid that contains DNA for which law enforcement officers may find use.

The use of blood-obtained information and bloodstain evidence will generally require expert collection, expert evaluation, and expert testimony.[83] In one murder case, the victim had been killed by an unknown assailant, but blood testing provided a way to determine the identity of the perpetrator. The body of a young woman was found by her sister in their home. A medical examiner determined, based on an examination of the body at the scene and an autopsy, that the deceased had been beaten and stabbed multiple times with a screwdriver. In addition, the doctor determined that she had been sexually assaulted. Evidence in the form of bloodstained clothes and a partial Walkman headset were found at the defendant's home. The headset part matched one part found under the body of the deceased. A Walkman and blood-stained underwear were found in the defendant's bedroom. The prosecution introduced DNA evidence obtained from blood at the crime scene. The DNA evidence demonstrated that the DNA profile of blood samples taken from the defendant's screwdriver and personal property found at his home matched the victim's DNA profile and that semen samples taken from the victim's body matched the defendant's DNA profile. With such overwhelming evidence arrayed against him, the defendant contended that the DNA testing process had not been shown to meet the general acceptance of the general scientific acceptance standard and should not have been admitted. The reviewing court

[79] A chemical compound that reacts with blood and semen and chemically changes to give off light.
[80] People v. Wooten, 283 A.D.2d 931, 933, 725 N.Y.S.2d 767, 770, 2001 N.Y. App. Div. LEXIS 4659 (N.Y. 2001).
[81] People v. Cumbee, 851 N.E.2d 934, 948, 2006 Ill. App. LEXIS 578 (2006).
[82] People v. Gonzales, 35 N.Y. 49 (1866).
[83] People v. Driver, 62 Ill. App. 3d 847, 379 N.E.2d 840 (1978).

rejected the recent approach taken by the Supreme Court of the United States and held that newer DNA testing must meet the general scientific acceptance standard that had been in effect for many years. The murder conviction was remanded for a hearing to decide whether the newest DNA testing was sufficiently reliable to be admitted in the state court system of Minnesota.[84] Following remand, the court determined that the testing met the general scientific acceptance standard followed by Minnesota.[85]

As a general rule, scientific evidence involving blood grouping and DNA analysis will be admissible once courts determine that the newest advances meet the requirements of relevancy and reliability. If the prosecution needs to explain bloodstain patterns as a way to prove how a crime occurred, expert witnesses will be essential. The prosecution is required to show that evidence concerning the impact of bloodstain evidence is based upon a well-recognized scientific principle or technique that has gained general acceptance in the particular field to which it belongs.[86] In an Alabama multiple homicide case, the trial court permitted a state medical examiner with the Alabama Department of Forensic Sciences to testify that, based on blood splatter analysis, one victim was turning his head and looking up when he received his fatal gunshot wound and that blood splatter analysis indicated that another victim was on the floor with the killer was standing over the victim at the time the victim was shot through the heart.[87]

Evaluating blood splatter patterns that remain at crime scenes helps to corroborate truthful oral evidence or challenge witness statements that may be false, misleading, or erroneous. Blood spatter analysis involves mechanical scrutiny based on the physics of fluid flow and an evaluation of impact angles at which the spatters hit other objects rather than only concerning microscopic scientific analysis. For example, a significant number of state jurisdictions have held that blood spatter analysis is reliable and may be admitted where the witness qualifies as an expert through training, education, and experience. Blood splatter analysis has been recognized as known and accepted scientific discipline by many courts because of its logical and scientific basis.[88] In a Virginia case involving expert testimony covering blood splash patterns, the high court accepted the principles on which bloodstain pattern interpretation has been based and noted that expert testimony is recognized to explain the pattern of bloodstains. The court observed that:

---

[84]   *See* Minnesota v. Roman Nose, 649 N.W.2d 815, 2002 Minn. LEXIS 554 (2002).

[85]   Minnesota v. Roman Nose, 667 N.W.2d 386, 2003 Minn. LEXIS 513 (2003).

[86]   *See* Frye v. United States, 54 App. D.C. 46, 293 F. 1013 (1923), which followed the general scientific acceptance approach and many state jurisdictions followed the logic. When the Supreme Court decided *Daubert v. Merrell Dow Pharmaceuticals*, 509 U.S. 579 (1993), it ruled that Federal Rule of Evidence 702 had superseded the *Frye* standard for federal courts.

[87]   Miller v. State, 913 So.2d 1148, 1156, 2004 Ala. Crim. App. LEXIS 239 (2004).

[88]   Hudson v. State, 95 Ark. 85, 102, 146 S.W.3d 380, 390, 2004 Ark. App. LEXIS 124 (2004). *See also* State v. Torres, 137 N.M. 607, 113 P.3d 877; 2005 N.M. App. LEXIS 56 (2005).

many of the specific physical elements of blood spatter analysis are capable of being tested using the laws of physics and chemistry, and by employing principles of gravity, inertia, and viscosity. In accordance with other jurisdictions, we adhere to the view that this form of scientific analysis can form a basis for admissible proof upon an appropriate foundation.[89]

The Virginia court held that a trial court committed no error when it permitted a blood pattern analyst to offer testimony that the victim had not been standing, when the defendant said that he shot her as she was standing and attacking him. The blood pattern expert assisted in refuting the defendant's claim of self-defense and helped prove that the victim was sitting when murdered.[90]

E. Narcotics and Narcotics Paraphernalia

Drug-related crimes involving major trafficking, possession with intent to sell, and simple possession have increased in the past 20 years to such an extent that a large percentage of local, state, and federal agents' time is devoted to investigating such crimes and testifying against the accused persons. Naturally, the high level of litigation that surrounds drug prosecutions generates a significant number of court decisions in which defendants test the rules for admission and exclusion of drug-related evidence. As a general rule, courts require a more conclusively established chain of custody for proof of authentication where interchangeable items like drugs or blood are involved,[91] a factor that may help some drug defendants.

While prosecutors can expect that narcotics evidence will be challenged by defendants when the government attempts to introduce narcotics or other controlled substances as evidence, state evidence codes and case law developed that require precise and documented steps to assure admissibility. Failure to comply with the rigorous procedures may result in evidence not being admitted. While the reviewing courts have generally approved the admissibility of narcotics in trial courts, there is a fine line between what is admissible and what is inadmissible for one reason or another. The following cases illustrate this point. In a Louisiana case, the appeals court agreed that a proper foundation was laid for cocaine seized during the arrest, and therefore such evidence was admissible in a prosecution for possession of more than 400 grams of cocaine, despite evidence that the cocaine was handed over at a crime laboratory to a person who was later arrested for stealing evidence in another case.[92] The court confirmed that the person who stole the evidence testified that the only cocaine he took was evidence from another case, the police officers traced the cocaine from the time of seizure to the time it was placed into

---

[89]   Smith v. Commonwealth, 265 Va. 250, 576 S.E.2d 465, 2003 Va. LEXIS 36 (2003).

[90]   *Id.*

[91]   Thompson v. State, 2006 Ark. App. LEXIS 364 (2006).

[92]   State v. Sais, 706 So. 2d 650 (La. 1998).

evidence, and the witness testified that the packages introduced into evidence were the same packages of cocaine she carried in her luggage.

In order to introduce seized drugs as evidence, federal and state courts require that the prosecutor prove a proper chain of custody as a prerequisite to admission in evidence. In one Illinois case, the defendant objected that the prosecution had offered inadequate proof of the chain of custody of drugs that allegedly had been in the defendant's possession and had been seized by a drug task force.[93] The trial court admitted the cocaine and the lab tests, but the appellate court had some concerns that the chain of custody had weak links or gaps in its proof. There was no evidence concerning what the seizing officer did with the plastic bag that he took from the defendant and proof was missing that police placed the seized bag in another sealed container and no proof that it was dated or initialed by the seizing officers. The reviewing court had concerns that "[n]o evidence showed how a bag taken from defendant ended up in a sealed evidence bag. No evidence showed this bag is different in any way from other bags of controlled substances that may have been handled by the task force, or transported to the lab, or stored. No evidence showed the bag presented as exhibit No. 1 is the same one recovered from defendant"[94] by one of the officers. However, the reviewing court upheld the authentication of the cocaine under the chain of custody theory because the court noted that the prosecution need not prove every single link in the chain of custody and the defendant failed to introduce any evidence that cast strong doubt on the chain of custody or proved some level of tampering.

However, in a Georgia case, an appellate court reversed a drug possession conviction based on incompetency of counsel who failed to contest the chain of custody of the drugs. Police testified to collection of the drug samples and the fact that they were placed in bags in the property room. No testimony was given that the samples were labeled, sealed, or otherwise made unique from other fungible samples in the property room. The drug analysis technician testified that she received the samples in a sealed state, but no showing was ever offered concerning how the suspected drug samples were transported from police custody to the analysis lab or how the lab received the samples. The court of appeals reversed the conviction because it believed that the chain of custody must be more closely proved in cases of fungible materials, like drugs, and there was not a reasonable certainty that the evidence seized was the evidence introduced against the defendant.[95]

Illinois courts have taken a less demanding position with respect to chain of custody in drug cases. One Illinois court, reviewing a conviction for possession of cocaine, noted that a flaw in the chain of custody does not necessarily mean that a reasonable doubt exists concerning the identity of the sub-

[93] People v. Echavarria, 362 Ill. App.3d 599, 607, 840 N.E.2d 815, 823, 2005 Ill. App. LEXIS 1284 (2005).
[94] Id. at 608.
[95] Wilson v. State, 271 Ga. App. 359, 362, 609 S.E.2d 703, 706, 2005 Ga. App. LEXIS 41 (2005).

stance tested.[96] Before drug evidence can be introduced, the government must lay a foundation that shows the police took reasonable precautions to assure that a recovered substance was the same substance delivered to the laboratory chemist. In the Illinois case, police left recovered substances contained in small plastic bags on the booking room table for a period of time before initializing them or placing them inside other labeled containers. When substances are not unique in appearance, it may be difficult to positively identify the objects as coming from a particular source if they are not immediately given an identifying mark or number. The reviewing court observed that the officers never did anything with the bags that might have created an imminent risk of undetected substitution or tampering, even though the procedure was not ideal. The defendant also contended that the prosecution did not offer testimony that proved every link in the chain of custody from collection until scientific testing had occurred, but the reviewing court stated that "it is well established that when no indication exists that evidence has been tampered with or its integrity otherwise compromised, the State need not present the testimony of every custodian of the evidence."[97] The reviewing court upheld the cocaine possession conviction with the observation that "[s]howing that evidence remained in official hands and in a sealed container and was tracked under a consistent identifying number or code effectively excludes the possibility of anything but deliberate tampering."[98]

Generally, courts have authorized the introduction of not only narcotics seized from the defendants or from their residences, but also related objects such as drug paraphernalia, containers used for packaging, records, pagers, and other "tools of the trade." Some examples will highlight the types of evidence that have been introduced and the conditions surrounding the introduction of the evidence.

In an Ohio case involving possession of nine ounces of cocaine, the trial court rejected the defendant's motion to exclude some items seized from his person and his home. The items allowed to be introduced at trial included guns, ammunition, a bulletproof vest, cash, and creatine[99] found during the consent search of his home. The appellate court held that there was no error admitting these items into evidence because:

> several witnesses testified that creatine is a "cutting agent" used to dilute cocaine and increase its sales value. Moreover, there was testimony that guns and large amounts of cash are tools of the drug dealers' trade. On this uncontroverted testimony, we cannot say that the items which were admitted were irrelevant or unfairly prejudicial.[100]

---

[96]   People v. Johnson, 361 Ill. App. 3d 430, 437, 837 N.E.2d 467, 473, 2005 Ill. App. LEXIS 1041 (2005).
[97]   *Id.*, at 442.
[98]   *Id.*, at 443.
[99]   A substance often used as 'cut' in the making of crack cocaine from powdered cocaine.
[100]   United States v. Brown, 16 F.3d 423 (D.C. Cir. 1994).

Similarly, in a Tennessee case involving drug-related evidence, a trial court admitted three aerosol cans that originally contained engine starting fluid, one component of which was ether, used in manufacturing methamphetamine. Police initially stopped the defendant's vehicle because he had been reported to have recently purchased large quantities of Sudafed, an over-the-counter decongestant that can be used to produce methamphetamine. A problem with admission of the three starter fluid cans occurred when one deputy sheriff checked two cans from the property room and used them to clean the carburetor on his personal boat motor. Because the original officer identified the three starting fluid cans at trial as being the ones he seized from the defendant, the appellate court did not find error in the chain of custody and stated, "The identification or chain of custody is sufficient if the facts establish a reasonable assurance of the identity of the evidence and its integrity."[101]

F. Other Types of Evidence

Other articles connected with a crime are also admissible if they meet the general tests. For example, in a Missouri homicide case in which the deceased had been the victim of a hit-and-run accident, police ascertained the type of vehicle from the debris at the scene of the impact and discovered the color from paint samples left on the body of the deceased. They eventually discovered the defendant's vehicle complete with front-end damage and paint scrapes and paint shards resting on the driveway. The police seized the paint shards and other evidence and eventually, through expert testimony, entered them into evidence in the murder prosecution. The trial court rejected the defendant's constitutional challenges to the collection of the evidence and the court of appeals affirmed the method of collection and the admission into evidence of the paint chips. [102]

In a sexual assault case in which there was insufficient violence to produce either the victim's blood or the defendant's blood, medical and evidence technicians obtained evidence from the victim to place in a rape kit that included saliva, blood, clothing, fingernail scrapings, and a hair sample.[103] The defendant objected to the introduction of various types of evidence derived from the rape kit that helped the prosecution convict him. His major contentions involved arguments that the chain of custody of the rape kit was not sufficiently proven, that the exhibits had not been properly preserved and that there was no proof that the exhibits contained the same specimen and evidence originally taken from the complainant. The reviewing court rejected the defendant's arguments because there was proof that the doctor took the personal material from the victim, transferred them to another health worker who sealed the envelopes and transferred them a police officer, who added his name to the chain of custody. The officer delivered the samples to the police department's secure property room. Later, an investigator for the district attor-

---

[101]   State v. Long, 2005 Tenn. Crim. App. LEXIS 199 (2005).
[102]   Missouri v. Pacheco, 101 S.W.3d 913, 2003 Mo. App. LEXIS 543 (2003).
[103]   Vinson v. State, 2006 Tex. App. LEXIS 1634 (2006).

ney's office took possession and delivered the rape kit to the testing laboratory. At no point did any custodian note that any tampering appeared visible. Evidence technicians followed a similar path and procedure in collecting buccal saliva swabs from the defendant. According to the appellate court, the prosecutor demonstrated "a complete chain of custody from the first step, the collection of evidence from the complainant and appellant, to the final step, turning the evidence over to the Identigene laboratory. As there was no evidence of tampering, any gaps alleged by appellant went to the weight of the evidence, not its admissibility."[104] The trial court committed no error in admitting the results of the rape kit into evidence.

In an unpublished California arson case, a court convicted a grandmother and her grandson of committing arson of their residential home and insurance fraud.[105] Firefighters responded to a report of the fire and discovered several old burn areas on floors and an active fire in a linen closet that they later concluded had been intentionally set. When other evidence aroused additional suspicion of firefighters that the fire might have been intentionally set, they procured a criminal search warrant. In executing the warrant, investigators

> found bills indicating [defendant] was past due on her mortgage and a credit card account. They also found receipts from Wal-Mart for the recent purchase of storage containers and garbage cans. In a motor home on the property, investigators found storage containers matching the type on the receipts. They also found several cats in small cages, clothing, food, and a computer. Further, they located receipts for three storage units at a self-storage facility. A search of these units revealed clothing, furniture, and household furnishings in good condition. Some items in the units were contained in storage bins matching the type on the receipts.[106]

The trial court permitted the evidence of pre-fire planning and other real evidence to be introduced against both defendants and a jury rendered a guilty verdict on all counts. The court of appeals upheld the convictions, noting that any rational trier of fact could have found that all the essential elements of the crimes had been proven beyond a reasonable doubt.

§ 14.5 View of the Scene

In almost all jurisdictions the trial court has the discretion to determine whether to allow a jury view of the scene of the alleged crime, and the trial court's decision will only be reversed on appeal based on a showing of an abuse of the judge's discretion.[107] Generally, the defendant and legal counsel

---

[104] *Id.*
[105] People v. Mead, 2006 Cal. App. Unpub. LEXIS 3150 (2006).
[106] *Id.*
[107] People v. Alston, 24 A.D.3d 391, 806 N.Y.S.2d 208, 209, 2005 N.Y. App. Div. LEXIS 14894 (2005).

must be permitted to accompany the jury to a view of the scene, and a failure to permit their presence may be reversible error.[108] The trial judge may act on a motion by either party or may order the jurors to be escorted to a place where a material fact occurred or an offense was committed, without a motion of either party. In deciding whether to allow a view of the scene, a judge may:

> consider the totality of the circumstances of the case, including, but not limited to, the timing of the request for the jury view, the difficulty and expense of arranging it, the importance of the information to be gained by it, the extent to which that information has been or could be secured from more convenient sources (e.g., photographs, videotapes, maps, or diagrams), and the extent to which the place or object to be viewed may have changed in appearance since the controversy began.[109]

The purpose of a view of the scene is to allow visual observation by the jury of the premises or place in question so that the jury may observe places or objects that are relevant to the case and thus to provide them with a mental picture of the locality.[110] As another court phrased it, "The purpose of a jury site visit is to help the jury understand existing evidence, not to take new evidence."[111] There exists a conflict in law as to whether a view constitutes independent evidence; however, the resulting difference in opinion has little operational effect because the jury has the power to give a view of the scene whatever weight it chooses.

The procedure for viewing the premises varies from state to state, and the manner of viewing the scene is often regulated by statute or rule of the court. Good practice dictates that the trial judge accompany the members of the jury to the viewing, although it may not constitute reversible error if the judge does not view the scene.[112] Usually the jury is escorted to the crime scene by an officer of the court who directs the jurors' attention to places, objects, or land features that will be or have been mentioned in testimony given in court. When a defendant attends the viewing of the scene, appropriate security will accompany the defendant and counsel. As a general rule, the parties and their counsel are allowed to be present; however, they are not permitted to discuss their case with members of the jury and jurors are not allowed to discuss the case among themselves. For example, Kansas criminal procedure holds that while conducting a view of the scene, generally "no person other than the officer and the person appointed to show them the place shall speak to them on any subject connected with the trial."[113]

---

[108] *See* People v. Garcia, 36 Cal. 4th 777, 115 P.3d 1191, 31 Cal. Rptr. 3d 541, 2005 Cal. LEXIS 8226 (Cal. 2005). *But see* State v. Engelhardt, 280 Kan. 113, 123, 119 P.3d 1148, 1159, 2005 Kan. LEXIS 462 (Kan. 2005), holding that a defendant may have no right to be present at a jury view of the scene.

[109] Andika v. State, 2005 Tex. App. LEXIS 4862 (2005).

[110] *See* NY CLS CPL § 270.50(3) Trial jury; viewing of premises (2006).

[111] State v. Dalluge, 2005 Wash. App. LEXIS 450 (2005).

[112] State v. Campbell, 2006 Tenn. Crim. App. LEXIS 584 (2006).

[113] K.S.A. § 22-3418 View of place of crime. (2006).

In criminal cases, some states permit the accused to be present; in others, allowing the accused to be present is within the discretion of the judge. Most jurisdictions do not permit jurors to ask questions at the scene, while there are situations in which a judge may permit juror questions. However, one court held that although the trial court allowed jurors to ask questions when viewing the crime scene, the defendant was not so prejudiced as to be deprived of a fair trial, given the fact that the defendant failed to object to the taking of questions prior to the jury viewing the crime scene.[114]

Inevitably, what the jurors see at a view of the scene will be used in reaching a verdict; therefore, viewing the scene must be carefully planned and the activities at the scene must be kept under close supervision. A defendant may base an appeal on crime scene views if prejudice to the case resulted from juror misconduct or outside influence by the public. However, the mere fact that the victim's family was present outside the house while the jury toured the house in a Louisiana case did not so prejudice the defendant as to deprive him of a fair trial, particularly because the victim's family had no contact with the jury.[115]

§ 14.6   Photographs

As mentioned in previous sections, it is often possible to exhibit the person of the victim to the jury or judge, to introduce articles connected with the crime, or to have the jury view the scene of the crime. In other instances, it is impracticable to bring all of the tangible evidence before the court. On the other hand, it is often impossible to define tangible evidence and properly convey its importance by words alone. Photographs, if properly taken and explained, bring this type of evidence into court in a more convenient fashion. Photographs frequently convey information to the court and jury more accurately than words. Although photos are merely graphic representations of the oral testimony of witnesses, they often have far greater value than words and may pose a risk of unfair prejudice because of the chance that jurors may be swayed by emotion or vindictiveness.

When a party desires to introduce photographs that have relevance to the case, the trial judge has discretion to admit or refuse the photo evidence based on the judge's evaluation of whether the photographs pose a danger of unfair prejudice or whether the probative value outweighs any potential for prejudice. Evidence (including photographs) can be excluded where there is a danger of creating a "confusion of the issues, or misleading the jury, or by considerations of undue delay, waste of time, or needless presentation of cumulative evidence."[116] Precisely how this calculation is made varies with the case, the need for the evidence, and the perception of the judge. In considering the admissibility of photographs, the Supreme Court of Arkansas suggested that:

---

[114]   State v. McKinney, 637 So. 2d 1120 (La. 1994).
[115]   *Id.*
[116]   FED. R. EVID. 403.

> When photographs are helpful to explain testimony, they are ordi-
> narily admissible. Further, the mere fact that a photograph is inflam-
> matory or is cumulative is not, standing alone, sufficient reason to
> exclude it. Even the most gruesome photographs may be admissible
> if they assist the trier of fact in any of the following ways: by shed-
> ding light on some issue, by proving a necessary element of the
> case, by enabling a witness to testify more effectively, by corrobo-
> rating testimony, or by enabling jurors to better understand the tes-
> timony. Other acceptable purposes are to show the condition of the
> victims' bodies, the probable type or location of the injuries, and the
> position in which the bodies were discovered. Absent an abuse of
> discretion, this court will not reverse a trial court for admitting pho-
> tographs into evidence.[117]

This passage offers some standards to judge whether to admit a photograph
and does not simply mean that any and all photographs should be admitted
into evidence. To be properly considered for admission, the trial judge must
evaluate the probative value and consider the prejudicial effect in the exercise
of judicial discretion.

Unless photographs were part of the crime such as would be the case in
child pornography or extortion by use of a photograph, photographs are generally inadmissible as original or substantive evidence. However, as demonstrative real evidence, photographs should be admissible where they help the witness explain testimony or assist the jury in understanding the testimony of a
witness. As one court noted, "Even the most gruesome photographs may be
admissible if they assist the trier of fact by shedding light on some issue, proving a necessary element of the case, enabling a witness to testify more effectively, corroborating testimony, or enabling jurors to better understand the testimony."[118] The same court upheld the admission of photographs of the victim's
dead body at the crime scene and two photographs taken during the victim's
autopsy. The reviewing court agreed with the admissibility of the photos because
the pictures at the crime scene were useful to show how the crime scene
appeared and the others demonstrated the nature of the victim's wounds.[119]

The proponent of photographic evidence must supply the court with a
proper foundation prior to admission into evidence. Federal Rule of Evidence
901 requires authentication or identification that an item of evidence is what
its proponent claims. In the case of a photograph, the person who took the
photo presumably could offer evidence concerning where, when, how, and
under what circumstances he or she took the photo. A competent witness who
has personal knowledge of the facts depicted within the photograph must testify that the picture is an accurate representation of the objects or persons contained within the photograph. A photo may be authenticated by anyone who
has sufficient knowledge to prove that the contents of a photo depict what it

---

[117]   Davis v. State, 350 Ark. 22, 35, 84 S.W.3d 427, 435, 2002 Ark. LEXIS 446 (2002).
[118]   Holloway v. State, 2005 Ark. LEXIS 497 (Ark. 2005).
[119]   *Id.*

purports to depict. For example, in a stabbing case, the defendant objected to the admission of photographs by a police officer who did not take the picture, but was able to state that he was present and observed the stab wounds and that they were accurately depicted in the photographs at issue.[120] Additionally, the prosecutor obtained the officer's testimony that he observed the victim's wounds when he first arrived at the crime location and when medical personnel treated the victim, both at the crime scene and at the hospital. The reviewing court rejected the defendant's arguments concerning lack of proper foundation and noted that the admission of photographic evidence lies within the sound discretion of the trial court. To be admissible, a photograph must first be made a part of a qualified person's testimony. Someone, often a law enforcement officer, must serve as its testimonial sponsor; in other words, it must be verified. A photograph may not be received by itself, but must be brought to court by a witness and authenticated as genuine and correctly representing what it purports to represent.[121]

The correctness of such a representation may be established by any witness who is familiar with the scene, object, or person portrayed, or who is competent to speak from personal observation. A witness qualifying a photograph does not have to be the photographer or see the picture taken; it is only necessary that the witness recognize and identify the object depicted and testify that the photograph fairly and correctly represents that object.[122] Whether there is sufficient evidence of the correctness of a photograph to render it competent to be used by a witness for the purpose of illustrating or explaining his or her testimony is a preliminary question of fact for the trial judge.[123]

A trial court has broad discretion to determine the admissibility of photographs and videotapes by weighing the probative value of such evidence against its unfair prejudicial effect.[124] For example, autopsy photographs may be admissible when they help explain the other evidence in the case. In a case in which a defendant was accused of strangling the victim and then setting fire to her apartment in an effort to cover up his crime, the judge allowed some gruesome photographs of the victim's body into evidence.[125] The defendant argued that no one was disputing the victim's death and the photos failed to show any injury to the throat of the victim. The prosecution contended that the autopsy photos helped to demonstrate the pathologist's testimony that the

---

[120]　State v. High Elk, 330 Mont. 259, 265, 127 P.3d 432, 436, 2006 Mont. LEXIS 6 (2006).

[121]　3 WIGMORE, EVIDENCE § 794 (3d ed. 1970); *see also* Phillips v. State, 550 N.E.2d 1290 (Ind. 1990), which held that photographs are generally admissible if they depict an object or scene that a witness would be permitted to describe in his or her testimony.

[122]　Kleveland v. United States, 345 F.2d 134 (2d Cir. 1965).

[123]　State v. Gardner, 228 N.C. 567, 46 S.E.2d 824 (1948). In this case, the trial judge, in admitting a photograph, instructed the jury: "You will not consider this photograph as substantive evidence—it is not competent for that purpose. It is only competent, and the court limits the evidence in the way of a photograph, to illustrate the testimony of the witness, and it is a question for you as to whether or not it does illustrate his testimony, and you will receive it and consider the photograph in no other way than as tending to illustrate the testimony of the witness, and not as substantive evidence."

[124]　State v. Davlin, 272 Neb. 139, 158, 719 N.W.2d 243, 2006 Neb. LEXIS 123 (2006).

[125]　*Id.*

deceased was dead prior to the fire because the photographs showed that her back, which was next to the floor, was not as badly burned as the rest of her body and they also indicated her prior death because if she had been attempting to escape the fire, her body would have been more evenly burned. The reviewing court upheld the admission of the somewhat gruesome photographs of the deceased murder victim noting that "If a photograph illustrates or makes clear some controverted issue in a homicide case, a proper foundation having been laid, it may be received, even if gruesome."[126]

In a homicide case in which the deceased had been shot, allegedly during a struggle with the defendant during a robbery, police noticed what appeared to be an entry wound on the forehead of the deceased. This theory appeared consistent with the defendant's initial story, but the autopsy indicated that the forehead wound was an exit wound and the cause of death had been an entrance wound at the rear of the head, execution-style. The doctor took photographs of the head wounds after shaving some hair away from the scalp and determined that the bullet entry wound was consistent with a contact gunshot. The trial court permitted the autopsy doctor, an expert in forensic pathology, to authenticate and introduce some of the photographs taken at the autopsy, which included some photos of the victim's face as well as the fatal injuries. The court excluded some photographs that were cumulative and admitted other photographs that met the tests for relevancy. In approving the admission of the photographs, the Supreme Court of Arkansas held that the photographs assisted the medical examiner in determining the manner of death and the actual cause of death and assisted in corroborating the testimony of the coroner and served to explain the police investigation. Although the photographs were somewhat gruesome and inflammatory, they had been properly authenticated and were relevant to the prosecution's case and thus were properly admitted.[127]

In addition to being properly verified or identified, photographic evidence will not be admitted unless it is relevant and necessary. Photographs are generally admissible to prove facts at issue in a criminal case, if they have a tendency to prove or disprove some disputed point or if the photographs offer corroboration of other evidence. Even photographs that might inflame the passions of the jury may be admissible where there is a need for the evidence and the prejudicial value is not outrageously high. In one case in which the court admitted extensive autopsy photographs that the defendant argued were unfairly prejudicial, the appellate court approved the introduction of the photographs because there were significant reasons to allow their use.[128] There was sufficient evidence in the case to prove that the defendant murdered the victim during a kidnapping and robbery spree, despite the defendant's claim of ineffective assistance of counsel based on not objecting to the introduction of the photographs. The photographs the court allowed included standard pictures taken from above the autopsy gurney, pictures of the victim's defensive

---

[126] *Id.*

[127] *See* Mathews v. Arkansas, 99 S.W.3d 403, 2003 Ark. LEXIS 122 (2003).

[128] Eggers v. State, 914 So. 2d 883, 914, 2004 Ala. Crim. App. LEXIS 266 (2004).

wounds to her left hand, and a close-up picture of an abdominal injury. In addition, the court admitted pictures the showed internal parts of the victim's skull that depicted extensive hemorrhaging from a blunt force wound to the head. The reviewing court stated that the pictures would have been admissible even if the defendant's attorney had lodged an objection with the court.[129] Autopsy photographs that may be cumulative are not always excluded.

A defendant cannot prevent the prosecution from using photographs by conceding or admitting that a deceased died from a gunshot wound, or from a beating, or from specific injuries. It has often been stated that the is no rule that requires a prosecutor to try a case based on stipulations,[130] so by removing some issues from the contest, a defendant cannot defeat the use of photographs by the prosecution. Even after an offer of a stipulation, the prosecution may introduce photographs because they help present the true story of a case and may be helpful to a jury in rendering a verdict or a sentence and therefore remain relevant.[131] As the same court noted in a different case, "the rule prohibiting the exhibition of inflammatory evidence to a jury does not preclude the revelation of the true facts surrounding the commission of a crime when these facts are relevant and necessary."[132]

In allowing admission of a photograph that arguably possessed strong prejudicial value, a federal trial court did not commit error when it permitted the prosecution to introduce a photograph of the defendant wearing jail clothes.[133] The prosecution contended that the defendant had killed a fellow American Indian but the defendant claimed self-defense, stating that the victim threw a punch, clipping him in the chin. Following the defendant's arrest, the government took his picture to help refute the self-defense argument because the picture demonstrated that the defendant was uninjured on the day of the killing. The trial court gave a limiting instruction to the jury concerning the jail clothing that the jury was not to infer guilt from the dress of the defendant in the picture. The Court of Appeals for the Eighth Circuit refused to disturb the conviction and held that the photograph, though somewhat prejudicial, had been properly admitted.

In several cases the question has arisen as to whether it is necessary to follow the rules relating to the chain of custody as discussed in § 14.2. Still photographs and video movies are treated differently from instrumentalities of the crime or fungible drugs that do not necessarily have unique qualities. In a prosecution in which a security camera captured the crime and getaway, the prosecution played the video for the jury and made a few still photos from the video that were introduced over the defendant's objection on chain of custody grounds. The video and the still photographs did not require any proof of chain

---

[129]   *Id.*
[130]   Green v. Commonwealth, 197 S.W.3d 76, 2006 Ky. LEXIS 140 (Ky. 2006), quoting Payne v. Commonwealth, 623 S.W.2d 867, 877 (Ky. 1981)
[131]   Green v. Commonwealth, 197 S.W.3d 76, 2006 Ky. LEXIS 140 (Ky. 2006).
[132]   Adkins v. Commonwealth, 96 S.W.3d 779, 2003 Ky. LEXIS 13 (Ky. 2003).
[133]   United States v. Two Crow, 178 Fed. Appx. 610, 2006 U.S. App. LEXIS 11165 (8th Cir. 2006).

of custody because witnesses authenticated the pictures by testifying to their genuine quality.[134] The fact that it is not necessary to establish the chain of custody of a photograph, however, does not mean that it may be used without authentication. Evidence must be introduced to demonstrate that the photograph constitutes a genuine representation of the object or scene depicted.

Not all photographs are admissible, even when a proper foundation is laid. If, in obtaining a photograph, the state violates the Constitution the defendant has constitutional grounds to object to its admissibility. In the case of *California v. Ciraolo*, police officers took an airplane flight over the defendant's backyard and photographed marijuana under cultivation.[135] The United States Supreme Court held that the photographs were lawfully taken from a public vantage point and no constitutional violation occurred. However, when officers use infrared photography without a warrant to scan a home or apartment for extra heat escaping from the building that might indicate marijuana production, the image produced can be suppressed from admission in court due to the Fourth Amendment violation.[136]

A. *Posed Photographs*

Some courts will allow the introduction into evidence of staged or posed photographs of attempted reproductions of crime scenes showing posed persons, dummies, or other objects. However, one court held that posed photographs of trial witnesses that were prepared for the sole purpose of allowing the jury to take them to the jury room to associate a name with a witness's face constituted error.[137] If based on facts admitted in the case, staged photographs can illustrate one party's theory of what occurred in the case at the time of the crime. In most jurisdictions where this question has arisen, the courts have held such photographs admissible when a proper foundation has been laid by preliminary testimony showing that the pictures are faithful representations of what actually took place. An Ohio court upheld a posed photo of a defendant handcuffed on his stomach with money and crack cocaine placed on his back by police. The Ohio Court of Appeals noted that "[w]e agree with appellant that the photographs had limited probative value but we do not find them misleading or prejudicial as argued by the appellant."[138] A Georgia trial court permitted the prosecution to introduce two staged photographs that had been designed to demonstrate the trajectory of a fatal bullet.[139] In that case, the Supreme Court of Georgia approved of the prosecutor's use of the staged photographs to test and determine whether a person could shoot through the roof of an automobile while sitting in the passenger seat. In a different case, the

---

[134]   State v. Thomas, 158 S.W.3d 361, 2005 Tenn. LEXIS 135 (Tenn. 2005).
[135]   California v. Ciraolo, 476 U.S. 267, 106 S. Ct. 1809, 90 L. Ed. 2d 210 (1986).
[136]   State v. Detroy, 102 Haw. 13, 72 P.3d 485, 2003 Haw. LEXIS 314 (Haw. 2003). *See also* Kyllo v. United States, 533 U.S. 27, 2001 U.S. LEXIS 4487 (2001).
[137]   State v. Chomnarith, 654 N.W.2d 660, 666, 2003 Minn. LEXIS 2 (Minn. 2003).
[138]   State v. Owings, 2006 Ohio 4281 (Ohio 2006).
[139]   Grier v. Georgia, 273 Ga. 363, 541 S.E.2d 369, 2001 Ga. LEXIS 56 (2001).

Supreme Court of Georgia approved the use of a staged photograph of a police officer holding a particular stance to demonstrate the trajectory of a fatal bullet. According to the court, there was no abuse of discretion by the trial court.[140] In recent years, posed photographs have seen diminished use in criminal trials, probably because of computer-generated animations and some reluctance of courts to admit posed photographs.

B. Gruesome Photographs

As a general rule, trial courts are rarely reversed based on abuse of discretion in the admission of photographs that might be classified as gruesome or inflammatory. There is the requirement that the probative value of the photographs outweigh the risk of unfair prejudice, but that measuring concept remains a rather subjective device so that appellate courts often choose to defer to the trial court judgment. An Arkansas court noted:

> Even the most gruesome photographs may be admissible if they assist the trier of fact by shedding light on some issue, by proving a necessary element of the case, by enabling a witness to testify more effectively, by corroborating testimony, or by enabling jurors to better understand the testimony. Other acceptable purposes are to show the condition of the victim's body, the probable type or location of the injuries, and the position in which the body was discovered.[141]

On the other hand, a different court held that photographs that are gruesome or inflammatory and lack any evidentiary purpose should be excluded.[142] After making this general observation, a Mississippi court noted that when deciding on the admissibility of gruesome photographs, the trial judge must consider: (1) whether the proof is absolute or in doubt as to the identity of the guilty party; (2) whether the photographs are necessary evidence or simply a ploy on the part of the prosecutor to arouse passion and prejudice in the jury. A New York appellate court approved the admission of photographs of a deceased victim as well as photographs of the crime scene because the trial court found the photographs were relevant to various trial issues and helped corroborate the testimony of a surviving victim.[143]

While many defendants base their appeals partially on alleged error in the admission of prejudicial photographs, few are ever successful on this ground. The example of a California case in which the prosecution introduced photographs demonstrating the locations and extent of wounds of the deceased proves the general rule that reversal for admitting photographs is rare. In this case the appellant contended that the introduction of four autopsy photographs of the deceased had minimal probative value because her attorney had offered

---

[140] Rowe v. State, 276 Ga. 800, 582 S.E.2d 119, 2003 Ga. LEXIS 549 (2003).
[141] Garcia v. State, 2005 Ark. LEXIS 559 (Ark. 2005).
[142] Underwood v. State, 708 So. 2d 18 (Miss. 1998). *See* case in Part II.
[143] New York v. Byrd, 303 A.D. 2d 184, 756 N.Y.S.2d 190, 2003 N.Y. App. Div. LEXIS 2223 (2003).

to stipulate to what the photographs depicted. Because none of the photos showed the face of the deceased, and the other photographs tended to demonstrate trajectories of the bullets as they entered the deceased, all the photographs were admitted for specific purposes. The crucial question for a trial court and for an appellate court concerns whether the probative value of the photograph is outweighed by the danger of unfair prejudice to the defendant. The court pointed out that only four photographs were used to show the deceased's injury; the photographs clarified the testimony of the deputy medical examiner, who was able to use the photographs to explain his placement of the trajectory rods to show that a single bullet caused multiple wounds; the photographs supported testimony on the cause of death; the photographs were not displayed; and only one reference was made to the photographs in the closing argument to the jury. The appellate court held that the trial court did not abuse its discretion in admitting the photographs.[144] Even when a court finds error in the admission of gruesome photographs, if the error is deemed to be "harmless error," the case will not be reversed.

The line between photographs that are inadmissible because they unduly arouse passion or prejudice and those that have sufficient probative value remains a gray area rather than a bright line. For example, a Michigan court allowed the admission of a black-and-white photograph of the female decedent's body lying naked on her back with her arms crossed, revealing a stab wound to her neck.[145] In a Kansas case involving a rough photo, the court held that a photograph of the victim's naked body on the autopsy table with the internal organs protruding from each end and the skin in a decomposed state with portions hanging on the table, was properly admitted, despite its gruesome nature, because its probative nature showed the condition in which the body was found, the manner in which the defendant disposed of the body, and premeditation. If photographs of this type do not result in reversal, it is difficult to predict which types of photographs will find favor with reviewing courts. Another court explained that photographs have evidentiary value in homicide cases, even if gruesome, when they assist in describing the circumstances of a killing, describe the location where the body was found, and describe the cause of death, and supplement or explain the clarity of witness testimony.[146]

On the other hand, a federal court held that photographs showing the defendant with his finger on the trigger of a gun pointed at the head of another person was potentially very inflammatory and was, at best, cumulative of four other photographs linking the defendant to the gun, and should not have been admitted.[147] But in a federal Virgin Islands case, where the federal district court sits as an appellate court for the local trial court, the district court upheld the admission in evidence of pictures of a severely decomposed corpse from various angles that showed a mummified section of the body that had

---

[144]   California v. Lovelace, 2003 Cal. App. Unpub. LEXIS 7538 (2003).

[145]   People v. Benore, 2005 Mich. App. LEXIS 2718 (2005).

[146]   McIntosh v. State, 917 So. 2d 78, 84, 2005 Miss. LEXIS 754 (Miss. 2005).

[147]   United States v. Rose, 104 F.3d 1408 (1st Cir. 1997).

been exposed to the sun and a hole near the right armpit that was a stab wound.[148] The reviewing court noted, "[t]he relevance of the photographs to the fact of death and the condition and location of the body as it was discovered, which were relevant to the manner and probable time of death, all militated in favor of admission of the evidence."[149]

The general rule that can be discerned from the case law suggests that if photographs are relevant to a fact in issue and are not so inflammatory or prejudicial as to outweigh their probative value, the mere fact that they are somewhat inflammatory or gruesome does not bar their admission. If, however, the photographs have the potential to distort the deliberative process and unfairly skew the trial's outcome, their prejudicial effect outweighs their probative value and admission is improper.

C. Time of Taking

In authenticating photographs for admission in criminal cases, the photograph must accurately depict what it purports to depict so that the picture is not misleading either because too much time has passed between the event in question and the time the photograph was taken because the picture may not accurately capture the situation as it existed on the relevant date. To be admissible, a photograph must be sufficiently identified as a true and accurate representation of what it is supposed to represent. Therefore, if the time between the incident and the taking of the photograph is so great as to make it unlikely that the photograph actually portrays the situation as it existed at the time of the incident, such a photograph cannot be authenticated as accurately portraying the reality of the original event or scene and should not be admissible. For example, if a body had been discovered in the spring before ground cover became extensive, admission of a late summer photograph of the same scene with lush foliage would potentially be very misleading.

In a murder case involving a six-month-old infant, the Supreme Court of Mississippi upheld the admission of a photograph of the baby, taken when the child was alive dressed in a Christmas outfit, for the purpose of proving identity. The court noted that the photo was not offered for the purposes of inflaming the jury but fell within accepted case law allowing photographs of victims for identity purposes.[150]

Demonstrative of the principle that pictures must be taken at the appropriate time, in a homicide case, officers took still pictures of scratches on the defendant's neck, and took still and video pictures of the home where the death occurred. Later, police took pictures of the defendant's injured hand for future use during the trial. The taking of the still and video pictures had the effect of "freezing" the crime scene for future reference, when, without the contempo-

---

[148]   Krepps v. Government of the Virgin Islands, 2006 U.S. Dist. LEXIS 24904 (D. V.I. 2006).

[149]   *Id.*

[150]   Havard v. State, 928 So. 2d 771, 2006 Miss. LEXIS 90 (Miss. 2006). *See also* Lamar v. Georgia, 256 Ga. App. 567, 571, 568 S.E.2d 837, 2002 Ga. App. LEXIS 957 (2002).

raneous pictures, the crime scene could not have been reconstructed.[151] A trial court did not abuse its discretion in admitting a photograph of a crime scene, even though the photograph was taken in the daytime and the alleged crime occurred at night, and the photograph was not authenticated as to the lighting, because the witness did not know whether the light fixtures shown in the photograph were working on the night of the incident.[152] The reviewing court explained that the photography was adequately authenticated as to the layout of the parking lot in which the shooting occurred, and the layout was more significant to the jury than the details of the lighting, because the officer testified that they watched the shooter continuously from the point of the shooting to the point of the arrest.

D. Color Photographs

Color photographs, color slides, PowerPoint presentations, and other methods of displaying photographs are admissible in evidence subject to the same limitations and restrictions placed on black-and-white photographs. Even though color photographs are often more lifelike and consequently may be more gruesome and revolting, this in itself does not constitute grounds for exclusion of color photographs.[153] In an aggravated assault case in which the prosecution used several enlarged color pictures of the victim's injuries, the defendant contended that the trial court committed reversible error in admitting the pictures.[154] The reviewing court rejected the contention because showing the nature and extent of the victim's injuries was relevant to proving the prosecution's case. The court noted that they were unpleasant to observe, but the probative value outweighed any prejudice. Because color photographs are subject to color distortion, however, it is more difficult to take photographs that show the actual colors as they existed at the scene, and the proponent is often subject to a strong cross-examination on the subject of distortion.

In a murder trial, where a sober driver led police officers on a high-speed chase in which one of the officers was killed, the defendant objected to the admission of color photographs from different angles taken of the deceased officer's body in the emergency room.[155] Because the defendant did not dispute that the officer died in a car accident, he contended that the gruesome pictures were introduced to prejudice the jury. The reviewing court disagreed, noting that the pictures had a legitimate purpose, that a stipulation does not relieve the government from proving all essential elements of the case, and that a government witness can use photographs to tell a more complete story. Color photographs of the deceased's body taken during an autopsy have been admitted to give the jury a clear understanding of the cause of death,[156] and

---

[151] Gracia v. State, 2006 Tex. Crim. App. LEXIS 1284 (2006).
[152] United States v. Crockett, 49 F.3d 1357 (8th Cir. 1995).
[153] State v. Fulcher, 20 N.C. App. 259 (1973).
[154] State v. Dunfee, 327 Mont. 335, 340, 114 P.3d 217, 221, 2005 Mont. LEXIS 225 (2005).
[155] State v. Betha, 167 N.C. App. 215, 223, 605 S.E.2d 173, 179, 2004 N.C. App. LEXIS 2150 (2004).
[156] State v. McClellan, 6 Ohio App. 2d 155, 217 N.E.2d 230 (1966).

color photographs of injuries were admitted in a case in which the attending doctors identified the photographs as a fair representation of the plaintiff's condition at the time they were taken.[157]

E. Enlargements and Aerial Photographs

Photographs that have been enlarged in the same aspect ratio generally will be admitted if a smaller print or a photo on a computer screen would have been admissible. Although a defendant will typically object to the use of an enlarged picture on the grounds that the larger picture may cause unfair prejudice, courts routinely admit enlarged pictures because they help the jury better understand the evidence. In a North Carolina murder case in which the deceased had been killed by a firearm and injured with a knife, the court permitted, over the defendant's objection, the prosecution to show enlarged autopsy photographs projected on a large courtroom screen. The court reasoned that the enlarged photos would help the jury understand the extent of the injuries received by the deceased. The photos showed two knife wounds to the deceased and the fatal gunshot wound. In upholding the use of the enlarged autopsy photos, the appellate court stated that the probative value outweighed any danger of unfair prejudice and then noted, "[t]he photographs were not used in a repetitive manner and it was not excessive to project them onto a screen for the purpose of making them more easily viewed."[158] Enlarged photographs are frequently used in cases involving the comparison of handwriting or to show the place of an accident or the scene of a crime.

In a case in which a man had been convicted of killing his brother, prosecutors introduced several photographic enlargements despite the defendant's objections. According to the prosecution, the enlargements demonstrated the defendant's extreme atrocity or cruelty in committing the homicide and demonstrated consciousness of guilt. According to the appellate court, where there is probative value to a material issue, an enlarged gruesome picture will not be excluded on that ground alone.[159]

There seems to be no distinction between aerial and other types of photographs insofar as their admissibility is concerned, but authentication may be an issue. In a case in which a defendant had been charged with dealing drugs within 1,000 feet of a church, an aerial photograph was authenticated and used to prove that the defendant's drug business had transpired within the 1,000-foot prohibited area.[160] In another case, the prosecution used an aerial photograph to show how far a defendant moved a victim to support a charge of kidnapping.[161] The admission of aerial photographs is not uncommon and they are

[157]   Jenkins v. Associated Transport, Inc., 330 F.2d 706 (6th Cir. 1964). *See also* State v. Sinchak, 703 A.2d 790 (Conn. 1998).

[158]   State v. Snider, 168 N.C. App. 701, 706, 609 S.E.2d 231, 235, 2005 N.C. App. LEXIS 395 (2005).

[159]   Commonwealth of Massachusetts v. Obershaw, 435 Mass. 794, 803, 762 N.E.2d 276, 286, 2002 Mass. LEXIS 70 (2002).

[160]   Illinois v. Sparks, 335 Ill. App. 3d 249, 253, 780 N.E.2d 781, 784, 2002 Ill. App. LEXIS 1132 (2002).

[161]   People v. Dominguez, 39 Cal. 4th 1141, 1153, 47 Cal. Rptr. 3d 575, 2006 Cal. LEXIS 9977 (Cal. 2006).

usually admitted into evidence for the purpose of giving the jury an accurate view of an object or geographic scene that is relevant to a fact in issue; however, they may be excluded from evidence at the discretion of the court when the court has previously admitted other evidence covering the same issues.[162]

§ 14.7 Motion Pictures and Videotapes

Motion pictures, videotape recordings, digital videodisc recordings and accurate copies are admissible in evidence "once a proper foundation has been laid if the tape is a true, authentic, and accurate representation of the event taped without distortions or deletions."[163] The proponent of admission of a videotape recording or of a traditional movie film must lay a foundation that demonstrates that the film or video properly depicts what it purports to depict. The questions concerning authenticity are similar to those involved when laying the foundation for admission of a still photograph. The party desiring to introduce recorded motion pictures must establish that the contents of the motion pictures are relevant to an issue and that they accurately demonstrate what they purport to show. The authentication process also must demonstrate that the pictures are accurate, genuine, and that no tampering has occurred. In some cases, the admissibility of motion pictures depends upon testimony by the operator of the camera that the film or video accurately portrays what he or she observed at the time and place of the action in question. Although modern evidence rules permit the admission of film, DVD, or still photos taken in sequence that some banks use, by permitting authentication by a person who can identify the contents of the recording,[164] some jurisdictions require a more formal presentation of a foundation. In one case involving forgery, an Indiana court noted the method of proving a foundation for film cameras requires that "there should be evidence as to how and when the camera was loaded, how frequently the camera was activated, when the photographs were taken, and the processing and chain of custody of the film after its removal from the camera."[165] In this forgery case, the bank camera recorded transactions and it included one from the defendant teller forging a withdrawal record from a customer's account. The appellate court approved the admission of the bank surveillance tape showing the defendant's crime because the bank manager removed the videotape and a police officer checked it to identify the proper date of the tape. The officer watched that same videotape to match transaction numbers to customer accounts with representations that were depicted on the video. In addition, the custodian of the bank's records signed an affidavit that the surveillance taping was a regularly conducted business activity of the bank

---

[162] *See* United States v. Chiquito, 175 Fed. Appx. 215, 2006 U.S. App. LEXIS 8724 (10th Cir. 2006) and Helmig v. Kemna, 2006 U.S. App. LEXIS 22564 (8th Cir. 2006).

[163] Parkinson v. Kelly, 2006 U.S. Dist. LEXIS 54661 (N.D.N.Y. 2006).

[164] *See* F. RULE. EVID. 901. Requirement of Authentication or Foundation.

[165] McHenry v. State, 820 N.E.2d 124, 128, 2005 Ind. LEXIS 4 (Ind. 2005), quoting Edwards v. State, 762 N.E.2d 128, 136, 2002 Ind. App. LEXIS 50 (2002).

and that the custodian had verified the trustworthiness of the tape. This evidence proved to sufficiently lay the foundation for the video evidence.[166]

In a Georgia case[167] the trial court held that a proper foundation had been laid for the introduction of videotape made by a security video recorder that ran automatically. The camera had caught two defendants in acts of shoplifting, but the defendants based their appeal partly on grounds that a police officer should not have been able to testify as to the relevant portions of the video and that the trial court erred in admitting the original crime scene videotape and the slow motion copy and alleged that the prosecutor failed to lay a proper foundation for admission into evidence of the videotape recording. The defendant complained that the tape was made on two different days and no operator actually produced the automatic recording. The appellate court rejected the allegations concerning the video on the grounds that the court properly admitted the video pursuant to proper process and state law. In authenticating the videotapes, the store employee previously had viewed both videotapes and was familiar with the cameras used to make the surveillance videotape. The clerk testified that the cameras ran automatically and the recording media were changed daily. Additionally, the clerk testified that she was familiar with the locations of the cameras and understood the sweep of their coverage areas. The store clerk testified that, except for their running speeds, there was no difference between the slow-motion videotape and the high-speed original. When asked whether the videotape evidence truly and accurately depicted what occurred on the date of the offense, she answered in the affirmative. In addition, the clerk testified under oath that the videotape had not been altered in any way.

After noting that the admissibility of a film or video rested with the sound discretion of the trial court, the appellate court cited a Georgia statute that helped ensure admissibility of videotapes under these circumstances. The court referred to the law concerning admissibility of photographs and similar articles:

> Subject to any other valid objection, photographs, motion pictures, videotapes, and audio recordings produced at a time when the device producing the items was not being operated by an individual person or was not under the personal control or in the presence of an individual operator shall be admissible in evidence when the court determines, based on competent evidence presented to the court, that such items tend to show reliably the fact or facts for which the items are offered, provided that prior to the admission of such evidence the date and time of such photograph, motion picture, or videotape recording shall be contained on such evidence and such date and time shall be shown to have been made contemporaneously with the events depicted in the photograph, videotape, or motion picture.[168]

---

[166] McHenry v. State, 820 N.E.2d 124, 128, 2005 Ind. LEXIS 4 (Ind. 2005). *See* case in Part II.

[167] Ross v. Georgia, 2003 Ga. App. LEXIS 908, 2003 Fulton County D. Rep. 2331 (2003).

[168] O.C.G.A. § 24-4-48 (c) Admissibility of photographs, motion pictures, videotapes, and audio recordings (2006).

According to the Georgia appellate court, the videotape had been properly authenticated and the trial judge had not abused his discretion. The weight of the video evidence was an issue for the jury, which, the appellate court noted, had been determined adversely to the defendants.

In a different Georgia case, the appellate court approved the introduction of a videotape made by three teenagers while engaging in sexual acts in a motel room. One victim proved to be somewhat unconscious during the taping, and was unavailable to authenticate the tape from personal knowledge, but she was able review the tape and to identify herself as appearing on the tape. The mother of another child identified her daughter engaging in sexual activities on the videotape. In a pretrial statement, the juvenile defendant admitted to activities that were depicted on the tape. According to the reviewing court, "[v]iewing the circumstances under which the videotape was discovered and considering its contents, the trial court did not abuse its discretion in ruling that there was sufficient competent evidence that it reliably showed the facts for which it was offered so that it was admissible in evidence to be given whatever weight the jury chose to accord it."[169]

With respect to authentication and introduction of videotapes made by an automatic surveillance system, an Ohio court admitted a surveillance tape that had been edited by police, but that was considered to be an accurate and true recording of what transpired.[170] In the case, police alleged that the defendant and others severely beat the victim in full view of a digital video security recorder. The owner of the apartment complex, who was licensed to install security cameras, testified that he installed the system at issue. The two cameras used in this case snap images that are identified and stored on an 80-gigabyte hard drive. Each image contains the date and time of day that the system recorded it. Police made four compact disc copies of the photo images from the hard drive and an officer who was a forensic video analyst used a process called "padding" to make a virtual movie of the events. In using "padding," the forensic analyst slows down the fast motion generated by the video images taken at set intervals and weaves the images into a final product that approximates real-time viewing. Duplicate images were used to make the appearance of a seamless movie that was transferred to videotape and a DVD. The victim proved to be little help in authenticating the pictures and the movie constructed from the stills. Using the knowledge of the officers concerning the physical layout of the crime scene, the information from the man who installed the system, and the recording of the defendant entering and leaving the apartment and pulling the victim from the bushes after having severely beaten him, police officers were able to help authenticate the result. The appellate court approved the admission of the reconstructed real time movie as accurately displaying the actual events as they really occurred. Under the "silent witness" method of authentication, the evidence speaks for itself and constitutes substantive evidence that is admissible despite not having a sponsoring witness.

---

[169]   Wilson v. State, 279 Ga. App. 459, 631 S.E.2d 391, 2006 Ga. App. LEXIS 483 (2006).
[170]   State v. Arafat, 2006 Ohio 1722, 2006 Ohio App. LEXIS 15 (Ohio 2006).

With respect to authentication of videotapes made by automatic process-es, an Illinois court adopted the theory that is implicit in the Georgia statute referred to above, the "silent witness" theory of authentication. A drug sting had been arranged by Illinois police officers, where police installed a camera and video recorder within a confidential informant's vehicle. The camera auto-matically recorded videotape evidence of a defendant selling drugs to the con-fidential informant. When the prosecutor introduced the videotape evidence against the drug dealer, he objected, citing improper authentication of the video, because the confidential informant did not testify. As the defendant alleged, no person who had knowledge testified concerning authentication. The Illinois court adopted the "silent witness" theory of authentication for films, pictures, and videotape recordings. The appellate court held that the "silent witness" theory may be used to admit photographic evidence in situa-tions in which the trial judge determines that the videotape is reliable after carefully considering the evidence establishing the time and date of the taping or the time of the making of the photographic evidence. The judge must con-sider whether there was any evidence of editing or tampering and must be sure that the operating condition ensured accuracy and reliability of the video or motion picture. The judge must be convinced that the procedure employed fol-lowed appropriate instructions concerning the preparation, testing, operation, and security of the equipment used to produce the motion picture or video. There should be testimony identifying the relevant participants depicted in the photographic evidence. On a proper review, the videotape will be admitted into evidence because it has been properly authenticated even though no per-son operated the camera at every moment during the taping. In the Illinois case, the appellate court held that the judge had not abused discretion in admitting the videotape against the defendants because the officers were able to assist in authentication along with the "silent witness." Therefore, the court upheld the convictions.[171]

In a capital murder prosecution, a Michigan trial court permitted a securi-ty videotape to be admitted on behalf of the prosecution that showed the vic-tim going into the defendant's apartment, after which she was never seen alive.[172] The defendant contended that a proper foundation had not been shown sufficient to authenticate the tape as genuine due to a lack of testimony con-cerning the acceptability of the recording methods. Michigan Rule of Evi-dence 901 accepts that authentication is satisfied when there has been evi-dence introduced sufficient to support the finding that the matter in question is what it purports to be. In this case, security technicians testified that the security tape system had been installed properly and was in good working order on the date in question. Other witnesses who were seen in the tape tes-tified that the tape accurately recorded their activities on the day in question. Because the reviewing court held the opinion that the proper foundation had

[171] 336 Ill. App. 3d 893, 899, 784 N.E.2d 410, 415, 2003 Ill. App. LEXIS 111 (2003).
[172] People v. Rocafort, 2005 Mich. App. LEXIS 3274 (2005), *appeal denied*, 475 Mich. 870, 714 N.W.2d 322, 2006 Mich. LEXIS 1151 (Mich. 2006).

been laid to introduce the videotape, the trial court did not abuse its discretion in admitting the video.

However, transcripts of tape recordings containing quotation marks around words that the government alleged were code words could not be provided to the jury in a prosecution for money laundering and conspiracy to possess with intent to distribute five or more kilograms of cocaine; the government could not bolster its argument by customizing the transcript to reflect its theory of the case.[173]

Newer cases may involve computer-generated animations (CGA) that incorporate the opinions of several expert witnesses in a manner that appears as a recreation of a how a crime happened. The use of CGAs in criminal cases requires that the jury be informed that the animation constitutes only a demonstrative exhibit or an illustration that will be used to demonstrate the prosecution's theory of a case that is based on interpretation of actual evidence in the case. In one Pennsylvania case that involved a police officer as a defendant in a homicide prosecution, the trial court permitted the commonwealth to show the jury a CGA that incorporated the expert opinion of a forensic pathologist and a crime scene reconstructionist that was based on the forensic and physical evidence found at the actual crime scene.[174] Following the police officer's conviction of the murder of his wife, he appealed, contending that the CGA was unfairly prejudicial, lacked authentication, presented cumulative evidence, and should not have been admitted. The Supreme Court of Pennsylvania concluded that the admission or exclusion of computer-generated animations should be governed by the concepts of authentication and relevancy, by weighing the chance for unfair prejudicial value against the probative effect of the evidence. The top Pennsylvania court noted that some concerns prior to the admission decision carry more weight and deserve closer scrutiny than when a court faces the admission or exclusion of more traditional evidence. The Supreme Court affirmed the police officer's conviction for first-degree murder because, among other issues, the admission of the CGA did not create unfair prejudice to his case and provided relevant evidence. The Court of Criminal Appeals of Oklahoma reversed a murder conviction in which a computer-generated animation attempted to demonstrate how the defendant killed her fiancé with a firearm.[175] The court overturned the conviction because the CGA failed to accurately and properly demonstrate what actually occurred. Insufficient data existed to tell which positions each person occupied during the event and there was no data to explain the trajectory of the bullet. Essentially, the CGA filled in the gaps of evidence with what amounted to speculation. The prejudicial effect clearly outweighed any probative value offered by the animation.

Traditional motion pictures, videotape recordings, DVD recordings, and virtual movies constructed by the use of "padding" must be authenticated as accurately portraying what they purport to depict, as a threshold for admission

---

[173]   United States v. Gonzales-Maldonado, 115 F.3d 9 (1st Cir. 1997).

[174]   Commonwealth v. Serge, 896 A.2d 1170, 1178, 2006 Pa. LEXIS 561 (Pa. 2006).

[175]   See Dunkle v. State, 2006 OKLA. CRIM. 29, 139 P.3d 228, 2006 Okla. Crim. App. LEXIS 29 (2006).

into evidence. Video evidence must be relevant to a fact that is at issue in the case and the prejudicial value cannot outweigh the probative value in order for a judge to allow the video evidence as proof in a case.

§ 14.8　X-rays

For purposes of admission, X-ray evidence generally is treated like other photographs,[176] although some slightly different admission problems may arise. The purpose of an X-ray "picture" is to reveal inner portions of the body that cannot be seen by the naked eye by passing X-ray radiation through the human body to place an image on film that is sensitive to radiation produced by X-rays. Because no person ever really sees the body part depicted on X-ray film, it cannot be verified in the same manner as an ordinary photograph— that is, by testimony that it is a correct representation of the object that it purports to depict.

In a recent decision involving the potential termination of a parent's rights due to extreme child abuse, the mother contended that X-ray images taken at a hospital should not have been admitted to show broken bones of her child because the government had not authenticated them properly. The X-rays were taken at a children's hospital that used film-less images that were viewed on computer monitors. The evaluating doctor testified that he is a specialist in the area of interpretation of pediatric imaging studies. He also testified that he was the radiologist who evaluated the child's X-ray images and that the images were appropriate for use. The doctor helped authenticate the X-rays by testifying that the images taken had the child's name and the date of the X-ray on them.[177] In this case, the radiologist who worked at the hospital that took the images, printed the X-ray image from a computer program that allowed but did not require slight alterations of the image. The radiologist testified that the computer program could alter the contrast, brightness, and could crop the edges of the X-ray but could not otherwise manipulate the X-ray image. The Supreme Court of Texas held that the trial court properly admitted the X-ray image stored on the computer and did not abuse its discretion.[178]

Some jurisdictions hold that an X-ray has been sufficiently authenticated if the evidence shows that the X-ray was taken by a qualified expert who is familiar with X-ray techniques and procedures, and that the X-ray is a true depiction of what it purports to represent. The foundation for an X-ray picture may be established when the physician or radiologist under whose supervision and control the picture was taken interprets it in court for the jury.

Professional medical witnesses may illustrate X-rays through a view screen, PowerPoint display or other projection device available in a courtroom. Using X-rays in a different manner, a computer tomography imaging system

---

[176]　FED. R. EVID. 1001(2).
[177]　In the Interest of J.P.B., 2005 Texas App. LEXIS 1159 (2005).
[178]　In the Interest of J.P.B, 180 S.W.3d 570, 575, 2005 Tex. LEXIS 912 (Tex. 2005).

(CAT scan) provides excellent images of living tissue, bone, and blood structures and the resulting images can be admitted into evidence upon a proper foundation. Magnetic resonance imaging (MRI) offers better views of living tissue and experts frequently testify once the doctor or other professional has provided a proper foundation. Similar issues of authentication arise with MRI and CAT data that accompany traditional X-ray evidence.

§ 14.9 Sound Recordings

Public sound recordings generally present few constitutional issues due to a lack of any Fourth Amendment or statutory expectation of privacy that exists when speaking in public[179] and sounds or speech voluntarily uttered generally do not implicate Fifth Amendment self-incrimination allegations. Surreptitious recordings may present both constitutional issues as well as concerns relating to authentication of the voices that may be present on a wiretap recording. Recording conversations with prior notice to at least one party,[180] such as recording a prisoner's non-lawyer phone calls, does not transgress state or federal law and the recording may be admissible against a prisoner.[181] Federal law and many state statutes regulate wiretapping and surreptitious recording of conversations, but provide for methods to properly record and to admit the fruits of a wiretap.[182] Through these laws and through constitutional protections, privacy rights are generally protected despite the advances in the ability of law enforcement agents and private citizens to record almost anything at anytime. Despite concerns that indiscriminate use of recording devices in law enforcement raises serious constitutional questions, sound recordings are frequently admitted into evidence.[183] In today's law enforcement world, tapes of 911 emergency telephone calls may provide an excellent source of evidence that should be admissible at criminal trials. In one case in which an intruder had murdered a woman's husband, neighbors began placing 911 calls that were later introduced against and over the objection of the accused murderer.[184] He contended that the calls had not been properly authenticated because the 911 operator should have testified and the 911 log book should have been introduced to properly authenticate the calls. The trial court permitted one of the 911 callers to testify that she had recently listened to the tape and that the recording was an accurate account of her call to the 911 oper-

---

[179] *See* Commonwealth v. Rivera, 445 Mass. 119, 833 N.E.2d 1113; 2005 Mass. LEXIS 491 (2005), in which a convenience store robbery suspect failed in his argument to suppress video and audio of his conduct and words during a murder.

[180] Some states require consent of both parties to a conversation.

[181] *See* Sanchez v. State, 2005 Tex. App. LEXIS 5084 (2005).

[182] *See* OHIO REV. CODE ANN. 2933.52 Interception of wire, oral or electronic communications (2006).

[183] Seymour v. State, 949 P.2d 881 (Wyo. 1997). In this case, the court noted that admission of tape-recordings is especially appropriate when the witness who heard the statements also testifies and the report gives an independent support to his testimony.

[184] Calhoun v. State, 932 So. 2d 923, 2005 Ala. Crim. App. LEXIS 101 (2005), *cert. denied*, 2006 U.S. LEXIS 5233 (2006).

ator. She identified her own voice and testified that she made a 911 call on the night of the killing. In approving the authentication process used for the 911 calls, the Alabama court noted that generally there were two methods of authenticating sound recordings. One, used in this case, requires that a competent witness testify that the sound or other medium accurately and reliably represents what she or he sensed at the time in question. Under this theory the witness must testify that the witness had sufficient personal knowledge of the scene or events pictured or recorded that the item of evidence accurately and reliably represents the actual sounds or scene.[185] The other method, called the "silent witness" foundation, requires:

1. a showing that the device or process or mechanism that produced the item being offered as evidence was capable of recording what a witness would have seen or heard had a witness been present at the scene or event recorded,

2. a showing that the operator of the device or process or mechanism was competent,

3. establishment of the authenticity and correctness of the resulting recording, photograph, videotape, etc.,

4. a showing that no changes, additions, or deletions have been made,

5. a showing of the manner in which the recording, photograph, videotape, etc., was preserved,

6. identification of the speakers, or persons pictured, and

7. for criminal cases only, a showing that any statement made in the recording, tape, etc., was voluntarily made without any kind of coercion or improper inducement.[186]

Authentication for 911 tapes may in actual practice be an easier task than authenticating recordings involving surreptitious audiotaping or wiretapping, where acquiring evidence to authenticate an unknown voice may prove difficult. The fact that the proponent of an audio recording has sufficiently authenticated it does not mean that the substantive content will be admissible; the concept of authentication is a preliminary hurdle that must be overcome prior to considerations of admission of the internal content.

Authenticating audiotapes and voices may pose problems when the law enforcement official has minimally dealt with criminal targets personally and talked on telephones sporadically when some conversations were taped and others were not recorded. In a drug investigation operation, a detective dealt frequently with a man named J.R., and for a large part of the investigation, did not know his true identity.[187] On several occasions, the detective met with the defendant, but did not know that he was really J.R. because the conversations

---

[185]   *Id.* at 954.

[186]   *Id.*

[187]   United States v. Bush, 405 F.3d 909, 2005 U.S. App. LEXIS 7114 (10th Cir. 2005).

were cryptic and short. Over the course of the investigation, the detective spoke with the defendant three times in person and began to believe that the defendant was J.R. The trial court permitted the detective to authenticate an incriminating audiotape of the defendant's voice as being the voice of J.R. and to state that the voiced belonged to the same person. The defendant voiced an objection that although the detective had 10 substantive conversations with J.R., the detective had insufficient understanding of the defendant's voice to authenticate that voice as the voice of J.R. The trial court rejected the defendant's argument that the authentication had to be done by precisely following the suggestions of Federal Rule of Evidence 901, while noting that voice identification only had to rise to a level involving minimal familiarity in order to be considered as proper identification of a voice or tape-recording. In affirming the trial court's finding of sufficient authentication, the Court of Appeals for the Tenth Circuit noted, "[o]nce minimal familiarity is satisfied, it is for the jury to assess any issues regarding the extent of the witness's familiarity with the voice."[188]

In determining whether to admit an audiotape recording, the judge must consider whether the probative value of the audiotape outweighs the danger of unfair prejudice to the defendant. In a federal kidnapping case in which the victim died, the trial court properly admitted an audiotape where, in remarking about the death of the victim, the defendant stated, "I feel bad about it but I'm not gonna let it ruin my life, you know what I mean. I didn't know her that well. . . . I hate to be so cold and heartless about it but who gives a shit, it happens every day."[189] The court concluded that the statement was relevant because the defendant was discussing the maid of honor at his wedding who was his child's babysitter and that it was not unfairly prejudicial to allow the audiotape to be played for the jury. However, in a different case, a reviewing court indicated that the trial court abused its discretion in admitting an unintelligible tape recording of a statement made by the defendant to a police officer and thereby prejudicing that defendant, because the jury may have believed that the tape contained incriminating statements made by the defendants based on the fact that the tape was introduced by the prosecution.[190] The mere fact that some portions of the tape recording are inaudible does not, by itself, require exclusion of the tape in criminal prosecutions.[191] In a case in which the defendants were accused of a strong-arm robbery, the 911 call made by the hysterical female occupant of an apartment was largely unintelligible after the defendants forcefully entered the apartment. The hysteria continued until long after the defendants left the scene of the crime. According to the reviewing court, the probative value of the audiotape consisted of what the caller stated before she became hysterical and the later hysteria was probative that the intruders had no permission to enter the apartment.

---

[188]   *Id.* at 919.
[189]   United States v. Gianakos, 415 F.3d 912, 925, 2005 U.S. App. LEXIS 15236 (8th Cir. 2005).
[190]   State v. Lane, 480 Ohio App. 3d 172, 549 N.E.2d 193 (1988).
[191]   Benavides v. State, 808 N.E.2d 708, 710, 2004 Ind. App. LEXIS 901 (2004).

An audiotape of which portions are inaudible may be admitted into evidence, assuming relevancy and a proper foundation. In one case, a police officer wore a wire to record the defendant, offering him $20,000 to kill her husband before her divorce was final, but portions of the recording could not be fully understood. In admitting the audiotape, the court correctly concluded that the probative value far exceeded any potential for unfair prejudice and noted that the inaudible sections affected the weight of the evidence.[192]

The use of recording devices to overhear conversations beyond the area in which they might normally be heard does not in itself require the evidence to be suppressed. Section 2511 of the United States Code states in detail the procedures that must be followed when using electronic surveillance devices to overhear and record conversations. Informants and undercover law enforcement agents may use hidden recorders or wear wire transmitters to tape or record a conversation and the same agents can invite unsuspecting criminals into bugged locations controlled by police without violating 18 U.S.C § 2515. In federal courts, as long as one party to the conversation consented to the electronic recording of the conversations, they will not be excluded unless other rules of evidence prevent admission.[193]

If one party does not agree to the recording of a conversation, the procedures specified in the statute must be followed to the letter if the recording is to be free from challenge on constitutional grounds.[194] Federal law prohibits the use of illegally seized audio information in court. For example:

§ 2515. Prohibition of use as evidence of intercepted wire or oral communications

Whenever any wire or oral communication has been intercepted, no part of the contents of such communication and no evidence derived therefrom may be received in evidence in any trial, hearing, or other proceeding in or before any court, grand jury, department, officer, agency, regulatory body, legislative committee, or other authority of the United States, a State, or a political subdivision thereof if the disclosure of that information would be in violation of this chapter [18 U.S.C. §§ 2515.].[195]

Noncompliance with the statute renders otherwise excellent evidence inadmissible in court. Even if the recordings meet federal constitutional standards, the evidence standards must also be met. Therefore, a taped confession was not admissible when a police captain admitted that the recorder on which the defendant's confession was originally recorded was not under his exclusive control and that some of the defendant's statements had not been recorded.[196]

Related to sound recordings are text messages, as well as e-mail correspondence that may be sent and received on cell phones, personal digital assistants,

---

[192] State v. Jackson, 2005 Tenn. Crim. App. LEXIS 193 (2005).
[193] See CHAPTER 119. WIRE AND ELECTRONIC COMMUNICATIONS INTERCEPTION AND INTERCEPTION OF ORAL COMMUNICATIONS National Institute for Trial Advocacy (2006).
[194] See 18 U.S.C. § 2511 (2006).
[195] See 18 U.S.C. § 2515 (2006).
[196] Monts v. State, 214 Tenn. 171, 379 S.W.2d 34 (1964).

and other devices. Criminals have embraced the new technology in an effort to make their operations more difficult to detect and to provide better communication to facilitate criminal activities, especially drug transactions. Generally, courts have determined that the Federal Wiretap Act, 18 U.S.C. §§ 2510 *et seq.*, governs only the "acquisition of the contents of electronic communications that occur contemporaneously with their transmission,"[197] and the Act does not regulate data that is acquired from electronic storage by information service providers. To obtain text messages and other stored electronic data, Title II of the Electronic Communications Privacy Act of 1986, 18 U.S.C. § 2701 *et seq.*, federal officials must apply for a warrant based on probable cause that is consistent with the Federal Rules of Criminal Procedure. The warrant requires that the provider or storing entity to disclose the contents of wire or electronic communication that the holder has in storage to the federal government. Congress made this type of information easier to obtain than information gathered by following the Federal Wiretap Act, whereby, for stored information, the government need not explain why the evidence could not be obtained by any other method, prior to being able to procure a warrant.[198]

§ 14.10   Diagrams, Maps, and Models

The propriety of permitting a witness to explain his or her testimony by visual illustration is now firmly established; however, unless the illustration is essential to an understanding of the testimony, it is largely cumulative in effect, and the admission or exclusion rests within the discretion of the trial judge. A prosecutor could use a map to help a witness illustrate his or her testimony and it could either be used only as a exhibit or the proponent could move for it to be admitted into evidence. In a murder case, the court permitted the prosecution to use a map that was not drawn to scale as an exhibit but the witness described it as essentially accurate. The trial court later admitted the map into evidence over the defendant's objection. The fact that the map was not a genuine map and was not to scale went to its weight and did not affect admissibility.[199]

The admissibility of a map is similar to the admissibility of photographs, in that the trial court should determine whether the exhibit aids the jury in understanding evidence, and any inaccuracy in the map does not raise questions of admissibility, but rather questions of what weight the jury will give it.[200]

Authenticated maps may be admissible to demonstrate drug-free zones around schools and other locations. In New Jersey, state law permits municipalities to produce maps for the purpose of depicting the 1,000-foot boundary

---

[197]   United States v. Jones, 2006 U.S. Dist. LEXIS 56473 (D.D.C. 2006), citing United States v. Steiger, 318 F.3d 1039, 1048-49 (11th Cir. 2003).

[198]   *Id.*

[199]   Calhoun v. State, 932 So. 2d 923, 951, 2005 Ala. Crim. App. LEXIS 101 (2005).

[200]   State v. Kirker, 47 Conn. App. 612, 707 A.2d 303 (1998).

around school properties or the 500-foot area near public housing that is drug-free. In one case, a prosecutor used a genuine municipal map but did not introduce the municipal ordinance that approved the map into evidence.[201] The reviewing court held that any map could be used to demonstrate the drug-free area if it was properly admitted under the rules of evidence. The officer who testified against the defendant was familiar with the area and the area maps in general and he testified that the sale of drugs was within the drug-free area. Another public official, who was a director of the public housing authority, authenticated the map as being genuine. He demonstrated his familiarity with the drug-free area and noted that a sale at a particular point would be within the 500-foot area. The reviewing court held that the map was properly introduced as evidence and upheld the conviction.[202]

There is a distinction between a diagram or chart that is in evidence or used for evidentiary purposes and one used only in counsel's argument; that is, the former may be exhibited throughout the trial or a portion thereof to which it is relevant, while the latter should be withdrawn from the jury's observation at the conclusion of the argument in which it is used. The chart used by counsel in his or her argument should refer only to matters that are in evidence or to inferences that may properly be drawn from the evidence.[203]

Charts may be used to show relationships and organizational structure if properly introduced and used for a limited purpose. Generally, charts should show factual data and not advocate one position or another. In an employment discrimination case, the plaintiff's attorney proffered charts that the judge viewed as advocacy charts and did not reflect what the plaintiff's attorney personally knew, but revealed what she advocated.[204] Federal courts may admit charts, summaries, or calculations at the discretion of the court under Federal Rule of Evidence 1006. The trial judge refused to admit her charts because they indicated how the attorney believed that other documents in the case should be interpreted.

Models, when properly identified and authenticated, may be used for illustration purposes if the evidence offered as a result of the use of a model is relevant and material to the ultimate fact to be demonstrated.[205] Neither an exact model nor a full-size model is required if the original is substantially represented so the model will not prove misleading to the jury or judge. If a replica of the original is used, the jury should be instructed that the object is not the one used in the crime and that it is to be considered as evidence that demonstrates or illustrates the object used in the crime. In a Virginia murder prosecution involving the Virginia, Maryland, and District of Columbia sniper

---

[201] State v. Trotman, 366 N.J. Super. 226, 234, 840 A.2d 952; 2004 N.J. Super. LEXIS 52 (N.J. 2004).
[202] *Id.*
[203] Ratner v. Arrington, 111 So. 2d 82 (Fla. 1959).
[204] Hutchins v. UPS, 2006 U.S. App. LEXIS 19885 (3d Cir. 2006).
[205] State v. Mitchel, 56 Wash. App. 610, 784 P.2d 568 (1990). *See also* Taylor v. State, 640 So. 2d 1227 (Fla. 1994), in which the court noted that demonstration exhibits may be used at the trial as an aid to the jury's understanding, but only if the exhibits constitute an accurate and reasonable reproduction of the object involved.

shootings of 2002, the prosecution used a model of the trunk of the car from which the commonwealth alleged the shooting took place. The defendant objected that the model was "not complete" and "was out of context." The appellate court upheld the trial judge's decision to allow the model of the car trunk to be used as demonstrative evidence because it sufficiently represented the original Caprice trunk in most important aspects.[206] In a different case, the state was properly allowed to use a knife and a styrofoam head as demonstrative exhibits in the prosecution of a defendant who was charged with stabbing the victim in the head.[207] The court noted that the knife and styrofoam were sufficiently accurate replicas of the objects involved in the crime.

Plastic models of the human skeleton and of the heart, brain, kidney, or other organs—when injury to one of them is involved—are frequently used to illustrate the testimony of a medical expert.

§ 14.11 Courtroom Demonstrations and Experiments

While it is usually more convenient to videotape or photograph demonstrations or experiments that are performed outside of court, in some instances courtroom demonstrations are logically permitted because they more convincingly depict the situation to the jury. In order for a courtroom demonstration to be admissible as evidence, the party wishing to conduct the demonstration must convince the trial judge that the demonstration will be relevant and will be conducted under conditions that are substantially the same as the actual event to which it relates.[208] As a general rule, virtually all of the same foundational and legal requirements and elements affecting the admissibility and use of demonstrative evidence apply to courtroom experiments and demonstrations.

An experiment or demonstration may be permitted by the judge where it clearly resembles the actual event and is not unfairly prejudicial while still offering relevant evidence connected to the issues in the case. In a case involving fraud in the federal agricultural support program, the court permitted the defendant to demonstrate how the moisture content of corn could be measured and later raised by misting it and then subjecting it to a Dickey John machine for a re-read of the moisture content. The person conducting the experiment was qualified because he used the Dickey John machine to measure the moisture content of corn that he actually purchased. The Court of Appeals upheld the use of the demonstration in the courtroom because it found the judge had not abused his discretion.[209]

To be legally relevant, demonstration or experiment must meet the test of "similarity of conditions," but it is not necessary that the conditions be exactly

---

[206] Muhammad v. Commonwealth, 611 S.E.2d 537, 576, 2005 Va. LEXIS 39 (Va. 2005).

[207] Brown v. State, 550 So. 2d 527 (Fla. 1989).

[208] United States v. Williams, 2006 U.S. App. LEXIS 21337 (4th Cir. 2006).

[209] United States v. Howard, 51 Fed. Appx. 118, 2002 U.S. App. LEXIS 23711 (4th Cir. 2002).

the same, because this would generally be difficult or impossible. In a Massachusetts drug case in which a police officer used a telescope to observe drug transactions at night illuminated by streetlights and business signs, the officer radioed other officers to make drug arrests.[210] The trial court permitted the officer to position the actual telescope for jurors to look from the courthouse to a distance approximating the distance used in the defendant's drug bust. Even though the jurors looked out during the daylight hours from a different vantage point at a different distance, the trial judge allowed the demonstration to proceed. He offered a cautionary note to the jury that the conditions were somewhat different. The appellate court approved the use of the demonstration as not abusing judicial discretion and because the defendant's trial objection only concerned the lighting differences.

In a Kentucky case, a prosecutor and a police officer reenacted the operative elements of a shooting case during closing arguments in a way that had not been sanctioned by the trial court. Even though the demonstration was highly improper and could have prejudiced the jury, because the facts were not in serious dispute, and the only issue concerned *mens rea*, the curative instruction given by the trial court cured any prejudice. The Supreme Court of Kentucky affirmed the conviction.[211]

§ 14.12   Preservation and Disclosure of Evidence Favorable to the Defense

In the classic case of *Brady v. Maryland*, the United States Supreme Court decided that a defendant has a due process right to request and obtain from the prosecution evidence that is either material to the guilt or innocence of the defendant or relevant to punishment to be imposed.[212] The *Brady* material that must be disclosed includes impeachment evidence that could be useful to a defendant.[213] In the *Brady* case, the prosecution knew of an extrajudicial confession to murder of Brady's accomplice and Brady was never informed. The rationale of disclosure supports the view that fundamental fairness requires that the government not affirmatively hide evidence known to it that could be helpful to the rendering of actual justice. The *Brady* Court cautioned that failure to disclose such evidence following a defense request denies due process—irrespective of the good or bad faith of the prosecutor.

According to the Supreme Court in *United States v. Agurs*, the prosecution has a duty to disclose evidence that might be exculpatory for the defendant, even if the defendant does not request discovery of exculpatory evidence. Fundamental fairness requires that the prosecution seek justice and not be inter-

---

[210] Commonwealth v. Perryman, 55 Mass. App. Ct. 187, 193, 770 N.E.2d 1, 6, 2002 Mass. App. LEXIS 8 (Mass. 2002).

[211] Price v. Commonwealth of Kentucky, 59 S.W.3d 878, 880, 881, 2001 Ky. LEXIS 200 (2001).

[212] Brady v. Maryland, 373 U.S. 83, 1963 U.S. LEXIS 1615 (1963).

[213] United States v. Bagley, 473 U.S. 667, 677, 1985 U.S. LEXIS 130 (1985).

ested in winning the case at the cost of injustice.[214] However, the Court at the same time rejected the argument that a "prosecutor has a constitutional duty routinely to deliver his entire file to the defense counsel,"[215] even though some prosecutors do have a completely open file policy toward defendants.

In *Moore v. Illinois*, the Court observed that:

> We know of no constitutional requirement that the prosecution make a complete and detailed accounting to the defense of all police investigatory work on a case.[216]

To prove a *Brady* violation, the Supreme Court noted in *Strickler v. Greene* that the defendant must demonstrate that: "The evidence at issue must be favorable to the accused, either because it is exculpatory, or because it is impeaching; that evidence must have been suppressed by the state, either willfully or inadvertently; and prejudice must have ensued."[217] The Supreme Court of the United States held that Greene proved everything necessary to show that a *Brady* violation existed, except that he was not prejudiced because the case against the defendant was so strong that the outcome would not have changed.[218] The Court explained that the police officers were acting "in good faith and in accord with their normal practice" and did not destroy the breath samples in a calculated effort to circumvent the due process requirement. Therefore, the conviction was affirmed.

In 2006, the Supreme Court considered a *Brady* discovery case from West Virginia that involved evidence known to a police officer but not known to the prosecution. The conviction involved a sexual assault conviction in which the defendant maintained his innocence consistently. Following the trial and conviction, a defense investigator discovered that two of the victims had written a graphically explicit note that taunted the defendant for being played for a fool and one "victim" thanked him for oral sex. The letter squarely supported the defendant's consent theory of the encounter and, if believed, could have changed the outcome of the case. A state trooper had seen the note, declined to take possession of it, and suggested that it be destroyed. Evidence favorable to the accused under *Brady* appeared to have been suppressed. The Supreme Court sent the case back for a determination of whether the exculpatory note required reversal of the conviction based on the *Brady* principles of discovery.[219]

From these cases emerges the rule that due process requires disclosure, upon the defendant's request, of evidence favorable to the defendant, but unless a criminal defendant can show bad faith on the part of the police, failure to preserve potentially useful evidence does not constitute a denial of due

---

[214] United State v. Agurs, 427 U.S. 97, 1976 U.S. LEXIS 72 (1976).
[215] *Id.* at 111.
[216] Moore v. Illinois, 408 U.S. 786, 92 S. Ct. 2562, 33 L. Ed. 2d 706 (1972).
[217] Strickler v. Greene, 527 U.S. 263, 282, 1999 U.S. LEXIS 4191 (1999).
[218] *Id.* at 296.
[219] Youngblood v. West Virginia, ___ U.S. ___, 2006 U.S. LEXIS 4884 (2006).

process of law. When the interests of justice clearly require it, the police and prosecutor have an obligation to preserve the evidence. If the evidence is destroyed through bad faith, the due process protection is violated.

§ 14.13   Summary

In addition to the use of oral testimony and documentary evidence, real evidence may be introduced to help the jury or other factfinders in determining what happened in a particular case. Real evidence may involve the actual objects from the crime or crime scene or they may be called demonstrative real evidence when they consist of duplicate items such as guns or knives or when the evidence was constructed for trial, such as models. The use of real evidence to assist the court and jury in determining the guilt or innocence of the accused in criminal cases has had the sanction of immemorial usage. In many instances, real evidence is more persuasive and aids the jury more in reaching a decision than does the testimony of the witness. The courts, recognizing the desirability of obtaining all the facts, have actually encouraged the use of real evidence.

With the use of real evidence, care must be taken to offer probative evidence that does not pose a risk of unfair prejudice. This may be a special concern when using demonstrative real evidence. To avoid unfair prejudice, certain rules have been established and must be followed if such evidence is to be admitted. For example, the prosecution must show that there is a connection between the instrument or article introduced and the accused, that the article is relevant to the particular case, and that the object is substantially in the same condition as it was when it was used in connection with the crime—or the change in condition, if any, is explained. Also, the prosecution must show a chain or continuity of custody concerning the article to be introduced, but a break in the chain may go more toward weight than admissibility. Alternatively, the proponent may properly identify the evidence by identifying a unique mark or serial number.

There are various types of real evidence that have been held admissible, and for each type, certain conditions must be met. In some instances, the exhibition of the person of the witness may be the best way to explain an injury. In this event, the judge in his discretion may allow such exhibition even though it may be somewhat gruesome.

Articles connected with the crime, such as weapons or clothing, may be introduced as real evidence if the prosecution can show that there was or is a connection between the properly authenticated article and the accused. Also, the judge may allow the jury to visit and view the scene of the incident if, in his or her discretion, this will help the jury in determining the facts of the case.

If it is not practicable to let the jury view the scene or to bring all of the evidence into court, photographs are admissible as a form of real evidence. Before a photograph may be introduced, a foundation must be laid; i.e., a competent witness who has personal knowledge of the area or thing photographed must testify that the picture is an accurate representation of the object or person depicted. In addition to still photographs, motion pictures, DVDs, X-rays, CT scans, MRI scans, and sound recordings may be introduced. As in the case of photographs, a foundation must be laid before such evidence is admitted into court.

With the use of demonstrative real evidence it is possible for witnesses to more effectively explain the events that occurred by using guns, knives, diagrams, maps, charts, and models. When references are made to such a diagram, map, or model, a witness must testify that it is a correct portrayal of the situation or thing represented.

Due process requires disclosure, upon the defendant's request, of evidence favorable to the defense and the prosecution has a duty to disclose exculpatory evidence even without a request. Evidence known to police or prosecutors, even where known only to one and not the other, is deemed to be known by the government for disclosure purposes.

Results of Examinations and Tests

15

It is now well established that a witness who qualifies as an expert in the science of ballistics, may identify a gun from which a particular bullet was fired by comparing the markings on that bullet with those on a test bullet fired by the witness through the suspect gun.

Roberts v. Florida, 164 So. 2d 817 (Fla. 1964)

Chapter Outline

```
┌─────────────────────────────────────────────────┐
│                                                   │
│  Key Terms and Concepts                           │
│                                                   │
│  ballistics experiments          implied consent  │
│  Breathalyzer test               radar            │
│  DNA                             scientific evidence │
│  horizontal gaze nystagmus test    admissibility test │
│                                                   │
└─────────────────────────────────────────────────┘
```

§ 15.1 Introduction

In Chapter 14, the general rules concerning the collection, protection, and introduction of real evidence were considered. Evidence is characterized as real evidence if it is the result of experiments and tests either in or out of court, even though in many cases the evidence is of little value unless it is accompanied by oral testimony.

Although a comparatively small part of the evidence produced at trial in the usual criminal case results from out-of-court tests and examinations, such evidence is often very convincing and is certainly important in helping the factfinders to determine what actually occurred. Convictions for drug possession and related activities are often decided on the results of tests administered out of court. Prosecutions are initiated following out-of-court tests—such as having a drug detection dog sniff a car and obtaining a positive result,[1] testing residue found in trash pulls that reveal the presence of illegal drugs,[2] and testing powders found in a prison cell that indicate the presence of drug contraband.[3] Juries and judges rely on the admission of these drug tests in deciding whether to convict because most tests prove to be quite convincing. Prosecutors use scientific testing results to prove that a vehicle driver has been driving under the influence of alcohol. Similarly, DNA testing in rape cases carries significant weight with factfinders in many cases, especially where a stranger has been charged with adult sexual assault or the test indicates illegal contact between relatives.[4]

---

[1]   Illinois v Caballes, 543 U.S. 405, 2005 U.S. LEXIS 769 (2005).
[2]   *See* United States v. Faust, 456 F.3d 1342, 2006 U.S. App. LEXIS 18366 (11th Cir. 2006).
[3]   *See* Garcia v. Martinez, 2006 U.S. App. LEXIS 24199 (7th Cir. 2006).
[4]   McGregor v. State, 2004 Tex. App. LEXIS 3365 (2004).

While evidence concerning the results of examinations and tests has a great impact in criminal cases, such evidence is admissible only when it clears several evidence hurdles. First, forensic evidence must meet the same tests as most other evidence, such as the tests of relevancy, materiality, and competency. Before such evidence is admitted, a foundation must be laid. For example, in a Georgia case, the foundation for admission of the results of scientific tests of a seized sample requires that care be taken that the correct sample is tested.

> Evidence such as suspected cocaine, seized from a crime scene, is typically placed in a sealable evidence bag that can be marked with the date, time, location, suspect, arresting officer, and other particulars. The evidence should be promptly delivered to a safe, suitable storage site that provides "reasonable assurance" that the evidence will not be tampered with or corrupted. Evidence may be sent by certified mail, return receipt requested, to a crime lab and sent to the prosecutor in the same manner. The mail receipts, once identified by the witness, are admissible to help prove the chain of custody. . . . For fungible evidence that has been tested, it generally is sufficient to provide the testimony of the police officer who seized and transported the evidence, according to the department's routine, and the lab technician who tested the evidence and recorded the results according to the crime lab's routine.[5]

If a sample is not labeled properly, a significant break in the chain of custody has occurred and a trial court may rule that the proper foundation has not been made for the introduction of the results of the scientific testing.[6]

If the courts have not previously accepted the results of a novel scientific test or a test that has not reached general scientific acceptance, the party seeking to introduce the evidence must demonstrate that the new or different test or experiment meets the test required for introduction in that particular jurisdiction.[7]

For many years, state and federal courts followed the *Frye* standard, which courts used for evaluating the admissibility of scientific tests and experiments. The test gradually gained national acceptability following the decision in *Frye v. United States*.[8] In that case, the court stated:

> Just when a scientific principle or discovery crosses these lines between the experimental and the demonstrable stages is difficult to define. Somewhere in this twilight zone the evidential force of the principle must be recognized, and while courts will go a long way in admitting expert testimony deduced from a well-recognized scientific principle or discovery, the thing from which the deduction is made must be sufficiently established to have gained general acceptance from the particular field in which it belongs.[9]

---

[5]   Wilson v. State, 271 Ga. App. 359, 362, 609 S.E.2d 703, 706, 2005 Ga. App. LEXIS 41 (2005).
[6]   *Id.*
[7]   Kanani v. Phillips, 2004 U.S. Dist. LEXIS 20444 (S.D.N.Y. 2004).
[8]   293 F. 1013 (D.C. Cir. 1923).
[9]   *Id.* at 1014.

In the ensuing years, the majority of state and federal jurisdictions adopted the *Frye* "general acceptance" test, discussing, defining, and attempting to refine it, as new and more complex forms of novel evidence have surfaced in the legal arena.[10] Many states have not adopted the different test for scientific evidence admissibility required in the federal courts by the Supreme Court decision in *Daubert v. Merrell Dow* and have retained the *Frye* standard. Among these states are Alabama and Florida, where the arguably slightly more rigorous *Frye* standard remains good law and is applied to the full range of scientific testing when court admissibility is desired.[11]

In the case of *Daubert v. Merrell Dow Pharmaceuticals, Inc.*, the United States Supreme Court held that the Federal Rules of Evidence supersede the *Frye* test for cases involving federal law.[12] The Court held that the admissibility of expert opinion testimony concerning novel scientific evidence no longer is limited solely to knowledge or evidence "generally accepted" as reliable in the relevant scientific community. The Court did not, however, sanction the wholesale abandonment of standards for admission of expert opinion or knowledge, but stated:

> that the *Frye* test was displaced by the Rules of Evidence does not mean, however, that the Rules themselves place no limits on the admissibility of purportedly scientific evidence. Nor is the trial judge disabled from screening such evidence. To the contrary, under the Rules the trial judge must ensure that any and all scientific testimony or evidence admitted is not only relevant but reliable.

The Court in *Daubert* held that Rule 702 is the "primary locus" of a trial judge's screening of purportedly scientific evidence for relevancy and reliability under Rule 104a for federal trials.[13] The *Daubert* Court stated, "'General acceptance' is not a necessary precondition to the admissibility of scientific evidence under the Federal Rules of Evidence, but the Rules of Evidence—especially Rule 702—do assign to the trial judge the task of ensuring that an expert's testimony both rests on a reliable foundation and is relevant to the task at hand. Pertinent evidence based on scientifically valid principles will satisfy those demands."[14] The concept of requiring proof of a scientific foundation guarantees that admissible evidence will have a firm grounding in scientific methods and practices.

---

[10] United States v. Martinez, 3 F.3d 1191 (8th Cir. 1993). *See also Fifty Years of Frye in Alabama: The Continuing Debate over Adopting the Test Established in Daubert v. Merrell Dow Pharmaceuticals,* 35 CUMB. L. REV. 231 (2004/2005).

[11] *See* Arnold v. Florida, 807 So. 2d 136, 2002 Fla. App. LEXIS 743 (2002) and Slay v. Keller Industries, 823 So. 2d 623; 2001 Ala. LEXIS 439 (Ala. 2002).

[12] Daubert v. Merrell Dow Pharmaceuticals, 509 U.S. 579, 1993 U.S. LEXIS 4408 (1993).

[13] Rule 702 provides that "if scientific, technical or other specialized knowledge will assist the trier of fact to understand the evidence or to determine a fact in issue, a witness qualified an expert by knowledge, skill, experience, training, or education may testify thereto."

[14] *Daubert* at 597.

The *Daubert* Court established the following nonexclusive list of non-exclusive factors to guide lower federal courts in assessing the reliability of scientific evidence:

1. Whether a scientific theory or technique can be (or has been) tested;

2. Whether the theory or technique has been subjected to peer review and publication;

3. The known or potential rate of error and the existence and maintenance of standards controlling the technique's operation;

4. Whether the technique is generally accepted or has widespread acceptance.[15]

The court in *Daubert* emphasized that the inquiry in determining the reliability of scientific evidence is a flexible one, focusing on the principles and methodology proffered as evidence rather than the conclusions they generate. The *Daubert* principles are to be read in conjunction with Rule 702, which permits expert scientific witness where their testimony "will assist the trier of fact to understand the evidence or to determine a fact in issue." In addition, the evidence must be based on reliable principles and scientific methods and the expert witness must be shown to have applied the scientific principles properly.[16] Under *Daubert*, scientific evidence brought to court by expert witnesses must be both relevant and reliable and meet the other standards in order to be properly admitted in evidence.[17]

A Colorado appeals court referred to both the *Frye* test and the Federal Rules of Evidence as links to the *Daubert* case and stated the applicable law in these terms:

> Under the *Frye* test, novel scientific evidence is not admissible unless its proponent shows that the theory supporting the proffered conclusion exists and is generally accepted in the scientific community, the techniques that are generally accepted in the scientific community exist and are capable of producing reliable results, and accepted scientific techniques were performed.[18]

The Colorado court noted that the *Daubert* test superseded the *Frye* test for federal trials.

> Under the federal counterpart of CRE 702, the admissibility of scientific evidence, "novel" or otherwise, now rests on several considerations, including: (1) whether the theory or technique is or can be tested; (2) whether a theory or technique has been subjected to peer review and publication; (3) whether a technique has a known or

---

[15]   *Daubert* at 593.

[16]   Smith v. Cangieter, 2006 U.S. App. LEXIS 23085 (8th Cir. 2006).

[17]   United States v. McGinnis, 2006 U.S. App. LEXIS 24451 (th Cir. 2006), quoting Pipitone v. Biomatrix, Inc., 288 F.3d 239, 244-45 (5th Cir. 2002).

[18]   People v. Brooks, 950 P.2d 649, 652, 1997 Colo. App. LEXIS 183 (1997).

potential rate of error; (4) whether a technique's operation is controlled by existing and maintained standards; and (5) whether the theory or technique is generally accepted in the scientific community.[19]

According to the Colorado court, where scientific expertise was not helpful or where the evidence could be presented by laypersons or non-scientific experts, any test for admissibility of scientific evidence did not apply. The Colorado court noted:

> If the proffered evidence does not depend upon any scientific device, method, or process, neither the *Frye* nor the *Daubert* test for admissibility applies. [20]

The proponent of the scientific evidence has the burden of proving its relevancy as well as its scientific reliability, both of which are deemed proven where a particular court has previously approved the use of a particular scientific test.[21]

Once a test for admissibility of scientific evidence has been approved in a substantial number of courts, the trial judge may judicially notice (without receiving evidence) that the procedure has been established with verifiable certainty, or that it rests on the laws of nature.[22]

§ 15.2   Examination of the Person

Examination of the body of the defendant in a criminal case in a reasonable manner is not considered violative of his or her constitutional right of privacy or his or her privilege against self-incrimination. Both federal and state courts have usually held that the privilege against self-incrimination as protected by the Fifth Amendment to the United States Constitution offers no protection against being compelled to submit to fingerprinting, photographing, or measurements; to write or speak for identification; to appear in court; to stand; to assume a stance; to walk; or to make a particular gesture.[23] The courts have allowed procedures that involve minor interferences—for purposes of identification—with the person of individuals charged with crimes. Numerous cases uphold reasonable out-of-court identification procedures against claims of violation of the Fifth Amendment; for example, requiring the prisoner to try on a blouse that fit him;[24] requiring the accused to submit to a lineup;[25] order-

---

[19]   *Id.*

[20]   *Id.*

[21]   United States v. Dien Vy Phung, 127 Fed. Appx. 594, 2005 U.S. App. LEXIS 6146 (3th Cir. 2005).

[22]   Gentry v. State, 443 S.E.2d 667 (Ga. Ct. App. 1994).

[23]   Schmerber v. California, 384 U.S. 757, 86 S. Ct. 1826, 16 L. Ed. 2d 908 (1966). *See* case in Part II at cases relating to Chapter 14. *See also* Chapter 16 for additional discussion of the privilege against self-incrimination.

[24]   Holt v. United States, 218 U.S. 245, 31 S. Ct. 2, 54 L. Ed. 1021 (1910); State v. Lerner, 308 A.2d 324 (R.I. 1973).

[25]   United States v. Gaines, 2006 U.S. App. LEXIS 22584 (7th Cir. 2006).

ing an accused to give a voice sample at trial for identification purposes;[26] examination of a defendant's body for traces of blood;[27] ordering a subject to give his name,[28] examination of the body for marks and bruises;[29] requiring the defendant to remove items of clothing or to assume poses;[30] and taking penis scrapings and saliva samples from the defendant.[31]

In a case of theft of and interfering with the mail, the federal government may force a defendant to give a saliva sample as a condition of receiving probation and the compulsion does not violate any federal constitutional provision.[32] As the record did not indicate that the samples were taken against the suspect's will, his rights were not violated.

In both homicide and wrongful death cases, the results of an autopsy of the body of the deceased by a trained pathologist can be introduced as evidence in a court. The pathologist may offer testimony concerning the condition of the body of the deceased, the cause of death, and the injuries sustained. Examination of the body generally includes photographs that the doctor may have taken during the autopsy. Crime scene pictures taken by the medical examiner may be introduced to illustrate the injuries sustained by a deceased and to support an expert opinion on the cause of death. The medical examiner's report is admissible as to his or her anatomical findings, anatomical diagnosis, and cause of death.

§ 15.3 Intoxication Tests

Intoxication may be scientifically determined by testing the subject's blood, breath, urine, or saliva. Evidence resulting from such out-of-court tests is usually admissible. Types of tests and limitations on the use of such evidence are discussed in the following paragraphs.

A. Blood Tests

Statutes in the several states have amended their driving while intoxicated statutes to hold that a driver is considered to be in violation of the law when the blood-alcohol content is .08 or higher. Many states formerly did not recognize intoxication until it reached .15 percent blood-alcohol content. Demonstrative of this change in state law is the Alaska statute.

---

[26] Hubanks v. Frank, 392 F.3d 926, 932, 2004 U.S. App. LEXIS 26791 (7th Cir. 2004).
[27] McFarland v. United States, 150 F.2d 593 (D.C. Cir. 1945); Brattain v. Herron, 309 N.E.2d 150 (Ind. 1974).
[28] *See* Hiibel v. Sixth Judicial District Court, 542 U.S. 177, 124 S. Ct. 2451, 159 L. Ed. 2d 292, 2004 U.S. LEXIS 4385 (2004) and United States v. Doe, 128 Fed. Appx. 179, 2005 U.S. App. LEXIS 5707 (2d Cir. 2005).
[29] Leeper v. Texas, 139 U.S. 462 (1891).
[30] Gilbert v. United States, 366 F.2d 923 (9th Cir. 1966); United States v. Robertson, 19 F.3d 1318 (10th Cir. 1994).
[31] Brent v. White, 276 F. Supp. 386 (E.D. La. 1967).
[32] *See* United States v. Hand, 2006 U.S. App. LEXIS 17715 (11th Cir. 2006).

Sec. 28.35.030. Operating a vehicle, aircraft or watercraft while under the influence of an alcoholic beverage, inhalant, or controlled substance

(a) A person commits the crime of driving while under the influence of an alcoholic beverage, inhalant, or controlled substance if the person operates or drives a motor vehicle or operates an aircraft or a watercraft

    (1) while under the influence of an alcoholic beverage, intoxicating liquor, inhalant, or any controlled substance, singly or in combination; or

    (2) and if, as determined by a chemical test taken within four hours after the alleged operating or driving, there is 0.08 percent or more by weight of alcohol in the person's blood or 80 milligrams or more of alcohol per 100 milliliters of blood, or if there is 0.08 grams or more of alcohol per 210 liters of the person's breath.[33]

A driver may be proven to violate the Alaska law by objective evidence that the driver was under the influence of an intoxicant by proving behavior consistent with impairment, even at levels below .08. This provision becomes particularly useful when a problem exists in a blood or breath test and the results are excluded from evidence. Alaska law has been interpreted to require that the .08 blood-alcohol content have existed at the time the person operated or had control over a motor vehicle and not at a later time.[34]

A number of cases involving blood tests and constitutional issues spawned by the collection of blood and introduction into evidence of blood results have reached the Supreme Court of the United States. Litigants complained of search-and-seizure and self-incrimination violations. Over last 50 years, most of the important constitutional issues have been decided with the result that legal issues involving driving while intoxicated cases have been determined and can be considered settled law.

In *Breithaupt v. Abram*,[35] police officers caused blood to be drawn from the driver of an automobile involved in an accident, and a blood-alcohol test was conducted. The Court found that there was ample justification for the conclusion that the driver was under the influence of alcohol. The Court determined that because a physician drew the blood in a medically acceptable manner in a hospital environment, there was no violation of the driver's constitutional rights, even though the driver was unconscious at the time the blood was drawn and had no opportunity to object to the procedure. The Court affirmed the conviction resulting from the use of the test, holding that under the circumstances, the withdrawal did not offend fundamental concepts of due process under the Fourteenth Amendment.

In a landmark case, *Schmerber v. California*,[36] the Supreme Court held that the extraction and testing of blood samples from the accused while he was

---

[33] ALASKA STAT. § 28.35.030 (2006).

[34] Conrad v. State, 54 P.3d 313, 2002 Alaska App. LEXIS 196 (2002).

[35] 352 U.S. 432, 77 S. Ct. 408, 1 L. Ed. 2d 448 (1957).

[36] 384 U.S. 757, 1966 U.S. LEXIS 1129 (1966). *See* case in Part II at cases relating to Chapter 14. *See also* Winston v. Lee, 470 U.S. 753, 105 S. Ct. 1611, 84 L. Ed. 2d 662 (1985), in which reference was made to the balancing test approved in the *Schmerber* case.

in the hospital after being arrested for driving under the influence of intoxicating liquor had been conducted in a reasonable manner and did not violate his rights under the Fourth Amendment to be free from unreasonable searches. The Court also decided that the physician's withdrawal of a blood sample at the direction of a police officer and the admission of the blood analysis against Schmerber did not deny him due process of law. Neither was the evidence excludable on the theory that it violated the defendant's Fifth Amendment privilege against self-incrimination, which states that a person should not be compelled in a criminal case to be a witness against himself. The Court held that the blood evidence was not of a testimonial nature, but was more of a scientific fact.

Proving impairment may be made by proof of objective conduct by the driver or by a finding of a prohibited level of alcohol in the driver's blood. In 2006, a Missouri court of appeals held that proof that a driver had a .08 percent or greater blood-alcohol content was sufficient for a license revocation. Under Missouri law, the driver may request a trial to litigate whether the blood-alcohol content was actually at, above, or below the .08 percent. Proof of a valid probable cause arrest and proof of a greater than .08 percent blood-alcohol content creates the presumption that the driver was intoxicated. In order to avoid a conviction, the driver has an opportunity to introduce evidence that the blood-alcohol content was less than .08 percent.[37]

B. Breath Tests

A doctor, chemist, or medical technician with the proper equipment can determine the level of alcohol in the blood from a blood sample. Due to the inconvenience and cost of obtaining and analyzing a blood sample, other means have been invented to determine blood-alcohol content without actually taking blood. The law enforcement use of breath samples has become common and has the advantage of being more convenient and less painful. In developing probable cause for arrest, many jurisdictions use a non-admissible preliminary blood-alcohol test that a motorist generally may refuse without consequence.[38] The breath test that police use that is more accurate than the preliminary one is admissible if conducted according to the manufacturer's instructions. The admissible breath test had the advantage of being administered by a law enforcement officer, while generally a physician or nurse is needed when blood is to be drawn.

In the use of devices such as "Breathalyzers," "drunkometers," and "alcometers," the blood-alcohol content is determined by a formula applied to a test of the breath of the subject, who is required to blow deep lung air into a collection device. The breath thus captured is allowed to expel itself through a tube containing a mixture of potassium permanganate and sulphuric acid until

[37] See Kaufman v. Director of Revenue, 193 S.W.3d 300, 2006 Mo. App. LEXIS 215 (2006).
[38] See Wis. Stat. § 343.303 Preliminary breath screening test.(2006). But see Blank v. State, 2006 Alaska App. LEXIS 144 (2006), where the preliminary test refers only to the time of administration and not to a diagnostic test to determine probable cause.

a certain shade or color is attained. By a measure of the water displaced by the breath that passed through this tube, it is determined how much air was required to create the color described above. This amount is determined from a reading of a calibrated scale. The number read from the calibrated scale must then be calculated and translated into a percentage of alcohol in the blood.[39]

The major emphasis on apprehending and punishing the drinking driver has led to novel methods of attacking the problem. While the traditional driving while intoxicated or driving under the influence of alcohol prosecution continues to be addressed criminally, some states have devised alternative methods to remove drinking drivers from the road. As an example, Illinois provides that a person suspected of driving under the influence may be asked to take a preliminary breath test that the driver may refuse. If the driver consents and takes the test with the results indicating a prohibited blood-alcohol level, that test may be used to permit an administrative suspension for three months. Because this is a civil matter, the motorist who contests the suspension in court carries the initial burden of proof and must show that there is reason to doubt the preliminary blood test results. Where the motorist fails to introduce credible evidence that the preliminary blood test was invalid, the administrative suspension of driving privileges stands. The results of the preliminary blood test are not admissible against the driver in a driving while intoxicated prosecution.[40]

Before evidence regarding breath test results is admissible in a criminal prosecution, the prosecution must establish a proper foundation.[41] The standards for each machine are somewhat different and states have protocols to assure that breath analysis machines are working properly. For example, Montana requires that breath analysis machines must be certified properly or a proper foundation for admission of the evidence cannot be established. Montana requires that each breath analysis machine be returned to the Department of Justice on an annual basis (once every 365 days) for a laboratory recertification. Failure to use a machine that is current in its certification renders the results of any test inadmissible in court.[42] The officer must use a certified machine according to the instructions and user protocols that are specific to that machine or the results will not be admissible.

Where blood is drawn for the purposes of conducting an alcohol analysis, most jurisdictions require that samples be preserved and often permit a defendant to split the sample for independent testing. In addition, the sample must be properly stored and a chain of custody must be proven prior to admitting

---

[39] JAMES R. RICHARDSON, MODERN SCIENTIFIC EVIDENCE § 13.5 (1974). *See* Frankvoort, Mulder, and Neuteboom, *The Laboratory Testing of Evidential Breath Testing Machines*, 35 FORENSIC SCIENCE INT'L 27 1987), in which researchers found that although the results of breath-testing machines in general were good, the machines tended to underestimate actual concentration. *See also Breathalyzer Accuracy in Actual Enforcement Practice*, 32 J. FORENSIC SCI. 1235 (1987), in which it was found that the blood-alcohol concentration tended to be underestimated by the Breathalyzer.

[40] *See* People v. Rozela, 345 Ill. App. 3d 217; 802 N.E.2d 372; 2003 Ill. App. LEXIS 1570 (2004).

[41] *See* Roze v. Department of Motor Vehicles, 141 Cal. App. 4th 1176, 46 Cal. Rptr. 3d 829, 2006 Cal. App. LEXIS 1188 (2006).

[42] *See* State v. Frickey, 332 Mont. 255, 136 P.3d 558, 2006 Mont. LEXIS 207 (2006).

the results in court. In one Massachusetts case,[43] an officer received the blood sample and stored it overnight in the common police station refrigerator until the sample could be taken to the laboratory that was to perform the analysis. Among other allegations, the defendant contended that the blood lost its chain of custody when stored where any police officer could have access to it. The prosecution must establish that the blood sample was taken from the defendant and arrived at the testing laboratory without tampering or contamination. The reviewing court noted that despite refrigerator access by other officers, there was not any proof of a break in the chain of custody. Massachusetts, like most jurisdictions, allows the accused to have the blood draw independently tested if a sufficient sample remains after the laboratory has concluded testing. This secondary testing allows a defendant to determine whether the original result was correct or if a problem in analysis exists.

There is no deprivation of constitutional rights involving search and seizure or the privilege against self-incrimination when a person, charged with the offense of operating a motor vehicle while under the influence of intoxicating liquor, voluntarily submits to a test to determine blood-alcohol level. States use the concept of implied consent to permit the collection of blood, breath, or urine samples for analysis. Statutes typically note that if a person has been driving on the roads within a jurisdiction and probable cause exists to believe that the person has operated or been in control of a motor vehicle while in violation of the statutes prohibiting impaired driving or other triggering conditions, the act of driving indicates that the driver has given prior consent to search that person for alcohol impairment or drug use by operation of law.[44]

When new or updated machines used to test blood-alcohol content come into use, defendants may attempt to question their reliability or accuracy. In one case involving an established machine, the defendant had concerns about whether the Intoxilyzer 5000 produced accurate readings from the deep lung air samples that it uses to compute a person's blood-alcohol level. The defendant wanted to obtain the algorithm that the machine used to convert the breath sample into a blood-alcohol level in order to analyze the algorithm to determine if there were any errors in computation. The trial court refused to require the prosecution to deliver the information because the data were not in the hands of the prosecution or the government. The court noted that the defendant was free to subpoena the manufacturer of the Intoxilyzer 5000 to obtain the information.[45] In a different case involving the Intoxilyzer 5000, the machine had been deemed to meet the state's requirements for accuracy as long as a state chemist certified that the machine was operating properly 30 days before and 30 days after the machine was used to test a subject. In Delaware, the results of the tests are admissible under the state's evidence code regulating business records hearsay exceptions. To be admissible, "the evi-

---

[43] *See* Commonwealth v. Pratt, 19 Mass. L. Rep. 425, 2005 Mass. Super. LEXIS 276 (Mass. 2005).

[44] *See* IOWA CODE § 321J.6 Implied consent to test. (2005). *See also* ALA. CODE § 32-5-192 Consent to testing; suspension of license; hearing. (2006).

[45] State v. Walters, 2006 Conn. Super. LEXIS 726 (Conn. 2006).

dence admitted must be: (1) prepared in the regular course of business; (2) made at or near the time of the event; (3) trustworthy; and (4) testified to by custodian of the record or other qualified person."[46] The officer must demonstrate that he or she possessed knowledge of how to properly operate the Intoxilyzer, was familiar with the calibration process, and knew how the certification sheets were maintained by the police agency.[47] These steps are designed to provide accurate information on the blood-alcohol level and to protect persons who are tested from having inaccurate information used against them.

In many jurisdictions, the test that has been designated the Preliminary Breath Test (PBT) has been considered sufficiently reliable to test for the presence of alcohol consumption but is considered insufficiently reliable to be admitted as substantive evidence.[48] However, the PBT can be used by a police officer as a screening tool to help determine whether probable cause exists.[49] The results of such tests are generally inadmissible at a criminal driving while intoxicated trial and are used to help determine probable cause for arrest.[50] The court held in this case that these tests, if positive, create a rebuttable presumption that the defendant has engaged in the prohibited activity.

C. Urine Tests

Although the use of urine to determine blood-alcohol content has some advantages, it also has disadvantages. One is that concentration of alcohol or drugs in the urine lags behind alcohol concentration in the blood. Demonstrative of this principle is a Kentucky case that showed the defendant's urine contained bare traces of drugs while a blood test indicated an absence of drugs.[51] Further, the test results are rendered unreliable by the fact that dilution is greater or lesser according to the amount of urine in the bladder, and the person conducting the test has no way of knowing this information. As contrasted with blood collection, obtaining a urine sample can be compromised by psychological stress or, in one case, physical problems. In an Ohio case, a breath machine indicated that suspect had a .07 percent blood-alcohol content, so the officer wanted a urine sample.[52] When the man was unable to provide a sample due to an enlarged prostate, an administrative revocation of his driving privileges occurred. On appeal, the court reversed the revocation, because the man did not refuse to provide a sample, but just was unable to produce a sample. Medical testimony supported the subject's position.

---

[46]   State v. Boyer, 2006 Del. C.P. LEXIS 67 (Del. 2006).

[47]   Id.

[48]   People v. Bock, 357 Ill. App. 3d 160, 168, 827 N.E.2d 1089, 1095, 2005 Ill. App. LEXIS 386 (2005).

[49]   Commonwealth v. Allen, 684 A.2d 633 (Pa. 1996).

[50]   People v. Kavanaugh, 362 Ill. App. 3d 690, 696 840 N.E.2d 807, 812, 2005 Ill. App. LEXIS 1282 (2005).

[51]   Thompson v. Commonwealth, 177 S.W.3d 782, 783, 2005 Ky. LEXIS 370 (Ky. 2005). *See also* State v. Smith, 2006 Tenn. Crim. App. LEXIS 145 (2006).

[52]   State v. Norman, 2006 Ohio 3362, 2006 Ohio App. LEXIS 3254 (2006).

Because of the doubts about blood-alcohol content estimated from urine, the National Highway Traffic Safety Administration has discouraged the use of such tests.[53] Some experts recommend that urinalysis be used only when a blood sample is unavailable or contaminated.[54]

D. *Horizontal Gaze Nystagmus Tests*

With the development of the Horizontal Gaze Nystagmus Test (HGN), police officers have one more field diagnostic test available to assist them in the determination of whether probable cause to arrest exists in a particular case. The basis of the test is the inability of the eyes to maintain visual fixation as they are turned to the side following consumption of alcohol. This test was described by the Supreme Court of New Hampshire in 2006 in these terms:

> In summary, it is a standardized field sobriety test designed to detect nystagmus, i.e., an involuntary, rapid, back-and-forth jerking of the eyes. The administering police officer positions a stimulus, such as a pen, penlight, or finger, approximately twelve to fifteen inches in front of the suspect's eyes and gradually moves the stimulus laterally towards the suspect's ear. The officer observes the suspect's eyeballs to detect the following three signs, which could indicate intoxication: (1) the inability of the eye to smoothly track the stimulus; (2) the presence of nystagmus at the eye's maximum horizontal deviation; and (3) the point at which nystagmus, if present, begins as the stimulus is moved. The officer tests each eye and gives the suspect a point for each sign observed; therefore, a total of six points is possible.[55]

Nystagmus is a well-known physiological phenomenon caused by, among other things, ingestion of alcohol. The Supreme Court of New Hampshire indicated that, as a majority of jurisdictions do, the horizonal gaze nystagmus test is based on scientific principles and is reliable and evidence obtained thereby is admissible. The officer must have been properly trained and the test properly administered, and when that has been shown, the evidence will be admissible.[56]

Therefore, as a general rule, an officer who has been properly trained in the use of the horizonal gaze nystagmus test is generally permitted to testify to a subject's performance and whether the test indicated intoxication. Although some evidence exists to demonstrate that a police office can estimate the blood-alcohol content from a subject's performance, a Georgia court excluded a defense expert's testimony that would have offered an estimated blood-alcohol reading. The court noted "[i]t may be an open question, how-

---

[53] NATIONAL HIGHWAY TRAFFIC AND SAFETY ADMINISTRATION HIGHWAY SAFETY PROGRAM MANUAL #8.

[54] Winek and Esposito, *Comparative Study of Ethanol Levels in Blood v. Bone Marrow*, 17 FORENSIC SCI. INTL. 27 (1981).

[55] State v. Cochrane, 897 A.2d 952, 955, 2006 N.H. LEXIS 48 (N.H. 2006).

[56] *Id.*

ever, whether the HGN test has reached a state of verifiable certainty in the scientific community as a basis for determining the numerical level of a driver's blood-alcohol level."[57]

In the case of *State v. Murphy*, the court noted that some courts have held that a police officer is not qualified to testify to the HGN test's scientific reliability.[58] Other courts hold that HGN evidence, although it is of a scientific nature, is reliable and admissible if preceded by a proper foundation as to the techniques used and the officer's ability to conduct the test.[59] Still other courts regard the HGN test as no more scientific than other field sobriety tests that require no expert interpretation.[60]

E. Implied Consent Statutes

Many states have enacted statutes that provide that a driver, whether licensed locally, unlicensed, or licensed in another state, is deemed to have given his consent, in return for the privilege of driving, to submit to an alcohol test if probable cause exists to believe that he or she is driving while intoxicated; if he or she refuses to take the test, his or her license may be suspended. In upholding the constitutionality of an early version of the implied consent law, the Supreme Court of Nebraska stated:

> The validity of a sample of blood or urine under the implied consent law is not impaired by a request for legal counsel, or the failure of defendant's counsel to appear before the sample is taken. . . . A defendant loses no rights subject to protection by legal counsel when he is requested and furnishes a sample of blood or urine for chemical analysis to be used as evidence against him under the implied consent law.[61]

Alaska takes the implied consent statute in a different direction than some states. In Alaska, a driver who refuses to take a blood-alcohol test when properly requested to do so commits a separate crime. The state must prove that the defendant was under arrest for driving while under the influence, that the arrestee knew that he had a legal duty to take the test, and that he or she refused to take an appropriate blood-alcohol test. Evidence properly admitted results in a conviction when the subject was warned that a refusal is a separate crime.[62]

In most jurisdictions, a driver who is advised of his or her rights under the implied consent law but declines to submit to a chemical test to determine his or her blood-alcohol content is deemed to have refused the test. Such a person

---

[57] Webb v. State, 277 Ga. App. 355, 359, 626 S.E.2d 545, 549, 2006 Ga. App. LEXIS 85 (2006).

[58] State v. Borchardt, 224 Neb. 47, 395 N.W.2d 551 (1986); Commonwealth v. Miller, 367 Pa. Super. 359, 532 A.2d 1186 (1987); State v. Barker, 366 S.E.2d 642 (W. Va. 1988). *See also* Hawkins v. State, 293 Ga. App. 34, 476 S.E.2d 803 (1996).

[59] State v. Superior Court, 149 Ariz. 269, 718 P.2d 171 (1986); State v. Clark, 762 P.2d 853 (Mont. 1988).

[60] State v. Nagel, 30 Ohio App. 3d 80, 506 N.E.2d 285 (1986).

[61] State v. Oleson, 180 Neb. 546, 143 N.W.2d 917 (1966).

[62] Olson v. State, 2006 Alaska App. LEXIS 20 (2006).

will have his or her driver's license administratively revoked.[63] According to a Pennsylvania law,[64] a suspension of a driver's license will follow a refusal to submit to a breath, urine, or blood test. The officer must have probable cause for arrest and the driver must have been arrested, and have refused to take the test suggested by the police officer. The general administrative suspension lasts for twelve months. This civil sanction is in addition to any criminal penalty that might result from the same conduct.

Drivers aggrieved by loss of license privileges litigated the concept of administrative suspensions on a variety of grounds. In the 1983 case of *South Dakota v. Neville*, the United States Supreme Court examined not only the implied consent statutes, but also the constitutionality of prosecutors using closing arguments to comment on the failure of defendants to take a blood-alcohol test.[65] In this case, the defendant was arrested for driving while intoxicated. The arresting officer asked him to submit to a blood-alcohol test and warned him that he would lose his license if he refused. The South Dakota trial court granted a motion to suppress all evidence, and the South Dakota Supreme Court affirmed on the ground that the statute, which allowed the introduction of evidence of refusal to take the blood-alcohol test, violated the Fifth Amendment privilege against self-incrimination as applied to the states. The prosecution asked for a review by the United States Supreme Court.

First, the United States Supreme Court pointed out the reason for the implied consent law: that, as part of the program to deter drinkers from driving, South Dakota made it easier for law enforcement officials to obtain evidence from the drinking driver. This statute, the Court explained, declares that any person operating a vehicle is deemed to have consented to a chemical test of the alcohol content of his or her blood if arrested for driving while intoxicated. In disagreeing with the South Dakota Supreme Court, the United States Supreme Court held that the self-incrimination clause was not implicated because the results of blood-alcohol tests were not testimonial in nature so it was permissible to introduce evidence of a refusal to take a blood-alcohol test and for a prosecutor to comment on that failure.

As to the constitutionality of commenting on the failure to take the test, the Court stated that it was not fundamentally unfair, or in violation of due process, to use a defendant's refusal to take a blood-alcohol test as evidence of guilt, even though the police failed to warn him that the refusal could be used against him at trial. In making this decision, the Court explained, "the offer of taking the blood-alcohol test is clearly legitimate, and the action becomes no less legitimate when the state offers a second option of refusing the test, with the attendant penalties for making that choice." Summarizing the opinion, the Court concluded:

---

[63]   People v. Kavanaugh, 362 Ill. App. 3d 690, 840 N.E.2d 807, 2005 Ill. App. LEXIS 1282 (2005).

[64]   *See* 75 PA. CONS. STAT. § 1547 Chemical testing to determine amount of alcohol or controlled substance (2006).

[65]   South Dakota v. Neville, 459 U.S. 553, 103 S. Ct. 916, 7 L. Ed. 2d 748 (1983).

We hold, therefore, that a refusal to take a blood-alcohol test, after a police officer has lawfully requested it, is not an act coerced by the officer, and thus is not protected by the privilege against self-incrimination.

§ 15.4 Blood Grouping Tests and Blood Comparisons

In the days prior to DNA testing and prior to the time that DNA testing became highly sophisticated and regularly admitted as evidence, general blood grouping tests often served a very useful identification purpose in criminal prosecutions for rape,[66] assault and battery,[67] or nonsupport. In a rape and murder case, the defendant argued on appeal that the trial court erred in admitting evidence of a serologist that the defendant was one of 35 percent of the male population who are Type O secretors.[68] The evidence was offered to show that the defendant could have had been the male who had sexual contact with the victim. The reviewing court agreed that this was not improper evidence, because it only indicated that the defendant fell into the suspect percentage of the population who could have been the perpetrator. This excluded the evidence because risk of unfair prejudice outweighed the probative value of the evidence.

Some other examples of the use of blood comparisons in criminal cases indicate the importance of this type of test. In a prosecution for kidnapping and for engaging in lewd and lascivious conduct with a child, blood grouping evidence taken from the victim's clothing indicated a high probability that it came from the defendant in the case. According to expert testimony that helped convict the defendant, the defendant's blood met the factors contained within the sample tested because the blood "had to have come from either an ABO Type B secretor or a nonsecretor who is PGM two plus."[69] DNA testing of semen from the victim's shirt matched the defendant's DNA profile.[70] In another case, the results from electrophoretic typing of aged, dried bloodstains were admissible in a murder prosecution in which evidence indicated that the testing was performed by competent analysts using sufficient controls.[71] In approving the use of this blood test, the court noted that a trained technician who had been working with serological electrophoresis for five years examined the samples in question, and his readings were controlled by second readings as required by protocol.

---

[66] Shanks v. State, 185 Md. 437, 45 A.2d 85 (1945).
[67] Commonwealth v. Statti, 16 Pa. Super. 577, 73 A.2d 688 (1950).
[68] State v. Duncan, 698 S.W.2d 63 (Tenn. 1985).
[69] California v. Funston, 2002 Cal. App. Unpub. LEXIS 3513 (2002).
[70] Id.
[71] State v. Fenney, 448 N.W.2d 54 (Minn. 1989).

A pre-DNA testing example of why blood grouping proves not to be sufficiently sophisticated for significant criminal justice needs can be demonstrated by the case of a man who was not excludable as the father of a child in 1978. Following a divorce, he was ordered to pay child support for a child that he may have not fathered, but blood testing had not emerged to the level of current DNA analysis.[72] Years later, when he was in arrears in paying child support, although newer blood testing would have revealed with mathematical precision whether he was the father of the child, under modern law, newer blood tests were unavailable for use because the court would not revist the paternity issue. Arguably, when incarceration or freedom may depend on a correct identification test, older, traditional blood grouping tests may not be what justice and due process demand.

Some older pre-DNA testing cases are still moving through the criminal justice system where convictions were obtained based on older blood grouping methodology. A California capital case is demonstrative of prosecutions involving older blood identification science that are continuing to be litigated.[73] In this case, police discovered the eight-year-old female child's body inside the defendant's apartment inside his suitcase. Ordinarily this type of evidence might prove to be devastating to a defendant, but police and the prosecutor's office pursued blood-grouping tests that were commonly available in 1994. Using older technology, one of the criminalists typed the victim's blood as ABO type A and another criminalist identified the defendant's blood as ABO type B. In the defendant's apartment, police found the sheet in which the victim had been wrapped and found bloodstains of ABO type AB, semen, and amylase, a component of saliva. A forensic serologist testified at trial that the sample, ABO type AB, could be a mixture of the defendant's blood and the victim's blood or it could have come from an unknown third person. Police found stained tissue paper in defendant's wastebasket that, upon analysis, revealed that the tissue paper exhibited semen stains consistent with the defendant and high amylase activity consistent with saliva from the victim. Expert testimony indicated that the stains were consistent with the result of oral copulation. The blood evidence alone might have been sufficient to convict, but with that evidence being less than certainly conclusive on the issue of identity, the evidence mentioned and other extensive evidence resulted in a guilty verdict and a death sentence.

Older science that provided much-needed evidence of identification has largely been supplanted by DNA testing because the DNA testing proves much more definitive in making identifications and is able to discriminate among different donors of blood and body material when human material becomes commingled.

---

[72]   Norris v. Norris, 2002 Ohio App. LEXIS 5322 (2002).

[73]   People v. Panah, 35 Cal. 4th 395, 414, 107 P.3d 790, 803, 25 Cal. Rptr. 3d 672, 689, 2005 Cal. LEXIS 2712 (Cal. 2005).

§ 15.5 Polygraph Examinations[74]

The polygraph, also known as the lie detector, is an electronic device that, when properly connected to the human body, graphically records changes in blood pressure, heart rate, and respiration. These basic features may be supplemented with a unit for recording what is known as the galvanic skin reflex, based on changes in the activity of the sweat pores in a subject's hands, and another unit for recording muscular movements and pressures. A galvanometer used alone is totally inadequate for lie detection.

As an investigative technique, the use of the polygraph is based on the assumption that lying leads to conflict; that conflict causes fear and anxiety; that this mental state is the direct cause of measurable physiological changes that can be accurately recorded; and that the polygraph operator, by a study of these reactions, can tell whether the subject is being deceptive or truthful. The polygraph presents problems concerning reliability, scientific acceptability, consistency, and accuracy among examiners, and operation of the polygraph still cannot answer the questions that it purports to answer without engaging detractors who present good arguments against admissibility. An early blow to the admissibility of polygraph evidence occurred in a famous case, *Frye v. United States*, where the court of appeals held that polygraph evidence was not admissible because the field of polygraph testing had not been "sufficiently established to have gained general acceptance in the particular field in which it belongs."[75] According to the Supreme Court of New Mexico, as of 2004, 27 states apply a per se rule of exclusion to the admission of polygraph evidence.[76] As the court noted, "These per se states ban polygraph evidence, including test results, offers to take the test, as well as refusals to take the test, for a variety of reasons. These courts found that the polygraph has not been proven valid or reliable or that it has not been generally accepted in the scientific community."[77] Echoing the view that polygraph evidence lacks reliability, one law review commentator compared the use of the polygraph to find the truth to the task of pinning the tail on a donkey at a child's birthday party.[78]

Taking a different view, the Supreme Court of New Mexico considered the admission of polygraph evidence and, in principle, approved the admission of polygraph evidence in the courts of the state.[79] The court reviewed the theory of the polygraph.

---

[74] *See* Chapter 6, *supra*, for discussion of admissibility of polygraph results on stipulation. *See also The Re-Lie-ability of Polygraph Evidence: An Evaluation of Whether Texas's Per Se Rule Against the Admissibility of Polygraph Evidence is Violative of the Texas Rules of Evidence*, 58 BAYLOR L. REV. 265 (2006).

[75] 293 F. 1013, 1014, 1923 U.S. App. LEXIS 1712 (D.C. Cir. 1923).

[76] Lee v. Martinez, 136 N.M. 166, 96 P.3d 291, 2004 N.M. LEXIS 378 (N.M. 2004).

[77] *Id.* at 185.

[78] *Playing "Pin the Tail on the Truth" in the Eleventh Circuit: Why Polygraph Evidence Should Be Excluded in Federal Courts*, 30 STETSON L. REV. 2000.

[79] Lee v. Martinez, 136 N.M. 166, 2004 NMSC 27, 96 P.3d 291, 2004 N.M. LEXIS 378 (N.M. 2004).

> The polygraph instrument records "physiological responses that are believed to be stronger during acts of deception than at other times." These physiological responses include cardiovascular activity, electrodermal activity (electrical conductance at the skin surface), and respiratory activity. In general, a polygraph examination consists of "a series of yes/no questions to which the examinee responds while connected to sensors that transmit data on these physiological phenomena by wire to the instrument, which uses analog or digital technology to record the data." "The record of physiological responses during the polygraph test is known as the polygraph chart." The polygraph examination is based on the theory that "a deceptive response to a question causes a reaction—such as fear of detection or psychological arousal—that changes respiration rate, heart rate, blood pressure, or skin conductance relative to what they were before the question was asked." [Internal citations omitted.][80]

The Supreme Court reviewed the three general types of polygraph examination techniques and eventually focused on the second theory for use in New Mexico courts.

> Three different polygraph questioning techniques have been developed. First, in the "relevant/irrelevant" technique, the examinee is asked two different types of questions—"the relevant questions are typically very specific and concern an event under investigation"; whereas, "the irrelevant questions may be completely unrelated to the event and may offer little temptation to deceive." A deceptive person is expected to have a stronger physiological response to the relevant questions than to the irrelevant questions. Second, in the "control question technique" or "comparison question technique," instead of coupling the relevant questions with irrelevant questions, the irrelevant questions are replaced with control questions "intended to generate physiological reactions even in nondeceptive examinees." An example of a control question might be, "Have you ever lied to a friend?" Truthful examinees are expected to experience stronger physiological responses to the control questions; whereas, deceptive examinees are expected to experience stronger physiological responses to the relevant questions. Third, in the "guilty knowledge polygraph test," the examinee is asked a number of "questions about details of an event under investigation that are known only to investigators and those with direct knowledge of the event." Examinees are expected to experience the greatest physiological responses to those questions that accurately describe the event. [Internal citations omitted.][81]

The Court noted that the case of *Daubert v. Merrell Dow Pharmaceuticals*, 509 U.S. 579 (1993), which liberalized the admission of scientific evidence in

---

[80]   *Id.* at 170.
[81]   *Id.*

federal courts, was in sync with the general approach concerning admissibility of evidence and the liberal thrust of the Federal Rules of Evidence. Under the New Mexico rules regulating the admission of evidence, the judge must assure that any and all scientific evidence or results meets the tests of reliability and relevancy. The trial judge must also determine whether the scientific methodology is really based on science and whether that science will support conclusions based on probability rather than mere guess or conjecture.

> In making this determination, we consider: "(1) whether a theory or technique can be (and has been) tested; (2) whether the theory or technique has been subjected to peer review and publication; (3) the known potential rate of error in using a particular scientific technique and the existence and maintenance of standards controlling the technique's operation; and (4) whether the theory or technique has been generally accepted in the particular scientific field." [Internal citations omitted.][82]

The court reviewed some of the reasons for admitting this sort of testimony and noted that the research that has been conducted shows that the basic science demonstrated support for the theories on which the polygraph examination is based. The court reviewed the perceived rate of error related to polygraph examinations and evaluated the fact that a number of polygraph validation studies had been conducted with adequate results. Additionally, the court surveyed some of the peer-reviewed scholarly publications that addressed polygraph issues and testing, some of which cautioned that polygraph studies have not reached the high level of research desired in scientific inquiry, but it noted that some studies have appeared in high-quality research journals. Professional standards have been developed by the leading professional association, the American Polygraph Association, which, when followed, should produce reliable evidence, according to the court. The court concluded that the control question polygraph examination technique proved to be appropriate to admit if general standards for admission of evidence were followed.[83]

An interesting factor to which the Supreme Court of New Mexico referred was the fact that the very groups and individuals wanting to keep polygraph evidence from admission in New Mexico courts were those who used polygraph examination results in their own governmental pursuits. "Often the same government officials who vigorously oppose the admission of exculpatory polygraphs of the accused find polygraph testing to be reliable enough to use in their own decisionmaking. Federal and state governments rely upon the results of polygraph examinations for a variety of law enforcement purposes, even in jurisdictions where polygraph evidence is inadmissible."[84] The court mentioned that polygraph results have been used to determine probable cause, whether to prosecute, whether to arrest, and judges have considered the results

---

[82]　　*Id.* at 173.
[83]　　*Id.* at 171.
[84]　　*Id.* at 181.

in deciding whether to issue an arrest warrant. In order for polygraph results to be admitted, each trial judge must evaluate the situation and make an individual determination based on the facts of each case, but the clear thrust of this case was to permit, and not to absolutely prohibit, the admission of polygraph evidence that has been conducted by licensed examiners who have followed the standards of the professional associations and meet the criteria established by the Supreme Court of New Mexico.

Prior to the *Lee* decision above, the Supreme Court of the United States had an opportunity to liberalize the admission of polygraph evidence in federal courts, but determined not to go in that direction. The case decided in 1998 involved an appeal from the Court of Appeals for the Armed Forces in which an airman had been accused of ingesting methamphetamine and he contended that he absolutely had not taken any drugs.[85] In the case, *United States v. Scheffer*, the trial court refused to admit polygraph evidence based on a unique military rule of evidence. Military Rule of Evidence 707 provides, among other things, that "[n]otwithstanding any other provision of law, the results of a polygraph examination, the opinion of a polygraph examiner, or any reference to an offer to take, failure to take, or taking of a polygraph examination, shall not be admitted into evidence."[86] The evidence available resulted in a conviction at court-martial. On appeal, the Court of Appeals reversed the conviction, noting that in that case, the per se exclusion of the polygraph evidence violated the Sixth Amendment right to put on a defense. The Supreme Court considered the case and rejected the Sixth Amendment argument while stating:

> Rule 707 serves several legitimate interests in the criminal trial process. These interests include ensuring that only reliable evidence is introduced at trial, preserving the jury's role in determining credibility, and avoiding litigation that is collateral to the primary purpose of the trial. The rule is neither arbitrary nor disproportionate in promoting these ends. Nor does it implicate a sufficiently weighty interest of the defendant to raise a constitutional concern under our precedents.[87]

The Supreme Court mentioned that the defendant was not categorically prohibited from introducing a defense because he could introduce any factual evidence he possessed and nothing prohibited him from taking the witness stand in his own defense. Justice Thomas, writing for the majority and speaking to the dissenter in the case, called the reliability of the polygraph into question as he noted, "[t]he contentions of respondent and the dissent notwithstanding, there is simply no consensus that polygraph evidence is reliable."[88] From the perspective of the Supreme Court, it appears that an approval for the admission of polygraph in federal courts may be a long time coming, if ever.

---

[85]   United States v. Scheffer, 523 U.S. 303, 1998 U.S. LEXIS 2303 (1998).
[86]   *Id.* at 306-307.
[87]   *Id.* at 309.
[88]   *Id.*

According to one law review article, when the Supreme Court heard arguments in the *Scheffer* case, "twenty-two states allowed for the admission of polygraph evidence to some degree, and twenty-seven states plus the District of Columbia did not allow for polygraph evidence in criminal trials."[89] The author noted that in 2000, only two federal circuits, the Fourth Circuit and the District of Columbia Circuit, continued to hold that polygraph evidence was per se inadmissible.[90] With customary inertia, jurisdictions that refuse to allow any polygraph evidence tend to continue on the same path, while jurisdictions that permit polygraph under some circumstances tend to remain open to polygraph evidence on a case-by-case basis.

For example, following the reasoning of the Supreme Court in *Scheffer*, in a 2006 case, the Court of Appeals for the Eighth Circuit upheld the exclusion from evidence of polygraph results in a drug case in which the defendant contended that he did not possess the gun in conjunction with the charged drug offense. The defendant had wanted to use the polygraph evidence to bolster his testimony that there was no link between his drug offense and the firearm. The trial court indicated that, absent a stipulation between the parties, it would not consider the polygraph evidence and cited the Supreme Court's view in *Scheffer* that the polygraph carries uncertainties concerning reliability.

In conformity with the practice that most state courts tend to exclude polygraph evidence, an Idaho trial court refused to permit a defendant to introduce polygraph evidence in a murder prosecution in the absence of a stipulation by the parties. The trial judge reasoned that the polygraph evidence did not help the jury but substituted decisions that the jury should be making. The Supreme Court of Idaho indicated that it supported the trial judge's decision by citing *United States v. Scheffer*, which held that, in non-military trials, admission of polygraph evidence was up to the trial judge's discretion.[91] When the case reached the federal district court in a petition for a writ of habeas corpus, the district court failed to find that the exclusion of polygraph evidence was cause for an unconstitutional conviction despite the defendant's allegation that the exclusion violated his Sixth Amendment right to put on a defense. The federal district court found that there was nothing that was contrary to established law that lawfully prevented the state trial judge from excluding polygraph evidence. As the district court noted, "[p]etitioner has not shown that the Idaho Supreme Court's decision affirming the trial court's refusal to admit Petitioner's own polygraph test is contrary to, or an unreasonable application of, United States Supreme Court precedent."[92]

A substantial minority of courts admit polygraph evidence upon stipulation of the parties subject to judicial discretion. For the most part, this result has been achieved by court decision, although statutory provisions may

---

[89]   *See* Dorian D. Peters, *Per Se Prohibitions of the Admission of Polygraph Evidence as Upheld in Scheffer are Both Violative of the Constitution and the Federal Rules of Evidence as Applied by Daubert*, 27 AM. J. CRIM. L. 249 (2000).

[90]   *Id.*

[91]   *See* State v. Trevino, 132 Idaho 888, 980 P.2d 552, 1999 Idaho LEXIS 54 (1999).

[92]   Trevino v. Hardison, 2006 U.S. Dist. LEXIS 27294 (D. Idaho 2006).

achieve the same result. A few courts recognize a trial court's discretion to admit polygraph evidence even in the absence of stipulation. The Seventh Circuit Court of Appeals has adopted this approach.

There are generally three identifiable approaches to the admissibility of polygraph evidence. The first holds that the evidence is inadmissible per se, the second approach allows the evidence upon the stipulation of all the parties, subject to the judge's discretion, and the third approach permits polygraph evidence in the absence of stipulation when certain circumstances exist such as impeachment or corroboration. The approaches in the various jurisdictions are discussed below with the caveat that the decisions of each jurisdiction must be examined to determine the law applicable in that jurisdiction.

1. *Some states take the position that polygraph evidence is inadmissible per se and under all circumstances.* Whether to impeach, corroborate, or use as substantive evidence, the results of a polygraph test cannot be used in court.[93] Evidence is not admissible by either party either as substantive evidence or as relating to the credibility of the witness. In an Arkansas case, the defendant wanted a mistrial because a prosecution witness had inadvertently mentioned that she had taken a polygraph test but no mention of the result was ever brought to the jury's attention.[94] Mere mention of a polygraph was not sufficient introduction of polygraph evidence to cause reversible error and the appellate court upheld the defendant's conviction. In a Connecticut case in which a father had been accused of two counts of first-degree sexual assault of his daughter, he indicated to police that he would be willing to take a lie detector test.[95] In Connecticut, polygraph results are not admissible. A police officer introduced part of the defendant's statement where he stated, "I did not touch my daughter like they say I did and I will go on the machine to tell the truth."[96] The court did not permit the full statement and excluded the part, "and I will go on the machine to tell the truth." The appellate court upheld the trial court's redaction of the full statement, noting that the willingness to take a polygraph is of little probative value.

2. *Use of polygraph evidence is admitted if both parties stipulate to the evidence's admissibility.* For example, in California courts, results of a polygraph exam or any reference to taking an exam or an offer to take an exam cannot be admitted in any criminal court, unless all parties stipulate to the admission of polygraph results.[97] In a South Dakota case, pursuant to a plea bargain, the defendant agreed to take a polygraph examination to determine whether he had committed arson in other places and in other years than the

---

[93]   A.C.A. § 12-12-704 Results inadmissible. (Ark. 2006). *But see* Rollins v. State, 2005 Ark. LEXIS 293 (Ark. 2005), in which stipulations by both parties have been admitted.

[94]   *See* Johnson v. State, 2006 Ark. LEXIS 215 (Ark. 2006).

[95]   State v. Antonio A., 90 Conn. App. 286, 295, 878 A.2d 358, 364, 2005 Conn. App. LEXIS 306 (2005).

[96]   *Id.*

[97]   *See* CAL EVID CODE § 351.1 Exclusion of results of polygraph examination. (2006).

crime for which he was pleading guilty. The state agreed to request a 17-year sentence if the defendant passed the polygraph and told the complete truth about his past arson activity. When the polygraph operator indicated that the defendant was being untruthful about his arson history and one specific fire in particular, the judge sentenced the defendant to the maximum 35-five year sentence. Because the parties had agreed to the use of the polygraph in the sentencing phase, the evidence could be used to enhance the sentence.[98]

3. *Polygraph evidence is admissible in the absence of stipulation when certain circumstances exist; for example, for impeachment where the defendant opened the door or corroboration or to determine whether a defendant's prior confession had been voluntarily offered.* An appellate court approved the mention by corrections officers during the penalty stage that the defendant knew how to beat a polygraph. Allowing the officer to mention the polygraph was appropriate because the defendant had "opened the door" when he had earlier testified that he passed the polygraph.[99] In a retrial of a New York criminal case, the defendant contended that his original statements given during a polygraph exam were not voluntary even though the police believed that probable cause to arrest him existed after hearing his answers to the polygraph test. The defendant contended that his statement was involuntary because it was based on misinformation given to him by police. In a ruling prior to the retrial, the judge permitted a limited use of polygraph evidence. As the judge noted, "while polygraph evidence is not admissible on the issue of guilt or innocence, if a proper foundation is established, such evidence may be admitted on the limited issue—which is central to this case—of the voluntariness of defendant's confession."[100]

In jurisdictions in which the results of polygraph examinations are inadmissible, police still use the polygraph during investigations and as a tool to encourage admissions and confessions. Even though the results are useless in court, statements made before, during, and after an examination may be admissible. In a Tennessee, where polygraph results are inadmissible, a suspect in a child rape case agreed to take a polygraph test concerning the facts.[101] After the examiner finished asking questions, the told the subject that he had observed deception on a few questions and stated to the subject that the child contended that she had been forced to engage in sexual intercourse. The subject noted to the examiner, "she was not forced." At the trial the court permitted the polygraph examiner to tell the court that the defendant stated that in reference to the sexual activity, that "she was not forced." The defendant appealed and offered the argument that "Tennessee courts have held repeatedly that polygraph test results, testimony concerning such results, and testi-

---

[98]   South Dakota v. Stevenson, 2002 S.D. 120, 652 N.W.2d 735, 2002 S.D. LEXIS 138 (S.D. 2002).

[99]   *See* Hinton v. State, 2006 Ala. Crim. App. LEXIS 72 (2006).

[100]   People v. Kogut, 2005 N.Y. Slip Op. 25412, 10 Misc. 3d 245, 805 N.Y.S.2d 789, 2005 N.Y. Misc. LEXIS 2142 (N.Y. 2005).

[101]   State v. Damron, 151 S.W.3d 510, 515, 2004 Tenn. LEXIS 993 (Tenn. 2004).

mony concerning a defendant's willingness or refusal to submit to a polygraph test are inadmissible."[102] The reviewing court held that the evidence had been properly introduced against the defendant because, according to the general rule followed in a majority of jurisdictions in the United States, the introduction of voluntary statements made during a polygraph examination are admissible because the reliability of a voluntary statement does not depend on the accuracy or reliability of the polygraph.

In order for stipulated polygraph results to be admitted, the defendant's participation in the examination must be free and voluntary.[103] In some jurisdictions, polygraph evidence may be admitted in criminal cases when, prior to taking the exam, the prosecution and the defendant enter into a stipulation that the results of a polygraph exam will be admissible.[104] The stipulation only binds the parties to the agreement and cannot bind other co-defendants.

Even if the state court has held that polygraph results are generally inadmissible, even for impeachment purposes, absent a stipulation of the parties, the prosecutor's failure to disclose to the defense that a key government witness had failed a polygraph test may be a due process violation.[105] In *Bartholomew v. Wood*, the defendant claimed that the state denied him due process by failing to disclose that a crucial witness on the issue of premeditation had failed a polygraph test. The Ninth Circuit Court of Appeals agreed with the defendant that failure to disclose to the defendant that the witness had failed the test was a due process violation of the kind condemned in *Brady v. Maryland*.[106]

Does a defendant have a constitutional right to tell a court-martial that he passed a lie detector test? This was the question that was submitted to the United States Supreme Court in the case of *United States v. Scheffer*.[107] The defendant was charged, among other things, with using a controlled substance. A lie detector test indicated that he answered truthfully when he denied taking drugs, but he was not allowed to use the lie detector result at the trial. The United States Court of Appeals for the Armed Services held that the mandatory rule of exclusion followed by the military violated Scheffer's right to put on a defense. In reversing, the Supreme Court said that a defendant's right to present evidence can be subject to reasonable restrictions and that the ban on the use of polygraph results in military trials is a valid means of limiting the admissibility of unreliable evidence. The ruling allows those who authorize the use of polygraph evidence to continue that use. Four dissenters agreed that the military rule did not violate the Constitution's Sixth Amendment right to present a defense, but these four justices indicated that a later case "might present a more compelling case for introduction of the testimony than this one does."[108]

---

[102]   *Id.* at 516.
[103]   State v. Fain, 774 P.2d 252 (Idaho 1989).
[104]   State v. Castagna, 187 N.J. 293, 311, 901 A.2d 363, 373, 2006 N.J. LEXIS 1081 (N.J. 2006), Miller v. State, 380 S.E.2d 690 (Ga. 1989).
[105]   Bartholomew v. Wood, 34 F.3d 870 (9th Cir. 1994).
[106]   Brady v. Maryland, 373 U.S. 83, 83 S. Ct. 1174, 10 L. Ed. 2d 215 (1963). *See* § 4.9 for a discussion of the *Brady* rule
[107]   United States v. Scheffer, 523 U.S. 303, 1998 U.S. LEXIS 2303 (1998).
[108]   *Id.* at 318.

Evidence or mention of the fact that the defendant either took or refused to take a lie detector examination is generally not admissible and can create reversible error if mentioned by the prosecutor.[109] In a Mississippi embezzlement case, the reviewing court reversed the conviction because it was held to be fundamental error for the prosecutor to improperly inquire about a witness's willingness to take a polygraph examination. In reversing the case, the court noted that reversal in such cases is not automatic, but in a close case, reversible error had been committed.[110]

The polygraph examiner should receive his or her training in the lie detector technique under the guidance of an experienced examiner with a sufficient volume of actual cases to permit the trainee to make frequent observations of lie detector tests and to conduct tests himself or herself under the instructor's personal supervision. In addition, the trainee should read and take courses in the pertinent areas of psychology and physiology and should examine and interpret a considerable number of lie detector test records in verified cases.[111] Some states now require licensing of polygraph operators. To practice in Illinois, the law requires that the examiner possess a state license. To qualify, an Illinois polygraph examiner must have earned an academic degree at least at the baccalaureate level, be of good moral character, have passed the licensing exam, and have satisfactorily completed six months of an internship.[112]

From the foregoing, it is apparent that the laws relating to the use of polygraph evidence in court are still changing. Some courts now hold that the polygraph has attained a degree of validity and reliability, and that such evidence may be admitted. Future cases and legislation will determine whether this recognition will be approved by the courts.

§ 15.6 "Truth Serum" Results

The term "truth serum" has no precise medical or scientific meaning.[113] To refer to sodium amytal or sodium pentothal as "truth serum" is a misnomer, as they have no propensity or chemical effect to cause a person "to speak the truth." These drugs do not induce a state of mind in which a person tells the truth, but instead causes the subject to speak more freely than he or she otherwise might. The use of sodium amytal can produce any one of four results:

---

[109] See CAL EVID CODE § 351.1 Exclusion of results of polygraph examination. (2006). See also People v. Lungberg, 2006 Cal. App. Unpub. LEXIS 3676 (Cal. 2006).

[110] Fagan v. State, 894 So. 2d 576, 580, 2004 Miss. LEXIS 1486 (Miss. 2004).

[111] Inbau, F.E. and J.E. Reid, The Lie-Detector Technique: A Reliable and Valuable Investigative Aid, 50 A.B.A.J. 470 (May 1964).

[112] 225 ILCS 430/11 Qualifications for licensure as an examiner (Ill. 2006). See also 26 V.S.A. § 2904 Qualifications for license (Vt. 2006).

[113] See Townsend v. Sain, 372 U.S. 293, 83 S. Ct. 745, 768, 9 L. Ed. 2d 770 (1963) (Stewart, J., dissenting).

truth, falsehood, fantasy, or response to suggestion.[114] One court refused to allow expert witnesses to use sodium amytal-influenced answers to questions posed to a defendant because all the experts in the case agreed that sodium amytal interviews are not scientifically reliable for ascertaining truth.[115] Constitutionally, any substance that might be administered as a way of recovering or discerning the truth will require the consent of the defendant and, as a result, if any truth serum drug is to be administered, it is the defense rather than the prosecution that has an opportunity to consider this avenue.

A confession induced by the administration of drugs is constitutionally inadmissible because it is not the product of a rational free will and intellect.[116] In a prosecution for murder in which police questioned the defendant at the hospital after he had been shot by police three times, he had been recovering from surgery hours earlier, he was on significant amounts of pain medication, he had not eaten for several days, he was in the intensive care unit, he had tubes in his nose and mouth, and he was suicidal. The interrogation conducted by police under these circumstances did not produce a free and voluntary confession. The defendant's answers to police questions were delusional and a doctor testified that he was not sane or competent to waive any rights. The officers alleged that the defendant did waive his *Miranda* rights, and continued to question him because he was responsive even though his answers were mostly unintelligible. Other medications were withheld from the defendant that led the federal district court to conclude that withholding medication must be considered coercive. The drugs given the defendant may have had "truth serum" properties, but the federal district court granted the writ of habeas corpus because of the dangers of interrogating a person in the drugged state in which the police found the defendant.

Although excessive alcohol causes people to talk and say things that ordinarily would not be said when sober, the mere fact that a subject is intoxicated, without more, does not make a waiver of rights improper or interrogation constitutionally suspect. In an Ohio case, a court of appeals upheld a conviction when the defendant made an allegation that he was too drunk to understand *Miranda* warnings.[117] The court reviewed the defendant's tape-recorded words that he understood his rights and that he had read them and held that the effects of alcohol did not render the statement invalid or coerced. The court contrasted the facts in this case with *Townsend v. Sain*, in which a police physician had given Townsend a drug with truth-serum properties and the

---

[114]   Freeman v. New York Central R. Co., 174 N.E.2d 550 (Ohio Ct. App. 1960), a civil action in which the plaintiff told his psychiatrist that he was unable to recall the events leading up to his accident, and asked the doctor to try to restore his memory. The doctor administered a treatment of sodium amytal, which placed the plaintiff in a hypnotic or semiconscious state during which the doctor conversed with the plaintiff and made a record of the questions and answers. At the trial, the plaintiff's testimony was based upon his medically refreshed memory. The court did not expressly decide on the propriety of this method of refreshing one's memory.

[115]   State v. Pitts, 116 N.J. 580, 625, 562 A.2d 1320, 1345, 1989 N.J. LEXIS 73 (N.J. 1989).

[116]   Hanna v. Price, 2005 U.S. Dist. LEXIS 30380 (W.D. Mich. 2005).

[117]   State v. Hill, 2006 Ohio 1408 (2006).

police who obtained a confession knew the defendant had been given drugs. This case was different, according to the court of appeals.

A judge in his or her discretion may exclude expert testimony by a psychiatrist explaining the effects of sodium amytal, especially when the psychiatrist admits that narcoanalysis does not reliably induce truthful statements.[118] However, the fact that the witness underwent a sodium amytal interview does not preclude testimony of that witness concerning his or her current recollection of events. The court in *United States v. Solomon* determined that the admission of the testimony of a witness concerning his current recollection of events was not an abuse of discretion, despite the claim that the witness's testimony could not be reliable after he underwent a sodium amytal interview. The court recognized that the defendant was not precluded from presenting evidence that the witness's testimony was enhanced by the use of sodium amytal during narcoanalysis.

In a California double murder case, the defendant offered a confession shortly after the killings.[119] The actual defense centered around his sexual and psychological abuse as a child, as well as being a victim of adult traumma. Ten months after his confession, the defendant underwent interrogation by his doctor while under the influence of sodium amytal, a short-acting barbiturate drug that has some truth-serum properties. The purpose in administering sodium amytal was to refresh the defendant's memory so that he could remember his conduct involving the alleged criminal activity. At the time the doctor began working with the defendant, he could not remember what he did to one of the deceased individuals from the time he shot her until he saw her dead in a pool of blood. According to the reviewing court opinion, "Dr. Glaser believed defendant's psychological profile was most consistent with the phenomenon of 'dissociative states' in which a person is not fully in control of his or her thoughts, feelings, or behavior. Individuals with dissociative disorders are aware of the occurrence of lost periods of time or memory lapses."[120] The defendant testified at the trial based on his viewing of the videotapes taken when his doctor questioned him while the defendant was under the influence of sodium amytal. The doctor testified on behalf of the defendant and offered the opinion, based on his examination of the defendant and on his questioning him under the influence of the truth serum, that the defendant had not planned or premeditated the killing of one of the prostitutes or weighed the consequences due to his mental problems. While the defendant attempted to use incompetence and other mental excuses along with his abuse as a child, the efforts by his doctor to use the truth serum to refresh the defendant's memory failed to convince the jury that he should be found not guilty of killing the two women. The use of the truth serum, sodium amytal, due to the defendant's alleged lack of memory, may not have influenced the jury because he made confessions after his arrest at a time when his memory did not seem impaired.

---

[118]   United States v. Solomon, 753 F.2d 1522 (9th Cir. 1985).
[119]   People v. Rogers, 39 Cal. 4th 826, 2006 Cal. LEXIS 9862 (Cal. 2006).
[120]   *Id.* at 843.

After careful review, the Supreme Court of California upheld the defendant's capital convictions and death sentences.

In an Idaho case, the defendant, in his motion to introduce statements made under the influence of sodium amytal, argued that such refreshed testimony should be admitted to the same extent that hypnotically refreshed testimony would be allowed.[121] The reviewing court agreed that the motion was properly denied, because there was no scientific basis to conclude that hypnosis and the use of sodium amytal produced comparable results. The court concluded that until the so-called "truth serum" test gains scientific acceptability, the results of such tests are inadmissible.

§ 15.7 Fingerprint Comparisons

The science of fingerprint comparison for identification purposes is as old as civilization itself. The courts take judicial notice of the fact that fingerprint identification is one of the surest methods of identification. The primary purpose of fingerprinting is the positive identification of an accused. Another purpose of fingerprinting is evidentiary, e.g., to compare the fingerprints of the defendant with fingerprints left at the scene of the crime or on an object connected to the crime. The evidentiary purpose may or may not be present in a given case.

The Fifth Amendment offers no protection against compulsion to submit to fingerprinting. Furthermore, fingerprinting of individuals who have been validly arrested or formally charged with a crime does not constitute an unreasonable search and seizure within the meaning of the Fourth Amendment.[122]

In a criminal case, an official police department fingerprint record may be authenticated for admission in evidence by the person who, having the duty to compile and file such records, is the lawful custodian thereof.[123] A fingerprint expert, to qualify as such, should have formal training in the science of fingerprinting and should be skilled in the photographic procedure of enlarging and developing photographs of fingerprints.[124] Thus, a woman who had been doing fingerprint identification for 24 years, who had compared more than three million fingerprints, and who had never misidentified a fingerprint match was qualified as an expert and was qualified to testify concerning fingerprint identification.[125] Whether a witness has the requisite qualifications of a fingerprint expert is a question within the discretion of the trial court.

---

[121] State v. Rosencrantz, 110 Idaho 124, 714 P.2d 93 (1986).

[122] United States v. Laub Baking Co., 283 F. Supp. 217 (N.D. Ohio 1968); Schmerber v. California, 384 U.S. 757, 86 S. Ct. 1826, 16 L. Ed. 2d 908 (1967); see KANOVITZ & KANOVITZ, CONSTITUTIONAL LAW (10th ed. 2005) and KLOTTER, WALKER & HEMMENS, LEGAL GUIDE FOR POLICE (7th ed. 2005). See also United States v. Snow, 82 F.3d 935 (10th Cir. 1996), in which the court held that asking a subject to sign a fingerprint identification card does not violate the Fifth Amendment privilege against self-incrimination and a suspect is not required to be Mirandized before signing the card, because there is no constitutional right not to be fingerprinted.

[123] State v. Shank, 115 Ohio App. 291, 185 N.E.2d 63 (1962).

[124] McGarry v. State, 82 Tex. Crim. 597, 200 S.W. 527 (1918).

[125] United States v. Cruz, 2006 U.S. App. LEXIS 18353 (10th Cir. 2006).

According to one court, evidence obtained through digital imaging enhancement of latent fingerprints and palm prints was admissible under the *Frye* test because there did not appear to be a significant dispute among qualified experts as to the validity of enhanced digital imaging performed by qualified experts using appropriate software.[126]

Evidence of palmprints left at the scene of a crime is admissible under the same standards and is just as reliable and accurate as fingerprints. In one case, the trial court permitted a latent print expert to testify that a bloody palmprint that the expert detected on the murder weapon compared favorably with a known sample of the defendant's palmprint and could have been made only when the blood on the handgun was wet.[127] In a different murder case, the trial court admitted evidence of bare footprints that matched the defendant's bare footprint, some of which were mingled with the blood of the deceased.[128] Some footprints may be latent and require the skills of a latent print specialist, while some are quite visible and photography will properly preserve them as evidence.

According to the general rule in Texas and in most other states, a witness who had made measurements of foot tracks or prints and measured the footprint of a defendant or who has made some comparison between the tracks and the shoes of a defendant or who has detailed any peculiarities of the footprint that corresponds to a defendant's shoe, that witness may give an opinion concerning the similarity of the tracks. This type of evidence is admissible either by lay or expert witness opinion.[129]

A court that orders a defendant to submit a fingerprint or palmprint after he or she has been indicted has not interfered with a defendant's rights under the Fourth Amendment or the Fifth Amendment. In a case involving illegal aliens who had been indicted for possession of a firearm by a felon and an indictment for possession of a firearm by an illegal alien, the prosecution moved that the defendants submit handprints for comparison purposes.[130] The defendants argued against having to produce a handprint, alleging that their rights to be free from unreasonable searches and seizures would be violated if they were forced to submit handprint samples. In rejecting the defendants' Fourth Amendment contention, the trial judge noted that prior cases held that there was no expectation of privacy in the quality of one's voice and a grand jury could order that a sample be given for consideration. This principle that privacy does not extend to personal characteristics held open to the public applied to photographs, measurements, and fingerprints. The judge rejected the defendants' arguments that the forced production of a palmprint violated their right not to incriminate themselves under the Fifth Amendment. Compelling a suspect to offer real or physical evidence to the prosecution fails to violate the Fifth Amendment because the self-incrimination clause only pro-

[126] State v. Hayden, 950 P.2d 1024 (Wash. 1998).

[127] People v. Valdez, 32 Cal. 4th 73, 84, 82 P.3d 296, 308, 8 Cal. Rptr. 3d 271, 2004 Cal. LEXIS 4 (Cal 2004).

[128] State v. Robinson, 2003 Iowa App. LEXIS 550 (Iowa 2003).

[129] Rogers v. State, 2006 Tex. Crim. App. LEXIS 852 (2006).

[130] United States v. Meza-Rodrigues, 2006 U.S. Dist. LEXIS 58619 (W.D. Mich. 2006).

tects against compelling verbal testimony or testimonial communications. Accordingly, the trial judge ordered the defendants to submit a sample of their handprints.

A search warrant is not necessary to take the fingerprints or palmprint of a person lawfully in custody. The fact that the person is under arrest permits the taking of a print as an incident of a lawful arrest and removes any Fourth Amendment search and seizure issue.[131]

Although the police may take fingerprints at the scene of the crime and an expert may make comparisons, the state is not required to gather fingerprint evidence.[132] Even if the defendant argues that the police were attempting to frame him or her, the state is not required to gather evidence from articles allegedly touched by the defendant, and it is not incumbent on the state to account for the absence of such fingerprint evidence.[133] However, according to one federal court, the fact that the government did not introduce fingerprint evidence properly could be argued to the jury during the closing argument.[134]

In the case of *United States v. Sanchez-Garcia*, the use of fingerprint evidence played a strong role in justifying an enhanced drug offense sentence.[135] Due to an informant's tip, police suspected that the subject had been and was dealing and smuggling drugs as well as being an illegal alien. Following a lawful traffic stop that revealed that the subject's name did not match his identification, police received permission to search the subject's car and apartment. A records check of the name offered by the subject returned a complete set of fingerprints, a list of his aliases, and a photograph. A consent-based search of the subject's residence revealed illegal drugs and a firearm with a latent fingerprint. Comparisons of that fingerprint with a fingerprint database revealed that the subject's print matched the fingerprint of an illegal alien who had prior drug offenses and who had been lawfully deported. Ultimately, the jury trial resulted in the defendant being convicted of a variety of drug- and weapons-related offenses. In order to enhance the penalties, the prosecution used photographs of one of the defendant's alias identities and compared that photo to his presence in court. Additionally, the court considered the testimony at trial that the defendant was the individual with a different name who had previously been convicted of drug-related offenses and concluded that the fingerprint evidence demonstrated that the alias identity and the defendant in court were the same person beyond a reasonable doubt. The reviewing court agreed that the trial judge acted properly when she imposed a heightened sentence because the current drug crimes were committed after a previous felony drug conviction.

---

[131] United States v. Johnson, 445 F.3d 793, 2006 U.S. App. LEXIS 85, n.1 (5th Cir. 2006).
[132] State v. Beck, 785 S.W.2d 714 (Mo. 1990).
[133] State v. Schneider, 736 S.W.2d 392 (Mo. 1987).
[134] United States v. Hoffman, 964 F.2d 21 (D.C. Cir. 1992). *See also* United States v. Poindexter, 942 F.2d 354 (6th Cir.), *cert. denied*, 502 U.S. 994, 112 S. Ct. 615, 116 L. Ed. 2d 637 (1991) and United States v. Day, 956 F.2d 124 (6th Cir. 1992).
[135] United States v. Sanchez-Garcia, 402 F.3d 175; 2005 U.S. App. LEXIS 4568 (8th Cir. 2006).

Courts have approved the use of fingerprint evidence for the purpose of enhancing sentences because a court may evaluate any evidence in making a sentencing determination as long as it has sufficient indicia of reliability.[136] State computer records and computer-based fingerprint evidence may be used as a tool to help determine a sentence or to enhance a sentence for other valid reasons.

§ 15.8   Ballistics Experiments

The science of forensic ballistics concerns the ability to determine whether a particular projectile was fired from a particular firearm and, among other factors, the analysis of the size or caliber of the projectile and of the weapon. The application of this science may be able to determine the brand or class of firearm by analyzing the remains of a projectile. The science of ballistics may involve test firings of recovered weapons to produce a sample projectile that can be the basis for comparison with a crime scene projectile. Rifled barrels produce markings on each projectile as it twists through the barrel during the firing sequence, but these markings will change over the life of the firearm depending on firearm care, how many rounds have been fired, and the type of projectile fired. These markings, called striations, often aid or enable the forensic examiner to determine which gun fired the questioned projectile. In addition to striation marks on a bullet, firearms leave marks on shells that are ejected from many guns by automatic extractors and even revolvers may sometime leave telltale signs and scratches on the cartridges used in the gun. An expert in ballistics may be permitted to offer testimony to show that the bullet that killed a person was fired from a weapon possessed by the defendant. Before a witness may testify in regard to the identification of firearms and bullets, the attorney for one of the parties must qualify the person as an expert by demonstrating the background, experience, and education of the proposed expert to give such scientific and opinion testimony. If the proponent of the expert demonstrated that the witness had specialized training and experience as an employee of a crime laboratory or can be qualified as an independent expert in forensic ballistics, the court will allow the witness to testify as an expert.

For example, in appealing a federal firearms conviction, the convicted defendant challenged the qualifications of a forensic ballistics expert and contended that his testimony should not have been admitted because he was unqualified as an expert.[137] To qualify to offer expert testimony, it must appear that the proposed witness has sufficient knowledge and/or experience in the particular field of science so that the witness's opinion and knowledge will assist the finder of fact in making proper determinations. In qualifying a witness as an expert on ballistics, testimony indicated that the proposed forensic

---

[136]   United States v. Urbina-Mejia, 450 F.3d 838, 840, 2006 U.S. App. LEXIS 15078 (8th Cir. 2006).

[137]   United States v. Hicks, 389 F.3d 514, 524, 2004 U.S. App. LEXIS 22688 (5th Cir. 2004).

ballistics expert had a degree in "chemistry, had received training in firearms comparisons testing from the FBI, and had done firearms examinations for over twenty years." In addition, the witness testified "he had performed more than a thousand cartridge-firearm comparisons in the course of his twenty-eight-year career with the Texas Department of Public Safety without a suggestion that any of his matches were incorrect."[138] The Court of Appeals ruled that because the witness applied accepted firearms comparison tests, followed the standard practices, and had virtually a zero error rate, the trial court did not abuse its discretion in allowing the officer to testify as a forensic ballistics expert.

A ballistics expert may testify that the firing-pin marking on cartridge shells remaining in a revolver or on spent cartridges found in a defendant's possession corresponds to the marking on a test shell fired from the defendant's revolver.[139] Ballistics evidence may be able to prove that a particular bullet had been fired from a specific gun due to microscopic markings placed on a bullet by the effect of the rifling lands and grooves as it twists down the barrel[140] or due to unique markings made on spent cartridges ejected from the gun.[141] Likewise, a ballistics expert witness who is also trained in toolmark analysis[142] may testify that an empty shotgun shell found at the scene of a homicide had been fired from the defendant's shotgun, and he or she may base that opinion on breechface markings revealed by a comparison microscope and photographs.[143] The brand of a firearm can often be identified, or sometimes excluded, by careful observation of the lands and grooves.[144] In some situations, ballistics experts will be permitted to offer expert opinion concerning the probable trajectory of a bullet fired from a firearm based on forensic evidence in a particular case.[145]

Gunpowder burn patterns on clothing or bare skin can be used by a qualified expert in some cases to determine whether a gun was fired at a close range or from a distance. The burn pattern can also determine whether a wound was an entry or an exit wound.[146] With respect to powder burns, a medical examiner often plays a collateral role along with the ballistics expert in estimating how far from an object or a person a gun was fired[147] or who fired the gun.[148] In a Tennessee murder prosecution, the court permitted the medical examiner to testify that an examination of the gunshot entrance wound in the

---

[138]   *Id.*

[139]   Sanchez v. State, 2005 Tex. App. LEXIS 5084 n.2 (2005).

[140]   Hinton v. State, 2006 Ala. Crim. App. LEXIS 72 (2006).

[141]   United States v. Hicks, 389 F.3d 514, 523, 2004 U.S. App. LEXIS 22688 (5th Cir. 2004).

[142]   United States v. Green, 405 F. Supp. 2d 104, 118, 2005 U.S. Dist. LEXIS 34273 n.26 (D. Mass. 2005).

[143]   Ferrell v. Commonwealth, 177 Va. 861, 14 S.E.2d 293 (1941); *see also* Holland v. State, 268 So. 2d 883 (Ala. Ct. App. 1972).

[144]   *See* Maine v. Cookson, 2002 Me. Super. LEXIS 256 (2002) for discussion of the merits and techniques of ballistics.

[145]   Ronquillo v. Washington, 2001 Wash. App. LEXIS 2615 (2001).

[146]   State v. Austin, 2005 Tenn. Crim. App. LEXIS 815 (2005).

[147]   Tennessee v. Croft, 2002 Tenn. Crim. App. LEXIS 1005 (2002).

[148]   State v. Georgekopoulos, 2005 Ohio 5106, 2005 Ohio App. LEXIS 4624 (2005).

victim's forehead revealed hardly any evidence of gunpowder burns. To the expert medical examiner, the absence of burn patterns indicated that the barrel of the gun was 18 to 21 inches from the victim's skin.[149]

In order for an expert to give opinion testimony concerning ballistics test results, the opinion must be based upon facts within the knowledge of the expert, or the expert may give an opinion based upon a hypothetical question that is itself based on facts already in evidence. This does not necessarily mean that real evidence itself must be admitted. For example, in the case of *Hinton v. State*, test bullets fired by the state's ballistics expert were compared with the bullets recovered from the crime scene. Even though the test bullets were not admitted into evidence, the reviewing court found that the decision of the lower court was not error because the experts used the test bullets only in analyzing the pieces of evidence that they were asked to examine.[150]

§ 15.9 Speed Detection Readings

The principle of Radio Detection and Ranging (RADAR) applies exact laws of science and nature in the measurement of distance and speed. The radar speed-detecting devices commonly used in traffic control operate on what is known as the Doppler effect and utilize a continuous beam of microwaves emitted at a fixed frequency. The Doppler effect can be experienced by noticing the sound of a train horn when it is approaching and listening for the sound change as the train and its horn pass the observer. The frequency shift in the sound of the horn is an example of the Doppler effect. The operation depends upon the physical law that when such waves are intercepted by a moving object, the frequency changes in such a ratio to the speed of the intercepted object that, by measuring the change of the frequency, the speed may be determined.[151] The scientific principle is so universally accepted that courts routinely take judicial notice of the reliability of the principles upon which radar is based.[152] Where difficulty in enforcing speed laws with radar units arises, defendants normally attack the operational techniques of the officers using the equipment or the calibration and maintenance of the machines, because the principles are not easily refuted.

In operation, traffic enforcement police use a vehicle in which the radar speed detection system has been installed in such a way as to beam radio waves toward the motoring public. Modern radar devices are designed to be calibrated at set intervals of time to assure that the units are operating properly. When a moving vehicle enters the radar unit's broadcast radio beam, the returned radio wave has a frequency shift that registers with the radar unit,

---

[149] Rogers v. State, 2004 Tenn. App. LEXIS 10735 (2004).
[150] *See* Hinton v. State, 2006 Ala. Crim. App. LEXIS 72 (2006).
[151] Kopper, *The Scientific Reliability of Radar Speedmeters*, 33 N.C.L. REV. 343 (1955).
[152] Cleveland Heights v. Katz, 2001 Ohio App.LEXIS 5394 (2001). *See* case in Part II.

where the speed of the vehicle is instantly computed. The office may initiate a stop or radio to another officer to make the traffic stop.

For many years, the public, especially those who have been ticketed, have been aware of the widespread use of radio, microwaves, and other electronic devices in detecting the speed of motor vehicles and other moving objects. While the intricacies of such devices are not fully understood by all drivers, their general accuracy and effectiveness had few scientific or legal challenges once courts in the several states accepted the basic scientific principles. Once the principles of radar as applied to speed detection gained general legal acceptance, courts then took judicial notice of the scientific principles and did not require expert testimony on the principles before admitting evidence produced by radar units. The logic was that radar produced speed readings that were accepted in evidence just as courts have accepted photographs, X-rays, speedometer readings, and the like without requiring expert testimony as to the scientific principles underlying them. To establish the foundation for admission of radar unit produced speed evidence, the state must prove that the actual unit used by the officer operated properly at the time the officer used the unit to obtain the speed of the motorist.[153]

In laying a proper foundation for admission of radar-produced evidence, the officer must explain his or her training, the calibration of the machine, and that it was used properly during the event being litigated. In one Nebraska case, the officer explained that he had used the same type of radar unit since becoming a trooper, he was certified to use the particular type of radar, and his training certificate was up to date.[154] The officer testified to the use of tuning forks to assure proper operation of the radar unit and that the radar unit itself had a current certificate of calibration. At the start of each shift, the officer presses a switch on the unit to conduct a self-test and the unit runs a self-test every 10 minutes while in operation. The unit indicated that it was functioning properly by a four-count beep. He also noted that a technician checks the accuracy of the tuning forks once a year and that the radar units are checked for accuracy by the technician on a yearly basis. The reviewing court held that the prosecution had established a sufficient foundation for admitting the evidence of speed produced by the Stalker Dual SL radar unit.

In an Ohio case,[155] a defendant mounted a fairly broad-based attack on the use of radar in an effort to reverse a conviction for speeding. A police officer, working traffic, had been alerted to the possibility that the defendant was speeding so he locked his radar unit on the defendant's vehicle to get a reading. When the unit indicated that the subject vehicle was exceeding the limit, the officer initiated a stop and issued a ticket. Following a trial, the court found the defendant guilty.

At the trial, the officer testified that he had received training, including eight hours of training at the police academy and 40 hours of supervised road

[153] Putman v. State, 270 Ga. App. 45, 46, 606 S.E.2d 50, 51, 2004 Ga. App. LEXIS 1337 (2004).
[154] State v. Huff, 2004 Neb. App. LEXIS 117 (2004).
[155] Cleveland Heights v. Katz, 2002 Ohio 4241, 2001 Ohio App. LEXIS 5394 (2001).

training, regarding operation of the particular model radar unit he was using. The office testified that his main career path as a police officer for 12 years had been operating radar equipment.

Concerning testing and calibration, the officer testified that prior to use, he performed a light-on test and both an internal and external calibration test sequence. The officer explained that the light-on test checked all the lights on the system and the internal calibration involved turning another button to pre-select a speed of 32 miles per hour. Then the tuning forks were activated; one was supposed to and did cause a readout of 35 miles per hour and the other one produced 65 miles per hour. These tests indicated that the unit was operating properly.

In putting the prosecution to its proof, the defense forced the prosecution to further justify the reliability of the equipment by having a communication and radar technician from the city to testify about the radar units. His job was to test the calibration of the radar units used by the police officers, including the unit used by the officer who cited the defendant. The technician testified concerning his training and education on the testing and calibrating of radar devices from the radar system manufacturer. The technician testified about how he used the manufacturer's testing equipment to test the radar units three times per year and that his testing equipment is shipped to the manufacturer for testing once per year. When the test equipment is returned, it carries a certificate attesting to accuracy.

The defendant argued that the testing equipment calibration certificate was not properly authenticated and should not have been admissible. The defense contended that without the certificates or any testimony by a representative of the manufacturer that the testing equipment had been properly calibrated, there was no way of knowing whether the equipment used by city technician to test the radar device used by the police officer had been properly calibrated. Because that calibration was not proven, there no way to know whether the actual radar device used by the police officer was accurate and operating properly. The speeding driver argued that the police officer's testimony regarding the defendant's speed, as determined by the radar device, was not admissible for consideration by the court.

On appeal, the defendant contended that the court should not have taken judicial notice of the principle of radar, but the appellate court rejected that contention as having been waived by not raising it at the trial on the merits. The defendant argued that the officer should have performed more testing because all the testing revealed with respect to the light was that the lights worked and that tuning forks could be emitting a different frequency if they had become bent or dropped. Further, the city failed to show that the test equipment worked properly and that its associated tuning forks were in good order.

The appellate court rejected the defendant's call for more extensive testing of the equipment and refused to speculate about any additional testing that could have been done. The appellate court referred to the decision of another court of appeals and noted that there are many different ways to prove the same thing and it would not require that a matter be proved in all possible ways before it found a fact to be established. In this case, the initial radar unit had recently been calibrated; it was further tested at the city shop by testing equipment that was regularly checked and calibrated by the manufacturer regularly during a recheck. Despite putting forth every possible avenue to attack the radar-based speeding conviction, the court upheld the defendant's speeding conviction. The officer performed properly and the equipment was properly maintained and calibrated, leaving no legal stone to throw at the conviction.

While the prosecution must establish that radar units were operating properly, the requirement of authentication is waived when the opponent fails to object on authentication grounds.[156] For example, the magistrate properly disallowed the use of radar evidence in a prosecution for speeding on federal property when the government did not provide certificates of accuracy for either the speedometer or the tuning forks that were used to calibrate the radar device, as was required under the Virginia statute governing the use of radar.[157]

While the courts have generally taken judicial notice of the scientific reliability of radar speed detection devices, an Ohio reviewing court warned that judicial notice of the accuracy of a specific model of a radar device cannot automatically be extended to warrant judicial notice of the accuracy of another model of a radar device.[158] That reviewing court found that the trial court erred in taking judicial notice of the construction, operation, and accuracy of the S-80 moving radar unit without the benefit of expert testimony before the trial court as to that specific model of moving radar. However, if a defendant fails to make a trial objection to a court's decision to take judicial notice of the reliability of a particular type of radar gun, the objection cannot be first raised on appeal.[159]

Although radar speed detection remains one of law enforcement's tools for regulating the speed of motorists, laser detection has become a strong companion tool for police officers. Laser detection of speed poses different challenges from the use of radar, and the theoretical accuracy may make this system a superior law enforcement tool. Before any new scientific tool may be used, the proponent must prove that it accurately does what it says it will do. In the case of laser detection, the courts initially had to be convinced by expert testimony that the principles were scientifically sound and that the device that purported to apply the science did so regularly and routinely.

To facilitate police use of laser equipment, some states have passed statutes that permit police use and court admissibility of laser-generated information concerning speed.[160] Georgia's legislature passed a statute that operates like a rule of evidence and, subject to some conditions, permits evidence of laser-detected speed to be admitted in court. The law provides:

---

[156] State v. Roberts, 867 P.2d 697 (Wash. 1994).

[157] United States v. Wornom, 754 F. Supp. 517 (W.D. Va. 1991).

[158] Village of Moreland Hills v. Gazdak, 49 Ohio App. 3d 22, 550 N.E.2d 203 (1988).

[159] State v. Brown, 2002 Ohio 6463, 2002 Ohio App. LEXIS 6294 (2002).

[160] Odum v. Georgia, 255 Ga. App. 70, 564 S.E.2d 490, 2002 Ga. App. LEXIS 478 (2002). The trial court admitted laser-generated evidence of speed upon proof that the officer and officer's use of the device met state standards.

§ 40-14-17. Laser devices; reliability and admissibility of evidence

Evidence of speed based on a speed detection device using the speed timing principle of laser which is of a model that has been approved by the Department of Public Safety shall be considered scientifically acceptable and reliable as a speed detection device and shall be admissible for all purposes in any court, judicial, or administrative proceedings in this state. A certified copy of the Department of Public Safety list of approved models of such laser devices shall be self-authenticating and shall be admissible for all purposes in any court, judicial, or administrative proceedings in this state.[161]

When a law enforcement officer operates the approved laser speed detection unit according to the manufacturer's instructions and uses a Georgia-approved laser speed detection device that has been properly calibrated according to the manufacturer's specifications, the evidence should be admissible. Similar procedures permit admissibility of the evidence in other jurisdictions. When a Georgia prosecutor failed to introduce the required list of approved laser speed detection models, a proper foundation for laser-generated speed evidence was lacking and the result of the laser unit was not admissible in evidence.[162]

In one speeding case that was contested because the evidence had been obtained by the use of a laser device, the prosecution introduced evidence of the defendant's speed from a laser device listed as certified by the Georgia Department of Public Safety. The officer testified that he had been trained on the Kustom ProLaser II, a model that was properly listed with the public safety department. He also noted that he had calibrated and checked the laser detector for accuracy before he used it. Under the circumstances, the evidence carried with it a presumption that an accurate detection of speed had been recorded and the evidence produced was considered to be scientifically acceptable and reliable for court use. The reviewing court upheld the defendant's speeding conviction based on the laser evidence.[163]

The Intermediate Court of Appeals of Hawai'i recently upheld the use of laser speed detection where the prosecution did not produce any expert witnesses to testify concerning how the laser speed detection system operates.[164] The defendant appealed her speeding conviction, contending that the trial court erred in admitting evidence of her speed obtained by a laser unit when the prosecution offered no expert testimony relative to the principles behind laser speed detection. The reviewing court noted that expert testimony may be required when a scientific technique is new and creates an issue of first impression for a court. The court observed that once a scientific principle or process has been fully vetted and established, expert testimony is no longer necessary because a court may take judicial notice of the validity of the prin-

---

[161]   GA. CODE ANN. § 40-14-17 (2006).

[162]   In the Interest of J. D. S., a child, 273 Ga. App. 576, 615 S.E.2d 627, 2005 Ga. App. LEXIS 579 (2005).

[163]   Van Nort v. Georgia, 250 Ga. App. 7, 550 S.E.2d 111, 2001 Ga. App. LEXIS 659 (2001).

[164]   State v. Stoa, 2006 Haw. App. LEXIS 397 (2006).

ciple. The defendant argued that no reviewing court "in Hawai'i has recognized widespread acceptance of the reliability or accuracy of laser technology as a means of measuring speed"[165] and that courts in other jurisdictions have held that using laser-based speed detection units had failed to reach sufficient scientific acceptance to be introduced in the absence of expert testimony. The Intermediate Court of Appeals of Hawai'i rejected the defendant's arguments that expert witnesses were required. The court noted that: (1) the science of laser speed detection is based on well-understood principles; (2) the accuracy and reliability of laser speed-detection devices for monitoring traffic speed have been approved in other jurisdictions (Maryland, Minnesota, and New Jersey as well as a municipal court in the state of Ohio); and (3) the laser device used in this case met all the requirements of the Hawai'i Supreme Court for accuracy. The officer in the case testified:

> that he performed the required functionality tests on the laser gun prior to beginning his patrol, and that the readings indicated that the device was functioning properly. He also testified that he possessed a valid certification for operating the laser gun and that he had twenty years' experience in performing traffic enforcement duties.[166]

The Intermediate Court noted that it joined other jurisdictions that have taken judicial notice of the scientific acceptance of the accuracy and reliability of the modern laser units for measuring the speed of motor vehicles.

The onboard computer of currently manufactured motor vehicles records the last few seconds of the vehicle's speed and stores the data. Recently manufactured motor vehicles often contain an onboard diagnostics computer system, OBD II, that captures various information about the performance of the individual motor vehicle, such as whether seat belts were fastened, when brakes were last applied, when the air bag deployed, and the speed of the motor vehicle. In General Motors cars since 1990, an SDM, or sensing diagnostic module, records, among other parameters, the:

> acceleration or deceleration and makes decisions every 10 milliseconds whether or not to deploy the passive restraint system in the vehicle. The system also stores vehicle data such as vehicle speed, engine RPM, throttle percentage and brake data, change in velocity or delta V and seat belt usage, all in one second increments for a period of five seconds.[167]

In a New York prosecution for speeding, hitting, and killing a pedestrian, a police officer downloaded the data from the car's onboard computer and SDM and obtained information about the last few seconds of the operation of defendant's car. The information included the fact that the car was going

---

[165] *Id.*
[166] *Id.*
[167] People v. Christmann, 3 Misc. 3d 309, 311, 776 N.Y.S.2d 437, 439, 2004 N.Y. Misc. LEXIS 45 (N.Y. 2004).

38 miles per hour. The officer, who was qualified as an accident reconstruction expert, used other data from the accident to determine and corroborate the defendant's speed. The appellate court found that no warrant was needed to capture the defendant's data and that, under the circumstances, the evidence of speeding was properly reliable and admissible against the defendant.[168]

Similarly, data from a General Motors event data recorder, the sensing and diagnostic module, recorded a defendant's Firebird speeding in a 30 m.p.h. zone.[169] The Florida trial court admitted the computer-generated speed evidence in a double manslaughter case involving the deaths of two 16-year-old girls whom the defendant killed while he was driving down a residential street at 114 miles per hour. An expert witness testified that the data from computer event data recorders are used by the auto industry to design automobiles, in crash testing analysis, and in the medical fields and in biomechanics. The prosecutor introduced evidence that insurance companies and accident crash investigators rely on this type of collected data because it is believed to be accurate and reliable. For these reasons, the Florida reviewing court upheld the admissibility of the data collected from the motor vehicle computer.

§ 15.10　Voice Identification

A scientific technique designed to identify persons by means of a voiceprint has presented evidentiary problems centering around reliability and scientific certainty. While 30 years ago voice spectrographic analysis seemed to have a promising future, admissibility in courts seems to be diminishing.[170] Voiceprints, also know as speech spectrograms, were first developed in the United States in the 1930s at the Bell Telephone laboratories. The speech spectrogram, broadly speaking, is a picture showing the distribution of speech energy over the audio frequency spectrum, plotted against time. According to those who favor the use of this technique, every person's voice is as unique and identifiable as a fingerprint.

In a Michigan State University Department of Information Service publication dated August 9, 1973, a Michigan State University audiology and speech scientist, Dr. Oscar Tosi, declared that in 39 cases, experts were authorized to testify in court for purposes of voice identification. In the paper, Dr. Tosi explained that, of 3,000 voice examinations made in cooperation with the Michigan State Police, 500 were positive identifications, 1,600 were probable identifications and positive eliminations, and 850 were no-decisions. In criticizing a California judge's ruling that rejected the voiceprint, Dr. Tosi pointed out that voice identification is effective, but only if strict guidelines are observed, including:

---

[168]　*Id.* at 316, 442.
[169]　Matos v. State, 899 So. 2d 403, 405-406, 2005 Fla. App. LEXIS 4359 (2005).
[170]　*See* Michelle McCarthy, *Admissibility and Weight of Voice Spectrographic Analysis Evidence*, A.L.R. 5TH 471 § 17 (2002).

1. The examination must include both aural and visual comparisons of the known voice with the unknown voice.

2. The examiner must be qualified, with at least two years of practical experience in an apprenticeship program.

3. In positively identifying the voice, the examiner cannot have the slightest hint of a doubt.

Although there are still arguments concerning the reliability and admissibility of the spectrogram to identify persons by showing similarities in spectrogram readings, more federal and state courts are moving away from admitting spectrographic voice analysis. Numerous questions about the validity of both the scientific theory and the ability to practice it within sufficiently accurate tolerances to be routinely admissible in court have arisen. Following the changes in scientific evidence admissibility in federal courts following *Daubert v. Merrell Dow Pharmaceuticals, Inc.*, 509 U.S. 579 (1993), many courts revisited scientific issues in general and such a reconsideration reached the voiceprint analysis testers.[171]

For example, in a case in which the convicted defendant contended that the trial court erred in refusing to hire a voice analysis expert for his drug sale and possession trial, a federal district court granted habeas corpus. According to the district court, the state should have paid for expert witnesses to evaluate the identity of a voice that the defendant stated was not his. The judge in the district court held a hearing at which a voice expert testified about the voice sample alleged to belong to the defendant. According to the voice expert, the procedures used in voice analysis and his own analysis of the government tapes indicated a good chance that the defendant could be eliminated as a possible speaker. The expert found that at least 80 percent of the comparable words in the samples were dissimilar aurally and spectrographically divergent. The defendant's voice expert testified that:

> there were published recommended procedures for conducting voice identification examinations, he also acknowledged several weaknesses in spectrographic analysis. Specifically, he testified that there was no set of objective criteria against which to check the accuracy of a particular expert's analysis and that voice identification analysis was largely subjective in that the examiner ultimately decides whether two spectrographs match one another.[172]

The court of appeals determined that there was no strong proof that if the defendant had been permitted to hire and use a voice expert that the outcome of his drug trial would have been any different. The court further noted that:

---

[171] *But see* Alaska v. Coon, 974 P.2d 386 (1999), in which the Supreme Court of Alaska is the only appellate court to approve the use of voice spectrographic analysis subsequent to the *Daubert* decision.

[172] United State v. Drones, 218 F.3d 496, 500, 2000 U.S. App. LEXIS 17765 (5th Cir. 2000), *cert. denied*, 531 U.S. 1151, 121 S. Ct. 1095, 148 L. Ed. 2d 968, 2001 U.S. LEXIS 1214 (2001).

In addition to the fact that the state of the law concerning expert voice identification was ambiguous, the expert testimony presented at the evidentiary hearing demonstrates that spectrographic analysis is—and was at the time of [defendant's] trial—of questionable scientific validity. Most notably, at the hearing, [the voice expert] testified that there is no proven theoretical basis for the basic underlying premise that one person's voice is truly unique and therefore identifiable. He further stated that this has resulted in a precipitous drop in the number of expert practitioners over the past few decades, from fifty to sixty practitioners in the 1970s to roughly a dozen experts at the time of [defendant's] trial. While [a different expert] testified that expert voice identification testimony has been used extensively in state and federal courts over the past thirty years, he also testified that he did not know if spectrographic evidence was widely accepted by the relevant scientific community. He also acknowledged that numerous factors—including a defendant's ability to disguise his own voice—could affect the reliability of expert analysis.[173]

The court concluded by noting that there remained sufficient uncertainty in the field and that there was no deficiency in the representation of the defendant by his attorney due to failure to pursue voice identification analysis.

A different court in 2003 refused to admit spectrographic voice analysis in a case in which a defendant disputed that his voice had been recorded while he made inculpatory statements. The proffered expert had excellent credentials within the field of voice identification analysis, but he could not isolate his error rate in identifying voices and did not introduce any supporting information to otherwise indicate error rates of the technique in general. The appellate court upheld the exclusion of voice identification evidence with the following statement and included citations:

The inconsistency in error rates clearly illustrates the uncertainty of this method, and a proper foundation has not been established pursuant to the factors listed within *Daubert*, 509 U.S. at 593-594. Moreover, other courts considering the uncertainty of the law regarding the reliability and admissibility of expert voice identification evidence have also concluded that there are problems concerning the reliability and scientific validity of the method.[174]

A federal district court in a 2003 pretrial memorandum refused to admit voice spectrographic analysis by an expert witness in a trial in which the defendant disputed the prosecution's assertion that his voice had been recorded on an audiotape.[175] The prosecutor's position was that the aural spectrographic method for voice identification and the expert's application of that

---

173 *Id.*
174 Louisiana v. Morrison, 2003 La. App. LEXIS 2479 (2003).
175 United States v. Angleton, 269 F. Supp. 2d 892, 2003 U.S. Dist. LEXIS 17046 (S.D. Tex. 2003).

method failed to meet the requirements of the federal evidentiary rules and the *Daubert* standards of admissibility. The expert's qualifications were impeccable in that he held two degrees in forensic science, had been trained in voice identification, had worked for the Secret Service in voice identification, and had trained with a voice identification expert with the Michigan State Police. The expert testified that he had evaluated the tape alleged to contain the defendant's voice and that he believed that the defendant's voice was not the one on the tape. In opposition, the prosecution presented and expert who had been working in speech recognition since 1977 including with the Los Angeles police. The district court noted, "[s]ince *Daubert*, no federal appellate court has approved the admission of voice spectrographic expert testimony into evidence."[176] The judge noted that it was not clear whether voice spectrographic analysis ever gained acceptance in the relevant scientific community and that there were doubts concerning the validity of the method. After the court reviewed error rates of the voice technology, peer review issues, and the fact that the concept had never gained general scientific acceptance, it refused to permit the defendant's spectrographic voice analyst testify on behalf of the defendant.

More recently, spectrographic analysis that had been admitted in a criminal trial in 1973 resulted in a new trial being ordered based on the withholding of evidence by the FBI.[177] Experts working for the FBI attempted to apply spectrographic voice analysis to an audiotape of a ransom message and had concluded that the Bureau could not state with any certainty that the voice on the ransom note belonged to the defendant. This important exculpatory evidence was kept from the defendant, despite his requests for any exculpatory evidence from the prosecution. Despite the FBI's lack of confidence in the voice identification, the prosecution had an expert from the Michigan State Police who testified that he believed that, after using spectrographic voice analysis on the audiotape, the voice belonged to the defendant. The reviewing court ordered a new trial for a kidnapping and murder case that had been originally tried in 1973.

Whatever the original promise that machine-assisted voice identification may have once held, the technique has fallen into disuse and presently plays virtually no role in identification of unknown voices in criminal cases.[178] In a federal drug prosecution for conspiracy to distribute illegal recreational pharmaceuticals, the Court of Appeals for the Fourth Circuit sustained a trial judge's refusal to admit expert testimony of a scientist in the field of spectrographic voice analysis. The appellate court determined that evidence concerning voice recognition had properly been excluded because the evidence lacked probative value and failed to make any fact that was important to the case either more or less likely to be proved.[179]

---

[176] *Id.*

[177] Commonwealth v. Lykus, 20 Mass. L. Rep. 598, 2005 Mass. Super. LEXIS 686 (Mass. 2005).

[178] *See* State v. Louisiana, 867 So. 2d 740, 2003 La. App. LEXIS 2479 (2003), in which a trial court's refusal to permit spectrographic voice analysis evidence due to lack of proof of reliability, among other reasons.

[179] United States v. Ricketts, 141 Fed. Appx. 93, 2005 U.S. App. LEXIS 14500 (4th Cir. 2005).

A low technology method of permitted voice identification involves a voice identification lineup conducted in much the same way as a traditional in-person lineup.[180] The procedure, as one court noted, has some differences from the traditional identification process:

> In determining the proper parameters in which to conduct a non-suggestive voice line-up, we believe it is important to distinguish between voice and traditional line-ups. Obviously, not all of the participants in a voice line-up can be evaluated at the same time; thus, the victim must listen to participant's statements individually. In doing so, it is impermissible for the authorities to unnecessarily focus attention upon the Defendant. One method of focusing such attention upon the Defendant would involve manipulating the characteristics of the participants' voices so that only the Defendant's voice would fit the description given by the victim. Here, the record contains no evidence of dissimilarity between the participants' voices.[181]

§ 15.11 Neutron Activation Analysis

Neutron activation analysis is a process by which the chemical composition of materials can be determined, but it has been eclipsed by some newer technologies. The admission of the results of this process was approved in a federal case that involved sending a package bomb through the mail.[182] In this case, the court approved the explanation of the process, which appeared in *American Jurisprudence's* "Proof of Facts," stating:

But we feel that the following description is the most understandable and succinct explanation which we have found available.

American Jurisprudence's "Proof of Facts" describes the process thus:

> One of the newest and most promising techniques of forensic science is neutron activation analysis. The ability of this nuclear method to detect traces of elements in minute samples enables it to solve many problems of identification that have heretofore been considered hopeless. . . . The process is essentially one whereby the material to be analyzed is first made radioactive—i.e., it is "charged" so that it will give off or emit radiation in the form of gamma rays. This radioactive sample is then exposed to a scintillation crystal; and every time a gamma ray from the radioactive material interacts with the crystal, it emits a flash of light, which is converted into an electrical pulse whose voltage is proportional to the energy of the gamma rays. An electronic device called a multi-channel differential analyzer then sorts the electrical impulses into different energy groups and adds up the pulses in each group. The

---

[180] *See* People v. Gray, 2006 Mich. App. LEXIS (2006).
[181] Louisiana v. Pickney, 714 So. 2d 854, 1998 La. App. LEXIS 1366 (1998).
[182] United States v. Stifel, 433 F.2d 431 (6th Cir. 1970).

result is a graph shown on an oscilloscope screen. The graph contains information related to the kind and amount of elements in the radioactive sample and can be transcribed immediately or stored on magnetic tape or punched paper tapes for future reference.

Virtually no sample of material is too small to be analyzed by activation analysis. A single hair, a shred of marijuana, or a fleck of automobile paint no longer than the period at the end of this sentence can be analyzed and correctly identified. Furthermore, activation analysis' high sensitivity allows quantitative measurement of elements in the parts per million and parts per billion range. For instance, if one thimbleful of arsenic poison were diluted in ten tankcars of water, the exact amount of arsenic present could be determined by activation analysis. In most cases, the analysis is also nondestructive, so that material evidence may be preserved for presentation in court or saved for analysis by another method.

A Florida case illustrates the limits of admissibility of neutron activation testing with respect to relevance. In a case in which a defendant had been charged with firing a weapon in the direction of two complaining witnesses, the state took swabs from the defendant's hand for analysis. Near the trial date, the results were not back from the state lab because the lab had not conducted the tests. The tests were delivered just as the trial ended so that little advance notice of admission of the tests to the defendant was possible. In addition, the tests were forensically inconclusive because only three particles of gunpowder residue were swabbed from the defendant and four particles were generally necessary to have a positive result for firing a firearm. The judge allowed the testimony even though an argument could have been made that the prejudicial value outweighed the probative value because the jury still might conclude, based on the science, that the defendant had fired a gun that day.[183]

Some crime scenes may not prove conducive to either neutron activation analysis or to a related test, atomic-absorption analysis. In a Tennessee case, numerous individuals were armed during a robbery that was drug-related and a significant number of gunshots were exchanged within a home, resulting in a homicide. From the police investigation, the proof indicated that the defendant had a gun and fired several shots at unarmed occupants and later changed clothes. No guns were found at the crime scene. A former police officer testified for the defense and suggested that neutron activation analysis or atomic-absorption testing should have been done to establish who fired weapons. A civilian expert testified for the state that neither test would be conclusive to isolate the shooter, even if done immediately, because the firing of so many weapons in a small space would have placed residue on everyone. As the expert offered his expertise on neutron activation analysis:

---

[183]   Southerland v. Florida, 816 So. 2d 154, 2002 Fla. App. LEXIS 7240 (2002).

It was his opinion that testing for gunshot residue would not have been helpful in this case. He explained that gunshot residue materials can be picked up from a variety of very common sources, such as car batteries. Dr. Smith stated that both false negatives and false positives are common with gunshot residue tests because the residue is easily transferred and removed. He added that his laboratory never performed gunshot residue testing when the victim has undergone significant medical intervention before death.[184]

The limits of the testing process indicate that it will not solve all gun-firing crime issues, but in a variety of contexts, neutron activation analysis testing will be able to indicate who has fired a weapon if the testing is conducted promptly.

Although the neutron activation analysis does not conclusively establish whether the subject has recently fired a gun, because the component chemicals could have had a different origin than firing a firearm or handling a gun, the test results are generally admissible in evidence despite this inherent inconclusiveness. The evidence is admissible as relevant because it shows a probability that the suspect did or did not fire a gun; its probative value is for the jury to determine.

A newer technology than neutron activation analysis that offers some promise is called inductively coupled plasma-optical emission spectroscopy (ICP).[185] The process is able to distinguish discrete components of different products, such as lead. The goal of distinguishing different components of lead would, in theory, allow scientists to compare lead from one batch of lead bullets to see if it matched other bullets possessed by a defendant. Comparative bullet lead analysis would permit a recovered bullet's chemical composition to be compared with remaining bullets contained in a defendant's remaining cartridges. Ultimately, the FBI abandoned the process because the science did not allow the reliable chemical bullet matching that had originally been anticipated.[186] In a case in which comparative bullet lead analysis had been admitted against a defendant to help prove that the bullets recovered from the homicide matched the lead in other bullets remaining in unfired cartridges, the reviewing court reversed. Using inductively coupled plasma-optical emission spectroscopy as a successor to neutron activation analysis might reveal the constituents of a lead bullet, but that information may still remain irrelevant. To make valid comparisons of lead in different bullets came from a common source would require that the common source be a completely homogenous source of lead. The best testimony indicated that within each run of lead used to make bullets, significant differences exist in the constituent trace metals.

---

[184]   State v. Mills, 2002 Tenn. Crim. App. LEXIS 405 (2002).

[185]   "In 1993, the technique of FBI choice was changed to inductively coupled plasma, atomic emission spectroscopy (ICP)." See State v. Behn, 375 N.J. Super. 409, 426, 868 A.2d 329, 341, 2005 N.J. Super. LEXIS 73 (N.J. 2005).

[186]   See Clemmons v. State, 392 Md. 339, 896 A.2d 1059, 2006 Md. LEXIS 192 n.8 (Md. 2006). See also Commonwealth v. Daye, 19 Mass. L. Rep. 674, 2005 Mass. Super. LEXIS 368 (Mass. 2005).

The reviewing court held that the use of any of the different methods of conducting comparative bullet lead analysis should not have been admitted because, under the *Frye* test for admission of scientific evidence, several fundamental assumptions were not generally accepted by the relevant scientific community.[187]

§ 15.12 Deoxyribonucleic Acid (DNA) Tests

Researchers have made a significant breakthrough in using the deoxyribonucleic acid (DNA) code present in human cells, blood, and other body fluids to link evidence, such as bloodstains or semen specimens, to a specific individual, while excluding all others. According to an article that appeared in a National Institute of Justice publication dated October 1987, DNA patterns are so different between people who are not identical twins so as to provide virtually definite identification. In recent years, smaller and smaller samples of fluids containing DNA have been required because the science has advanced in the area of amplification of samples to usable levels.

A California case demonstrates the significant advances that have occurred in the years since the DNA testing revolution changed criminal investigations forever. In this case, a woman was raped by someone she knew. The rapist injured the woman sufficiently that her DNA and the attacker's DNA became mixed together so that the rape testing kit contained multisource DNA. Blood samples were taken from the victim and from the attacker and, along with DNA samples collected from a sexual assault kit, were sent to a DNA laboratory.

As the court explained the theory of DNA testing:

> Deoxyribonucleic acid is material present in each cell of the human body that determines an individual's characteristics. Virtually all deoxyribonucleic acid is the same from one human to another. However, a small percentage of the deoxyribonucleic acid is different in each individual. Cellmark Diagnostics tests deoxyribonucleic acid by comparing an unknown sample from a crime scene to that from known individuals. The tests serve to either include or exclude an individual as a possible source of the biological sample. As will be explained in more detail below, the polymerase chain reaction is a technique that has been used in the field of molecular biology since the 1980s to copy small specific regions of deoxyribonucleic acid. The deoxyribonucleic acid is isolated into a form that can be copied. Then copies of that deoxyribonucleic acid sequence are copied. Finally, the actual deoxyribonucleic acid types are examined and compared to other samples to determine whether they could be included or excluded as a donor source for the sample.[188]

---

[187] *Id.*

[188] California v Smith, 107 Cal. App. 4th 646, 131 Cal. Rptr. 2d 230, 2003 Cal. App. LEXIS 475 (2003), *petition for review denied*, 2003 Cal. LEXIS 3547 (2003). For additional enlightenment, this case has a scientifically interesting account of DNA information contained within the opinion.

The evidence demonstrated that the lab followed extremely strict protocols to avoid contamination of samples or inaccurate results. The results demonstrated that the nonsperm DNA fraction had a primary source that was female and was consistent with the profile from the victim, while the sample of DNA taken from the sperm faction indicated the source was from a male. In addition, the interpretation of the results demonstrated that the defendant was the source of the male fraction taken from the victim using the sexual assault kit.

In a hearing consolidated from several California cases with similar issues, a judge made a determination that the science has progressed to the point that DNA at a crime scene can properly be compared with samples donated by suspects and victims to see if a match can be declared and such results would be admissible. The evidence discussed included STR (short tandem repeat) testing and PCR (polymerase chain reaction) testing and found that both theories had scientific validity for the purposes in question. The defendant wanted a hearing to determine whether mixed samples could be analyzed to determine the individual sources. The court analyzed the testimony of the various experts to determine whether the mixed sample could be analyzed and whether the results would meet the necessary reliability standards. The court ruled that the deoxyribonucleic acid evidence, based on analysis of mixed samples, was properly found to be generally accepted in the scientific community and could be admitted against the defendant in the rape case.[189]

With the general admissibility of DNA evidence permitted under the *Daubert* or the *Frye* standards for admission of scientific evidence, the battle for prosecutors and for the defense bar moved from challenging the concept to challenging the methodology and admissibility of the newest advances in DNA testing. For example, in a quadruple murder case involving four rapes and strangulations, the defendant mounted an attack on the admissibility of the DNA evidence that the defense expected would be offered by the prosecution.[190] He challenged the testing laboratory's methodology in dealing with mixed DNA samples and alleged that the lab violated generally accepted protocols. The defendant alleged that the laboratory failed to perform its tests properly and to report them accurately. In addition, the defendant contended that the lab failed to adhere to the conservative protocols of the DNA test kit manufacturer. In the math area of DNA testing, he contended that the use of the product rule to make frequency calculations for mixed samples was faulty. Finally, the defendant contended that the database used by the lab proved inadequate for frequency calculations. The Supreme Judicial Court of Massachusetts serially addressed each of the defendant's contentions and upheld the trial court's rejection of all of his arguments. The posture of this type of case demonstrates that defendants are contesting the application of the science of DNA testing rather than arguing about the basic validity of the concept that each person (except identical twins) carries a unique DNA profile.

---

[189]   *Id.*

[190]   Commonwealth v. Gaynor, 443 Mass. 245, 263, 820 N.E.2d 233, 249, 2005 Mass. LEXIS 7 (Mass. 2005). *See* case in Part II.

As courts approved the admission of DNA results and approved different types of testing procedures, the prosecution and defense bars have embraced the use of DNA evidence where appropriate. The defense bar quickly adopted the concept of DNA testing for the purpose of establishing actual innocence in older death penalty cases in which a convicted defendant alleged that the wrong person had been convicted. DNA testing has resulted in some people being removed from death row by excluding them as the source of DNA at homicide scenes. In a Tennessee case, a jury convicted a defendant of the murder of another man's wife.[191] At the trial, an FBI serologist testified that a secretor belonging to the ABO blood group was the one who deposited the semen on the victim's nightgown and on her underwear. The evidence showed that the defendant was a member of that blood grouping. Although the government neither alleged nor proved any sexual offense, the prosecution argued that implication during the closing argument. The defendant had blood on his jeans that did not belong to him and that was consistent with the blood type of the deceased victim. With the advent of DNA testing and with the newer refinements to the testing process, DNA evidence demonstrated that the semen came from the deceased woman's husband and that the defendant could not have been the depositor. Evidence existed that the deceased wife's husband had made a drunken confession to her murder. Armed with the new DNA results, a federal district court held a hearing but ruled that all claims had been procedurally defaulted and that the defendant had failed to demonstrate actual innocence. The Court of Appeals for the Sixth Circuit eventually affirmed the federal district court's decision. The Supreme Court of the United States reversed the defendant's conviction and remanded the case on the strength of the DNA testing that did not exist at the time of the original trial.[192]

As the science of DNA testing has become more accepted and admissible, other legal challenges involve proper collection, storing, and preventing contamination of samples[193] rather than arguing against the science. Proper handling of deoxyribonucleic acid (DNA) samples in conformity with established procedures is essential before DNA evidence can be considered reliable.[194]

A collateral issue concerning the collection and use of DNA data arises when former convicts, probationers, and parolees are ordered to submit a DNA sample to be added to state and local DNA databanks or the federal databank, the Combined DNA Index System of the Federal Bureau of Investigation (CODIS). Most jurisdictions require persons convicted of felonies or sexual offenses to submit a DNA sample for inclusion in national and state databanks.

In a case from the District of Columbia, government agents ordered that a probationer give a DNA sample for inclusion in the CODIS databank.[195] The authority for the order came from a federal statute stating that officials "shall

[191] *See* House v. Bell, ___ U.S. ___, 2006 U.S. LEXIS 4675 (2006).
[192] *Id.*
[193] United States v. Morrow, 374 F. Supp. 42, 46 (D.D.C. 2005).
[194] Commonwealth v. Blasioli, 685 A.2d 151 (Pa. 1996).
[195] Johnson v. Quander, 370 U.S. App. D.C. 167, 440 F.3d 489, 499, 2006 U.S. App. LEXIS 6601 (D.C. Cir. 2006). *Accord*, United States v. Sczubelek, 402 F.3d 175, 2005 U.S. App. LEXIS 4568 (3d Cir. 2006).

collect a DNA sample from each individual under the supervision of the Agency who is on supervised release, parole, or probation who is, or has been, convicted of a qualifying District of Columbia offense . . ." The agents had neither warrant nor probable cause to believe that the probationer had committed any new crimes. Under the DNA Analysis Backlog Elimination Act of 2000, persons with former convictions were expected to contribute to the growing database of DNA profiles. When his probation was about to be revoked for failure to give a DNA sample, the former probationer sued in federal court and asked for a restraining order to prevent his DNA from being added to the databank. The probationer contended that the forced collection violated his rights to be free from unreasonable searches and seizures under the Fourth Amendment and that it was unconstitutional for the government to keep his sample and research it in the database at any time after his probationary period expired. The trial court found in favor of the government and the Court of Appeals for the District of Columbia agreed. The reviewing court concluded that the collection of DNA constituted a search under the Fourth Amendment but that such a search was not unreasonable because it was a well-settled concept that probationers have a reduced expectation of privacy and have to give consent to some searches as a condition of receiving probation. Additionally, the Court of Appeals held that retaining the DNA profile and searching it at will does not constitute a Fourth Amendment search because the process of matching one government record against another government record is not a search of the defendant. Because DNA profiles can be collected from probationers, it can also be collected from parolees because they are similarly situated for Fourth Amendment purposes.

§ 15.13 Other Examinations and Tests

As other techniques and procedures have met the requirements for admission by way of expert testimony, courts have recognized the new tests and have admitted evidence based on those tests. For example, in a New Jersey case, the trial court permitted an expert witness to testify that the bullets taken from the crime scene were tested using the Plasma Atomic Emission Spectroscopy testing process along with bullets from live cartridges possessed by the defendant and their lead composition was the same. The plasma atomic emission spectroscopy testing method determines what trace elements are contained in a lead sample and compares that result to another sample bullet. If they are of the same composition, the conclusion is that they came from the same original source. On a petition for habeas corpus, the federal district court held that the admission of the expert testimony did not violate any federal constitutional right.[196] The process of using plasma atomic emission spectroscopy probably analyzes the trace metals in lead properly but there has been some concern in

---

[196] *See* Noel v. Hendricks, 2006 U.S. Dist. LEXIS 41374 (D.N.J. 2006).

other jurisdictions and among some experts that the original sources of lead for bullets fails to have the consistency of composition that is required for this type of bullet matching to be valid.[197]

Another court, in discussing the reliability of procedures, noted that Fourier Transform Infrared Spectrophotometer (FTIR) analysis is a scientific procedure based upon scientific principles that are generally accepted as reliable within the relevant scientific community, as required for test results to be admissible in criminal proceedings.[198] The process at issue used advanced materials science analysis to compare safe cement linings that deposited its dust on a safecracker's tools, clothing, and other articles personal to the alleged safecracker. The expert testimony evidence tended to prove that cement dust samples taken from the crime scene, from the remains of the victims' safe, and from the defendant's tools, were all consistent with safe lining cement, which could have come from the victims' safe, was sufficiently reliable to be admissible in a burglary prosecution.

§ 15.14   Summary

Real evidence is often not admitted directly into court but is used for experiments and tests conducted out of court. General rules have been established regarding the admissibility of testimony concerning the results of experiments and tests, and the use of evidence such as charts and graphs resulting from experiments and tests. In recent years, the trend has been for the courts to allow and encourage the use of such evidence, and this has been held to be consistent with the rights of the accused.

As a general rule, examination of the body for evidence such as marks and bruises, and the taking of samples (such as saliva, urine, and blood) from the body do not violate the privilege against self-incrimination. Such evidence is admissible if proper standards concerning the testing of this type of evidence are met. Also, the common practice of determining blood-alcohol content by testing the suspect's blood, breath, or urine has been approved when law enforcement officials meet the conditions dictated by the Constitution, by the courts, and by legislative bodies.

Blood grouping test results provide useful information, but are increasingly being replaced by DNA testing, which is both more reliable and very precise. Blood-based evidence is generally used for purposes of identification when that element is at issue in criminal prosecutions involving rape, assault, homicide, and in civil and criminal paternity actions. For the results of blood-based testing to be admissible, it must be demonstrated that a qualified person conducted the test, that the qualified technician observed proper protocols

---

[197]   *See* Clemmons v. State, 392 Md. 339, 896 A.2d 1059, 2006 Md. LEXIS 192 n.8 (Md. 2006). *See also* State v. Behn, 375 N.J. Super. 409, 868 A.2d 329, 2005 N.J. Super. LEXIS 73 (N.J. 2005).

[198]   People v. Roraback, 666 N.Y.S.2d 397 (1997).

during the testing procedure, and that the testing methods revealed no discrepancies in the results.

Courts are divided concerning the admissibility of polygraph evidence with a strong bias in favor of exclusion. Three approaches have been taken by various federal and state courts: (1) the traditional approach of per se inadmissibility; (2) polygraph evidence is admissible only when both parties so stipulate; and (3) polygraph evidence is admissible even in the absence of stipulation when special circumstances exist.

The reasoning that has been applied in the use of the polygraph is similar to that of most courts in finding that so-called "truth serum" tests are not admissible for or against the defendant in a criminal case because of the lack of scientific certainty about the results. However, the courts take an entirely different view as to fingerprint comparisons. The results of fingerprint comparisons made out of court may be introduced to compare the fingerprints of the defendant with fingerprints left at the scene of the crime. This procedure has become so well recognized that the courts will take judicial notice of the fact that fingerprint identification is one of the most accurate methods of personal identification.

The science of forensic ballistics is also a well-recognized subject of expert testimony. The courts will generally allow such expert testimony to show, for example, that the bullet that entered the body was fired from a weapon belonging to the defendant in the case. Before such evidence is admissible, the introducing party must show that approved procedures were followed and that the person testifying is qualified as an expert in the field.

The use of speed detection devices using the principle of radar are universally approved, and testimony concerning the readings on such devices is generally accepted in evidence. However, test results are not admissible in court unless there is proof that the equipment was properly calibrated and the witness is qualified to testify concerning the meaning of such tests. Many jurisdictions have approved the use of laser-based speed detection, as long as police use approved laser units and follow proper protocols provided by the manufacturer.

Another identification technique is voice identification through the use of the spectrogram. Although the majority rule is that such evidence will be excluded if offered by either party, a few courts may permit admission where there is a strong showing of particular applicability in a particular case.

Neutron activation analysis provided strong evidence to detect trace compounds but has fallen into disuse in criminal cases in recent times. Evidence concerning the results of such analysis is generally admissible, but here, too, the use of the equipment and the qualifications of the user must comply with strict standards. In a proper case, courts will admit inductively coupled plasma-optical emission spectroscopy where evidence of trace metals or elements is relevant.

Recent research has resulted in the development of forensic DNA analysis as a scientific technique that reveals distinctive patterns in human genetic material in blood and other body fluids, hair, and tissue. Courts routinely admit the results of this "DNA fingerprint" test to prove identity and to exclude suspects because this science has general acceptance by the experts in the field. Generally, proof that the experts have properly applied the technology assures admission into evidence.

Because criminal justice personnel conduct many of the out-of-court examinations and tests, it is essential that such personnel be aware of the value of such evidence and be familiar with the requirements designed to protect the rights of those who are accused of crime.

Exclusion of Evidence on Constitutional Grounds

Evidence
Unconstitutionally
Obtained   16

Today we once again examine Wolf's *constitutional documentation of the right of privacy free from unreasonable state intrusions, and, after its dozen years on our books, are led by it to close the only courtroom door remaining open to evidence secured by official lawlessness in flagrant abuse of that basic right, reserved to all persons as a specific guarantee against that very same unlawful conduct. We hold that all evidence obtained by searches and seizures in violation of the Constitution is, by that same authority, inadmissible in a state court.*

Mapp v. Ohio, 367 U.S. 643, 81 S. Ct. 1684,
6 L. Ed. 2d 1081 (1961)

Chapter Outline

Key Terms and Concepts

delay in arraignment rule	impoundment
due process	plain view doctrine
eavesdropping	self-incrimination
exclusionary rule	wiretapping
free and voluntary rule	

§ 16.1 Introduction

In a democracy where the rule of law is of paramount importance, the government must follow the law so that fundamental fairness and predictability of behavior serve as the norm for both the government and its citizens. Fair dealing is a rough equivalent to due process, which everyone should be able to expect and all are entitled to receive from government. On the rare occasion when a local, state, or the federal government fails to follow the policy of due process and fairness, a remedy should be readily accessible for the constitutional violation. In the discussion of the rules of evidence in Chapter 2, the text indicated that some judicially created rules exclude evidence that has been obtained in violation of the rights protected by the Constitution. This is not because the evidence is not relevant or material; it is to remove any incentive for future improper governmental behavior so that the executive branch law enforcers observe the rule the next time the situation arises. In fact, in many instances, the evidence obtained in violation of the constitutional provisions as interpreted by the courts is highly relevant and material and would be admissible under the traditional rules of evidence. The courts have reasoned that even though the evidence is otherwise admissible and would help prove or disprove a fact at issue, illegally obtained evidence should not be admitted because authorizing the use of illegally obtained evidence would encourage violation of citizens' rights as enumerated in the Constitution and give a judicial stamp of approval for future law enforcement violations of the Constitution.

Although the exclusionary rules relating to the various types of evidence have been extended greatly in recent years, much doubt remains as to what evidence will be excluded and what will be admissible. Under recent United States Supreme Court decisions, evidence is primarily excluded when the seizure of evidence violates the rights protected by the Fourth, Fifth, or Sixth Amendments to the Constitution. The general rules concerning search and seizure, self-incrimination, right to counsel, and other constitutional provisions cannot be discussed comprehensively due to space limitations. However, rules relating to the admission or exclusion of the evidence obtained by conduct that infringes on these rights will be discussed briefly.[1]

§ 16.2   Development of the Exclusionary Rule

Comparatively speaking, the search and seizure exclusionary rule is of recent origin. This rule provides very succinctly that when evidence has been illegally obtained, or obtained in violation of the Constitution, it will be excluded from use in court.

First, it should be pointed out that this exclusionary rule is not universally applied. Today in England and in most other countries that follow Anglo-Saxon legal tradition evidence is admitted even if obtained illegally. The principle that evidence should not be excluded merely because the constable has blundered in obtaining evidence was followed in about one-half of the states as late as 1961. This rule, also known as the common law "English Rule," was justified by an English judge, who explained:[2]

> I think it would be a dangerous obstacle to the administration of justice if we were to hold that because evidence was obtained by illegal means, it could not be used against the party charged with an offense. It therefore seems to me that the interests of the state must excuse the seizure of documents, which seizure would otherwise be unlawful, if it appears in fact that such documents were evidence of a crime committed by anyone.

Although the exclusionary rule as it relates to searches in violation of the Constitution was mentioned as far back as 1886 by the United States Supreme Court, it was not until 1914 that the Supreme Court, in the case of *Weeks v. United States*,[3] made the exclusionary rule applicable in federal courts in this country. The Supreme Court held that, in a federal prosecution, the Fourth Amendment barred the use of evidence secured through an illegal search and seizure.

---

[1]   For a more comprehensive discussion of the constitutional limitations, *see* KANOVITZ & KANOVITZ, CONSTITUTIONAL LAW (10th ed. 2005) and KLOTTER, WALKER & HEMMERS, LEGAL GUIDE FOR POLICE (7th ed. 2005).

[2]   Elias v. Pasmore, 2 K.B. 65 (1934).

[3]   232 U.S. 383, 34 S. Ct. 341, 58 L. Ed. 652 (1914).

The reason for adopting the exclusionary rule is that the rule (according to the court) is the only way for the judiciary to ensure that police and prosecutors will not violate or encourage violation of the rights protected by the Constitution and its amendments. If courts allowed illegally seized evidence to be introduced for jury consideration, the courts could be considered tainted by the illegality that they would be condoning. The situation becomes more clear when one lawbreaker, the criminal, is prosecuted by evidence obtained by another lawbreaker, the police officer, who obtained evidence illegally. While the English courts argue that the remedy is action against the officer who violates these provisions, the courts in this country emphasize that only by excluding the evidence can these privileges be sufficiently protected. By removing illegally seized evidence from admissibility, the incentive for law enforcement agents to violate the law or constitution is substantially diminished. A civil action for damages against the offending officer by the injured party may be a possibility under state law or pursuant to a federal *Bivens* action, which may allow a civil suit against federal officers.[4]

"The ordinary remedy in a criminal case for violation of the Fourth Amendment is suppression of any evidence obtained by the illegal police conduct."[5] Exclusion of evidence serves as a judicially created sanction that indirectly enforces the Fourth Amendment by removing any reward for its violation.[6] The primary purpose of the exclusionary rule is to remove the incentive for police to disregard the provisions of the Fourth Amendment.[7] When the illegally seized evidence is excluded, the prosecutor may have no prosecutable case that remains, the degree of seriousness of the case may be reduced, or the case may have sufficient legal evidence remaining to enable a successful prosecution.

Although the exclusionary rule based on illegal searches and seizures has been applied in federal courts since 1914,[8] it was not until 1961 that the Supreme Court determined that the Fourth Amendment and the exclusionary rule were applicable against the states in search and seizure cases.[9] A reason for the extension of the exclusionary rule to the states has to do with the doctrine of selective incorporation of many of the rights contained in the Bill of Rights into the due process clause of the Fourteenth Amendment.

Partially on the basis of the Fourth Amendment and the exclusionary rule, but probably more as a result of legislation, wiretapping and eavesdropping evidence is often excluded if statutory requirements are not met. However, if the wire or telephone intercept meets the requirements of state and federal wiretap laws, evidence obtained by wiretapping and eavesdropping is admissible.[10]

---

[4]　Bivens v. Six Unknown Named Agents of Federal Bureau of Narcotics, 403 U.S. 388, 1971 U.S. LEXIS 23 (1971)

[5]　United States v. Olivares-Rangel, 2006 U.S. App. LEXIS 20595 (10th Cir. 2006).

[6]　State v. Klosterman, 114 Ohio App. 3d 327, 683 N.E.2d 100 (1996).

[7]　Hudson v. Michigan, ___ U.S. ___, 2006 U.S. LEXIS 4677 (2006).

[8]　Weeks v. United States, 232 U.S. 383, 1914 U.S. LEXIS 1368 (1914).

[9]　Mapp v. Ohio, 367 U.S. 643, 81 S. Ct. 1684, 6 L. Ed. 2d 1081 (1961).

[10]　*See* United States v. Moore, 452 F.3d. 382, 2006 U.S. App. LEXIS 14152 (5th Cir. 2006), for a case in which wiretapping in a federal prison did not require suppression of evidence seized since it complied with the Federal Wiretap Act.

The United States Supreme Court has determined that involuntary confessions and statements taken in violation of the *Miranda* warnings may not be admitted in court. Coerced confessions violate the concept of due process and the Fifth Amendment protections against self-incrimination and coerced statements call into question the reliability and truthfulness of a confession. Statements taken in violation of *Miranda* may be reliable but are excluded under public policy decisions made by the Supreme Court. More recently, the courts have applied exclusionary reasoning to exclude evidence obtained in violation of the right to counsel provisions of the Sixth Amendment to the Constitution.

Before leaving the general discussion of the exclusionary rule, it is important to emphasize that the rule applies not only to evidence obtained directly as a result of unlawful action by enforcement personnel, but also to "derivative evidence." Whenever an original search proved to be unlawful, but the results pointed toward other evidence that would only have been discovered because of the original illegality, that other evidence is also excluded[11] in order to ensure that the prosecution is not put in a better position that it would have been if no illegality had transpired.[12] However, if the prosecution can show that the evidence ultimately or inevitably would have been discovered by lawful means,[13] the exclusionary rule serves no deterrent purpose and does not apply.[14] The degree of application of these rules of exclusion is discussed in the following sections.

§ 16.3 Search and Seizure Exclusions

The Fourth Amendment to the Constitution provides:

> The right of the people to be secure in their persons, houses, papers, and effects, against unreasonable searches and seizures, shall not be violated, and no Warrants shall issue, but upon probable cause, supported by Oath or affirmation, and particularly describing the place to be searched, and the persons or things to be seized.[15]

The amendment that is now known as the Fourth Amendment was part of the first 10 amendments that were proposed as a means of inducing the necessary number of states to ratify the proposed Constitution of the United States. The first 10 amendments became known as the Bill of Rights and were designed to place limitations on the national government. At this point in history, the Fourth Amendment and the other amendments in the Bill of Rights did not apply to state officials, but were added to prohibit the officials of a strong central government from abridging the rights of the citizens of the various states.

---

[11] Wong Sun v. United States, 371 U.S. 471 (1963).

[12] State v. Seager, 571 N.W.2d 204 (Iowa 1997). *See also* United States v. Watson, 118 F.3d 1315 (9th Cir. 1997).

[13] *See* Murray v. United States, 487 U.S. 533 (1988) and Nix v. Williams, 467 U.S. 431 (1984).

[14] State v. Ballon, 703 So. 2d 130 (La. 1997).

[15] U.S. CONST. amend. IV.

Initially, in the case of *Weeks v. United States*,[16] the Supreme Court of the United States devised the exclusionary rule to help enforce the Fourth Amendment by excluding evidence from federal courts when federal officials had obtained evidence through illegal searches. In a later reconsideration of the coverage of the Fourth Amendment, the Supreme Court in *Mapp v. Ohio* (1961) extended the rule to cover state and local courts because the Court believed that the rule was needed to enforce the due process clause of the Fourteenth Amendment.[17] By making the exclusionary rule applicable to the states, the Court made it necessary for state prosecutors and judges to consider the decisions of the Supreme Court of the United States for minimum federal constitutional standards that must be met by state officials.

In the *Mapp* case, the Supreme Court indicated that the decision closed the last door to the use of illegally seized evidence. However, in 1984, the Supreme Court adopted the good faith exception to the exclusionary rule. In the case of *United States v. Leon*, police officers acting in good faith executed a search warrant instructing them to search residences for controlled substances.[18] Although it was later determined that the search warrant was invalid due to lack of probable cause, the evidence seized pursuant to the warrant could be admitted in court. The *Leon* Court made this comment:

> We conclude that the marginal or nonexistent benefits produced by suppressing evidence obtained in objectively reasonable reliance on a subsequently invalidated search warrant cannot justify the substantial costs of exclusion.

The Supreme Court acknowledged that the exclusionary rule had been modified, but included this warning:

> We do not suggest, however, that exclusion is always inappropriate in cases where an officer has obtained a warrant and abided by its terms. . . . Nevertheless, the officer's reliance on the magistrate's probable cause determination and on the technical sufficiency of the warrant he issues must be objectively reasonable . . . and it is clear that in some circumstances the officer will have no reasonable grounds for believing that the warrant was properly issued.

The original intent of the Fourth Amendment's exclusionary rule was to deter illegal police conduct. When the wrong did not come from the police but came from a judge, the police could not have been deterred by using a facially valid search warrant. When, under particular circumstances, there was no deterrent effect on the police, there is no rationale for applying the exclusionary rule.

In *Massachusetts v. Shepherd*, which was decided on the same day as *Leon*, the Supreme Court upheld a search for real evidence when the search

---

[16]   232 U.S. 383, 1914 U.S. LEXIS 1368 (1914).
[17]   367 U.S. 643, 1961 U.S. LEXIS 812 (1961).

was executed in good faith by the officers.[19] The Court determined that the evidence should be admitted even though a reviewing court later found that the description in the search warrant did not meet constitutional standards and the error had been made by the judge.

In both the *Leon* and *Shepherd* cases, police officers executed what they reasonably believed to be valid warrants. Soon after these cases were decided, the question arose as to whether the "good faith" rationale would be applied to situations in which officers acted without a warrant. In the case of *Illinois v. Krull*, officers acting pursuant to a statute inspected an automobile wrecking yard and discovered several stolen cars.[20] The state statute, similar to those in many other states, regulated the business of buying and selling motor vehicles, parts, and scrap metal. The day after the warrantless search, a federal court ruled that such a statute was unconstitutional, and at the trial a motion was made to exclude the evidence obtained by the officers, even though the officers acted in good faith under the statute. On review, the United States Supreme Court reversed the lower court decision and decided that the evidence should have been admitted, as the application of the exclusionary rule in these circumstances would have little deterrent effect on police conduct because police cannot foretell which laws might be later ruled unconstitutional. In fact, the police made no error; the Illinois legislature erred in passing the unconstitutional statute. In both *Leon* and *Shepherd* the basic deterrent effect would not operate to affect judicial behavior because the intent of the exclusionary rule was to modify police behavior. As Justice O'Connor once stated, "Where the rule's deterrent effect is likely to be marginal, or where its application offends other values central to our system of constitutional governance or the judicial process, we have declined to extend the rule to that context."[21]

Although the court in the Krull case did not extend the "good faith" exception to a considerable extent, it did clarify the reasoning concerning the exclusionary rule with these comments:

> Application of the Exclusionary Rule "is neither intended nor able to cure the invasion of the defendant's rights which he has already suffered". . . . Rather, the rule "operates as a judicially created remedy designed to safeguard Fourth Amendment rights generally through its deterrent effect, rather than as a personal constitutional right of the party aggrieved". . . . As with any remedial device, application of the exclusionary rule properly has been restricted to those situations in which its remedial purpose is effectively advanced.

---

[18]   104 S. Ct. 3405, 82 L. Ed. 2d 677 (1984). *See* case in Part II.
[19]   Massachusetts v. Shepherd, 468 U.S. 897, 104 S. Ct. 3424, 82 L. Ed. 2d 677 (1984).
[20]   Illinois v. Krull, 475 U.S. 868, 107 S. Ct. 1160, 94 L. Ed. 2d 364 (1987). *See* KANOVITZ & KANOVITZ, CONSTITUTIONAL LAW (10th ed. 2005) for a more thorough discussion of the search and seizure requirements.
[21]   Duckworth v. Eagan, 492 U.S. 195, 208 (1989).

These cases indicate a trend by the Supreme Court to apply less technical rules in search and seizure cases. However, the exclusionary rule still applies in a majority of cases when evidence has been obtained illegally. Therefore, it is essential that the rules concerning the constitutionality of searches be followed.

Stops and brief searches on less than probable cause may create constitutional issues when police were looking for drugs rather than impaired drivers. In *Indianapolis v. Edmond*, the defendant had been stopped based on absolutely no suspicion at a citywide checkpoint in an effort to locate drivers with illegal substances. The court held that while brief stops to detect drunk drivers was a reasonable approach under the Fourth Amendment,[22] stopping people for general crime control on absolutely no suspicion could not be squared with the Constitution.[23] However, for a specific important purpose, such as a roadblock designed to obtain more information about a recent hit-and-run offense and not to investigate any particular driver, a checkpoint can be reasonable under the Fourth Amendment.[24] Police contact with motorists consisted of an information request and they gave each motorist an informational flyer.

When police proceed without probable cause or a warrant, there may be some limitations. Clearly, entering a private residence in the absence of a warrant, exigent circumstances, or probable cause may run afoul of the doctrine of the *Mapp* case, but the thermal imaging of a dwelling involves no physical intrusion. However, evidence obtained from heat scans of residential buildings should not be used as part of probable cause to obtain a warrant. In *Kyllo v. United States*, the Court held that using a thermal-imaging device to take a scan of the heat signature from a residence that indicated the possibility that there was marijuana growing inside constituted a Fourth Amendment search for which a warrant or a substitute was constitutionally required.[25]

Exigent or emergency circumstances permit police to enter a home or other location without a warrant to save a life or to prevent serious bodily injury. In a Utah case, police responded to a call about a loud party at 3:00 A.M. to find juveniles drinking alcoholic beverages in the yard and a fight going on inside the home among four adults and a juvenile.[26] Officers observed the fight and blood from outside and announced their presence, but no one responded to the officers. The police entered the kitchen fight area and arrested various adults for contributing to the delinquency of a minor. The Supreme Court of the United States held that the situation fell into the exigent or emergency circumstances category of an exception to the warrant requirement, where police may enter a home when they have an objectively reasonable basis to believe a person may be seriously injured or is threatened with death or serious bodily injury. Evidence so acquired is admissible and is not excluded by the *Mapp* doctrine.

---

22   *See* Michigan v. Sitz, 496 U.S. 444 (1990).
23   Indianapolis v. Edmond, 531 U.S. 32 (2000).
24   *See* Illinois v. Lidster, 540 U.S. 419, 2004 U.S. LEXIS 656 (2004).
25   Kyllo v. United States, 533 U.S. 27 (2001).
26   Brigham City v. Stuart, ___ U.S. ___, 2006 U.S. LEXIS 4155 (2006).

Other exceptions to the exclusionary rule include the *independent source rule*, in which evidence is admitted when the Fourth Amendment has been violated but there is a separate avenue by which the evidence could be legally obtained.[27] In one case, officers illegally entered a building to determine whether the evidence remained inside, but they used only good, untainted evidence on an affidavit for a warrant. The illegal entry did not taint the warrant because there was a good independent source for probable cause.[28] Evidence may be admitted when it will be inevitably discovered by lawful means within a reasonable time[29] that is not tainted by Fourth Amendment illegality. In this case, an officer violated the principles of *Miranda* to obtain the location of a murder victim, but the evidence of the body was not excluded because the police were searching in the area and would inevitably have found the body lawfully within a reasonable time. When the illegality is separated or attenuated from the illegal collection of evidence by time and distance, the evidence is not excluded.[30] In this case, the defendants went to police to confess and make a deal several days after an alleged illegal search of their homes. The confession evidence was separated by an independent act of free will and by time and distance, and would not be excluded on Fourth Amendment grounds.

One type of search, which is universally recognized as legal, is a search with a warrant. Both the United States Constitution and the constitutions of the various states describe the circumstances under which search warrants may be issued.

In order for a search warrant to to be valid, it must meet certain requirements. Some of the requirements are enumerated in the Constitution. Others have been added by legislation or court interpretation. In order for a search warrant to to be enforceable, the following requirements must be met:

1. The warrant must be issued on probable cause.

2. The warrant must be supported by oath or affirmation.

3. The proper judicial official must issue the warrant.

4. The place to be searched and the things to be seized must be particularly described.[31]

The United States Supreme Court, as well as other courts, has encouraged the use of a search warrant in making a search. In 1983, the Court, in reinforcing this preference and in indicating a trend to approve less technical procedures, modified the probable cause requirements for a search warrant. In previous cases, the Court had approved the use of undisclosed informants in determining probable cause and had established what was known as the "two-

---

27   Murray v. United States, 468 U.S. 796 (1984).
28   *Id.*
29   Nix v. Williams, 467 U.S. 431, 1984 U.S. LEXIS 101 (1984).
30   *See* Wong Sun v. United States, 371 U.S. 471, 1963 U.S. LEXIS 2431 (1963).
31   *See* KLOTTER, WALKER & HEMMENS, LEGAL GUIDE FOR POLICE: CONSTITUTIONAL ISSUES (7th ed. 2005) and the Fourth Amendment.

pronged" test.[32] Under this test, the judge must be given facts from an informant that equal probable cause and the judge must have clear reasons why the informant is to be believed. This standard for testing the credibility of an informant's tip upon which a magistrate is asked to rely was: (1) that the magistrate must be given some of the underlying circumstances from which the affiant concluded that the informant was credible or that his or her information was reliable; and (2) that the magistrate must be given some of the underlying circumstances from which the informant reached the conclusion conveyed in the tip.

In a reconsideration of the use of informants to help establish probable cause, in *Illinois v. Gates* the Supreme Court abandoned the two-pronged test in which probable cause must be based on informant information and established the "totality of circumstances" test.[33] While agreeing with the Illinois Supreme Court that an informant's veracity, reliability, and basis of knowledge were all highly relevant in determining whether an informant's report equals probable cause, the Court indicated that the totality of circumstances approach was far more consistent with the Court's prior treatment of probable cause. Under this test, the issuing judicial official must make a practical, common-sense decision, given all the circumstances set forth in the affidavit, that there is a fair probability that contraband or evidence of a crime will be found in a particular place. State courts are free to require a higher standard for informant-based probable cause under state laws or constitutions.[34]

Even though a warrant has been issued correctly, the evidence can be made inadmissible by improper execution of the warrant. In executing the warrant, the officer must follow these guidelines:

1. The warrant must be executed by the officer named or the officer must come within the class designated.

2. The warrant must be executed within certain time limitations.

3. Only necessary force may be used in executing the warrant.

4. Prior notice and demand shall usually precede forcible entry.

5. Only the property described may to be seized under the warrant.

One of the requirements of the Fourth Amendment is that searches and seizures must be reasonable in the way they are executed. One of the common law hallmarks indicating reasonableness was the concept that the officers should knock and announce before resorting to breaking into a house. The knock-and-announce rule serves to protect the privacy of the individual, avoids needless destruction of property, and reduces confusion, shielding police and occupiers from attack by each other. Notwithstanding the statutes

---

[32] Aguilar v. Texas, 378 U.S. 108, 84 S. Ct. 1509, 12 L. Ed. 2d 723 (1964).

[33] 462 U.S. 213, 103 S. Ct. 2317, 76 L. Ed. 2d 527 (1983). *See also* People v. Jack, 70 Cal. Rptr. 2d 676 (1997).

[34] *See* People v. Tarver, 292 A.D.2d 110, 741 N.Y.S.2d 130, 2002 N.Y. App. Div. LEXIS 3631 (N.Y. 2002) and People v. Williams, 284 A.D.2d 564, 726 N.Y.S.2d 740, 2001 N.Y. App. Div. LEXIS 11474, n.1 (N.Y. 2001).

and case law requiring prior notice and demand, the courts have recognized an exception for exigent circumstances, such as immediate physical danger, flight, or clear potential for destruction of evidence. In the case of *Wilson v. Arkansas*, the United States Supreme Court noted that "this Court has little doubt that the Amendments' framers thought that whether the officers announced their presence and authority before entering a dwelling was among the factors to be considered in assessing a search's reasonableness."[35] The court recognized, however, that there are exceptions to the rule, "including the threat of physical harm to the police, the fact that an officer is pursuing a recently escaped arrestee, and the existence of reason to believe that evidence would likely be destroyed if advance notice were given may establish the reasonableness of unannounced entry."

The Court retreated from a preference for the knock-and-announce requirement when faced with a clearly guilty defendant who wanted evidence suppressed based on an imperfect knock and announce by police. In this case,[36] under the authority of a search warrant, the police announced their presence and entered, all within the space of three to five seconds. The defendant's door was unlocked at the time the police entered to find narcotics and illegal guns. The prosecution conceded that the police had violated the *Wilson v. Arkansas* rule, but contended that suppression of the evidence was not the appropriate remedy. The Supreme Court noted, "[t]he common-law principle that law enforcement officers must announce their presence and provide residents an opportunity to open the door is an ancient one,"[37] but the Court was not inclined to suppress the evidence just because there was a Fourth Amendment violation. It noted that the knock and announce rule did not protect the citizen from keeping the government from seeing evidence described in a warrant. The deterrence effect on police must outweigh the substantial social costs of suppression and the Court believed that the deterrent effect was small and every litigant would be contesting the failure to knock and announce if the result of a win would be suppression of all the evidence. What the Court stated in *Wilson v. Arkansas* had been difficult to apply in practice and the Court no longer requires that police knock and announce. The present rule seems to suggest that knock and announce may be proper but that if police fail to knock and announce, they run little risk of having the evidence suppressed from use by the prosecutor.

Although preference is given to the search warrant as a means of making a search, and the search warrant is the only such means mentioned in the Constitution as proper, Supreme Court jurisprudence has recognized the necessity of conducting some searches without warrants, especially in emergency situations[38] or when the officer might be facing an unclear danger.[39] Case law illu-

---

[35]   Wilson v. Arkansas, 514 U.S. 927, 115 S. Ct. 1914, 131 L. Ed. 2d 976 (1995).
[36]   Hudson v. Michigan, ___ U.S. ___, 2006 U.S. LEXIS 4677 (2006).
[37]   *Id.*
[38]   *See* Warden v. Hayden, 387 U.S. 294 (1967) and New York v. Quarles, 467 U.S. 649 (1984).
[39]   *See* United States v. Arellano-Ochoa, 2006 U.S. App. LEXIS 22466 (9th Cir. 2006), in which the court permitted a warrantless entry where an officer could not see through the screen of a house trailer door under circumstances in which the officer might have been dealing with an armed drug trafficker.

minates and illustrates the typical exceptions to the general necessity of a warrant. In each instance, an exception applies only when certain requirements are met. The paragraphs that follow discuss the most important examples of these exceptions.

A. Search Incident to a Lawful Arrest

The right to make a search incident to a lawful arrest has been recognized by all courts, including the United States Supreme Court,[40] but does require an actual lawful arrest prior to conducting a valid search.[41] In addition to a valid arrest, the search incident to arrest requires that the search be made contemporaneously with the arrest and that the search be reasonable in scope. Naturally, the arrest must be made in good faith that probable cause exists.[42] In emphasizing that the arrest must be lawful, the Court of Appeals of Florida suppressed the fruits of a search incident to the defendant's arrest in his own motel room because the defendant was entitled to remain in his room and police were not permitted to make a warrantless arrest under the circumstances. Because the arrest was unlawful, the search incident to the arrest was an unlawful search and the evidence had to be suppressed.[43]

While the United States Supreme Court has left no doubt that a search of the person incident to a lawful arrest may occur slightly before the actual arrest if the arrest occurs contemporaneously with the search, it is preferable to conduct a search incident to an arrest following the arrest.[44] In the case of *Smith v. Ohio*, the United States Supreme Court was asked to answer the single question of "whether a warrantless search, which provides probable cause for an arrest, can nonetheless be justified as an incident of that arrest."[45] In this case, the defendant, when asked by an officer to "come here a minute," threw onto the hood of his car a paper grocery sack that he was carrying. The officer, before making the arrest, pushed the defendant's hand away and opened the bag, which contained drug paraphernalia.

The search was illegal because the defendant was not arrested until after the contraband was discovered. Therefore, the contraband could not serve as a part of the justification for a lawful arrest and could not support a lawful search incident to an arrest. The Court reversed the conviction and concluded that:

> The exception for searches incident to arrest permits the police to search a lawfully arrested person and areas within his immediate control . . . it does not permit police to search any citizen without a warrant or probable cause so long as an arrest immediately follows.

---

[40] Chimel v. California, 395 U.S. 752, 89 S. Ct. 2034, 23 L. Ed. 2d 685 (1969).

[41] *See* Knowles v. Iowa, 525 U.S. 113, 1998 U.S. LEXIS 8068 (1998).

[42] Arizona v. Evans, 514 U.S. 1, 1995 U.S. LEXIS 1806 (1995). *See also* United States v. Miller, 382 F. Supp. 2d 350 (N.D. N.Y. 2005).

[43] Brown v. State, 891 So. 2d 1120, 2004 Fla. App. LEXIS 20023 (Fla. 2004).

[44] Rawlings v. Kentucky, 448 U.S. 98, 111, 1980 U.S. LEXIS 142 (1980). *Accord*, United States v. Montgomery, 377 F. 3d 582, 2004 U. S. App. LEXIS 15438 (6th Cir. 2004)

[45] Smith v. Ohio, 494 U.S. 541, 110 S. Ct. 1288, 108 L. Ed. 2d. 464 (1990).

Because a search incident to a lawful arrest is intended to protect the searching officer and to prevent the destruction of evidence, the scope of the area of the search is limited generally to the lunge area where a weapon could be obtained or evidence destroyed. In the case of *Chimel v. California*, the area of search was defined as "the area within his immediate control—construing that phrase to mean the area from which he might gain possession of a weapon or destructible evidence."[46]

However, in applying the *Chimel* rule when the search is made of a residence incident to a lawful arrest, police may not search the interior of the arrestee's home when the arrest occurred on the sidewalk outside of the home. In one case, the search of the arrestee's home was unreasonable because it was not conducted incident to his arrest and was not confined to a cursory inspection. The Fourth Amendment allows a sweep if the officers lawfully enter an arrestee's home but where the officers have no right to enter, there can be no lawful sweep.[47] If an arrest is made in one part of the house, the Fourth Amendment permits a properly limited protective sweep in conjunction with the in-home arrest when the searching officers possess a reasonable belief, based on specific and articulable facts, that the area to be swept harbors an individual posing a danger to those on the arrest scene. However, the fact that an arrest is made in the living room does not justify a full search of the whole house without a warrant unless there is consent by one who has authority to consent.[48]

In summarizing the scope of a "sweep search," a federal appeals court indicated that a "sweep search" is narrowly confined to a cursory visual inspection of places in a building where a person might be hiding.[49] The court continued by noting that officers are permitted to take reasonable steps to ensure their safety, and may, without probable cause or reasonable suspicion, look in closets or other spaces immediately adjoining the places of arrest from which an attack could be immediately launched. A protective sweep became an unreasonable search when officers conducted a sweep of an apartment where they could see all the rooms of the apartment from the foyer and the defendant was not the target of the officer's attentions. The defendant was not under arrest and the bedroom where the illegal drugs were discovered was not within the lunge area of the defendant. From the view that the officers originally had in the foyer, there was no need for a protective sweep and the drugs were suppressed as fruits of an illegal "sweep search."[50]

Following a lawful arrest of a driver or passenger who was located in or near a motor vehicle, police may search the interior passenger compartment and any containers as an incident to a lawful arrest, whether the arrestee

---

[46] Chimel v. California, 395 U.S. 762, 89 S. Ct. 2034, 23 L. Ed. 2d 685 (1969); *see also* United States v. Robinson, 414 U.S. 218 (1973), which held that the authority to search incident to a lawful arrest includes the right to search the person arrested for evidence not related to the crime.

[47] *See* United States v. Rios-Ramirez, 2004 U.S. Dist. LEXIS 26573 (D. P.R. 2004).

[48] Maryland v. Buie, 494 U.S. 325, 110 S. Ct. 1093, 108 L. Ed. 2d 276 (1990).

[49] United States v. Barnett, 989 F.2d 546 (1st Cir.), *cert. denied*, 510 U.S. 850, 114 S. Ct. 148, 126 L. Ed. 2d 110 (1993). *See also* United States v. Hutchings, 127 F.3d 1255 (10th Cir. 1997).

[50] United States v. Ali, 2006 U.S. Dist. LEXIS 21543 (E.D.N.Y. 2006).

remains near the vehicle or has been removed some distance.[51] According to the general rule, "when a policeman has made a lawful custodial arrest of the occupant of an automobile, he may, as a contemporaneous incident of that arrest, search the passenger compartment of that automobile."[52] In explaining the scope of a search incident to a lawful arrest, a different court upheld the search of the passenger compartment of the defendant's automobile even though he was arrested some distance from the vehicle.[53] The fact that an arrestee may be too far from the vehicle to lunge and grab a weapon, may have exited the vehicle prior to the arrest,[54] or may be handcuffed, does not prevent police officers from searching a motor vehicle recently occupied by an arrestee as incident to a law arrest.

B. Search After a Waiver of Constitutional Right

In accordance with the general principles that allow a person to waive his or her constitutional rights, the rights protected by the Fourth Amendment to the Constitution and state provisions concerning search and seizure may be waived. In order for this exception to the warrant rule to apply, the prosecution must show that the consent was voluntarily and freely given, and that the person who gave the consent had the capacity and authority to consent. The general rule is that the consent of one who has dominion and control over the premises or effects is the proper person and may give valid consent against the absent nonconsenting person with whom the authority is shared,[55] unless the nonconsenting person is present and refuses to grant consent.[56] In this latter situation, a couple shared dominion and control over the marital residence and a domestic dispute brought the police. The wife alleged that the defendant had drugs within the home and consented to a police search of the marital home. The husband refused to grant consent to search and the Supreme Court held that one spouse had no recognized authority in law or in social practice to prevail over the other one who was present and refused consent to search. The police had no better claim to being able to reasonably enter the marital premises than anyone else when joint consent was not available.[57] Apparent shared authority over real or personal property will permit one of the persons to give lawful consent to search where police act in an objectively reasonable manner and the other person with authority is not present or does not object.[58] But where a wife was asked to consent to a search of a home computer for which the non-present husband had already denied police consent, the wife's

---

[51]　New York v. Belton, 453 U.S. 454, 101 S. Ct. 2960, 69 L. Ed. 2d 768 (1981).

[52]　*Belton*, 453 U.S. at 460.

[53]　United States v. Jones, 155 Fed. Appx. 204, 2005 U.S. App. LEXIS 25303 (6th Cir. 2005).

[54]　*See* Thornton v. United States, 541 U.S. 615, 2004 U.S. LEXIS 3681 (2004).

[55]　United States v. Matlock, 415 U.S. 164, 94 S. Ct. 988, 39 L. Ed. 2d 242 (1974). *See* KANOVITZ & KANOVITZ, CONSTITUTIONAL LAW (10th ed. 2005) for a discussion of the authority of a spouse, a minor child, and a parent to consent to a search.

[56]　Georgia v. Randolph, ___ U.S. ___, 2006 U.S. LEXIS 2498 (2006).

[57]　*Id.*

[58]　Illinois v. Rodriguez, 497 U.S. 177 (1990).

consent was not controlling and the evidence should have been suppressed.[59] The test for a waiver of consent encompasses the totality of the circumstances—in which the age, education, legal education, if any, coerciveness of the atmosphere, whether the person was under arrest or threatened with arrest, and whether the person knew of the right to refuse without facing adverse consequences—are considered.[60]

In considering the waiver of constitutional rights, the police and the courts must carefully observe any limitations placed upon the consent. A general consent to search for drugs in a vehicle generally extends to any part of the vehicle where the drugs might reasonably be hidden[61] in the absence of some limitation by the consenting party.[62] There is some authority stating that a person may revoke the consent during the process of the search.[63] If the consent is revoked, evidence obtained from a continuing search is not admissible unless justified on other grounds.

To be constitutionally adequate, the consent must be given without force, duress, or compulsion of any kind.[64] Where the government agent used subtle coercion, the consent may be ruled as inadequate and involuntary. In a case in which an officer used pressure to gain consent to search a car, the consent was not valid.[65] Where a high school student merely acquiesced to a police officer's command to come to the police officer and the officer ordered him to show the contents of his backpack containing marijuana, such conduct of submission to authority does not produce a valid consent to search.[66] The government has the burden of proving that the consent was truly voluntary, unfettered by coercion, whether express or implied.[67] However, the Fourth Amendment does not require that a lawfully seized detainee be affirmatively advised that he or she is "free to go" before his or her consent to search will be recognized as voluntary.[68]

Some situations exist when the consent to search may not be completely voluntarily given but evidence seized remains admissible. In the context of probation or parole, a convict may be forced to agree to a reduction or waiver of some Fourth Amendment rights as a condition of release. In one California case,[69] as a condition of release, the parolee was forced to agree in writing to allow a search and seizure of his person, property, place of residence, and any other location where he might have an expectation of privacy, to search any-

[59] United States v. Hudspeth 2006 U.S. App. LEXIS 21664 (8th Cir. 2006).
[60] *See* Schneckloth v. Bustamonte, 412 U.S. 218 (1973).
[61] Florida v. Jimeno, 500 U.S. 248, 1991 U.S. LEXIS 2910 (1991).
[62] United States v. Gregoire, 425 F.3d 872, 880, 2005 U.S. App. LEXIS 21398 (10th Cir. 2005).
[63] *Id.* at 881. *See also* United States v. Flores-Ocampo, 173 Fed. Appx. 688, 691, 2006 U.S. App. LEXIS 8367 (10th Cir. 2006), in which a general consent to search a car included gas tank and sun roof area.
[64] Schneckloth v. Bustamonte, 412 U.S. 218 (1973).
[65] Ohio v. Robinette, 519 U.S. 33 (1996).
[66] People v. Kveton, 362 Ill. App. 3d 822, 831, 840 N.E.2d 714, 722, 2005 Ill. App. LEXIS 1195 (2005). *See also* Florida v. Bostick, 501 U.S. 429, 111 S. Ct. 2382, 115 L. Ed. 2d 389 (1991).
[67] Commonwealth v. Rogers, 444 Mass. 234, 344, 827 N.E.2d 669, 677, 2005 Mass. LEXIS 216 (Mass. 2005).
[68] Ohio v. Robinette, 517 U.S. 33, 177 S. Ct. 417, 136 L. Ed. 2d 347 (1996).
[69] Samson v. California, ___ U.S. ___, 2006 U.S. LEXIS 4885 (2006).

time, with or without a warrant, by any probation officer or law enforcement officer. A police officer conducted a warrantless search of the parolee's person and found methamphetamine, which was a violation of his parole. The convict argued that the Fourth Amendment could not be construed to force him to give up his rights in exchange for conditional freedom. The Supreme Court held that a condition of release can constitutionally diminish a parolee's expectation of privacy to permit a suspicionless search and the evidence discovered is not subject to exclusion from court.

The court looks at the totality of circumstances to determine whether a consent to search has been voluntary in fact,[70] and if consent is not sufficiently an act of the free will to purge the primary taint of the illegal search warrant, then the results of the search must to be suppressed as "fruit of poisonous tree."[71]

C. Search of a Vehicle That Is Moving or about to Be Moved

Recognizing a difference between the search of a dwelling house, for which a warrant can be readily obtained, and the search of an automobile, ship, wagon, airplane, or other movable object, for which securing a warrant may not be practical because of the mobility of the vehicle, courts have determined that some vehicles may be searched without a warrant as long as probable cause exists.[72] Two requirements that must be met in order for a search of this type to be valid are: (1) the officer must have probable cause that would justify the issuance of a search warrant if the facts were presented to a judge and (2) the vehicle must be readily movable. In such a case, the decision concerning whether to seize the vehicle while a warrant is obtained or conduct an immediate warrantless search is left to the determination of the officer involved. According to the Supreme Court, either course of action is reasonable.

In a subsequent case, the United States Supreme Court reexamined the scope of the search under the moving vehicle doctrine and held that police acting under the automobile exception to the Fourth Amendment warrant requirement may search every part of the vehicle, including closed containers in the trunk, that might conceal the contraband for which the police have probable cause.[73] However, officers may not search the trunk of a vehicle where there is no probable cause to believe that seizable property is contained within.[74]

---

[70]　*See* United States v. Drayton, 536 U.S. 194, 2002 U.S. LEXIS 4420 (2002), in which officers were "working the buses" and obtained consent to search luggage from interstate bus passengers.

[71]　United States v. Cowdin, 984 F. Supp. 1374 (D. Kan. 1997). In this case, a revolver obtained as a result of a search without voluntary consent was held inadmissible. *See also* Wong Sun v. United States, 371 U.S. 471 (1963).

[72]　Chambers v. Maroney, 339 U.S. 42, 90 S. Ct. 1975, 26 L. Ed. 2d 419 (1970). The genesis for this theory seems to have been *Carroll v. United States*, 267 U.S. 132, 1925 U.S. LEXIS 361 (1925), in which police conducted a warrantless search of a moving automobile that had been stopped where there was probable cause to search. *See also Wyoming v. Houghton*, 526 U.S. 295 (1999), in which the United States Supreme Court, after referring to United States v. Ross, held that police officers with probable cause to search a car may inspect passengers' belongings found in the car that are capable of concealing the object of the search.

[73]　United States v. Ross, 456 U.S. 798, 1982 U.S. LEXIS 18 (1982).

Under the stop-and-frisk standard, officers may briefly stop, ask questions, and request consent to search when there is a reasonable basis to suspect that criminal activity might be afoot.[75] When subjects fit a drug courier profile, police may stop and talk to occupants of automobiles.[76]

The scope of the search under the moving vehicle doctrine depends upon the object of the search and the places in which there is probable cause to believe the object may be found.[77] Where there is probable cause to search an entire car, it would be permissible to search a woman's purse found within the car.[78] For example, if probable cause exists to believe that a container placed in the trunk of an automobile contains contraband, this does not justify a search of the entire car under that doctrine.[79] A search of other parts of the car might be justified under the search incidental to a lawful arrest theory, the vehicle inventory search theory, or if consent is given by the person in possession of the automobile.

As a general rule, the movable vehicle doctrine, which authorizes the search of a vehicle that is in movable condition, applies to automobiles, boats, and airplanes if the criteria are met. A federal court of appeals reversed a trial court holding that a particular moveable vehicle could be searched without a warrant. Police searched the subject's home pursuant to a warrant and also searched a Suburban SUV for which probable cause existed. Police searched a Cadillac owned by the subject that was parked in the apartment complex lot, by relying on the fact that there had been an allegation that drugs had been stored in the Suburban SUV. In rejecting the legality of the search of the Cadillac, the appellate court noted that the vehicle exception did not apply to the movable Cadillac and observed:

> The Cadillac was not subject to a valid warrantless search under the automobile exception since Appellees had no probable cause to believe that marijuana would be found in the Cadillac. *See United States v. Hogan* (determining that the seizure of a vehicle was invalid for lack of probable cause because all of the evidence indicated that drugs would be found in the defendant's home or in a different vehicle, and none of the evidence indicated that drugs would be found in the particular vehicle that was seized). Here, the informant reported to Appellees [police] only that Appellant sometimes kept marijuana in his Suburban, not the Cadillac. Furthermore, upon looking into the vehicle, Appellees do not claim they saw or smelled something that might lead to probable cause. Therefore, no search of the Cadillac was allowed under the automobile exception.

---

[74]   United States v. Jackson, 367 U.S. App. D.C. 320, 415 F.3d 88, 92, 2005 U.S. App. LEXIS 14951 (D.C. Cir. 2005).

[75]   *See* Alabama v. White, 496 U.S. 325 (1990).

[76]   Orlenas v. United States, 517 U.S. 690 (1996).

[77]   United States v. Gastfiaburo, 16 F.3d 582 (4th Cir. 1994).

[78]   Wyoming v. Houghton, 526 U.S. 295 (1999).

[79]   California v. Acevedo, 500 U.S. 565 (1991).

The exception to the warrant requirement under the movable vehicle doctrine allows warrantless searches of motor vehicles, provided probable cause to search exists at the moment the search begins. Where the vehicle is movable, but not moving and no probable cause exists, no lawful search of a vehicle may be conducted unless some other legal theory provides the rationale for the search.

Some vehicle stops may be initiated on less than probable cause[80] and some cursory searches may mature into full probable cause vehicle searches. In one case, border patrol officials determined that a vehicle had tripped a sensor on a road typically used by drug smugglers. As a federal official interdicted the minivan, he noticed that the occupants did not want to look at him and the children had their legs up on some cargo on the backseat floorboards. Probable cause to search did not exist, but the officer followed the *Terry* stop-and-frisk protocol as applied to motor vehicles to make a stop and brief inquiry. Following the stop, the story offered by the driver of the heavily loaded minivan did not make sense, and eventually probable cause developed, allowing a warrantless search that revealed that the driver was smuggling recreational drugs.[81] Various factors considered on an individual basis may not lead to a reasonable basis to suspect criminal activity under the stop-and-frisk standard or to probable cause for a search or arrest, but when considered under a totality of the circumstances, the stop-and-frisk standard may mature or probable cause for a vehicle search may be present.[82]

D. The Seizure of Evidence When No Search Is Required (Plain View)

The plain view doctrine allows seizures of objects that either offend the law by their mere presence or are objects that, under the circumstances, appear to constitute criminal evidence. In an earlier case, *Coolidge v. New Hampshire*, the Court seemed to require that seizures under the plain view doctrine must have been discovered inadvertently from a vantage point where the police officer had the legal right to be.[83] In one sense, the plain view doctrine does not involve a search; the law enforcement officer merely observes the seizable object in full view without any need to conduct a search. The officer must legally be in the place from which the clear view was available. For example, in one case, a police officer was lawfully inside an apartment investigating a gunshot when he observed expensive electronic equipment that looked out-of-place in the shabby apartment. He moved one item to secure a serial number from the rear of the unit. This was held to be a search and could not be justified under the plain view doctrine.[84] In a typical situation, the officer is merely on the premises and, unexpectedly, the officer observes an object that seems to indicate that a crime has been committed. The plain view doctrine comes into

---

[80]   Alabama v. White, 496 U.S. 325, 1990 U.S. LEXIS 3053 (1990).
[81]   United States v. Arvizu, 534 U.S. 266, 2002 U.S. LEXIS 490 (2002).
[82]   *Id.*
[83]   403 U.S. 443, 469, 1971 U.S. LEXIS 25 (1971).
[84]   *See* Arizona v. Hicks, 480 U.S. 321, 1987 U.S. LEXIS 1056 (1987).

play when an officer on a domestic call observes white powder and a scale or when a parole officer, when meeting with the parolee, observes a gun on a bed.

The gloss of inadvertence as a requirement of the plain view doctrine ended when the Supreme Court decided *Horton v. California*.[85] In that case, the police executed a warrant at Horton's home for proceeds from an armed robbery. The warrant mentioned some objects but did not describe a gun that the officers expected to find and did find. The *Horton* Court held that while inadvertence was a characteristic of most plain view seizures, inadvertence was not a necessary condition under this warrant exception. The Court considered the gun to have been lawfully seized, even though its presence was expected. The United States Supreme Court reiterated that the warrantless seizure of an object in plain view is valid if the following conditions are met: (1) the officer did not violate the Fourth Amendment in entering the place where the object was seen; (2) the object's incriminating character was immediately apparent, and (3) the officer had lawful access to the object itself. The *Horton* Court added that the concept of inadvertency as part of this warrant exception was never an essential part of the holding in *Coolidge v. New Hampshire* even though most plain view doctrine seizures occur due to the unexpected finding of contraband. "The normal Fourth Amendment rule is that items discovered in plain view are admissible if the officers were legitimately on the premises"[86] as long as there was probable cause to seize the evidence at the time it was encountered.

The plain view doctrine permitted a police officer to seize a gun from an automobile that the officer observed while getting into a lawful position to read the vehicle identification number (VIN) of a vehicle lawfully stopped. The Supreme Court held such evidence admissible even when the officer had to remove some papers that obscured the area on the dashboard where the manufacturer affixed the VIN plate.[87] The Court cautioned, however, that the decision "does not authorize police officers to enter a vehicle to obtain a dashboard-mounted VIN when the VIN is visible from outside the automobile."

In a Colorado case that involved the plain view doctrine,[88] officers observed a syringe containing a clear liquid in a partially opened bedside table in a motel room. The police used a tactic known as a "knock and talk" in which they approach the door of a place of interest and ask the occupant if they might talk to the person inside the building. The defendant permitted four officers to enter her motel room to talk to her, resulting in the plain view sighting and seizure of the syringe and drugs. The trial court refused to suppress the drug evidence that resulted in the defendant's conviction. The reviewing court held that the officers were in the motel room lawfully due to the defendant's consent and they observed the syringe by looking around the room without conducting a search.

---

[85]   496 U.S. 128, 141, 1990 U.S. LEXIS 2937 (1990).

[86]   Georgia v. Randolph, ___ U.S. ___, ___, 2006 U.S. LEXIS 2498 (2006). *See* case in Part II.

[87]   New York v. Class, 475 U.S. 106, 106 S. Ct. 960, 89 L. Ed. 2d 81 (1986).

[88]   People v. Bostic, 2006 Colo. App. LEXIS 622 (2006).

Generally, state and federal courts have agreed that the use of an officer's flashlight to illuminate a darkened area in an automobile does not constitute a search, and thus triggers no Fourth Amendment protection.[89] One court reasoned that an officer who peers into the interior of a vehicle during a traffic stop, and who uses a flashlight for illumination and safety, commits no Fourth Amendment wrong.[90]

E. Seizure of Evidence from Premises Not Protected by the Fourth Amendment (Open Fields)

In 1984, the United States Supreme Court confirmed the rule that only "houses, papers, and effects" are protected by the Constitution and that a search of open fields does not violate the Fourth Amendment.[91] The closing paragraph of the Supreme Court opinion in this case summarizes the decision with these words:

> We conclude that the open fields doctrine, as enunciated in *Hester*, is consistent with the plain language of the Fourth Amendment and its historical purposes.

While the Constitution protects houses, including the curtilage,[92] evidence obtained from outside the curtilage is admissible even if entry amounts to a trespass in the civil or criminal sense. In the case of *United States v. Dunn*, the United States Supreme Court suggested some guidelines that could be applied in determining whether an area is within the curtilage for Fourth Amendment purposes.[93] The Dunn Court enumerated four factors to be considered in determining extent-of-curtilage questions:

1. The proximity of the area to the home;

2. Whether the area is within an enclosure surrounding the home;

3. The nature and uses to which the area is put; and

4. The steps taken by the resident to protect the area from observation by passersby.

Applying these criteria, the Court ruled that a barn, located 50 yards from the house, behind several animal fences, and not within the area enclosed by a fence surrounding the house, was not within the curtilage of the home. Additionally, the government had evidence that the barn was not being used for intimate family purposes.

---

[89] People v. Brown, 2006 Cal. App. Unpub. LEXIS 4196 (2006).

[90] State v. Young, 895 So. 2d 753, 757, 2005 La. App. LEXIS 536 (2005).

[91] Oliver v. United States, 466 U.S. 170, 104 S. Ct. 1735, 80 L. Ed. 2d 214 (1984), reaffirming Hester v. United States, 265 U.S. 57 (1924).

[92] Black's Law Dictionary (2004) defines curtilage as "[t]he land or yard adjoining a house, usu. within an enclosure." Commonly the curtilage is the area around an individual home that might be reasonably fenced if a fence were installed.

In a Florida federal case, officers responded after an emergency operator received two 911 hangup calls.[94] They found a subject who walked toward them after he exited a barn located 130 feet from the home. He indicated that he had had a fight with his girlfriend and that he had made the calls before the girlfriend left. The subject gave consent to look around the barn area but officers went 100 feet farther, where they found a backpack and later a gun in a foot of pond water. The trial court permitted the gun to be introduced against the subject, a former felon, because the pond and the area immediately around the pond were beyond the curtilage and there was no fence that enclosed both the house and the pond area. In addition, the land around the pond was considered to be an "open field" for which the defendant had taken no steps to protect the pond and its area against view. Because there was no expectation of privacy, in seizing the gun, the officers had not violated the defendant's rights under the Fourth Amendment.

After a long debate in the lower courts, the United States Supreme Court concluded that the Fourth Amendment does not prohibit the warrantless seizure of garbage and trash left for collection outside of the curtilage of the home.[95] In addition to the trash being beyond the curtilage, the defendants had indicated that they wanted no additional use of the trash and had abandoned it by placing it out for the trash haulers. When the police arranged to have private trash haulers collect the evidence from the curb in front of the defendant's home, they committed no Fourth Amendment wrong and the evidence of drug possession and use was properly admitted against the home's occupiers.

F. Search by a Private Individual

The Fourth Amendment provisions apply to government officials, not to private individuals who are not acting as agents of the government or with participation or knowledge of any government official. In the case of *United States v. Jacobsen* in 1984, the Supreme Court held that employees of a private carrier who examined a package did not violate the Fourth Amendment; therefore, the evidence obtained in the examination was admissible.[96]

This exception to the warrant requirement applies to private conduct when there is either no official governmental involvement or only minimal entanglement. In order to show that private activity in conducting searches has so much government connection that it cannot be deemed private, "two elements must be shown in order to treat ostensibly private action as a state-sponsored search: (1) the police must have instigated, encouraged, or participated in the search; and (2) the private individual must have engaged in the search with the intent of assisting the police."[97] Private conduct that did not affect the Fourth

---

93 United States v. Dunn, 480 U.S. 294, 107 S. Ct. 1134, 94 L. Ed. 2d 326 (1987). *See also* State v. Moley, 490 N.W.2d 764 (Wis. 1992).

94 United States v. Taylor, 2006 U.S. App. LEXIS 18931 (11th Cir. 2006).

95 California v. Greenwood, 486 U.S. 35, 1988 U.S. LEXIS 2279 (1988). *See* the case for a review of lower court decisions.

96 466 U.S. 109, 104 S. Ct. 1652, 80 L. Ed. 2d 85 (1984).

97 United States v. Bruce, 396 F.3d 697, 705, 2005 U.S. App. LEXIS 1712 (6th Cir. 2005).

Amendment was held to exist when hotel employees smelled burning mari-juana and reported it to supervisory staff, who contacted the local police. The police requested that the trash from each room be kept separate and labeled. After police inspected the trash, they obtained a search warrant, using the evi-dence from the trash pulls. The defendant contended that the hotel employees were acting as police agents but the reviewing court noted that the hotel employees were asked by the police only to label and not commingle the trash from the respective rooms. In addition, private individuals working at the hotel first contacted the police and not the other way around. The court held that the evidence obtained had been properly admitted because only private conduct had been involved in obtaining the evidence.[98] However, if the government ini-tiated the searching process, the activity would probably be considered to be governmental conduct and the Fourth Amendment would apply.

If a private individual, without the knowledge of a law enforcement agent, makes a private search of a person's personal computer and indirectly sends the information to a local police agency, the search of the hard drive may not be considered a search by a government agency.[99] The informant attached a Trojan horse virus to downloadable child pornography that the defendant vol-untarily placed on his computer. The virus enabled the virus's author to have full access to files on the defendant's computer. The illegal materials were copied and sent to a private anti-child porn agency. The child pornography files found their way to the defendant's local police department, which had no idea who originally discovered the illegal photos on the defendant's computer. The Ninth Circuit Court of Appeals reversed a district court decision that sup-pressed the evidence because the appellate court believed that because the prosecuting agency and local police had nothing to do with the virus and pri-vate search of the defendant's hard drive, the search was a private one and did not implicate the Fourth Amendment.

In an early case concerning the status of public school officials, the United States Supreme Court held that teachers and administrators are considered government officials for Fourth Amendment purposes. The Court justified the search of students when there are reasonable grounds for suspecting that the search would turn up evidence that either the law or a rule of the school had been violated.[100] With parental consent, public schoolchildren can be tested for drugs as a condition of participating in extracurricular sports or related acad-emic activities, even in the absence of any individualized suspicion.[101] As a general rule, these results are not used for purposes of criminal prosecution. Even though the Fourth Amendment applies, these searches are considered "reasonable" because the tests cannot be performed unless parents consent and because the purpose of the testing was to reduce drug use by public school

---

[98]   *Id.*
[99]   United States v. Kline, 112 Fed. Appx. 562, 2004 U.S. App. LEXIS 20759 (9th Cir. 2004), *cert. denied*, 544 U.S. 950, 2005 U.S. LEXIS 2818 (2005).
[100] New Jersey v. T.L.O., 469 U.S. 325, 105 S. Ct. 733, 83 L. Ed. 2d 720 (1985).
[101] Board of Education v. Earls, 536 U.S. 822, 2002 U.S. LEXIS 4882 (2002).

students. Private schools are not limited by the Fourth Amendment and may test in the way that the school officials prefer.

Probation officers are also considered government officials for Fourth Amendment purposes. As one court recognized, "[i]t is well-settled that conditions that allow probation officers to conduct visits to and searches of the residences of probationers are valid under the Fourth Amendment."[102] In order to be reasonable, the entry must be authorized by law, a regulation, or an agreed-upon condition of probation. The reason may be routine or may involve suspicion or probable cause to believe that the probationer has violated some condition of probation.[103]

In some jurisdictions, a private police officer may carry sufficient authority of the state so that the officer must comply with the Fourth Amendment. In a Michigan casino, private security officers employed by the casino had the power from the state to detain errant patrons as well as full arrest powers. When a dispute involving the Fourth Amendment arose, the trial court held that, as a matter of law, the security officer was a state actor subject to the restraints of the Fourth Amendment.[104]

G. Search after Lawful Impoundment

Inventory searches have been approved when objects or vehicles come into the control of police, but inventory searches are improper and will not produce admissible evidence unless the police department has a policy regulating such searches.[105] The general rule is that "[e]vidence discovered during an inventory search conducted pursuant to standardized procedures is admissible, unless the police acted in bad faith or for the sole purpose of investigation."[106] Often the police have the duty and responsibility to impound a car that has been abandoned, is blocking traffic, is illegally parked, or has been left without a driver after the driver has been arrested. In such instances, the officer is usually required, either by law or departmental regulations, to search the vehicle and make a list of its contents before impounding it. Provided that the police department has and follows an inventory policy routinely and not just when police think something incriminating might be discovered, evidence seized during an inventory search will be admissible against the occupier of the vehicle.[107] The issues of the reasonableness of inventory seizures reached

---

[102] Cass v. County of Suffolk, 2005 U.S. Dist. LEXIS 8623 (E.D.N.Y. 2005).

[103] *Id.*

[104] Romanski v. Detroit Entertainment, L.L.C., 428 F.3d 629, 635, 2005 U.S. App. LEXIS 23336 (6th Cir. 2005).

[105] Florida v. Wells, 495 U.S. 1 (1990). *See also* State v. Hensley, 2005 Minn. App. LEXIS 233 (2005), in which an inventory search did not produce admissible evidence because the sheriff's department had no inventory policy.

[106] United States v. Thompson, 2006 U.S. App. LEXIS 12734 (3d Cir. 2006).

[107] South Dakota v. Opperman, 328 U.S. 364, 96 S. Ct. 3092, 49 L. Ed. 2d 1000 (1976); Arkansas v. Sullivan, 532 U.S. 769, 2001 U.S. LEXIS 4118 (2001), in which the court approved an inventory search following the driver's arrest.

the United States Supreme Court in the case of *Colorado v. Bertine* in 1987.[108] In approving the opening of closed containers found in a van that was lawfully impounded, the Court held that important government interests were served by inventory searches. An inventory search protects the citizen from loss of property by police or their agents while it protects the police from false claims of loss. In addition, an inventory search prevents police from harboring a vehicle that might contain harmful cargo, contraband, or dangerous items and it prevents vandalism to the vehicle. Two caveats apply here:

1. The police must follow standard procedures in carrying out the search, and

2. The police must perform the inventory search for the purpose of actually obtaining an inventory and not for the sole purpose of conducting a criminal investigation.[109]

In following a departmental inventory search policy, police may look for incriminating items that might be present as long as their sole purpose is not to investigate a crime.[110] Therefore, police may not use the inventory search theory as a justification for supporting a search that was simply a search for incriminating evidence.

H. Stop-and-Frisk Search

To complete the discussion concerning the admissibility of search and seizure evidence, the stop-and-frisk limited search must be mentioned. In 1968, the United States Supreme Court authorized the admission of evidence obtained by a police officer who articulated his reasons for "frisking" a person that he suspected was "casing a job."[111] The Court explained the limitation of such a seizure in this language:

> The sole justification of the search in the present situation is the protection of the police officer and others nearby, and it must, therefore, be confined in scope to an intrusion reasonably designed to discover guns, knives, clubs, or other hidden instruments for the assault of the police officer.

The frisk that is authorized by the *Terry v. Ohio* case is limited to a frisk for weapons when an officer has reasonable suspicion that the person with whom he is dealing may be armed and dangerous. When there is no reasonable suspicion that a subject may be armed and dangerous, a frisk does not appear to

---

[108]   Colorado v. Bertine, 479 U.S. 367, 107 S. Ct. 738, 93 L. Ed. 2d 739 (1987). *See also* Florida v. Wells, 495 U.S. 1, 110 S. Ct. 1632, 109 L. Ed. 2d 1 (1990), in which the United States Supreme Court discussed the necessity of having a departmental policy regarding inventory searches, and United States v. McKnight, 17 F.3d 1139 (8th Cir. 1994).

[109]   State v. Hensley, 2005 Minn. App. Lexis 233 (2005).

[110]   United States v. Kennedy, 427 F.3d 1136, 1143, 2005 U.S. App. LEXIS 23962 (8th Cir. 2005).

[111]   Terry v. Ohio, 392 U.S. 1, 88 S. Ct. 1868, 20 L. Ed. 2d 720 (1968).

be warranted. When an officer who has made a valid *Terry* stop has reasonable suspicion that the person with whom he or she is dealing may be armed, the officer may frisk the outer garments of the detainee to search for weaponlike lumps. Applying the *Terry* reasoning, the Supreme Court upheld the investigatory stop of a motorist and the search of a paper bag located in his car.[112] The Court reasoned that the protective search of the passenger compartment of an automobile was reasonable under the principles articulated in *Terry*. According to *Michigan v. Long*, when an officer stops a car to issue a traffic citation, he or she may, for his or her protection, order the driver to step out of the car and, if the facts available warrant a person of reasonable caution to conclude that the person may be armed and poses a serious and present danger to the safety of the officer, the officer may frisk the person for weapons. If weapons are found under these circumstances, they may be introduced into evidence. The Supreme Court held that if a *Terry* detainee refuses to identify him- or herself, and where state law permits, the detainee may be arrested and subjected to a search incident to a lawful arrest.[113] In that case, a police officer received a phone call reporting that a man was engaged in an assault on a woman inside a red and silver pick-up truck on a particular road. When he arrived, the male subject was not cooperative, said that he had done nothing wrong, and refused to produce any identification or orally identify himself. The officer arrested the driver for refusing to produce identification. According to the Court, the arrest was proper and any evidence obtained in a search incident to an arrest would be admissible against the motorist.

The *Terry* rule was also applied in holding that law enforcement agents may temporarily detain luggage on reasonable suspicion amounting to less than probable cause that the luggage contains narcotics.[114] The Supreme Court noted that if an officer's observation leads him or her reasonably to suspect that a traveler may be carrying luggage that contains narcotics, the officer may detain the luggage briefly to investigate the circumstances that aroused his or her suspicion, provided that the investigative detention is properly limited in scope. In this case, the 90-minute time span between the luggage seizure and its exposure to a search by a trained narcotics detection dog was unreasonable under the circumstances; therefore, the court suppressed the evidence.

In the *Terry* case, the United States Supreme Court approved the practice of frisking suspects on less than probable cause when there were reasonable grounds to believe that criminal activity might be afoot. The court noted, however, that the frisk had to be confined in scope to an intrusion reasonably designed to discover guns, clubs, knives, or other hidden instruments for the assault of the police officer. Several years after that decision was handed down by the Supreme Court, the question the Supreme Court was asked to answer was whether, while in the process of searching for a weapon on a person, offi-

---

[112]   Michigan v. Long, 463 U.S. 1032, 103 S. Ct. 3469, 77 L. Ed. 2d 1201 (1983); *and see* California v. Acevedo, 500 U.S. 565 (1991).

[113]   *See* Hiibel v. Sixth Judicial District Court, 542 U.S. 960, 2004 U.S. LEXIS 4385 (2004).

[114]   United States v. Place, 462 U.S. 696, 103 S. Ct. 2637, 77 L. Ed. 2d 110 (1983).

cers could seize other articles that were not dangerous if the other articles came into plain view or under the "plain feel" doctrine as a result of the frisk for weapons.[115]

In the case of *Minnesota v. Dickerson,* the officer, upon observing the suspect's seemingly evasive actions when approached by police officers and the fact that he had just left a building known for narcotics trafficking, decided to investigate further and ordered the suspect to submit to a pat-down search because a drug trafficker might be armed. The search revealed no weapons, but the officer who conducted the search testified that he felt a small lump in the suspect's jacket, believed it to be a lump of crack cocaine, and after rolling it between his fingers, reached into the pocket and retrieved a small bag of cocaine. The pat-down was within lawful limits, but the rolling of the crack between the thumb and index finger constituted a search beyond the scope of a stop and frisk and the Supreme Court agreed with the defendant that the rock of cocaine should not have been admitted at his trial.[116] In a different case,[117] an officer who had reason to suspect that a detainee might be an armed burglar frisked him and discovered metal car keys in his pocket. The officer removed the keys but returned them almost immediately. When it became necessary to connect the defendant to a car at a crime scene, the officer took the keys a second time. The reviewing court held that the keys originally were lawfully removed under the *Terry* stop and frisk standard because metal in a pocket could be a weapon and to take them back later did not infringe on any privacy right because the officer already knew the keys were in the subject's pants.

From the foregoing, it is obvious that some evidence, such as the rock of cocaine in the *Dickerson* case, obtained in an illegal search is logically relevant and material to a case, and would be admissible under the rules of evidence if no other considerations were involved. For constitutional reasons and consistent with court-generated rules designed to enforce constitutional provisions some evidence cannot be admitted. Evidence will be excluded if the search is illegal or if the search does not come within one of the recognized exceptions.

§ 16.4   Exclusion of Evidence Obtained by Illegal Wiretapping or Eavesdropping

At one time, the United States Supreme Court refused to include wiretapping within the scope of the Fourth Amendment. In the case of *Olmstead v. United States,*[118] after reviewing the historical context in which the Fourth Amendment was adopted, the Court concluded that the proscription was limited to search and seizure of material things, and did not apply to evidence procured by the sense of hearing. However, in a later decision, *Nardone v. United*

---

[115]   Minnesota v. Dickerson, 508 U.S. 366, 1993 U.S. LEXIS 4018 (1993).

[116]   *Id.*

[117]   People v. Sanders, 2006 Mich. App. LEXIS 2 (2006).

[118]   277 U.S. 438, 48 S. Ct. 564, 72 L. Ed. 944 (1928).

States,[119] the Supreme Court held that although wiretapping did not violate the Constitution, it did violate the Federal Communications Act of 1934, and the Court ruled that evidence obtained by officers who violated the provisions of this Act was inadmissible in federal court. This rule was not originally applied to the state courts, but many states adopted the rule, either by legislation or by court interpretation. In a landmark decision in 1967, *Katz v. United States,*[120] the Supreme Court rejected the contention that surveillance without trespass and without the seizure of material fell outside the purview of the Constitution. This and other decisions make it clear that wiretapping and electronic or mechanical eavesdropping are within the protection of the Fourth Amendment.

After several efforts, Congress in 1968 finally enacted a comprehensive scheme designed to regulate eavesdropping and wiretapping on a uniform nationwide basis.[121] This law, as amended, must be studied thoroughly in order to understand the requirements for wiretapping or eavesdropping. Broadly speaking, the interception of wire or oral communications is illegal unless conducted in conformity with statutory procedures. To be admissible, evidence obtained by wiretapping or eavesdropping must comply with the standards established by federal law as interpreted by the courts.

Title 18 United States Code §§ 3121-3126 sets forth the procedures for wiretapping and eavesdropping. Section 2511 prohibits the interception and disclosure of wire, oral, or electronic communications except when in compliance with a detailed statutory procedure. Section 2516 lists the procedures by which an investigative agency may apply for an order authorizing the interception of a wire or oral communication. In effect, this portion of the statute authorizes designated federal and state officers to apply for a court order, similar to a search warrant, to intercept wire or oral communications when the crimes charged are specifically enumerated.

In addition, some evidence obtained by means of wiretapping and eavesdropping is admissible if one party to the conversation consents. Section 2511(2)(c) authorizes federal law enforcement officers to intercept wire, oral, or electronic communications with the consent of one party without a court order unless a state statute prohibits such interception.

While federal law and some state laws include an exception that allows interception of communications if one party consents, the consent must be voluntary.[122] It is not voluntary if it is coerced by either explicit or implicit means or by an implied threat or covert force. Where federal prisoners are permitted to make telephone calls, the prisoner must consent to having the calls recorded or telephone privileges will not be extended. In one case, the prisoner continued to run a heroin importation ring using a prison phone following his

---

[119] 302 U.S. 379, 58 S. Ct. 275, 82 L. Ed. 314 (1937).
[120] 389 U.S. 347, 88 S. Ct. 507, 19 L. Ed. 2d 576 (1967).
[121] *See* Chapter 119 of the Omnibus Crime Control Act of 1968, 18 U.S.C. § 2510 (amended in 1986 by Pub. L. No. 99-508, and codified at 18 U.S.C. § 2510 *et seq.*)
[122] United States v. Antoon, 933 F.2d 200 (3d Cir.), *cert. denied,* 502 U.S. 907, 112 S. Ct. 300, 116 L. Ed. 2d 243 (1991).

imprisonment for prior crimes.[123] The phone calls that the prisoner made were monitored with his consent and some of the tapes of the calls were used at his subsequent trial for conspiracy to distribute heroin. The trial court and the court of appeals rejected his contention that the government taping violated § 2515 of the Federal Wiretap Act[124] and the phone evidence should have been excluded from his trial. The defendant offered the theory that consent was not sufficient to allow admission and the conversations should have been excluded because they were not collected in the ordinary course of law enforcement. According to the Court of Appeals for the Fifth Circuit, consent by one party is all that is required to render a telephone recording admissible in a federal court.

Cases interpreting and explaining the provisions of the federal law have been voluminous. When law enforcement officers circumvent the requirements of the wiretap authorization statute, courts must suppress evidence obtained from the illegal wiretap. For example, in a drug conspiracy case, a state judge had issued a wiretap order for the defendants' digital beepers, which required the police to record and store the data recovered on tape or another storage device. The police did not follow the court order, and recorded the data recovered in handwriting. Due to the disregard of the judge's order, the evidence was suppressed. The federal government wanted to try the defendants for the same act under federal law and the defendants contended that the evidence should be suppressed because 18 U.S.C. § 2510 contains virtually identical language to the state statute violated by state officers and suppression is a remedy when the government violates the law. The federal district judge suppressed the evidence because the government failed to follow the judicial order and if the evidence were allowed it could encourage law enforcement officials to sidestep other requirements in electronic eavesdropping.[125]

While states may enact wiretap and eavesdrop statutes that are more restrictive than the federal statutes, they may not enforce statutes that are less restrictive. But if the federal government's wiretap procedure complied with the federal law, evidence obtained thereby is admissible in federal courts, even if those procedures violated the state law.[126]

In an older case, the Supreme Court of the United States ruled that individuals have no expectation of privacy when they transmit a requested telephone number to the phone service provider and have no privacy concerning personal phone numbers.[127] At that point in history, state and federal law enforcement officials did not violate the Fourth Amendment and did not need a warrant when they used pen registers and trap-and-trace devices to collect telephone numbers dialed to or from phones as long as substantive content was

---

[123]   United States v. Moore, 452 F.3d 382; 2006 U.S. App. LEXIS 14152 (5th Cir. 2006).
[124]   18 U.S.C. § 2515.
[125]   United States v. Amanuel, 418 F. Supp. 2d 244; 2005 U.S. Dist. LEXIS 30108 (W.D.N.Y. 2005), Adhered to, On reconsideration by United States v. Amanuel, 418 F. Supp. 2d 244, 2006 U.S. Dist. LEXIS 3890 (W.D.N.Y. 2006).
[126]   United States v. Padilla-Pena, 129 F.3d 457 (8th Cir. 1997).
[127]   Smith v. Maryland, 442 U.S. 375 (1979).

not collected. Subsequently, Congress addressed the pen register and the trap-and-trace device issue to prohibit the warrantless use of such devices making the prior practice, approved in the *Smith* case, illegal. Later, Congress modified 18 U.S.C. § 3121 as part of the USA PATRIOT Act by expanding the coverage of pen registers and similar devices by redefining a pen register. Under the revised statute, "the term 'pen register' means a device or process which records or decodes dialing, routing, addressing, or signaling information transmitted by an instrument or facility from which a wire or electronic communication is transmitted, provided, however, that such information shall not include the contents of any communication."[128] Presently, the pen register may be used with a court order to reveal cell phone numbers, Web site addresses, e-mail addresses, and similar noncontent data. One limitation that may exist concerns cell phone tower usage, which could reveal where the person making or taking the call was located. In a federal case, the government sought such evidence but was rebuffed in a federal district court in 2005.[129]

Bumper beepers that can track automobiles and GPS tracking devices may require probable cause in some federal jurisdictions and in others, a reduced level of reasonable suspicion may suffice. In a Wisconsin methamphetamine prosecution, officers without a warrant attached a GPS tracking device to the defendant's automobile to see where it traveled and periodically retrieved it to download the information. All this was done without a warrant but with at least reasonable suspicion and perhaps probable cause. The federal district magistrate judge recommended that the evidence be admitted because he found that a warrant was not needed, but that the minimum standard of reasonable suspicion had to be proved by the government or the evidence would be suppressed. The government's evidence proved that there was reasonable suspicion that the defendant was engaged in methamphetamine manufacturing and that probable cause also existed. The magistrate judge's recommendation to the federal district court was to admit the evidence obtained as a result of the GPS device as well as the derivative evidence discovered.[130] At this point, the Supreme Court has not ruled on the level of proof required and has not determined whether a prior warrant based on probable cause will be required when it settles the divergent views of the various federal circuits concerning GPS and other tracking devices.

Because the state laws are still inconsistent, one must look to the statutes and decisions of the various states as well as the federal statutes to determine whether wiretapping, eavesdropping are permissible in a particular state and if permitted, under what circumstances. Federal law remains in a state of flux because of the tension between the need for national security and the desire to protect civil liberties. If the evidence is obtained in violation of federal or state laws or decisions, it usually may not be admitted into court.[131]

---

[128]   18 U.S.C. § 3127

[129]   In re Application of the United States of America for an Order Authorizing the Installation and Use of a Pen Register, 402 F. Supp. 2d 597 (D. Md. 2005).

[130]   United States v. Garcia, 2006 U.S. Dist. LEXIS 29596 (W.D. Wis. 2006).

[131]   For further discussions of the use of wiretap and eavesdrop evidence *see* KANOVITZ & KANOVITZ, CONSTITUTIONAL LAW (10th ed. 2005). *See also* KLOTTER, WALKER & HEMMENS, LEGAL GUIDE FOR POLICE: CONSTITUTIONAL ISSUES (7th ed. 2005).

§ 16.5　Exclusion of Confessions Obtained in Violation of Constitutional Provisions

Although a confession or an admission of guilt would seem to be the best kind of relevant evidence, in many instances evidence of a confession is not admissible because the officer obtaining the confession violated certain constitutional provisions. In making a determination of whether a confession has been voluntarily taken consistent with the Fifth Amendment, the ultimate question to be answered is "whether, under the totality of the circumstances, the challenged confession was obtained in a manner compatible with the requirements of the Constitution."[132] A confession that has been secured following a violation of the Fourth Amendment generally cannot be used against the person due to the Fourth Amendment exclusionary rule unless the confession can be shown to be an act of free will sufficient to purge the taint of the original illegality.[133]

It is essential that both federal and state laws be examined when considering the admissibility rules. Although the federal courts have established minimum standards to be applied, states may employ more stringent standards concerning the admissibility of confessions than the due process requirements pronounced in federal cases, but less stringent state standards are prohibited.[134]

A. The Free and Voluntary Rule

At early common law, courts permitted the use of admissions or confessions as evidence of guilt despite the fact that they were products of force or duress. The rule allowing the admissibility of such evidence was abandoned because it was found by experience that persons accused of a crime would admit to committing the crime in order to avoid torture. As a result, the courts developed what came to be known as the "free and voluntary" rule.

The free and voluntary rule states that the confession of a person accused of crime is admissible against the accused only if freely and voluntarily made, without fear, duress, or compulsion in its inducement. Excluding coerced confessions made logical sense because involuntary confessions might not be reliable and courts insisted on the requirement of voluntariness because the Fifth Amendment requirement that no person shall be compelled in a criminal case to be a witness against himself seemed to dictate the rejection of coerced confessions.[135] When a defendant raises the issue concerning voluntariness of a confession, the burden to prove whether the confession was voluntarily and

---

[132]　Miller v. Fenton, 474 U.S. 104, 112, 1985 U.S. LEXIS 144 (1985).

[133]　Kaupp v. Texas, 538 U.S. 626, 632, 2003 U.S. LEXIS 3670 (2003). An illegal arrest without probable cause quickly followed by a confession will ordinarily result in the confession being suppressed under the Fourth Amendment.

[134]　Griffin v. State, 230 Ga. App. 318, 496 S.E.2d 480 (1998).

[135]　Bram v. United States, 168 U.S. 532, 18 S. Ct. 187, 42 L. Ed. 568 (1897).

freely given rests upon the prosecution.[136] A determination of voluntariness of a confession requires that the trial court consider various factors, including the defendant's age, intelligence, and level of education. The court must factor into the decision the length of the defendant's detention and the length and nature of the interrogation, whether the police advised the defendant of constitutional rights, and whether the defendant had been subject to any physical coercion.[137]

Although the "free and voluntary rule" was formulated more than a century ago, the courts continue to define the rule. In 1991, the Supreme Court upheld the Supreme Court of Arizona's reversal of a murder conviction of a man who had been coerced into a confession. A fellow inmate, who was working for the government inside the prison, offered protection from harm from other inmates if the defendant confessed to the government's inmate agent. The Supreme Court of Arizona held that the first confession had been involuntarily given under coercion.[138] In 1993, a federal court stated that in evaluating the voluntariness of a confession, the court looks to the totality of the circumstances in which the confession was given to determine whether the government agent's conduct was such as to overbear the defendant's will to resist and to bring about confessions not freely self-determined.[139]

The test for the voluntariness of a confession is whether, under the totality of circumstances, the statement was made freely, without compulsion or inducement, with consideration given to the characteristics of the accused and the details of the interrogation. Under the totality of the circumstances, the "[f]actors to be considered include: the defendant's age, intelligence, background, experience, mental capacity, education and physical condition at the time of questioning, the legality and duration of the detention, the duration of the questioning, and any physical or mental abuse by the police, including any threats or promises. No single factor is dispositive."[140]

The United States Supreme Court in 1985 reaffirmed its authority to review state cases in which the confession was admitted as part of the evidence. The Court noted that the voluntariness of a confession is a matter that is subject to review by federal courts.[141] Although in this case the New Jersey Supreme Court had determined that the petitioner's confession was voluntary, the United States Supreme Court announced that it was not bound by a state court finding as to voluntariness.

Regardless of which historical approach is most persuasive, a confession obtained by force or duress, or by promises of reward, whether the confession

---

[136]   United States v. Jett, 2006 U.S. Dist. LEXIS 27829 (N.D. Ind. 2006), citing Lego v. Twomey, 404 U.S. 477, 489, 1972 U.S. LEXIS 100 (1972).

[137]   United States v. Lopez, 437 F.3d 1059, 1063, 2006 U.S. App. LEXIS 4052 (2006).

[138]   Arizona v. Fulminante, 499 U.S. 279 (1991).

[139]   United States v. Kaba, 999 F.2d 47 (2d Cir.), *cert. denied*, 510 U.S. 1002, 114 S. Ct. 577, 126 L. Ed. 2d 476 (1993).

[140]   Bridges v. Chambers, 447 F.3d 994, 997, 2006 U.S. App. LEXIS 11763 (7th Cir. 2006), quoting People v. Bridges, 2003 Ill. App. LEXIS 888).

[141]   Miller v. Fenton, 474 U.S. 104, 106 S. Ct. 445, 88 L. Ed. 2d 405 (1985).

is a judicial confession or an extrajudicial confession, should not be admitted.[142] The issue to be determined in each case is whether the defendant's will was overborne at the time that the defendant made the confession.[143] For example, a defendant's will was overborne when officers falsely told him that a gunpowder residue test was positive and that they had six eyewitnesses when they had only two. The officers told the defendant that if he cooperated he could get six years instead of 60, the difference between murder and a mistake. The appellate court upheld the trial court decision that suppressed the two confessions in the case because the misrepresentations of the evidence, together with the promise of leniency, were powerful enough to make the confessions involuntary.[144] However, in the event that a confession has been erroneously admitted, any conviction resulting from the admission of an improper confession should be tested by the harmless error standard.

Judges in various courts have often disagreed as to the amount of evidence required to determine whether a confession is voluntary. When an allegation has been made and some evidence demonstrated, the prosecution has the burden of proof to demonstrate that the confession was given freely and voluntarily. In *Lego v. Twomey*,[145] the judge in the lower court had not found the confession voluntary "beyond a reasonable doubt" and the defendant argued that this made the admission of the confession erroneous. The Supreme Court disagreed, however. The Court explained that the defendant is presumed innocent, and that the burden falls on the prosecution to prove guilt beyond a reasonable doubt; however, the Court continued, "[t]his is not the same burden that applies in determining the admissibility of a confession." The Court agreed that the prosecution must prove the confession to be free and voluntary by a preponderance of the evidence, but that it was not required to prove the confession to be free and voluntary "beyond a reasonable doubt."

B. The Delay in Arraignment Rule

Under *Riverside v. McLaughlin*, when police make a warrantless arrest, the arrestee must be taken before a judicial official for a determination of probable cause within 48 hours. If a warrant has been the basis for arrest or if the arrest followed an indictment by a grand jury, a second determination of probable cause is not necessary. When a person has been arrested without any judicial involvement or grand jury action, it becomes imperative that a judicial

---

[142]   The United States Supreme Court in the case of Arizona v. Fulminante, 499 U.S. 279, 113 L. Ed. 2d 302, 111 S. Ct. 1246 (1991) ruled that defendants whose coerced confessions were improperly used as evidence are not always entitled to a new trial. The use of such confessions may be considered "harmless error" if other trial evidence was sufficient to convict the defendant. In this case, the Supreme Court affirmed the decision of the Arizona Supreme Court that the harmless error analysis could not be used to save the conviction because a second confession that would have been admissible was tainted by the first one that was deemed illegally taken. The Court remanded the case for a new trial without the use of the first confession.

[143]   United States v. Yukins, 444 F.3d 713, 719, 2006 U.S. App. LEXIS 8160 (6th Cir. 2006).

[144]   *See* United States v. Lopez, 437 F.3d 1059, 2006 U.S. App. LEXIS 4052 (10th Cir. 2006).

[145]   Lego v. Twomey, 404 U.S. 477, 92 S. Ct. 619, 30 L. Ed. 2d 618 (1972).

official make a decision regarding whether probable cause exists within the allotted time.[146] Failure to seek judicial approval, where necessary, may result in civil suits against police officers or their jurisdiction,[147] but does not generally result in a dismissal of the criminal charge, may not result in suppressed evidence, and will not void a subsequent conviction.[148]

C. The Miranda Rule

The restrictions concerning the use of unwarned confessions and admissions as evidence were broadened in 1966. The confessions in *Miranda v. Arizona* and its three companion cases were declared inadmissible by the Supreme Court because the suspects were not given the constitutionally required warnings prior to being interrogated. The Supreme Court held that for a confession or an inculpatory statement to be deemed admissible, the person who has been taken into custody or otherwise deprived of his or her freedom of action in any significant way must be warned before questioning that: (1) the individual has a right to remain silent; (2) if the subject does make a statement, anything he or she says can and will be used against him or her in court; (3) the individual has the right to have an attorney present or to consult with an attorney; and (4) if he or she cannot afford an attorney, one will be appointed prior to any questioning if he or she so desires.[149]

Although the earlier cases interpreting the requirements of *Miranda* held that the warning must be given in the exact terms as stated in the case, the Supreme Court has retreated from that position in recent cases. In the case of *Duckworth v. Eagan*, the United States Supreme Court found that the warning need not be given in the exact terms as stated in *Miranda*, but that the warning must reasonably convey to a suspect his or her rights as required by *Miranda*.[150] To produce admissible evidence, the warnings must be given, even where the person in custody states that he "knows" the warnings, otherwise the oral evidence obtained will generally be suppressed for use in proving guilt.[151]

The *Miranda* warnings are not required unless the individual has been placed in custody and the police anticipate interrogating the subject. The ultimate inquiry in determining whether a suspect is in custody for *Miranda* purposes is simply whether there is a formal arrest or restraint of the freedom of movement of the degree associated with a formal arrest. In determining whether the suspect was in custody for *Miranda* purposes, the courts should inquire how a reasonable person in the suspect's position would have understood his or her situation.[152] In *Thompson v. Keohane*, the police interrogated the defendant for a period of time and allowed him to leave the police station

---

[146] Riverside v. McLaughlin, 500 U.S. 44 (1991).

[147] *See* Turner v. City of Taylor, 412 F.3d 629; 2005 U.S. App. LEXIS 11233 (6th Cir. 2005) and Young v. Graham, 2005 U.S. Dist. LEXIS 20882 (S.D. Ga. 2005).

[148] *See* United States v. Arnett, 2005 U.S. Dist. LEXIS 23741 (E.D. Cal. 2005).

[149] Miranda v. Arizona, 384 U.S. 436, 16 L. Ed. 2d 694, 86 S. Ct. 1602 (1966).

[150] 492 U.S. 195, 109 S. Ct. 2875, 106 L. Ed. 2d 166 (1989).

[151] United States v. Patane, 542 U.S. 630, 639, 2004 U.S. LEXIS 4577 (2004).

[152] United States v. Hicks, 967 F. Supp. 242 (E.D. Mich. 1997).

after he admitted killing his ex-wife. Following his allegation that he had been in custody for *Miranda* purposes, the Supreme Court sent the case back for a decision concerning custody[153] and the Ninth Circuit found that Keohane was not in custody and *Miranda* warnings were not necessary.[154] In another case, the police wanted to talk to a suspect in an axe murder who willingly rode with police to the stationhouse. She voluntarily entered the police station and was told that she was free to leave at any time and that she was not under arrest during the officer's polite interrogation. The reviewing court concluded that the interrogation only became custodial after the suspect confessed to her participation.[155] Only then would the *Miranda* warnings have been required.

The fact of custody and the desire to interrogate dictate that the initial warnings be given but the subject must understand that the right to cease talking or to consult an attorney may be exercised at any time during questioning. If the accused indicates in an unambiguous manner that he or she wants to speak with an attorney, interrogation must cease immediately and not be attempted later.[156]

Also, at any stage of the questioning, the person in custody may waive his or her rights and make a statement. There has been some question as to what constitutes a waiver and whether an express waiver is an essential requirement or whether the facts taken as a whole indicate that the waiver has been made. When an arrestee responds to additional police-initiated interrogation following an initial request for counsel, there has been no valid waiver.[157] The burden is on the prosecution to show that the defendant has waived his or her rights to silence and to an attorney. If an accused, after invoking his right to counsel under *Miranda*, does not begin new discussions with law enforcement agents, any later statement procured by law enforcement efforts is not admissible for proof of guilt. In one case, an inmate who was in Florida custody wanted an attorney and Florida officers had ceased attempts at interrogation. Ohio police officers violated the principles of *Miranda* when they arrived at the Florida lockup and began a new interrogation. The Ohio officers knew the suspect had requested an attorney and chose to interrogate him anyway. Because the Ohio officers took the statements in violation of *Miranda* and because the Ohio prosecutors could not show a waiver by the defendant, the evidence should not have been used against him.[158] If an arrestee clearly initiates new contact and wants to talk, the conduct indicates a waiver of *Miranda*. In a case in which the subject wants to talk and answer questions, but refuses to sign or make a written statement, the oral statements constituted admissible evidence.

---

153   Thompson v. Keohane, 516 U.S. 99 (1995).
154   Thompson v. Keohane, 1998 U.S. App. LEXIS 9432 (9th Cir. 1998).
155   Slwooko v. State, 2006 Alaska App. LEXIS 114 (2006).
156   Edwards v. Arizona, 451 U.S. 477 (1981).
157   *Id.*
158   Van Hook v. Anderson, 444 F.3d 830, 834, 2006 U.S. App. LEXIS 9628 (6th Cir. 2006).

Despite the rules that restrict how confessions and inculpatory statements may be obtained, confessions continue to be an useful investigative tool and provide evidence that a prosecutor can use during the government's case-in-chief. In fact, the Supreme Court in the *Miranda* case stated that confessions remained a proper element in law enforcement and that any statement given freely and voluntarily without any compelling influence was admissible in evidence.[159] In a subsequent case, the Court held that a person may volunteer any statement, even one prompted by mental problems, and the statement will not be excluded on *Miranda* grounds as long as the police did not coerce the subject.[160] In this case, when a person with mental problems approached a police officer to confess to a homicide, the officer properly listened to the confession and it was not considered to have been involuntarily taken under *Miranda*. The Court held that "coercive police activity is a necessary predicate to the finding that a confession is not 'voluntary' within the meaning of the Due Process Clause of the Fourteenth Amendment."[161] Therefore, it is clear that confessions continue to be admitted into evidence, and the skilled and informed investigator can obtain confessions or statements and still comply with the requirements established by the courts. Even if police fail to meet the strict requirements of *Miranda*, as long as the confession is voluntarily given, the evidence may be admitted for impeachment purposes where a defendant takes the stand and offers testimony contradictory to an otherwise inadmissible *Miranda* statement.[162]

In the case of *Harris v. New York*, the defendant was charged with selling heroin, and at the trial he took the stand in his own defense. The prosecution did not offer a confession made by the defendant during its case-in-chief because it appeared to have been taken in violation of the principles of *Miranda*. After the defendant testified by telling a story that was in direct conflict with his voluntary statement taken in violation of *Miranda*, the prosecution offered the original confession to impeach the testimony of the defendant. The United States Supreme Court allowed the admission of the confession even though *Miranda* warnings had not been given, explaining that a confession may be used for impeachment purposes if it is freely and voluntarily made. In so doing, the Court reasoned that:

> Having voluntarily taken the stand, petitioner was under an obligation to speak truthfully and accurately, and the prosecution did no more than utilize the traditional truth-testing devices of the adversary process.

In a more recent application of the *Harris* principle, a defendant accused of having a firearm under a disability had admitted to a police officer that he had

---

[159] Miranda v. Arizona, 384 U.S. 436, 1966 U.S. LEXIS 2817 (1966).

[160] Colorado v. Connelly, 479 U.S. 157, 1986 U.S. LEXIS 23 (1986).

[161] *Id.* at 167.

[162] Harris v. New York, 401 U.S. 222, 91 S. Ct. 643, 28 L. Ed. 2d 1 (1971); Oregon v. Hass, 420 U.S. 714, 91 S. Ct. 1215, 43 L. Ed. 2d 570 (1975).

possessed the gun.[163] At the time of the admission, he had not received his custodial *Miranda* warnings, so the statement could not be used to prove guilt. However, in a pretrial motion, the defendant wanted the statement suppressed and not used at trial even if he took the stand and contradicted the first unwarned statement. In a ruling citing *Harris v. New York*, the trial court refused to prevent the prosecution from impeaching the defendant if he chose to commit perjury during trial. The ruling noted that the benefit of excluding such evidence could not be used as a license to commit perjury, free from the risk of being confronted with prior inconsistent non-Mirandized statements.

Alternatively, if a confession has been coerced and was not voluntarily made even though *Miranda* warnings were given, the confession is not admissible in evidence even for impeachment purposes.[164]

In 1984, the Supreme Court decided a case involving an emergency situation in which a suspect's incriminating answer to a police officer's question was admitted even though the *Miranda* warnings were not administered prior to the suspect's emergency interrogation. The Supreme Court recognized a "narrow exception" to the *Miranda* rule, which stated that statements elicited from an arrestee, as well as real evidence obtained from exploiting such statements, may be admitted against the arrestee-defendant even if the officers failed to recite the *Miranda* warnings before asking the questions, as long as the officer's safety or the safety of others appeared to be in jeopardy.[165] In recognizing a "public safety" exception to the *Miranda* rule, the Court concluded that if the officer or the public may be in life-threatening danger, the threat to the public safety outweighs the need for the rule protecting the Fifth Amendment privilege against self-incrimination, and evidence resulting from questions not preceded by *Miranda* warnings is admissible under these limited circumstances. In a newer case, police questioned a domestic dispute subject concerning guns in plain view on a living room couch after having gained custody of the subject in a bedroom.[166] The officer asked, "What are those doing there?" and the subject admitted that he was trying to hide them because he knew the police were coming. The subject had a prior felony conviction and was not lawfully permitted to have the firearms. Under the circumstances, the subject's answer to the officer's pre-*Miranda* question constituted admissible evidence against him due to the emergency in getting control of the domestic dispute situation.

Following the original *Miranda* decision, the Congress demonstrated its disagreement with the ruling by passing the Omnibus Crime Control and Safe Streets Act of 1968, which contained a provision intended to reverse the effects of the *Miranda* decision in federal courts. The applicable part of this Act is 18 U.S.C. § 3501(c), which reads as follows:

163   United States v. Jenkins, 2003 U.S. Dist. LEXIS 4312 (S.D.N.Y. 2003).
164   Mincey v. Arizona, 437 U.S. 385, 98 S. Ct. 2408, 57 L. Ed. 2d 290 (1978).
165   New York v. Quarles, 467 U.S. 649, 104 S. Ct. 2626, 81 L. Ed. 2d 550 (1984).
166   *See* United States v. Martinez, 406 F.3d 1160, 1163, 2005 U.S. App. LEXIS 8624 (9th Cir. 2002).

> In any criminal prosecution by the United States or by the District of Columbia, a confession made or given by a person who is a defendant therein, while such person was under arrest or other detention in the custody of any law enforcement officer or law enforcement agency, shall not be inadmissible solely because of delay in bringing such person before a commissioner or other officer empowered to commit persons charged with offenses against the laws of the United States or of the District of Columbia if such confession is found by the trial judge to have been made voluntarily . . .[167]

The clear intention of the statute was to undermine the *Miranda* warnings by statutorily overruling the Supreme Court. Congress may change laws that it has passed and nullify Supreme Court decisions that have interpreted those laws, but it has no power to overrule Supreme Court decisions when the Court has interpreted a provision of the Constitution of the United States. In the case of *Dickerson v. United States*, the Supreme Court found that § 3501 was an unconstitutional exercise by Congress of its powers because the Court held that the *Miranda* decision and its accompanying warnings were of constitutional dimension.[168] That is to say, the Court held that the *Miranda* warnings were required by the Constitution and that Congress had no power to attempt to change a decision of constitutional dimensions. In the *Dickerson* case, the defendant, a bank robber, had been arrested by federal agents and interrogated voluntarily without being given his *Miranda* warnings. By all objective measures, the interrogation and incriminating statements were given in a completely voluntary manner; the only problem with their use was the *Miranda* decision. The trial court suppressed the statement but the Court of Appeals for the Fourth Circuit, by reversing and remanding the case, noted that the requirements of § 3501 had been met and that the confession was voluntarily made. After granting certiorari, the Supreme Court reversed the Fourth Circuit, holding that *Miranda* warnings were required by the Constitution and that any voluntariness standard suggested by the statute would not square with the *Miranda* decision and the federal constitution.[169] The attempt by Congress to overturn the *Miranda* decision failed and the accused robber's confession could not be used in court.

It is apparent from this discussion concerning confessions and other statements that although courts have established strict rules concerning how to evaluate their admissibility, confessions and admissions constitute admissible evidence and continue to be valuable tools in the prosecution of criminal activity. Generally, voluntary statements obtained in accordance with the requirements of the Fifth Amendment, *Miranda,* and other rules established by the Supreme Court will be admissible evidence.

---

[167] A delay in bringing an arrestee before a judge or magistrate may cause a detainee to file a civil suit, but generally, it does not seem to have resulted in the dismissal of a criminal case. *See* Turner v. City of Taylor, 412 F.3d 629, 2005 U.S. App. LEXIS 11233 (6th Cir. 2005) and Bryant v. City of New York, 404 F.3d 128, 2005 U.S. App. LEXIS 5376 (2d Cir. 2005).

[168] Dickerson v. United States, 530 U.S. 428, 440, 2000 U.S. LEXIS 4305 (2000).

[169] *Id.*

§ 16.6   Self-Incrimination and Related Protections

Often evidence is challenged because the officer, in obtaining the evidence, violated the Fifth Amendment privilege against self-incrimination. The pertinent section concerning self-incrimination provides that: "No person . . . shall be compelled in any criminal case to be a witness against himself." This provision, like the Fourth Amendment search and seizure provision, was included as a part of the Bill of Rights and became a part of the Constitution in 1791. The Fifth Amendment restrictions were not made applicable to the states until 1964 when the Supreme Court held that the due process clause of the Fourteenth Amendment included protections against self-incrimination.[170] The United States Supreme Court, in the case of *Malloy v. Hogan*, stated in its decision:

> We hold today that the Fifth Amendment's exception from compulsory self-incrimination is also protected by the Fourteenth Amendment against abridgement by the states.

This means that the Fifth Amendment standards to be applied in the states are the same standards as determined by the Supreme Court for federal courts and not the standards that were developed by state courts. After many conflicting decisions, the Supreme Court in the case of *Schmerber v. California*[171] clearly limited the application of the privilege against self-incrimination to evidence that can be categorized as "testimonial" in nature.

> We hold that the privilege protects the accused only from being compelled to testify against himself, or otherwise provide the state with evidence of a testimonial or communicative nature, and that the withdrawal of blood and use of the analysis in question in this case did not involve compulsion to these ends.

Following this interpretation, obtaining physical evidence from a defendant's person, such as evidence from a lineup, taking blood or DNA samples, and taking handwriting samples, does not constitute testimonial self-incrimination. As the *Schmerber* Court noted, the Fifth Amendment as applied to the states "offers no protection against compulsion to submit to fingerprinting, photographing, or measurements, to write or speak for identification, to appear in court, to stand, to assume a stance, to walk, or to make a particular gesture."[172] On the other hand, if an accused was forced to take a lie detector test or was coerced to give other evidence of a testimonial or communicative nature, such as being required to produce a response to a subpoena that has hallmarks of being testimonial in nature,[173] the Fifth Amendment's self-

---

[170]   Malloy v. Hogan, 378 U.S. 1, 84 S. Ct. 1489, 12 L. Ed. 2d 653 (1964).
[171]   384 U.S. 757, 86 S. Ct. 1826, 16 L. Ed. 2d 908 (1966). *See* case in Part II in Cases Relating to Chapter 14.
[172]   *Id.* at 764.
[173]   United States v. Ponds, 454 F.3d 313, 319, 2006 U.S. App. LEXIS 17718 (D.C. Cir. 2006).

incrimination provisions can be violated, and evidence so obtained may be ruled as inadmissible.

As a general rule, when a defendant invokes a constitutional right, the claim of right cannot be used as a sword against the defendant by commenting on it or highlighting its invocation. However, when there is no constitutional right to withhold evidence under the Fifth Amendment, a prosecutor may properly mention the fact to the jury during closing arguments. In the case of *South Dakota v. Neville*, the United States Supreme Court approved the admission of evidence that the defendant refused to submit to a blood-alcohol test.[174] Summarizing its opinion, the Court stated:

> We hold, therefore, that a refusal to take a blood alcohol test, after a police officer has lawfully requested it, is not an act coerced by the officer, and thus is not protected by the privilege against self-incrimination.

The Fifth Amendment self-incrimination provision neither prohibits the compelled display of identifiable physical characteristics such as tattoos, bodily scars, or deformities that help identify a person, nor does it protect against having to provide saliva and hair samples to a grand jury.[175] Echoing the *Schmerber* case, the Supreme Court of New Hampshire held in a sexual assault case that neither the state constitution nor the federal Fifth Amendment were violated by requiring a defendant to provide DNA samples that were introduced with blood evidence against him, because the evidence was non-testimonial in nature.[176] Requiring a handwriting sample from a defendant does not violate the Fifth Amendment or a similar state provision because the sample is an identifying physical fact and nothing more.[177]

While it is not generally a violation of the Fifth Amendment self-incrimination provision to require a suspect to give handwriting specimens or voice exemplars for identification purposes and it is not a violation for a prosecutor to comment on the failure to provide such sample, but it constitutes a violation of the Fifth Amendment for a prosecutor to comment to the jury on the failure of the accused to testify.[178]

In Arizona, when reasonable suspicion exists that an individual may be driving impaired, there is no right to refuse to take field sobriety tests and the tests do not violate the privilege against self-incrimination. Therefore, a driver who refuses to allow a search to determine whether he or she is impaired may be mentioned to the jury by police witnesses and used in closing arguments.[179] Following a similar logic, requiring an arrestee to comply with an officer's

[174] South Dakota v. Neville, 459 U.S. 553, 103 S. Ct. 916, 75 L. Ed. 2d 748 (1983).
[175] *See* People v. Watson, 214 Ill. 2d 271, 825 N.E.2d 257, 2005 Ill. LEXIS 2 (Ill. 2005).
[176] State v. Hearns, 151 N.H. 226, 855 A.2d 549, 2004 N.H. LEXIS 129 (N.H. 2004).
[177] State v. Wiggins, 2004 Del. Super. LEXIS 64 (Del. 2004). The Delaware courts have interpreted the Delaware Constitution of 1897, art. I, § 7, dealing with self-incrimination to be coextensive with the federal Fifth Amendment.
[178] Griffin v. California, 380 U.S. 609, 85 S. Ct. 1229, 14 L. Ed. 2d 106 (1965).
[179] State ex rel. Verburg v. Jones, 211 Ariz. 413, 121 P.3d 1283, 1285, 2005 Ariz. App. LEXIS 148 (2005).

request for a urine sample did not violate his Fifth Amendment privilege against self-incrimination, inasmuch as a sample was not evidence of a testimonial or communicative nature.[180] Likewise, where a defendant refused to give a urine sample in a drug possession case, the prosecution may comment on the defendant's refusal and the jury may give it whatever weight it chooses to give.[181]

All defendants have the privilege against self-incrimination based on state constitutions or on the federal Fifth Amendment, but it can successfully be asserted only when the evidence would be considered testimonial in nature. Evidence that involves physical attributes, personal characteristics, and scientific data about the defendant may implicate Fourth Amendment search and seizures issues, but rarely involve a violation of the Fifth Amendment.

§ 16.7 Due Process Exclusions

Closely related to the self-incrimination protections are the limitations that the due process clause of the Fourteenth Amendment imposes on the conduct of criminal proceedings of the states. If investigators, in obtaining evidence, violate the due process clause of the Fifth Amendment (in federal cases) or of the Fourteenth Amendment (in state cases), evidence obtained thereby will not be admissible. The reasoning here, as in other instances involving constitutional violations, is that to allow the admission of such evidence would encourage conduct that is prohibited by the Constitution.

Although the courts have refused to specifically define what is included in the due process protection, police and law enforcement actions that violate concepts of "fundamental fairness" generally violate the concept of due process.

For example, evidence obtained as a result of an improper lineup is inadmissible. If a lineup or other confrontation for identification is held in such a way as to be unduly suggestive, i.e., to suggest to the witnesses who make the identification which person in the lineup is the suspect, then the in-court identification would be contaminated.[182] For example, where the suspect wore dreadlocks, it did not violate due process when no more than two other men in the lineup appeared in dreadlocks.[183] The argument can be made that when photographs are shown to victims for identification purposes in such a way as to be unduly suggestive, the procedure denies due process to the suspect. Therefore, evidence obtained in this way may be inadmissible on due process grounds, but the Supreme Court has recognized that the due process clause does not always require a blanket rule of exclusion, suppressing testimony following an impermissibly suggestive identification procedure.[184] However, the

---

[180]   United States v. Edmo, 140 F.3d 1289 (9th Cir. 1998).

[181]   State v. Mattson, 2005 S.D. 71, 698 N.W.2d 538, 552, 2005 S.D. LEXIS 73 (S.D. 2005).

[182]   Foster v. California, 394 U.S. 440, 89 S. Ct. 1127, 22 L. Ed. 2d 402 (1969).

[183]   Dobson v. Walker, 150 Fed. Appx. 49, 50, 2005 U.S. App. LEXIS 21294 (2d Cir. 2005).

[184]   Amador v. Dretke, 2005 U.S. Dist. LEXIS 6072 (W.D. Tex. 2005), aff'd sub nom. by Amador v. Quarterman, 2006 U.S. App. LEXIS 19301 (5th Cir. 2006).

taking of blood, breath, saliva or urine samples—if done properly—does not violate the due process clause, and such evidence is admissible if other conditions are met.[185]

To summarize, if evidence is obtained by federal agents in violation of the due process clause of the Fifth Amendment, or by state agents in violation of the due process clause of the Fourteenth Amendment, courts will generally exclude such evidence when used for proof of guilt.

§ 16.8 Right to Counsel as It Relates to the Exclusion of Evidence

One of the protections of the Bill of Rights that has been very broadly interpreted in recent years is the section of the Sixth Amendment that provides: "In all criminal prosecutions, the accused shall enjoy the right . . . to have the assistance of counsel for his defense." In early decisions, this right was made available to the accused only at the trial if a defendant could afford an attorney but later was extended to indigents who were charged with felonies.[186] Subsequently, the Supreme Court determined that the Sixth Amendment right to the assistance of counsel applied during the early stages of criminal investigations when a focus on individual suspects occured.

As a means of enforcing the right to counsel provisions, a confession or statement obtained when the right to counsel is not protected will be excluded from evidence. For example, in *Escobedo v. Illinois*, the defendant moved to suppress the use of incriminating statements taken after he had requested counsel and had been refused. In this pre-*Miranda* right to counsel case, the Supreme Court held that the Sixth Amendment right to counsel attaches once the police have narrowed their inquiry to a specific subject, have taken the subject into custody, the subject has requested the assistance of an attorney, and police have embarked on efforts to question and elicit incriminating statements. Because Escobedo had been denied his right to the assistance of counsel who might have helped him assert his constitutional rigts, his convictions were reversed and the case remanded.[187] If Escobedo had originally been granted the assistance of counsel, presumably, he would not have assisted the government in obtaining evidence to be used against him.

Although in the *Escobedo* case the accused requested counsel, the Supreme Court in *Miranda*[188] stated that such a request was unnecessary because police must inform the person in custody of constitutional rights. Under the *Miranda* ruling, if the suspect is in custody when the police desire to conduct interrogation, the burden is placed on the police to inform the sus-

---

[185] Davis v. District of Columbia, 247 A.2d 417 (D.C. Ct. App. 1968).
[186] Gideon v. Wainwright, 372 U.S. 335, 1963 U.S. LEXIS 1942 (1963).
[187] *See* Escobedo v. Illinois, 378 U.S. 478, 1964 U.S. LEXIS 827 (1964).
[188] Miranda v. Arizona, 384 U.S. 436, 1966 U.S. LEXIS 2817 (1966).

pect of his or her constitutional rights and to refrain from asking any questions unless the accused knowingly waives his or her right to counsel.

From these and other cases, it is obvious that if custody exists and the accused requests counsel prior to or during the interrogation and counsel is not allowed, any statements obtained will not be admissible for proof of guilt. The *Miranda* Court reasoned that there are compelling pressures that exist in any custodial police interrogation and in order to help a suspect "to combat these pressures and to permit a full opportunity to exercise the privilege against self-incrimination, the accused must be adequately and effectively appraised of his rights and the exercise of those rights must be fully honored."[189] Under the *Miranda* reasoning, if police take a suspect into custody and question him or her with a view to obtaining incriminating statements, the police must advise him or her of his or her right to counsel and to silence or any evidence obtained will be excluded from trial to prove guilt.

The suspect may waive the right to counsel provided the waiver is made voluntarily, knowingly, and intelligently. However, the Supreme Court in *Edwards v. Arizona* determined that if the accused has clearly requested the assistance of counsel, interrogation must cease until counsel has been made available to the accused or until the accused initiates additional communication.[190] Although the Court in *Edwards* did not define "initiation of further communications," the Court in a later case determined that the question from the suspect, "Well, what is going to happen to me now?" really amounted to an attempt by the defendant to initiate further questioning, and that ensuing statements given by the defendant, even after he was warned further of his rights, were admissible.[191]

The rationale that was framed in *Edwards v. Arizona* was applied when the Supreme Court decided that if police initiate an interrogation after a defendant's assertion of his or her right to counsel at the arraignment or similar proceedings, a waiver of that right after police-initiated interrogation is invalid unless counsel is present. Once a suspect has been arraigned and has requested counsel at the arraignment or preliminary hearing, a police officer may not initiate questioning. The suspect may initiate additional communication with the police, but the burden is on the prosecution to show that the suspect did, in fact, initiate further questioning.[192] In *Michigan v. Jackson*, the arrestee initially requested the appointment of counsel, but before the attorney had a chance to meet with the arrestee, police had initiated interrogation and obtained a confession. The Supreme Court agreed with the state supreme court that the defendant's conviction must be reversed. According to the Supreme Court of the United States, "[i]f police initiate an interrogation after a defendant's assertion of his right to counsel at an arraignment or similar proceed-

---

[189]	*Id.* at 467.
[190]	Edwards v. Arizona, 451 U.S. 477, 101 S. Ct. 1880, 68 L. Ed. 2d 378 (1981).
[191]	Oregon v Bradshaw, 463 U.S. 1039, 103 S. Ct. 2830, 77 L. Ed. 2d 405 (1983).
[192]	Michigan v. Jackson, 475 U.S. 625, 1986 U.S. LEXIS 91 (1986). *See also* Poynter v. Murray, 964 F.2d 1404 (4th Cir.), *cert. denied*, 506 U.S. 958, 113 S. Ct. 419, 121 L. Ed. 2d 342 (1992).

ing, as in these cases, any waiver of that right for that police-initiated interrogation is invalid."[193] The prosecution does not get a chance to argue otherwise, even if the waiver might have honestly been a valid waiver.

In determining whether events subsequent to the accused's exercise of the right to be silent or have counsel present during a custodial interrogation constitute a waiver of the previously asserted right, the court must first determine whether the accused actually invoked the right, and, if so, the court must then determine whether the accused initiated further discussion with the police and knowingly and intelligently waived the previously asserted rights.[194]

Statements that might not be admissible under the *Edwards* case or the *Michigan v. Jackson* case may be used for impeachment purposes to cast doubt on a defendant's false or inconsistent testimony if a defendant takes the witness stand and offers testimony that is materially different from what the defendant stated to investigators during the illegal interrogation.[195] The court explained that while the Sixth Amendment prohibits the use of evidence obtained after the defendant has invoked his or her Sixth Amendment right to counsel for his or her case-in-chief, this shield should not be perverted into a license defensive perjury, free from the risk of confrontation with prior inconsistent utterances.

Another case that has had influence on the admissibility of evidence when the right to counsel is at issue is *United States v. Wade*.[196] This case concerned the right to counsel during a police lineup. In *Wade*, the Supreme Court stated that both the defendant *Wade* and his counsel should have been notified of the impending post-indictment lineup and that counsel's presence should have been a requisite to the conduct of the lineup, absent an intelligent waiver. The Court asserted that the best method of enforcing this right to counsel at the lineup is to prohibit in-court identification by witnesses if the court finds that the pretrial confrontation or lineup tainted the in-court identification. In other words, the Court reasoned that the post-indictment in-person lineup was a critical stage of the proceedings and that counsel should be present—unless the right is waived—if the identifying witness is to testify in court. In justifying this stand, the Court stated:

> Since it appears that there is a grave potential for prejudice, intentional or not, in the pretrial lineup, which may not be capable of reconstruction at trial, and since presence of counsel itself can often avert prejudice and assure a meaningful confrontation at trial, there can be little doubt that for *Wade* the post-indictment lineup was a critical stage of the prosecution.

If the accused's attorney is present or if the accused intelligently waives the right to an attorney, then a witness who made an identification of the

---

[193] *Id.* at 636.
[194] State v. Lane, 262 Kan. 373, 940 P.2d 422 (1997).
[195] Michigan v. Harvey, 494 U.S. 344, 110 S. Ct. 1176, 108 L. Ed. 2d 293 (1990).
[196] 388 U.S. 218, 87 S. Ct. 1926, 18 L. Ed. 2d 1149 (1967).

accused at the lineup may be called upon in court to identify the accused in court. However, if the attorney was not present at a post-information or post-indictment lineup and the defendant did not waive the right to counsel, the witness may not be permitted to make an in-court identification of the defendant. If the prosecution can establish that an in-court identification will not be based on or tainted by the uncounseled lineup and will be based on a crime scene identification by clear and convincing proof, the identification evidence can be admitted.[197] In such circumstances, the in-court identification may be admissible even though counsel was not present at the pretrial confrontation.

In an Illinois case, the United States Supreme Court eased the requirement of counsel at some lineup situations.[198] After reiterating the opinion that subjecting a person to a lineup does not deprive the accused of the right to protection from self-incrimination, the Court further explained that counsel is not required at a prearrest, preindictment identification confrontation. The Court distinguished this situation from the *Wade* post-indictment confrontation for identification, explaining:

> The initiation of judicial criminal proceedings is far from a mere formalism. It is the starting point of our whole system of adversary criminal justice. For it is only then that the government has committed itself to prosecute, and only then that the adverse positions of government and defendant have solidified. . . . It is this point, therefore, that marks the commencement of the "criminal prosecution" to which alone the explicit guarantees of the Sixth Amendment are applicable.

The modified rule, therefore, is that the post-indictment lineup or confrontation for identification is a critical stage, and the right to counsel attaches if the witness is to identify the accused at trial. However, the pre-arrest, pre-indictment, pre-information confrontation is not a critical stage for Sixth Amendment purposes, and identification evidence may be offered at trial even if counsel was not present at the lineup or showup. Case law in some states helps clarify when the right to counsel attaches in state prosecutions. For example, in New York, a suspect does not have a right to counsel when police conduct a pre-arraignment lineup[199] where there has been no indictment. And in Michigan, the right to counsel for in-person lineups does not attach until adversarial judicial proceedings have been initiated.[200] In an additional limitation of the right to counsel at identification procedures, the Supreme Court held that "the Sixth Amendment does not require that defense counsel be pre-

[197]   Moore v. Illinois, 434 U.S. 220, 225, 1977 U.S. LEXIS 163 (1977).

[198]   Kirby v. Illinois, 406 U.S. 682, 92 S. Ct. 1877, 32 L. Ed. 2d 411 (1972).

[199]   People v. Woolcock, 2005 NY Slip Op 25045 (N.Y. 2005).

[200]   People v. Harris, 2005 Mich. App. LEXIS 3264 (2005). Michigan grants the right to counsel for corporeal identifications only at or after the initiation of adversarial judicial proceedings and there is no right to counsel at photographic arrays. *See* People v. Hickman, 470 Mich. 602, 684 N.W.2d 267, 2004 Mich. LEXIS 1544 (Mich. 2004).

sent when a witness views police or prosecution photographic arrays[,]"[201] although a state would be free to require them. Due process still dictates that a photographic array or photo lineup cannot be unduly suggestive if police want to have the evidence admitted at a defendant's trial.

§ 16.9 Summary

Although the traditional common law doctrine is that evidence is admissible if relevant even though obtained illegally, much evidence is not admissible if a federal or state constitutional provision has been violated. Exclusionary rules have developed over time and have been made applicable both to federal and state courts on a piecemeal basis.

Under the present rules as established by the United States Supreme Court and lower courts, most evidence obtained by search and seizure in violation of the Constitution is inadmissible in both federal and state courts. The cases must be examined thoroughly to determine what is considered an illegal search and under what circumstances the exclusionary rules apply.

Although wiretap evidence at first was not considered to be within the protection of the constitutional provisions, recent cases have held that wiretapping and eavesdropping fall within the protection of the Fourth Amendment as well as state and federal law. Under the Omnibus Crime Control Act of 1968, certain wiretap and eavesdrop evidence is admissible if the statutory requirements are met or if one party to the conversation consents. Evidence obtained in violation of the statute will not be admitted into court. The Patriot Act expanded the definition of a pen register so that newer methods of transmitting data and communication may be covered when the executive branch obtains a warrant.

As a means of ensuring that confessions will be obtained freely and voluntarily, courts have established rules that prohibit the admissibility of confessions obtained in violation of established standards. Although evidence continues to be challenged with arguments that the admission of physical facts or scientific evidence results in a violation of the Fifth Amendment self-incrimination privilege, this protection has been interpreted to apply only to evidence of a testimonial or a communicative nature. Evidence that is of a testimonial or communicative nature is inadmissible unless this protection is waived.

Evidence acquired in violation of the due process clauses of the Fifth and Fourteenth Amendments is also inadmissible. While most due process arguments for excluding evidence fall under specific provisions of the Bill of Rights, some evidence is subject to exclusion under due process standards. Court opinions must be studied to determine what activities constitute a violation, keeping in mind that some states offer greater protection under due process than is required by the federal constitution.

---

[201] United States v. Ash, 413 U.S. 300, 1973 U.S. LEXIS 45 (1973).

Evidence is also excluded if the right to counsel provisions of the Sixth Amendment are violated. Again, it is essential that cases be studied carefully to determine the various courts' interpretations concerning what is a violation of the Sixth Amendment.

Although courts exclude certain evidence to enforce constitutional provisions that have been violated, criminal justice personnel should not take a negative attitude, because these limitations uphold the rule of law. Proper investigation that follows constitutional requirements and interpretations will result in both protecting the rights of the individual and successful prosecutions of wrongdoers with admissible evidence.

Part II:
Judicial Decisions
Relating To Part I

Part II: Table of Cases

(for a complete Table of Cases in Part I, see page ???)

Cases Relating to Chapter 1

History and Development of Rules of Evidence

FUNK

v.

UNITED STATES

Supreme Court of the United States
290 U.S. 371, 54 S. Ct. 212 (1933)

JUSTICE SUTHERLAND delivered the opinion of the Court.

The sole inquiry to be made in this case is whether in a federal court the wife of the defendant on trial for a criminal offense is a competent witness in his behalf. Her competency to testify against him is not involved.

The petitioner was twice tried and convicted in a federal district court upon an indictment for conspiracy to violate the prohibition law. His conviction on the first trial was reversed by the circuit court of appeals upon a ground not material here. 46 F.2d 417. Upon the second trial, as upon the first, defendant called his wife to testify in his behalf. At both trials she was excluded upon the ground of incompetency. The circuit court of appeals sustained this ruling upon the first appeal, and also upon the appeal which followed the second trial. 66 F.2d 70. We granted certiorari, limited to the question as to what law is applicable to the determination of the competency of the wife of the petitioner as a witness.

Both the petitioner and the government, in presenting the case here, put their chief reliance on prior decisions of this court. The government relies on United States v. Reid, 12 How. 361; Logan v. United States, 144 U.S. 263; Hendrix v. United States, 219 U.S. 79; and Jin Fuey Moy v. United States, 254 U.S. 189. Petitioner contends that these cases, if not directly contrary to the decisions in Benson v. United States, 146 U.S. 325, and Rosen v. United States, 245 U.S. 467, are so in principle. We shall first briefly review these cases, with the exception of the Hendrix case and the Jin Fuey Moy case, which we leave for consideration until a later point in this opinion.

In the Reid case, two persons had been jointly indicted for a murder committed upon the high seas. They were tried separately, and it was held that one of them was not a competent witness in behalf of the other who was first tried. The trial was had in Virginia; and by a statute of that state passed in 1849, if applicable in a federal court, the evidence would have been competent. Section 34 of the Judiciary Act of 1789 declares that the laws of the several states, except where the Constitution, treaties or statutes of the United States otherwise provide, shall be regarded as rules of decision in trials at common law in the courts of the United States in cases where they apply; but the court said that this referred only to civil cases and did not apply in the trial of criminal offenses against the United States. It was conceded that there was no act of Congress prescribing in express words the rule by which the federal courts would be governed in the admission of testimony in criminal cases. "But," the court said (p. 363), "we think it may be found with sufficient certainty, not indeed in direct terms, but by necessary implication, in the acts of

1789 and 1790, establishing the courts of the United States, and providing for the punishment of certain offences."

The court pointed out that the Judiciary Act regulated certain proceedings to be had prior to impaneling the jury, but contained no express provision concerning the mode of conducting the trial after the jury was sworn, and prescribed no rule in respect of the testimony to be taken. Obviously however, it was said, some certain and established rule upon the subject was necessary to enable the courts to administer the criminal jurisprudence of the United States, and Congress must have intended to refer them to some known and established rule "which was supposed to be so familiar and well understood in the trial by jury that legislation upon the subject would be deemed superfluous. This is necessarily to be implied from what these acts of Congress omit, as well as from what they contain." (p. 365.) The court concluded that this could not be the common law as it existed at the time of the emigration of the colonists, or the rule which then prevailed in England, and [therefore] the only known rule which could be supposed to have been in the mind of Congress was that which was in force in the respective states when the federal courts were established by the Judiciary Act of 1789. Applying this rule, it was decided that the witness was incompetent.

In the Logan case it was held that the competency of a witness to testify in a federal court sitting in one state, was not affected by his conviction and sentence for felony in another state; and that the competency of another witness was not affected by his conviction of felony in a Texas state court, where the witness had since been pardoned. The indictment was for an offense committed in Texas and there tried. The decision was based not upon any statute of the United States, but upon the ground that the subject "is governed by the common law, which, as has been seen, was the law of Texas . . . at the time of the admission of Texas into the Union as a State." (p. 303.)

We next consider the two cases upon which petitioner relies. In the Benson case two persons were jointly indicted for murder. On motion of the government there was a severance, and Benson was first tried. His codefendant was called as a witness on behalf of the government. The Reid case had been cited as practically decisive of the question. But the court, after pointing out what it conceived to be distinguishing features in that case, said (p. 335), "We do not feel ourselves, therefore, precluded by that case from examining this question in the light of general authority and sound reason."

The alleged incompetency of the codefendant was rested upon two reasons, first, that he was interested, and second, that he was a party to the record, the basis for the exclusion at common law being fear of perjury. "Nor," the court said, "were those named the only grounds of exclusion from the witness stand; conviction of crime, want of religious belief, and other matters were held sufficient. Indeed, the theory of the common law was to admit to the witness stand only those presumably honest, appreciating the sanctity of an oath, unaffected as a party by the result, and free from any of the temptations of interest. The courts were afraid to trust the intelligence of jurors. But the last fifty years have wrought a great change in these respects, and to-day the tendency is to enlarge the domain of competency and to submit to the jury for their consideration as to the credibility of the witness those matters which heretofore were ruled sufficient to justify his exclusion. This change has been wrought partially by legislation and partially by judicial construction." Attention then is called to the fact that Congress in 1864 had enacted that no witness should be excluded from testifying in any civil action, with certain exceptions, because he was a party to or interested in the issue tried; and that in 1878 (c. 37, 20 Stat. 30) Congress made the defendant in any criminal case a competent witness at his own request. The opinion then continues (p. 337):

Legislation of similar import prevails in most of the States. The spirit of this legislation has controlled the decisions of the courts, and steadily, one by one, the merely technical barriers which excluded witnesses from the stand have been removed, till now it is generally, though perhaps not universally, true that no one is excluded therefrom unless the lips of the originally adverse party are closed by death, or

unless some one of those peculiarly confidential relations, like that of husband and
wife, forbids the breaking of silence.

. . . If interest and being party to the record
do not exclude a defendant on trial from
the witness stand, upon what reasoning can
a codefendant, not on trial, be adjudged
incompetent?

That case was decided December 5, 1892.
Twenty-five years later this court had before
it for consideration the case of Rosen v. United States, supra. Rosen had been tried and
convicted in a federal district court for conspiracy. A person jointly indicted with Rosen,
who had been convicted upon his plea of
guilty, was called as a witness by the government and allowed to testify over Rosen's
objection. This court sustained the competency of the witness. After saying that while the
decision in the Reid case had not been specifically overruled, its authority was seriously
shaken by the decisions in both the Logan
and Benson cases, the court proceeded to dispose of the question, as it had been disposed
of in the Benson case, "in the light of general authority and sound reason."

"In the almost twenty [twenty-five] years,"
the court said [pp. 471, 472], "which have
elapsed since the decision of the Benson
Case, the disposition of courts and of legislative bodies to remove disabilities from
witnesses has continued, as that decision
shows it had been going forward before,
under dominance of the conviction of our
time that the truth is more likely to be
arrived at by hearing the testimony of all
persons of competent understanding who
may seem to have knowledge of the facts
involved in a case, leaving the credit and
weight of such testimony to be determined
by the jury or by the court, rather than by
rejecting witnesses as incompetent, with
the result that this principle has come to be
widely, almost universally, accepted in this
country and in Great Britain.

"Since the decision in the Benson Case we
have significant evidence of the trend of
congressional opinion upon this subject in
the removal of the disability of witnesses

convicted of perjury, Rev. Stats., § 5392,
by the enactment of the Federal Criminal
Code in 1909 with this provision omitted
and § 5392 repealed. This is significant,
because the disability to testify, of persons
convicted of perjury, survived in some
jurisdictions much longer than many of the
other common-law disabilities, for the reason that the offense concerns directly the
giving of testimony in a court of justice,
and conviction of it was accepted as showing a greater disregard for the truth than it
was thought should be implied from a conviction of other crime.

"Satisfied as we are that the legislation and
the very great weight of judicial authority
which have developed in support of this
modern rule, especially as applied to the
competency of witnesses convicted of
crime, proceed upon sound principle, we
conclude that the dead hand of the common-law rule of 1789 should no longer be
applied to such cases as we have here, and
that the ruling of the lower courts on this
first claim of error should be approved."

It is well to pause at this point to state a little more concisely what was held in these
cases. It will be noted, in the first place, that
the decision in the Reid case was not based
upon any express statutory provision. The
court found from what the congressional legislation omitted to say, as well as from what
it actually said, that in establishing the federal courts in 1789 some definite rule in
respect to the testimony to be taken in criminal cases must have been in the mind of Congress; and the rule which the court thought
was in the mind of that body was that of the
common law as it existed in the thirteen original states in 1789. The Logan Case in part
rejected that view and held that the controlling rule was that of the common law in force
at the time of the admission of the state in
which the particular trial was had. Taking the
two cases together, it is plain enough that the
ultimate doctrine announced is that in the
taking of testimony in criminal cases, the
federal courts are bound by the rules of the
common law as they existed at a definitely
specified time in the respective states, unless
Congress has otherwise provided.

With the conclusion that the controlling rule is that of the common law, the Benson case and the Rosen case do not conflict; but both cases reject the notion, which the two earlier ones seem to accept, that the courts, in the face of greatly changed conditions, are still chained to the ancient formulae and are powerless to declare and enforce modifications deemed to have been wrought in the common law itself by force of these changed conditions. Thus, as we have seen, the court in the Benson case pointed to the tendency during the preceding years to enlarge the domain of competency, significantly saying that the changes had been wrought not only by legislation but also "partially by judicial construction"; and that it was the spirit (not the letter, be it observed) of this legislation which had controlled the decisions of the courts and steadily removed the merely technical barriers in respect of incompetency, until generally no one was excluded from giving testimony, except under certain peculiar conditions which are set forth. It seems difficult to escape the conclusion that the specific ground upon which the court there rested its determination as to the competency of a codefendant was that, since the defendant had been rendered competent, the competency of the codefendant followed as a natural consequence.

This view of the matter is made more positive by the decision in the Rosen case. The question of the testimonial competency of a person jointly indicted with the defendant was disposed of, as the question had been in the Benson case, "in the light of general authority and sound reason." The conclusion which the court reached was based not upon any definite act of legislation, but upon the trend of congressional opinion and of legislation (that is to say of legislation generally), and upon the great weight of judicial authority which, since the earlier decisions, had developed in support of a more modern rule. In both cases the court necessarily proceeded upon the theory that the resultant modification which these important considerations had wrought in the rules of the old common law was within the power of the courts to declare and make operative.

That the present case falls within the principles of the Benson and Rosen cases, and especially of the latter, we think does not reasonably admit of doubt.

The rules of the common law which disqualified as witnesses persons having an interest, long since, in the main, have been abolished both in England and in this country; and what was once regarded as a sufficient ground for excluding the testimony of such persons altogether has come to be uniformly and more sensibly regarded as affecting the credit of the witness only. Whatever was the danger that an interested witness would not speak the truth—and the danger never was as great as claimed—its effect has been minimized almost to the vanishing point by the test of cross-examination, the increased intelligence of jurors, and perhaps other circumstances. The modern rule which has removed the disqualification from persons accused of crime gradually came into force after the middle of the last century, and is today universally accepted. The exclusion of the husband or wife is said by this court to be based upon his or her interest in the event. Jin Fuey Moy v. United States, supra. And whether by this is meant a practical interest in the result of the prosecution or merely a sentimental interest because of the marital relationship, makes little difference. In either case, a refusal to permit the wife upon the ground of interest to testify in behalf of her husband, while permitting him, who has the greater interest, to testify for himself, presents a manifest incongruity.

Nor can the exclusion of the wife's testimony, in the face of the broad and liberal extension of the rules in respect of the competency of witnesses generally, be any longer justified, if it ever was justified, on any ground of public policy. It has been said that to admit such testimony is against public policy because it would endanger the harmony and confidence of marital relations, and, moreover, would subject the witness to the temptation to commit perjury. Modern legislation, in making either spouse competent to testify in behalf of the other in criminal cases, has definitely rejected these notions, and in the light of such legislation and of modern thought they seem to be altogether fanciful. The public policy of one generation may not, under changed conditions, be the public policy of another. Patton v. United States, 281 U.S. 276, 306.

The fundamental basis upon which all rules of evidence must rest—if they are to rest upon reason—is their adaptation to the successful development of the truth. And since experience is of all teachers the most dependable, and since experience also is a continuous process, it follows that a rule of evidence at one time thought necessary to the ascertainment of truth should yield to the experience of a succeeding generation whenever that experience has clearly demonstrated the fallacy or unwisdom of the old rule.

It may be said that the court should continue to enforce the old rule, however contrary to modern experience and thought, and however opposed, in principle, to the general current of legislation and of judicial opinion, it may have become, leaving to Congress the responsibility of changing it. Of course, Congress has that power; but if Congress fail to act, as it has failed in respect of the matter now under review, and the court be called upon to decide the question, is it not the duty of the court, if it possess the power, to decide it in accordance with present day standards of wisdom and justice rather than in accordance with some outworn and antiquated rule of the past? That this court has the power to do so is necessarily implicit in the opinions delivered in deciding the Benson and Rosen cases. And that implication, we think, rests upon substantial ground. The rule of the common law which denies the competency of one spouse to testify in behalf of the other in a criminal prosecution has not been modified by congressional legislation; nor has Congress directed the federal courts to follow state law upon that subject, as it has in respect of some other subjects. That this court and the other federal courts, in this situation and by right of their own powers, may decline to enforce the ancient rule of the common law under conditions as they now exist we think is not fairly open to doubt.

In Hurtado v. California, 110 U.S. 516, 530, this court, after suggesting that it was better not to go too far back into antiquity for the best securities of our liberties, said:

It is more consonant to the true philosophy of our historical legal institutions to say that the spirit of personal liberty and individual right, which they embodied, was preserved and developed by a progressive growth and wise adaptation to new circumstances and situations of the forms and processes found fit to give, from time to time, new expression and greater effect to modern ideas of self-government.

This flexibility and capacity for growth and adaptation is the peculiar boast and excellence of the common law. . . . and as it was the characteristic principle of the common law to draw its inspiration from every fountain of justice, we are not to assume that the sources of its supply have been exhausted. On the contrary, we should expect that the new and various experiences of our own situation and system will mould and shape it into new and not less useful forms.

Compare Holden v. Hardy, 169 U.S. 366, 385-387.

To concede this capacity for growth and change in the common law by drawing "its inspiration from every fountain of justice," and at the same time to say that the courts of this country are forever bound to perpetuate such of its rules as, by every reasonable test, are found to be neither wise nor just, because we have once adopted them as suited to our situation and institutions at a particular time, is to deny to the common law in the place of its adoption a "flexibility and capacity for growth and adaptation" which was "the peculiar boast and excellence" of the system in the place of its origin.

The final question to which we are thus brought is not that of the power of the federal courts to amend or repeal any given rule or principle of the common law, for they neither have nor claim that power, but it is the question of the power of these courts, in the complete absence of congressional legislation on the subject, to declare and effectuate, upon common law principles, what is the present rule upon a given subject in the light of fundamentally altered conditions, without regard to what has previously been declared and practiced. It has been said so often as to have become axiomatic that the common law is not immutable but flexible, and by its own principles adapts itself to varying conditions. In Ketelsen v. Stilz, 184 Ind. 702; 111 N. E. 423, the supreme court of that state, after pointing out that the common law of England was based upon usages, customs and institutions of the English people as declared from time to time by the courts, said (p. 707):

The rules so deduced from this system, however, were continually changing and expanding with the progress of society in the application of this system to more diversified circumstances and under more advanced periods. The common law by its own principles adapted itself to varying conditions and modified its own rules so as to serve the ends of justice as prompted by a course of reasoning which was guided by these generally accepted truths. One of its oldest maxims was that where the reason of a rule ceased, the rule also ceased, and it logically followed that when it occurred to the courts that a particular rule had never been founded upon reason, and that no reason existed in support thereof, that rule likewise ceased, and perhaps another sprang up in its place which was based upon reason and justice as then conceived. No rule of the common law could survive the reason on which it was founded. It needed no statute to change it but abrogated itself.

That court then refers to the settled doctrine that an adoption of the common law in general terms does not require, without regard to local circumstances, an unqualified application of all its rules; that the rules, as declared by the English courts at one period or another, have been controlling in this country only so far as they were suited to and in harmony with the genius, spirit and objects of American institutions; and that the rules of the common law considered proper in the eighteenth century are not necessarily so considered in the twentieth. "Since courts have had an existence in America," that court said (p. 708), "they have never hesitated to take upon themselves the responsibility of saying what are the proper rules of the common law."

And the Virginia Supreme Court of Appeals, in Hanriot v. Sherwood, 82 Va. 1, 15, after pointing to the fact that the common law of England is the law of that commonwealth except so far as it has been altered by statute, or so far as its principles are inapplicable to the state of the country, and that the rules of the common law had undergone modification in the courts of England, notes with obvious approval that "the rules of evidence have been in the courts of this country undergoing such modification and changes, according to the circumstances of the country and the manner and genius of the people."

The supreme court of Connecticut, in Beardsley v. Hartford, 50 Conn. 529, 541-542, after quoting the maxim of the common law, cessante ratione legis, cessat ipsa lex, said:

This means that no law can survive the reasons on which it is founded. It needs no statute to change it; it abrogates itself. If the reasons on which a law rests are overborne by opposing reasons, which in the progress of society gain a controlling force, the old law, though still good as an abstract principle, and good in its application to some circumstances, must cease to apply as a controlling principle to the new circumstances.

The same thought is expressed in People v. Randolph, 2 Park. Cr. Rep. (N. Y.) 174, 177:

Its rules [the rules of the common law] are modified upon its own principles and not in violation of them. Those rules being founded in reason, one of its oldest maxims is, that where the reason of the rule ceases the rule also ceases. * * *

Judgment reversed.

MR. JUSTICE CARDOZO concurs in the result.

MR. JUSTICE McREYNOLDS and MR. JUSTICE BUTLER are of opinion that the judgment of the court below is right and should be affirmed.

Cases Relating to Chapter 2

Approach to the Study of Criminal Evidence

STATE

v.

PERKINS

130 W. Va. 708, 45 S.E.2d 17 (1947)

KENNA, Judge.

Katherine Perkins was indicted by a grand jury of Wayne County for the Murder of her husband, P.P. Perkins. She pleaded not guilty, was tried and convicted of murder of the second degree, and sentenced to imprisonment for a term of five to eighteen years. She brings the case here by writ of error.

On the evening of September 1, 1944, defendant, while riding in the automobile of a friend on Monroe Avenue in the City of Huntington, observed her husband in his automobile embracing a woman. At the request of the defendant, the automobile was stopped, and defendant then went to the vehicle in which her husband and companion were seated, and there engaged a fight with the woman. The husband interfered in the struggle, enjoined defendant not to hurt his companion and finally hit and kicked defendant several times. The defendant reentered her friend's automobile and returned to her home in the town of Ceredo.

About ten o'clock p.m. of the same day, the husband returned to his home, and, according to defendant's testimony, he was angry and inclined to be violent. The quarrel between defendant and her husband was renewed and ended by the husband striking and kicking the defendant. After committing the second assault on defendant, the husband left his home and did not return until about

midnight. Upon his return home he occupied a room on the second floor of his residence different from that which he and defendant had been wont to occupy. The defendant slept for the greater portion of the night in the room of her son and daughter-in-law.

On the morning of September 2, 1944, defendant prepared breakfast for a boarder, herself and her family. She and her daughter-in-law ate breakfast together, after which defendant went to the business section of the town for the purpose of paying a grocery bill. At some time during the morning defendant went to the home of a witness who testified for the State, where the witness said she saw a firearm in the possession of defendant, and that defendant indicated that trouble was about to occur.

Defendant returned to her home, went to an upstairs bedroom, and began combing her hair. While doing so her husband came to the door; severely criticized defendant on her conduct in fighting the night before; said in substance that he was not further interested as he was leaving and started toward defendant, saying "I will break your God damned neck."

The record is not clear as to what took place after the threat had been made by the husband. Defendant does not admit shooting her husband, but it is a reasonable inference, well supported by the facts, that she shot the deceased three times. One bullet entered his shoulder, one about the middle of his right thigh, and another at the ninth dorsal vertebra. All bullets entered from the back. It is also a reasonable inference that defendant shot herself in the forehead, a pistol having been found near her body in the upstairs hall, and she was bleeding from a gunshot wound in her head.

The pistol found near defendant's body was offered as an exhibit, and was fairly well identified as belonging to a boarder and roomer, who stayed at the home of defendant and her husband, and whose room was on the first floor thereof. The neighbors of defendant were summoned upon their arrival at the scene of the shooting, the husband, who had fallen down the stairway to the first floor, requested them to go upstairs and see about "Kate", adding that he was to blame for the shooting. Another witness testified that on the way to the hospital in the ambulance defendant stated she was sorry she had not killed her husband and applied to him a vile epithet.

The husband was taken to a hospital, where he remained under treatment until the 8th day of April, 1945, when he left the hospital and returned to his home, where he died on April 16, 1945.

Defendant contends that the court committed the following errors: (1) In permitting an attending physician, prior to any proof of the cause of death, to give in evidence his opinion as to the cause of the decedent's death; (2) in refusing to give defendant's instruction No. 3; and (3) by overruling defendant's objection to the cross-examination of defendant by the judge.

* * *

Instruction No. 3 embodied a statement of the law of self-defense. The instruction was refused on the ground that there was no evidence, either on the part of the State or defendant, supporting an instruction on self-defense. The record in this case has been carefully examined. The acts of violence perpetrated by the deceased on defendant on the night preceding the shooting, as well as the threat made by the deceased just prior to thereto, have been considered. Mere words, unaccompanied by an overt act, are not sufficient to justify an instruction to the jury on the theory of self-defense. State v. Snider, 81 W. Va. 522, 94 S.E. 981. Defendant was probably smarting from the indignities occa-

sioned by the two assaults committed on her prior to the shooting, but when the deceased encountered defendant at the the time of the shooting, there was no overt act committed by deceased. There is testimony that he started toward defendant at the time of the threat but that fact does not constitute an overt act. The record does not disclose what took place after the threat was made, as the defendant states that her mind is blank as to what was done by her or the deceased after the threat. Instruction No. 3 assumes that deceased made an attack on defendant. There is no showing of such fact in the record, nor is there sufficient evidence which tends to prove that such attack was made. The instruction comes within the rule laid down in the third point of the syllabus in State v. Barker, 92 W. Va. 583, 115 S.E. 421. See State v. Weissengoff, 89 W. Va. 279, 109 S.E. 707; State v. Frank Zinn, 95 W. Va. 148, 120 S.E. 387; State v. Newman, 101 W. Va. 356, 132 S.E. 728.

Facts necessary to support the theory of self-defense are not shown in this record. On the contrary, it is undisputed that all of the bullets inflicting wounds on deceased entered from the rear, which militates against the idea that deceased had assumed an aggressive attitude toward defendant at the time of the shooting. The refusal of the trial court to give defendant's instruction No. 3 is not error.

Defendant testified in her own behalf. At the commencement of her re-direct examination, her counsel asked one question, which she did not answer. At that time the judge of the trial court commenced to cross-examine defendant in the presence of the jury and asked, without intermission, forty-one questions. It would unduly prolong this opinion to quote all the questions asked by the judge and answered by defendant. Such questions related to the ownership of the revolver, and also how the revolver came to be on the second floor when the room of the owner thereof was on the first floor. The cross-examination also elicited the fact that defendant had made the roomer's bed on the morning of the shooting; that deceased was shot three times in the back; and that defendant also suffered a gunshot wound.

After developing these two subjects, the judge of the trial court then asked defendant the following questions:

"Q. Mrs. Perkins, you have told the jury you had a blackout up there on the evening when you found your husband with this woman and you don't remember anything except what your husband did to you, is that right?

"A. That is right, exactly right.

"Q. You remember everything that happened from then on until this shooting?

"A. Yes, sir.

"Q. You remember your husband standing with a flashlight in his hand and his gun in his hand?

"A. Yes, sir.

"Q. You remember that?

"A. Yes, sir.

"Q. Then you testified to the jury that you had a blackout from that time on, is that right?

"A. Yes, sir.

"Q. You don't remember what happened?

"A. I don't remember anything that happened until late that evening in the hospital.

"Q. When that blackout struck you where were you standing?

"A. In the doorway.

"Q. Room No. 2?

"A. Yes, sir.

"Q. Where was he?

"A. In the hall.

"Q. Facing each other?

"A. Yes.

"Q. And you don't know how that gun which has been exhibited in evidence got there in the hallway and found there after you were shot?

"A. I don't remember ever having that gun in my hands.

"Q. You didn't have a blackout except on those two occasions, is that right?

"A. I don't understand what you mean.

"Q. You told the jury your mind was a blank at the time of the trouble with this woman, now you tell the jury your mind was a blank from the time your husband was standing there in the hall and you were in the room facing him.

"A. I guess I was so mad, I don't know anything else."

Thereupon defendant objected to the questions asked by the trial judge and rested her case.

The question presented by the third assignment of error has been before this Court several times. In disposing of a similar question presented in the case of State v. Hurst, 11 W. Va. 54, this Court laid down the following rule: "It is error for a court in the trial of a criminal cause, to make a remark to, or in the presence of the jury, in reference to matters of fact, which might in any degree influence them in their verdict." In the case of State v. Thompson, 21 W. Va. 741, 756, this Court again adverted to the rule laid down in the Hurst case.

The rule is amplified and restated in the seventh point of the syllabus in the case of State v. Austin, 93 W. Va. 704, 117 S.E. 607, as follows: "In the trial of a criminal case, the jurors, not the court, are the triers of the facts, and the court should be extremely cautious not to intimate in any manner, by word, tone, or demeanor, his opinion of any fact in issue." In the case of State v. Hively, 103 W. Va. 237, 136 S.E. 862, this Court held: "Under the practice in this State, the trial judge should express to the jury no opinion on the testimony, either directly or by innuendo.

The action of the trial judge in the case of State v. Songer, 117 W. Va. 529, 186 S.E. 118, was somewhat similar to that of the trial judge in the instant case. In the Songer case, this Court, citing with approval the case of State v. Austin, supra, reversed the trial court, using the following language: "Edgar Martin was a witness for the state though friendly to defendant. The court virtually conducted his examination in chief by asking him in all, sixty questions. Reed Mullens was a witness for the defendant. Reed testified (without objection) that he did not know they were stealing the car; that Martin told him Bias had the car borrowed. (Martin was not questioned on that point). While Reed's examination in chief was in progress, the court interposed and asked him thirty-three questions. Upon Reed's cross examination, the court again asked a number of questions. Some of the court's questions were brusque and his interrogations generally, both of Martin and Mullens, tended to indicate to the jury that he did not credit the innocence of the defendant. This was prejudicial error.

* * *

In this case the demeanor of the trial judge is not portrayed by the record, nor is it shown whether the questions were brusque or otherwise. But it suffices to say that the trial judge in this case conducted a vigorous, searching and sustained cross-examination of the defendant. Upon consideration of any single question, we could not say that there was prejudice. But upon consideration of forty-one questions asked the defendant by the trial judge, the conclusion is inescapable that the trial judge by such cross-examination of the defendant in the manner here shown intimated to the jury his opinion upon the facts in issue.

We cannot say to what extent the minds of the jurors who tried defendant were influenced by the cross-examination conducted by the trial judge, but we must assume that if the trial judge indicated to the jury his belief in her guilt, such belief influenced the jury in arriving at its verdict.

We do not intend to say that a trial judge should not ask questions during the progress of a criminal trial at proper times and in a proper manner. Clarifying questions are necessary, but we see no occasion for the trial judge to take over the duties of a prosecuting officer.

In accordance with the foregoing we reverse the judgment of the Circuit Court of Wayne County, set aside the verdict, and award the defendant a new trial.

Judgment reversed; verdict set aside; new trial awarded.

HAYMOND, Judge (dissenting).

Though I fully agree with the principle stated in the syllabus, it does not apply to the situation which existed, as shown by the record, in the trial of this case. For that reason I dissent from the decision of the majority.

In my opinion the defendant had a fair trial which was free from prejudicial error and in which the evidence was ample to support the verdict of the jury in finding her guilty of murder of the second degree. The sole ground upon which the majority sets aside that verdict and reverses the judgment is the action of the trial judge in propounding certain questions to the defendant while she was testifying in her own behalf after examination by her attorney and cross-examination by the prosecuting attorney had not succeeded in developing pertinent facts relative to her conduct shortly before or at the time she shot and killed her husband. I emphatically disapprove any act or conduct of a judge of any trial court which indicates the slightest bias or unfairness toward any party or any opinion entertained by him with respect to any factual question, and I would promptly act to reverse the judgment and award a new trial whenever behavior of that nature occurs. But I would not require a judge of a trial court to act the part of a mere umpire in charge of a game between contestants or deprive him of his unquestioned right and duty to exercise his judicial power to direct and conduct the trial of a case. A trial is not a game. It is a solemn judicial inquiry to determine the merits of the conflicting claims of the parties for the sole purpose of administering justice between them according to law and the right of the case.

The judge of a trial court should, at all times, carefully refrain from encroachment upon the function of the attorneys who represent the litigants. Rarely should he engage in the examination of witnesses. That is the work of counsel. When, however, a witness is unwilling to tell the facts within his knowledge, and counsel are not disposed, or are unable, to elicit the facts, it may be proper for the judge, within recognized limits, to interrogate a witness. In such instances his failure to do so would risk his proper control of the case or require him to submit to the whim of an unruly witness. He is not required to do either.

* * *

I am unable to find, in this record, any act of the circuit judge who conducted the trial of this case indicative of any partiality or lack of fairness upon his part toward either party, or any conduct by which any opinion entertained by him concerning the guilt or innocence of the defendant, or as to any other fact, was or could have been communicated or disclosed to the jury. Nothing prejudicial to any right of the defendant appears to have resulted from the conduct of the trial judge.

The defendant was fairly tried. The verdict of guilty of murder of the second degree was fully warranted by the evidence. In fact, upon the evidence, a verdict for any offense less than murder, or of not guilty, would not have been justified. The verdict was approved by the court and a proper judgment was rendered upon it. Perceiving no prejudice or injustice to the defendant, I am unwilling to disturb that judgment.

I am authorized to say that Judge FOX concurs in the views expressed in this dissent.

TRAMMEL

v.

UNITED STATES

Supreme Court of the United States
445 U.S. 40, 100 S. Ct. 906,
63 L. Ed. 2d 186 (1980)

MR. CHIEF JUSTICE BURGER delivered the opinion of the Court.

We granted certiorari to consider whether an accused may invoke the privilege against adverse spousal testimony so as to exclude the voluntary testimony of his wife. 440 U.S. 934 (1979). This calls for a re-examination of Hawkins v. United States, 358 U.S. 74 (1958).

I.

On March 10, 1976, petitioner Otis Trammel was indicted with two others, Edwin Lee Roberts and Joseph Freeman, for importing heroin into the United States from Thailand and the Philippine Islands and for conspiracy to import heroin in violation of 21 U. S. C.§§ 952 (a), 962 (a), and 963. The indictment also named six unindicted co-conspirators, including petitioner's wife Elizabeth Ann Trammel.

According to the indictment, petitioner and his wife flew from the Philippines to California in August 1975, carrying with

them a quantity of heroin. Freeman and Roberts assisted them in its distribution. Elizabeth Trammel then ounsello to Thailand where she purchased another supply of the drug. On November 3, 1975, with four ounces of heroin on her person, she boarded a plane for the United States. During a routine customs search in Hawaii, she was searched, the heroin was discovered, and she was arrested. After discussions with Drug Enforcement Administration agents, she agreed to cooperate with the Government.

Prior to trial on this indictment, petitioner moved to sever his case from that of Roberts and Freeman. He advised the court that the Government intended to call his wife as an adverse witness and asserted his claim to a privilege to prevent her from testifying against him. At a hearing on the motion, Mrs. Trammel was called as a Government witness under a grant of use immunity. She testified that she and petitioner were married in May 1975 and that they remained married. She explained that her cooperation with the Government was based on assurances that she would be given lenient treatment. She then described, in considerable detail, her role and that of her husband in the heroin distribution conspiracy.

After hearing this testimony, the District Court ruled that Mrs. Trammel could testify in support of the Government's case to any act she observed during the marriage and to any communication "made in the presence of a third person"; however, confidential communications between petitioner and his wife were held to be privileged and inadmissible. The motion to sever was denied.

At trial, Elizabeth Trammel testified within the limits of the court's pretrial ruling; her testimony, as the Government concedes, constituted virtually its entire case against petitioner. He was found guilty on both the substantive and conspiracy charges and sentenced to an indeterminate term of years pursuant to the Federal Youth Corrections Act, 18 U. S. C. § 5010 (b).

In the Court of Appeals petitioner's only claim of error was that the admission of the adverse testimony of his wife, over his objection, contravened this Court's teaching in Hawkins v. United States, supra, and therefore constituted reversible error. The Court of

Appeals rejected this contention. It concluded that Hawkins did not prohibit "the voluntary testimony of a spouse who appears as an unindicted co-conspirator under grant of immunity from the Government in return for her testimony." 583 F.2d 1166, 1168 (CA10 1978).

II.

The privilege claimed by petitioner has ancient roots. Writing in 1628, Lord Coke observed that "it hath been resolved by the Justices that a wife cannot be produced either against or for her husband." 1 E. Coke, A Commentarie upon Littleton 6b (1628). See, generally, 8 J. Wigmore, Evidence § 2227 (McNaughton rev. 1961). This spousal disqualification sprang from two canons of medieval jurisprudence: first, the rule that an accused was not permitted to testify in his own behalf because of his interest in the proceeding; second, the concept that husband and wife were one, and that since the woman had no recognized separate legal existence, the husband was that one. From those two now long-abandoned doctrines, it followed that what was inadmissible from the lips of the defendant-husband was also inadmissible from his wife.

Despite its medieval origins, this rule of spousal disqualification remained intact in most common-law jurisdictions well into the 19th century. See id., § 2333. It was applied by this Court in Stein v. Bowman, 13 Pet. 209, 220-223 (1839), in Graves v. United States, 150 U.S. 118 (1893), and again in Jin Fuey Moy v. United States, 254 U.S. 189, 195 (1920), where it was deemed so well established a proposition as to "hardly [require] mention." Indeed, it was not until 1933, in Funk v. United States, 290 U.S. 371, that this Court abolished the testimonial disqualification in the federal courts, so as to permit the spouse of a defendant to testify in the defendant's behalf. Funk, however, left undisturbed the rule that either spouse could prevent the other from giving adverse testimony. Id., at 373. The rule thus evolved into one of privilege rather than one of absolute disqualification. See J. Maguire, Evidence, Common Sense and Common Law 78-92 (1947).

The modern justification for this privilege against adverse spousal testimony is its per-

ceived role in fostering the harmony and sanctity of the marriage relationship. Notwithstanding this benign purpose, the rule was sharply criticized. Professor Wigmore termed it "the merest anachronism in legal theory and an indefensible obstruction to truth in practice." 8 Wigmore § 2228, at 221. The Committee on Improvements in the Law of Evidence of the American Bar Association called for its abolition. 63 American Bar Association Reports 594-595 (1938). In its place, Wigmore and others suggested a privilege protecting only private marital communications, ounsell on the privilege between priest and penitent, attorney and client, and physician and patient. See 8 Wigmore § 2332 et seq.

These criticisms influenced the American Law Institute, which, in its 1942 Model Code of Evidence, advocated a privilege for marital confidences, but expressly rejected a rule vesting in the defendant the right to exclude all adverse testimony of his spouse. See American Law Institute, Model Code of Evidence, Rule 215 (1942). In 1953 the Uniform Rules of Evidence, drafted by the National Conference of Commissioners on Uniform State Laws, followed a similar course; it limited the privilege to confidential communications and "[abolished] the rule, still existing in some states, and largely a sentimental relic, of not requiring one spouse to testify against the other in a criminal action." See Rule 23 (2) and comments. Several state legislatures enacted similarly patterned provisions into law.

In Hawkins v. United States, 358 U.S. 74 (1958), this Court considered the continued vitality of the privilege against adverse spousal testimony in the federal courts. There the District Court had permitted petitioner's wife, over his objection, to testify against him. With one questioning concurring opinion, the Court held the wife's testimony inadmissible; it took note of the critical comments that the common-law rule had engendered, id., at 76, and n. 4, but chose not to abandon it. Also rejected was the Government's suggestion that the Court modify the privilege by vesting it in the witness-spouse, with freedom to testify or not independent of the defendant's control. The Court viewed this proposed modification as antithetical to the widespread belief, evidenced in the rules then in effect in a majority of the States and in England, "that the law should not force or encourage testimony which might alienate husband and wife, or further inflame existing domestic differences." Id., at 79.

Hawkins, then, left the federal privilege for adverse spousal testimony where it found it, continuing "a rule which bars the testimony of one spouse against the other unless both consent." Id., at 78. Accord, Wyatt v. United States, 362 U.S. 525, 528 (1960). However, in so doing, the Court made clear that its decision was not meant to "foreclose whatever changes in the rule may eventually be dictated by 'reason and experience.' " 358 U.S., at 79.

III.

A.

The Federal Rules of Evidence acknowledge the authority of the federal courts to continue the evolutionary development of testimonial privileges in federal criminal trials "governed by the principles of the common law as they may be interpreted . . . in the light of reason and experience." Fed. Rule Evid. 501. Cf. Wolfle v. United States, 291 U.S. 7, 12 (1934). The general mandate of Rule 501 was substituted by the Congress for a set of privilege rules drafted by the Judicial Conference Advisory Committee on Rules of Evidence and approved by the Judicial Conference of the United States and by this Court. That proposal defined nine specific privileges, including a husband-wife privilege which would have codified the Hawkins rule and eliminated the privilege for confidential marital communications. See proposed Fed. Rule Evid. 505. In rejecting the proposed Rules and enacting Rule 501, Congress manifested an affirmative intention not to freeze the law of privilege. Its purpose rather was to "provide the courts with the flexibility to develop rules of privilege on a case-by-case basis," 120 Cong. Rec. 40891 (1974) (statement of Rep. Hungate), and to leave the door open to change. See also S. Rep. No. 93-1277, p. 11 (1974); H. R. Rep. No. 93-650, p. 8 (1973).

Although Rule 501 confirms the authority of the federal courts to reconsider the continued validity of the Hawkins rule, the long history of the privilege suggests that it ought not to be casually cast aside. That the privilege is one affecting marriage, home, and family relationships—already subject to much erosion in our day—also counsels caution. At the same time, we cannot escape the reality that the law on occasion adheres to doctrinal concepts long after the reasons which gave them birth have disappeared and after experience suggests the need for change. This was recognized in Funk where the Court "[declined] to enforce . . . ancient [rules] of the common law under conditions as they now exist." 290 U.S., at 382. For, as Mr. Justice Black admonished in another setting, "[when] precedent and precedent alone is all the argument that can be made to support a court-fashioned rule, it is time for the rule's creator to destroy it." Francis v. Southern Pacific Co., 333 U.S. 445, 471 (1948) (dissenting opinion).

B.

Since 1958, when Hawkins was decided, support for the privilege against adverse spousal testimony has been eroded further. Thirty-one jurisdictions, including Alaska and Hawaii, then allowed an accused a privilege to prevent adverse spousal testimony. 358 U.S., at 81, n. 3 (STEWART, J., concurring). The number has now declined to 24.[1] In

---

[1] Eight States provide that one spouse is incompetent to testify against the other in a criminal proceeding: see Haw. Rev. Stat. § 621-18 (1976); Iowa Code § 622.7 (1979); Miss. Code Ann. § 13-1-5 (Supp. 1979); N. C. Gen. Stat. § 8-57 (Supp. 1977); Ohio Rev. Code Ann. § 2945.42 (Supp. 1979); Pa. Stat. Ann., Tit. 42, §§ 5913, 5915 (Purdon Supp. 1979); Tex. Crim. Proc. Code Ann., Art. 38.11 (Vernon 1979); Wyo. Stat. § 1-12-104 (1977).

Sixteen States provide a privilege against adverse spousal testimony and vest the privilege in both spouses or in the defendant-spouse alone: see Alaska Crim. Proc. Rule 26 (b)(2); Colo. Rev. Stat. § 13-90-107 (1973); Idaho Code § 9-203 (Supp. 1979); Mich. Comp. Laws § 600.2162 (1968); Minn. Stat. § 595.02 (1978); Mo. Rev. Stat. § 546.260 (1978); Mont. Code Ann. § 46-16-212 (1979); Neb. Rev. Stat. § 27-505 (1975); Nev. Rev. Stat. § 49.295 (1977); N.J. Stat. Ann. § 2A:84A-17 (West 1976); N. M. Stat. Ann. § 20-4-505 (Supp. 1977); Ore. Rev.

Stat. § 44.040 (1977); Utah Code Ann. § 78-24-8 (1977); Va. Code § 19.2-271.2 (Supp. 1979); Wash. Rev. Code § 5.60.060 (Supp. 1979); W. Va. Code § 57-3-3 (1966).

Nine States entitle the witness-spouse alone to assert a privilege against adverse spousal testimony: see Ala. Code § 12-21-227 (1975); Cal. Evid. Code Ann. §§ 970-973 (West 1966 and Supp. 1979); Conn. Gen. Stat. § 54-84 (1979); Ga. Code § 38-1604 (1978); Ky. Rev. Stat. § 421.210 (Supp. 1978); La. Rev. Stat. Ann. § 15:461 (West 1967); Md. Cts. & Jud. Proc. Code Ann. §§ 9-101, 9-106 (1974); Mass. Gen. Laws Ann., ch. 233, § 20 (West Supp. 1979); R. I. Gen. Laws.

The remaining 17 States have abolished the privilege in criminal cases: see Ariz. Rev. Stat. Ann. § 12-2231 (Supp. 1978); Ark. Stat. Ann. § 28-101, Rules 501 and 504 (1979); Del. Code Ann., Tit. 11, § 3502 (1975); Fla. Stat. §§ 90.501, 90.504 (1979); Ill. Rev. Stat., ch. 38, § 155-1 (1977); Ind. Code §§ 34-1-14-4, 34-1-14-5 (1976); Kan. Stat. Ann. §§ 60-407, 60-428 (1976); Maine Rules of Evidence 501, 504; N.H. Rev. Stat. Ann. § 516.27 (1974); N.Y. Crim. Proc. Law § 60.10 (McKinney 1971); N.Y. Civ. Proc. Law §§ 4502, 4512 (McKinney 1963); N.D. Rules of Evidence 501, 504; Okla. Stat., Tit. 12, §§ 2103, 2501, 2504 (West Supp. 1979); S. C. Code § 19-11-30 (1976); S. D. Comp. Laws Ann. §§ 19-13-1, 19-13-12 to 19-13-15 (1979); Tenn. Code Ann. § 40-2404 (1975); Vt. Stat. Ann., Tit. 12, § 1605 (1973); Wis. Stat. §§ 905.01, 905.05 (1975).

In 1901, Congress enacted a rule of evidence for the District of Columbia that made husband and wife "competent but not compellable to testify for or against each other," except as to confidential communications. This provision, which vests the privilege against adverse spousal testimony in the witness-spouse, remains in effect. See 31 Stat. 1358, §§ 1068, 1069, recodified as D. C. Code § 14-306 (1973).

1974, the National Conference on Uniform State Laws revised its Uniform Rules of Evidence, but again rejected the Hawkins rule in favor of a limited privilege for confidential communications. See Uniform Rules of Evidence, Rule 504. That proposed rule has been enacted in Arkansas, North Dakota, and Oklahoma—each of which in 1958 permitted an accused to exclude adverse spousal testimony.[2] The trend in state law toward divesting the accused of the privilege to bar adverse spousal testimony has special relevance because the laws of marriage and domestic relations are concerns traditionally reserved to the states. See Sosna v. Iowa, 419 U.S. 393, 404 (1975). Scholarly criticism of the Hawkins rule has also continued unabated.

Support for the common-law rule has also diminished in England. In 1972, a study group there proposed giving the privilege to the witness-spouse, on the ground that "if [the wife] is willing to give evidence . . . the law would be showing excessive concern for the preservation of marital harmony if it were to say that she must not do so." Criminal Law Revision Committee, Eleventh Report, Evidence (General) 93.

C.

Testimonial exclusionary rules and privileges contravene the fundamental principle that "the public . . . has a right to every man's evidence." United States v. Bryan, 339 U.S. 323, 331 (1950). As such, they must be strictly construed and accepted "only to the very limited extent that permitting a refusal to testify or excluding relevant evidence has a pub-

---

[2]   In 1965, California took the privilege from the defendant-spouse and vested it in the witness-spouse, accepting a study commission recommendation that the "latter [was] more likely than the former to determine whether or not to claim the privilege on the basis of the probable effect on the marital relationship." See Cal. Evid. Code Ann. §§ 970-973 (West 1966 and Supp. 1979) and 1 California Law Revision Commission, Recommendation and Study relating to The Marital "For and Against" Testimonial Privilege, at F-5 (1956). See also 6 California Law Revision Commission, Tentative Privileges Recommendation—Rule 27.5, pp. 243-244 (1964).

lic good transcending the normally predominant principle of utilizing all rational means for ascertaining truth." Elkins v. United States, 364 U.S. 206, 234 (1960) (Frankfurter, J., dissenting). Accord, United States v. Nixon, 418 U.S. 683, 709-710 (1974). Here we must decide whether the privilege against adverse spousal testimony promotes sufficiently important interests to outweigh the need for probative evidence in the administration of criminal justice.

It is essential to remember that the Hawkins privilege is not needed to protect information privately disclosed between husband and wife in the confidence of the marital relationship—once described by this Court as "the best solace of human existence." Stein v. Bowman, 13 Pet., at 223. Those confidences are privileged under the independent rule protecting confidential marital communications. Blau v. United States, 340 U.S. 332 (1951); see n. 5, supra. The Hawkins privilege is invoked, not to exclude private marital communications, but rather to exclude evidence of criminal acts and of communications made in the presence of third persons.

No other testimonial privilege sweeps so broadly. The privileges between priest and penitent, attorney and client, and physician and patient limit protection to private communications. These privileges are rooted in the imperative need for confidence and trust. The priest-penitent privilege recognizes the human need to disclose to a spiritual ounsellor, in total and absolute confidence, what are believed to be flawed acts or thoughts and to receive priestly consolation and guidance in return. The lawyer-client privilege rests on the need for the advocate and ounsellor to know all that relates to the client's reasons for seeking representation if the professional mission is to be carried out. Similarly, the physician must know all that a patient can articulate in order to identify and to treat disease; barriers to full disclosure would impair diagnosis and treatment.

The Hawkins rule stands in marked contrast to these three privileges. Its protection is not limited to confidential communications; rather it permits an accused to exclude all adverse spousal testimony. As Jeremy Bentham observed more than a century and a half ago, such a privilege goes far beyond making "every man's house his castle," and permits a person to convert his house into "a den of thieves." 5 Rationale of Judicial Evidence 340 (1827). It "secures, to every man, one safe and unquestionable and ever ready accomplice for every imaginable crime." Id., at 338.

The ancient foundations for so sweeping a privilege have long since disappeared. Nowhere in the common-law world—indeed in any modern society—is a woman regarded as chattel or demeaned by denial of a separate legal identity and the dignity associated with recognition as a whole human being. Chip by chip, over the years those archaic notions have been cast aside so that "[no] longer is the female destined solely for the home and the rearing of the family, and only the male for the marketplace and the world of ideas." Stanton v. Stanton, 421 U.S. 7, 14-15 (1975).

The contemporary justification for affording an accused such a privilege is also unpersuasive. When one spouse is willing to testify against the other in a criminal proceeding—whatever the motivation—their relationship is almost certainly in disrepair; there is probably little in the way of marital harmony for the privilege to preserve. In these circumstances, a rule of evidence that permits an accused to prevent adverse spousal testimony seems far more likely to frustrate justice than to foster family peace. Indeed, there is reason to believe that vesting the privilege in the accused could actually undermine the marital relationship. For example, in a case such as this, the Government is unlikely to offer a wife immunity and lenient treatment if it knows that her husband can prevent her from giving adverse testimony. If the Government is dissuaded from making such an offer, the privilege can have the untoward effect of permitting one spouse to escape justice at the expense of the other. It hardly seems conducive to the preservation of the marital relation to place a wife in jeopardy solely by virtue of her husband's control over her testimony.

IV.

Our consideration of the foundations for the privilege and its history satisfy us that "reason and experience" no longer justify so sweeping a rule as that found acceptable by the Court in Hawkins. Accordingly, we conclude that the existing rule should be modified so that the witness-spouse alone has a privilege to refuse to testify adversely; the witness may be neither compelled to testify nor foreclosed from testifying. This modification—vesting the privilege in the witness-spouse—furthers the important public interest in marital harmony without unduly burdening legitimate law enforcement needs.

Here, petitioner's spouse chose to testify against him. That she did so after a grant of immunity and assurances of lenient treatment does not render her testimony involuntary. Cf. Bordenkircher v. Hayes, 434 U.S. 357 (1978). Accordingly, the District Court and the Court of Appeals were correct in rejecting petitioner's claim of privilege, and the judgment of the Court of Appeals is

Affirmed. MR. JUSTICE STEWART, concurring in the judgment.

Although agreeing with much of what the Court has to say, I cannot join an opinion that implies that "reason and experience" have worked a vast change since the Hawkins case was decided in 1958. In that case the Court upheld the privilege of a defendant in a criminal case to prevent adverse spousal testimony, in an all-but-unanimous opinion by Mr. Justice Black. Today the Court, in another all-but-unanimous opinion, obliterates that privilege because of the purported change in perception that "reason and experience" have wrought.

The fact of the matter is that the Court in this case simply accepts the very same arguments that the Court rejected when the Government first made them in the Hawkins case in 1958. I thought those arguments were valid then, and I think so now.

The Court is correct when it says that "[the] ancient foundations for so sweeping a privilege have long since disappeared." Ante, at 52. But those foundations had disappeared well before 1958; their disappearance certainly did not occur in the few years that have elapsed between the Hawkins decision and this one. To paraphrase what Mr. Justice Jackson once said in another context, there is reason to believe that today's opinion of the Court will be of greater interest to students of human psychology than to students of law.

WASHINGTON
v.
ABD-RAHMAAN

**Supreme Court of Washington
154 Wash. 2d 280, 111 P.3d 1157,
2005 Wash. LEXIS 461 (2005)**

C. Johnson, J. This case involves the issue of the admissibility of hearsay statements of unavailable witnesses in a sentencing modification hearing. Petitioner Khatib Abd-Rahmaan argues that the United States Supreme Court ruling in *Crawford v. Washington*, 541 U.S. 36, 124 S. Ct. 1354, 158 L. Ed. 2d 177 (2004), applies here and requires the exclusion of hearsay evidence because Abd-Rahmaan did not have a prior opportunity to cross-examine the witnesses. In the alternative, Abd-Rahmaan argues the trial court erred in admitting hearsay evidence without making specific findings of good cause. We hold that *Crawford* does not apply here. Though we agree with the analytical framework employed by the Court of Appeals, we do not find the record made by the trial court sufficient to establish good cause to admit the hearsay evidence. Therefore, we reverse the decision of the Court of Appeals.

FACTS AND PROCEDURAL HISTORY

In June 1999, Abd-Rahmaan pleaded guilty pursuant to an *Alford* plea to delivery of cocaine. Adb-Rahmaan was sentenced to 38 months in custody and 12 months community placement.

In January 2003, the State sought to modify Abd-Rahmaan's sentence, alleging violations of three conditions of his community placement: (1) that Abd-Rahmaan failed to report to his community corrections officer (CCO), (2) that Abd-Rahmaan failed to provide truthful answers to a polygraph test, and (3) that Abd-Rahmaan consumed a con-

trolled substance. At the sentence modification hearing, the State conceded that there
was no order for the polygraph test in the
judgment and sentence, and the court found
nothing to support the allegation that Abd-
Rahmaan consumed a controlled substance.
Regarding the allegation that Abd-Rahmaan
failed to report, the trial court heard testimony from Chris Salatka, Abd-Rahmaan's CCO.
Salatka stated:

> Mr. Abd-Rahmaan was instructed to report
> on all days he does not work at the Mil-
> lionaires' [sic] Club. When I discovered,
> after he took his polygraph, he disclosed
> what he had been doing or had not been
> doing. I followed up at the Millionaires'
> [sic] Club. They reported to me that he had
> not been working on the days that I have
> listed on December 4th, 10th, 11th, the
> 12th and 13th. . . .
>
> He was terminated from the Federal
> Express on the first day he was working
> for them. And the reason why he was ter-
> minated was because they claimed he was
> dropping products. And he was, I guess he
> was. It was his job to carry the expensive
> boxes of alcohol, and he dropped several
> boxes. So they requested of him to leave.
> And at that time Mr. Abd-Rahmaan,
> according to this particular person at Fed-
> eral Express, accused him of making
> threatening and intimidating gestures.
> They told him they felt unsafe and wanted
> him out of there. Now, when I followed up
> with what happened, after the polygraph,
> the Millionaires' [sic] Club reported to me
> that he was not allowed to work through
> the service of the Millionaires' [sic] Club
> because of what he did at the Federal
> Express. And, in addition, because Mr.
> Abd-Rahmaan did not disclose his status.

The court overruled Abd-Rahmaan's
objection to these statements as unreliable
hearsay, but did not specifically state the reasons for admitting the hearsay evidence.
Abd-Rahmaan was then given an opportunity to present his version of the events. After
hearing both accounts, the trial court found
that Abd-Rahmaan violated the conditions of
his sentence by failing to report to his CCO
and ordered 60 days of confinement.

On appeal, Division One of the Court of
Appeals addressed whether the right to confrontation necessitates a specific written
finding that hearsay evidence is reliable.
State v. Abd-Rahmaan, 120 Wn. App. 284, 84
P.3d 944 (2004). That court found sentence
modification hearings to be substantially
similar to other revocation hearings, requiring the minimum due process protections
articulated in *Morrissey v. Brewer*, 408 U.S.
471, 92 S. Ct. 2593, 33 L. Ed. 2d 484 (1972).
Finding that *Morrissey* does not provide an
absolute right to confrontation, the Court of
Appeals held that hearsay evidence is admissible in a sentence modification hearing
where the hearsay is reliable and where there
is good cause to allow it. The court found the
testimony provided by the CCO regarding
Abd-Rahmaan's employment status presented adequate indicia of reliability based on the
detailed accounts of Abd-Rahmaan's employment given to the CCO by the Millionair
Club and Federal Express. In further assessing the reliability of the hearsay statements,
the court found it persuasive that Abd-Rahmaan participated in the hearing, was able to
give his version of the events, and had the
opportunity to call witnesses to rebut the
CCO's testimony and present corroborative
evidence had he wished to do so. Additionally, the Court of Appeals held the trial court
had good cause to allow the hearsay evidence, inferring that there was difficulty and
expense in providing the live witnesses.
While the Court of Appeals noted that it preferred trial courts to make specific, written
findings regarding the reliability of the evidence and the difficulty or expense of presenting live witnesses, it found the trial court
record sufficient to understand the reasons
for admitting the hearsay evidence.

After Abd-Rahmaan's motion for reconsideration was denied in the Court of
Appeals, we granted limited review to determine whether the trial court erred in admitting the hearsay evidence.

ANALYSIS

Conceding that probationers do not have
the same due process protections as criminal
defendants, Abd-Rahmaan contends that on
the basis of the United States Supreme Court
decision in *Crawford*, cross-examination is

the only permissible means of assessing the reliability of hearsay evidence. Because the due process required at a parole revocation hearing or sentencing modification hearing parallels the Sixth Amendment right to confrontation, Abd-Rahmaan argues the requirements set forth in *Crawford* should be applied in those settings. Alternatively, if we find that *Crawford* does not apply here, Abd-Rahmaan argues the trial court erred in admitting the hearsay because there was no finding of the reliability of the hearsay evidence or good cause to admit it.

* * *

In March 2004, the United States Supreme Court ruled in *Crawford* that a defendant's right to confrontation under the Sixth Amendment is violated where testimonial hearsay is admitted at trial and the defendant has not been afforded the prior opportunity to cross-examine the witness. *Crawford* overruled the United States Supreme Court's prior decision in *Ohio v. Roberts*, 448 U.S. 56, 66, 100 S. Ct. 2531, 65 L. Ed. 2d 597 (1980), which held that, under the confrontation clause, statements of a witness unavailable at trial may be admitted only if the hearsay bears adequate indicia of reliability. The *Crawford* Court rejected this conclusion, stating that "where testimonial statements are involved, we do not think the Framers meant to leave the Sixth Amendment's protection to the vagaries of the rules of evidence, much less to amorphous notions of 'reliability.'" *Crawford*, 541 U.S. at 61. The Court noted that the confrontation clause itself reflects both a judgment of the desirability of reliable evidence and the sense that reliability is best determined in criminal prosecutions by confrontation. Under this analysis, accordingly, testimonial evidence is inadmissible at a criminal trial where a witness is unavailable and the defendant has not been afforded the prior opportunity to cross-examine the witness.

Abd-Rahmaan argues that the rule articulated in *Crawford* should apply to the right to confront witnesses at a sentence modification hearing because the right to confront a witness in a parole revocation hearing under *Morrissey* incorporates the guaranties of the Sixth Amendment. He contends that no constitutionally permissible means exist to

assess the reliability of testimonial evidence absent confrontation. We disagree.

The confrontation clause of the Sixth Amendment explicitly applies to "criminal prosecutions." The United States Supreme Court and this court have recognized the different due process requirements existing in parole revocation hearings as opposed to the right to confrontation in criminal prosecutions. For the purposes of confrontation, the former are analyzed under the Fourteenth Amendment, while the latter are analyzed under the Sixth Amendment. By its own terms, the guaranties of the Sixth Amendment do not apply in these post-conviction settings, but to "criminal prosecutions." We also note that in *Crawford*, the United States Supreme Court analyzed the right to cross-examine witnesses exclusively within the context of the confrontation clause of the Sixth Amendment. Congruent with the explicit terms of the Sixth Amendment, the *Crawford* holding applies to criminal prosecutions and does not require prior cross-examination of testimonial evidence in civil proceedings or in post-conviction hearings.

While the United States Supreme Court overruled *Roberts* in *Crawford*, we find no indication that it overruled the decisions in *Morrissey* and *Scarpelli*. The minimum rights guaranteed an individual in a parole revocation hearing as outlined in *Morrissey* are grounded in the due process clause of the Fourteenth Amendment, not the Sixth Amendment.

* * *

We find that *Crawford* does not apply in sentence modification hearings. In these postconviction settings, we continue to apply the two-prong test of *Dahl* to establish good cause where we consider the reliability of the hearsay in light of the difficulty in procuring the live witness.

Even if *Crawford* does not apply here, Abd-Rahmaan urges us to reverse the Court of Appeals' decision in this case and find that the trial court erred in admitting the hearsay evidence. He contends that there was no finding of good cause by the trial court to admit the evidence as required under *Dahl*.

"Good cause has thus far been defined in terms of the difficulty and expense of procuring witnesses in combination with 'demon-strably reliable' or 'clearly reliable' evidence." *State v. Nelson*, 103 Wn.2d 760, 765, 697 P.2d 579 (1985). The trial court here made no record to support a conclusion that there was good cause to admit the hearsay evidence. There was neither a showing in the record that the hearsay evidence was demonstrably reliable nor was there any comment on the difficulty or cost in procuring live witnesses. Although written findings are useful, trial courts are not required to make written findings establishing good cause to admit hearsay evidence in sentence modification hearings; however, appellate courts require some record explaining the evidence on which the trial court relied and the reasons for the admission of the hearsay evidence. These requirements are necessary in order for an appellate court to ascertain whether there is substantial evidence to support the trial court's decision to modify a sentence. Unlike the Court of Appeals, we find the record below insufficient to establish good cause for the admission of the hearsay evidence or the reasons for the trial court's decision. The modification of Abd-Rahmaan's sentence is invalid to the extent the trial court admitted and relied on the hearsay evidence provided by the CCO's testimony.

CONCLUSION

We reverse the Court of Appeals' decision. While we note that relief for Abd-Rahmaan here is moot because he has already served his time, we issue this opinion to clarify the rule for future sentence modification hearings. We hold that *Crawford* does not apply in sentence modification hearings. Under *Morrissey* and *Dahl*, the right to confront witnesses at sentence modification hearings exists unless good cause is established by the trial court to admit the hearsay evidence. When admitting hearsay on a finding of good cause, trial courts are required to articulate the basis on which they are admitting the hearsay testimony by either oral or written findings in order to facilitate appellate review. While we agree with the Court of Appeals that trial courts should articulate the reasons for admitting hearsay evidence in these hearings, we disagree that the record here is sufficient to review the trial court's reasoning.

Cases Relating to Chapter 3

Burden of Proof

IN RE WINSHIP

Supreme Court of the United States
397 U.S. 358, 90 S. Ct. 1068,
25 L. Ed. 2d 368 (1970)

MR. JUSTICE BRENNAN delivered the opinion of the Court.

Constitutional questions decided by this Court concerning the juvenile process have centered on the adjudicatory stage at "which a determination is made as to whether a juvenile is a 'delinquent' as a result of alleged misconduct on his part, with the consequence that he may be committed to a state institution." In re Gault, 387 U.S. 1, 13 (1967). Gault decided that, although the Fourteenth Amendment does not require that the hearing at this stage conform with all the requirements of a criminal trial or even of the usual administrative proceeding, the Due Process Clause does require application during the adjudicatory hearing of " 'the essentials of due process and fair treatment.' " Id., at 30. This case presents the single, narrow question whether proof beyond a reasonable doubt is among the "essentials of due process and fair treatment" required during the adjudicatory stage when a juvenile is charged with an act which would constitute a crime if committed by an adult.

Section 712 of the New York Family Court Act defines a juvenile delinquent as "a person over seven and less than sixteen years of age who does any act which, if done by an adult, would constitute a crime." During a 1967 adjudicatory hearing, conducted pursuant to § 742 of the Act, a judge in New York Family Court found that appellant, then a 12-year-old boy, had entered a locker and stolen $112 from a woman's pocketbook. The petition which charged appellant with delinquency alleged that his act, "if done by an adult, would constitute the crime or crimes of Larceny." The judge acknowledged that the proof might not establish guilt beyond a reasonable doubt, but rejected appellant's contention that such proof was required by the Fourteenth Amendment. The judge relied instead on § 744 (b) of the New York Family Court Act which provides that "any determination at the conclusion of [an adjudicatory] hearing that a [juvenile] did an act or acts must be based on a preponderance of the evidence." During a subsequent dispositional hearing, appellant was ordered placed in a training school for an initial period of 18 months, subject to annual extensions of his commitment until his 18th birthday—six years in appellant's case. The Appellate Division of the New York Supreme Court, First Judicial Department, affirmed without opinion, 30 App. Div. 2d 781, 291 N.Y.S.2d 1005 (1968). The New York Court of Appeals then affirmed by a four-to-three vote, expressly sustaining the constitutionality of § 744 (b), 24 N.Y.2d 196, 247 N.E.2d 253 (1969). We noted probable jurisdiction, 396 U.S. 885 (1969). We reverse.

I.

The requirement that guilt of a criminal charge be established by proof beyond a reasonable doubt dates at least from our early years as a Nation. The "demand for a higher degree of persuasion in criminal cases was recurrently expressed from ancient times, [though] its crystallization into the formula 'beyond a reasonable doubt' seems to have occurred as late as 1798. It is now accepted in common law jurisdictions as the measure of persuasion by which the prosecution must convince the trier of all the essential elements of guilt." C. McCormick, Evidence § 321, pp. 681-682 (1954); see also 9 J. Wigmore, Evidence § 2497 (3d ed. 1940). Although virtually unanimous adherence to the reasonable-doubt standard in common-law jurisdictions may not conclusively establish it as a requirement of due process, such adherence does "reflect a profound judgment about the way in which law should be enforced and justice administered." Duncan v. Louisiana, 391 U.S. 145, 155 (1968).

Expressions in many opinions of this Court indicate that it has long been assumed that proof of a criminal charge beyond a reasonable doubt is constitutionally required. See, for example, Miles v. United States, 103 U.S. 304, 312 (1881); Davis v. United States, 160 U.S. 469, 488 (1895); Holt v. United States, 218 U.S. 245, 253 (1910); Wilson v. United States, 232 U.S. 563, 569-570 (1914); Brinegar v. United States, 338 U.S. 160, 174 (1949); Leland v. Oregon, 343 U.S. 790, 795 (1952); Holland v. United States, 348 U.S. 121, 138 (1954); Speiser v. Randall, 357 U.S. 513, 525-526 (1958). Cf. Coffin v. United States, 156 U.S. 432 (1895). Mr. Justice Frankfurter stated that "it is the duty of the Government to establish . . . guilt beyond a reasonable doubt. This notion—basic in our law and rightly one of the boasts of a free society—is a requirement and a safeguard of due process of law in the historic, procedural content of 'due process.'" Leland v. Oregon, supra, at 802-803 (dissenting opinion). In a similar vein, the Court said in Brinegar v. United States, supra, at 174, that "guilt in a criminal case must be proved beyond a reasonable doubt and by evidence confined to that which long experience in the common-law tradition, to some extent embodied in the Constitution, has crystallized into rules of evidence consistent with that standard. These rules are historically grounded rights of our system, developed to safeguard men from dubious and unjust convictions, with resulting forfeitures of life, liberty and property." Davis v. United States, supra, at 488, stated that the requirement is implicit in "constitutions . . . [which] recognize the fundamental principles that are deemed essential for the protection of life and liberty." In Davis a murder conviction was reversed because the trial judge instructed the jury that it was their duty to convict when the evidence was equally balanced regarding the sanity of the accused. This Court said: "On the contrary, he is entitled to an acquittal of the specific crime charged if upon all the evidence there is reasonable doubt whether he was capable in law of committing crime. . . . No man should be deprived of his life under the forms of law unless the jurors who try him are able, upon their consciences, to say that the evidence before them . . . is sufficient to show beyond a reasonable doubt the existence of every fact necessary to constitute the crime charged." Id., at 484, 493.

The reasonable-doubt standard plays a vital role in the American scheme of criminal procedure. It is a prime instrument for reducing the risk of convictions resting on factual error. The standard provides concrete substance for the presumption of innocence—that bedrock "axiomatic and elementary" principle whose "enforcement lies at the foundation of the administration of our criminal law." Coffin v. United States, supra, at 453. As the dissenters in the New York Court of Appeals observed, and we agree, "a person accused of a crime . . . would be at a severe disadvantage, a disadvantage amounting to a lack of fundamental fairness, if he could be adjudged guilty and imprisoned for years on the strength of the same evidence as would suffice in a civil case." 24 N.Y.2d, at 205, 247 N.E.2d, at 259.

The requirement of proof beyond a reasonable doubt has this vital role in our criminal procedure for cogent reasons. The accused during a criminal prosecution has at stake interests of immense importance, both because of the possibility that he may lose his liberty upon conviction and because of the certainty that he would be stigmatized by the conviction. Accordingly, a society that values the good name and freedom of every individual should not condemn a man for commission of a crime when there is reasonable doubt about his guilt. As we said in Speiser v. Randall, supra, at 525-526: "There is always in litigation a margin of error, representing error in factfinding, which both parties must take into account. Where one party has at stake an interest of transcending value—as a criminal defendant his liberty—this margin of error is reduced as to him by the process of placing on the other party the burden of . . . persuading the factfinder at the conclusion of the trial of his guilt beyond a reasonable doubt. Due process commands that no man shall lose his liberty unless the Government has borne the burden of . . . convincing the factfinder of his guilt." To this end, the reasonable-doubt standard is indispensable, for it "impresses on the trier of fact the necessity of reaching a subjective state of certitude of the facts in issue." Dorsen & Rezneck, In Re Gault and the Future of Juvenile Law, 1 Family Law Quarterly, No. 4, pp. 1, 26 (1967).

Moreover, use of the reasonable-doubt standard is indispensable to command the respect and confidence of the community in applications of the criminal law. It is critical that the moral force of the criminal law not be diluted by a standard of proof that leaves people in doubt whether innocent men are being condemned. It is also important in our free society that every individual going about his ordinary affairs have confidence that his government cannot adjudge him guilty of a criminal offense without convincing a proper factfinder of his guilt with utmost certainty.

Lest there remain any doubt about the constitutional stature of the reasonable-doubt standard, we explicitly hold that the Due Process Clause protects the accused against conviction except upon proof beyond a reasonable doubt of every fact necessary to constitute the crime with which he is charged.

II.

We turn to the question whether juveniles, like adults, are constitutionally entitled to proof beyond a reasonable doubt when they are charged with violation of a criminal law. The same considerations that demand extreme caution in factfinding to protect the innocent adult apply as well to the innocent child. We do not find convincing the contrary arguments of the New York Court of Appeals. Gault rendered untenable much of the reasoning relied upon by that court to sustain the constitutionality of § 744 (b). The Court of Appeals indicated that a delinquency adjudication "is not a 'conviction' (§ 781); that it affects no right or privilege, including the right to hold public office or to obtain a license (§ 782); and a cloak of protective confidentiality is thrown around all the proceedings (§§ 783-784)." 24 N.Y.2d, at 200, 247 N.E.2d, at 255-256. The court said further: "The delinquency status is not made a crime; and the proceedings are not criminal. There is, hence, no deprivation of due process in the statutory provision [challenged by appellant] . . . ." 24 N.Y.2d, at 203, 247 N.E.2d, at 257. In effect the Court of Appeals distinguished the proceedings in question here from a criminal prosecution by use of what Gault called the "'civil' label-of-convenience which has been attached to juvenile proceedings." 387 U.S., at 50. But Gault expressly rejected that distinction as a reason for holding the Due Process Clause inapplicable to a juvenile proceeding. 387 U.S., at 50-51. The Court of Appeals also attempted to justify the preponderance standard on the related ground that juvenile proceedings are designed "not to punish, but to save the child." 24 N.Y.2d, at 197, 247 N.E.2d, at 254. Again, however, Gault expressly rejected this justification. 387 U.S., at 27. We made clear in that decision that civil labels and good intentions do not themselves obviate the need for criminal due process safeguards in juvenile courts, for "[a] proceeding where the issue is whether the child will be found to be 'delinquent' and subjected to the loss of his liberty for years is comparable in seriousness to a felony prosecution." Id., at 36.

Nor do we perceive any merit in the argument that to afford juveniles the protection of proof beyond a reasonable doubt would risk destruction of beneficial aspects of the juvenile process. Use of the reasonable-doubt standard during the adjudicatory hearing will not disturb New York's policies that a finding that a child has violated a criminal law does not constitute a criminal conviction, that such a finding does not deprive the child of his civil rights, and that juvenile proceedings are confidential. Nor will there be any effect on the informality, flexibility, or speed of the hearing at which the factfinding takes place. And the opportunity during the post-adjudicatory or dispositional hearing for a wide-ranging review of the child's social history and for his individualized treatment will remain unimpaired. Similarly, there will be no effect on the procedures distinctive to juvenile proceedings that are employed prior to the adjudicatory hearing.

The Court of Appeals observed that "a child's best interest is not necessarily, or even probably, promoted if he wins in the particular inquiry which may bring him to the juvenile court." 24 N.Y.2d, at 199, 247 N.E.2d, at 255. It is true, of course, that the juvenile may be engaging in a general course of conduct inimical to his welfare that calls for judicial intervention. But that intervention cannot take the form of subjecting the child to the stigma of a finding that he violated a criminal law and to the possibility of institutional confinement on proof insufficient to convict him were he an adult.

We conclude, as we concluded regarding the essential due process safeguards applied in Gault, that the observance of the standard of proof beyond a reasonable doubt "will not compel the States to abandon or displace any of the substantive benefits of the juvenile process." Gault, supra, at 21.

Finally, we reject the Court of Appeals' suggestion that there is, in any event, only a "tenuous difference" between the reasonable-doubt and preponderance standards. The suggestion is singularly unpersuasive. In this very case, the trial judge's ability to distinguish between the two standards enabled him to make a finding of guilt that he conceded he might not have made under the standard of proof beyond a reasonable doubt. Indeed, the trial judge's action evidences the accuracy of the observation of commentators that "the preponderance test is susceptible to the misinterpretation that it calls on the trier of fact merely to perform an abstract weighing of the evidence in order to determine which side has produced the greater quantum, without regard to its effect in convincing his mind of the truth of the proposition asserted." Dorsen & Rezneck, supra, at 26-27.

III.

In sum, the constitutional safeguard of proof beyond a reasonable doubt is as much required during the adjudicatory stage of a delinquency proceeding as are those constitutional safeguards applied in Gault—notice of charges, right to counsel, the rights of confrontation and examination, and the privilege against self-incrimination. We therefore hold, in agreement with Chief Judge Fuld in dissent in the Court of Appeals, "that, where a 12-year-old child is charged with an act of stealing which renders him liable to confinement for as long as six years, then, as a matter of due process . . . the case against him must be proved beyond a reasonable doubt." 24 N.Y.2d, at 207, 247 N.E.2d, at 260.

Reversed.

* * *

[Concurring and dissenting opinions omitted.]

VICTOR
v.
NEBRASKA

Supreme Court of the United States
511 U.S. 1, 114 S. Ct. 1239,
127 L. Ed. 2d 583 (1994)

SYLLABUS:
The government must prove beyond a reasonable doubt every element of a charged offense. In re Winship, 397 U.S. 358. In upholding the first degree murder convictions and death sentences of petitioners Sandoval and Victor, the Supreme Courts of California and Nebraska, respectively, rejected contentions that due process was violated by the pattern jury instructions defining "reasonable doubt" that were given in both cases.

Held: Taken as a whole, the instructions in question correctly conveyed the concept of reasonable doubt, and there is no reasonable likelihood that the jurors understood the instructions to allow convictions based on proof insufficient to meet the Winship standard. Pp. 1-20.

(a) The Constitution does not dictate that any particular form of words be used in advising the jury of the government's burden of proof, so long as "taken as a whole, the instructions correctly convey the concept of reasonable doubt," Holland v. United States, 348 U.S. 121, 140. In invalidating a charge declaring, among other things, that a reasonable doubt "must be such . . . as would give rise to a grave uncertainty," "is an actual substantial doubt," and requires "a moral certainty," the Court, in Cage v. Louisiana, 498 U.S. 39, 40, observed that a reasonable juror could have interpreted the instruction to allow a finding of guilt based on a degree of proof below that which is constitutionally required. However, in Estelle v. McGuire, 502 U.S. __, __, and n. 4, the Court made clear that the proper inquiry is not whether the instruction "could have" been applied unconstitutionally, but whether there is a reasonable likelihood that the jury did so apply it. Pp. 1-3.

(b) The instructions given in Sandoval's case defined reasonable doubt as, among other things, "not a mere possible doubt," but one "depending on moral evidence," such that the jurors could not say they felt an abiding conviction, "to a moral certainty," of the truth of the charge. Pp. 3-6.

(c) Sandoval's objection to the charge's use of the 19th century phrases "moral evidence" and "moral certainty" is rejected. Although the former phrase is not a mainstay of the modern lexicon, its meaning today is consistent with its original meaning: evidence based on the general observation of people, rather than on what is demonstrable. Its use here is unproblematic because the instructions given correctly pointed the jurors' attention to the facts of the case before them, not (as Sandoval contends) the ethics or morality of his criminal acts. For example, in the instruction declaring that "everything relating to human affairs, and depending on moral evidence, is open to some possible or imaginary doubt," moral evidence can only mean empirical evidence offered to prove matters relating to human affairs—the proof introduced at trial. Similarly, whereas "moral certainty," standing alone, might not be recognized by modern jurors as a synonym for "proof beyond a reasonable doubt," its use in

conjunction with the abiding conviction language must be viewed as having impressed upon the jury the need to reach the subjective state of near certitude of guilt, see Jackson v. Virginia, 443 U.S. 307, 315, and thus as not having invited conviction on less than the constitutionally required proof. Moreover, in contrast to the situation in Cage, there is no reasonable likelihood that the jury here would have understood moral certainty to be disassociated from the evidence in the case, since the instruction explicitly told the jurors, among other things, that their conclusion had to be based upon such evidence. Accordingly, although this Court does not condone the use of the antiquated "moral certainty" phrase, its use in the context of the instructions as a whole cannot be said to have rendered those instructions unconstitutional. Pp. 6-14.

(d) Sandoval's objection to the portion of the charge declaring that a reasonable doubt is "not a mere possible doubt" is also rejected. That the instruction properly uses "possible" in the sense of fanciful is made clear by the fact that it also notes that everything "is open to some possible or imaginary doubt." P. 14.

(e) The instructions given in Victor's case defined reasonable doubt as, among other things, a doubt that will not permit an abiding conviction, "to a moral certainty," of the accused's guilt, and an "actual and substantial doubt" that is not excluded by the "strong probabilities of the case." Pp. 14-16.

(f) Victor's primary argument—that equating a reasonable doubt with a "substantial doubt" overstated the degree of doubt necessary for acquittal—is rejected. Any ambiguity is removed by reading the phrase in question in context: The Victor charge immediately distinguished an "actual and substantial doubt" from one "arising from mere possibility, from bare imagination, or from fanciful conjecture," and thereby informed the jury that a reasonable doubt is something more than a speculative one, which is an unexceptionable proposition. Cage, supra, at 41, distinguished. Moreover, the instruction defined a reasonable doubt alternatively as a doubt that would cause a reasonable person to hesitate to act, a formulation which this Court has repeatedly approved and which gives a common-sense benchmark for just how substantial a reasonable doubt must be. Pp. 16-18.

(g) The inclusion of the "moral certainty" phrase in the Victor charge did not render the instruction unconstitutional. In contrast to the situation in Cage, a sufficient context to lend meaning to the phrase was provided by the rest of the Victor charge, which equated a doubt sufficient to preclude moral certainty with a doubt that would cause a reasonable person to hesitate to act, and told the jurors that they must have an abiding conviction of Victor's guilt, must be convinced of such guilt "after full, fair, and impartial consideration of all the evidence," should be governed solely by that evidence in determining factual issues, and should not indulge in speculation, conjectures, or unsupported inferences. Pp. 18-19.

(h) The reference to "strong probabilities" in the Victor charge does not unconstitutionally understate the government's burden, since the charge also informs the jury that the probabilities must be strong enough to prove guilt beyond a reasonable doubt. See Dunbar v. United States, 156 U.S. 185, 199. P. 19.

No. 92-8894, 242 Neb. 306, 494 N.W.2d 565, and No. 92-9049, 4 Cal. 4th 155, modified, 4 Cal. 4th 928a, 841 P.2d 862, affirmed.

STATE
v.
EICHELBERGER

Court of Appeals of Washington, Division One
2005 Wash. App. LEXIS 2429 (2005)

APPELWICK, J.—Donald Eichelberger was convicted of two counts of trafficking in stolen property in the second degree after he found a suitcase full of compact discs. One count was charged for selling 35 of the CDs the day he found them, and the other count for attempting to sell additional CDs two days later. Eichelberger argues that his conviction for two counts violated his protection against double jeopardy because he committed only one unit of crime, that the State failed to meet its burden of proof beyond a reasonable doubt, and that the trial court erred in determining his offender score

because it included a point based on a fact that should have been presented to the jury and found beyond a reasonable doubt. Finding no error, we affirm.

FACTS

Donald Eichelberger was walking through the University District of Seattle in the late afternoon of May 20, 2003. He spotted a black suitcase lying on the ground, in an alley close to a dumpster. There were no people or vehicles around. Eichelberger opened the suitcase and saw that it contained many CDs. He did not inspect the CDs, and from the way they were arranged in the suitcase he could see only the spines of the CDs. Having been a University of Washington student himself, Eichelberger knew that students often move out of their residences and leave behind items that they no longer consider valuable, but that others might. He thought that the former owner of the suitcase had abandoned it and that he was thus entitled to take it. Eichelberger did not notice any identifying information on the CDs or the suitcase, did not attempt to ascertain who owned the CDs, and did not notify the police. Instead, Eichelberger took the bus to CD Trader, a used CD store in Queen Anne where he had previously sold CDs. He sold 35 of the CDs that day for $92. The record contains conflicting evidence about whether Eichelberger left because he was short on time and decided to return later to sell the remaining CDs, or whether he left because the clerk asked him to return later in the week to sell the remaining CDs.

It turns out that many of the CDs had been stolen from Stuart Sanderson during a burglary on May 20. Sanderson had affixed a sticker on many of his CDs that included his name and driver's license number. Sanderson filed a police report after the theft. The police investigation turned up no fingerprints at his home. On May 21, Sanderson called several used CD stores to see if his CDs had turned up. The manager at CD Trader informed Sanderson that several CDs with his sticker on them had been sold to the store the previous day. Sanderson went to the store and identified all 35 of the CDs Eichelberger had sold to CD Trader as his CDs. The manager took the CDs out of inventory and eventually turned them over to the police. Eichelberger returned to CD Trader on May 22 to sell more of the CDs. The manager recognized Eichelberger's name and came up with a ruse to keep Eichelberger in the store while he called the police. The police arrived and arrested Eichelberger. He was charged with two counts of trafficking in stolen property in the second degree. The State had no evidence to link Eichelberger to the burglary of Sanderson's home, and the court specifically instructed the jury not to make any such inference from the evidence or allow it to influence their verdict. The jury convicted Eichelberger on both counts. All parties agreed that Eichelberger's offender score was 3, which included one point because Eichelberger was on community custody at the time of the current offenses. Eichelberger received a low-end, standard range sentence based on this offender score.

ANALYSIS

I. Eichelberger's Two Convictions Did Not Violate His Protection Against Double Jeopardy.

* * *

We hold that the State was entitled to charge Eichelberger with two counts of trafficking in stolen property in the second degree, and that there was no double jeopardy violation.

II. Eichelberger's Convictions Were Supported By Sufficient Evidence

The test for sufficiency is whether, viewing the evidence in a light most favorable to the State, any rational trier of fact could have found each essential element of the charge beyond a reasonable doubt. State v. Salinas, 119 Wn.2d 192, 201, 829 P.2d 1068 (1992). "A claim of insufficiency admits the truth of the State's evidence and all inferences that reasonably can be drawn therefrom." Salinas, 119 Wn.2d at 201. A reviewing court neither weighs the evidence nor needs to be convinced that it established guilt beyond a reasonable doubt. State v. Green, 94 Wn.2d 216, 221, 616 P.2d 628 (1980). A trier of fact may properly render a guilty verdict based on circumstantial evidence alone, even if the evi-

dence is also consistent with the hypothesis of innocence. State v. Kovac, 50 Wn. App. 117, 119, 747 P.2d 484 (1987). A conviction will not be overturned unless there is no substantial evidence to support it. Lamborn v. Phillips Pac. Chem. Co., 89 Wn.2d 701, 709-10, 575 P.2d 215 (1978).

To find Eichelberger guilty of trafficking in stolen property in the second degree, the jury had to be satisfied beyond a reasonable doubt that he recklessly trafficked in stolen property. A person "acts recklessly when he knows of and disregards a substantial risk that a wrongful act may occur and his disregard of such substantial risk is a gross deviation from conduct that a reasonable man would exercise in the same situation." RCW 9A.08.010(1)(c). Reckless conduct therefore includes both a subjective and an objective component. State v. R.H.S., 94 Wn. App. 844, 847, 974 P.2d 1253 (1999). A trier of fact is permitted to find actual subjective knowledge if there is sufficient information that would lead a reasonable person to believe that a fact exists. RCW 9A.08.010(1)(b)(ii); R.H.S., 94 Wn App. at 847.

The evidence here was that Eichelberger came upon a suitcase. He opened the suitcase and saw that it contained CDs. When he saw the CDs, he thought that he would cash them in for money. His next act was to wheel the suitcase down the street, get on the bus, and go to Queen Anne to sell the CDs to CD Trader. He did not notify the police and did not check the CDs to see if they had anyone's name on them. He did not attempt to find out if they actually belonged to someone and were lost. Many of the CDs were labeled with the owner's name and driver's license number, which would have allowed a reasonable person to easily ascertain whether they were actually abandoned, or whether they were in fact lost or stolen.

Taking all inferences in the light most favorable to the state, the evidence was sufficient to permit the jury to find actual subjective knowledge. A reasonable person faced with similar circumstances would know that there was a substantial risk that the CDs were stolen or lost, and would take some steps to determine who the owner was prior to selling the CDs. Thus, the jury was entitled to find that Eichelberger had subjective knowledge of and disregarded the substantial risk that a wrongful act would occur when he converted the CDs to his own use. And, as the court instructed the jury when it asked for the definition of gross deviation, "[t]he law provides no precise definitions of these terms. The jury should rely on their understanding of the common meaning of 'gross deviation.'"

Eichelberger presents plausible explanations for the appearance of the suitcase other than that it was lost or stolen property, and testified that he thought the suitcase was abandoned. But the test is whether there was sufficient evidence to support the jury's verdict, not whether the jury could have reached a different result. We conclude that sufficient evidence supported the jury's verdict.

III. The Trial Court Did Not Err in
   Calculating Eichelberger's Offender
   Score

* * *

We affirm.

MARTIN
v.
OHIO

**Supreme Court of the United States
480 U.S. 228, 107 S. Ct. 1098,
94 L. Ed. 2d 267 (1987)**

JUSTICE WHITE delivered the opinion of the Court.

The Ohio Code provides that "[every] person accused of an offense is presumed innocent until proven guilty beyond a reasonable doubt, and the burden of proof for all elements of the offense is upon the prosecution. The burden of going forward with the evidence of an affirmative defense, and the burden of proof by a preponderance of the evidence, for an affirmative defense, is upon the accused." Ohio Rev. Code Ann. § 2901.05(A)(1982). An affirmative defense is one involving "an excuse or justification peculiarly within the knowledge of the accused, on which he can fairly be required to adduce supporting evidence." Ohio Rev.

Code Ann. § 2901.05(C)(2)(1982). The Ohio courts have "long determined that self-defense is an affirmative defense," 21 Ohio St. 3d 91, 93, 488 N.E.2d 166, 168 (1986), and that the defendant has the burden of proving it as required by § 2901.05(A).

As defined by the trial court in its instructions in this case, the elements of self-defense that the defendant must prove are that (1) the defendant was not at fault in creating the situation giving rise to the argument; (2) the defendant had an honest belief that she was in imminent danger of death or great bodily harm, and that her only means of escape from such danger was in the use of such force; and (3) the defendant did not violate any duty to retreat or avoid danger. App. 19. The question before us is whether the Due Process Clause of the Fourteenth Amendment forbids placing the burden of proving self-defense on the defendant when she is charged by the State of Ohio with committing the crime of aggravated murder, which, as relevant to this case, is defined by the Revised Code of Ohio as "purposely, and with prior calculation and design, [causing] the death of another." Ohio Rev. Code Ann. § 2903.01 (1982).

The facts of the case, taken from the opinions of the courts below, may be succinctly stated. On July 21, 1983, petitioner Earline Martin and her husband, Walter Martin, argued over grocery money. Petitioner claimed that her husband struck her in the head during the argument. Petitioner's version of what then transpired was that she went upstairs, put on a robe, and later came back down with her husband's gun which she intended to dispose of. Her husband saw something in her hand and questioned her about it. He came at her, and she lost her head and fired the gun at him. Five or six shots were fired, three of them striking and killing Mr. Martin. She was charged with and tried for aggravated murder. She pleaded self-defense and testified in her own defense. The judge charged the jury with respect to the elements of the crime and of self-defense and rejected petitioner's Due Process Clause challenge to the charge placing on her the burden of proving self-defense. The jury found her guilty.

Both the Ohio Court of Appeals and the Supreme Court of Ohio affirmed the conviction. Both rejected the constitutional challenge to the instruction requiring petitioner to prove self-defense. The latter court, relying upon our opinion in Patterson v. New York, 432 U.S. 197 (1977), concluded that the State was required to prove the three elements of aggravated murder but that Patterson did not require it to disprove self-defense, which is a separate issue that did not require Mrs. Martin to disprove any element of the offense with which she was charged. The court said, "the state proved beyond a reasonable doubt that appellant purposely, and with prior calculation and design, caused the death of her husband. Appellant did not dispute the existence of these elements, but rather sought to justify her actions on grounds she acted in self defense." 21 Ohio St. 3d, at 94, 488 N.E.2d, at 168. There was thus no infirmity in her conviction. We granted certiorari, 475 U.S. 1119 (1986), and affirm the decision of the Supreme Court of Ohio.

In re Winship, 397 U.S. 358, 364 (1970), declared that the Due Process Clause "protects the accused against conviction except upon proof beyond a reasonable doubt of every fact necessary to constitute the crime with which he is charged." A few years later, we held that Winship's mandate was fully satisfied where the State of New York had proved beyond reasonable doubt each of the elements of murder, but placed on the defendant the burden of proving the affirmative defense of extreme emotional disturbance, which, if proved, would have reduced the crime from murder to manslaughter. Patterson v. New York, supra. We there emphasized the preeminent role of the States in preventing and dealing with crime and the reluctance of the Court to disturb a State's decision with respect to the definition of criminal conduct and the procedures by which the criminal laws are to be enforced in the courts, including the burden of producing evidence and allocating the burden of persuasion. 432 U.S., at 201-202. New York had the authority to define murder as the intentional killing of another person. It had chosen, however, to reduce the crime to manslaughter if the defendant proved by a preponderance of the evidence that he had acted under the influence of extreme emotional distress. To convict of murder, the jury was required to find beyond a reasonable doubt, based on all the evidence, including that related to the defendant's mental state at the time of the crime, each of the elements of murder and also to conclude that the defendant had not proved his affirmative defense. The jury convicted Patterson, and we held there was no violation of the Fourteenth Amendment as construed in Winship. Referring to Leland v. Oregon, 343 U.S. 790 (1952), and Rivera v. Delaware, 429 U.S. 877 (1976), we added that New York "did no more than Leland and Rivera permitted it to do without violating the Due Process Clause" and declined to reconsider those cases. 432 U.S., at 206, 207. It was also observed that "the fact that a majority of the States have now assumed the burden of disproving affirmative defenses—for whatever reasons—[does not] mean that those States that strike a different balance are in violation of the Constitution." Id., at 211.

As in Patterson, the jury was here instructed that to convict it must find, in light of all the evidence, that each of the elements of the crime of aggravated murder has been proved by the State beyond reasonable doubt, and that the burden of proof with respect to these elements did not shift. To find guilt, the jury had to be convinced that none of the evidence, whether offered by the State or by Martin in connection with her plea of self-defense, raised a reasonable doubt that Martin had killed her husband, that she had the specific purpose and intent to cause his death, or that she had done so with prior calculation and design. It was also told, however, that it could acquit if it found by a preponderance of the evidence that Martin had not precipitated the confrontation, that she had an honest belief that she was in imminent danger of death or great bodily harm, and that she had satisfied any duty to retreat or avoid danger. The jury convicted Martin.

We agree with the State and its Supreme Court that this conviction did not violate the Due Process Clause. The State did not exceed its authority in defining the crime of murder as purposely causing the death of another with prior calculation or design. It did not seek to shift to Martin the burden of proving any of those elements, and the jury's verdict reflects that none of her self-defense evidence raised a reasonable doubt about the State's proof that she purposefully killed with prior calculation and design. She nevertheless had the opportunity under state law and the instructions given to justify the killing and show herself to be blameless by proving that she acted in self-defense. The jury thought she had failed to do so, and Ohio is as entitled to punish Martin as one guilty of murder as New York was to punish Patterson.

It would be quite different if the jury had been instructed that self-defense evidence could not be considered in determining whether there was a reasonable doubt about the State's case, i.e., that self-defense evidence must be put aside for all purposes unless it satisfied the preponderance standard. Such an instruction would relieve the State of its burden and plainly run afoul of Winship's mandate. 397 U.S., at 364. The instructions in this case could be clearer in this respect, but when read as a whole, we think they are adequate to convey to the jury that all of the evidence, including the evidence going to self-defense, must be considered in deciding whether there was a reasonable doubt about the sufficiency of the State's proof of the elements of the crime.

We are thus not moved by assertions that the elements of aggravated murder and self-defense overlap in the sense that evidence to prove the latter will often tend to negate the former. It may be that most encounters in which self-defense is claimed arise suddenly and involve no prior plan or specific purpose to take life. In those cases, evidence offered to support the defense may negate a purposeful killing by prior calculation and design, but Ohio does not shift to the defendant the burden of disproving any element of the state's case. When the prosecution has made out a prima facie case and survives a motion to acquit, the jury may nevertheless not convict if the evidence offered by the defendant raises any reasonable doubt about the existence of any fact necessary for the finding of guilt. Evidence creating a reasonable doubt could easily fall far short of proving self-defense by a preponderance of the evidence. Of course, if such doubt is not raised in the jury's mind and each juror is convinced that the defendant purposely and with prior calculation and

design took life, the killing will still be excused if the elements of the defense are satisfactorily established. We note here, but need not rely on, the observation of the Supreme Court of Ohio that "[appellant] did not dispute the existence of [the elements of aggravated murder], but rather sought to justify her actions on grounds she acted in self-defense." 21 Ohio St. 3d, at 94, 488 N.E.2d, at 168.

Petitioner submits that there can be no conviction under Ohio law unless the defendant's conduct is unlawful, and that because self-defense renders lawful what would otherwise be a crime, unlawfulness is an element of the offense that the state must prove by disproving self-defense. This argument founders on state law, for it has been rejected by the Ohio Supreme Court and by the Court of Appeals for the Sixth Circuit. White v. Arn, 788 F.2d 338, 346-347 (1986); State v. Morris, 8 Ohio App. 3d 12, 18-19, 455 N.E.2d 1352, 1359-1360 (1982). It is true that unlawfulness is essential for conviction, but the Ohio courts hold that the unlawfulness in cases like this is the conduct satisfying the elements of aggravated murder—an interpretation of state law that we are not in a position to dispute. The same is true of the claim that it is necessary to prove a "criminal" intent to convict for serious crimes, which cannot occur if self-defense is shown: the necessary mental state for aggravated murder under Ohio law is the specific purpose to take life pursuant to prior calculation and design. See White v. Arn, supra, at 346.

As we noted in Patterson, the common-law rule was that affirmative defenses, including self-defense, were matters for the defendant to prove. "This was the rule when the Fifth Amendment was adopted, and it was the American rule when the Fourteenth Amendment was ratified." 432 U.S., at 202. Indeed, well into this century, a number of States followed the common-law rule and required a defendant to shoulder the burden of proving that he acted in self-defense. Fletcher, Two Kinds of Legal Rules: A Comparative Study of Burden-of-Persuasion Practices in Criminal Cases, 77 Yale L. J. 880, 882, and n. 10 (1968). We are aware that all but two of the States, Ohio and South Carolina, have abandoned the common-law rule and require the prosecution to prove the absence of self-defense when it is properly raised by the defendant. But the question remains whether those States are in violation of the Constitution; and, as we observed in Patterson, that question is not answered by cataloging the practices of other States. We are no more convinced that the Ohio practice of requiring self-defense to be proved by the defendant is unconstitutional than we are that the Constitution requires the prosecution to prove the sanity of a defendant who pleads not guilty by reason of insanity. We have had the opportunity to depart from Leland v. Oregon, 343 U.S. 790 (1952), but have refused to do so. Rivera v. Delaware, 429 U.S. 877 (1976). These cases were important to the Patterson decision and they, along with Patterson, are authority for our decision today.

The judgment of the Ohio Supreme Court is accordingly

Affirmed.

JUSTICE POWELL, with whom JUSTICE BRENNAN and JUSTICE MARSHALL join, and with whom JUSTICE BLACK-MUN joins with respect to Parts I and III, dissenting.

Today the Court holds that a defendant can be convicted of aggravated murder even though the jury may have a reasonable doubt whether the accused acted in self-defense, and thus whether he is guilty of a crime. Because I think this decision is inconsistent with both precedent and fundamental fairness, I dissent.

I.

Petitioner Earline Martin was tried in state court for the aggravated murder of her husband. Under Ohio law, the elements of the crime are that the defendant has purposely killed another with "prior calculation and design." Ohio Rev. Code Ann. § 2903.01 (1982). Martin admitted that she shot her husband, but claimed that she acted in self-defense. Because self-defense is classified as an "affirmative" defense in Ohio, the jury was instructed that Martin had the burden of proving her claim by a preponderance of the evidence. Martin apparently failed to carry this burden, and the jury found her guilty.

The Ohio Supreme Court upheld the conviction, relying in part on this Court's opinion in Patterson v. New York, 432 U.S. 197 (1977). The Court today also relies on the Patterson reasoning in affirming the Ohio decision. If one accepts Patterson as the proper method of analysis for this case, I believe that the Court's opinion ignores its central meaning.

In Patterson, the Court upheld a state statute that shifted the burden of proof for an affirmative defense to the accused. New York law required the prosecutor to prove all of the statutorily defined elements of murder beyond a reasonable doubt, but permitted a defendant to reduce the charge to manslaughter by showing that he acted while suffering an "extreme emotional disturbance." See N.Y. Penal Law §§ 125.25, 125.20 (McKinney 1975 and Supp. 1987). The Court found that this burden shifting did not violate due process, largely because the affirmative defense did "not serve to negative any facts of the crime which the State is to prove in order to convict of murder." 432 U.S., at 207. The clear implication of this ruling is that when an affirmative defense does negate an element of the crime, the state may not shift the burden. See White v. Arn, 788 F.2d 338, 344-345 (CA6 1986). In such a case, In re Winship, 397 U.S. 358 (1970), requires the state to prove the nonexistence of the defense beyond a reasonable doubt.

The reason for treating a defense that negates an element of the crime differently from other affirmative defenses is plain. If the jury is told that the prosecution has the burden of proving all the elements of a crime, but then also is instructed that the defendant has the burden of disproving one of those same elements, there is a danger that the jurors will resolve the inconsistency in a way that lessens the presumption of innocence. For example, the jury might reasonably believe that by raising the defense, the accused has assumed the ultimate burden of proving that particular element. Or, it might reconcile the instructions simply by balancing the evidence that supports the prosecutor's case against the evidence supporting the affirmative defense, and conclude that the state has satisfied its burden if the prosecution's version is more persuasive. In either case, the jury is given the unmistakable but erroneous impression that the defendant shares the risk of nonpersuasion as to a fact necessary for conviction.[1]

Given these principles, the Court's reliance on Patterson is puzzling. Under Ohio law, the element of "prior calculation and design" is satisfied only when the accused has engaged in a "definite process of reasoning in advance of the killing," i.e., when he has given the plan at least some "studied consideration." App. 14 (jury instructions) (emphasis added). In contrast, when a defendant such as Martin raises a claim of self-defense, the jury also is instructed that the accused must prove that she "had an honest belief that she was in imminent danger of death or great bodily harm." Id., at 19 (emphasis added). In many cases, a defendant who finds himself in immediate danger and reacts with deadly force will not have formed a prior intent to kill. The Court recognizes this when it states:

It may be that most encounters in which self-defense is claimed arise suddenly and involve no prior plan or specific purpose to take life. In those cases, evidence offered to support the defense may negate a purposeful killing by prior calculation and design. . . .

---

[1]   Indeed, this type of instruction has an inherently illogical aspect. It makes no sense to say that the prosecution has the burden of proving an element beyond a reasonable doubt and that the defense has the burden of proving the contrary by a preponderance of the evidence. If the jury finds that the prosecutor has not met his burden, it of course will have no occasion to consider the affirmative defense. And if the jury finds that each element of the crime has been proved beyond a reasonable doubt, it necessarily has decided that the defendant has not disproved an element of the crime. In either situation the instructions on the affirmative defense are surplusage. Because a reasonable jury will attempt to ascribe some significance to the court's instructions, the likelihood that it will impermissibly shift the burden is increased.

Of course, whether the jury will in fact improperly shift the burden away from the state is uncertain. But it is "settled law . . . that when there exists a reasonable possibility that the jury relied on an unconstitutional understanding of the law in reaching a guilty verdict, that verdict must be set aside." Francis v. Franklin, 471 U.S. 307, 323, n. 8 (1985).

Ante, at 234. Under Patterson, this conclusion should suggest that Ohio is precluded from shifting the burden as to self-defense. The Court nevertheless concludes that Martin was properly required to prove self-defense, simply because "Ohio does not shift to the defendant the burden of disproving any element of the state's case." Ibid.

The Court gives no explanation for this apparent rejection of Patterson. The only justification advanced for the Court's decision is that the jury could have used the evidence of self-defense to find that the State failed to carry its burden of proof. Because the jurors were free to consider both Martin's and the State's evidence, the argument goes, the verdict of guilt necessarily means that they were convinced that the defendant acted with prior calculation and design, and were unpersuaded that she acted in self-defense. Ante, at 233. The Court thus seems to conclude that as long as the jury is told that the state has the burden of proving all elements of the crime, the overlap between the offense and defense is immaterial.

This reasoning is flawed in two respects. First, it simply ignores the problem that arises from inconsistent jury instructions in a criminal case. The Court's holding implicitly assumes that the jury in fact understands that the ultimate burden remains with the prosecutor at all times, despite a conflicting instruction that places the burden on the accused to disprove the same element. But as pointed out above, the Patterson distinction between defenses that negate an element of the crime and those that do not is based on the legitimate concern that the jury will mistakenly lower the state's burden. In short, the Court's rationale fails to explain why the overlap in this case does not create the risk that Patterson suggested was unacceptable.

Second, the Court significantly, and without explanation, extends the deference granted to state legislatures in this area. Today's decision could be read to say that virtually all state attempts to shift the burden of proof for affirmative defenses will be upheld, regardless of the relationship between the elements of the defense and the elements of the crime. As I understand it, Patterson allowed burden shifting because evidence of an extreme emotional disturbance did not negate the mens rea of the underlying offense. After today's decision, however, even if proof of the defense does negate an element of the offense, burden shifting still may be permitted because the jury can consider the defendant's evidence when reaching its verdict.

I agree, of course, that States must have substantial leeway in defining their criminal laws and administering their criminal justice systems. But none of our precedents suggests that courts must give complete deference to a State's judgment about whether a shift in the burden of proof is consistent with the presumption of innocence. In the past we have emphasized that in some circumstances it may be necessary to look beyond the text of the State's burden-shifting laws to satisfy ourselves that the requirements of Winship have been satisfied. In Mullaney v. Wilbur, 421 U.S. 684, 698-699 (1975) we explicitly noted the danger of granting the State unchecked discretion to shift the burden as to any element of proof in a criminal case. The Court today fails to discuss or even cite Mullaney, despite our unanimous agreement in that case that this danger would justify judicial intervention in some cases. Even Patterson, from which I dissented, recognized that "there are obviously constitutional limits beyond which the States may not go [in labeling elements of a crime as an affirmative defense]." 432 U.S., at 210. Today, however, the Court simply asserts that Ohio law properly allocates the burdens, without giving any indication of where those limits lie.

Because our precedent establishes that the burden of proof may not be shifted when the elements of the defense and the elements of the offense conflict, and because it seems clear that they do so in this case, I would reverse the decision of the Ohio Supreme Court.

II.

Although I believe that this case is wrongly decided even under the principles set forth in Patterson, my differences with the Court's approach are more fundamental. I continue to believe that the better method for deciding when a State may shift the burden of proof is outlined in the Court's opinion in Mullaney and in my dissenting opinion in Patterson. In Mullaney, we emphasized that the state's obligation to prove certain facts beyond a reasonable doubt was not necessarily restricted to legislative distinctions between offenses and affirmative defenses. The boundaries of the state's authority in this respect were elaborated in the Patterson dissent, where I proposed a two-part inquiry:

> The Due Process Clause requires that the prosecutor bear the burden of persuasion beyond a reasonable doubt only if the factor at issue makes a substantial difference in punishment and stigma. The requirement of course applies a fortiori if the factor makes the difference between guilt and innocence. . . . It also must be shown that in the Anglo-American legal tradition the factor in question historically has held that level of importance. If either branch of the test is not met, then the legislature retains its traditional authority over matters of proof. 432 U.S., at 226-227 (footnotes omitted).

Cf. McMillan v. Pennsylvania, 477 U.S. 79, 103 (1986) (STEVENS, J., dissenting) ("[If] a State provides that a specific component of a prohibited transaction shall give rise both to a special stigma and to a special punishment, that component must be treated as a 'fact necessary to constitute the crime' within the meaning of our holding in In re Winship").

There are at least two benefits to this approach. First, it ensures that the critical facts necessary to sustain a conviction will be proved by the state. Because the Court would be willing to look beyond the text of a state statute, legislatures would have no incentive to redefine essential elements of an offense to make them part of an affirmative defense, thereby shifting the burden of proof in a manner inconsistent with Winship and Mullaney. Second, it would leave the States free in all other respects to recognize new factors that may mitigate the degree of criminality or punishment, without requiring that they also bear the burden of disproving these defenses. See Patterson v. New York, 432 U.S., at 229-230 (POWELL, J., dissenting) ("New ameliorative affirmative defenses . . . generally remain undisturbed by the holdings in Winship and Mullaney" (footnote omitted)).

Under this analysis, it plainly is impermissible to require the accused to prove self-defense. If petitioner could have carried her burden, the result would have been decisive-ly different as to both guilt and punishment. There also is no dispute that self-defense his-torically is one of the primary justifications for otherwise unlawful conduct. See, e.g., Beard v. United States, 158 U.S. 550, 562 (1895). Thus, while I acknowledge that the two-part test may be difficult to apply at times, it is hard to imagine a more clear-cut application than the one presented here.

III.

In its willingness to defer to the State's leg-islative definitions of crimes and defenses, the Court apparently has failed to recognize the practical effect of its decision. Martin alleged that she was innocent because she acted in self-defense, a complete justification under Ohio law. See State v. Nolton, 19 Ohio St. 2d 133, 249 N.E.2d 797 (1969). Because she had the burden of proof on this issue, the jury could have believed that it was just as likely as not that Martin's conduct was justi-fied, and yet still have voted to convict. In other words, even though the jury may have had a substantial doubt whether Martin com-mitted a crime, she was found guilty under Ohio law. I do not agree that the Court's authority to review state legislative choices is so limited that it justifies increasing the risk of convicting a person who may not be blameworthy. See Patterson v. New York, supra, at 201-202 (state definition of crimi-nal law must yield when it " 'offends some principle of justice so rooted in the traditions and conscience of our people as to be ranked as fundamental' " (quoting Speiser v. Ran-dall, 357 U.S. 513, 523 (1958))). The com-plexity of the inquiry as to when a State may shift the burden of proof should not lead the Court to fashion simple rules of deference that could lead to such unjust results.

Cases Relating to Chapter 4

Proof via Evidence

MADDOX
v.
MONTGOMERY

**United States Court of Appeals,
Eleventh Circuit 718 F.2d 1033
(11th Cir. 1983)**

Fay, Vance and Kravitch, Circuit Judges.

PER CURIAM

Appellant Jimmy Maddox was convicted of rape in a Georgia state court and sentenced to life imprisonment. At the trial, appellant and the alleged victim, Kathy Elder, gave radically different accounts of the events in question. Elder testified that on a number of occasions prior to the alleged rape, appellant had approached her purportedly seeking to sell her an insurance policy. On the morning in question, while Elder was dressing her two sons, appellant appeared at her apartment and again asked whether she wanted the insurance. After explaining that she had discovered that she could get insurance at work, Elder went into the bedroom to retrieve coats for the boys. Elder testified that appellant followed her into the room and forcibly raped her on the bed. Another witness for the prosecution, Debbie Phillips, testified that she had once taken out insurance with appellant, but had dropped it after he had come to her home on a Saturday night. Appellant testified that he and Elder had had voluntary sexual relations on several occasions prior to the alleged rape and that Elder had consented to their sexual relations on the morning in question.

Having unsuccessfully pursued his direct appeal and the state post-conviction remedy, appellant filed a federal habeas corpus peti-tion alleging prosecutorial suppression of exculpatory evidence in violation of the doctrine of Brady v. Maryland, 373 U.S. 83, 83 S. Ct. 1194, 10 L. Ed. 2d 215 (1963). Specifically, appellant asserted that his right to due process was violated by the state's failure to disclose (1) a photograph taken by the police shortly after the alleged rape showing Elder's bed neatly made, (2) the results of a police examination of the bedspread which revealed no blood, semen or other fluid, and (3) a written statement by another witness, Brenda Phelps, that Debbie Phillips had stated that she dropped her insurance with appellant for financial reasons. Appellant appeals the denial of habeas relief. We affirm.

There are four types of situations in which the Brady doctrine applies: (1) the prosecutor has not disclosed information despite a specific defense request; (2) the prosecutor has not disclosed information despite a general defense request for all exculpatory information or without any defense request at all; (3) the prosecutor knows or should know that the conviction is based on false evidence[; (4)] the prosecutor fails to disclose purely impeaching evidence not concerning a substantive issue, in the absence of a specific defense request. United States v. Anderson, 574 F.2d 1347, 1353 (5th Cir. 1978). Inasmuch as appellant filed no pretrial request—specific or general—for exculpatory information, the present case falls within the second category with respect to the photograph of the bed and the results of the police examination of the bedspread and within the fourth category with respect to Phelps' statement.

In order to prevail on a Brady claim, one must establish the materiality of the exculpatory information suppressed by the prosecution. United States v. Kopituk, 690 F.2d 1289, 1339 (11th Cir.1982), cert. denied, 461 U.S. 928, 103 S. Ct. 2089, 77 L. Ed. 2d 300 (1983); Anderson, 574 F.2d at 1353. The applicable threshold of materiality, however, varies depending on the type of situation. Where, as here, the state failed to disclose substantive evidence favorable to the defendant for which there was no specific request, the standard set forth in United States v. Agurs, 427 U.S. 97, 96 S. Ct. 2392, 49 L. Ed. 2d 342 (1976), governs. In Agurs, the Supreme Court stated that such a failure to disclose violates due process only "if the omitted evidence creates a reasonable doubt that did not otherwise exist." Id. at 112, 96 S. Ct. at 2401; accord United States v. Kubiak, 704 F.2d 1545, 1551 (11th Cir.1983). In Cannon v. Alabama, 558 F.2d 1211 (5th Cir. 1977), cert. denied, 434 U.S. 1087, 98 S. Ct. 1281, 55 L. Ed. 2d 792 (1978), the former Fifth Circuit explained: Applying this standard requires an analysis of the evidence adduced at trial and of the probable impact of the undisclosed information. In this context, we cannot merely consider the evidence in the light most favorable to the government but must instead evaluate all the evidence as it would bear on the deliberations of a factfinder. Id. at 1213-14.

With regard to the photograph of the bed, we agree with the district court that "the undisclosed photograph does not create a reasonable doubt as to [appellant's] guilt that did not otherwise exist," Order, p. 8, and thus is not material under Agurs. Similarly, the results of the police examination of the bedspread do not give rise to a reasonable doubt and again are immaterial under Agurs. Although both pieces of evidence, if admitted at trial, might conceivably have affected the jury's verdict, the constitutional threshold of materiality is higher. See Agurs, 427 U.S. at 108-09, 96 S. Ct. at 2400. Insofar as this information is merely consistent with appellant's version of the incident and scarcely contradicts the alleged victim's testimony, and in view of the substantial inculpatory evidence in the record, the evidence at issue is not sufficiently material to render the state's failure to disclose unconstitutional.

The standard of materiality in a case, such as this one, involving the prosecution's suppression of impeaching evidence absent a specific request was recently discussed in United States v. Blasco, 702 F.2d 1315 (11th Cir.), cert. denied, 464 U.S. 914, 104 S. Ct. 275, 78 L. Ed. 2d 256 (1983). There this Court noted, "if the suppressed evidence is purely impeaching evidence and no defense request has been made, the suppressed evidence is material only if its introduction probably would have resulted in acquittal." Id. at 1328; accord Anderson, 574 F.2d at 1354. Given the relatively minor role of Phillips' testimony and the limited impact that Phelps' statement would likely have had on the jury's assessment of Phillips' credibility, appellant is unable to demonstrate that the undisclosed evidence probably would have resulted in an acquittal. Accordingly, the evidence is immaterial under Blasco, and its suppression did not violate appellant's due process right.

For the foregoing reasons, the district court's dismissal of appellant's habeas petition is AFFIRMED.

BROWN
v.
STATE

Supreme Court of Delaware
897 A.2d 748, 2006 Del.
LEXIS 163 (2006)

Before STEELE, Chief Justice, HOLLAND and JACOBS, Justices.

HOLLAND, Justice:

The defendant-appellant, Jeron Brown, appeals from his convictions of Burglary in the Second Degree, Theft, two counts of Receiving Stolen Property, and Criminal Mischief. In this appeal, Brown alleges that the Superior Court erred by: first, denying his motion to suppress evidence obtained during a search incident to his arrest because the police did not have probable cause to arrest him; second, denying his request for a mistrial after the State disclosed potentially exculpatory evidence during the trial; and third, failing to provide, *sua sponte*, a missing evidence jury instruction because a witness was unavailable to testify at trial. We conclude that there was no reversible error. Therefore, the judgments of the Superior Court must be affirmed.

Facts

On January 20, 2004, the Del-Mar Appliance store and two private residences in Dover, Delaware, were burglarized. After the third burglary, the police reviewed a video surveillance tape from a local 7-11 store that showed an African American male and female attempting to sell items to the store clerk. Anwar Al-Rasul, the third burglary victim, had earlier identified the items on the tape as items that were stolen from his home. Later that day, the police received a tip from Mr. Al-Rasul's wife that an African American man would soon attempt to sell items similar to those stolen from her home at a nearby store, named the Closet.

The police set up surveillance outside the Closet. Jeron Brown approached the store carrying a duffel bag and wearing a jacket similar to the jacket worn by the man whose image was captured in the 7-11 video surveillance tape. Brown was also the same race, height, and build of the man shown in the tape. Brown entered the Closet and left shortly thereafter.

As he exited the store, the police approached Brown and immediately handcuffed him. The officers asked Brown if they could pat him down. They also asked Brown if they could search his jacket and duffel bag. Brown consented to both requests. Mr. Al-Rasul identified the items found by the police in Brown's jacket and duffel bag as his stolen property. The police then obtained a search warrant for Brown's residence, where they searched and seized more stolen property.

Probable Cause Established

[The appellate court agreed that probable cause was properly established.]

Mistrial Properly Denied

On the morning of the third day of Brown's trial, his defense counsel moved for a mistrial because alleged *Brady* material[1] was not disclosed by the prosecution until the preceding Friday, following two days of Brown's trial. The alleged *Brady* material at issue was a laptop computer stolen during the January 20, 2004 burglary of the Del-Mar Appliance store in Dover. The stolen laptop computer was recovered by the Delaware Probation Department from an individual named Moustapha Bobbo. After a probation officer took the laptop from Bobbo, it was turned over to Detective Virdin of the Dover Police Department. Detective Virdin then returned the computer to its rightful owner, Bruce Nygard.

Brown contends that, because the State did not inform him of information regarding Nygard's recovered laptop computer and because the computer was found in the possession of Bobbo, not Brown, this prevented Brown from introducing witnesses at trial to trace the whereabouts of the computer after it was stolen from the Del-Mar Appliance store. In denying the mistrial motion, the trial judge noted that Brown's contention concerning the laptop computer related to only one of his three pending burglary charges.

The State tried to mitigate any potential prejudice to Brown by the late disclosure of the information regarding the laptop computer. The State was able to locate both Moustapha Bobbo and Antonio Medina, another witness who had some information as to how the laptop computer came to be in the possession of Bobbo. Both Bobbo and Medina appeared at Brown's trial and testified as defense witnesses.

The Superior Court has a variety of remedies available for a discovery violation under Superior Court Criminal Rule 16(d)(2). As this Court has noted, "In determining the

---

[1] Brady v. Maryland, 373 U.S. 83, 1963 U.S. LEXIS 16 (1963), requires that the prosecution disclose and not suppress evidence that would be material to a defendant's guilt or punishment where the defendant has made a request. Good faith or bad faith on the part of the prosecution makes no difference in the requirement of disclosure.

question of whether sanctions should be imposed, the trial court should weigh all relevant factors, such as the reason for the State's delay and the extent of prejudice to the defendant." As we pointed out in *Doran*, "Superior Court Criminal Rule 16 sets forth four alternative sanctions: 1) order prompt compliance with the discovery rule; 2) 'grant a continuance;' 3) 'prohibit the party from introducing in evidence material not disclosed;' or 4) such other order the Court 'deems just under the circumstances.'"

Whether a mistrial should be declared is a matter entrusted to the trial judge's discretion. The trial judge is in the best position to assess the risk of any prejudice resulting from trial events. n16 "A trial judge should grant a mistrial only where there is 'manifest necessity' or the 'ends of public justice would be otherwise defeated.'" The remedy of a mistrial is "mandated only when there are 'no meaningful and practical alternatives' to that remedy."

In this case, the practical alternative to granting a mistrial was to permit Brown to present the testimony of both Moustapha Bobbo and Antonio Medina regarding the stolen laptop computer. Both could testify that Jeron Brown had no ostensible connection with that particular item of stolen property before its seizure by a probation officer and ultimate return to the true owner. In fact, Brown presented testimony to that effect by both of those witnesses.

Brown argues on appeal that, had he known about this information at an earlier date, his trial examinations of Medina and Bobbo would have been different. He fails to explain, however, how their examinations would have been different and how the difference(s), if any, would have mattered. The record reflects that there was no abuse of discretion in the trial judge's refusal to grant Brown's motion for a mistrial.

No Plain Error

Finally, Brown contends that the trial judge, *sua sponte*, should have given a missing evidence instruction pursuant to *Deberry v. State*. Brown's request for the *Deberry* missing evidence jury instruction did not involve the physical evidence at issue (the laptop computer), but, rather, related to a missing witness, Laura Johansen, who was not available to testify at Brown's trial. Johansen was the person who gave the stolen laptop computer to Bobbo and presumably could have testified that she purchased the laptop computer from someone other than Brown.

Brown made no request at trial for a *Deberry* missing evidence jury instruction. Therefore, that claim has been waived by Brown and may now be reviewed on appeal only for plain error. To be plain, the alleged error must affect substantial rights, generally meaning that it must have affected the outcome of Brown's trial. In demonstrating that a forfeited error is prejudicial, the burden of persuasion is on Brown.

Brown was found in possession of a digital camera and camera printer taken from the Del-Mar Appliance store when he was arrested by the police. The digital camera and printer that the police discovered in Brown's possession linked him to the stolen property from the Del-Mar appliance burglary. Accordingly, there was an independent evidentiary basis for the jury to conclude that Brown was guilty of receiving that other stolen property.

Brown was not convicted of the Del-Mar Appliance store burglary. He was convicted only of receiving stolen property resulting from that burglary, property that included the digital camera and the printer. Consequently, Brown cannot demonstrate plain error, because even if Johanson had appeared at trial and testified that she purchased the stolen laptop computer from someone other than Brown, the ultimate result at trial would have been the same.

Conclusion

The judgments of the Superior Court are affirmed.

STATE

v.

JORDAN

COURT OF APPEALS OF OHIO, THIRD APPELLATE DISTRICT

2002 Ohio 1418, 2002 Ohio App. LEXIS 1469 (2002)

HADLEY, J. The defendant/appellant, Neil L. Jordan ("the appellant"), appeals his conviction by the Seneca County Municipal Court, finding him guilty of three counts of vehicular manslaughter, in violation of R.C. 2903.06(A)(4). Based on the following, we reverse the judgment of the trial court.

Mr. Jordan was returning home from a basketball game on January 21, 2001 when, at approximately 8:30 p.m., his auto collided with another at the intersection of U.S. Route 224 and Hopewell Township Road 113 in Hopewell Township, Seneca County, Ohio. As a result of that accident, Lisa M. Johnson and Daniel P. Shaver, the occupants of the other auto, were killed. The eight to twelve week old fetus that Ms. Johnson was carrying also perished.

The appellant was charged with three counts of vehicular manslaughter. The state alleged that he violated R.C. 4511.43(A), in that he failed to stop at the point nearest the intersecting roadway where he had clear view of approaching traffic on the intersecting roadway before entering it, and that he consequently caused the deaths of Lisa M. Johnson, Daniel P. Shaver, and the unlawful termination of Ms. Johnson's pregnancy, in violation of R.C. 2903.06(A)(4). The appellant was found guilty of all three counts by a jury. He was sentenced to 45 days in jail on each count, to be served consecutively, and fined $ 375.00, plus costs.

The appellant now appeals his convictions, raising three assignments of error for our review.

ASSIGNMENT OF ERROR NO. I

As a matter of law, the trial judge committed error prejudicial to the defendant-appellant by denying his motion for judgment of acquittal at the conclusion of the State's case

[Trial Transcript, p. 222], at the conclusion of all of the evidence [Trial Transcript, p. 230], and after the return of the verdict [Ruling of August 13, 2001], since the State failed to provide any evidence (direct, circumstantial, or otherwise) that the defendant-appellant failed to stop in violation of Revised Code § 4511.43(A).

* * *

The appellant asserts in his first assignment of error that the trial court erred in failing to grant his motions for judgment of acquittal at various stages of his trial because, he alleges, the state failed to prove a material element of the charges against him. We agree with the appellant.

Crim.R. 29 prohibits a court from entering an order of judgment of acquittal if the evidence is such that reasonable minds can reach different conclusions as to whether each material element of a crime has been proved beyond a reasonable doubt. Furthermore, in reviewing a ruling on a Crim.R. 29 motion for judgment of acquittal, a reviewing court must construe the evidence in a light most favorable to the prosecution. Thus, we must determine if, construing the evidence in the light most favorable to the state, evidence was presented before the trial court which would allow reasonable minds to reach different conclusions as to whether the state proved all the material elements of vehicular manslaughter beyond a reasonable doubt.

The portion of R.C. 2903.06 under which the appellant was charged reads, in relevant part:

(A) No person, while operating or participating in the operation of a motor vehicle, motorcycle, snowmobile, locomotive, watercraft, or aircraft, shall cause the death of another or the unlawful termination of another's pregnancy in any of the following ways:

* * *

(4) As the proximate result of committing a violation of any provision of any section contained in Title XLV of the Revised Code that is a minor misdemeanor or of a

municipal ordinance that, regardless of the penalty set by ordinance for the violation, is substantially equivalent to any provision of any section contained in Title XLV of the Revised Code that is a minor misdemeanor.

The underlying minor misdemeanor the appellant was found to have violated is R.C. 4511.43(A), which states:

Except when directed to proceed by a law enforcement officer, every driver of a vehicle or trackless trolley approaching a stop sign shall stop at a clearly marked stop line, but if none, before entering the crosswalk on the near side of the intersection, or, if none, then at the point nearest the intersecting roadway where the driver has a view of approaching traffic on the intersecting roadway before entering it. After having stopped, the driver shall yield the right-of-way to any vehicle in the intersection or approaching on another roadway so closely as to constitute an immediate hazard during the time the driver is moving across or within the intersection or junction of roadways.

The appellant argues that the state presented no evidence that he failed to stop in violation of R.C. 4511.43(A). Rather, he argues, in order for the jury to find that he failed to stop, it had to draw an inference from another inference.

It is impermissible for a trier of fact to draw "an inference based * * * entirely upon another inference, unsupported by any additional fact or another inference from other facts[.]" If, however, the second inference is based in part upon another inference and in part upon facts, it is a parallel inference and, if reasonable, is permissible. Likewise, a trier of fact may draw multiple inferences from the same set of facts.

There was no direct evidence presented at the trial regarding whether the appellant failed to stop at the stop sign. What follows is a summary of the relevant evidence that was presented:

1. Pictures and descriptive testimony of the crash scene, including evidence that the victims' car was wrapped around a telephone pole and torn almost in half;

2. testimony regarding the position of the stop sign;

3. testimony about the point nearest the intersecting roadway where the appellant had a clear view of approaching traffic on the intersecting roadway, which was identified as the point where the fog line on U.S. 224 would traverse 113 if projected into the intersection, and testimony as to the distance between that point and the point of impact;

4. testimony that the appellant's car was traveling southbound at the time of the accident and the victims' car was traveling westbound;

5. testimony that the cars traveled in a basically southerly direction after the initial impact;

6. testimony that no evasive action was taken by either driver prior to impact;

7. testimony that the final resting point of both cars was the southwest corner of the intersection of U.S. 224 and Township Road 113;

8. and testimony regarding the injuries to and causes of death of the victims.

We agree with the appellant that the only way the jury could have concluded that he failed to stop in accordance with [state law] R.C. 4511.43(A) was to first infer from the evidence that his vehicle was traveling at a high rate of speed at the time of impact. Any further inference beyond this must have been supported by additional facts. The record reveals no other evidence to support an inference that the appellant failed to stop, nor do the facts that were presented independently support it. Thus, the inference that the appellant failed to stop could only be based on an inference that his vehicle was traveling at a high rate of speed, which amounts to an impermissible inference built upon another inference. Thus, we find that the appellant's Crim.R. 29 motion should have been granted because reasonable minds could only find that the State failed to prove beyond a reasonable doubt that the appellant violated R.C. 4511.43(A).

The crucial flaw in the state's case was the lack of expert testimony and scientific evidence, which, if properly presented, would have assisted the jury in understanding the significance of the state's demonstrative evidence. The limited accident reconstruction testimony in this case, in conjunction with photographs and diagrams, established the extent of damage to the vehicles, points of impact, and relative positions of the vehicles following the collision. While this evidence is significant, in order to use it as the cornerstone of their case, the state needed to establish that based on the evidence: 1) the appellant's vehicle must have been traveling at a minimum speed and 2) this speed was greater than the appellant's vehicle could have achieved in any acceleration from a proper stop at either the stop sign or the fog line.

No scientific evidence or expert opinion was placed before the jury to assist them in establishing the speed of appellant's vehicle at the point of impact with the other car. In addition, no scientific evidence or expert opinion was placed before the jury to properly assist them in ascertaining the acceleration capability of appellant's vehicle from either the fog line (approximately three feet from the point of impact) or the stop sign (some 24-27 feet from the point of impact), to the point of impact. In fact there was brief testimony from the state's expert that the acceleration capability of appellant's vehicle to the point of impact might have been anywhere from zero to thirty miles per hour or possibly even zero to sixty miles per hour from a stop at the fog line.

As a result, from the crash scene evidence alone, the jury in this case was permitted to determine for itself, without any expert or other supporting testimony: 1) that the appellant had to be traveling at a certain minimum speed sufficient to create the existing crash scene and 2) that this speed exceeded the capability of appellant's car to accelerate from a lawful stop at the stop sign or the fog line—in order to then determine that appellant did not stop at either location prior to the collision.

In addition to requiring an improper stacking of inferences, the impact-speed and acceleration determinations described above are beyond the knowledge or experience of lay persons and therefore constitute determinations which are not permissible for a jury to make from crash scene evidence alone, without the assistance of expert testimony.

Because we find for the appellant on this assignment of error, we need not address his second or third assignments of error.

Accordingly, the appellant's first assignment of error is well taken and hereby affirmed.

Having found error prejudicial to the appellant herein, in the particulars assigned and argued, we reverse the judgment of the trial court and remand the matter for further proceedings consistent with this opinion.

Judgment Reversed.

SHAW, P.J., and WALTERS, J., concur.

Cases Relating to Chapter 5

Judicial Notice

STATE
v.
VEJVODA

231 Neb. 668, 438 N.W.2d 461
(1989)

Hastings, C.J., Boslaugh, White, Caporale, Shanahan, and Fahrnbruch, J.J. White, J., dissenting.

SHANAHAN, OPINION:

In a bench trial in the county court for Hall County, Mark Vejvoda was convicted of drunk driving and received an enhanced sentence as the result of his second conviction for drunk driving. See Neb. Rev. Stat. § 39-669.07 (Reissue 1988). On appeal, the district court affirmed Vejvoda's conviction and sentence. Vejvoda contends that the evidence is insufficient to sustain his conviction for drunk driving and that the State failed to prove that Hall County was the venue for his trial because the court improperly took judicial notice that locations mentioned in Vejvoda's trial were within Hall County.

VEJVODA'S TRIAL

Officer Elmer Edwards of the Grand Island Police Department was the sole witness at Vejvoda's trial. Edwards testified that on May 1, 1987, at 2:14 A.M., he was in the vicinity of 7th and Vine Streets and noticed a vehicle proceeding west on 7th Street, "weaving back and forth across the entire width of the street." Edwards had observed the vehicle for "21/2 to 3 blocks," when the

car commenced a right turn from 7th Street onto Oak Street and "ran over the curb section located at the . . . northeast corner of the intersection." In pursuit, Edwards followed the car northbound on Oak Street to 8th Street, where Edwards stopped the pursued vehicle.

On confronting the car's driver, whom Edwards eventually identified as Vejvoda, Edwards observed that Vejvoda's eyes were bloodshot and watery, and a strong odor of alcohol emanated from Vejvoda's car. According to Edwards, Vejvoda's reactions were "slow and sluggish" while he fumbled to produce a driver's license. Edwards then asked Vejvoda to step out of his car for field sobriety tests. Vejvoda was "swaying and wobbling" and had difficulty maintaining his balance during the field sobriety tests. In Edwards' opinion, Vejvoda was under the influence of alcohol when stopped by the officer, who later arrested Vejvoda for drunk driving. In all his testimony concerning his observations, pursuit, and stop of the vehicle, Edwards never mentioned the city or county where the events occurred. Defense counsel did not cross-examine Edwards, and the prosecution rested.

After Vejvoda offered no evidence, the prosecutor apparently realized that Edwards had not testified that the events involving Vejvoda occurred in Hall County. When the prosecutor asked leave to recall Edwards for testimony concerning the location of events, the court responded, "The Court will take judicial notice of the fact that all of the addresses and areas described are those—are those within the city limits of the city of

Grand Island which lies wholly within Hall County." Vejvoda objected to the court's "taking judicial notice after the . . . State has rested." In closing argument, Vejvoda argued, among other things, that the State had failed to prove proper venue. The court then found Vejvoda guilty of drunk driving. Vejvoda contends, first, that there is insufficient evidence to sustain his conviction for drunk driving, and, second, the court improperly took judicial notice of facts establishing the site of the events on which his conviction is based. In essence, Vejvoda's venue claim is an assertion that the court improperly took judicial notice that Grand Island in Hall County was the site of the events in question and, as the result of the improper judicial notice, determined that venue was evidentially established as Hall County.

SUFFICIENCY OF EVIDENCE

In determining whether evidence is sufficient to sustain a conviction in a bench trial, the Supreme Court does not resolve conflicts of evidence, pass on credibility of witnesses, evaluate explanations, or reweigh evidence presented, which are within a fact finder's province for disposition. A conviction in a bench trial of a criminal case is sustained if the evidence, viewed and construed most favorably to the State, is sufficient to support that conviction. See State v. Brown, 225 Neb. 418, 405 N.W.2d 600 (1987).

With no explanation for the obvious or further comment necessary, we find that the evidence supports Vejvoda's conviction for drunk driving, the substantive offense charged against Vejvoda.

GUARANTEE OF VENUE

The venue problem in this appeal could have been easily avoided by the court's merely granting the State's motion to withdraw its rest and present evidence on venue. "Even in criminal prosecutions the withdrawal of a rest in a trial on the merits is within the discretion of the trial court." State v. Putnam, 178 Neb. 445, 448-49, 133 N.W.2d 605, 608 (1965). Unfortunately, however, instead of allowing the State to recall Edwards to answer a single, simple question identifying venue, the court chose to try to remedy the

evidential situation and created the venue problem presented in Vejvoda's appeal.

Vejvoda claims that "an accused is guaranteed the right to be tried in the county where the offense is committed by Article 1, Section 11 of the Constitution of the State of Nebraska." Brief for appellant at 3. Vejvoda, however, incorrectly interprets the constitutional guarantee in article I, § 11, of the Nebraska Constitution, which grants to a criminal defendant the right to "a speedy public trial by an impartial jury of the county or district in which the offense is alleged to have been committed." We have characterized the preceding constitutional language as "too plain to require interpretation." Marino v. State, 111 Neb. 623, 625, 197 N.W. 396, 397 (1924). Article I, § 11, of the Nebraska Constitution relates to an impartial jury in a criminal case for which a jury trial is constitutionally guaranteed, but does not grant a defendant a constitutional right to be tried in a particular county. In the present case, Vejvoda was convicted in a bench trial. Therefore, article I, § 11, of the Nebraska Constitution concerning a jury trial is inapplicable to Vejvoda's case.

Vejvoda's right to be tried in the county in which the criminal offense is alleged to have been committed is secured by statute rather than by the Nebraska Constitution. Neb. Rev. Stat. § 29-1301 (Reissue 1985) provides that "[a]ll criminal cases shall be tried in the county where the offense was committed . . . unless it shall appear to the court by affidavits that a fair and impartial trial cannot be had therein." While proper venue in a criminal case may be established by circumstantial evidence, we have held that the State must prove proper venue beyond a reasonable doubt. Union P. R. Co. v. State, 88 Neb. 547, 130 N.W. 277 (1911); Keeler v. State, 73 Neb. 441, 103 N.W. 64 (1905). It is clear from Nebraska decisions that a defendant may waive the statutorily designated venue for the trial of a criminal case in accordance with § 29-1301 concerning a change of venue. See Kennison v. State, 83 Neb. 391, 119 N.W. 768 (1909). Whether venue is an element of the substantive offense charged against an accused is apparently an unresolved issue in Nebraska. See, however, State v. Harris, 48 Wash. App. 279, 281-82, 738 P.2d 1059, 1061 (1987): "As a general rule, proof of venue is necessary in a criminal prosecution. [Citations omitted.] However, venue is not an element of the crime [citations omitted], and it need not be proved beyond a reasonable doubt [citation omitted]." See, further, State v. Graycek, 335 N.W.2d 572, 574 (S.D. 1983): "Venue, not being an integral part of a criminal offense, does not affect the question of the guilt or innocence of the accused [and may be proved] by a preponderance of the evidence . . . ." Cf., State v. Barnes, 7 Ohio App. 3d 83, 84, 454 N.E.2d 572, 574 (1982): "Venue with respect to the situs of a crime is ordinarily considered an element of the offense which must be proved along with the other elements"; State v. Hester, 145 Ariz. 574, 703 P.2d 518 (1985) (venue is an essential element).

WAIVER OF VENUE

If the rules regarding waiver of venue in a civil action were applicable in the present appeal, Vejvoda's appellate claim based on venue would undoubtedly fail. At the risk of waiver, to preserve a claim of improper venue in a civil case, a defendant must raise the venue issue before or in the defendant's answer. In a civil action, if a defendant fails to timely raise the issue of proper venue, the defendant waives any venue question. See, In re Interest of Adams, 230 Neb. 109, 430 N.W.2d 295 (1988) (venue under the Nebraska Mental Health Commitment Act waived by failure to request transfer at appropriate time); Blitzkie v. State, 228 Neb. 409, 422 N.W.2d 773 (1988) (venue in a transitory civil action under the State Tort Claims Act waived unless raised in the answer or earlier). Unlike venue in a civil case, however, a statutorily designated venue in a criminal case may not be waived by a defendant's failure to raise the venue issue before or at trial. Union P. R. Co. v. State, supra; State v. Lindsey, 193 Neb. 442, 227 N.W.2d 599 (1975). In Union P. R. Co. v. State, supra, involving a prosecution for violation of the state's "anti-pass law" regarding railroads, the court was faced with a situation in which "the matter of venue was entirely overlooked by both the prosecutor and the trial court . . . ." Union P. R. Co., supra at 550, 130 N.W. at 278. Despite the fact that the defendant apparently did not raise the venue issue at trial, the court held,

over dissent, that the defendant's conviction should be reversed "[f]or the sole reason that the state failed to prove the venue . . . ." Union P. R. Co., supra at 551, 130 N.W. at 279. (In Union P. R. Co. v. State, supra, the dissent argued that the "ancient rule" that venue must be proved beyond a reasonable doubt was not "based upon reason," and further noted that "the rule that a defendant may waive the right to insist upon a trial in any particular county, and that if he goes to trial without objection he does so, is in accord with reason and modern conditions . . . ." (Sedgwick, J., dissenting.) Union P. R. Co., supra at 552, 130 N.W. at 279.) Thus, Nebraska cases indicate that a defendant in a criminal case may waive the issue of a statutorily designated venue by requesting a change of venue in accordance with § 29-1301, but a defendant does not waive the venue issue by failure to raise the issue before or during trial. See State v. Lindsey, supra. In the absence of a defendant's waiver of venue, the State has the burden to prove proper venue beyond a reasonable doubt. State v. Lindsey, supra; Union P. R. Co. v. State, supra; Keeler v. State, supra. With this in mind, we turn to Vejvoda's claim that proper venue was not sufficiently proved in his case.

PROOF OF VENUE

The venue of an offense may be proven like any other fact in a criminal case. It need not be established by positive testimony, nor in the words of the information; but if from the facts appearing in evidence the only rational conclusion which can be drawn is that the offense was committed in the county alleged, it is sufficient. Weinecke v. State, 34 Neb. 14, 24, 51 N.W. 307, 310 (1892). See, also, Gates v. State, 160 Neb. 722, 71 N.W.2d 460 (1955); State v. Liberator, 197 Neb. 857, 251 N.W.2d 709 (1977); State v. Laflin, 201 Neb. 824, 272 N.W.2d 376 (1978); State v. Ellis, 208 Neb. 379, 303 N.W.2d 741 (1981).

The only testimony regarding venue was that of Edwards, a Grand Island police officer, who observed Vejvoda's car at "7th and Vine Streets" and later apprehended Vejvoda on a street called "Oak." Edwards never identified the city or county where he observed and apprehended Vejvoda. As this court noted in State v. Bouwens, 167 Neb. 244, 247, 92 N.W.2d 564, 566 (1958), the fact that a defendant was arrested by policemen of a particular city "is not proof that the offense was committed within the jurisdiction . . . of the city . . . ." When the judicial notice in question is disregarded, the evidence offered in Vejvoda's case fails to establish that either a Vine Street or an Oak Street exists in Grand Island or Hall County. A defendant's arrest by a law enforcement officer of a particular political subdivision does not identify or establish the political subdivision as the proper venue in a criminal case. State v. Bouwens, supra. Therefore, without the court's judicial notice that events concerning Vejvoda occurred in Grand Island within Hall County, the evidence fails to establish venue.

In this appeal, the State does not challenge the current Nebraska rule that a waiver does not result from a defendant's inaction on a venue question in a criminal case, nor does the State take issue with the necessity of evidence beyond a reasonable doubt regarding proof of venue.

JUDICIAL NOTICE

Neb. Evid. R. 201(2), Neb. Rev. Stat. § 27-201(2) (Reissue 1985), pertains to judicial notice of adjudicative facts and states: "A judicially noticed fact must be one not subject to reasonable dispute in that it is either (a) generally known within the territorial jurisdiction of the trial court or (b) capable of accurate and ready determination by resort to sources whose accuracy cannot reasonably be questioned."

A fact is adjudicative if the fact affects the determination of a controverted issue in litigation, or, as one author has characterized adjudicative facts:

When a court or an agency finds facts concerning the immediate parties—who did what, where, when, how, and with what motive or intent—the court or agency is performing an adjudicative function, and the facts so determined are conveniently called adjudicative facts. . . .

Stated in other terms, the adjudicative facts are those to which the law is applied

in the process of adjudication. They are the facts that normally go to the jury in a jury case. They relate to the parties, their activities, their properties, their businesses. Davis, Judicial Notice, 55 Colum. L. Rev. 945, 952 (1955).

Concerning judicial notice of adjudicative facts, Weinstein observes:

The obvious cost of establishing adjudicative facts in an adversary proceeding—in terms of time, energy and money—justifies dispensing with formal proof when a matter is not really disputable. . . . When facts do not possess this requisite degree of certainty, our traditional procedure has been to require proof within the framework of the adversary system for reasons well-expressed by Professor Davis: "The reason we use trial-type procedure, I think, is that we make the practical judgment, on the basis of experience, that taking evidence subject to cross-examination and rebuttal, is the best way to resolve controversies involving disputes of adjudicative facts, that is, facts pertaining to the parties. The reason we require a determination on the record is that we think fair procedure in resolving disputes of adjudicative facts calls for giving each party a chance to meet in the appropriate fashion the facts that come to the tribunal's attention, and the appropriate fashion for meeting disputed adjudicative facts includes rebuttal evidence, cross-examination, usually confrontation, and argument (either written or oral or both)." [Quoting from K. Davis, A System of Judicial Notice Based on Fairness and Convenience, in Perspectives of Law 69 (1964).] 1 J. Weinstein & M. Berger, Weinstein's Evidence para. 201[03] at 201-23 to 201-24 (1988).

When neither of the alternative tests prescribed in Neb. Evid. R. 201(2) is satisfied, judicial notice of an adjudicative fact is improper. See Cardio-Medical Assoc. v. Crozer-Chester Med. Ctr., 721 F.2d 68 (3d Cir. 1983). See, also, 1 J. Weinstein & M. Berger, supra.

A judge or court may take judicial notice, whether requested or not. Neb. Evid. R.

201(3). Judicial notice of an adjudicative fact may be taken at any stage of the proceedings. Neb. Evid. R. 201(6).

JUDICIAL NOTICE: A SPECIES OF EVIDENCE

Judicial notice of an adjudicative fact is a species of evidence, which, if relevant as an ultimate fact or a fact from which an ultimate fact may be inferred, is received without adherence to the Nebraska Evidence Rules otherwise applicable to admissibility of evidence and establishes a fact without formal evidentiary proof. See, In re Samaha, 130 Cal. App. 116, 19 P.2d 839 (1933) (judicial notice is a form of evidence); Moss v. Aetna Life Ins. Co., 267 S.C. 370, 377, 228 S.E.2d 108, 112 (1976): judicial notice "means that the court will admit into evidence and consider, without proof of the facts, matters of common and general knowledge"; National Aircraft Leasing v. American Airlines, *** 74 Ill. App. 3d 1014, 1017, 394 N.E.2d 470, 474 (1979): "Judicial notice is an evidentiary concept which operates to admit matters into evidence without formal proof . . . ." Although Neb. Evid. R. 201 does not expressly require relevance for judicial notice, an irrelevant fact cannot be validly classified as an "adjudicative fact," the only type of fact noticeable under Neb. Evid. R. 201. See, Blank v. Kirwan, 39 Cal. 3d 311, 703 P.2d 58, 216 Cal. Rptr. 718 (1985); United States v. Byrnes, 644 F.2d 107 (2d Cir. 1981); 21 C. Wright & K. Graham, Federal Practice and Procedure § 5104 (1977).

JUDICIAL NOTICE v. A JUDGE'S PERSONAL KNOWLEDGE

Judicial notice, however, is not the same as extrajudicial or personal knowledge of a judge. "What a judge knows and what facts a judge may judicially notice are not identical data banks. . . . [A]ctual private knowledge by the judge is no sufficient ground for taking judicial notice of a fact as a basis for a finding or a final judgment . . . ." McCormick on Evidence § 329 at 922-23 (E. Cleary 3d ed. 1984). As Wigmore observes:

There is a real but elusive line between the judge's personal knowledge as a private man and these matters of which he takes judicial notice as a judge. The latter does not necessarily include the former; as a judge, indeed, he may have to ignore what he knows as a man and contrariwise. . . .

It is therefore plainly accepted that the judge is not to use from the bench, under the guise of judicial knowledge, that which he knows only as an individual observer outside of court. The former is in truth "known" to him merely in the fictional sense that it is known and notorious to all men, and the dilemma is only the result of using the term "knowledge" in two senses. Where to draw the line between knowledge by notoriety and knowledge by personal observation may sometimes be difficult but the principle is plain. (Emphasis in original.) 9 J. Wigmore, Evidence in Trials at Common Law § 2569(a) at 722-23 (J. Chadbourn rev. 1981). See, also, Government of Virgin Islands v. Gereau, 523 F.2d 140 (3d Cir. 1975).

JUDICIAL NOTICE IN CRIMINAL CASES

In function and effect, judicial notice in a civil action is fundamentally different from judicial notice in a criminal case. "In a civil action or proceeding, the judge shall instruct the jury to accept as conclusive any fact judicially noticed. In a criminal case, the judge shall instruct the jury that it may, but is not required to, accept as conclusive any fact judicially noticed." Neb. Evid. R. 201(7). In a civil action, the adjudicative fact judicially noticed is conclusively established and binds the jury, whereas in a criminal case a jury ultimately has the freedom to find that an adjudicative fact has not been established notwithstanding judicial notice by the trial court. If the conclusive effect of judicial notice in a civil action were transposed to the trial of a criminal case, judicial notice might supply proof of an element in the charge against an accused and thereby have the practical effect of a directed verdict on the issue of the defendant's guilt. The actual danger of judicial notice as a directed verdict against an accused was carefully considered in State v.

Lawrence, 120 Utah 323, 234 P.2d 600 (1951), which involved a conviction of grand larceny, that is, theft of property with value in excess of $50. As recounted by the court in Lawrence:

At the conclusion of the evidence, the defendant's counsel moved the court for a directed verdict on the ground that there had been no evidence of value of the stolen car. The State's attorney might properly and with little difficulty have moved to re-open and supply the missing evidence. He did not do so but instead argued that judicial notice could be taken of the value of the car. The court denied defendant's motion and included in its instructions to the jury the following:

. . . .

In this case you will take the value of this property as being in excess of $50.00 and therefore the defendant, if he is guilty at all, is guilty of grand larceny." 120 Utah at 326, 234 P.2d at 601.

In that setting, the Lawrence court directed its attention to the prosecution's argument that the court could take judicial notice of the automobile's value and instruct the jury accordingly. Rejecting the State's argument, the court concluded:

It is to be admitted that upon the surface there doesn't appear to be much logic to the thought that a jury would not be bound to find that the car involved here (1947 Ford 2-Door Sedan) is worth more than $50. However, under our jury system, it is traditional that in criminal cases juries can, and sometimes do, make findings which are not based on logic, nor even common sense. No matter how positive the evidence of a man's guilt may be, the jury may find him not guilty and no court has any power to do anything about it. Notwithstanding the occasional incongruous result, this system of submitting all of the facts in criminal cases to the jury and letting them be the exclusive judges thereof has lasted for some little time now and with a fair degree of success. If the result

in individual cases at times seems illogical, we can be consoled by the words of Mr. Justice Holmes, that in some areas of the law, "a page of history is worth a volume of logic." We, who live with it, have a fervent devotion to the jury system, in spite of its faults. We would not like to see it destroyed nor whittled away. If a court can take one important element of an offense from the jury and determine the facts for them because such fact seems plain enough to him, then which element cannot be similarly taken away, and where would the process stop? 120 Utah at 330-31, 234 P.2d at 603. The court then reversed Lawrence's conviction and ordered a new trial.

In U.S. v. Mentz, 840 F.2d 315 (6th Cir. 1988), the government prosecuted Mentz in a jury trial on charges of bank robbery. To convict Mentz, the government had to prove that Mentz robbed a financial institution insured by the Federal Deposit Insurance Corporation. See 18 U.S.C. § 2113(a) and (f) (1982). When Mentz moved for dismissal of the charges at the close of the government's case, claiming that evidence failed to establish that the banks were FDIC-insured at the time of the robberies, the court overruled Mentz' motion and, although there was no evidence of FDIC insurance, instructed the jury that each of the banks, which Mentz was accused of robbing, was "insured by the Federal Deposit Insurance Corporation at the time of the offense alleged in the indictment." (Emphasis omitted.) 840 F.2d at 318-19. In reversing Mentz' conviction, the court stated:

Regardless of how overwhelming the evidence may be, the Constitution delegates to the jury, not to the trial judge, the important task of deciding guilt or innocence. "[The jury's] overriding responsibility is to stand between the accused and a potentially arbitrary or abusive Government that is in command of the criminal sanction. For this reason, a trial judge is prohibited from entering a judgment of conviction or directing the jury to come forward with such a verdict, regardless of how overwhelming the evidence may point in that direction. The trial judge is thereby barred from attempting to override or interfere with the jurors' independent judgment in a manner contrary to the interests of the accused." United States v. Martin Linen Supply Co. [citation omitted]. 840 F.2d at 319.

The Mentz court continued:

We agree with Mentz that the trial judge invaded the jury's province by instructing that body, in clear and unequivocal language, that the banks were FDIC insured at the time the robberies occurred. His conclusive statement left no room for the jury to believe otherwise. The judge improperly cast himself in the role of trier of fact, and directed a verdict on an essential element of the bank robbery charge. His instructions had the effect of relieving the government of its burden of proving, beyond the jury's reasonable doubt, that the accused committed the crimes charged. . . .

It is not important that the jury might have reached a similar conclusion had it been given an opportunity to decide the issue under a correct instruction. A plea of not guilty places all issues in dispute, "even the most patent truths." [Citations omitted.] The First Circuit has succinctly stated this point: "Whatever probative force the government's proof possessed, the jury had the power to accept or reject it—or to find it insufficiently persuasive. The defendant had a correlative right to free and unhampered exercise by the jury of all its powers." [Quoting from U.S. v. Argentine, 814 F.2d 783 (1st Cir. 1987).] 840 F.2d at 320.

The court in Mentz then noted: "Since the government's evidence on this issue consisted mainly of witness testimony, the trial judge replaced the jury by reaching a conclusion based on assessing the credibility of witnesses and weighing the probative value of the evidence." 840 F.2d at 320 n.8.

Specifically referring to judicial notice under Fed. R. Evid. 201(g), the counterpart to Neb. Evid. R. 201(7), the court concluded in Mentz:

A court may take judicial notice of adjudicative facts in a criminal case, whether requested or not. Rule 201(c), (f), Fed.R.Evid. When the court does so, however, there will normally be a record of this. "Care should be taken by the court to identify the fact it is noticing, and its justification for doing so." Colonial Leasing Company of New England v. Logistics Control Group International, 762 F.2d 454, 459 (5th Cir. 1985). This facilitates intelligent appellate review, and is particularly necessary when the fact noticed is an essential element of the crime charged. . . .

. . . In a criminal case, a trial court that takes judicial notice of an adjudicative fact must "instruct the jury that it may, but is not required to, accept as conclusive any fact judicially noticed." Rule 201(g), Fed.R.Evid. *** This provision "contemplates that the jury in a criminal case [will] pass upon facts which are judicially noticed." United States v. Jones, 580 F.2d 219, 224 (6th Cir. 1978). As so construed, Rule 201(g) preserves the jury's "traditional prerogative to ignore even uncontroverted facts in reaching a verdict," and thereby prevents the trial court from transgressing the spirit, if not the letter, of the Sixth Amendment right to a jury trial by directing a partial verdict as to the facts. [Citations omitted.]

A trial court commits constitutional error when it takes judicial notice of facts constituting an essential element of the crime charged, but fails to instruct the jury according to Rule 201(g). The court's decision to accept the element as established conflicts with the bedrock principle that the government must prove, beyond the jury's reasonable doubt, every essential element of the crime. [Citation omitted.]

Even assuming the district court in this case judicially noticed the insurance coverage by the FDIC, it was obligated to inform the jury that it could disregard the facts noticed. The court's failure to make such a statement permitted the jury to convict Mentz without ever examining the evidence concerning an element of the crime charged, and thus violated his Sixth Amendment right to a jury trial. 840 F.2d at 322-23.

As one commentator has remarked concerning judicial notice and Fed. R. Evid. 201(g), which remark is equally applicable to Neb. Evid. R. 201(7):

With respect to criminal cases, Rule 201(g) apparently contemplates that contrary evidence is admissible, which of course means that evidence, if any, in support of the fact judicially noticed may also be admitted. Problems arising with respect to the court considering inadmissible evidence in determining the propriety of taking judicial notice coupled with the confusion that naturally would be expected to arise in the jury's mind when presented with judicial notice accompanied by conflicting evidence, makes resort to judicial notice in criminal cases where the opposing party is prepared to introduce contrary evidence highly undesirable. M. Graham, Handbook of Federal Evidence § 201.7 at 83 (2d ed. 1986).

JUDICIAL NOTICE IN A BENCH TRIAL

Potential problems from judicial notice in a bench trial are discussed in 21 C. Wright & K. Graham, Federal Practice and Procedure § 5104 at 488 (1977):

[T]he high degree of indisputability required before a fact can be judicially noticed applies to both forms of litigation [jury trials and court or bench trials]. However, the procedural context in which notice is taken makes the process quite different in court trials. Since the judge is not insulated, as the jury is, from the material consulted in deciding whether or not to take notice, it may make little difference whether he takes formal judicial notice based on the material or whether he is simply convinced of the fact as a result of having examined the sources. Technically, the source material is not in evidence, and thus a finding that was without other support in the record could not stand unless the mat-

ter was properly noticeable; but otherwise, the line between judicial notice and proof-taking is blurred in court trials.

From all the foregoing observations, we believe, and for that reason suggest, that judicial notice should be sparingly used in a criminal case lest prejudicial error result from denial of a defendant's constitutional or statutory rights in the trial of a criminal case.

JUDICIAL NOTICE IN VEJVODA'S CASE

Under the Nebraska Evidence Rules, the trial court's sua sponte judicial notice was permissible at the point in Vejvoda's trial where adduction of evidence had been concluded and the case was ready for submission to the factfinding process. See Neb. Evid. R. 201(4): "A judge or court shall take judicial notice if requested by a party and supplied with the necessary information." See, also, Neb. Evid. R. 201(6): "Judicial notice may be taken at any stage of the proceeding."

However, from the record in Vejvoda's case, one cannot conclude that the location of the municipal microcosm known as Vine Street or 8th and Oak Streets was known throughout the length and breadth of Hall County and, therefore, a fact "known within the territorial jurisdiction of the trial court." Neb. Evid. R. 201(2)(a). Consequently, we must focus on the alternative expressed in Neb. Evid. R. 201(2)(b), that is, whether the location of Vine and Oak Streets in Grand Island and the site of Vejvoda's arrest are adjudicative facts "capable of accurate and ready determination by resort to sources whose accuracy cannot reasonably be questioned."

For resolution of Vejvoda's claim regarding the impropriety of the trial court's judicial notice, we must first identify and characterize the scope of the trial court's "judicial notice," which actually has two components: (1) Vine, Oak, 7th, and 8th Streets exist in Grand Island, which is located in Hall County, and (2) Vejvoda's drunk driving occurred at 8th and Oak in Grand Island. Thus, existence of Grand Island streets is inferentially correlated with Edwards' testimony, producing a conclusion judicially noticed by the trial court, namely, the judicially noticed streets are the same streets mentioned in Edwards' testimony, and, therefore, Vejvoda was arrested in Grand Island.

An inference may be entirely reasonable, yet nevertheless an improper subject for judicial notice[.] [Neb. Evid. R. 201] puts judges and attorneys on notice that underlying assumptions must be analyzed to ascertain whether their validity can be verified and placed beyond practical dispute. Attorneys must be alert to instances . . . where a court's statement, although plausible on the surface, may be based on unverified [and unverifiable] hypotheses. 1 J. Weinstein & M. Berger, Weinstein's Evidence para. 201[03] at 201-34 (1988).

When a fact is not generally known within the territorial jurisdiction of the trial court, judicial notice may be taken only if an adjudicative fact can be verified by "sources whose accuracy cannot reasonably be questioned." Neb. Evid. R. 201(2)(b). The inference that Vejvoda was arrested in Grand Island is not "capable of accurate and ready determination by resort to sources whose accuracy cannot reasonably be questioned." Neb. Evid. R. 201(2)(b). We cannot imagine any unimpeachable source or sources which quickly and accurately verify the trial court's inferential determination that Vejvoda's drunk driving occurred in Grand Island. While a map of Grand Island would verify existence of Vine and Oak Streets within the city, a Grand Island map would not indisputably establish that Vejvoda was driving in that city.

As a matter of judicial notice, the trial court's conclusion that Vejvoda's drunk driving occurred in Grand Island is verifiable only by the cumbersome process of examining all locations outside Grand Island, which might match Edwards' description of a site with "Vine" and "Oak" streets, and then eliminating those locations which are inconsistent with Edwards' testimony about the direction traveled by Vejvoda's vehicle, for example, Vejvoda's car traveled west on 7th Street, turned right from 7th Street onto Oak Street, and stopped at 8th and Oak Streets. In the foregoing process of comparison and elimination, a court would have to consult not only a map of Grand Island, but also maps of cities and towns outside Grand

Island and Hall County which have streets designated "Vine," "Oak," "7th," and "8th." Although a court might, after a laborious comparison of virtually innumerable city maps, confirm Edwards' identification of "Vine" and "Oak" as the streets traveled by Vejvoda within Grand Island, such an unavoidably burdensome procedure is not only impracticable but contrary to Neb. Evid. R. 201(2)(b), which specifies that a judicially noticed adjudicative fact must be "capable of . . . ready determination."

A court may take judicial notice concerning the location of streets in a particular political subdivision within the court's jurisdiction. State v. Scramuzza, 408 So. 2d 1316 (La. 1982); Evans Associated Industries, Inc. v. Evans, 493 S.W.2d 547 (Tex. Civ. App. 1973); State v. Martin, 270 N.C. 286, 154 S.E.2d 96 (1967); Cascio v. State, 213 Ark. 418, 210 S.W.2d 897 (1948); United States v. Hughes, 542 F.2d 246 (5th Cir. 1976). See, also, Annot., Judicial Notice as to Location of Street Address Within Particular Political Subdivision, 86 A.L.R.3d 485 (1978). In the trial of a criminal case, whether a political subdivision has a street identified by a particular name used in evidence is an adjudicative fact for judicial notice, but whether the street location mentioned in testimony is actually within the political subdivision is a matter of reasonable inference by the fact finder. United States v. Mendell, 447 F.2d 639 (7th Cir. 1971).

In Vejvoda's case, the trial court could properly take judicial notice that Grand Island, which is wholly within Hall County, has streets named "Vine" and "Oak." Furthermore, by simply referring to a map of Grand Island, the court could properly take judicial notice that the intersection of 7th and Vine Streets is within two blocks of the intersection of 8th and Oak Streets. At that point the site of the offense was an issue submissible to the trier of fact.

Although the location of streets within Grand Island is readily verifiable by reference to a city map, a source capable of ready verification and a cartographic source of information which cannot reasonably be questioned, the county court took another and impermissible step by judicially noticing the inference that Vejvoda was driving in

Grand Island. The court's locational inference necessary for venue was not an adjudicative fact "capable of accurate and ready determination by resort to sources whose accuracy cannot reasonably be questioned." The county court erred in taking judicial notice of the inference that Vejvoda was driving in Grand Island and, therefore, that Vejvoda's drunk driving occurred in Grand Island. If Vejvoda had been convicted in a jury trial, we would reverse Vejvoda's conviction on account of the trial court's invasion of the factfinding process within a jury's province in the trial of a criminal case. However, as mentioned, Vejvoda's case was tried to the court. Although Vejvoda's arrest by Edwards, a Grand Island police officer, does not establish venue, Edwards' official affiliation as a Grand Island police officer was a circumstance bearing on the issue of venue. When combined with other evidence, namely, the trial court's judicial notice of "Vine" and "Oak" as streets in Grand Island, Edwards' testimony supplied a sufficient evidentiary basis for a fact finder's determination that Vejvoda's drunk driving occurred in Grand Island, Hall County, Nebraska. "Harmless error exists in a jury trial of a criminal case when there is some incorrect conduct by the trial court which, on review of the entire record, did not materially influence the jury in a verdict adverse to a substantial right of the defendant." State v. Watkins, 227 Neb. 677, 686, 419 N.W.2d 660, 666 (1988). The preceding principle applicable in a jury trial of a criminal case is equally applicable to a judgment embodying factfinding in the bench trial of a criminal case.

Therefore, the trial court's error in judicially noticing the inferential location of Vejvoda's conduct, namely, drunk driving, is harmless error beyond a reasonable doubt. Vejvoda's conviction is affirmed.

Affirmed.

White, J., dissenting.

Today, the majority holds that harmless error occurred during a bench trial of a criminal case when the trial court took judicial notice of venue.

Today's holding conflicts with our holding in State v. Bouwens, 167 Neb. 244, 92 N.W.2d 564 (1958). In Bouwens, this court affirmed the decision of the district court which dismissed a complaint against the defendant for disturbing the peace. While noting that "[i]t is fundamental that venue must be proven as any other essential fact," id. at 246, 92 N.W.2d at 566, the court held that the mere reference to streets and addresses in an unnamed city, standing alone, will not be deemed sufficient evidence for the court to take judicial notice of venue.

Second, as I first noted in my dissent in State v. Foster, 230 Neb. 607, 433 N.W.2d 167 (1988), today's holding is another step in the continuing process of making the trial court an active participant in criminal proceedings. Again, I submit that this active participation offends notions of fairness and due process.

ROBINSON
v.
STATE

**Court of Appeals of Georgia,
Second Division**

**260 Ga. App. 186, 2003 Ga. App.
LEXIS 366 (2003)**

JUDGES: MIKELL, Judge. Johnson, P. J., and Eldridge, J., concur.

OPINION: MIKELL, Judge.

On December 15, 2001, Christina Robinson was charged with driving under the influence of alcohol. A bench trial was conducted on March 28, 2002, in the City of Jonesboro Municipal Court. The court convicted Robinson of DUI and sentenced her to one day in jail, a $963 fine, and sixty hours of community service. The Superior Court of Clayton County affirmed the conviction. Robinson appeals, arguing that her conviction cannot stand because the state failed to prove venue beyond a reasonable doubt. We agree and reverse the conviction.

Our Supreme Court has mandated that "venue is more than a mere procedural nicety; it is a [Georgia] constitutional requirement that all criminal cases be conducted in the county in which the crimes are alleged to have occurred. Graham v. State, 275 Ga. 290,

292 (2) (565 S.E.2d 467) (2002). In Jones v. State, 272 Ga. 900 (537 S.E.2d 80) (2000), the Supreme Court held that the state's failure to prove venue beyond a reasonable doubt warranted reversal of a defendant's felony murder conviction. Id. at 904 (3). The Court reasoned that:

Our Georgia Constitution requires that venue in all criminal cases must be laid in the county in which the crime was allegedly committed. Ga. Const. (1983), Art. VI, Sec. II, Par. VI; O.C.G.A. § 17-2-2 . Venue is a jurisdictional fact, and is an essential element in proving that one is guilty of the crime charged. Like every other material allegation in the indictment, venue must be proved by the prosecution beyond a reasonable doubt. Proof of venue is a part of the State's case, and the State's failure to prove venue beyond a reasonable doubt renders the verdict contrary to law, without a sufficient evidentiary basis, and warrants reversal.

(Punctuation and footnotes omitted.) Id. at 901-902 (2). Accord Walker v. State, 258 Ga. App. 354 (2) (574 S.E.2d 317) (2002) (even when evidence demonstrated that the crimes were committed in the City of Atlanta, convictions must be reversed because the state failed to prove the county in which venue was proper).

We note that this Court is bound by decisions of the Supreme Court; therefore, we are without authority to overlook the requirement that venue be expressly proven, even in a case such as this where the City of Jonesboro is entirely within Clayton County. "The application of the doctrine of stare decisis is essential to the performance of a well-ordered system of jurisprudence." Etkind v. Suarez, 271 Ga. 352, 357 (5) (519 S.E.2d 210) (1999), citing Cobb v. State, 187 Ga. 448, 452 (200 SE 796) (1939).

The only evidence of venue presented in the case sub judice was the testimony of Sergeant Pat Cauchy of the City of Jonesboro Police Department that he observed Robinson driving within the city limits of Jonesboro. "By long-standing precedent, proving that a crime took place within a city without also proving that the city is entirely within a county does not establish venue." (Footnote omitted.) Graham, supra at 293 (2). Our research reveals no authority for the pre-

sumption that the trial court, acting as the finder of fact in a bench trial, took judicial notice of venue, nor is there any indication in the record that such judicial notice was taken in this case. Accordingly, because the state did not establish the county in which the crime was committed, we reverse Robinson's conviction. We note that retrial would not be barred by the Double Jeopardy Clause. See Jones, supra at 905 (4).

Judgment reversed. Johnson, P. J., and Eldridge, J., concur.

STATE
v.
RICHARDSON

COURT OF APPEALS OF LOUISIANA, SECOND CIRCUIT

811 So. 2d 154, 2002 La. App. LEXIS 467 (2002)

JUDGES: Before BROWN, WILLIAMS and GASKINS, JJ.

OPINION: WILLIAMS, J.

The defendant, Sammie Jean Richardson, was tried by a jury and convicted as charged of distribution of a Schedule II controlled dangerous substance (cocaine), a violation of LSA-R.S. 40:967(A). She was sentenced to serve five years at hard labor without the benefit of probation, parole or suspension of sentence. The defendant appeals. For the following reasons, we affirm.

FACTS

In September 1997, Ricky Bridges, a narcotics officer with the Bienville Parish Sheriff's Department, contacted Agent Evelyn Miller of the Magnolia Police Department and requested her assistance in undercover narcotics purchases in Bienville. When they met, Bridges provided Miller with money for the purchases. Miller was introduced to a confidential informant and proceeded with the informant to different locations to make narcotics purchases.

On September 7, 1997, Miller and the informant drove to the residence of the defendant, Sammie Jean Richardson, with Bridges following shortly behind them in his vehicle. The defendant's residence was located in Arcadia, Bienville Parish, Louisiana. While Bridges watched from some distance away, Miller and the informant approached the defendant's residence and encountered Rayfield McGee and the defendant. McGee was living in the defendant's residence because of his relationship with Sammy K., the defendant's daughter. Agent Miller told the defendant that she wanted to buy some crack cocaine. The defendant gave McGee her keys and instructed McGee to get the "dope" from her blue Cadillac. McGee returned [Pg 3] from the car and gave the crack cocaine to Miller. Miller then gave McGee forty dollars, which he later gave to the defendant. McGee described his role in the transaction as that of a "middle man."

Immediately after the transaction, Officer Bridges and Agent Miller met again. Miller produced two off-white rocks and gave them to Bridges, which he immediately placed in an evidence envelope and sealed. Randall Robillard, a forensic chemist from the North Louisiana Crime Laboratory, later determined that these rocks were crack cocaine.

As a result of the information obtained from Miller, Bridges obtained arrest warrants for the defendant and Rayfield McGee. Both suspects were arrested approximately a month and a half later for distribution of cocaine. As a result of a plea bargain, and in exchange for his agreement to testify truthfully in proceedings against the defendant, McGee received a five-year suspended sentence and was placed on probation.

At trial, the defendant's daughter, Yolanda Tate, testified that she never saw the defendant with any cocaine. She also stated that the defendant had not owned a car in the last five years, and defendant did not have a driver's license. Tate could not recall the 1978 blue Cadillac that McGee testified was parked outside the defendant's home at the time of the crime. The state and the defense stipulated that the defendant had a driver's license, which expired on April 9, 1996.

On rebuttal, the state questioned Donald Byrd, an employee of the Department of Motor Vehicles for the State of Louisiana. Byrd worked primarily in the driver's license division. Byrd identified computer generated documents, which showed, among other things, that ownership of a 1978 Cadillac El Dorado automobile was transferred from McGee to the defendant on October 1, 1996. The document also showed that the defendant was stopped on September 5, 1997 while driving this vehicle without insurance. Byrd testified that it is a common practice for people to transfer titles to vehicles back and forth within a household or among friends to avoid paying fines for insurance cancellations.

The defendant was convicted of distribution of cocaine. She was sentenced to serve five years imprisonment at hard labor without the benefit of probation, parole or suspension of sentence. The defendant now appeals.

DISCUSSION

Assignment of Error No.1:

By this assignment of error, the defendant contends the trial court erred in denying her motion for a "judgment of acquittal." She argues that jurisdiction and venue in Bienville Parish was never proved by the state. She also contends that the evidence was insufficient to support her conviction. In particular, she argues that the testimony given by Bridges and Miller was contradictory, and Miller's written report, which allegedly supported her testimony, was not produced by the state.

The state argues that the trial testimony established that the crime occurred at the defendant's residence located off of Hill Street in Arcadia, Bienville Parish. Moreover, the state contends that the trial court may take judicial notice that a recognizable location is inside a parish even though the parish is never specifically mentioned by name, citing State v. Adams, 394 So. 2d 1204 (La. 1981) and LSA-C.E. art. 201 B.

The state further argues that Miller's testimony was sufficient to prove the defendant's guilt. It contends that Bridges never claimed to witness the transaction, and any alleged discrepancy between his testimony and Miller's testimony was inconsequential.

JURISDICTION AND VENUE:

LSA-C.Cr.P. art. 611 provides that all trials shall take place in the parish where the offense has been committed unless a change of venue is obtained. The Louisiana Supreme Court has held that in order for a conviction to stand, venue must be proved during the course of the trial. *State v. Adams, supra;* State v. Hollingsworth, 292 So. 2d 516 (La. 1974). However, because venue is a special question, the scope of appellate review on that question is limited to determining whether there was some evidence, no matter how little, submitted to the jury to establish venue. *State v. Adams, supra;* State v. Rheams, 352 So. 2d 615 (La. 1977); State v. West, 319 So. 2d 901 (La. 1975). To sustain this proof, a trial court may take judicial notice of a fact that is not subject to reasonable dispute in that it is either generally known within the territorial jurisdiction of the trial court, or capable of accurate and ready determination by resort to sources whose accuracy cannot reasonably be questioned. In this case, the court could apply the judicial notice rule to find that geographical locations mentioned by witnesses are within a particular parish, even if the parish is never specifically mentioned in the testimony. LSA-C.E. art. 201 ; *State v. Adams, supra;* Rheams, supra; State v. Batiste, 327 So. 2d 420 (La. 1976).

The record does not support the defendant's contention that jurisdiction and venue were never proved by the state. Both Bridges and Miller testified that Miller met Bridges in Arcadia and that Miller went to the defendant's residence [Pg 6] on Hill Street in Arcadia to make the cocaine purchase. The trial court was able to take judicial notice that the defendant's residence at Hill Street in Arcadia was located in Bienville Parish. LSA-C.E. art. 201 ; *State v. Adams, supra;* Rheams, supra; Therefore, this argument is without merit.

* * *

CONCLUSION

For the foregoing reasons, the defendant's conviction and sentence are affirmed.

STATE
v.
SMITH

**Court of Common Pleas
of Delaware, Sussex**
2006 Del. C.P. LEXIS 34 (2006)

Rosemary Betts Beauregard

DECISION ON STATE'S APPEAL

Pending before this Court is an appeal by the State of Delaware ("State") from a decision by the Justice of the Peace Court ("J.P. Court") suppressing evidence in favor of the defendant, Mack K. Smith ("Defendant") because it found that the arresting officer did not have probable cause to arrest. This Court set a schedule for briefing on the State's appeal. After reviewing the briefs provided, the Court finds and determines as follows outlined below.

PROCEDURAL BACKGROUND

The Defendant was arrested for committing a violation of 21Del. C. § 4177(a), Driving Under the Influence ("DUI"), and for committing a violation of 21 Del. C. § 4169, Speeding, on November 27, 2004. The State filed the Information in J.P. Court. Thereafter, the court scheduled the motion to suppress and trial for hearing on April 20, 2005. At the hearing, the court granted the Defendant's motion to suppress, and the State certified that the evidence was essential to the prosecution of the case, in accordance with 10 Del. C. § 9902(b). However, the court did not dismiss the case at the conclusion of the hearing. Instead, upon further inquiry by the State via letter on May 6, 2005, the court properly dismissed the case on May 24, 2005. The State timely filed its appeal pursuant to 10 Del. C. § 9902(c) on June 3, 2005.

STATEMENT OF FACTS

Trooper Mark Little ("Officer") stopped the Defendant on State Route 26 ("SR 26"), west of Dagsboro, Delaware, at 2:52 p.m. on November 27, 2004. The Officer testified that SR 26 has portions that curve and wind and portions that are straight. The Officer stated that he observed and stopped the vehicle as it traveled on a long, straight stretch of the roadway in the opposite direction that the Officer was traveling. Just prior to stopping the Defendant, the Officer observed his vehicle passing several other vehicles. According to the Officer's radar, the Defendant's vehicle was speeding, thus, the Officer stopped the Defendant, who appropriately pulled his vehicle over to the shoulder of the roadway. Upon approaching the vehicle and informing the Defendant that he had stopped him for speeding, the Officer observed that the Defendant had rosy cheeks, bloodshot eyes and that he omitted a moderate odor of alcohol, however, the Defendant spoke well and he appeared to have no trouble producing his license and registration. The Defendant admitted to the Officer that he had been speeding and that he had consumed approximately two beers earlier in the day.

Upon making his observations, the Officer administered a number of routine field sobriety tests to determine whether the Defendant was driving under the influence. First, the Officer administered the alphabet test, wherein the Defendant did not begin or end at the instructed letters and he recited other letters out of order. Second, the Officer asked the Defendant to count backwards from 100 to 85. The Defendant failed to stop at the appropriate number. Next, the Officer had the Defendant perform a finger dexterity test, which the Defendant successfully completed. Thereafter, the Officer asked the Defendant to exit his vehicle, which he did without any visible problem.

Once the Defendant was out of his vehicle, the Officer administered the horizontal gaze nystagmus test ("HGN"), a test on which he had received training during his education with the police academy in 1995, and as a field officer. Additionally, in 2001, the Officer became a certified HGN instructor, which enabled him to assist in instruction at the academy and a special event devised to educate certain members of the legal community. At the hearing, the Officer testified as to how the HGN test is administered, signals that the administrator looks for while conducting the test, and what factors other than alcohol consumption might create nystagmus in the subject, including strobe lights, rotating lights and rapidly moving traffic within close proximity. Furthermore, the Officer testified that when he performed the HGN test on the Defendant, he observed six out of six clues. On cross examination, the Officer admitted that while looking for nystagmus at maximum deviation, which was the second part of the three part test, he only caused the Defendant's eye to be held at the maximum deviation position for two to three seconds, rather than four seconds, which is required by the NHTSA manual. Additionally, the Officer acknowledged that the NHTSA manual states that the HGN test is only validated when it is administered in the prescribed fashion. The Officer also stated that strobe lights, rotating lights and some moving traffic in close proximity where all present when he administered the test.

After conducting the HGN test, the Officer then administered the walk and turn test. Although it is preferred that the test be conducted on a painted line, the Officer had the Defendant complete the test on the side of the road for safety reasons. Thus, the test was administered in an area, which the Officer described as grassy, with a slight slope designed for drainage purposes. According to the Officer, the slight grade did not affect the results of the test. The Officer described the weather as "windy and clear" at the time of the stop. While the Officer explained the test to the Defendant, he observed that the Defendant was unable to maintain his balance while standing with one foot in front of the other. When the Defendant completed the walk and turn test, the Officer perceived that the Defendant took ten steps instead of nine, and he took one large step instead of a series of small steps to make the turn, as instructed. The Defendant accurately took a second series of nine steps back to his original starting point.

Next, the Officer administered the one leg stand test. At that time, the Defendant informed the Officer that one of his feet was weaker than the other. Thus, the Officer suggested that he complete the test using his stronger foot for balance. The Officer observed that the Defendant raised his arms for balance, swayed, and put his foot down at different points throughout the test. Lastly, the Officer administered a portable breath test ("PBT") on the Defendant. Although the J.P. Court permitted such evidence, the State never established the results of that test.

After the court admitted the foregoing evidence, it ruled that the Officer lacked probable cause to arrest. In its decision, the court relied heavily on its personal knowledge of the roadway where a number of the field sobriety tests were administered to find that the area was not an acceptable place to administer the tests.

DISCUSSION

An appeal by the State pursuant to 10 Del. C. § 9902(c) shall be heard on the record. CCP Crim. R. 39(f). When addressing appeals from the J.P. Court this Court sits as an intermediate appellate court. The function of the Court in this capacity is to 'correct errors of law and to review the factual findings of the court below to determine if they are sufficiently supported by the record and are the product of an orderly and logical deductive process.' *State v. Richards*, 1998 WL 732960, *1 (Del. Super.)(citing Baker v. Connell, 488 A.2d 1303 (Del. 1985). Therefore, the Court must apply a *de novo* standard of review to the lower court's legal determinations and a clearly erroneous standard to findings of fact. State v. Arnold, 2001 WL 985101, *2 (Del. Super.).

The State argues that the J.P. Court inappropriately relied on information outside of the record, and applied the wrong legal standard in its decision on the Defendant's motion to suppress. Accordingly, the first question presented is whether the J.P. Court erred when it considered facts that were not in evidence. The second question at issue is whether the J.P. Court erred when it decided that the Officer did not have probable cause to arrest the Defendant.

The J.P. Court Inappropriately Relied on Facts Not in Evidence

The transcript reflects that as the J.P. Court considered the evidence admitted for purposes of establishing probable cause, the court enlarged the record with its own personal knowledge. The sole witness at the hearing, the Officer who administered the tests, provided that the testing area was grassy, with a slight grade, but hard, not muddy and not rocky. However, upon ruling on the motion, the Court interjected its own knowledge of the area and disregarded the Officer's testimony. Specifically, when determining the probative value of the walk and turn test and the one leg stand test, the court spoke as to its personal knowledge of the roadway. The court noted that the tests were improper because they were conducted,

"on the side of a road, on a road that I know, and everyone else in Sussex County, knows it is not only a grass shoulder road but a very tapered grass shoulder road into a heavy ditch in low lying swamp ground. We know what that road is. We know why they call it a Nine Foot Road. It was a miraculous piece of construction when they put that concrete road on that piece of road on 26 because it is a low lying piece of swamp that was drained off to put into agriculture. I mean I know all these things. And this is not the place to do that test."

Because the facts depended on by the J.P. Court were not admitted into evidence, the question arises whether reliance on those facts constituted error. The Delaware Rules of Evidence provide that courts are permitted to take judicial notice of an adjudicative fact. D.R.E. 202. However, courts may only take judicial notice of a fact that is not subject to reasonable dispute in that it either is generally known within the territorial jurisdiction of the court, or it is capable of accurate and ready determination in sources whose accuracy cannot reasonably be questioned. D.R.E. 202(b). The doctrine of judicial notice should be applied with due care because if there is even a mere possibility of dispute as to whether the fact asserted is accurate, or of common knowledge, judicial notice is inappropriate and evidence is required to establish the fact. Fawcett v. State, 697 A.2d 385, 388 (Del. 1997).

Although the court stated that "everyone in Sussex County, knows [the area] is not only a grass shoulder road but a very tapered grass shoulder road into a heavy ditch in low lying swamp ground," the Officer's contrary testimony wherein he described the testing area as grassy, with a slight grade, but hard, not muddy and not rocky indicates that the conditions of that area at the time of administration were indeed subject to reasonable dispute. The court did not indicate that it determined the Officer was untrustworthy. Rather, the court relied solely on its own opinion of the conditions that may or may not have been present in the testing area to discredit the tests. The court's opinion is therefore not an adjudicative fact. Accordingly, I find that the J.P. Court committed plain error when it relied on evidence that was outside of the record in its decision finding that the Officer did not have probable cause to arrest the Defendant.

Probable Cause Existed

The State argues that the court improperly "diluted each [of the Officer's probable cause] observation[s] with hypothetically innocent explanations and then rejected them," without considering the Officer's observations under the totality of the circumstances.

* * *

[The Court reviewed the facts supporting a finding of probable cause.]

In conclusion, the Officer made the following observations of the Defendant (1) blood shot eyes, (2) rosy cheeks, (3) moderate odor of alcohol, (4) admission of consuming alcohol, (5) failure to follow instruction and properly perform the alphabet, counting and walk and turn tests, (6) trouble maintaining balance on the walk and turn and one leg stand tests, (7) several clues present upon application of the HGN test and (8) Speeding. Case law suggests that such factors are adequate to establish probable case.

* * *

CONCLUSION

This Court concludes that the J.P. Court inappropriately relied on facts not in evidence. Furthermore, this Court finds that the Officer had probable cause to believe that the Defendant had been driving under the influence when he arrested the Defendant. Thus, the Court hereby reverses the J.P. Court's decision on the Defendant's motion to suppress and remands the case for further proceeding consistent with this Order.

IT IS SO ORDERED, this 6th day of June 2006.
The Honorable Rosemary Betts Beauregard

Cases Relating to Chapter 6

Presumptions, Inferences, and Stipulations

STATE

v.

JACKSON

112 Wash. 2d 867, 774 P.2d 1211
(1989)

En Banc. Callow, C.J. Utter, Dolliver, Dore, Pearson, and Andersen, J.J., concur. Smith, J., concurs in the result only; Durham and Brachtenbach, JJ., dissent by separate opinion.

CALLOW, OPINION:

The defendant, Destin L. Jackson, was convicted of attempted second degree burglary. He contends the trial court erred in giving an inference of intent instruction.

The issues presented are:

1. In an attempted burglary case, is it error to instruct the jury that it may infer the defendant acted with intent to commit a crime within the building from the fact that the defendant may attempted entrance into the building?

2. Is malicious mischief in the third degree a lesser included offense within attempted burglary in the second degree, where a substantial step taken in the furtherance of the burglary is the malicious destruction of property?

3. Does federal due process require the State to plead the nature of the crime a defendant intended to commit inside the building he tried to enter? See and compare State v. Bergeron, 105 Wn.2d 1, 711 P.2d 1000 (1985), overruling State v. Johnson, 100 Wn.2d 607, 674 P.2d 145 (1983).

We hold the trial court cannot instruct the jury, where the charge is attempted burglary, that it may infer the defendant acted with intent to commit a crime within a building, where the evidence is that the defendant may have attempted entrance into a building, but there exist other equally reasonable conclusions which follow from the circumstances.

On the evening of February 2, 1986, a Seattle police officer received a dispatch call to proceed to Neal's Tailoring and Beverage Shop. As the officer was coming around a corner he saw the defendant kicking the front door of the shop. The defendant was taking short running kicks at the door and bouncing off. The kicks were aimed at the window area of the door. Once the defendant spotted the officer, he proceeded to briskly walk away. The officer placed the defendant under arrest. The officer testified that no one else was in the vicinity and that the defendant was constantly in his sight. When the door was examined it was found that about 10 inches of Plexiglas had been pushed inward and part of the wood stock around the Plexiglas was broken out of its frame. Footprints existed on the Plexiglas and they appeared to match the shoes of the defendant. The Plexiglas was not taken into custody, even though the right edge had been pushed inward, as it still prevented entry into the business. The molding which holds the glass in the door was broken on the inside, and there was wood on the floor. The pressure from the outside tore the molding off on the inside.

The defendant was charged with attempted second degree burglary. At trial, the defendant denied kicking the door. He claimed he noticed the broken door as he was walking by the shop and was arrested as he continued on his way.

At the conclusion of the State's case, the defendant moved for a dismissal asserting:

This may get to attempting malicious mischief, but to stack inferences of intent as to what was intended in terms of kicking or knocking out the door, then another inference if he intended to break in, he intended to commit a crime is beyond the limits of reasonable inferences. One inference is not enough. There is evidence to support one inference that he intended to break in, but you are asking, or the State would be asking, your honor, for the jury to do is to stack inferences. First of all, you have to infer he intended to break in based on his conduct. If you believe that once—that he did it, then that he intended to commit a crime. Stacking inferences is something that is beyond a prima facie case. Therefore, the case should proceed only on attempted criminal trespass or malicious mischief.

The trial court denied the motion. At the conclusion of the trial, the court heard exceptions to the proposed instructions to the jury.

[Defense Counsel] The defense would except to your Honor's failure to give the lesser included. The defense would suggest that the attempt statute is so broad. When you get down to what is alleged, namely, Destin Jackson broke the door in an attempt to get in that, indeed, legally and factually you would have to commit malicious mischief, or attempted burglary, which in a manner which has been charged in this case. For that reason, I would except to your Honor's failure to give that lesser included instruction. . . .

[Defense Counsel] In addition, the defense would except to your Honor's giving the inference Instruction No. 10. Factually, the cases do not support that inference. The instruction reads, "A person who remains unlawfully in a building with intent to commit a crime." However, the record does not support the allegation Mr. Jack-

son even if you assume it was Mr. Jackson who entered or remained unlawfully, he is charged with attempting to do so. Again, in the motion to dismiss at the end of the State's case, you are asking the jury first to infer what his intent is, then asking them to infer what his intent was assuming the inference, that is inappropriate. It is clear on the face of the instruction it doesn't apply here because no injury was or entry was actually made. That is the reason this instruction is inappropriate and the defense would except to it being given.

. . . [Defense Counsel] Your Honor, in terms of our record, then having changed that, the defense would still suggest it is inappropriate because it stacks inferences. It requires the jury to make one conclusion, then, based on that conclusion, suggests they make another inference. It is a permissive inference as outlined here, but it is a comment on the evidence, if you find this then you can find that, then move on from there. The defense believes it is stacking inferences and would rely on that as previously explained.

Over the defendant's objection the court gave the following jury instruction:

A person who attempts to enter or remain unlawfully in a building may be inferred to have acted with intent to commit a crime against a person or property therein unless such entering or remaining shall be explained by evidence satisfactory to the jury to have been made without such criminal intent. This inference is not binding upon you and it is for you to determine what weight, if any, such inference is to be given.

(Italics ours.) WPIC 60.05 does not include the italicized words "attempts to". The defendant objected to the trial court's failure to give a lesser included instruction. (See WPIC 4.11.) However, the defendant did not propose an instruction setting out the crime, nor did he except to the instruction which defined burglary. These issues were not raised in the petition for review; only the objection to the inference of intent instruction and whether there is evidence of an actual entry are raised before us. The jury found the defendant guilty as charged.

In ruling on the motion for new trial the trial court stated in part:

> The Court: [C]ounsel reminded me that there was a motion for a new trial brought by the defense in regard to an instruction, . . . which I gave to the jury, in regard to the inference of intent to commit a crime therein, this being an attempted burglary in the second degree in which the jury found defendant was guilty of the crime of attempted burglary in the second degree.

The trial court denied the motion for new trial, the defendant appealed and we granted a petition for review after the Court of Appeals affirmed his conviction.

I.

Quaere: What Is the Function of an Inference and When Is an Inference Permissible?

"'"Presumptions" . . . "may be looked on as the bats of the law, flitting in the twilight but disappearing in the sunshine of actual facts." . . .'" Bradley v. S.L. Savidge, Inc. 13 Wn.2d 28, 123 P.2d 780 (1942) (citing Beeman v. Puget Sound Traction, Light & Power Co., 79 Wash. 137, 139, 139 P. 1087 (1914) (quoting Paul v. United Rys. Co., 152 Mo. App. 577, 134 S.W. 3 (1911))).

The basic notions upon which presumptions are grounded are simple. When fact A (the basic fact) is proved at a trial the courts will by rule assume that fact B (the presumed fact) exists for certain purposes and with certain limitations. This specific assumption or inference by application of a general rule is a presumption. 5 K. Tegland, Wash. Prac., Evidence § 65, at 127 (2d ed. 1982).

Most presumptions have come into existence primarily because the judges have believed that proof of fact B renders the inference of the existence of fact A so probable that it is sensible and timesaving to assume the truth of the fact A until the adversary disproves it. E. Cleary, McCormick on Evidence § 343, at 969 (3d ed. 1984).

We follow Bradley v. S.L. Savidge, Inc., supra, in quoting the definition of presumption as defined in Heidelbach v. Campbell, 95 Wash. 661, 668, 164 P. 247 (1917):

> A presumption is an inference, affirmative or disaffirmative, of the truth of a proposition of fact which is drawn by a process of reasoning from some one or more matters of known fact. The presumption arises from a want of knowledge of the truth of the proposition. It is in the nature of evidence, and if it be known whether the given proposition is true or false, there can be no presumption because the fact is established which the presumption tends to prove or disprove.

Presumptions are one thing; inferences another. Presumptions are assumptions of fact which the law requires to be made from another fact or group of facts; inferences are logical deductions or conclusions from an established fact. Presumptions deal with legal processes, whereas inferences deal with mental processes. Lappin v. Lucurell, 13 Wn. App. 277, 284, 534 P.2d 1038, 94 A.L.R.3d 594 (1975). "An inference is simply a logical deduction or conclusion which the law allows, but does not require, following the establishment of the basic facts." 5 K. Tegland, at 127-28.

RCW 9A.52.040 creates an "inference of intent" as applied to burglary and trespass as follows:

> In any prosecution for burglary, any person who enters or remains unlawfully in a building may be inferred to have acted with intent to commit a crime against a person or property therein, unless such entering or remaining shall be explained by evidence satisfactory to the trier of fact to have been made without such criminal intent.

RCW 9A.52.040 is reflected in WPIC 60.05 to read:

> A person who enters or remains unlawfully in a building may be inferred to have acted with intent to commit a crime against a person or property therein [unless such entering or remaining shall be explained by evidence satisfactory to the

jury to have been made without such criminal intent]. This inference is not binding
upon you and it is for you to determine
what weight, if any, such inference is to be
given.

Both RCW 9A.52.040 and WPIC 60.05
permit the inference of one fact from another
as a presumption. Burglary consists of two
elements; entry or unlawfully remaining upon
another's premises, and intent. RCW
9A.52.030. RCW 9A.52.040 provides that a
burglary may be inferred (intent exists) if one
either unlawfully remains upon another's
premises or an entry occurs. "Inferences and
presumptions are a staple of our adversary
system of factfinding. It is often necessary for
the trier of fact to determine the existence of
an element of the crime—that is, an 'ultimate'
or 'elemental' fact—from the existence of one
or more 'evidentiary' or 'basic' facts." County
Court of Ulster Cy. v. Allen, 442 U.S. 140,
156, 60 L. Ed. 2d 777, 99 S. Ct. 2213 (1979).
"The most common evidentiary device is the
entirely permissive inference or presumption,
which allows—but does not require—the trier
of fact to infer the elemental fact from proof
by the prosecutor of the basic one and which
places no burden of any kind on the defendant." Ulster Cy. Court, at 157.

WPIC 60.05 provides for a permissive
inference or presumption, which allows the
trier of fact to either infer the elemental fact
from proof by the prosecutor, or reject the
inference. WPIC 60.05 does not apply to
those attempting to enter or remain unlawfully "unless it can at least be said with substantial assurance that the presumed fact is
more likely than not to flow from the proved
fact on which it is made to depend." Leary v.
United States, 395 U.S. 6, 36, 23 L. Ed. 2d
57, 89 S. Ct. 1532 (1969). See also Sandstrom v. Montana, 442 U.S. 510, 61 L. Ed. 2d
39, 99 S. Ct. 2450 (1979).

For a trier of fact to draw inferences from
proven circumstances, the inferences must be
"rationally related" to the proven facts. State
v. Jeffries, 105 Wn.2d 398, 442, 717 P.2d 722,
cert. denied, 479 U.S. 922 (1986). A rational
connection must exist between the initial fact
proven and the further fact presumed. "The
jury is permitted to infer from one fact the
existence of another essential to guilt, if reason and experience support the inference."

Tot v. United States, 319 U.S. 463, 467, 87 L.
Ed. 1519, 63 S. Ct. 1241 (1943).

For a criminal statutory presumption to
meet the test of constitutionality the presumed fact must follow beyond a reasonable
doubt from the proven fact. State v. Blight,
89 Wn.2d 38, 569 P.2d 1129 (1977). See also
State v. Odom, 83 Wn.2d 541, 520 P.2d 152,
cert. denied, 419 U.S. 1013 (1974); State v.
Rogers, 83 Wn.2d 553, 520 P.2d 159, cert.
denied, 419 U.S. 1053 (1974).

WPIC 60.05 may be given as a proper
instruction in a burglary case. However,
where the State pleads and proves only
attempted burglary, as here, this instruction is
improper. In State v. Bergeron, supra, the
defendant signed a statement wherein he
admitted that when he threw a rock through a
window he intended to enter the premises. In
Bergeron we reasoned that while intent may
be inferred from all the facts and circumstances surrounding the commission of an
act, intent may not be inferred "from conduct
that is patently equivocal." In order to give an
instruction that an inference of an intent to
commit a crime existed in a burglary case,
there must be evidence of entering or remaining unlawfully in a building. The instruction
on intent cannot be given without evidence to
support it and that must place the defendant
within a building. State v. Ogden, 21 Wn.
App. 44, 49, 584 P.2d 957 (1978).

A presumption is only permissible when
no more than one conclusion can be drawn
from any set of circumstances. An inference
should not arise where there exist other reasonable conclusions that would follow from
the circumstances. Here the inferences are
twofold: (1) attempted burglary or (2) vandalism or malicious destruction. Therefore,
an inference cannot follow that there was
intent to commit a crime within the building
just by the defendants' shattering of the window in the door. This evidence is consistent
with two different interpretations; one indicating attempted burglary, a felony; and the
other malicious mischief, a misdemeanor.

II.

Quaere: Could the Giving of the Instruction Be Considered Harmless Error?

"A 'harmless error' is one which is "trivial,
or formal, or merely academic, and was not

prejudicial to the substantial rights of the party assigning it, and in no way affected the final outcome of the case.'" State v. Pam, 98 Wn.2d 748, 754, 659 P.2d 454 (1983) (quoting State v. Wanrow, 88 Wn.2d 221, 237, 559 P.2d 548 (1977)). Here, the giving of the instruction could not be harmless error since it tended to prove an element of the commission of a crime. The instruction coming from the trial judge indicated that the defendant had entered the building and did so with the intent to commit a crime against the property therein. We do not need to determine whether the "overwhelming evidence" test would be applicable since we are convinced the inference of intent instruction was not harmless. See State v. Guloy, 104 Wn.2d 412, 426, 705 P.2d 1182 (1985).

III.

Quaere: Is Malicious Mischief a Lesser Included Offense of Attempted Burglary?

"Under the Washington rule, a defendant is entitled to an instruction on a lesser included offense if two conditions are met. First, each of the elements of the lesser offense must be a necessary element of the offense charged. Second, the evidence in the case must support an inference that the lesser crime was committed." (Citations omitted.) State v. Workman, 90 Wn.2d 443, 447-48, 548 P.2d 382 (1978). Here, the defendant contends that an instruction defining malicious mischief in the third degree should have been given to the jury. RCW 9A.48.090 defines malicious mischief in the third degree as:

(1) A person is guilty of malicious mischief in the third degree if he knowingly and maliciously causes physical damage to the property of another, . . . (2) Malicious mischief in the third degree is a gross misdemeanor if the damage to the property is in an amount exceeding fifty dollars; otherwise, it is a misdemeanor.

The defendant is charged with attempted burglary. RCW 9A.52.030 defines burglary in the second degree as:

(1) A person is guilty of burglary in the second degree if, with intent to commit a

crime against a person or property therein, he enters or remains unlawfully in a building other than a vehicle.

Criminal attempt is defined by RCW 9A.28.020 as:

(1) A person is guilty of an attempt to commit crime if, with intent to commit a specific crime, he does any act which is a substantial step toward the commission of that crime.

(2) If the conduct in which a person engages otherwise constitutes an attempt to commit a crime, it is no defense to a prosecution of such attempt that the crime charged to have been attempted was, under the attendant circumstances, factually or legally impossible of commission.

Since the first condition of the test has not been met, we need not go any further in determining whether the second condition applies. Malicious mischief is not a lesser included offense of attempted burglary because one does not invariably cause physical damage while attempting a burglary. One who enters a premises through an unlocked door without permission may be committing burglary, but he has not physically damaged property. The prosecution should have charged the defendant in the alternative; by not doing so the prosecution's choice was to seek a conviction of attempted burglary or nothing.

IV.

Quaere: Must the State Specify the Crime a Defendant Intended To Commit Upon Entry Into Property?

We have held that our burglary statutes simply require an intent to commit a crime against a person or property inside the burglarized premises. As stated in State v. Bergeron, 105 Wn.2d 1, 4, 711 P.2d 1000 (1985):

The intent to commit a specific named crime inside the burglarized premises is not an "element" of the crime of burglary in the State of Washington. . . . The intent required by our burglary statutes is simply the intent to commit any crime against a person or property inside the burglarized premises.

We adhere to the decision in Bergeron. The conviction of attempted second degree burglary is reversed and the cause is remanded for a new trial.

Durham, J. (Dissenting) The majority remands for a new trial after concluding that the trial court committed reversible error by giving the following jury instruction in a prosecution for attempted burglary:

A person who attempts to enter or remain unlawfully in a building may be inferred to have acted with intent to commit a crime against a person or property therein unless such entering or remaining shall be explained by evidence satisfactory to the jury to have been made without such criminal intent. This inference is not binding upon you and it is for you to determine what weight, if any, such inference is to be given.

This instruction is derived from a Washington pattern jury instruction, WPIC 60.05, which in turn is based on RCW 9A.52.040. Both WPIC 60.05 and RCW 9A.52.040 allow juries in burglary prosecutions to infer that a defendant intended to commit a crime on the premises when he unlawfully entered or remained in a building. An instruction of this nature is appropriate not only in a burglary case, but also in a prosecution for attempted burglary where the evidence shows that the defendant illegally entered the building. State v. Bassett, 50 Wn. App. 23, 26, 746 P.2d 1240 (1987), review denied, 110 Wn.2d 1016 (1988). The Legislature has broadly defined an entry in this context to include "the insertion of any part of [a person's] body" into a building. RCW 9A.52.010(2); see also Bassett, at 26 (insertion of finger through window constitutes entry); State v. Couch, 44 Wn. App. 26, 31-32, 720 P.2d 1387 (1986) (pushing open a trap door constitutes entry). Because the jury reasonably could have found that an entry occurred in the present case—Jackson kicked the Plexiglas window some 10 inches back into the building—the instruction was proper. So reasoned the Court of Appeals in this case, and so should we. See State v. Jack-

son, 51 Wn. App. 100, 102-05, 751 P.2d 1248 (1988).

Instead, the majority engages in an abstract and protracted discussion of the nature of presumptions and inferences. Unfortunately, the court does not discuss the case that addresses presumptions and inferences in the very context at issue here, jury instructions based on RCW 9A.52.040. In State v. Johnson, 100 Wn.2d 607, 674 P.2d 145 (1983), overruled on other grounds in State v. Bergeron, 105 Wn.2d 1, 711 P.2d 1000 (1985), this court explained that there are four fundamental types of presumptions: conclusive presumptions, persuasion-shifting presumptions, production-shifting presumptions, and permissive inferences. Instructions based on RCW 9A.52.040 are analyzed as permissive inferences when the defendant presents evidence in his own case, as occurred here. Johnson, at 616-20. Permissive inferences are "constitutionally impermissible only when 'under the facts of the case, there is no rational way the trier could make the connection permitted by the inference.'" Johnson, at 616 (quoting County Court of Ulster Cy. v. Allen, 442 U.S. 140, 157, 60 L. Ed. 2d 777, 99 S. Ct. 2213 (1979)).

By contrast, the majority concludes that "[a]n inference should not arise where there exist other reasonable conclusions that would follow from the circumstances." Majority, at 876. The majority's conclusion conflicts with the well-accepted notion that juries are not bound to find for the defendant merely because reasonable inferences can be drawn either in favor of guilt or innocence. See State v. Gosby, 85 Wn.2d 758, 764-68, 539 P.2d 680 (1975) (rejecting the requirement of a multiple-hypothesis instruction); State v. Randecker, 79 Wn.2d 512, 517, 487 P.2d 1295 (1971). The mere existence of contrary reasonable inferences does not necessarily preclude juries from finding guilt. Randecker, at 517. The Johnson standard recognizes these principles, the majority's does not.

Applying the Johnson standard to the present case is not difficult. There is, of course, a rational connection between Jackson's act of kicking in a window and an inference of an intent to commit a crime inside the building. Because the requisite rational connection exists in this case regardless of the existence of other rational inferences, the instruction was properly given to the jury.

The majority concludes not only that the trial court erred in using this instruction, but that the error was prejudicial, requiring a reversal of the conviction below. The majority presents the basis for its holding as follows:

> Here, the giving of the instruction could not be harmless error since it tended to prove an element of the commission of a crime. The instruction coming from the trial judge indicated that the defendant had entered the building and did so with the intent to commit a crime against the property therein. We do not need to determine whether the "overwhelming evidence" test would be applicable since we are convinced the inference of intent instruction was not harmless. Majority, at 877.

I disagree both with the majority's interpretation of the instruction, and with its application of the law of harmless error. The instruction in no way "indicated" that Jackson intended to commit another crime; it merely informed the jurors that they were permitted to infer this intent from the evidence presented. As for the test of harmless error, the majority implies that an error relating to presumptions or inferences can never be harmless when it relates to an element of the crime. The case law holds directly to the contrary. See Rose v. Clark, 478 U.S. 570, 579-82, 92 L. Ed. 2d 460, 106 S. Ct. 3101 (1986); State v. Johnson, supra at 620-21.

If I were to reach the issue of harmless error, I would adopt the approach taken by the Court of Appeals in this case. The Court of Appeals reasoned that any error in instructing the jury based on RCW 9A.52.040 would be harmless because the jury would have been permitted to make the inference as to Jackson's intent even if the RCW 9A.52.040 instruction were not used. See Jackson, at 104 n.3.

Accordingly, I dissent from the majority's holdings in sections I and II of its opinion. I would affirm the Court of Appeals in upholding the conviction below.

STATE
v.
PURCELL

APPELLATE COURT OF ILLINOIS, SECOND DISTRICT

325 Ill. App. 3d 551, 758 N.E.2d 895, 2001 Ill. App. LEXIS 837 (2001)

JUDGES: JUSTICE GEIGER delivered the opinion of the court. HUTCHINSON, P.J., and McLAREN, J., concur.

The defendant, Willard Purcell, has filed the instant appeal pursuant to Supreme Court Rule 604(c) (188 Ill. 2d R. 604(c)), seeking review of the September 10, 2001, order of the circuit court of Winnebago County denying bail. On appeal, the defendant argues (1) that section 110-4(b) of the Code of Criminal Procedure of 1963 (the Code) (725 ILCS 5/110-4(b) (West 2000)) is unconstitutional; and (2) that the trial court erred in denying his request for pretrial bail.

On August 2001, the defendant was arrested and indicted on four counts of first-degree murder (720 ILCS 5/9-1(a)(2) (a)(3), (b)(19) (West 2000)). The defendant was alleged to have killed his wife, Barbara Purcell, by striking her repeatedly in the head with a blunt object. If convicted of the charged offense, the defendant may receive a sentence of life imprisonment. 730 ILCS 5/5-8-1(a)(1)(b) (West 2000).

Following his arrest, the defendant filed a motion requesting bail. The defendant also filed a motion seeking a determination that section 110-4 of the Code (725 ILCS 5/110-4 (West 2000)) is unconstitutional. Section 110-4(a) provides that a defendant may not obtain bail where "the proof is evident or the presumption great" that the defendant committed a capital offense or an offense for which he may be sentenced to life imprisonment. 725 ILCS 5/110-4(a) (West 2000). Section 110-4(b) places the burden of demonstrating that the proof of guilt is not evident and the presumption of guilt not great upon the individual seeking release on bail. 725 ILCS 5/110-4(b) (West 2000). In his motion before the trial court, the defendant argued that subsection (b) violates the presumption of innocence accorded to criminal defendants while awaiting trial. See Stack v. Boyle, 342 U.S. 1, 96 L. Ed. 3, 72 S. Ct. 1 (1951).

On August 15, 2001, the trial court denied the defendant's motion to declare section 110-4(b) of the Code unconstitutional. Then, on September 10, 2001, following a hearing, the trial court denied the defendant's motion for pretrial bail. The trial court found that the defendant did not meet his burden of demonstrating that the proof of his guilt was not evident and that the presumption of his guilt was not great. The defendant then filed the instant appeal pursuant to Supreme Court Rule 604(c).

We will first address the defendant's constitutional argument. The right of an accused to obtain pretrial bail is governed by article I, section 9, of the Illinois Constitution of 1970. Ill. Const. 1970, art. I, § 9. That section provides:

"All persons shall be bailable by sufficient sureties, except the following offenses where the proof is evident or the presumption great: capital offenses and offenses for which a sentence of life imprisonment may be imposed as a consequence of conviction ***." Ill. Const. 1970, art. I, § 9.

Section 110-4 of the Code is a codification of this constitutional provision. That section provides:

"(a) All persons shall be bailable before conviction, except the following offenses where the proof is evident or the presumption great that the defendant is guilty of the offense: capital offenses and offenses for which a sentence of life imprisonment may be imposed as a consequence of conviction ***.

(b) A person seeking release on bail who is charged with a capital offense or an offense for which a sentence of life imprisonment may be imposed shall not be bailable until a hearing is held wherein such person has the burden of demonstrating that the proof of his guilt is not evident and the presumption is not great." 725 ILCS 5/110-4 (West 2000).

Subsection (b) goes beyond the language of article I, section 9, and was added to clarify the issues of proof that might arise during bail proceedings. 725 ILCS Ann. 5/110-4, Committee Comments 1963, at 48 (Smith-Hurd 1992). The language contained in this subsection was taken from section 68(2) of the Code of Criminal Procedure promulgated by the American Law Institute in 1930. ALI Code of Criminal Procedure § 68(2) (1930). Under this provision, the burden falls upon the defendant seeking pretrial bail to establish that the proof of his guilt is not substantial.

As the defendant correctly notes, the due process clauses of both the United States and the Illinois Constitutions guarantee the accused that he will not be convicted on proof less than reasonable doubt of every fact necessary to constitute the crime with which he is charged. U.S. Const., amend. XIV; Ill. Const. 1970, art. I, § 2; Sullivan v. Louisiana, 508 U.S. 275, 277-78, 124 L. Ed. 2d 182, 187-88, 113 S. Ct. 2078, 2080 (1993). The complement to this guarantee is that the State bears the burden of proof and that the accused is presumed innocent. People v. Devine, 295 Ill. App. 3d 537, 544, 229 Ill. Dec. 796, 692 N.E.2d 785 (1998). The presumption of innocence attaches to the accused from the onset of the proceedings and is one of the underpinnings of an accused's right to bail. See Stack, 342 U.S. at 4, 96 L. Ed. at 6, 72 S. Ct. at 3. The traditional right to freedom before conviction permits the unhampered preparation of a defense and serves to prevent the infliction of punishment prior to conviction. Stack, 342 U.S. at 4, 96 L. Ed. at 6, 72 S. Ct. at 3.

The question of whether section 110-4(b) infringes upon an accused's presumption of innocence has not previously been addressed by an Illinois court. However, Illinois' constitutional bail provision is not unique; the constitutions of most states contain similar provisions guaranteeing bail to the accused, except in cases punishable by death or life imprisonment where the proof is evident or the presumption great. As a result, there are a number of reported cases nationwide in which courts have considered the question of whether the State or the accused bears the burden during a bail hearing for an offense for which death or life imprisonment may be imposed, to show, or to disprove, that the proof is evident or the presumption great. See H. Hirschberg, Annotation, Upon Whom Rests Burden of Proof, Where Bail is Sought Before Judgment But After Indictment in Capital Case, as to Whether Proof is Evident or the Presumption Great, 89 A.L.R.2d 355 (1963). The decisions in these cases have been conflicting, some holding that the State has the burden, and others holding that the burden falls on the accused.

In those cases placing the burden upon the State to prove that the accused's guilt is evident or that the presumption of such guilt is great, the courts have relied upon the presumption of innocence. See Orona v. District Court, 184 Colo. 55, 518 P.2d 839 (1974); In re Steigler, 250 A.2d 379 (Del. 1969); State v. Arthur, 390 So. 2d 717 (Fla. 1980); Young v. Russell, 332 S.W.2d 629 (Ky. 1960); Application of Wheeler, 81 Nev. 495, 406 P.2d 713 (1965); Fountaine v. Mullen, 117 R.I. 262, 366 A.2d 1138 (1976). These courts have explained that the presumption of innocence precludes any inference that the accused committed the charged offense. Finding that an indictment has no evidentiary value, these courts have held that the indictment does not raise a presumption, prima facie or otherwise, that the accused is guilty. See, e.g., Arthur, 390 So. 2d at 719-20. Additionally, in placing the burden of proof on the State, these courts have explained that the right to bail is constitutionally guaranteed, subject only to exceptions for certain designated offenses. These courts hold that the State has the burden to show the existence of one of the exceptions and prove that the defendant is not entitled to bail. See Beck v. State, 648 S.W.2d 7 (Tex. Crim. App. 1983).

For example, in Arthur, the Florida Supreme Court held that the presumption of innocence protected the accused for all purposes while awaiting trial and that it was the State's burden to prove the facts which removed the accused's entitlement to bail. Arthur, 390 So. 2d at 719-20. The court explained that, under the State's constitution, bail could only be denied when the accused was charged with a crime punishable by death of life imprisonment and that the proof of guilt was evident or the presumption great. The court therefore held that the indictment or information, standing alone, could not

serve as proof or a presumption of guilt. Arthur, 390 So. 2d at 719. Rather, the court held that the State was required to come forward with an independent showing that the proof of guilt was evident or the presumption of guilt great. Arthur, 390 So. 2d at 720. The court also noted that, as a matter of convenience, fairness, and practicality, it was preferable that the State carry the burden of proof, as it was presumably in a better position to present to the court the evidence upon which it intended to rely. Arthur, 390 So. 2d at 720.

In Wheeler, the Nevada Supreme Court similarly concluded that the State bears the burden to show that the accused should not be admitted bail. Wheeler, 81 Nev. at 499, 406 P.2d at 716. The Nevada constitution provides that "all persons shall be bailable by sufficient sureties; unless for Capital Offenses when the proof is evident, or the presumption great." Nev. Const., art. 1, § 7. Construing this language, the court concluded that all offenses are bailable, including capital offenses, as a matter of right. However, the court noted that the right to bail in a capital case could be limited upon a showing that the proof of guilt is evident or the presumption great. Wheeler, 81 Nev. at 499, 406 P.2d at 715. Explaining that the accused is presumed innocent of the charged offense until proven guilty, the court held that the burden rests on the State to show that the right to bail is limited rather than absolute. Wheeler, 81 Nev. at 499, 406 P.2d at 716.

In Steigler, the Delaware Supreme Court considered the effect of a statute similar to section 110-4(b) of the Code. Steigler, 250 A.2d at 382. That statute placed the burden upon the accused seeking pretrial bail in a capital case to demonstrate that "there is good ground to doubt the truth of the accusation." Steigler, 250 A.2d at 382. Although the court did not hold the statute unconstitutional, it nonetheless found that the burden of going forward with evidence at a bail hearing could not be placed upon the accused. The court explained:

"Delaware seemingly [is] among the states holding that the indictment raises a prima facie presumption of proof positive or presumption great. We think, however, the rule, if indeed it has been the rule of this State, offends against a basic concept of our criminal law—the presumption of innocence until found guilty after trial. There is something inherently contradictory in maintaining the presumption of innocence until final conviction and, at the same time, presuming probable guilt from the fact of indictment when the accused seeks to exercise his constitutional right to bail.

The right to bail is constitutionally conferred in all offenses with one exception—a capital offense where the proof is positive or the presumption great. Since the general rule is admission to bail, the State, if it seeks to invoke the exception to the rule, must bear the burden of going forward with the evidence to produce facts to warrant the invocation of the exception." Steigler, 250 A.2d at 382-83.

The court therefore held that the State must go forward with evidence tending to show "proof positive or presumption great." The court explained that, once this has been done, the State has sufficiently laid the basis for the application of the exception to the constitutional right to bail and the burden of proof then falls upon the accused to demonstrate the contrary. Steigler, 250 A.2d at 383.

Other jurisdictions have held that the burden to show that the proof of guilt is not evident or the presumption of guilt not great falls upon the accused seeking bail. The courts in these jurisdictions have found that the indictment raises a prima facie presumption of guilt that the accused must overcome by sufficient rebuttal evidence. See Partlow v. State, 453 N.E.2d 259 (Ind. 1983); State v. Green, 275 So. 2d 184 (La. 1973); Fischer v. Ball, 212 Md. 517, 129 A.2d 822 (1957). This presumption is held to create an inference of guilt for all purposes except the actual trial. As already noted, this was the view taken by the American Law Institute in its 1930 Code of Criminal Procedure. ALI Code of Criminal Procedure § 68(2) (1930).

For example, in Green, the Louisiana Supreme Court held that a state statute that placed the burden of proof on the accused seeking to obtain pretrial bail in capital cases did not violate the presumption of innocence or the due process clause of the fourteenth amendment to the United States Constitu-

tion. Green, 275 So. 2d at 186. The statute provided that "after indictment [the burden of proof] is on the defendant to show that the proof is not evident nor the presumption great that he is guilty of the capital offense." Green, 275 So. 2d at 185, citing La. Code Crim. Proc. art. 313 . The court explained:

"The presumption of innocence is a guide to the jury. If it were absolute and operative at every stage of a prosecution, the defendant could never be jailed until conviction. It does not prevent arrest. There is little relationship between the right to bail and the presumption of innocence. The presumption of innocence is operative and protects against conviction, not against arrest (which is taking into custody). We find no merit in defendant's argument that La.C.Cr.P. art. 313 is unconstitutional." Green, 275 So. 2d at 186.

In Fischer, a Maryland court also concluded that the finding of the indictment created, at the very least, a prima facie presumption of guilt. Fischer, 212 Md. at 523-24, 129 A.2d at 826. The court held that the State had the right to rely on this presumption during a hearing to determine pretrial bond. Thus, the court held that, when the accused seeks to remain at liberty on bail, the burden is upon him to rebut the presumption by introducing evidence that the proof of guilt is not positive and the presumption not great. Fischer, 212 Md. at 523-24, 129 A.2d at 826. Accord Partlow v. State, 453 N.E.2d 259 (Ind. 1983); State v. Monroe, 397 So. 2d 1258 (La. 1981).

After careful consideration of the foregoing authorities, we conclude that the correct approach is taken by those jurisdictions that place the burden upon the State to prove that the proof of the accused's guilt is evident and the presumption great. We believe that such an approach is required by the due process guarantees of both the United States and Illinois Constitutions. As noted above, the United States Supreme Court has held that the presumption of innocence applies during bail proceedings and is a primary underpinning of allowing pretrial bail. See Stack, 342 U.S. at 4, 96 L. Ed. at 6, 72 S. Ct. at 3. Accordingly, we must disagree with those jurisdictions that have held the presumption of innocence is not operative until the time of trial.

Because the presumption of innocence is operative during pretrial bail proceedings, we fail to see how an accused can be constitutionally required to prove that the evidence of his guilt is not great. Such a burden plainly flies in the face of the presumption of innocence and impermissibly shifts the evidentiary burden from the State to the accused. See Arthur, 390 So. 2d at 720. The presumption of innocence guarantees that the accused has no obligation to come forward with any evidence concerning the proof, or lack thereof, of any of the elements of the charged offense. Rather, as both the federal and state constitutions protect the right to bail, we believe that the State must have the burden of demonstrating that the defendant should be deprived of such a right.

Additionally, we note that principles of basic fairness also require that the burden of proof fall upon the State. See Arthur, 390 So. 2d at 720. As a practical matter, the accused is not in a good position to gather and present evidence during a bail hearing, as the criminal proceeding has been only recently initiated and the accused is in jail. The State, on the other hand, has ready access to the evidence of the alleged offense and is in a better position to present such evidence during a bail hearing. Indeed, in most cases, the State already will have presented evidence in order to secure an indictment from the grand jury.

* * *

We therefore hold that, in those cases where bail may be denied, the burden falls upon the State to show that the defendant is not entitled to bail because the proof of his guilt is evident and the presumption great. Accordingly, we find that section 110-4(b) of the Code is unconstitutional.

We further hold that invalidity of subsection (b) is not fatal to the remainder of the statute. This court has an obligation to uphold legislative enactments whenever reasonably possible, and we may excuse an offending provision of a statute and preserve the remainder provided the remainder is complete in and of itself and is capable of being executed wholly independently of the severed portion. People v. Sanders, 182 Ill.

2d 524, 534, 231 Ill. Dec. 573, 696 N.E.2d 1144 (1998).

* * *

For the foregoing reasons, we vacate the trial court's September 10, 2001, order, and we remand the cause for a new hearing upon the defendant's motion for pretrial bail conducted in conformity with the views expressed herein.

Order vacated; cause remanded.
HUTCHINSON, P.J., and McLAREN, J., concur.

BOZEMAN
v.
STATE

Court of Appeal of Florida,
Fourth District
931 So. 2d 1006, 2006 Fla. App.
LEXIS 8986 (2006)

Taylor, J. Gunther, J., concurs. Farmer, J., dissents with opinion.

Taylor, J.

Appellant Oliver Bozeman was tried by jury and convicted of grand theft of an automobile. He appeals, arguing that the trial court erred in instructing the jury on the inference to be drawn from possession of recently stolen property. He argues that the evidence was insufficient to show the exclusive possession required for the instruction. We disagree and affirm appellant's conviction.

While on routine patrol in Lauderdale Lakes shortly after midnight, Deputy William Leffew observed a 1990 Mazda pushing a 1967 Chevrolet Malibu. The deputy stopped the two vehicles. Appellant was driving the Mazda. His brother, Antoine McIntyre, was in the front passenger seat. Appellant was using the Mazda to push the Chevrolet Malibu. The Malibu had been stolen from a residence earlier that evening. Joe Bolling was in the driver's seat of the stolen Malibu. The Malibu's headlights were not on and the engine was not running. There was no vehicle tag on the Malibu. Inside, the vehicle's steering wheel column was damaged and there was no key in the ignition. The Malibu's driver side window was shattered and broken glass was on that side of the floorboard. When stopped, appellant told the deputy that McIntyre had purchased the Malibu and that he was merely helping him transport it to McIntyre's house. All three men were arrested at the scene for theft of the Chevrolet Malibu.

Co-defendant Bolling pled guilty to grand theft and possession of burglary tools. When he was sentenced, he told the judge that appellant had nothing to do with the crime. Bolling also testified at appellant's trial. He said that he and McIntyre elicited appellant's help in moving the car without telling appellant that the car was stolen.

During the jury charge conference, defense counsel argued that the standard instruction allowing the jury to infer that the defendant knew that the property was stolen based on his possession of the recently stolen property should not be given because it did not apply. The trial court disagreed and instructed the jury, as follows:

Proof of possession of recently stolen property, unless satisfactorily explained, gives rise to an inference that the person in possession of the property knew or should have known that the property had been stolen.

Fla. Std. Jury Instr. (Crim.) 14.1 at 270.

The jury found appellant guilty of grand theft. He was sentenced to ten years in prison as a habitual felony offender. On appeal, he challenges the above instruction and his sentence.

Appellant argues that the trial court erred in instructing the jury on the inference arising from possession of recently stolen property because the evidence did not demonstrate that appellant possessed the stolen vehicle or that he possessed the vehicle to the extent that he exercised any dominion and control over it.

A defendant to have a jury determine whether he has the requisite predicate convictions for a habitual felony offender sentence"), and *Washington v. State*, 895 So. 2d 1141, 1143 (Fla. 4th DCA 2005) (holding that "shotgun" notice of intent to seek habitual offender sentence is valid).

At trial, appellant's defense to the grand theft charge was that he did not know that the

car was stolen. The jury instruction at issue isl a standard jury instruction in theft cases that permits the prosecution to prove by inference that a defendant knew or should have known that property in his possession was stolen. *See Scobee v. State*, 488 So. 2d 595, 598 (Fla. 1st DCA 1986). However, before the prosecution can receive the benefit of this jury instruction, it must first produce evidence that the defendant possessed the property. *Chamberland v. State*, 429 So. 2d 842, 843 (Fla. 4th DCA 1983); *Ridley v. State*, 407 So. 2d 1000 (Fla. 5th DCA 1981). The state must demonstrate that the possession was personal, i.e., involved a distinct and conscious assertion of possession by the accused, and that the possession was exclusive. *Chamberland*, 429 So. 2d at 843; *Garcia v. State*, 899 So. 2d 447 (Fla. 4th DCA 2005); *Boone v. State*, 711 So. 2d 594, 596 (Fla. 1st DCA 1998); *King v. State*, 431 So. 2d 272 (Fla. 5th DCA 1983).

As the first district explained in *Scobee*:

The "exclusive" requirement does not mean that defendant's possession must be separate from the possession of all other persons. The joint possession of two or more persons acting in concert is "exclusive" as to any one of them.

Scobee, 488 So. 2d at 598; *see also Walker v. State*, 896 So. 2d 712, 720 n.5 (Fla. 2005) (approving *Scobee's* analysis of the "exclusive" requirement in joint possession cases).

In *People v. White*, 99 Ill. App. 2d 270, 240 N.E.2d 342 (Ill. App. 1968), officers observed the defendant pushing a recently stolen automobile into an alley at 3:00 a.m., and another person sitting at the wheel of the vehicle. When the officers approached, the man at the steering wheel fled. The court stated that the evidence established that "the car was in the joint possession of the defendant and his partner." *Id.* at 343. In finding the facts sufficient to raise a presumption of guilt and warrant a conviction for theft, the court explained that "[a]lthough the defendant was not inside the vehicle, he was exerting control over it by pushing in into the alley." *Id.*

Similarly, in this case, the evidence showed that appellant exercised dominion and control over the Malibu by pushing it while Bolling controlled the car's steering and braking. Without appellant's actions, the car could not have been moved. The two men jointly controlled the car and jointly possessed it. Because this was the sort of possession necessary to support the instruction on inference of knowledge, the trial court did not abuse its discretion in giving this instruction to the jury. It was up to the jury to weigh appellant's explanation for possessing the car and decide whether to accept the correctness of the inference. *See Scobee*, 488 So. 2d at 599.

* * *

Affirmed.

Gunther, J., concurs.
Farmer, J., dissents with opinion.
Farmer, J., dissenting.

The standard of review in this case is not only abuse of discretion. It is a mixture of de novo and abuse of discretion. Whether to instruct the jury on a specific subject begins as a rule bound exercise. Initially, the rule is that if there is evidence on the subject the party is entitled to an instruction. *See Bradley v. State*, 82 Fla. 108, 89 So. 359, 359 (Fla. 1921) ("Charges of the court must be based upon facts in proof, and if not so based upon the facts in proof it is error to give them; and the court below erred in giving the quoted charge."); *Diggs v. State*, 489 So. 2d 1228, 1228 (Fla. 5th DCA 1986) (like defendant, state "is entitled to all applicable jury instructions"); *Griffin v. State*, 370 So. 2d 860, 861 (Fla. 1st DCA 1979) ("the giving of this charge absent appropriate factual basis in the record is reversible error."). Discretion then may arise as to its content, as when there is no standard instruction on the subject, or the standard instruction is circumstantially inappropriate. *Card v. State*, 803 So. 2d 613, 624 (Fla. 2001) (holding that decision as to "whether to give a *particular* jury instruction is within trial court's discretion").

I cannot agree that there is any evidence that this defendant had possession of a stolen automobile when he was simply pushing it with his vehicle.

Cases Relating to Chapter 7

Relevancy and Materiality

COMMONWEALTH

v.

PRASHAW

**APPEALS COURT OF
MASSACHUSETTS**

**57 Mass. App. Ct. 19, 781 N.E.2d 19,
2003 Mass. App. LEXIS 5 (2003)**

JUDGES: Present: Lenk, Mason, & Berry, JJ.

BERRY, J. In this appeal, the defendant challenges the admission in evidence of photographs depicting her naked in various sexually provocative positions. Balancing the minimal probative value of the pictures with respect to the nonsex-related offenses being tried against the marked prejudice, we conclude that this is one of those exceptional cases where the bounds of the usual grant of wide discretion to a trial judge concerning the admission of photographic evidence were exceeded. Accordingly, we reverse the judgments of conviction.

1. Background facts. On December 26, 1999, a fire broke out in the house in which the defendant and her husband resided. During a "cause-and-origin" survey of the house after the blaze, an investigator saw in plain view in an upstairs bedroom a twelve-gauge shotgun standing in a corner against the wall, and marijuana "roaches" in an ashtray. The shotgun was immediately confiscated. Based

on these sightings, the police applied for a warrant to search the house.

The defendant's husband was present in the house both when the fire started and during the fire investigation. The defendant was not at home and had left the house a few days before Christmas following an altercation with her husband during which he beat her and hit her face (this abuse was of a continuing pattern over many years, including past incidents of domestic violence requiring hospital treatment). Following this incident of violence, the defendant sought shelter at her mother's house in New York State. On the day after Christmas, she returned home, only to see the house smouldering from the fire and firefighters and police on the scene.

The defendant entered the house, spoke to an officer, gathered some belongings, and described the assault that had led to her fleeing from the house. The defendant's face had not healed and still bore a bruise from that assault. One of the officers escorted the defendant to the police station, where she applied for, and was granted, a protective order under G.L.C. 209A. Thereafter, she returned to the house, even though she had been previously told by an officer that she could not enter because the police were seeking a search warrant. There were curious aspects surrounding the circumstances of the defendant's return and her explanation of the reasons why she came back to the house. The details do not matter, but of moment is that, when she returned, there was a man with her (whom the officers throughout the trial only described as a black man) and that she had a plan to reenter the house with this man, notwithstanding the police directive not to do so.

While waiting for the search warrant application to be processed, the police had cordoned off the house and stationed an officer as sentry in an unmarked cruiser in front of the house. It was during this time that the defendant and the unidentified man returned to the burned-out house. The man entered the house through the back. When the entry was discovered, another officer was dispatched to the scene to investigate the break-in. A witness, a neighbor, identified the defendant, who was standing nearby, as having "had something to do with this" break-in. The officer approached the defendant, handcuffed her, and conducted a patfrisk. A "crack" cocaine pipe containing cocaine residue was found in her pocket. The defendant was arrested. The man who had entered the house had been arrested by the officer stationed in front of the house.

Thereafter, two search warrants—one for the house and one for a Toyota Four-Runner sport utility vehicle—were executed. Seized from the Toyota were a knife with a seven-inch blade, a small quantity of marijuana, and rolling papers. Seized from the upstairs bedroom were marijuana roaches, a small amount of marijuana in a plastic bag, two bottles that had been crafted into crack cocaine pipes, aluminum foil with marijuana residue, a nonworking postal scale, another scale, the defendant's driver's license and firearm identification card, a joint tax return, and eighteen Polaroid photographs. The photographs depicted the defendant in various sexually explicit poses. In another upstairs room, in a gun cabinet, the police seized two packages of fireworks.

2. The introduction of the photographs. The Commonwealth indicated prior to trial that it would seek to admit all eighteen photographs. In response, the defendant filed a motion in limine. Following a hearing, the trial judge excluded all but three photographs. Although the Commonwealth sought to introduce the three photographs as exhibits, after an unrecorded sidebar conference, only two of the photographs were marked as exhibits and admitted in evidence for the jury's deliberations. In each of the two photographs, the defendant is naked, posing with an object in her hands and displaying the object vis-a-vis her body in a sexually provocative way. The objects being held appear blurry in the pictures. When confronted with the photographs during cross-examination, the defendant described the objects as a cigarette lighter and a billy club; the Commonwealth inferred from its scrutiny that the objects were a handgun and a shotgun. However, as to the latter, the Commonwealth concedes that, even assuming that the object is a shotgun, it is not the same shotgun that was standing in the bedroom and which was the subject of the unlawful storage charge.

The overarching principle is that "the admissibility of photographic evidence is left to the discretion of the trial judge, and [an appellate court] will overturn the judge's decision only where a defendant is able to bear the heavy burden of demonstrating an abuse of that discretion." Commonwealth v. Waters, 399 Mass. 708, 715, 506 N.E.2d 859 (1987). Such judicial discretion has a wide berth, as the trial judge is best positioned to determine evidentiary value and to balance the probative value and relevancy against prejudicial effect. However, notwithstanding this wide latitude, there still are "rare instances in which the probative value of the evidence is overwhelmed by its inflammatory potential." Commonwealth v. Repoza, 382 Mass. 119, 128, 414 N.E.2d 591 (1980). In this case, we determine "whether sexually explicit photographs . . . '[were] so inflammatory as to outweigh their probative value.'" Commonwealth v. Halsey, 41 Mass. App. Ct. 200, 203, 669 N.E.2d 774 (1996), quoting from Commonwealth v. Hrycenko, 31 Mass. App. Ct. 425, 431, 578 N.E.2d 809 (1991). The defendant objected to the admission of the photographs, and, thereby, preserved the issue for appeal. Accordingly, we seek to determine whether there was prejudicial error. We conclude that the answer to that question is in the affirmative. In the balance to be struck, the extraordinary prejudice far overbore the minimal probativeness.

A. Probative value. We begin with an assessment of the evidentiary probativeness of the photographs. As noted, the objects being held by the defendant in the photographs are murky, but, even if viewed by the Commonwealth's lights, and even assuming such additional candle power would have led the beholder to perceive a shotgun of some sort being held in one photograph, it is not, as the Commonwealth concedes, the shotgun identified in the improper storage charge. n3 The Commonwealth, therefore, concedes that neither photograph was relevant to the wrongful storage of a firearm charge and concedes error in admission on that basis. Instead, the Commonwealth argues on appeal, as the sole basis for admission, that the photographs were probative of the defendant's control of the upstairs bedroom where the marijuana, scales, and crack pipes were found.

We note at the outset that there was no dispute that the room was the defendant's bedroom and, in effect, belonged to her. As the prosecutor put it in the closing: "This, ladies and gentlemen, is her room; and there's no question about that. And these things were found in her closet; there's no questions about that, in her bureau, throughout her things; there's no question about the possession, ladies and gentlemen, no question." Precisely so, the defendant's general control over, and association with, the bedroom was well-established by abundant evidence—wholly apart from the photographs. This other evidence included the defendant's clothing, both stored in bureaus and strewn about the bedroom, as well as her driver's license, firearm identification card, and tax return, all of which were found within the bedroom. See Commonwealth v. Rarick, 23 Mass. App. Ct. 912, 912-913, 499 N.E.2d 1233 (1986) (personal effects belonging to the defendant linked her to contraband found in proximity to those effects even though multiple persons shared the dwelling). The strength of this other connective evidence substantially diminished the probative need for introduction of the sexually explicit pictures on the issue of general control of the bedroom, which was not even being disputed. Put another way, that this was the defendant's bedroom was fairly obvious, and the photographs added little but prejudice.

The principal issue with respect to control was limited to the defendant's absence from the house for the five days she stayed with her mother. Given this sojourn, there was a question, it appears from the evidence, as to whether someone else may have used the bedroom for some sort of partying and drinking spree. Indeed, that someone else was in the bedroom during this period might have been inferred from an empty bottle of whiskey and a pizza box which, according to the defendant, were not there before she left for New York, and the fact that, before she left, the photographs were kept in her locked closet. This and other evidence suggest that the defendant did not have control of the room during her absence and that the defendant's estranged, alcoholic husband may well have gone on a drinking binge in that room.

Given this lapse in the defendant's control, the probative value of the photographs, if any, is to be analyzed with respect to this five-day period. Any such probative link between the photographs and this period of time was extremely weak. There was no evidence, and the four corners of the photographs do not manifest, that the pictures were taken within the five-day time frame. Nor was there any evidence that the photographs were taken in the bedroom area where either the drugs or paraphernalia were found or in the corner of the room where the shotgun was standing. Further undercutting the Commonwealth's contention that the photographs showed the defendant's association with, and control over, the bedroom is a handwritten notation, "George's house," on the face of one of the photographs, which suggests that the pictures were taken someplace else. In fact, there was no substantive evidence whatsoever linking the photographs to control of the bedroom by the defendant during her five-day absence. Rather than such authentication, the photographs were simply dropped in evidence as items seized in the search and were not further authenticated by time, place, or manner during the course of trial."To be admissible in evidence, a photograph must be shown to be accurate and bear enough similarity to circumstances at the time in dispute to be relevant and helpful to the jury in its deliberations." Henderson v. D'Annolfo, 15 Mass. App. Ct. 413, 428, 446 N.E.2d 103 (1983). Thus, on a sliding scale, the probative value of the photographs was minimal. We next consider the prejudice.

B. Prejudicial effect. In this case, the prejudicial effect was depicting the defendant as "a lewd [woman] and to lead the jury to believe that a [woman] of [her] character would be likely to commit the crimes charged." Commonwealth v. Ellis, 321 Mass. 669, 670, 75 N.E.2d 241 (1947). It does not take much imagination to conjure that the purpose and effect of the introduction of the pictures was so that the jury, appalled by the defendant's posing in such a manner, might be swayed to perceive the defendant as not of good moral character and more likely to have committed criminal offenses. See Liacos, Brodin & Avery, Massachusetts Evidence § 11.6, at 708 (7th ed. 1999). Such a prejudicial effect, inherent in sexually explicit depictions, was amplified in this case because the trial did not involve a sex-related offense. Moreover, although only two photographs were published to the jury, one of the officers testified that there were eighteen such Polaroid photographs seized. See, e.g., Commonwealth v. Allen, 377 Mass. 674, 680, 387 N.E.2d 553 (1979) (photograph of the victim's bloody crotch, which was due to natural decomposition, possessed "great potential for inciting jury speculation about possible sexual overtones to the crime" in a murder trial); Commonwealth v. Darby, 37 Mass. App. Ct. 650, 654, 642 N.E.2d 303 (1994) (photograph of the male defendant in a sexually turgid state was unduly prejudicial where impotence or sexual dysfunction was not "directly or inferentially" relevant to the case). As a last resort, the Commonwealth suggests harmless error should cause us to affirm the convictions, but we are unable to say the photographs did not unduly and unfairly influence the jury, or had just a slight effect. In sum, the risk was great that the sexually suggestive pictures, which had little to do with the case at hand, unduly swayed the jury. For these reasons, we conclude that it was error to admit the photographs.

* * *

The judgments of convictions on all the complaints tried are reversed and the verdicts are set aside. The denial of the motion to suppress is affirmed.

So ordered.

JACKSON
v.
UNITED STATES

District of Columbia Court of Appeals
856 A.2d 1111, 2004 D.C. App.
LEXIS 413 (2004)

Before STEADMAN and SCHWELB, Associate Judges, and NEBEKER, Senior Judge.

STEADMAN, *Associate Judge*: Appellant and his co-defendant were selling music compact discs ("CDs") from a table they had set up on the sidewalk near Union Station. The CDs were "counterfeit"; that is, they were manufactured without the authorization of the copyright owner. Appellant was convicted at a bench trial of attempted deceptive labeling of a sound recording, in violation of D.C. Code §§ 22-103 (attempt) and -3814.1 (deceptive labeling) (1996).

The only issue on appeal is whether the trial court erred in admitting, in the government's case in chief, evidence of prior criminal conduct in violation of the strictures of the case law emanating from *Drew v. United States*, 118 U.S. App. D.C. 11, 331 F.2d 85 (1964). Specifically, evidence was introduced that five weeks prior to the date of the offense for which he was on trial, appellant had been arrested, also in the vicinity of Union Station, when he was also vending counterfeit CDs and was warned at that time that he was selling counterfeit CDs. (The actual arrest in that prior case was for vending without a license.) The government takes the position that the evidence went to the issue of appellant's knowledge that the CDs were counterfeit at the time of the offense for which he was on trial. Appellant argues that his knowledge was not then a materially contested issue, and his defense, in fact, was that he was not selling the CDs at all but rather just happened to be passing by at the time. The introduction of the evidence, he asserts, thus violated the prohibition that he reads into *Thompson v. United States*, 546 A.2d 414 (D.C. 1988), against the introduction of *Drew* evidence which bore only upon issues not genuinely in dispute. We conclude that this is far too broad a reading of *Thompson* and affirm the conviction.

I.

The principal government witness in its case in chief was Officer Tracey Hanbury. He testified that he saw two men selling compact discs from a table they had set up on the sidewalk near Union Station. He saw both men sell CDs to customers. When he confronted the two individuals, he realized they were the same two men whom he had arrested some five weeks previously after witnessing them selling CDs outside Union Station. Although the prior arrest was for vending without a license, Officer Hanbury had advised appellant that the CDs he was selling were counterfeit.

Officer Hanbury further testified that the CDs he observed in appellant's possession at the time of the second arrest were "obviously counterfeits." He noted: "The front of the CD [was] just a thin piece of paper . . . that was copied on the CD and . . was cut with a pair of scissors where some of them don't have perfectly straight lines. . . They were also wrapped in saran wrap type wrapping and that wasn't consistent with what you would see in a music CD store."

The government presented an expert witness, Phillip Brooks, who testified that counterfeit CDs often have "poor shrink wrappings . . . poorly folded corners . . . while a legitimate compact disc is characterized by tight corners, [and] tightly sealed." He further explained that "the insert card on a counterfeit disc will be a thin piece of paper . . . of poor quality," while the insert cards on a legitimate compact disc "are one of the more expensive aspects of the disc." He also said that the playing side of a counterfeit compact disc "will be greenish or bluish in tint which indicates it's a CD recordable," while "the legitimate compact disc will be silver and . . . legitimate record companies do not manufacture their compact disc on CD recordables." Mr. Brooks identified as counterfeits a random selection of discs from the box of 62 CDs seized from appellant.

Testifying in his own defense, appellant said he had come to Union Station for a dinner and movie with his common-law wife. After he parked his car and was walking toward the entrance, a police car came speeding towards him, two officers jumped out and escorted appellant over to the co-defendant and placed them under arrest. Appellant testified he was not selling any CDs and didn't receive any money from any customers. Appellant stated that he had never sold CDs in the District, but had other people sell CDs for him. Appellant acknowledged that he had been previously arrested and was then informed that the CDs being sold at his vending table were counterfeit but he said that at the time he had no idea that they were counterfeit. Once he found this out, he stopped carrying CDs at his vending table. Appellant's co-defendant testified that all of the property on the table belonged to him and that he had not given appellant any money that evening and, in fact, the co-defendant had not made a single sale all evening.

In rebuttal, the government called Officer Aisha Jackson, who testified that on several previous occasions she had "shut down" appellant for selling CDs without a vending license in the vicinity of Union Station. She accompanied Officer Hanbury at the time of the prior arrest when the warning was given to appellant that the CDs that he was selling were counterfeit. On that occasion, appellant acknowledged that the CDs were his and stated, "Yeah, these are mine, everybody is doing it."

II.

"If evidence of prior bad acts that are criminal in nature and independent of the crime charged is offered to prove predisposition to commit the charged crime, it is inadmissible. . . . 'It is a principle of long standing in our law that evidence of one crime is inadmissible to prove disposition to commit crime, from which the jury may infer that the defendant committed the crime charged. Since the likelihood that juries will make such an improper inference is high, courts presume prejudice and exclude evidence of other crimes unless that evidence can be admitted for some substantial, legitimate purpose.'" *Johnson v. United States*, 683 A.2d 1087, 1092 (D.C. 1996) (en banc) (quoting *Drew, supra,* 331 F.2d at 89-90) (other citations omitted), *cert. denied*, 520 U.S. 1148, 137 L. Ed. 2d 484, 117 S. Ct. 1323 (1997). This presumption of prejudice may be overcome if "the [other crimes] evidence [is] offered for a substantial, legitimate purpose," n4 and "the court. . . considers the relative probative value of the evidence and the danger of unfair prejudice that it poses, and concludes that the balance favors admission." *Id.* at 1092-93 (citations omitted). Moreover, *Drew* does not apply at all where "such evidence (1) is direct and substantial proof of the charged crime, (2) is closely intertwined with the evidence of the charged crime, or (3) is necessary to place the charged crime in an understandable context." *Id.* at 1098.

The government first contends that *Drew* is inapplicable to the disputed evidence because the circumstances surrounding appellant's prior arrest provided "direct and substantial proof" of a constituent element of the crime charged, by demonstrating his knowledge of the counterfeit nature of the CDs at issue. The government's argument, that a factor in a previous crime which tends to make more probable an element of the current crime charged is therefore direct and substantial proof of the current crime charged, if too broadly read could threaten to swallow up the very protection that *Drew* endeavors to provide. *Drew* places upon other crime evidence a presumption of prejudice not because such evidence is "irrelevant; on the contrary, it is said to weigh too much with the jury and to . . . overpersuade them. . . ." *Thompson, supra,* 546 A.2d at 418 (quoting *Michelson v. United States,* 335 U.S. 469, 475-76, 93 L. Ed. 168, 69 S. Ct. 213 (1948)). The difficulty is that *Drew* evidence often itself operates as "direct and substantial proof" of an element of a charged crime, such as with, for example, the intent and identity exceptions. It is no easy task to articulate the line that divides evidence subject to *Drew* from evidence not subject to *Drew* on the ground that the latter is "direct and substantial proof" of the offense.

A substantial portion of our cases declaring other crimes evidence to be "direct and substantial proof" of the crime charged involve the admission of evidence of prior possession of a weapon, which was also used in the charged crime. [Citations omitted.] We have held such determinations to be "consistent with the principle that 'an accused person's prior possession of the physical means of committing the crime is some evidence of the probability of his guilt, and is therefore admissible.'" [Citations omitted.] Other crimes evidence has also fallen outside the strictures of *Drew* in cases involving a shared

"evidentiary stream" between the prior and the charged crime, [Citation omitted.], and involving evidence of an attempt to conceal the charged crime. [Citations omitted.] We need not, here, explore the issue further because, even if we assume the disputed evidence does fall within the purview of *Drew,* its admission was not error.

III.

The government argues, and we agree, that applying *Drew,* the evidence in question was properly admitted to prove appellant's knowledge that the CDs were counterfeit.

We have not previously expressly recognized "knowledge" as a legitimate purpose for which other crimes evidence may be offered and, thereby, escape *Drew's* prohibition. In *Johnson,* we enumerated substantial and legitimate purposes warranting admission of other crimes evidence, which "included, but [were] *not limited* to . . . (1) motive; (2) intent; (3) absence of mistake or accident; (4) common scheme or plan; [and] (5) identity." *Johnson, supra,* 683 A.2d at 1092 (emphasis added). Furthermore, we have identified as "consistent with District of Columbia law" the following language from Federal Rule of Evidence 404(b): "Evidence of other crimes, wrongs, or acts is not admissible to prove the character of a person in order to show action in conformity therewith. It may, however, be admissible for other purposes, such as proof of motive, opportunity, intent, preparation, plan, *knowledge,* identity, or absence of mistake or accident." *Id.* at 1100 n.17 (emphasis added). Knowledge is widely accepted as a non-propensity purpose for which other crimes evidence may be admitted. *See generally, e.g.,* 29 AM. JUR. 2D. Evidence § 443 (1994); EDWARD J. IMWINKELREID, UNCHARGED MISCONDUCT EVIDENCE §§ 5:24, 5:26 (2004); Randall, *Acquittals in Jeopardy: Criminal Collateral Estoppel and the Use of Acquitted Act Evidence,* 141 U. Pa. L. Rev. 283, 307 n.114 (1992) (citing RICHARD O. LEMPERT & STEPHEN A. SALTZBURG, A MODERN APPROACH TO EVIDENCE 215-16 (2d ed. 1982)). Thus, we now explicitly hold that other crimes or bad acts evidence may be offered for the purpose of demonstrating "knowledge" and, absent a finding that the prejudicial effect of the evidence substantially outweighs its probative value, evidence offered for such purpose will overcome *Drew's* presumption of inadmissibility.

Given our adoption of this further exception to *Drew*, we must evaluate whether the evidence of appellant's previous arrest for the purpose of showing his knowledge was properly admitted. "A decision on the admissibility of evidence, of course, is committed to the sound discretion of the trial court." *Sanders, supra,* 809 A.2d at 590 (citation omitted). Moreover, "the evaluation and weighing of evidence for relevance and potential prejudice is quintessentially a discretionary function of the trial court, and we owe a great degree of deference to its decision." *Johnson, supra,* 683 A.2d at 1095.

Appellant was convicted of attempted deceptive labeling. "A person commits the offense of deceptive labeling if, for commercial advantage or private financial gain, that person *knowingly* advertises, offers for sale, resale, or rental, or sells, resells, rents, distributes, or transports, or possesses for such purposes, a sound recording or audiovisual work, the label, cover, or jacket of which does not clearly and conspicuously disclose the true name and address of the manufacturer thereof." D.C. Code § 22-3814.1(b) (emphasis added). Thus, to secure a conviction for deceptive labeling, the government was required to prove that appellant knew that "the label, cover, or jacket of [the CDs in question]. . . [did] not clearly and conspicuously disclose the true name and address of the manufacturer thereof." Such knowledge would be implicit if appellant knew the CDs were counterfeit, and therefore could not reflect the true name of the manufacturer. Testimony that appellant had been previously warned that the CDs he was selling were counterfeit went to the issue of whether he knew the CDs at issue were counterfeit. Although the government presented no direct evidence that the appearance of the CDs at issue was the same as the CDs about which appellant was warned, a fair inference to that effect could be made from the expert's general description of counterfeit CDs and the testimony of Officer Hanbury, the same individual who had previously warned the appellant about counterfeit CDs, that he immediately recognized that the CDs at issue were coun-

terfeit. Thus, the trial court did not abuse its discretion in admitting evidence that appellant had previously sold counterfeit CDs because the evidence was not admitted to establish appellant's criminal propensity but to demonstrate appellant's knowledge as to the counterfeit nature of the discs, an essential element of the crime charged.

* * *

IV.

* * *

V.

The trial court did not err in permitting, in the government's case in chief, the introduction of other crime evidence for the purpose of demonstrating appellant's knowledge of the counterfeit nature of the CDs, even where he had not at that time disputed, nor did he later dispute, that issue. Accordingly, the judgment appealed from is hereby

Affirmed.

Cases Relating to Chapter 8

Competency of Evidence and Witnesses

UNITED STATES

v.

PHIBBS

**United States Court of Appeals,
Sixth Circuit
999 F.2d 1053 (1993)**

Before: GUY and SUHRHEINRICH, Circuit Judges; and DOWD, District Judge.

RALPH B. GUY, JR., Circuit Judge.

Defendants, Raymond Huckelby, Diane Whited, Robert Phibbs, Victor Rojas, and Robert Murr appeal their convictions arising from their participation in a cocaine distribution ring operating in Tennessee and Kentucky. In addition, Phibbs and Rojas challenge the appropriateness of their sentences.

* * *

E. Competency of Jerry Parks and Tommy McKeehan

Whited claims that witnesses Jerry Parks and Tommy McKeehan were incompetent to give testimony on grounds of mental incapacity. In the case of Parks, he had previously been found incompetent to stand trial, had a history of auditory delusions, and had spent time in mental health facilities. As for McKeehan, Whited cites an affidavit filed with the district court by his treating psychiatrist that he could not assist his counsel in an upcoming trial because he suffered from "confusion, agitation, paranoia and hallucinations." This affidavit was dated four days

prior to McKeehan having entered into a plea agreement with the government. Because of such information, Whited contends that, at the very least, it was error for the court not to conduct a preliminary examination of Parks' and McKeehan's competency as witnesses.

Under Rule 601 of the Federal Rules of Evidence (General Rule of Competency), "every person is competent to be a witness except as otherwise provided in these rules." The Advisory Committee Notes to Rule 601 explain that "this general ground-clearing eliminates all grounds of incompetency not specifically recognized in the rules of this Article." Accordingly, "no mental or moral qualifications for testifying as a witness" are specified. Id. This is because "standards of mental capacity have proved elusive in actual application." Id.

Thus, the Federal Rules of Evidence strongly disfavor barring witnesses on competency grounds due to mental incapacity. As we wrote in United States v. Ramirez, 871 F.2d 582, 584 (6th Cir.), cert. denied, 493 U.S. 841, 107 L. Ed. 2d 88, 110 S. Ct. 127 (1989):

What must be remembered, and is often confused, is that "competency" is a matter of status not ability. Thus, the only two groups of persons specifically rendered incompetent as witnesses by the Federal Rules of Evidence are judges (Rule 605) and jurors (Rule 606). The authority of the court to control the admissibility of the testimony of persons so impaired in some manner that they cannot give meaningful testimony is to be found outside of Rule

791

601. For example, the judge always has the authority under Rule 403 to balance the probative value of testimony against its prejudicial effect. Similarly, under Rule 603, the inability of a witness to take or comprehend an oath or affirmation will allow the judge to exclude that person's testimony. An argument can also be constructed that a person might be impaired to the point that he would not be able to satisfy the "personal knowledge" requirement of Rule 602. Again though, it is important to remember that such decisions by a trial judge to either admit or exclude testimony will only be reversed for a clear abuse of discretion.

(Footnote omitted.)

The district court did not rule on Parks' competency before he took the stand; later, in considering a motion for judgment of acquittal, the court indicated that Parks and McKeehan "were not crazy witnesses." Likewise, it addressed the question of McKeehan's mental capacity during a bench conference held after he had begun to testify. The court stated that it had "observed Mr. McKeehan, and he appears to the Court to be sober, cogent. He appears to the Court to know exactly where he is and what he is doing. His testimony has been direct, and his testimony has not been confused." When pressed concerning the psychiatrist's affidavit that McKeehan could not help in his own defense, the court opined that "he sure has made a remarkable recovery . . . [His condition is] fodder for cross-examination, and it would appear that either the psychiatrist made an inaccurate diagnosis September the 5th or the witness has made a remarkable recovery. And the Court observes that—repeats that he does not appear to be confused today."

At a hearing on defendants' post-trial motions, the district court supplemented its findings regarding Parks' and McKeehan's competency, and the need for a special examination of their mental faculties. The court noted that

one of the reasons I overlooked stating as to my belief that an independent evaluation at this time would be a waste of time

is that—is that such a finding, even if they found that they were incompetent here in April of 1992, would not be dispositive as to their competence or mental state when they testified in September of 1991 at the trial of this case or at the hearings that we held in August.

. . . .

Similarly, even if I had such an opinion from a psychiatrist or psychologist or whoever that gave us an independent opinion that these people were—Mr. Parks and McKeehan were total screwballs, I would—I would find those opinions to have little probative value and of little weight, and I would not—I would not accept them as being—as being conclusive on the matter. And I would not let such opinions override my own judgment after having seen—personally witnessed their performance in court.

Hence, the district court did not find that Parks and McKeehan were incapable of understanding their oath and obligation to testify truthfully. Nor did the court find, based on its observations, that their mental abilities were so limited that they did not have sufficient capacity to perceive events, to remember them, and to describe them for the benefit of the trier of fact. See Fed. R. Evid. 602. The court was not required, as Whited would have it, to conduct a special examination into their competency. If either Parks' or McKeehan's behavior raised concerns stemming from Rule 602 or 603, it could have excluded their testimony (or portions thereof) without any examination whatsoever. Furthermore, the court had the additional authority, pursuant to Rule 403, to exclude their testimony in light of their past or present mental state. The court chose not to take any of these measures in the circumstances. Instead, it permitted defense counsel to use the psychiatric records of Parks and McKeehan, as well as other indicia of their mental capacity, to vigorously attack their credibility.

After carefully reviewing the record, we conclude that the district court did not abuse its discretion in doing so. As long as a witness appreciates his duty to tell the truth, and is minimally capable of observing, recalling, and communicating events, his testimony should come in for whatever it is worth. It is then up to the opposing party to dispute the witness' powers of apprehension, which well may be impaired by mental illness or other factors. As we are persuaded that Parks and McKeehan were at least minimally capable of offering reliable evidence, the possible weaknesses in their testimony went to its credibility, and so were to be assessed by the jury. See United States v. Moreno, 899 F.2d 465, 469 (6th Cir. 1990).

Whited also argues that defendants should have been allowed to introduce the psychiatric records of Parks and McKeehan as substantive evidence. They were ruled inadmissible hearsay by the district court. Whited alleges, however, that they were not put forward for the truth of the matters asserted within, but to show how manipulative Parks and McKeehan could be if they were not, in fact, mentally unbalanced. Such use of the records during cross-examination to challenge Parks' and McKeehan's credibility was appropriate. However, we believe that they would have constituted hearsay if employed as part of a substantive defense. They would have to have been offered to show that the psychiatrists making the records actually concluded that Parks and McKeehan were mentally ill. Otherwise, Parks' and McKeehan's deception would have no basis in fact. Consequently, the district court did not err in declining to admit the psychiatric records.

* * *

B. The Presence of Government Agents in the Courtroom

Phibbs also asserts that defendants did not receive a fair trial because FBI Special Agent Clyde Merryman and DEA Special Agent Frank Finken, both of whom appeared as witnesses, were allowed to remain in the courtroom throughout the proceedings.

Rule 615 of the Federal Rules of Evidence (Exclusion of Witnesses) provides:

At the request of a party the court shall order witnesses excluded so that they cannot hear the testimony of other witnesses, and it may make the order of its own

motion. The rule does not authorize exclusion of (1) a party who is a natural person, or (2) an officer or employee of a party which is not a natural person designated as its representative by its attorney, or (3) a person whose presence is shown by a party to be essential to the presentation of the party's cause.

In the instant case, the government sought to designate both Merryman and Finken as its representatives during the trial. After a defense objection, the district court replied:

I think the rule provides that anyone that was necessary to assist counsel in the presentation of the case would be—would be permitted to remain in the courtroom. Inasmuch as this is an extended trial, boxes of documents both from the Eastern District of Kentucky and the Eastern District [of] Tennessee, it would be unduly burdensome on the Court and time consuming if we just had one case agent. So the request of the Government is not unreasonable, so the motion is overruled.

The court then engaged in a colloquy with one of the counsel for the defense, inviting him to bring contrary authority to its attention before any witnesses were called. Counsel did not do so.

Hence, the court initially treated both Merryman and Finken as "essential" witnesses under Rule 615(3). Later, however, the court requested that the government designate one of the two as its representative pursuant to Rule 615(2); it would then consider whether the other agent was an "essential" witness. The government responded by selecting Merryman as its representative, and the court found that Finken's presence in the courtroom was also needed for the government to effectively present its case.

Phibbs concedes that one of the agents could have stayed in the courtroom, despite the fact that he would later testify. However, he argues that the government had the burden to show that the presence of more than one agent was "essential" to it laying out its case. See Fed. R. Evid. 615.

The district court followed our procedure, as set out in United States v. Pulley, 922 F.2d

1283 (6th Cir.), cert. denied, Pulley v. United States, U.S. __, 112 S. Ct. 61 (1991), to be used when the government seeks to have two agent-witnesses in the courtroom for assistance. Rule 615(2) affords the government the right to designate only one representative for such a purpose. Id. at 1286. However, certain prosecutions may be complex enough that the aid of more than one law enforcement officer is needed to sort through extensive, technical evidence, and to help "map out strategy." See United States v. Martin, 920 F.2d 393, 397 (6th Cir. 1990). When the government wants to have two agent-witnesses in attendance throughout a trial, "it is always free to designate one agent as its representative under subpart (2) [to Rule 615] and to try to show under subpart (3) that the presence of the second agent is "essential" to the presentation of its case." Pulley, 922 F.2d at 1286.

Demonstrating that an additional agent is, in fact, "essential" is no easy task. Criminal defendants, as do all persons caught up in the legal process, have a substantial interest in "discouraging and exposing fabrication, inaccuracy, and collusion" related to in-court testimony. Advisory Committee Notes to Fed. R. Evid. 615. This interest was recognized in the text of Rule 615, which made the exclusion of witnesses by the parties a matter of right, subject to exceptions that are narrowly defined.

The "essential" witness exception set out in Rule 615(3) "contemplates such persons as an agent who handled the transaction being litigated or an expert needed to advise counsel in the management of the litigation." Advisory Committee Notes to Fed. R. Evid. 615. We are persuaded that Finken fell within this category due to the particular circumstances of the case at bar. This was a trial that was scheduled for approximately one month, involving several defendants and a great deal of evidence, not all of which was readily accessible. After Merryman was designated the government's representative in accordance with Rule 615(2), the court determined that Finken, who was intimately familiar with portions of the evidence, was also needed to advise the government in its handling of the prosecution. As Merryman and Finken were, for the most part, responsible for distinct aspects of a far-flung investigation, this was not an abuse of discretion.

We note that the district court took steps to guarantee that Merryman and Finken would not parrot each other's testimony. It directed that, when one of them was on the stand, the other was to be outside the courtroom. Such a measure could be taken, not only on the basis of the court's inherent powers of trial oversight, but also in reliance upon Rule 615 itself. See, e.g., United States v. Womack, 654 F.2d 1034 (5th Cir. 1981), cert. denied, 454 U.S. 1156, 71 L. Ed. 2d 314, 102 S. Ct. 1029 (1982) (breach of conditions placed on sequestration constitutes violation of Fed. R. Evid. 615).

Phibbs, however, asserts that government counsel really wanted Finken and Merryman in court so that they might be in a position to coach Parks during recesses, or to otherwise guide his testimony. He claims that defendants were prejudiced because Merryman had substantial contact with Parks, "and the clear purpose and effect of allowing Agent Merryman to remain in the courtroom was to be able to listen to all of the testimony and to, in fact, cumulatively correct any questionable credibility problems and to bolster the credibility of Mr. Parks[.]" As for Finken, he "also had the opportunity to sit through this testimony and assist Agent Merryman in the 'correction' of Mr. Parks' testimony." Phibbs offers nothing to support his charges, and we find them to be rank speculation.

Despite the possibility of improper influence, Rule 615(2) allows the government to have any law enforcement officer it wants at its counsel table. Similarly, Rule 615(3) does not categorically bar any class of agents from assuming "essential" witness status. Ordinarily, if there are concerns about coaching by an agent-witness, the court may order him not to discuss the case with any other witness. If the agent fails to adhere to such an order, the court has a variety of remedies at its disposal, ranging from commenting on the transgression to the jury, to holding the agent in contempt, or disqualifying him as a witness, or even declaring a mistrial.

In addition, the defense is free to cross-examine both the agent-witness and the alleged object of his coaching efforts, subject to the control of the court. See Geders v.

United States, 425 U.S. 80, 89-91, 47 L. Ed. 2d 592, 96 S. Ct. 1330 (1976). See also M. Graham, Federal Practice and Procedure: Evidence § 6611 at 217-221 (West 1992). Here, defendants engaged in spirited cross-examination of Parks, Merryman, and Finken, touching upon the question of coaching.

* * *

AFFIRMED.

STATE
v.
WELLS

COURT OF APPEALS OF OHIO, NINTH APPELLATE DISTRICT, SUMMIT COUNTY

2003 Ohio 3162, 2003 Ohio App. LEXIS 2840 (2003)

JUDGES: LYNN C. SLABY. SLABY, P. J. CONCURS. BATCHELDER, J. CONCURS. CARR, J. DISSENTS.

This cause was heard upon the record in the trial court. Each error assigned has been reviewed and the following disposition is made:

Per curiam.

Appellant, Jerome Wells, appeals from his conviction in the Summit County Court of Common Pleas of one count of gross sexual imposition. This Court reverses and remands for a new trial.

Wells was indicted on one count of rape, in violation of R.C. 2907.02(A)(1)(b). He allegedly engaged in sexual conduct with a child under thirteen years of age on or about December 9, 2001. The alleged victim of his crime, T.V., was five years old at the time the case proceeded to trial during May 2002. Prior to trial, because T.V. was less than ten years old, a hearing was held to determine whether she was competent to testify. Following an examination by the trial judge, the prosecutor and defense counsel, the trial court determined that T.V. was competent to testify.

Following a jury trial, Wells was convicted of the lesser included offense of gross sexual imposition. Wells appeals and raises five assignments of error.

FIRST ASSIGNMENT OF ERROR

"THE TRIAL COURT ERRED AND ABUSED ITS DISCRETION BY FINDING A FIVE (5) YEAR OLD CHILD COMPETENT TO TESTIFY PURSUANT TO EVID.R. 601 WHERE SHE CLEARLY WAS INCAPABLE OF RECEIVING JUST IMPRESSIONS OF FACTS AND DID NOT COMPREHEND THE CONCEPT OF A LIE OR ITS CONSEQUENCES."

Wells contends that the trial court erred in determining that five-year-old T.V., the alleged victim, was competent to testify because she was not capable of receiving just impressions of fact and did not understand the concept of a lie or the consequences of lying. Evid.R. 601(A) provides:

"Every person is competent to be a witness except * * * children under ten years of age, who appear incapable of receiving just impressions of the facts and transactions respecting which they are examined, or of relating them truly."

The burden falls on the proponent of the witness to establish that the witness exhibits "certain indicia of competency." State v. Clark (1994), 71 Ohio St.3d 466, 469, 1994 Ohio 43, 644 N.E.2d 331. In State v. Frazier (1991), 61 Ohio St.3d 247, 574 N.E.2d 483 , syllabus, the Supreme Court of Ohio set forth five factors that the trial court "must take into consideration" when determining whether a child under the age of ten is competent to testify:

"(1) the child's ability to receive accurate impressions of fact or to observe acts about which he or she will testify, (2) the child's ability to recollect those impressions or observations, (3) the child's ability to communicate what was observed, (4) the child's understanding of truth and falsity and (5) the child's appreciation of his or her responsibility to be truthful."

These factors "are aimed at protecting the accused by ascertaining that a child witness is trustworthy." State v. Ulch (Apr. 19, 2002), 6th Dist. No. L-00-1355, 2002 Ohio App. LEXIS 1866.

At the hearing to determine whether T.V. was competent to testify in this case, the State failed to meet its burden of presenting sufficient evidence of T.V.'s competency. Specifically, there was not a sufficient inquiry into the fourth or fifth Frazier competency factors: the child's understanding of truth and falsity and the child's appreciation of his or her responsibility to be truthful. "[A] child may be competent to testify even though the child *** initially does not recognize the concept of truth, so long as the voir dire continues on to demonstrate that the child *** generally *** understands the concept of truthfulness." State v. Brooks (Oct. 26, 2001), 2nd Dist. No. 18502, 2001 Ohio 1650 , quoting State v. Boyd (Oct. 31, 1997), 2d Dist. No. 97 CA 1, 1997 Ohio App. LEXIS 4748.

In this case, however, after T.V. initially demonstrated that she did not understand the concepts of truth and falsity, the further voir dire on this issue was not sufficient to demonstrate that T.V. did, in fact, generally understand the concept of truthfulness or that she appreciated her responsibility to tell the truth. The trial court errs in finding a child witness competent without sufficient evidence before it to consider each of the five Frazier factors. See State v. Wilson (Feb. 18, 2000), 4th Dist. No. 99CA672, 2000 Ohio App. LEXIS 677. Because there was not an adequate demonstration on the fourth and fifth Frazier factors, the trial court erred in finding T.V. competent to testify.

It has been held that such a deficiency in the hearing on the child's competency can be cured if the child's subsequent testimony at trial demonstrates that the trial court was justified in finding the child competent to testify. See State v. Wilson, citing State v. Lewis (1982), 4 Ohio App.3d 275, 4 Ohio B. 494, 448 N.E.2d 487. At the time T.V. testified at trial, however, the State failed to elicit any further testimony regarding her understanding of the concept of truthfulness. Consequently, the error could not have been cured by her later testimony.

Because there was insufficient evidence before the trial court to demonstrate that T.V. had an understanding of the concepts of truth and falsity or that she appreciated her responsibility to be truthful, the trial court exceeded the scope of its discretion by finding that she was competent to testify. See Frazier, 61 Ohio St.3d at 247, syllabus. The first assignment of error is sustained and the judgment is reversed and remanded for a retrial.

The remaining assignments of error have been rendered moot and will not be reached. See App.R. 12(A)(1)(c). The judgment of the trial court is reversed and the cause is remanded for a new trial.

Judgment reversed and the cause remanded.

CONCUR: BATCHELDER, J.

Although I agree with the reasoning of the principal opinion, I write separately to emphasize the lack of the evidence before the trial court regarding T.V.'s competency to testify. There was almost no evidence on the fourth Frazier factor, "the child's understanding of truth and falsity" and there was a complete lack of evidence on the fifth factor, "the child's appreciation of his or her responsibility to be truthful." See Frazier, 61 Ohio St.3d at 247, syllabus. As indicated above, the trial judge had an mandatory obligation to consider all five factors. See id.

At the competency hearing, the testimony elicited by the prosecutor from T.V. regarding her understanding of truth and falsity and her appreciation of her responsibility to be truthful was the following:

"Q. Okay. [T,] do you know what it means to have to tell the truth?
"A. (Witness shook head.)
"Q. Okay. You are shaking your head. Which do you mean? If you tell the truth, what do you have to do? Let me ask you a different way. You are wearing a jump suit today, aren't you?
"A. (Witness nodded.)
"Q. Is that a yes?
"A. Yes.
"Q. Okay. If I said your jump suit was green, is that right?
"A. (Witness shook head.) No.
"Q. No? What color is your jump suit?

"A. Pink.

"Q. It is pink. You are right, it is pink.

"A. Pink and white.

"Q. Pink and white, you are right. Yes, it is. And who is this right here?

"A. My bear.

"Q. That's a bear. If I told you that this was a kitty cat; is that right?

"A. No.

"Q. No, it is not right, is it. Did you talk with me about having to come to the courtroom today?

"A. Yes.

"Q. Okay. And did I tell you that you would have to tell the truth when you came here?

"A. Yes.

"Q. Okay. And did your mom tell you that, too?

"A. Yes.

"Q. Okay. Did we tell you that that means that you have to tell us what happened and you can't make it up?

"A. Yes.

"Q. Yes, okay."

After T.V. indicated that she did not understand what it meant to have to tell the truth, the prosecutor did not ask any follow-up questions on that specific issue. Instead, the prosecutor asked T.V. questions about what is "right" and "not right," never linking those two concepts to truth and/or falsity. Equating right and not right with truth and falsity is not necessarily something that a five-year-old child is able to do and, absent some demonstration to that effect, the trial court had no reason to presume that this child was able to do so. Further questioning of T.V. failed to even suggest that this child had such an understanding. Although, at the conclusion of the prosecutor's questioning, T.V. agreed that she had been told to tell "the truth" when she came to court, there had been no demonstration that she understood what "the truth" was.

Defense counsel's subsequent questioning of the child only served to demonstrate that the child remained confused:

"Q. [T,] do you remember when [the prosecutor] asked you if you understood what telling the truth was?

"A. Yes.

"Q. Did you shake your head back and forth like a no?

"A. (Witness nodded.)

"Q. You did shake your head back and forth from side to side?

"A. Yes.

"Q. [T.,] do you know what a lie is?

"A. No.

"Q. No? Is that what you are saying?

"A. (Witness nodded.)"

T.V. again indicated a lack of understanding of the concepts of truth and falsity. After these responses by T.V. to direct questions on the issue, there was no follow-up questioning by defense counsel or anyone else to demonstrate that the child was not, in fact, completely confused about the issue.

The trial judge concluded with the following line of questioning:

"Q: [T.,] I am going to ask you a question right now. What you said to me and to [the prosecutor] so far today, have you been telling the truth? She asked you about what the truth is. You have told the truth in this court to this Judge?

"A: Yes.

"Q: Everything you said now is the truth?

"A: (Witness nodded.)

"Q: Is there any question about that in your mind as to whether it is true or not?

"A: Yes.

"Q: There is a question?

"[Prosecutor]: I don't think she understood the question, Judge.

"Q: Okay. You told the truth as far as what happened?

"A. Yes.

"Q: All the questions you answered are—were the truth, right?

"A: Yes.

"Q: And you know what it is to tell the truth, you already answered that.

"A: Yes.

"Q: It is something that really happened, right?

"A: Yes.

"Q: Not something you make up, right?

"A: Yes.

"Q: So you are going to keep telling the truth now from here on, and what you are going to say is what really happened, right?

"A: Yes."

T.V.'s answers to the trial judge's questions might seem appropriate, if viewed in isolation. Given the confusion that T.V. had already demonstrated, however, her answers to the judge's questions failed to demonstrate that she did, in fact, have a general understanding of the concepts of truth and falsity.

Moreover, even if the judge's questioning somehow cured the shortcomings of the con-

fused testimony elicited from T.V. on the fourth Frazier factor, there was absolutely no testimony elicited from T.V. on the fifth mandatory *Frazier* factor, an appreciation of her responsibility to be truthful.

The trial judge had the discretion to find the child competent to testify only upon a consideration of all five of the Frazier factors. Because there was not adequate evidence before the trial court on all five factors, I agree with the principal opinion that the trial judge exceeded the scope of his discretion by finding that this child was competent to testify and I would reverse the judgment of the trial court on that basis.

Cases Relating to Chapter 9

Examination of Witnesses

UNITED STATES
v.
DRUMMOND

UNITED STATES COURT OF APPEAL, THIRD CIRCUIT

___ F.3d ___, 2003 U.S. App. LEXIS 14819 (2003)

OPINION: OPINION OF THE COURT

ROSENN, Circuit Judge:

This case raises the issue of whether the District Court committed reversible error when it denied the motion *in limine* of defendant, Alvin Drummond, to compel the Government's case agent to testify first at trial. The purpose of the motion was to prevent the possibility that the case agent might endeavor, when called as a witness, to conform his testimony to that of the preceding Government witness.

On reviewing the matter de novo, we hold that, under the circumstances of this case, the harm to the Government's case that would have resulted from granting Drummond's motion far outweighs any possible harm to Drummond from denying the motion. The District Court did not abuse its discretion in denying the motion. We affirm. Drummond timely appealed.

I

A jury convicted Drummond on two counts of cocaine distribution. The trial court sentenced him to a 327-month prison term. Before his trial began, he filed a Motion in Limine requesting that the Court order the Government to call its case agent, Detective Ronald Marzec, as its first witness at trial. The District Court denied the motion, holding that, under Federal Rule of Evidence 615, it was outside its authority to control the sequence of the Government's witnesses.

At trial, the Government first called Detective Marvin Charles Mailey, Jr., who testified that, while he was working undercover, Drummond sold him cocaine. Mailey testified to his close contact with Drummond, and unequivocally identified him as the person who sold him cocaine on multiple occasions. Agent Marzec then testified that he witnessed some of the drug-sales transactions between Drummond and Mailey from a distance, sometimes aided by binoculars. Marzec verified that the person present at these transactions was Drummond and, in that respect, his testimony was consistent with Mailey's. Drummond's defense was primarily based on a challenge to the prosecution's identification of Drummond. Drummond's witnesses testified, *inter alia*, that Drummond had brothers who closely resembled him, and that he often loaned one of his cars—the car in which Mailey and Marzec testified some of the drug sales had occurred in—to others.

Drummond now challenges the District Court's denial of his motion to compel Marzec to testify first.

II

Our review here is plenary. The District Court is alleged to have misinterpreted the Rules of Evidence. This is a question of whether it correctly understood the scope of its authority under the Rules. We review the District Court's refusal to require the case agent to testify first for abuse of discretion.

The District Court erred in its exclusive reliance on Rule 615. Rule 615 provides that a court shall order the sequestration of witnesses, upon the request of a party. However, Rule 615 does not permit the exclusion from trial of "an officer or employee of a party which is not a natural person designated as its representative by its attorney." Fed. R. Evid. 615(2). We have held that a case agent for the Government falls within this exemption, and ordinarily cannot be sequestered pursuant to Rule 615. United States v. Gonzalez, 918 F.2d 1129, 1138 (3d Cir. 1990). Thus, Marzec, as the case agent, could not have been validly sequestered under this Rule. The District Court apparently believed that Rule 615 somehow protected the Government against judicial intervention in its sequence of trial witnesses.

However, Rule 611(a) does not exempt case agents. It merely provides: "The court shall exercise reasonable control over the mode and order of interrogating witnesses and presenting evidence so as to (1) make the interrogation and presentation effective for the ascertainment of the truth, (2) avoid needless consumption of time, and (3) protect witnesses from harassment or undue embarrassment." Fed. R. Evid. 611(a). There is no obvious reason why the Rule 615 case agent exemption, designed to allow a representative of the Government to be in the courtroom at all times, would have any relevance to Rule 611.

Accordingly, other courts of appeals have held that case agents, ineligible for sequestration under Rule 615, might nonetheless be forced to testify first at trial, to avoid giving the prosecution unfair advantage. See United States v. Parodi, 703 F.2d 768, 774 (4th Cir. 1983). (permission for the investigating officer to remain in court at trial under Rule 615 may be conditioned on requirement that the officer be forced to testify first); In Re United States, 584 F.2d 666, 667 (5th Cir. 1978) ("The District Court may, in the exercise of its discretion under [Rule 611(a), conclude that the government should be required to present [its case agent's] testimony at an early stage of

the government's case."). Thus, the District Court's sole reliance on Rule 615 was error; the language of the Rules of Evidence and the persuasive holdings of our sister courts suggest that Rule 611(a) was applicable.

Drummond next urges that, in determining the standard under which a district court should evaluate a request to have the case agent testify first, we should adopt a rule promulgated by the Court of Appeals for the Fourth Circuit. Under its rule, a Government case agent "should ordinarily be called first so as to avoid giving the prosecution unfair advantage or the appearance that the prosecution is being favored." United States v. Frazier, 417 F.2d 1138, 1139 (4th Cir. 1969). That court went on to state that "this should be the order of presentation unless, in the judge's considered opinion, it would unduly break the continuity and seriously impair the coherence of the Government's proof." Id. At the opposite interpretive pole is the Court of Appeals for the First Circuit. In United States v. Machor, 879 F.2d 945, 954 (1st Cir. 1989), the court held that "good reason should exist before the court intervenes [as to the sequence of witnesses] in what is essentially a matter of trial strategy."

Drummond insists that regardless of the standard we choose, we must set forth some interpretive benchmark as to Rule 611 motions or any other motion regarding the sequencing of case agent witnesses. Because this court has not previously ruled on this issue, he asserts that we must remand to the District Court so that it can apply whatever standard we announce. However, Drummond was not entitled to have Marzec testify first. The Government has an interest in the order of its presentation, cf. (sequencing of witnesses is "essentially a matter of trial strategy"), and here the chief witness was Mailey. It would have been confusing to the jury and harmful to the Government case to force it to have its secondary witness testify first.

Furthermore, in Gonzalez, we observed that there was no prejudice in declining to sequester a case agent, because "[the defendant's] argument that [two Government] agents could coordinate their testimony does not pose a likelihood of prejudice since they had ample time before trial to do that, were they so inclined." 918 F.2d at 1138. Here, the two witnesses were both law enforcement officers, who had worked closely together throughout the investigation, and Drummond gave no other reason for his motion than to prevent deliberate conformity of testimony. If the witnesses were so inclined, and we have confidence that they were not, the two easily could have discussed their testimony before trial.

Therefore, the Government's interests in the orderly presentation of its case far outweighs the negligible possibility of prejudice to Drummond. Although this might be a more difficult issue if Marzec's testimony were not clearly subsidiary to Mailey's, or if there were non-Government witnesses involved for whom pre-trial coordination of testimony would be more difficult, in this case there was no justification for ordering Marzec to testify first. Moreover, Rule 611 only calls for an ordering of witnesses to maximize the "ascertainment of the truth." While there may be instances where the defense is hamstrung by its inability to sequester a case agent, and where it may be justified in requesting that the case agent to testify first, such a measure is not warranted here and would not further the trial's truth-seeking function. The judgment of conviction and sentence is affirmed.

Max Rosenn, Circuit Judge

PEOPLE
v.
MELENDEZ

Supreme Court of Colorado
102 P.3d 315, 2004 Colo. LEXIS 1006 (2004).

JUSTICE HOBBS delivered the Opinion of the Court.

EN BANC

We granted certiorari under C.A.R. 49 to review the court of appeals' decision in People v. Melendez, 80 P.3d 883 (Colo. App. 2003). The trial court precluded the testimony of a defense witness who allegedly violated a sequestration order. Because the record does not demonstrate an adequate inquiry by the trial court into whether the sequestration violation actually occurred and because preclusion of the witness's testimony was not harmless error, we affirm the judgment of the court of appeals.

I.

A jury convicted Jorge Melendez of multiple counts of sexual assault in the first and second degrees, aggravated incest, sexual assault on a child, sexual assault on a child-pattern of abuse, and sexual assault on a child under fifteen by one in a position of trust.

Melendez's former step-daughter, a seven-year-old girl, reported to her grandparents that he had sexually assaulted her on several occasions when he was married to her mother. Melendez defended on the basis that the child fabricated the allegations due to emotional problems with her mother, Melendez, and the divorce.

The trial court issued a sequestration order barring witnesses from the courtroom while other witnesses were testifying at trial, but made an exception for Detective Kenneth Brecko, a prosecution advisory witness.

The prosecution proceeded with testimony by Jodi Curtin, the child advocacy center interviewer who had interviewed the child after the police began investigating the allegations. The prosecution showed a videotape of Curtin's interview with the child to the jury. Curtin testified about her observations of the child's behavior during the interview, emphasizing a change in her demeanor when the alleged assaults were mentioned. On cross examination, defense counsel asked Curtin whether false allegations are more common in "high conflict" situations and she answered that they may be. She also said false accusations can occur in interviews but not often, in her experience.

After Curtin's testimony, Brecko, the detective assigned to the Melendez case, testified about general procedures used in investigating sexual assault cases.

* * *

[T]he defense presented testimony from its expert witness, Dr. Spiegle. Spiegle criticized the manner in which Curtin conducted her interview, opining that she had used inappropriately suggestive and leading questions with the child, which may have affected the reliability of the child's answers. He also testified about a study showing that some twenty-three percent of sexual assault allegations by children in the Denver area in a particular time period proved to be false. Spiegle also testified about his evaluation of the child's behavior as seen on the videotaped interview. His view was that various pre-allegation events in her life may have impacted her emotional wellbeing and behavior.

Following Spiegle's testimony, the defense called the director of the child advocacy center where Curtin worked, followed by the officer who had responded to the neglect call. This testimony concluded at the end of the business day.

The defense planned to call Robert Curry the next day. Curry, a friend of Melendez, would have testified to his observations of the child's relationship with Melendez, as well as her behavior with her mother. The trial court precluded Curry from testifying.

The trial court based its preclusion order solely on the prosecution's assertion that Brecko had reported seeing Curry in the courtroom during portions of Curtin's testimony and during bench discussions after the recess.

Defense counsel responded that he was not aware of Curry's presence in the courtroom. He argued that Curry's testimony would not have been tainted by any of Curtin's testimony that he may have overheard, because Curry was planning to testify to completely different matters. Defense counsel made the following offer of proof regarding Curry's testimony:

Judge, the expected nature of the testimony of Mr. Curry would essentially be that he has observed Mr. Melendez with the alleged victim in this case. He has seen him with the mother in this case. He has seen interactions between parent/child, Mr. Melendez and child. This is essentially the scope of his testimony.

Counsel also asserted that "having [Curry] stricken as a defense witness I believe is a really severe sanction in this case. I think that the Court could inquire or admonish or ask questions of Mr. Curry but not allowing him to testify I think would be a severe prejudice to the defendant. "

The prosecutor answered that Curtin testified about the child's behavior and the kinds of behavioral changes to be expected after sexual assaults. The prosecutor argued that this testimony could taint Curry's testimony because it suggested ways to show that the child was emotionally disturbed before she made her allegations. The prosecutor also noted that Brecko had subsequently told her that he had seen Curry talking to the defendant during a break and it sounded as if they were discussing the case. The trial court delayed ruling on the issue until the following morning.

The next day, defense counsel and the prosecutor made essentially the same arguments. The court precluded Curry's testimony, ruling that,

considering argument of both the defense and the prosecution, noting the length of time the defendant (sic) was in the courtroom, paying particular attention that the witness was in the courtroom during the testimony of Ms. Curtin, the Court is going to not allow the witness to be called for the defense.

The trial court did not ask any questions of Brecko, Curry, or Melendez concerning the alleged sequestration violation.

Defense counsel rested his case after Melendez testified. The jury convicted Melendez on several counts.

On appeal, Melendez argued, inter alia, that the trial court abused its discretion by precluding Curry's testimony and that the error was not harmless. We agree and affirm the court of appeals' judgment.

II.

Because the record does not demonstrate an adequate inquiry by the trial court into whether the sequestration violation actually occurred, and because preclusion of the witness's testimony was not harmless error, we affirm the judgment of the court of appeals.

A. Standard of Review

In proper circumstances, the trial court may sequester witnesses, find that a witness has violated the sequestration order, and impose sanctions for the sequestration violation. See People v. Wood, 743 P.2d 422, 429-30 (Colo. 1987); People v. P.R.G., 729 P.2d 380, 382 (Colo. App. 1986). We review the trial court's determinations for abuse of discretion. People v. Stewart, 55 P.3d 107, 122 (Colo. 2002). If an abuse of discretion occurred, we must then determine whether the error is reversible. See Salcedo v. People, 999 P.2d 833, 841 (Colo. 2000).

B. Sequestration Order Violations

Trial courts shall impose sequestration orders on witnesses at the request of either party. Martin v. Porak, 638 P.2d 853, 854 (Colo. App. 1981); CRE 615. The court may order witnesses to remain outside the courtroom and not discuss the case with each other. People v. Brinson, 739 P.2d 897, 899 (Colo. App. 1987).

* * *

Before it considers sanctions for a sequestration violation, the trial court must first determine that a violation has actually occurred and prejudice will result from unrestricted admission of the testimony. See Wood, 743 P.2d at 429-30.

Sanctions for violations of sequestration orders fall into three general categories: (1) citing the witness for contempt; (2) permitting counsel or the court to comment to the jury on the witness's noncompliance as a reflection on his or her credibility; and (3) precluding the witness's testimony. P.R.G., 729 P.2d at 382; see also J. Weinstein & M. Berger, 4 Weinstein's Federal Evidence § 615.07[2] (2d ed. 2004). Additionally, mistrial is a possible but rarely justified sanction. P.R.G., 729 P.2d at 382.

Disqualifying witness testimony is a severe sanction to be imposed only after careful consideration.

* * *

We have allowed prosecution witnesses to testify despite the allegation of a sequestration violation. See Wood, 743 P.2d at 429 (finding no prejudice to defendant requiring exclusion of witness for sequestration violation); cf. People v. Gomez, 632 P.2d 586, 594 (Colo. 1981) (approving trial court's limitation on scope of testimony by witness who violated sequestration order).

We have not had occasion for over one hundred years to consider the implications of precluding a defense witness from testifying due to a sequestration violation. See Vickers v. People, 31 Colo. 491, 73 P. 845 (Colo. 1903).

Sanctioning a defense witness for violating a sequestration order implicates important rights of the criminal defendant. See Washington v. Texas, 388 U.S. 14, 19, 18 L. Ed. 2d 1019, 87 S. Ct. 1920 (1967) ("The right to offer the testimony of witnesses . . . is in plain terms the right to present a defense, the right to present the defendant's version of the facts as well as the prosecution's to the [fact finder] so it may decide where the truth lies."); People v. Chastain, 733 P.2d 1206, 1212 (Colo. 1987) (noting that a defendant's right to offer testimony at trial is a "fundamental element of due process of law") (internal citations omitted).

While fundamental, the right to present defense evidence is not absolute. A defendant must "make some plausible showing of how [the] testimony would have been both material and favorable to his defense."

* * *

Nevertheless, cumulative evidence that may corroborate the defendant's own statement should ordinarily be admitted. See People v. Green, 38 Colo. App. 165, 553 P.2d 839, 840 (Colo. App. 1976) ("It is manifest that [evidence which is cumulative to some degree] should not be prohibited when it is sought to be introduced to corroborate [the defendant's] statement, which . . . may be, and often is, looked upon by the jury with some degree of suspicion.") (internal quotations omitted); Towner v. State, 685 P.2d 45, 50 (Wyo. 1984) (the only evidence offered to corroborate defendant's testimony was admissible even though duplicative to defendant's own statement).

C. Trial Court's Duty of Inquiry

The trial court has a duty of diligent inquiry into allegations of a sequestration violation. The trial court must first determine whether the violation actually occurred and, if so, whether prejudice will result from allowing the testimony.

* * *

In 1986, the Colorado Court of Appeals . . . set forth three principal factors for trial court consideration in determining a sanction. P.R.G., 729 P.2d at 382. First, the trial court must consider the involvement, or lack thereof, of a party or counsel in the violation of the order by the witness. Id. Second, the trial court should consider the witness's actions and state of mind in his or her violation of the sequestration order, and whether the violation was inadvertent or deliberate. Id. Finally, the trial court should consider the subject matter of the violation in conjunction with the substance of the disobedient witness's testimony and if the testimony is unrelated in substance to the violation of the sequestration order, the court enjoys wide discretion in its ability to allow the witness to testify. Id. We agree, but modify the first factor to require evidence of the party's or counsel's consent, connivance, procurement, or knowledge regarding the violation before a sanction can be imposed against that party. We base adoption of these factors, as modified, on our review of the case law.

* * *

D. Application to This Case

In the case before us, the trial court did not make an adequate inquiry into whether the sequestration violation actually occurred. It simply accepted the prosecution's assertions. The record contains no verification that Curry was actually in the courtroom, let alone any facts regarding the length of his presence or what he heard. Similarly, the record is devoid of any indication that the trial court considered the factors applicable to the choice of appropriate sanction.

* * *

E. Not Harmless Error

The defendant objected to the preclusion of Curry's testimony. Defense counsel argued to the court that: 1) an inquiry could be made to determine the severity of the violation; 2) other sanctions might be imposed, such as admonishment; and 3) that exclusion of Curry would be prejudicial to his client.

We do not require that parties use "talismanic language" to preserve particular arguments for appeal, but the trial court must be presented with an adequate opportunity to make findings of fact and conclusions of law on any issue before we will review it. [Citations omitted.]

Here, defense counsel offered the trial court an adequate opportunity to commence a sufficient inquiry into the violation and the possible prejudice resulting from its exclusion order. Curry's was the only evidence offered to corroborate the defendant's own testimony, as well as the only evidence offered that would link the expert's testimony about factors leading to false allegations with the case at hand. Our review of the record reveals that Curry's evidence would have materially assisted Melendez's case.

A defendant has a fundamental constitutional right to present his or her version of the facts and favorable evidence. See Washington, 388 U.S. at 19. Here, a constitutional error was properly preserved for appeal, and the constitutional harmless error standard applies. See Blecha v. People, 962 P.2d 931, 942 (Colo. 1998). We cannot say beyond a reasonable doubt that the exclusion of Curry's testimony did not contribute to the guilty verdict.

III.

Accordingly, we affirm the court of appeals' judgment. [Reversing the convictions.]

UNITED STATES
v.
SPIVEY

United States Court of Appeals,
Seventh Circuit
841 F.2d 799 (1988)

Bauer, Chief Judge, Ripple and Manion, Circuit Judges.

BAUER, Chief Judge.

Anthony Spivey appeals from his convictions for conspiracy to possess and actual possession of goods stolen from an interstate shipment, knowing that the goods were stolen. 18 U.S.C. §§ 371, 659. He contends on appeal that the district court violated his sixth amendment right to confront witnesses against him by limiting the cross-examination of his co-conspirator, and that the district court's treatment of his trial counsel deprived him of a fair trial. We reject both claims and affirm Spivey's conviction.

I.

A.

Spivey and Albert "Rick" Crumble were long-time friends. Both men frequented a tavern on Chicago's West Side called "The Karate Club," which was owned by the family of their mutual friends David, Randy, and Tom Johnson. Spivey apparently worked sporadically as a volunteer bouncer at the club. In September, 1984, Crumble was a truck driver for Cargo, Incorporated, a Chicago trucking company.

On Friday, September 21, 1984, Crumble invited Spivey to join him in looking for a trailerload of goods to steal. Spivey accepted the invitation, so Crumble went to work that night, picked up his tractor, then picked up Spivey. After Crumble delivered one load of goods, the two men drove around the Santa Fe rail yard in Chicago looking for a trailer to steal. Finding nothing that suited their fancy, they drove to the Burlington rail yard. There they found an overseas trailer, which Crumble attached to his tractor.

Crumble and Spivey drove the trailer back to Cargo's yard, parked in a secluded spot, and broke the trailer's seal. Inside was a thief's dream: Sharp Electronics calculators, turntables, speakers, receivers, and cassette decks. Spivey and Crumble agreed that it was a good load, then began contemplating what to do with it. Spivey contacted a fence of stolen goods, who met with Spivey and Crumble, then left with Spivey to look for another fence, to whom they would offer the load. After nothing came of that idea, Spivey and the fence drove to a warehouse to see if they could hide the stolen goods there. The warehouse door was too low for the trailer, however, and they went back to tell Crumble the bad news. Apparently, they left the trailer at Cargo's yard.

On Saturday, September 22, 1984, Crumble went back to work at Cargo, taking Spivey with him. After work, the two men went to the Karate Club Lounge, where they told David Johnson and another friend, Pierre Cameron, of their theft, and recruited Johnson and Cameron to help unload the trailer. The four men then returned to Cargo, got the trailer of stolen goods, stole another empty trailer marked "AVAZ" from the yard across the street from Cargo, and began transferring the goods from one trailer to the other. The four men unloaded all of the Sharp stereo equipment and calculators from the overseas trailer until they reached copying equipment. At that point, the men moved the AVAZ trailer, now loaded with the stolen stereo equipment and calculators, to a secluded spot. Next, they loaded David Johnson's truck with some of the stolen goods, which each would try to sell individually.

Late Sunday or early Monday, during the night of September 23 and 24, 1984, Crumble moved the AVAZ trailer, first to a restaurant parking lot in Chicago and then back to the Cargo yard, while David Johnson and Spivey followed in Johnson's pickup. At the Cargo yard, the three men loaded more of the loot into Johnson's truck and departed. Unfortunately for them, another Cargo employee who was waiting for the return of his tractor saw Crumble, Spivey, and Johnson leave in Johnson's pickup.

B.

FBI Agent Thomas Dillon, brought into the investigation by the Chicago police, spoke to Crumble about the theft on September 28, 1984. Crumble denied everything in a lengthy, elaborate statement, all of it lies. On October 4, 1984, the Chicago police arrested Crumble. While in custody, he asked to speak to Agent Dillon. This time Crumble admitted his participation in the theft and gave Dillon the names of several others he said were involved in taking, unloading, and fencing the merchandise. He also agreed to cooperate with the government. In November, 1984, Crumble was indicted on federal charges of theft and conspiracy. On March 8, 1985, he pled guilty pursuant to a plea agreement and the court, aware that Crumble was cooperating with the government, gave him a suspended sentence of five years plus five years probation, the first six months to be spent in custody.

Spivey admitted his participation in the theft in a written statement taken by Agent Dillon on February 22, 1985. Spivey's statement was substantially similar to Crumble's confession, except that Spivey said he thought that the theft of the goods and the subsequent transfer into the empty AVAZ container all may have occurred on Saturday (and not Friday) night, September 22, 1984, although he was not sure. Spivey was indicted in September, 1985. At trial, he proffered an alibi defense. Randy Johnson, one of the Johnson brothers, testified that Spivey was working at the Karate Club Lounge on Saturday, September 22, 1984. Johnson said he remembered that night because there was a large birthday party held that evening for one of the club's regulars. Thomas Johnson, the club's manager, testified, however, that that birthday party had been cancelled. Other members of the Johnson family testified that Spivey was working at the club on the night of the theft. The key witness for the government was, of course, Crumble.

II.

A.

Spivey first argues that the district court violated his sixth amendment right to con-

front witnesses against him by terminating his cross-examination of Crumble before he was able to question Crumble about prior convictions and other bad acts. The government called Crumble to the stand on the afternoon of January 14, 1987. On direct examination, Crumble testified about the events of September 22 through 24, 1984. He also testified that he had pled guilty and served a jail term for his role in the theft, that he was testifying under a grant of immunity, and that he had lied to Agent Dillon on September 28, 1984 when he denied his involvement in the theft.

Defense counsel's cross-examination of Crumble lasted the remainder of the afternoon and early evening. During the cross-examination, defense counsel elicited the following information: that Crumble would not have testified unless granted immunity; that Crumble's September 28, 1984 statement to Agent Dillon was "all lies"; that Crumble admitted his participation in the crime to the FBI only after the Chicago police had arrested and jailed him; that the FBI never charged Crumble with the crime of giving a false statement; that after the government informed the court of his cooperation, Crumble was sentenced to only six months of incarceration; that the government had interviewed Crumble three or four times for up to seven hours before trial; and that during these interviews, Crumble overcame his confusion about when the theft actually occurred.

Late in the day, after defense counsel repeatedly asked Crumble whether he had ever attempted to sell any of the stolen merchandise at the Karate Club, to which Crumble repeatedly answered "no," counsel informed the court in a sidebar that he had an additional half-hour of cross-examination concerning prior bad acts. It was approximately 5:20 P.M. Although the government asked the court to limit defense counsel's questioning concerning Crumble's prior acts, the court refused to do so, stating that it was "going to allow a lot of latitude on the cross-examination of [Crumble] in light of the grant of immunity and other matters brought to the attention of the jury." The court then denied defense counsel's request to continue Crumble's cross-examination the next morning.

Defense counsel then questioned Crumble for twenty minutes concerning his second statement to Agent Dillon, after which counsel pointed out that it was 5:40 and that he was now going to delve into whether Crumble had lied to the FBI in other earlier investigations. The court ruled that counsel could inquire into these areas but that he could not prove any lies with extrinsic evidence. Defense counsel then twice more asked to continue the cross-examination until the following morning, but the court refused, stating that "you cannot move as slowly as you are and then say you're not getting enough time."

Defense counsel then questioned Crumble about statements made to the FBI in May, 1984 regarding a trailer Crumble owned in which some stolen Craig radios were found. Crumble admitted on the stand that he knew of the theft of the radios, but said he was not involved in the theft. He also admitted that he had lied to the FBI about his knowledge of the theft. Defense counsel then started taking Crumble through the May, 1984 statement line by line, asking which statements were and were not lies. The court sustained a government objection, advising counsel that "the jury has heard enough about this conversation. . . . Move to another area of inquiry, if any." After informing the court that he had an additional half-hour to forty-five minutes worth of cross-examination, defense counsel proceeded to ask more questions about the Craig merchandise theft. After a number of such questions, the court sua sponte terminated the cross-examination. The following morning, defense counsel arrived after the 10:00 A.M. starting time, and the court refused to hear his motion to reopen the cross-examination of Crumble. The jury subsequently convicted Spivey.

B.

The sixth amendment guarantees a defendant the right to cross-examine hostile witnesses. Davis v. Alaska, 415 U.S. 308, 315, 39 L. Ed. 2d 347, 94 S. Ct. 1105 (1973). Thus, a defendant must be granted the opportunity to expose facts from which a defendant could argue that the witness is incredible, Delaware v. Van Arsdall, 475 U.S. 673, 106 S. Ct. 1431, 1435, 89 L. Ed. 2d 674 (1986) (citing Davis v. Alaska, 415 U.S. at

316-17), and we have stated that defense counsel should be afforded every opportunity to effectively cross-examine a government witness. United States v. Castro, 788 F.2d 1240, 1244 (7th Cir. 1986).

This does not mean, however, that the right to cross-examine is unlimited. "The Confrontation Clause guarantees an opportunity for effective cross-examination, not cross-examination that is effective in whatever way, and to whatever extent, the defense might wish." Delaware v. Fensterer, 474 U.S. 15, 106 S. Ct. 292, 295, 88 L. Ed. 2d 15 (1986) (emphasis in original). Hence, the trial court has discretion to impose reasonable limitations on cross-examination based upon concerns about, inter alia, harassment, confusion of issues, and repetitive or marginally relevant interrogation. Delaware v. Van Arsdall, 106 S. Ct. at 1435; see also United States v. Silva, 781 F.2d 106, 110 (7th Cir. 1986). The question on review is whether the jury had sufficient information to make a discriminating appraisal of the witness's motive or bias. United States v. Rodgers, 755 F.2d 533, 548 (7th Cir.), cert. denied, 473 U.S. 907, 105 S. Ct. 3532, 87 L. Ed. 2d 656 (1985).

In this case, we believe the answer to that question is an obvious affirmative. Before the court terminated the Crumble cross-examination, defense counsel exposed facts showing virtually every possible motive or bias Crumble might have for testifying against Spivey. Defense counsel elicited that Crumble would not have testified but for his grant of immunity, that Crumble cooperated with the FBI only after he was arrested by Chicago police, that thereafter Crumble's state criminal case disappeared, that the government had interviewed Crumble extensively before trial, and that, during these interviews, Crumble crystallized in his mind the times and dates of the theft. Defense counsel also exposed that Crumble's first statement to the FBI was "all lies," and that Crumble had lied to the FBI during the 1984 investigation of the stolen Craig merchandise. Together, this was sufficient information for the jury to make a discriminating appraisal of Crumble's possible motives and biases. That Spivey was not able to pursue certain other avenues of impeachment does not change this conclusion.

Thus, the district court's termination of defense counsel's cross-examination of Crumble did not violate Spivey's sixth amendment rights. Defense counsel had cross-examined Crumble for most of the afternoon and evening. It was only after defense counsel backtracked, persistently asked improper questions, and repeatedly revised his estimates of how much cross-examination he had left that the court interceded. Even at the court's prodding, defense counsel refused to move on to new areas of inquiry. When it became clear that defense counsel was stalling, the court terminated the cross-examination. Cutting off the repetitive interrogation was within the court's discretion. Indeed, our review of the record indicates that the district court allowed defense counsel a good deal of latitude in his questioning of Crumble, and carefully weighed the consequences of terminating the cross-examination before doing so. In short, there was no sixth amendment violation.

III.

Spivey next argues that, by terminating defense counsel's cross-examination of Crumble and another witness, Agent Dillon, and by making certain other statements to defense counsel during the trial, the court destroyed the credibility of Spivey's attorney in the eyes of the jury and deprived Spivey of a fair trial. A judge, of course, "should be and be seen to be even-handed." United States v. Kwiat, 817 F.2d 440, 470 (7th Cir. 1987). Because "the influence of the trial judge on the jury is necessarily and properly of great weight," United States v. Dellinger, 472 F.2d 340, 386 (7th Cir.), cert. denied, 410 U.S. 970, 35 L. Ed. 2d 706, 93 S. Ct. 1443 (1972),

"the judge should reserve extensive and harsh criticism of counsel for times when the jury is absent," Kwiat, 817 F.2d at 447. Where the trial judge's remarks effectively destroy counsel's credibility in the eyes of the jury, we will reverse a criminal conviction. United States v. Blakey, 607 F.2d 779, 788 (7th Cir. 1979). Our review of the record, however, indicates that no such thing occurred in this case.

Spivey argues that the court's termination of defense counsel's cross-examinations of both Crumble and Dillon, coupled with other, for the most part unidentified, remarks addressed to defense counsel destroyed counsel's credibility. We disagree. We have already found no fault with the court's handling of the cross-examination of Crumble, and Spivey does not argue on appeal that the court's termination of defense counsel's cross-examination of Dillon was improper. As to the other remarks, Spivey points to none that fall outside the court's discretion to regulate the conduct of the trial, which, at certain points, requires the court to take positions and remind counsel, sometimes repeatedly, to ask proper questions. Kwiat, 817 F.2d at 447; see also Blakey, 607 F.2d at 788. Obviously, some of defense counsel's tactics taxed the court's patience below, but the record does not reveal any overt display of contempt for the defense that occurred in the presence of the jury. What our review shows is a no-nonsense judge properly controlling the tempo of the trial before him. In short, the court was doing its job, not prejudicing the jury.

For the foregoing reasons, the defendant-appellant's conviction is
AFFIRMED.

Cases Relating to Chapter 10

Privileges

ST. CLAIR

v.

COMMONWEALTH

Supreme Court of Kentucky
174 S.W.3d 474, 2005
Ky. LEXIS 334 (2005)

OPINION OF THE COURT BY CHIEF
JUSTICE LAMBERT
REVERSING AND REMANDING

FACTS

Appellant, Michael D. St. Clair, was convicted of two counts of receiving stolen property over $ 100, criminal attempt to commit murder, second-degree arson, and capital kidnapping. He was sentenced to death for the kidnapping of Frank Brady, during which Brady was murdered. Appellant waived his right to jury sentencing on the non-capital charges, and agreed to a sentence of twenty years for attempted murder, twenty years for second-degree arson, and five years on each count of receiving stolen property over $ 100, for a total of fifty years. Appellant now appeals to this Court as a matter of right.

This is not the first time this particular defendant is before this Court. In February of 1992, a Bullitt County Grand Jury indicted Appellant for the Capital Murder of Frank Brady. He was tried and convicted in August, and sentenced to death in September of 1998. This Court in a recent decision, St. Clair v. Commonwealth, (hereinafter "St. Clair I"), reversed and remanded for a new penalty phase hearing on Appellant's death sentence.

Prior to trial in Hardin County, this Court rendered St. Clair v. Roark, (St. Clair II), in which St. Clair's petition for extraordinary relief to prevent his prosecution for capital kidnapping in Hardin County was denied. In large part a complete recitation of the facts is contained in St. Clair I and St. Clair II, and is relied upon to illustrate the facts relevant to this appeal.

According to the evidence, Appellant escaped from Oklahoma authorities in September of 1991 while awaiting final sentencing for two Oklahoma murder convictions. St. Clair and Dennis Gene Reese stole a pickup truck from a jail employee and fled from the jail in Durant, Oklahoma. The pickup truck eventually ran out of gas and Reese and St. Clair stole another pickup truck, a handgun, and some ammunition from the home of Vernon Stephens and headed for the suburbs of Dallas, Texas. St. Clair's wife at the time, Bylynn St. Clair n4 ("Bylynn"), met with her husband and Reese in Texas, and provided them with money, clothing, and other items. Reese was arrested several months later in Las Vegas, Nevada, and confessed to his involvement in the Kentucky events detailed below.

According to Reese, after escaping from jail in Oklahoma, he and St. Clair traveled to Colorado where they kidnapped Timothy Keeling and stole Keeling's pickup truck. Keeling was later murdered in New Mexico. St. Clair and Reese proceeded to drive Keeling's truck to New Orleans, Louisiana, then through Arkansas and Tennessee before arriving at a rest stop in southern Hardin County, Kentucky. While in Hardin County, they decided to steal Frank Brady's late model pickup truck. They kidnapped Brady and drove him from Hardin County to Bullitt County where St. Clair shot and killed Brady. St. Clair and Reese then returned to Hardin County and set fire to Keeling's truck.

Witnesses to the arson gave the Kentucky State Police a description of the Brady truck seen near the location where Keeling's truck was on fire. Based on that description, Trooper Herbert Bennett stopped Reese and St. Clair while they were still driving Brady's truck through Hardin County. St. Clair fired two shots at Trooper Bennett, one of which penetrated the radiator of the police cruiser. A high-speed chase followed, but Reese and St. Clair escaped when Bennett's cruiser became disabled. Reese was arrested two weeks later in Las Vegas and waived extradition to Kentucky. St. Clair was arrested about two months later in Hugo, Oklahoma.

On December 20, 1991, St. Clair was indicted for two counts of receiving stolen property, criminal attempt to commit murder, and second-degree arson. On January 17, 1992, the Hardin County Grand Jury indicted St. Clair for capital kidnapping. On June 19, 1998, the Commonwealth filed its Notice of Intent to Seek Death Penalty. St. Clair was convicted in February of 2001 of the Capital Kidnapping of Frank Brady, and he was sentenced to death. Additional facts will be presented as necessary. St. Clair argues that his wife Bylynn was improperly allowed to testify to four privileged conversations, and that those conversations should have been excluded by his assertion of the marital privilege under KRE 504. When the statements were made, St. Clair and Bylynn were married.

I. Marital Privilege

The first contested statement given by Bylynn was that when she met St. Clair in Texas before St. Clair reached Kentucky, she hugged him and felt something hard on his belt. Over St. Clair's objection, she testified that when she asked if he had a gun, she testified that he, St. Clair, told her he took a gun off that old man whose house he had broken into (the home of Vernon Stephens in Oklahoma).

Bylynn's second statement concerned her meeting St. Clair in Oklahoma at Frost's Farm in December of 1991, the night before he was arrested. It was there that St. Clair stated to Bylynn that St. Clair and Reese had to leave their belongings and that they burned a truck. St. Clair told Bylynn that he returned to Oklahoma by riding with truck drivers. St. Clair objected and moved for a mistrial on the grounds that this latter statement had not been included in the Commonwealth's notice, and that it was privileged under the marital privilege.

Bylynn's third statement at trial concerned a telephone conversation between her and St. Clair. She testified that St. Clair called her from Louisiana and that Reese was in the bathroom while he was calling. The Commonwealth then elicited that St. Clair told Bylynn that he had to leave some of his things behind in the truck, and that he said something about being in Louisiana. St. Clair objected on the grounds that he was not provided notice of the Commonwealth's intention to introduce evidence relating to his travel to Louisiana, and that it was not an unexpected answer since the Commonwealth asked her if St. Clair had ever said anything about being in Louisiana. The Commonwealth responded that this testimony was not new information since Bylynn had testified to it at the Bullitt County trial.

Bylynn's fourth statement is that St. Clair told her that he was in Louisiana, and that he had told her he had been in Oklahoma for a few weeks before he saw her in December at a friend's house in Durant County, Oklahoma. She stated that he had told her that the Oklahoma State Bureau of Investigation (OSBI) had searched the place, but that he was hiding under some hay and they never saw him. The Commonwealth then asked Bylynn how long St. Clair had told her he had been in Oklahoma and the date of the conversation when he did so. She responded that it was December 17, 1991, the day before his arrest. This testimony was elicited to contradict Reese's anticipated testimony that St. Clair had arrived at his farm on October 1, 1991.

St. Clair objected to the testimony, and the trial court overruled the objection on the grounds that the Commonwealth could cross-examine Bylynn about any subject to which she had previously testified. St. Clair now argues that the introduction of this testimony violated due process, his right to a fair trial and that Bylynn's testimony was admitted in violation of the marital privilege. St. Clair also argues that at the time of trial, KRS 421.210(1) was applicable and allowed one spouse to prohibit the other from testifying to communications made during their marriage, which are confidential in nature. Finally, St. Clair argues that Bylynn's statements that incriminated St. Clair were also inadmissible since they violated RCr 7.24(1).

The Commonwealth contends that the marital privilege does not apply in this case for two reasons. First, the Commonwealth argues that Bylynn and St. Clair were involved in joint criminal activity under KRE 504(c)(1). It posits that no privilege is applicable since the communications testified to occurred during St. Clair's escape from the Bryan County Jail in Oklahoma and that Bylynn provided him with items which he later used to kidnap and kill Brady. Second, the Commonwealth argues that these communications were not confidential because they were made in the presence of Reese.

KRE 504 contains a spousal testimonial privilege, KRE 504(a), a confidential marital communications privilege, KRE 504(b), and exceptions to those privileges in KRE 504(c). Both privileges are designed to protect and enhance the marital relationship at the expense of otherwise useful evidence. KRE 504(c)(1) codifies preexisting law, KRS 421.210(1). KRE 504 provides:

(a) Spousal testimony. The spouse of a party has a privilege to refuse to testify against the party as to events occurring after the date of their marriage. A party has a privilege to prevent his or her spouse from testifying against the party as to events occurring after the date of their marriage.

(b) Marital communications. An individual has a privilege to refuse to testify and to prevent another from testifying to any confidential communication made by the individual to his or her spouse during their marriage. The privilege may be asserted only by the

individual holding the privilege or by the holder's guardian, conservator, or personal representative. A communication is confidential if it is made privately by an individual to his or her spouse and is not intended for disclosure to any other person.

(c) Exceptions. There is no privilege under this rule:

(1) In any criminal proceeding in which sufficient evidence is introduced to support a finding that the spouses conspired or acted jointly in the commission of the crime charged;

(2) * * *

(3) In any proceeding in which the spouses are adverse parties.

KRE 504(a) and (b) changed the spousal privilege from KRS 421.210(1) in two significant respects. First, the testimonial privilege in KRE 504(a) was expanded to enable a party spouse to preclude a witness spouse from testifying against him. Second, the marital communications privilege in KRE 504(b) was narrowed by defining the term "confidential" to require that the communication was not intended for disclosure to any other person, i.e., there must have been a positive expectation of confidentiality.

The issue we must first address is whether subsection (c)(1) applies in this situation. We begin our analysis by examining the plain language of KRE 504(c)(1). The plain language of the exception states that there must be "sufficient evidence" to "support a finding that the spouse conspired or acted jointly in the commission of the crime charged." Plainly, this exception to the privilege applies only if each spouse has contributed to or participated in the crime charged. In Gill v. Commonwealth, this Court discussed the application of the marital communications privilege and its exceptions as they existed under KRS 421.210(1). In Gill, testimony of one spouse was held not privileged where both spouses were accused of being *particeps criminis* with the wife having been indicted for the same crime that her husband had been convicted of committing.

In this case, Bylynn facilitated St. Clair's flight after his prison escape, but there was no evidence that Bylynn conspired or acted jointly in the commission of the crimes with which St. Clair was charged (two counts of receiving stolen property over $ 100, criminal attempt to commit murder, second-degree arson, or capital kidnapping).

This Court has reviewed the record extensively. Statements two and three were undoubtedly made outside the presence of Reese or any other person. Bylynn acknowledged on the stand that statement two occurred in private when she and St. Clair were in a barn loft. She also confirmed that statement three occurred during a phone conversation with St. Clair while Reese was out of the room. As stated in KRE 504(b), "[a] communication is confidential if it is made privately by an individual to his or her spouse and is not intended for disclosure to any other person." St. Clair was running from the authorities, and confided certain information to his wife. His statements implicated him in various crimes, and their sensitive nature combined with the circumstances of their disclosure rendered them confidential. For these reasons statements two and three fall within the ambit of a confidential communication, and should have been excluded by virtue of the marital privilege.

Upon review, there is some doubt as to the confidential nature of statements one and four. Statement one took place at a fair, and apparently was made in full view of the public eye. Moreover, based on the testimony of Bylynn, it is unclear whether St. Clair was alone or with Reese at the time of this statement. However, confidential statements need not be given behind closed doors to retain their confidential character. A hushed or whispered statement from one spouse to another may be considered confidential depending on the circumstances of its disclosure. In this case, the record is insufficient to make a definitive determination as to the confidential nature of statement one. Therefore, upon remand the trial judge should hear additional evidence regarding the circumstances of statement one and make a factual finding.

Whether statement four was confidential is equally unclear. At trial, Bylynn seemed to relate the statement four disclosure to the same telephone conversation in which the statement three disclosure was made. If this is the case, statement four would enjoy the same privileged status as statement three. However, review of the record leaves the Court with enough doubt to require a hearing on the statement four issue.

Accordingly, statements two and three were privileged and should have been excluded at trial. As to statements one and four, a hearing should be held on remand to determine their status.

The admission of the privileged statements was prejudicial because the Commonwealth used this testimony to corroborate Reese's testimony that St. Clair was the ringleader and the shooter. Bylynn was a critical witness as her testimony repeated the details of the jail escape and that St. Clair had stolen the alleged murder weapon. It revealed that she felt a gun on Appellant's person when she met him in Dallas, and her testimony contradicted St. Clair's defense that he had never been in Kentucky because he told her he had burned a truck in Kentucky. Bylynn's testimony was crucial because it contained the only admission by St. Clair of guilt, and one of a few pieces of evidence that placed St. Clair in Kentucky at the time of the kidnapping and murder. Consequently, the admission of Bylynn's testimony was prejudicial error and retrial is required.

II. Jury Instructions

III. Various Other Claims

For the forgoing reasons, we reverse and remand.

DISSENTING OPINION BY JUSTICE WINTERSHEIMER

I must respectfully dissent from the majority opinion because there was no error on the part of the trial judge in permitting the testimony of the ex-wife concerning communications between the accused and her during his escape and other patently criminal activities. The majority opinion construes the marital privilege too broadly.

The marital communications privilege does not apply in this situation because the communications involved aiding St. Clair in patently criminal activity and because the communications sought to be privileged were likely intended to be shared with a third party. Furthermore, the wife's testimony has substantial probative value thereby outweighing the minimal prejudicial effect.

Thus, the majority has interpreted the confidential marital communications privilege too broadly. Privileges are to be interpreted narrowly. [Citation omitted.] Porter, supra, states that "privileges 'must be strictly construed and accepted only to the very limited extent that permitting a refusal to testify or excluding relevant evidence has a public good transcending the normally predominate principle of utilizing all rational means for ascertaining truth." 986 F.2d at 1019 citing Trammel v. United States, 445 U.S. 40, 50, 100 S. Ct. 906, 63 L. Ed. 2d 186 (1980); United States v. Nixon, 418 U.S. 683, 709-10, 94 S. Ct. 3090, 41 L. Ed. 2d 1039 (1974).

In concluding that statements two and three were confidential, the majority opinion fails to analyze whether the information shared between St. Clair and his wife were "not intended for disclosure to any other person." KRE 504(b). Because St. Clair and Reese escaped and stole a pickup truck together, it is reasonable to infer that they made plans on securing the means to continue their escape. For instance, communications to the wife concerning the need for clothing, money, and other items would be expected to be non confidential because St. Clair would tell Reese from where aid to their escape would come. Accordingly, statements from St. Clair to his wife concerning his and Reese's location, future location, and plans would also fail the "not intended for disclosure to another person" test because Bylynn was a source of aid to them.

KRE 504(c)(1) states that the privilege is excepted "in any criminal proceeding in which sufficient evidence is introduced to support a finding that the spouses conspired or acted jointly in the commission of the crime charged." The majority interprets this to mean that Bylynn must have directly aided in receiving stolen property, criminal attempt to commit murder, or second-degree arson. It is arguable whether aiding and abetting the escape results in conspiring for the purposes of rendering the privilege. Gill v. Commonwealth, 374 S.W.2d 848 (Ky. 1964) states, "when husband and wife are co-conspirators, or when the evidence justifies such a conclusion, a declaration of the husband or wife at the time of the act in question is not privileged". Certainly, under the situation described in these facts, the wife became some part of the criminal activities by her assistance. Furthermore, this analysis is more consistent with the 6th Circuit's interpretation of the joint participation exception to the confidential marital communications privilege. See United States v. Sims, 755 F.2d 1239 (6th Cir. 1985) (Exception to privilege for confidential marital communications arising out of joint criminal activity exists for conversations that pertain to patently illegal activity.). Even though this part of the analysis may be a close call in this case, the communications were not confidential.

The majority opinion states that the evidence of the wife's testimony would be prejudicial. This analysis is incorrect under KRE 403. KRE 403 disallows evidence whose prejudicial value outweighs the probative value. Because her testimony corroborated some other evidence, and especially because her testimony was the critical key to place St. Clair in Kentucky at the time of the criminal commissions, it has significant probative value. Accordingly, the trial judge did not err in admitting the testimony after disallowing the confidential marital communications privilege to apply.

Therefore, there was no confidential marital communications privilege here. The trial judge properly instructed the jury. I would affirm the conviction in all respects.

Graves and Scott, JJ., join this dissent.

STATE
v.
DeMARCO

275 N.J. Super. 311,
646 A.2d 431 (1994)

Before Judges Gaulkin, D'Annunzio and Wallace:

PER CURIAM

The issue is whether the State may compel discovery of reports prepared by the defendant's expert witness for other clients in unrelated cases. The issue arises on the appeal of the expert witness, pursuant to leave granted, from an order denying his motion to quash a subpoena. We now reverse that order.

Defendant's first trial for capital murder and other related crimes, held in March 1993, ended in a mistrial due to the jury's deadlock during the guilt phase. Jury selection for defendant's retrial was interrupted when we granted leave to appeal.

Defendant John DeMarco is charged with the murder of his girlfriend, Karen DeStefanis. The victim's nude body was found by a hunter in a remote area of Hillsborough Township in December, 1990. She had been stabbed at least twenty times.

During the autopsy, the medical examiner took specimens from the victim's body for microscopic analysis. Among those specimens were fluids obtained by swabbing the oral, vaginal and anal orifices. One of the oral swabs revealed the presence of semen. These results were reported to the Somerset County Prosecutor's Office, which subsequently forwarded the swabs and slides to the FBI for DNA analysis. See United States v. Jakobetz, 955 F.2d 786 (2d Cir.), cert. denied, U.S. 113 S.Ct. 104, 121 L. Ed. 2d 63 (1992), and State v. Cauthron, 120 Wash. 2d 879, 846 P.2d 502 (Wash. 1993), for explanations of DNA typing for purposes of identification.

The FBI utilized what is known as the RFLP DNA test procedure. This procedure examines the cells which are contained in the evidence samples and requires a relatively large amount of specimen to obtain a useful result. On May 23, 1991, the FBI issued a report concluding that the semen specimen could not be analyzed because the DNA was "degraded and/or insufficient." The exhibits were returned to the Somerset County Prosecutor's office and made available to defense counsel by order of the trial court.

Defense counsel retained the services of Dr. Edward Blake of Forensic Science Associates, Richmond, California, to conduct DNA testing on the sperm-bearing swab. Dr. Blake used a technique known as Polymerase Chain Reaction (PCR). The PCR technique involves extraction of DNA material from the evidence, and amplification of the DNA material to obtain a sample sufficient for typing purposes. See State v. Williams, 252 N.J. Super. 369, 599 A.2d 960 (Law Div. 1991), for a description of the PCR technique and Dr. Blake's role in that case in behalf of the State.

Dr. Blake identified semen on the oral swab, extracted a minute amount of DNA material from the swab, amplified the extracted DNA material and examined it. As a result of his analysis, Dr. Blake concluded in his report that defendant "can not be the source of the sperm recovered from the DeStefanis oral swab." Dr. Blake's report was received by defense counsel in September 1992.

Dr. Blake testified in defendant's behalf at the first trial in March 1993. On June 18, 1993, Assistant Prosecutor James Wronko, who had tried the case for the State, wrote to Dr. Blake requesting that he provide the State with "copies of your reports for all criminal cases in which you have conducted PCR DQ Alpha testing on behalf of either the State or the defense." By letter dated June 21, 1993, Dr. Blake responded that he would not honor this demand as it was an "inappropriate invasion of my professional practice."

On June 25, 1993, Wronko, without notice to Dr. Blake, issued a subpoena duces tecum to Roche Molecular Systems, Inc. (Roche), requesting that it turn over case file reports prepared by Dr. Blake and in Roche's possession. The State sought the reports "specifically to locate additional cases wherein Blake's test results indicated the existence of unexplained contamination in either evidentiary or reference samples."

The reports were apparently in the possession of Dr. Henry Erlich, the current director of Roche's Department of Human Genetics. Dr. Erlich and his colleagues developed the DNA technology utilized by Blake in this case. See State v. Williams, supra, 252 N.J. Super. at 381. Between 1987 and 1991, Blake "scientifically collaborated" with Erlich and other members of his laboratory with respect to the PCR HLA DQ Alpha technique and its relationship to forensic casework, and Blake would often send Erlich copies of his case-work reports. The collaborations resulted in several articles on the topic. Dr. Erlich and his colleagues also acted as consultants to Dr. Blake on several occasions. Roche responded to the subpoena by turning over 234 case files to the State on September 13, 1993.

On September 29, 1993, Blake moved to quash the subpoena, arguing that the case reports were protected from disclosure as work product and also under the attorney-client privilege. The trial court rejected these arguments, stating:

> even if we accept as true that an attorney-client privilege, or some right of confidentiality exists, when these case reports were prepared by Dr. Blake and held by him, that right of confidentiality ceased when Dr. Blake sent those reports to Dr. Erlich, to Roche, or to other scientists who were not part of his staff and office.

> When he delivered those case reports to another scientist, or another office outside of his own office, in my view, they enter the public domain, and they become subject to a subpoena duces tecum.

* * *

The Defendant here suggests that the disclosure of this data would severely jeopardize other capital Defendants, but no such case has been brought to the attention of this court. And if there were to be any such cases in which the disclosure of this material would severely jeopardize other capital Defendants or other Defendants, and that information was brought to my attention, I think that matter could easily be resolved by redacting the names of those particular Defendants, or litigants, from the files that could be used by the Prosecutor in this case.

* * *

Accordingly, we find that there is no basis for Dr. Blake to bring this motion. We are unaware of any privilege given to Dr. Blake, once he has disseminated the information to other parties.

The court further held that Blake did not have standing to bring a motion to quash the subpoena. However, the court granted the motion to quash with respect to those "two or three" case reports where Mr. Scheck (Blake's attorney) was the attorney of record. The court stated that this was done to "protect his [Scheck's] right of privilege."

As previously indicated, we granted Dr. Blake's motion for leave to appeal. We also permitted counsel for DeMarco to participate in the appeal by filing a brief and presenting oral argument. The State's cross-motion for leave to appeal from that part of the order quashing the subpoena as to reports rendered to Mr. Scheck was also granted.

Counsel for Dr. Blake contends on appeal that his clients' case reports are privileged as attorney work product and are protected from disclosure by the attorney-client privilege. He also contends that disclosure of these reports would violate the Sixth Amendment right to effective assistance of counsel and that the reports prepared on behalf of law enforcement agencies are protected by a "law enforcement investigatory privilege."

Although we do not decide whether the asserted privileges apply in this case, we deem it necessary to discuss them and the policy considerations on which they are founded.

The attorney work product privilege prohibits disclosure of certain materials prepared by an attorney in anticipation of litigation, and thereby "creates a zone of privacy in which an attorney can investigate, prepare, and analyze a case." In re Grand Jury Subpoena Dated November 8, 1979, 622 F.2d 933, 935 (6th Cir. 1980).

The work product privilege was recognized by the United States Supreme Court in Hickman v. Taylor, 329 U.S. 495, 67 S.Ct. 385, 91 L.Ed. 451 (1947). The Court observed that

> it is essential that a lawyer work with a certain degree of privacy, free from unnecessary intrusion by opposing parties and

their counsel. Proper presentation of a client's case demands that he assemble information, sift what he considers to be the relevant from the irrelevant facts, prepare his legal theories and plan his strategy without undue and needless interference.

[Id. at 510-11, 67 S.Ct. at 393, 91 L.Ed. at 462.]

In United States v. Nobles, 422 U.S. 225, 95 S.Ct. 2160, 45 L. Ed. 2d 141 (1975), the Court acknowledged that the work product doctrine applies in criminal cases, and succinctly explained:

At its core, the work product doctrine shelters the mental processes of the attorney, providing a privileged area within which he can analyze and prepare his client's case. The doctrine is an intensely practical one, grounded in the realities of litigation in our adversary system. One of those realities is that attorneys often must rely on the assistance of investigators and other agents in the compilation of materials in preparation for trial. It is therefore necessary that the doctrine protect material prepared by agents for the attorney as well as those prepared by the attorney himself.

[Id. at 238-39, 95 S.Ct. at 2170, 45 L. Ed. 2d at 154.]

In New Jersey, the attorney work product privilege applicable to criminal cases is codified in R. 3:13-3(c), which provides:

Documents Not Subject to Discovery. This rule does not require discovery of a party's work product consisting of internal reports, memoranda or documents made by that party or his attorney or agents, in connection with the investigation, prosecution or defense of the matter nor does it require discovery by the State of records or statements, signed or unsigned, of defendant made to defendant's attorney or agents.

The privilege protects materials prepared by the attorney, as well as those prepared by agents of the attorney retained to aid in the preparation of a case. R. 3:13(c); Nobles, supra, 422 U.S. at 238-39, 95 S.Ct. at 2170, 45 L. Ed. 2d at 154. In New Jersey, however, it has been held that "true work product" is

material that is "inherently inadmissible." State v. Mingo, 77 N.J. 576, 585, 392 A.2d 590 (1978); accord State v. Montague, 55 N.J. 387, 402, 262 A.2d 398 (1970) ("the internal office materials which embody the attorney's private thoughts and impressions, as distinguished from the statements of witnesses, would be nonevidential and protected by the [work product] privilege"). Thus, a report of a defendant's handwriting expert, whom defendant did not intend to call as a witness, was not privileged work product "as it constitutes a species of evidence admissible under some circumstances." Mingo, supra, 77 N.J. at 585. Dr. Blake's case reports fall into the same category and it is unlikely, therefore, that they would be protected work product under New Jersey law. But cf. State v. Williams, 80 N.J. 472, 479, 404 A.2d 34 (1979) (memoranda by defense counsel summarizing interview of victim, and photographs used in interview, constituted protected work product when defendant did not intend to use those items at trial).

Dr. Blake and defendant also contend that disclosure of the 234 case reports would violate the attorney-client privilege that exists between the attorneys who retained Dr. Blake to prepare those reports and their clients. Dr. Blake is seeking to assert the privilege as an agent of the attorneys who retained him. The State counters that "the material reflected in the reports could not possibly be considered protected communications under the attorney-client privilege."

The attorney-client privilege protects against disclosure of confidential communications between the client and the attorney, made in the course of the professional relationship. See N.J.R.E. 504. The primary purpose of the privilege is to encourage full and frank communication of information from the client to the attorney. In re Advisory Opinion No. 544 of the New Jersey Supreme Court Advisory Committee on Professional Ethics, 103 N.J. 399, 405, 511 A.2d 609 (1986).

The privilege extends to necessary communications made by the client to an agent of the attorney, such as a scientific expert retained to aid in the preparation and presentation of the defense. State v. Kociolek, 23 N.J. 400, 413, 129 A.2d 417 (1957). Similarly, the privilege is broad enough to shield communications made between the attorney and client which the attorney shares with the agent or scientific expert. Coyle v. Estate of Simon, 247 N.J. Super. 277, 281-82, 588 A.2d 1293 (App. Div. 1991). It is on this ground that Dr. Blake and defendant claim that the reports are protected by the attorney-client privilege. Dr. Blake and defendant suggest that the attorneys, in retaining Dr. Blake's services, necessarily must relay attorney-client communications to Blake to enable him to perform his analysis.

To the extent that confidential attorney-client communications are contained in Dr. Blake's reports, those communications would be privileged. See Coyle, supra, 247 N.J. Super. at 281-82. It appears that Dr. Blake's reports follow a uniform format. They begin with a restatement of the "background" provided to Dr. Blake by the client's attorney, followed by a description of the physical evidence supplied by the attorney. Dr. Blake then discusses his examination of the physical evidence, describes his genetic analysis and reports his conclusions. Although we have examined only two sample reports, there is a risk that the "background" may contain confidential communications between the attorney and client. Similarly, the physical evidence supplied to Dr. Blake in a particular case may also implicate confidential disclosures by the client.

Our Supreme Court has recognized a relationship between the work product and attorney-client privileges and the Sixth Amendment right to effective assistance of counsel. See State v. Mingo, supra, 77 N.J. at 583-84. Relying on Mingo, Dr. Blake and defendant contend that disclosure of Dr. Blake's unrelated reports violates the Sixth Amendment rights of Dr. Blake's clients. Of course, this contention applies only to those clients who are defendants or suspects; it does not apply to law enforcement agencies.

In Mingo, defendant was charged with rape and attempted robbery. The victim, prior to being attacked, was given a handwritten note from her assailant. The defendant was subsequently brought into police custody and instructed to provide a handwriting sample containing the exact words written in the rapist's note. Prior to trial, defendant's counsel sought production of the rapist's note in order to have it examined by his own hand-

writing expert to aid in preparing a defense. Id. at 579. The court granted defendant's request on the condition that defense counsel would furnish the prosector with a copy of any reports rendered by the expert regarding the handwriting, "irrespective of whether the defense intended to use the expert as a witness at trial." Ibid. Defendant's expert concluded that the same person had written each note, and, therefore, the defense attorney determined he would not use this expert at trial. Id. at 580. The prosecutor obtained a copy of the report pursuant to the discovery order and subsequently subpoenaed the expert to testify on the State's behalf. Ibid.

Although the New Jersey Supreme Court affirmed Mingo's conviction, it ruled that "the report and testimony of a defense-retained expert consultant who will not testify as a defense witness and whose report will not be utilized as evidence are not available to the State." Id. at 587. The Court relied primarily on the right to effective assistance of counsel guaranteed by the Sixth Amendment and the New Jersey Constitution Art. I, par.10. The Court explained:

This rule will safeguard the internal strategic processes of the defense. The protection such a rule affords will enhance the ability of the defense attorney to provide effective representation by affording him the maximum freedom to seek the guidance of expert advice in assessing the soundness and advisability of offering a particular defense without the fear that any unfavorable material so obtained can be used against his client. . . . Reliance upon the confidentiality of an expert's advice itself is a crucial aspect of a defense attorney's ability to consult with and advise his client. If the confidentiality of that advice cannot be anticipated, the attorney might well forego seeking such assistance, to the consequent detriment of his client's cause. The protection from unwarranted disclosure we today mandate is an indispensable element of a criminal defendant's constitutional right to the effective assistance of counsel.

[Ibid.]

In the case at bar, Dr. Blake asserts that many of the case reports at issue contain test results which incriminate defendants in pending cases. If this is correct, the attorney presumably would not utilize that report at trial, and, therefore, in New Jersey, under Mingo, the report would not be subject to disclosure. Id. at 585-86; State v. Williams, supra, 80 N.J. at 480-81.

Dr. Blake also asserts that public disclosure of his reports to law enforcement agencies would jeopardize many ongoing homicide investigations across the country. Blake contends that these reports are privileged in their controlling jurisdiction, and then, relying on N.J.R.E. 515, the "official information" privilege, asserts that "simple principles of comity alone would dictate that New Jersey courts ought to protect case reports prepared by Dr. Blake for prosecutors and law enforcement personnel in other jurisdictions."

N.J.R.E. 515 provides:

No person shall disclose official information of this State or of the United States (a) if disclosure is forbidden by or pursuant to any Act of Congress or of this State, or (b) if the judge finds that disclosure of the information in the action will be harmful to the interests of the public.

However, the comment accompanying this rule limits the rule's scope. It states that "this privilege does not apply to the official information of other states, countries or jurisdictions. If such official information is to be privileged from disclosure, the protection would have to rest upon some justification independent of N.J.R.E. 515. . . ." Biunno, Current N.J. Rules of Evidence, comment 1 on N.J.R.E. 515 (1993-94 ed.).

Application of the work product and attorney-client privileges, as well as Mingo's Sixth Amendment analysis, to the reports at issue is problematic. As previously indicated, it is unlikely that the work product privilege applies. Application of the attorney-client privilege would require examination of each report and probably the development of a record of the context in which each report was produced. Most of the reports were generated outside New Jersey and it would be necessary to determine the law of each rele-

vant jurisdiction regarding the claimed privileges. Moreover, we do not know the extent to which applicable privileges have been waived by Dr. Blake's clients through prior disclosure. In the great majority of cases, Dr. Blake's clients and their lawyers are unaware of this controversy and have not been given the opportunity to be heard.

Although we do not determine the applicability of the privileges or Mingo's Sixth Amendment analysis, their underlying policies inform our view of the issue. Dr. Blake's reports contain private and critical information which should be shielded from undue public exposure. Moreover, litigators, public and private, should have access to the assistance of retained experts with a minimum of risk that their reports, which otherwise have not been placed in the public domain, will surface in unrelated litigation. We are persuaded that these concerns are "relevant considerations" within the meaning of R. 3:13-3(d)(1), which provides:

(d) Protective Orders. (1) Grounds. Upon motion and for good cause shown the court may at any time order that the discovery or inspection sought pursuant to this rule be denied, restricted, or deferred or make such other order as is appropriate. In determining the motion, the court may consider the following: protection of witnesses and others from physical harm, threats of harm, bribes, economic reprisals and other intimidation; maintenance of such secrecy regarding informants as is required for effective investigation of criminal activity; protection of confidential relationships and privileges recognized by law; any other relevant considerations.

Need is the touchstone of our analysis. Cf. State v. Garcia, 131 N.J. 67, 81, 618 A.2d 326 (1993) (disclosure of police surveillance site requires a substantial showing of need); State v. Cusick, 219 N.J. Super. 452, 459, 530 A.2d 806 (App. Div. 1987) (defendant's need for DYFS' records regarding victim did not outweigh need for confidentiality of records). The State contends that it wants the unrelated reports "to locate additional cases wherein Blake's test results indicated the existence of unexplained contamination in either evidentiary or reference samples." We do not know how many of the subpoenaed reports support an inference of contamination or include an acknowledgement of contamination by Dr. Blake. The record indicates, however, that such reports would tend to be cumulative because Dr. Blake conceded during cross-examination at the first trial that contamination is a risk in DNA analysis.

In preparation for the first trial, the State had access to approximately twenty case reports prepared by Dr. Blake which were in the public domain. The State cross-examined Dr. Blake as to several of them in which contamination had been present. In addition, the State informed us at oral argument that it now has access to an additional twenty case reports other than the reports at issue. Thus, the State has a total of forty reports, and we were further informed that approximately fifteen of them reveal or suggest contamination.

Obviously, the reports at issue will not establish that the DeMarco specimens were contaminated. They may demonstrate that contamination does occur. But Dr. Blake did not testify that contamination does not occur; he denied that the specimens he examined in the DeMarco case were contaminated. We are persuaded, therefore, that the State has not demonstrated a need for the material sufficient to outweigh the legitimate privacy and confidentiality concerns which attach to the subpoenaed material. Consequently, we conclude that the trial court mistakenly exercised its discretion under R. 3:13-3(d)(1) by failing to quash the subpoena.

That part of the order dated September 30, 1993, denying Dr. Blake's application to quash the subpoena is reversed. We affirm that part of the order quashing the subpoena as to "case reports and/or materials in which clients of Barry C. Scheck, Esq. are involved." The matter is remanded for further proceedings.

NEW YORK CITY HEALTH
v.
MORGENTHAU

COURT OF APPEALS OF NEW YORK

**98 N.Y.2d 525, 779 N.E.2d 173,
749 N.Y.S.2d 462,
2002 N.Y. LEXIS 3140 (2002)**

JUDGES: Opinion by Judge Rosenblatt. Chief Judge Kaye and Judges Smith, Levine, Ciparick, Wesley and Graffeo concur.

OPINIONBY: ROSENBLATT

Hospitals may assert a physician-patient privilege under CPLR 4504 (a) to maintain the confidentiality of patient medical records. The case before us involves the extent to which grand juries may, compatibly with CPLR 4504 (a), acquire medical records for the purpose of identifying criminal assailants.

On May 25, 1998, an unidentified assailant stabbed a man to death in Manhattan. Police could determine only that the assailant was a Caucasian male in his 30s or early 40s and that he may have been bleeding when he fled the scene. Over $2^{1}/_{2}$ years later, still unable to identify him, the District Attorney of New York County conjectured that the assailant may have sought medical treatment at a local hospital shortly after the homicide. In early 2001, the District Attorney served grand jury subpoenas duces tecum on 23 hospitals, including four facilities operated by the New York City Health and Hospitals Corporation (HHC). Those subpoenas sought:

"any and all records pertaining to any male Caucasian patient between the ages of 30 to 45 years, who was treated or who sought treatment on May 25th, 1998 through May 26th, 1998 for a laceration, puncture wound or slash, or other injury caused by or possibly caused by a cutting instrument and/or sharp object, said injury being plainly observable to a lay person without expert or professional knowledge; said records including but not limited to said patient's name, date of birth, address, telephone number, social security number and other identifying information, except any and all information acquired by a physician, registered nurse or licensed practical nurse in attending said patient in a professional capacity and which was necessary to enable said doctor and/or nurse to act in that capacity."

Citing CPLR 4504 (a), n1 HHC invoked the physician-patient privilege and refused to turn over emergency room triage logs potentially responsive to these subpoenas, claiming that compliance would necessarily breach patient confidentiality in violation of the statute. After the District Attorney moved to hold HHC in contempt, HHC cross-moved for an order quashing the subpoenas. Supreme Court denied both motions but ordered HHC to submit the records for in camera inspection. The Appellate Division unanimously reversed and granted the motion to quash, holding that compliance with the subpoenas would violate the physician-patient privilege because "the assessment of the nature and cause of the injuries triggering production of the relevant documents involves an inherently medical evaluation" (287 AD2d 287, 288, 731 N.Y.S.2d 17 [2001]). This Court granted the District Attorney leave to appeal, and we now affirm.

Our analysis begins with the history and purpose of the physician-patient privilege. Common law did not recognize any confidentiality in communications between patients and medical professionals. New York was the first state to enact a physician-patient privilege statute (see 2 Rev Stat of NY, part III, ch VII, tit III, § 73 [1st ed 1829]; see also Dillenbeck v Hess, 73 NY2d 278, 284, 536 N.E.2d 1126, 539 N.Y.S.2d 707 [1989]; Fisch, New York Evidence § 541, at 356 [2d ed 1977]). The modern codification of the privilege, CPLR 4504 (a), serves three core policy objectives implicated on this appeal (see generally Prince, Richardson on Evidence §§5-301, 5-302, at 246-249 [Farrell 11th ed]). First, the physician-patient privilege seeks to maximize unfettered patient communication with medical professionals, so that any potential embarrassment arising from public disclosure will not "deter people from seeking medical help and securing adequate diagnosis and treatment" (Dillenbeck at 285, quoting Williams v Roosevelt Hosp., 66 N.Y.2d 391, 395, 497 N.Y.S.2d 348, 488

N.E.2d 94 [1985]; see also Matter of Grand Jury Proceedings [Doe], 56 N.Y.2d 348, 352, 437 N.E.2d 1118, 452 N.Y.S.2d 361 [1982]). Second, the privilege encourages medical professionals to be candid in recording confidential information in patient medical records, and thereby averts a choice "between their legal duty to testify and their professional obligation to honor their patients' confidences" (Dillenbeck at 285, citing Fisch § 541; see also Revisers' Reports and Notes, 3 Rev Stat of NY, at 737 [2d ed 1836]). Third, the privilege protects patients' reasonable privacy expectations against disclosure of sensitive personal information (see Martin, Capra & Rossi, New York Evidence Handbook § 5.3.1, at 367 [1997]; Developments in the Law—Privileged Communications, Medical and Counseling Privileges, 98 Harv L Rev 1530, 1544-1548 [1985]).

Though in derogation of the common law, the physician-patient privilege is to be given a "broad and liberal construction to carry out its policy" (Matter of Grand Jury Investigation of Onondaga County, 59 NY2d 130, 134, 450 N.E.2d 678, 463 N.Y.S.2d 758 [1983]; Matter of City Council of the City of N.Y. v Goldwater, 284 NY 296, 300, 31 N.E.2d 31 [1940]).

On this appeal, the District Attorney contends that enforcement of the subpoenas would not offend these policies or violate CPLR 4504 (a). The prosecutor argues that the subpoenas do not seek information acquired by means of medical diagnosis, treatment or expertise, and should be enforced because they purport to seek records only of injuries "plainly observable to a lay person without expert or professional knowledge." We disagree.

The physician-patient privilege generally does not extend to information obtained outside the realms of medical diagnosis and treatment. Indeed, because the policies underlying the physician-patient privilege implicate confidential patient relationships with medical professionals as medical professionals, we have generally limited the privilege to information acquired by the medical professional "through the application of professional skill or knowledge" (Dillenbeck, 73 N.Y.2d at 284 n 4). Accordingly, notwithstanding CPLR 4504 (a), medical professionals have been authorized to disclose observations of a heroin packet falling from a patient's sock (see People v Capra, 17 NY2d 670, 216 N.E.2d 610, 269 N.Y.S.2d 451 [1966]), injuries on a patient's cheek and lip (see People v Giordano, 274 A.D.2d 748, 711 N.Y.S.2d 557 [2000]), and a patient's slurred speech and alcohol-laced breath incident to intoxication (see People v Hedges, 98 A.D.2d 950, 470 N.Y.S.2d 61 [1983]). Likewise, photographs of methadone-treatment patients taken to prevent unauthorized individuals from obtaining the drug (see People v Newman, 32 NY2d 379, 384, 298 N.E.2d 651, 345 N.Y.S.2d 502 [1973], cert denied 414 U.S. 1163, 39 L. Ed. 2d 116, 94 S. Ct. 927 [1974]) and the names and addresses of a medical professional's patients (see In Matter of Albert Lindley Lee Mem. Hosp., 115 F. Supp. 643 [ND NY 1953], affd 209 F.2d 122 [2d Cir], cert denied sub nom. Cincotta v United States, 347 U.S. 960, 98 L. Ed. 1104, 74 S. Ct. 709 [1954]) are outside the ambit of CPLR 4504 (a) and must be surrendered pursuant to a valid subpoena.

We conclude, however, that Onondaga County controls this appeal and directs that the challenged subpoenas be quashed. In Onondaga County, as in the instant case, the victim was stabbed to death under circumstances that led investigators to conclude that the assailant may have left the scene bleeding. Endeavoring to identify the assailant, the District Attorney of Onondaga County issued a grand jury subpoena on a hospital, seeking "all medical records pertaining to treatment of any person with stab wounds or other wounds caused by a knife" (Onondaga County, 59 N.Y.2d at 133). In quashing the subpoena, the Court held that compliance might have "required the hospital to which it is addressed to divulge information protected by the physician-patient privilege" (59 N.Y.2d at 132). The Court concluded that under those circumstances, it was "not . . . possible to comply with a demand for names and addresses of all persons treated for a knife wound without disclosing privileged information concerning diagnosis and treatment" (59 N.Y.2d. at 135).

We perceive no difference of any actual substance between the subpoena quashed in Onondaga County and the ones challenged here. The records potentially responsive to

the HHC subpoenas are precisely the same as those sought in Onondaga County. Though the District Attorney crafted the instant subpoenas with Onondaga County in mind by broadening their scope (to include most bleeding wounds rather than only knife wounds) and narrowing their reach (to include only wounds "plainly observable to a lay person"), the subpoenas still run afoul of Onondaga County.

Here, much as in Onondaga County, the challenged subpoenas define the class of records sought by the "cause or potential cause" of injury. Thus, the subpoenas inevitably call for a medical determination as to causation "through the application of professional skill or knowledge" (Dillenbeck, 73 N.Y.2d at 284 n 4). It is precisely this intrusion into the physician-patient relationship that CPLR 4504 (a) seeks to prevent. The inherently medical nature of this judgment is not obviated by attempting to qualify it in terms of what a layperson might plainly observe.

By merely reviewing hospital records after patients obtain emergency medical treatment, hospitals cannot reasonably determine whether particular injuries and their causes would have been obvious to a layperson. Medical records are not organized on the basis of what laypersons—as opposed to medical professionals—might discern. Even if a particular medical record does state the cause of injury, the record may not indicate reliably how the hospital ascertained the cause. Medical professionals may have learned the cause from the patient, or discovered it based on their medical expertise. Hospitals should not face contempt proceedings merely because they cannot distinguish the indistinguishable.

This result is further justified by the policy objectives of the physician-patient privilege and the broad construction of CPLR 4504 (a) required to achieve them. Patients should not fear that merely by obtaining emergency medical care they may lose the confidentiality of their medical records and their physicians' medical determinations. A contrary result would discourage critical emergency care, intrude on patients' confidential medical relationships and undermine patients' reasonable expectations of privacy.

Finally, we note that none of the Legislature's many statutory exceptions to the physician-patient privilege apply here. For example, notwithstanding CPLR 4504 (a), Public Health Law § 2101 (1) obliges physicians to disclose immediately any case of communicable disease (see Thomas v Morris, 286 NY 266, 268-270, 36 N.E.2d 141 [1941]), and Social Services Law § 413 (1) requires all medical professionals to report actual or suspected cases of child abuse (see People v Trester, 190 Misc 2d 46, 48, 737 N.Y.S.2d 522 [2002]). CPLR 4504 (b) exempts from the privilege "information indicating that a patient who is under the age of sixteen years has been the victim of a crime." Likewise, Penal Law § 265.26 requires hospitals and medical professionals to report to law enforcement authorities certain cases of serious burns (see Rea v Pardo, 132 A.D.2d 442, 446, 522 N.Y.S.2d 393 [1987]), and Penal Law § 265.25 obliges hospitals and medical professionals to report every case of a bullet wound, gunshot wound, powder burn and "every case of a wound which is likely to or may result in death and is actually or apparently inflicted by a knife, icepick or other sharp or pointed instrument" (emphasis added; see also Onondaga County, 59 N.Y.2d at 133, 135-136; Donnino, Practice Commentaries, McKinney's Cons Laws of NY, Book 39, Penal Law §§ 265.25, 265.26, at 220, 222).

Inasmuch as the Legislature enacted an exception to CPLR 4504 (a) directing the reporting of potentially life-threatening stab wounds (see Penal Law § 265.25), we reaffirm our conclusion that the Legislature intended CPLR 4504 (a) to protect against disclosure those medical records of patients whose stab wounds are less severe (see Onondaga County, 59 N.Y.2d at 136). Thus, because none of the Legislature's other exceptions to the privilege apply, the records the District Attorney seeks remain privileged under CPLR 4504 (a), and the subpoenas seeking their disclosure must be quashed.

Accordingly, the order of the Appellate Division should be affirmed, without costs.

Chief Judge Kaye and Judges Smith, Levine, Ciparick, Wesley and Graffeo concur.

Order affirmed, without costs.

Cases Relating to Chapter 11

Opinions and Expert Testimony

BOWLING
v.
STATE

Court of Appeals of Georgia
275 Ga. App. 45, 619 S.E.2d 688,
2005 Ga. App. LEXIS 808 (2005)

Writ of certiorari denied, 2006 Ga. LEXIS 51 (Ga. 2006)

Johnson, Presiding Judge. Ruffin, C. J., and Barnes, J., concur.

Johnson, Presiding Judge.

A jury found Daniel Bowling guilty of operating a boat while under the influence of alcohol to the extent it was less safe for him to do so. He appeals from his conviction, claiming the evidence was insufficient to show that he was a less safe driver, or that he was less safe as a result of being under the influence of alcohol. We disagree and affirm his conviction.

On appeal the evidence is viewed in a light most favorable to the verdict, and an appellant no longer enjoys a presumption of innocence; moreover, this Court determines evidence sufficiency and does not weigh the evidence or determine the credibility of witnesses. The jury's verdict must be upheld if any rational trier of fact could have found the essential elements of the crime beyond a reasonable doubt.

Viewing the evidence in the proper light, it shows that an officer with the Georgia Department of Natural Resources was patrolling Lake Lanier when he observed a boat traveling at night without a stern light.

The officer pulled alongside the vessel and told the driver, Bowling, that he was stopping the boat because of the light violation. The officer proceeded to conduct a safety inspection, and asked Bowling to produce a lifejacket for each person on board, a "throwable" lifesaving device, a fire extinguisher, and the boat's registration. Bowling had difficulty trying to find some of the items, and was unable to produce the registration or a throwable lifesaving device. The officer testified that Bowling seemed confused while looking for the items. Bowling said he thought the registration card was in the glove compartment, but instead of looking there, he looked around the driver's seat for the card. The officer testified that Bowling asked to use the officer's flashlight, even though Bowling had just looked straight at the floor where there was a large spotlight. The officer noticed an empty wine glass on the floorboard of the boat, and detected an odor of alcohol coming from the boat. He asked Bowling if he had been drinking. Bowling said he had not.

Based on his observations, as well as Bowling's mannerisms and demeanor, the officer asked Bowling to perform field sobriety tests to determine if he was under the influence of alcohol.

With Bowling in his own boat and the officer in the patrol boat, the officer administered the horizontal gaze nystagmus (HGN) test, testing for involuntary jerking of the eyes. Bowling was unable to perform the test properly because he kept moving his head after being told not to do so. The officer testified that Bowling exhibited all six "clues" on the HGN test, though he did not explain for the jury what that meant in terms of intoxication.

The officer asked Bowling to step over into the patrol boat. He noted that Bowling stumbled badly when doing so. The officer noticed an odor of alcohol coming from Bowling's person. When the officer asked Bowling to recite the alphabet without singing, Bowling started reciting it, then stopped, started over, repeated letters, laughed and sang part of the test. He omitted several letters. Bowling was unable to do a finger dexterity exercise or a hand pat exercise as instructed. Bowling refused to submit to an alco-sensor test.

The officer placed Bowling under arrest for boating under the influence, and then read the implied consent notice. Bowling became hostile and demanded to be returned to his boat. Instead, the officer took Bowling to the police station. Once there, Bowling refused to take a breath test. According to the officer, Bowling displayed mood swings throughout the incident, going from belligerent and irritated to calm. When the officer was asked at trial where he believed the odor of alcohol was coming from, he stated that there was a strong odor of alcohol coming from the boat, and a moderate odor of alcohol coming from Bowling. *When asked whether he determined that Bowling "was under the influence to the extent that [it] was less safe to operate that vessel," the officer testified that he concluded after conducting field sobriety tests that Bowling "was a less safe boat operator."* [Emphasis added.]

Bowling contends that the evidence was insufficient to prove beyond a reasonable doubt that he was a less safe driver, or that he was a less safe driver due to the presence of alcohol. He urges that the officer could not recall whether the life jackets and fire extinguisher were eventually found, did not know whether the boat's spotlight worked (which would explain why Bowling asked for a flashlight), and admitted that some operators cannot locate registration documents. He argues further that there was no evidence that he was operating the boat in an unsafe manner, that the hand pat and finger dexterity tests are not part of standard field sobriety exercises, that argumentativeness does not necessarily prove that someone is under the

influence of alcohol, that the officer failed to give his opinion of what the six clues of the HGN test indicate about a person's level of intoxication, that a counting test was performed correctly, and that the officer gave inconsistent statements regarding the source and strength of the alcohol odor. Reversal is not required.

In order to obtain a conviction for driving under the influence of alcohol to the extent it is less safe to drive, the state must prove that the defendant had impaired driving ability as a result of drinking alcohol. A trier of fact can find that a driver was "less safe" based on circumstantial evidence, such as where the driver exhibited signs of intoxication. Field sobriety tests are not designed to detect the mere presence of alcohol, but to produce information regarding whether alcohol is present at an impairing level such that the driver is less safe.

Bowling's refusal to submit to chemical tests of his breath is circumstantial evidence of intoxication. And, a jury could have found from Bowling's performances on several of the sobriety tests that he was not as alert or physically capable and was a less safe driver than he would have been had he not consumed alcohol. Moreover, there was evidence that the smell of alcohol emanated from Bowling's person, that he stumbled badly while trying to board the patrol boat, that an empty wine glass lay on the floorboard, and that Bowling was confused. There was also opinion testimony from the officer that Bowling was under the influence to the extent he was a less safe boat operator. This testimony followed a series of questions regarding the officer's detection of the odor of alcohol emanating from the boat and from Bowling's person. A police officer may offer opinion evidence that a person was a less safe driver. We add that, contrary to Bowling's position, the state was not required to prove that he committed an unsafe act in order to show it was "less safe" for him to operate the vessel.

A rational trier of fact could have found from evidence of alcohol on the boat, the odor of alcohol emanating from Bowling's person, Bowling's refusal to submit to chemical tests of his breath, his demeanor and conduct, and his performance on several sobriety tests, that he was impaired and that the impairment was a result of alcohol consumption. The evidence was sufficient for a rational trier of fact to find Bowling guilty beyond a reasonable doubt of operating a boat while under the influence of alcohol to the extent it was less safe for him to do so.

Judgment affirmed. Ruffin, C. J., and Barnes, J., concur.

OSBOURN
v.
STATE

COURT OF CRIMINAL APPEALS
OF TEXAS

92 S.W.3d 531, 2002 Tex. Crim. App. LEXIS 236 (2002)

JUDGES: Meyers, J., delivered the unanimous opinion of the Court.

OPINION BY: Meyers

Appellant was convicted in a bench trial of possession of marihuana, a usable amount of less than two ounces. Punishment was assessed at twenty days' confinement in the county jail. The Court of Appeals affirmed the trial court's conviction. We granted review to decide whether the Court of Appeals erred when it held that the arresting officer's identification of marihuana was admissible as a lay opinion under Texas Rule of Evidence 701. We will affirm.

Appellant was the passenger in a vehicle that was stopped by Officer Nicole Saval. During the traffic stop, Saval smelled alcohol and the odor of burning marihuana emanating from the vehicle and suspected that the driver of the vehicle was under the influence. While Saval questioned appellant, another officer performed a field sobriety test on the driver who was subsequently arrested. Saval asked appellant if she and the driver had been smoking marihuana. Appellant first denied that she had been smoking marihuana and claimed that the odor was cigarettes. After Saval explained to appellant that cigarette smoke does not smell like marihuana smoke, appellant admitted that she and the driver had been smoking marihuana. Appellant then told the officer that there was more marihua-

na in the vehicle, which Saval found in a clear plastic bag between the two front seats.

Saval documented her identification of the marihuana in the offense report that was given to appellant before trial. After receiving the offense report, appellant requested and the court ordered the State to provide notice of its intent to offer expert testimony pursuant to Article 39.14(b) of the Texas Code of Criminal Procedure. The State did not respond to the order.

At trial, Saval testified about her police academy training. She stated that the trainees were shown what different drugs looked like and were able to smell marihuana both before and after it was burned. She stated that although she was not a drug recognition expert and was not certified as one, based on her training at the academy and her experience on the police force, she was able to identify what marihuana looks and smells like.

During Saval's testimony, appellant objected claiming that the State was attempting to qualify Saval as an expert without providing notice. The State responded that Saval was not being offered as an expert under Rule 702, rather as an individual who can identify what marihuana looks and smells like. The court withheld ruling on the admissibility and allowed the testimony to continue. At the end of the trial, the court concluded that the officer was testifying as an expert due to her specialized knowledge, however, the testimony was admissible because the offense report was adequate notice.

On appeal, appellant claimed that the testimony of the officer was improperly admitted due to the State's failure to provide notice of intent to offer expert testimony. Appellant also claimed that without this testimony, the evidence was legally insufficient to support a conviction.

The Court of Appeals concluded that the testimony was admissible as lay opinion testimony under Rule of Evidence 701. Osbourn v. State, 59 S.W.3d 809, 815 (Tex. App.- Austin 2001). Because Saval's testimony was personal knowledge that was rationally based on her perceptions, inferences, and impressions, the Court of Appeals held that she was not testifying as an expert. Id. at 814. Because the trial court found the evidence admissible under the alternative theory that Saval was testifying as an expert, the Court of Appeals also addressed the issue of notice. The court found that because the offense report was made available to appellant prior to the request for notice, appellant could anticipate the content of the testimony of the arresting officer. Since appellant was not surprised by the testimony and the State's actions did not constitute bad faith, the Court of Appeals reviewed the trial court's admission of the testimony for abuse of discretion. Id. at 816. Finding no abuse, the court declined to disturb the trial court's ruling.

Appellant advances two grounds for review but in view of our disposition of the case only ground two will require discussion. The issue raised by the determinative ground of error is whether the Court of Appeals erred when it held that a police officer's identification of marihuana is admissible as a lay opinion under Texas Rule of Evidence 701.

Appellant argues that the Court of Appeals erred when it held that the officer's testimony regarding the identification of marihuana was admissible under Rule of Evidence 701. Because Saval's opinion was based on the training she received at the police academy and the experience she gained during her three years as a police officer, appellant contends that she was an expert witness under Rule 702. Appellant claims that only a witness who testifies based on personal knowledge, rather than experience and training, can identify marihuana as a lay witness under Rule 701.

The State counters appellant's assertion by claiming that expert testimony is not necessary to identify marihuana because appellant herself identified the substance as marihuana. Additionally, the fact that all police officers have training and experience does not necessarily make them expert witnesses. The State contends that since Saval personally observed the marihuana, she was not testifying as an expert.

Both lay and expert witnesses can offer opinion testimony. Rule 701 covers the more traditional witness—one who "witnessed" or participated in the events about which he or she is testifying—while Rule 702 allows for a witness who was brought in as an expert to testify. A witness can testify in the form of an opinion under Rule 701 if the opinions or inferences are (a) rationally based on his or her perceptions and (b) helpful to the clear understanding of the testimony or the determination of a fact in issue. Fairow v. State, 943 S.W.2d 895, 898 (Tex. Crim. App. 1997). Perceptions refer to a witness's interpretation of information acquired through his or her own senses or experiences at the time of the event (i.e., things the witness saw, heard, smelled, touched, felt, or tasted). Since Rule 701 requires the testimony to be based on the witness's perception, it is necessary that the witness personally observed or experienced the events about which he or she is testifying. Id. at 898. Thus, the witness's testimony can include opinions, beliefs, or inferences as long as they are drawn from his or her own experiences or observations. This also incorporates the personal knowledge requirement of Rule 602 which states that a witness may not testify to a matter unless he or she has personal knowledge of the matter. Bigby v. State, 892 S.W.2d 864, 889 (Tex. Crim. App.1994). There is, however, a provision in Rule 602 for opinion testimony by expert witnesses which allows a person testifying as an expert under Rule 702 to base his or her opinion on facts and data that are of a type reasonably relied upon by experts in the field. TEX. R. CRIM. EVID. 703. Thus, expert testimony serves the purpose of allowing certain types of relevant, helpful testimony by a witness who does not possess personal knowledge of the events about which he or she is testifying.

When a witness who is capable of being qualified as an expert testifies regarding events which he or she personally perceived, the evidence may be admissible as both Rule 701 opinion testimony and Rule 702 expert testimony. A person with specialized knowledge may testify about his or her own observations under Rule 701 and may also testify about the theories, facts and data used in his or her area of expertise under Rule 702. Texas Rules of Evidence Manual art. VII-6-7 (6th ed. 2002) states that: "A witness may qualify to give testimony both under Rule 702-because of his or her superior experiential capacity-and under Rule 701, if the witness's testimony and opinion are based upon firsthand knowledge." This court has never addressed the issue of whether someone with training and experience can testify as a lay witness but the Courts of Appeals have admitted such testimony as both lay and expert opinion. See e.g., Harnett v. State, 38 S.W.3d 650, 659 (Tex. App.-Austin 2000, pet. ref'd) (a social worker was permitted to testify under Rule 701 based on her personal observations of the appellant and under Rule 702 based on her training and experience); Thomas v. State, 916 S.W.2d 578, 581 (Tex. App.-San Antonio 1996, no pet.) (police officer qualified as both lay opinion and expert witness to testify regarding the operation of a "crack" house); Ventroy v. State, 917 S.W.2d 419, 422 (Tex. App.-San Antonio 1996, pet. ref'd) (police officer was permitted to testify under Rules 701 and 702 based on his experience and personal knowledge about the scene of an accident); Yohey v. State, 801 S.W.2d 232, 243 (Tex. App.-San Antonio 1990, pet. ref'd) (police officer's testimony regarding time of death was admissible under both Rule 701 and 702); Austin v. State, 794 S.W.2d 408, 409-411, (Tex. App.-Austin 1990, pet. ref'd) (police officer testified under Rules 701 and 702 that, based on his experience and observation, "Swedish Deep Muscle Rub" was a term for prostitution). Thus, although police officers have training and experience, they are not precluded from offering lay testimony regarding events which they have personally observed. See e.g., Reece v. State, 878 S.W.2d 320, 325 (Tex. App.-Houston [1 dist.] 1994, no pet.) (police officer testified that, in his opinion, based on his experience, the actions he observed were consistent with someone selling drugs); State v. Welton, 774 S.W.2d 341, 343 (Tex. App.-Austin 1989, pet. ref'd) (police officer permitted to testify as non-expert opinion witness regarding intoxication based in part on smelling the odor of alcohol).

The ninth circuit has addressed the issue of whether a police officer with experience and training can testify as a lay witness. In United States v. Von Willie, 59 F.3d 922, 929 (9th Cir. 1995) the ninth circuit allowed a police officer who searched appellant's residence to testify as a lay witness about the nexus between drug trafficking and the possession of the type of weapons found during the search. The court stated that "these observations are common enough and require such a limited amount of expertise, if any, that they can, indeed, be deemed lay witness opinion." Id. At 929. Thus, although the police officer

testified based on his experience, his testimony was admitted as a lay opinion under Rule 701 because it was rationally based on his perceptions during the search and was helpful to the determination of a fact in issue. Id. at 929. However, not all observations by witnesses with experience and training can be admitted as lay opinion testimony. This Court, in Emerson v. State, 880 S.W.2d 759, 763 (Tex. Crim. App. 1994) declined to admit as a lay opinion an officer's testimony regarding appellant's intoxication. Because the officer's opinion was based on his observations while administering the horizontal gaze nystagmus (HGN) test, this Court held that the testimony could only be admissible as expert testimony under Rule 702. Id. at 763. Although the officer personally perceived the appellant's eye movements during the HGN test, we held that his observations were not considered mere lay opinion because the test is based on a scientific theory. Id. at 763.

A distinct line cannot be drawn between lay opinion and expert testimony because all perceptions are evaluated based on experiences. However, as a general rule, observations which do not require significant expertise to interpret and which are not based on a scientific theory can be admitted as lay opinions if the requirements of Rule 701 are met. This is true even when the witness has experience or training. Additionally, even events not normally encountered by most people in everyday life do not necessarily require the testimony of an expert. The personal experience and knowledge of a lay witness may establish that he or she is capable, without qualification as an expert, of expressing an opinion on a subject outside the realm of common knowledge. United States v. James Earl Paiva, 892 F.2d 148, 157 (1st Cir. 1989). It is only when the fact-finder may not fully understand the evidence or be able to determine the fact in issue without the assistance of someone with specialized knowledge that a witness must be qualified as an expert.

It does not take an expert to identify the smell of marihuana smoke. Testimony as to the identity of an odor is admissible in some instances even though the person testifying is not an expert. Chess v. State, 172 Tex. Crim. 412, 357 S.W.2d 386, 387-388 (1962). While smelling the odor of marihuana smoke may not be an event normally encountered in daily life, it requires limited, if any, expertise to identify. See e.g., Kemner v. State, 589 S.W.2d 403 (Tex. Crim. App. 1979) (airline employee recognized odor of marihuana emanating from appellant's suitcase and informed DEA); Chaires v. State, 480 S.W.2d 196 (Tex. Crim. App. 1972) (airline baggage agent smelled odor of marihuana in appellant's suitcase, opened the suitcase and identified the grassy substance it contained as marihuana); Hattersley v. State, 487 S.W.2d 354 (Tex. Crim. App. 1972) (airline employee determined by sight and smell that appellant's suitcase contained marihuana); Sorensen v. State, 478 S.W.2d 532 (Tex. Crim. App. 1972) (appellant's mother testified that she recognized the odor of marihuana when she found it in her son's room); Mumphrey v. State, 774 S.W.2d 75 (Tex. App.-Beaumont 1989, pet. ref'd) (13 year old rape victim testified that she smelled the odor of marihuana on the clothes of appellant). Although it cannot be presumed that everyone is capable of identifying marihuana by smell, a witness who is familiar with the odor of marihuana smoke through past experiences can testify as a lay witness that he or she was able to recognize the odor.

The admissibility of evidence is within the discretion of the trial court and will not be reversed absent an abuse of discretion. Powell v. State, 63 S.W.3d 435, 438 (Tex. Crim. App. 200; Harnett, 38 S.W.3d at 657 ; Ventroy, 917 S.W.2d at 422. If there is evidence supporting the trial court's decision to admit evidence, there is no abuse and the appellate court must defer to that decision. Powell, 63 S.W.3d at 438; Fairow, 943 S.W.2d at 901. Even when the trial judge gives the wrong reason for his decision, Salas v. State, 629 S.W.2d 796, 799 (Tex. Crim. App. 1981), if the decision is correct on any theory of law applicable to the case it will be sustained. Romero v. State, 800 S.W.2d 539, 543 (Tex. Crim. App. 1990); Moreno v. State, 170 Tex. Crim. 410, 411, 341 S.W.2d 455, 456 (Tex. Crim. App. 1961); Calloway v. State, 743 S.W.2d 645, 651-652 (Tex. Crim. App. 1988). This is especially true with regard to the admission of evidence. Dugard v. State, 688 S.W.2d 524 (Tex. Crim. App. 1985), overruled by Williams v. State, 780 S.W.2d

802 (Tex. Crim. App. 1989); Sewell v. State 629 S.W.2d 42, 45 (Tex. Crim. App. 1982). Taking this into account, we will now determine whether the Court of Appeals erred in upholding the trial court's admission of Saval's testimony.

Using the standard set out above, Saval's observation that the odor she smelled was marihuana did not require significant expertise to interpret. And, her observations were not interpreted based on a scientific theory. Thus, if her testimony meets the requirements of Rule 701, it is admissible as a lay opinion. Rule 701 allows a lay witness to give testimony in the form of opinions or inferences that are rationally based on the witness' perception and helpful to a clear understanding of the witness' testimony or the determination of a fact in issue. Thus, if the witness perceived events and formed an opinion that a reasonable person could draw from the facts, then the first part of the rule is met. If the opinion is also helpful for the trier of fact to understand the witness's testimony or aids in the determination of a fact in issue, then the opinion is admissible under Rule 701. Here, Saval participated in the events about which she testified and her opinion was based on what she perceived at the scene of the traffic stop. That is, she smelled an odor that she recognized as marihuana smoke. And, the testimony was helpful to the determination of a fact in issue (i.e., whether appellant was in possession of marihuana). Her belief or inference that the substance was marihuana was based on identifiable facts that were within her personal knowledge such as the green, leafy appearance and the distinct odor. Unlike other drugs that may require chemical analysis, marihuana has a distinct appearance and odor that are familiar and easily recognizable to anyone who has encountered it. So Saval's opinion that appellant possessed marihuana, based on the odor she smelled and the green, leafy substance she saw, was one that a reasonable person could draw from the circumstances. Her testimony regarding the identification of the marihuana was admissible as a lay opinion under Rule 701.

The record also indicates that appellant objected to Saval's testimony on the basis that her opinion was based on her training and experience as a police officer, making her a Rule 702 expert witness. There are certain fields where a witness may qualify as an expert based upon experience and training, however, use of the terms "training" and "experience" do not automatically make someone an expert. All opinions are formed by evaluating facts based on life experiences including education, background, training, occupation, etc. While Saval may have had the potential to be qualified as an expert because she possessed knowledge, skill, experience and education, she was not testifying as an expert when she identified the marihuana. Rather, she was testifying based on her firsthand sensory experiences. Saval herself smelled the odor that she perceived to be burnt marihuana. The fact that she had smelled marihuana before in the course of her employment as a police officer does not necessarily make her an expert. And, again, even if she was an expert, that would not preclude her from offering a lay opinion about something she personally perceived.

Although the trial court admitted Saval's testimony under a different theory, because evidence supports admission of the testimony under Rule 701, the trial court did not abuse its discretion. Consequently, the Court of Appeals correctly upheld the trial court's admission of the testimony. The judgment of the Court of Appeals is affirmed.

Meyers, J.

UNITED STATES
v.
DE SOTO

United States Court of Appeals, Seventh Circuit

885 F.2d 354 (1989)

[Only the part of the case that relates to opinion and expert testimony is included here.]

RIPPLE, Circuit Judge.

The defendants—Gustavo Chaverra Cardona, Ruth Urrego Chaverra, and Maria Urrego de Soto—appeal their convictions for various drug trafficking offenses; a jury found each defendant guilty of conspiring to distribute cocaine in violation of 21 U.S.C. § 846 and of several counts of possession of cocaine with intent to distribute in violation of 21 U.S.C. § 841(a)(1). The defendants appeal on a multitude of grounds. We affirm.

I.

Facts

A tangled web of actions, spun by the three defendants and a number of their associates in a north Chicago neighborhood over the course of 1986, forms the basis of the case now before us. The three defendants are all related to each other: Gustavo Chaverra Cardona and Ruth Urrego Chaverra are husband and wife, and Maria Urrego de Soto is Ruth Urrego Chaverra's sister.[1] Other participants in the conspiracy were also closely tied to the defendants by bonds of family or friendship: Alvaro Chaverra (Alvaro) is Mr. Chaverra's brother and Ramon Sanchez (Sanchez) is a close associate of the family members. Also involved in the organization was Fanny Bertha Altamirano, who served in the Chaverra and de Soto homes as a housekeeper, and later became a principal government witness in the case against her former employers. The locations used by the conspiracy were proximate to each other. The conspiracy operated out of three primary households: (1) Alvaro's apartment at 5752 North Campbell Avenue, which served as a stash house; (2) Ms. de Soto's apartment at 5812 North Campbell Avenue, which served as a meeting place to carry out the transactions; and (3) Mr. and Mrs. Chaverra's former home at 5306 North California Avenue. (Just prior to Mr. Chaverra's arrest, the Chaverras moved to a new home at 5143 North Oakley Avenue.)

In August 1984, Mrs. Altamirano started working as a housekeeper for the Chaverras. Ms. de Soto often came to visit her sister and brother-in-law's home, and thus Mrs. Altamirano came to know Ms. de Soto as well. After becoming acquainted, Ms. de Soto occasionally hired Mrs. Altamirano to do household

---

[1] In this opinion, we shall refer to Gustavo Chaverra Cardona as Mr. Chaverra, Ruth Urrego Chaverra as Mrs. Chaverra, and Maria Urrego de Soto as Ms. de Soto.

chores at her home. In early 1986, Mrs. Altamirano testified, she came to notice large amounts of cash in the Chaverra home. This money was stacked in a closet to which Mr. Chaverra would go often, and alone, during each day; she also noticed a safe in a closet of another room. By the month of May 1986, Mrs. Altamirano began to see even larger amounts of cash in the Chaverra home. For example, she saw Mrs. Chaverra and Ms. de Soto counting stacks of money and separating them by denomination. At Ms. de Soto's apartment, Mrs. Altamirano witnessed similar activity—once, the money counting occurred immediately before the visit of a woman named Mona, who was a friend of Ms. de Soto's. Another time, while she was cleaning Ms. de Soto's dresser, Mrs. Altamirano found a box containing a white powdery substance. Mrs. Altamirano later observed Ms. de Soto sell the powder to an unidentified man for $900.

Mrs. Altamirano was not simply a detached observer of the goings-on in the Chaverra and de Soto homes. She herself sold cocaine, supplied by Mrs. Chaverra, to a confidential informer. Sometime in early May 1986, this confidential informer introduced undercover FBI Agent Gregorio Rodriguez to Mrs. Altamirano. After negotiations, she agreed to sell cocaine to Agent Rodriguez—then known to her as Jorge Castro. On May 28, Agent Rodriguez met Mrs. Altamirano to purchase a sample of the cocaine that she said she could provide through her Colombian employers—the Chaverras. He paid her $150, and she entered the Chaverra home; a short time later, Mrs. Altamirano returned with a small packet of cocaine. Mrs. Altamirano testified that Mrs. Chaverra provided her with the cocaine and instructed her to use the code word "movies" for any future cocaine purchases. On May 30, Agent Rodriguez arranged another purchase through Mrs. Altamirano. First, she called Mrs. Chaverra and told her she wanted a "movie"; then, Agent Rodriguez gave her $1,200 to buy an ounce of cocaine. At 3:00 P.M., Mrs. Altamirano went into the Chaverra house and soon returned to Agent Rodriguez' car with a plastic bag containing 28 grams of 93 percent pure cocaine. Mrs. Altamirano testified that Mrs. Chaverra provided her

with the cocaine and that Mrs. Chaverra gave her $50 for arranging the deal.

On June 3, Agent Rodriguez again met with Mrs. Altamirano to buy another ounce of cocaine. They again drove to the same area, Agent Rodriguez paid $1,200, and Mrs. Altamirano went into the Chaverra home. On this occasion, however, the transaction did not proceed as smoothly as on May 30. Upon entering the Chaverra home, Mrs. Altamirano was told by Mrs. Chaverra that the cocaine was not ready. Mr. Chaverra then arrived; he and Mrs. Chaverra had a conversation. Mrs. Chaverra soon broke down in tears and explained that Alvaro had not yet delivered "it." Mr. Chaverra was not satisfied with his wife's response and called Alvaro on the phone, telling Mrs. Chaverra that Alvaro "has to obey." Alvaro soon arrived, carrying a paper bag containing one ounce of cocaine, which was given to Mrs. Altamirano. She then returned to Agent Rodriguez and delivered the drugs. Agent Rodriguez made a third one-ounce purchase on June 11. This time the transaction proceeded without incident. Mrs. Altamirano told her undercover customer that Mrs. Chaverra was her supplier and that the Chaverra house contained a stash of cocaine and large amounts of cash. With regard to this cocaine sale, Mrs. Altamirano testified that Alvaro delivered the cocaine, which Mrs. Chaverra then turned over to her housekeeper. Mr. Chaverra observed the transaction.

On June 21, 1986, Agent Rodriguez visited Mrs. Altamirano at her home. She indicated that she had just returned from Ecuador carrying one kilogram of cocaine. Agent Rodriguez testified that Mrs. Altamirano then explained how Maria de Soto's home at 5812 North California was used as a cocaine selling place, and that, at another apartment one-half block away, Ms. de Soto and some friends stored, packaged, and weighed cocaine. According to Agent Rodriguez, Mrs. Altamirano also told him that she would continue to deal with him directly because Ms. de Soto and Mrs. Chaverra did not want to deal with Agent Rodriguez.

The government offered as evidence numerous telephone pen register records from the telephone numbers of the Chaverras, Ms. de Soto, and Alvaro covering the period between April and October 1986. These records revealed numerous calls of short duration from the various residences to Florida and Colombia. For example, Ms. de Soto called numbers in Florida 300 times and numbers in Colombia 142 times during this period. One of her monthly phone bills totaled $1,596.

The investigation conducted by Agent Rodriguez did not bear immediate fruit because the investigation was not approved by his supervisors as a "Group 2 undercover operation" until January 1987. See Tr. IV at 68. Consequently, the relevant facts of this case next occur in mid-October 1986. On October 15, 1986, several officers from the Chicago Police Department-Drug Enforcement Administration Task Force (Task Force) were conducting a surveillance of Ms. de Soto's building at 5812 North Campbell because they had received an informer's tip that a cocaine delivery would soon be made to that address. That afternoon, they observed Mr. Chaverra drive up in front of the building in a gray Mercury Cougar, enter the building, and then exit ten minutes later. Agents attempted to follow him, but they eventually lost him in traffic.

At approximately 5:00 A.M. the following morning, the agents spotted a brown Mercury Marquis slowly circling the block. After three tours of the area, the car stopped in front of Ms. de Soto's building. Two persons got out of the car and went into the building; the agents could not tell which apartment they entered in the two-apartment building. Suspecting that this was the delivery vehicle, Chicago Police Lt. Maurice Dailey radioed for a canine narcotics team to inspect the car. A narcotics dog named Rex was walked by the car; its handler reported that Rex reacted positively to the presence of drugs in the rear of the Marquis.

About an hour later, 5812 North Campbell started bustling with activity. First, Sanchez was dropped off by a passing car and entered the building. Next, an Hispanic man arrived, walked up the stoop, and entered. About fifteen minutes later, an empty-handed Sanchez walked out of 5812 North Campbell and stopped on the stoop. He looked up and down the street and then walked to Alvaro's building—5752 North Campbell. Five to ten min-

utes later, Sanchez returned to 5812 North Campbell carrying a small paper bag. However, moments after entering the building, Sanchez again left. This time, he was accompanied by Ms. de Soto. The two looked up and down the street, and then together walked to and entered 5752 North Campbell. Ten to fifteen minutes later, Sanchez and Ms. de Soto, now toting a gray flight bag, left 5752 North Campbell and returned to 5812 North Campbell. The Hispanic man who had earlier entered Ms. de Soto's building then left, carrying a brown paper bag.

At around 12:15 P.M., Ms. de Soto left her building with two children and a man. They all entered the brown Marquis to which Rex had earlier reacted positively. Members of the surveillance team stopped the car and arrested Ms. de Soto and the man. A later search of the car revealed a secret compartment hidden in the interior of the gas tank. Inside that compartment was discovered more than ten kilograms of 91 percent pure cocaine.

At around 12:30-12:45 P.M., Mr. Chaverra, accompanied by two other men, arrived at 5812 North Campbell. They were stopped by the police. Upon their indicating that they were entering Ms. de Soto's building, they were arrested.

Members of the Task Force secured Ms. de Soto's apartment at 5812 North Campbell and Alvaro's apartment at 5752 North Campbell. Subsequently, the officers executed searches of these premises pursuant to search warrants. These searches produced a variety of incriminating evidence, including, from Ms. de Soto's apartment, large amounts of cash and ledgers and journals listing names and information later interpreted as being drug related. A triple-beam scale, a revolver, a safe, and four kilograms of cocaine were recovered from Alvaro's apartment.

In October 1986, just before the arrests at Ms. de Soto's apartment, Agent Rodriguez re-established contact with Mrs. Altamirano, who still did not know his undercover status. After the arrest of Mr. Chaverra and Ms. de Soto, a number of conversations between Agent Rodriguez and Mrs. Altamirano were recorded. In those conversations, she described the organization of the distribution operation and stated that Mrs. Chaverra was still willing and able to sell cocaine despite the arrest of her husband and her sister. No further undercover purchases ever occurred, however.

II.

Analysis

Each defendant raises a number of issues on appeal. We shall address each defendant's arguments separately.

A. Mr. Chaverra's Appeal

1. Admission of Testimony of Lt. Dailey
Mr. Chaverra submits that the district court abused its discretion in allowing Lt. Dailey to testify as an expert witness. Specifically, he contends that the district court erred in allowing Lt. Dailey to testify as to (1) his opinion on the manner in which drug dealers operate, including countersurveillance activities, (2) his opinion on the true nature of certain activities that he observed, and (3) his interpretation of certain documents seized at Ms. de Soto's apartment. See Mr. Chaverra's Br. with Counsel at 16-17.

We begin our evaluation of these contentions by stating the basic principles that must guide our inquiry:

1. Federal Rule of Evidence 702, governing the admission of expert testimony in federal courts, states that:

> If scientific, technical, or other specialized knowledge will assist the trier of fact to understand the evidence or to determine a fact in issue, a witness qualified as an expert by knowledge, skill, experience, training, or education, may testify thereto in the form of an opinion or otherwise.

Fed.R.Evid. 702. Courts have recognized that "the subject matter of the expert testimony here, i.e., the clandestine manner in which drugs are bought and sold, is unlikely to be within the knowledge of the average layman." United States v. Carson, 702 F.2d 351, 369 (2d Cir.), cert. denied, 462 U.S. 1108, 103 S. Ct. 2456, 77 L. Ed. 2d 1335 (1983); see also United States v. Young, 745 F.2d 733, 760 (2d Cir. 1984), cert. denied, 470 U.S. 1084, 85 L. Ed. 2d 142, 105 S. Ct. 1842

(1985); United States v. Borrone-Iglar, 468 F.2d 419, 421 (2d Cir. 1972), cert. denied, 410 U.S. 927, 35 L. Ed. 2d 588, 93 S. Ct. 1360 (1973). Therefore, law enforcement experts may testify in order to assist the jury in understanding particular transactions. However, like all expert testimony, this testimony must be evaluated under the qualification and helpfulness requirements of Rule 702. In short, each witness must be qualified as an expert and the district court must determine that the testimony "will assist the trier of fact to understand the evidence or to determine a fact in issue." Fed.R.Evid. 702; see also United States v. Dicker, 853 F.2d 1103, 1109 (3d Cir. 1988) ("interpretation of clear statements is not permissible, and is barred by the helpfulness requirement of . . . Fed.R.Evid. 702"); United States v. Devine, 787 F.2d 1086, 1088 (7th Cir.) (affirmed district court's refusal to admit proffered testimony dealing with subject understandable by jury without help of expert), cert. denied, 479 U.S. 848, 93 L. Ed. 2d 107, 107 S. Ct. 170 (1986).

2. The admission of expert testimony, like all evidentiary determinations, constitutes a ground for reversal by a court of appeals "only where the district court commits a clear abuse of discretion." United States v. Marshall, 856 F.2d 896, 901 (7th Cir. 1988); see also United States v. Peco, 784 F.2d 798, 800 (7th Cir.), cert. denied, 476 U.S. 1160, 106 S. Ct. 2281, 90 L. Ed. 2d 723 (1986). However, the abuse of discretion standard of review does not mean the absence of any review at all. See In re Ronco, Inc., 838 F.2d 212, 217 (7th Cir. 1988) ("Review under an abuse of discretion standard does not mean no appellate review."). An appellate court always must be mindful of the context in which an evidentiary decision is made. When the litigation context presents circumstances particularly susceptible to abuse, we must be especially alert to the possibility of prejudice. Such a situation exists here. Lieutenant Dailey was called by the government to testify both as an eyewitness to the events of October 16 and as an expert on law enforcement and drug dealer methodology. Testifying as both eyewitness and expert is permissible. See Young, 745 F.2d at 760; Carson, 702 F.2d at 369. However, when these two roles are intertwined, the possibility of juror

confusion is increased. Here, for instance, this intermingling of the two roles increased the possibility that the jurors would not distinguish between Lt. Dailey's role as eyewitness and his role as expert. This situation placed an especially heavy burden on the district court to ensure that the jury understood its function in evaluating the evidence. In reviewing the record, we must pay special attention to the manner in which the district court discharged this responsibility. We now turn to the precise situations presented for our review.

a. Countersurveillance Testimony

Lieutenant Dailey testified as an expert with respect to "countersurveillance" techniques employed by drug dealers to avoid detection by competitors or the police. As an example of such a technique, the Lieutenant noted that when "on the street when they are on foot they constantly stop and look back and forth at the street traffic to see if anyone is watching them." Tr. II at 123. Later on in his testimony, while describing the events of October 16, Lt. Dailey recounted how he twice witnessed Sanchez emerge from Ms. de Soto's building (once accompanied by Ms. de Soto) and look up and down the street while standing on the stoop. When asked by the prosecutor to describe Sanchez' activity more precisely, Lt. Dailey stated that Sanchez "was looking for either us, the police, or any type agents or, again, competitors that may be concerned what his activities were." Id. at 137. Sanchez' actions "definitely" constituted countersurveillance, in Lt. Dailey's opinion. Id.; see also id. at 140. Mr. Chaverra now submits that Lt. Dailey's interpretation of these outwardly commonplace and innocuous actions—looking up and down a street—was based on mere speculation and improperly imposed the imprimatur of expert testimony on an otherwise straightforward narrative. Mr. Chaverra's Br. with Counsel at 20-21. Therefore, the defendant further argues, Lt. Dailey's testimony should have been excluded as intruding on the exclusive province of the jury. Under the circumstances set forth in this record, we cannot agree.

As we have noted earlier, testimony by law enforcement officers regarding drug counter-surveillance may be admitted as expert testimony. For example, in United States v. Stewart, 770 F.2d 825, 831 (9th Cir. 1985), cert. denied, 474 U.S. 1103, 88 L. Ed. 2d 922, 106 S. Ct. 888 (1986), the Ninth Circuit "upheld admission of DEA agents' opinion testimony that the defendant's activities were similar to the modus operandi of persons conducting counter-surveillance while transporting drugs." See also United States v. Maher, 645 F.2d 780, 783-84 (9th Cir. 1981) (testimony regarding modus operandi). The particular conduct as to which the agents testified in Stewart and Maher was the manner in which the defendants drove their cars—circuitously touring the drop-off point several times before stopping. Such activity, especially in city streets with congested parking spaces, may appear, to the outside observer, to be perfectly normal and innocent—just like looking up and down a street. As the Ninth Circuit concluded, however, the everyday appearance of the activity is not an automatic bar to the admission of expert testimony which may attribute a more sinister motive to the actions. See also United States v. Patterson, 819 F.2d 1495, 1507 (9th Cir. 1987) (testimony of heroin street distribution; some individuals acted as lookouts for police or customers, others collected payments, while others collected cash); Carson, 702 F.2d at 369 (testimony of street-corner sales as being drug transactions); Borrone-Iglar, 468 F.2d at 421 (testimony of code words in conversation as actually representing drug orders).

However, because such activities are usually innocent, the district court must be especially vigilant in ensuring that a law enforcement expert's testimony does not unfairly prejudice the defendant or usurp the jury's function. Consequently, there are limits to admission of this type of testimony: the expert must not base his opinion on mere speculation; nor can he speak, as an expert, to matters that the jury can evaluate for itself. See United States v. Arenal, 768 F.2d 263, 269 (8th Cir. 1985), law enforcement expert "testimony is still subject to exclusion if the subject matter is within the knowledge or experience of the jury, because the testimony does not meet the helpfulness requirement of

Rule 702"); Young, 745 F.2d at 760 (court questioned need to have expert police testimony that "25 to 30 people milling around outside a building" indicated presence of heroin den).

Our review of the record convinces us that, in this case, the district court was well aware of its special responsibilities and proceeded with the utmost caution. Immediately before Lt. Dailey testified, the district court carefully considered the defendants' arguments to exclude this expert testimony. Tr. II at 5-10. It stated that:

> What we're dealing with here, as I understand it, is the projected testimony of someone who has observed a lot of narcotics transactions, and has observed conduct that might, to someone who has not had that as part of his or her common experience, appear either perfectly innocuous or perhaps with argument might view that with some degree of suspicion.

Id. at 8. After that characterization of Lt. Dailey's proposed testimony, the court allowed admission of the evidence. However, later on, during the testimony of Lt. Dailey, the district court admonished the jury "that the fact that an expert has given an opinion does not mean that it's binding on you. . . . You should assess the weight that's to be accorded to this expert opinion in the light of all of the evidence in the case." Id. at 164. This instruction was repeated to the jury at the conclusion of the trial. Tr. IX at 165. Finally, and most importantly, the jury had an opportunity to hear the defendants' arguments, which cast all these activities in an innocent light. Id. at 108-112; see also id. at 108 ("An American jury needs something more than a policeman saying looking up and down a street is countersurveillance and he was engaged in countersurveillance and that's it."). On this record, we cannot say that the district court abused its discretion in admitting Lt. Dailey's testimony regarding countersurveillance.

b. "Dope Deals" Testimony

The district court's concern that the jury appreciate its role in evaluating Lt. Dailey's testimony is further illustrated by its decision to strike his opinion that two of the defendants were conducting "dope deals" in Ms. de Soto's building. Tr. II at 150. In the course of his narrative, Lt. Dailey had testified that he saw Ms. de Soto and Sanchez enter Ms. de Soto's building carrying a gray flight bag, and, shortly afterwards, an Hispanic man, who previously had entered the building empty-handed, emerged carrying a paper bag. Lieutenant Dailey did not see whether the Hispanic man had entered Ms. de Soto's apartment. When asked to describe the nature of the activities inside the building, Lt. Dailey testified that they were "dope deals or drug sales, purchases." Id. The district court struck the answer. Even though the answer was stricken and the jury was cautioned to disregard the statement, id. at 149-50, Mr. Chaverra now submits that the comment nevertheless constituted reversible error. See Mr. Chaverra's Br. with Counsel at 18. The government responds that the district court erred in striking the statement. See Government Br. at 26. Relying on Young, 745 F.2d at 760 (court affirmed admission of eyewitness police officer's opinion that certain activities constituted drug sales), and Carson, 702 F.2d at 369-70 (court affirmed admission of eyewitness agent's opinion that street-corner deals "appeared to him to be drug transactions"), the government suggests that the district court was overly cautious and that Lt. Dailey should have been permitted to testify that he regarded the pattern of activity he witnessed to be a "dope deal." See generally Fed.R.Evid. 704 (opinion testimony on ultimate issue permitted).

There does appear to be authority for the government's position—at least in the abstract. However, a district court must be given great latitude in any evidentiary judgment call and, in a context as delicate as the one before us, we should certainly be most circumspect about second-guessing a district court's determination to proceed cautiously. Here, where Lt. Dailey was unable to see the activities within Ms. de Soto's apartment, the court's conservative approach is certainly understandable and we certainly shall not express disapproval of its judgment. Nor shall we presume that the jury ignored the court's explicit cautionary instruction. In making this determination, we note that, like the district court's decision regarding the proper scope of Lt. Dailey's countersurveillance testimony, this evidentiary decision was informed and careful. Prior to the government's embarking on this line of questioning, the court held a prolonged sidebar discussion, see Tr. II at 142-49; when the government persisted in pursuing this improper evidence, apparently through a misunderstanding, the court made its evidentiary ruling and then called another conference, outside the hearing of the jury, to explain its decision and stress that Lt. Dailey's testimony must be restricted to matters within his past experience. Id. at 151-59. It is clear that no reversible error was committed.

c. Testimony Regarding Documents Retrieved from Ms. de Soto's Apartment

As a final evidentiary challenge, Mr. Chaverra also submits that Lt. Dailey's testimony interpreting documents seized at Ms. de Soto's apartment constituted plain error. See Mr. Chaverra's Br. with Counsel at 19; see also id. at A-2 et seq. (copies of the seized records). These documents appear to be informal business records: all but one contain numbers and most also contain names and comments cryptically entered, in Spanish, in the margins. Names including "Gustavo," "Ruth," and "Mona" appear on some of the documents. For example, on the most formal ledger-type sheet, there is an entry for "Gustavo's rent" and a corresponding figure. See Mr. Chaverra's Br. with Counsel at A-8. Mr. Chaverra now challenges Lt. Dailey's tying the records to drug sales, despite no mention of the words drugs, cocaine, heroin, or similar terminology in the

records, and his explanation of numbers listed on certain documents as representing records of drug sales in quantities of kilograms or ounces. When testifying, Lt. Dailey stated that drug dealers often drop the zeros in thousand-dollar calculations, and he referred to various numerals as representing kilograms or ounces of cocaine. Tr. VII at 126-32. He also stated that he did not know who authored these documents.

The admission of this testimony was not plain error. The seized records were quite obscure and Lt. Dailey's expert interpretation could be considered helpful to the jury. See Fed.R.Evid. 702. Additionally, we note that the witness himself never linked these documents to the defendants on trial; the government argued that connection during its closing statement. Furthermore, Lt. Dailey's interpretation received some corroboration: Government Exhibit 16T features a notation for a $345 expense for the repair of a brown car; also found in the search of Ms. de Soto's apartment was a $345 car repair receipt for repairs made on the Mercury Marquis—a brown car. See Tr. III at 75; Mr. Chaverra's Br. with Counsel at A-5. Accordingly, we refuse to hold that the admission of Lt. Dailey's testimony interpreting these seized documents constituted plain error.

* * *

CONCLUSION

For the preceding reasons, we affirm the convictions of Gustavo Cardona Chaverra, Ruth Urrego Chaverra, and Maria Urrego de Soto.

AFFIRMED.

Cases Relating to Chapter 12

Hearsay Rule and Exceptions

BELL

v

STATE

COURT OF APPEAL OF FLORIDA, THIRD DISTRICT

847 So. 2d 558, 2003 Fla. App. LEXIS 8767 (2003)

COPE, J.

Gary Paul Bell appeals his conviction and sentence for attempted kidnapping. We affirm.

Defendant-appellant Bell argues that the trial court should have excluded as hearsay the officer's testimony regarding the victim's account of the crime. The trial court admitted the testimony under the hearsay exception for excited utterances.

The victim testified that she was walking along the street during the daytime when the defendant twice drove up to her in his van and offered to give her a ride to her destination. She refused. When the victim next saw the defendant he was standing on the sidewalk with his van parked nearby. He grabbed her around the neck, held a gun to her head, and attempted to force her into the van. She broke free, ran into traffic, pounded on cars, and asked for help in getting away. The defendant, standing nearby, pointed his gun and threatened to shoot her.

The victim returned to her house and called the police. They found the victim to be hysterical and very fearful that the defendant may have followed her home. The victim was so upset that she could not speak. It took the officers fifteen or twenty minutes to calm the victim down to the point where she could give them a statement.

The hearsay exception for excited utterances applies to "[a] statement or excited utterance relating to a startling event or condition made while the declarant was under the stress of excitement caused by the event or condition." § 90.803(2), Fla. Stat. (2001).

The Florida Supreme Court has said:

> The essential elements necessary to fall within the excited utterance exception are that (1) there must be an event startling enough to cause nervous excitement; (2) the statement must have been made before there was time to contrive or misrepresent; and (3) the statement must be made while the person is under the stress of excitement caused by the event.

The spontaneous statement exception and the excited utterance exception often overlap. However, as noted by Professor Ehrhardt:

> The two exceptions differ mainly in the amount of time that may lapse between the event and the statement describing the event. Under Section 90.803(2) it is not necessary that there be contemporaneity between the event and the statement. As long as the excited state of mind is present when the statement is made, the statement is admissible if it meets the other requirements of Section 90.803(2). This excited state may exist a substantial length of time after the event. Factors that the trial judge

can consider in determining whether the necessary state of stress or excitement is present are the age of the declarant, the physical and mental condition of the declarant, the characteristics of the event and the subject matter of the statements. Whether the necessary state of mind is present is a preliminary fact for the court to determine pursuant to Section 90.104. (citation omitted).

The defendant argues that the victim's statements in this case fail the excited utterance test because there was a time delay of approximately 50 minutes between the time of the incident and the time the victim became calm enough to speak. According to the defendant, this was sufficient time for the victim to contrive or misrepresent.

As the Jano decision indicates, however, points two and three of the test are interwoven. The theory of this hearsay exception is that so long as the declarant remains under the stress of excitement caused by the event, the declarant is unlikely to contrive or misrepresent.

In this case the investigating officer described the victim as hysterical when he first reached the house. She kept going to the window and looking outside to be sure that the defendant was not there. She was so upset she could not speak at all. The trial court permissibly concluded that the victim remained sufficiently under the stress of excitement of the event to make this an excited utterance for purposes of the hearsay exception. Henyard v. State, 689 So. 2d 239, 251 (Fla. 1996). Even if there were any error here, and we do not think there is any, we fail to see any harm as the victim herself testified and was subject to defense cross-examination on all of this.

* * *

Affirmed.

GONZALEZ
v.
STATE

**Court of Criminal Appeals of Texas
195 S.W.3d 114, 2006 Tex. Crim.
App. LEXIS 1129 (2006)**

COCHRAN

The question presented in this case of first impression is whether appellant forfeited, by his own misconduct of fatally shooting Maria Herrera during a robbery or the burglary of her home, his right to confront Maria in court about hearsay statements she made before she died. We find that he did, and we therefore affirm the judgment of the court of appeals which held the same.

I.

San Antonio police officers, responding to 911 calls, arrived at Maria and Baldomero Herrera's home shortly after 6:00 P.M. on May 3, 2002, and found that both of them had been shot. Maria lay near the front door. She was in shock, scared and bleeding, but she was still conscious and asking for help. Baldomero was sprawled unconscious in an easy chair. When officers asked her what had happened, Maria excitedly said that she and her husband had been shot by "a Latin male, blondish colored hair, and he was about 18 years old." She said "the person that did it is related to the people that live across the street in the rock house." Maria kept repeating that he had colored or bleached hair. She stated "that the guy that shot her took her truck" and "she had recognized him from—from the house across the street that had a rock wall in front of it." Maria said it was "just one person." Baldomero died at their home; Maria died at the hospital a few hours later.

Officers found the license plate number of the Herreras' new white Nissan truck and broadcast it over the police radio. There was only one house with a rock face across the street; appellant's grandmother lived there. Appellant's aunt had left him there earlier in the day. His hair was spiky and blonde on top.

* * *

While appellant was at Sylvia's apartment, a police officer on routine patrol, who had heard the broadcast about the Herreras' stolen truck, saw it parked at [appellant's cousin's] apartment complex. He radioed for assistance, and undercover officers in unmarked cars soon arrived and set up surveillance. Around 7:45 p.m., undercover officers noticed a "bleach blonde Latin," later identified as appellant, and another male walk out to the truck, then they both went back inside. At 9:20 p.m., three people, including appellant, came out of the apartment.

Appellant got into the Herreras' Nissan; the other two people got into the Ford truck. The Nissan then followed the Ford out of the apartment complex. When the SWAT officers followed behind him, appellant raced off in the stolen truck, leading officers on a sometimes high-speed chase that lasted about 15 minutes. Eventually, appellant drove down a one-way street and was blocked in by police cars. Appellant refused to get out of the truck, so he was pulled out, handcuffed, and searched. Officers found a black address book, containing Baldomero's credit cards, in his pocket. Appellant was taken to jail and his clothes, a white shirt, jeans and tennis shoes, were collected. Maria's blood was found on the tennis shoes.

The medical examiner testified that Baldomero died from a single gunshot wound to the chest; Maria, who had been shot from three to five times, died from a gunshot wound to the abdomen.

Appellant was charged with capital murder. In a motion *in limine*, and again at trial, appellant objected to the admission of Maria's statements to the police officers as hearsay and as violating his confrontation rights. The trial court held a hearing outside the presence of the jury to determine if Maria's statements to three different officers were admissible. The State argued that Maria's statements, though hearsay, were admissible under the excited utterance and dying declaration exceptions. Appellant argued that the statements were not dying declarations; he pointed to the officers' testimony that Maria was not aware of the gravity of her condition. He also argued that her statements were not excited utterances because they were not spontaneous; instead,

they were answers to police questions. The trial judge doubted that the statements were dying declarations, but he admitted them "mainly under the excited utterance" exception, noting that they also fell under the hearsay exceptions for present-sense impression and then-existing physical condition. The jury convicted appellant of capital murder and sentenced him to life imprisonment.

One of appellant's claims on appeal was that the admission of Maria's out-of-court "testimonial" statements violated his right to confrontation under *Crawford v. Washington*, which the Supreme Court had delivered during the pendency of his appeal. The court of appeals held that Maria's statements were excited utterances and decided that it need not resolve whether they were also testimonial because appellant had forfeited his right to confrontation under the doctrine of forfeiture by wrongdoing. Noting that the Supreme Court had stated in *Crawford* that it would continue to recognize the doctrine of forfeiture by wrongdoing, which "extinguishes confrontation claims on essentially equitable grounds," the court of appeals held that "Gonzalez is precluded from objecting to the introduction of Maria's statements on Confrontation Clause grounds because it was his own criminal conduct (in this case, murder) that rendered Maria unavailable for cross-examination."

II.

In all criminal prosecutions, the accused has a Sixth Amendment right to be confronted with the witnesses against him. Even when hearsay offered against a defendant is admissible under evidentiary rules, that evidence may implicate the Confrontation Clause of the Sixth Amendment if the defendant is not afforded the opportunity to confront the out-of-court declarant. In *Crawford v. Washington,* the Supreme Court held that "where testimonial statements are at issue, the only indicium of reliability sufficient to satisfy constitutional demands is the one the Constitution actually prescribes: Confrontation." Nevertheless, the Supreme Court recognized that equitable exceptions to the Confrontation Clause may still apply, and it specifically mentioned the doctrine of forfeiture by wrongdoing which "extinguishes confrontation claims on essentially equitable grounds" as one that it accepts.

The doctrine of forfeiture by wrongdoing has been a part of the common law since at least 1666. In early English cases, the doctrine allowed a witness's deposition testimony to be admitted instead of live testimony if the defendant caused the witness's absence from trial. The doctrine is based on the principle that "any tampering with a witness should once for all estop the tamperer from making any objection based on the results of his own chicanery." In other words, the rule is based on "common honesty" and the maxim that "no one shall be permitted to take advantage of his own wrong."

* * *

In 1997, the "forfeiture by wrongdoing" doctrine was codified in the Federal Rules of Evidence as a hearsay exception. By that time every circuit that had addressed the issue had recognized the doctrine of forfeiture by misconduct. The doctrine was added to Rule 804 to clarify that a party forfeits the right to object, on hearsay grounds, to the admission of a declarant's prior statement when that party's deliberate wrongdoing procured the unavailability of the declarant as a witness. As the advisory committee note explained:

> The most obvious situation for employing this exception is where a criminal defendant kills a witness, or has him killed, to prevent him from testifying; by engaging in this conduct, the defendant has forfeited the right to object on hearsay grounds to any of the victim's statements. The Rule was derived from cases that have held that a criminal defendant forfeits his right to confrontation if he causes or acquiesces in the witness' unavailability. If the defendant's conduct is such as to cause a forfeiture of the constitutional objection, it should *a fortiori* be enough to cause a forfeiture of the parallel hearsay objection.

Before the Rule 804(b)(6) hearsay exception can apply, the offering party must show that the opposing party committed the wrongdoing with the intent to prevent the declarant's testimony:

> Under the Rule, it must be shown that the party against whom the evidence is offered acted with intent to procure the unavailability of the declarant as a witness. If the defendant kills a declarant simply because he didn't like him, or because he was burned in a drug deal by him, then the defendant has not forfeited his right to object to the declarant's hearsay statement. It follows that the defendant in a murder case cannot be held to have forfeited his objection to hearsay statements made by the victim. The defendant might have murdered the victim, but he undoubtedly didn't murder the victim to prevent him from testifying in the murder trial.

Some version of the forfeiture doctrine has been adopted in various state courts. While courts have widely accepted the doctrine of forfeiture by wrongdoing to reject both hearsay objections and confrontation claims, the test for determining whether there is a forfeiture has varied. Courts have agreed that forfeiture requires (1) the declarant's unavailability, (2) as a result of the defendant's act of misconduct. Courts have disagreed on whether the defendant must intend that his act of misconduct silence the witness. Courts also have disagreed on whether evidence inadmissible under Federal Rule 804(b)(6) (*i.e.* when the predicate wrongdoing is the same crime for which the defendant is being tried) might nonetheless be admissible over a confrontation clause objection under the forfeiture doctrine.

This debate has taken on new life since the *Crawford* decision. Several courts have used the language in *Crawford* to apply the forfeiture doctrine expansively—when the wrongdoing is the same crime for which the defendant is being tried and without regard to whether the defendant intended to silence the witness. Other courts have held that the forfeiture doctrine does not apply in those situations because (1) the defendant's wrongdoing only indirectly "procured" the witness's absence; (2) the wrongful act was not done with the intent to prevent the witness from testifying; or (3) it is the same wrongful act for which the defendant is on trial.

In *United States v. Mayhew*, the district court cited to the amicus brief filed by a group of law school professors in *Crawford* to apply the forfeiture doctrine even though the defendant was on trial for the very act of murder that caused the declarant's unavailability. In their brief, the professors did not mention the role of the wrongdoer's intent. They simply stated,

If the trial court determines as a threshold matter that the reason the victim cannot testify at trial is that the accused murdered her, then the accused should be deemed to have forfeited the confrontation right, even though the act with which the accused is charged is the same as the one by which he allegedly rendered the witness unavailable.

* * *

In the present case, the San Antonio Court of Appeals cited state-court decisions that have held the same, including the Kansas Supreme Court in *State v. Meeks* as well as Colorado and California appellate courts in *State v. Moore,* and *People v. Giles*. Some post-*Crawford* decisions have declined to apply the forfeiture doctrine when the defendant's actions did not directly cause the witness's absence or were not intended to make his testimony unavailable. For example, in *People v. Melchor*, the evidence showed that the defendant had intentionally absconded and engaged in an elaborate scheme to avoid the law for ten years, during which time the sole eyewitness to the shooting, Ortiz, died from a drug overdose. The forfeiture doctrine did not apply because there was no causal link between the defendant's misconduct and the witness's unavailability.

In sum, the majority of post-*Crawford* cases have applied the forfeiture by wrongdoing doctrine when the trial court makes a preliminary finding under Rule 104(a) that the defendant's act of misconduct caused the witness's unavailability, although some have also required that the defendant acted with the intent to prevent the witness's testimony.

III.

The determination of whether the forfeiture doctrine applies in the present case appears, at first glance, to depend upon an interpretation of the scope of the "forfeiture by wrongdoing" doctrine. We have been favored with thorough briefing by both the State and appellant. The State cites to the language in *Crawford* and in the law professors' amicus brief, and argues that the court of appeals correctly applied the forfeiture doctrine because forfeiture by wrongdoing, as an equitable doctrine, does not require the prosecution to establish the defendant's motive. Appellant, on the other hand, asserts that the doctrine cannot apply unless the State shows that the defendant engaged in the wrongdoing for the purpose of preventing the witness from testifying at a future trial. Appellant notes that pre-*Crawford*, the doctrine was generally applied only in the context of witness tampering, and that the Supreme Courts in Pennsylvania, Alaska, and New York had expressly held that the doctrine does not apply where the defendant murders the declarant for personal reasons rather than to prevent the declarant from testifying. Appellant faults post-*Crawford* cases applying the doctrine as the court of appeals did in this case for fastening on language in *Crawford* and [another case],without sufficient analysis of the history and intent of the rule.

We need not settle that dispute in this case. An examination of the entire record clearly supports the inference that appellant shot the Herreras to silence them. They knew him. They lived across the street from his grandmother and were friends with her and other members of her family. Appellant entered the Herreras' home without a disguise and with a very distinguishing characteristic—his dark hair dyed blonde. Indeed, there was no sign of forced entry, so he was either welcomed or walked through an unlocked door. Appellant entered the Herreras' home armed. And he shot to kill. Baldomero, who had not even gotten up from his easy chair, was shot through the heart. Maria was also shot in the chest—and when she did not die appellant shot her again and again. Both were shot from beyond two feet. Both were left for dead.

A logical inference is that appellant killed the Herreras because he wanted to steal their truck and their money, and he didn't want any witnesses to his crime—especially witnesses that knew him, and knew where to find him. This case is factually different from the post-

Crawford cases that the court of appeals relied on. Those cases involved passion or revenge killings—killings for personal reasons. There was no evidence in this case that appellant had any personal grudge against the Herreras; the evidence strongly supports the inference that appellant committed burglary or robbery for financial gain and then murdered the two witnesses who could identify him.

We agree with those post-*Crawford* cases and the *Crawford* amicus brief that the doctrine of forfeiture by wrongdoing may apply even though the act with which the accused is charged is the same as the one by which he allegedly rendered the witness unavailable. The trial court in this case did not make a preliminary ruling on whether appellant killed Maria, at least in part, to prevent her from testifying against him because this case was tried before *Crawford* was decided. Nonetheless, an evidentiary ruling, such as the one admitting Maria's out-of-court statements, will be upheld on appeal if it is correct on any theory of law that finds support in the record. We agree with the court of appeals that the record provides ample support for the admission of Maria's out-of-court statements, despite appellant's Confrontation Clause objection, because appellant forfeited his right to confront Maria by his own wrongful act. The evidence strongly suggests that the procurement of Maria's absence was motivated, at least in part, by appellant's desire to permanently silence her and prevent her from identifying him. We express no opinion on the court of appeals's broader holding that the procurement of a witness's absence need not be motivated by a desire to silence the declarant for the forfeiture by wrongdoing doctrine to apply.

We affirm the judgment of the court of appeals.

Johnson, J., *filed a concurring opinion.*

I concur in the judgment of the Court. First, I think that Mrs. Herrera's statements were admissible as a dying declaration. Despite the police officers' assertions that she was not aware of the gravity of her situation, no one seems to have inquired of her what her perception of her injuries was. Certainly she was aware that she had been shot multiple times, including a gunshot wound to the abdomen. Under such circumstances, it is probable that she understood quite clearly the gravity of her situation. The *Crawford* Court conceded that dying declarations may, by historical imperative, be admissible, despite the lack of an opportunity to cross-examine.

There is also the argument that Mrs. Herrera's statements were not testimonial. Depending on the circumstances, a police officer asking, "What happened?" may or may not be interrogation. Even if her statements were testimonial and the trial court erred in admitting them, I would find the error harmless. The Herreras' truck was missing, a fact easily ascertained from sources other than Mrs. Herrera's statements. The license plate number was also easily ascertainable by law officers. A bulletin about the missing truck was broadcast to police officers. An officer on routine patrol saw the truck and called for assistance. After a chase, officers stopped the truck and arrested appellant, the driver, who had Mr. Herrera's credit cards in his pocket and Mrs. Herrera's blood on his shoes. With such evidence, Mrs. Herrera's statements were superfluous.

I do not think that this is the right case in which to consider expanding the concept of forfeiture by wrongdoing. The basis for such an expansion seems to be based on federal Rule of Evidence 804(b)(4), which by its very terms does not apply in this case. In addition, there is a logical disconnect in saying that a defendant killed a person to prevent them from testifying at the defendant's trial for killing that person; if the defendant did not kill the person, there would be no murder trial and hence no need to suppress damaging testimony, so killing the person creates the reason for killing the person. Such reasoning is circular and should not be incorporated into the law.

COX
v.
STATE

**COURT OF APPEALS OF INDIANA,
SECOND DISTRICT**

**774 N.E.2d 1025, 2002 Ind. App.
LEXIS 1533 (2002)**

JUDGES: ROBB, Judge. RILEY, J., and
MATTINGLY-MAY, J., concur.

James Cox was convicted following a
bench trial of domestic battery, a Class A
misdemeanor. Cox appeals his conviction.
We affirm.

Issues

Cox raises two issues for our review,
which we restate as follows:

1. Whether the trial court properly admitted
   hearsay testimony under the excited utterance hearsay exception; and
2. Whether the State presented sufficient evidence to support his conviction.

Facts and Procedural History

Deputy Sheriff Daniel Herrick responded
to a radio dispatch of a reported battery on
October 12, 2001. When he arrived at the
scene, he observed Cox standing in front of
an apartment building talking to another
police officer. Deputy Herrick found Denise
Hogan inside the apartment building a few
minutes later. He noticed that she was crying
and shaking and appeared to be very upset.
He also noticed that she was talking very
quickly and showed signs of a fresh injury.
Hogan had a cut above her eye which was
bleeding, her left eye was swollen and she
was holding an ice pack to her eye. Additionally, she had marks on her neck that appeared
to have been caused by someone grabbing
her on her neck.

Hogan told Deputy Herrick how she sustained the injuries and that it was Cox who
injured her. At trial, Deputy Herrick testified
to the statements Hogan made to him. Cox
objected, asserting that Herrick's testimony

was hearsay. The State responded that the
statements were being offered under the
"excited utterance" exception. The trial court
allowed the testimony.

Following the trial, the trial court found
Cox guilty of domestic battery. This appeal
ensued.

Discussion and Decision

I. Admission of Testimony

A. Standard of Review

Our standard of review in this area is well
settled. The admission of evidence is within
the sound discretion of the trial court, and the
decision whether to admit evidence will not
be reversed absent a showing of manifest
abuse of the trial court's discretion resulting
in the denial of a fair trial. Prewitt v. State,
761 N.E.2d 862, 869 (Ind. Ct. App. 2002).
An abuse of discretion involves a decision
that is clearly against the logic and effect of
the facts and circumstances before the court.
Id. In determining the admissibility of evidence, the reviewing court will only consider
the evidence in favor of the trial court's ruling and any unrefuted evidence in the defendant's favor. Id.

B. Admission of Deputy Herrick's Testimony

Hearsay is a statement made out-of-court
that is offered into evidence to prove the fact
or facts asserted in the statement itself. Ind.
Evidence Rule 801(c); Craig v. State, 630
N.E.2d 207, 209 (Ind. 1994). In the present
case, the contested portions of Deputy Herrick's testimony constitute hearsay. Hogan
made the statements out-of-court and Deputy
Herrick repeated the statements at trial, for
the purpose of proving the facts asserted in
the out-of- court statements, namely that Cox
struck and choked Hogan. Such hearsay is
not admissible at trial unless it fits within
some exception to the hearsay rule. Craig,
630 N.E.2d at 207.

Cox contends that the hearsay testimony of
Deputy Herrick is inadmissible because it
does not fit into any hearsay exception and
because Hogan did not appear for trial. Alternatively, he contends that, if the testimony

falls under the excited utterance exception, then the State failed to lay a proper foundation for the evidence. We disagree.

The excited utterance exception is found in Evidence Rule 803(2). The rule provides that:

> The following are not excluded from the hearsay rule, even though the declarant is available as a witness.
>
> * * *
>
> (2) A statement relating to a startling event or condition made while the declarant was under the stress of excitement caused by the event or condition.

For a hearsay statement to be admitted as an excited utterance under Evidence Rule 803(2), three elements must be shown: (1) a startling event occurs; (2) a statement is made by a declarant while under the stress of excitement caused by the event; and (3) the statement relates to the event. Jenkins v. State, 725 N.E.2d 66, 68 (Ind. 2000). This is not a mechanical test; it turns on whether the statement was inherently reliable because the witness was under the stress of an event and unlikely to make deliberate falsifications. Id. Additionally, while the time period between the startling event and a subsequent statement is, of course, one factor to consider in determining whether the statement was an excited utterance, no precise length of time is required. Simmons v. State, 760 N.E.2d 1154, 1161 (Ind. Ct. App. 2002).

Cox argues that Hogan's absence makes her statement inadmissible hearsay. However, the language of Rule 803 makes it clear that the exceptions listed are not excluded from the hearsay rule, "even though the declarant is available as a witness." Evid. R. 803. Therefore, Rule 803 lists exceptions which are not hearsay regardless of whether the declarant is available. The fact that Hogan did not appear for trial has no effect on Deputy Herrick's testimony. Hogan's statements to Deputy Herrick fit squarely within the excited utterance exception and were admissible at trial.

Cox also argues that the State failed to lay a proper foundation for the excited utterance exception. We disagree.

We have recently held that a victim's statement made to a police officer after a battery constituted an excited utterance. Gordon v. State, 743 N.E.2d 376, 378 (Ind. Ct. App. 2001). In Gordon, a police officer was dispatched to an apartment complex where he found a woman who was shaking and had redness about her neck. The woman told the officer that her boyfriend had struck her. Because the woman did not testify at trial, Gordon argued that the police officer's testimony was inadmissible hearsay. This court examined the circumstances surrounding the statements made by the victim and held that it was reasonable to infer that the woman was upset because of a startling event and that the event was the physical altercation she described to the officer. Id.

As in Gordon, we find that Hogan's statements to Deputy Herrick satisfy the conditions for excited utterances. The record reflects that Hogan placed a 911 call at 2:21 a.m., that Deputy Herrick was dispatched to the scene at approximately 2:33 a.m., and that he arrived there within minutes of receiving the dispatch. n1 Deputy Herrick testified that Hogan was crying and shaking and appeared to be upset when he spoke with her. It is clear that Hogan was still upset by a startling event, which she had reported in the 911 call only minutes before; it is also reasonable to infer that the startling event that caused her visible distress was the physical altercation with Cox that she described to Deputy Herrick.

Cox also contends that the State failed to lay a proper foundation for the excited utterance exception because he asserts that Hogan was capable of thoughtful reflection when she made the statements to Deputy Herrick. In support of this, Cox compares Hogan's voice on the 911 call with Deputy Herrick's testimony regarding Hogan's emotional state when he interviewed her. Specifically, Cox seems to be arguing that Deputy Herrick testified that Hogan was calm when he interviewed her. However, our review of the record reveals that Deputy Herrick testified that Hogan was upset and crying. The trial court did not abuse its discretion in finding that the State had laid a proper foundation through Deputy Herrick's testimony regarding Hogan's emotional state.

Additionally, Cox cites Montgomery v. State, 694 N.E.2d 1137 (Ind. 1998), asserting that all circumstances must be considered when determining whether a hearsay statement can be admitted as an excited utterance. n2 In Montgomery, a police officer twice asked a gunshot victim who shot him. Both times, the victim merely stated that he needed to go home. After calming the man down, the officer asked again and the victim named Montgomery as the shooter. About one minute passed from the time of the officer's arrival at the scene to the time of the victim's statement. The man later died from the gunshot wound and the officer testified at trial regarding the victim's statement over Montgomery's hearsay objections.

Our supreme court examined the requirements for a statement to be considered an excited utterance and found the victim's statement met these requirements. 694 N.E. 2d at 1140-41. The main question was whether the victim's statement met the requirements for an excited utterance because the victim was answering questions from the officer rather than making his own statements. 694 N.E. 2d at 1141. The court noted that the officer did not suggest who the shooter was and there was no evidence that someone had coerced the victim to falsely name Montgomery. Id. Therefore, the court held that the hearsay testimony was properly admitted under the excited utterance exception.

We are presented with facts similar to Montgomery in the present case. Deputy Herrick was the first person at the scene to talk with Hogan. He asked her questions and she identified Cox as the person who had hit her. Cox has presented no evidence that Deputy Herrick suggested Cox's name to Hogan or that someone had coerced Hogan to Identify Cox as her assailant. Therefore, because Hogan's statements to Deputy Herrick satisfy the requirements for excited utterances and Cox has presented no evidence of coercion, the trial court did not abuse its discretion in admitting Deputy Herrick's testimony under the excited utterance hearsay exception.

II. Sufficiency of the Evidence

A. Standard of Review

Our standard of review for sufficiency claims is well settled. We will not reweigh the evidence or assess the credibility of witnesses. Smith v. State, 725 N.E.2d 160, 161 (Ind. Ct. App. 2000). We consider only the evidence most favorable to the judgment, together with all reasonable inferences that can be drawn therefrom. Alspach v. State, 755 N.E.2d 209, 210 (Ind. Ct. App. 2001), trans. denied. If a reasonable trier of fact could have found the defendant guilty based on the probative evidence and reasonable inferences drawn therefrom, then a conviction will be affirmed. Smith, 725 N.E.2d at 161.

B. Evidence of Domestic Battery

Cox next contends that there is insufficient evidence to sustain his domestic battery conviction. To convict Cox of this offense, the State was required to prove that he knowingly or intentionally touched Hogan, a person that he was living with as if she were his spouse, in a rude, insolent, or angry manner that resulted in bodily injury. Ind. Code § 35-42-2-1.3.

Cox seems to argue that because he testified that he did not strike Hogan out of anger and Hogan did not testify, the trial court erroneously convicted him. However, Deputy Herrick testified that Hogan had injuries to her face and neck when he arrived at the scene. Deputy Herrick also testified that Hogan told him that Cox struck her in the face and choked her. Additionally, Cox testified that he was angry at Hogan, that Hogan lived with him and that she was two months pregnant with his child at the time of the incident. This testimony is sufficient to support Cox's conviction. A reasonable trier of fact could have convicted Cox of domestic battery based on the probative evidence and reasonable inferences drawn therefrom.

Conclusion

The trial court did not abuse its discretion in admitting Deputy Herrick's testimony under the excited utterance hearsay exception. Additionally, there was sufficient evidence to support Cox's conviction. Therefore, Cox's conviction is affirmed.

MORGAN
v.
STATE

SUPREME COURT OF GEORGIA

275 Ga. 222, 564 S.E.2d 192, 2002 Ga. LEXIS 448 (2002)

JUDGES: Carley, Justice. All the Justices concur.

OPINION BY: Carley, Justice.

A jury found Felix Morgan guilty of the felony murder of Lawrence Hendrix while in the commission of an aggravated assault. The trial court entered judgment of conviction and sentenced him to life imprisonment. A motion for new trial was denied, and he appeals.

Construed in support of the verdict, the evidence shows that the victim and Morgan were visiting Hannelore Boose on the patio of her home. Ms. Boose was Morgan's girlfriend and the victim's close friend. When the victim questioned Morgan about his physical abuse of Ms. Boose, the two men began to argue. Ms. Boose and the victim went into the house. Morgan followed and fatally shot the victim, who was unarmed and who did not threaten or charge at Morgan. Immediately afterwards, Morgan tried to persuade Ms. Boose to say that his actions were self-defense. When he later called her to ask again and she refused, he threatened her. According to her testimony at trial, the assault on the victim was unprovoked. The evidence was sufficient to authorize a rational trier of fact to find beyond a reasonable doubt that Morgan did not act in self-defense in shooting the victim and that he was guilty of felony murder while in the commission of an aggravated assault. Jackson v. Virginia, 443 U.S. 307 (99 S. Ct. 2781, 61 L. Ed. 2d 560) (1979); Breland v. State, 269 Ga. 834 (504 S.E.2d 193) (1998).

Morgan contends that the trial court erred by denying certain motions in limine and allowing the State to present evidence of his previous altercation with the victim and of his prior fighting with and shooting at Ms. Boose. According to Morgan, the only purpose of such evidence was to prove that, because of his bad character, he was more likely to have committed the crime. However, the prior difficulties with the victim were clearly admissible to show Morgan's motive, intent, and bent of mind. Givens v. State, 273 Ga. 818, 823 (4) (546 S.E.2d 509) (2001). Morgan's physical abuse of Ms. Boose was relevant to the motive for the murder, because the evidence showed that the victim talked to Morgan about the mistreatment on prior occasions, and it was also the subject of their argument just prior to the shooting. Cummings v. State, 273 Ga. 547, 548 (2) (544 S.E.2d 429) (2001). See also Vaughns v. State, 274 Ga. 13, 14 (2) (549 S.E.2d 86) (2001); Givens v. State, supra at 821 (2).

Morgan complains that the trial court allowed the State to explore the subject of his parole status. On direct examination, however, he brought up that subject. Although Morgan did not thereby place his character in issue, he did raise "an issue which may be fully explored by the State on cross-examination. [Cit.]" Jones v. State, 257 Ga. 753, 759 (1) (b) (363 S.E.2d 529) (1988). The prosecutor here could have, but did not, question Morgan about the conviction for which he was on parole. Jones v. State, supra at 760 (2), fn. 10. Instead, the prosecutor merely confirmed that Morgan was on parole at the time of the crime and inquired whether he violated the conditions of his parole when he obtained the weapon which he used to shoot the victim. See Dowdy v. State, 209 Ga. App. 95, 96 (2) (432 S.E.2d 827) (1993) (parole documents admitted).

"Since . . . the appellant . . . introduced the topic on direct examination, he cannot now complain that the prosecutor followed up on cross-examination. [Cit.]" Willis v. State, 214 Ga. App. 659, 661 (3) (448 S.E.2d 755) (1994).

Morgan enumerates as error the admission of his custodial statement. Prior to making the statement, he signed a waiver of rights form, but informed the officer that he did not want to talk. When the officer prepared to leave, Morgan said that he would talk if there was no tape recorder or note-taking. The officer then sat down and, without any questioning, listened to Morgan's version of the events. Contrary to the argument on appeal, neither the transcript of the Jackson-Denno hearing nor the record shows that Morgan ever invoked his right to counsel. "Thus, we are not guided by Edwards[v. Arizona, 451 U.S. 477 (101 S. Ct. 1880, 68 L. Ed. 2d 378) (1981)], but by Michigan v. Mosley, 423 U.S. 96 (96 S. Ct. 321, 46 L. Ed. 2d 313) (1975). [Cit.]" Fields v. State, 266 Ga. 241, 242 (1) (466 S.E.2d 202) (1996). Mosley permits further dialogue with a suspect after his invocation of the right to remain silent, so long as certain requirements are met, even if the police reinitiate the interrogation. Bright v. State, 251 Ga. 440, 445-446 (2) (306 S.E.2d 293) (1983). In this case, Morgan himself initiated his statement, after previously expressing a different desire, thereby "clearly evincing his intent not to remain silent. [Cit.]" Larry v. State, 266 Ga. 284, 286 (2) (a) (466 S.E.2d 850) (1996). Morgan did not equivocate in his decision merely by specifying the absence of any immediate recording method as a condition. See Larry v. State, supra. Moreover, there was never an attempt to wear down his resistance and make him change his mind. Screws v. State, 245 Ga. App. 664, 666 (2) (538 S.E.2d 547) (2000). Accordingly, we find that the trial court did not err in admitting Morgan's custodial statement into evidence.

After being transported to the hospital, the victim told a police officer that Morgan "just shot me" and "we weren't fighting." The officer who took the statement testified that the victim was in great pain from the gunshot wound to his abdomen and asked the officer "if he was going to die." The officer told him "no, that the doctor was working on him now." Morgan contends that this testimony shows that the victim was not conscious of imminent death and, thus, that the trial court erroneously admitted the victim's statement as a dying declaration.

One of the requirements for a statement to be admissible as a dying declaration is that the deceased must have been "conscious of his condition. . . ." O.C.G.A. § 24-3-6. "It need only appear to the court from the circumstances of the case that there was a probability that the deceased was conscious of his condition at the time he made the statement . . ." Walton v. State, 79 Ga. 446, 450 (2) (5 S.E. 203) (1888). The testimony introduced as dying declarations need not "contain any statement by the deceased to the effect that he was conscious of impending death at the time the declarations were made, since this may be inferred from the nature of the wounds and other circumstances. [Cits.]" Morakes v. State, 201 Ga. 425, 436 (5) (40 S.E.2d 120) (1946). See also Norris v. State, 258 Ga. 889, 890 (2) (376 S.E.2d 653) (1989), overruled on other grounds, Johnson v. State, 272 Ga. 254 (526 S.E.2d 549) (2000). In this case, the fact that the victim asked whether he was going to die, his knowledge of the serious gunshot wound, the occurrence of his death within a matter of hours, and his great pain established a prima facie case that he realized that death was impending and, therefore, the ultimate determination was for the jury. See Morakes v. State, supra. The officer's reassurance of the victim did not preclude admission of the dying declaration. Morakes v. State, supra at 436, 437 (5). "To discount the statement as a dying declaration, the record must indicate that a negative response to the question 'Am I going to die?' relieved the declarant's fears and belief of [his] imminent death. [Cit.]" Charles v. State, 955 S.W.2d 400, 404 (Tex. App. 1997). The transcript does not show that the officer's response to the victim relieved his fears. Therefore, the trial court did not err in admitting the victim's statement as a dying declaration.

Moreover, even if a decedent's statement is not admissible as a dying declaration, it may be admitted under the res gestae exception to the hearsay rule. Andrews v. State, 249 Ga. 223 (290 S.E.2d 71) (1982). The trial court here correctly also relied on that exception, because the victim made his statement while receiving emergency treatment just 25 to 30 minutes after the shooting. See Jay v. State, 232 Ga. App. 661, 663 (3) (503 S.E.2d 563) (1998); Brinson v. State, 208 Ga. App. 556 (1) (430 S.E.2d 875) (1993); Salleywhite v. State, 133 Ga. App. 170 (1) (210 S.E.2d 334) (1974).

* * *

Judgment affirmed. All the Justices concur.

STATE
v.
WASHINGTON

SUPREME COURT OF MICHIGAN

664 N.W.2d 203; 2003 Mich. LEXIS 1465 (2003)

JUDGES: Chief Justice Maura D. Corrigan, Justices Michael F. Cavanagh, Elizabeth A. Weaver, Marilyn Kelly, Clifford W. Taylor, Robert P. Young, Jr., Stephen J. Markman. KELLY, J. (dissenting).

OPINION: PER CURIAM
Defendant was convicted of armed robbery and assault with intent to do great bodily harm less than murder. The Court of Appeals reversed the convictions because the accomplice's statement, in which the accomplice identified himself as the shooter, was improperly admitted against defendant. 251 Mich. App. 520; 650 N.W.2d 708 (2002). It also found that the trial court abused its discretion in denying defense counsel the opportunity to conduct voir dire of a juror in mid-trial. We reverse the judgment of the Court of Appeals and reinstate the verdict.

I

On May 8, 1998, two men robbed James Turner while he was using a public pay phone at a Detroit gas station. One of the men pulled a gun, pointed it at Turner's head, and demanded money. The other went through Turner's pockets and took his watch and pager. When Turner told his assailants that he didn't have anything else of value, he was shot in the back.

A few minutes later, two police officers saw a car containing defendant and Daniel Mathis drive into an alley behind a gas station that was approximately a mile from the scene of the robbery. The officers decided to investigate because the area was known for drug sales and prostitution. Defendant was uncooperative with the officers and, following a scuffle, he was handcuffed pending further investigation. As the officers returned to talk to Mathis, who had remained in the car, the report of the Turner robbery and a

description of his assailants were broadcast over the police radio. When one of the officers asked to have the description repeated, Mathis blurted out, "I did it—I'm the shooter." Turner identified defendant in a lineup as one of his assailants. He failed to identify Mathis.

Defendant and Mathis were charged with armed robbery, MCL 750.529, and assault with intent to murder, MCL 750.83. They were tried separately. On the morning of defendant's trial, the issue whether Mathis's statement was admissible was raised. Without elaboration, the trial court decided that the statement would be allowed into evidence. Defendant was convicted of armed robbery and assault with intent to do great bodily harm less than murder, MCL 750.84.

The Court of Appeals reversed defendant's convictions. It concluded that Mathis's statement was improperly admitted as a statement against penal interest because it was not reliable. According to assertions made by defense counsel, Mathis was mentally ill. n1 In addition, the panel found that the trial court should have allowed defense counsel to question a juror in mid-trial.

II

The decision to admit evidence is reviewed for an abuse of discretion. People v Starr, 457 Mich. 490, 494; 577 N.W.2d 673 (1998). When the decision regarding the admission of evidence involves a preliminary question of law, such as whether a statute or rule of evidence precludes admissibility of the evidence, the issue is reviewed de novo. People v Lukity, 460 Mich. 484, 488; 596 N.W.2d 607 (1999).

III

Declarations against penal interest constitute an exception to the general proscription against hearsay provided by MRE 802. MRE 804(b)(3),in pertinent part, defines a declaration against penal interest as

[a] statement which was at the time of its making . . . so far tended to subject the declarant to civil or criminal liability . . . that a reasonable person in the declarant's

position would not have made the statement unless believing it to be true. A statement tending to expose the declarant to criminal liability and offered to exculpate the accused is not admissible unless corroborating circumstances clearly indicate the trustworthiness of the statement.

The exception is based on the assumption that people do not generally make statements about themselves that are damaging unless they are true. People v Poole, 444 Mich. 151, 161; 506 N.W.2d 505 (1993), citing the comment of the Advisory Committee on Federal Rules of Evidence relating to FRE 804(b)(3). Mathis's statement is against his penal interest and, therefore, is admissible.

The inquiry, however, does not stop there because the Confrontation Clauses of the federal and state constitutions are implicated. US Const, Am VI; Const 1963, art 1, § 20. The admission of Mathis's statement as substantive evidence does not violate the Confrontation Clause if the prosecution can establish that Mathis was unavailable as a witness and that his statement bore adequate indicia of reliability. Alternatively, the Confrontation Clause is not violated if the statement fell within a firmly rooted hearsay exception. Poole, supra at 163.

Some jurisdictions have held that the hearsay exception for statements against penal interest is a firmly rooted hearsay exception. See, e.g., United States v McKeeve, 131 F.3d 1, 9 (CA 1, 1997), People v Wilson, 17 Cal App 4th 271, 278; 21 Cal.Rptr.2d 420 (1993), and State v Tucker, 109 Ore. App. 519, 526; 820 P.2d 834 (1991). However, we need not decide that issue because Mathis had been charged with the crimes and was considered unavailable because it was expected that he would assert his Fifth Amendment right not to testify. Additionally, Mathis's statement bears adequate indicia of reliability.

In Poole, supra at 165, we instructed:

In evaluating whether a statement against penal interest that inculpates a person in addition to the declarant bears sufficient indicia of reliability to allow it to be admitted as substantive evidence against the other person, courts must evaluate the circumstances surrounding the making of the statement as well as its content.

The presence of the following factors would favor admission of such a statement: whether the statement was (1) voluntarily given, (2) made contemporaneously with the events referenced, (3) made to family, friends, colleagues, or confederates—that is, to someone to whom the declarant would likely speak the truth, and (4) uttered spontaneously at the initiation of the declarant and without prompting or inquiry by the listener.

On the other hand, the presence of the following factors would favor a finding of inadmissibility: whether the statement (1) was made to law enforcement officers or at the prompting or inquiry of the listener, (2) minimizes the role or responsibility of the declarant or shifts blame to the accomplice, (3) was made to avenge the declarant or to curry favor, and (4) whether the declarant had a motive to lie or distort the truth.

Courts should also consider any other circumstance bearing on the reliability of the statement at issue. See, generally, United States v Layton, 855 F.2d 1388, 1404-1406 (CA 9, 1988). While the foregoing factors are not exclusive, and the presence or absence of a particular factor is not decisive, the totality of the circumstances must indicate that the statement is sufficiently reliable to allow its admission as substantive evidence although the defendant is unable to cross-examine the declarant.

When those precepts are applied to the facts at bar, we find that Mathis's statement to the police officers bears sufficient indicia of reliability to satisfy Confrontation Clause concerns and to allow its admission as substantive evidence at trial. The statement was voluntarily given and made contemporaneously with the events referenced. It was uttered spontaneously by Mathis and without prompting or inquiry by the officers. In fact, the officers had just heard of the robbery when Mathis made the statement. Mathis did not minimize his role in the crimes, admitting that he shot the victim, and he had no motive to lie or distort the truth. In addition, there is nothing in the statement indicating that the declarant was attempting to curry favor at the time he made the statement.

We agree with the dissenting judge of the Court of Appeals that there was no record evidence establishing that Mathis "suffered from mental illness." The unsubstantiated assertions of defense counsel are not substantive evidence and cannot be used to undermine the indicia of reliability contained in the accomplice's statement.

IV

* * *

V

We conclude that the accomplice's statement contains sufficient "particularized guarantees of trustworthiness," considering the totality of the circumstances surrounding its utterance, to justify its admission. Poole, supra at 164.

* * * Accordingly, we reverse the judgment of the Court of Appeals and reinstate the judgment of the circuit court. MCR 7.302(F)(1).

KELLY, J. (dissenting).

I disagree that the indicia of reliability surrounding codefendant's statement were sufficient to support admission of the statement into evidence in defiance of the confrontation clauses of the state and federal constitutions. Rather, I agree with the Court of Appeals majority that the circuit court should not have admitted the statement. The majority, Judge Kirsten Frank Kelly and Judge Harold Hood, aptly stated:

A review of the record reveals an assertion by defense counsel that codefendant Mathis suffered from mental illness and that he had a history of psychiatric and psychological treatment. Certainly, an inculpatory statement made by a mentally ill codefendant that tacitly inculpates defendant as his accomplice is not a statement that contains "particularized guarantees of trustworthiness" sufficient to introduce the statement as substantive evidence against defendant without the opportunity for cross-examination. Permitting codefendant's statement to come in as substantive evidence against defendant, while depriving defendant the opportunity to challenge that statement through the adver-

sarial process, violates the bedrock principles underlying the Confrontation Clause itself. Indeed, "'the Confrontation Clause is generally satisfied when the defense is given a full and fair opportunity to probe and expose . . . infirmities through cross-examination, thereby calling to the attention of the factfinder the reasons for giving scant weight to the witness' testimony.'" [People v Gearns, 457 Mich. 170, 186; 577 N.W.2d 422 (1998)] quoting Delaware v Fensterer, 474 U.S. 15, 22; 106 S. Ct. 292; 88 L. Ed. 2d 15 (1985) (emphasis omitted).

The trial court's admission of codefendant's inculpatory statement as substantive evidence against defendant without providing defendant any opportunity to challenge the statement through cross-examination is not harmless error. Based on the evidence presented at trial, it is more probable than not that a different outcome would have resulted without the admission of codefendant's statement.

On appeal, the prosecution asserts that defendant ran from the police officers, but neither the testimony of defendant nor the officers supports this assertion. Also, the prosecution contends that defendant tried to drive away. However, the testimony of the officers actually indicates that the car was never started and that they were not even sure if defendant attempted to insert the keys into the ignition. Furthermore, defendant was alleged to have stolen $ 71, but, when apprehended, he had over $ 500 on his person. Neither he nor codefendant had a gun, the stolen pager, the stolen watch, and these items were not found in the car in which they were traveling. The fact that defendant was found within minutes of the robbery within one mile of the crime scene does not tend to establish his guilt any more than any other person who lives in the area and was also at the gas station at the same time. Finally, the description the victim gave to the police was "quite vague" and did not match either the defendant or codefendant.

Although we acknowledge the victim identified defendant in a lineup, we do not believe this, standing alone, clothes the codefendant's statement with "adequate indicia of reliability." The lineup was conducted ten days after the robbery and after the victim had been sedated and medicated in the hospital for five days. The victim identified the defendant as the man who shot him, but defendant was tried as the accomplice of the shooter. In addition, the victim did not identify the codefendant.

As we noted People v Spinks, 206 Mich. App. 488, 493; 522 N.W.2d 875 (1994), quoting People v Banks, 438 Mich. 408, 430; 475 N.W.2d 769 (1991), if the ""'minds of an average jury" would have found the prosecution's case "significantly less persuasive" had the statement of the [accomplice] been excluded,'" then the error is not harmless. Considering that codefendant's statement is the only concrete evidence linking defendant to the crime for which he now stands con-

victed, we find that had the statement been properly excluded, the prosecution's case would have been significantly less persuasive in "the minds of an average jury". Accordingly, we find that the trial court abused its discretion by admitting the statement. [251 Mich. App. 520, 527-529; 650 N.W.2d 708 (2002).]

For the reasons expressed by the Court of Appeals majority, I would hold the codefendant's statement inadmissible. Accordingly, I would affirm the decision of the Court of Appeals and allow the case to be remanded for a new trial.

Cases Relating to Chapter 13

Documentary Evidence

WILKERSON

v.

STATE

Court of Appeals of Arkansas,
Division Two
2005 Ark. App. LEXIS 12 (2005)

ROBERT J. GLADWIN, Judge. HART
and BAKER, JJ., agree.

ROBERT J. GLADWIN, Judge

Appellant Jeffery Scott Wilkerson seeks
the reversal of his conviction for delivering a
Schedule VI controlled substance—marijuana. On appeal, appellant argues that the trial
court erred: (1) by denying his motion for a
directed verdict because there was insufficient evidence to support the conviction; (2)
in admitting into evidence a tape recording
between a confidential informant and appellant that was not properly authenticated; (3)
in failing to suppress evidence where the
application for search warrant failed to set
forth particular facts bearing on the informant's reliability; (4) by denying his motion
to suppress where the search warrant did not
indicate that it was based upon either recorded testimony or sworn affidavits. We affirm.

Lonnie Cogburn testified that while he was
working as a confidential informant for Officer Chris Martin, he contacted appellant in an
effort to purchase marijuana. Officer Martin
equipped Cogburn with a micro-cassette
recorder and gave him a twenty-dollar bill and
a ten-dollar bill as buy money, both of which
were photocopied by the police for verification purposes. On or about January 15, 2003,

Cogburn met appellant on the road and asked
him about the drugs, at which time appellant
handed him the marijuana through the car
window in exchange for the thirty dollars.
Cogburn then returned to Officer Martin and
gave him the quarter-bag of marijuana and the
micro-cassette recorder and tape.

On or about January 23, 2003, appellant
was charged with the delivery of a Schedule
VI controlled substance, a Class C felony,
pursuant to Ark. Code Ann. § 5-64-
401(a)(1)(iv) for allegedly delivering to a
confidential informant, directly supervised
by an officer with the 18th West Judicial District Drug Task Force, marijuana, the aggre-
gate weight of which, including adulterants
or dilutents, was less than one ounce. A trial
was held on September 2, 2003, and appellant was convicted by a Montgomery County
jury, sentenced to six years in the Arkansas
Department of Correction, and ordered to
pay a $ 5000 fine. This appeal followed.

Denial of motion for directed verdict

The standard of review in cases challenging the sufficiency of the evidence is well
established. We treat a motion for a directed
verdict as a challenge to the sufficiency of
the evidence. *Fairchild v. State*, 349 Ark.
147, 76 S.W.3d 884 (2002); *Branscum v.
State*, 345 Ark. 21, 43 S.W.3d 148 (2001).
This court has repeatedly held that, in
reviewing a challenge to the sufficiency of
the evidence, we view the evidence in a light
most favorable to the State and consider only
the evidence that supports the verdict. *Stone
v. State*, 348 Ark. 661, 74 S.W.3d 591 (2002).

We affirm a conviction if substantial evidence exists to support it. *Id.* Substantial evidence is that which is of sufficient force and character that it will, with reasonable certainty, compel a conclusion one way or the other, without resorting to speculation or conjecture. *Jones v. State*, 336 Ark. 191, 984 S.W.2d 432 (1999). The testimony of one eyewitness alone is sufficient to sustain a conviction. *See Lenoir v. State*, 77 Ark. App. 250, 72 S.W.3d 899 (2002). Moreover, the appellate court does not weigh the evidence presented at trial or weigh the credibility of witnesses, as these are matters to be resolved by the finder of fact. *Id.*

Arkansas Code Annotated section 5-64-401 provides that it is unlawful for any person to deliver a controlled substance. "Delivery" is defined as the actual, constructive, or attempted transfer of a controlled substance or counterfeit substance in exchange for money or anything of value. *See* Ark. Code Ann. § 5-64-101(f). There was testimony from Cogburn, the confidential informant who supposedly bought the marijuana, describing the details of the "buy" from appellant. There was also a tape recording of the transaction; however, no written transcript of the tape is available to confirm its corroboration of Cogburn's testimony. There was also evidence that the specific twenty-dollar bill and ten-dollar bill that were given to Cogburn as buy money were found in appellant's wallet at the time of his arrest, as verified by the photocopies previously made by the police and by testimony from Officer Martin. Resolution of conflicts in testimony and assessment of witness credibility is for the fact-finder. *Slater v. State*, 76 Ark. App. 365, 65 S.W.3d 481 (2002). There was substantial evidence to support appellant's conviction for delivery of a controlled substance.

Admitting into evidence a tape recording between the a confidential informant and appellant that allegedly was not properly authenticated

Appellant alleges that the micro-cassette recording purporting to corroborate Cogburn's description of the drug buy was erroneously allowed into evidence without proper authentication under Rule 901 of the Arkansas Rules of Evidence. Rule 901(a)

specifically states that the requirement of authentication or identification as a condition precedent to admissibility is satisfied by evidence sufficient to support a finding that the matter in question is what its proponent claims. Appellant argues that prior to the admission of the recording, none of the parties speaking on the recording testified that it was a true and accurate depiction of the conversation, and he further contends that Officer Martin was not present when that conversation took place.

Officer Martin testified that after Cogburn left with the thirty dollars and the micro-cassette recorder, there were numerous times during the course of the drug buy that Cogburn was out of his sight. Appellant attempts to distinguish the facts of this case from those in *Smithey v. State*, 269 Ark. 538, 602 S.W.2d 676 (Ark. App. 1980), where the Arkansas Supreme Court found proper authentication where the officer involved testified that he saw the informant talking with the defendant while the officer listened to the conversation electronically and watched a videotape of the parties. In the instant case, Cogburn was the only witness for the State who was present when the recording was made, and he testified that he had never listened to it.

Additionally, Officer Martin testified that he had limited knowledge about the recording, in that he only knew what the recording itself told him about the interaction between Cogburn and appellant. Appellant maintains that this scenario is markedly different from the facts in *Walker v. State*, 13 Ark. App. 124, 680 S.W.2d 915 (1984), where the supreme court found that where one of the undercover officers who was present when the tapes were recorded testified as to their accuracy and authenticity, the officer's testimony was sufficient to authenticate the recordings.

Officer Martin testified that he gave Cogburn the micro-cassette recorder and then followed him around "as best as [he] could" until Cogburn returned with the recorder and the marijuana he purchased from appellant. Officer Martin explained that there were times Cogburn was out of his sight because he could not follow Cogburn too closely, considering that everyone knew the vehicle he drove and that he did not want to put either Cogburn or himself in danger. Officer Martin stated that after receiving the tape and recorder back from Cogburn, he took it to the police department and logged it into the evidence vault. He testified that the transaction lasted only seconds and that he had listened to the tape many times since receiving it from Cogburn. The State reiterates that the tape recording is corroborated by Cogburn's testimony regarding the transaction. The State argues that the authentication requirement of Rule 901(a) is satisfied where a trial judge, in his discretion, is satisfied that the physical evidence presented is genuine and in reasonable probability has not been tampered with. *Guydon v. State*, 344 Ark. 251, 39 S.W.3d 767 (2001).

In evidentiary determinations, a trial court has wide discretion, and we will not reverse a trial court's ruling on the admission of the evidence absent an abuse of discretion. *See Davis v. State*, 350 Ark. 22, 86 S.W.3d 872 (2002). Further, we do not reverse a trial court's evidentiary decision absent a showing of prejudice. *Id.* The tape was properly introduced, and the content of the recording goes to the weight of the evidence rather than to its admissibility. There is also substantial evidence of appellant's guilt, including Cogburn's eyewitness account of the buy, as well as the "buy money" being recovered from appellant's wallet upon his arrest. The tape recording of the drug buy is cumulative, and any error occasioned by the trial court's admission of the recording was rendered harmless beyond a reasonable doubt by the admission of the other evidence. *See Jackson v. State*, ___ Ark. ___, ___ S.W.3d ___, 2004 Ark. LEXIS 638 (Nov. 4, 2004).

* * *

[The defendant's other arguments possessed insufficient merit to obtain a reversal of his conviction.]

Affirmed.
HART and BAKER, JJ., agree.

McKEEHAN
v.
STATE

COURT OF APPEAL OF FLORIDA, FIFTH DISTRICT

838 So. 2d 1257, 2003 Fla. App. LEXIS 3367 (2003)

JUDGES: MONACO, J. THOMPSON, C.J., and SAWAYA, J., concur.

The defendant, Ronald McKeehan, was found guilty after jury trial of robbery with a firearm, grand theft, aggravated assault with a firearm, and kidnapping with intent to commit a felony. All of these crimes were purportedly committed at a Sleep Inn Motel in Orlando. McKeehan asserts that the trial court committed error by allowing the State to prove the contents of a videotape with oral testimony, rather than with the tape itself.

During the course of the trial, the State introduced collateral crime evidence of a robbery of an Extended Stay America Hotel that was close to the site of the Sleep Inn that occurred a few days before the crimes related to the present case. A clerk who worked at the Extended Stay Hotel testified and identified McKeehan as the perpetrator of the robbery there. The State then called an investigator with the sheriff's office who investigated both robberies. He testified that he had seen a surveillance videotape of the Extended Stay robbery. When the prosecutor asked him if he saw the defendant on the tape, the defense objected, citing the best evidence rule, and pointed out that the State should be required to introduce the tape. The objection, however, was overruled, and the investigator was permitted to testify that the defendant was shown on the videotape.

During jury deliberations, the jury asked the court by written inquiry two questions concerning the evidence. First, the jury asked why the videotape had not been introduced into evidence. The jury also asked if it was permitted to consider the investigator's testimony concerning his observation of the defendant on the tape "as evidence." The trial judge explained to the jury that he could not answer why the videotape had not been introduced, but that the jury was permitted to consider the testimony of the investigator with regard to the tape.

The best evidence rule is set forth in section 90.952, Florida Statutes (2002), as follows:

Except as otherwise provided by statute, an original writing, recording, or photograph is required in order to prove the contents of the writing, recording, or photograph.

Section 90.954, Florida Statutes, amplifies the preceding statute by providing that:

The original of a writing, recording, or photograph is not required, except as provided in s. 90.953 [concerning duplicates], and other evidence of its contents is admissible when:

(1) All originals are lost or destroyed, unless the proponent lost or destroyed them in bad faith.
(2) An original cannot be obtained in this state by any judicial process or procedure.
(3) An original was under the control of the party against whom offered at a time when that party was put on notice by the pleadings or by written notice from the adverse party that the contents of such original would be subject to proof at the hearing, and such original is not produced at the hearing.
(4) The writing, recording, or photograph is not related to a controlling issue.

The best evidence rule, as codified by statute, requires that if the original evidence or a statutorily authorized alternative n1 is available, no evidence should be received which is merely "substitutionary in nature." Liddon v. Bd. of Pub. Instruction for Jackson County, 128 Fla. 838, 175 So. 806, 808 (Fla. 1937); Sun Bank of St. Lucie County v. Oliver, 403 So. 2d 583, 584 (Fla. 4th DCA 1981). Thus, evidence which indicates that a more original source of information is available should be excluded. Id. In short, unless otherwise excused by the evidence code, the original must be produced unless it is shown to be unavailable for a reason other than the serious fault of the proponent. See Williams v. State, 386 So. 2d 538, 540 (Fla. 1980); Firestone Serv. Stores, Inc. of Gainesville v. Wynn, 131 Fla. 94, 179 So. 175 (Fla. 1938).

This rule is predicated on the principle that if the original evidence is available, that evidence should [**5] be presented to ensure accurate transmittal of the critical facts contained within it. See Williams; State v. Eubanks, 609 So. 2d 107 (Fla. 4th DCA 1992). Thus, in Williams it was found to be error for the trial court to permit introduction of oral evidence of what the victim of an attempted murder wrote (which implicated the defendant in the crime), while at a hospital awaiting treatment. The supreme court noted that no effort had been made by the state to explain the absence of the original writing.

The same is true in the instant case concerning the videotape of the Extended Stay Hotel robbery. The State sought to prove the contents of the videotape not by introduction of the tape, but by oral testimony of its contents without ever establishing the videotape's unavailability. Accordingly, the admission of the testimony violated the best evidence rule.

A violation of the best evidence rule may, however, constitute harmless error. In Williams, the supreme court affirmed despite the error, explaining:

Rather than contesting the accuracy of the terms contained in Ms. Marshall's note, appellant's objection was directed to the reliability of the out-of-court identification, an issue not addressed by the best evidence rule. Moreover, counsel had ample opportunity to discredit the identification by cross-examining Ms. Marshall about the events at the hospital. Given this posture, we do not believe that the trial court's technical error injuriously affected the substantial rights of appellant. § 59.041, Fla. Stat. (1975). 386 So. 2d at 540 (footnote omitted).

Under a harmless error analysis, the state must show beyond a reasonable doubt that the error complained of did not contribute to the verdict, or, stated alternatively, that there is no reasonable possibility that the error contributed to the conviction. State v. DiGuilio, 491 So. 2d 1129, 1136 (Fla. 1986); Stires v. State, 824 So. 2d 943 (Fla. 5th DCA 2002). Application of the rule "requires an examination of the entire record by the appellate court including a close examination of the permissible evidence on which the jury could have legitimately relied and, in addition, an even closer examination of the impermissible evidence which might have possibly influenced the jury verdict." DiGuilio, 491 So. 2d at 1135. [**7] As our supreme court has noted, "the harmless error analysis focuses on the effect of the error on the trier of fact." Goodwin v. State, 751 So. 2d 537, 542 (Fla. 1999) (quoting State v. Lee, 531 So. 2d 133, 137 (Fla. 1988)).

The question, therefore, is not whether the evidence against the defendant was overwhelming. Lee, 531 So. 2d at 136-37; Jones v. State, 754 So. 2d 792 (Fla. 1st DCA 2000). A reviewing court "must resist the temptation to make its own determination of whether a guilty verdict could be sustained by excluding the impermissible evidence and examining only the permissible evidence." Goodwin, 751 So. 2d at 542.

In the instant case, the pivotal issue at trial concerned identification of the perpetrator of the Sleep Inn robbery. The sole evidence directly tying the defendant to the Sleep Inn robbery was the desk clerk's eyewitness testimony. The State attempted to bolster the desk clerk's identification with Williams rule evidence linking the defendant to another recent and very similar hotel robbery in the same vicinity. The victim of the second robbery identified McKeehan as the perpetrator of that crime.

The State then presented an investigator's identification of the defendant from the videotape. As this identification confirmed the identification of the defendant made by the victim, it might appear to amount to the erroneous admission of cumulative evidence that would constitute harmless error. [Citations omitted.]

In the present case, however, the jury's inquiry of the court relating, first, to the absence of the videotape, and then to the investigator's identification testimony based on his examination of the tape, makes it quite evident that the jury seriously considered that particular testimony in reaching its verdict. Moreover, the use by the State in this case of evidence less than the original, when there was no demonstration that the original was unavailable, authorizes an inference that the proponent's position would have been defeated if the best evidence had been furnished. Liddon, 175 So. at 808. Under the circum-

stances, therefore, we cannot say that there is no reasonable possibility that the inadmissible testimony contributed to the conviction. DiGuilio, 491 So. 2d at 1135. Given the questions from the jury, in fact, it is far more likely that the erroneously admitted testimony had an influence on the jury verdict. Accordingly, we reverse the convictions and order a new trial.

REVERSED and REMANDED.
THOMPSON, C.J., and SAWAYA, J., concur.

STATE
v.
HUEHN

COURT OF APPEALS OF COLORADO, DIVISION FIVE

53 P.3d 733, 2002 Colo. App. LEXIS 21 (2002)

JUDGES: Opinion by JUDGE VOGT. Kapelke and Erickson, JJ., concur.

Defendant, Daniel Huehn, appeals the judgment of conviction entered on a jury verdict finding him guilty of theft. We affirm.

On December 24, 1998, technicians responding to a call to service a Key Bank automated teller machine (ATM) discovered that the safe at the bottom of the machine was unlocked and the money cassettes normally found there were missing. The cassettes had been in the safe when the ATM was serviced on the morning of December 23, and customers had withdrawn money from the machine throughout that day. Computer records showed that the safe had been opened at approximately 9:30 p.m. on December 23, although there had been no call for service at that hour.

Defendant, one of the ATM technicians who had access to this machine, admitted in a written statement to his employer that he had opened the safe sometime between 8:30 and 9:30 p.m. on December 23 while at the site on a call regarding another ATM. He claimed, however, that the cassettes were still in the safe at that time.

I.

Defendant first contends that the trial court abused its discretion in admitting into evidence certain computer-generated records that were not sufficiently authenticated. We disagree.

The exhibits at issue are computer records reflecting customer transactions and technician servicing at the ATM on December 23 and 24, 1998. Four of the exhibits were records generated for Key Bank by Money Access Services (MAC), with whom Key Bank had contracted to process its ATM transactions. Defendant objected to admission of these records on the grounds that there was an insufficient foundation for their admission as business records under CRE 803(6) and the records were not authenticated in accordance with CRE 901(b)(9). The trial court overruled the objections and admitted the exhibits.

Although he did not object on this basis at trial, defendant also contends on appeal that Exhibit 14, a portion of a status tape that recorded the openings and closings of the ATM vault on a hard drive inside the machine, should have been excluded for lack of authentication.

A.

As an initial matter, we reject defendant's contention that, because computer-generated evidence is "a species of scientific evidence," the prosecution had to make the showing required under Frye v. United States, 54 App. D.C. 46, 293 F. 1013 (D.C. Cir. 1923), or Daubert v. Merrell Dow Pharmaceuticals, Inc., 509 U.S. 579, 113 S. Ct. 2786, 125 L. Ed. 2d 469 (1993), before the evidence could be admitted. See People v. Shreck, 22 P.3d 68 (Colo. 2001)(CRE 702, rather than Frye, governs admissibility of scientific evidence).

In support of his contention, defendant cites R. Bailin et. al., Colorado Evidentiary Foundations (Miche 1997). However, that authority itself recognizes that, while presentation of scientific evidence usually requires proof of the validity of the underlying theory and the reliability of the instrument, "computers are so widely accepted and used that the proponent of computer evidence need not

prove those two elements of the foundation." Colorado Evidentiary Foundations, supra, ch. 4(C)(2), at 52; see also Brooks v. People, 975 P.2d 1105, 1112 n.7 (Colo. 1999)(rejecting view that "whenever one can find 'science' by scratching beneath the surface of expert testimony, the validation rules governing scientific evidence would have to apply").

The trial court in this case properly focused its inquiry on whether a sufficient foundation had been laid to warrant admission of the proffered records under the applicable rules of evidence.

B.

The admissibility of a computer printout is governed by the rules of relevancy, authentication, and hearsay. Benham v. Pryke, 703 P.2d 644 (Colo. App. 1985), rev'd on other grounds, 744 P.2d 67 (Colo. 1987). The relevancy of the computer records in this case is not disputed.

The requirement of authentication as a condition precedent to admissibility is satisfied by evidence sufficient to support a finding that the matter in question is what its proponent claims. CRE 901(a). Whether a proper foundation has been established is a matter within the sound discretion of the trial court, whose decision will not be disturbed absent a clear abuse of that discretion. People v. Slusher, 844 P.2d 1222 (Colo. App. 1992).

The hearsay objection to the admissibility of computer-generated records may be overcome by, among other methods, showing that such records are admissible under CRE 803(6), the business records exception to the hearsay rule. Material and relevant computer records are admissible under this exception if: (1) the computer entries are made in the regular course of business; (2) those participating in the record making were acting in the routine course of business; (3) the input procedures were accurate; (4) the entries were made within a reasonable time after the transaction involved; and (5) the information was transmitted by a reliable person with knowledge of the event reported. Palmer v. A.H. Robins Co., 684 P.2d 187 (Colo. 1984); Benham v. Pryke, supra.

C.

Here, Key Bank's ATM accounting supervisor testified that transactions at the bank's ATMs are electronically communicated to, and recorded by, MAC, which handles the processing of the transactions. MAC's computer-generated reports for each ATM are transmitted daily to Key Bank, stored for three months in Key Bank's computer, then transferred to fiche. The witness testified that Key Bank received and stored the records in the ordinary course of its business, and he identified the exhibits at issue as accurate copies of Key Bank's fiche record of activity at the ATM on the relevant dates.

A representative of the company that serviced Key Bank's ATMs testified similarly that the status tapes for the ATMs are kept inside the ATMs on the hard drive and automatically record each opening and closing of the safe.

It was undisputed that the entries on all the exhibits were made within a reasonable time of the transactions involved.

Defendant contends that this testimony was insufficient to satisfy the requirements for admitting computer records under CRE 803(6) because (1) the first four exhibits were MAC records but were not introduced by anyone from MAC, and (2) the prosecution did not show that the computer input procedures were accurate by complying with the authentication procedure in CRE 901(b)(9). We reject both contentions.

1.

The fact that the records created by MAC were introduced through the Key Bank officer, whose department received and kept the records, did not preclude their admission under CRE 803(6). See Hauser v. Rose Health Care Systems, 857 P.2d 524 (Colo. App. 1993)(documents created by one business but regularly received, maintained, and relied upon by another may be admitted as business records of the latter); Teac Corp. v. Bauer, 678 P.2d 3 (Colo. App. 1984)(records prepared by another source that are adopted and integrated in regular course of established business procedures into records sought to be introduced are admissible under

CRE 803(6), even if identity of person whose first-hand knowledge was the basis of a particular entry is not established).

2.

Defendant also argues that, to establish the accuracy of the input procedures, the prosecution was required to proceed in accordance with CRE 901(b)(9), which permits authentication by "evidence describing a process or system used to produce a result and showing that the process or system produces an accurate result." This showing was not made, he contends, because the Key Bank foundation witness admitted on cross-examination that he did not know how or when the MAC computer had been programmed, whether it had been repaired, or whether procedures were used to ensure the accuracy of the program. Nor did the authentication witness for Exhibit 14, the status list, testify that the system that generated the list produced an accurate result.

Defendant acknowledges that Colorado cases have not previously required compliance with CRE 901(b)(9) as a condition of admitting computer-generated business records. However, he cites Colorado Evidentiary Foundations, supra, for the proposition that Colorado courts have been "lax" in applying the authentication requirement to computer records, admitting them with "minimal analysis of authenticity issues," and he argues that we should require such further authentication in this case. We decline to do so.

First, although CRE 901(b)(9) may be used to authenticate computer records, there is no requirement, either in the rule itself or in Colorado case law construing the rule, that computer records be authenticated only in this way.

Second, computer business records have a greater level of trustworthiness than an individually generated computer document such as that at issue in People v. Slusher, supra, relied on by defendant, in which a division of this court upheld the exclusion of a purported lease agreement that was apparently created by the defendant on his computer.

Finally, courts have generally declined to require testimony regarding the functioning and accuracy of the computer process where, as here, the records at issue are bank records reflecting data entered automatically rather than manually. See United States v. Moore, 923 F.2d 910 (1st Cir. 1991) (testimony by bank's loan officer was sufficient to authenticate computer-generated loan histories); State v. Veres, 7 Ariz. App. 117, 436 P.2d 629 (Ariz. Ct. App. 1968)(fact that bank's foundation witness was unfamiliar with operation of encoding machine that generated bank records did not preclude their admission as business records), overruled by State v. Osborn, 107 Ariz. 295, 486 P.2d 777 (Ariz. 1971); People v. Lugashi, 205 Cal. App. 3d 632, 252 Cal. Rptr. 434 (Cal. Ct. App. 1988) (where computer record consists of retrieval of automatic inputs rather than computations based on manual entries, testimony on acceptability, accuracy, maintenance, and reliability of computer hardware and software need not be produced for purposes of admitting record into evidence).

In People v. Lugashi, microfiche copies of computer tapes containing credit card account information were introduced in a prosecution for grand theft. In rejecting an authentication argument similar to that made here, the Lugashi court observed that bank statements prepared in the regular course of banking business, in accordance with banking regulations, are in a different category than ordinary business and financial records of a private enterprise. The court also noted that the "bulk of other jurisdictions" had similarly declined to require more extensive authentication of such records. People v. Lugashi, supra, 252 Cal. Rptr. at 442 (collecting cases).

We agree with the rationale of those decisions upholding the admission of computer-generated bank records without the additional authentication urged by defendant, and accordingly conclude that the trial court did not abuse its discretion in declining to exclude the computer records in this case based on lack of authentication.

II.

Defendant next contends that admission of an incomplete copy of the status tape that recorded openings and closings of the ATM safe violated the best evidence rule. We disagree.

Under CRE 1002 and 1003, the so-called "best evidence rules," an original is generally required to prove the contents of a writing, but a duplicate is admissible to the same extent as an original unless (1) a genuine question is raised as to the authenticity of the original, or (2) under the circumstances, it would be unfair to admit the duplicate in lieu of the original. CRE 1004(1) further provides that an original is not required if it has been lost or destroyed, unless it was lost or destroyed in bad faith.

Determining the admissibility of evidence offered in lieu of an original writing under these rules is within the trial court's discretion, and that court's determination will not be disturbed absent clear evidence of mistake amounting to an error of law. United Cable Television of Jeffco, Inc. v. Montgomery LC, Inc., 942 P.2d 1230 (Colo. App. 1996).

Mere speculation or supposition that an original document may have contained information that the duplicate did not, or vice versa, does not amount to a showing that it would be unfair to admit the duplicate and thus does not preclude admission of the duplicate under CRE 1003. Equico Lessors, Inc. v. Tak's Automotive Service, 680 P.2d 854 (Colo. App. 1984).

The prosecution's foundation witness for Exhibit 14 identified it as a copy of a portion of the status tape that was kept inside the ATM on the hard drive. The tape was retrieved by a technician who took it off the machine in the presence of the witness. The witness then took the original tape roll and photocopied the portions offered into evidence. At the time of trial, he did not know where the original tape was.

Defendant objected to admission of the copy on the basis that it was incomplete and portions of some entries were cut off at the bottom of the page. He argued that the original tape was required. The trial court disagreed, noting that the critical portion, showing entry into the safe at 9:30 p.m. on December 23, was not cut off.

Admission of the duplicate was not an abuse of discretion. The foundation witness testified that the location of the original tape was unknown, and there was nothing to indicate that the original had been lost or destroyed in bad faith. For the reasons set forth in Part I, above, there is no genuine question as to the authenticity of the original tape. Finally, defendant has not shown that it was unfair to admit the duplicate in lieu of the original. He argues that a cut-off entry at the bottom of the first page of the exhibit might have shown a door opening at 6:56 p.m. on December 23, thereby establishing that the theft could have occurred then. This argument is not only speculative, see Equico Lessors, Inc. v. Tak's Automotive Service, supra, but also contradicts defendant's own written statement that the cassettes were in the safe when he opened it between 8:30 and 9:30 p.m. on December 23.

* * *

The judgment is affirmed.

Cases Relating to Chapter 14

Real Evidence

SCHMERBER
v.
CALIFORNIA

**Supreme Court of the United States
384 U.S. 757, 86 S. Ct. 1826,
16 L. Ed. 2d 908 (1966)**

MR. JUSTICE BRENNAN delivered the opinion of the Court.

Petitioner was convicted in Los Angeles Municipal Court of the criminal offense of driving an automobile while under the influence of intoxicating liquor. He had been arrested at a hospital while receiving treatment for injuries suffered in an accident involving the automobile that he had apparently been driving. At the direction of a police officer, a physician at the hospital then withdrew a blood sample from petitioner's body. The chemical analysis of this sample revealed a percent by weight of alcohol in his blood at the time of the offense which indicated intoxication, and the report of this analysis was admitted in evidence at the trial. Petitioner objected to receipt of this evidence of the analysis on the ground that the blood had been withdrawn despite his refusal, on the advice of his counsel, to consent to the test. He contended that in that circumstance the withdrawal of the blood and the admission of the analysis in evidence denied him due process of law under the Fourteenth Amendment, as well as specific guarantees of the Bill of Rights secured against the States by that Amendment; his privilege against self-incrimination under the Fifth Amendment; his right to counsel under the Sixth Amendment; and his right not to be subjected to unreasonable searches and seizures in violation of the Fourth Amendment. The Appellate Department of the California Superior Court rejected these contentions and affirmed the conviction. In view of constitutional decisions since we last considered these issues in Breithaupt v. Abram, 352 U.S. 432—see Escobedo v. Illinois, 378 U.S. 478; Malloy v. Hogan, 378 U.S. 1, and Mapp v. Ohio, 367 U.S. 643—we granted certiorari. 382 U.S. 971. We affirm.

I.

The Due Process Clause Claim

Breithaupt was also a case in which police officers caused blood to be withdrawn from the driver of an automobile involved in an accident, and in which there was ample justification for the officer's conclusion that the driver was under the influence of alcohol. There, as here, the extraction was made by a physician in a simple, medically acceptable manner in a hospital environment. There, however, the driver was unconscious at the time the blood was withdrawn and hence had no opportunity to object to the procedure. We affirmed the conviction there resulting from the use of the test in evidence, holding that under such circumstances the withdrawal did not offend "that 'sense of justice' of which we spoke in Rochin v. California, 342 U.S. 165." 352 U.S., at 435. Breithaupt thus requires the rejection of petitioner's due process argument, and nothing in the circumstances of this case or in supervening events persuades us that this aspect of Breithaupt should be overruled.

II.

The Privilege Against
Self-Incrimination Claim

Breithaupt summarily rejected an argument that the withdrawal of blood and the admission of the analysis report involved in that state case violated the Fifth Amendment privilege of any person not to "be compelled in any criminal case to be a witness against himself," citing Twining v. New Jersey, 211 U.S. 78. But that case, holding that the protections of the Fourteenth Amendment do not embrace this Fifth Amendment privilege, has been succeeded by Malloy v. Hogan, 378 U.S. 1, 8. We there held that "the Fourteenth Amendment secures against state invasion the same privilege that the Fifth Amendment guarantees against federal infringement—the right of a person to remain silent unless he chooses to speak in the unfettered exercise of his own will, and to suffer no penalty . . . for such silence." We therefore must now decide whether the withdrawal of the blood and admission in evidence of the analysis involved in this case violated petitioner's privilege. We hold that the privilege protects an accused only from being compelled to testify against himself, or otherwise provide the State with evidence of a testimonial or communicative nature, and that the withdrawal of blood and use of the analysis in question in this case did not involve compulsion to these ends.

It could not be denied that in requiring petitioner to submit to the withdrawal and chemical analysis of his blood the State compelled him to submit to an attempt to discover evidence that might be used to prosecute him for a criminal offense. He submitted only after the police officer rejected his objection and directed the physician to proceed. The officer's direction to the physician to administer the test over petitioner's objection constituted compulsion for the purposes of the privilege. The critical question, then, is whether petitioner was thus compelled "to be a witness against himself."

If the scope of the privilege coincided with the complex of values it helps to protect, we might be obliged to conclude that the privilege was violated. In Miranda v. Arizona, ante, at 460, the Court said of the interests protected by the privilege: "All these policies point to one overriding thought: the constitutional foundation underlying the privilege is the respect a government—state or federal—must accord to the dignity and integrity of its citizens. To maintain a 'fair state-individual balance,' to require the government 'to shoulder the entire load' . . . to respect the inviolability of the human personality, our accusatory system of criminal justice demands that the government seeking to punish an individual produce the evidence against him by its own independent labors, rather than by the cruel, simple expedient of compelling it from his own mouth." The withdrawal of blood necessarily involves puncturing the skin for extraction, and the percent by weight of alcohol in that blood, as established by chemical analysis, is evidence of criminal guilt. Compelled submission fails on one view to respect the "inviolability of the human personality." Moreover, since it enables the State to rely on evidence forced from the accused, the compulsion violates at least one meaning of the requirement that the State procure the evidence against an accused "by its own independent labors."

As the passage in Miranda implicitly recognizes, however, the privilege has never been given the full scope which the values it helps to protect suggest. History and a long line of authorities in lower courts have consistently limited its protection to situations in which the State seeks to submerge those values by obtaining the evidence against an accused through "the cruel, simple expedient of compelling it from his own mouth. . . . In sum, the privilege is fulfilled only when the person is guaranteed the right 'to remain silent unless he chooses to speak in the unfettered exercise of his own will.'" Ibid. The leading case in this Court is Holt v. United States, 218 U.S. 245. There the question was whether evidence was admissible that the accused, prior to trial and over his protest, put on a blouse that fitted him. It was contended that compelling the accused to submit to the demand that he model the blouse violated the privilege. Mr. Justice Holmes, speaking for the Court, rejected the argument as "based upon an extravagant extension of the Fifth Amendment," and went on to say: "The prohibition of compelling a man in a criminal court to be witness against himself is a prohibition of the use of physical or moral compulsion to extort communications from him, not an exclusion of his body as evidence when it may be material. The objection in principle would forbid a jury to look at a prisoner and compare his features with a photograph in proof." 218 U.S., at 252-253.

It is clear that the protection of the privilege reaches an accused's communications, whatever form they might take, and the compulsion of responses which are also communications, for example, compliance with a subpoena to produce one's papers. Boyd v. United States, 116 U.S. 616. On the other hand, both federal and state courts have usually held that it offers no protection against compulsion to submit to fingerprinting, photographing, or measurements, to write or speak for identification, to appear in court, to stand, to assume a stance, to walk, or to make a particular gesture. The distinction which has emerged, often expressed in different ways, is that the privilege is a bar against compelling "communications" or "testimony," but that compulsion which makes a suspect or accused the source of "real or physical evidence" does not violate it.

Although we agree that this distinction is a helpful framework for analysis, we are not to be understood to agree with past applications in all instances. There will be many cases in which such a distinction is not readily drawn. Some tests seemingly directed to obtain "physical evidence," for example, lie detector tests measuring changes in body function during interrogation, may actually be directed to eliciting responses which are essentially testimonial. To compel a person to submit to testing in which an effort will be made to determine his guilt or innocence on the basis of physiological responses, whether willed or not, is to evoke the spirit and history of the Fifth Amendment. Such situations call to mind the principle that the protection of the privilege "is as broad as the mischief against which it seeks to guard," Counselman v. Hitchcock, 142 U.S. 547, 562.

In the present case, however, no such problem of application is presented. Not even a shadow of testimonial compulsion upon or enforced communication by the accused was involved either in the extraction or in the chemical analysis. Petitioner's testimonial capacities were in no way implicated; indeed, his participation, except as a donor, was irrelevant to the results of the test, which depend on chemical analysis and on that alone. Since the blood test evidence, although an incriminating product of compulsion, was neither petitioner's testimony nor evidence relating to some communicative act or writing by the petitioner, it was not inadmissible on privilege grounds.

* * *

Affirmed. MR. JUSTICE HARLAN, whom MR. JUSTICE STEWART joins, concurring.

In joining the Court's opinion I desire to add the following comment. While agreeing with the Court that the taking of this blood test involved no testimonial compulsion, I would go further and hold that apart from this consideration the case in no way implicates the Fifth Amendment. Cf. my dissenting opinion and that of MR. JUSTICE WHITE in Miranda v. Arizona, ante, pp. 504, 526.

MR. CHIEF JUSTICE WARREN, dissenting.

While there are other important constitutional issues in this case, I believe it is sufficient for me to reiterate my dissenting opinion in Breithaupt v. Abram, 352 U.S. 432, 440, as the basis on which to reverse this conviction.

MR. JUSTICE BLACK with whom MR. JUSTICE DOUGLAS joins, dissenting.

I would reverse petitioner's conviction. I agree with the Court that the Fourteenth Amendment made applicable to the States the Fifth Amendment's provision that "No person . . . shall be compelled in any criminal case to be a witness against himself. . . ." But I disagree with the Court's holding that California did not violate petitioner's constitutional right against self-incrimination when it compelled him, against his will, to allow a doctor to puncture his blood vessels in order to extract a sample of blood and analyze it for alcoholic content, and then used that analysis as evidence to convict petitioner of a crime.

* * *

MR. JUSTICE DOUGLAS, dissenting.

I adhere to the views of THE CHIEF JUSTICE in his dissent in Breithaupt v. Abram, 352 U.S. 432, 440, and to the views I stated in my dissent in that case (id., 442) and add only a word.

We are dealing with the right of privacy which, since the Breithaupt case, we have held to be within the penumbra of some specific guarantees of the Bill of Rights. Griswold v. Connecticut, 381 U.S. 479. Thus, the Fifth Amendment marks "a zone of privacy" which the Government may not force a person to surrender. Id., 484. Likewise the Fourth Amendment recognizes that right when it guarantees the right of the people to be secure "in their persons." Ibid. No clearer invasion of this right of privacy can be imagined than forcible bloodletting of the kind involved here.

MR. JUSTICE FORTAS, dissenting.

I would reverse. In my view, petitioner's privilege against self-incrimination applies. I would add that, under the Due Process Clause, the State, in its role as prosecutor, has no right to extract blood from an accused or anyone else, over his protest. As prosecutor, the State has no right to commit any kind of violence upon the person, or to utilize the results of such a tort, and the extraction of blood, over protest, is an act of violence. Cf. CHIEF JUSTICE WARREN's dissenting opinion in Breithaupt v. Abram, 352 U.S. 432, 440.

STATE
v.
COWANS

APPELLATE COURT OF ILLINOIS, FIRST DISTRICT, SIXTH DIVISION

336 Ill. App. 3d 173, 782 N.E.2d 779, 2002 Ill. App. LEXIS 1170 Appeal denied by People v. Cowans, 2003 Ill. LEXIS 649 (Ill., Apr. 2, 2003)

JUDGES: JUSTICE O'MARA FROSSARD delivered the opinion of the court. O'BRIEN, P.J., and GALLAGHER, J., concur.

Following a bench trial defendant was found guilty of one count of possession of a controlled substance with intent to deliver. The trial court sentenced defendant to seven years in the Illinois Department of Corrections. On appeal, defendant challenges the sufficiency of the evidence and contends the stipulated facts, together with the entire trial record, fail to establish a complete chain of custody for the controlled substance.

BACKGROUND

The State called Officer McCarthy as a witness and introduced additional evidence through two stipulations. McCarthy testified that around 9:45 p.m. on January 22, 2000, near 4936 West Huron Street, he observed defendant with the aid of binoculars. During a five-minute surveillance McCarthy saw four individuals approach defendant, engage in a brief conversation, and give defendant money. Defendant placed the money in his pants pocket and gave a small object to each individual. When McCarthy was about 15 feet away, defendant looked in his direction and threw a number of small plastic bags to the ground. McCarthy recovered from the ground nine small plastic bags containing what he suspected to be cocaine. Defendant was arrested. McCarthy searched defendant and recovered $ 190 from his pants pocket. McCarthy testified that he later inventoried the nine small plastic bags under inventory number 2295494 and the money under inventory number 2295495. The Nash School was located about one block away.

The State offered two stipulations agreed to by defense counsel. By way of stipulation it was agreed that if Investigator Tansy were to testify he would state that he measured the distance from 4936 West Huron Street to the Nash School and found it was 742 feet. It was further stipulated that if forensic scientist Maureen Dully were to testify she would state that she received nine items under inventory number 2295494 and tested five of the nine items, which she found contained 1.2 grams of cocaine.

Defendant and Lonniece Young-Frazier testified in the defense case. Frazier testified that she knows defendant, but does not know him personally. On January 22, 2000, between 9 p.m. and 10 p.m., she was a passenger in a car in front of 4935 West Huron Street. She saw the defendant walking westbound on the north side of Huron Street when two uniformed officers, a male and female, approached him. Defendant put his hands up in the air. Frazier testified that she did not see defendant drop anything on the ground and did not see anyone passing objects for money. She testified that the officers searched defendant, handcuffed him, and placed him in the police car. Frazier testified that the male officer had a flashlight and was looking on the ground all over the area, including under porches two or three houses away.

Defendant testified that he was walking home from the store after playing the lottery. He was on the north side of Huron Street. Officer McCarthy and a female police officer pulled up in a marked squad car. Defendant denied he had anything in his hands or dropped anything; he denied selling drugs or possessing any drugs. Defendant stated that McCarthy searched him, found money, and told the female officer that defendant must be doing something. Defendant was handcuffed and placed in the squad car. McCarthy searched the area with a flashlight. Defendant testified that when McCarthy got into the car he showed defendant a plastic pouch and then drove to the police station.

ANALYSIS

Defendant stipulated to certain facts at trial. Generally, a defendant is precluded from attacking any facts previously agreed to

in a stipulation. Defendant does not attack the specific facts agreed to in the stipulation. Defendant, relying on In re R.F., 298 Ill. App. 3d 13, 16, 232 Ill. Dec. 519, 698 N.E.2d 610 (1998), challenges the sufficiency of the evidence and argues that the stipulated facts, together with the entire trial record, fail to establish a sufficiently complete chain of custody.

When a defendant challenges the sufficiency of the evidence, the relevant inquiry is whether, after viewing the evidence in the light most favorable to the prosecution, any rational trier of fact could have found the essential elements of the crime beyond a reasonable doubt. [Citations omitted.] A challenge to the sufficiency of the evidence is not subject to the waiver rule and may be raised for the first time on direct appeal. People v. Enoch, 122 Ill. 2d 176, 119 Ill. Dec. 265, 522 N.E.2d 1124 (1988).

Before real evidence may be admitted at trial, the State must provide an adequate foundation either by way of live testimony or stipulation which establishes that the item sought to be introduced is the actual item involved in the alleged offense and that its condition is substantially unchanged. People v. Cole, 29 Ill. App. 3d 369, 375, 329 N.E.2d 880 (1975). Where an item possesses unique and readily identifiable characteristics and its substance is relatively impervious to change, testimony at trial that the item sought to be admitted in evidence is the same one recovered and in substantially the same condition as when recovered is sufficient to establish an adequate foundation. People v. Gilbert, 58 Ill. App. 3d 387, 15 Ill. Dec. 956, 374 N.E.2d 739 (1978). If the item is not readily identifiable or if it is susceptible to alteration by tampering or contamination, its chain of custody must be established by the State with sufficient completeness to render it improbable that the original item has either been exchanged, contaminated, or subjected to tampering. People v. Winters, 97 Ill. App. 3d 288, 289, 52 Ill. Dec. 763, 422 N.E.2d 972 (1981).

The character of the item determines which method for laying an adequate foundation must be used. [Citation omitted.] Based on the character of the evidence in this case, the chain of custody must be established by the State with sufficient completeness to render it improbable that the original item has either been exchanged, contaminated, or subjected to tampering. Thus, the State was required to establish a chain of custody to demonstrate the connection between the items recovered from the ground by Officer McCarthy after discarded by defendant and the items tested by forensic scientist Maureen Dully.

Regarding that connection, the record contained the testimony of Officer McCarthy and the stipulated testimony of forensic scientist Maureen Dully. The testimony of Officer McCarthy on direct examination by the State regarding recovering and handling the controlled substance was as follows:

"Q. What happened as you were approaching the defendant?

A. He looked in my direction, and he threw to the ground numerous plastic bags. I recovered these bags and found them to be nine clear, plastic bags each containing white, rocky substance that I believed to be crack cocaine.

***

Q. Officer, did you later inventory the U.S. currency and the suspect rock cocaine?

A. Yes.

Q. And did you inventory the nine, clear baggies containing the suspect rock cocaine under inventory number 2295494?

A. Yes."

On cross-examination McCarthy testified as follows:

"Q. And you were 15 feet away from him, and that's when he threw these things down on the ground?

A. I said approximately 15 feet.

Q. And could you see then what those things were?

A. I could tell they were, at least, clear, plastic bags.

Q. Were they tinted at all?

A. Yes.

Q. What color tint?

A. Green."

The agreed stipulation between the State and defense regarding the testimony of forensic scientist Duffy was as follows:

"[711 LAW CLERK FOR THE STATE]: Also, that if Maureen Dully, a forensic scientist employed by the Illinois State Police Division of Forensic Services were to be called, she would testify that on February 7, 2000, she received the following inventory number, 2295494, which contained nine items, and that she tested five of those nine items and that she has determined that—with a reasonable degree of scientific certainty that the five tested items tested positive for 1.2 grams of cocaine. So stipulated? [DEFENSE ATTORNEY]: Yes."

The testimony of Officer McCarthy and the stipulation regarding the testimony of forensic scientist Dully was in total the evidence produced by the State regarding chain of custody.

In order to prove its case, the State is required to prove a connection between the defendant and the illegal contraband. In doing so the State is required to establish a proper chain of custody. A sufficient chain of custody does not require that every person involved in the chain testify, nor must the State exclude all possibilities that the evidence may have been subject to tampering. Winters, 97 Ill. App. 3d at 295. The State must demonstrate that the evidence has not been changed in any important respect. People v. Hominick, 177 Ill. App. 3d 18, 29, 126 Ill. Dec. 422, 531 N.E.2d 1049 (1988). The State is required to establish that it took reasonable protective measures since the substance was seized. People v. Hermann, 180 Ill. App. 3d 939, 944, 129 Ill. Dec. 656, 536 N.E.2d 706 (1988). The purpose of the protective measures is to ensure that the substance taken from the defendant was the same as the substance tested by the forensic chemist. People v. Ryan, 129 Ill. App. 3d 915, 919, 85 Ill. Dec. 93, 473 N.E.2d 461 (1984).

We are mindful that unless the defendant produces actual evidence of tampering, substitution, or contamination, the State need only establish a probability that tampering, substitution or contamination did not occur, and any deficiencies go to the weight rather than the admissibility of the evidence. Hominick, 177 Ill. App. 3d at 29. In the instant case, defendant did not produce actual evidence of tampering, substitution, or contamination. Therefore, the State is only required to establish a probability that reasonable protective measures were employed to protect the evidence from the time it was seized and that it was improbable the evidence was altered. People v. Bynum, 257 Ill. App. 3d 502, 510, 196 Ill. Dec. 179, 629 N.E.2d 724 (1994). To establish a sufficiently complete chain of custody, the State is required to prove delivery, presence, and safekeeping of the evidence. People v. Gibson, 287 Ill. App. 3d 878, 882, 223 Ill. Dec. 234, 679 N.E.2d 419 (1997).

The State, relying on People v. Irpino, 122 Ill. App. 3d 767, 78 Ill. Dec. 165, 461 N.E.2d 999 (1984), contends that the chain of custody was sufficiently established in this case because the "testimony clearly demonstrated that the evidence seized 'matched' the evidence subjected to chemical analysis." We recognize that if one link in the chain is missing, but there is evidence describing the condition of the evidence when delivered which matches the description of the evidence when examined, the evidence can be sufficient to establish chain of custody. Irpino, 122 Ill. App. 3d at 775.

Officer McCarthy testified he recovered from the ground nine small plastic bags with a green tint that contained suspected crack cocaine after being discarded by the defendant. The record reflects by way of stipulation that the forensic scientist received nine items and tested the contents of five items, which she found to contain 1.2 grams of cocaine. The officer's description includes details about the color, shape and packaging of the items, but not the weight. The forensic scientist's stipulation contains no corresponding details about the color, shape and packaging of the items. The forensic scientist's stipulation includes a weight estimate, but in no way further describes the items.

Here, the only common features in the testimony describing the condition of the evidence when seized and the description of the evidence when tested are the number of items and the inventory number. The stipulation of the testimony provided by the forensic scientist did not include whether the items she received were in plastic bags or whether the bags were colored or clear. The stipulation of the testimony provided by the forensic scien-

tist did not include any description as to size, shape, or color of the items received. Officer McCarthy described the evidence as a white, rocky substance. However, there was no corresponding or "matching" description provided by the forensic scientist in the stipulation as to the shape and color of the substance. While there was evidence that the nine plastic bags retrieved from the ground by Officer McCarthy were distinctive in color, that distinctive color was not included in the description of the items tested by the forensic scientist provided by the State's stipulation. Rather, the stipulation referenced the evidence by use of the generic term "items." The "items" received by forensic scientist Duffy were given no further description in the stipulation.

As noted, where there is evidence describing the condition of the evidence when seized, which matches the description of the evidence when examined, the evidence can be sufficient to establish chain of custody. Irpino, 122 Ill. App. 3d at 775. For the reasons previously discussed, we cannot conclude that the record reflects the condition of the evidence when seized sufficiently matches the description of the evidence when tested. This gap in the chain of custody is not resolved by the record.

Moreover, the record reflects several additional missing links in the chain of custody regarding proof of handling, delivery, presence, and safekeeping of the evidence. To establish a sufficiently complete chain of custody, the State is required to prove delivery, presence, and safekeeping of the evidence. Gibson, 287 Ill. App. 3d at 882. The record reflects no reasonable protective techniques regarding custody, handling, delivery, presence, and safekeeping of the alleged contraband. The State presented no evidence of what procedures, if any, were used in the handling and safekeeping of the evidence between Officer McCarthy's recovery of the plastic bags and the receipt of the evidence by forensic scientist Dully 16 days later. The record contains no evidence either by live testimony or stipulation as to what Officer McCarthy did with the plastic bags he retrieved from the ground after defendant allegedly discarded them, other than the fact that McCarthy inventoried those items under an inventory number. There is no evidence that the plastic bags recovered from the ground from Officer McCarthy were placed in any closed or sealed container or envelope or were initialed or dated by Officer McCarthy; no evidence as to what condition the items were kept in during the 16 days that passed before forensic scientist Dully received them; no evidence that the items received at the crime laboratory were received sealed; and no evidence of the whereabouts of the plastic bags for the 16 days that passed from the time Officer McCarthy recovered the plastic bags on January 22, 2000, and February 7, 2000, when forensic scientist Duffy received the items.

Regarding chain of custody, the State relies on People v. Leemon, 66 Ill. 2d 170, 172, 5 Ill. Dec. 250, 361 N.E.2d 573 (1977), and argues "the court held in Leemon that the police officer's testimony identifying the bag he recovered from the defendant, together with a stipulation between the parties that the contents of the bag were LSD, made a sufficient showing of continuity of possession of custody." In Leemon, Officer Edwards described the bag of LSD he purchased from defendant which he had marked with the date and his initials. That plastic bag containing LSD was received in evidence. Unlike Leemon, the record in this case contains no testimony by Officer McCarthy during trial identifying the baggies he recovered from the defendant, either in the form of live testimony or by way of stipulation. There is no evidence that Officer McCarthy marked the baggies with the date and his initials. In Leemon, the plastic bag containing LSD recovered by the police officer from the defendant was received in evidence. Unlike Leemon, in the instant case the baggies containing the controlled substance recovered by Officer McCarthy were not offered into evidence by the State or received into evidence by the court either through live testimony or by way of stipulation. The controlled substance in this case was never given an exhibit number. Here, the State not only failed to provide an adequate foundation to introduce the contraband into evidence, but it never sought to introduce into evidence the controlled substance either by live testimony or stipulation.

As previously noted, the State must provide an adequate foundation demonstrating the item sought to be offered into evidence is the actual item involved in the alleged offense and its condition is substantially unchanged. McCarthy never identified the narcotics as those retrieved after being discarded by defendant nor did the State establish that fact by way of stipulation. McCarthy never testified that, at the time of trial, the controlled substance was in substantially the same condition as when he inventoried it, nor did the State establish that fact by way of stipulation. The record reflects no evidence by way of live testimony or stipulation that the items recovered by McCarthy were substantially unchanged from the time of the offense to the time of trial. The record contains no evidence either by live testimony or stipulation that Officer McCarthy would identify the items tested by Dully and would testify that these items were in the same or substantially the same condition as when he recovered these items from the ground after they were allegedly discarded by defendant on January 22, 2000. These gaps in the chain of custody are not resolved by the record.

There are additional gaps in the chain of custody. There is no evidence either by way of direct testimony or stipulation regarding delivery of the items to the crime laboratory. The stipulation indicates the items were received on February 7, 2000. However, there is no evidence in the record as to where those "items" were for 16 days from January 22, 2000, until February 7, 2000. There is no testimony, live or stipulated, describing the condition of the items when delivered to the crime laboratory. There is no evidence the items were delivered in a closed or sealed container. There is no evidence of any protective measures the State took from the point the substance was recovered by Officer McCarthy until the point the items were received 16 days later at the crime laboratory by forensic scientist Duffy.

Reversal for evidentiary insufficiency is required when the State fails to prove its case. As recently noted in People v. Moore, "When the issue is one which concerns the sufficiency of the evidence, we are required to reverse outright, whereas the erroneous admission of evidence is a procedural error which allows us to remand for a new trial." People v. Moore, 335 Ill. App. 3d 616, 781 N.E.2d 493, 2002 Ill. App. LEXIS 1058, (November 15, 2002), citing People v. Olivera, 164 Ill. 2d 382, 393, 207 Ill. Dec. 433, 647 N.E.2d 926 (1995). In this case, defendant challenges the sufficiency of the evidence. There is no issue regarding the erroneous admission of the controlled substance, because the State never sought to admit the controlled substance either by live testimony or stipulation.

Moreover, in this case there is no challenge to the stipulated facts and no contention that the stipulations were misstated. See People v. Maurice, 31 Ill. 2d 456, 457-59, 202 N.E.2d 480 (1964) (where stipulation was misstated, court concluded admission of heroin into evidence without sufficient chain of custody required reversal and remand for new trial). Rather, in the instant case, the defendant challenges the sufficiency of the evidence and argues that the stipulated facts, considered together with the entire trial record, fail to establish a sufficiently complete chain of custody. See In re R.F., 298 Ill. App. 3d at 15 (insufficient foundation provided by State for admission of controlled substance required outright reversal).

CONCLUSION

The evidence was insufficient to sustain defendant's conviction because the State failed to establish a sufficient chain of custody for the controlled substance. The State failed to demonstrate that the police took reasonable protective measures to ensure that the substance recovered by Officer McCarthy from the ground after abandoned by defendant was the same or substantially the same as the items tested by forensic chemist Dully. There was no evidence regarding the handling and safekeeping of the controlled substance from the point in time when Officer McCarthy recovered the evidence until the point in time when forensic scientist Dully received the evidence 16 days later.

Other than the testimony of Officer McCarthy that he inventoried the evidence under inventory number 2295494, the only other evidence offered to prove the chain of custody was the stipulation, which merely established that Duffy tested five of nine "items" assigned to inventory number 2295494, which tested positive for 1.2 grams of cocaine. The State failed to establish a sufficiently complete chain of custody by proof of delivery, presence and safekeeping of the controlled substance. The State failed to establish a probability that reasonable measures were used to protect the evidence from the time that it was seized and that it was improbable the evidence was altered.

For the reasons previously discussed, we find the evidence was insufficient to prove defendant guilty beyond a reasonable doubt.

Reversed.

O'BRIEN, P.J., and GALLAGHER, J., concur.

UNDERWOOD
v.
STATE

Supreme Court of Mississippi
708 So. 2d 18 (1998)

En Banc.
SULLIVAN, Presiding Justice, for the Court:

PART ONE: GUILT PHASE

1. Justin Underwood was indicted for capital murder by the grand jury for Madison County during the March Term of 1994. The indictment charged that Underwood had murdered Virginia Ann Harris on or about February 15, 1994, by shooting her with a pistol, during the course of kidnapping, in violation of Miss. Code Ann. § 97-3-19(2)(e). Underwood pleaded not guilty and proceeded to trial on May 22, 1995, in the Circuit Court of Madison County. The jury returned a verdict of guilty on the charge of capital murder on May 24. The sentencing phase of the trial was held on the following day, and the jury found that Underwood should be sentenced to death. Circuit Judge John B. Toney entered the final judgment of conviction and sentence on May 25, and ordered that Underwood be put to death by lethal injection on July 7, 1995. Following

denial of his motion for judgment notwith-standing the verdict, or in the alternative for a new trial, Underwood perfected his appeal to this Court.

STATEMENT OF THE FACTS

2. On February 15, 1994, Lindsay Harris spoke with his wife, Virginia Ann Harris, before leaving their home in Flora to travel to his produce business at the Farmer's Market in Jackson. Mrs. Harris asked her husband to eat dinner in Jackson on his way home from work, because she planned to do some shopping in Jackson that day. Mr. Harris agreed, told his wife goodbye, and left for work at about 6:00 A.M. He worked from 6:30 A.M. until closing time at 4:00 P.M., when he loaded a delivery order in his truck and left for Flora at about 4:30 P.M.

3. When Mr. Harris arrived at his house, he saw his wife's car, a blue Lincoln Towncar, in the garage, but when he entered the home and called her name, there was no answer. He noticed that the lights and television were on in the den, and the curtains were drawn. Walking back to their bedroom, Mr. Harris saw that Mrs. Harris's makeup drawer was pulled open, the lights were on, and a make-up bottle was left upside down on the counter. Mr. Harris and his son Kyle both testified that it was unlike Mrs. Harris to leave the house in such a condition.

4. At about 5:00 P.M., Mr. Harris changed clothes and left to go feed his cattle. When he returned, Mrs. Harris still wasn't home. He showered and dressed for bed, and by 8:00 P.M. he was extremely worried about his wife. He started calling family and friends, but no one knew where she was. At midnight Mr. Harris called the police and reported Mrs. Harris as a missing person. At 12:30 or 1:00 A.M., Officer Ogden Wilson arrived at the Harris home and filled out a missing person report, which he forwarded to the sheriff's department.

5. At 1:30 A.M. Mr. Harris called his son Kyle and told him that Mrs. Harris was still missing. Kyle came over immediately, and the two conducted a search of the house and yard. On their way back into the house through the garage, Kyle noticed that the keys to Mrs. Harris's Lincoln were in the ignition. They also discovered Mrs. Harris's purse on the floor of the front passenger side of the car, which was not Mrs. Harris's custom. Kyle testified that his mother normally kept her purse on the seat beside her. There was no money in the purse, which was unusual for Mrs. Harris, who usually carried at least $40 with her at all times. The only unlocked car door was the driver's door, indicating that only one person had exited the car, because when the ignition was turned, all of the doors automatically locked. The front seat of the car was pushed back to its furthermost position, which was also out of character for Mrs. Harris. Mr. Harris testified that he was 5'9", and his feet didn't touch the pedals in Mrs. Harris's car with the seat that far back. Charles Scarborough, Master Sergeant Trooper with the Mississippi Highway Patrol, testified that he was 5'11" and would not be comfortable with the seat in that position. Mr. Harris also testified that he believed the Lincoln was parked in the garage differently than Mrs. Harris usually parked it. Nothing was missing from the house, other than possibly some cash from Mrs. Harris's purse. At this point, Mr. Harris and Kyle agreed that Mrs. Harris must have been kidnapped.

6. At 6:00 A.M. on February 16, the highway patrol, police, and sheriff's department were contacted, and detectives began arriving at the Harris home to take over the investigation. Sergeant Scarborough lifted fingerprints and fibers from Mrs. Harris's Lincoln and took pictures of the car. Only two latent prints of value were lifted from the car, and neither were matched with anyone, including the defendant, Justin Underwood. The fibers taken from Mrs. Harris's car similarly were not linked to anyone, including Underwood. Sergeant Judy Tucker with the Mississippi Highway Patrol Investigation Bureau was called to head up the investigation. Mr. Harris described to Sergeant Tucker the state of the house as he found it on the evening of February 15. He also showed her Mrs. Harris's pill box with two of five pills missing from her February 15 doses, her diet log book showing that she had consumed only two glasses of water on the morning of February 15, and a shopping list left on the kitchen counter of items that Mrs. Harris planned to buy in Jackson on February 15. Based upon the state of the house when Mr.

Harris arrived home on February 15, Sergeant Tucker determined that Mrs. Harris had not left the house of her own free will.

7. Sergeant Tucker contacted her supervisors for further instructions, and a search of the area was organized, including an aerial search. The investigators discovered that Mrs. Harris had missed her 11:15 appointment at Jenny Craig Weight Loss Centre and her afternoon nail appointment at Mona's Nails in Jackson. Mona's had called the Harris home at 2:30 P.M. on February 15 with no response. With the help of Mrs. Harris's daughter-in-law, Lynette Harris, they determined that Mrs. Harris's red house shoes, blue robe, and a wide black belt were missing.

8. Around 4:40 P.M. in the afternoon on February 16, Webb Bozeman informed authorities that two of his employees had seen Mrs. Harris's car backed into a cattle gap on his property on old Highway 49, approximately 1.5 miles from the Harris home, between 9:00 and 10:00 A.M. on February 15. Testimony at trial placed Underwood's car, or one very similar to it, in a driveway near the Harris home on February 15 at approximately 10:00 or 10:30 A.M. Based upon the tip from Mr. Bozeman's employees, Sergeant Tucker and other law enforcement officers went to the cattle gap and began searching. At about 5:10, Officer Donny Spell found a black belt in a fire lane on the Bozeman property near Bozeman Lake. Continuing on around the lake shore, at about 5:20, Sergeant Tucker discovered Mrs. Harris's body, clothed in a blue pleated shirt, black knit pants, and red house shoes. Clumps of grass and weeds were clutched in her hands. Mrs. Harris only had foundation makeup on the right side of her face. At trial, Mr. Harris testified that in more than forty years of marriage, his wife had never left the house without having makeup on or without being properly dressed. After contacting the crime scene unit, Sergeant Tucker accompanied Dudley Bozeman to notify Mr. Harris and his family.

9. Mrs. Harris had been shot four times. Two of the bullets did not exit Mrs. Harris's body, and these were sent to the Mississippi Crime Lab for testing following the autopsy. One bullet traveled from her back through her right lung, diaphragm, and liver. A second bullet struck the right side of her back and penetrated her right lung. Dr. Steven Hayne, who performed the autopsy, testified that either of these first two gunshot wounds would have individually caused death due to extensive internal bleeding. A third bullet struck Mrs. Harris's left ear, went through the ear, struck and went through the left side of her neck, and struck her front right shoulder. Dr. Hayne testified that this gunshot would not have caused death by itself. The fourth bullet entered the front of Mrs. Harris's left arm and exited the inner arm. This gunshot wound was also nonlethal. All four of the gunshot wounds were distant, meaning that the shots were fired more than 1 to 2 feet away, and they occurred at or about the same time. The angles of the gunshot wounds were consistent with Mrs. Harris being on her knees and the shooter standing behind her. Dr. Hayne testified that the manner of Mrs. Harris's death was homicide, and that it would have taken a minimum of fifteen to twenty minutes for Mrs. Harris to die from her wounds.

10. When Mrs. Harris's body was discovered, rigor mortis had set in, indicating that Mrs. Harris had been dead for at least two hours, but no more than forty eight hours. Fly larvae, or maggots, were in both of Mrs. Harris's ears, indicating that she had been dead for at least twelve to twenty four hours. Based upon Sergeant Tucker's testimony that the body was discovered at about 5:20 P.M. on February 16, and Mr. Harris's testimony that he saw his wife alive at about 6:00 A.M. on February 15, this evidence would place the time of death between approximately 6:00 A.M. on February 15, and 5:20 A.M. on February 16. One of the Harris's neighbors, Bill Richardson, testified that he heard three gunshots near Bozeman Lake around 10:15 or 10:20 A.M. on February 15.

11. In late January or February of 1994, Charlie Palmer, Justin Underwood's uncle, discovered that some items were missing from his home, including his pistol and some tools. Mr. Palmer spoke with Chief Deputy Hubert Roberts of the Madison County Sheriff's Department about the stolen items, but did not file an official report, because he thought that his ex-wife might have used the spare keys to enter his home. Mr. Palmer

decided to check his nephew's home to find out if Underwood had taken the items. Underwood let his uncle search his car, a light yellow Oldsmobile Cutlass, in which Mr. Palmer found his tools and his pistol. On March 7 or 8, Mr. Palmer went to see Deputy Roberts again, and this time Deputy Roberts filled out a report on the items that Mr. Palmer had discovered were missing over the last month. Included in this report was the RG blue steel .32 caliber revolver, serial number 0207090, that Mr. Palmer had recovered. Although Mr. Palmer was somewhat confused about exactly when he noticed that his pistol was missing, he was certain that it was missing before March 7 or 8, when he gave this report to Deputy Roberts. The statement says that the pistol was missing in late January or early February.

12. When Mr. Palmer gave his statement to Deputy Roberts, he also turned over the pistol and the box of .32 caliber revolver bullets that he used with the gun to the deputy. Deputy Roberts then wrote down the gun's serial number and gave the pistol and bullets to Sergeant Tucker on March 8. No attempts were made to lift fingerprints from the gun, because it had already been handled by Charlie Palmer and Deputy Roberts before he handed it over to Sergeant Tucker. However, Steve Byrd, a forensic scientist specializing in firearms examinations at the crime lab, concluded from his examination that the bullets taken from Mrs. Harris's body were fired from Charlie Palmer's pistol. His conclusion was corroborated by the findings of a second analyst who initialed Byrd's report.

13. On March 9, Deputy Roberts arrested Underwood for the burglary of Charlie Palmer's residence. Later that afternoon, Underwood gave his statement to Terry Barfield, an investigator with the Madison County Sheriff's Office, and W.H. Hathcock with the Mississippi Highway Patrol. In his statement, Underwood admitted to breaking into Charlie Palmer's home on February 5 and taking items, including the pistol that Charlie Palmer retrieved from Underwood's car on March 7.

14. The next day, March 10, Underwood gave another statement to Officer Barfield and Investigator Larry Saxton in which he admitted to killing Mrs. Harris by shooting her at Bozeman Lake. However, he stated that Mrs. Harris had asked him to kill her because her husband had given her AIDS. Both parties stipulated at trial that Mrs. Harris never had AIDS or HIV. Evidence was presented at trial showing that Mrs. Harris was taking amitriptyline, a medication commonly prescribed for depression. However, Mrs. Harris had undergone a radical mastectomy, so it wouldn't be unusual for her doctor to prescribe an antidepressant. Dr. George Allard, Mrs. Harris's primary care physician testified that amitriptyline could also be prescribed for an intestinal tract problem, which would be consistent with Mrs. Harris's medical history.

15. According to Underwood's March 10 statement made to Officers Barfield and Saxton, Mrs. Harris saw Underwood drive by on February 15 and waved for him to come to her house. Mrs. Harris knew Underwood, because he had done some yard work for her. When he came into the house, Underwood said that Mrs. Harris asked if he had a gun, so he went and got it out of his car, and she offered him money to kill her. Underwood stated that she drove them to the cattle gap, where they got out of the car and walked to the lake, stopping periodically for Mrs. Harris to catch her breath. He said that Mrs. Harris got down on her knees and started praying, so Underwood got down on his knees, and then Mrs. Harris said, "Do it." Underwood got up, closed his eyes, and shot the pistol six times. The pistol was the same one that he had taken from Charlie Palmer's house. Then he left Mrs. Harris lying on the ground, drove her car back to her house, and left in his own car.

16. After presenting the foregoing evidence, the State rested its case. The defense rested without calling any witnesses. Following closing arguments and jury instructions, the jury convicted Underwood of capital murder. At the close of the sentencing phase, the jury found that Underwood should be sentenced to death.

* * *

V.

**THE PREJUDICIAL EFFECT OF THE
INTRODUCTION OF THE VIDEO
TAPE OF THE CRIME SCENE
DEPICTING THE VICTIM'S BODY
OUTWEIGHED THE TAPE'S
PROBATIVE VALUE.**

VI.

**THE PREJUDICIAL EFFECT OF THE
INTRODUCTION OF NUMEROUS
GRUESOME PHOTOGRAPHS
OUTWEIGHED THEIR PROBATIVE
VALUE AND CONSTITUTES
REVERSIBLE ERROR BY THE
LOWER COURT.**

44. Underwood's next two assignments of error are directed toward the trial court's allowing photographs and a video tape of Mrs. Harris's body at the crime scene and photographs of the body prior to the autopsy to be shown to the jury. "Although relevant, evidence may be excluded if its probative value is substantially outweighed by the danger of unfair prejudice, confusion of the issues, or misleading the jury, or by considerations of undue delay, waste of time, or needless presentation of cumulative evidence." Miss. R. Evid. 403. Underwood argues that the photographs and video tape created unfair prejudice in the minds of the jury that outweighed any probative value.

A general rule of this court leaves the admission of photographs into evidence to the sound discretion of the trial judge. Her decision is upheld unless there has been an abuse of that discretion. Stringer v. State, 548 So.2d 125, 134 (Miss. 1989). " '[P]hotographs which are gruesome or inflammatory and lack an evidentiary purpose are always inadmissible as evidence.' " McNeal v. State, 551 So.2d 151, 159 (Miss. 1989) quoting McFee v. State, 511 So.2d 130, 135 (Miss. 1987). Mackbee v. State, 575 So.2d 16, 31 (Miss. 1990).

When deciding on the admissibility of gruesome photos, trial judges must consider: "(1) whether the proof is absolute or in doubt as to identity of the guilty party, [and] (2) whether the photos are necessary evidence or simply a ploy on the part of the prosecutor to arouse the passion and prejudice of the jury." Holland v. State, 587 So.2d 848, 864 (Miss.1991) (quoting McNeal, 551 So.2d at 159).

[T]he lower court's judgment will not be reversed on the ground that photographs are gruesome and prejudicial, unless the lower court has abused its discretion.

Moreover, in a slaying such as the instant case, in which the only eyewitness was the defendant, and it was argued that the slaying was something other than murder, the relevancy of photographs showing the scene and victim is increased. Griffin v. State, 557 So.2d 542, 549-50 (Miss. 1990) (internal citations omitted). "The same standards applicable to determining the admissibility of photographs are applicable to video tapes." Blue v. State, 674 So.2d 1184, 1210 (Miss. 1996) (citing Holland, 587 So.2d at 864).

45. Over Underwood's objection, Judge Toney allowed the prosecution to enter five pictures of Mrs. Harris's body into evidence. State's Exhibit 5 is an 8x10 color photograph of Mrs. Harris's body as found by the lakeshore. It shows the body face down on the ground, wearing a blue shirt, black pants and belt, and red house shoes. There are patches of blood visible on the blue shirt. State's Exhibits 10, 11, and 12 are all 8x10 color photographs of the body just before the autopsy, showing the gunshot wounds. Little or no blood is evident in any of the autopsy photographs. Exhibit 10 shows Mrs. Harris's back with the two gunshot wounds, Exhibit 11 depicts the two arm wounds, and Exhibit 12 is a photograph of the gunshot wound to Mrs. Harris's neck and to the shoulder. State's Exhibit 17 is a 3x4 color photograph taken at the autopsy of Mrs. Harris's hand showing abrasions on her palm and fingers. These pictures are not particularly gruesome or inflammatory so as to shock or prejudice the jury in this case. The photographs were all relevant to show the victim's injuries and to help the jury visualize the crime and crime scene, corroborating the testimony of the investigators and partially corroborating Underwood's confession. Photographs showing Mrs. Harris's body wearing the red house shoes and the scratches on her hands from clutching weeds and grass were relevant to support the prosecution's theory of kidnapping, to refute any

theory of assisted suicide, and to corroborate Dr. Hayne's testimony that Mrs. Harris did not die immediately. The trial court did not abuse its discretion in allowing these photographs to be admitted into evidence.

46. Also over Underwood's objection, Judge Toney allowed the prosecution to play a video tape for the jury of Mrs. Harris's body as it was found by investigators. After hearing the arguments from counsel, the judge determined that the jury would not be allowed to take the tape into deliberations, because he instructed the prosecutor to stop the tape before the body was turned over. The portion of the video tape shown to the jury depicts little more than State's Exhibit 5, the photograph of Mrs. Harris's body at the crime scene. The only additional footage is a shot of Mrs. Harris's ear, revealing that maggots had infested her ear. Judge Toney allowed the prosecution to show the tape through a closeup of the ear, because that evidence was used to help establish the time of death. Out of precaution, however, Judge Toney ruled that the remainder of the video tape, showing the investigators' further examination of the body after turning it over, would not be shown to the jury.

47. Underwood specifically points to this Court's decision in McNeal, supra, to support his argument that the video depicting maggots in Mrs. Harris's ear was inflammatory and lacked any evidentiary purpose. In McNeal, we held that the admission of close-up color photographs of the victim's decomposed, maggot-infested skull was an abuse of discretion. McNeal, 551 So.2d at 159. However, the Court described those photographs as "some of the most gruesome photographs ever presented to this Court." Id. Here, the short segment of video tape showing the inside of Mrs. Harris's ear is not exceptionally gruesome, particularly since there is no visual evidence of decomposition. Furthermore, unlike the photographs in McNeal, the video of the maggots in Mrs. Harris's ear is relevant, because the evidence was used to establish the time of death. Judge Toney properly reviewed this evidence under Rule 403, and did not abuse his discretion in allowing the jury to view that portion of the prosecution's video tape.

* * *

Conviction of murder affirmed.
[Parts of case omitted]

McHENRY
v.
STATE

Supreme Court of Indiana
820 N.E.2d 124, 2005 Ind.
LEXIS 4 (2005)

Dickson, Justice. Shepard, C.J., and Sullivan, Boehm, and Rucker, JJ., concur.

Dickson, Justice.

Following a jury trial, the defendant, Mirtha McHenry, a bank teller, was convicted of forgery, a class C felony, and theft, a class D felony, as a result of her actions relating to an unauthorized withdrawal of $6,500 from the account of a bank customer. Concluding that the evidence was insufficient to establish her guilt of either crime, the Court of Appeals reversed the convictions and remanded with instructions that she be discharged.

We grant transfer and affirm the trial court.

In her appeal from the convictions, the defendant alleges three grounds for reversal: (1) insufficient evidence; (2) refusal to strike two jurors for cause; and (3) erroneous admission of surveillance videotape.

1. Sufficiency of Evidence

The defendant contends that neither of her convictions were supported by sufficient evidence. Upon a challenge to the sufficiency of evidence to support a conviction, a reviewing court does not reweigh the evidence or judge the credibility of the witnesses, and respects "the jury's exclusive province to weigh conflicting evidence." We have often emphasized that appellate courts must consider only the probative evidence and reasonable inferences supporting the verdict. Expressed another way, we have stated that appellate courts must affirm "if the probative evidence and reasonable inferences drawn from the evidence could have allowed a reasonable trier of fact to find the defendant guilty beyond a reasonable doubt."

Evidence at her jury trial established that the defendant, a bank teller, withdrew $6,500 from the account of Charles Landes. The defendant testified that someone had come to her wanting to make this withdrawal, that she had filled in the withdrawal slip, and that she had the customer sign it and gave him the money. Upon receiving his bank statement and discovering a $6,500 withdrawal from his account, Landes immediately reported the error to the bank and signed an affidavit of forgery stating that the signature on the withdrawal slip was not his and that he did not receive any of the proceeds. The withdrawal slip was time-stamped 4:44 p.m. The bank's videotape showed no one at the defendant's teller window when the transaction occurred. Bank records also disclosed that the defendant had accessed and viewed this customer's account records twice during the two weeks before the withdrawal.

Although reciting that "in reviewing the sufficiency of the evidence, we will not reweigh the evidence or judge the credibility of witnesses," the Court of Appeals reversed the convictions, speculating that the withdrawal slip "*may have been* received earlier and only stamped at 4:44 p.m." and that the defendant's prior inquiries into the customer's account balance "*may have been* precipitated by a phone call request."

In reversing the jury's verdict, the Court of Appeals failed to restrict its consideration to only the evidence and reasonable inferences favorable to the trial court's verdict, but instead reweighed the evidence, improperly substituting its own judgment for that of the jury. While the jury could have drawn the same inferences as the Court of Appeals, they did not. They returned a unanimous verdict of guilt on each count.

The defendant urges that the State failed to present evidence that she intended to defraud the customer or the bank or that she took the money. The State responds (and the defendant concedes) that intent to defraud may be proven by circumstantial evidence, and the State argues that the defendant acknowledged accessing the customer's account and performing the transaction that removed

$6,500 from the account—money that the customer did not receive. And the videotape enabled the jury to infer that there was no customer at the defendant's teller window when the withdrawal was made.

Finding that the probative evidence and reasonable inferences drawn from the evidence could have allowed a reasonable trier of fact to find the defendant guilty beyond a reasonable doubt, we conclude that the evidence was sufficient to support the judgment.

2. Failure to Exclude Jurors for Cause

* * *

3. Surveillance Videotape

The defendant also contends that the trial court committed reversible error in admitting the bank's surveillance video. The video shows that no person was at the defendant's teller window at the time she entered the questioned transaction. The defendant's objection at trial was that the videotape was not a business record and that there was an inadequate foundation, the particulars of which were not specified. On appeal, the defendant does not present argument as to the business record issue but rather argues generally that because the state did not present information to support the reliability of the surveillance tape other than the affidavit of a records custodian, it failed to lay a proper foundation for the admission of the video.

The parties agree that under a "silent witness" theory, videotapes may be admitted as substantive evidence, but "there must be a strong showing of authenticity and competency" and that when automatic cameras are involved, "there should be evidence as to how and when the camera was loaded, how frequently the camera was activated, when the photographs were taken, and the processing and changing of custody of the film after its removal from the camera."

The State argues that witness testimony established the videotape's authenticity. The bank manager removed the videotape, and a police detective checked it to assure that it was the tape covering the date in question. The detective then watched the tape to match the transactions and customers' account numbers with the representations on the videotape. In addition, the bank's custodian of records verified by affidavit that the tape was a regularly conducted activity of the bank and that she had examined the records to verify its trustworthiness.

Rulings on the admission of evidence are subject to appellate review for abuse of discretion. We are not persuaded that the trial court abused its discretion in admitting the videotape.

Conclusion

We grant transfer and affirm the judgment of the trial court. [Reversed the Court of Appeals.]

Shepard, C.J., and Sullivan, Boehm, and Rucker, JJ., concur.

COMMONWEALTH
v.
GAYNOR

**Supreme Judicial Court
of Massachusetts
443 Mass. 245, 820 N.E.2d 233,
2005 Mass. LEXIS 7 (2005)**

Judges Present: Marshall, C.J., Greaney, Spina, & Sosman JJ.

SPINA, J. The defendant was convicted of the aggravated rape and murder of four women in Springfield between November 1, 1997, and March 11, 1998. The jury returned verdicts under all three theories of murder in the first degree in each case. On appeal, the defendant asserts error in certain pretrial rulings, including . . . rulings that deoxyribonucleic acid (DNA) evidence taken from mixed DNA samples was sufficiently reliable to be admitted in evidence, and that the database on which Cellmark Diagnostics based its frequency calculations was adequate. . . . Finally, the defendant asks us to grant him a new trial under G. L. c. 278, § 33E. We affirm the convictions and decline to grant relief under § 33E.

1. *Facts.* The jury could have found the following facts.

a. *Victim no. 1.* The victim put her children to bed at 10 P.M. on October 31, 1997. Sometime between midnight and 12:30 A.M., the first-floor tenant at 866 Worthington Street in Springfield heard a "scream of pain" followed by a "thud" from the victim's second-floor apartment. The victim's son discovered her body on the living room couch after he awoke at 7 A.M.. on November 1. Her naked body was covered by a blanket and a towel had been placed over her head. Her hands were bound behind her back.

An autopsy revealed that death was caused by asphyxia due to manual strangulation. The victim's blood tested positive for metabolites of cocaine and alcohol. Her anus was widely dilated, consistent with penetration.

The defendant's thumb print was identified on a broken ashtray found in the living room, and his palm print was identified on a hair gel container, also in the living room. Fecal matter was found on a sock and inside the rim of a small vase recovered from the victim's living room. The defendant told his brother that he had had anal intercourse with women he met in the Worthington-Federal Streets section of Springfield, an area known for prostitutes and "crack" cocaine. The defendant's brother had driven him several times in October and November, 1997, to the neighborhood where the victim lived.

Several items collected from the scene and all biological evidence recovered from the first victim's body, as well as blood samples given by the defendant were sent to Cellmark for DNA analysis. Cellmark performed two series of polymerase chain reaction (PCR) tests on DNA samples taken from items submitted in all four cases. The first series of tests were performed at nine genetic loci: DQ Alpha, five polymarker (PM) loci, and three (TPOX, THO1, and CSF) short tandem repeat (STR) loci. In some instances testing was done at a tenth locus, identified as D1S80. Some of these tests were witnessed by a defense expert. A second series of PCR tests was done on some samples at thirteen core STR loci (including the three STR loci where testing previously had been done) designated for inclusion in the national database that contains DNA profiles n1 of convicted felons, known as the combined DNA index system, or CODIS. See G. L. c. 22E, § 1 (definitions). A defense expert was present during the second series of tests. DNA samples from seven other suspects were examined and all seven were excluded as contributors in each case.

* * *

[Three other murder victims presented similar DNA evidence from murder scenes.]

* * *

5. *Admissibility of DNA evidence.* The defendant filed a pretrial motion in which he requested a "*Daubert-Lanigan* hearing" with respect to the admissibility of DNA evidence the Commonwealth was expected to offer in all four cases. See Daubert v. Merrell Dow Pharmaceuticals, Inc., 509 U.S. 579, 125 L. Ed. 2d 469, 113 S. Ct. 2786 (1993); Commonwealth v. Lanigan, 419 Mass. 15, 641 N.E.2d 1342 (1994). Hearings were conducted as to both the first and second series of tests, and the defendant now appeals from rulings that (1) Cellmark's methodology in dealing with mixtures and technical artifacts is generally accepted within the scientific community; (2) Cellmark both performed its tests properly and reported the results accurately; (3) Cellmark's election not to stay within conservative recommendations of test kit manufacturers regarding the minimum quantity of DNA tested did not invalidate the studies; (4) the use of the product rule to make frequency calculations for identifiable primary contributors in a mixed DNA sample is acceptable; and (5) the database used by Cellmark to make frequency calculations is adequate and common within the field.

a. *Mixtures and artifacts.* The defendant first claims that the evidence does not support the judge's conclusion that Cellmark can reliably distinguish technical artifacts from true alleles, or primary from secondary con-

tributors in mixed samples of DNA. He does not challenge the scientific validity of PCR testing. We previously have held that PCR-based DNA analysis, both generally and at the DQ Alpha locus, the PM loci, and the D1S80 locus, is a scientifically valid methodology for developing DNA profile evidence. See Commonwealth v. Vao Sok, 425 Mass. 787, 799, 801-802, 683 N.E.2d 671 (1997). We reached the same conclusion with respect to PCR testing at STR loci identified as CSF1P0, TPOX, and TH01. Commonwealth v. Rosier, 425 Mass. 807, 812-813, 685 N.E.2d 739 (1997). The defendant does not challenge the scientific validity of PCR testing at the other STR loci designated under CODIS. His challenge focuses on the second, or reliability prong of the *Daubert-Lanigan* inquiry.

A determination of the reliability of the testing process entails a fact-based inquiry, including questions of credibility. See Commonwealth v. Vao Sok, supra at 797, 798. The analysis calls on a judge to determine whether testing was properly performed, Commonwealth v. McNickles, 434 Mass. 839, 850, 753 N.E.2d 131 (2001), and whether an expert's conclusions based on clinical experience and observations were sufficiently reliable. Canavan's Case, 432 Mass. 304, 313, 733 N.E.2d 1042 (2000). The judge's decision under the reliability prong is reviewed under the abuse of discretion standard. Id. at 312.

Testimony indicated that it is not unusual to find mixtures of DNA (a sample containing DNA from two or more persons) in cases of sexual assault. The presence of a mixture of DNA can create difficulties in interpreting test results. For example, where DNA from two contributors is present in a mixture in relatively equal amounts, the dots or bands (depending on the particular test) produced by the two samples during the testing process will display comparable intensity (darkness). In such cases the Cellmark analyst will report the existence of a combination without attempting to interpret the results.

Similar interpretive challenges arise from the presence of technical artifacts: mistakes in the PCR amplification process that replicates a defined segment of DNA through the use of enzymes. Artifacts typically give faint readings. When a test result suggests either an artifact or a secondary contributor and the difference in intensity between readings is slight, the Cellmark analyst will not attempt to distinguish them but will report the result as not interpretable.

Where DNA from two contributors is present in a mixture in unequal amounts, readings produced by the larger sample will be darker than those of the smaller sample, roughly in direct proportion to the difference between the amounts of the samples. Where the differences are such that intensity readings from the greater sample are dark and those from the lesser sample are faint, the Cellmark analyst may conclude that the darker reading is produced by a primary contributor and report her conclusion in the same way she reports a single source sample, conformably with the recommendation of the National Resource Council (NRC), The Evaluation of Forensic DNA Evidence (1996) at 129. We have treated the reports of the NRC as authoritative works for purposes of determining generally accepted standards within the scientific community for (a) the validity of the underlying scientific theory, or (b) the reliability of the underlying process for developing forensic DNA evidence. See Commonwealth v. Rosier, supra at 815; Commonwealth v. Vao Sok, supra at 801.

Here, only test results based on a single source of DNA, or, where there appeared to be a mixture, only test results that yielded strong evidence (dark bands or dots) of a primary contributor were used. Consequently, a weak reading of a secondary contributor or technical artifact had no effect on Cellmark's ability to report the result of the primary contributor and calculate a statistic of the probability of a random match to the defendant's DNA profile. The judge's findings that Cellmark's methodology in reporting tests of a mixed sample with an identifiable primary contributor in the same way it reports tests of a single source sample conforms to the recommendation of the NRC, and that Cellmark's methodology in dealing with the presence of mixtures or technical artifacts is generally accepted within the scientific community, were made with record support and well within his discretion.

b. *Conduct of tests.* The defendant suggests other known conditions that could affect the accuracy and reliability of test results, including contamination, loci dropout, allele dropout, differential amplification, stochastic effect, spikes, and peak imbalances. We need not engage in a lengthy discussion about these conditions. For purposes of this appeal, it is sufficient to note that Cellmark analysts considered each of these issues and factored them into their test results. The judge accepted the testimony of Dr. Robin Cotton, Cellmark's forensic laboratory director, with respect to the many controls and safeguards that Cellmark uses to adjust for these challenges, including threshold control dots to detect minimum sample size at the DQ Alpha locus, the use of two different manufacturers' test kits that test DNA at four of the same loci for CODIS testing, controls to ensure against contamination at the PM and D1S80 loci, and others. The judge found that Cellmark follows the standards adopted by the DNA advisory board, a group of individuals authorized by Congress to advise the Federal Bureau of Investigation on DNA testing, and the guidelines published by the Technical Working Group for DNA Analysis Methods (TWGDAM) in 1995, except in cases where those guidelines have been superseded by the DNA advisory board standards. The judge did not abuse his discretion in ruling that the test results were sufficiently reliable to be put before the jury and that the questions raised by the defendant were more appropriately addressed to the weight of the evidence. See Commonwealth v. McNickles, 434 Mass. 839, 850-854, 753 N.E.2d 131 (2001).

c. *Manufacturer's recommendations.* There is no merit to the defendant's contention that Cellmark's failure to comply with the minimum standards for DNA sample sizes set by the test kit manufacturers invalidated the test results. The user's manuals for the Profiler Plus and Cofiler kits, both manufactured by PerkinElmer, Inc., recommended that they not be used with less than one to 2.5 nanograms (one-billionth of a gram) of questioned DNA, but many of the tests were conducted with less than the recommended amounts. The judge found that the manufacturers' recommendations were just that, recommendations. They were intended to ensure optimal results. He found, with record support, that Cellmark had conducted validation studies that supported the reliability of testing based on amounts smaller than recommended by the manufacturers, amounts as small as one-half nanogram. Cellmark had also conducted validation studies indicating that analysts could reliably interpret computerized test results (the second series of tests performed under CODIS) based on readings as low as forty relative fluorescent units (RFUs) rather than the conservative level of 150 RFUs recommended by the manufacturers, and the judge found that Cellmark's readings were reliable. There was no abuse of discretion.

The defendant's expert, Dr. Donald E. Riley, ultimately conceded Cellmark's conclusions (that test results matched the defendant's profile) were supported by the data and that the defendant's and the victims' identified alleles matched those identified by Cellmark's testing. The judge observed that "[a]ll that Dr. Riley can really say is that there is a 'potential' for this system of analysis to miss alleles and distort results. I recognize that the potential for error exists in *any* scientific testing, but I am satisfied that Cellmark has done all that is reasonably possible to eliminate that potential" (emphasis in original). He correctly noted that the issues raised by the defendant went to the weight of the evidence, not its admissibility.

d. *Use of the product rule.* The defendant argues that the judge erred by accepting the proposition that if an analyst can distinguish between a primary contributor and a secondary contributor in a mixed DNA sample, the analyst may properly treat the primary contributor as a single source for statistical purposes. His argument, essentially, is that [HN22]the "product rule," which has been held to be a scientifically acceptable method for calculating frequency profiles based on results of PCR testing of single source samples, see Commonwealth v. Rosier, supra at 816-817, produces unreliable results in mixed samples; and that a "likelihood ratio," which has been held to be a scientifically acceptable method of calculating frequency profiles based on results of testing of mixed

samples, should have been used. See Commonwealth v. McNickles, supra at 845-848.

Likelihood ratio analysis is appropriate for test results of mixed samples when the primary and secondary contributors cannot be distinguished. Id. at 846. It need not be applied when a primary contributor can be identified. Contrary to the defendant's view, the use of the product rule is scientifically acceptable where the analyst can distinguish between a primary and a secondary contributor in a mixed sample, and thereafter treat the primary contributor as a single source for statistical purposes. See NRC, Evaluation of Forensic DNA Evidence (1996), Executive Summary Recommendation 4.1 at 5; State v. Roman Nose, 667 N.W.2d 386, 398 (Minn. 2003). In any event, at trial, Dr. Christopher Basten, the Commonwealth's statistician in the field of population genetics, recalculated the profile frequencies using likelihood ratios and reached results comparable to those obtained under the product rule.

e. *Cellmark's database.* Finally, the defendant contends that the judge erred in ruling that Cellmark's database was adequate, that the absence of data on African-Americans from Springfield in Cellmark's database was not a matter of concern, and that the results of Cellmark's profile frequency calculations through use of the product rule were reliable and accurate.

The product rule refers to the product, or multiplication, of the frequencies (probabilities) with which each allele in a tested sample of DNA occurs in the population included in the database. The resulting number is the probability of someone's having the same characteristics as the sample tested. See Commonwealth v. Curnin, 409 Mass. 218, 224, 565 N.E.2d 440 (1991). The product rule is based on two assumptions about the nature of genetic variants in the population. Those assumptions are known as the condition of Hardy-Weinberg equilibrium, and the condition of linkage equilibrium. Hardy-Weinberg equilibrium is a condition that is achieved when there is no particular relationship between the occurrence of alleles within a single genetic marker. That is, when a person's parents meet randomly in the general population. Linkage equilibrium is a condition that is achieved when there is no partic-ular relationship between genes. That is, when genes are inherited independently, and not linked to other genes. See id. at 225 n.11; NRC, Evaluation of Forensic DNA Evidence (1996) at 90-91, 106-107.

Dr. Basten testified that he had conducted a study of fifty databases, including Cell-mark's, to determine whether the frequencies of alleles at particular loci varied between databases or between racial groups within the databases for the population of the United States. He had presented the details and the results of his study at two scientific conven-tions. Dr. Basten concluded that there was consistency of allelic frequency between the various databases and within the various racial groups, but that allelic frequency var-ied between racial groups. He also concluded that the size of Cellmark's database, 103 per-sons, is adequate and common within the field, and that a database larger than Cell-mark's would produce no significant differ-ence in result. He explained that the reliabil-ity of profiling depends more on the number of alleles in the database than the number of persons in the database. Dr. Basten discount-ed the absence of data on any African-Amer-ican from Springfield in Cellmark's database because his study of the fifty databases indi-cated that the African-American population is fairly homogeneous across the United States. He endorsed Cellmark's use of the product rule in making its profile frequency calculations, and verified Cellmark's test results through the use of the theta factor, a statistical adjustment recommended by the NRC when dealing with possible subgroups, or small isolated populations. See NRC, Evaluation of Forensic DNA Evidence (1996) at 29-30. Dr. Basten employed the more conservative of the two theta factors recommended by the NRC. Verification also was made through the use of "confidence intervals." See Commonwealth v. Rosier, supra at 814 n.14.

The judge found that Dr. Basten's use of the conservative theta factor and confidence intervals were an "appropriate corrective measure" to account for any possible sub-structure with the African-American commu-nity in Springfield. He acted within his dis-cretion in ruling that Cellmark's database was adequate and that the use of the product

rule produced reliable results. See Common-wealth v. Rosier, supra at 813-814.

* * *

Relief under G. L. c. 278, § 33E. We have reviewed the transcript, the record, and the briefs, and conclude that there is no reason to reduce the verdicts or grant a new trial pur-suant to our power under G. L. c. 278, § 33E.

Judgments affirmed.

UNITED STATES
v.
GILLIARD

United States Court of Appeals, Eleventh Circuit
133 F.3d 809 (11th Cir. 1998)

[Some footnotes omitted.]

BLACK, Circuit Judge:

The sole issue in this appeal is whether the district court erred when it excluded evi-dence of a polygraph examination offered into evidence by Appellant Fred Emerson Gilliard. The district court excluded the poly-graph evidence under Fed. R. Evid. 702 and, alternatively, under Fed. R. Evid. 403. Gilliard contends that the district court's rul-ing constituted an abuse of discretion. We hold that the district court did not abuse its discretion, and affirm the judgment entered by the district court.

I. BACKGROUND

On March 8, 1996, a grand jury indicted Gilliard on 100 counts of submitting false claims to Medicare and Medicaid, in viola-tion of 18 U.S.C. § 287, while he was chief executive officer of Penn-Teck Diagnostics, Inc. (Penn-Teck); 1 count of obstructing jus-tice in violation of 18 U.S.C. § 1503 by influ-encing a witness to make false statements pertaining to the Medicare and Medicaid claim submissions; and 1 count of making false declarations to a grand jury in violation of 18 U.S.C. § 1623. On June 24, 1996, Gilliard submitted to a polygraph examina-tion administered by Charles R. Honts, Ph.D.

(the Honts Polygraph). Dr. Honts is an associate professor of psychology at Boise State University whose training is in psychophysiology, the science of how the mind and body interact. The Honts Polygraph consisted of four relevant questions:

1. While you were employed by Penn-Teck, did you develop a scheme designed to defraud Medicare or Medicaid through the use of incorrect billing codes?

2. When the incorrect billings were filed with Medicare or Medicaid, did you know that they were incorrect?

3. While you were employed by Penn-Teck, did you deliberately cause incorrect billings to be filed with Medicare or Medicaid?

4. To the best of your knowledge, were the incorrect billings to Medicare and Medicaid made unintentionally?

Gilliard denied any wrongdoing. Dr. Honts scored the examination using two different methods, and concluded that the results indicated that Gilliard was not being deceptive when he answered the relevant questions. Gilliard notified the Government of the results of the Honts Polygraph. The Government never conducted its own polygraph examination of Gilliard, but instead moved for the exclusion of the Honts Polygraph evidence.

On July 11, 1996, the magistrate judge held an evidentiary hearing, and on August 14, 1996, he issued an order holding the Honts Polygraph evidence to be admissible. The Government appealed that ruling to the district court. The district court recognized that under this Court's en banc decision in United States v. Piccinonna, 885 F.2d 1529 (11th Cir. 1989), polygraph evidence is no longer per se inadmissible. After performing the analysis required by our holding in Piccinonna, the district court sustained the Government's objection and held that the Honts Polygraph evidence was inadmissible under Fed. R. Evid. 702, as well as under Fed. R. Evid. 403.

The jury convicted Gilliard on all 102 counts of the indictment, and the district court sentenced Gilliard to imprisonment. Gilliard now appeals the exclusion of the Honts Polygraph evidence.

II. ANALYSIS

Prior to this Court's en banc decision in Piccinonna, polygraph evidence was per se inadmissible in this Circuit. Piccinonna, 885 F.2d at 1531-32. In Piccinonna, however, this Court concluded that the per se rule was unwarranted in light of the advances that had been made in the field of polygraphy and the lack of evidence that juries are unduly swayed by polygraph evidence. Id. at 1535. Specifically, we held that a district court can admit polygraph evidence in two circumstances: (1) when the parties stipulate in advance as to the circumstances of the test and as to the scope of its admissibility; and (2) to impeach or corroborate the testimony of a witness at trial. Id. at 1536. We were careful to note, however, that neither modification to the per se exclusionary rule "preempt[s] or limit[s] in any way the trial court's discretion to exclude polygraph expert testimony on other grounds under the Federal Rules of Evidence." Id.

As the parties did not stipulate to the circumstances and admissibility of the Honts Polygraph, the issue here is whether the Honts Polygraph evidence should have been admitted to corroborate Gilliard's trial testimony. There are three prerequisites to the admission of polygraph evidence for the purpose of corroborating the trial testimony of a witness: (1) "the party planning to use the evidence at trial must provide adequate notice to the opposing party that the expert testimony will be offered;" (2) the opposing party must be given a "reasonable opportunity to have its own polygraph expert administer a test covering substantially the same questions;" and (3) the polygraph administrator's testimony must be admissible under the Federal Rules of Evidence governing the admissibility of corroboration testimony. Id. Again, however, even if a party satisfies these prerequisites, a district court can exercise its discretion to exclude the polygraph evidence under other applicable rules of evidence. Id.

In this case, the district court assumed that Gilliard satisfied the three prerequisites to the admission of the polygraph testimony for the purpose of corroborating Gilliard's trial testimony. The court concluded, however, that the evidence was not admissible expert testimony under Fed. R. Evid. 702 and, alternatively, that the evidence was inadmissible under Fed. R. Evid. 403.

A. *Rule 702*

1. *Standard of Review*

A district court's decision to admit or exclude expert testimony under Rule 702 is reviewed for abuse of discretion. General Elec. Co. v. Joiner, __ U.S. __, __, 118 S. Ct. 512, 517 (1997).

2. *Daubert v. Merrell Dow Pharmaceuticals, Inc.*

In Daubert v. Merrell Dow Pharmaceuticals, Inc., 509 U.S. 579, 113 S. Ct. 2786 (1993), the Supreme Court set out a two-prong analysis for determining whether expert scientific testimony is admissible under Fed. R. Evid. 702: (1) whether the evidence constitutes scientific knowledge; and (2) whether the evidence is relevant, i.e., whether it would "assist the trier of fact to understand the evidence or to determine a fact in issue." Id. at 589-591, 113 S. Ct. at 2794-96. Factors relevant to the determination of whether a technique constitutes scientific knowledge include: (1) whether the technique can be and has been tested; (2) whether the technique "has been subjected to peer review and publication;" (3) "the known or potential rate of error;" (4) "the existence and maintenance of standards controlling the technique's operation;" and (5) whether the technique has attained general acceptance within the relevant scientific community. Id. at 593-94, 113 S. Ct. at 2796-97.

3. *Polygraph Techniques*

"[P]olygraphy is a developing and inexact science." Piccinonna, 885 F.2d at 1535. Resolution of the issue presented in this case requires an understanding of the various techniques that can be used to administer a polygraph examination.[3]

---

[3]   The information set forth in this opinion pertaining to the various techniques that can be used to administer a polygraph examination is culled from the testimony presented to the magistrate judge. The parties do not dispute the general nature of the various techniques.

a. *Relevant/Irrelevant Technique*

One method of conducting a polygraph examination is the relevant/irrelevant technique, in which the examiner asks both questions that are relevant to the purpose of the test and questions that are irrelevant to the purpose of the test. In theory, an individual will have a unique response associated with lying. The relevant/irrelevant technique generally has been rejected by the scientific community.

b. *Concealed or Guilty Knowledge Technique*

A second method of conducting a polygraph examination is the concealed or guilty knowledge technique. In this type of polygraph, an examiner tests the examinee's response to information that only the perpetrator of the crime would know. For example, if a ruby ring was stolen, the examiner would ask: Did you steal a diamond ring? Did you steal a sapphire ring? Did you steal a ruby ring? In theory, a guilty individual will recognize the critical item, or question, and will show a psychophysiological response to that item. The difficulty with using this technique is that the examiner must be sure that the information tested (i.e., that the stolen ring was a ruby ring) is not known generally and would not be known by the individual being tested unless he was the perpetrator of the crime.

c. *Control Question Techniques*

Most polygraph examiners employ a control question format in conducting polygraph examinations. At least three different techniques fall within this general format. In a control question polygraph, the examiner generally asks questions relevant to the purpose of the examination and so-called control questions. The control questions address issues unrelated to the purpose of the examination. Depending on the particular technique used, the examinee will either be tricked into giving or directed to give a false answer to each control question. The premise underlying the control question format is that an innocent examinee will have a stronger physiological response to his false responses to the control questions than to his truthful answers to the relevant questions in which he denies wrongdoing, and that the reverse will be true for a guilty examinee.

Three control question techniques are pertinent to this case. The first, and apparently the most tested and most widely used, is called the probable lie control question technique. The Government concedes that this technique, if properly utilized, has been recognized in the scientific community as being "good science."[4] In administering a probable lie control question polygraph, the examiner asks the examinee a question that is designed to elicit a probable lie about a matter unrelated to the matter under investigation. For example, the examiner might ask an examinee whether he ever did anything illegal, dishonest, or immoral prior to the incident at issue. The examiner "tricks" the examinee into denying any such conduct by conducting a pretest interview of the examinee such that during the examination the examinee will be too embarrassed to admit such conduct or will be unsure as to the truth of his answer. The premise is that virtually everyone has done something that could be considered to be illegal, dishonest, or immoral.

The second technique is the directed lie control question technique. The directed lie control question technique involves the examiner instructing the examinee to give a false response to the control questions. In

theory, the examinee will exhibit a physiological response to the control questions because the examiner has emphasized the questions by telling the examinee that it is important that he responds appropriately when he lies.

The third technique is a hybrid control question technique, in which the examiner uses both probable lie and directed lie control questions. Dr. Honts used a hybrid control question technique in examining Gilliard.

4. *The Honts Polygraph*

The polygraph examination that Dr. Honts administered to Gilliard consisted of four relevant questions, one probable lie control question, three irrelevant or neutral questions, and two directed lie control questions. Before the polygraph examination, Dr. Honts discussed the questions with Gilliard. During the course of the polygraph examination, Dr. Honts posed the questions to Gilliard in an order determined by the computerized polygraph machine. After Dr. Honts asked the questions one time through, he permitted Gilliard to take a break and he and Gilliard discussed the questions and Gilliard's responses. Dr. Honts asked the questions a second time, and he again permitted Gilliard to take a break and he and Gilliard again discussed the questions and Gilliard's responses. Dr. Honts then asked the questions one final time.

In scoring the examination, Dr. Honts looked at Gilliard's physiological responses to each relevant question in the five response areas measured by the polygraph machine, and compared those responses to the strongest control response for each of the five tested response areas.[5]

5. *Analysis of Daubert factors*

The evidence presented to the district court showed that the hybrid control question technique has been the subject of only one scientific study, a field study conducted by Dr. Honts and Professor David Raskin that was

---

4   Although it is unclear what technique was used to conduct the polygraph examination in Piccinonna, the opinion and the studies cited in footnote 8 of that opinion strongly suggest that it was the probable lie control question technique. See, e.g., John A. Podlesny and David C. Raskin, Effectiveness of Techniques and Physiological Measures in the Detection of Deception, 15 Psychophysiology 344 (1978) (published laboratory study in which the probable lie control question technique and the guilty knowledge technique were used; authors concluded that although the accuracy rates for the control question technique and the guilty knowledge technique were similar, the control question technique was the "current method of choice in criminal investigations" due to the limited applicability of the guilty knowledge technique); Gordon H. Barland and David C. Raskin, An Evaluation of Field Techniques in Detection of Deception, 12 Psychophysiology 321 (1975) (published laboratory study involving the probable lie control question technique).

5   Two channels measured Gilliard's respiration, one channel measured Gilliard's galvanic skin response, one channel measured Gilliard's blood pressure, and one channel measured Gilliard's pulse.

published in 1988. This 1988 field study included 25 subjects, 13 of whom were innocent and 12 of whom were guilty. The guilt or innocence of the individuals was confirmed by confession (by either the individual or another individual), physical evidence, or recantation by the alleged victim. Dr. Honts testified that his field study showed the hybrid technique to be 100% accurate with respect to detecting innocent subjects and 92% accurate with respect to detecting guilty subjects.

The Government, however, presented evidence suggesting that the addition of directed lie control questions would skew the results of a polygraph examination in favor of a guilty examinee. One of the Government's experts, Dr. Stanley Abrams, testified that he performed a study in which he compared the probable lie control question technique to the directed lie control question technique. Dr. Abrams found that people appeared more truthful under the directed lie control question technique than under the probable lie control question technique, and has concluded that the directed lie control question technique is substantially less than 90% accurate. Dr. Abrams testified that although using the directed lie control question technique reduced the number of false positives, i.e., innocent people appearing to be lying, it increased the number of false negatives, i.e., guilty people appearing to be innocent.

With respect to whether the hybrid technique has attained general acceptance within the relevant scientific community, Dr. Honts testified that the hybrid method is used by himself, Professor Raskin, the Arizona School of Polygraph, the Arizona State Police, and four other individual polygraphers. The Government, on the other hand, presented evidence that the hybrid technique is disfavored not only by the Government's experts, but also by federal government agencies. Dr. Abrams testified that the Internal Revenue Service and the Drug Enforcement Agency do not use the hybrid technique, and that according to the Department of Defense Polygraph Institute, none of the federal agencies is able to use it.

Considering the paucity of tests and published studies addressing the validity of the hybrid technique, and Gilliard's failure to

show that the hybrid technique has gained general acceptance within the relevant scientific community, the district court did not abuse its discretion in finding the Honts Polygraph evidence to be inadmissible under Fed. R. Evid. 702. Furthermore, due to the lack of corroboration by other studies and polygraphers, the district court did not err in declining to assign much weight to the rate of accuracy that Dr. Honts attributed to the hybrid technique.

B. *Rule 403*

1. *Standard of Review*

A district court's decision to exclude evidence under Fed. R. Evid. 403 is reviewed for clear abuse of discretion. United States v. Taylor, 17 F.3d 333, 338 (11th Cir. 1994). A trial court may exclude otherwise admissible evidence "if its probative value is substantially outweighed by the danger of unfair prejudice, confusion of the issues, or misleading the jury. . . ." Fed. R. Evid. 403. "Expert evidence can be both powerful and quite misleading because of the difficulty in evaluating it. Because of this risk, the judge in weighing possible prejudice against probative force under Rule 403 of the present rules exercises more control over experts than over lay witnesses." Daubert, 509 U.S. at 595, 113 S. Ct. at 2798 (internal quotations and citation omitted).

2. *Analysis*

Although the district court held that the Honts Polygraph evidence was not admissible under Fed. R. Evid. 702, the district court also addressed the Government's argument that, assuming the evidence was admissible under Fed. R. Evid. 702, it should nonetheless be excluded under Fed. R. Evid. 403. In performing the Rule 403 analysis, the district court's primary concerns centered around the amount of time it would have taken the parties to present evidence pertaining to the Honts Polygraph, the fact that the questions posed to Gilliard during the Honts Polygraph did not address all counts in the indictment, and the fact that a Government representative was not present during the administration of the Honts Polygraph.[6] The district court concluded that the probative value of the Honts Polygraph evidence was substantially outweighed by the potential for unfair prejudice, confusion of the issues, and misleading the jury.

The district court was concerned about the amount of time it would have taken the parties to present evidence pertaining to the Honts Polygraph, and the way in which it would have affected the focus of the trial. Although the actual number of hours and minutes it would take to put on expert testimony should not ordinarily be a controlling factor, a court may consider whether the amount of time needed to present the evidence would shift the focus of a criminal trial from determining guilt or innocence to determining the validity of the scientific method at issue.

In this case, the district court determined that the four-day trial would have taken an additional one-half to two days had both sides presented evidence pertaining to the Honts Polygraph. In light of the degree to which the validity of the hybrid technique was disputed, it was not unreasonable for the district court to assume for purposes of its analysis that the time needed would have been at least one day. The district court did not err in concluding that the devotion of so much time to the presentation of the Honts Polygraph evidence likely would have diverted the jury's attention from the real issue in the case, that of guilt or innocence, to the issue of the validity of polygraph evidence in general and the validity of the hybrid technique in particular.

The district court also expressed concern about the fact that the Honts Polygraph addressed only the false claims counts of the indictment. If the jurors heard one to two days of evidence on a polygraph examination pertaining to only one of the three categories of charges against Gilliard, they may have viewed the obstruction of justice and perjury charges as secondary in nature. Moreover,

the three categories of charges in this case were so intertwined it is possible, if not probable, that if the jurors believed the Honts Polygraph evidence, they would have determined Gilliard also was not guilty of the obstruction of justice and perjury charges without looking at the evidence specifically addressing those two counts.

The district court expressed further concern with respect to the fact that a Government representative was not present during the administration of the Honts Polygraph. Although a party is not required to give an adverse party advance notice of, and the opportunity to be present at, a polygraph examination, the absence of such notice and opportunity may be a factor in determining whether admission of the polygraph evidence would unduly prejudice the adverse party. In this case, even though the Government had the opportunity to view a videotape of the Honts Polygraph examination, viewing a videotape is not the same as being present at the examination. The district court could reasonably have concluded that the unilateral nature of the Honts Polygraph hindered the Government's ability to cross examine Gilliard's experts and to have its own experts conduct an independent review of the Honts Polygraph results.

Based on these considerations of the danger of unfair prejudice, confusion of the issues, and misleading the jury, we conclude that the district court did not abuse its discretion in excluding the Honts Polygraph evidence under Fed. R. Evid. 403.

III. CONCLUSION

For the reasons set forth above, the district court did not abuse its discretion in excluding the Honts Polygraph evidence under Fed. R. Evid. 702 or under Fed. R. Evid. 403.

AFFIRMED.

---

[6]   The district court also expressed concern about the scope of the questions that the Government could have asked had it conducted its own polygraph examination.

CITY OF CLEVELAND HEIGHTS

v.

KATZ

COURT OF APPEALS OF OHIO, EIGHTH APPELLATE DISTRICT, CUYAHOGA COUNTY

2002 Ohio 4241, 2001 Ohio App. LEXIS 5394 (2001)

TIMOTHY E. McMONAGLE, P.J.:

Defendant-appellant, Daniel Katz, appeals the judgment of the Cleveland Heights Municipal Court, entered after a bench trial, finding him guilty of speeding, in violation of Section 333.03 of the Codified Ordinances of Cleveland Heights, and fining him $55.

Cleveland Heights Police Officer Don Roach testified at appellant's trial that at approximately 8:37 p.m. on February 7, 2001, he was parked in a police cruiser in the median at the intersection of Fairmount and Arlington Boulevards in Cleveland Heights. Roach was facing west, monitoring the speed of eastbound vehicles on Fairmount with a radar device. Roach testified that he observed appellant's SUV pulling away from a huge group of cars and approaching him at a pretty good rate. According to Roach, he locked in the radar device on appellant's SUV and then heard a high-pitched tone, which confirmed his visual sighting of appellant's high speed. The reading on the radar unit indicated that appellant was traveling 47 miles per hour in a zone marked 35 miles per hour. Roach testified that appellant's speed was unreasonable for the conditions.

Roach testified that he had received specialized training, including 8 hours of training at the police academy and 40 hours of on-the-road training, regarding operation of the model 96-11 KR-10 radar unit he was using on September 7, 2001. Roach also testified that his main function as a police officer since his graduation from the police academy twelve years prior had been operating radar equipment.

Roach testified that he performed a light test, an internal calibration test and an external calibration test on the radar unit prior to using it on September 7, 2001. The light test involved pressing a special button on the unit

to make sure that all the lights on the unit were working properly. According to Roach, the internal calibration test involved pressing another designated button on the unit to elicit a preset reading of 32 miles per hour. Roach then used two tuning forks to test the external calibration of the unit. According to Roach, one fork is set at 35 miles per hour and the other is set at 65 miles per hour. When he tapped the forks against a nonmetallic object and then placed them in front of the radar unit, they gave readings of 35 miles per hour and 65 miles per hour respectively. Roach testified that the three tests he performed indicated that the radar unit was working properly on September 7, 2001.

Scott Whitmer, a communications and radar technician for the City of Cleveland Heights Police Department, also testified at appellant's trial.

Whitmer testified that one of his job responsibilities was to test the calibration of the radar units used by City of Cleveland Heights police officers, including the unit used by Roach on February 7, 2001. Whitmer testified further that he had received extensive training regarding testing and calibrating radar devices from Simco Electronics, the manufacturer of the devices, and through his service in the United States Air Force.

Whitmer testified that he tests and calibrates all of the radar devices once a year, using three pieces of equipment specifically designed for testing radar equipment.

Whitmer testified that on September 20 and 21, 2000, he calibrated the radar device used by Roach according to the manufacturer's instructions and when the machinery left our precinct, it was working true and accurate. Whitmer testified further that he had no records reflecting that any repairs had been completed on the unit after that time.

The trial court admitted four records created by Whitmer concerning his tests on the unit: 1) an inventory sheet reflecting the model and serial numbers of the unit and its associated tuning forks; 2) a certificate reflecting that Whitmer calibrated the unit on September 21, 2000 at 35 miles per hour, 50 miles per hour and 65 miles per hour; 3) a certificate of accuracy reflecting that one tuning fork associated with the unit was properly calibrated at 35 miles per hour; and 4) a certificate of accuracy reflecting that the other tuning fork associated with the unit was properly calibrated at 65 miles per hour.

Whitmer also testified that the equipment he used to test Roach's radar unit was shipped to Simco Electronics in August 2000 for testing and calibrating.

According to Whitmer, Simco subsequently returned the equipment with certificates of calibration indicating that the test equipment was properly calibrated.

Defense counsel objected to the admission of the certificates of calibration, however, arguing that they were not authenticated. Defense counsel argued further that without the certificates or any testimony by a representative of Simco Electronics that the testing equipment had been properly calibrated, there was no way of knowing whether the equipment used by Whitmer to test the radar device used by Roach was properly calibrated and, therefore, no way of knowing whether the radar device used by Roach to determine that appellant was speeding was accurate. Accordingly, defense counsel asserted that Officer Roach's testimony regarding appellant's speed, as determined by the radar device, was not admissible for consideration by the trier of fact.

In a journal entry filed on April 4, 2001, the trial court ruled that Officer Roach's testimony regarding the radar reading was admissible, finding that the level of proof proposed by appellant, i.e., that evidence of a radar reading is not admissible absent evidence that the equipment used to calibrate the radar device has itself been properly calibrated, was not necessary to the radar reading.

In light of Officer Roach's testimony, the trial court found that appellant was traveling at 47 miles per hour in a zone marked 35 miles per hour and that the speed was unreasonable for the conditions. On April 9, 2001, the trial court fined appellant $ 55 plus costs but stayed the sentence pending appeal.

Appellant raises two assignments of error for our review:

I. THE CONVICTION AGAINST DANIEL KATZ SHOULD BE REVERSED SINCE THERE WAS INSUFFICIENT TESTIMONY AS TO THE PROPER CALIBRATION OF OFFICER DONALD ROACH'S RADAR EQUIPMENT.

II. THE CONVICTION AGAINST DANIEL KATZ SHOULD BE REVERSED WHERE THE TRIAL COURT DECISION WAS AGAINST THE MANIFEST WEIGHT OF THE EVIDENCE.

In his first assignment of error, appellant asserts that the trial court erred in admitting Officer Roach's testimony regarding his speed because there was insufficient testimony regarding the calibration of Officer Roach's radar equipment.

A court may take judicial notice of the technical theory of operation and the scientific reliability of stationary radar devices. East Cleveland v. Ferell (1958), 168 Ohio St. 298, 154 N.E.2d 630; Cleveland Heights v. Bartell, 1987 Ohio App. LEXIS 7152, (Feb. 19, 1987), Cuyahoga App. No. 51719, unreported. Although not raised in his brief on appeal, at oral argument appellant asserted that the trial court improperly took judicial notice of the scientific reliability of the KR-10 stationary radar device used by Officer Roach. Appellant did not raise this issue in the trial court, however, and therefore has waived it on appeal.

In Cleveland Heights v. Bartell (1987), Cuyahoga App. No. 51719, unreported, the trial court took judicial notice of the scientific reliability of the KR-10 radar unit and this court upheld that finding. Contrary to appellant's argument, our holding did not preclude appellant from further challenging the unit's reliability at trial. If appellant had wanted to challenge the reliability of the KR-10 unit at trial, he could have subpoenaed representatives from the manufacturer of the device and questioned them regarding its reliability. As counsel admitted in oral argument, however, appellant did not do so, and accordingly, there is no evidence in the record to indicate the unit is not reliable. Therefore, the trial court did not err in taking judicial notice of the scientific reliability of the KR-10 radar unit, in reliance on Bartell.

Once judicial notice of the operation and reliability of a radar device is taken, the court must further determine 1) that the radar device was in good operating condition and properly calibrated at the time of use; 2) that the operator of the radar device was properly qualified to use the device; and 3) that the police officer properly operated and read the radar device. Id.

Although appellant concedes that a court may take judicial notice of the reliability and operation of a radar device, as the trial court did here, appellant asks this Court to find that the City failed to prove that the radar device at issue was calibrated properly because 1) Officer Roach should have performed more than three tests on his unit to ascertain its accuracy; and 2) the City did not produce evidence that the equipment used by Whitmer to calibrate the unit and its associated tuning forks was itself properly calibrated.

Appellant argues that the trial court should have required evidence that more than three tests had been performed on Officer Roach's radar unit before concluding that it was properly calibrated because there are limitations to the three tests performed by Officer Roach. Appellant asserts that the light test performed by Roach was insufficient because it merely determined that the light fixtures inside the radar unit were functioning properly. He also asserts that tuning forks may get dented or bent and, if used on a radar unit that is out of calibration, could possibly indicate accuracy when, in fact, the unit is out of calibration.

We refuse to speculate, however, about possible problems with the tests. This court has previously held that as few as two tests (an internal calibration test and an external calibration test) are sufficient to demonstrate that a radar unit is properly calibrated. Lyndhurst v. Danvers, 1988 Ohio App. LEXIS 4621, (Nov. 23, 1988), Cuyahoga App. No. 55537, unreported; Cleveland Heights v. Bartell, supra. Moreover, appellant offered no evidence whatsoever that any of the three tests performed by Officer Roach on February 7, 2001 were flawed or produced inaccurate results. Accordingly, there was no reason for the trial court to require evidence of more tests before concluding that Roach's radar unit was accurate.

Appellant also contends that there was insufficient evidence that Roach's radar unit was properly calibrated at the time of use because the City failed to show that Simco Electronics properly calibrated the equipment used by Whitmer to subsequently test and calibrate the unit. Appellant asserts that Whitmer's calibrations of Roach's radar unit were accurate only if the test equipment used to perform the calibrations was itself properly calibrated. Therefore, appellant contends, without testimony from a representative of the manufacturer that the test equipment was properly calibrated, there was no evidence that the radar device used by Roach was functioning properly and, accordingly, Roach's testimony regarding appellant's speed was inadmissible.

Appellant's argument was squarely rejected, however, in State v. Ellison, 1987 Ohio App. LEXIS 5688, (Jan. 30, 1987), Auglaize App. No. 2-85-35. In Ellison, the defendant was convicted of operating a motor vehicle at a speed of 70 miles per hour in a 55 miles per hour zone. The defendant challenged the trial court's finding that the radar device was in proper working order because the State had not presented evidence of certification from the manufacturer as to the accuracy of the tuning forks used to test the calibration of the unit.

The Third Appellate District rejected the defendant's argument, stating:

Like most matters of proof, however, there may be various ways to prove the same thing, or a point is reached in the matter of proof, beyond which no further proof is needed and presumptions of regularity pertain. Thus, in determining that a mechanism is in proper working order, it might become absurd to require that each component part be also proved to be in working order, or, for example, that a testing mechanism, which is not itself a component part, is itself in working order. The sufficiency of proof will, as to individual things which must be proved in a specific case, vary as to the circumstances involved and the availability of other proof, and generally will be left to the sound discretion of the trial court, particularly where there is no showing, as here, that the testing device is, in some respect, not in proper working order.

*** Thus, once it is determined that a device is generally reliable when properly operated by a properly trained operator to prove a certain thing, such as speed, dependent upon the individual circumstances of the case, it may not be necessary for the State, in the absence of evidence to the contrary, to offer any evidence of the similar proper working order of another device used to test the first device.

The circumstances of this case demonstrate that it was not necessary for the City to prove that the test equipment used by Whitmer to calibrate Roach's radar unit was itself properly calibrated. First, appellant presented no evidence whatsoever that the testing equipment was not in proper working order. Accordingly, as in Ellison, supra, there was no need for the City to produce evidence that the testing equipment was properly calibrated.

Moreover, although no one from Simco Electronics testified regarding the accuracy of the testing equipment, Scott Whitmer testified that the testing equipment was sent to Simco in August 2000 to be tested and calibrated and was subsequently returned with certificates of calibration indicating that the test equipment was properly calibrated. Therefore, contrary to appellant's assertion, there was, in fact, evidence that the testing equipment was in proper working order.

Appellant contends that his argument that the City must demonstrate that the testing equipment was itself properly calibrated has been suggested and followed by the Ohio Supreme Court in State v. Bonar (1973), 40 Ohio App. 2d 360, 319 N.E.2d 388. Appellant's reliance on Bonar, however, is misplaced. First, Bonar was decided by the Seventh Appellate District Court of Appeals, not the Supreme Court of Ohio.

Moreover, Bonar clearly does not support appellant's argument. In Bonar, the defendant was convicted of operating a motor vehicle at a speed of 75 miles per hour in a 60 miles per hour zone. The defendant appealed his conviction, arguing that the State had put on no evidence to indicate that the radar unit that had clocked his speed was functioning prop-erly. The Seventh Appellate District Court of Appeals reversed the defendant's conviction, finding that there was *** no testimony as to whether the radar measuring equipment was properly installed, set up or operating correctly. Accordingly, the Seventh District held that the trial court should have granted the defendant's motion for a directed verdict.

The Seventh Appellate District did not hold, as appellant contends, that in any case involving a radar detector, the State must prove that the equipment used to calibrate the radar detector has itself been properly calibrated. Rather, the Bonar court held that the State must demonstrate, as it did here, that the unit was properly set up, tested and functioning properly.

In State v. Bechtel (1985), 24 Ohio App. 3d 72, 493 N.E.2d 318, the defendant appealed his conviction for speeding, arguing that the trial court erred in admitting testimony regarding the tuning forks used to test the calibration of the radar unit because there was no testimony regarding the accuracy of the tuning forks. The Ninth Appellate District disagreed, however, stating:

While generally the accuracy of the radar unit and the accuracy of the testing apparatus are essential to a speeding conviction based solely on the radar evidence, the weight of the authority holds that when two tuning forks are used to ascertain the accuracy of the radar unit, additional proof of the accuracy of the tuning forks is not necessary. This is because each tuning fork corroborates the accuracy of the other, and it is highly unlikely that the radar unit and each tuning fork would be inaccurate to the same degree. Id. at 73. (Citations omitted).

Here, in addition to the light test and internal calibration tests, Officer Roach used two individually-calibrated tuning forks to test the external calibration of his radar unit. If in Bechtel the use of two tuning forks was sufficient to demonstrate the accuracy of a radar device, we see no reason in this case to require further proof that the equipment used to calibrate the radar device and tuning forks was itself properly calibrated, especially where there was no evidence that the testing equipment was not functioning properly.

Appellant's first assignment of error is therefore overruled.

In his second assignment of error, appellant contends that because the City failed to prove that the testing equipment used to calibrate Roach's radar unit was itself properly calibrated, it failed to demonstrate the accuracy of Roach's unit and, therefore, Roach's testimony regarding appellant's speed as determined by the radar device was not admissible at trial. Appellant further contends that without Roach's testimony there was no competent evidence produced at trial to establish that he was speeding and, therefore, his conviction was against the manifest weight of the evidence. We disagree.

As set forth in our discussion regarding appellant's first assignment of error, the City was not required to prove that the equipment used to calibrate Officer Roach's radar unit was itself properly calibrated. Rather, Officer Roach's testimony regarding appellant's speed as determined by the radar unit was admissible if the City demonstrated that the radar device was in good operating condition and properly calibrated at the time of use, the operator of the device was properly trained and qualified to use it and did, in fact, properly operate the radar device. See State v. Bechtel, supra.

Scott Whitmer testified for the City that Roach's unit had been tested and calibrated on September 20 and 21, 2000 and no repairs were made to the unit after that time. Officer Roach testified that he performed three tests on the unit on February 7, 2001 prior to apprehending appellant and all three tests indicated that the unit was operating properly. He testified further that he had been specially trained in operating the radar device used to determine appellant's speed on February 7, 2001 and that he was properly operating the device at the time of appellant's speeding violation.

This testimony laid a sufficient foundation to establish the accuracy of Roach's radar unit and, therefore, Roach's testimony regarding appellant's speed as established through the radar unit was properly admissible.

In light of this testimony, the trial court did not err in finding appellant guilty of speeding.

Appellant's second assignment of error is therefore overruled.

*** The defendant's conviction having been affirmed, any bail pending appeal is terminated. Case remanded to the trial court for execution of sentence.

Cases Relating to Chapter 16

Evidence Unconstitutionally Obtained

UNITED STATES
v.
LEON

**Supreme Court of the United States
468 U.S. 897, 104 S. Ct. 3405,
82 L. Ed. 2d 677 (1984)**

JUSTICE WHITE delivered the opinion of the Court.

This case presents the question whether the Fourth Amendment exclusionary rule should be modified so as not to bar the use in the prosecution's case in chief of evidence obtained by officers acting in reasonable reliance on a search warrant issued by a detached and neutral magistrate but ultimately found to be unsupported by probable cause. To resolve this question, we must consider once again the tension between the sometimes competing goals of, on the one hand, deterring official misconduct and removing inducements to unreasonable invasions of privacy and, on the other, establishing procedures under which criminal defendants are "acquitted or convicted on the basis of all the evidence which exposes the truth." Alderman v. United States, 394 U.S. 165, 175 (1969).

I.

In August 1981, a confidential informant of unproven reliability informed an officer of the Burbank Police Department that two persons known to him as "Armando" and "Patsy" were selling large quantities of cocaine and methaqualone from their resi-

dence at 620 Price Drive in Burbank, Cal. The informant also indicated that he had witnessed a sale of methaqualone by "Patsy" at the residence approximately five months earlier and had observed at that time a shoebox containing a large amount of cash that belonged to "Patsy." He further declared that "Armando" and "Patsy" generally kept only small quantities of drugs at their residence and stored the remainder at another location in Burbank.

On the basis of this information, the Burbank police initiated an extensive investigation focusing first on the Price Drive residence and later on two other residences as well. Cars parked at the Price Drive residence were determined to belong to respondents Armando Sanchez, who had previously been arrested for possession of marihuana, and Patsy Stewart, who had no criminal record. During the course of the investigation, officers observed an automobile belonging to respondent Ricardo Del Castillo, who had previously been arrested for possession of 50 pounds of marihuana, arrive at the Price Drive residence. The driver of that car entered the house, exited shortly thereafter carrying a small paper sack, and drove away. A check of Del Castillo's probation records led the officers to respondent Alberto Leon, whose telephone number Del Castillo had listed as his employer's. Leon had been arrested in 1980 on drug charges, and a companion had informed the police at that time that Leon was heavily involved in the importation of drugs into this country. Before the current investigation began, the Burbank officers had learned that an informant had told a Glendale police officer that Leon stored a large quantity of methaqualone at his residence in Glendale. During the course of this investigation, the Burbank officers learned that Leon was living at 716 South Sunset Canyon in Burbank.

Subsequently, the officers observed several persons, at least one of whom had prior drug involvement, arriving at the Price Drive residence and leaving with small packages; observed a variety of other material activity at the two residences as well as at a condominium at 7902 Via Magdalena; and witnessed a variety of relevant activity involving respondents' automobiles. The officers also observed respondents Sanchez and Stewart board separate flights for Miami. The pair later returned to Los Angeles together, consented to a search of their luggage that revealed only a small amount of marihuana, and left the airport. Based on these and other observations summarized in the affidavit, App. 34, Officer Cyril Rombach of the Burbank Police Department, an experienced and well-trained narcotics investigator, prepared an application for a warrant to search 620 Price Drive, 716 South Sunset Canyon, 7902 Via Magdalena, and automobiles registered to each of the respondents for an extensive list of items believed to be related to respondents' drug-trafficking activities. Officer Rombach's extensive application was reviewed by several Deputy District Attorneys.

A facially valid search warrant was issued in September 1981 by a State Superior Court Judge. The ensuing searches produced large quantities of drugs at the Via Magdalena and Sunset Canyon addresses and a small quantity at the Price Drive residence. Other evidence was discovered at each of the residences and in Stewart's and Del Castillo's automobiles. Respondents were indicted by a grand jury in the District Court for the Central District of California and charged with conspiracy to possess and distribute cocaine and a variety of substantive counts.

The respondents then filed motions to suppress the evidence seized pursuant to the warrant. The District Court held an evidentiary hearing and, while recognizing that the case was a close one, see id., at 131, granted the motions to suppress in part. It concluded that the affidavit was insufficient to establish probable cause, but did not suppress all of the evidence as to all of the respondents because none of the respondents had standing to challenge all of the searches. In response to a request from the Government, the court made clear that Officer Rombach had acted in good faith, but it rejected the Government's suggestion that the Fourth Amendment exclusionary rule should not apply where evidence is seized in reasonable, good-faith reliance on a search warrant.

The District Court denied the Government's motion for reconsideration, id., at 147, and a divided panel of the Court of Appeals for the Ninth Circuit affirmed, judgt. order reported at 701 F.2d 187 (1983). The Court of Appeals first concluded that Officer Rombach's affidavit could not establish probable cause to search the Price Drive residence. To the extent that the affidavit set forth facts demonstrating the basis of the informant's knowledge of criminal activity, the information included was fatally stale. The affidavit, moreover, failed to establish the informant's credibility. Accordingly, the Court of Appeals concluded that the information provided by the informant was inadequate under both prongs of the two-part test established in Aguilar v. Texas, 378 U.S. 108 (1964), and Spinelli v. United States, 393 U.S. 410 (1969). The officers' independent investigation neither cured the staleness nor corroborated the details of the informant's declarations. The Court of Appeals then considered whether the affidavit formed a proper basis for the search of the Sunset Canyon residence. In its view, the affidavit included no facts indicating the basis for the informants' statements concerning respondent Leon's criminal activities and was devoid of information establishing the informants' reliability. Because these deficiencies had not been cured by the police investigation, the District Court properly suppressed the fruits of the search. The Court of Appeals refused the Government's invitation to recognize a good-faith exception to the Fourth Amendment exclusionary rule. App. to Pet. for Cert. 4a.

The Government's petition for certiorari expressly declined to seek review of the lower courts' determinations that the search warrant was unsupported by probable cause and presented only the question "[whether] the Fourth Amendment exclusionary rule should be modified so as not to bar the admission of evidence seized in reasonable, good-faith reliance on a search warrant that is subsequently held to be defective." We granted certiorari to consider the propriety of such a modification. 463 U.S. 1206 (1983). Although it undoubtedly is within our power to consider the question whether probable cause existed under the "totality of the circumstances" test announced last Term in Illinois v. Gates, 462 U.S. 213 (1983), that question has not been briefed or argued; and it is also within our authority, which we choose to exercise, to take the case as it comes to us, accepting the Court of Appeals' conclusion that probable cause was lacking under the prevailing legal standards. See this Court's Rule 21.1(a).

We have concluded that, in the Fourth Amendment context, the exclusionary rule can be modified somewhat without jeopardizing its ability to perform its intended functions. Accordingly, we reverse the judgment of the Court of Appeals.

II.

Language in opinions of this Court and of individual Justices has sometimes implied that the exclusionary rule is a necessary corollary of the Fourth Amendment, Mapp v. Ohio, 367 U.S. 643, 651, 655-657 (1961); Olmstead v. United States, 277 U.S. 438, 462-463 (1928), or that the rule is required by the conjunction of the Fourth and Fifth Amendments. Mapp v. Ohio, supra, at 661-662 (Black, J., concurring); Agnello v. United States, 269 U.S. 20, 33-34 (1925). These implications need not detain us long. The Fifth Amendment theory has not withstood critical analysis or the test of time, see Andresen v. Maryland, 427 U.S. 463 (1976), and the Fourth Amendment "has never been interpreted to proscribe the introduction of illegally seized evidence in all proceedings or against all persons." Stone v. Powell, 428 U.S. 465, 486 (1976).

A.

The Fourth Amendment contains no provision expressly precluding the use of evidence obtained in violation of its commands, and an examination of its origin and purposes

makes clear that the use of fruits of a past unlawful search or seizure "[works] no new Fourth Amendment wrong." United States v. Calandra, 414 U.S. 338, 354 (1974). The wrong condemned by the Amendment is "fully accomplished" by the unlawful search or seizure itself, ibid., and the exclusionary rule is neither intended nor able to "cure the invasion of the defendant's rights which he has already suffered." Stone v. Powell, supra, at 540 (WHITE, J., dissenting). The rule thus operates as "a judicially created remedy designed to safeguard Fourth Amendment rights generally through its deterrent effect, rather than a personal constitutional right of the party aggrieved." United States v. Calandra, supra, at 348.

Whether the exclusionary sanction is appropriately imposed in a particular case, our decisions make clear, is "an issue separate from the question whether the Fourth Amendment rights of the party seeking to invoke the rule were violated by police conduct." Illinois v. Gates, supra, at 223. Only the former question is currently before us, and it must be resolved by weighing the costs and benefits of preventing the use in the prosecution's case in chief of inherently trustworthy tangible evidence obtained in reliance on a search warrant issued by a detached and neutral magistrate that ultimately is found to be defective.

The substantial social costs exacted by the exclusionary rule for the vindication of Fourth Amendment rights have long been a source of concern. "Our cases have consistently recognized that unbending application of the exclusionary sanction to enforce ideals of governmental rectitude would impede unacceptably the truth-finding functions of judge and jury." United States v. Payner, 447 U.S. 727, 734 (1980). An objectionable collateral consequence of this interference with the criminal justice system's truth-finding function is that some guilty defendants may go free or receive reduced sentences as a result of favorable plea bargains. Particularly when law enforcement officers have acted in objective good faith or their transgressions have been minor, the magnitude of the benefit conferred on such guilty defendants offends basic concepts of the criminal justice system. Stone v. Powell, 428 U.S., at 490.

Indiscriminate application of the exclusionary rule, therefore, may well "[generate] disrespect for the law and administration of justice." Id., at 491. Accordingly, "[as] with any remedial device, the application of the rule has been restricted to those areas where its remedial objectives are thought most efficaciously served." United States v. Calandra, supra, at 348; see Stone v. Powell, supra, at 486-487; United States v. Janis, 428 U.S. 433, 447 (1976).

B.

Close attention to those remedial objectives has characterized our recent decisions concerning the scope of the Fourth Amendment exclusionary rule. The Court has, to be sure, not seriously questioned, "in the absence of a more efficacious sanction, the continued application of the rule to suppress evidence from the [prosecution's] case where a Fourth Amendment violation has been substantial and deliberate. . . ." Franks v. Delaware, 438 U.S. 154, 171 (1978); Stone v. Powell, supra, at 492. Nevertheless, the balancing approach that has evolved in various contexts—including criminal trials—"forcefully [suggests] that the exclusionary rule be more generally modified to permit the introduction of evidence obtained in the reasonable good-faith belief that a search or seizure was in accord with the Fourth Amendment." Illinois v. Gates, 462 U.S., at 255 (WHITE, J., concurring in judgment).

In Stone v. Powell, supra, the Court emphasized the costs of the exclusionary rule, expressed its view that limiting the circumstances under which Fourth Amendment claims could be raised in federal habeas corpus proceedings would not reduce the rule's deterrent effect, id., at 489-495, and held that a state prisoner who has been afforded a full and fair opportunity to litigate a Fourth Amendment claim may not obtain federal habeas relief on the ground that unlawfully obtained evidence had been introduced at his trial. Cf. Rose v. Mitchell, 443 U.S. 545, 560-563 (1979). Proposed extensions of the exclusionary rule to proceedings other than the criminal trial itself have been evaluated and rejected under the same analytic approach. In United States v. Calandra, for example, we declined to allow grand jury

witnesses to refuse to answer questions based on evidence obtained from an unlawful search or seizure since "[any] incremental deterrent effect which might be achieved by extending the rule to grand jury proceedings is uncertain at best." 414 U.S., at 348. Similarly, in United States v. Janis, supra, we permitted the use in federal civil proceedings of evidence illegally seized by state officials since the likelihood of deterring police misconduct through such an extension of the exclusionary rule was insufficient to outweigh its substantial social costs. In so doing, we declared that, "[if] . . . the exclusionary rule does not result in appreciable deterrence, then, clearly, its use in the instant situation is unwarranted." Id., at 454.

As cases considering the use of unlawfully obtained evidence in criminal trials themselves make clear, it does not follow from the emphasis on the exclusionary rule's deterrent value that "anything which deters illegal searches is thereby commanded by the Fourth Amendment." Alderman v. United States, 394 U.S., at 174. In determining whether persons aggrieved solely by the introduction of damaging evidence unlawfully obtained from their co-conspirators or codefendants could seek suppression, for example, we found that the additional benefits of such an extension of the exclusionary rule would not outweigh its costs. Id., at 174-175. Standing to invoke the rule has thus been limited to cases in which the prosecution seeks to use the fruits of an illegal search or seizure against the victim of police misconduct. Rakas v. Illinois, 439 U.S. 128 (1978); Brown v. United States, 411 U.S. 223 (1973); Wong Sun v. United States, 371 U.S. 471, 491-492 (1963). Cf. United States v. Payner, 447 U.S. 727 (1980).

Even defendants with standing to challenge the introduction in their criminal trials of unlawfully obtained evidence cannot prevent every conceivable use of such evidence. Evidence obtained in violation of the Fourth Amendment and inadmissible in the prosecution's case in chief may be used to impeach a defendant's direct testimony. Walder v. United States, 347 U.S. 62 (1954). See also Oregon v. Hass, 420 U.S. 714 (1975); Harris v. New York, 401 U.S. 222 (1971). A similar assessment of the "incremental furthering" of the ends of the exclusionary rule led us to conclude in United States v. Havens, 446 U.S. 620, 627 (1980), that evidence inadmissible in the prosecution's case in chief or otherwise as substantive evidence of guilt may be used to impeach statements made by a defendant in response to "proper cross-examination reasonably suggested by the defendant's direct examination." Id., at 627-628.

When considering the use of evidence obtained in violation of the Fourth Amendment in the prosecution's case in chief, moreover, we have declined to adopt a per se or "but for" rule that would render inadmissible any evidence that came to light through a chain of causation that began with an illegal arrest. Brown v. Illinois, 422 U.S. 590 (1975); Wong Sun v. United States, supra, at 487-488. We also have held that a witness' testimony may be admitted even when his identity was discovered in an unconstitutional search. United States v. Ceccolini, 435 U.S. 268 (1978). The perception underlying these decisions—that the connection between police misconduct and evidence of crime may be sufficiently attenuated to permit the use of that evidence at trial—is a product of considerations relating to the exclusionary rule and the constitutional principles it is designed to protect. Dunaway v. New York, 442 U.S. 200, 217-218 (1979); United States v. Ceccolini, supra, at 279. In short, the "dissipation of the taint" concept that the Court has applied in deciding whether exclusion is appropriate in a particular case "attempts to mark the point at which the detrimental consequences of illegal police action become so attenuated that the deterrent effect of the exclusionary rule no longer justifies its cost." Brown v. Illinois, supra, at 609 (POWELL, J., concurring in part). Not surprisingly in view of this purpose, an assessment of the flagrancy of the police misconduct constitutes an important step in the calculus. Dunaway v. New York, supra, at 218; Brown v. Illinois, supra, at 603-604.

The same attention to the purposes underlying the exclusionary rule also has characterized decisions not involving the scope of the rule itself. We have not required suppression of the fruits of a search incident to an arrest made in good-faith reliance on a substantive criminal statute that subsequently is declared unconstitutional. Michigan v. DeFillippo, 443 U.S. 31 (1979). Similarly, although the Court

has been unwilling to conclude that new Fourth Amendment principles are always to have only prospective effect, United States v. Johnson, 457 U.S. 537, 560 (1982), no Fourth Amendment decision marking a "clear break with the past" has been applied retroactively. See United States v. Peltier, 422 U.S. 531 (1975); Desist v. United States, 394 U.S. 244 (1969); Linkletter v. Walker, 381 U.S. 618 (1965). The propriety of retroactive application of a newly announced Fourth Amendment principle, moreover, has been assessed largely in terms of the contribution retroactivity might make to the deterrence of police misconduct. United States v. Johnson, supra, at 560-561; United States v. Peltier, supra, at 536-539, 542.

As yet, we have not recognized any form of good-faith exception to the Fourth Amendment exclusionary rule. But the balancing approach that has evolved during the years of experience with the rule provides strong support for the modification currently urged upon us. As we discuss below, our evaluation of the costs and benefits of suppressing reliable physical evidence seized by officers reasonably relying on a warrant issued by a detached and neutral magistrate leads to the conclusion that such evidence should be admissible in the prosecution's case in chief.

III.

A.

Because a search warrant "provides the detached scrutiny of a neutral magistrate, which is a more reliable safeguard against improper searches than the hurried judgment of a law enforcement officer 'engaged in the often competitive enterprise of ferreting out crime,'" United States v. Chadwick, 433 U.S. 1, 9 (1977) (quoting Johnson v. United States, 333 U.S. 10, 14 (1948)), we have expressed a strong preference for warrants and declared that "in a doubtful or marginal case a search under a warrant may be sustainable where without one it would fall." United States v. Ventresca, 380 U.S. 102, 106 (1965). See Aguilar v. Texas, 378 U.S., at 111. Reasonable minds frequently may differ on the question whether a particular affidavit establishes probable cause, and we have thus concluded that the preference for warrants is most appropriately effectuated by according "great deference" to a magistrate's determination. Spinelli v. United States, 393 U.S., at 419. See Illinois v. Gates, 462 U.S., at 236; United States v. Ventresca, supra, at 108-109.

Deference to the magistrate, however, is not boundless. It is clear, first, that the deference accorded to a magistrate's finding of probable cause does not preclude inquiry into the knowing or reckless falsity of the affidavit on which that determination was based. Franks v. Delaware, 438 U.S. 154 (1978). Second, the courts must also insist that the magistrate purport to "perform his 'neutral and detached' function and not serve merely as a rubber stamp for the police." Aguilar v. Texas, supra, at 111. See Illinois v. Gates, supra, at 239. A magistrate failing to "manifest that neutrality and detachment demanded of a judicial officer when presented with a warrant application" and who acts instead as "an adjunct law enforcement officer" cannot provide valid authorization for an otherwise unconstitutional search. Lo-Ji Sales, Inc. v. New York, 442 U.S. 319, 326-327 (1979).

Third, reviewing courts will not defer to a warrant based on an affidavit that does not "provide the magistrate with a substantial basis for determining the existence of probable cause." Illinois v. Gates, 462 U.S., at 239. "Sufficient information must be presented to the magistrate to allow that official to determine probable cause; his action cannot be a mere ratification of the bare conclusions of others." Ibid. See Aguilar v. Texas, supra, at 114-115; Giordenello v. United States, 357 U.S. 480 (1958); Nathanson v. United States, 290 U.S. 41 (1933). Even if the warrant application was supported by more than a "bare bones" affidavit, a reviewing court may properly conclude that, notwithstanding the deference that magistrates deserve, the warrant was invalid because the magistrate's probable-cause determination reflected an improper analysis of the totality of the circumstances, Illinois v. Gates, supra, at 238-239, or because the form of the warrant was improper in some respect.

Only in the first of these three situations, however, has the Court set forth a rationale for suppressing evidence obtained pursuant to a search warrant; in the other areas, it has simply excluded such evidence without considering whether Fourth Amendment interests will be advanced. To the extent that proponents of exclusion rely on its behavioral effects on judges and magistrates in these areas, their reliance is misplaced. First, the exclusionary rule is designed to deter police misconduct rather than to punish the errors of judges and magistrates. Second, there exists no evidence suggesting that judges and magistrates are inclined to ignore or subvert the Fourth Amendment or that lawlessness among these actors requires application of the extreme sanction of exclusion.

Third, and most important, we discern no basis, and are offered none, for believing that exclusion of evidence seized pursuant to a warrant will have a significant deterrent effect on the issuing judge or magistrate. Many of the factors that indicate that the exclusionary rule cannot provide an effective "special" or "general" deterrent for individual offending law enforcement officers apply as well to judges or magistrates. And, to the extent that the rule is thought to operate as a "systemic" deterrent on a wider audience, it clearly can have no such effect on individuals empowered to issue search warrants. Judges and magistrates are not adjuncts to the law enforcement team; as neutral judicial officers, they have no stake in the outcome of particular criminal prosecutions. The threat of exclusion thus cannot be expected significantly to deter them. Imposition of the exclusionary sanction is not necessary meaningfully to inform judicial officers of their errors, and we cannot conclude that admitting evidence obtained pursuant to a warrant while at the same time declaring that the warrant was somehow defective will in any way reduce judicial officers' professional incentives to comply with the Fourth Amendment, encourage them to repeat their mistakes, or lead to the granting of all colorable warrant requests.

B.

If exclusion of evidence obtained pursuant to a subsequently invalidated warrant is to have any deterrent effect, therefore, it must alter the behavior of individual law enforcement officers or the policies of their departments. One could argue that applying the exclusionary rule in cases where the police failed to demonstrate probable cause in the warrant application deters future inadequate presentations or "magistrate shopping" and thus promotes the ends of the Fourth Amendment. Suppressing evidence obtained pursuant to a technically defective warrant supported by probable cause also might encourage officers to scrutinize more closely the form of the warrant and to point out suspected judicial errors. We find such arguments speculative and conclude that suppression of evidence obtained pursuant to a warrant should be ordered only on a case-by-case basis and only in those unusual cases in which exclusion will further the purposes of the exclusionary rule.

We have frequently questioned whether the exclusionary rule can have any deterrent effect when the offending officers acted in the objectively reasonable belief that their conduct did not violate the Fourth Amendment. "No empirical researcher, proponent or opponent of the rule, has yet been able to establish with any assurance whether the rule has a deterrent effect. . . ." United States v. Janis, 428 U.S., at 452, n. 22. But even assuming that the rule effectively deters some police misconduct and provides incentives for the law enforcement profession as a whole to conduct itself in accord with the Fourth Amendment, it cannot be expected, and should not be applied, to deter objectively reasonable law enforcement activity.

As we observed in Michigan v. Tucker, 417 U.S. 433, 447 (1974), and reiterated in United States v. Peltier, 422 U.S., at 539:

> "The deterrent purpose of the exclusionary rule necessarily assumes that the police have engaged in willful, or at the very least negligent, conduct which has deprived the defendant of some right. By refusing to admit evidence gained as a result of such conduct, the courts hope to instill in those particular investigating officers, or in their future counterparts, a greater degree of care toward the rights of an accused. Where the official action was pursued in complete good faith, however, the deterrence rationale loses much of its force."

The Peltier Court continued, id., at 542:

"If the purpose of the exclusionary rule is to deter unlawful police conduct, then evidence obtained from a search should be suppressed only if it can be said that the law enforcement officer had knowledge, or may properly be charged with knowledge, that the search was unconstitutional under the Fourth Amendment." See also Illinois v. Gates, 462 U.S., at 260-261 (WHITE, J., concurring in judgment); United States v. Janis, supra, at 459; Brown v. Illinois, 422 U.S., at 610-611 (POWELL, J., concurring in part).

In short, where the officer's conduct is objectively reasonable, "excluding the evidence will not further the ends of the exclusionary rule in any appreciable way; for it is painfully apparent that . . . the officer is acting as a reasonable officer would and should act in similar circumstances. Excluding the evidence can in no way affect his future conduct unless it is to make him less willing to do his duty." Stone v. Powell, 428 U.S., at 539-540 (WHITE, J., dissenting).

This is particularly true, we believe, when an officer acting with objective good faith has obtained a search warrant from a judge or magistrate and acted within its scope. In most such cases, there is no police illegality and thus nothing to deter. It is the magistrate's responsibility to determine whether the officer's allegations establish probable cause and, if so, to issue a warrant comporting in form with the requirements of the Fourth Amendment. In the ordinary case, an officer cannot be expected to question the magistrate's probable-cause determination or his judgment that the form of the warrant is technically sufficient. "[Once] the warrant issues, there is literally nothing more the policeman can do in seeking to comply with the law." Id., at 498 (BURGER, C. J., concurring). Penalizing the officer for the magistrate's error, rather than his own, cannot logically contribute to the deterrence of Fourth Amendment violations.

C.

We conclude that the marginal or nonexistent benefits produced by suppressing evidence obtained in objectively reasonable reliance on a subsequently invalidated search warrant cannot justify the substantial costs of exclusion. We do not suggest, however, that exclusion is always inappropriate in cases where an officer has obtained a warrant and abided by its terms. "[Searches] pursuant to a warrant will rarely require any deep inquiry into reasonableness," Illinois v. Gates, 462 U.S., at 267 (WHITE, J., concurring in judgment), for "a warrant issued by a magistrate normally suffices to establish" that a law enforcement officer has "acted in good faith in conducting the search." United States v. Ross, 456 U.S. 798, 823, n. 32 (1982). Nevertheless, the officer's reliance on the magistrate's probable-cause determination and on the technical sufficiency of the warrant he issues must be objectively reasonable, cf. Harlow v. Fitzgerald, 457 U.S. 800, 815-819 (1982), and it is clear that in some circumstances the officer will have no reasonable grounds for believing that the warrant was properly issued.

Suppression therefore remains an appropriate remedy if the magistrate or judge in issuing a warrant was misled by information in an affidavit that the affiant knew was false or would have known was false except for his reckless disregard of the truth. Franks v. Delaware, 438 U.S. 154 (1978). The exception we recognize today will also not apply in cases where the issuing magistrate wholly abandoned his judicial role in the manner condemned in Lo-Ji Sales, Inc. v. New York, 442 U.S. 319 (1979); in such circumstances, no reasonably well trained officer should rely on the warrant. Nor would an officer manifest objective good faith in relying on a warrant based on an affidavit "so lacking in indicia of probable cause as to render official belief in its existence entirely unreasonable." Brown v. Illinois, 422 U.S., at 610-611 (POWELL, J., concurring in part); see Illinois v. Gates, supra, at 263-264 (WHITE, J., concurring in judgment). Finally, depending on the circumstances of the particular case, a warrant may be so facially deficient—i.e., in failing to particularize the place to be searched or the things to be seized—that the executing officers cannot reasonably presume it to be valid. Cf. Massachusetts v. Sheppard, post, at 988-991.

In so limiting the suppression remedy, we leave untouched the probable-cause standard and the various requirements for a valid warrant. Other objections to the modification of the Fourth Amendment exclusionary rule we consider to be insubstantial. The good-faith exception for searches conducted pursuant to warrants is not intended to signal our unwillingness strictly to enforce the requirements of the Fourth Amendment, and we do not believe that it will have this effect. As we have already suggested, the good-faith exception, turning as it does on objective reasonableness, should not be difficult to apply in practice. When officers have acted pursuant to a warrant, the prosecution should ordinarily be able to establish objective good faith without a substantial expenditure of judicial time.

Nor are we persuaded that application of a good-faith exception to searches conducted pursuant to warrants will preclude review of the constitutionality of the search or seizure, deny needed guidance from the courts, or freeze Fourth Amendment law in its present state. There is no need for courts to adopt the inflexible practice of always deciding whether the officers' conduct manifested objective good faith before turning to the question whether the Fourth Amendment has been violated. Defendants seeking suppression of the fruits of allegedly unconstitutional searches or seizures undoubtedly raise live controversies which Art. III empowers federal courts to adjudicate. As cases addressing questions of good-faith immunity under 42 U. S. C. § 1983, compare O'Connor v. Donaldson, 422 U.S. 563 (1975), with Procunier v. Navarette, 434 U.S. 555, 566, n. 14 (1978), and cases involving the harmless-error doctrine, compare Milton v. Wainwright, 407 U.S. 371, 372 (1972), with Coleman v. Alabama, 399 U.S. 1 (1970), make clear, courts have considerable discretion in conforming their decisionmaking processes to the exigencies of particular cases.

If the resolution of a particular Fourth Amendment question is necessary to guide future action by law enforcement officers and magistrates, nothing will prevent reviewing courts from deciding that question before turning to the good-faith issue. Indeed, it frequently will be difficult to determine whether the officers acted reasonably without resolving the Fourth Amendment issue. Even if the Fourth Amendment question is not one of broad import, reviewing courts could decide in particular cases that magistrates under their supervision need to be informed of their errors and so evaluate the officers' good faith only after finding a violation. In other circumstances, those courts could reject suppression motions posing no important Fourth Amendment questions by turning immediately to a consideration of the officers' good faith. We have no reason to believe that our Fourth Amendment jurisprudence would suffer by allowing reviewing courts to exercise an informed discretion in making this choice.

IV.

When the principles we have enunciated today are applied to the facts of this case, it is apparent that the judgment of the Court of Appeals cannot stand. The Court of Appeals applied the prevailing legal standards to Officer Rombach's warrant application and concluded that the application could not support the magistrate's probable-cause determination. In so doing, the court clearly informed the magistrate that he had erred in issuing the challenged warrant. This aspect of the court's judgment is not under attack in this proceeding.

Having determined that the warrant should not have issued, the Court of Appeals understandably declined to adopt a modification of the Fourth Amendment exclusionary rule that this Court had not previously sanctioned. Although the modification finds strong support in our previous cases, the Court of Appeals' commendable self-restraint is not to be criticized. We have now reexamined the purposes of the exclusionary rule and the propriety of its application in cases where officers have relied on a subsequently invalidated search warrant. Our conclusion is that the rule's purposes will only rarely be served by applying it in such circumstances.

In the absence of an allegation that the magistrate abandoned his detached and neutral role, suppression is appropriate only if the officers were dishonest or reckless in preparing their affidavit or could not have harbored an objectively reasonable belief in the existence of probable cause. Only respondent Leon has contended that no reasonably

well trained police officer could have believed that there existed probable cause to search his house; significantly, the other respondents advance no comparable argument. Officer Rombach's application for a warrant clearly was supported by much more than a "bare bones" affidavit. The affidavit related the results of an extensive investigation and, as the opinions of the divided panel of the Court of Appeals make clear, provided evidence sufficient to create disagreement among thoughtful and competent judges as to the existence of probable cause. Under these circumstances, the officers' reliance on the magistrate's determination of probable cause was objectively reasonable, and application of the extreme sanction of exclusion is inappropriate.

Accordingly, the judgment of the Court of Appeals is
Reversed.

* * *

UNITED STATES
v.
THORNTON

UNITED STATES COURT OF APPEAL, FOURTH CIRCUIT

325 F.3d 189, 2003 U.S. App. LEXIS 6367 (2003)

JUDGES: Before WIDENER, WILLIAMS, and MOTZ, Circuit Judges. Judge Motz wrote the opinion, in which Judge Widener and Judge Williams joined.

OPINION: DIANA GRIBBON MOTZ, Circuit Judge:

A jury convicted Marcus Thornton of possession with intent to distribute cocaine base and two firearm offenses. On appeal, he challenges only the district court's refusal to suppress a firearm found in his automobile, maintaining that it was not legally obtained pursuant to a "search incident to arrest." For the reasons that follow, we affirm.

I.

At a pretrial suppression hearing, the parties produced the following evidence.

On July 21, 2001, Officer Deion L. Nichols, of the Norfolk, Virginia Police Department, driving in an unmarked police cruiser, observed a gold Lincoln Town Car pull to his left that "wouldn't come all the way up to [him]." Assuming that the driver of the Lincoln suspected that he was a police officer, Officer Nichols pulled over to a side street and made a right turn. After the Lincoln passed him, Officer Nichols ran a check on the tags. The check revealed that the tags had been issued to a 1982 Chevy two-door car rather than a Lincoln Town Car. Officer Nichols followed the Lincoln, intending to pull it over. The Lincoln was driven into a parking lot, however, before Officer Nichols "had a chance to do so." Thornton parked the Lincoln and exited the vehicle. Officer Nichols "pulled in behind him and exited [his] vehicle." Officer Nichols, who was in uniform, then approached Thornton, asked him for his driver's license, and told him that his tags did not match the registered vehicle.

Thornton "appeared nervous" and "right away started rambling," "licking his lips," and "sweating." He told Officer Nichols that "someone had just given him the car." "For officer safety," Officer Nichols asked Thornton if he had any narcotics or weapons on him. Thornton said no. The officer then asked him if there were any weapons or narcotics in the car. Thornton again said no. Officer Nichols, "again for officer safety," patted Thornton down, after asking if he could do so. Officer Nichols felt a "bulge" in Thornton's front left pocket. The officer "didn't know what it was, so [he] just kind of casually asked Thornton, 'Do you have any illegal narcotics on you?'" Thornton said that he had "a bag of weed." Officer Nichols then asked him if he could have the bag. Thornton "reached into his pocket" and "pulled out two individual bags," one containing three bags of a "green leafy material consistent with marijuana" and the other with a "large amount of an off-white rocklike substance consistent with crack cocaine."

At that point, Officer Nichols handcuffed Thornton and advised him that he was under arrest. (At trial, Officer Nichols testified that he immediately thereafter put Thornton in the back of the patrol car.) Then, "incident to that arrest," the officer searched the vehicle and found a "BryCo .9-millimeter handgun" under the front driver's seat, where he had observed Thornton sitting. On the way to the police station, Thornton told Officer Nichols, "without any provocation," that he had "just robbed some cat out at Ocean View, and that's where he got the dope."

On December 12, 2001, a grand jury charged Thornton with possession with intent to distribute cocaine base,, possession of a firearm after having been previously convicted of a crime punishable by a term of imprisonment exceeding one year, and possession of a firearm in furtherance of a drug trafficking crime.

Thornton moved to suppress the drugs, his statement, and the firearm on various grounds. After a hearing, the district court denied the motion, finding, inter alia, that Officer Nichols lawfully searched Thornton's automobile incident to his arrest and, alternatively, that Officer Nichols could have conducted an inventory search of the automobile.

On February 8, 2002, a jury convicted Thornton on all three counts. Thornton moved for a new trial, again arguing that the automobile search was unlawful. The district court denied the motion based on the earlier suppression ruling. On May 3, 2002, the district court sentenced Thornton to 180 months imprisonment and eight years of supervised release. Thornton appeals, challenging only the district court's refusal to suppress the firearm; he does not challenge the refusal to suppress the drugs or his statement.

II.

* * *

Thornton's sole contention on appeal is that the search incident to arrest doctrine, as applied to searches of automobiles in *New York v. Belton*, 453 U.S. 454, 69 L. Ed. 2d 768, 101 S. Ct. 2860 (1981), required Officer Nichols to "initiate . . . contact with Thornton, either by actually confronting Thornton, or signaling confrontation with Thornton, while Thornton was still in his vehicle."

A.

It is a well-settled "first principle of Fourth Amendment jurisprudence that the police may not conduct a search unless they first convince a neutral magistrate that there is probable cause to do so." Belton, 453 U.S. at 457. In Chimel v. California, 395 U.S. 752, 23 L. Ed. 2d 685, 89 S. Ct. 2034 (1969), the Court discussed the rationale for and limitations of the "search incident to arrest" exception to that warrant requirement:

When an arrest is made, it is reasonable for the arresting officer to search the person arrested in order to remove any weapons that the latter might seek to use in order to resist arrest or effect his escape. Otherwise, the officer's safety might well be endangered, and the arrest itself frustrated. In addition, it is entirely reasonable for the arresting officer to search for and seize any evidence on the arrestee's person in order to prevent its concealment or destruction. And the area into which an arrestee might reach in order to grab a weapon or evidentiary items must, of course, be governed by a like rule. A gun on a table or in a drawer in front of one who is arrested can be as dangerous to the arresting officer as one concealed in the clothing of the person arrested. There is ample justification, therefore, for a search of the arrestee's person and the area "within his immediate control" —construing that phrase to mean the area from within which he might gain possession of a weapon or destructible evidence.

Chimel, 395 U.S. at 762-63. The Court has often reiterated the "two historical rationales for the 'search incident to arrest' exception: (1) the need to disarm the suspect in order to take him into custody, and (2) the need to preserve evidence for later use at trial." [Citations omitted.]

The Court in Belton applied those rationales to the arrest of an "occupant" of an automobile. See Belton, 453 U.S. at 460. In Belton, a police officer stopped four men, who had sped past the officer. Id. at 455. The officer "gave chase, overtook the speeding vehicle, and ordered its driver to pull it over to the side of the road and stop." Id. After examining the driver's license and the vehicle registration, the officer determined that none of the men owned the vehicle. Id. During that time, the officer also smelled burnt marijuana and saw, on the floor of the car, an envelope marked "Supergold," which he associated with marijuana. Id. at 455-56. Accordingly, the officer directed the men to get out of the car and arrested them for unlawful possession of marijuana. Id. at 456. After they exited the vehicle, the officer patted down each of them and "'split them into four separate areas of the Thruway . . . so they would not be in physical touching area of each other.'" Id. The officer then searched the passenger compartment; he found Belton's jacket on the back seat, unzipped one of the pockets of the jacket, and found cocaine. Id.

The Supreme Court rejected Belton's argument that the search of the passenger compartment of the car exceeded the permissible scope of the search incident to his arrest. The Court began its analysis by observing that for the protection of the Fourth and Fourteenth Amendments to be realized, courts must fashion a clear set of rules that allow police officers to easily determine in most situations "whether an invasion of privacy is justified in the interest of law enforcement." Id. at 458 (internal quotation marks omitted). Thus, the Court reasoned, "[a] single, familiar standard is essential to guide police officers, who have only limited time and expertise to reflect on and balance the social and individual interests involved in the specific circumstances they confront." Id. (internal quotation marks omitted).

The Court then noted the difficulty courts had experienced in fashioning such a rule in the context of an automobile search incident to an arrest:

While the Chimel case established that a search incident to an arrest may not stray beyond the area within the immediate control of the arrestee, courts have found no workable definition of "the area within the immediate control of the arrestee" when that area arguably includes the interior of an automobile and the arrestee is its recent occupant.

Id. at 460. Because articles within a car's passenger compartment "are in fact generally, even if not inevitably, within 'the area into which an arrestee might reach in order to grab a weapon or evidentiary item,'" the Belton Court established the "workable rule" that "when a policeman has made a lawful custodial arrest of the occupant of an automobile, he may, as a contemporaneous incident of that arrest, search the passenger compartment of that automobile." Id. at 460 (quoting Chimel, 395 U.S. at 763) (footnotes omitted).

B.

Thornton contends that the Belton rule does not govern this case because he was not an "occupant of an automobile" when Officer Nichols confronted him. In support of this contention, Thornton relies primarily on a line of authority from the United States Court of Appeals for the Sixth Circuit. See, e.g., United States v. Hudgins, 52 F.3d 115, 119 (6th Cir. 1995); United States v. Strahan, 984 F.2d 155, 159 (6th Cir. 1993). In Hudgins, the court elaborated on the principle that Thornton urges us to adopt:

> Where the officer initiates contact with the defendant, either by actually confronting the defendant or by signaling confrontation with the defendant, while the defendant is still in the automobile, and the officer subsequently arrests the defendant (regardless of whether the defendant has been removed from or has exited the automobile), a subsequent search of the automobile's passenger compartment falls within the scope of Belton and will be upheld as reasonable. . . . . . . However, where the defendant has voluntarily exited the automobile and begun walking away from the automobile before the officer has initiated contact with him, the case does not fit within Belton's bright-line rule, and a case by-case analysis of the reasonableness of the search under Chimel becomes necessary.

52 F.3d at 119 (emphasis added). See also Strahan, 984 F.2d at 15657, 159 (following this rule and finding that Belton did not apply because police silently observed the defendant park and exit his automobile and then immediately apprehended him approximately 30 feet away).

This court has not previously addressed the Sixth Circuit's limitation on the Belton rule in a published opinion. We note, however, that other courts of appeals have considered the question. Although one court previously embraced a rule consistent with the Sixth Circuit's limitation, see United States v. Fafowora, 275 U.S. App. D.C. 141, 865 F.2d 360, 362 (D.C. Cir. 1989) (holding that "ambiguity" necessitating Belton's bright-line rule does not apply "where the police come upon the arrestees outside of an automobile"), three others have refused to do so. See United States v. Sholola, 124 F.3d 803, 817 (7th Cir. 1997) (holding that defendant who was next to open car door ready to enter it, was "'positively linked to [car] prior to his arrest'") (quoting United States v. Adams, 26 F.3d 702, 705 (7th Cir. 1994)); United States v. Snook, 88 F.3d 605, 606 (8th Cir. 1996) (holding that fact that defendant "had just stepped out of his vehicle as the officer arrived and before his arrest does not alter his status as an 'occupant' of the vehicle"); United States v. Franco, 981 F.2d 470, 473 (10th Cir. 1992) (declining to adopt rule, advanced by defendant, that "unless an arrest was made in the arrestee's automobile, a search of the automobile was not 'incident to the arrest' for the purpose of that exception to the warrant requirement").

State courts have also struggled with this issue. Compare, e.g., State v. Stehman, 203 Ill. 2d 26, 783 N.E.2d 1, 6 (Ill. 2002) ("We find the . . . analysis of the Sixth Circuit Court of Appeals in [Hudgins] persuasive."), with State v. Wanzek, 1999 ND 163, 598 N.W.2d 811, 815 (N.D. 1999) ("We are not persuaded by the line of cases which hold an arrestee is an occupant only when arrested inside the vehicle or where the police initiate contact with the arrestee before the arrestee exits the vehicle."); Glasco v. Commonwealth, 257 Va. 433, 513 S.E.2d 137, 141-42 (Va. 1999) (same).

* * *

After carefully considering the question and the conflicting authority, we join those courts that have rejected the limitation of Belton to situations in which "the officer initiates contact with the defendant, either by actually confronting the defendant or by signaling confrontation with the defendant, while the defendant is still in the automobile." Hudgins, 52 F.3d at 119. We do so for a number of reasons.

First, the Supreme Court has clearly indicated, albeit in dicta, that an officer may search an automobile incident to an arrest, even if the officer has not initiated contact while the arrestee was still in the automobile. In Michigan v. Long, 463 U.S. 1032, 77 L. Ed. 2d 1201, 103 S. Ct. 3469 (1983), officers on patrol in a rural area observed a speeding car turn down a road and swerve into a shallow ditch. Id. at 1035. When the officers arrived at the scene, they met Long, the sole occupant of the vehicle, "at the rear of the car, which was protruding from the ditch onto the road," with the driver's side door open. Id. at 1035-36. Although affirming a subsequent search of the car's passenger compartment as a protective one under Terry v. Ohio, 392 U.S. 1, 20 L. Ed. 2d 889, 88 S. Ct. 1868 (1968), the Court noted at the outset that "it is clear, and the respondent concedes, that if the officers had arrested Long . . . they could have searched the passenger compartment [under Belton]." Id. at 1035 n.1. The Court further explained:

We stress that our decision does not mean that the police may conduct automobile searches whenever they conduct an investigative stop, although the"bright line" that we drew in Belton clearly authorizes such a search whenever officers effect a custodial arrest. An additional interest exists in the arrest context, i.e., preservation of evidence, and this justifies an "automatic" search.

Id. at 1049 n.14 (emphasis in original); see also Thomas, 532 U.S. at 776 (emphasizing the "bright-line" nature of the Belton rule).

Further, the historical rationales for the search incident to arrest doctrine — "the need to disarm the suspect in order to take him into custody" and "the need to preserve evidence for later use at trial" -do not permit the limitation on the Belton rule that the Sixth Circuit has adopted and Thornton espouses. Knowles, 525 U.S. at 116. "'Danger to an officer'" from an arrest and the

"need to discover and preserve evidence" continue to be concerns regardless of whether the arrestee exits the automobile voluntarily or because of confrontation with an officer. Id. at 117-18 (quoting Robinson, 414 U.S. at 234-35). Neither the Sixth Circuit nor Thornton suggest otherwise.

Indeed, we believe that Thornton's proposed limitation of the Belton rule would raise serious safety concerns for law enforcement personnel. A rule that requires officers to actually confront or signal confrontation with an arrestee while the arrestee is in the automobile, in order to justify a search of the automobile incident to arrest, could very well endanger an officer. For instance, we can certainly imagine the hesitancy of an officer to activate his lights and sirens if the officer encounters the arrestee while conducting undercover surveillance in an area. Moreover, when encountering a dangerous suspect, it may often be much safer for officers to wait until the suspect has exited a vehicle before signaling their presence, thereby depriving the suspect of any weapons he may have in his vehicle, the protective cover of the vehicle, and the possibility of using the vehicle itself as either a weapon or a means of flight. Mandating that officers alert a suspect to their presence before he sheds the protective confines of his vehicle would force officers to choose between forfeiting the opportunity to preserve evidence for later use at trial and increasing the risk to their own lives and the lives of others. We decline to require officers to make this choice. See Wanzek, 598 N.W.2d at 815 (The cases adopting the proposed limitation "raise grave public policy issues because they create serious concerns for the safety of officers and others."); Thomas, 761 So. 2d at 1014-15 (Wells, J., dissenting) "The reason for this bright-line rule is officer safety, which is equally as much a concern whether the officer initiates the contact, actually confronts the person, or the person voluntarily exits the vehicle as long as the connection with the vehicle is proximate to the arrest."); Stehman, 783 N.E.2d at 11 (Thomas, J., dissenting) ("Whether the defendant exits voluntarily or involuntarily, there is always a danger to the officer associated with the subsequent arrest and the proximity of the vehicle.").

Additionally, the limitation on the Belton rule that Thornton urges could "encourage individuals to avoid lawful searches of their vehicles by rapidly exiting or moving away from the vehicle as officers approached." Wanzek, 598 N.W.2d at 815. Surely, "police officers should not have to race from their vehicles to the arrestee's vehicle to prevent the arrestee from getting out of the vehicle in order to conduct a valid search." Id.

Nonetheless, we recognize the concerns of those courts that have attempted to limit the scope of Belton to situations in which officers have initiated contact with arrestees while still in the automobile. The Belton rule cannot be stretched so as to render it limitless by permitting officers to search any vehicle from which an arrestee has emerged, regardless of how much time has elapsed since his exit or how far he is from the vehicle when arrested.

In the case at hand, however, we note that Thornton concedes that he was in close proximity to his vehicle when Officer Nichols approached him. His concession is well-taken. Although the record is not clear as to the precise distance between Thornton and his automobile when Officer Nichols confronted him, the record does conclusively show that Officer Nichols observed Thornton park and exit his automobile and then approached Thornton within moments.

Thus, "no doubt exists that the car was within [Thornton's] immediate control at the beginning of his encounter with" Officer Nichols. * * * Stated differently, Thornton "was 'positively linked' to the searched vehicle prior to his arrest." Sholola, 124 F.3d at 817 (quoting Adams, 26 F.3d at 705); id. at 823 (Wood, J., concurring) ("The 'positive link' required must, in keeping with Belton, be one that requires physical proximity that is the equivalent of occupancy of the automobile."); see also Franco, 981 F.2d at 473 (affirming validity of search under Belton because defendant "was a recent occupant of his vehicle[,]" "the arrest was made in close proximity to his vehicle[,]" and "during the illegal transaction [defendant] exercised control over his vehicle and its contents"). The conceded close proximity, both temporally and spatially, of Thornton and his car at the time of his arrest provides adequate assurance that application of the Belton rule to cases like this one does not render that rule limitless. Accordingly, we hold that Officer Nichols lawfully searched Thornton's automobile incident to the arrest. Because we affirm on this ground, we decline to reach the district court's alternative holding that Officer Nichols could have conducted a lawful inventory search.

Affirmed.

GEORGIA
v.
RANDOLPH

SUPREME COURT
OF THE UNITED STATES
126 S. Ct. 1515, 164 L. Ed. 2d 208.
2006 U.S. LEXIS 2498 (2006)

Justice Souter delivered the opinion of the Court.

The Fourth Amendment recognizes a valid warrantless entry and search of premises when police obtain the voluntary consent of an occupant who shares, or is reasonably believed to share, authority over the area in common with a co-occupant who later objects to the use of evidence so obtained. Illinois v. Rodriguez, 497 U.S. 177, 110 S. Ct. 2793, 111 L. Ed. 2d 148 (1990); United States v. Matlock, 415 U.S. 164, 94 S. Ct. 988, 39 L. Ed. 2d 242 (1974). The question here is whether such an evidentiary seizure is likewise lawful with the permission of one occupant when the other, who later seeks to suppress the evidence, is present at the scene and expressly refuses to consent. We hold that, in the circumstances here at issue, a physically present co-occupant's stated refusal to permit entry prevails, rendering the warrantless search unreasonable and invalid as to him.

I

Respondent Scott Randolph and his wife, Janet, separated in late May 2001, when she left the marital residence in Americus, Georgia, and went to stay with her parents in Canada, taking their son and some belongings. In July, she returned to the Americus house with the child, though the record does not reveal whether her object was reconciliation or retrieval of remaining possessions.

On the morning of July 6, she complained to the police that after a domestic dispute her husband took their son away, and when officers reached the house she told them that her husband was a cocaine user whose habit had caused financial troubles. She mentioned the marital problems and said that she and their son had only recently returned after a stay of several weeks with her parents. Shortly after the police arrived, Scott Randolph returned and explained that he had removed the child to a neighbor's house out of concern that his wife might take the boy out of the country again; he denied cocaine use, and countered that it was in fact his wife who abused drugs and alcohol.

One of the officers, Sergeant Murray, went with Janet Randolph to reclaim the child, and when they returned she not only renewed her complaints about her husband's drug use, but also volunteered that there were "'items of drug evidence'" in the house. Brief for Petitioner 3. Sergeant Murray asked Scott Randolph for permission to search the house, which he unequivocally refused.

The sergeant turned to Janet Randolph for consent to search, which she readily gave. She led the officer upstairs to a bedroom that she identified as Scott's, where the sergeant noticed a section of a drinking straw with a powdery residue he suspected was cocaine. He then left the house to get an evidence bag from his car and to call the district attorney's office, which instructed him to stop the search and apply for a warrant. When Sergeant Murray returned to the house, Janet Randolph withdrew her consent. The police took the straw to the police station, along with the Randolphs. After getting a search warrant, they returned to the house and seized further evidence of drug use, on the basis of which Scott Randolph was indicted for possession of cocaine.

He moved to suppress the evidence, as products of a warrantless search of his house unauthorized by his wife's consent over his

express refusal. The trial court denied the motion, ruling that Janet Randolph had common authority to consent to the search.

The Court of Appeals of Georgia reversed, 264 Ga. App. 396, 590 S. E. 2d 834 (2003), and was itself sustained by the State Supreme Court, principally on the ground that "the consent to conduct a warrantless search of a residence given by one occupant is not valid in the face of the refusal of another occupant who is physically present at the scene to permit a warrantless search." 278 Ga. 614, 604 S. E. 2d 835, 836 (2004). The Supreme Court of Georgia acknowledged this Court's holding in *Matlock,* 415 U.S. 164, 94 S. Ct. 988, 39 L. Ed. 2d 242, that "the consent of one who possesses common authority over premises or effects is valid as against the absent, nonconsenting person with whom that authority is shared," id., at 170, 94 S. Ct. 988, 39 L. Ed. 2d 242, and found *Matlock* distinguishable just because Scott Randolph was not "absent" from the colloquy on which the police relied for consent to make the search. The State Supreme Court stressed that the officers in *Matlock* had not been "faced with the physical presence of joint occupants, with one consenting to the search and the other objecting." 278 Ga., at 615, 604 S. E. 2d, at 837. It held that an individual who chooses to live with another assumes a risk no greater than "'an inability to control access to the premises during [his] absence,'" ibid. (quoting 3 W. LaFave, Search and Seizure § 8.3(d), p 731 (3d ed. 1996) (hereinafter LaFave)), and does not contemplate that his objection to a request to search commonly shared premises, if made, will be overlooked.

We granted certiorari to resolve a split of authority on whether one occupant may give law enforcement effective consent to search shared premises, as against a co-tenant who is present and states a refusal to permit the search. 544 U.S. 973, 544 U.S. 973, 125 S. Ct. 1840, 161 L. Ed. 2d 722 (2005). We now affirm.

* * *

II

To the Fourth Amendment rule ordinarily prohibiting the warrantless entry of a person's house as unreasonable per se, Payton v. New York, 445 U.S. 573, 586 (1980);Coolidge v. New Hampshire, 403 U.S. 443, 454-455 (1971), one "jealously and carefully drawn" exception, Jones v. United States, 357 U.S. 493, 499 (1958), recognizes the validity of searches with the voluntary consent of an individual possessing authority, Rodriguez, 497 U.S., at 181. That person might be the householder against whom evidence is sought, Schneckloth v. Bustamonte, 412 U.S. 218, 222 (1973), or a fellow occupant who shares common authority over property, when the suspect is absent, [United States v.] Matlock, supra, at 170, and the exception for consent extends even to entries and searches with the permission of a co-occupant whom the police reasonably, but erroneously, believe to possess shared authority as an occupant, Rodriguez, supra, at 186. None of our co-occupant consent-to-search cases, however, has presented the further fact of a second occupant physically present and refusing permission to search, and later moving to suppress evidence so obtained. The significance of such a refusal turns on the underpinnings of the co-occupant consent rule, as recognized since Matlock.

A

The defendant in that case was arrested in the yard of a house where he lived with a Mrs. Graff and several of her relatives, and was detained in a squad car parked nearby. When the police went to the door, Mrs. Graff admitted them and consented to a search of the house. In resolving the defendant's objection to use of the evidence taken in the warrantless search, we said that "the consent of one who possesses common authority over premises or effects is valid as against the absent, nonconsenting person with whom that authority is shared." Id., at 170. Consistent with our prior understanding that Fourth Amendment rights are not limited by the law of property, we explained that the third party's "common authority" is not synonymous with a technical property interest:

"The authority which justified the third-party consent does not rest upon the law of property, with its attendant historical and legal refinement, but rests rather on mutual use of the property by persons generally having joint access or control for most purposes, so that it is reasonable to recognize that any of the co-inhabitants has the right to permit the inspection in his own right and that the others have assumed the risk that one of their number might permit the common area to be searched." 415 U.S., at 171, n. 7 (citations omitted).

* * *

The constant element in assessing Fourth Amendment reasonableness in the consent cases, then, is the great significance given to widely shared social expectations, which are naturally enough influenced by the law of property, but not controlled by its rules. Matlock accordingly not only holds that a solitary co-inhabitant may sometimes consent to a search of shared premises, but stands for the proposition that the reasonableness of such a search is in significant part a function of commonly held understanding about the authority that co-inhabitants may exercise in ways that affect each other's interests.

B

Matlock 's example of common understanding is readily apparent. When someone comes to the door of a domestic dwelling with a baby at her hip, as Mrs. Graff did, she shows that she belongs there, and that fact standing alone is enough to tell a law enforcement officer or any other visitor that if she occupies the place along with others, she probably lives there subject to the assumption tenants usually make about their common authority when they share quarters. They understand that any one of them may admit visitors, with the consequence that a guest obnoxious to one may nevertheless be admitted in his absence by another.

* * *

C

Although we have not dealt directly with the reasonableness of police entry in reliance on consent by one occupant subject to immediate challenge by another, we took a step toward the issue in an earlier case dealing with the Fourth Amendment rights of a social guest arrested at premises the police entered without a warrant or the benefit of any exception to the warrant requirement. Minnesota v. Olson, 495 U.S. 91 (1990), held that overnight houseguests have a legitimate expectation of privacy in their temporary quarters because "it is unlikely that [the host] will admit someone who wants to see or meet with the guest over the objection of the guest," id., at 99. If that customary expectation of courtesy or deference is a foundation of Fourth Amendment rights of a houseguest, it presumably should follow that an inhabitant of shared premises may claim at least as much, and it turns out that the co-inhabitant naturally has an even stronger claim.

To begin with, it is fair to say that a caller standing at the door of shared premises would have no confidence that one occupant's invitation was a sufficiently good reason to enter when a fellow tenant stood there saying, "stay out." Without some very good reason, no sensible person would go inside under those conditions. Fear for the safety of the occupant issuing the invitation, or of someone else inside, would be thought to justify entry, but the justification then would be the personal risk, the threats to life or limb, not the disputed invitation.

* * *

D

Since the co-tenant wishing to open the door to a third party has no recognized authority in law or social practice to prevail over a present and objecting co-tenant, his disputed invitation, without more, gives a police officer no better claim to reasonableness in entering than the officer would have in the absence of any consent at all. Accordingly, in the balancing of competing individual and governmental interests entailed by the bar to unreasonable searches, the cooper-

ative occupant's invitation adds nothing to the government's side to counter the force of an objecting individual's claim to security against the government's intrusion into his dwelling place. Since we hold to the "centuries-old principle of respect for the privacy of the home," Wilson v. Layne, 526 U.S. 603, 610 (1999), "it is beyond dispute that the home is entitled to special protection as the center of the private lives of our people," Minnesota v. Carter, 525 U.S. 83, 99 (1998) (KENNEDY, J., concurring). We have, after all, lived our whole national history with an understanding of "the ancient adage that a man's home is his castle [to the point that t]he poorest man may in his cottage bid defiance to all the forces of the Crown," Miller v. United States, 357 U.S. 301, 307 (1958) (internal quotation marks omitted).

Disputed permission is thus no match for this central value of the Fourth Amendment, and the State's other countervailing claims do not add up to outweigh it.

* * *

E

There are two loose ends, the first being the explanation given in Matlock for the constitutional sufficiency of a co-tenant's consent to enter and search: it "rests . . . on mutual use of the property by persons generally having joint access or control for most purposes, so that it is reasonable to recognize that any of the co-inhabitants has the right to permit the inspection in his own right. . . ." 415 U.S., at 171, n. 7. If Matlock's co-tenant is giving permission "in his own right," how can his "own right" be eliminated by another tenant's objection? The answer appears in the very footnote from which the quoted statement is taken: the "right" to admit the police to which Matlock refers is not an enduring and enforceable ownership right as understood by the private law of property, but is instead the authority recognized by customary social usage as having a substantial bearing on Fourth Amendment reasonableness in specific circumstances. Thus, to ask whether the consenting tenant has the right to admit the police when a physically present fellow tenant objects is not to question whether some property right may be divested by the mere objection of another. It is, rather, the question whether customary social understanding accords the consenting tenant authority powerful enough to prevail over the co-tenant's objection. The Matlock Court did not purport to answer this question, a point made clear by another statement: the Court described the co-tenant's consent as good against "the absent, nonconsenting" resident." Id., at 170.

The second loose end is the significance of Matlock and Rodriguez after today's decision. Although the Matlock defendant was not present with the opportunity to object, he was in a squad car not far away; the Rodriguez defendant was actually asleep in the apartment, and the police might have roused him with a knock on the door before they entered with only the consent of an apparent co-tenant. If those cases are not to be undercut by today's holding, we have to admit that we are drawing a fine line; if a potential defendant with self-interest in objecting is in fact at the door and objects, the co-tenant's permission does not suffice for a reasonable search, whereas the potential objector, nearby but not invited to take part in the threshold colloquy, loses out.

This is the line we draw, and we think the formalism is justified. So long as there is no evidence that the police have removed the potentially objecting tenant from the entrance for the sake of avoiding a possible objection, there is practical value in the simple clarity of complementary rules, one recognizing the co-tenant's permission when there is no fellow occupant on hand, the other according dispositive weight to the fellow occupant's contrary indication when he expresses it.

* * *

III

This case invites a straightforward application of the rule that a physically present inhabitant's express refusal of consent to a police search is dispositive as to him, regardless of the consent of a fellow occupant. Scott Randolph's refusal is clear, and nothing in the record justifies the search on grounds

independent of Janet Randolph's consent. The State does not argue that she gave any indication to the police of a need for protection inside the house that might have justified entry into the portion of the premises where the police found the powdery straw (which, if lawfully seized, could have been used when attempting to establish probable cause for the warrant issued later). Nor does the State claim that the entry and search should be upheld under the rubric of exigent circumstances, owing to some apprehension by the police officers that Scott Randolph would destroy evidence of drug use before any warrant could be obtained.

The judgment of the Supreme Court of Georgia is therefore affirmed.

It is so ordered.

Justice Alito took no part in the consideration or decision of this case.

HORTON

v.

CALIFORNIA

Supreme Court of the United States
496 U.S. 128, 10 S. Ct. 2301, 110 L.
Ed. 2d 112 (1990)

SYLLABUS:

A California policeman determined that there was probable cause to search petitioner Horton's home for the proceeds of a robbery and the robbers' weapons. His search warrant affidavit referred to police reports that described both the weapons and the proceeds, but the warrant issued by the Magistrate only authorized a search for the proceeds. Upon executing the warrant, the officer did not find the stolen property but did find the weapons in plain view and seized them. The trial court refused to suppress the seized evidence, and Horton was convicted of armed robbery. The California Court of Appeals affirmed. Since the officer had testified that while he was searching Horton's home for the stolen property he was also interested in finding other evidence connecting Horton to the robbery, the seized evidence was not discovered "inadvertently."

However, in rejecting Horton's argument that Coolidge v. New Hampshire, 403 U.S. 443, therefore required suppression of that evidence, the Court of Appeal relied on a State Supreme Court decision holding that Coolidge's discussion of the inadvertence limitation on the "plain view" doctrine was not binding because it was contained in a four-Justice plurality opinion. Held: The Fourth Amendment does not prohibit the warrantless seizure of evidence in plain view even though the discovery of the evidence was not inadvertent. Although inadvertence is a characteristic of most legitimate plain view seizures, it is not a necessary condition. Pp. 4-13.

(a) Coolidge is a binding precedent. However, the second of the Coolidge plurality's two limitations on the plain view doctrine—that the discovery of evidence in plain view must be inadvertent, id., at 469—was not essential to the Court's rejection of the State's plain view argument in that case. Rather, the first limitation—that plain view alone is never enough to justify a warrantless seizure, id., at 468—adequately supports the Court's holding that gunpowder found in vacuum sweepings from one of the automobiles seized in plain view on the defendant's driveway in the course of his arrest could not be introduced against him because the warrantless seizures violated the Fourth Amendment. In order for a warrantless seizure of an object in plain view to be valid, two conditions must be satisfied in addition to the essential predicate that the officer did not violate the Fourth Amendment in arriving at the place from which the object could be plainly viewed. First, the object's incriminating character must be "immediately apparent," id., at 466. Although the cars in Coolidge were obviously in plain view, their probative value remained uncertain until after their interiors were swept and examined microscopically. Second, the officer must have a lawful right of access to the object itself. Justice Harlan, who concurred in the Coolidge judgment but did not join the plurality's plain view discussion, may well have rested his vote on the fact that the cars' seizure was accomplished by means of a warrantless trespass on the defendant's property. Pp. 4-8.

(b) There are two flaws in the Coolidge plurality's conclusion that the inadvertence requirement was necessary to avoid a violation of the Fourth Amendment's mandate that a valid warrant "'particularly describe . . . [the] . . . things to be seized,'" id., at 469-471. First, evenhanded law enforcement is best achieved by applying objective standards of conduct, rather than standards that depend upon the officer's subjective state of mind. The fact that an officer is interested in an item and fully expects to find it should not invalidate its seizure if the search is confined in area and duration by a warrant's terms or by a valid exception to the warrant requirement. Second, the suggestion that the inadvertence requirement is necessary to prevent the police from conducting general searches, or from converting specific warrants into general warrants, is not persuasive because that interest is already served by the requirements that an unparticularized warrant not be issued and that a warrantless search be circumscribed by the exigencies which justify its initiation. Here, the search's scope was not enlarged by the warrant's omission of reference to the weapons; indeed, no search for the weapons could have taken place if the named items had been found or surrendered at the outset. The prohibition against general searches and warrants is based on privacy concerns, which are not implicated when an officer with a lawful right of access to an item in plain view seizes it without a warrant. Pp. 8-13. JUDGES: Stevens, J., delivered the opinion of the Court, in which Rehnquist, C. J., and White, Blackmun, O'Connor, Scalia, and Kennedy, JJ. joined. Brennan, J., filed a dissenting opinion, in which Marshall, J., joined.

Glossary

Adjudicative facts Facts that concern the immediate parties and are determinative of the outcome of the case.

Affirmation A solemn declaration without oath. The privilege of affirming in judicial proceedings is now generally extended to all persons who object to taking an oath.

Affirmative defense A response to a claim for relief that states information not otherwise before the court, e.g., a plea of self-defense, defense of another, or an insanity defense. (2) A justification or avoidance.

Alibi A defense resorted to where the party accused, in order to prove that he or she could not have committed the crime with which he or she is charged, offers evidence that he or she was in a different place at the time the offense was committed.

Authentication An attestation made by a proper officer, by which he or she certifies that a record is in due form of law, and that the person who certifies it is the officer appointed so to do. In the admission of evidence, evidence that proves the item is what it purports to be or proves that the item is the genuine article.

Ballistics experiments The science of gun examination, frequently used in criminal cases, especially cases of homicide, to determine the firing capacity of a weapon, its fireability, and whether a given bullet was fired from a particular gun.

Best evidence rule Also called the original document rule. The proof that provides the greatest certainty of the fact to be proven; the most reliable evidence. Under the best evidence rule, which is ordinarily applied to documents and writings sought to be proven, usually the highest degree of proof, i.e., the original document, must be presented if it is available.

Beyond a reasonable doubt Fully satisfied, entirely convinced, satisfied to a moral certainty.

Breathalyzer test Test to determine alcohol content of blood in one arrested for operating a motor vehicle under the influence of alcohol. The results of such tests, if properly administered, constitute admissible evidence.

Burden of going forward Refers to the obligation resting upon a party to produce prima facie evidence on a particular issue.

Burden of persuasion Refers to the burden of persuading the factfinder of the truth of the evidence produced by one side or the other.

Burden of proof The duty of proving facts disputed on the trial of a case by the proper weight of the evidence.

Chain of custody In evidence, one who offers real evidence (such as narcotics in the trial of a drug case) must account for the custody of the evidence from the moment when it reaches his or her custody until the moment when it is offered in evidence, and such evidence goes to the weight, not the admissibility, of the evidence.

Circumstantial evidence Evidence of one fact from which a second fact is reasonably inferred, although not directly proven. It is often introduced when direct evidence is not available.

Clear and convincing evidence A flexible term concerning the degree of proof required for certain issues in some civil cases. It is less than the degree required in criminal cases, but more than required in the ordinary civil action.

Competency The legal fitness or capacity of a witness to testify on the trial of a case that requires an oath, original perception, recollection, and an ability to communicate. (2) Freedom from mental illness or defect because of which a person is unable to understand in a reasonable manner the nature and consequences of a transaction, or he or she is unable to act in a reasonable manner in relation to the transaction. The quality of evidence offered, that makes it proper to be received.

Competent evidence The quality of evidence offered that makes it proper to be received.

Corroborative evidence Additional testimony to reinforce a point that was previously the subject of proof.

Cross-examination The questioning of a witness by the party opposed to the party who called the witness for direct examination. This usually occurs after the direct examination but on occasion may be otherwise allowed.

Cumulative evidence Testimony that is offered to prove what has already been proven by other evidence.

Delay in arraignment rule This rule provides that if there has been a delay in bringing the accused person before a magistrate, and if a confession has been obtained during this unnecessary delay, the confession may not be admitted, even though voluntarily made.

Direct evidence Testimony or other proof that expressly or straightforwardly proves the existence of a fact; opposite of circumstantial evidence.

Direct examination The initial questioning of a witness by the party who calls him or her.

DNA Deoxyribonucleic acid. A long, threadlike chain of molecules found in the nucleus of virtually every cell of the body. The DNA chains are tightly coiled into bodies called chromosomes of which humans have 23. No two individuals (except for identical twins) have identical DNA. Within a given person, however, DNA does not vary from cell to cell.

Documentary evidence Evidence that is furnished by written documents, records, and computer-generated reports.

Due process A flexible term for the compliance with the fundamental rules for fair and orderly legal proceedings, e.g., the right to be informed of the nature and cause of the accusation, to be confronted with the witnesses against you, to have compulsory process for obtaining witnesses in your favor, to have the assistance of counsel for your defense, and to have a fair and impartial jury. (2) Legal proceedings that observe the rules designed for the protection and enforcement of individual rights and liberties.

Dying declaration Hearsay evidence of what a person said when he or she was aware that his or her death was imminent that must relate to the way the declarant received final injuries. Under particular circumstances and in certain cases, it is competent evidence in some courts. (2) In a prosecution for homicide or in a civil action or proceeding, a statement made by a declarant while believing that his or her death was imminent, concerning the cause or circumstances of what he or she believed to be his or her impending death. It is not excluded by the hearsay rule if the declarant is unavailable as a witness. Fed. R. Evid. 804(b)(2).

Eavesdropping Knowingly and without authority entering into a private place with the intent to surreptitiously listen to a private conversation or to observe the personal conduct of any other person or persons therein conducted by personal listening or electronic collection of sounds.

Evidence Proof, either written or unwritten, of allegations at issue between parties.

Evidence-in-chief Proof that a party primarily relies upon in order to support his claim or defense.

Exception A form of objection to a ruling or order of a trial court, which has as its purpose the preservation of the point at issue for adjudication on appeal. Under modern rules of civil procedure, formal exceptions to court rulings or orders are unnecessary.

Exclusionary rule This rule requires that when evidence has been obtained in violation of the privileges guaranteed by the United States Constitution, the evidence must be excluded at the trial. Evidence that is obtained by an unreasonable search and seizure is excluded from evidence under the Fourth Amendment to the U.S. Constitution, and this rule applies to the states.

Exculpatory circumstances Exonerative facts; excusing evidence; facts tending to clear from a charge of fault or guilt.

Expert witness A person who has acquired by special study, practice, and experience, peculiar skill and knowledge in relation to some particular science, art, or trade. (2) A witness who, because of such special knowledge, is called to testify or give his or her opinion in cases depending on questions peculiar to such science, art, or trade.

Federal Rules of Evidence Rules governing the admissibility of evidence at trials in federal courts and before United States Magistrate judges.

Former testimony Testimony given by a witness at another hearing of the same or a different proceeding, or in a deposition taken in compliance with law in the course of the same or another proceeding, if the party against whom the testimony is now offered, or in a civil action or proceeding, a predecessor in interest, had an opportunity and similar motive to develop the testimony by direct, cross, or redirect examination. It is not excluded by the hearsay rule if the declarant is unavailable as a witness. Fed. R. Evid. 804(b)(1)

Free and voluntary rule The confession of a person accused of crime is admissible against the accused only if freely and voluntarily made, without fear, duress, or compulsion in its inducement and with full knowledge of the nature and consequences of the confession.

Hearsay evidence Statements offered by a witness, based upon what someone else has told him or her, and not upon personal knowledge or observation. Usually, such evidence is inadmissible, but exceptions are made, e.g., in questions of pedigree, custom, reputation, dying declarations, and statements made against the interest of the declarant. (2) A statement, other than one made by the declarant while testifying at the trial or hearing, offered in evidence to prove the truth of the matter asserted. Fed. R. Evid. 801(c).

Hearsay rule Rule prohibiting the admission of hearsay evidence—evidence of a statement that was made other than by a witness while testifying at the hearing and that is offered to prove the truth of the matter stated.

Horizontal gaze nystagmus test Horizontal gaze nystagmus is the inability of the eyes to maintain visual fixation as they are turned to the side. Nystagmus is a physiological phenomenon that is caused by, among other things, the ingestion of alcohol and is used to determine whether a person is intoxicated.

Hostile witness A person who is called to give evidence and is unfriendly or inimical to the party whose attorney called him and is really allied with the opposing party. Such a person is subject to cross-examination by the party calling him or her.

Impeachment of witness To prove that a witness has a bad reputation for truth and veracity and is therefore unworthy of belief.

Implied consent Various state laws that provide that any person who operates a motorized vehicle in the state is deemed to have given his or her consent to a chemical test, e.g., of his or her blood, breath, urine or saliva, for the purpose of determining the alcoholic content of his or her blood, if committed while driving, or in any physical control of, a motor vehicle in the state while under the influence of intoxicating beverages.

Impoundment Seizing and taking into custody of the law or a court, such as the police duty and responsibility to impound an automobile that has been abandoned, is illegally parked, or has been left without a driver when the driver has been arrested.

Incriminating circumstances Facts or circumstances, collateral to the fact of the commission of a crime, that tend to show either that such a crime has been committed and/or that some particular person committed it.

Inference A rational conclusion deduced from facts proved.

Judicial notice The acceptance by the court of certain notorious facts without proof. (2) A judicially noticed adjudicative fact must be one not subject to reasonable dispute in that it is either (a) generally known within the territorial jurisdiction of the trial court, or (b) capable of accurate and ready determination by resort to sources whose accuracy cannot reasonably be questioned. Fed. R. Evid. 201(b)

Lay witness Any witness that is not an expert. A lay witness simply must have the general capacity to testify, record, recollect, narrate, attest to, and affirm certain conditions and facts. Additionally, he or she must have the requisite level of mental capacity and emotional competency to outline in some logical and sensible sequence the facts, conditions, and events before the trier.

Leading question An inquiry of a witness that by its form suggests the answer that the attorney would prefer. A question in which the substance of the correct answer is embedded within the question and suggests the answer. The type of question that is generally permissible on cross-examination.

Legal evidence General term meaning all admissible evidence, both oral and documentary, that is of such a character that tends reasonably and substantially to prove the point, not to raise a mere suspicion or conjecture.

Material evidence Evidence that goes to the substantial matters in dispute or has a legitimate and effective influence or bearing on the decision of the case. Evidence that may tend to prove or disprove a fact that is at issue in a case.

Materiality Importance; relevance; capable of properly influencing the result of a lawsuit.

Motive The purpose underlying a defendant's conduct; the reason a person forms a criminal intent prior to engaging in a criminal act.

Negative evidence Testimony that an alleged fact does not exist; an absence of evidence.

Neutron activation analysis A testing procedure that determines the presence and amount of certain trace chemical elements.

Oath Various solemn affirmations, declarations or promises, made under a sense of responsibility to God, for the truth of what is stated or the faithful performance of what is undertaken.

Objection A resistance or protest on legal grounds, e.g., to the admissibility of evidence, or to the entry of an order or judgment.

Opinion evidence An inference or a conclusion, formed or entertained by a witness, as opposed to facts directly seen, heard, or perceived by him. Usually, a person's opinions are not competent testimony in a case unless the person has qualified as an expert witness.

Past recollection recorded A memorandum or record concerning a matter about which a witness once had knowledge but now has insufficient recollection to enable him or her to testify fully and accurately, shown to have been made or adopted by the witness when the matter was fresh in his or her memory and to reflect that knowledge correctly, is not excluded by the hearsay rule, even though the declarant is available as a witness. If admitted, the memorandum or record may be read into evidence but may not itself be received as an exhibit unless offered by an adverse party. Fed. R. Evid. 803(5).

Pecuniary interest A direct interest related to money in an action or case as would, for example, require a judge to disqualify him- or herself from sitting on a case if he or she owned stock in a corporate party.

Penal interest Pertaining to or respecting punishment.

Plain view doctrine A rule of law creating an exception to the requirement that police officers have a search warrant, when the police, while conducting themselves lawfully, e.g., while patrolling the streets or executing a search warrant for something else, observe incriminating evidence, and it is immediately apparent to the police that they have evidence of a crime. In such a situation, the evidence may be seized without a warrant if the officer physically occupies the place where the contraband is situated.

Polygraph examination An electromechanical instrument that simultaneously records certain physiological changes in the human body, which are believed to be involuntarily caused by an examinee's conscious attempts to deceive an interrogator while responding to a carefully prepared set of questions.

Preponderance of the evidence The greater weight of the evidence, in merit and in worth. (2) Sufficient evidence to overcome doubt or speculation. (3) Any evidence whose weight is greater than 50 percent.

Present memory revived The act of a witness who consults his or her documents, memoranda, or books, to clarify his or her recollection the details of past events or transactions, concerning which he or she is testifying. The witness testifies from present memory.

Presumption A conclusion or inference drawn from the proven existence of some fact or group of facts.

Presumption of fact Not the subject of a fixed rule, but merely natural presumptions, such as appear from common experience, that arise from particular circumstances of any case.

Presumption of law An inference or deduction that, in the absence of direct evidence on the subject, the law requires to be drawn from the existence of certain established facts in civil case but a deduction that cannot be enforced in criminal cases.

Prima facie evidence Proof of a fact or collection of facts that creates a presumption of the existence of other facts, or from which some conclusion may be legally drawn, but which presumption or conclusion may be discredited or overcome by other relevant proof.

Prior inconsistent statement In evidence, prior statements made by the witness that contradict statements made on the witness stand may be introduced to impeach the witness after a foundation has been laid concerning where and when the inconsistent statement was uttered and an opportunity given to the witness to affirm or deny whether such prior statements were made.

Privileged communications Statements made by one person to another when there is a necessary relation of trust and confidence between them, which the person receiving them cannot be legally compelled to disclose, e.g., the statements made by a husband to his wife, or a client to his or her attorney.

Proof Establishing the truth of an allegation by evidence. (2) The evidence itself. The person claiming the affirmative of an allegation ordinarily has the necessity of proving it. (3) The affidavits made to support a claim or statement of fact, which is doubted or disputed or of which a person acting in a representative capacity requires evidence under oath.

Radar Radio Detection and Ranging. Used in law enforcement to measure distance and speed of motor vehicles.

Real evidence Evidence that has physical essence; evidence provided by the physical items themselves as opposed to descriptions of the evidence.

Rebuttal Proof that is given by one party in a lawsuit to explain or disprove evidence produced by the other party.

Recross-examination An examination of a witness by a cross-examiner subsequent to a redirect examination of the witness.

Redirect examination An examination of a witness by the direct examiner following the cross-examination.

Rejoinder The opportunity to introduce evidence contrary to that introduced by the prosecution during the rebuttal.

Relevancy The connection between a fact tendered in evidence and the issue to be proved.

Relevant evidence Evidence having any tendency to make the existence of any fact that is of consequence to the determination of the action more probable or less probable than it would be without the evidence. Fed. R. Evid. 401.

Scientific evidence admissibility test Admissibility of scientific evidence rests on several considerations: whether a scientific theory or technique can or has been tested; whether the theory or technique has been subjected to peer review and publication; the known or potential rate of error and the existence and maintenance of standards controlling the technique's operation; whether the technique is generally accepted. A proponent of the scientific evidence has the burden of proving its relevancy as well as the scientific reliability by clear and convincing evidence.

Secondary evidence Evidence that is inferior to primary or best evidence. It becomes admissible when the primary or best evidence of the fact in question has been lost, destroyed, or is inaccessible through no fault of the offering party.

Self-authentication Instrument or document in which authenticity is taken as sufficiently established for purposes of admissibility without extrinsic evidence to that effect. Statutes frequently provide that certain classes of writings will be received in evidence "without further proof." Bank videotapes can be self-authenticating by their content and time and date stamp.

Self-defense The protection of one's person and property from injury. A person may defend himself when attacked, repel force by force, and even commit homicide in resisting an attempted felony involving a risk of death or serious injury, e.g., murder, rape, robbery, burglary, and the like.

Self-incrimination An act or declaration either as testimony at trial or prior to trial by which one implicates oneself in a crime.

Sequestration Separating or setting apart; excluding witnesses from the courtroom except when testifying, to prevent one witness from being influenced deliberately or subconsciously by hearing what another witness says.

Spontaneous utterance A statement relating to a startling event or condition made while the declarant was under the stress of excitement cause by the event or condition. It is not excluded from evidence as hearsay, even though the declarant is available as a witness. Fed. R. Evid. 803(2)

Stipulation An agreement; a bargain, proviso, or condition, e.g., an agreement between opposing litigants that certain facts are true and are not in dispute. It is binding without consideration if it complies with an applicable statute or rule of court.

Sufficiency of the evidence In a criminal case, whether the evidence is such that a jury could logically have found that a defendant was guilty beyond a reasonable doubt or that an affirmative defense was properly proven.

Summaries The contents of voluminous writings, recordings, computer-generated data or photographs that cannot be conveniently examined in court may be presented in the form of a chart, summary, or calculation. The originals, or duplicates, shall be made available for examination or copying, or both, by other parties at a reasonable time and place. The court may order that they be produced in court. Fed. R. Evid. 1006

Ultimate issue The questions that must finally be answered, such as the defendant's guilt in a criminal action.

Unfair prejudice A prejudgment, or bias, that interferes with a person's impartiality and sense of justice.

Uniform Rules of Evidence Prepared by the National Conference of Commissioners on Uniform State Laws, these are patterned after the Federal Rules and have consistent numbering with the Federal Rules. They are designed for adoption by legislatures of the states.

Voiceprint identification Once promising technology, now in disrepute, used in trial of cases that require voice identification. An instrument known as a spectrograph produces "prints" of a person's voice for use in comparing such readings with the actual voice of the person involved, to determine whether such person uttered the material words.

Waiver A positive act by which a legal right is relinquished.

Weight of evidence The balance or preponderance of evidence; the inclination of the greater amount of evidence, offered in trial, to support one side of the issue rather than the other.

Wiretapping A form of electronic eavesdropping in which, upon a court order, law enforcement officials surreptitiously listen to land and cell phone conversations, e-mail, text messages, and similar communications.

APPENDIX I

FEDERAL RULES OF EVIDENCE

As amended through December 1, 2006
The Committee on the Judiciary
House of Representatives

FEDERAL RULES OF EVIDENCE

Effective July 1, 1975, as amended to December 1, 2006

ARTICLE I: GENERAL PROVISIONS

RULE 101. Scope

These rules govern proceedings in the courts of the United States and before United States bankruptcy judges and United States magistrate judges, to the extent and with the exceptions stated in rule 1101.

(Amended, eff. Dec. 1993).

RULE 102. Purpose and Construction

These rules shall be construed to secure fairness in administration, elimination of unjustifiable expense and delay, and promotion of growth and development of the law of evidence to the end that the truth may be ascertained and proceedings justly determined.

RULE 103. Rulings on Evidence

(a) Effect of erroneous ruling. Error may not be predicated upon a ruling which admits or excludes evidence unless a substantial right of the party is affected, and

(1) Objection. In case the ruling is one admitting evidence, a timely objection or motion to strike appears of record stating the specific ground of objection, if the specific ground was not apparent from the context; or

(2) Offer of proof. In case the ruling is one excluding evidence, the substance of the evidence was made known to the court by offer or was apparent from the context within which questions were asked.

Once the court makes a definitive ruling on the record admitting or excluding evidence, either at or before trial, a party need not renew an objection or offer of proof to preserve a claim of error for appeal.

(b) Record of offer and ruling. The court may add any other or further statement which shows the character of the evidence, the form in which it was offered, the objection made, and the ruling thereon. It may direct the making of an offer in question and answer form.

(c) Hearing of jury. In jury cases, proceedings shall be conducted, to the extent practicable, so as to prevent inadmissible evidence from being suggested to the jury by any means, such as making statements or offers of proof or asking questions in the hearing of the jury.

(d) Plain error. Nothing in this rule precludes taking notice of plain errors affecting substantial rights although they were not brought to the attention of the court.

(As amended Apr. 17, 2000, eff. Dec. 1 2000.)

RULE 104. Preliminary Questions

(a) Questions of admissibility generally. Preliminary questions concerning the qualification of a person to be a witness, the existence of a privilege, or the admissibility of evidence shall be determined by the court, subject to the provisions of subdivision (b). In making its determination it is not bound by the rules of evidence except those with respect to privileges.

(b) Relevancy conditioned on fact. When the relevancy evidence depends upon the fulfillment of a condition of fact, the court shall admit it upon, or subject to, the introduction of evidence sufficient to support a finding of the fulfillment of the condition.

(c) Hearing of jury. Hearings on the admissibility of confessions shall in all cases be conducted out of the hearing of the jury. Hearings on other preliminary matters shall be so conducted when the interests of justice require, or when an accused is a witness and so requests.

(d) Testimony by accused. The accused does not, by testifying upon a preliminary matter, become subject to cross-examination as to other issues in the case.

(e) Weight and credibility. This rule does not limit the right of a party to introduce before the jury evidence relevant to weight or credibility.

(Amended, eff. 10-1-87)

RULE 105. Limited Admissibility

When evidence which is admissible as to one party or for one purpose but not admissible as to another party or for another purpose is admitted, the court, upon request, shall restrict the evidence to its proper scope and instruct the jury accordingly.

RULE 106. Remainder of or Related Writings or Recorded Statements

When a writing or recorded statement or part thereof is introduced by a party, an adverse party may require the introduction at that time of any other party or any other writing or recorded statement which ought in fairness to be considered contemporaneously with it.

(Amended, eff. 10-1-87)

ARTICLE II. JUDICIAL NOTICE

RULE 201. Judicial Notice of Adjudicative Facts

(a) Scope of rule. This rule governs only judicial notice of adjudicative facts.

(b) Kinds of facts. A judicially noticed fact must be one not subject to reasonable dispute in that it is either (1) generally known within the territorial jurisdiction of the trial court or (2) capable of accurate and ready determination by resort to sources whose accuracy cannot readily be questioned.

(c) When discretionary. A court may take judicial notice, whether requested or not.

(d) When mandatory. A court shall take judicial notice if requested by a party and supplied with the necessary information.

(e) Opportunity to be heard. A party is entitled upon timely request to an opportunity to be heard as to the propriety of taking judicial notice and the tenor of the matter noticed. In the absence of prior notification, the request may be made after judicial notice has been taken.

(f) Time of taking notice. Judicial notice may be taken at any stage of the proceeding.

(g) Instructing jury. In a civil action or proceeding, the court shall instruct the jury to accept as conclusive any fact judicially noticed. In a criminal case, the court shall instruct the jury that it may, but is not required to, accept as conclusive any fact judicially noticed.

ARTICLE III. PRESUMPTIONS IN CIVIL ACTIONS AND PROCEEDINGS

RULE 301. Presumptions in General in Civil Actions and Proceedings

In all civil actions and proceedings not otherwise provided for by Act of Congress or by these rules, a presumption imposes on the party against whom it is directed the burden of going forward with evidence to rebut or meet the presumption, but does not shift to such party the burden of proof in the sense of the risk of nonpersuasion, which remains throughout the trial upon the party on whom it was originally cast.

RULE 302. Applicability of State Law in Civil Actions and Proceedings

In civil actions and proceedings, the effect of a presumption respecting a fact which is an element of a claim or defense as to which State law supplies the rule of decision is determined in accordance with State law.

ARTICLE IV. RELEVANCY AND ITS LIMITS

RULE 401. Definition of "Relevant Evidence"

"Relevant evidence" means evidence having any tendency to make the existence of any fact that is of consequence to the determination of the action more probable or less probable than it would be without the evidence.

RULE 402. Relevant Evidence Generally Admissible; Irrelevant Evidence Inadmissible

All relevant evidence is admissible, except as otherwise provided by the Constitution of the United States, by Act of Congress, by these rules, or by other rules prescribed by the Supreme Court pursuant to statutory authority. Evidence which is not relevant is not admissible.

RULE 403. Exclusion of Relevant Evidence on Grounds of Prejudice, Confusion, or Waste of Time

Although relevant evidence may be excluded if its probative value is substantially outweighed by the danger of unfair prejudice, confusion of the issues, or misleading the jury, or by considerations of undue delay, waste of time, or needless presentation of cumulative service.

RULE 404. Character Evidence Not Admissible To Prove Conduct; Exceptions; Other Crimes

(a) Character evidence generally. Evidence of a person's character or trait of character is not admissible for the purpose of proving action in conforming therewith on a particular occasion, except:

(1) Character of accused. In a criminal case, evidence of a pertinent trait of character offered by an accused, or by the prosecution to rebut the same, or if evidence of a trait of character of the alleged victim of the crime is offered by an accused and admitted under Rule 404 (a)(2), evidence of the same trait of character of the accused offered by the prosecution;

(2) Character of victim. In a criminal case, and subject to the limitations imposed by Rule 412, evidence of a pertinent trait of character of the alleged victim of the crime offered by an accused, or by the prosecution to rebut the same, or evidence of a character trait of peacefulness of the victim offered by the prosecution in a homicide case to rebut evidence that the victim was the first aggressor;

(3) Character of witness. Evidence of the character of witness, as provided in Rules 607, 608 and 609.

(b) Other crimes, wrongs, or acts. Evidence of other crimes, wrongs, or acts is not admissible to prove the character of a person in order to show action in conformity therewith. It may, however, be admissible for other purposes, such as proof of motive, opportunity, intent, preparation, plan, knowledge, identity, or absence of mistake or accident, provided that upon request by the accused, the prosecution in a criminal case shall provide reasonable notice in advance of trial, or during trial if the court excuses pretrial notice on good cause shown, of the general nature of any such evidence it intends to introduce at trial.

(Amended, eff. Dec. 1991; Apr 17, 2000, eff. Dec. 1 2000; eff. 12-1-06)

RULE 405. Methods of Proving Character

(a) Reputation or opinion. In all cases in which evidence of character or trait of character of a person is admissible, proof may be made by testimony as to reputation or by testimony in the form of an opinion. On cross-examination, inquiry is allowable into relevant instances of conduct.

(b) Specific instances of conduct. In cases in which character or a trait of character of a person is an essential element of a charge, claim, or defense, proof may also be made of specific instances of that person's conduct.

(Amended, eff. 10-1-87)

RULE 406. Habit; Routine Practice

Evidence of the habit of a person or of the routine practices of an organization, whether corroborated or not and regardless of the presence of eyewitnesses, is relevant to prove that the conduct of the person or organization on a particular occasion was in conformity with the habit or routine practice.

RULE 407. Subsequent Remedial Measures

When, after an injury or harm allegedly caused by an event, measures are taken that, if taken previously, would have made the injury or harm less likely to occur, evidence of the subsequent measures is not admissible to prove negligence, culpable conduct, a defect in a product, a defect in a product's design, or a need for a warning or instruction. This rule does not require the exclusion of evidence of subsequent measures when offered for another purpose, such as proving ownership, control, or feasibility of precautionary measures, if controverted, or impeachment.

(As amended, Apr. 11, 1997, eff. Dec. 1, 1997.)

RULE 408. Compromise and Offers to Compromise

(a) Prohibited uses. Evidence of the following is not admissible on behalf of any party, when offered to prove liability for, invalidity of, or amount of a claim that was disputed as to validity or amount, or to impeach through a prior inconsistent statement or contradiction:

(1) furnishing or offering or promising to furnish or offering or promising to accept a valuable consideration in compromising or attempting to compromise the claim; and

(2) conduct or statements made in compromise negotiations regarding the claim, except when offered in a criminal case and the negotiations related to a claim by a public office or agency in the exercise of regulatory, investigative, or enforcement authority.

(b) Permitted uses. This rule does not require exclusion if the evidence is offered for purposes not prohibited by subdivision (a). Examples of permissible purposes include proving a witness' bias or prejudice; negating a contention of undue delay and proving an effort to obstruct a criminal investigation or prosecution. (Eff. 12-1-06)

RULE 409. Payment of Medical and Similar Expenses

Evidence of furnishing or offering or promising to pay medical, hospital, or similar expenses occasioned by an injury is not admissible to prove liability for the injury.

RULE 410. Inadmissibility of Pleas, Plea Discussions, and Related Statements

Except as otherwise provided in this rule, evidence of the following is not, in any civil or criminal proceeding, admissible against the defendant who made the plea or was a participant in the plea discussions:

(1) a plea of guilty which was later withdrawn;

(2) a plea of nolo contendere;

(3) any statement made in the course of any proceedings under Rule 11 of the Federal Rules of Criminal Procedure or comparable state procedure regarding either of the foregoing pleas; or

(4) any statement made in the course of plea discussions with an attorney for the prosecuting authority which do not result in a plea of guilty or which result in a plea of guilty later withdrawn.

However, such a statement is admissible (i) in any proceeding wherein another statement made in the course of the same plea or plea discussions has been introduced and the statement ought in fairness be considered contemporaneously with it, or (ii) in a criminal proceeding for perjury or false statement if the statement was made by the defendant under oath, on the record and in the presence of counsel.

(Amended, 12-12-75; 4-30-79, eff. 12-1-80)

RULE 411. Liability Insurance

Evidence that a person was or was not insured against liability is not admissible upon the issue whether the person acted negligently or otherwise wrongfully. This rule does not require the exclusion of evidence of insurance against liability when offered for another purpose, such as proof of agency, ownership, or control, or bias or prejudice of witness.

(Amended, eff. 10-1-87)

RULE 412. Sex Offense Cases; Relevance of Alleged Victim's Past Sexual Behavior or Alleged Sexual Predisposition

(a)Evidence generally inadmissible. The following evidence is not admissible in any civil or criminal proceeding involving alleged sexual misconduct except as provided in subdivisions (b) and (c):

(1) Evidence offered to prove that any alleged victim engaged in other sexual behavior.

(2) Evidence offered to prove any alleged victim's sexual predisposition.

(b) Exceptions.

(1) In a criminal case, the following evidence is admissible, if otherwise admissible under these rules:

(A) evidence of specific instances of sexual behavior by the alleged victim offered to prove that a person other than the accused was the source of semen, injury, or other physical evidence;

(B) evidence of specific instances of sexual behavior by the alleged victim with respect to the person accused of the sexual misconduct offered by the accused to prove consent or by the prosecution; and

(C) evidence the exclusion of which would violate the constitutional rights of the defendant.

(2) In a civil case, evidence offered to prove the sexual behavior or sexual predisposition of any alleged victim is admissible if it is otherwise admissible under these rules and its probative value substantially outweighs the danger of harm to any victim and of unfair prejudice to any party. Evidence of an alleged victim's reputation is admissible only if it has been placed in controversy by the alleged victim.

(c) Procedure to determine admissibility.

(1) A party intending to offer evidence under subdivision (b) must—

(A) file a written motion at least 14 days before trial specifically describing the evidence and stating the purpose for which it is offered unless the court, for good cause requires a different time for filing or permits filing during trial; and

(B) serve the motion on all parties and notify the alleged victim or, when appropriate, the alleged victim's guardian or representative.

(2) Before admitting evidence under this rule the court must conduct a hearing in camera and afford the victim and parties a right to attend and be heard. The motion, related papers, and the record of the hearing must be sealed and remain under seal unless the court orders otherwise.

(As added Oct. 28, 1978, eff. Nov. 28, 1978' amended Nov. 18, 1988; Apr. 29, 1994, eff. Dec. 1 1994; Sept. 13, 1994, eff. Dec. 1, 1994.)

RULE 413. Evidence of Similar Crimes in Sexual Assault Cases

(a) In a criminal case in which the defendant is accused of an offense of sexual assault, evidence of the defendant's commission of another offense or offenses of sexual assault is admissible, and may be considered for its bearing on any matter to which it is relevant.

(b) In a case in which the Government intends to offer evidence under this rule, the attorney for the Government shall disclose the evidence to the defendant, including statements of witnesses or a summary of the substance of any testimony that is expected to be offered, at least fifteen days before the scheduled date of trial or at such later time as the court may allow for good cause.

(c) This rule shall not be construed to limit the admission or consideration of evidence under any other rule.

(d) For purposes of this rule and Rule 415, "offense of sexual assault" means a crime under Federal law or the law of a State (as defined in section 513 of title 18, United States Code) that involved—

(1) any conduct proscribed by chapter 109A of title 18, United States Code;

(2) contact, without consent, between any part of the defendant's body or an object and the genitals or anus of another person;

(3) contact, without consent, between the genitals or anus of the defendant and any part of another person's body;

(4) deriving sexual pleasure or gratification from the infliction of death, bodily injury, or physical pain on another person; or

(5) an attempt or conspiracy to engage in conduct described in paragraphs (1)-(4).

RULE 414. Evidence of Similar Crimes in ChildMolestation Cases

(a) In a criminal case in which the defendant is accused of an offense of child molestation, evidence of the defendant's commission of another offense or offenses of child molestation is admissible, and may be considered for its bearing on any matter to which it is relevant.

(b) In a case in which the Government intends to offer evidence under this rule, the attorney for the Government shall disclose the evidence to the defendant, including statements of witnesses or a summary of the substance of any testimony that is expected to be offered, at least fifteen days before the scheduled date of trial or at such later time as the court may allow for good cause.

(c) This rule shall not be construed to limit the admission or consideration of evidence under any other rule.

(d) For purposes of this rule and Rule 415, "child" means a person below the age of fourteen, and "offense of child molestation" means a crime under Federal law or the law of a State (as defined in section 513 of title 18, United States Code) that involved—

(1) any conduct proscribed by chapter 109A of title 18, United States Code, that was committed in relation to a child;

(2) any conduct proscribed by chapter 110 of title 18, United States Code;

(3) contact between any part of the defendant's body or an object and the genitals or anus of a child;

(4) contact between the genitals or anus of the defendant and any part of the body of a child;

(5) deriving sexual pleasure or gratification from the infliction of death, bodily injury, or physical pain on a child; or

(6) an attempt or conspiracy to engage in conduct described in paragraphs (1)-(5).

(Added Sept. 13, 1994, eff. July 9, 1995.)

RULE 415. Evidence of Similar Acts in Civil Cases Concerning Sexual Assault or Child Molestation

(a) In a civil case in which a claim for damages or other relief is predicated on a party's alleged commission of conduct constituting an offense of sexual assault or child molestation, evidence of that party's commission of another offense or offenses of sexual assault or child molestation is admissible and may be considered as provided in Rule 413 and Rule 414 of these rules.

(b) A party who intends to offer evidence under this Rule shall disclose the evidence to the party against whom it will be offered, including statements of witnesses or a summary of the substance of any testimony that is expected to be offered, at least fifteen days before the scheduled date of trial or at such later time as the court may allow for good cause.

(c) This rule shall not be construed to limit the admission or consideration of evidence under any other rule.

(Added Sept. 13, 1994, eff. July 9, 1995.)

ARTICLE V. PRIVILEGES

RULE 501. General Rule

Except as otherwise required by the Constitution of the United States or provided by Act of Congress or in rules prescribed by the Supreme Court pursuant to statutory authority, the privilege of a witness, person, government, State, or political subdivision thereof shall be governed by the principles of the common law as they may be interpreted by the courts of the United States in the light of reason and experience. However, in civil actions and proceedings, with respect to an element of a claim or defense as to which State law supplies the rule of decision, the privilege of a witness, person, government, State, or political subdivision thereof shall be determined in accordance with State law.

ARTICLE VI. WITNESSES

RULE 601. General Rule of Competency

Every person is competent to be a witness except as otherwise provided in these rules. However, in civil actions and proceedings, with respect to an element of a claim or defense as to which State law supplies the rule of decision, the competency of a witness shall be determined in accordance with State law.

RULE 602. Lack of Personal Knowledge

A witness may not testify to a matter unless evidence is introduced sufficient to support a finding that the witness has personal knowledge of the matter. Evidence to prove personal knowledge may, but need not, consist of the witness' own testimony. This rule is subject to the provisions of rule 703, relating to opinion testimony by expert witnesses.

(Amended, eff. 10-1-87; 11-1-88)

RULE 603. Oath or Affirmation

Before testifying, every witness shall be required to declare that the witness will testify truthfully, by oath or affirmation administered in a form calculated to awaken the witness' conscience and impress the witness' mind with the duty to do so.

(Amended, eff. 10-1-87)

RULE 604. Interpreters

An interpreter is subject to the provisions of these rules relating to qualification as an expert and the administration of an oath or affirmation to make a true translation.

(Amended, eff. 10-1-87)

RULE 605. Competency of Judge as Witness

The judge presiding at the trial may not testify in that trial as a witness. No objection need be made in order to preserve the point.

RULE 606. Competency of Juror as Witness

(a) At the trial. A member of the jury may not testify as a witness before that jury in the trial of the case in which the juror is sitting. If the juror is called so to testify, the opposing party shall be afforded an opportunity to object out of the presence of the jury.

(b) Inquiry into validity of verdict or indictment. Upon an inquiry into the validity of a verdict or indictment, a juror may not testify as to any matter or statement occurring during the course of the jury's deliberations or the effect of anything upon that or any other juror's mind or emotions as influencing the juror to assent to or dissent from the verdict or indictment or concerning the juror's mental processes in connection therewith. But a juror may testify about (1) whether extraneous prejudicial information was improperly brought to the jury's attention, (2) whether any outside influence was improperly brought to bear upon any juror or whether there was a mistake in entering the verdict onto the verdict form. A juror's affidavit or evidence of any statement by the juror may not be received on a matter about which the juror would be precluded from testifying.

(Amended, eff. 12-12-75; 10-1-87; eff. 12-1-06)

RULE 607. Who May Impeach

The credibility of a witness may be attacked by any party, including the party calling the witness.

(Amended, eff. 10-1-87)

RULE 608. Evidence of Character and Conduct of Witness

(a) Opinion and reputation evidence of character. The credibility of a witness may be attacked or supported by evidence in the form of opinion or reputation, but subject to these limitations: (1) the evidence may refer only to character for truthfulness or untruthfulness, and (2) evidence of truthful character is admissible only after the character of the witness for truthfulness has been attacked by opinion or reputation evidence or otherwise.

(b) Specific instances of conduct. Specific instances of the conduct of a witness, for the purpose of attacking or supporting the witness' credibility, other than conviction of crime as provided in rule 609, may not be proved by extrinsic evidence. They may, however, in the discretion of the court, if probative of truthfulness or untruthfulness, be inquired into on cross-examination of the witness (1) concerning the witness' character for truthfulness or untruthfulness, or (2) concerning the character for truthfulness or untruthfulness of another witness as to which character the witness being cross-examined has testified.

The giving of testimony, whether by an accused or by any other witness, does not operate as a waiver of the accused's or the witness' privilege against self-incrimination when examined with respect to matters which relate only to character for truthfulness.

(Amended, eff. 3-27-03; 12-1-03)

RULE 609. Impeachment by Evidence of Conviction of Crime

(a) General rule. For the purpose of attacking the character for truthfulness of a witness, (1) evidence that a witness other than an accused has been convicted of a crime shall be admitted, subject to Rule 403, if the crime was punishable by death or imprisonment in excess of one year under the law under which the witness was convicted, and evidence that an accused has been convicted of such a crime shall be admitted if the court determines that the probative value of admitting this evidence outweighs its prejudicial effect to the accused; and (2) evidence that any witness has been convicted of a crime shall be admitted regardless of the punishment, if it can be determined that establishing the elements of the crime required proof of admission of an act of dishonesty or false statement by the witness.

(b) Time limit. Evidence of a conviction under this rule is not admissible if a period of more than ten years has elapsed since the date of the conviction or of the release of the witness from the confinement imposed for that conviction, whichever is the later date, unless the court determined, in the interests of justice, that the probative value of the conviction supported by specific facts and circumstances substantially outweighs its prejudicial effect. However, evidence of a conviction more than 10 years old as calculated herein, is not admissible unless the proponent gives to the adverse party sufficient advance written notice of intent to use such evidence to provide the adverse party with a fair opportunity to contest the use of such evidence.

(c) Effect of pardon, annulment, or certificate of rehabilitation. Evidence of a conviction is not admissible under this rule if (1) the conviction has been the subject of a pardon, annulment, certificate of rehabilitation, or other equivalent procedure based on a finding of the rehabilitation of the person convicted, and that person has not been convicted of a subsequent crime which was punishable by death or imprisonment in excess of one year, or (2) the conviction has been the subject of a pardon, annulment or other equivalent procedure based on a finding of innocence.

(d) Juvenile adjudications. Evidence of juvenile adjudications is generally not admissible under this rule. The court may, however, in a criminal case allow evidence of a juvenile adjudication of a witness other than the accused if conviction of the offense would be admissible to attack the credibility of an adult and the court is satisfied that admission in evidence is necessary for a fair determination of the issue of guilt or innocence.

(e) Pendency of appeal. The pendency of an appeal therefrom does not render evidence of a conviction inadmissible. Evidence of the pendency of an appeal is admissible.

(Eff. 12-1-06)

RULE 610. Religious Beliefs or Opinions

Evidence of the beliefs or opinions of a witness on matters of religion is not admissible for the purpose of showing that by reason of their nature the witness' credibility is impaired or enhanced.

(Amended, eff. 10-1-87)

RULE 611. Mode and Order of Interrogation and Presentation

(a) Control by court. The Court shall exercise reasonable control over the mode and order of interrogating witnesses and presenting evidence so as to (1) make the interrogation and presentation effective for the ascertainment of the truth, (2) avoid needless consumption of time and, (3) protect witnesses from harassment or undue embarrassment.

(b) Scope of cross-examination. Cross-examination should be limited to the subject matter of the direct examination and matters affecting the credibility of the witness. The court may, in the exercise of discretion, permit inquiry into additional matters as if on direct examination.

(c) Leading questions. Leading questions should not be used on the direct examination of a witness except as may be necessary to develop the witness' testimony. Ordinarily leading questions should be permitted on cross-examination. When a party calls a hostile witness, an adverse party, or a witness identified with an adverse party, interrogation may be by leading questions.

(Amended, eff. 10-1-87)

RULE 612. Writing Used To Refresh Memory

Except as otherwise provided in criminal proceedings by section 3500 of title 18, United States Code, if a witness uses a writing to refresh memory for the purpose of testifying, either—

(1) while testifying, or

(2) before testifying, if the court in its discretion determines it is necessary in the interests of justice,

an adverse party is entitled to have the writing produced at the hearing, to inspect it, to cross-examine the witness thereon, and to introduce in evidence those portions which relate to the testimony of the witness. If it is claimed that the writing contains matters not related to the subject matter of the testimony the court shall examine the writing in camera, excise any portions not so related, and order delivery of the remainder to the party entitled thereto. Any portion withheld over objections shall be preserved and made available to the appellate court in the event of an appeal. If a writing is not produced or delivered pursuant to order under this rule, the court shall make any order justice requires, except that in criminal cases when the prosecution elects not to comply, the order shall be one striking the testimony or, if the court in its discretion determines that the interests of justice so require, declaring a mistrial.

(Amended, eff. 10-1-87)

RULE 613. Prior Statements of Witnesses

(a) Examining witness concerning prior statement. In examining a witness concerning a prior statement made by the witness, whether written or not, the statement need not be shown nor its contents disclosed to the witness at that time, but on request the same shall be shown or disclosed to opposing counsel.

(b) Extrinsic evidence of prior inconsistent statement of witness. Extrinsic evidence of a prior inconsistent statement by a witness is not admissible unless the witness is afforded an opportunity to explain or deny the same and the opposite party is afforded an opportunity to interrogate the witness thereon, or the interests of justice otherwise require. This provision does not apply to admissions of a party-opponent as defined in rule 801(d)(2).

(Amended, eff. 10-1-87; 11-1-88)

RULE 614. Calling and Interrogation of Witnesses by Court

(a) Calling by court. The court may, on its own motion or at the suggestion of a party, call witnesses, and all parties are entitled to cross-examine witnesses thus called.

(b) Interrogation by court. The court may interrogate witnesses, whether called by itself or by a party.

(c) Objections. Objections to the calling of witnesses by the court or to interrogation by it may be made at the time or at the next available opportunity when the jury is not present.

At the request of a party the court shall order witnesses excluded so that they cannot hear the testimony of other witnesses, and it may make the order of its own motion. This rule does not authorize exclusion of (1) a party who is a natural person, or (2) an officer or employee of a party which is not a natural person designat4ed as its representative by its attorney, or (3)a person whose presence is shown by a party to be essential to the presentation of the party's cause, or (4) a person authorized by statute to be present.

RULE 615. Exclusion of Witnesses

At the request of a party the court shall order witnesses excluded so that they cannot hear the testimony of other witnesses, and it may make the order of its own motion. This rule does not authorize exclusion of (1) a party who is a natural person, or (2) an officer or employee of a party which is not a natural person designat4ed as its representative by its attorney, or (3)a person whose presence is shown by a party to be essential to the presentation of the party's cause, or (4) a person authorized by statute to be present.

(Amended, eff. 4-24-98; 12-1-98)

ARTICLE VII. OPINIONS AND EXPERT TESTIMONY

RULE 701. Opinion Testimony by Lay Witnesses

If the witness is not testifying as an expert, the witness' testimony in the form of opinions or inferences is limited to those opinions or inferences which are (a) rationally based on the perception of the witness and (b) helpful to a clear understanding of the witness' testimony or the determination of a fact in issue, and (c) not based on scientific, technical, or other specialized knowledge within the scope of Rule 702.

(Amended, eff. 10-1-87; Apr. 17, 2000, eff. Dec. 1, 2000.)

RULE 702. Testimony by Experts

If scientific, technical, or other specialized knowledge can assist the trier of fact to understand the evidence or to determine a fact in issue, a witness qualified as an expert by knowledge, skill, experience, training, or education, may testify thereto in the form of an opinion or otherwise, if (1)the testimony is based upon sufficient facts or data, (2) the testimony is the product of reliable principles and methods, and (3) the witness has applied the principles and methods reliably to the facts of the case.

(As amended, Apr. 17, 2000, eff. Dec. 1, 2000.)

RULE 703. Bases of Opinion Testimony

The facts or data in the particular case upon which an expert bases an opinion or inference may be those perceived by or made known to the expert at or before the hearing. If of a type reasonably relied upon by experts in the particular field in forming opinions or inferences upon the subject, the facts or data need not be admissible in evidence in order for the opinion or inference to be admitted. Facts or data that are otherwise inadmissible shall not be disclosed to the jury by the proponent of the opinion or the inference unless the court determines that their probative value in assisting the jury to evaluate the expert's opinion substantially outweighs their prejudicial effect.

(Amended, eff. 10-1-87; As amended, Apr. 17, 2000, eff. Dec. 1, 2000.)

RULE 704. Opinion on Ultimate Issue

(a) Except as provided in subdivision (b), testimony in the form of an opinion or inference otherwise admissible is not objectionable because it embraces an ultimate issue to be decided by the trier of fact.

(b) No expert witness testifying with respect to the mental state or condition of a defendant in a criminal case may state an opinion or inference as to whether the defendant did or did not have the mental state or condition constituting an element of the crime charged or of a defense thereto. Such ultimate issues are matters for the trier of fact alone.

(Amended, eff. 10-12-84)

RULE 705. Disclosure of Facts or Data Underlying Expert Opinion

The expert may testify in terms of opinion or inference and give reasons therefor without first testifying to the underlying facts or data, unless the court requires otherwise. The expert may in any event be required to disclose the underlying facts or data on cross-examination.

(Amended, eff. 12-1-93)

RULE 706. Court Appointed Experts

(a) Appointment. The court may on its own motion or on the motion of any party enter an order to show cause why expert witnesses should not be appointed, and may request the parties to submit nominations. The court may appoint any expert witnesses agreed upon by the parties, and may appoint expert witnesses of its own selection. An expert witness shall not be appointed by the court unless the witness consents to act. A witness so appointed shall be informed of the witness' duties by the court in writing, a copy of which shall be filed with the clerk, or at a conference in which the parties shall have opportunity to participate. A witness so appointed shall advise the parties of the witness' findings, if any; the witness' deposition may be taken by any party; and the witness may be called to testify by the court or any party. The witness shall be subject to cross-examination by each party, including a party calling the witness.

(b) Compensation. Expert witnesses so appointed are entitled to reasonable compensation in whatever sum the court may allow. The compensation thus fixed is payable from funds which may be provided by law in criminal cases and civil actions and proceedings involving just compensation under the fifth amendment. In other civil actions and proceedings the compensation shall be paid by the parties in such proportion and at such time as the court directs, and thereafter charged in like manner as other costs.

(c) Disclosure of appointment. In the exercise of its discretion, the court may authorize disclosure to the jury of the fact that the court appointed the expert witness.

(d) Parties' experts of own selection. Nothing in this rule limits the parties in calling expert witnesses of their own selection.

(Amended, eff. 10-1-87)

ARTICLE VII. HEARSAY

RULE 801. Definitions

The following definitions apply under this article:

(a) Statement. A "statement" is (1) an oral or written assertion or (2) non-verbal conduct of a person, if it is intended by the person as an assertion.

(b) Declarant. A "declarant" is a person who makes a statement.

(c) Hearsay. "Hearsay" is a statement, other than one made by the declarant while testifying at the trial or hearing, offered in evidence to prove the truth of the matter asserted.

(d) Statements which are not hearsay. A statement is not hearsay if—

(1) Prior statement by witness. The declarant testifies at trial or hearing and is subject to cross-examination concerning the statement, and the statement is (A) inconsistent with the declarant's testimony, and was given under oath subject to the penalty of perjury at a trial hearing, or other proceeding, or in a deposition, or (B) consistent with the declarant's testimony and is offered to rebut an express or implied charge against the declarant of recent fabrication or improper influence or motive, or (C) one of identification of a person made after perceiving the person; or

(2) Admission by party-opponent. The statement is offered against a party and is (A) the party's own statement, in either an individual or a representative capacity or (B) a statement of which the party has manifested an adoption or belief in its truth, or (C) a statement by a person authorized by the party to make a statement concerning the subject, or (D) a statement by the party's agent or servant concerning a matter within the scope of the agency or employment, made during the existence of the relationship, or (E) a statement by a coconspirator of a party during the course and in furtherance of the conspiracy. The contents of the statement shall be considered but are not alone sufficient to establish the declarant's authority under subdivision (C), the agency or employment relationship and scope thereof under subdivision (D), or the existence of the conspiracy and the party against whom the statement is offered under subdivision (E).

(Amended, eff. 10-31-75; 10-1-87; Apr. 11, 1997, eff. Dec. 1, 1997.)

RULE 802. Hearsay Rule

Hearsay is not admissible except as provided by these rules or by other rules prescribed by the Supreme Court pursuant to statutory authority or by Act of Congress.

RULE 803. Hearsay Exceptions; Availability of Declarant Immaterial

The following are not excluded by the hearsay rule, even though the declarant is available as a witness:

(1) Present sense impression. A statement describing or explaining an event or condition made while the declarant was perceiving the event or condition, or immediately thereafter.

(2) Excited utterance. A statement relating to a startling event or condition made while the _declarant was under the stress of excitement caused by the event or condition.

(3) Then existing, mental, emotional, or physical condition. Statement of the declarant's then existing state of mind, emotion, sensation, or physical condition (such as intent, plan, motive, design, mental feeling, pain, and bodily health), but not including a statement of memory or belief to prove the fact remembered or believed unless it relates to the execution, revocation, identification, or terms of declarant's will.

(4) Statements for purposes of medical diagnosis or treatment. Statements made for purposes of medical diagnosis or treatment and describing medical history, or past or present symptoms, pain, or sensations, or the inception or general character of the cause or external source thereof insofar as reasonably pertinent to diagnosis or treatment.

(5) Recorded recollection. A memorandum or record concerning a matter about which a witness once had knowledge but now has insufficient recollection to enable the witness to testify fully and accurately, shown to have been made or adopted by the witness when the matter was fresh in the witness' memory and to reflect that knowledge correctly. If admitted, the memorandum or record may be read into evidence but may not itself be received as an exhibit unless offered by an adverse party.

(6) Records of regularly conducted activity. A memorandum, report, record, or data compilation, in any form, of acts, events, conditions, opinions, or diagnoses, made at or near the time by, or from information transmitted by, a person with knowledge, if kept in the course of a regularly conducted business activity, and if it was the regular practice of that business activity to make the memorandum, report, record, or data compilation, all as shown by the testimony of the custodian or other qualified witness, or by certification that complies with Rule 902 (11), Rule 902 (12), or a statute permitting certification, unless the source of information or the method or circumstances of preparation indicate lack of trustworthiness. The term "business" as used in this paragraph includes business, institution, association, profession, occupation, and calling of every kind, whether or not conducted for profit.

(7) Absence of entry in records kept in accordance with the provisions of paragraph (6). Evidence that a matter is not included in the memoranda, reports, records, or data compilations, in any form, kept in accordance with the provisions of paragraph (6) to prove nonoccurrence or nonexistence of the matter, if the matter was of a kind of which a memorandum, report, record, or data compilation was regularly made and preserved, unless the sources of information or other circumstances indicate lack of trustworthiness.

(8) Public records and reports. Records, reports, statements, or data compilations, in any form, of public offices or agencies, setting forth (A) the activities of the office or agency, or (B) matters observed pursuant to duty imposed by law as to which matters there was a duty to report, excluding, however, in criminal cases matters observed by police officers and other law enforcement personnel, or (C) in civil actions and proceedings and against the government in criminal cases, factual findings resulting from an investigation made pursuant to authority granted by law, unless the sources of information or other circumstances indicate lack of trustworthiness.

(9) Records of vital statistics. Records or data compilations, in any form, of births, fetal deaths, deaths, or marriages, if the report thereof was made to a public office pursuant to requirements of law.

(10) Absence of public record or entry. To prove the absence of a record, report, statement, or data compilation, in any form, or the nonoccurrence or nonexistence of a matter of which a record, report, statement, or data compilation, in any form, was regularly made and preserved by a public office or agency, evidence in the form of a certification in accordance with Rule 902, or testimony, that diligent search failed to disclose the record, report, statement, or data compilation, or entry.

(11) Records of religious organizations. Statements of births, marriages, divorces, deaths, legitimacy, ancestry, relationship by blood or marriage, or other similar facts of personal or family history, contained in a regularly kept record of a religious organization.

(12) Marriage, baptismal, and similar certificates. Statements of fact contained in a certificate that the maker performed a marriage or other ceremony or administered a sacrament, made by a clergyman, public official, or other person authorized by the rules or practices of a religious organization or by law to perform the act certified, and purporting to have been issued at the time of the act or within a reasonable time thereafter.

(13) Family records. Statements of fact concerning personal or family history contained in family Bibles, genealogies, charts, engravings on rings, inscriptions on family portraits, engravings on urns, crypts, or tombstones, or the like.

(14) Records of documents affecting an interest in property. The record of a document purporting to establish or affect an interest in property, as proof of the content of the original document and its execution and delivery by each person by whom it purports to have been executed, if the record is a record of a public office and an applicable statute authorizes the recording of documents of that kind in that office.

(15) Statements in documents affecting an interest in property. A statement contained in a document purporting to establish or affect an interest in property if the matter stated was relevant to the purpose of the document, unless dealings made with the property since the document was made have been inconsistent with the truth of the statement or the purport of the document.

(16) Statements in ancient documents. Statements in a document in existence twenty years or more the authenticity of which is established.

(17) Market reports, commercial publications. Market quotations, tabulations, lists, directories, or other published compilations, generally used and relied upon by the public or by persons in particular occupations.

(18) Learned Treatises. To the extent called to the attention of an expert witness upon cross-examination or relied upon by the expert witness in direct examination, statements contained in published treatises, periodicals, or pamphlets on a subject of history, medicine, or other science or art, established as a reliable authority by the testimony or admission of the witness or by other expert testimony or by judicial notice. If admitted, the statements may be read into evidence but may not be received as exhibits.

(19) Reputation concerning personal or family history. Reputation among members of a person's family by blood, adoption, or marriage or among a person's associates, or in the community, concerning a person's birth, adoption, marriage, divorce, death, legitimacy, relationship by blood, adoption, or marriage, ancestry, or other similar fact of personal or family history.

(20) Reputation concerning boundaries or general history. Reputation in a community, arising before the controversy, as to boundaries of or customs affecting lands in the community, and reputation as to events of general history important to the community or State or nation in which located.

(21) Reputation as to character. Reputation of a person's character among associates or in the community.

(22) Judgment of previous conviction. Evidence of a final judgment, entered after a trial or upon a plea of guilty (but not upon a plea of nolo contendere), adjudging a person guilty of a crime punishable by death or imprisonment in excess of one year, to prove any fact essential to sustain the judgment, but not including, when offered by the Government in a criminal prosecution for purposes other than impeachment, judgments against persons other than the accused. The pendency of an appeal may be shown but does not affect admissibility.

(23) Judgment as to personal, family, or general history, or boundaries. Judgments as proof of matters of personal family, or general history, or boundaries, essential to the judgment, if the same would be provable by evidence of reputation.

(24) [Other exceptions.] [Transferred to Rule 807]

(Amended, eff. 12-12-75; 10-1-87; Apr. 11, 1997, eff. Dec. 1, 1997; Apr. 17, 2000, eff. Dec. 1, 2000)

RULE 804. Hearsay Exceptions: Declarant Unavailable

(a) Definition of unavailability. "Unavailability as a witness" includes situations in which the declarant—

(1) is exempted by ruling of the court on the ground of privilege from testifying concerning the subject matter of the declarant's statement; or

(2) persists in refusing to testify concerning the subject matter of the declarant's statement despite an order of the court to do so; or

(3) testifies to a lack of memory of the subject matter of the declarant's statement; or

(4) is unable to be present or to testify at the hearing because of death or then existing physical or mental illness or infirmity; or

(5) is absent from the hearing and the proponent of a statement has been unable to procure the declarant's attendance (or in the case of a hearsay exception under subdivision (b)(2), (3), or (4), the declarant's attendance or testimony) by process or other reasonable means.

A declarant is not unavailable as a witness if exemption, refusal, claim of lack of memory, inability, or absence is due to the procurement or wrongdoing of the proponent of a statement for the purpose of preventing the witness from attending or testifying.

(b) Hearsay exceptions.

The following are not excluded by the hearsay rule if the declarant is unavailable as a witness:

(1) Former testimony. Testimony given as a witness at another hearing of the same or a different proceeding, or in a deposition taken in compliance with law in the course of the same or another proceeding, if the party against whom the testimony is now offered, or, in a civil action or proceeding, a predecessor in interest, had an opportunity and similar motive to develop the testimony by direct, cross, or redirect examination.

(2) Statement under belief of impending death. In a prosecution for homicide or in a civil action or proceeding, a statement made by a declarant while believing that the declarant's death was imminent, concerning the cause or circumstances of what the declarant believed to be impending death.

(3) Statement against interest. A statement which was at the time of its making so far contrary to the declarant's pecuniary or proprietary interest, or so far tended to subject the declarant to civil or criminal liability, or to render invalid a claim by the declarant against another, that a reasonable person in the declarant's position would not have made the statement unless believing it to be true. A statement tending to expose the declarant to criminal liability and offered to exculpate the accused is not admissible unless corroborating circumstances clearly indicate the trustworthiness of the statement.

(4) Statement of personal or family history. (A) A statement concerning the declarant's own birth, adoption, marriage, divorce, legitimacy, relationship by blood, adoption, or marriage, ancestry, or other similar fact of personal or family history, even though declarant had no means of acquiring personal knowledge of the matter stated; or (B) a statement concerning the foregoing matters, and death also, of another person, if the declarant was related to the other by blood, adoption, or marriage or was so intimately associated with the other's family as to be likely to have accurate information concerning the matter declared.

(5) [Other exceptions.] [Transferred to Rule 807]

(6) Forfeiture by wrongdoing. A statement offered against a party that has engaged or acquiesced in wrongdoing that was intended to, and did, procure the unavailability of the declarant as a witness.

(As amended Dec. 12, 1975; Mar. 2, 1987, eff. Oct. 1, 1987; Nov. 18, 1988; Apr. 11, 1997, eff. Dec. 1, 1997.)

RULE 805. Hearsay Within Hearsay

Hearsay included within hearsay is not excluded under the hearsay rule if each part of the combined statements conforms with an exception to the hearsay rule provided in these rules.

RULE 806. Attacking and Supporting Credibility of Declarant

When a hearsay statement, or a statement defined in Rule 801(d)(2)(C), (D), or (E), has been admitted in evidence, the credibility of the declarant may be attacked, and if attacked may be supported, by any evidence which would be admissible for those purposes if declarant had testified as a witness. Evidence of a statement or conduct by the declarant at any time, inconsistent with the declarant's hearsay statement, is not subject to any requirement that the declarant may have been afforded an opportunity to deny or explain. If the party against whom a hearsay statement has been admitted calls the declarant as a witness, the party is entitled to examine the declarant on the statement as if under cross-examination.

(Jan. 2, 1975, P.L. 93-595, § 1, 88 Stat. 1943; Mar. 2, 1987, eff. Oct. 1, 1987; Apr. 11, 1997, eff. Dec. 1, 1997.)

RULE 807. Residual Exceptions

A statement not specifically covered by Rule 803 or Rule 804 but having equivalent circumstantial guarantees of trustworthiness, is not excluded by the hearsay rule, if the court determines that (A) the statement is offered as evidence of a material fact; (B) the statement is more probative on the point for which it is offered than any other evidence which the proponent can procure through reasonable efforts; and (C) the general purposes of these rules and the interests of justice will best be served by admission of the statement into evidence. However, a statement may not be admitted under this exception unless the proponent of it makes known to the adverse party sufficiently in advance of the trial or hearing to provide the adverse party with a fair opportunity to prepare to meet it, the proponent's intention to offer the statement and the particulars of it, including the name and address of the declarant.

(Added Apr. 11, 1997, eff. Dec. 1, 1997.)

ARTICLE IX. AUTHENTICATION AND IDENTIFICATION

RULE 901. Requirement of Authentication or Identification

(a) General provision. The requirement of authentication or identification as a condition precedent to admissibility is satisfied by evidence sufficient to support a finding that the matter in question is what its proponent claims.

(b) Illustrations. By way of illustration only, and not by way of limitation, the following are examples of authentication or identification conforming with the requirements of this rule:

(1) Testimony of witness with knowledge. Testimony that a matter is what it is claimed to be.

(2) Nonexpert opinion on handwriting. Nonexpert opinion as to the genuineness of handwriting, based upon familiarity not acquired for purposes of the litigation.

(3) Comparison by trier or expert witness. Comparison by the trier of fact or by expert witnesses with specimens which have been authenticated.

(4) Distinctive characteristics and the like. Appearance, contents, substance, internal patterns, or other distinctive characteristics, taken in conjunction with circumstances.

(5) Voice Identification. Identification of a voice, whether heard firsthand or through mechanical or electronic transmission or recording, by opinion based upon hearing the voice at any time under circumstances connecting it with the alleged speaker.

(6) Telephone conversations. Telephone conversations, by evidence that a call was made to the number assigned at the time by the telephone company to a particular person or business, if (A) in the case of a person, circumstances, including self-identification, show the person answering to be the one called, or (B) in the case of a business, the call was made to a place of business and the conversation related to business reasonably transacted over the telephone.

(7) Public records or reports. Evidence that a writing authorized by law to be recorded or filed and in fact recorded or filed in a public office, or a purported public record, report, statement, or data compilation, in any form, is from the public office where items of this nature are kept.

(8) Ancient documents or data compilation. Evidence that a document or data compilation, in any form, (A) is in such condition as to create no suspicion concerning its authenticity, (B) was in a place where it, if authentic, would likely be, and (C) has been in existence twenty years or more at the time it is offered.

(9) Process or system. Evidence describing a process or system used to produce a result and showing that the process or system produces an accurate result.

(10) Methods provided by statute or rule. Any method of authentication or identification provided by Act of Congress or by other rules prescribed by the Supreme Court pursuant to statutory authority.

RULE 902. Self-authentication

Extrinsic evidence of authenticity as a condition precedent to admissibility is not required with respect to the following:

(1) Domestic public documents under seal. A document bearing a seal purporting to be that of the United States, or of any State, district, Commonwealth, territory, or insular possession thereof, or the Panama Canal Zone, or the Trust Territory of the Pacific Islands, or of a political subdivision, department, officer or agency thereof, and a signature purporting to be an attestation or execution.

(2) Domestic public documents not under seal. A document purporting to bear the signature in the official capacity of an officer or employee of any entity included in paragraph (1) hereof, having no seal, if a public officer having a seal and having official duties in the district or political subdivision of the officer or employee certifies under seal that the signer has the official capacity and that the signature is genuine.

(3) Foreign public documents. A document purporting to be executed or attested in an official capacity by a person authorized by the laws of a foreign country to make the execution or attestation, and accompanied by a final certification as to the genuineness of the signature and official position (A) of the executing or attesting person, or (B) of any foreign official whose certificate of genuineness of signature and official position relates to the execution or attestation or is in a chain of certificates of genuineness of signature and official position relating to the execution or attestation. A final certification may be made by a secretary of an embassy or legation, consul general, consul, vice consul, or consular agent of the United States, or a diplomatic or consular official of the foreign country assigned or accredited to the United States. If reasonable opportunity has been given to all parties to investigate the authenticity and accuracy of official documents, the court may, for good cause shown, order that they be treated as presumptively authentic without final certification or permit them to be evidenced by an attested summary with or without final certification.

(4) Certified copies of public records. A copy of an official record or report or entry therein; or of a document authorized by law to be recorded or filed and actually recorded and filed a public office, including data compilations in any form, certified as correct by the custodian or other person authorized to make the certification, by certificate complying with paragraph (1), (2), or (3) of this rule or complying with any Act of Congress or rule prescribed by the Supreme Court pursuant to statutory authority.

(5) Official publications. Books, pamphlets, or other publications purporting to be issued by public authority.

(6) Newspapers and periodicals. Printed material purporting to be newspapers or periodicals.

(7) Trade inscriptions and the like. Inscriptions, signs, tags, or labels purporting to have been affixed the course of business and indicating ownership, control, or origin.

(8) Acknowledged documents. Documents accompanied by a certificate of acknowledgment executed in the manner provided by a law by a notary public or other officer authorized by law to take acknowledgments.

(9) Commercial paper and related documents. Commercial paper, signatures thereon, and documents relating thereto to the extent provided by general commercial law.

(10) Presumptions under Acts of Congress. Any signature, document, or other matter declared by Act of Congress to be presumptively or prima facie genuine or authentic.

(11) Certified domestic records of regularly conducted activity. The original or a duplicate of a domestic record of regularly conducted activity that would be admissible under Rule 803(6) if accompanied by a written declaration of its custodian or other qualified person, in a manner complying with any Act of Congress or rule prescribed by the Supreme Court pursuant to statutory authority, certifying that the record:

(A) was made at or near the time of the occurrence of the matters set forth by, or from information transmitted by, a person with knowledge of those matters;

(B) was kept in the course of the regularly conducted activity; and

(C) was made by the regularly conducted activity as a regular practice.

A party intending to offer a record into evidence under this paragraph must provide written notice of that intention to all adverse parties, and must make the record and declaration available for inspection sufficiently in advance of their offer into evidence to provide an adverse party with a fair opportunity to challenge them.

(12) Certified foreign records of regularly conducted activity. In a civil case, the original or a duplicate of a foreign record of regularly conducted activity that would be admissible under Rule 803(6) if accompanied by a written declaration by its custodian or other qualified person certifying that the record:

(A) was made at or near the time of the occurrence of the matters set forth by, or from information transmitted by, a person with knowledge of those matters;

(B) was kept in the course of the regularly conducted activity; and

(C) was made by the regularly conducted activity as a regular practice.

The declaration must be signed in a manner that, if falsely made, would subject the maker to criminal penalty under the laws of the country where the declaration is signed. A party intending to offer a record into evidence under this paragraph must provide written notice of that intention to all adverse parties, and must make the record and declaration available for inspection sufficiently in advance of their offer into evidence to provide an adverse party with a fair opportunity to challenge them.

(Amended, eff. 10-1-87; Apr. 25, 1988, eff. Nov. 1, 1988; Apr. 7, 2000, eff. Dec. 1, 2000.)

RULE 903. Subscribing Witness' Testimony Unnecessary.

The testimony of a subscribing witness is not necessary to authenticate a writing unless required by the laws of the jurisdiction whose laws govern the validity of the writing.

ARTICLE X. CONTENTS OF WRITINGS, RECORDINGS, AND PHOTOGRAPHS

RULE 1001. Definitions

For purposes of this article the following definitions are applicable.

(1) Writings and recordings. "Writings" and "recordings" consist of letters, words, or numbers, or their equivalent, set down by handwriting, type-writing, printing, Photostatting, photographing, magnetic impulse, mechanical or electronic recording, or other forms of data compilation.

(2) Photographs. "Photographs" include still pictures, X-ray films, video tapes, and motion pictures.

(3) Original. An "original" of a writing or recording is the writing or recording itself or any counterpart intended to have the same effect by a person executing or issuing it. An "original" of a photograph included the negative or any print therefrom. If data are stored in a computer or similar device, any printout or other output readable by sight, shown to reflect the data accurately, is an "original."

(4) Duplicate. A "duplicate" is a counterpart produced by the same impression as the original, or from the same matrix, or by means of photography, including enlargements and miniatures, or by mechanical or electronic rerecording, or by chemical reproduction, or by other equivalent techniques which accurately reproduces the original.

RULE 1002. Requirement of Original

To prove the content of a writing, recording or photograph, the original writing, recording, or photograph is required, except as otherwise provided in these rules or by Act of Congress.

RULE 1003. Admissibility of Duplicates

A duplicate is admissible to the same extent as an original unless (1) a genuine question is raised as to the authenticity of the original or (2) in the circumstances it would be unfair to admit the duplicate in lieu of the original.

RULE 1004. Admissibility of Other Evidence of Contents

The original is not required, and other evidence of the contents of a writing, recording, or photograph is admissible if—

(1) Originals have been lost or destroyed. All originals are lost or have been destroyed, unless the proponent lost or destroyed them in bad faith; or

(2) Original not obtainable. No original can be obtained by any available judicial process or procedure; or

(3) Original in possession of opponent. At time when an original was under the control of the party against whom offered, that party was put on notice, by the pleadings or otherwise, that the contents would be a subject of proof at the hearing, and that party does not produce the original at the hearing; or

(4) Collateral matters. The writing, recording, or photograph is not closely related to a controlling issue.

(Amended, eff. 10-1-87)

RULE 1005. Public Records

The contents of an official record, or of a document authorized to be recorded or filed and actually recorded or filed, including data compilations in any form, if otherwise admissible, may be proved by copy, certified as correct in accordance with Rule 902 or testified to be correct by a witness who has compared it with the original. If a copy which complies with the foregoing cannot be obtained by the exercise of reasonable diligence, then other evidence of the contents may be given.

RULE 1006. Summaries

The contents of voluminous writings, recordings, or photographs which cannot conveniently be examined in court may be presented in the form of a chart, summary, or calculation. The originals, or duplicates, shall be made available for examination or copying, or both, by other parties at reasonable time and place. The court may order that they be produced in court.

RULE 1007. Testimony or Written Admission of a Party

Contents of writings, recordings, or photographs may be proved by the testimony or deposition of the party against whom offered or by that party's written admission, without accounting for the nonproduction of the original.

(Amended, eff. 10-1-87)

RULE 1008. Functions of Court and Jury

When the admissibility of other evidence of contents of writings, recordings, or photographs under these rules depends upon the fulfillment of a condition of fact, the question whether the condition has been fulfilled is ordinarily for the court to determine in accordance with the provisions of Rule 104. However, when an issue is raised (a) whether the asserted writing ever existed, or (b) whether another writing, recording, or photograph produced at the trial is the original, or (c) whether other evidence of contents correctly reflects the contents, the issue is for trier of fact to determine as in the case of other issues of fact.

ARTICLE XI. MISCELLANEOUS RULES

RULE 1101. Applicability of Rules

(a) Courts and judges. These rules apply to the United States district courts, the District Court of Guam, the District Court of the Virgin Islands, the District Court for the Northern Mariana Islands, the United States Courts of Appeals, the United States Claims Court, and to United States bankruptcy judges and United States magistrate judges, in the actions, cases, and proceedings and to the extent hereinafter set forth. The terms "judge" and "court" in these rules include United States bankruptcy judges and United States magistrate judges.

(b) Proceedings generally. These rules apply generally to civil actions and proceedings, including admiralty and maritime cases, to criminal cases and proceedings, to contempt proceedings except those in which the court may act similarly, and to proceedings and cases under title 11, United States Code.

(c) Rule of privilege. The rule with respect to privileges applies at all stages of all actions, cases, and proceedings.

(d) Rules inapplicable. The rules (other than with respect to privileges) do not apply in the following situations:

(1) Preliminary question of fact. The determination of questions of fact preliminary to admissibility of evidence when the issue is to be determined by the court under Rule 104.

(2) Grand jury. Proceedings before grand juries.

(3) Miscellaneous proceedings. Proceedings for extradition or rendition; preliminary examinations in criminal cases; sentencing, or granting or revoking probation; issuance of warrants for arrest, criminal summonses, and search warrants; and proceedings with respect to release on bail or otherwise.

(e) Rules applicable in part. In the following proceedings these rules apply to the extent that matters of evidence are not provided for in statutes which govern procedure therein or in other rules prescribed by the Supreme Court pursuant to statutory authority: the trial of misdemeanors and other petty offenses before United States magistrate judges; review of agency actions when the facts are subject to trial de novo under section 706(2)(F) of title 5, United States Code; review of orders of the Secretary of Agriculture under section 2 of the Act entitled "An Act to authorize association of producers of agricultural products" approved February 18, 1922 (7 U.S.C. 292), and under sections 6 and 7(c) of the Perishable Agricultural Commodities Act, 1930 (7 U.S.C. 499f, 499g(c); naturalization and revocation of naturalization under sections 310-318 of the Immigration and Nationality Act (8 U.S.C. 1421-1429); prize proceedings in admiralty under sections 7651-7681 of title 10, United States Code; review of orders of the Secretary of the Interior under section 2 of the Act entitled "An Act authorizing associations of producers of aquatic products" approved June 25, 1934 (15 U.S.C. 522); review of orders of petroleum control boards under section 5 of

the Act entitled "An Act to regulate interstate and foreign commerce in petroleum and its products by prohibiting the shipment in such commerce of petroleum and its products produced in violation of State law, and for other purposes," approved February 22, 1935 (15 U.S.C. 715d); actions for fines, penalties, or forfeitures under part V of title IV of the Tariff Act of 1930 (19 U.S.C. 1581-1624), or under the Anti-Smuggling Act (19 U.S.C. 1701-1711); criminal libel for condemnation, exclusion of imports, or other proceedings under the Federal Food, Drug, and Cosmetic Act (21 U.S.C. 301-392); disputes between seamen under sections 4079, 4080, and 4081 of the Revised Statutes (22 U.S.C. 256-258); habeas corpus under sections 2241-2254 of title 28, United States Code; motions to vacate, set aside or correct sentence under section 2255 of title 28, United States Code; actions for penalties for refusal to transport destitute seamen under section 4578 of the Revised Statutes (46 U.S.C. 679); actions against the United States under the Act entitled "An Act authorizing suits against the United States in admiralty for damage caused by and salvage service rendered to public vessels belonging to the United States, and for other purposes," approved March 3, 1925 (46 U.S.C. 781-790), as implemented by section 7730 of title 10, United States Code. (Amended, eff. 12-1-93)

RULE 1102. Amendments

Amendments to the Federal Rules of Evidence may be made as provided in section 2072 of title 28 of the United States Code.

(As amended, Apr. 30. 1991, eff. Dec. 1, 1991.)

RULE 1103. Title

These rules may be known and cited as the Federal Rules of Evidence.

APPENDIX II

Table of Jurisdictions in which
Uniform Rules of Evidence
Have Been Adopted—2003[1]

Jurisdiction	Laws	Effective Date	Statutory Citation
Alaska	Sup.Ct.Order 364	8-1-1979	A.R.E. Rules 101 to 1101.
Arizona		9-1-1977	17A A.R.S. Rules of Evid., Rules 101 to 1103.
Arkansas	1975, No. 1143	7-1-1976	A.C.A. § 16-41-101
Colorado		1-1-1980	West's C.R.S.A., Title 13 App., Evid. 101-1102.
Delaware		7-1-1980	D.R.E. 101 to 1103.
Florida	1976, c. 76-237	7-1-1977	West's F.S.A. §§ 90.101 to 90.958.
Hawai'i	1980, c. 164	1-1-1981	HRS §§ 626-1 (Hawaii Rules of Evidence, Rules 100 to 1102) to 626-3.
Idaho		7-1-1985	Rules of Evidence, Rules 101 to 1103.
Indiana	Sup.Ct.Order 8-24-1993	1-1-1994	Rules of Evidence, Rules 101 to 1101.
Iowa		7-1-1983	Iowa R.Evid., Rules 101 to 1103.
Kentucky	1990, c. 88 Sup.Ct. Order	7-1-1992	KRE 101 to 1104
Louisiana	1988 Act 515	1-1-1989	LSAEvid.Code, arts. 101 to 1103.
Maine		2-2-1976	Rules of Evidence, Rules 101 to 1102.
Michigan		3-1-1978	Rules of Evidence, Rules 101 to 1102.
Minnesota		7-1-1977	50 M.S.A.Evid. Rules 101 to 1101.
Mississippi	Sup.Ct.Order 9-24-1985	1-1-1986	M.R.E. 101 to 1103.
Montana	1976, En. Sup.Ct. Ord. 12729	7-1-1977	Rules of Evidence, Rules 100 to 1008.
Nebraska	1975, L.B. 279	8-24-1975	R.R.S.1943, §§ 27-101 to 27-1103.
Nevada	1971, c. 775		N.R.S. § 47.929 et seq.
New Hampshire	7-1-1985		Rules of Evidence, Rules 100 to 1103.
New Jersey			New Jersey Rules of Evidence Rules 101-1103.
New Mexico	1973, S.C.Order	7-1-1973	N.M.R.Evid., Rules 101 to 1102.
North Carolina	1983, c. 701	7-1-1984	G.S. § 8C-1, Rules 101 to 1102.
North Dakota		2-15-1977	NDR Evid.Rules 101 to 1103.
Ohio		7-1-1980	Rules of Evidence, Rules 101 to 1103.
Oklahoma	1978, c. 285	10-1-1978	12 Okl.St.Ann. §§ 2101 to 3103.
Oregon	1981, c. 892	1-1-1982	ORS 40.010 to 40.585.
Rhode Island		1986*	Rules of Evidence, Rules 100 to 1008.
South Dakota			SDCL 19-9-1 to 19-18-8.
Tennessee		1-1-1990	Rules of Evidence, Rules 101 to 1008.
Texas[1]		9-1-1983	Rules of Civil Evidence, Rules 101 to 1008.
		9-1-1986	Rules of Criminal Evidence, Rules 101 to 1101.
Utah		9-1-1983	Rules of Evidence, Rules 101 to 1103.
Vermont		4-1-1983	Titled: Vermont Court Rules, Rules 101 to 1103.
Washington		4-2-1979	Rules of Evidence, Rules 101 to 1103.
West Virginia		2-1-1985	W.V.R.E., Rules 101 to 1102.
Wisconsin	Sup.Ct.Order, 59 W.(2d), page R9	1-1-1974	W.S.A. 901.01 to 911.02.
Wyoming		1-1-1978	Rules of Evidence, Rules 101 to 1104.

[1] Legal Information Institute, http://www.law.cornell.edu/uniform/evidence.html (10-13-2006).

APPENDIX III

TABLE OF CONTENTS
UNIFORM RULES OF EVIDENCE
(1974) WITH 1986 AND 1988 AMENDMENTS[1]

Article I

GENERAL PROVISIONS

Article II

JUDICIAL NOTICE

Article III

PRESUMPTIONS

Article IV

RELEVANCY AND ITS LIMITS

---

[1] Full text of the Uniform Rules of Evidence with 1998 amendments is available at http://www.law.upenn.edu/bll/ulc/ure/evid1200.htm (10-13-2006).

Article VIII

HEARSAY

Article IX

AUTHENTICATION AND IDENTIFICATION

Article X

CONTENTS OF WRITINGS, RECORDINGS, AND PHOTOGRAPHS

Article XI

MISCELLANEOUS RULES

Table of Cases

Index